THE ENDURING AUTHORITY OF THE CHRISTIAN SCRIPTURES

The Enduring Authority of the Christian Scriptures

Edited by

D. A. Carson

William B. Eerdmans Publishing Company
Grand Rapids, Michigan / Cambridge, U.K.

© 2016 D. A. Carson
All rights reserved

Published 2016 by
Wm. B. Eerdmans Publishing Co.
2140 Oak Industrial Drive N.E., Grand Rapids, Michigan 49505 /
P.O. Box 163, Cambridge CB3 9PU U.K.

Printed in the United States of America

22 21 20 19 18 17 16 7 6 5 4 3 2 1

Library of Congress Cataloging-in-Publication Data

Names: Carson, D. A., editor.
Title: The enduring authority of the Christian scriptures / edited by D. A. Carson.
Description: Grand Rapids, Michigan : Eerdmans Publishing Company, 2016. |
Includes bibliographical references and indexes.
Identifiers: LCCN 2015038502 | ISBN 9780802865762 (cloth: alk. paper)
Subjects: LCSH: Bible — Evidences, authority, etc.
Classification: LCC BS480 .E53 2016 | DDC 220.1 — dc23
LC record available at http://lccn.loc.gov/2015038502

www.eerdmans.com

Contents

COMPARATIVE RELIGIONS TOPICS

THINKING HOLISTICALLY

FAQS

Abbreviations

AAR	American Academy of Religion
AB	Anchor Bible
ABD	*Anchor Bible Dictionary*
ABH	Long, *The Art of Biblical History*
ACW	Ancient Christian Writers
adv. Marc.	Tertullian, *Adversus Marcionem*
AGJU	Arbeiten zur Geschichte des antiken Judentums und des Urchristentums
A.H.	After Hegira = Anno Hegirae (Muslim calendar)
AH	Irenaeus, *Adversus Haereses*
AJT	*Asia Journal of Theology*
AnBib	Analecta Biblica
ANF	*Ante-Nicene Fathers*
Ant.	Josephus, *Antiquities of the Jews*
A of F	Articles of Faith (Mormon)
1 Apol.	Justin Martyr, *The First Apology*
ARN	Avot of Rabbi Natan
Asc. Isa.	*The Ascension of Isaiah*
ASNU	Acta Seminarii Neotestamentici Upsaliensis
ASV	American Standard Version
ATANT	Abhandlungen zur Theologie des Alten und Neuen Testaments
AThR	*Anglican Theological Review*
BAR	*Biblical Archaeology Review*
B&C	*Books & Culture*
B&H	Broadman & Holman
Barn.	*Epistle of Barnabas*
BBB	Bonner Biblische Beiträge
BBR	*Bulletin for Biblical Research*
BC	*The Book of Concord*

B.C.E.	Before the Common Era
BECNT	Baker Exegetical Commentary on the New Testament
BETL	Bibliotheca Ephemeridum Theologicarum Lovaniensium
BHI	Provan, Long, Longman, *A Biblical History*
BI	*Biblical Interpretation*
Bib	*Biblica*
BSLK	*Die Bekenntnisschriften der evangelisch-lutherischen Kirche*
BST	*Bible Speaks Today*
BZAW	Beihefte zur Zeitschrift alttestamentliche Wissenschaft
Cahiers de l'A.P.F.	*Cahiers de l'Association des Pasteurs de France*
CApion	Josephus, *Contra Apion*
CBQ	*Catholic Biblical Quarterly*
CCels.	*Contra Celsum*
CCSL	*Corpus Christianorum Series Latina*
CD	*Church Dogmatics*
CD	Cairo Genizah copy of the *Damascus Document*
CD-B	*Damascus Document* — Recension B
CDV	*Commentary on the Documents of Vatican II*
C.E.	Common Era
CFaust.	Augustine, *Contra Faustum*
CivDei	Augustine, *De civitate Dei*
1 Clem.	*1 Clement*
2 Clem.	*2 Clement*
CNTC	*Calvin's New Testament Commentaries*
CO	*Ioannis Calvini Opera Quae Supersunt Omnia*
CR	Corpus Reformatorum
CRINT	Compendium rerum iudaicarum ad Novum Testamentum
CT	Codex Tchacos
CTM	*Currents in Theology and Mission*
CTR	*Criswell Theological Review*
DBSup	*Dictionnaire de la Bible: Supplément*
DEC	*Decrees of the Ecumenical Councils*
Dial.	*Dialogue with Trypho*
DJD	Discoveries in the Judean Desert
EDT	*Evangelical Dictionary of Theology*
Ep.	*Epistle*
Eph.	Ignatius, *To the Ephesians*
Ep. Ptol. Fl.	Ptolemaeus Gnosticus, *Epistula ad Floram*
ERT	*Evangelical Review of Theology*
esp.	especially
ESV	English Standard Version
ET	English Translation

EurJTh	*European Journal of Theology*
Eus.	Eusebius
EvQ	*Evangelical Quarterly*
ExAud	*Ex Auditu*
ExpT	*The Expository Times*
FAT	Forschungen zum Alten Testament
FOC	Fathers of the Church Patristic Series
FRLANT	Forschungen zur Religion und Literatur des Alten und Neuen Testaments
FTC	The Fathers of the Church
FWD	Free Will Defense
GCS	Die Griechischen Christlichen Schriftsteller
GD	*The Göttingen Dogmatics*
G. Jud.	*Gospel of Judas*
GNT	Grundrisse zum Neuen Testament
Gos. Thom.	*Gospel of Thomas*
GOTR	*Greek Orthodox Theological Review*
HAT	Handkommentar zum Alten Testament
HBT	*Horizons in Biblical Theology*
HC	*History of the Church* (Mormon; 2nd edition, 1950; 7 vols.)
HCSB	Holman Christian Standard Bible
HE	*Historia Ecclesiastica*
HNT	Handbuch zum Neuen Testament
HSM	Harvard Semitic Monographs
HTR	*Harvard Theological Review*
HUCA	*Hebrew Union College Annual*
IBC	Interpretation: A Bible Commentary for Teaching and Preaching
ICC	International Critical Commentary
In Apoc.	Victorinus, *Commentary on the Apocalypse*
Inst.	John Calvin, *The Institutes of the Christian Religion*
Int	*Interpretation*
ISBE	*International Standard Bible Encyclopedia*
JBR	*Journal of Bible and Religion*
JETS	*Journal of the Evangelical Theological Society*
JGRChJ	*Journal of Greco-Roman Christianity and Judaism*
JR	*Journal of Religion*
JSJ	*Journal for the Study of Judaism*
JSNT	*Journal for the Study of the New Testament*
JSOT	*Journal for the Study of the Old Testament*
JSOTSS	Journal for the Study of the Old Testament Supplement Series
JSP	*Journal for the Study of the Pseudepigrapha*
JSPSS	Journal for the Study of the Pseudepigrapha Supplement Series

JSS	*Journal of Semitic Studies*
JTS	*Journal of Theological Studies*
KEK	Kritisch-exegetischer Kommentar über das Neue Testament (Meyer-Kommentar)
KJV	King James Version
LCL	Loeb Classical Library
LNTS	Library of New Testament Studies
LRB	*London Review of Books*
LW	*Luther's Works*
LXX	Septuagint
Magn.	Ignatius, *To the Magnesians*
MeyerK	Meyer Kommentar
MF	*Muratorian Fragment*
MG	Migne Patrologia Graeca
MT	Masoretic Text
NAB	New American Bible
NAE	National Association of Evangelicals
NASB	New American Standard Bible
NBCLC	National Biblical Confessional and Liturgical Centre (Bangalore)
NBD	*New Bible Dictionary*
NEB	New English Bible
Neot	*Neotestamentica*
NET	New English Translation
NH	Nag Hammadi
NICNT	New International Commentary on the New Testament
NICOT	New International Commentary on the Old Testament
NIGTC	New International Greek Testament Commentary
NIV	New International Version
NJB	New Jerusalem Bible
NKJV	New King James Version
NLT	New Living Translation
NovT	*Novum Testamentum*
NovTSup	Supplements to Novum Testamentum
NPNF	Nicene and Post-Nicene Fathers
NRSV	New Revised Standard Version
NSBT	New Studies in Biblical Theology
NRSV	New Revised Standard Version
NT	New Testament
NTOA	Novum Testamentum et Orbis Antiquus
NTS	*New Testament Studies*
NTTSD	New Testament Tools, Studies and Documents
OCD	*Oxford Classical Dictionary*

OED	*Oxford English Dictionary*
OT	Old Testament
OTS	*Oudtestamentische Studiën/Old Testament Studies*
P&R	Presbyterian & Reformed
Paed.	Clement of Alexandria, *Paidagogus*
Panar.	Epiphanius, *Panarion*
PG	Patrologia Graeca
Phil.	Polycarp, *To the Philadelphians*
Phld.	Ignatius, *To the Philadelphians*
PL	Patrologia Latina
PNTC	Pillar New Testament Commentary
Polyc.	Polycarp
P.Oxy.	Oxyrhynchus Papyri
Praesc.	Tertullian, *De Praescriptione Haereticorum*
Princ.	Origen, *De Principiis*
Protr.	Clement of Alexandria, *Exhortation to the Heathen*
PRS	*Perspectives in Religious Studies*
Ps-Barn.	*Pseudo-Barnabas*
Ps.Sol.	Psalms of Solomon
PTS	Patristic and Text-Critical Studies
1QpHab	*Pesher* commentary on Habakkuk
1QS	*Rule of the Community*
4Q521	*Messianic Apocalypse* (= 4QMessAp)
11QT	*Temple Scroll*
Quis. div. sal.	Clement of Alexandria, *Quis Dives Salvetur*
Quis rer. div. her.	Philo, *Quis Rerum Divinarum Heres*
RB	*Revue Biblique*
RC	Roman Catholic(ism)
Ref.	Hippolytus, *Refutatio Haereses*
RestQ	*Restoration Quarterly*
Rom.	Ignatius, *To the Romans*
RSV	Revised Standard Version
SBAW	*Sitzungsberichte der Bayerischen Akademie der Wissenschaften*
SBJT	*The Southern Baptist Journal of Theology*
SBL	Society of Biblical Literature
SBS	Stuttgarter Bibelstudien
SBT	Studies in Biblical Theology
SC	Sources chrétiennes
SEP	*The Stanford Encyclopedia of Philosophy*
SJOT	*Scandinavian Journal of the Old Testament*
SJSJ	Supplements to the Journal for the Study of Judaism
SJT	*Scottish Journal of Theology*

Smyrn.	Ignatius, *To the Smyrneans*
SNT	Studien zum Neuen Testament
SNTSMS	Society of New Testament Studies Monograph Series
SP	Sacra Pagina
SPCK	Society for the Promotion of Christian Knowledge
Spec. Laws	Philo, *The Special Laws*
ST	*Studia Theologica*
Str-B	H. L. Strack & P. Billerbeck, *Kommentar zum Neuen Testament aus Talmud und Midrash*
Strom.	Clement of Alexandria, *Stromata*
SUNY	State University of New York
SuppVC	Supplements to Vigiliae Christianae
Targ. On.	Targum Onkelos
Targ. Ps.-Jon.	Targum Pseudo-Jonathan
TDNT	*Theological Dictionary of the New Testament*
TDOT	*Theological Dictionary of the Old Testament*
Test. Abr.	Testament of Abraham
Them	*Themelios*
Theol	*Theology*
TNIV	Today's New International Version
TNTC	Tyndale New Testament Commentary
TOTC	Tyndale Old Testament Commentary
Trall.	Ignatius, *To the Trallians*
TrinJ	*Trinity Journal*
TS	*Theological Studies*
TSAJ	Texts and Studies in Ancient Judaism
TynB	*Tyndale Bulletin*
UBSGNT	United Bible Societies' *Greek New Testament*
VC	*Vigiliae Christianae*
VT	*Vetus Testamentum*
VTS	Vetus Testamentum Supplements
WA	*D. Martin Luthers Werke*
WADB	*D. Martin Luthers Werke: Kritische Gesamtausgabe, Deutsche Bibel*
WBC	Word Bible Commentary
WCF	*Westminster Confession of Faith*
WJK	Westminster John Knox
WTJ	*Westminster Theological Journal*
WUNT	Wissenschaftliche Untersuchungen zum Neuen Testament
ZKG	*Zeitschrift für Kirchengeschichte*
ZNW	*Zeitschrift für die neutestamentliche Wissenschaft*

Preface

In the past, evangelicalism has often been said to turn on a formal principle and a material principle. The formal principle is the authority of the Bible, from which everything else derives. As necessary as the formal principle is, however, it is not sufficient to define evangelicalism. After all, many other groups and movements adhere to some sort of high view of Scripture: consider (to go no further) the Jehovah's Witnesses. So coupled with the formal principle is the material principle — a right understanding of the gospel.

This volume focuses on the formal principle. Few topics touch more issues than the topic of biblical authority: the nature of revelation, different ways of understanding truth, the locus of authority (located in the text or in the teaching office of the church), historical-critical considerations, continuity and discontinuity between the Testaments, the use of the Old Testament in the Old and in the New, the relationship between Scripture and canon, the formation of the canon, epistemology, the nature of inspiration, the notion of double authorship, the claims of Scriptural authority in an age dominated by a vision of science that widely presupposes philosophical materialism, Jesus' own view of the authority of antecedent Scripture, assorted hermeneutical challenges, the impact of certain intellectual giants (e.g., Calvin, Barth), complex histories of the doctrine of Scripture, the Bible's relation to history (and what "history" means), the coherence of certain shibboleth words like "inerrancy," the Western cultural suspicion of all voices of authority in what Charles Taylor calls "the age of authenticity," the perspicuity of Scripture, the way Scripture should and should not be used in the formation of doctrine, and, in an age of globalism, how the Christian doctrine of Scripture is and is not like the way other world religions view their sacred writings. To make matters still more complex, all of these related fields that bear on the nature and authority of the Bible have their own conceptual minefields. Not surprisingly, then, they too throw up challenging debates. Moreover, to survey the topics just listed is to remind oneself how the formal principle can never be completely isolated from the material principle: e.g., if one is wrestling with hermeneutical challenges, the discussion is bound to intrude into the territories of both principles.

About thirty years ago, some of the writers in this volume worked together and with others to produce a pair of volumes that is still in print: *Scripture and Truth* (1983) and *Hermeneutics, Authority, and Canon* (1986 — both edited by D. A. Carson and John D. Woodbridge, and both published by Zondervan). The two volumes played their parts in the then-current debates. Some of today's topics are similar, even though the debates have moved on; others are new. Recognizing that Scripture and its authority are being challenged and defended with renewed vigor, a handful of us put our heads together and laid down the topics you will find in this volume. Funded by the Henry Center for Theological Understanding (one of three Centers operated by Trinity Evangelical Divinity School), the project took on life. Scholars agreed to write these essays, and then their papers were circulated among the contributors. In June 2010, thirty-three of the thirty-seven contributors flew to Chicago from their various posts around the world, and spent an intense but hugely enjoyable week working through their essays. On every topic there were at least two or three people in the room who were competent on that subject, and sometimes more. This led to many debates, corrections, modifications, and to much subsequent rewriting. The hours were long, the discussions candid, but a rare camaraderie developed. Most of us went away, I think, holding to the opinion that we had never enjoyed theological discussion more. Not a few new friendships were forged.

For various reasons, rewriting (some of it major) and the writing of a couple of new essays that were not ready at the time of the conference took up three years. The final major revision showed up in January 2015. Probably I should have pushed harder; the blame for some of the delay must be placed squarely at my door. Nevertheless most of these papers are sufficiently weighty and robust that they will not quickly become dated.

It remains to thank the Henry Center for the funding that made this project possible, and for the logistical competence that smoothly and expertly arranged the details of the week of discussion, from transportation to food to acoustics. Special mention must be made of the skillful work of Hans Madueme, then a doctoral student at TEDS, who took detailed notes of these discussions and circulated them to all the participants, making it possible to follow up certain points with ongoing exchanges and clarifications. Warm thanks go to Eerdmans not only for taking on this project, but because (if I may resort to an expression now eclipsed), while they waited and encouraged, they composed their souls in peace. And abundant thanks to Daniel Ahn, Daniel Cole, and Wang Chi-Ying, who prepared the indexes, without which this volume would have been far less useful than it is.

"These are the ones I look on with favor: those who are humble and contrite in spirit and who tremble at my word" (Isa. 66:2).

Soli Deo gloria.

D. A. Carson

Introduction

ONE

The Many Facets of the Current Discussion

D. A. Carson

The last three decades or so have seen a plethora of books and articles on the nature of Scripture. Some of these, on both the confessional side and the more liberal side, have merely refreshed (rehashed?) old positions. That is not necessarily a bad thing, in exactly the same way that publishing more commentaries on biblical books is not necessarily a bad thing. We need new commentaries not only because new questions continue to be asked, and new audiences addressed, but also because we need a steady supply of new commentators — people who work carefully through the biblical texts and try to explain them to others. In exactly the same way, we constantly need a new supply of Christian scholars who think about the nature of Scripture, not only because new questions are raised from time to time, but also because we need a steady supply of new theologians who work through the fundamentals of every doctrine. Some of the many recent works on Scripture go beyond this, and, for better or for worse, break fresh ground. It is hard to keep up with all of it. This chapter is an attempt to survey and briefly evaluate some of it, while sometimes serving as an introduction to the rest of this volume.

One of my former students, Dr. Andy Naselli, found 337 items of new material on Scripture published between 1980 and 2010. A good deal of it is repetitive or not particularly significant. On the other hand, many more items could be added to the list if we included writings that do not directly address the doctrine of Scripture but that have a powerful (if unstated) bearing on our understanding of what Scripture is. I have not counted the number of new entries since 2010. In other words, this is fair warning that the survey that follows is far from exhaustive; I hope it is broadly representative.

The Diversity of Stances toward the Bible: A Sweeping Survey

Perhaps the place to begin is the insightful recent essay by Robert W. Yarbrough.[1] Yarbrough, who has made himself an expert on the history of (especially German) biblical criticism in the last two and a half centuries, briefly summarizes some of this terrain, and then surveys and interacts with three recent books that express their unease with the current situation. All three scholars sketch parts of the movement that progressively saw the Bible as text to be mastered and deployed to various social and academic ends, making it more and more difficult for the church to see it as the revelation of God, God's Word to sinners to bring about their redemption.

The first of these books is by Michael Legaspi, a Harvard-trained Hebrew scholar.[2] In Legaspi's take on the rise of biblical criticism, the figure on which he fastens is Johann David Michaelis (1717-1791), who with his contemporaries did not so much disown the Bible as co-opt it away from its own theological themes bound up with the gospel, to serve the social and political goals of progressive conservative Enlightenment interests. Biblical scholarship was incorporated into the humanities; the reconstruction of the history of ancient Israel was accomplished so as to be intelligible to and in line with contemporary vision rather than a God-given account to establish the knowledge of God. The newly created history made Moses an obsolete figure with little relevance to church life in the modern world. What might be called the academic Bible was progressively detached from the Bible of the church. The academic Bible became a domain where scholars exercised assorted methods to re-create its distant message; the scriptural Bible calls people to repentance and faith in the crucified and risen Christ. Legaspi finds space for both approaches. He holds that the modern critical approach may have some social and political usefulness, and he insists on the intellectual value of academic criticism, but concludes that such criticism cannot offer an intellectually compelling account of what such work serves. In the end, Legaspi is left with unresolved tension, but he is convinced that the academic Bible has been afforded much more authority in the church than it deserves.

The next two books that Yarbrough surveys were written by German New Testament scholars who, after a lifetime of critical study, in their senior years articulate their reservations over historical-critical methods. Ulrich Wilckens, emeritus at the University of Hamburg, offers a fairly tepid criticism of biblical criticism;[3] the criticisms of Klaus Berger, emeritus at the University of Hei-

1. "Bye-bye Bible? Progress Report on the Death of Scripture," *Them* 39 (2014): 415-27; available online at thegospelcoalition.org.

2. *The Death of Scripture and the Rise of Biblical Studies* (Oxford: Oxford University Press, 2011).

3. *Kritik der Bibelkritik: Wie die Bibel wieder zur Heiligen Schrift werden kann* (Neukirchen-Vluyn: Neukirchener, 2012).

delberg, are angry and sweeping.[4] Wilckens's first hundred pages provide an engaging history of historical-critical exegesis, and Wilckens is fair and frank. In his outline of the eight moves that constitute the skeletal outline of the period, Wilckens candidly points out the flawed assumptions that drove so many of the critics (a bias against supernaturalism, the controlling commitment to German Idealist philosophy), and discusses the influence of several key figures, including F. C. Baur, David Friedrich Strauss, Immanuel Kant, F. D. E. Schleiermacher, Ernst Troeltsch, and Rudolf Bultmann. Wilckens argues that contemporary biblical exegesis is stuck in the liberal trajectory, and needs not reformation but to be overcome *(Überwendung)*. After so broad an appeal, however, the rest of the book is rather timid. True, Wilckens insists that Jesus' resurrection takes place in history, that the atonement saves men and women from their sins, that New Testament ethics are normative, and much more. Nevertheless he leaves in place most of the higher-critical consensus regarding the dating and authorship of the documents, doing nothing to tie eyewitness accounts to the New Testament documents, and when he asks how the historically interpreted New Testament can become Holy Scripture again, his answers are anemic and without force. By contrast, Berger's volume — no mere tract but a sustained expostulation, for it is twice as long as Wilckens's book — opens by arguing that two centuries of biblical research have decimated our churches. The universities provide the pastors for most German churches, and these pastors are systematically taught a "hermeneutic of mistrust." Here Berger interacts forcefully with several of the most egregious examples of historical skepticism advanced by, among others, Rudolf Bultmann and Gerd Theissen. German exegesis is chained by the philosophical anthropology of Martin Heidegger, by psychology, sociology, religious theory, and politics, crushing theology with their entirely godless systems.[5] The result is that scholars who identify as Catholics or Protestants feel entirely free to disavow any allegiance to historic Christian teaching even though the Bible teaches it. As an example, Berger refers to Rudolf Pesch, a Catholic scholar who denies the virgin birth.[6] Today he could add the New Testament scholar Andrew T. Lincoln.[7] Much of the rest of Berger's book (pp. 43-296) is devoted to nine sections that outline how contemporary historical-critical liberal exegesis contributes to the destruction *(Zerstörung)* of the New Testament, and how he would respond to them. I list them using the Yarbrough translation:[8]

4. *Die Bibelfälscher: Wie wir um die Wahrheit betrogen warden* (Munich: Pattlock, 2013).

5. *Die Bibelfälscher*, 35-36.

6. See his two-volume commentary on Mark in the Herder series (1989, 1991).

7. *Born of a Virgin? Reconceiving Jesus in the Bible, Tradition, and Theology* (Grand Rapids: Eerdmans, 2013). Yarbrough makes the same connection, and draws attention to the review in *Them* 39 (2014): 367-69, while he himself provides the review in *BBR* 24 (2014): 581-82.

8. "Bye-bye Bible?" 425-46.

1. The demolition of Christianity in the classroom and from the pulpit
2. The most important errors of liberal exegesis
3. The preliminary assumptions of the opponents [of Scripture's truth]
4. Manipulation of the passion texts
5. Ruthless secularization
6. The domestication of the apostle Paul
7. The infancy narratives as a playground for radical biblical criticism (Jesus' childhood, like the passion narratives, is full of legends; Mary was not a virgin; Bethlehem was not Jesus' birthplace; there was no fleeing to Egypt by the holy family)
8. Rewriting history at will (Jesus was married; no hell but universal redemption; Jesus did not institute the Lord's Supper; Jesus did not pray the Lord's Prayer)
9. How did this exegesis ever get started?

Berger concludes by insisting that historical criticism in Germany has promoted atheism, splintered churches, and converted no one to Christ.[9] In the near term, Berger finds little hope; the trajectories of acceptable scholarship are discouraging. He quotes the [now former] Roman Catholic archbishop of Chicago, Francis Cardinal George, who wrote: "I expect to die in bed, my successor will die in prison and his successor will die a martyr in the public square."[10]

Whether the bleak outlook envisaged by George and Berger will come to pass or not, who can say? Two things are clear. *First,* many people perceive the importance of the doctrine of Scripture, and many voices insist that the well-being of the church and faithfulness to the gospel are at stake. *Second,* there is a very wide range of opinions as to the way ahead. It may be helpful to indicate a few of these.

Some voices are as destructive of Scripture as they are of the Christian faith. They operate with the conviction that there is nothing unique or revelatory in the New Testament documents. In addition to some work by Bart Ehrman to be mentioned later, one might point to *A New New Testament: A Bible for the 21st Century Combining Traditional and Newly Discovered Texts.*[11] Produced by the same people in the Jesus Seminar who wrote a volume on the gospels where they decided which verses were authentic (and found very few of them), this book adds the following to the traditional twenty-seven documents of the NT: *The Prayer of Thanksgiving; The Prayer of the Apostle Paul; The Thunder: Perfect*

9. *Die Bibelfälscher,* 345.

10. *Die Bibelfälscher,* 346. In his original address (2012), George adds: "His successor will pick up the shards of a ruined society and slowly help rebuild civilization, as the church has done so often in human history" (http://www.catholicnewworldcom/cnwonline/2012/1021/cardinal.aspx), cited at greater length by Yarbrough, "Bye-bye Bible?" 427.

11. Ed. Hal Taussig (New York: Houghton Mifflin Harcourt, 2013).

Mind; The Gospel of Thomas; The Gospel of Mary; The Gospel of Truth; The Acts of Paul and Thecla; The Letter of Peter to Philip; The Secret Revelation of John; The First, Second, Third, and Fourth Books of the Odes of Solomon. Remarkably, they include nothing from the Apostolic Fathers — *Didache,* for instance, or *The Shepherd of Hermas,* or *First Clement.* All the books chosen either support Gnosticism or promote women or both. It is hard not to detect an agenda when there is no serious discussion about claims to canonicity.

Then there is the book by Thom Stark, *The Human Faces of God: What Scripture Reveals When It Gets God Wrong.*[12] Its thesis is that the biblical text, taken on its own terms, is "evil" and has a "devilish nature" that reveals God to be a "genocidal dictator."[13] The Bible's usefulness is that it should be read as "condemned texts":[14] we condemn them in our encounter with them so that we can discover the dark side in our own lives.

A somewhat different contribution, but one that steers its slightly snide condescension in a different direction, is the recent essay by Stephen L. Young.[15] Young "examines how Evangelical Christian inerrantist scholars theorize their biblical scholarship." He highlights "their self-representation as true academics" and "the ways they modulate historical methods" to generate the answers they want, deploying "protective strategies" and "privileging" insider claims. These "characteristics of inerrantist religiosity" he then explores from the vantage point of "Practice Theory."[16] I confess I was sorely tempted to draft a response that examined how anti-evangelical scholars display their self-representation as academics, highlighting how instead of engaging with the issues themselves they modulate their sociological analyses and exercise Practice Theory so as to cast up protective strategies that privilege the characteristics of liberal religiosity. Mercifully, however, I decided that the target was too easy.

Nominally less destructive and certainly less constrained by an assumed antisupernaturalism than the scholars connected with the Jesus Seminar are works like those represented by A. E. Harvey, *Is Scripture Still Holy? Coming of Age with the New Testament.*[17] Here the unbelief is more selective. Harvey recognizes that the Bible's authority is irrefragably tied to its holiness, but argues that we need a new approach to what is "holy," one that can be accepted by modern readers. If we rethink the Bible as a holy text, decoupling what is "holy" from notions like

12. Thom Stark, *The Human Faces of God: What Scripture Reveals When It Gets God Wrong* (Eugene, OR: Wipf & Stock, 2011).

13. Stark, *The Human Faces of God,* 218, 219.

14. Stark, *The Human Faces of God,* 218.

15. "Protective Strategies and the Prestige of the 'Academic': A Religious Studies and Practice Theory Redescription of Evangelical Inerrantist Scholarship," *BI* 23 (2015): 1-35.

16. "Protective Strategies," 1.

17. A. E. Harvey, *Is Scripture Still Holy? Coming of Age with the New Testament* (Grand Rapids: Eerdmans, 2012).

inspiration and inerrancy, we may begin to perceive that the Bible offers a weak model of authority constantly in need of being reassessed, in much the same way that democratic societies keep assessing their leaders. In this way the Bible shows itself to be "holy." Harvey argues that this new model of authority has seven requirements:[18] (1) alignment with modern principles of equality, altruism, and compassion; (2) coherence with good moral character; (3) adherence to notions of historical accuracy appropriate to its time; (4) "a necessary intelligibility and consistency"; (5) "linguistic and imaginative depth"; (6) "its stance on moral questions must continue to be found relevant"; (7) "it reliably relates [its adherents] to their past and points them toward a credible and inspiring future." For Harvey, this works out in his wrestling with how we can speak of the reliability of the Gospels despite their contradictions. He presents Jesus as a prophet who announced the kingdom but who never claimed that its dawning was imminent. Paul is inconsistent in what he says, and in any case must be read through the lens of the new perspective. Early Christian eschatological expectations he finesses by treating them as if they are "as if" statements. In other words, Harvey is in line with the many critics who find they cannot accept what the Bible says, but who want to preserve some sort of inner meaning after the historically unacceptable has been stripped away. Exactly how this generates a new and authoritative "holiness" in Scripture is less than transparently obvious.

Somewhat similarly, David Crump, *Encountering Jesus, Encountering Scripture: Reading the Bible Critically in Faith,*[19] observing how many divinity students abandon the faith entirely once they are exposed to mainstream historical criticism, does not find something suspiciously wrong with such criticism, but calls for a Kierkegaardian leap of faith. He wants believers, including these students, to have a personal encounter with Jesus that has no fundamental biblical support, indeed no support except the act of faith itself: "ultimately every individual stands alone."[20] Textually speaking, nothing in the messianic expectation of the Old Testament is genuinely fulfilled in Jesus, but when people have an encounter with Jesus they are justified seeing the good news found in Jesus. Paul is converted through his Damascus Road experience, and only subsequently works out how he will henceforth read the old covenant texts. This, of course, is to confuse the psychological steps by which at least some people (like Paul) come to grips with the good news of Jesus the Messiah, and the manner in which that good news is tied to antecedent Scripture. Once converted, Paul is convinced that before his conversion he *mis*understood Scripture. That is why in his evangelistic efforts with Jews he does not say, in effect, "What you really need is your own private

18. Harvey, *Is Scripture Still Holy?* 15-19.

19. David Crump, *Encountering Jesus, Encountering Scripture: Reading the Bible Critically in Faith* (Grand Rapids: Eerdmans, 2013).

20. Crump, *Encountering Jesus, Encountering Scripture,* 14.

Damascus Road experience; otherwise you can never understand," but rather, "Let's read these texts together. Don't you see? Rightly understood, they really do point us to Jesus and his cross and resurrection." Even when Paul appeals to the work of the Spirit in conversion (e.g., 1 Cor. 2:10b-16), he does not envisage the Spirit's work as establishing a text-free revelatory insight, but as enabling sin-blinded sinners to see what is actually there in the text. Failure to understand this is why Crump avows that Bultmann is one of the heroes, precisely *because* Bultmann's appeal to faith is so dramatically cut off from substantive content — from everything except the forlorn "dass."

Another volume that maintains something of a hiatus between historical-critical exegesis and the actual object of faith, but in a considerably more conservative fashion than the book by Crump, is the recent work edited by Christopher R. Seitz and Kent Harold Richards, *The Bible as Christian Scripture: The Work of Brevard S. Childs.*[21] It contains an interesting mix of essays. Some directly interact with the work of Childs, especially his understanding of biblical theology and his uneasy interaction with historical-critical issues; others are meant to be independent pieces that are in line with Childs's heritage.

Diametrically opposed to the critique of historical criticism offered by Legaspi and Berger, yet equally unhappy with approaches to faith that sidestep or ignore the results of historical-critical method, is the important book by Roy A. Harrisville, *Pandora's Box Opened: An Examination and Defense of Historical-Critical Method and Its Master Practitioners.*[22] In the extended metaphor Harrisville deploys, the period *before* Pandora's box is opened was the period before the dawning of historical criticism, when scholars thought the Bible, because it is the Word of God, should be read in a unique way. As one reviewer puts it, "The relatively recent asking of historical-critical questions has engendered a host of answers pestilential in their effect on many people's faith in the Bible as God's Word, or even as containing or becoming the Word of God."[23] Harrisville candidly depicts the many questions that cannot now be put back into the box. Moreover, they *shouldn't* be put back into the box. More worrisome to Harrisville, however, is the fact that these developments have raised vast armadas of additional questions — questions that touch on whether the notion of canon remains useful; on the ways the Old Testament is taken up by the New; on complex issues surrounding accommodation, naturalism, truth, and perspicuity; on the interplay between revelation and reason; on the role of the Spirit; on a complex array of hermeneutical issues, including allegory and typology; on interpretive grids that offer, say, Marxist readings of the gospel, postcolonial readings, and feminist readings; and much, much, more (this is a very partial list). The opening of Pandora's box, in

21. Atlanta: SBL, 2013.

22. Grand Rapids: Eerdmans, 2014.

23. Robert Gundry, "Thinking Outside the Box," *B&C* 21, no. 1 (Jan./Feb. 2015): 34.

other words, has led to vast methodological disarray. One sympathizes with the depth of Harrisville's dismay. At the end of the day, although he acknowledges that the opening of Pandora's box must largely be laid at the door of the rise of the historical-critical method, it is futile to try to reverse history. As his subtitle makes clear, Harrisville is launching a defense of historical-critical method over against the open-ended questions frequently raised by scholars primarily concerned with their own agendas; one must hope for help from the box itself, Harrisville insists, from the kind of relatively conservative historical-critical approach exemplified in Harrisville's teacher, Otto Piper. He does not seriously consider the kind of historical probing that faithfully recognizes the historical particularity of biblical texts, while integrating confessional stances that recognize some of the entailments of treating the Bible as the Word of God. A glance at some of the chapter titles in this present work discloses how a number of issues that Harrisville raises are discussed in the following pages (though of course all of these pages were written before the publication of Harrisville's work).

The thrust of Harrisville's thesis is both admirably right and disturbingly weak. It is right in that Harrisville perceives that the biblical revelation is very frequently enmeshed in historical events, so that to ignore the historical narrative and the critical study of that narrative is to turn away from huge swaths of Scripture. This is a salutary reminder to pay attention to the text, to be suspicious of multiplying contemporary agendas, and to remember that God has disclosed himself *in history* — not least in the incarnation and in the resurrection events, which claim to take place *in history.* The Harrisville thesis is weak, however, in that the history that many liberal forms of historical criticism reconstruct is so destructive of what the historical narrative of Scripture actually says that the faith that Harrisville wants to encourage cannot have as its object what Scripture says. Scripture's authority has been leached out. To put this another way, the faith that Harrisville (and Crump, too) enjoins is not grounded in Scripture and its authority but is held out as a *desideratum* despite the critical reconstructions of Scripture that have undermined its objects.

No less important for our purposes are the volumes and essays that espouse supernatural Christian religion, and that want Scripture itself to be authoritative in *some* sense, but that disavow traditional formulations of Scripture. They are of many kinds. Some of the writers of these books (though certainly not all) identify themselves with the evangelical heritage from which they spring, a heritage whose doctrine of Scripture, they aver, badly needs correcting. Some of these authors offer thoughtful proposals; others belong to the "angry young man" heritage (irrespective of the ages of these authors!).

A volume by Kenton L. Sparks, *God's Word in Human Words: An Evangelical Appropriation of Critical Biblical Scholarship,*[24] and another by Peter E. Enns,

24. Grand Rapids: Baker, 2008.

Inspiration and Incarnation: Evangelicals and the Problem of the Old Testament,[25] both slightly angry and slightly self-righteous, have been admirably discussed in many reviews and in a fine book edited by James K. Hoffmeier and Dennis R. Magary, *Do Historical Matters Matter to Faith? A Critical Appraisal of Modern and Postmodern Approaches to Scripture.*[26] The volume by Sparks raises many questions about how to think of God as the author of Scripture and of Scripture's human authors, but his discussion lacks the rigorous theological reflection displayed by Henri Blocher in his essay in this volume (about which more will be said below).[27] The volume by Enns engages in prolonged parallels between the inspiration of Scripture and the incarnation of Christ, and these and related matters have been discussed at length.[28] One of the things that characterize both of these books, and more recent ones that have flowed from the same authors, is that both Sparks and Enns seem to be more certain of what version of inspiration and authority they are against than of what version of inspiration and authority they are actually advocating. It is difficult to delineate in their writings a stable positive construction.

Rather sophisticated is the thesis of Craig D. Allert,[29] who argues that for the early Christians "Scripture" was not coterminous with "canon" — that many more books were thought to be Scripture and "inspired" that were not listed as canonical. The notion of canon, Allert insists, was a late development. But Charles Hill, whom we shall mention later, convincingly demonstrates that canonical thought is very early. Yes, Allert is right to say that "inspiration" is occasionally used more loosely than it is by, say, the Reformers, and can refer to more books than the canonical ones. The sermons of Chrysostom, for instance, are said by some to be inspired. But the Fathers claim freedom from error only for the canonical books. In any case, what is meant by "canon" is something to which we shall return.

Although he does not disavow the importance of exegesis, Joel Green[30] adopts a kind of reader-response hermeneutic. The "model reader" (shades of Umberto Eco) is one whose theological location lies within the church, the historic and global church. The community reads the Bible as God-revealing Scripture, and is thereby shaped by it. When one looks around at what the church,

25. Grand Rapids: Baker, 2005.

26. Wheaton: Crossway, 2012. Full disclosure: I too have written a lengthy review of Enns: cf. D. A. Carson, "Three More Books on the Bible: A Critical Review," *TrinJ* 27 (2006): 1-62.

27. "God and the Scripture Writers: The Question of Double Authorship" (ch. 17 in this collection).

28. Cf. the review article by Carson, "Three More Books on the Bible: A Critical Review," and especially the lengthy exchange between G. K. Beale and Peter Enns, *JETS* 49 (2006): 287-312, 313-26.

29. *A High View of Scripture? The Authority of the Bible and the Formation of the New Testament Canon* (Grand Rapids: Baker, 2007).

30. *Seized by Truth: Reading the Bible as Scripture* (Nashville: Abingdon, 2007).

however, whether local or global, is allegedly "finding" to be the central message of Scripture, one could easily conclude that there is little hope for renewal along such lines: the agendas of the churches soon domesticate hearing the Word of God.[31] Meaning is being abstracted a little too far from the intentions of the authors (human and divine) as disclosed in the text.

Yet something must be put in place to enable us to reflect helpfully on the relationship between the believing interpreter and the believing community. For a start, one must recognize that there can be disadvantages as well as advantages to communal handling of Scripture. One thinks, for instance, of Jeremiah 8:8: "How can you say, 'We are the wise, for we have the law of the LORD,' when actually the lying pen of the scribes has handled it falsely?" Moreover, those who champion communal interpretation do not obviously check out and submit to community thought in a way that others do not. Does, say, a Joel Green or a Stanley Grenz, who emphasize the importance of community in the interpretive process, actually reflect a community or submit his findings to a community in a way in which, say, Millard Erickson or I. Howard Marshall does not? Most theologians and biblical scholars recognize that all interpretation of Scripture is in some measure shaped by the interpreters, including the interpretive communities from which they spring. Nevertheless to suspend all the weight of meaning from this solitary insight would mean it is impossible for different individuals and communities to study common texts with a view, so far as it is possible, to come to a meeting of minds as to what those texts say.

Consider a telling example: When the *Africa Bible Commentary* was published a few years ago,[32] its publishers and promoters kept insisting that at last we could hear the voices of Christians living in another continent reaching their own conclusions as to the meaning of Scripture, thus contributing to worldwide mutual Christian enrichment. In some measure, of course, this is wonderfully true. The *Africa Bible Commentary* devotes more attention than do Western one-volume Bible commentaries to exorcism, to questions surrounding ancestor worship, and to challenging the "health, wealth, and prosperity gospel." But what is most striking about the volume is that 90 or 95 percent of its content could be read and understood by, and could have been written by, believing Christians in virtually any part of the world. That should not surprise us: after all, we do share the same Book. Before we become too enamored with a narrowly conceived reader-response hermeneutic, we must ask ourselves in what ways the *Africa Bible Commentary* is *not* innovative, and *shouldn't* be. An essay by Richard Lints helps us with these questions.[33]

31. E.g., Cynthia Briggs Kittredge, Ellen Bradshaw Aitken, and Jonathan A. Draper, eds., *The Bible in the Public Square: Reading the Signs of the Times* (Minneapolis: Fortress, 2008).

32. Ed. Tokunboh Adeyomo (Grand Rapids: Zondervan, 2006).

33. "To Whom Does the Text Belong? Communities of Interpretation and the Interpretation of Communities" (ch. 29 in this collection).

Harder to classify is one of the recent books by Christian Smith, *The Bible Made Impossible: Why Biblicism Is Not a Truly Evangelical Reading of Scripture.*[34] The work has convinced some of us that Smith is a better sociologist than he is a theologian.[35] But sometimes the person who is trying to modify a longstanding position on Scripture is not a sociologist but a mature theologian: we might mention A. T. B. McGowan, *The Divine Spiration of Scripture: Challenging Evangelical Perspectives.*[36] In the central section of the book, McGowan wants to redefine and thus correct evangelical use of a number of words, including inspiration (he prefers spiration), illumination (he prefers recognition), perspicuity (he prefers comprehension), and inerrancy (he prefers a carefully qualified infallibility) — with more dangers afoot than he seems to realize. Doubtless the most informed and penetrating review is that of John Frame, available online.[37]

Or consider the 2005 volume by N. T. Wright, *The Last Word.*[38] The subtitle in the American edition is *Beyond the Bible Wars to a New Understanding of the Authority of Scripture.* While he ably defends, say, the resurrection of Jesus, and treats the Jesus Seminar with the dismissal it deserves, Wright nevertheless argues that categories like "truth" which demand an antithetical response of either belief or unbelief, are rendered unimportant if we understand the context of Scripture. He cannot possibly be rejecting all antitheses, as he himself constructs an antithesis elsewhere (as we shall see). The context of Scripture, he avers, is the authority of God. He argues that "the phrase 'authority of Scripture' can make Christian sense only if it is shorthand for 'the authority of the triune God, exercised somehow *through* Scripture.'"[39] Read very sympathetically, the assertion could almost be applauded. Nevertheless the word "somehow" niggles a little, and "through" is wonderfully ambiguous.[40] How does God exercise his authority *through* the Bible? Wright answers that God's authority is "his sover-

34. Grand Rapids: Brazos, 2011.

35. There are penetrating reviews by Kevin DeYoung on his blog (http://www.thegospelcoalition.org/blogs/kevindeyoung/2011/08/02/christian-smith-makes-the-bible-impossible/), and by Robert Gundry in *B&C* 17, no. 5 (Sept./Oct. 2011): 9-11.

36. Nottingham: Inter-Varsity, 2007. In the American version, the title is *The Divine Authenticity of Scripture: Retrieving an Evangelical Heritage,* in which "Spiration" is changed to "Authenticity," and the subtitle is no longer challenging anything but claiming to reproduce what evangelicals have apparently abandoned (Downers Grove, IL: InterVarsity, 2007), which has the advantage of being simultaneously untrue and good marketing.

37. http://www.frame-poythress.org/review-of-andrew-mcgowans-the-divine-spiration-of-scripture/.

38. N. T. Wright, *The Last Word* (San Francisco: HarperSanFrancisco, 2005). In the United Kingdom the book was titled *Scripture and the Authority of God* (London: SPCK, 2004).

39. Wright, *The Last Word,* 23.

40. See the careful review article by John Frame, "N. T. Wright and the Authority of Scripture," in *Did God Really Say? Affirming the Truthfulness and Trustworthiness of Scripture,* ed. David B. Garner (Phillipsburg, NJ: P&R, 2012), 107-27.

eign power accomplishing the renewal of all creation."[41] Scripture, then, is the narrative of that authority, of that power. And then Wright's antithesis: Scripture is not to be interpreted as a "list of rules" or a "compendium of true doctrines," even though rules and doctrines are found in it.[42] Thus he has managed to relegate "rules" (law? ethics?) and doctrines to at best subsidiary importance — subsidiary, that is, to narrative. Inerrancy he has occasionally dismissed as an American aberration — a conclusion that can be sustained only by the most remarkable ignorance of the history of the doctrine. Instead of adding the importance of the Bible's storyline to older emphases on law, truth, confessionalism, and the like, it trumps everything, and establishes an antithesis that leaves young pilgrims happy to avoid technical discussions of the nature of Scripture that have occupied the church for two millennia, and feeling quite superior as they do so.

And so we could continue describing this book or that. Yet it may be helpful to pause and offer a generalizing impression. It is fair to say that although there are many fine voices espousing a traditional view of Scripture (more on them in a moment), and although there are many competent scholars who ably defend a more skeptical tradition, one of the most striking tendencies is the rising number of students and scholars who seek to blur as many distinctions as possible. They publicly adhere to a high view of Scripture, but are entirely comfortable with multiple Isaiahs, a very late date for Deuteronomy, and the deuterocanonical status of the Pastorals. They may even begrudgingly adhere to that bugaboo "inerrancy" (especially if the institutions where they teach require it), while arguing that the label is late, unfortunate, unnecessary, and American. One thinks, for example, of several of the writers in the book edited by Christopher M. Hays and Christopher B. Ansberry, *Evangelical Faith and the Challenge of Historical Criticism,* who espouse a form of historical criticism that is happy to get rid of Adam and Eve and the fall, and very loose on whether the exodus took place, and comfortable with great swaths of pseudonymity and with Jesus making predictions that are erroneous. Not to buy into these conclusions means (we are told) that evangelicals are not using historical criticism honestly.[43] For some authors, the move away from the traditional understanding of the nature of Scripture is accompanied by, or even generated by, the move to postconservatism.[44] It is easy to sympathize with Greg Beale's observations on *The Erosion of Inerrancy in Evangelicalism.*[45]

41. Frame, "N. T. Wright and the Authority of Scripture," 29.

42. Frame, "N. T. Wright and the Authority of Scripture," 25-26.

43. London: SPCK, 2013. See the penetrating review article by Robert W. Yarbrough in *Them* 39 (2014): 37-52. Similar proposals to those of Hays-Ansberry are not uncommon: e.g., Siegfried Zimmer, *Schadet die Bibelwissenschaft dem Glauben? Klärung eines Konflikts* (Göttingen: Vandenhoeck & Ruprecht, 2012).

44. See Osvaldo Padilla, "Scripture and Authority in Postconservative Evangelical Theologians" (ch. 21 in this collection).

45. Wheaton: Crossway, 2008. See also J. Merrick and Stephen M. Garrett, eds., *Five Views*

Before leaving this opening survey, it would be a mistake to ignore some of the books and essays that have in recent years attempted to defend a traditional view of Scripture and its authority, sometimes in pretty traditional ways, sometimes by carefully reviewing what Christian thinkers have said in the past, and sometimes by careful interaction with the most recent discussions. More such works will be introduced in the pages that follow, but a smattering must be noticed here.

Some approaches are broadly traditional. One thinks of the book edited by Steven B. Cowan and Terry L. Wilder, *In Defense of the Bible: A Comprehensive Apologetic for the Authority of Scripture,*[46] cast at a semi-popular level. Perhaps the volume that has the greatest potential for serving as the heir and successor to *"Fundamentalism" and the Word of God,* the influential paperback of J. I. Packer fifty years ago,[47] is the compelling and readable little book by Kevin DeYoung, *Taking God at His Word.*[48] Similarly cast at the popular level is Sinclair B. Ferguson, *From the Mouth of God: Trusting, Reading and Applying the Bible.*[49]

Another group of books cuts fresher paths. Though they agree in their support of the trustworthiness of Scripture that dominates the church across the centuries, these books, in smaller or larger ways, go about their task with an enviable freshness of purpose or tone. In the realm of systematic theology, pride of place goes to John Frame, *The Doctrine of the Word of God,*[50] part of the series A Theology of Lordship. The essays edited by Paul Helm and Carl Trueman[51] ask, among other things, what it means for God to be trustworthy, and then probe the ways in which the Bible fits into such categories. Many of the essays are characterized by fresh and rigorous thought. Rather unusually, the book provides two stimulating responses (by Colin Gunton and Francis Watson). Similarly, the book edited by David B. Garner[52] provides only seven essays, but all of them address issues or writers that control much of the current discussion. Equally contemporary is the engaging book by Craig L. Blomberg, *Can We Still Believe the Bible? An Evangelical Engagement with Contemporary Questions.*[53] Several chapters engage primarily with Bart Ehrman (on whom more, below). Blomberg's notes are rich and invaluable (though it is more than a little frustrating to find them

---

on Biblical Inerrancy (Grand Rapids: Zondervan, 2013) for a remarkable spread of opinions among those who would call themselves evangelicals.

46. Nashville: B&H, 2013.

47. Grand Rapids: Eerdmans, 1958.

48. Wheaton, IL: Crossway, 2014.

49. Edinburgh: Banner of Truth, 2014.

50. Phillipsburg, NJ: P&R, 2010.

51. *The Trustworthiness of God: Perspectives on the Nature of Scripture* (Leicester: Apollos; Grand Rapids: Eerdmans, 2002).

52. Garner, ed., *Did God Really Say?*

53. Grand Rapids: Brazos, 2014.

collected as endnotes in double columns). I have already briefly mentioned the lengthy volume edited by James Hoffmeier and Dennis Magary.[54] The volume by John Douglas Morrison, *Has God Said? Scripture, the Word of God, and the Crisis of Theological Authority,*[55] is both stimulating and sometimes frustrating: stimulating, because Morrison paints on a large canvas and interacts with substantial numbers of scholars, and frustrating for the same reason: Morrison's own proposal, integrating as it does some of Einstein, some of Torrance, and some of Calvin, elicits praise for parts of the creative integration, and frank uncertainty over the credibility of some of the leaps. Shorter but more polished is the book by Timothy Ward.[56] Reflecting on the frequency with which Scripture connects God and his words, Ward writes:

> God has *invested* himself in words, or we could say that God has so *identified* himself with his words that whatever someone does to God's words (whether it is to obey or disobey) they do directly to God himself. Obvious though this may seem, in the following pages we shall discover that its implications are enormous. When they are overlooked, it is always detrimental to our understanding of Scripture. To ask why or how this can be, that words and persons can be so intimately related, is to enter deep theological and philosophical waters. . . .[57]

Another creative thinker is Vern S. Poythress, who has contributed two important books on this subject: *Inerrancy and Worldview: Answering Modern Challenges to the Bible,*[58] and *Inerrancy and the Gospels: A God-Centered Approach to the Challenges of Harmonization.*[59] Poythress invites us, courteously but firmly, to think theologically and worldviewishly, as well as historically, when we give ourselves to try to articulate the nature of Scripture. Two further volumes sustain this commitment to worldviewish thinking. Written from a confessional Lutheran perspective, one volume attempts to anchor the authority of Scripture in the transforming gospel of Christ.[60] Another seeks to repristinate the influence of the six-volume work of Carl F. H. Henry.[61] But perhaps the most stimulating and

54. Hoffmeier and Magary, eds., *Do Historical Matters Matter to Faith?*

55. Eugene, OR: Pickwick, 2006.

56. Timothy Ward, *Words of Life: Scripture as the Living and Active Word of God* (Nottingham: Inter-Varsity; Downers Grove, IL: InterVarsity, 2009).

57. Ward, *Words of Life,* 27.

58. Wheaton, IL: Crossway, 2012.

59. Wheaton, IL: Crossway, 2012.

60. Peter H. Nafzger, *"These Are Written": Toward a Cruciform Theology of Scripture* (Eugene, OR: Pickwick, 2013).

61. Gregory Alan Thornbury, *Recovering Classic Evangelicalism: Applying the Wisdom and Vision of Carl F. H. Henry* (Wheaton: Crossway, 2013) — referring, of course, to Henry's *God,*

creative of the recent books on Scripture is a volume by Andrew G. Shead, *A Mouth Full of Fire: The Word of God in the words of Jeremiah.*[62] By a careful and cogent reading of one biblical book (a form of biblical theology), combined with a judicious use of speech-act theory, Shead contributes rigorous theological construction that is exegetically based in one biblical book. Perhaps this is the place to mention the more popular work of Tim Meadowcroft, *The Message of the Word of God.*[63] Instead of working out the nature of Scripture in some sort of systematic fashion, Meadowcroft expounds twenty passages that unfold important things about the Word of God — e.g., the glory of God made known (Psalm 19), the Word made flesh (John 1:1-14), and so forth.

Several books focus on what former generations of thinkers have said about Scripture. This is important because, as the next section of this paper observes, various revisionist readings of the history of the doctrine of Scripture have sought to marginalize those with a high view of Scripture by insisting that their views are late and therefore erroneous. The massive volume edited by Peter A. Lillback and Richard B. Gaffin Jr., pulls together into one place the *Essential Writings on the Doctrine of Scripture from the Reformation to Today* (as the subtitle puts it).[64] The volume includes essays and excerpts from Luther, Calvin, Monod, Owen, Turretin, Gaussen, Edwards, Spurgeon, Hengstenberg, Machen, and more — including some of the debates of the past half-century. Conceptually similar but much more modest is the book by Stephen J. Nichols and Eric T. Brandt.[65] More historically focused yet is Gaffin's exposition of the thought of Abraham Kuyper and Herman Bavinck.[66]

Finally, a little hunting turns up many essays that are either wise and admirable summaries of important aspects of what the Bible is (e.g., Carl Trueman on "The Sufficiency of Scripture"[67]) or provocative pieces that stimulate fresh thought (e.g., Roland Deines, "Did Matthew Know He was Writing Scripture?"[68]).

We turn, then, from this survey of the diversity of recent books and essays on the Bible and its authority, and focus attention on a handful of storm centers.

Revelation and Authority, 6 vols. (Waco, TX: Word, 1976-83; repr., Wheaton, IL: Crossway, 1999).

62. NSBT 29; Nottingham: Apollos; Downers Grove, IL: InterVarsity, 2012.

63. BST; Nottingham: Apollos; Downers Grove, IL: InterVarsity 2011.

64. *Thy Word Is Still Truth: Essential Writings on the Doctrine of Scripture from the Reformation to Today* (Phillipsburg, NJ: P&R, 2013).

65. *Ancient Word, Changing Worlds: The Doctrine of Scripture in a Modern Age* (Wheaton, IL: Crossway, 2009).

66. Richard B. Gaffin Jr., *God's Word in Servant-Form: Abraham Kuyper and Herman Bavinck on the Doctrine of Scripture* (Jackson, MS: Reformed Academic Press, 2008).

67. http://9marks.org/article/journalsufficiency-scripture/.

68. *EurJTh* Part 1: 22, no. 2 (2013): 101-9; Part 2: 23, no. 1 (2014): 3-9.

Historical Revisionism That Seeks to Become the New Orthodoxy

In the last half-century, many periods in the history of the church have been churned over afresh to demonstrate either that (a) historical criticism goes back a lot farther than many people think, or, more commonly, that (b) orthodoxy, and especially an orthodox view of Scripture, are rather late developments, so they can, and perhaps should, be held rather lightly. A fine example of the former view — that biblical criticism goes back a lot farther than many people think — is found in John Barton's *The Nature of Biblical Criticism.*[69] In his fifth chapter, Barton argues that biblical criticism finds its roots not in the Enlightenment, but earlier, in the Reformation, better in the Renaissance, and even in the ancient premodern world. In part, he is able to sustain his thesis by denying that the historical-critical method is central to biblical criticism, opting instead for semantics and textual understanding. Failing to recognize how central the notion of revelation was to the patristic fathers and the Reformers alike, Barton does not see that their embrace of the authority of Scripture was grounded in their perception of the truthfulness of that revelation. Sometimes Barton pitches his argument as an either/or: for example, *either* the Enlightenment *or* the Renaissance. But few of the thinkers of the Renaissance, indeed few in the early Enlightenment, and none of the Reformers, entertained the kind of skepticism needed for the rise of modern biblical criticism. Such criticism becomes strong as the Enlightenment progresses, along the way adopting Troeltschian assumptions.

But we shall leave Barton to one side, and focus on the much more prevalent result of contemporary research into the history of the church, viz., that orthodoxy, and especially an orthodox view of Scripture, is a rather late development, so it can, and perhaps should, be held rather loosely.

(1) At least four interlocking arguments, drawn from a revisionist history of the early church, are commonly advanced to undermine confidence in the Christian Scriptures.

(a) Bart Ehrman has been at the forefront of those who argue that during the first few centuries of the Christian era the orthodox themselves were primarily responsible for the corruption of their own Scriptures.[70] The most telling response lies in the series of essays in the book edited by Daniel B.

69. Louisville: Westminster John Knox, 2007.

70. *The Orthodox Corruption of Scripture: The Effect of the Early Christological Controversies on the Text of the New Testament,* 2nd edition (New York: Oxford University Press, 2011). Ehrman is, of course, a highly skilled text critic, and when he is not on one of his crusades to destroy Christianity, his work is a model of text-critical scholarship. For an up-to-date assessment of contemporary text criticism of the NT, see, *inter alia,* Bart D. Ehrman and Michael W. Holmes, eds., *The Text of the New Testament in Contemporary Research: Essays on the* Status Quaestionis, NTTSD, 2nd edition (Leiden: Brill, 2013).

Wallace.[71] Most recently, after assuming that the New Testament books commonly thought to be deuterocanonical are in fact pseudonymous, Ehrman strenuously argues that this was a self-conscious deceit and thus a moral failure.[72] Ehrman labels about half the canonical New Testament books "counterfeit" (viz. Ephesians, Colossians, 2 Thessalonians, the Pastorals, James, 1 Peter, 2 Peter, Jude, 1 John, Acts, and Hebrews). The latter two, Acts and Hebrews, he calls "non-pseudepigraphic forgeries" because Acts, though anonymous, incorporates "we" sections in the book to establish verisimilitude designed, falsely, to validate the authority of the record, while Hebrews, also anonymous, deploys a closing paragraph that was taken to imply, quite wrongly, Pauline authorship. At no point in this 628-page book does Ehrman engage critics who deny that these books are forgeries; indeed, one supportive reviewer, J. K. Elliott, says that Ehrman "rightly refuses to engage with such ostriches."[73] Ehrman's sole concern is to insist that pseudepigraphy was *meant* to deceive, and therefore could not be innocuous and benign. For myself, I should say that I agree with that conclusion, but disagree that pseudonymity is found in the NT.[74]

(b) A vociferous handful of scholars insists that originally Christianity was diverse and tolerant, and that other "scriptures," other gospels and "acts" and apocalypses, were once considered no less authoritative than the books that make up our New Testament. It was the narrow intolerance and bigotry of the "orthodox" who, as they grew stronger, shut down this delightful diversity.[75] It is well worth reading the robust response of Craig Evans[76] and the carefully understated volume by C. E. Hill.[77] Transparently this reconstruction of a very broad or open early Christianity is tied to the old thesis of Walter Bauer,[78] a thesis that has been hit on the head repeatedly, like the beast that receives a "fatal wound" in Revela-

71. *Revisiting the Corruption of the New Testament: Manuscript, Patristic, and Apocryphal Evidence* (Grand Rapids: Kregel, 2011).

72. Bart D. Ehrman, *Forgery and Counter Forgery: The Use of Literary Deceit in Early Christian Polemics* (New York: Oxford University Press, 2013).

73. *ExpT* 125 (2013): 74.

74. Cf. D. A. Carson, "Pseudonymity and Pseudepigraphy," *Dictionary of New Testament Background,* ed. Craig A. Evans and Stanley E. Porter (Downers Grove, IL: InterVarsity, 2000), 856-64.

75. See, for example, Bart D. Ehrman, *Lost Scriptures: Books That Did Not Make It into the New Testament* (New York: Oxford University Press, 2003); Elaine Pagels, *Beyond Belief: The Secret Gospel of Thomas* (New York: Random House, 2003).

76. Craig A. Evans, *Fabricating Jesus: How Modern Scholars Distort the Gospels* (Downers Grove, IL: InterVarsity, 2006).

77. *Who Chose the Gospels? Probing the Great Gospel Conspiracy* (New York: Oxford University Press, 2010).

78. *Orthodoxy and Heresy in Earliest Christianity* (Philadelphia: Fortress, 1971 [German orig. 1934]).

tion 13 and nevertheless keeps coming back, resurfacing again and again.[79] The essay by Simon Gathercole in this collection is extraordinarily helpful.[80]

(c) Many have argued that the early fathers were sloppy with their texts and sloppier with their exegesis, demonstrating complete freedom from any notion that might be dubbed "inerrancy." The riposte of James Kugel, recently retired from Harvard, is much more in line with reality. He demonstrates that all ancient readers of Scripture operated with four assumptions. The fourth is that the Bible is a divinely given book in which God speaks directly through its pages. Hence (third assumption) the Bible has no mistakes or contradictions, so that when *apparent* difficulties are uncovered, they must be explained away by clever exegesis; and, indeed, the Bible's meanings must be dug out by various interpretive strategies (second assumption).[81] This is not to say that the church fathers got everything right; it is to say that they operated with a very high view of Scripture, with what would today be called an inerrantist view of Scripture.[82]

(d) More broadly, an array of writers has argued that patristic and gnostic disputes over interpretation, and the lack of systematic reflection on the doctrine of Scripture, not to mention the delay in defining the New Testament canon, demonstrate that a high view of Scripture is a late Protestant preoccupation. Here the essay by C. E. Hill brings needed clarity. By carefully working through the patristic period he demonstrates "the foundational role which Scripture played in Christian intellectual and spiritual life, even from the earliest times and even in the midst of conflict."[83] The Fathers thought of Scripture "as divine, as God's self-attesting word, and as consistent, harmonious, or inerrant."[84] Along the way he explores the rise of the New Testament canon, and the relations between Scripture and the *analogia fidei.* In the words of Augustine, "Let us treat scripture like scripture: like God speaking."[85]

(2) One of the most confusing areas of historical debate concerns the doctrine of accommodation. The language of accommodation is used in every extended period of the church's life. This can scarcely be surprising, for every generation must wrestle with what it means to confess that the God who inhabits eternity

79. Cf. I. Howard Marshall, "Orthodoxy and Heresy in Earlier Christianity," *Them* 2, no. 1 (1976): 5-14; Paul Trebilco, "Christian Communities in Western Asia Minor into the Early Second Century: Ignatius and Others as Witnesses Against Bauer," *JETS* 49 (2006): 17-44.

80. "*E pluribus unum?* Apostolic Unity and Early Christian Literature."

81. James L. Kugel, *How to Read the Bible: A Guide to Scripture, Then and Now* (New York: Free Press, 2007).

82. See Michael Graves, *The Inspiration and Interpretation of Scripture: What the Early Church Can Teach Us* (Grand Rapids: Eerdmans, 2014).

83. " 'The Truth above All Demonstration': Scripture in the Patristic Period to Augustine" (ch. 2 in this collection).

84. " 'The Truth above All Demonstration'," 44, below.

85. Sermon 162C.15.

and who has no vocal cords speaks through the words of human beings who inhabit time, speak in various languages, and communicate with sounds and letters. The strength of Glenn S. Sunshine's essay[86] is that it carefully analyzes the shape of accommodation in the patristic period, the medieval scholastic period, the Reformation, and the later rationalist period, and shows that only in the latter period did accommodation extend to the notion of God accommodating himself to allow errors, theological mistakes, and the like. To read this second and radically different understanding of accommodation back into the understanding of accommodation before the rationalist period is to perpetuate a major historical blunder. It is to claim that the contemporary notion of accommodation, one that anachronistically insists that errors and moral failures are a necessary component of Scripture owing to the necessity of divine accommodation to human limitations and failures, has always been the church's position, when transparently earlier understanding of accommodation allowed no such lapses. Moreover, the modern view of accommodation presupposes that error is essential to being human. It is difficult to adopt that assumption when one contemplates the incarnation.

(3) The need to understand a little better the relation between natural philosophy (what we would today call "science") and Scripture in the seventeenth century becomes obvious when we recall how often the church is set up as ignorant, authoritarian, and anti-science. Historians of science are aware that the situation was a little more complicated than the popular press makes it out to be.[87] By working through the contributions of Kepler, Copernicus, and Galileo, and especially the responses to them by many informed Christians, including John Ray of Trinity College, Cambridge, Rodney Stiling demonstrates how seriously Christians at the time wrestled with the phenomenological language used in Scripture.[88]

(4) Several other periods of church history attract the attention of those who are convinced that a truly high view of Scripture is a very late development. Perhaps the Reformers limited the authority of Scripture to matters of "faith and practice," excluding other matters; perhaps Jakob Spener and the German Pietists had nothing vested in an infallible Scripture; perhaps Wesley's quadrilateral demonstrates that for Wesleyans Scripture does not have quite the same claim to truth that it enjoys among the followers of Calvin. In each case, excellent studies have worked through the primary material to recognize how tendentious such arguments are.[89]

86. "Accommodation Historically Considered" (ch. 8 in this collection).

87. Cf. Denis Alexander, *Rebuilding the Matrix: Science and Faith in the 21st Century* (Oxford: Lion, 2001).

88. "Natural Philosophy and Biblical Authority in the Seventeenth Century" (ch. 4 in this collection).

89. See chs. 3, 5, and 6 of this collection: respectively, Robert Kolb, "The Bible in the Reformation and Protestant Orthodoxy"; John D. Woodbridge, "German Pietism and Scriptural Authority: The Question of Biblical Inerrancy"; and Thomas H. McCall, "Wesleyan Theology and the Authority of Scripture: Historic Affirmations and Some Contemporary Issues."

(5) Bebbington argues that British evangelicals held unformed views on biblical authority as late as the 1850s, and that Robert Haldane concocted inerrancy and brought it to Geneva where it was developed and promulgated by Gaussen.[90] But we have already glimpsed how inerrancy has been a primary belief of Christians since the early church. It was not constructed a mere 250 years ago. More pointedly, in his hugely influential work on Scripture (1841), Gaussen himself leans on French authorities to defend his views on biblical infallibility.[91] Gaussen insists that the biblical books "contain no errors; all their writings are inspired of God," the Spirit himself guiding the human writers "even in the employment of the words they were to use, and to preserve them from all error, as well as from every omission."[92] Kenneth J. Stewart's published dissertation on the Swiss *Réveil* draws similar conclusions about Gaussen.[93] A check on the men who delivered the prestigious Bampton Lectures at the University of Oxford during this period shows them to be staunch inerrantists.[94] More telling yet, Samuel Taylor Coleridge, intending to dismantle what he perceived to be the dominant views on the doctrine of Scripture in his day, wrote a revealing book with the title *Confessions of an Inquiring Spirit,* published posthumously in 1841.[95] Setting forth the need for his work, Coleridge asserts that he has listened to clergy from every denomination, Calvinist and Arminian, Quaker and Methodist and Established Church, and everywhere "their principal arguments were grounded on the position, that the Bible throughout was dictated by Omniscience, and therefore in all its parts infallibly true and obligatory, and that the men, whose names are prefixed to the several books or chapters, were in fact but as different pens in the hand of one and the same Writer, and the words the words of God himself."[96] And so, Coleridge concludes, "What could I say to this? — I could neither deny the fact, nor evade the conclusion, — namely, that such is at present the popular belief."[97] Small wonder, then, this book by Coleridge stirred up a hornet's nest of controversy on both sides of the Atlantic. What is certainly

90. David W. Bebbington, *Evangelicalism in Modern Britain: A History from the 1730s to the 1980s* (London: Allen & Unwin, 1989), especially ch. 3, and developed in more recent publications.

91. Louis Gaussen, *Theopneusty, or the Plenary Inspiration of the Holy Scriptures,* trans. Edward Kirk (New York: John S. Taylor and Co, 1845 [1841]).

92. Gaussen, *Theopneusty,* 44-45.

93. *Restoring the Reformation: British Evangelicalism and the Francophone* Réveil *1815-1849* (Milton Keynes, UK: Paternoster, 2006).

94. Cf. John D. Woodbridge, *Biblical Authority: Infallibility and Inerrancy in the Christian Tradition* (Grand Rapids: Zondervan, 1982), 143-45.

95. Samuel Taylor Coleridge, *Confessions of an Inquiring Spirit* (Boston: James Monroe and Company).

96. Coleridge, *Confessions of an Inquiring Spirit,* 79-80. Cited by Woodbridge, *Biblical Authority,* 122.

97. Coleridge, *Confessions of an Inquiring Spirit,* 81.

clear is that Bebbington is wrong to say that British views on Scripture were inchoate until the rise of the influence of Haldane and Gaussen. It is past time that scholars stopped trying to knock out the word "inerrancy" on the ground that it is a late addition to the discussion. Doubtless it would be unprofitable to speculate why this "narrative" is constantly shored up when the hard evidence is so consistently against it.

(6) A number of scholars have tried to position Charles Hodge and Benjamin B. Warfield of Old Princeton as the innovators in the field — innovators so much influenced by Thomas Reid and Scottish Common Sense Realism that they introduced notions like inerrancy that had not been part of the church's heritage before their time. Doubtless the most influential book defending that thesis was written by Jack B. Rogers and Donald K. McKim.[98] They relied overly much on the work of Ernest Sandeen, who argued for a trajectory toward greater confidence in inerrancy, passing from Archibald Alexander through Charles Hodge to Benjamin Warfield.[99] It appears that the formidable historian George Marsden supports the view that Hodge and Warfield were so influenced by Thomas Reid and his Scottish Common Sense Realism that their high view of Scripture became paradigm-dependent on Common Sense — such that not only were they innovating, but now that Common Sense commands little respect among those concerned with epistemology, the Old Princeton stance on Scripture is similarly weakened.[100] Today, however, most recognize that the thesis of Sandeen has been dismantled.[101] Woodbridge has demonstrated that Common Sense influenced Warfield's opponents as much as Warfield; that although both Hodge and Warfield leaned on Common Sense, neither was uncritical of the movement and carefully distanced themselves from it, not least when discussing the nature of Scripture; that many writers in the nineteenth century other than Hodge and Warfield shared their view; and that in any case their high view of Scripture is remarkably paradigm-independent across the history of the church, not unlike some other major doctrines (e.g., the deity of Christ, and Jesus' resurrection from the dead).[102] Now the careful essay by Bradley N. Seeman, who has worked through the Princeton archives, brings additional clarity.[103]

98. *The Authority and Interpretation of the Bible: An Historical Approach* (San Francisco: Harper & Row, 1979).

99. *The Roots of Fundamentalism: British and American Millenarianism, 1800-1930* (Grand Rapids: Baker, 1978).

100. *Fundamentalism and American Culture: The Shaping of Twentieth Century Evangelicalism 1870-1925* (New York: Oxford University Press, 1980).

101. John D. Woodbridge and Randall H. Balmer, "The Princetonians and Biblical Authority: An Assessment of the Ernest Sandeen Proposal," in *Scripture and Truth,* ed. D. A. Carson and John D. Woodbridge (Grand Rapids: Zondervan, 1983), 251-79.

102. Woodbridge, *Biblical Authority.*

103. "The 'Old Princetonians' on Biblical Authority" (ch. 7 in this collection).

(7) To bring history a little closer to our own time, scholars continue to work through the implications of Vatican II for Roman Catholic understanding of Scripture. Three decades after Vatican II, the *Catechism of the Catholic Church* asserts, in line with pre–Vatican II stances, that the biblical documents teach truth for salvation "firmly, faithfully, and without error."[104] This *Catechism* is in fact citing Vatican II's *Dei Verbum* 11, which more fully reads: ". . . we must acknowledge that the books of Scripture firmly, faithfully, and without error teach that truth which God, *for the sake of our salvation,* wished to see confided to the Sacred Scriptures" (italics added).[105] The italicized words have generated a certain amount of discussion among Catholic authorities. The inerrantists focus on the words "firmly, faithfully, and without error"; the non-inerrantists focus on "for the sake of our salvation," and insist *Dei Verbum* allows for errors of history and perhaps other domains, but affirms inerrancy solely in matters pertaining to salvation. The most recent treatment of Scripture by the Pontifical Biblical Commission,[106] though it is in many respects a remarkably conservative document, apparently betrays this ongoing intramural debate (though it does not deploy terms like inerrancy and non-inerrancy) when it approaches what presents itself as history in the Old Testament and decides it is not: e.g., "we must understand the entire event of the conquest as a sort of symbol, analogous to what we read in certain gospel parables of judgment."[107] This is a kind of *Sachkritik:* we find it difficult to make sense of the ostensible history, so declare it to be a different genre and thereby domesticate it. It is difficult to imagine pre–Vatican II documents making the same move.[108] Anthony N. S. Lane argues convincingly that Vatican II moved the Roman Catholic Church from a largely formal acknowledgment of the human authorship of Scripture to a stance that makes human authorship more significant. That shift has brought Catholic scholars increasingly into line with mainline Protestant liberal scholarship. Such a shift would surely have doctrinal implications for Protestants, but apparently has fewer for Catholicism, since for Catholics the ultimate teaching authority is not Scripture but the teaching of the church.[109]

On the Protestant side, there has been a renewed interest in the view of Scripture found in the voluminous writings of Karl Barth. Probably no one has been so ardent and so articulate a defender of Barth's view of Scripture as John

104. (New York: Doubleday, 1995), 107.

105. Cf. similarly Gregg R. Allison, *Roman Catholic Theology and Practice: An Evangelical Assessment* (Wheaton, IL: Crossway, 2014), 96.

106. Pontifical Biblical Commission, *The Inspiration and Truth of Sacred Scripture* (Collegeville, MN: Liturgical Press, 2014).

107. Pontifical Biblical Commission, *The Inspiration and Truth of Sacred Scripture,* 147.

108. E.g., the Council of Trent, Leo XIII's encyclical *Providentissimus Deus,* and Pius XII's encyclical *Divino Afflante Spiritus.*

109. Anthony N. S. Lane, "Roman Catholic Views of Biblical Authority from the Late Nineteenth Century to the Present" (ch. 10 in this collection).

Webster, who in turn has influenced many of his own students in a similar direction.[110] One can easily detect the diversity of reactions to Barth by reading the book edited by George Hunsinger, *Thy Word Is Truth: Barth on Scripture.*[111] In his assessment of Barth, David Gibson holds that Barth's impassioned invitation to read and reread the Bible, precisely in his work as a dogmatician, is sometimes undermined by his exegetical handling of text — not least those texts that formulate his understanding of the nature of Scripture.[112]

The "Inerrancy" Dragon

In discussions about the nature of Holy Scripture, no word evokes such strong responses as the word "inerrancy," among both inerrancy-affirmers and inerrancy-deniers. On the one hand, it is the shibboleth that, provided you affirm it, provides you with the keys to the (evangelical) kingdom. On the other hand, authors like Peter Enns repeatedly blog about people they know who were brought up with inerrancy but who have now "moved on," still smarting under various "burns." J. R. Daniel Kirk seems to think that an inerrantist must hold to a young earth, such that if you tell a high schooler "inerrancy or bust" this is an invitation to bust.[113] Citing Lesslie Newbigin, Enns says that inerrancy is sub-Christian, and is more Muslim in its theology than Christian.[114]

Clearly the important question is the *meaning* of the word "inerrancy." If it is associated with certain interpretive schemes that critics dislike, then the critics may disavow the word because they dislike the interpretive schemes. One ought to begin, then, with a more sophisticated definition of "inerrancy." To claim that the Bible is inerrant is to focus on the Bible's truthfulness wherever it is making a truth claim. The word is not to be confused with degrees of precision or with hermeneutical stipulation; it happily acknowledges that there are complex issues of literary genre with which to wrestle, and that not every sentence is a falsifiable proposition. This and much more have been treated in an essay by Paul Feinberg that deserves reprinting and wide circulation.[115] A more recent

110. See his *Holy Scripture: A Dogmatic Sketch* (Cambridge: Cambridge University Press, 2003). Cf. my review, "Three More Books on the Bible: A Critical Review" (cited in note 26 above).

111. Grand Rapids: Eerdmans, 2012.

112. "The Answering Speech of Men: Karl Barth on Holy Scripture" (ch. 9 in this collection).

113. "Creating Space," quoted on the *patheos* website: http://www.patheos.com/blogs/slacktivist/2012/08/18/inerrancy-is-not-a-victimless-crime/. Cf. also Carlos R. Bovell, *Inerrancy and the Spiritual Formation of Younger Evangelicals* (Eugene: Wipf & Stock, 2007).

114. E.g., http://www.patheos.com/blogs/peterenns/2013/08/inerrantism-is-more-muslim-than-christian-a-thought-from-lesslie-newbigin/.

115. "The Meaning of Inerrancy," in *Inerrancy,* ed. Norman L. Geisler (Grand Rapids:

essay by Paul Helm extends the discussion to think through how inerrancy is tied to indexicality, assertion, speech-act theory, and kinds of error.[116] Another essay by Peter J. Williams homes in on the nuanced and exegetically grounded arguments for inerrancy that are regularly misinterpreted because some of the key terms have come to mean different things in different camps, causing remarkable confusion.[117]

If someone were to ask what is the use of a word that requires so much careful definition and discussion, we might respond by asking what significant word in the theological arena is *not* subject to careful definition and discussion. Justification? God? Truth?

The Authority of Jesus, the Biblical Writings, and the Canon

The issues, like certain kinds of demons, are legion. Not a few are admirably discussed in books already mentioned.[118] Here we restrict ourselves to a handful of issues.

(1) Transparently there is a voluminous literature on the historical Jesus. Little of that literature is written with questions about the nature of Scripture in mind. It would take a book merely to usefully categorize that discussion over the last thirty years and more. Nevertheless it is worth reflecting on one of the constantly slippery elements in contemporary discussion, viz. what is meant by "historicity" or "historical event." Many a New Testament scholar, including some who designate themselves evangelical, hold that an event is "historical" only if it meets the criteria of the historians' guild for historical events — and such criteria are invariably universal and naturalistic. Under such a definition, the transfiguration of Jesus, say, or his resurrection, is not "historical," but it may still be a "real" event, one that is accessible only to faith. Yet this is an intellectualist's playground. Try preaching that the resurrection of Jesus is not historical yet nonetheless real. The overwhelming majority of our hearers will either misunderstand what is being said, or confess they do not understand the claim. If, by contrast, we allow an event to be called "historical" if it takes place in space-time history, even if it does not fall within the limitations of philosophical naturalism and appeals to

Zondervan, 1979), 367-404. It is not unfair to observe that critics such as Peter Enns and Carlos Bovell tend to be much more precise on what they do *not* like about traditional formulations of the doctrine of Scripture, than exactly what they would put in its place. In addition to the literature already cited, see Bovell, *Rehabilitating Inerrancy in a Culture of Fear* (Eugene, OR: Wipf & Stock, 2012).

116. "The Idea of Inerrancy" (ch. 28 in this collection).

117. Peter J. Williams, "Ehrman's Equivocation and the Inerrancy of the Original Text" (ch. 13 in this collection).

118. E.g., Hoffmeier and Magary, eds., *Do Historical Matters Matter to Faith?*

universal criteria, then clearly the New Testament writers are convinced that both the transfiguration and the resurrection are indeed "historical" events.

(2) Not only are there wildly different scholarly assessments of the historical value of the Old Testament documents — all the way from "minimalist" schools to highly maximalist readings of almost all genres — but where different documents cover the same period (e.g., 1 and 2 Chronicles over against Samuel and Kings) some posit not complementary or progressive understandings but mutually contradictory communities. V. Philips Long has devoted a lengthy essay to bringing clarity to the issues.[119]

Some authors have attempted to address the way the Bible speaks the truth by thinking about what might be called the "genre" of the Bible writ large. In a stimulating essay Luke Timothy Johnson asserts that his premise is that, "like the character in the song who is 'looking for love in all the wrong places,' readers of the Bible . . . have been looking for truth in all the wrong places."[120] In particular, the American culture wars have insisted that the truth of the Bible lies in the past, in what the Bible says to have taken place in history, or in its future, as various Christian groups read the future off the face of Revelation. Unfortunately for both claims, Johnson asserts, historical criticism has destroyed confidence in the Bible's ostensible "history," and a learned grasp of apocalyptic literature makes future-casting from the Book of Revelation a dubious exercise. Johnson proposes that the truth of the Bible "works in and through literary imagination."[121] He asks, "How, then, is the Bible true? I believe that this question grows richer and more pertinent to our lives when we begin to imagine the world Scripture itself imagines, through its literary art; when we ask what is the shape of that world and its rules and how we might embody it. . . ."[122]

But one must ask some questions. (a) Assuming it has been given by God, does the Bible *intend* primarily to incite the human imagination? Even at the human level, avoiding appealing to God as the Bible's ultimate author: Do the human biblical writers primarily *intend* to spark human beings to exercise their imaginations? Or would it be more accurate to say that they have a variety of goals, including provoking imagination, but also providing moral exhortation, disclosing the nature of God, making historical claims, and much more? What precisely sanctions such a high valuation of imagination *set over against* other ways of conveying truth? Certainly one might argue that heavily symbol-laden literature, such as apocalyptic, is more vested in sparking the imagination than,

119. "Competing Histories, Competing Theologies? Reflections on the Unity and Diversity of the Old Testament('s Readers)" (ch. 12 in this collection).

120. Luke Timothy Johnson, "How Is the Bible True? Let Me Count the Ways," *Commonweal* 36, no. 10 (22 May 2009): 12.

121. Johnson, "How Is the Bible True?" 14.

122. Johnson, "How Is the Bible True?" 16.

say, genealogical lists. But even apocalyptic demonstrably has other intentions built into the genre. In other words, Johnson is short-circuiting serious discussion of the complex functions of diverse literary genres. Granted that, say, the book of Proverbs is not primarily interested in making historical claims, what forms of Scripture *are* interested in making historical claims? How does one decide? Johnson's essay begins to appear like a whimsical piece of reductionism. (b) More importantly, the Bible occasionally underscores the importance of what has taken place *in history,* observed by attested witnesses. Doubtless the prime example is the resurrection of Jesus. The apostle insists that if one avers it has happened (*sc.* in history), when in fact it has *not* happened (*sc.* in history), then we remain in our sins, the apostles are liars, our faith is futile, and we are of all people most to be pitied. In other words, there are crucial contexts when one of the factors that validates faith is the truthfulness of faith's object, viz. the claim regarding what has happened in history. Must we not similarly say something similar about the *historical* nature of the incarnation? Moreover, there are several theologically rich, imagination-empowering arguments in the Bible that depend *absolutely* on the validity of a certain *historical* sequence (e.g., Galatians 3; Heb. 4:1-13 [if the Pentateuch is not telling the truth about entering into the "rest" of the promised land *after* the failure in the time of Moses but *before* the writing of Psalm 95, then the argument in Hebrews 4 makes no sense]; 7:1-25). (c) The treatment of "truth" in Johnson's essay is thoroughly unclear. What is the relationship between truthful text and authoritative text? Both "authority" and "truth" call forth countless books and essays. By focusing on their relationship, we narrow the topic down to a focus on realism and anti-realism, and on the ease with which difficult matters of consistency and coherence (not necessarily the same thing) are readily sacrificed in the service of an unprincipled infatuation with eclecticism. The essay by Michael Rea in this collection clarifies many of the issues.[123] (d) Johnson's argument is profoundly intellectualist; try preaching it in the real world. More importantly, we are not saved by imagination-stirring ideas about the death and resurrection of the incarnate Son of God, but by the death and resurrection of the incarnate Son of God. What saves us is not a set of ideas that fire the imagination, and call us to share a similarly imagined world, but the extra-textual realities to which the text points. The Bible casts up many ideas, of course, but not because ideas themselves reconcile us to God, but because the ideas are about Jesus Christ, and he reconciles us to God. Once we get such matters clear in our minds, then of course we can say all sorts of useful things about the power of the imagination, the use of words and images to stir and shape us, and so forth: that is, in part, what good preaching does. But if one says such things *at the expense* of the extra-textual referentiality, it's a bit like building a skyscraper after destroying the foundation. Only intellectuals can accommodate such nonsense. If you are a Buddhist, of course, and someone

123. "Authority and Truth" (ch. 27 in this collection).

"proves" that Gautama the Buddha never lived, it would not devastate your Buddhism: Buddhism depends for its believability very little on historical claims. But that cannot be said of Christianity. Prove that Jesus never lived, never died, and never rose from the dead, or declare that historical details are unimportant provided our imaginations are fired up, and you have utterly destroyed Christianity.

The same sort of miss-step appears in the literature in several different guises. For example, in a very recent book Peter Enns offers a slightly different antithesis to the one adopted by Luke Timothy Johnson. Enns insists that the Bible is not a cookbook but an ancient spiritual journey, full of mystery.[124] Andrew Wilson has done an admirable job indicating where Enns makes some useful points, and where his analysis is hopelessly lacking.[125] One of the most plastic of words regularly deployed in discussion of biblical (especially Old Testament) texts is "myth." Bruce K. Waltke has brought some order to the discussion.[126]

(3) For many years John Wenham's little book *Christ and the Bible*[127] has been a staple for young (and some not so young) Christians, who need to learn what Jesus thought of antecedent Scripture. Wenham made a strong and effective case for Jesus being convinced that what we call the Old Testament is in truth the Word of God, authoritative, and without error. An essay by Craig L. Blomberg[128] updates Wenham's thought by wrestling with the ways in which Jesus, while upholding the God-givenness of the Old Testament, maintains his own authority to interpret it, frequently deploying a typological reading of it that we must understand and learn if we are to read Old Testament texts in line with him.

(4) Despite the plethora of books and essays advocating or presupposing an extraordinarily skeptical approach to the canonical Gospels, several scholars stand out for the work they have done on the historical credibility of the Gospels. This does not mean they necessarily align with traditional understandings of the nature of Scripture, but their work is extraordinarily helpful for many readers. One thinks, for instance, of many of the historical essays authored by Roland Deines,[129] the volume on eyewitnesses by Richard Bauckham,[130] and some of

124. *The Bible Tells Me So: Why Defending the Bible Has Made Us Unable to Read It* (New York: HarperOne, 2014).

125. http://www.christianitytoday.com/ct/2014/september-web-only/bible-is-more-than-mystery.html.

126. "Myth, History, and the Bible: With Focus on the Old Testament" (ch. 18 in this collection).

127. Third edition (Grand Rapids: Baker, 1994).

128. "Reflections on Jesus' View of the Old Testament" (ch. 22 in this collection).

129. See, for example, his *Acts of God in History: Studies Towards Recovering a Theological Historiography,* WUNT 317, ed. Christoph Ochs and Peter Watts (Tübingen: Mohr Siebeck, 2013).

130. *Jesus and the Eyewitnesses: The Gospels as Eyewitness Testimony* (Grand Rapids: Eerdmans, 2006).

the voluminous writings of N. T. Wright, one or two of them simultaneously percipient and wonderfully funny.[131]

(5) The first book written by my *Doktorvater* Barnabas Lindars was titled *New Testament Apologetic: The Doctrinal Significance of the Old Testament Quotations.*[132] Its thesis was quite simple. The New Testament writers regularly ripped OT texts out of their contexts in order to "prove" their Christian claims. That was the very nature of the apologetic that New Testament writers undertook.

The strongest form of that sort of argument is of course utterly incompatible with any notion of a high view of Scripture. A less violent but slightly mystical version might say that God himself intended multiple meanings in those Old Testament texts that the human authors did not see or intend. More conservative scholars will try, in one fashion or another, to show that the New Testament use of the Old Testament rests on a handful of hermeneutical axioms and carefully formed typologies that most early Christians shared. Some have argued, for instance, that Paul's mode of citation probably depends on his complex educational background, both Jewish and Greco-Roman.[133] In any case, the last three decades have witnessed an amazing jump in the number and quality of studies on the New Testament use of the Old Testament. Though few intend to address directly the question of the nature of Scripture, such topics sometimes stand behind the work: see, for example, the large volume that Greg Beale and I edited.[134] But it is an essay by Doug Moo and Andy Naselli that thoughtfully explores these issues within the context of our understanding of what Scripture is.[135]

(6) Recent decades have spawned a complicated literature regarding the very notion of canon.[136] This literature touches both Testaments. So far as the Old Testament is concerned, it pertains to different Hebrew text types, their relation to the so-called LXX, the very meaning of "Hebrew canon," and, even when the meaning is agreed, the date by which "canonical" notions come into play. At issue, too, are disputed passages in the literature of Second Temple Juda-

131. In particular, see his "Taking the Text with Her Pleasure: A Post-Post-Modernist Response to J. Dominic Crossan, *The Historical Jesus: The Life of a Mediterranean Jewish Peasant* (T. & T. Clark, HarperSanFrancisco 1991) (With apologies to A. A. Milne, St Paul and James Joyce)," *Theol* 96 (1993): 303-10.

132. London: SCM, 1961.

133. E.g., Stanley E. Porter and Andrew W. Pitts, "Paul's Bible, His Education and His Access to the Scriptures of Israel," *JGRChJ* 5 (2008): 9-41.

134. *Commentary on the New Testament Use of the Old* (Grand Rapids: Baker, 2007).

135. "The Problem of the New Testament's Use of the Old Testament" (ch. 23 in this collection).

136. See especially Eve-Marie Becker and Stefan Scholz, eds., *Kanon in Konstruktion und Dekonstruktion: Kanonisierungsprocesse religiöser Texte von der Antike bis zur Gegenwart: Ein Handbuch* (Berlin and Boston: De Gruyter, 2012) — though the coverage is pretty much restricted to German literature.

ism with regard to the twenty-two-book canon. In the past, many of us have consulted Roger Beckwith.[137] The detailed work of Chapman, influenced not least by Brevard Childs, focuses on the formation of the Old Testament canon: we must read the inspired documents not only as "Scripture" but as books that preserve and generate the interpretive framework that shapes further texts. "In other words, because the goal of the canonical process was to transmit a framework for interpretation (or 'grammar') along with the sacred writings themselves the received form of the text contains literary features which act as hermeneutical guides for present-day readers."[138] The work of Seitz is not entirely dissimilar, though the focus of his attention lies rather heavily on the way this canonical process must not be short-changed by allowing Paul, say, or some other New Testament figure to constrain the exegesis of the Old Testament texts.[139] Now we have a splendid essay by Stephen G. Dempster giving these questions some fresh thought.[140]

Much discussion regarding the New Testament canon has revolved around the question as to when books so came together in the mind of believers that they constituted a widely recognized canon. In other words, the focus has commonly been on the *historical* evidence, primarily from the patristic period. What has been lacking is a *theology* of the canon. This lacuna has now been nicely filled by two books written by Michael Kruger[141] and a long essay by Graham A. Cole.[142] Both Kruger and Cole argue persuasively that there are compelling intrinsic reasons why, owing to the communicative act of the God who speaks, the notion of canon was early and formative. Kruger outlines and responds to the five planks commonly advanced in support of the very common opposite view, viz., that the New Testament notion of canon arose haphazardly and late.[143] Michael Thate

137. *The Old Testament Canon of the New Testament Church and Its Background in Early Judaism* (London: SPCK, 1985).

138. Steven B. Chapman, *The Law and the Prophets: A Study in Old Testament Canon Formation,* FAT 27 (Tübingen: Mohr Siebeck, 2000), 109.

139. Christopher R. Seitz, *The Character of Christian Scripture: The Significance of a Two-Testament Bible* (Grand Rapids: Baker 2011). At a more popular level, see his *The Goodly Fellowship of the Prophets: The Achievement of Association in Canon Formation* (Grand Rapids: Baker, 2009).

140. "The Old Testament Canon, Josephus, and Cognitive Environment" (ch. 11 in this collection).

141. Viz., *Canon Revisited: Establishing the Origins and Authority of the New Testament Books* (Wheaton, IL: Crossway, 2012); idem, *The Question of Canon: Challenging the Status Quo in the New Testament Debate* (Downers Grove, IL: InterVarsity, 2013).

142. "Why a Book? Why This Book? Why the Particular Order within This Book? Some Theological Reflections on the Canon" (ch. 15 in this collection).

143. Certainly Kruger has been strenuously challenged (see especially John C. Poirier, "An Ontological Definition of 'Canon'?" *BBR* 24 [2014]: 457-66), but one suspects that the different approaches are at least partly generated by fundamentally different readings of the fathers.

sent me the lovely quote from Tom Shippey: "[M]yths are still in fashion, and canons are not."[144]

Some Epistemological, Philosophical, and Theological Issues

Under this heading I include several topics on which there has arisen extensive literature.

(1) One of the striking lessons to learn from the fact that a high view of the authority of Scripture — indeed, a view that embraces inerrancy — has prevailed in the Christian church across the centuries, is that this view of Scripture, like many central Christian doctrines, keeps showing up in many lands, in many cultures, in many epistemological structures, even in many theological systems. If it could be shown that, say, inerrancy is utterly dependent on one particular epistemological structure — say, Cartesian foundationalism — then with the abandonment of that epistemological structure, inerrancy would necessarily fall. Indeed, this is the argument of Carlos Bovell,[145] who for his approach to Scripture prefers a Husserlian emphasis on origins. But apart from incidental weaknesses to his argument (e.g., he provides very little evidence that the Westminster divines were in any way influenced by Descartes),[146] the widespread acceptance of the doctrine across the centuries and across diverse structures of thought argues against monocausational analyses. In other words (as we saw earlier with respect to Scottish Common Sense Realism), high views of Scripture are surprisingly paradigm-independent — or, better put, they have a habit of surfacing in many philosophical and theological contexts.

That is why, among those who defend a traditional view of Scripture, substantial differences in their respective understandings of epistemology remain — just as there are, of course, substantial differences in epistemology among those who critique those with a high view of Scripture. In an essay in this collection, James Beilby surveys some of the epistemological issues irrefragably bound up with discussion of such issues as inspiration, revelation, and epistemology.[147] He himself strongly commends a relational-dynamic view of inspiration, but he would be among the first to recognize that other models exist. While Bovell, just discussed, condemns inerrancy for its (ostensible) dependence on Cartesian foundationalism, R. Scott Smith, in this collection, is suspicious of non-foundational episte-

144. Tom Shippey, "Gloomy/Cheerful," *LRB* 30, no. 1 (3 Jan. 2008): 23.

145. *By Good and Necessary Consequence: A Preliminary Genealogy of Biblicist Foundationalism* (Eugene, OR: Wipf & Stock, 2009).

146. See the insightful review article by Russell W. Howell, "Inerrancy: A Cartesian Faux-Pas?" *B&C* 20, no. 6 (Sept./Oct. 2014): 8-10.

147. "Contemporary Religious Epistemology: Some Key Aspects" (ch. 25 in this collection).

mologies,[148] while Randall Hauser, writing from a non-inerrancy perspective, attacks attempts to defend inerrancy from any non-foundationalist perspective.[149] An increasingly widespread perception is that a modest, chastened foundationalism and a modest, chastened realism are not far from reaching out and touching similarly chastened non-foundational epistemologies. Cultural-linguistic models of doing theology, along with cognitive-propositionalist models and experiential-expressivist models, are all in danger, if any one of them is given unfettered sway, of subordinating and domesticating Scripture. Tied to these issues is the way in which one goes about constructing theology and making sense of doctrinal development. All sides of orthodox Christianity will acknowledge that in some ways the Trinitarian formulations of the third and fourth centuries go "beyond what is written,"[150] yet articulate the nature of God in responsible and faithful ways that are, if not mandated by Scripture, made virtually necessary by Scripture. Kevin J. Vanhoozer helps us think through what bearing such discussions have on the nature of biblical authority.[151]

(2) What is the relationship between God and his Word — between the authority of God and the authority of his Word? This topic has many facets. For some authors, the issue revolves around the question of whether, in one's systematic theology, one should begin with epistemology and the nature of Scripture, or with God himself. Because the Word comes to us in our historical location, complex issues are immediately raised regarding the ontological Trinity and the economic Trinity. Moreover, if there is one God, one divine Mind, behind the whole of Scripture, one must ask how that one Mind establishes the unity of all of Scripture, even while we take pains to observe the many diversities of form, language, style, vocabulary, author, purpose, genre, and length. Peter Jensen works out many of these intricacies by tying the diverse words that constitute Scripture into the one divine storyline, making the connection between the authority of God and the authority of Scripture irrefragably tight.[152]

(3) The issues surrounding the double authorship of Scripture continue to command wide discussion. Transparently, if all the emphasis is placed on God while the human authors are little more than organic recording devices, the differences in Scripture from book to book are impossible to understand, and the

148. "Non-Foundational Epistemologies and the Truth of Scripture" (ch. 26).

149. *Theology in Search of Foundations* (New York: Oxford University Press, 2009).

150. In the original context, of course, the exhortation "Do not go beyond what is written" (1 Cor 4:6) is not intended to undermine the legitimacy of teasing out necessary inferences from the Scriptural texts, but to rebuke the Corinthian factionalists who were going "beyond what is written" by identifying themselves in arrogant fashion with Peter, Paul, Apollos, or even (in some partisan fashion) with Christ (cf. 1:11-13; 3:4-15).

151. "May We Go Beyond What Is Written After All? The Pattern of Theological Authority and the Problem of Doctrinal Development" (ch. 24 in this collection).

152. Peter F. Jensen, "God and the Bible" (ch. 16 in this collection).

Bible becomes akin to the Qur'an or the Book of Mormon.[153] Alternatively, if all the emphasis is placed on the human authors and God is no more than a ghostly cipher lurking some distance away, or if he could get up and take himself to another universe while leaving behind no sense of loss in our understanding of what Scripture *is,* then there are few if any constraints against purely naturalistic interpretations of the Bible,[154] and the Bible's own self-understanding (if I may strain language a bit) collapses.

Some scholars address the issues by exploring what double agency might mean in a particular cultural context — the context of Paul, for instance.[155] Some in the charismatic tradition fragment the discussion, especially in the context of the Book of Acts, and pit Scripture over against acts of God and the authoritative voices of individuals who interpret those acts without appealing to Scripture.[156] The most sophisticated treatment of the subject I have read for years is the lengthy essay by Henri Blocher.[157]

(4) An age that is uncomfortable with definite and clear meanings of texts, preferring polyvalence and ambiguity, will be uncomfortable with any insistence on the perspicuity of Scripture. Put another way, any defense of the perspicuity of Scripture is going to have to be informed and sophisticated — and this we have in an essay by Mark D. Thompson.[158]

(5) The popular writings of Richard Dawkins[159] and others among the new atheists have strengthened the widespread perception that the Bible is not reliable, not truthful, especially when it bears, even tangentially, on scientific matters. Here it is imperative to wrestle with such thinkers as a theist like John Polkinghorne and a panentheist like Arthur Peacocke — not because they espouse a well-articulated view of Scripture, but because they are scientists who reject the philosophical naturalism of the new atheists, and find ways to think about the integration of scientific learning and fundamental Christian claims, including supernatural claims.[160]

153. Cf. Vishal Mangalwadi, "The Bible: Is It a Fax from Heaven?" *ERT* 36 (2012): 78-87.

154. For example, some of the chapters in the recent book edited by Christopher M. Hays and Christopher B. Ansberry, *Evangelical Faith and the Challenge of Historical Criticism* (London: SPCK, 2013), briefly discussed above, seem to flirt with this side of the pendulum.

155. So John M. G. Barclay and Simon J. Gathercole, eds., *Divine and Human Agency in Paul and His Cultural Environment,* LNTS 335 (London: T. & T. Clark, 2006).

156. E.g., Graham H. Twelftree, "Is 'Holy Scripture' Christian? A Lucan Perspective," *Theol* 116 (2013): 351-60.

157. "God and the Scripture Writers: The Question of Double Authorship" (ch. 17 in this collection).

158. "The Generous Gift of a Gracious Father: Towards a Theological Account of the Clarity of Scripture" (ch. 20 in this collection).

159. See especially his *The Blind Watchmaker* (New York: W. W. Norton, 1986) and his *The God Delusion* (Boston: Houghton Mifflin, 2006).

160. See, for example, Arthur Peacocke, *Paths from Science towards God: The End of All*

We need to adopt a certain cautious skepticism along two fronts. First, we ought to be skeptical regarding some of the claims of science, even when those claims command almost universal approbation. Not that many decades ago, phrenology and eugenics were both almost universally espoused and commonly practiced. They were, after all, "scientific." Today they are equally universally dismissed. Of course it is difficult to know exactly what scientific claims are least well supported and most deserving of skepticism. A careful reading of *Scientific Mythologies* is a good place to begin.[161] Scientists and non-scientists alike need to proceed cautiously — but it is important to recognize how even some commonly supported and widely attested theories may someday come crashing down. For example, although one hesitates to mention it, theoretical physicists have begun to raise new scientific doubts about the big bang theory (not the TV program of the same name!). It is too early to guess what other theoretical physicists and cosmologists will make of them.[162] But what is clear is twofold: specifically, that serious and competent physicists may call in question something as widely assumed as the big bang, once again reminding us that many of the "facts" of science are provisional until a better theory comes along; and more generally, that scientists and non-scientists alike should be prepared to maintain a cautious skepticism over some scientific claims. This stance does not sanction arrogant dismissal; it mandates respect, careful listening, evaluation, and sometimes patient uncertainty, as we refuse to be intimidated by the overconfident claims of some scientists or by the popularity of some nearly universally adopted theories. Second, Christians should also maintain a certain cautious skepticism with respect to the hermeneutical reductionism advocated by some Christian thinkers. Some scholars appear to be utterly certain about how to read every line

---

Our Exploring (Oxford: Oneworld, 2001); idem, *Creation and the World of Science: The Reshaping of Belief* (Oxford: Oxford University Press, 2004); John Polkinghorne, *Faith, Science and Understanding* (London: SPCK, 2000); *Science and the Trinity: The Christian Encounter with Reality* (New Haven: Yale University Press, 2005); idem, *Quantum Physics and Theology: An Unexpected Kinship* (New Haven: Yale University Press, 2007).

161. James A. Herrick, *Scientific Mythologies: How Science and Science Fiction Forge New Religious Beliefs* (Downers Grove, IL: InterVarsity, 2013).

162. The crucial papers, written by Canadian and Egyptian physicists, are Ahmed Farag Ali and Saurya Das, "Cosmology from Quantum Potential," *Physics Letters B* 741 (4 Feb. 2014): 276-79, also available at arXiv:1404.3093[gr-qc]; and Saurya Das and Rajat K. Bhaduri, "Dark Matter and Dark Energy from Bose-Einstein Condensate," arXiv:1411.0753[gr-qc]. The big bang falls out from the mathematics of general relativity, but because it necessitates a singularity at the beginning, where the laws of physics do not apply, some theoreticians have always been slightly uncomfortable with the theory. In removing the singularity, this model, itself based on earlier work by David Bohm, gets rid of the big bang and dark matter (said to make up about 70 percent of the universe), replacing them with a fluid of quantum particles. At a popular level, see Lisa Zyga, "No Big Bang? Quantum Equation Predicts Universe Has No Beginning," accessed 11 March 2015 at phys.org/news/2015-02-big-quantum-equan-universe.html.

of Genesis 1–11. The recent book by Walton and Sandy[163] is aimed at destroying traditional certainties; unfortunately, the authors are equally certain about their alternative hermeneutical constructions. Frankly, in the light of the complexity of the hermeneutical issues raised by these opening chapters of Scripture, the question posed by Francis A. Schaeffer forty years ago is still the most pertinent one: What is the least that Genesis 1–11 must be saying in order for the book of Genesis, and the rest of the Bible, to be coherent and true?[164] In any case, Kirsten Birkett wisely helps Christians think through some of the slippery issues surrounding "Science and Scripture."[165]

Comparative Religious Topics

The globalization of the world has its corollary in the globalization of Christianity. In missions, for example, it is no longer "from the West to the rest," but from everywhere to everywhere. As the sheer numbers of believers in the Majority World continue to climb, many have observed that these believers largely accept the authority of the Bible, holding to a theology that, by Western standards, is orthodox, conservative, even traditionalist.[166] By the same token, more and more Christians are compelled to think through how what we mean by Scripture and the authority of Scripture stands in relation to the scriptures of other world religions and their respective claims to authority. This cannot possibly be a neutral discussion. For example, Christians evaluate such matters out of the framework of utter confidence that Christ has taken away their sins, that God has revealed Christ in them and to them and promised them resurrection existence in the new heaven and the new earth. All that they know of the triune God and his providential purposes in the world and the church has been mediated to them by the Bible, so inevitably they think of the Bible within that confessional stance.[167] At the same time, when Christians speak of the self-attestation of Scripture, they are referring neither to a fideistic leap of faith, nor to a mystical inner voice, but to the Bible's own testimony to itself.[168]

163. John H. Walton and D. Brent Sandy, *The Lost World of Scripture: Ancient Literary Culture and Biblical Authority* (Downers Grove, IL: InterVarsity, 2013).

164. *Genesis in Space and Time* (London: Hodder & Stoughton, 1972).

165. Ch. 30 in this collection.

166. See, for example, Timothy C. Tennent, *Theology in the Context of World Christianity: How the Global Church Is Influencing the Way We Think about and Discuss Theology* (Grand Rapids: Zondervan, 2007).

167. See, for instance, John Piper, "Why I Trust the Scriptures," available at http://www.desiringgod.org/conference-messages/why-i-trust-the-scriptures.

168. Cf. Paul Helm, "The Self-Attestation of Scripture," *Modern Reformation* 19, no. 2 (Mar./Apr. 2010): 45-57. More broadly, see Te-Li Lau, "Knowing the Bible Is the Word of God Despite Competing Claims" (ch. 31 in this collection).

One of the striking contrasts between the way Christians view the Bible and the way Muslims view the Qur'an is that, although both religions are in certain respects "missionary" religions, the ways they propagate their respective holy books are quite different. For Muslims, the only way to read the Qur'an is in Arabic, the language in which Muhammad wrote it. Correspondingly, translations of the Qur'an are therefore not the Word of God, but interpretation of it, or commentary upon it. By contrast, Christians have since earliest times busied themselves with producing versions of their sacred Scriptures. Inevitably, this generates a great deal of discussion about how to translate the Word of God, how to communicate it not only in another language but in another culture — discussion that varies between the wise and the unwise, between the probing and the compromised.[169] More fundamentally, it generates discussion about what it means to locate divine inspiration (and, consequentially, divine authority) in autographs written in Hebrew, Aramaic, and Greek, while preaching and teaching our English versions of the Bible as the authoritative Word of God. Much has been written on this subject, of course, but the best recent contribution is an essay by Karen Jobes.[170]

Although there are books and essays that compare and contrast the Bible and, say, the Qur'an — whether written from the Muslim perspective or from the Christian — most of these are very general introductions. Missionaries, cultural anthropologists, historians, and other scholars sometimes compare and contrast roughly common themes in the Bible and the Qur'an — the people of God and the *ummah,* for instance, or disparate notions of the kingdom of God,[171] or the nature of forgiveness.[172] But relatively little has been written by biblical scholars on specific textual parallels,[173] doubtless because the world of the Qur'an is largely closed to most readers of the Bible. In any case, the essay by Ida Glaser in this collection is designed to help Bible readers understand how Muslims think of the Qur'an.[174]

At least Christianity and Islam are both monotheistic religions. It is at least feasible to compare the Bible and the Qur'an. It is far more challenging to com-

169. For examples of both, see R. Daniel Shaw and Charles E. Van Engen, *Communicating God's Word in a Complex World: God's Truth or Hocus Pocus?* (Lanham, MD: Rowman & Littlefield, 2003).

170. "Relevance Theory and the Translation of Scripture," *JETS* 50 (2007): 773-97.

171. E.g., Shabbir Akhtar, *Islam as Political Religion: The Future of an Imperial Faith* (New York: Routledge, 2011).

172. E.g., Sigvad von Sicard, "Forgiveness and Reconciliation Through the Lenses of the Bible and the Qur'an," *World Christianity in Muslim Encounter,* vol. 2, ed. Stephen R. Goodwin (London: Continuum, 2009), ch. 3.

173. But see, for example, Michael A. Haller, "Forgiving Your Neighbour: A Comparative Reading of Matthew 6:12 and Surah 3:134," *ERT* 39 (2015): 61-75.

174. "Qur'anic Challenges for the Bible Reader" (ch. 32).

pare the Bible with the sacred writings of a theoretically non-theistic religion like Buddhism, or of a polytheistic religion like Hinduism. In the one case, what is required is a fundamental explanation of Buddhism itself;[175] in the other, while an explanation of the extraordinary diversity and complexity of Hinduism's sacred texts is helpful,[176] Timothy C. Tennent goes further, drawing us into careful evaluation by asking whether there is any sense, from a Christian perspective, that Hinduism's sacred writings, or at least some of them, might serve as a kind of Hindu Old Testament.[177]

Conclusion: Thinking Holistically

Although the topics undertaken by the essays in this volume are important and deserve serious treatment, nevertheless there is a sense in which the exercise is in at least some danger of serving as a distraction. As soon as I had written that sentence, I immediately said to myself, "No, that's not fair. The topics addressed are hugely important; 'distraction' is not the right word." Yet all of the focus of the essays in this volume is on the nature of the Bible, the authority of the Bible, the way the Bible has been viewed in various parts of the history of the church, the nature of inspiration and of truth, epistemology, the comparison of the Christian Scriptures with the sacred texts of other traditions, and much more — and nothing about how the Bible shapes us, what value lies in bowing to its authority, and how to read it. One does not want to give the impression that faithfulness to the Bible is primarily about defending the Bible. One remembers the quip universally attributed to C. H. Spurgeon: "Defend the Bible? I would as soon defend a lion. Unchain it and it will defend itself." Moreover, if inerrancy or any other high view of Scripture drives us to think the Bible is all about the provision of mere information, we have swallowed a massive reductionism.

The challenge is all the more acute now that we live in *A Secular Age*.[178] This does not mean that our age demands the abandonment of religion, but the squeezing of religion to the periphery, to the private. It means we live in a time when it is no longer almost unthinkable to be an atheist, as was once the case;

175. Harold Netland and Alex G. Smith, "Buddhist Sutras and Christian Revelation" (ch. 34 in this collection); cf. Naomi Appleton, "Buddhist Scriptures: An Overview," *ExpT* 125 (2014): 573-82.

176. See Robert Leach, "A Religion of the Book? On Sacred Texts in Hinduism," *ExpT* 126 (2014): 15-27.

177. Timothy C. Tennent, "Can Hindu Scriptures Serve as a 'Tutor' to Christ?" (ch. 33 in this collection).

178. The penetrating volume by Charles Taylor (Cambridge, MA: Belknap, 2007). The 900-page masterwork has been beautifully summarized by James K. A. Smith, *How (Not) to Be Secular: Reading Charles Taylor* (Grand Rapids: Eerdmans, 2014).

indeed, in many sectors of Western culture, a practical atheism is the default position. It means we live in a time of "expressive individualism," in the "age of authenticity" (both are recurring phrases in Taylor) — a time when all authority is viewed with suspicion, when "authentic" living demands the sidelining of authority. We no longer think in terms of what everything *means,* in which we must *find* the order that is already built into the universe; rather, the "buffered self" must bring order and meaning *to* the universe. In the face of such assumptions, only the closest and most faithful reading of Scripture will have the temerity to construct an alternative world, a Christian world, that is deeply grounded in, and permeated by, Holy Scripture.

One of the things that is required is what Yarbrough calls "cognitive reverence,"[179] which is more important, and more demanding, than *merely* insisting on propositional truth. It is what makes it possible for inerrancy to become "a place to live,"[180] not just a position to hold. And it authorizes the preacher.

Today there are growing calls to reform life, culture, and theology by the Word of God.[181] Some appeals for the greater integration of biblical studies and the life and conduct of the church seem to be driven by political and social agendas, or by rather too much respect for the "orthodoxies" of classic liberalism.[182] Nevertheless the appeals themselves are reminders that debates about the authority of the Bible cannot substitute for unfeigned submission to the authority of the Bible. A friend[183] sent me a quote from Martin Sheen, the actor who played the President in the television serial *The West Wing.* Commenting on Aaron Sorkin as a writer and the tendency of the actors to improvise, Sheen writes:

> In the beginning, I have to say frankly, my discipline was not in line with the program. I was a bit too cavalier, and I was not always attentive to the very letter of the word. But gradually I came to realize that I was in the wrong. And when I surrendered to the word and was ruled specifically by the text, I learned a wonderful freedom. Aaron Sorkin is a masterful composer. You can do your

179. Robert W. Yarbrough, "The Future of Cognitive Reverence for the Bible," *JETS* 57 (2014): 5-18.

180. Cf. the winsome picture painted by John M. Frame, "Inerrancy: A Place to Live," *JETS* 47 (2014): 29-39.

181. E.g., Miroslav Volf, *Captive to the Word of God: Engaging the Scriptures for Contemporary Theological Reflection* (Grand Rapids: Eerdmans, 2010); Kevin J. Vanhoozer, "Interpreting Scripture Between the Rock of Biblical Studies and the Hard Place of Systematic Theology: The State of the Evangelical (dis)Union," in *Renewing the Evangelical Mission,* ed. Richard Lints (Grand Rapids: Eerdmans, 2013), 201-25.

182. E.g., Cynthia Briggs Kittredge, Ellen Bradshaw Aitken, and Jonathan A. Draper, eds., *The Bible in the Public Square: Reading the Signs of the Times* (Minneapolis: Fortress, 2008); George G. Nicol, "Biblical Studies — Between Academy and Church," *ExpT* 125 (2013): 105-16.

183. Melvin Tinker.

own riff and you can improvise — but it's not the same composition. And the end result is different. I think all the cast came to that realization at different stages in the production. And now we're all in sync.[184]

So now Daniel Doriani, who gave us what is the best book on faithful application in biblical preaching,[185] provides us with a stimulating closing essay on what it means to read the Bible faithfully.[186] After all, we serve the God who says, "These are the ones I look on with favor: those who are humble and contrite in spirit and who tremble at my word" (Isa. 66:2).

184. Ian Jackman and Paul Ruditis, *The West Wing: The Official Companion* (New York: Pocket Books, 2002), viii.

185. *Putting the Truth to Work: The Theory and Practice of Biblical Application* (Phillipsburg, NJ: P&R, 2001).

186. "Take, Read" (ch. 35 in this collection).

Historical Topics

TWO

"The Truth Above All Demonstration": Scripture in the Patristic Period to Augustine

Charles E. Hill

Nearly two millennia after their latest constituent member saw the light of day, the books that make up the Christian Bible continue to play an indispensable role in the spiritual lives of churches and individual believers. Yet today, many who wish to honor Scripture as the word of God can scarcely do so unaware that nearly every aspect of the study and use of their prized volume is under dispute. Whether the topic be the origins of Scripture's individual books, the early scribal transmission of those books, their eventual collection into an exclusive "canon," their interpretation, their reliability or truthfulness, or the role they play in the church's attempt to define itself (and others), the reader of Scripture faces no lack of critical scrutiny. It is not surprising, then, that many should think of looking to the "pre-critical" past and should hark back specifically to the early centuries of the Christian era, when the foundations for scriptural exegesis in the Christian tradition were being laid and when Scripture was finding its place in the worshiping life of the church.

Such a pursuit is surely healthy and, in my view, much to be encouraged. Two preliminary considerations, however, may be mentioned. First, even in the patristic period one may look in vain for an idyllic past when scriptural exegesis flourished entirely unencumbered by criticism. From the very beginning there was strife with fellow Jews over the rightful interpretation of Scripture; gnostic, Marcionite, and Valentinian exegesis of the church's books quickly added an array of serious challenges for Christian expositors. And if these somewhat "intramural" problems were not enough, just about as soon as Christians could lift their heads and venture into the public arena, their sacred writings were hit with the literary-cultural criticism of Greco-Roman intellectuals such as Celsus, Galen, Lucian, and, most devastatingly, Porphyry of Tyre. Second, the general dearth of lengthy systematic reflection on the doctrine of Scripture in this period, and the historical delay and disorder in achieving a consensus on the canon, have convinced some that a high respect for Scripture and a conviction of its central importance for the life of the church is a Protestant thing, or more narrowly, a product of Protestant evangelicalism and therefore very much a historically circumscribed phenomenon. In the patristic period, it is thought, there was no canon of Scripture to appeal to, only a canon or rule of faith. And while the Scriptures, particularly the Jewish Scriptures, were regarded as authoritative, they were not consulted as much as were the various creedal summaries and an authoritative church hierarchy. The growing influence of specifically Christian writings (later called the New Testament) is often depicted as gradual, as is the slow dawn of the idea that there ought to be a limit to the number of books to which authoritative appeal in the church should be made.

What I hope to show in this brief foray into the patristic period is, first of all, something of the foundational role that Scripture played in Christian intellectual and spiritual life, even from the earliest times and even in the midst of conflict. This chapter will first seek to summarize how Christians conceived of Scripture as divine, as God's self-attesting word, and as consistent, harmonious, or inerrant. The second part will consider the rise of the New Testament canon, engaging some of the current controversy about this subject. Then follow an examination of the relationship between Scripture and tradition (including the rule of faith) in one important writer, Irenaeus of Lyons; an exploration of Scripture's inspiration in relation to certain "inspired" alternatives; and, finally, a glimpse at the path by which Scripture came to be part of the day-to-day spiritual lives of Christian clergy and even of laypeople.

Conception (Doctrine) of Scripture

Divinity

The Christian church did not so much construct a doctrine of Scripture as inherit one. It succeeded to its conception of the divinity and authority of Holy Scripture, one might say, as bequeathed to it from the broad Jewish heritage in general. As the Alexandrian Jewish philosopher Philo said, "all men are eager to preserve their own customs and laws, and the Jewish nation above all others; for looking upon their laws as oracles (*logia*) directly given to them by God himself, and having been instructed in this doctrine from early youth, they bear in their souls the images of the commandments contained in these laws as sacred" (*On the Embassy to Gaius,* 210).[1] Yet it would also be correct to say that the church received its conception of Scripture from Scripture itself, and from Jesus and his apostles in what soon became a new body of Scripture. "Until heaven and

1. Translation modified from C. D. Yonge, *The Works of Philo, Complete and Unabridged,* new updated edition (Peabody, MA: Hendrickson, 1993). Cf. Paul's words about Timothy's upbringing in 2 Tim. 3:15.

earth pass away, not an iota, not a dot, will pass from the Law until all is accomplished"; "Scripture cannot be broken"; "Thy word is truth"; "All Scripture is breathed out by God and profitable"; "no prophecy was ever produced by the will of man, but men spoke from God as they were carried along by the Holy Spirit." Such conceptions were taught and received by the first Christians. Throughout subsequent Christian history the divinity of Scripture, that is, its ultimate divine authorship, sanctity, and authority, is the common assumption of the faith. Two examples from the third century will give a taste of the doctrine that undergirded Christian thought.

Origen:

> The sacred books (*tas hieras biblous*)[2] are not the compositions of men, but . . . composed by inspiration of the Holy Spirit (*ex epipnoias tou hagiou pneumatos . . . anagegraphthai*), agreeably to the will of the Father of all things through Jesus Christ, and they have come down to us. (*De Principiis* 4.1.9)

Hippolytus:

> There is, brethren, one God, the knowledge of whom we gain from the Holy Scriptures (*tōn hagiōn graphōn*),[3] and from no other source. For just as a man, if he wishes to be skilled in the wisdom of this world, will find himself unable to get at it in any other way than by mastering the dogmas of philosophers, so all of us who wish to practise piety will be unable to learn its practice from any other quarter than the oracles (*tōn logiōn*) of God. Whatever things, then, the divine Scriptures (*hai theiai graphai*) declare, at these let us look; and whatsoever things they teach, these let us learn; and as the Father wills our belief to be, let us believe; and as He wills the Son to be glorified, let us glorify Him; and as He wills the Holy Spirit to be bestowed, let us receive Him. Not according to our own will, nor according to our own mind, nor yet as using violently those things which are given by God, but even as He has chosen to teach them by the Holy Scriptures, so let us discern them. (*Contra Noetum* 9)

Even schismatics and heretics used, and had to use, the Holy Scriptures, for all knew the final court of appeal among the churches was the voice of God speaking in the Scriptures. The arguments were not about whether to use Scripture, or (with notable exceptions)[4] about which Scriptures to use, but about the in-

2. The Greek of *De Principiis* is taken from J. Armitage Robinson, *The Philocalia of Origen: The Text Revised with a Critical Introduction and Indices* (Cambridge: Cambridge University Press, 1893).

3. Greek text from E. Schwartz, "Zwei Predigten Hippolyts," *SBAW* 1936, no. 3: 3-51.

4. As when Athanasius, in his thirty-ninth festal letter and elsewhere, accused the Melitians

terpretation of the Scriptures given by God. Novatian, widely criticized for his schism in Rome in the third century, appeals to "the heavenly Scripture," "the divine Scripture" (*De Trinitate* 6), as did every other church leader. In the fourth century, before controversy broke out over his theological statements, Arius had become famous for his commentaries on Scripture.[5] All the great doctrinal debates were at their cores debates about the meaning of Scripture. Eusebius gives an interesting report to his somewhat skeptical home church in Caesarea after his participation in the Council at Nicea:

> I had no criticism of the anathemas which were put after the creed. It forbade the use of un-Scriptural terms, which has been the cause of nearly all the confusion and anarchy in the Church. Because sacred Scripture makes no use of the term "out of nothing" or of "there was once a time when He was not" or of like words, it did not seem right to say these things or to teach them.

The Criterion of Truth: Scripture as Indemonstrable First Principle

The high confidence Christians placed in the divine writings was not at that time, as it is still not today, well understood or appreciated by outsiders. While Christians responded to numerous attacks on Scripture by defending it against charges of falsehood of various kinds, the divine origin and authority of their Scriptures was not, generally speaking, something they could or needed to "prove," but was that by which they proved all things.

It is true that Christian writers throughout the period frequently turned to the "proof from prophecy." The fulfillment of the prophets' words was very often pointed to as showing that their written words truly were inspired by God's Spirit (e.g., Origen, *Princ.* 4.1.6; Eusebius, *Proof of the Gospel* 1.1). But even this is best seen as an appeal to the way Scripture manifested its own divinity and not as a humanly constructed argument for its divinity "from the ground up," so to speak. Though often lost sight of today, the self-authenticating quality of Scripture was perhaps surprisingly well recognized, especially among some early Greek writers.

---

of using Apocryphal writings. See David Brakke, "Canon Formation and Social Conflict in Fourth-Century Egypt: Athanasius of Alexandria's Thirty-Ninth *Festal Letter*," *HTR* 87 (1994): 395-419 at 410-17.

5. See, e.g., Charles Kannengiesser, "The Bible in the Arian Crisis," in *The Bible in Greek Christian Antiquity,* ed. and trans. Paul M. Blowers (Notre Dame: University of Notre Dame Press, 1997), 217-28; "[T]he oldest chroniclers of Christianity felt confident to declare that Arius had become famous in his lifetime for commentaries on Scripture he delivered in preaching to the Alexandrian parish for which he had become responsible under Bishop Alexander. His congregation was astounded by the originality of his interpretations" (218).

Justin, Ps. Justin, and an Old Man

The conversion of the philosopher Justin to Christianity, probably sometime before about 130 C.E., occurred after his encounter with an older man whose name Justin never reveals. In the course of their conversation, as Justin relates it, the old man introduced Justin to the Hebrew prophets,[6] who in their writings spoke, he asserted, by the divine and Holy Spirit. One derives more help on philosophical matters, he said to the young philosopher, from the prophets than from the philosophers themselves. For these prophets "did not use demonstration (*apodeixeōs*) in their treatises, seeing that they were witnesses to the truth above all demonstration (*anōterō pasēs apodeixeōs*), and worthy of belief (*axiopistoi*)" (*Dial.* 7.2).[7]

It is important to observe that, though the old man spoke specifically of the Hebrew prophets, this same quality of self-authentication apparently applied to "the words of the Saviour," which, Justin later came to see, also "possess a terrible power in themselves, and are sufficient to inspire those who turn aside from the path of rectitude with awe; while the sweetest rest is afforded those who make a diligent practice of them" (*Dial.* 8.2). These words, "filled with the Spirit of God, and big with power, and flourishing with grace" (*Dial.* 9.1),[8] are words Justin knew from the memoirs of Jesus' apostles, books otherwise known as Gospels (cf. *Dial.* 10.2).[9]

After exhorting Justin to believe the prophets' testimony about the Creator and "his Son, the Christ," the old man counseled him also to pray for light, "for these things cannot be perceived or understood by all, but only by the man to whom God and His Christ have imparted wisdom" (*Dial.* 7.3, cf. Matt. 11:25-27). Thereafter a love for the prophets and for the "friends of Christ" (no doubt his apostles) was indeed kindled in Justin's soul.

These two principles, that Scripture is divine and therefore not in need of philosophical defense or demonstration, and that it could only be truly and fully apprehended through divine aid, would often recur together.

A treatise *On the Resurrection,*[10] once attributed to Justin but probably deriv-

6. Justin's student, Tatian the Syrian, too would later testify that it was his reading of the Hebrew Scriptures that led him to faith (*Address to the Greeks* 29).

7. Greek of the *Dialogue* from Miroslav Marcovich, ed., *Iustini Martyris Dialogus cum Tryphone,* PTS 47 (Berlin/New York: Walter de Gruyter, 1997).

8. The apologist Aristides hopes that the emperor will be able to "judge the glory of his [Christ's] presence from the holy gospel writing" (15.1).

9. See C. E. Hill, "Was John's Gospel among the Apostolic Memoirs?" in *Justin Martyr and His Worlds,* ed. Sara Parvis and Paul Foster (Minneapolis: Fortress, 2007), 88-93.

10. Attributed by John of Damascus to Justin, this anonymous treatise, according to Claudio Moreschini and Enrico Norelli, *Early Christian Greek and Latin Literature: A Literary History,* 2 vols.: vol. 1, *From Paul to the Age of Constantine,* trans. Matthew J. O'Connell (Peabody, MA:

ing from another second- or early-third-century writer, shares the old man's idea that the truth, because it is from God, is self-attesting and beyond demonstration. This author opens his work in this way:

> The word of truth is free, and carries its own authority (*autexousios*),[11] disdaining to fall under any skilful argument, or to endure the logical scrutiny (*di' apodeixeōs exetasin hypomenein*) of its hearers. But it would be believed for its own nobility, and for the confidence due to him who sends it. Now the word of truth is sent from God; wherefore the freedom claimed by the truth is not arrogant. For being sent with authority, it were not fit that it should be required to produce proof of what is said; since neither is there any proof beyond itself, which is God. For every proof (*apodeixis*) is more powerful and trustworthy than that which it proves. . . . But nothing is either more powerful or more trustworthy than the truth. (*Res.* 1.1-6)

Clement of Alexandria

Such ideas may have been quite common among Christians, for they (or caricatures of them) are noted, though not appreciated, even by outsiders. Writing in about 180, the physician Galen complained about Jews and Christians not using demonstration in their treatises but relying on faith instead.[12] Galen had evidently read Moses, whose method, he judges, was "to write without offering proofs, saying 'God commanded, God spake.'" The schools of Moses and Christ speak of "undemonstrated laws" and order their followers "to accept everything on faith."[13] He clearly did not much admire the Christians' intellectual achievements, as he knew them: "Most people are unable to follow any demonstrative argument consecutively; hence they need parables, and benefit from them . . . just as now we see the people called Christians drawing their faith from parables and miracles and yet sometimes acting in the same way [as those who philosophize]."[14]

Hendrickson, 2005; Italian original 1995), 202, "fits perfectly into the debates at the end of the second century." A. Whealey, "Pseudo-Justin's *De Resurrectione:* Athenagoras or Hippolytus?" *VC* 60 (2006): 420-30, argues it is the work of Hippolytus of Rome or someone in his circle.

11. Greek text from Martin Heimgartner, *Pseudojustin — Über die Auferstehung. Text und Studie,* PTS 54 (Berlin/New York: Walter de Gruyter, 2001).

12. See R. Walzer, *Galen on Jews and Christians* (London: Oxford University Press, 1949), 11-15.

13. The citations, in order, are from *On His Own Books* 1; *On the Differences of Pulses* 2.4: *On the Prime Unmoved Mover* (Arabic). All of these, and the next, have been taken from Robert M. Grant, *Second-Century Christianity: A Collection of Fragments,* 2nd edition (Louisville/London: Westminster John Knox, 2003), 11-12, which see for more quotations.

14. Arabic excerpt from Galen's lost summary of Plato's *Republic.*

In the next decade, Clement of Alexandria would write very much aware of this kind of disdain. Clement's understanding of Greek philosophy, and in particular its discussions of logic (including epistemology) is quite impressive and he does not shy away from the issue of demonstration. His response to charges such as those leveled by Galen is not to deny them by asserting that Christians do indeed demonstrate everything before believing. Rather, he defends the priority of faith[15] by pointing out that some things (both ideas and material objects) do not stand in need of demonstration. In several places in the *Stromateis* Clement discusses what Aristotle had called "first principles" (*archai*), things that are true and primary, and "convincing on the strength not of anything else but of themselves."[16] Clement found this concept conducive to explaining the role of Christian faith to critics like Galen: "Should one say that knowledge is founded on demonstration by a process of reasoning, let him hear that first principles are incapable of demonstration" (*ei de tis legoi tēn epistēmēn apodeiktikēn einai meta logou, akousatō hoti kai hai archai anapodeiktoi*) (*Stromateis* 2.4.13.4).[17] What is paramount here is to recognize that for Clement, whatever God says in Scripture has, perforce, the character of an indemonstrable first principle. Not only is this first principle indemonstrable by human reasoning, it is at the same time irrefutably demonstrated by God himself: "If a person has faith in the divine Scriptures and a firm judgment, then he receives as an irrefutable demonstration (*apodeixin anantirrhēton*) the voice of the God who has granted him those Scriptures. The faith no longer requires the confirmation of a demonstration (*di' apodeixeōs oxyrōmenē*). 'Blessed are those who without seeing have believed' (John 20:29)" (*Strom.* 2.2.9.6).[18] While his most comprehensive work on logic and demonstra-

15. Faith here is a "preconception by the will, an act of consenting to religion" (*Stromateis* 2.2.8.4).

16. Aristotle, *Topics* 100b19, cited from Silke-Petra Bergjan, "Logic and Theology in Clement of Alexandria: The Purpose of the 8th Book of the *Stromata*," *Zeitschrift für antikes Christentum* 12 (2008): 396-413 at 405. On the background in philosophical thought, see Salvatore R. C. Lilla, *Clement of Alexandria: A Study in Christian Platonism and Gnosticism* (Oxford: Oxford University Press, 1971), 118-31; more recently, Andrew C. Itter, *Esoteric Teaching in the* Stromateis *of Clement of Alexandria,* SuppVC 97 (Leiden/Boston: Brill, 2009), 94-104; and the fine discussion in Andrew Radde-Gallwitz, *Basil of Caesarea, Gregory of Nyssa, and the Transformation of Divine Simplicity,* Oxford Early Christian Studies (Oxford: Oxford University Press, 2009), 40-49. Itter points out that Clement is close to Aristotle in his exposition of first principles but that he "primarily develops his own Christian thesis" on them (94).

17. Here he may be invoking against Christianity's critics the authority of Aristotle himself, who, in a discussion of philosophy, said that first principles were indemonstrable (*hai d' archai anapodeiktoi*), *Magna Moralia* 1197a 23-29.

18. *Clement of Alexandria* Stromateis *Books One to Three,* FTC 85, trans. John Ferguson (Washington, DC: Catholic University of America Press, 1991). Greek text of Clement from Otto Stählin, *Clemens Alexandrinus,* vol. 2, *Stromata Buch I-VI,* GCS 15 (Leipzig: J. C. Hinrichs'sche Buchhandlung, 1906).

tion (*apodeixis*) comes in the enigmatic book 8, the discussion most relevant to Scripture specifically comes in book 7.

> For in the Lord we have the first principle (*tēn archēn*) of instruction, guiding us to knowledge from first to last "in divers ways and divers portions" (Heb. 1:1) through the prophets and the gospel and the blessed apostles. And, if any one were to suppose that the first principle stood in need of something else, it could no longer be really maintained as a first principle. He then who of himself believes the Lord's Scripture and his actual voice (*tē kyriakē graphē te kai phōnē*) is worthy of belief. . . . Certainly we use it [Scripture] as a criterion (*kriteriō*) for the discovery of the real facts. But whatever comes into judgment is not to be believed before it is judged, so that what is in need of judgment cannot be a first principle. With good reason therefore having apprehended our first principle by faith without proof (*anapodeikton*), we get our proofs (*apodeixeis*) about the first principle *ex abundanti* from the principle itself, and are thus trained by the voice of the Lord for the knowledge of the truth. For we pay no attention to the mere assertions of men, which may be met by equally valid assertions on the other side. If, however, it is not enough just simply to state one's opinion, but we are bound to prove (*pistōsasthai*) what is said, then we do not wait for the witness of men, but we prove the point (*pistoumetha*) in question by the voice of the Lord, which is more to be relied on than any demonstration or rather which is the only real demonstration (*apodeixis*). (*Stromateis* 7.16.95)[19]

> So too we, obtaining from the Scriptures themselves a perfect demonstration concerning the Scriptures, derive from faith a conviction which has the force of demonstration (*apodeiktikōs*). (*Stromateis* 7.16.96)

God himself, of course, is the ultimate first principle, and Scripture, God's voice, therefore gives us sure knowledge that proves other things but is not itself subject to proof. As Eric Osborn observes, this "foundationalism" is certainly not "naïve."[20] For Clement, the Bible was "divine oracle and . . . true philosophy,

19. Translation from Henry Chadwick and J. E. L. Oulton, eds., *Alexandrian Christianity: Selected Translations of Clement and Origen* (Louisville and London: Westminster John Knox, 1954), 155. Greek from Otto Stählin, ed., *Clemens Alexandrinus,* vol. 3, *Stromata Buch VII und VIII, Excerpta ex Theodoto, Eclogae Propheticae, Quis Dives Salvetur, Fragmente,* GCS 17 (Leipzig: J. C. Hinrichs'sche Buchhandlung, 1909).

20. Eric Osborn, "Clement and the Bible," in Gilles Dorival and Alain Le Boulluec, *Origeniana Sexta. Origène et la Bible/Origen and the Bible. Actes du Colloquium Origenianum Sextum, Chantilly, 30 août–3 septembre 1993* (Leuven: Leuven University Press, 1995), 121-32 at 121. He believes "Clement confronted and overcame the kind of divide which exists today between post-modernist and analytic philosopher" (122 n. 3).

which always included argument."[21] Argument, however, is secondary, for investigating, understanding, and explicating what is received through an act of faith. Clement the teacher was all about investigation. But he held that investigation to be best which "accompanies faith and which builds the magnificent knowledge of the truth on the base represented by faith" (*Strom.* 5.1.5.2).

We note that Clement's description of Scripture, God's voice, as a first principle that does not submit to human demonstration applies not only to the words of prophets, but to "the gospel and the blessed apostles."

Origen

Origen continues the theme and derives support for it from the apostle Paul. Near the beginning of his great work against Celsus, written ca. 246, he wrote,

> We have to say, moreover, that the Gospel has a demonstration (*apodeixis*) of its own (*oikeia*), more divine (*theiotera*) than any established by Grecian dialectics. And this diviner method is called by the apostle the "manifestation (or demonstration, *apodeixin*) of the Spirit and of power" (1 Cor. 2:4): of "the Spirit," on account of the prophecies, which are sufficient to produce faith in any one who reads them, especially in those things that relate to Christ; and of "power," because of the signs and wonders that we must believe to have been performed, both on many other grounds, and on this, that traces of them are still preserved among those that regulate their lives by the precepts of the Gospel. (*CCels.* 1.2)

Almost twenty years earlier, Origen had begun his treatise *On First Principles* with a statement of his Christian epistemology. All who are assured that grace and truth came in Jesus Christ "derive the knowledge which incites men to a good and happy life from no other source than from the very words and teaching of Christ." This does not mean merely those words Jesus uttered while on earth. For Christ, the Word of God, spoke in Moses and the prophets (citing Heb. 11:24-26). Jesus spoke also in his apostles, as "is shown by Paul in these words: 'Or do you seek a proof (*dokimēn*) of Christ, who speaketh in me?' " (2 Cor. 13:3). Thus, that knowledge which leads to a good and happy life comes from Christ alone, through the Scriptures of the Old and New Testaments. Of the several teachings that Origen regards as first principles, derived from apostolic preaching, is that the Scriptures come from God,[22] and that there is a spiritual meaning to Scripture that often lies hidden behind the material (*Princ.* praef. 8).

21. Osborn, "Clement and the Bible," 122.

22. Moreschini and Norelli, *Early Christian Greek and Latin Literature,* vol. 1, *From Paul to*

Origen does not ignore the subjective effects that Justin and his teacher had spoken of, which Reformation theologians would call the inward testimony of the Holy Spirit: "And he who reads the words of the prophets with care and attention, feeling by the very perusal the traces of the divinity (*ichnos enthousiasmou*)[23] that is in them, will be led by his own emotions to believe that those words which have been deemed to be the words of God are not the compositions of men (*ouk anthrōpōn*)" (*Princ.* 4.1.6).

Eusebius

Of course, not all readers of Scripture were so led. Christianity's intellectual opponents were evidently not placated by the appeal to Scripture's self-authenticating divinity — though it is certainly questionable how seriously this appeal was ever engaged by those opponents. The written refutations by people like Hierocles, a Roman official who helped instigate the great persecution, and especially of Porphyry,[24] who struck hard at Scripture, had gone deep, but their essential criticism of Christian thought apparently had not moved much beyond Galen's.

> As we have such a mob of slanderers flooding us with the accusation that we are unable logically to present a clear demonstration of the truth we hold, and think it enough to retain those who come to us by faith alone, and as they say that we only teach our followers like irrational animals to shut their eyes and staunchly obey what we say without examining it at all, and call them therefore "the faithful" because of their faith as distinct from reason. (*Proof* 1.1.10)[25]

With these criticisms in mind, Eusebius wrote his great two-volume defense, *Preparation for the Gospel* and *Demonstration of the Gospel,* to show that "our

---

the Age of Constantine, 285, observe that Origen "intends to take as his point of departure and justificatory criterion the data of the Scriptures. On that foundation he will develop rational arguments, but without forgetting those who reject such proofs, claiming that they wish to restrict themselves to the biblical data." As John Behr, *The Formation of Christian Theology,* vol. 1, *The Way to Nicaea* (Crestwood, NY: St. Vladimir's Seminary Press, 2001), 33, summarizes, "These first principles, grasped by faith, are the basis for subsequent demonstrations, and are also subsequently used to evaluate other claims to truth, acting thus as a 'canon.' "

23. This word often carries the connotation of ecstatic frenzy, but here "divinity" is a better translation, as will become clear in the section on "Inspiration and Frenzy," 81-83 below.

24. See Lactantius, *On the Death of the Persecutors* 16.4; *The Divine Institutes* 5.2; Macarius, *Apocriticus.*

25. Robert M. Berchman, *Porphyry against the Christians,* Ancient Mediterranean and Medieval Texts and Contexts, Studies in Platonism, Neoplatonism, and the Platonic Tradition 1 (Leiden/Boston: Brill, 2005), 137 n. 16, notes that this was "an authentic critique likely raised by Porphyry."

devotion to the oracles of the Hebrews thus had the support of judgment and sound reason" (*Proof* 1.1.10). Scripture certainly functioned for Eusebius as supreme authority, as God's own voice, though it does not appear that Eusebius stated so clearly as some of his predecessors did the principle of Scripture as the indemonstrable first principle of knowledge, due perhaps to the pressure he felt to answer the specific charges of Porphyry. But the principle is indeed alive and seems to cast a shadow over his entire work. At one point Eusebius observes that Plato himself said "we must in obedience to the law believe, even though . . . without certain or probable proofs (*apodeixeiōn*)" (Timaeus 40e; *Preparation* 2.7.76b).

Eusebius does refer to some predecessors, who gave "demonstrations without number" in written defenses, and refers to commentaries on "the sacred and inspired Scriptures (*hieras kai entheous graphas*), showing by mathematical demonstrations (*apodeixesi*) the unerring (*adiaptōton*) truthfulness of those who from the beginning preached to us the word of godliness"[26] (*Preparation* 1.3.7c). Like Origen, Eusebius appealed to the man he says was the first Christian to deprecate "deceitful and sophistical plausibilities, and to use proofs (*apodeixesin*) free from ambiguity . . . the holy Apostle Paul, who says in one place, 'And our speech and our preaching was not in persuasive words of wisdom, but in demonstration of the Spirit and of power'" (1 Cor. 2:4, *Preparation* 1.3.7b, citing then 1 Cor. 3:5; 2 Cor. 3:5). Eusebius's substantial apologetic work is his attempt to keep Peter's exhortation "to be ready to give an answer to every man that asketh a reason concerning the hope that is in us" (1 Pet. 3:15), and to show that Christians have not devoted themselves to an "unreasoning faith, but to wise and profitable doctrines which contain the way of true religion" (*Preparation* 1.5.14b). But in line with Christians before him, Eusebius places no ultimate confidence in the force of logical demonstrations but depends on "the help which comes down from the God of the universe" supplying "to the teaching and name of our Saviour its irresistible and invincible force, and its victorious power against its enemies" (*Preparation* 1.4.9d-10a).

Even when not stated in terms of an "indemonstrable first principle," Scripture's divine and foundational authority appears to be the common assumption and the common confession of the church. Gregory of Nyssa, more than perhaps any other fourth-century Christian author, absorbed Greek philosophy. He has been accused of merely applying Christian names to Plato's doctrines and calling it Christian theology.[27] Nonetheless, Gregory affirmed "We are not able to affirm what we please. We make Holy Scripture the rule and the measure of every tenet. We approve of that alone which may be made to harmonize with the intention

26. I take it he means the apostles.

27. The charge is that of H. F. Cherniss, *The Platonism of Gregory of Nyssa,* University of California Publications in Classical Philology 11.1 (Berkeley, 1930), 62; see Quasten, 3, 283-84.

of those writings" (*De anima et resurr.*, MG 46, 49B). Scripture is "the guide of reason" (*Contra Eunom.* I, 114, 126), "the criterion of truth" (107).[28]

Two things perhaps need emphasizing here. On the one hand, the assertion that Scripture's truth and divinity are beyond human demonstration, despite the carping of critics, cannot not be regarded as anti-intellectual. The charges leveled by Galen in the second century have echoed through the centuries right up to the present, but they ring no less hollow. Quite obviously, none of the Christian writers treated above found that faith in the teachings of Scripture impeded the robust and exacting employment of logic, historical study, philosophy, or any other tool of human erudition. For them, this view of Scripture provided the only sure foundation for intellectual endeavors of any kind. From Justin and his unnamed Christian teacher, to Clement, Origen, Gregory, and Augustine in our period, through the intellectual achievements of the Middle Ages, right up to Reformed Epistemology in the present, a Scripture-based Christianity has not avoided the encounter with non-Christian philosophies nor has it shirked a responsibility to "lead every thought captive to Christ" (2 Cor. 10:5) and to do the positive labor of ordering human thought in accordance with Scripture. The words of Scripture, the voice of God, have been the criterion of truth that has legitimized human intellectual activity. Ultimately, Galen's disparagement has proved to be reactionary and misinformed.

On the other hand, the adoption of terminology and ideas from the Greek philosophical tradition could be viewed as a sign of the church's abandonment of Hebrew thought and its rapid capitulation to Hellenistic thought. While in some areas of Christian theology this charge might be made more or less compellingly, I would argue that in what we have seen regarding the doctrine of Scripture, the adoption of terms was essentially defensive and reciprocal. Adopting the philosophical term "first principle" for the privileging of Scripture was a way of "plundering the Egyptians," or, of hoisting the critic with his own petard. The entire fabric of the effort from the Christian side was designed to assert the priority of divine revelation, and faith in that revelation, to syllogistic human reasoning exemplified in the demand for external "demonstration." These early authors saw their approach as a working-out of what was implicit in scriptural passages such as John 20:29 and 1 Corinthians 2:4.

Scripture's Internal Harmony, Consistency, and Inerrancy

Because Scripture was divine and sacred, it was also received as internally consistent, harmonious, and a faultless expression of the divine will. We saw

28. All these cited from J. Quasten, *Patrology*, 3 vols., vol. 3, *The Golden Age of Greek Patristic Literature* (Westminster, MD: Christian Classics Inc., 1984 repr. of 1950 orig.), 284.

above Eusebius's allusion to the apostles' unerring truthfulness (*to apseudēs kai adiaptōton*), which could plausibly be seen as one testimony to a belief in scriptural inerrancy. Most of the explicit expressions along these lines, though, have to do with Scripture's consistency or harmony.

Following directly the claims made by NT authors themselves, the first noncanonical writers maintain Scripture's truthfulness and harmony. Before referencing a string of scriptural passages Clement of Rome reminds his readers, "You have searched the holy scriptures (*tas hieras graphas*), which are true, which were given by the Holy Spirit; you know that nothing unrighteous (*adikon*) or counterfeit (*parapepoiēmenon*) is written in them" (*1 Clem.* 45.2-3). Justin at one point scolds his opponent:

> If you spoke these words, Trypho, in order that I might say the Scriptures contradicted each other (*enantias . . . allēlais*), you have erred. But I shall not venture to suppose or to say such a thing; and if a Scripture which appears to be of such a kind be brought forward, and if there be a pretext [for saying] that it is contrary [to some other] (*hōs enantia ousa*), since I am entirely convinced that no Scripture contradicts another (*hoti oudemia graphē tē hetera enantia estin*), I shall admit rather that I do not understand what is recorded, and shall strive to persuade those who imagine that the Scriptures are contradictory, to be rather of the same opinion as myself. (*Dial.* 65)

Irenaeus too was confident that "the entire Scriptures, the prophets, and the Gospels, can be clearly, unambiguously, and harmoniously understood by all, although all do not believe them" (*AH* 2.27.2), that "the Scriptures are indeed perfect, since they were spoken by the Word of God and His Spirit" (2.28.2). Such confidence in Scripture's divinity, harmony, and perfection promoted a hermeneutic by which the ambiguous passages could be interpreted by reference to the clear: "all Scripture, which has been given to us by God, shall be found by us perfectly consistent; and the parables shall harmonize with those passages which are perfectly plain; and those statements the meaning of which is clear, shall serve to explain the parables; and through the many diversified utterances [of Scripture] there shall be heard one harmonious melody in us, praising in hymns that God who created all things" (2.28.4).

While it may be true that not all the difficulties unearthed by critics since the Enlightenment were known to or acknowledged by the ancients, I dare to say that a great many of them were. The ancients were not ignorant of "the phenomena" of Scripture. Because of their relatively greater accessibility and their centrality to the evangelistic and apologetic task, the four Gospels became a very public forum for attack, defense, and discussion of the harmony of Christian Scripture. From at least the time of Papias's elder, probably ca. 100, discrepancies between the narratives of the Gospels were known and treated by Christians. The elder defended Mark's "order" (*taxis*), or lack thereof, on the basis of his intention to record simply but faithfully what he had heard from Peter (Eusebius, *HE* 3.39.15-16). The author of the *Muratorian Fragment*,[29] too, acknowledged differences, but credited the Gospels with a Spirit-authored unity.

> And so, though various elements [or beginnings] may be taught in the individual books of the Gospels, nevertheless this makes no difference to the faith of believers, since by the one sovereign Spirit all things have been declared in all [the Gospels]: concerning the nativity, concerning the passion, concerning the resurrection, concerning life with his disciples, and concerning his twofold coming; the first in lowliness when he was despised, which has taken place, the second glorious in royal power, which is still in the future.[30]

Confidence in this harmony between the Gospels had already resulted in a new literary form, the *Diatessaron,* which attempted to combine all four Gospel accounts into a single harmonized narrative. We know of at least two before Irenaeus, one by Theophilus of Antioch and the more famous one by Tatian the Syrian. The name given to these productions, diatessaron, itself was a musical term for the interval we call "a fourth" and may well have been chosen because of a conception of harmony that was quite in keeping with that which Irenaeus would soon articulate concerning the four Gospels (*AH* 3.11.8) and Scripture in general. This conviction of an underlying harmony between the evangelists is no doubt also responsible for a significant number of "harmonizations" introduced by "well-meaning" scribes into the textual tradition of the Gospels, and of the NT generally.

The analogy with musical harmony is seen in Origen as well. Those who claim to find disharmony in Scripture, he says, are like those who do not recognize harmony in music. The blessed peacemaker (Matt. 5:9) "knows that all the Scripture

29. The traditional date of the *MF* (late second or early third century) has been contested in favor of a date in the second half of the fourth century. The main arguments for the later date have been made by A. C. Sundberg, "Towards a Revised History of the New Testament Canon," *Studia Evangelica* 4, no. 1 (1968): 452-61; "Canon Muratori: A Fourth-Century List," *HTR* 66 (1973): 1-41; and G. M. Hahneman, *The Muratorian Fragment and the Development of the Canon* (Oxford: Oxford University Press, 1992). The theory fails, however, to account adequately for the fragment's dating of itself not long after Hermas's *The Shepherd,* and ignores much of the evidence for a late-second-century context; see C. E. Hill, *The Johannine Corpus in the Early Church* (Oxford: Oxford University Press, 2004), 129-34. The most thorough response to Sundberg/Hahneman is Joseph Verheyden, "The Canon Muratori: A Matter of Dispute," in J.-M. Auwers and H. J. de Jonge, *The Biblical Canons,* BETL 163 (Leuven: Leuven University Press, 2003), 487-556.

30. The translation of Bruce Metzger, *The Canon of the New Testament* (Oxford: Oxford University Press, 1987), 305-6.

is the one perfect and harmonized [or fitted] instrument of God, which from different sounds gives forth one saving voice to those willing to learn, which stops and restrains every working of an evil spirit, just as the music of David laid to rest the evil spirit in Saul, which also was choking him (1 Sam. 16:14)" (*Comm. Matt.* 2).[31] In Origen, however, we encounter a more complex musicology; Scripture's perfect harmony did not mean that it contained no "errors," on the material (as opposed to spiritual) level. "The chief concern of the evangelists," he wrote, "was related to the mysteries; they did not so much care to report the accurate history of the events as to set forth the mystery of those things that derive from the historical facts. . . . The evangelists sometimes changed historical circumstances to the benefit of the spiritual purpose, so that they reported that something happened in a determined place and time, although in fact it happened in another place and time" (*Comm. John* 10.5.19). Michael Holmes summarizes Origen's statements: "in order to accomplish its primary goal the Word utilized whenever possible actual historical events. But when these were not suitable, the Word worked fictional elements into the narrative in order to get the desired message across."[32] This applied to both the OT and the NT.

Holmes observes that Origen might be called an inerrantist with respect to the spiritual meaning of Scripture, but certainly not with respect to its literal meaning, at least not as inerrancy is usually understood. One might also observe that these things in Scripture that in Origen's view "are not true according to the bodily sense" (*Princ.* 4.2.9) may be historically inaccurate or factually false, but are not exactly mistakes or "errors," for they are deliberately placed there by the Spirit, intended not to deceive but to lead into deeper spiritual truth. It is only the sensual man who is led astray by focusing on the mere letter (*Hom. Gen.* 10.5).

Origen's openness to recognizing historical untruths "according to the letter"[33] cannot be separated from his particular hermeneutical approach and his enthusiasm to get to the "spiritual realities" of which the bodily realities are fig-

31. *ANF* 10, 413.

32. Michael Holmes, "Origen and the Inerrancy of Scripture," *JETS* 24 (1981): 221-31 at 227. See also Enrique Nardoni, "Origen's Concept of Biblical Inspiration," *Second Century* 4 (1984): 9-23 at 18. He cites S. Laeuchli, "The Polarity of the Gospels in the Exegesis of Origen," *Church History* 21 (1952): 215, "In definitive contrast to Tatian and Theophilus of Antioch, here for the first time a theologian of the church realizes the full impossibility of any historical harmonization of the gospels."

33. Origen sometimes drew distinctions between those parts of Scripture that had the quality of direct revelation, and those that came from the mind of the writer. Though all the Scriptures current in the church "are believed to be divine" (*Comm. John* 1.14), Origen also sometimes speaks as though there is a hierarchy among them: "we must say that the apostolic writings are wise and trustworthy and most beneficial; they are not, to be sure, on a par with 'Thus says the Lord almighty'" (*Comm. John* 1.15). Because of his many assertions of the divinity, sanctity, and authority of all the Scriptures, one imagines that the distinctions he has in mind here are much like genre distinctions.

ures. Historical irregularities merely alert the reader that there is a deeper spiritual meaning to be found. Thus, one can understand how the hunt to discover spiritual treasures for the church[34] might not only dampen interest in resolving an apparent discrepancy, but perhaps even magnify the discrepancy. This appears, for example, in his exposition of Genesis 24:16, where Origen explains, "history is not being narrated, but mysteries are interwoven" (*Hom. Gen.* 10.4). Precisely this tendency has been observed in Origen's predecessor and "mentor" in allegorical method, Philo of Alexandria. Maren Niehoff writes that Philo "stresses problems in the literal text in order to make room for allegory. . . . The literal dimension of Scripture is thus not altogether dismissed, but shown to be problematic to a degree that renders the allegorical meaning plausible."[35] A desire to showcase the benefits of spiritual exegesis can open one's eyes to literal contradictions where others may not see them.

In Origen's Christian context, when it came to admitting factual or historical untruths in Scripture, it may be that he was not "an isolated example."[36] Yet it is not easy to find even among his many admirers[37] any who were as quick to concede the presence of "inerrant errors" in Scripture as he was, or as willing to abandon the attempt to reconcile Scripture with reason or history or itself (even Origen, of course, did this at times). Recall the comment of Eusebius, one of Origen's most enthusiastic supporters,[38] about the apostles' unerring truthfulness. We know that Origen was opposed even in his lifetime by Christians who believed he had exceeded the bounds of responsible exegesis. But another reason for the general failure of other Christian writers to match Origen's boldness in this regard had to be the publication of a work called *Against the Christians* by a neo-Platonist critic who claimed that, as a young man, he had known the great Christian teacher.[39] Porphyry of Tyre, says Kofsky, "sharply criticized the ten-

34. By his allegorical treatment of Genesis 24:15-16, he aims to "edify the Church of God" and to challenge "very sluggish and inactive hearers with the examples of the saints and mystical explanations" (*Hom. Gen.* 10.5).

35. See Maren R. Niehoff, "Philo's Scholarly Inquiries into the Story of Paradise," in *Paradise in Antiquity: Jewish and Christian Views,* ed. Markus Bockmuehl and Guy G. Stroumsa (Cambridge: Cambridge University Press, 2010), 28-42 at 37. Niehoff notes as well some of the earlier background in pagan allegorizations of Homer.

36. So Holmes, "Inerrancy," 230.

37. For an example of one of his critics (Epiphanius), see Hill, *Johannine Corpus,* 186-90.

38. See Charles Kannengiesser, "Eusebius of Caesarea, Origenist," in *Eusebius, Christianity, and Judaism,* ed. Harold W. Attridge and Gohei Hata (Detroit: Wayne State University Press, 1992), 435-66 at 459.

39. See Eusebius, *HE* 6.19.3-8. It has of course been questioned whether Porphyry was referring to Origen the Christian or another man by that name. But Porphyry's description, given by Eusebius (*HE* 6.19.3-8), makes it hard to think it was not the famous biblical scholar we know. See also R. M. Berchman, "In the Shadow of Origen: Porphyry and the Patristic Origins of New Testament Criticism," in G. Dorival and A. Le Boulluec, *Origeniana Sexta: Origène et la Bible/*

dency to allegorical interpretation popular among Christians. He was well aware that this exegetical approach offered a solution to difficulties presented by the Scriptures. . . . By ruling out allegorical interpretation one exposed the difficulties presented by the text."[40] Porphyry specifically named Origen as the one who took from the Greeks the absurdity (*atopia*) which is the allegorical method (*ton metalēptikon tropon*) and introduced it to the Christians (Fr. 39).[41]

Despite the best efforts of Diodorus of Tarsus and other teachers of the Antiochene school, Christians of course never completely discarded the allegorical method. Yet its vulnerability to abuse, particularly when used as a facile way to avoid exegetical difficulties, came to be widely recognized. Particularly after the withering critique of Porphyry, Christian scholars in general would not be so blithe as Origen sometimes seemed to be about the historical, factual, or internal consistency problems in Scripture. Apologetic responses to informed attacks on Scripture required greater sophistication and facility with the tools employed by the critics. According to Berchman, Porphyry's critique "led Christians to a defense of scripture on historical and literary grounds. They became higher critics of scripture themselves."[42] The use of literary and historical methods by Christian writers perennially raises questions among Christian communities about compromise and corruption from without. But it would be wrong to surmise that even the appropriation of the methods of ancient higher criticism by Christian scholars meant or must mean a weakening of faith in the transcendent power and veracity of Scripture.

"If we are perplexed by an apparent contradiction in Scripture," wrote Augustine in his response to Faustus (397-400), "it is not allowable to say, The author of this book is mistaken; but either the manuscript is faulty,[43] or the translation is wrong, or you have not understood" (*CFaust.* 11.5). Faustus had rejected the Gospel testimonies because of the different genealogies of Jesus given in Matthew and Luke (a problem also observed by Porphyry). Augustine points out that many able and learned men had seen the obvious inconsistency and had found that "there is more in it than appears at first sight" (11.2). "But with a due regard to the high authority of Scripture, they believed that there was something here which would be given to those that ask, and denied to those that snarl; would be found by those that seek, and taken away from those that criticise; would be open

---

Origen and the Bible. Actes du Colloquium Origenianum Sextum Chantilly, 30 août–3 septembre 1993 (Leuven: Leuven University Press, 1995), 657-73.

40. Aryeh Kofsky, *Eusebius of Caesarea Against Paganism* (Boston/Leiden: Brill, 2002), 29. See also Berchman, *Porphyry,* 58: "What angered Porphyry was the way in which Christians used allegory to explain away, as he saw it, the difficulties in the Jewish Bible."

41. Kofsky, *Eusebius,* 58.

42. Berchman, *Porphyry,* 60.

43. Berchman is mistaken when claiming (*Porphyry,* 69) that Augustine never appealed to copyist error in resolving difficulties. E.g., *On the Harmony of the Evangelists* 3.7.29.

to those that knock, and shut against those that contradict. They asked, sought, and knocked; they received, found, and entered in" (*CFaust.* 3.2). As he would say elsewhere, "It is a wonderful and beneficial thing that the Holy Spirit organized the holy scripture so as to satisfy hunger by means of its plainer passages and remove boredom by means of its obscurer ones" (*OCD* 2.15, Green's translation).

What Augustine found when he sought concerning this difficulty was not a spiritual lesson derived by allegory, but simply that one evangelist's account gave Joseph's biological father, the other his adoptive father. Augustine then summarizes his dealings with the variations between the evangelists: "if one says one thing, and another another, or one in one way and another in another, still they all speak truth, and in no way contradict one another; only let the reader be reverent and humble, not in an heretical spirit seeking occasion for strife, but with a believing heart desiring edification" (*CFaust.* 3.5).[44]

Well aware of the critical attacks of Porphyry and others,[45] Augustine could assert that the evangelists "in no way contradict one another." In about the year 400 Augustine wrote a laborious treatise *On the Harmony of the Evangelists.* While his solutions may not always completely satisfy, he remained faithful to his conviction of Scripture's truthfulness, harmony, and consistency. We even have in his letter to Jerome (*Ep.* 82.1.3) dated to 404/405 (PL 33) at least one statement of inerrancy proper.[46]

> I have learned to yield this respect and honour only to the canonical books of Scripture: of these alone do I most firmly believe that the authors were completely free from error *(ut nullum eorum auctorem scribendo aliquid errasse firmissime credam).*[47] And if in these writings I am perplexed by anything which appears to me opposed to truth, I do not hesitate to suppose that either the Ms. *(codicem)* is faulty, or the translator has not caught the meaning of what

44. Faustus, like many who would follow, showed a tendency to declare inauthentic those portions of the New Testament that did not support his doctrines. This ploy, in Augustine's view, "is the last gasp of a heretic in the clutches of truth; or rather it is the breath of corruption itself" (*CFaustum* 10.3).

45. Berchman, *Porphyry,* 224-25, "By employing the very critical approaches Porphyry used to ridicule the truth claims of the Bible, Augustine turned Porphyry on his head. He defended the truth claims of scripture by demonstrating them efficacious — in reference to correspondence theories of truth." Berchman speaks of Augustine's approach as necessitating an abandonment of "Origen's coherence interpretation of the Bible, which was based on allegorical and symbolic interpretations of scripture" (225 n. 8).

46. It is evident that Augustine is thinking not merely of intentional deception when he says he believes that Scripture's authors are completely free from error. On the assertions of Rogers and McKim to the contrary, see John Woodbridge, *Biblical Authority: A Critique of the Rogers/McKim Proposal* (Grand Rapids: Zondervan, 1982), 44-46.

47. I have taken the Latin text of Augustine's writings from the *S. Aurelii Augustini Opera Omnia — edition latina* at http://www.augustinus.it/index2.htm.

was said, or I myself have failed to understand it. As to all other writings, in reading them, however great the superiority of the authors to myself in sanctity and learning, I do not accept their teaching as true on the mere ground of the opinion being held by them; but only because they have succeeded in convincing my judgment of its truth either by means of these canonical writings themselves, or by arguments addressed to my reason.

Identity (Canon) of Scripture

Self-Authenticating and Self-Delimiting?

One advantage of considering the kinds of materials we have reviewed in the first section of this essay is that it helps us to comprehend how differently the ancients viewed the Scriptures from the way moderns do.[48] It is widely taught today that the Scripture "selection process" began in the second century,[49] arising out of the churches' felt needs for a new set of authoritative Scriptures,[50] and was pursued through criteria developed by the church over time. Any conviction that there were or ought to be boundaries for this new set of Scriptures, we are often told, came fairly late: "In the early church there appears to be no interest in fixed collections of scriptures much before the fourth century."[51]

But the confession of early church leaders presents a problem for this ap-

48. Much of the material in this section will be found in expanded form in C. E. Hill, "God's Speech in These Last Days: The New Testament Canon as an Eschatological Phenomenon," in *Resurrection and Eschatology: Theology in Service of the Church. Essays in Honor of Richard B. Gaffin Jr.*, ed. Lane G. Tipton and Jeffrey C. Waddington (Phillipsburg, NJ: P&R, 2008), 203-54, and "The New Testament Canon: *Deconstructio ad Absurdum?" JETS* 52 (2009): 101-19.

49. As representing this view, see, e.g., Lee Martin McDonald, *The Biblical Canon: Its Origin, Transmission, and Authority* (Peabody, MA: Hendrickson, 2007); David L. Dungan, *Constantine's Bible: Politics and the Making of the New Testament* (Minneapolis: Fortress, 2007); Craig Allert, *A High View of Scripture? The Authority of the Bible and the Formation of the New Testament Canon* (Grand Rapids: Baker Academic, 2007).

50. If the first century is mentioned, it is often only to say how the church at that time felt no need for any new Scriptures, let alone any closed canon of Scripture: McDonald, *Biblical Canon,* 422; Dungan, *Constantine's Bible,* 79. Allert, *High View,* 125, following von Campenhausen and Kurt Aland, extends this claim through the second century as well, saying the church had no need of a canon because it had the rule of faith. But if this is true, it had no need of Scripture either. On the rule of faith, see the section on "Scripture, Tradition, and Authority," 72-76 below.

51. Lee Martin McDonald, "What Do We Mean by Canon? Ancient and Modern Questions," in *Jewish and Christian Scriptures: The Function of "Canonical" and "Non-Canonical" Religious Texts,* ed. James H. Charlesworth and Lee Martin McDonald (Edinburgh: T. & T. Clark, 2010), 8-40 at 11.

proach. Clement's statement, quoted above, rings in the ear: "whatever comes into judgment is not to be believed before it is judged, so that what is in need of judgment cannot be a first principle." How could a church which confessed that Scripture is the self-authenticating voice of God presume to determine *if* it needed a new set (or even the old set) of Scriptures? How could it presume to *select* what books it thought it needed as Scripture?[52] I would argue that there is no reason to think that it did either of these things. If Scripture is its own interpreter, should it not also be its own delimiter? There are of course no canonical lists contained in Scripture itself (though Jesus in Luke 24 gives the three categories of the OT writings). But Scripture did provide the principle for a canon of new Scripture, and this seems to have been recognized by second-century writers.

For Justin, the same prophetic Scriptures that proclaimed beforehand the identity of the Christ, his deeds, his sufferings, his resurrection, and the founding of his church, also predicted an authoritative new word to be delivered to all nations.[53] The mighty scepter of Psalm 110:2, by which the LORD would rule in the midst of his foes, is, according to Justin, the word of Jesus' apostles, which went forth from Zion and is preached everywhere (*1 Apol.* 45.5). Perhaps the single most influential passage in this regard came from the prophet Isaiah, echoed by Micah, "For out of Zion shall go forth the law, and the word of the LORD from Jerusalem" (Isa. 2:3; cf. Mic. 4:2).[54] This prophecy, Justin affirms, predicted the apostolic preaching: "For from Jerusalem there went out into the world men, twelve in number, and these illiterate, of no ability in speaking: but by the power of God they proclaimed to every race of men that they were sent by Christ to teach to all the word of God" (*1 Apol.* 39.3; cf. *Dial.* 24.1, 3). Irenaeus too interprets this law which goes forth from Zion in Isaiah's prophecy as "the word of God, preached by the apostles, who went forth from Jerusalem."[55] But the appeal to Isaiah 2:3 (Mic. 4:2) did not originate in the second century. Jesus in Luke and

52. Or, as McDonald prefers to say, as a resource "for Christian identity and guidance" (McDonald, *Biblical Canon,* 422).

53. See C. E. Hill, "Justin and the New Testament Writings," in *Studia Patristica* 30, ed. E. Livingstone (Leuven: Peeters, 1997), 42-48, at 46. Justin also sees the preaching ministry of the apostles predicted in Ps. 110:2 (*1 Apol.* 45.5); Exod. 28:33 (*Dial.* 42.1); and Ps. 19:2 (*Dial.* 64.8).

54. Reidar Hvalvik says that "in the early church Isa 2:3 (Mic 4:2) is the central proof-text for the apostolic mission." Reidar Hvalvik, "Christ Proclaiming His Law to the Apostles: The *Traditio Legis*-Motif in Early Christian Art and Literature," in *The New Testament and Early Christian Literature in Greco-Roman Context: Studies in Honor of David E. Aune,* ed. John Fotopoulos, NovTSup 122 (Leiden: Brill, 2006), 419; cf. Oskar Skarsaune, *The Proof from Prophecy: A Study in Justin Martyr's Proof-Text Tradition: Text-Type, Provenance, Theological Profile,* NovTSup 56 (Leiden: Brill, 1987), 160; cf. also 356ff. Among other instances, Hvalvik discusses Augustine, *City of God* 10.32, which directly links Isa. 2:2-3 to Jesus' words in Luke 24:44-47.

55. *AH* 4.34.4; see also *Proof of Apostolic Preaching* 86; Melito of Sardis, *Peri Pascha* 7.

Acts alludes to this passage in the founding of the apostles' mission to be his witnesses in all the world, "beginning from Jerusalem" (Luke 24:47; Acts 1:8).[56]

These and other prophetic texts constituted, for Jesus and the apostles and for early church writers, the scriptural authorization for the apostolic preaching, a new law and word of the Lord; in effect, these texts also limited that new law and word of the Lord to what the apostles and their assistants would produce in the original apostolic mission.[57] The upshot of this is that the constant appeal in the church to the apostles and their authority was not the result of any church's decision to adopt "apostolicity" as one of its "criteria" for selecting its books of sacred Scripture. Apostolicity was the authorizing and delimiting principle given by Scripture itself.

The teaching authority conferred by Jesus on his apostles permeates the apostolic ministry as it is related in Acts and the New Testament epistles. Though the practice of public reading of Scripture in the synagogues was taken over in Christian meetings for worship, a new source arose immediately to take its place alongside the Hebrew Scriptures. On the day of Pentecost, after Peter had finished preaching, which preaching included exposition of Joel and the Psalms, we read, "And they devoted themselves to the apostles' teaching and fellowship, to the breaking of bread and the prayers" (Acts 2:42). The oral teaching of Jesus' apostles continued to center, no doubt, on the words and deeds of Jesus to which they were commissioned witnesses. In the next decades written "Gospels" containing their remembered accounts would appear, and the apostle Paul would instruct that letters containing his teaching be read out to the congregations (Col. 4:16; cf. 2 Cor. 10:10; Eph. 3:4; 2 Thess. 2:15; 3:14). This of itself need not indicate a scriptural status for Paul's letters. But the authority with which he wrote as an apostle and the obedience he expected to his written word (1 Cor. 14:37-38; 2 Thess. 3:14) tell in favor of such a recognition from the first. In any case, 1 Peter seems to use phrases and concepts from some of Paul's letters, and 2 Peter 3:15-16 refers to a known collection of Paul's letters as Scripture. A collection was made either by Paul himself or, at any rate, not long after his death.[58]

56. For more on this, see Hill, "God's Speech."

57. This conception of apostolicity was not, of course, so restricted as to apply to only what an apostle personally spoke or penned. The reference here to "assistants" is intentional and reflects the universal recognition of the legitimate apostolicity of writers like Mark and Luke, the author of Hebrews (if he was not Paul), and even the Lord's brothers (Gal. 1:18; Jude 1) James and Jude, the former of whom, at least, is known to have been visited by the risen Christ (1 Cor. 15:7) and is explicitly aligned with the apostles in apostolic ministry in New Testament writings (Acts 12:17; 15:13-21; 21:18; Gal. 1:19, etc.).

58. See, among others, David Trobisch, his *Die Entstehung der Paulusbriefsammlung: Studien zu den Anfängen christlicher Publizistik,* NTOA 10 (Freiburg/Göttingen, 1989), summarized in his *Paul's Letter Collection: Tracing the Origins* (Minneapolis: Fortress, 1994); Harry Y. Gamble, *Books and Readers in the Early Church: A History of Early Christian Texts* (New Haven and London: Yale University Press, 1995), 100.

There is a remarkably clean continuity between the NT writings and the early non-canonical writings on the understanding of the apostles as the authoritative custodians and publishers of the gospel of Jesus. Still in the first century, Clement of Rome writes, "The apostles received the gospel for us from the Lord Jesus Christ; Jesus the Christ was sent forth from God. So then Christ is from God, and the apostles are from Christ" (*1 Clem.* 42.1-2). The same understanding is present in the thought of Ignatius (*Magn.* 6.1; 7.1; *Smyrn.* 8.1),[59] Polycarp (*Phil.* 6.3), Ps. Barnabas (5.9; 8.3) and is generally assumed among non-orthodox writers as well. From here it becomes virtually the universal Christian tradition (until modern times).

The Second Century

In the last half of the second century, church leaders in such disparate parts of the empire as Lyons, Antioch, and Alexandria would speak of the Gospels and other literature as what had been handed down to them (Irenaeus; Serapion; Clement).[60] This denotes the very tangible aspect of the reception of the scriptural writings as a process that took place in real life: church leaders knew the collections that they had inherited from their predecessors, collections they perceived as going back to the apostles.[61] The collections in these churches must indeed have developed from the actual artifacts of the original apostolic mission, particularly in the churches founded during that mission, judging from the early date by which we find some of these records in use. Echoes of Jesus' teaching, sometimes actual quotations from the written Gospels, reverberate throughout the works of the Apostolic Fathers. And just as quickly, the letters of Paul are explicitly referenced (2 Peter; *1 Clem.;* Ignatius; Polycarp), and letters of Peter, John, and "To the Hebrews" are used in the composition of early inter-ecclesial correspondence (*1 Clem.;* Polycarp).[62]

There is a recognizable continuity between the apostolic sources used in Antioch (Ignatius), Asia Minor (Polycarp), Rome (Clement), and elsewhere (Ps. Barnabas — Alexandria?) at the beginning of the second century. It was surely

59. C. E. Hill, "Ignatius and the Apostolate: The Witness of Ignatius to the Emergence of Christian Scripture," in *Studia Patristica* 36, ed. M. F. Wiles and E. J. Yarnold (Leuven: Peeters, 2001), 226-48.

60. Irenaeus, *AH* 3.1.1, etc.; Clement, *Strom.* 3.13.93; Serapion in Eusebius, *HE* 6.12.3-6.

61. Tertullian (*Praescr.* 36) refers to the apostolic churches, "in which the very thrones of the apostles are still pre-eminent in their places, in which their own authentic writings are read *(authenticate litterae eorum recitantur)*." These churches, he claims, held "as a sacred deposit *(sacrosanctum)*" the apostolic letters (*adv. Marc.* 4.5).

62. For recent critical evaluations see A. Gregory and C. Tuckett, eds., *The Reception of the New Testament in the Apostolic Fathers* (Oxford: Oxford University Press, 2005).

inevitable, however, there should also be variation and imperfection in the process of preserving, collecting, and handing down what Jesus' apostles and their companions left behind. Confusion would arise as well from the appearance of other books that had no direct or indirect historical connection with apostles, but which in form or in content (some also in title) resembled those that had.

While by the end of the second century discrepancies in the collections of certain churches were coming to light, it is at least the case that, as far as we can tell, they all had collections. As we begin to hear that some doubted the Pauline authorship of Hebrews, or did not want *The Shepherd* read in church, etc., we hear of no church that regarded *no* Christian writings as Scripture or as authoritative. There are no reports of anybody protesting, "the orally-transmitted-words-of-Jesus, and the orally-transmitted-words-of-Jesus alone! If they were good enough for Peter and Paul . . ." Nor do the collections appear to be greatly at variance, as one might expect they would be, if indeed the diversity among the churches and the blurriness of lines of demarcation were as great as many current scholars allege.

As early as Ignatius, writing probably in about 107/108,[63] we have a Christian using the categories of "gospel" and "apostles." When it is seen that he uses these categories of religious authority alongside the canonical categories for the OT Scriptures, "the prophecies . . . the law of Moses," etc. (*Smyrn.* 5.1; cf. *Phld.* 5.1-2; 8.2; 9.1-2; *Smyrn.* 7.2), it appears as if Ignatius may be thinking of the written collection in the church at Antioch.[64] As early as Papias's elder (c. 100), we have reference to the titles of at least two of the Gospels, Matthew and Mark (Eusebius, *HE* 3.39.15-16), and very possibly to all four (*HE* 3.24.5-17).[65] The brief excerpt from Papias's work preserved by Eusebius in *HE* 3.39.15-16 shows us that churches in Asia Minor already at the dawn of the second century were interested to have information about their written apostolic sources for the words and acts of Jesus.

In Justin we see that it is not only the words of Jesus, contained in the "Memoirs of the Apostles," which are recognized as being "big with power." The words of his apostles too were recognized as the words of God (*Dial.* 119.6). Though Justin does not mention apostolic epistles, the effects of Paul's letters to the Romans and to the Galatians, and possibly others, in his writings are well known to scholars.[66] He also considers the Apocalypse of John to be the work of the

63. Some date Ignatius's writings two or more decades later.

64. C. E. Hill, "Ignatius, 'the Gospel' and the Gospels," in *Trajectories through the New Testament and the Apostolic Fathers,* ed. Andrew F. Gregory and Christopher M. Tuckett (Oxford: Oxford University Press, 2005), 267-85, esp. 280, and the chart on 284-85, which notes other uses of the categories in the second century.

65. C. E. Hill, "What Papias Said about John (and Luke): A 'New' Papian Fragment," *JTS* 49 (1998): 582-629; "'The Orthodox Gospel': The Reception of John in the Great Church prior to Irenaeus," in *The Legacy of John,* ed. Tuomas Rasimus (Leiden: Brill, 2009), 233-300 at 285-94.

66. See Oskar Skarsaune, "Justin and His Bible," in *Justin Martyr and His Worlds,* ed. Sara

apostle (*Dial.* 81.4). Skarsaune is right that in Justin's writings, all of which were addressed to outsiders, "there is not yet any clear delimitation of exactly which documents should be considered authoritative above others, once we are outside the category of *Memoirs* or Gospels."[67] Skarsaune is also right when he continues, "On the other hand, Justin has an incipient canon in the way he refers to the Gospels, exactly as *Memoirs,* and he has a kind of implicit canon in the decisive role he accords to the apostles."[68]

Two opposing tendencies seem to be visible in the second century. There was an ideal of unity throughout the universal church. Contrary to what some have said, this was not an ideal that originated only with Eusebius or with Constantine in the fourth century. The term "catholic," in use since at least Ignatius, depicts the ideal, and a self-conception. But at the same time there was also a respect paid to individual churches and their traditions, particularly if those traditions were held to go back to the apostles. We see this in one of the most divisive debates of the second century, the quartodeciman controversy. Victor of Rome, apparently motivated by a desire for uniformity, went to the extreme of cutting off fellowship with the churches of Asia Minor who had a distinctive Easter practice (Eusebius, *HE* 5.24.9). Irenaeus's cool-headed approach would eventually prevail. He respected the antiquity of both practices, and the claim that each side made that it had received these practices from the times of the apostles. Irenaeus's judgment was that, in this case, diversity must be allowed: "the disagreement in the fast confirms our agreement in the faith" (*HE* 5.24.13). It would be wrong to conclude, based on this diversity of practice, that at the time of the controversy there was no Easter observance at all in Christianity, or no concern about it, only that there was no *universally* established Easter practice. It is similar, I would suggest, to conceptions of a NT canon.

By the end of the second century, judging from the writings of Justin, Melito, the *Muratorian Fragment,* Theophilus, Irenaeus, Serapion, Clement, Tertullian, and Hippolytus in particular, a four-Gospel canon, Acts, a corpus of thirteen or fourteen of Paul's letters (with or without Hebrews), the Revelation of John and at least 1 Peter and 1 John and probably Jude must have been in collections of new covenant Scripture throughout the empire. It is hard to discern the status of the other Catholic Epistles at this time, as their attestation is infrequent. It may be that it was the Syrian church which was the main holdout against other members of this corpus. Even in the late fourth century and afterwards the churches in that region omitted the Catholic Epistles from their canon. There are in addition

---

Parvis and Paul Foster (Minneapolis: Fortress, 2007), 53-76, 179-87, at 74, and his list of studies establishing this in n. 91. He notes the possible, though debatable, traces of James, 1 Peter, and 1 John.

67. Skarsaune, "Justin and His Bible," 76.

68. Skarsaune, "Justin and His Bible," 76.

a few other popular books that could boast some support early on, chiefly the *Apocalypse of Peter* and *The Shepherd,* and to a lesser extent Ps. Barnabas, and the *Didache* (all cited favorably or as Scripture by Clement of Alexandria). There is no support among the writers listed above for the *Gospel of Thomas* or any of the so-called gnostic Gospels.

The third century would see at least the following three developments. First, we hear less and less of the *Apocalypse of Peter, The Shepherd* (after the *MF* and Tertullian in particular), Ps. Barnabas, and the *Didache.* Second, the book of Revelation took a hit. After widespread use as Scripture for a century in both east and west, it came under suspicion due to the way it was being interpreted. The criticism evidently began in Rome, in relation especially to the Montanist controversy, but also to chiliasm.[69] The issue seems to have been quickly resolved there, however. Doubt took root in the east, after Dionysius of Alexandria rejected on critical grounds the book's apostolic authorship (though not its revelatory status, Eusebius *HE* 7.25.7). It was probably Eusebius's equivocation about the book in his widely read *Ecclesiastical History* (3.25.1-7) however, which was most responsible for several eastern sources in the fourth and fifth centuries not including Revelation in their canonical lists.[70] Third, by at least sometime in the late third century the collection of seven catholic letters existed as a corpus (Eusebius, *HE* 2.23-24-25).

That there was variation, beyond the "core" books, and at least no successful, far-reaching attempt to impose any strict limitation, accompanied by the promulgation of authoritative lists, has been widely interpreted to mean that there was no conception at all of Scripture as a definite or closed set of books.[71] The evidence shows, however, not the absence of a notion of delimitation but rather a level of disagreement or simply uncertainty about what belonged in that delimited body of writings. First of all, it does not seem to be the case that no attempts were made to achieve agreement, even by the beginning of the third century. Tertullian mentions church councils that had deliberated on canon issues at least

69. It is possible that the attack of Gaius, which alleged that Revelation had been authored by the heretic Cerinthus, also pertained to the Gospel of John. But the evidence for this is quite debatable. For more see Hill, *Johannine Corpus,* 172-204.

70. Cyril of Jerusalem, ca. 350, *Catech. Lect.* 4.33; Synod of Laodicea, 363; first Council of Carthage, 397.

71. Cf. Sundberg, "Revised History"; Hahneman, *Muratorian Fragment;* McDonald, *Biblical Canon;* Dungan, *Constantine's Bible;* Allert, *High View,* 144-45, states, "No matter how one looks at the history, it is difficult to maintain that the church had a closed New Testament canon for the first four hundred years of its existence. This means that an appeal to the 'Bible' as the early church's sole rule for faith and life is anachronistic." One will find an ancient writer, Hippolytus, caught in a display of "anachronism" in his *Contra Noetum* 9, when he says, "There is, brethren, one God, the knowledge of whom we gain from the Holy Scriptures, and from no other source." See the entire quote on p. 45 above.

far enough to reject *The Shepherd* (*De Pudicitia* 10).[72] Despite the lack of treatment it has received, this reference will not disappear simply through neglect, or by a flippant attribution to Tertullian's "rhetoric."[73] In my opinion, the *Muratorian Fragment* shows signs of being related to one of these councils; it speaks more prescriptively for the church, as a council would, than does Origen or Eusebius.[74]

Elsewhere I have shown several other indications that churches and individuals well before the fourth century did assume that even the NT Scriptures were a closed body of writings.[75] Another such indication is contained in the records of the quartodeciman controversy just mentioned (probably in the early 190s). Eusebius preserves portions of a letter written by Polycrates, bishop of Ephesus, who at one point protested, "I have studied all holy Scripture (*pasan hagian graphēn dielēlythōs*), I am not afraid of threats." If, as Dungan says, "*scripture* is a boundless living mass of heterogenous sacred texts,"[76] how did Polycrates know when to stop studying?

More evidence that Christians had a notion of a limited collection of authoritative, new covenant books by the end of the second century has come to light recently.[77] At some point in the early history of Christian scribal culture, some Christian scribes began to place a *siglum* in the left-hand margins of books they were copying to mark quotations from Scripture. This *siglum,* an arrow or wedge-shaped sign known as a *diplē* (pl. *diplai*), had been adapted from Greek scholarship where it had served for some time as a multipurpose marginal marking to indicate some textual or paratextual feature. The sign is used (though not consistently) in the great fourth- and fifth-century uncial manuscripts of the Bible, ℵ, A, B, C, and D[e], to mark where NT writers quote the OT. But our earliest evidence so far for this practice occurs in Christian, non-Biblical manuscripts where an author quotes Scripture (I have not yet found the marking used by Christian scribes for any citations not presumed to be scriptural).[78] Clearly, the scribes who used this *siglum* (and not all did) had to know in advance which quotations to mark and which ones not to mark; that is, they must have had some notion of a lim-

72. Perhaps what Tertullian says about the book of Hebrews (which he ascribes to Barnabas, accepting the denial of Pauline authorship) reflects the concerns of one or more of these councils.

73. *Pace* Hahneman, *Muratorian Fragment,* 63, followed by several others.

74. See Hill, *Johannine Corpus,* 132-34.

75. C. E. Hill, "The Debate over the Muratorian Fragment and the Development of the Canon," *WTJ* 57 (1995): 437-52; *"Deconstructio ad Absurdum."*

76. Dungan, *Constantine's Bible,* 132-33.

77. For a full presentation of the evidence, see Charles E. Hill, "Irenaeus, the Scribes, and the Scriptures. Papyrological and Theological Observations from P.Oxy 3.405," in *Irenaeus: Life, Scripture, Legacy,* ed. Sara Parvis and Paul Foster (Minneapolis: Fortress, 2012), 119-30.

78. The only explicit statement I have found concerning the use of this sign in antiquity comes from Isidore of Seville (560-636) in his *Etymologies* 1.21.13: "Our scribes place this in books of churchmen to separate or to make clear the citations of Sacred Scriptures."

ited corpus of Scripture. For instance, the scribe of Codex Alexandrinus (5th c.) does *not* use *diplai* for Paul's citations of two pagan authors at Acts 17:28, nor for the citation of Enoch in Jude 14–15, nor for the citation of Epimenides in Titus 1:12. When did Christian scribes begin using this sign to mark scriptural quotations? We do not know, but we have two instances that may date from the end of the second century or the early third century. One is a fragment of Irenaeus's *Against Heresies* (P.Oxy. 3.405, from book 3), which papyrologist Colin Roberts confidently dated to the end of the second century.[79] In the fragment Irenaeus quotes Matthew 3:16. The other early example is a fragment from an unidentified Christian theological work, P.Mich. xviii.764, dated by its editor to the second or third century.[80] The left margin of the right-hand column of the fragment contains *diplai* marking citations of Jeremiah 18:3-6 and 1 Corinthians 3:13.

What is most significant for our purposes is that each of these early examples uses the *diplai* to mark quotations not simply from an OT book but from a NT book (Matthew and 1 Corinthians). The occurrence of this scribal convention as early as the late second or early third century is one more indication that Christians had a conception of Scripture as a distinct set of sacred texts, so much so that they could mark them out visually in their writings.

The Twenty-Seven-Book Canon

In his *On Christian Doctrine* 2.8.13 Augustine gave a list of the canonical books of the Old and New Testaments. The OT books are the traditional Protestant Canon plus six others: Tobias, Judith, 1 and 2 Maccabees, Wisdom, and Ecclesiasticus (this corresponds to the contents of Codex Sinaiticus).[81] The NT books are exactly the twenty-seven books that make up the NT now accepted by the three major branches of Christianity. Before naming the books, Augustine notes that the skillful interpreter of the sacred writings will know all of these books and in regard to the canonical Scriptures will follow the judgment of the majority of churches, and those in particular that had apostolic foundations.

> Accordingly, among the canonical Scriptures he will judge according to the following standard: to prefer those that are received by all the catholic churches to those which some do not receive. Among those, again, which are not received

79. C. H. Roberts, *Manuscript, Society and Belief in Early Christian Egypt,* The Schweich Lectures of the British Academy 1977 (London, 1979), 23.

80. Cornelia Eva Römer, "7.64. Gemeinderbrief, Predigt oder Homilie über den Menschen im Angesicht des Jüngsten Gerichts," in *P. Michigan Koenen (= P. Mich. Xviii): Michigan Texts Published in Honor of Ludwig Koenen,* ed. Cornelia E. Römer and Traianos Gagos (Amsterdam: J. C. Gieben, 1996), 35-43.

81. See Stephen Dempster's chapter in this volume.

> by all, he will prefer such as have the sanction of the greater number and those of greater authority, to such as are held by the smaller number and those of less authority. If, however, he shall find that some books are held by the greater number of churches, and others by the churches of greater authority (though this is not a very likely thing to happen), I think that in such a case the authority on the two sides is to be looked upon as equal. (*On Christian Doctrine* 2.8.12)[82]

By those books "not received by all," he may have had in mind the OT books outside the list acknowledged by the Jews. It at least seems that virtually all the canon lists from the fourth and fifth centuries agree on that smaller canon, beyond which there is variation in the lists. When Augustine says to *prefer*[83] the books received by all, he might mean that the extra six might not be used with the same level of authority as the rest in the construction of Christian doctrine, and this would form an analogy with the way these (and other) books are termed "deuterocanonical" even by contemporary Roman Catholic and Eastern Orthodox churches.

It is possible that Augustine might also have had some NT books in mind as "not received by all." We know that at this time there were churches which did not receive one or more of the books 2 Peter, 2-3 John, Jude,[84] James, Hebrews, Revelation. Yet in the decade of the 390s these same twenty-seven books would be acknowledged by Augustine (here) and by a council in Hippo, by a synod in Carthage, by Rufinus in Rome, by Jerome in Bethlehem (*Ep.* 53.9; 394), and by Amphilocius of Iconium in Asia Minor *(Iambi ad Seleucum)*. These are the books Jerome translated for his new Latin edition, and this would have a decisive effect on Western Christianity. As is well known, this same list had been claimed by Athanasius thirty years earlier in Alexandria in his Easter letter of 367 (the same list minus Revelation had been promulgated by the Council of Laodicea in 363). It is often stated that Athanasius's letter in 367 signifies the first time a definite NT canon with exactly these twenty-seven books appears. But on the contrary, it seems that by the time Athanasius identified it, this twenty-seven-book New Testament had already had a long history of acceptance in the church.

These same twenty-seven books are the ones which Eusebius, fifty or more years earlier, noted were either "recognized" (*homologoumenoi*) by all or "dis-

82. See Anne-Marie la Bonnardière, "Le canon des divines Ecritures," in *Saint Augustin et la Bible,* ed. Anne-Marie la Bonnardière (Paris: Beauchesne, 1986), 287-301.

83. I take it he does not mean "preferring" them in the sense of including them in the canon, as he indicates that they are canonical, but preferring them in the sense of building Christian doctrine from them.

84. At least by the time of Jerome, Jude was questioned because of its citation of 1 Enoch: "Jude the brother of James, left a short epistle which is reckoned among the seven catholic epistles, and because in it he quotes from the apocryphal book of Enoch it is rejected by many. Nevertheless by age and use it has gained authority and is reckoned among the Holy Scriptures." See Jerome, *De Viris Illustribus* 4. Cf. Eusebius, *HE* 2.23.25.

puted (*antilegoumenoi*)" but known to most (*HE* 3.25).[85] It is true that Eusebius only regards the books in the first category as "covenanted," which appears to be his terminology for "in the New Testament" or what we might call "canonical." In the second category are the five books, James, Jude, 2 Peter, 2-3 John. It is the "disputed" label that has drawn most of the critical attention, while not so much attention has been paid to the rest of Eusebius's description: "disputed but nevertheless known to most."[86] In another passage he says these books are "disputed yet nevertheless used publicly by many in most churches" (*HE* 3.31.6).[87] And when he elsewhere mentions James and Jude as belonging to the group of "the so-called Catholic Epistles," he notes, "we know that these have been read publicly along with the remaining epistles in most churches" (2.23.24-25). Besides these five, he places no other books in the same category. Consequently, no matter where we judge Eusebius's own preferences to lie in the matter of these five,[88] according to his researches it would appear that all twenty-seven books (with the possible exception of Revelation) *were* the New Testament Scriptures for *most* of the churches when he wrote, early in the fourth century.

Just how long this might have been the case is impossible to tell. The same twenty-seven books, however, do appear in an even earlier but usually neglected list given by Origen in about 240 in his *Homilies on Joshua* 7.1.

> But when our Lord Jesus Christ comes, whose arrival that prior son of Nun designated, he sends priests, his apostles, bearing "trumpets hammered thin," the magnificent and heavenly instruction of proclamation. Matthew first sounded the priestly trumpet in his Gospel; Mark also; Luke and John each played their own priestly trumpets. Even Peter cries out with trumpets in two of his epistles; also James and Jude. In addition, John also sounds the trumpet through his epistles [and Apocalypse],[89] and Luke, as he describes the Acts of the Apostles. And now that last one comes, the one who said, "I think God displays us

85. This is noted by Dungan, *Constantine's Bible,* 78. Of the books in the disputed-but-known-to-most category, he says Eusebius "like a good philosopher reporting the state of the question, is content to leave them perched squarely on the fence, neither in or out." On the contrary, what Eusebius reports shows that they were in for most, and out for some.

86. There were, of course, several other books that were disputed, but which Eusebius knows had not been used by the majority.

87. *tōn antilegomenōn men, homōs d' en pleistais ekklēsiais para pollois dedēmosieumenōn.* Cf. also 2.23.25, where he mentions that the authenticity of James and Jude is denied by some, since few of the ancients quote them. At this point he mentions no doubts about 2-3 John, but in 3.25.3 he lists them among the disputed and mentions the possibility that they were written by another John.

88. Everett R. Kalin, "The New Testament Canon of Eusebius," in *The Canon Debate,* ed. Lee M. McDonald and James A. Sanders (Peabody, MA: Hendrickson, 2002), 386-404, believes that he did not wish to include them; others believe that he did.

89. Some of the manuscripts omit the Apocalypse, though there is copious evidence that Origen considered this book both inspired and Scripture.

> apostles last," and in fourteen of his epistles, thundering with trumpets, he casts down the walls of Jericho and all the devices of idolatry and dogmas of philosophers, all the way to the foundations.

Unfortunately, suspicion exists here because, first, we do not have these homilies in Greek but only in the Latin translation of Rufinus, who has been known to "correct" Origen at some points, and second, Origen elsewhere notes that some of these books were disputed.[90] It is hardly likely, however, that Rufinus fabricated the entire analogy between the trumpets and the NT books. And even if we should allow for the most generous emendation, Origen's original list could not have been much different. What is most significant, in the light of current attempts to maintain that the church had no conception of a limited canon until well into the fourth century, is that Origen would give a list of the NT "trumpets" at all. And despite his reporting elsewhere that the authenticity of 2 Peter and 2 and 3 John was doubted *(Comm. John),* and that the Pauline authorship of Hebrews was disputed (Eus. *HE* 6.25.3-14), Origen himself appears to have accepted and used all these books. He routinely used Hebrews as Paul's,[91] and where he acknowledges that "God only knows" who wrote it, he says it is "not inferior" to Paul. In his *Homilies on Leviticus* 4.4.2 he used 2 Peter and attributed it without qualification to the apostle. He used James and Jude in his *Commentary on Matthew.* As Metzger has observed, it is entirely credible that Origen would give his own view (probably too the view of his church in Caesarea) in a sermon in an unqualified way while qualifying a report in his more scholarly writings.[92]

Scripture, Tradition, and Authority

In a recent book, Craig Allert writes at length on the relationship of tradition and Scripture.[93] There are a few points that surface in his interpretation of the

90. E. Kalin's article, "Re-examining New Testament Canon History: 1. The Canon of Origen," *CTM* 17 (1990): 274-82, denies the authenticity of the list. But Everett Ferguson, "Factors Leading to the Selection and Closure of the New Testament Canon: A Survey of Some Recent Studies," in *The Canon Debate,* ed. Lee M. McDonald and James A. Sanders (Peabody, MA: Hendrickson, 2002), 295-320, at 319 n. 104, says Kalin's position "depends on discrediting Rufinus's translation . . . and not considering the sequence of Origen's writings and the possibility that Origen changed his views." Ferguson cites Otto Bardenhewer, *Geschichte der altkirchlichen Literatur* (Freiburg: Herder, 1914), 2:152-56, "who defends the reliability of Rufinus's translation of Origen's passages on the canon."

91. Barbara J. Bruce, trans., Cynthia White, ed., *Origen: Homilies on Joshua,* Fathers of the Church (Washington, DC: Catholic University of America Press, 2002), 75 n. 5.

92. So Metzger, *Canon,* 140.

93. Allert, *High View.*

important witness of Irenaeus in particular which, because they resemble the views of other scholars as well, might be profitably considered here.

Irenaeus's advocacy of a four-Gospel canon is well known, but Allert seeks to show that Irenaeus's support for these Gospels as Scripture is not as absolute as one might think. Allert points, first, to the fact that Irenaeus does not always cite these Gospels accurately, and second, to Irenaeus's advocacy also of the rule of truth or rule of faith, a somewhat flexible creed-like summary of Christian doctrine (*AH* 1.10.1; 1.221. 5.20.1).[94] The first objection, however, rests on a mistaken assumption about citations in antiquity. Full or consistent accuracy in citation is simply not a reliable measure of the respect a writer has for a text, and cannot provide a refutation of a writer's explicit statements about that text.[95] Allert's second reason calls for more attention.

He cites a passage from the third book of *Against Heresies* in which Irenaeus says that if the apostles had not left us writings, we would have to have recourse to the churches they founded in order to ascertain the truth. Irenaeus even asserts that there are illiterate Christians who are saved (without Scripture) through their knowledge of the truth as symbolized in the church's rule of faith. Allert deduces from this that "[t]he true doctrine of the church has been faithfully passed on and is sufficient to lead people to salvation. Irenaeus confirms that the church of the second century really had no need of a written canon because it already had a canon of truth. It was this Rule of Faith against which everything was measured in the second century — even the writings of the developing New Testament."[96] He says we cannot push this so far as to say that "Christian writings were relatively unimportant in the early church." But he cites with approval two other scholars who seem nearly to push this far: Hans von Campenhausen, who writes that Scripture "never suppresses or replaces the living, public proclamation of the church, which holds the original 'canon of truth'";[97] and Annette Yoshiko Reed, who says that for Irenaeus the canon functions as an "extra-textual criterion for

94. Allert, *High View,* 121-26.

95. See, e.g., John Whittaker, "The Value of Indirect Tradition in the Establishment of Greek Philosophical Texts or the Art of Misquotation," in *Editing Greek and Latin Texts: Papers Given at the Twenty-Third Annual Conference on Editorial Problems, University of Toronto 6-7 November 1987,* ed. John Grant (New York, 1989), 63-95; Christopher D. Stanley, *Paul and the Language of Scripture: Citation Technique in the Pauline Epistles and Contemporary Literature,* SNTSMS 69 (Cambridge: Cambridge University Press, 1992); Sabrina Inowlocki, *Eusebius and the Jewish Authors: His Citation Technique in an Apologetic Context,* AGJU 64 (Leiden: Brill, 2006); C. E. Hill, "'In These Very Words': Methods and Standards of Literary Borrowing in the Second Century," in *The Early Text of the New Testament,* ed. C. E. Hill and M. J. Kruger (Oxford: Oxford University Press, 2012), 261-81.

96. Allert, *High View,* 125.

97. Allert, *High View,* 125, citing Hans von Campenhausen, *The Formation of the Christian Bible,* trans. J. A. Baker (Philadelphia: Fortress, 1972), 329.

distinguishing true doctrine from heretical speculations, authentic texts from spurious compositions, and proper Scriptural interpretation from 'evil exegesis.'"[98] Allert's conclusion, which he believes is consonant with that of other scholars, is that the rule of faith "tempers the exclusivity of the four Gospels as canon in Irenaeus."[99] On this basis he writes at an earlier point in the book that "even the Christian writings eventually included in the New Testament canon were subjected to this Rule of Faith."[100]

The rule of faith was a summary of apostolic teaching based on the Trinitarian baptismal statement enjoined by Jesus (Matt. 28:19), with elaborations under "Father, Son, and Holy Spirit." The baptismal injunction (given in Scripture) was a natural framework on which to base catechetical teaching and to formulate creedal statements. As elaborated in the church, informed by the rest of the New Testament revelation, it also became a hermeneutic for the proper interpretation of Scripture.

Reading the entire context of the opening chapters of Book 3, however, shows that Irenaeus's first appeal is not to "tradition" or the rule of faith but in fact to Scripture. It is only the heretics who posit a hierarchy that subordinates Scripture to their tradition. At the beginning of 3.1.1, Irenaeus writes, "We have learned from none others the plan of our salvation, than from those through whom the Gospel has come down to us, which they did at one time proclaim in public, and, at a later period, by the will of God, handed down to us in the Scriptures, to be the ground and pillar of our faith." The apostles, invested with the Holy Spirit and with perfect knowledge, proclaimed, and then they published. Their writings declare the truth about God the Creator and Christ his Son. Irenaeus is here constructing an apologetic for the authority of the apostles and their writings, against the heretics. The apostles represent Jesus: "For the Lord of all gave to His apostles the power of the Gospel, through whom also we have known the truth, that is, the doctrine of the Son of God; to whom also did the Lord declare: 'He that heareth you, heareth Me; and he that despiseth you, despiseth Me, and Him that sent Me'" (*AH* 3.praef.). Thus if any gnostic, Marcionite, or Valentinian does not agree to the truths taught by the apostles "he despises the companions of the Lord; nay more, he despises Christ Himself the Lord; yea, he despises the Father also, and stands self-condemned" (3.1.2).

98. Allert, *High View,* 126, citing Reed, "ΕΥΑΓΓΕΛΙΟΝ: Orality, Textuality, and Christian Truth in *Adversus haereses,*" *VC* 65 (2002): 11-46.

99. Allert, *High View,* 121.

100. Allert, *High View,* 55. It is true of course that certain writings were judged not to be Scripture because they were deemed heretical. But this does not mean that those that were recognized had endured an ecclesiastical screening process before being used. When questions arose about books already in use, as with Hebrews or Revelation, judgments were made about their orthodoxy. But for these two books the deliberation took place after they had been received and used in church settings.

Irenaeus continues, "When, however, they are confuted from the Scriptures, they turn round and accuse these same Scriptures as not being correct, nor of authority, and that they are ambiguous, and that the truth cannot be derived from them by those who are ignorant of tradition" (*AH* 3.2.1). It is only at this point, after the heretics have made their escape from Scripture, after they have invoked their own secret and unwritten tradition, that the appeal to true, apostolic tradition preserved in the churches is made. For Irenaeus, the true tradition of faith exists plentifully, having been preserved in the churches which the apostles themselves founded. It had been faithfully passed down from presbyters like Clement in Rome and Polycarp in Smyrna, and those in Ephesus who knew the apostle John. It is this tradition, summarized in Irenaeus's rule of truth, which confirms the right interpretation of Scripture and the faith that Irenaeus is trying to give.

According to Irenaeus (and Allert agrees with this), there can be no dichotomy between Scripture and tradition, for both derive from the same source: the apostles of Jesus. Not only Scripture but "the faith" itself had been handed down from the apostles. Scripture in this sense *is* tradition, for Scripture is handed down. Yet this does not make "tradition" the more ultimate category. Tradition is authoritative not because it is tradition, but because it, like Scripture, is apostolic. As Tertullian would later say, "In the Lord's apostles we possess our authority; for even they did not of themselves choose to introduce anything, but faithfully delivered to the nations (of mankind) the doctrine which they had received from Christ" (*Praescr.* 6). And what is apostolic is authoritative because it derives from Jesus, and Jesus was sent from God (*1 Clem.* 42.1-2). John Behr provides a fitting summary:

> So, for Irenaeus, both the true apostolic tradition maintained by the churches, and the apostolic writings themselves, derive from the same apostles, and have one and the same content, the Gospel, which is itself . . . "according to the Scriptures." "Tradition" for the early Church is, as Florovsky put it, "Scripture rightly understood."[101] Irenaeus's appeal to tradition is thus fundamentally different to that of his opponents. While they appealed to tradition precisely for that which was not in Scripture, Irenaeus, in his appeal to tradition, was not appealing to anything else that was not also in Scripture. Thus Irenaeus can appeal to tradition, to establish his case, and at the same time maintain that Scripture cannot be understood except on the basis of Scripture itself, using its own hypothesis and canon.[102]

101. Citing G. Florovsky, "The Function of Tradition in the Early Church," *GOTR* 9, no. 2 (1963): 182; repr. in Florovsky, *Bible, Church, Tradition* (Vaduz, Liechtenstein: Büchervertriebsanstalt, 1987), 75.

102. Behr, *The Way to Nicaea,* 45.

When Irenaeus says that we would have to revert to the apostles' successors *if* the apostles had not left us writings, he is making a point from a contrary-to-fact hypothetical.[103] The example Irenaeus cites to prove his point is the existence of those who are "barbarians" in speech, who have not read Scripture but who believe the truth that had been preached to them. They either cannot read or do not have Scriptures in their language (or both). One imagines that Irenaeus may have had certain believers in his own communities in Gaul in mind (cf. *AH* 1.praef.3). In which case, those who preach to these people still have the Scriptures to guide their preaching. Irenaeus of course knew that one could be saved by hearing and learning the saving message without having Scripture. But this does not mean Irenaeus would agree with the statement that "the church of the second century really had no need of a written canon because it already had a canon of truth." After showing that the church did possess the true tradition from the apostles, he continues, "let us revert to the Scriptural proof furnished by those apostles who did also write the Gospel, in which they recorded the doctrine regarding God, pointing out that our Lord Jesus Christ is the truth, and that no lie is in Him" (3.5.1). Thus we come full circle, back to the Scriptures, and Irenaeus goes on to fulfill the purpose of his third book, as he says in its preface, "In this, the third book, I shall adduce proofs from the Scriptures."

The appeal to tradition and the rule of faith in Irenaeus, Tertullian, Cyprian, Augustine, and others occurs largely in the context of the clash with heretical alternatives. This aspect of the use of tradition is thus essentially hermeneutical: Where does one go to find the correct interpretation of Scripture when Scripture is interpreted in a false but "plausible" manner, or when Scripture's testimony is rejected in preference to sectarian tradition? One goes to the churches where the living faith, handed down from the same apostles who gave us the Scriptures, still flourished.

The "Inspiration" of Scripture and Non-Scripture: Of Preachers, Prophets, Pseudepigraphers, and Sibyls

No one would contest that early Christianity received the books of Scripture as "inspired." 2 Timothy 3:16 and 2 Peter 1:20-21 are among the *loci classici* which even in early times both reflected and guided Christian thought about the divine

103. Tertullian in his *Prescription* uses but also modifies Irenaeus's argument. To tell who had the right interpretation all one had to do was to ascertain where the true Christian faith resided, and this search must lead to the churches founded by the apostles (*Praescr.* 19). One did not and *should* not use Scripture in debate with heretics, for the heretics had no legitimate right to it. This was rhetorically brilliant, but in the end it could have the effect of inserting something in front of Scripture as representative of the divine will.

origins of Scripture.[104] It is often observed these days, however, that the early Christians had a broader view of inspired speech and writing than that which would develop later in the history of the church. It at least cannot be said that the ancients believed that Scripture and only Scripture was, in any sense, truly "inspired." The author of 1 Clement may have believed that he penned his letter for the Roman church to the Corinthian church "through the Spirit" (*1 Clem.* 63.2).[105] Ignatius of Antioch claims to have cried out "with God's own voice," at an emotional meeting in Philadelphia (*Phld.* 7.1-2). The work of the Septuagint translators was inspired, according to Irenaeus (*AH* 3.21.2). According to Clement of Alexandria, even Plato and other philosophers, when they confessed that there was only one true God, did so "through his inspiration (*kat' epipnoian autou*)" (*Protr.* 6.71.1).[106]

Since inspiration of some kind seems to pertain to a great deal more oral and written materials than are scriptural,[107] many contemporary writers have pointed out that inspiration was not a "criterion" but a "corollary" of canonicity. This may be true, as far as it goes. It is probably going too far, though, to claim, as Lee McDonald does, that "The Christian community believed that God continued to inspire individuals in their proclamation, just as God inspired the writers of the New Testament literature. They believed the Spirit was the gift of God to the whole church, not just its writers of sacred literature."[108] That the Spirit was the gift to the whole church was indeed the church's confession. But if the Spirit's

104. On *theopneustos* in 2 Tim. 3:16, a word that Paul may have coined, see the still-authoritative work of B. B. Warfield, "God-Inspired Scripture," chapter 7 in B. B. Warfield, *Revelation and Inspiration* (Oxford: Oxford University Press, 1927, repr. Baker, 1981), 229-80, the lexicons, and the commentaries.

105. This may well be the correct translation. If so, perhaps Clement was mindful of 1 Cor. 12:8 and regarded his letter as a word of wisdom or word of knowledge. Lindemann thinks this "does not mean that the text claims to be 'inspired'; however, it may well mean that the expressions here are not simply of personal convictions" (Andreas Lindemann, "The First Epistle of Clement," in *The Apostolic Fathers: An Introduction,* ed. Wilhelm Pratscher [Waco, TX: Baylor University Press, 2010], 47-69 at 63). It is possible, however, that the sentence should be translated with "through the Holy Spirit" referring not to Clement's writing but to the means by which the Corinthians are expected to root out their jealousy, as in *ANF* 10 translation: "Joy and gladness will ye afford us, if ye become obedient to the words written by us and through the Holy Spirit root out the lawless wrath of your jealousy." It may then be related to verses like Rom. 8:13, "but if by the Spirit you put to death the deeds of the body, you will live." Given Clement's words in 8.1; 22.1 (where the phrase *dia* [*tou*] *pneumatou hagiou,* as in 63.2, also precedes the verb it modifies) and 45.2 in particular, I am inclined to the latter alternative.

106. *epipnoia,* a word not used in the NT or the LXX, means a breathing out, or inspiration.

107. See, e.g., the collection of witnesses in Allert, *High View,* 177-88.

108. Lee Martin McDonald, "Identifying Scripture and Canon in the Early Church: The Criteria Question," in *The Canon Debate,* ed. Lee Martin McDonald and James A. Sanders (Peabody, MA: Hendrickson, 2002), 416-39 at 438.

work was, and was understood to be, "just the same" in all Christians alike, it would be incomprehensible why nearly all of the pseudepigrapha needed to claim authorship by one or another of the apostles.

Was there anything that distinguished Scripture from other speech and literature said to be inspired? This is a subject much too large for full treatment here, but it might be profitable nevertheless to ask how Christian writers spoke about Scripture in ways that set it apart from other forms of "inspired" speech or writing. A few preliminary points: first, this is not a subject on which there was a common, agreed-upon, technical vocabulary among Christians in the early centuries. The vocabulary of inspiration, deriving partly from the sacred writings themselves, partly from the larger Greco-Roman culture,[109] encompassed a number of different words, each with a history and with its own set of associations. Second, many of the examples cited by Allert in particular of the attribution of inspiration or scriptural status to works that are not in Scripture concern books of the so-called OT Apocrypha or Deuterocanonical writings. There are well-known debates from the early centuries about these books and their place among or alongside the sacred Scriptures. We cannot enter into these here (though see "Identity [Canon] of Scripture" above), only to observe that this is a special category, due to the fluctuating judgments about them in the early church. Third, I strongly suspect that in some cases inspiration words are used in laudatory and hyperbolic ways (as when one of the Cappadocians praises another as "God-breathed" (*theopneustos*) or as "a second Moses" or the like.[110] I do not think such statements were meant or were taken as straightforward, prosaic speech. Finally, some of the distinctions I will broach below occur together in various places, so segregating them is for convenience.

Inspiration and the Holy Spirit

A number of references to inspiration in people or non-scriptural writings arguably involve an inspiration of a different order. Whereas the inspiration of Scripture is consistently attributed to the Holy Spirit, to God, or to Christ (sometimes as Logos or Wisdom), this is not always true of other "inspired" literature. It was, of course, culturally speaking, much more natural for people in antiquity to acknowledge the occurrence of inspired speech. Most of Greco-Roman society

109. Robert J. Hauck, *The More Divine Proof: Prophecy and Inspiration in Celsus and Origen*, AAR Academy Series 69 (Atlanta: Scholars, 1989), 138: "Pagan understandings of prophecy, inspiration and revelation provided the theory and language for the discussion of the experience of prophecy, visions, dreams, and the knowledge of God."

110. See Basil, *On the Spirit* 74; Gregory of Nazianzus, *Orations* 21.33; Gregory of Nyssa, *Apologia in Hexaemeron* (PG 44, 61-62). This might apply to certain other instances as well.

in general regarded reality as punctuated through and through with elements of the supernatural. The second-century anti-Christian critic Celsus despairs of recounting "all the oracular responses, which have been delivered with a divine voice by priests and priestesses, as well as by others . . . who were under a divine influence (*entheō phōnē*)"; indeed "the world is full of such instances" (*CCels.* 8.45). Of course, Christians often regarded such things as the effects of evil demons. But even New Testament writers speak not strictly of the work of the Holy Spirit but presume the involvement of plural "spirits" in forms of non-scriptural, divine-human interaction (1 Cor. 12:10;[111] 14:22; 1 John 4:2; Rev. 22:6).

An instructive test case is the Sibyl. The collection of Sibylline oracles that has survived from antiquity is a fictitious and apologetically motivated Jewish production, which has been further interpolated and supplemented by one or more Christian hands. This seems plain to modern students, but was not so plain to all early Christian writers. Nor, for that matter, was it clear to many Christians living much later, such as Michelangelo, who depicted the four main Sibyls on the Sistine Chapel ceiling along with the Hebrew prophets. Clearly, some Christian writers did not know quite what to do with the Sibyl. For who could, or would want to, deny that she spoke beforehand of the coming of Christ, much like the Hebrew prophets? As perplexing as her "inspiration" might be to us, we note that she did present early Christians an undeniable apologetic opportunity.

In his *Protreptikos,* Clement calls the Sibyl a prophetess (*prophētis*).[112] This already reminds us that for early Christians, not every "true" prophet or prophetess gave revelations that were scriptural, and this may provide some insight into, among other texts,[113] Jude 14, where the author regards Enoch as a prophet. The Sibyl, Clement says, speaks "very much in an inspired way" (*entheōn sphodra*), using a word (*entheōs*, full of God, inspired, or possessed) not used in the LXX or the NT but used, as we saw above, by Celsus for pagan oracles of various kinds.[114] He then begins quoting from the prophets of Scripture, whose words he attributes in a conspicuous way to the Holy Spirit, "Now Jeremiah, the all-wise prophet, or rather the Holy Spirit in Jeremiah, shows what God is." "Once again, the same Spirit says through Isaiah. . . . What says the Holy Spirit to them through Hosea?" (*Protr.* 8). Clement never ascribes the Sibyl's words to the Holy Spirit, nor, I believe, do any Christian writers do so.

The treatise *Cohortatio ad Graecos,* at one time attributed to Justin but now ascribed to a third-century writer,[115] acknowledges that the Sibyl spoke "by some

111. Here it is the one Spirit who gives the gift of distinguishing spirits.

112. 2 Peter 1:20, on the other hand, speaks of "prophecy of Scripture."

113. Such as *Ps-Barn.* 11.10 and 12.1, which attribute to a "prophet" words from *2 Baruch* and *4 Ezra* respectively.

114. Josephus speaks of himself as *entheos* in *Wars* 3.353.

115. Moreschini and Norelli, *Early Christian Greek and Latin Literature,* 1:202-3. The translation used is from *ANF* 1; the Greek text is from Miroslav Marcovich, ed., *Pseudo-Iustinus*

kind of potent inspiration (*ek tinos dynatēs epipnoias*) . . . truths which seem to be much akin to the teaching of the prophets" (37.1; 38.2). She even predicted "in a clear and patent manner, the advent of our Saviour Jesus Christ" (38.1). Yet the author never attributes her inspiration to the Holy Spirit or equates her writings with Scripture. Instead, he tells his pagan readers that her prophecies "will constitute your necessary preparatory training (*progymnasma*) for the study of the prophecies of the sacred writers (*tēs tōn hierōn andrōn prophēteias*)" (*Cohort.* 38.2; so also Clement, *Protr.* 8.1). This author concludes, "From every point of view, therefore, it must be seen that in no other way than only from the prophets who teach us by divine inspiration (*dia tēs theias epipnoias*), is it at all possible to learn anything concerning God and the true religion" (*Cohort.* 38.2). Whatever was the source of the Sibyl's "potent inspiration," it was not divine in the sense that the scriptural prophets' inspiration was.

In sum, many early Christians held notions of inspiration that accommodated the interaction of a variety of supernatural or otherworldly influences on a human subject, for ends that might be good or evil or mixed (see below). For these phenomena they made use of a "religious" vocabulary that was shared with the larger culture. But when it comes to the Hebrew and Christian Scriptures, we are met with an unparalleled clarity and consistency in the Christian confession of these books as "inspired" or "breathed out" by God, or specifically by the Holy Spirit (*De Principiis* 4.1.9).

Full or Partial Inspiration

The attribution of Scripture to the Holy Spirit entailed something else that apparently separated Scripture from other forms of inspired speech, and that was its plenary nature. "All Scripture," wrote Paul, "is breathed out by God" (2 Tim. 3:16). Clement of Rome told the Corinthians, "You have studied the Holy Scriptures which are true, and given by the Holy Spirit (*dia tou pneumatos tou hagiou*). You know that nothing unjust or counterfeit (*ouden adikon ouden parapeipoiēmenon*) is written in them" (45.2-3). Irenaeus is assured that "the Scriptures are indeed perfect, since they were spoken by the Word of God and His Spirit" (*AH* 2.28.2). But other speakers or writings could apparently be unevenly inspired. Justin could say that the Logos spoke through Socrates when he exposed the daemons (*1 Apol.* 5) and Clement of Alexandria could say that Plato and other philosophers spoke through God's inspiration (*kat' epipnoian autou*) when they confessed that there was only one true God (*Protr.* 6.71.1). But clearly, little if anything else these Greeks said or wrote could be so described.

Cohortatio ad Graecos, De Monarchia, Oratio ad Graecos, PTS 32 (Berlin/New York: Walter de Gruyter, 1990).

Augustine in the *City of God* also evinces a similar understanding of certain apocryphal Jewish writings:

> There is indeed some truth to be found in these Apocrypha; but they have no canonical authority *(nulla est canonica auctoritas)* on account of the many falsehoods they contain. Certainly, we cannot deny that Enoch (the seventh in descent from Adam) wrote a number of things by divine inspiration,[116] since the apostle Jude says as much in a canonical epistle. But there was good reason for the exclusion of these writings from the canon of the Scriptures. (*CivDei* 15.23.4)

He goes on to observe that, unlike the scriptural books, Enoch and other writings were not preserved by the priests in the temple, and then cites Enoch's story of angels mating with women as indicative of its falsehoods.

Inspiration and Frenzy

One important way in which the Sibyl's inspiration distinguished itself from that of the scriptural prophets had to do with her psychological state. The very first literary reference to the Sibyl has her prophesying "with raging mouth" (Heraclitus, fr. 75),[117] and depictions of her speaking in mantic frenzy are common, in non-Christian and Christian sources. The Sibyl, says the author of the *Cohortatio,* "was filled indeed with prophecy at the time of the inspiration (*epipnoias*), but as soon as the inspiration ceased, there ceased also the remembrance of all she had said" (37.2).[118]

Though one might find an occasional representation of the OT prophets in similar terms, the state of mental ecstasy was generally not understood to be the genuine mode of true prophecy by church writers.[119] The common view of mantic speech is seen in an offhand remark by Justin, *Dial.* 9.1, who chides Trypho for speaking nonsense when he condemned Christians, "For you know not what you say . . . and you speak, like a diviner (*apomanteuomenos*) whatever comes into your mind." Irenaeus describes the process by which Marcus the Valentinian deluded his disciples/victims:

116. There is no separate word for "inspiration" here, simply *divine,* "divinely."

117. See J. L. Lightfoot, *The Sibylline Oracles: With Introduction, Translation, and Commentary on the First and Second Books* (Oxford: Oxford University Press, 2007), 9.

118. See also Origen, *CCels.* 7.3.

119. It is sometimes held that Justin is an exception, for he speaks in *Dial.* 115 of Zechariah prophesying "in a trance." I am not convinced that this is an exception, for Justin's point here is simply that Zechariah was not describing what he was seeing with his eyes but was reporting what he saw in a vision. The key seems to be that he was in possession of his senses as he wrote or dictated.

> He says to her, "Open thy mouth, speak whatsoever occurs to thee, and thou shalt prophesy." She then, vainly puffed up and elated by these words, and greatly excited in soul by the expectation that it is herself who is to prophesy, her heart beating violently [from emotion], reaches the requisite pitch of audacity, and idly as well as impudently utters some nonsense as it happens to occur to her, such as might be expected from one heated by an empty spirit. . . . Henceforth she reckons herself a prophetess.

The general recognition that the true prophet spoke while in control of his/her own senses, would become important in the evaluations of Montanist prophecy.[120] The New Prophets were disqualified in the eyes of many not only because some of their prophecies proved false, but also because they came through mantic or ecstatic speech (the Anonymous, Eusebius, *HE* 5.17.1-4; Epiphanius, *Panar.* 48). Origen was one who offered several reflections on the "mechanics" of true, prophetic inspiration. Distancing himself from the views of Philo[121] and of the Montanists, including Tertullian,[122] Origen took up and explicitly refuted the opinion that the Hebrew prophets spoke in ecstasy.

> For it is not the case, as some people surmise, that the prophets were out of their minds and spoke by the Spirit's compulsion. The Apostle says: "If a revelation is made to another who is sitting there, let the first one be silent" (1 Cor 14:30). That shows that the one who speaks has control over when he wants to speak and when he wants to be silent. Also, to Balaam it is said: "But there is a word that I am sending into your mouth, take care to speak this" (Num 23:5, 16).[123] This implies that he has the power, once he has received the word of God, to speak or to be silent. (*Hom. Ezek.* 6.1.1)

He then cites Jonah as an example of a prophet who was told what to say by God and did not want to say it (*Hom. Ezek.* 6.1.2). Origen saw the Holy Spirit's work as effecting a clarity of mind, rather than ecstasy (*CCels.* 7.4) and that this constituted a "new way which had nothing in common with the divination inspired by daemons" (*CCels.* 7.7). The inspired prophet Moses, in fact, wrote his five books "like a distinguished orator who pays attention to outward form" (*CCels.* 1.18). As

120. See, e.g., Christine Trevett, *Montanism: Gender, Authority and the New Prophecy* (Cambridge: Cambridge University Press, 1996), 86-95.

121. Nardoni, "Origen's Concept," 11, citing Philo, *Quis rer. div. her.* 259 (LCL 261, 416-17); Hauck, *More Divine Proof,* 120.

122. Tertullian defends ecstasy or rapture *(amentia)* of the New Prophecy in *Adv. Marc.* 4.22 (cf. the ecstasy of dreams in *De Anima* 45 and note that he wrote a now lost work *On Ecstasy*).

123. *Origen: Homilies 1-14 on Ezekiel,* ACW 62, translation and introduction by Thomas P. Scheck (New York/Mahwah, NJ: Newman Press, 2010).

to the Sibyl, the ambiguity as to the source of her inspiration in earlier Christian writers is removed by Origen: it is "of the race of daemons" (*CCels.* 7.4).[124]

Authority and Apostolicity

Ignatius believed that he spoke an exhortation at Philadelphia in an oracular way, with the voice of God. But when he wrote his letters, he recognized a categorical difference between his words and those of an apostle: "I do not order you like Peter and Paul. They were apostles: I am a convict" (Rom. 4:3; cf. *Trall.* 3.3). An extemporaneous burst of what he deemed divine insight might produce an utterance fit for the moment. But as we have seen, it was apostolicity that was the defining human characteristic of the new Scriptures to be passed down in the church. For apostolicity denoted, indeed, an investment by the Holy Spirit (Luke 24:49; John 20:21-22; Acts 1:8, etc.), but also an authority bestowed by Christ and predicted in the prophets, an authority to pass down authoritative teaching that is permanently relevant for the church (Irenaeus, *AH* 3.1.1).

It is no surprise, then, that another reason for the church's rejection of Montanist claims to inspiration by the promised Paraclete was that their prophecies were portrayed as something equal to, or greater than, the apostolic revelation. Whereas one may find early Christian writers who countenanced the possibility of the episodic appearance of the prophetic charism, the New Prophets crossed a line and so brought forth further reflections on the limits of legitimate prophecy. A Montanist named Themiso, we are told, impudently "composed a general epistle in imitation of the apostle" (Eusebius, *HE* 5.18.5); Eusebius reports that the Roman controversialist Gaius, in his *Dialogue with Proclus,* curbed the recklessness and audacity of his Montanist opponents who composed new "Scriptures" (*HE* 6.20). The comment of an anonymous anti-Montanist critic has the same import. With a touch of sarcasm, he says that he had refrained from writing a response earlier "from fear and concern lest in any way I appear to some to add a new writing or add to the word of the new covenant of the gospel to which one who has chosen to live according to the gospel itself can neither add nor subtract" (Eusebius, *HE* 5.16.3).[125] Clearly it was perceived that some were presuming to add something. I have a hard time reading these statements in any other way than as indicating that these church leaders at the end of the second century held that the new covenant was represented by a known body of writings that could not be added to or subtracted from.

Even the rightful use of the prophetic gift was determined, by some at least,

124. See Hauck, *More Divine Proof,* 121.

125. Translation from Heine, ed., *The Montanist Oracles and Testimonia* (Macon, GA: Mercer University Press, 1989).

to have ceased with apostolic times, for true prophecy is only that which was approved by apostles.[126] This forms a kind of parallel to what Josephus and the rabbis considered to be a "prophetic epoch" that had ended with Haggai, Zechariah, and Malachi in the time of Artaxerxes.[127] "From Artaxerxes up to our own time every event has been recorded but this is not judged worthy of the same trust, since the exact line of succession of the prophets did not continue" (*CApion* 1.8.41). Even an occasional prophetic utterance could be acknowledged, but whatever it produced was not considered to be on the same level as Scripture, because the succession of the prophets had come to an end. For Christians it was the time of the apostles which was the epoch of "canonical" revelation. This is seen also in the *Muratorian Fragment* when it prohibits *The Shepherd* from being read in church, not because it was not "inspired" but because it was after the apostles' time (lines 79-80).

Augustine in *Contra Faustum* 11.5 (usually dated between 397 and 400) offers some reflection on the divide that separates scriptural and non-scriptural books:

> [T]here is a distinct boundary line separating all productions subsequent to apostolic times from the authoritative canonical books of the Old and New Testaments *(libris . . . canonicae auctoritatis Veteris et Novi Testamenti).* The authority of these books has come down to us from the apostles through the successions of bishops and the extension of the Church, and, from a position of lofty supremacy, claims the submission of every faithful and pious mind.

Even if innumerable books should be written containing the same truths as Scripture, "there is not the same authority *(auctoritas),*" says Augustine, for "Scripture has a sacredness peculiar to itself" (*CFaustum* 11.5). We are free to agree or disagree with portions of any other book, depending on whether that portion can be clearly demonstrated, or shown to agree with a canonical book. But because of "the distinctive peculiarity of the sacred writings *(in illa vero canonica eminentia sacrarum Litterarum),* we are bound to receive as true whatever the canon shows to have been said by even one prophet, or apostle, or evangelist. Otherwise, not a single page will be left for the guidance of human fallibility" (*CFaustum* 11.5).

In these reflections we see multiple ways in which Scripture distinguishes itself from all other books. Its properties of sacredness and authority are internal properties by which Scripture manifests itself to be what it is: the word of God. Originating with prophet, apostle, or evangelist, the writings of Scripture have come down from the apostles as from a fountainhead, flowing through the hands of successive generations of church leaders. All these things form a distinct boundary line for Augustine.

126. Epiphanius's anonymous source, *Panarion* 48.2.1-3. See Heine, *Montanist Oracles,* 29.
127. See Stephen Dempster's chapter in this volume.

Inspiration, Inscripturation, and Copying

The Sibyl's words were often thought to have been inspired by some sort of spiritual power. But the taking down of her words was another matter. Their written form sometimes lacks proper meter, says the author of the *Cohortatio,* because those who took them down were illiterate (an interesting use of the word "illiterate") and often went astray. The Sibyl could not later correct the meter for she could not remember what she had spoken in ecstasy (37.3). By contrast, Origen speaks of the scriptural prophets' inspiration as pertaining not only to their experience and to their speech, but also to the writing process. "It was by a more divine spirit not only that they (the prophetic visions) were seen by the prophet, but also that they were described verbally and in writing" (*CCels.* 1.43).[128] Thus even the writing down of Scripture is due to the divine Spirit.

This understanding of the inscripturation process, as also attributable to the working of the Holy Spirit, was probably assumed by Christians in general. The same did not extend, of course, to the discrete copying process by scribes after the original, for Irenaeus, Origen, Jerome, and others complain from time to time about the faults of scribes.[129] For ancient readers, the need to inspect and correct handwritten manuscripts was a fact of life. Well aware of the imperfections inherent in the process of transcription, early Christian users of these manuscripts did not despair of their access to the word of God (unlike some modern counterparts). They seemed to have confidence that in doubtful cases the original text was there to be found, if sought for.

In conclusion, it is certainly the case that "inspiration" had a broader meaning and a somewhat expanded vocabulary in the patristic period than would later be the case in Christian theology. Yet there were several ways in which the inspiration of the sacred texts by the Holy Spirit was perceived to be distinctive, such that the Spirit's activity in producing Scripture was not "just the same" in the speech and writing of individual believers.

The Private Use of Scripture

In Deuteronomy 17:18-19 the future king, assumed to have the ability to read, is instructed to "write for himself in a book a copy of this law, from that which is in charge of the Levitical priests; and it shall be with him, and he shall read in it all

128. *hypo theioterou pneumatos ou monon hōramenois tō prophētē alla kai eirēmenois kai anagegrammenois.* Greek from *Origène. Contre Celse,* vol. 1, *Introduction, Texte Critique, Traduction et notes,* by Marcel Borret, SC 132 (Paris: Éditions du Cerf, 1967). Translation modified from Henry Chadwick, *Origen,* Contra Celsum (Oxford: Oxford University Press, 1980), 40.

129. E.g., Irenaeus, *AH* 5.30.1; Origen, *In Matth.* 15.14.

the days of his life, that he may learn to fear the LORD his God by keeping all the words of this law and these statutes, and doing them." We live like kings today, with the ability to read daily from even several translations of the Bible, in copies we did not have to write out for ourselves. In antiquity, however, both books and people who could read them were much less readily available. Yet Christians were very much given to the reading and the study of their books, more so, it seems to me, than they are sometimes given credit for,[130] and it apparently did not take long for the demand for Christian books to grow.

Throughout the period under review, the codex form is developing, enabling the binding together of (progressively larger) groups of scriptural books. One effect of the transition from the roll to the codex was the relatively greater affordability and portability of scriptural texts, thus making private possession and use of them an increasing possibility. Irenaeus must have thought there were many who could heed his advice when he advocated "daily study" *(diuturno studio)* of the things God has revealed in the sacred Scriptures (*AH* 2.27.1). Only a little later Clement of Alexandria could assume that many Christians not only could read but also had their own copies of at least some of the Scriptures. He wrote of the true, "gnostic" Christian, "His sacrifices are prayers, and praises, and readings in the Scriptures before meals, and psalms and hymns during meals and before bed, and prayers also again during night" (*Strom.* 7.7.49). For others, the churches often provided daily public reading and exposition of the Scriptures. The practice of daily Bible reading, whether public or private, is mentioned in *Apostolic Tradition* 36 (traditionally assigned to Hippolytus) in the early third century: "And if there is a day on which there is no instruction let each one at home take a holy book and read in it sufficiently what seems profitable."[131]

For three years in the 240s, Origen preached almost every day in Caesarea. In some of the homilies that survive (mostly in Latin translation), we find Origen exhorting catechumens to devote themselves to daily hearing of the Law read publicly (*Hom. Josh.* 4.1). While preaching on Genesis 24:15-16, he urges his hearers, "come daily to the wells," that is, to the wells of Scripture (*Hom. Gen* 10.3). Origen reproaches those who come to church and hear Scripture read but do

130. *Pace* Roger Bagnall, *Early Christian Books in Egypt* (Princeton/Oxford: Princeton University Press, 2009), 21: "[W]e have little evidence for the private lay ownership of biblical texts at any early date, and even later, ownership of Christian books by individuals may not have been extensive," and 23, "There is no reason to suppose that Christians were disproportionately more likely than other people to own books."

131. Gamble rightly cautions that "it can hardly be supposed that every Christian had personal copies of scripture" (*Books and Readers,* 232; see also Alistair Stewart-Sykes, *Hippolytus: On the Apostolic Tradition* [Crestwood, NY: St. Vladimir's Seminary Press, 2001], 166). Yet he concedes that this reflects an ideal, and the injunction means that at least some people had their own copies and could read. The words of Clement and Origen (see below) may indicate that personal ownership of at least some Scriptural texts by laypeople was becoming more common.

not pay close attention, complaining, "There is no mutual investigation of these words which have been read, no comparison" (*Hom. Exod.* 12.2). He exhorts the faithful to "read the text again and inquire into it" and mentions those who are "neither occupied at home in the word of God nor frequently enter the church to hear the word" (*Hom. Gen.* 11.3). These last excerpts assume that many laypeople had their own copies of scriptural books and could read them at home and bring them to church. The growing availability of scriptural texts for a burgeoning reading laity is corroborated by the discovery of several early NT and OT papyri, including miniature codices and opisthographs, which show signs of having been copied for private, not public, use.[132]

The line between the recognition of Scripture's spiritual power, and a superstitious regard for it, may, however, have been too fine for many lay believers. As a sacred object, Scripture was sometimes treated as possessing magical powers, as manifested in the amulets,[133] incantations, examples of bibliomancy, and hermeneia, which have survived from antiquity.[134] Gamble cites Augustine's words about one magical practice: "Regarding those who draw lots from the pages of the Gospel, although it could be wished that they would do this rather than run about consulting demons, I do not like this custom of wishing to turn the divine oracles to worldly business and the vanity of this life, when their object is another life" (*Ep.* 55.37).[135] Gamble concludes his treatment of this subject by saying, "But behind the sundry magical uses of these books lies the regular solemn reading and hearing of scripture in Christian worship, in which the power of scripture was experienced and emphasized as the source of divine revelation — a power that belonged to words, but no less to the books in which they stood."[136]

Conclusion

Churches and individual Christians today who seek to give rightful place to Scripture as God's word face multiple challenges, many of which have real precedents in the ancient world. It is not too much to hope that we may still learn from the constructive ways in which our forebears responded to the challenges they faced,

132. For instance, P45 and P72, the latter being in fact a miscellany that included 1 and 2 Peter and Jude mixed in with sundry non-biblical books. This drive for accessibility of the Scriptures is one significant reason for the entry of many errors into the manuscript tradition as copies were often made outside the direct auspices of church scriptoria.

133. Many Psalm texts have been found in amulets used apparently for magical purposes. The *incipits,* or first words, of the Gospels were also popular. The practice was prohibited in canon 36 of the Council of Laodicea of 360.

134. Gamble, *Books and Readers,* 237.

135. Gamble, *Books and Readers,* 240.

136. Gamble, *Books and Readers,* 241.

and that, like many of them, we too might persevere and contribute constructively to the ongoing ministry of the word of God in the world. In that spirit, it is fitting to conclude with the advice of Theonas of Alexandria writing to a younger colleague about the year 300:

> Let no day pass by without reading some portion of the Sacred Scriptures, at such convenient hour as offers, and giving some space to meditation. And never cast off the habit of reading in the Holy Scriptures; for nothing feeds the soul and enriches the mind so well as those sacred studies do. (*Letter to Lucianus* 9; *ANF* 6, 160-61)

THREE

The Bible in the Reformation and Protestant Orthodoxy

Robert Kolb

The Bible played a key role in the unfolding of the Protestant Reformation; countless volumes have analyzed the many aspects of this truism.[1] This chapter focuses on Luther and Calvin and their "schools," particularly on their views of the nature of Scripture and its authority, in the context of their practice in comment and proclamation.

Recent scholarship reaffirms that Scripture supplied the raw material from which medieval Christian theology was constructed. Lectures on biblical books concluded the student's learning theology after the dogmatic structure composed by Peter Lombard and commented on by countless instructors over three centuries provided a foundation. Even throughout Lombard's questions Scripture and its interpretation in the Fathers gave answers to questions of dogma and life, of natural science, politics, and the social order.[2] Nonetheless, Protestant reformers were convinced that Scripture's clay had been mixed with

1. Cf. overviews of the topic in *A History of Biblical Interpretation,* vol. 2, *The Medieval through the Reformation Periods,* ed. Alan J. Hauser and Duane F. Watson (Grand Rapids: Eerdmans, 2009): Mark D. Thompson, "Biblical Interpretation in the Works of Martin Luther," 299-318; Timothy J. Wengert, "Biblical Interpretation in the Works of Philip Melanchthon," 319-40; Barbara Pitkin, "John Calvin and the Interpretation of the Bible," 341-71; Lee W. Gibbs, "Biblical Interpretation in Medieval England and the English Reformation," 372-402; Scott Murray, "Biblical Interpretation among the Anabaptist Reformers," 403-27; Guy Bedouelle, "Biblical Interpretation in the Catholic Reformation," 428-49. Cf. Richard A. Muller, *Post-Reformation Reformed Dogmatics: The Rise and Development of Reformed Orthodoxy, ca. 1520 to ca. 1725,* vol. 2, *Holy Scripture,* 2nd edition (Grand Rapids: Eerdmans, 2003), 63-94.

2. Muller, *Post-Reformation Reformed Dogmatics,* 2:23-62; Gillian R. Evans, *The Language and Logic of the Bible: The Road to Reformation* (Cambridge: Cambridge University Press, 1985); Beryl Smalley, *The Study of the Bible in the Middle Ages* (Oxford: Clarendon, 1941).

I am grateful to several other authors in this volume, particularly David Gibson, for their helpful suggestions.

a good deal of alien dung, in part because of the authority over interpretation exercised by the pope.[3] Scholastic commentators at the universities tended to press biblical concepts into Aristotelian forms, which lacked a concept of a Creator God, forcing a focus on human performance that seriously weakened a truly scriptural worldview. Insufficient theological resources and a lack of personnel equipped to teach the biblical message in local leadership also permitted certain basic pagan rhythms to remain in place and twist the biblical superstructure at its foundations. Therefore, as prominent as it was in the church's practice, Scripture had played far too restricted a role in medieval thinking, according to the reformers.

They certainly did not come upon a world devoid of the Bible. Alongside the university exegetical lectures that provided the crown of the medieval theological enterprise (although its robes were Lombard's doctrinal discourses), monasteries provided lectures on Scripture that often employed serious historical study of the text and also cultivated piety. Such instruction, which coupled with allegorical interpretations a serious consideration and application of the literal meaning of the text, nursed Martin Luther, for instance, as a theologian.[4]

Luther and Scripture

When Luther became a *doctor in Biblia* in 1512, he had already absorbed Bible stories and content from the limited preaching and catechesis of his home village, from the primary and secondary school curriculum that had prepared him for university study, and from daily praying the psalms and reading the lessons in the monastery. One predecessor in his Augustinian monastery in Erfurt, two centuries earlier, Hermann von Schildesche, had developed an exegetical method that studied both historical and non-historical elements of the Bible's literal sense and the application of figurative interpretation in both.[5] Luther never mentioned Hermann, but throughout his lectures he critically though often appreciatively cited the Parisian Franciscan Nicholas of Lyra (ca. 1270-1341) and Paul of Burgos (ca. 1351-1435), whose commentary on Lyra argued for a prophetic interpretation of the Old Testament which focused on Christ, an approach Luther adopted.

Doctorate in hand, Luther continued his teaching career in Wittenberg with exegetical lectures treating the texts he knew best, the psalms, 1513-1515. He em-

3. Scott Hendrix, *Recultivating the Vineyard* (Louisville: Westminster John Knox, 2004), 1-35.

4. Christopher Ocker, *Biblical Poetics before Humanism and Reformation* (Cambridge: Cambridge University Press, 2002), 15-30.

5. Ocker, *Biblical Poetics,* 94-106.

ployed linguistic and exegetical helps from the best biblical humanists, Johannes Reuchlin, Jacques Lefevre d'Étaples, and, for the New Testament, Erasmus.[6] The psalms' message of God's judgment upon those who oppose him and his mercy for his chosen people shaped Luther's conception of what God is doing in addressing fallen humankind in Scripture, and it reshaped his method of interpretation. Luther's Psalms lectures and those on Romans, Galatians, and Hebrews in 1515-1518 reveal his striving for linguistic and conceptual clarity. Scholars have often described Luther's "revolution" in exegesis as the discarding of allegory, but this is not the case. First, he did not discard it (though he largely discounted its use and importance). Second, his most significant alteration in biblical study involved his abandonment of the medieval diachronic understanding of the course of biblical revelation as a progression from law and prophecy as preparation for Christ to fulfillment in Christ, who introduced a higher law and the grace to perform its demands. In place of this interpretative schema Luther used throughout Scripture his own distinction of "law" as God's expectations for human performance from "gospel" as God's promise of new life in Christ. This "law/gospel" application employed "law" primarily for the crushing accusation that leads to repentance, "gospel" for the bestowing of God's unconditional promise of new life in Christ, grasped by trust in him.[7]

Luther looms large in the history of exegesis not because he made a sharp break with his entire medieval heritage but because his distinction of law and gospel offered what Christopher Ocker says no biblical humanist or pious monk before him had found: "a literary method for handling the narrative construction of the Bible as a whole . . . where discrete biblical meanings congealed in a coherent body of knowledge."[8] Luther believed that "the whole life of the Christian is a life of repentance,"[9] and therefore God continually addresses his people with his law's demand for human righteousness and the gospel's promise of forgiveness and life. Deliverance from sin and delivery of new life come through the Holy Spirit's bestowal of the benefits of Christ, anchored in Scripture, conveyed in its Word as formulated in oral, written, and sacramental forms.[10] His distinction of

6. Helmar Junghans, *Der junge Luther und die Humanisten* (Göttingen: Vandenhoeck & Ruprecht, 1985), 240-87.

7. Gerhard Ebeling, "The Beginnings of Luther's Hermeneutics," *Lutheran Quarterly* 17 (1993): 129-58, 315-38, 451-68. Cf. Erik Herrmann, " 'Why Then the Law?' Salvation History and the Law in Martin Luther's Interpretation of Galatians 1513-1522" (Ph.D. dissertation, Concordia Seminary, Saint Louis, 2005), 147-247.

8. Ocker, *Biblical Poetics,* 211.

9. *D. Martin Luthers Werke* (Weimar: Böhlau, 1883-1993 [henceforth WA]), 1:233,10-11; *Luther's Works* (Saint Louis: Concordia; Philadelphia: Fortress, 1958-1986 [henceforth LW]), 31:25.

10. Robert Kolb and Charles P. Arand, *The Genius of Luther's Theology: A Wittenberg Way of Thinking for the Contemporary Church* (Grand Rapids: Baker, 2008), 175-203; Robert Kolb, *Martin Luther, Confessor of the Faith* (Oxford: Oxford University Press, 2009), 131-51.

law and gospel in the service of preaching repentance and faith embraced all God does in and with Scripture.

Luther's "metanarrative," based on creation, fall, redemption through Christ's death and resurrection, and the activity of the Holy Spirit, moving toward the Last Day, within the framework of the call to repentance and faith-filled living comprehended in law and gospel, provided the hermeneutic for his lifelong activity as biblical interpreter. Perhaps his most influential biblical comment over the centuries has been his postils, sermons on the appointed pericopes for each Sunday and festival, issued as his Church Postil (1521/22, 1525-1528, 1544), and his House Postil (1544, 1559). Preaching often in the main Sunday service, he treated these pericopes; he also preached sermon series on Genesis, Exodus, Matthew, John, 1 and 2 Peter, and Jude. As university lecturer, he guided future pastors through many psalms after he had completed the Hebrews lectures in 1518 and later returned to psalm texts for lectures several times. He treated the minor prophets, Exodus, Deuteronomy, sections of Isaiah, 1 John, and individual passages, including 1 Corinthians 7 and 15. Perhaps his two most important lecture courses occurred in 1531-1532 (Galatians) and 1535-1545 (Genesis). As an Augustinian he had learned to preach and apparently preached well. Often accused of being a one-book theologian — Romans! — or at least a Pauline theologian, he in fact loved John's Gospel and epistles, lectured mostly on Old Testament books, and the pericopal system impelled him to treat synoptic texts extensively.

Throughout his career Luther often simply stated that Scripture is the Word of God.[11] His concept of God's Word extended beyond Scripture to what later Lutheran dogmaticians called the Word's uncreated forms, the Word made flesh, Jesus Christ, and the creative speech of Genesis 1 that brought the whole created order into existence. God extends his "created Word" out of Scripture's pages into the ways he chose to apply it to hearers and readers, in oral, written, and sacramental[12] forms that deliver Scripture's message and power. That God deals with

11. E.g., "Sermon on the Mount" (1532), WA 32:305,22-30; LW 21:10; "1 Corinthians 15" (1532), WA 36:500,25–501,10; LW 28:76-77; "Johannine Epistles" (1537), WA 46:542,6, 548,32-33; LW 22:6, 14; Armin Buchholz, *Schrift Gottes im Lehrstreit: Luthers Schriftverständnis und Schriftauslegung in seinen drei großen Lehrstreitigkeiten der Jahre 1521-28* (Frankfurt: Lang, 1993), 15-38, 61-74. Mark D. Thompson, *A Sure Ground on Which to Stand: The Relation of Authority and Interpretive Method in Luther's Approach to Scripture* (Carlisle: Paternoster, 2004), 47-90; Paul Althaus, *The Theology of Martin Luther,* trans. Robert Schultz (Philadelphia: Fortress, 1966), 1-8; Oswald Bayer, *Martin Luther's Theology: A Contemporary Interpretation,* trans. Thomas Trapp (Grand Rapids: Eerdmans, 2008), 66-90; Bernhard Lohse, *Martin Luther's Theology,* trans. Roy Harrisville (Minneapolis: Fortress, 1999), 187-95.

12. E.g., in his *Small Catechism,* Luther answers the questions of how baptism and the Lord's Supper can bestow forgiveness of sins, life, and salvation: e.g., "Clearly the water does not do it, but the Word of God, which is with and alongside the water, and faith, which trusts this Word of God in the water," *Die Bekenntnisschriften der Evangelisch-Lutherischen Kirche,* ed. Irene Dingel (Göttingen: Vandenhoeck & Ruprecht, 2014 [henceforth BSELK]),

human beings through his Word seemed natural, reflecting God's essence, for the first chapters of Genesis made it clear to Luther that God is a God of conversation and community. He knew that this God, who had spoken of old through prophets and then through his Son, had delivered his Word authoritatively in the Bible. For him Scripture held unique, supreme authority in dispensing God's Word and delivering its life-changing impact to sinners. It alone served as the ultimate source and criterion for faith and proclamation.[13] "Scripture, too, must remain master and judge, for when we follow the brooks [that flow out of the spring of Scripture, the origin of God's Word; namely, pious writings of Christians, especially the church fathers] too far, they lead us too far away from the spring and lose both their taste and nourishment."[14]

This view of Scripture rested upon his belief that God's Word, as the agent of his creating power, established and still determines reality. Hans-Martin Barth summarizes Luther's view: "God's Word is the original reality, which lies at the basis of all reality."[15] Luther believed that "by speaking God created all things and worked through his Word. All his works are words of God, created by the uncreated Word."[16] God's way of speaking "is a language different from ours. When the sun rises, when the sun sets, God is speaking. Accordingly, the words of God are not empty air but things very great and wonderful, which we see with our eyes and feel with our hands." When the Creator sends forth his Word, things occur. His Word accomplishes his purposes.[17] Luther confessed, "our building and promotion of the church is not the result of our works but of the Word of God which we preach . . . everything comes forth [*provenire*] from the Word. . . . The mouth of Paul, of the apostles and preachers, is called the mouth of God."[18]

God's Word is much more than typical human language although it is that, too: "the Scriptures, although they too were written by men, are neither of nor from human beings but from God."[19] In Scripture and the contemporary delivery of its message, human language stands under the creative direction of the Holy Spirit: "what is written and proclaimed [*verkundigt*] in the prophets, says Peter, is not of human invention or devising; but pious and holy men have spoken [*geredt*] it as they were moved by the Holy Spirit" (2 Pet. 1:21).[20] "The

---

516; *The Book of Concord,* ed. Robert Kolb and Timothy J. Wengert (Minneapolis: Fortress, 2000 [henceforth BC]), 359.

13. WA 10,2:139,14-18. *Three Symbols* (1538), WA 50:282,11-17; LW 34:227-28.

14. *On the Councils and the Church* (1539), WA 50:520,6-10; LW 41:20.

15. Hans-Martin Barth, *Die Theologie Martin Luthers, eine kritische Würdigung* (Gütersloh: Gütersloher Verlagshaus, 2009), 147.

16. "Genesis Lectures" (1535), WA 42:353,8-40; LW 1:47.

17. "Lecture on Psalm 2" (1532), WA 40,2:230,20–231,28; LW 12:32-33.

18. WA 31,2:460,7-20, 26-28; LW 17:257-58.

19. WA 10,2:92,6-8; LW 35:153.

20. "2 Peter," WA 14:31,25-27; LW 30:167. Cf. similar passages: *Avoiding the Doctrines*

Holy Spirit has comprehended his wisdom and counsel and all his secrets in the Word and revealed them in Scripture."[21] Indeed, "whoever has the grace to recognize [the book=Scripture] as the Word of God rather than a human word, will also think of it more highly and dearly."[22] As a form of human communication the Bible's language relates the true, factual story of God's intervention in human history.

Sensitive to literary genre, Luther could recognize what different authors were doing with different literary forms in different passages. His brief introduction to the Psalms, penned in 1531, labeled the psalms by genre: "Trostpsalm" [psalm of comfort], "weissagung von Christo" [prophecy of Christ], "Dankpsalm" [psalm of thanks], among others.[23] However, he believed it of utmost importance that the narrative of God's discourse with his people be seen as historical. He found the book of Judith "a beautiful religious fiction by a holy, ingenious man who wanted to sketch and depict therein the fortunes of the whole Jewish people and the victory God always miraculously granted them over all their enemies." But it was not Scripture because "it hardly squares with the historical accounts of Holy Scriptures."[24]

Luther did work with the traditional canon minus the "apocryphal books," but did not lay much weight on canonical questions. For him they seem to have resolved themselves simply by the impact and conviction individual books wrought. Like ancient fathers, he distinguished those books that addressed the central questions of the faith more clearly. He contended that "John's gospel and his first epistle, Saint Paul's epistles, especially Romans, Galatians, and Ephesians, and Saint Peter's first epistle are the books that show you Christ and teach you all that is necessary and salutary for you to know." In this context he characterized James's epistle as "an epistle of straw."[25] But within the same body of prefaces to New Testament books he deemed James "a good book because it sets up no human teaching but vigorously promulgates the law of God" even though the ancients rejected it as canonical and it fails to teach justification, Christ's passion and resurrection, and the Holy Spirit.[26] The "epistle of straw" passage is sometimes used to suggest that Luther could play fast and loose with biblical texts that did not suit his fancy; the contrary is true, but his evaluation of them fit them into his Christ-centered reading in the context of distinguishing law and gospel. Luther regarded God's revelation of himself in Jesus Christ and

---

of Men (1522), WA 10,2:91,12–92,7; LW 35:152-53; *On the Councils and the Church* (1539), WA 50:545,35–547,11; LW 41:51-52; Althaus, *Theology*, 35-42, 72-102, 338-41.

21. "1 Corinthians 15" (1533), WA 36:501,11-13; LW 28:76-77.

22. "Sermon on the Mount" (1532), WA 32:305,27-30; LW 21:10.

23. WA 38:8-69.

24. WADB 12:4-7; LW 35:337-38.

25. Preface to the New Testament (1522), WADB 6:20,33-35; LW 35:362.

26. Preface to James (1522), WADB 7:384,1/385,1–386,30/387,30; LW 35:395-97.

his atonement through death and resurrection as the center and sum of what God gives in Scripture.[27]

His Ockhamist instructors had made him comfortable with God's material world; his Augustinian spiritualizing platonic tendencies gradually receded during the 1520s and early 1530s. From early on, indeed, he recognized that God had selected certain elements of the created order as special instruments for his re-creation of sinners into saints. The Word as the second person of the Trinity was made flesh (John 1:1-14), and God continues to commission human language and the mouths that speak it, as well as the baptismal water and the bread-body and wine-blood of the Lord's Supper — Word-accompanying and Word-delivering signs. Each form of God's Word plays a unique role in his economy of salvation. Because Scripture is God's Word, God is present in its pages and uses it as an instrument of his power, to condemn sin and evil, and, especially, to re-create sinners into his chosen people. The biblical Word of forgiveness and life, in human language, not only points to a heavenly reality but actually conveys or delivers God's power, Luther argued. God's promise of salvation in Christ functions as God's re-creating Word because his promise not only teaches but also actually performs or executes his saving will.[28]

Because God's Word is not a magical device used in incantations or ritual manipulation but rather his communication with his people, it was important for Luther that the Word of God be clear. God neither contradicts himself nor confuses his people.[29] Luther conceded that some passages of Scripture may seem obscure to those who read apart from the Holy Spirit; however, the faithful understand the message, even if not always in every detail and even as the mysteries of God remain beyond the comprehension of all creatures.[30]

Thus, Luther rejected ideas that imagined God's presence and power could come through other than external communication. "Stick to God's external Word, and listen to it. It tells you that God is your gracious Father. This is how the Father draws you."[31] In 1 Corinthians 15:3-7, Paul "adduces Scripture as his strongest proof, for there is no other enduring way of preserving our doctrine and our faith than the physical or written Word, poured into letters and preached orally by him or others, for here we find it stated clearly, 'Scripture!

27. WA 45:653,19–655,8; LW 24:211-13.

28. WA 4:321,35-36; 284,32-33.

29. Thompson, *Sure Ground,* 147-90.

30. WA 18:606,1–609,14; LW 33:24-28; Steven D. Paulson, "Internal Clarity of Scripture and the Modern World: Luther and Erasmus Revisited," in *Hermeneutica Sacra: Studien zur Auslegung der Heiligen Schrift im 16. und 17. Jahrhundert, Bengt Hägglund zum 90. Geburtstag,* ed. Tobjørn Johansson et al. (Berlin: De Gruyter, 2010), 85-109; Friedrich Beißer, *Claritas scripturae bei Martin Luther* (Göttingen: Vandenhoeck & Ruprecht, 1966), passim; Buchholz, *Schriftverständnis,* 74-138; Thompson, *Sure Ground,* 191-247.

31. "John 6, 45-46" (1531), WA 33:141,9-17; LW 23:93.

Scripture!' "[32] In 1538 Luther condemned the "ravers" who attempted to hear the Holy Spirit within their own imaginations rather than in the external Word in its various forms, "as if the Spirit could not come through the Scriptures or the spoken word of the apostles. . . . For both those who believe prior to baptism and those who become believers in baptism have everything through the external word that precedes [*durchs äußerliche vorgehende Wort*]."[33] Perhaps a variation on the scholastic concept "prevenient grace," Luther formulated the concept of the prevenient Word, God's initiation of his grace in sinners' lives.

Luther's reliance on Scripture alone as the only authoritative source for all teaching did not lead him to ignore the tradition of the church or its contemporary delivery in preaching, teaching, and writing, as well as the sacraments.[34] The "sola scriptura" principle meant for him that tradition and his own delivery of the biblical Word had always to be dependent on, subject to, and faithful to Scripture. He told the Wittenberg congregation, "If I am to stand my ground, I must constantly adhere to Scripture. . . . These articles of faith which we preach are not based on human reason and understanding, but on Scripture; it follows that they must not be sought anywhere but in Scripture or explained otherwise than with Scripture."[35] In regard to tradition, he commented, without Scripture "the church, had it depended on councils and the fathers, would not have lasted long."[36]

This Word of God that is above all, for Luther, a word from the cross, cannot be mastered by human conceptualization. His "theology of the cross," based on 1 Corinthians 1 and 2, insisted upon that. His student and editor Veit Dietrich captured that when he transformed Luther's claim "our theology is a theology of the cross" into "theology is properly called the profession of the holy cross."[37] Paul said that what seems to human minds that demand mastery over the truth through empirical signs or rational logic as weakness and foolishness is actually God's power and wisdom (1 Cor. 1:18-25). Luther believed that God's power comes through the word of the cross, foundationally in Scripture and then in all oral, written, and sacramental forms that deliver its message. Born into a semi-literate cultural setting, Luther emphasized the oral delivery of the biblical message — and none other! — to his hearers.[38] As vital to his reformation as the medium of print was, the reformation was fundamentally an oral event.[39] Writing his first postil, he told priest-readers that the gospel of Christ "should

32. "1 Corinthians 15" (1533), WA 36:500,21–501,10; LW 28:76-77.

33. Smalcald Articles 3.8.6-7, BSELK 772-73; BC 322.

34. Thompson, *Sure Ground,* 249-87.

35. "1 Corinthians 15" (1533), WA 36:504,13-32; LW 28:79-80.

36. *On the Councils and the Church* (1539), WA 50:547,2-4; LW 41:52.

37. WA 40,3:193,19-20.

38. WA 33:147,26–148,1; LW 23:97. Cf. Thompson, *Sure Ground,* 76-78.

39. Mark U. Edwards, *Printing, Propaganda, and Martin Luther* (Berkeley: University of California Press, 1994), 37, 11.

really not be [regarded as] something written, but a spoken word that produced the Scriptures." Furthermore, the good news Scripture delivers is "spread not by pen but by word of mouth" (truer in his culture than today).[40] Conversation with God, through his active, power-filled Word, creates faith and bestows salvation.[41] Luther's own lectures on biblical books departed from the medieval methods of analysis; in 1519, in the preface to the printed versions of his Galatian lectures of 1516/1517, he announced that this volume would not conform to their expectations for a commentary but was instead his "testimony," his confession of faith.[42] Such was the nature of God's Word and of his human creatures, who in his image confess their faith to others. Luther described this activity often as "preaching" or "proclaiming" but most often as "teaching." He viewed *doctrina* as an active agent of God's revelation of himself in his Word. Peter Fraenkel described Melanchthon's usage of nouns such as "teaching" and "tradition" as "verbal nouns" because the action of conveying the content must accompany the content being taught or handed down.[43] Luther's usage is the same.

Luther and Melanchthon not only regarded "teaching," "proclamation," and "confession" as involving human action; they served as instruments of God's action of killing and making alive as well. In 1520 Luther noted that "three things are necessary to know to be saved: first, what he should do and not do; second, when he sees that he cannot do or not do these things by his own strength, that he know where to seek and find it, so that he may do and not do these things; third, that he know how to see and gain it." Sick people must diagnose their illness, then seek the remedy, and consequently desire and strive for healing.[44] The law reveals sin; the gospel reveals God's help and deliverance; those who trust the gospel proceed to practice the life of faith. This distinction is less a definition of terms than a lively guideline to their use.[45] They were designed as God's address of sinners, to bestow on them Christ's benefits through God's telling hearers that Christ had died and risen "for you."[46] For this reason Gerhard Forde has regarded

40. WA 10,1,1:17,15-20; LW 35:123. On Luther's view of the Word in the postil, see Makito Masaki, "Luther's Two Kinds of Righteousness and His Wartburg Postil" (Ph.D. dissertation, Concordia Seminary, 2008), 11-16.

41. WA 33:147,10–148,9; LW 23:97.

42. WA 2:449,16-31; LW 27:159.

43. Peter Fraenkel, "Revelation and Tradition, Notes on Some Aspects of Doctrinal Continuity in the Theology of Philip Melanchthon," *Studia Theologica* 13 (1959): 97-133.

44. WA 7:204,13-27. Cf. Luther's *Prayerbook* (1522), WA 10,2:376,12–377,14; Althaus, *Theology*, 251-73.

45. Bayer, *Theology*, 56-62; Gerhard Ebeling, *Luther, an Introduction to His Thought*, trans. R. Wilson (Philadelphia: Fortress, 1970), 110-24; Lohse, *Theology*, 267-76; Kolb and Arand, *Genius*, 148-59.

46. Guntis Kalme, "'Words Written in Golden Letters' — a Lutheran Reading of the Ecumenical Creeds" (Ph.D. dissertation, Concordia Seminary, Saint Louis, 2006), 54-138.

absolution as the native form of God's Word, for it delivers forgiveness, life, and salvation most directly to the person who must hear that the message is "for you."[47] Thus, Luther found Christ as the central focus of Scripture's revelation of who God is and what he does for humankind. Luther's preface to the Old Testament (1523) reminded readers that Christ directed people to the Scriptures and their testimony of him (John 5:39) as did Paul (1 Tim. 4:13; Rom. 1:2; 1 Cor. 15:3-4).[48] This approach to Scripture informed Luther's hermeneutic for the epistle to the Romans in 1522, which was to guide readers through the entire Scripture. It consisted of contrasting definitions of fundamental concepts, above all "law" and "gospel."[49] This hermeneutic elicited echoes and elaborations in the works of Melanchthon[50] and their student, Cyriakus Spangenberg.[51]

Luther urged his students to follow an adaptation of the monastic pattern of reading *(lectio)*, prayer, and meditation with his prescription of prayer *(oratio)*, meditation *(meditatio)*, and spiritual struggle *(tentatio)* in their Bible study. He knew that readers of Scripture depend on the Holy Spirit's guidance and need to pray as they approach its text. They need to turn over its words in their minds. But they also bring life's burdens to the text and encounter there Satan's diversions and attacks.[52] For Luther knew that the battle between God's truth and Satan's deception never ceases (John 8:44). All heresies try to find their basis in Scripture, so its interpretation must be carefully guarded.[53] "By God's grace I have learned to know much about Satan. If he can twist and pervert the Word of God and the Scriptures, what will he not be able to do with my or someone else's words?"[54]

This understanding of Scripture as weapon against Satan and God's tool to effect repentance and faith by killing sinful identities and raising up dead sinners to life in Christ never disappeared from view for Luther's successors, even when polemic pressures caused them to focus on the nature of Scripture as the inspired Word of God in the following century.

47. Gerhard Forde, *Theology Is for Proclamation* (Minneapolis: Fortress, 1990), esp. 147-90.

48. WADB 8:10,1/11,1–12,22/13,22; LW 35:235-37. See Kolb and Arand, *Genius*, 161-66.

49. WADB 7:2,18/3,20–12,26/13,26; LW 35:366-72. Cf. the pioneering study of Gerhard Ebeling, *Evangelische Evangelienauslegung: Eine Untersuchung zu Luthers Hermeneutic*, 3rd edition (Tübingen: Mohr/Siebeck, 1991).

50. Cf. his *Commentary on Romans*, trans. Fred Kramer (Saint Louis: Concordia, 1992), 15-35; *Melanchthons Werke in Auswahl*, vol. 5, ed. Robert Stupperich and Rolf Schäfer (Gütersloh: Mohn, 1965), 39-56.

51. Robert Kolb, "Learning to Drink from the Foundations of Israel: The Biblical Exegesis of Cyriakus Spangenberg," in *Luther's Heirs Define His Legacy: Studies on Lutheran Confessionalization* (Aldershot, UK: Variorum, 1996), 13:3-12.

52. WA 50:658,29–661,8; LW 34:285-88; Bayer, *Theology*, 13-41.

53. WA 45:647,14–649,37; LW 24:204-7.

54. WA 26:499,7–500,26; LW 37:360-61.

Lutherans and Scripture

Luther, Melanchthon, and their colleagues recognized in various ways the hermeneutical challenge posed by disagreements on the text. They regarded their own formulations of Christian teaching, such as the Augsburg Confession and Luther's catechisms, as a "body of doctrine," the functional equivalent of the ancient "rule of faith," as a summary based totally on Scripture which could serve as the fundamental hermeneutical guide to its further interpretation.[55] This *"corpus doctrinae,"* defined with some variation by various of their students, continued to shape Lutheran biblical interpretation in subsequent generations.

Wittenberg training and publishing elicited a wealth of biblical comment. Melanchthon's influence on the exegesis of successive generations may have been as great as Luther's,[56] certainly in terms of method greater.[57] His exegetical lectures were less homiletical than Luther's but provided rhetorical, linguistic, and theological aids for preaching the biblical message. His method embraced more of Aristotle's mode of analysis than Luther used. His pioneering effort at reformulating how Reformation theologians presented public doctrine, *Loci communes theologici,* originally took shape as a reader's guide to Romans (1521).

Though he never studied there and thought somewhat independently, Johannes Brenz's preaching produced widely read commentaries that arose from fundamentally the Wittenberg view of Scripture and its hermeneutic.[58] Though he wrote no commentaries except his *Gloss on the New Testament,* the work of Matthias Flacius Illyricus in hermeneutics is recognized yet today as pioneering new paths for hermeneutics, based upon Wittenberg linguistic training and the law/gospel distinction.[59] Building upon what he had learned from Luther and Melanchthon,

55. Irene Dingel, "Philip Melanchthon and the Establishment of Confessional Norms," *Lutheran Quarterly* 20 (2006): 146-69.

56. See the work of Timothy J. Wengert, summarized in "Biblical Interpretation in the Works of Philip Melanchthon," 319-40: *Philip Melanchthon's* Annotationes in Johannem *in Relation to Its Predecessors and Contemporaries* (Geneva: Droz, 1987); *Law and Gospel: Philip Melanchthon's Debate with John Agricola of Eisleben over Poenitentia* (Grand Rapids: Baker, 1997); *Human Freedom, Christian Righteousness: Philip Melanchthon's Exegetical Dispute with Erasmus of Rotterdam* (Oxford/New York: Oxford University Press, 1998).

57. Robert Kolb, "Philipp's Foes but Followers Nonetheless: Late Humanism among the Gnesio-Lutherans," in *The Harvest of Humanism in Central Europe: Essays in Honor of Lewis W. Spitz,* ed. Manfred P. Fleischer (Saint Louis: Concordia, 1992), 159-77; "Teaching the Text: The Commonplace Method in Sixteenth Century Lutheran Biblical Commentary," *Bibliothèque d'Humanisme et Renaissance* 49 (1987): 571-85; "Melanchthon's Influence on the Exegesis of His Students: The Case of Romans 9," *Philip Melanchthon (1497-1560) and the Commentary,* ed. M. Patrick Graham and Timothy J. Wengert (Sheffield: Sheffield Academic Press, 1997), 198-217.

58. Cf. Robert L. Rosin, *Reformers, the Preacher, and Skepticism: Luther, Brenz, Melanchthon, and Ecclesiastes* (Mainz: Zabern, 1997), 151-214.

59. His *Glossa Compendaria* (Basel, 1570); *Clavis Scripturae Sacrae* (Basel, 1567); cf. Bengt

in both doctrine and method, and on other attempts at formulating hermeneutical principles, such as that of Andreas Hyperius, Flacius regarded Christ, "the lamb who was slain," as the key to understanding all Scripture (Rev. 5:12). He paid close attention to linguistic and rhetorical forms in order to help readers recognize the clarity that the Holy Spirit gives the text as he uses it as his instrument to kill sinners and bring them alive as God's children. His emphasis on the Spirit's inspiration of the text (including Hebrew vowel points) and his general hermeneutical principles shaped Lutheran biblical interpretation for over a century.

Thus, the reformers and their students passed a lively tradition of biblical interpretation on to the subsequent generations. The historiography of Lutheran "Orthodoxy" emphasizes the massive dogmatic works of university theologians, but even those theologians, like others, produced commentaries aimed at cultivating good preaching, with as much positive result as professors usually produce. Among many examples are the commentaries of Jena professor Johann Gerhard (1582-1637) on Genesis, Deuteronomy, Matthew, Luke/Acts, Romans, 1 and 2 Timothy, Hebrews, 1 and 2 Peter, and Revelation. The *Biblia Illustrata* (1672/1676) of Wittenberg professor Abraham Calov (1612-1686), "the most significant commentary on the whole Bible of seventeenth-century Lutheran theology," exhibited the same concerns for delivering the gospel to readers that marked Gerhard's exegesis.[60] Both grounded their dogmatics in extensive exegetical argument and regarded Scripture not just as a depository of information on God's work in the world but also the Holy Spirit's tool for killing and making alive.[61] Their dogmatics found precisely this use in their readers' preaching.[62]

The reformers' theological great-grandchildren continued their confidence in the authority and power of Scripture, albeit, as is usually the case with great-grandchildren, with some different linguistic formulations, arising out of new concerns as they discussed questions of authority and doctrine with other Christians, and out of new methods of teaching and public discourse. "In their entire treatment of Scripture the orthodox Lutherans, like Luther himself, really have only two basic concerns. First, they desire to maintain the principle of *sola Scriptura:* only Sacred Scripture can establish articles of faith; all theology is to

---

Hägglund, "Pre-Kantian Hermeneutics in Lutheran Orthodoxy," *Lutheran Quarterly* 20 (2006): 318-22; Rudolf Keller, *Der Schlüssel zur Schrift: Die Lehre vom Wort Gottes bei Matthias Flacius Illyricus* (Hannover: Lutherisches Verlagshaus, 1984); Günther Moldaenke, *Schriftverständnis und Schriftdeutung im Zeitalter der Reformation: Matthias Flacius Illyricus* (Stuttgart: Kohlhammer, 1936).

60. Volker Jung, *Das Ganze der Heiligen Schrift: Hermeneutik und Schriftauslegung bei Abraham Calov* (Stuttgart: Calwer, 1999), 129-226, on 129.

61. Jung, *Das Ganze der Heiligen Schrift,* 276-90; Kenneth G. Appold, *Abraham Calov's Doctrine of Vocatio in Its Systematic Context* (Tübingen: Mohr/Siebeck, 1998), esp. 117-69.

62. Bernhard Liess, *Johann Heerman (1585-1647): Prediger in Schlesien zur Zeit des Dreißigjährigen Krieges* (Münster: LIT, 2003), 186-91.

be drawn from the written Word of God alone. Second, they are intent on emphasizing the power and efficacy of Scripture as God's Word of Law and Gospel; Scripture possesses the power of very God, the power to judge and to save, to kill and to make alive."[63]

Seventeenth-century Lutheran views of Scripture's nature as God's Word and its authority were formed in part in polemical exchange with Roman Catholics; one critical stage took place in a colloquy in Regensburg in 1601, in which Wittenberg professor Aegidius Hunnius and his colleagues insisted on the sole authority of Scripture and wrestled with questions relating to secondary authority that adjudicates matters of dispute.[64] Forced to attempt to answer the theodical question concerning the means by which the Holy Spirit governs the church and its teaching, they formulated answers that could not meet Roman Catholic objections, because, as with other questions about evil in God's world, Lutherans tended to believe, no satisfactory answer devised by human reason is possible. Thus, the Lutheran Orthodox theologians also rejected the Socinian view of revelation that designated "the Holy Scriptures, especially those of the New Testament" as the source of instruction for attaining eternal life but placed the hermeneutical key to understanding them in human reason and the evidence it provides.[65]

The "Orthodox" theologians insisted that the Holy Spirit speaks from Scripture's pages and effects his saving will, bringing sinners to repentance, faith, and new obedience.[66] They employed Aristotelian categories to discuss its nature and saving activity,[67] but they preserved Luther's convictions regarding God's presence and power that it conveys to its hearers and readers. Scholars have different estimates of the role the concept of inspiration itself played in seventeenth-century Lutheran theology. Hägglund notes that, without depending on the term "inspiration" extensively, Gerhard viewed Scripture as God speaking, present in its pages in his condemning and redeeming power.[68] Preus and Ratschow concluded that "Orthodox" authors emphasized more and more that the Spirit's inspiration of every Word in Scripture gave it its authority[69] as they described the Spirit's inspiration of the words of the biblical text (emphasizing it more than

63. Robert D. Preus, *The Theology of Post-Reformation Lutheranism,* 2 vols. (Saint Louis: Concordia, 1970, 1972), 1:256; *The Inspiration of Scripture* (Edinburgh: Oliver & Boyd, 1957), 88-146, 170-92.

64. Wilhelm Herbst, *Das Regensburger Religionsgespräch von 1601* (Gütersloh: Bertelsmann, 1928).

65. E.g., *The Racovian Catechism . . . ,* ed. Thomas Rees (London: Longman, 1818; repr. Lexington: ATKA, 1962), 1-13. Cf. Preus, *Theology,* 1:189-90, 355-56.

66. Preus, *Inspiration,* 170-92.

67. Bengt Hägglund, *Die Heilige Schrift und ihre Deutung in der Theologie Johann Gerhards: Eine Untersuchung über das altlutherische Schriftverständnis* (Lund: Gleerup, 1951), 105-18.

68. Hägglund, *Schrift,* 64-81.

69. Hägglund, *Schrift,* 118-27.

the inspiration of the writers).[70] They drew from this inspiration the Scripture's characteristics of perfection or sufficiency as God's revelation, its clarity, efficacy, and utter reliability, and its authority for the church's teaching and life. They believed that the Holy Spirit remains present in Scripture and guides the church's use in applying it to the hearers' and readers' lives in every age.[71] That gave it unchallengeable authority.[72] In any case Karl Barth drives a false wedge between the reformers and their successors in terms of the substance of their views of the relationship between Scripture and the Holy Spirit.[73]

Orthodox theologians held that the Spirit not only gave the text through the holy writers; he enlightens believers and guides the church in absorbing Scripture throughout history, working through their internal clarity to bestow trust in Christ and thus forgiveness and life.[74] Wittenberg professor Wolfgang Franz (1564-1628) and Gerhard's successor in Jena Salomon Glassius (1591-1656) continued his hermeneutical work; Glassius's *Philologia sacra* (1623) concentrated on the significance of grammar, rhetorical forms, and genre while emphasizing that Scripture depends on "a demonstration of the Spirit and power" rather than human wisdom (1 Cor. 2:1, 4). Like Gerhard, he sought the mystical sense of Scripture in applying its insights to faith while anchoring biblical study in the literal meaning of the text.[75] Well aware of the implications of genre and rhetoric for the ways in which biblical texts communicate, these theologians presumed that, as God's voice, Scripture is without error.[76]

For all the differences in nuance and focus between Luther and seventeenth-century theologians, the fundamental elements of his understanding of Scripture remained.

Reformed Theologians and Scripture

The roots of the Reformed tradition also lie deep and firm in Scripture. Against the same medieval background as Luther, Ulrich Zwingli and his contemporaries developed their theology on the basis of a *sola Scriptura* principle.[77] The *Confessio*

70. Carl Heinz Ratschow, *Lutherische Dogmatik zwischen Reformation und Aufklärung*, 2 vols. (Gütersloh: Mohn, 1964, 1966), 71-132; Preus, *Theology* 1:265-95; Preus, *Inspiration*, esp. 26-49.

71. Preus, *Theology*, 265-67, 309-15, 362-78; Preus, *Inspiration*, 88-192.

72. Preus, *Inspiration*, 81-105.

73. *Church Dogmatics* I/2, ed. G. W. Bromiley and T. F. Torrance, trans. G. T. Thomson and Harold Knight (Edinburgh: T. & T. Clark, 1956), 520-22 [*Die Kirchliche Dogmatik* I/2, 4th edition (Zollikon-Zürich: Evangelischer Verlag, 1948), 577-80].

74. Hägglund, "Hermeneutics," 322-25.

75. Hägglund, "Hermeneutics," 325-30; cf. Preus, *Theology*, 1:315-39.

76. Preus, *Theology*, 339-62; Preus, *Inspiration*, 76-87.

77. Most essays in *Biblical Interpretation in the Era of the Reformation: Essays Presented to*

Tetrapolitana (1530) staked its confession on Scripture given by the Holy Spirit (2 Tim. 3:16), through which he fashions godly people and equips them for every good work.[78]

In Zurich Heinrich Bullinger actively searched the Scriptures in his commentaries on all the New Testament epistles, including Revelation, on John's Gospel[79] and Acts, and, in homiletical comment on Isaiah, Jeremiah, Lamentations, and Daniel.[80] He recognized Scripture as God's authoritative, inspired Word.[81] His catechetical sermons, the *Decades* (1549), began by treating "God's Word." God's Word signifies, first, God's power, then the second person of the Trinity, and then the revelation of God's will through Christ, the prophets, and the apostles, "and after that registered in writings, which are rightly called 'holy and divine scriptures.'" As God's Word, their word is "true, just, without deceit and guile, without error or evil affection, holy, pure, good, immortal, and everlasting," the truth (John 17:17).[82] This echoed the *First Helvetic Confession* (1536), which Bullinger, Oswald Myconius, and Simon Grynaeus composed; it confessed that "the holy, divine, biblical Scripture, which is the Word of God, inspired by the Holy Spirit and presented to the world through the prophets and apostles, is the most ancient, most perfect, and loftiest teaching, comprehending everything that serves the true knowledge, love, and honor of God, proper, true piety, and the living of a pious, upright, blessed life." "The holy divine Scripture shall be interpreted and explained by nothing than itself through the rule of faith and love."[83] Bullinger's *Second Helvetic Confession* (1562) elaborated this statement, affirming that the canonical Scriptures of the prophets and apostles of both testaments are truly God's

---

David C. Steinmetz in Honor of His Sixtieth Birthday, ed. Richard A. Muller and John L. Thompson (Grand Rapids: Eerdmans, 1996) deal with Reformed exegetes, including Bucer, Bullinger, Musculus, Vermigli, Zanchi, and Zwingli.

78. *Reformierte Bekenntnisschriften,* ed. Heiner Faulenbach and Eberhard Busch (Neukirchen: Neukirchener, 2002-), 2/2:460-61.

79. Ulrich Gäbler, "Bullingers Vorlesung über das Johannesevangelium aus dem Jahre 1523," in *Heinrich Bullinger 1504-1575: Gesammelte Aufsätze zum 400. Todestag,* ed. Ulrich Gäbler and Erland Herkenrath (Zurich: Theologischer Verlag, 1975), 1:13-27.

80. Alexandre Ganoczy and Stefan Scheld, *Die Hermeneutik Calvins: Geistesgeschichtliche Voraussetzungen und Grundzüge* (Wiesbaden: Steiner, 1983), 71.

81. See his *De Scripturae sanctae authoritate, certitudine, firmitate et absoluta perfectione* (Zurich: Forschauer, 1538). Cf. István Tökés, "Bullingers hermeneutische Lehre," in *Bullinger, Gesammelte Aufsätze,* 1:161-89, and Susi Hausammann, "Anfragen zum Schriftverstaendnis des jungen Bullinger im Zusammenhang einer Interpretation von 'De Scripturae negatio,'" in *Bullinger, Gesammelte Aufsätze,* 1:29-48. Particularly through his catechetical sermons in the *Decades,* Bullinger cultivated the biblical understanding of countless pastors, especially in England and Hungary.

82. *The Decades of Henry Bullinger, the First and Second Decades,* trans. H. I. (Cambridge: Cambridge University Press, 1849), 37.

83. *Reformierte Bekenntnisschriften,* 1/2:44.

Word. God spoke through them and "speaks to us through the Holy Scriptures." Preachers of the biblical message deliver God's Word to their hearers.[84]

Bullinger did not believe, however, that the biblical Word actually delivers God's power. Although he affirmed the need for the external Word against those who focus on the Holy Spirit's inner working, his reaction against the medieval sacerdotal system and his metaphysic based on Realist presuppositions denied the power of the pronounced word of absolution to bestow forgiveness of sins; that happens only at the right hand of God in heaven, where the Lord Jesus sits in the true tabernacle.[85] Nonetheless, Bullinger believed that Scripture alone provides God's revelation and norms its proclamation in the church. He had confidence that the faithful in the communion of the saints could interpret Scripture clearly and purely.[86]

Calvin and Scripture

Bullinger's colleague in Geneva, John Calvin, held much the same position; the two worked with unique gifts parallel to each other.[87] The 1559 edition of Calvin's *Institutes* taught that knowledge of God, who is faintly perceived through nature, can truly come only through Scripture. The patriarchs knew God as Creator, but to be illuminated to the hope of eternal life, they needed to know God as Redeemer as well. To ensure that this unambiguous faith "might abide forever in the world with a continuing succession of teaching . . . the same oracles he had given to the patriarchs it was his pleasure to have recorded, as it were, on public tablets."[88] Indeed, the Word of God had come to the patriarchs before Scripture was written, in dreams, visions, and other modes of communication, but once the Scriptures were in place, they alone, as God's Word, "obtain full authority among believers only when men regard them as having sprung from heaven, as if there the living words of God were heard." Calvin rejected the medieval concept that the church exercises power over Scripture. That idea mocks the Holy Spirit. The church is instead grounded upon Scripture (Eph. 2:20).[89]

Calvin practiced exegesis at the lectern and in the pulpit, in conversation

84. *Die Bekenntnisschriften der reformierten Kirche,* ed. E. F. Karl Müller (Leipzig: Deichert, 1903), 170-71.

85. Bullinger, *Decades: The Fifth Decade* (Cambridge: Cambridge University Press, 1852), 96-98.

86. Ganoczy and Scheld, *Hermeneutik,* 74-75.

87. Joel E. Kok, "Heinrich Bullinger's Exegetical Method: The Model for Calvin?" in *Biblical Interpretation,* 241-54.

88. *Calvin: Institutes of the Christian Religion,* Library of Christian Classics 20-21, ed. John T. McNeill, trans. Ford Lewis Battles (Philadelphia: Westminster, 1960), 1:70-71 (1.6.1).

89. *Calvin: Institutes of the Christian Religion,* 1:74-76 (1.7.1-2). Cf. Ganoczy and Scheld, *Hermeneutik,* 90-92.

with the exegetes of all ages, including his own, his friend Martin Bucer in Strasbourg among them. Bucer produced significant exegetical work himself (on the four Gospels, all Pauline epistles, and the psalms[90]), on the basis of his view that Scripture was written by the Holy Spirit, through human authors as his amanuenses, who, in the process of the Spirit's inspiration, remained individual personalities. The Spirit gave Scripture authority and thus certitude. The Spirit always works in tandem with Scripture, which is God's Word and depends on his using it for its proper interpretation and impact.[91] God's Word moves from Scripture by the Holy Spirit's power to address the congregation as the minister of the Word preaches, although Bucer "explicitly rejects the dogma that God does not give faith and the Holy Spirit, unless the word and sacrament go before."[92] While he could define the sacraments as "visible words," he wished to avoid any *ex opere operato* view of their working and therefore did not define them as means or instruments of bestowing grace.[93]

Under Bucer's tutelage, Calvin, who had lectured on Romans and perhaps other Pauline epistles before leaving Geneva, lectured on John's gospel at the Strasbourg Academy (1539-1541).[94] At this time he was also studying Romans. Richard Muller notes that the chronological and thematic proximity of the publication of his commentary on Paul's epistle (1540) and the appearance of the first major revision of his *Institutes of the Christian Religion* (1539, Latin; 1541, French) was more than coincidental: "Calvin himself indicated that his thought was rooted in two parallel exercises — in the ongoing work of preaching, lecturing, and commenting through the text of Scripture and in the related work of developing disputations and *loci* based on exegetical insight and presented to particular contexts of positive thought and debate. The *Institutes* cannot be rightly understood apart from Calvin's exegetical and expository efforts, nor can his exegetical and expository efforts be divorced from his work of compiling the *Institutes*."[95] The biblical text shaped his formulation of public doctrine significantly, which, in turn, the rhetorical formulation of the *"argumentum," "dispositio," "scopus,"* or *"methodus"* of the epistle reflects.[96] This interplay between public treatment of Scripture in

90. Bernard Roussel, "Bucer Exegete," in *Martin Bucer and Sixteenth Century Europe,* ed. Christian Krieger and Marc Lienhard (Leiden: Brill, 1993), 39-54.

91. W. Peter Stephens, *The Holy Spirit in the Theology of Martin Bucer* (Cambridge: Cambridge University Press, 1970), 129-55. Cf. Johannes Müller, *Martin Bucers Hermeneutik* (Gütersloh: Mohn, 1965), 72-80; Ganoczy and Scheld, *Hermeneutik,* 76-89.

92. Stephens, *Spirit,* 201, cf. 196-212.

93. Stephens, *Spirit,* 213-59.

94. Barbara Pitkin, "Calvin as Commentator on the Gospel of John," in *Calvin and the Bible,* ed. Donald K. McKim (Cambridge: Cambridge University Press, 2006), 164-98.

95. Richard A. Muller, *The Unaccommodated Calvin: Studies in the Foundation of a Theological Tradition* (Oxford: Oxford University Press, 2000), 186.

96. Muller, *The Unaccommodated Calvin,* 28; cf. 108, 140. On Calvin's polemic in his ex-

exegetical lectures and sermons and articulation of the church's doctrine continued throughout Calvin's life. His exegesis reflects his polemical and catechetical concerns, and his dogma was grounded on careful study of the biblical text.[97] Nonetheless, it is important to note the balance between Calvin's "dogmatic" work and his exegetical work: "The *Institutes* is equaled in size by Calvin's sermons on Job and dwarfed by the sermons on Deuteronomy, as well as by the individual commentaries on Psalms, Isaiah, Jeremiah, and the Pentateuch."[98] His lectures were directed at the church's pastors and teachers, but he also commented on biblical books to a wider audience on Fridays in the *congregations.* His sermons, usually serial expositions of an entire book, addressed the text to the general population of Geneva. From 1549 to his death in 1564 one scribe, appointed by the city, Denis Raguenier, transcribed the sermons for publication. Others, including Jean Budé, took notes on his lectures.[99]

Calvin followed the publication of his Romans commentary in 1540 with nearly a quarter century of biblical interpretation, in three forms of exposition: sermons, lectures (which often turned into commentaries), and works written as commentaries, though in the last category only his *Harmony of the Last Four Books of Moses* and his treatments of the Psalms and Joshua fit.[100] He deliberately worked his way through the Bible, publishing finally expositions of almost every book.[101] He held strictly to the new Protestant canon of sixty-six books.[102] His exegetical work reflects his ongoing conversation with the tradition of biblical comment. He knew, used, criticized, and amplified insights from many patristic writers, some medieval commentators, Jewish scholarship, and a range of contemporaries, including Luther, Melanchthon, Sebastian Münster, Bullinger, Bucer, and Wolfgang Musculus.[103]

---

egesis, see Wilhelmus H. Th. Moehn, *"God Calls Us to His Service": The Relation between God and His Audience in Calvin's Sermons on Acts* (Geneva: Droz, 2001), 125-75.

97. Muller, *The Unaccommodated Calvin,* 148-52.

98. Muller, *The Unaccommodated Calvin,* 5.

99. Muller, *The Unaccommodated Calvin,* 32, 146; cf. T. H. L. Parker, *Calvin's Old Testament Commentaries* (Edinburgh: T. & T. Clark, 1986), 10-12.

100. Parker, *Calvin's Old Testament Commentaries,* 9-41.

101. Muller, *The Unaccommodated Calvin,* 145-48.

102. Ward Holder, *John Calvin and the Grounding of Interpretation: Calvin's First Commentaries* (Leiden: Brill, 2006), 21; cf. T. H. L. Parker, *Calvin's New Testament Commentaries* (Grand Rapids: Eerdmans, 1971), 69-78.

103. See David C. Steinmetz, "Calvin and Abraham: The Interpretation of Romans 4 in the Sixteenth Century," *Church History* 57 (1988): 443-55; "Calvin and the Patristic Exegesis of Paul," in *The Bible in the Sixteenth Century,* ed. David Steinmetz (Durham, NC: Duke University Press, 1990), 100-118; and essays in *Calvin in Context* (New York: Oxford University Press, 1995); and A. N. S. Lane's studies, particularly *John Calvin: Student of the Church Fathers* (Grand Rapids: Baker, 1999). Cf. also Susan E. Schreiner, *Where Shall Wisdom Be Found? Calvin's Exegesis of Job from Medieval and Modern Perspectives* (Chicago: University of Chicago Press, 1994); Randall C.

Particularly his usage of ancient commentators, along with his careful philological work, indicates that Calvin's training in biblical humanism played a large role in making him the exegete he was. He applied this education in careful textual criticism,[104] rhetorical analysis,[105] and historical study of the context.[106] Muller notes the "close relationship between Calvin's theology of the Word and his humanist understanding of the dynamics of language — in the context of a detailed discussion of the rhetorical tradition and the contemporary rhetorical training on which Calvin drew."[107] Although he urged a proper use of God's gift of reason, Calvin submitted human reason to the authority of Scripture and insisted that Scripture alone can truly interpret Scripture.[108]

Calvin regarded the Bible as God's Word while simultaneously honoring its human authorship. God accommodates his language and message to sinners whose reason is sufficiently damaged to cloud their understanding of the mysteries of God, but he nonetheless conveys his will and disposition toward them in human language.[109] Calvin took seriously the "mind" or intention, purpose, and goal of individual authors, holding that "the proper task of the interpreter is to reveal the mind of the author, and the mind of the author is disclosed by context."[110] Calvin's exposition elucidated various levels of context, including the fundamental "argument" or purpose of a book or author, the individual author's linguistic usage, including his peculiar vocabulary, and the larger historical, cultural setting of a book.[111] Authors retained "their own marks of style, and the peculiarities of their textual manner" despite the Holy Spirit's dictation of their language, the inspiring agent of every biblical author.[112]

Zachmann, "Calvin as Commentator on Genesis," in McKim, ed., *Calvin and the Bible,* 16-21; Wulfert de Greef, "Calvin as Commentator on the Psalms," 87-90; Darlene K. Fleming, "Calvin as Commentator on the Synoptic Gospels," 136-42; Parker, *New Testament,* 30-48; and Thomas F. Torrance, *The Hermeneutics of John Calvin* (Edinburgh: Scottish Academic Press, 1988), 73-95.

104. Ganoczy and Scheld, *Hermeneutik,* 136-42.

105. Ganoczy and Scheld, *Hermeneutik,* 142-44. See particularly Olivier Millet, *Calvin et la dynamique de la parole: Étude de rhétorique réformée* (Paris: Campion, 1992).

106. Ganoczy and Scheld, *Hermeneutik,* 144-54; on, e.g., his use of Josephus to elucidate the context of Acts, see Wilhelmus H. Th. Moehn, "Calvin as Commentator on the Acts of the Apostles," in McKim, ed., *Calvin and the Bible,* 205-9.

107. Muller, *The Unaccommodated Calvin,* 11. Cf. Torrance, *Hermeneutics,* 95-155.

108. Holder, *Grounding,* 108-17.

109. Commentary on Psalm 69:28, *Corpus Reformatorum, Calvini Opera* (Braunschweig/Berlin: Schwetschke, 1864-1900) [henceforth CR/CO], 59/31:650; cf. H. Jackson Forstman, *Word and Spirit: Calvin's Doctrine of Biblical Authority* (Stanford: Stanford University Press, 1962), 107; Holder, *Grounding,* 45-50.

110. Zachmann, "Genesis," 11; cf. Zachmann, "Gathering Meaning from the Context: Calvin's Exegetical Method," *The Journal of Religion* 82 (2002): 1-26.

111. Holder, *Grounding,* 98-108.

112. Holder, *Grounding,* 60.

This lively engagement with the human side of Scripture, in both origin and use, in no way alters Calvin's confidence that the Bible's human words were also God's words, given by the Holy Spirit. Scripture comes to its hearers "from the very mouth of God."[113] God's Spirit "meant by the mouth of David to instruct the whole church."[114] "Calvin can therefore speak of two authors of Genesis: Moses and the Holy Spirit."[115] God designed the entire Scripture, and he is responsible for the coordination, for example, of John's Gospel with the Synoptics: "God dictated to the four Evangelists what they should write, in such a manner, that, while each had his own part assigned to him, the whole might be collected into one body. . . . It is now our duty to blend the four by a mutual relation, so that we may permit ourselves to be taught by all of them, as by one mouth." However, the canonical ordering need not determine how Christians read the New Testament: Calvin preferred beginning with John, followed by Matthew, in order to see Christ more clearly.[116] This combination of respect for the Holy Spirit's words and the freedom to apply it to the actual hearers or readers before him exhibited itself also in Calvin's *Harmony of the Four Last Books of Moses* (1559). Calvin admitted that he had not "inconsiderately . . . altered the order which the Holy Spirit himself has prescribed" but, in Muller's words, "only offered an aid to the 'unpracticed reader' to facilitate the understanding of the object and plan of Moses' work." Calvin believed that the biblical books ought still to be studied separately, as written.[117]

Calvin "operated with a conception of scripture as authoritative and errorless," even though it is prescriptive.[118] He contrasted the Bible's historicity to the fables of Greek and Roman poets.[119] Because it is God's Word, Scripture is clear, both in its use of human language and its conveying God's will and ways to the person whom the Holy Spirit moves to faith.[120]

Calvin perceived "manifest signs of God speaking in Scripture," which authenticates itself and makes it "clear that the teaching of Scripture is from heaven." Scripture proves its authenticity and authority by its superior wisdom, antiquity, truthfulness, and through miracles, fulfillment of its prophecies, its simplicity and heavenly character, and the fact that martyrs have died for its message.[121] None-

113. Holder, *Grounding,* 58-68, and Calvin on 2 Timothy 3:16, CR80/CO52:283.

114. Commentary on Acts 1:20, CR76/CO48:20. Forstman, *Word,* supplies other such citations, 50-62.

115. Zachman, "Genesis," 3, quoting *Institutes,* 2:1153-54 (4.8.6).

116. Commentary on John's Gospel, argument, CR75/CO47:viii, 1-2. Cf. Muller, *The Unaccommodated Calvin,* 33.

117. Muller, *The Unaccommodated Calvin,* 36-37, from Preface to the Harmony, CR52/CO24:6-7.

118. Forstman, *Word,* 122.

119. Zachmann, "Genesis," 3-4.

120. Ganoczy and Scheld, *Hermeneutik,* 95-101.

121. *Institutes,* 1:81-92 (1.8.1-13).

theless, in the final analysis, Calvin believed that the divinity of Scripture must be found in a source higher than anything human, "the secret testimony of the Holy Spirit," which is "God's sufficient witness of himself in his word."[122] Muller sets aside the "neo-orthodox or Barthian notion of the Bible as a 'witness' to the Word" as an inaccurate appraisal of Calvin's understanding of Scripture squarely, just as false as the view that he was "an antagonist of all things medieval and a clear predecessor of the historical-critical method," both wishful thinking of scholars eager to enlist him for their purposes.[123]

Though sensitive to the different settings and usage of Old Testament and New Testament writers, Calvin read the Bible as a whole, calling on other books to illuminate a text with confirming proofs, parallels that clarified or expanded a point, analogies, and other comparisons, while always trying to keep the original historical setting of the text in view. His treatment of Old Testament prophets often examined a passage in light of its immediate historical context, its significance in understanding Christ and the apostolic era, and the course of history to the Last Day.[124] Holder notes,

> For Calvin, the functional unity of the two testaments is a result of a more basic statement of his theology and theological hermeneutics. . . . "God is the same yesterday and today, and always acts toward humanity in the same manner." God speaks with one voice through the whole of the scripture, so that scripture cannot finally contradict itself. With that as a touchstone of his theology, any other relationship between the Old and New Testaments would be preposterous, positing a God who used to have a different relationship to his followers than he does now. This can also be seen in the realization that the final import

122. *Institutes,* 1:78-81 (1.7.4-5); cf. Forstmann, *Word,* 17-19, 68-71; Ganoczy and Scheld, *Hermeneutik,* 93-94, 100-101, 111-20.

123. Muller, *The Unaccommodated Calvin,* 12. Karl Barth's reading of both the reformers, including Luther and Calvin, and the Orthodox theologians of the seventeenth century is anachronistic and ahistorical. His treatment of the inspiration of Scripture according to Luther and Calvin is indeed nuanced, but insufficiently distinguishes their view of the nature of the text, as inspired in the human writers, from the impact or effect of the text when the Holy Spirit uses it as his means or instrument of creating faith; *Church Dogmatics* I/2, 520-22. Barth strays further when he accuses "the post-Reformation period" of destroying the mystery of the reformers' views and leading to a "denial of the sovereignty of the Word of God and therefore of the Word of God itself," or when he charges the Orthodox treatment of inspiration with leading to the loss of "the knowledge of the free grace of God as the unity of Scripture and revelation" (*Church Dogmatics* I/2, 526, cf. 523-26 [*Dogmatik,* 581-85]). Muller has criticized this misreading of the actual state of affairs in Orthodoxy in the light of its texts; see *Post-Reformation Reformed Dogmatics,* 230-61. For one example of how this false myth influences scholars to this day, see John Webster, *Holy Scripture: A Dogmatic Sketch* (Cambridge: Cambridge University Press, 2003), 31.

124. Pete Wilcox, "Calvin as Commentator on the Prophets," in McKim, ed., *Calvin and the Bible,* 121-22.

> of the whole scripture was the manifestation of Christ. The whole of scripture, thus, is tied together not only by a single author who is the Holy Spirit but also by its single message, who is Christ, sent from the one fountain of all goods, God the Father.[125]

The center of the Holy Spirit's message is Christ, the *scopus* of the entire Scriptures, in Calvin's opinion.[126] He defined the gospel as the "clear manifestation of the mystery of Christ."[127] That mystery centered on Christ's justifying work, given to the elect through faith in him.[128] In interpreting John's Gospel Calvin found its focus not in its teaching Christ's divinity but in its presentation of his saving work in dying and rising.[129] The book of Acts is dedicated, in Calvin's mind, to "the fruit of the acts of Christ."[130]

Christ and his fruits must be conveyed to sinners. In Holder's words, "*doctrina* is the taught form of faith . . . always takes on the character of application of interpretation. This is the teaching which must edify, and when understood, has a dispositional force."[131] Calvin believed that the commonalities of human experience permitted Genevans to recognize God's working and will in the biblical stories and that the biblical stories illuminated and guided life in sixteenth-century Geneva.[132] Cultivating this engagement with Scripture depended on teaching and, for most of the people of God, preaching. "For Calvin preaching was God himself speaking with the preacher as the instrument of the Holy Spirit. . . . Calvin considered preaching to be the handing on of the Word of God and to possess the authority of God himself. Since Scripture is 'the Word of God,' the preacher bore the heavy responsibility of being the humble servant of that Word. He must, therefore, preach the 'pure Word without intruding his own opinions into the text.' "[133] Calvin viewed preaching as God's instrument or weapon in his never-ending battle against Satan.[134]

For the church's preaching and teaching to function correctly, Calvin be-

125. Holder, *Grounding*, 57-58; cf. 50-58; Parker, *Old Testament*, 42-56; and Richard A. Muller, "The Hermeneutic of Promise and Fulfillment in Calvin's Exegesis of the Old Testament Prophecies of the Kingdom," in *Bible in the Sixteenth Century*, 68-99.

126. Holder, *Grounding*, 140-63; Muller, *The Unaccommodated Calvin*, 23.

127. *Institutes*, 1:424-25 (2.9.2).

128. Holder, "Pauline Epistles," 225.

129. Pitkin, "John," 181.

130. Commentary on Acts 1:1-2, CR76/CO48:2; cf. Moehn, "Acts," 201.

131. Holder, *Grounding*, 22-23.

132. K. Greene-McCreight, " 'We Are Companions of the Patriarchs' or Scripture Absorbs Calvin's World," *Modern Theology* 14 (1998): 213-24.

133. Schreiner, "Calvin as Interpreter of Job," in McKim, ed., *Calvin and the Bible*, 54. Cf. Calvin's Commentary on Job, CR63/CO 35:43-44; T. H. L. Parker, *Calvin's Preaching* (Louisville: Westminster John Knox, 1992), 1-56; and Holder, *Grounding*, 168-77.

134. Moehn, *Sermons on Acts*, 80-86.

lieved, it must use something comparable to the rule of faith, which he intended to summarize in his *Institutes,* an intention parallel to Melanchthon's in his first *Loci communes theologici.* The *Institutes* was to serve as "a key that unlocks the door to a right understanding of Scripture."[135] "Although the Holy Scripture contains perfect doctrine, to which one can add nothing, because our Lord meant to display the infinite treasures of his wisdom in it, on the other hand a person who has not much practice in it has good reason for some guidance and direction, in order to know what he ought to look for in it, so that he will not wander here and there, but will hold to a sure path, in order to attain the goal to which the Holy Spirit calls him."[136]

Calvin did not assign power to Scripture as an agent of God but saw it as mutually bound with the Holy Spirit, who "so inheres in Scripture in his truth, which he expresses in Scripture, that only when its proper reverence and dignity are given to the Word does the Holy Spirit show forth his power. . . . For by a kind of mutual bond the Lord has joined together the certainty of his Word and of his Spirit so that the perfect religion of the Word may abide in our minds when the Spirit, who causes us to contemplate God's face, shines; and that we may embrace the Spirit with no fear of being deceived when we recognize him in his own image, namely in the Word."[137] The Spirit who dispensed the Word efficaciously confirms the Word, but, in contrast to Luther's view, does not actually effect his bestowal of forgiveness through it. Nonetheless, the two shared the conviction that Scripture is God's Word and alone is authoritative for the church's faith and life.

Reformed Orthodoxy

Muller notes that the "Orthodox" treatment of Scripture among Calvin's followers developed in two phases, the first beginning about 1565, ending with the Synod of Dordrecht (1618), the second running to the early eighteenth century. In the 1560s and 1570s Zacharias Ursinus, Hieronymus Zanchi, and others developed arguments that asserted biblical authority; Scripture alone is worthy of faith and provides the rule of faith. They maintained that Jesus Christ is the *"scopus"* or center of Scripture; its goal belief in Christ and holy living.[138] Muller concludes that while later Orthodox theology stated its teachings on Scripture "more dogmatically, more technically, and in more strictly defined terms" than had the reform-

135. *Institutes,* 1:7 ("Argument of the Present Book").

136. *Institutes,* 1:6, cited by Holder, *Grounding,* 72. Cf. Torrance, *Hermeneutics,* 63-72.

137. *Institutes,* 1:95 (1.9.3).

138. Muller, *Post-Reformation Reformed Dogmatics,* 94-95, 103-5. Hereafter page references from this book will be given in parentheses in the text.

ers, the difference should be attributed not to different fundamental concerns — both wished to produce Scripture's claims for itself and both strove to defend exclusive biblical authority against Roman Catholic objections — but rather to the development of new theological methods and terminology (114).[139] Muller believes that later Orthodox theologians presented their understanding of Scripture with less polemic and more positive exposition than had the reformers, and that the oft-alleged conflict of the Orthodox with developing natural scientific theories, such as Copernican and Galilean cosmology, has been exaggerated since many treated Scripture with a sophisticated historical and literary sensitivity that did not drive them to interpret, for instance, the sun's standing still (Josh. 10:13) as scientific language (126-29).

Parallel to developments within contemporary Lutheran theology, in the last third of the sixteenth-century Reformed teachers altered the order of doctrinal topics, which Melanchthon had begun with "On God." Instead, they proceeded epistemologically, introducing theology by discussing its foundations in "the Word of God," usually equated solely or in part with Scripture. Leiden professor Lucas Trelcatius defined the Bible as "a holy instrument concerning the truth necessary to salvation, faithfully and perfectly written in the canonical books by the prophets and the apostles [acting as] the secretaries of God for the salvific instruction of the church" (225).[140] Franciscus Gomarus of Leiden defined the efficient cause of Scripture as both God, who divinely directed and inspired the amanuenses, and these servants who received the dictation and put God's Word in biblical words (226).[141] Yet Petrus van Mastricht, for example, argued that individual authors functioned differently, treating specific topics under the Spirit's inspiration. The human characteristics of the human authors were in no way voided by the Spirit's employment of their minds and hands (244-55).

Indeed, Trelcatius and Gomarus recognized that the Word of God is first of all the term for the second person of the Trinity; this essential word must be distinguished from the Word set forth in God's work within the finite order of creation. There God's Word comes as unwritten and written, immediate and mediate, and external and internal. Scripture is indeed God's Word, given through the inspiration of the Holy Spirit. The Holy Spirit works with the text he inspired throughout the church's history as he brings the external proclamation of the biblical message to ears and hearts, in which he works the internal hearing of faith. Scripture is God's immediate Word, having proceeded from his mouth or voice; proclamation is his mediate Word (161-203). Scripture stood, in the Orthodox

139. Olivier Fatio argues similarly regarding Calvinist Orthodoxy's faithfulness to Calvin's approach to Scripture, *Méthode et théologie: Lambert Daneau et les débuts de la scolastique réformée* (Geneva: Droz, 1976), esp. ix-xiii.

140. Quoting *Schol. Meth.* 1.1-2 (p. 12); cf. Muller, 151-61, 230-55.

141. Quoting *Disputationes* 2.12-14.

theologians as it had in the reformers, at the center of God's revelation of his saving will for humankind.

As God's Word Scripture exercised ultimate authority for the Orthodox. Like Calvin and other reformers, they appealed for its authority to the inner testimony that the Holy Spirit effects through believers' reading of Scripture as well as external testimonies, including its truth, consistency, and prophetic power (255-85; cf. 340-70). This authority existed in words open to rational analysis, so long as reason retained its ministerial position and served rather than dominated understanding the text. The Socinian hermeneutic of the accord of reason and what is true in Scripture, like that of Hugo Grotius, aroused Reformed critique, as it did in Lutheran circles (140-41, 253, 335-38). Only toward the end of the seventeenth century was the relationship between biblical revelation and reason seen somewhat differently, for example by Jean-Alphonse Turretin, whose more positive assessment of reason over against revelation was meant to meet growing societal reliance on reason (161-82).

Throughout the sixteenth and seventeenth centuries the divinity of Scripture was asserted on the basis of its truthfulness, certainty, infallibility, perfection, sufficiency, and perspicacity. Orthodox theologians may have used different expressions for such convictions than had the reformers, but similar views are found in both (300-340).

Orthodox theologians continued, in part, to echo Calvin in teaching that the *scopus* or center of Scripture is Christ, but some developed a broader definition of that center, including an orientation of all theology around God's covenants with his people, his eternal decree of predestination, and his establishing communion between the believer and Christ, with individual theologians designing their *scopus* in different ways (206-23).

Seventeenth-century Reformed theologians, like their Lutheran counterparts, focused considerable attention both on linguistic studies, textual criticism, and hermeneutics.[142] Theodore Beza's *Annotationes in Novum Testamentum* (1556) heralded an extensive series of such works on the entire Bible across the Reformed landscape. Linguistic scholars such as Johannes Buxtorf Senior contributed to deepening knowledge of the Hebrew language and writings. Despite the prominence of dogmatic works in the historiography of the period, many theological professors and preachers composed commentaries, widely used by preachers throughout Europe and in the North American colonies.

Roman Catholic challenges to the sufficiency and reliability of the biblical text were interwoven with polemic over the canon; Reformed confessions of faith and theologians taught a sixty-six-book canon of those books "not historically

142. The following examples are gleaned from Richard A. Muller, "Biblical Interpretation in the 16th and 17th Centuries," in *Historical Handbook of Major Biblical Interpreters,* ed. Donald K. McKim (Downers Grove, IL: InterVarsity, 1998), 123-52.

challenged" (371-441). Mid-century debates over the relationship between exegesis and dogmatics took place within the framework of two sides, represented, for instance, in Holland, by Johannes Cocceius and Gisbert Voetius (120-23, 130-48). Several seventeenth-century theologians followed in Andreas Hyperius's footsteps in developing hermeneutical principles, within the context of their dogmatics texts or in separate treatises. Andreas Rivetus's *Isagogics, or General Introduction to Holy Scripture* and John Weemse's *The Christian Synagogue* are examples (118). Muller views the "strain" placed upon seventeenth-century Reformed exegesis as stemming not from the exegetes' departing from "the perceptions of the Reformers [that] so radically and rigidly identified Word as Scripture" and thus reduced God's Word to biblical text. Instead, their increasing study of ancient versions and cognate languages and their reliance on historical, literal, grammatical, rather than allegorical or typological models of interpretation based on developing presuppositions regarding history and language, made it more difficult to keep their understanding of God in Christ and all the words of the Bible together in one unified system of explanation (206).

* * *

Following certain medieval precedents, Protestant reformers took seriously a literal-prophetic sense of Scripture, reducing the use of allegory to pedagogical-homiletical purposes. They embraced Scripture's authority as the absolute authority of God's Word, from which the Holy Spirit, who brought the texts into being through human authors, still speaks. Ockhamist presuppositions directed Luther toward teaching that the Holy Spirit is actually present in the text he caused to be written by human authors and that his power to retain and forgive sins flows from its pages into the church's proclamation in other written as well as oral and sacramental forms. Calvin did not share Luther's background in Ockhamism, and his humanistic education did not give him a basis for seeing the Spirit's presence and power in the text itself. But he viewed Scripture as the Spirit's instrument for addressing sinners and eliciting faith in Christ in them. "Orthodox" theologians continued these views as they defined them against Roman Catholic polemic. The eighteenth century witnessed a new, different way of using and interpreting Scripture, in part proceeding from the reformers' insistence on the human as well as divine nature of Scripture, in part from Orthodoxy's increasing reliance on reason, but with a spirit that no longer believed that God spoke and speaks in the biblical text. The legacy of the reformers was largely set aside in this process.

FOUR

Natural Philosophy and Biblical Authority in the Seventeenth Century

Rodney L. Stiling

Seventeenth-century European natural philosophers participated in the exhilarating expansion of their disciplines in the context of new physical discoveries, new instruments, new theoretical insights, and new institutional structures, to say nothing of the broader context of continued international turmoil, political adjustments and realignments, and theological and ecclesiastical upheavals. The European project of settling and development of the "New" World accelerated as Britain joined Spain, Portugal, France, and the Netherlands in planting permanent commercial enterprises and colonies in the western hemisphere, in the process presenting European natural philosophers with countless unfamiliar forms of plants, animals, and humans. It was the age of the "establishing" of the study of nature: The *Accadèmia dei Lincei* was founded in Italy in 1603, the Royal Society of London took its charter in 1662, the French *Académie des Sciences* was established in 1666 in Paris, and the *Preußische Akademie der Wissenschaften* launched in Berlin in 1700. Throughout the century, kings, queens, emperors, grand dukes, and other nobility of Europe increasingly provided patronage and support to court philosophers and mathematicians.

In 1596 Johannes Kepler dazzled philosophical minds in Europe with the geometrical "solution" to the secret structure of the universe revealed in his *Mysterium Cosmographicum.* By 1704 Isaac Newton had published his *Opticks* with its magnificent insights on the nature of light and color. In the intervening century, heliocentrism had been mathematically and observationally confirmed, the circulation of the blood (and true motion and function of the heart) had been established, the microscope and telescope had each been invented (revealing stunning new worlds minuscule and vast), the possibility of vacuum had been demonstrated (and the vacuum pump invented), fossils were confirmed as relics of real formerly living organic beings, extinction was acknowledged as factual, hundreds of new life forms from the western hemisphere were discovered and studied, calculus was invented (twice), the geological principle of superposition was adopted, the laws of motion and gravitation were developed, the relationships of pressure, volume, and temperature of gases became evident, and momentum and kinetic energy (then known as *vis viva*) were quantified, to enumerate but a few of the significant accomplishments wrought by natural philosophy in that century.

These scientific accomplishments grew in the productive intellectual soil of a Christian "Reformation" that was entering its second century with no apparent end of the attendant theological changes and political turmoil in sight. Religion was inescapably woven into every aspect of cultural life, and most Europeans of the era (and with certainty every character in this study) would have professed some version of Christian faith, including an affirmation of the divine character and authority of the Bible. In this environment, it became quite normal and common that the various disciplines and branches of both theology and natural philosophy would interact in meaningful ways. Among the patterns, trends, and claims that emerged in the seventeenth century as a direct result of the encounters of Christian faith and natural philosophy, three stand out as particularly significant. First, some natural philosophers and theologians increasingly believed that the study of natural philosophy (especially those investigations that lent themselves to mathematical analysis) could mitigate the noetic effect of Adam's Fall both for the individual person and for humanity collectively. This developing view represented a major factor in the unfolding of "modern" science and constitutes the subject of a major new appraisal by historian of science Peter Harrison. Protestants, beginning with Luther, Harrison suggests, believed that individuals could reduce the intellectually damaging results of the Fall by focusing on mathematical approaches to study since these rest on "self-evident axioms" and may have been "uniquely insulated from the corrupting effects of the Fall."[1] In the latter case, the collective study of nature could help humanity recover that vast and superior body of knowledge that Adam had by tradition commanded and enjoyed in prelapsarian Eden. The prospect of such a "grand restoration" greatly motivated Francis Bacon and also seemed to constitute a large part of the rationale for the establishment of the Royal Society in 1662.[2]

A second major theme that developed over the course of the seventeenth century was that the study of nature steadily shifted toward the investigation of "natural" or "secondary" causes, with an increased emphasis on the concept of natural law. This trend was evident among natural philosophers throughout the century, from Bacon to Newton, and became evident in theological circles, as well. For example, in chapter 5 ("Of Providence") of the *Confession of Faith* (1646), the Westminster Assembly specifically identified God as "the first Cause," and affirmed that while "God the great Creator of all things does uphold, direct,

1. Peter Harrison, *The Fall of Man and the Foundations of Science* (Cambridge: Cambridge University Press, 2007), 97.

2. Harrison, *The Fall of Man*, 4.

dispose, and govern all creatures, actions, and things, from the greatest even to the least, by His most wise and holy providence, . . . yet, by the same providence, He orders them to fall out, according to the nature of second causes, either necessarily, freely, or contingently." The footnote leads the reader through a half-dozen supporting texts, all of which constitute clear biblical descriptions of ordinary cause-and-effect relations in the natural world. That the Westminster divines would employ Scripture to emphasize that the creation runs according to "second causes" seemed to represent a kind of invitation to "look to nature to understand nature."[3]

The use of Scripture to characterize the actions and conduct of the natural world constitutes the third major development and the subject of this essay. Among seventeenth-century natural philosophers, the conviction grew that when the Holy Scriptures speak of nature, the words speak descriptively, theologically, poetically, artistically, visually, metaphorically, and the like, but not scientifically or philosophically. Since the primary purposes of Scripture are theological, natural philosophers argued, biblical descriptions of nature also reflect that essential purpose. I contend in these pages that throughout the seventeenth century natural philosophers increasingly believed (i.e., actually operated on the belief) that when the Scriptures refer to natural phenomena or realities, they express descriptive, aesthetic, and/or doxological declarations (and often in "accommodated" terms) — but not technical or scientific ones. That is, on the one hand, the biblical authors, in the view of numerous seventeenth-century natural philosophers, did not intend what was written about nature to be taken as philosophical or scientific instruction about how nature is actually constituted or how it actually functions. On the other hand, however, natural philosophers also believed that the philosophical or systematic study of nature as nature, as creature or creation, could and would draw attention to the Creator, would glorify and honor the Creator, and would invite the observer of nature to consider the attributes and power of God. Indeed the study of nature constituted one of the highest privileges and duties of humankind.

* * *

The German mathematician Johannes Kepler (1571-1630) appeared on the European astronomical stage with the publication of his strange but beautiful *Mysterium Cosmographicum* (1596) in which he confidently revealed the most significant cosmological secret of all time. "Nothing is more precious," he wrote in the dedicatory letter to the volume, "nothing is more splendid than this in the brilliant temple of God." And, he added, nothing "has been more closely con-

3. Robert Shaw, *The Reformed Faith: An Exposition of the Westminster Confession of Faith* (Inverness, Scotland: Christian Focus Publications, 1974 [1845]), 65 and 68.

cealed." As a private Copernican in the process of becoming a very public one, the young Kepler knew that in addition to the obvious philosophical objections to a shift from an earth-centered cosmology to a sun-centered one, the Copernican model held only six planets (of which the earth was now one) instead of the usual (and richly symbolic) seven. The mystery that Kepler unveiled proved to be a remarkable and creative geometric rationale (interleaved orbital spheres and regular polyhedra) for the number, the spacing, and the sizes of orbits of the six circumsolar planets. Kepler could scarcely contain his delight in having discovered such beauty and wonder in "the book of Nature, so greatly celebrated in the sacred writings." After a discourse on the apostle Paul and the first chapter of Romans, furthered by a development of Psalm 19 and other Davidic psalms, Kepler drew two remarkable conclusions in this introductory letter. First, he asked, what else can it mean for the inaudible voice of the heavens to praise God, "unless, when they supply men with cause to praise God, they themselves are said to praise God." Second, Kepler observed, "just as other animals, and the human body, are sustained by food and drink, so the very spirit of Man, which is something distinct from Man, is nourished, is increased, and in a sense grows up on this diet of knowledge," and that "fresh nourishment should never be lacking for the human mind" since it has "in this universe an inexhaustible workshop in which to busy itself."[4] Separately, Kepler had written to an esteemed teacher that God "wishes to be recognized from the Book of Nature";[5] to another friend he wrote concerning the operations of the material world that "those laws are within the grasp of the human mind; God wanted us to recognize them by creating us in his own image so that we could share in his own thoughts."[6]

Present in these musings of the early Kepler are hints about a growing conviction that the human intellect possessed the capacity for discovering physical truth in nature and that this quest for natural truth would prove spiritually nourishing and that God intended it to be thus. Scripture even testifies to this. Kepler's quiet suggestion here is that Holy Scripture says that it is spiritually and theologically essential for humankind to study nature — doing so constitutes a worshipful acknowledgment of nature's Creator and provides a kind of spiritual nourishment. Scripture's messages about nature, therefore, do not primarily instruct humanity in the physical workings or mathematical principles of nature, but rather remind us that the creation speaks of the Creator. For these reasons, Kepler saw astronomy as the highest, most noble, and most divine of the disciplines of natural philosophy. He believed the heavens themselves to be the most

4. Johannes Kepler, *Mysterium Cosmographicum: The Secret of the Universe* (Tübingen, 1596; New York: Abaris Books, 1981), 53, 55.

5. Kepler to Michael Maestlin, 3 October 1595. Carola Baumgardt, *Johannes Kepler: Life and Letters* (New York: Philosophical Library, 1951), 31.

6. Kepler to Herwart von Hohenburg, 9/10 April 1599. Baumgardt, *Johannes Kepler,* 50.

noble and most divinely evocative aspect of the creation, and could not help but notice "the splendid harmony of those things that are at rest, the Sun, the fixed stars, and the intermediate space, with God the Father, and the Son, and the Holy Spirit," the Holy Trinity, revealed in the heavens.[7]

If his *Mysterium Cosmographicum* brought Kepler to the attention of other interested (and bemused) professional astronomers and mathematicians, his 1609 *Astronomia Nova* brought him wider fame and deeper personal satisfaction. The *Mysterium Cosmographicum* attracted the attention of the famed Danish astronomer Tycho Brahe (1546-1601), who at the time was about to assume the post of Imperial Mathematician for the Holy Roman Emperor Rudolph II in Prague. Kepler joined Tycho in Prague at the latter's invitation, but Tycho unexpectedly died very soon thereafter, leaving Kepler with a vast store of highly accurate astronomical data, plus a large number of latest-state-of-the-art astronomical instruments (excluding telescopes, which had not yet been devised). With these ample resources, Kepler made some startling discoveries as he studied the orbit of Mars. The "new" in the *New Astronomy* proved not to be yet another promotional advertisement for the "new" Copernican cosmology — by now Kepler took this as a given. The "new" lay rather in Kepler's abandonment of the two-thousand-year-old, deeply held, and philosophically rational commitment to the idea that every moving object in the celestial region moved at a uniform speed in a perfect circle, or in some combination of perfectly uniform circular motions. Kepler calculated that Mars, and then the other planets, move in very slight, yet undeniably very real, ellipses instead of circles. This critical discovery and the accompanying so-called "Area Law" were later dubbed by Isaac Newton as "Kepler's First and Second Laws of Planetary Motion." The *New Astronomy* included an extended passage outlining Kepler's views on the relation of scriptural narrative to the study of astronomy. Kepler had not drawn upon biblical resources to discern and calculate that the planetary paths traced out ellipses. That the Bible did not speak of ellipses, planetary distances, orbital periods, or other mathematical or physical specifications did not in the least diminish Kepler's regard for the holy inspired text. He simply did not consider the teaching of mathematical or physical principles to be the province or the purpose of Scripture; its purposes were theological and ethical.

There is little doubt, however, that Kepler, a very serious and devout Lutheran who had once even harbored hopes for a career as a theologian, worried about how sincere but less-informed readers might respond to his ideas and to Copernicanism in general. "There are," he noted in the Introduction to *New Astronomy,* "many more people who are moved by piety to withhold assent from Copernicus, fearing that falsehood might be charged against the Holy Spirit speaking in scriptures if we say that the earth is moved and the sun stands still."

7. Kepler, *Mysterium Cosmographicum,* 63.

Did affirming Copernicanism amount to denying the truth of Scripture? It was precisely this worry that Kepler sought to allay in his Introduction.[8]

* * *

The worry was registered as early as 1543. In that year, the Polish astronomer Nicolaus Copernicus (1473-1543) unveiled his mathematical defense of the heliocentric cosmology with his *De Revolutionibus Orbium Coelestium.* Copernicus made every effort to convince his readers with the overwhelming power of exhaustive mathematical and geometrical calculations that understanding the universe as sun-centered made sense philosophically. In addition, the heliocentric system made sense aesthetically, he argued, suggesting that the universe constituted "this most beautiful of temples" in which the sun served as the central "lamp" or "lantern" or, by an alternative metaphor, the reigning sun "seated on a royal throne governs his household of Stars as they circle around him."[9] The manifest "marvelous symmetry" and "sure linking together in harmony" of the heavens reveal the divine handiwork of "this structure of the Almighty's."[10] This "best possible arrangement" is "directed by divine ordinance" and elevates the observer to "feel wonder for the Maker of all." No surprise, Copernicus reflected, that when the psalmist "delighted in the creations of God and in the work of His hands," he was drawn to the "contemplation of the highest Good."[11]

Though the currents of Protestant Reformation and religious turmoil were running rapidly and dangerously at the time, Copernicus's quiet loyalty to the Roman Church and Christian teaching remained unshaken. Far from the theological front lines, Copernicus had no problem dedicating his treatise to the sitting Roman Catholic Pope (Paul III; pontiff 1534-1549), and then handing the manuscript over to a young Protestant scholar (Georg Joachim Rheticus, 1514-1574) from the University of Wittenberg (of all places!) to be hand-carried from Poland to Nuremberg to be printed on a Protestant press. His proposal was not intended to stir the theological pot. And yet, he seemed to fear that it could. Missing from all the soaring references to divinity, order, beauty, God's work, and so on, was any specific reference to biblical material, especially biblical passages that could prove problematic for his proposal. Copernicus claimed not to be worried. While it is possible, he conceded, that there might be "triflers" who could possibly deploy "some passage of Scripture wrongly twisted . . . to criticize and censure this

8. Johannes Kepler, *New Astronomy* (1609), trans. William H. Donahue (Cambridge: Cambridge University Press, 1992), 59.

9. Nicolaus Copernicus, *On the Revolutions of the Heavenly Spheres,* translated from the Latin *De Revolutionibus Orbium Coelestium* (1543) by A. M. Duncan (London: David & Charles, 1976), 50.

10. Copernicus, *On the Revolutions of the Heavenly Spheres,* 51.

11. Copernicus, *On the Revolutions of the Heavenly Spheres,* 35.

undertaking of mine," he would "waste no time on them" and would "despise their judgement as thoughtless."[12]

Copernicus himself feared no conflict between the facts about the natural world discovered by natural philosophy and the theological intent of the Bible. But the telling "triflers" taunt in his dedicatory letter suggested a more sober assessment that Scripture could indeed be interpreted in "wrongly twisted" ways that could inhibit the actual discovery of real truth about nature or could in fact lead people into error. To add visual emphasis to verbal, Copernicus intentionally employed the Greek word *mataiologoi* ("triflers"; "empty talkers"), a rather direct allusion, it strongly appears, to Titus 1:10 where Paul warns that such people are deceivers who must be silenced.[13]

De Revolutionibus appeared in limited numbers (approximately 500 copies)[14] and before the Council of Trent convened (thus the renewed emphasis on literal biblical interpretation in the Catholic Church was not yet formalized). There was virtually no formal opposition to the Copernican proposal in the remaining decades of the sixteenth century, and Copernican principles were even adopted for the 1582 calendar reforms.[15] And since he passed away in the very year his volume appeared, Copernicus himself never faced a test from anyone who opposed his idea on biblical grounds. The few clues available, however, clearly and strongly indicate that Copernicus would have considered such opposition to be in the wrong: the teaching of Natural Philosophy *per se* he would not have regarded as the intent or province of the Scriptures.

If Copernicus's "triflers" constituted a potentially deliberate threat worth mentioning but not answering, Kepler saw a much greater danger in "thoughtless persons" (*incogitantes;* unthinking)[16] whose lack of knowledge and understanding

12. Copernicus, *On the Revolutions of the Heavenly Spheres,* 26. The English expression "idle babblers" appears at this point in other English translations. See Nicolaus Copernicus, *De Revolutionibus: Preface and Book I,* trans. John F. Dobson (London: Royal Astronomical Society, 1947), 6.

13. Nicolaus Copernicus, *De Revolutionibus Orbium Coelestium* (Norimbergae: Joh. Petrieum, Anno MDXLIII; facsimile reprint of the first edition 1543 with an introduction by Professor Johannes Müller; Leipzig. New York: Johnson Reprint Corporation, 1965), Praefatio, p. [8]. In 1 Timothy 1:6 the same expression is used in a slightly different form (to refer to "fruitless discussion"). Admittedly, Copernicus may be alluding to a classical Greek expression, but his use of the rather specialized expression *scripturae* in this sentence strongly signals an intentional biblical reference. See also R. Hooykaas, *G. J. Rheticus' Treatise on Holy Scripture and the Motion of the Earth* (Amsterdam: North Holland Publishing Company, 1984), 17.

14. See Owen Gingerich, *The Book Nobody Read: Chasing the Revolutions of Nicolaus Copernicus* (New York: Walker & Company, 2004), 121-29.

15. Thomas S. Kuhn, *The Copernican Revolution: Planetary Astronomy in Western Thought* (Cambridge, MA: Harvard University Press, 1957), 125-26.

16. Kepler, *New Astronomy,* 61. Johannes Kepler, "Introductio in hoc opus," in *Astronomia Nova* (Prague, 1609), facsimile edition (Brussels: Impression Anastaltique, 1968), 7.

of the interpretation of Scripture presented a very real threat that most certainly did merit an intentional and systematic response. In the carefully argued passage in the Introduction of *Astronomia Nova,* Kepler presented what would become a very influential framework for understanding Holy Scripture when it speaks of "common things" whose purposes are not to "instruct humanity" in spiritual matters.[17]

First, Kepler argued, since human verbal and narrative descriptions of nature are drawn from human sensory observation, especially "through the sense of sight, it is impossible for us to abstract our speech from this ocular sense." It is quite natural and normal for us to write or speak this way, Kepler suggested, offering an example from Virgil's widely known *Aeneid:* "We are carried from the port, and the land and cities recede." Kepler was not arguing here specifically for the relativity of motion, but for the accepted and understood difference between physical appearances and physical realities. Of course, everyone understands that the cities and the land are not moving, but the motion of the actual mover (the ship) makes it *look as if* the land is moving away.[18] Likewise when one speaks of vistas opening up before one, when one speaks of the rising and setting of stars, when one refers to the "solstice" (literally, "sun standing"), one speaks according to the commonplace appearances of things, with no loss of meaning and no sense of compromise of truth. After all, a single movement of the sun constitutes one person's sun*set* and another person's sun*rise,* depending on where one is situated on the globe. It is a way of speaking.[19]

When it comes to descriptions of physical nature, Kepler contended, the Bible communicates in just this way: "Now the Holy Scriptures, too, when treating common things," Kepler writes, "speak with humans in the human manner, in order to be understood by them. They make use of what is generally acknowledged, in order to weave in other things more lofty and divine." It should not be surprising, then, when sometimes "scripture also speaks in accordance with human perception when the truth of things is at odds with the senses." Thus Psalm 19 speaks figuratively about the movement of the sun to describe "the spreading of the Gospel and even the sojourn of Christ the Lord in this world on our behalf." Further, Kepler suggested, the point of Joshua's request that the daytime be lengthened was not to initiate a discussion over "the verbal contradiction, 'the sun stood still' versus 'the earth stood still'" (only the aforementioned "thoughtless ones" maintain an interest in that discussion), but simply "that the mountains

17. Kepler, *New Astronomy,* 60.

18. Kepler, *New Astronomy,* 59. The reference to Virgil's *Aeneid* may be "loaded" in the sense that Copernicus cites precisely the same passage in Book I, Section 8 of *De Revolutionibus,* when arguing that mere appearances cannot disprove his proposed motions of the earth. Kepler likely means to signal this connection to knowing readers.

19. Kepler, *New Astronomy,* 60.

not remove the sunlight from him." Humorously (to our ears; mine anyway!), Kepler assured readers that "God easily understood from Joshua's words what he meant and responded by stopping the motion of the earth, so that the sun might appear to him to stop."[20]

Genesis chapter 1, Jeremiah chapter 31, Job chapter 38, and like passages extol the grandeur and glory of the creation by means of beautiful descriptions and suggestive figures of speech. No one, Kepler observed, would argue from Psalm 24 "the absurd philosophical conclusion that earth floats upon rivers." Here Kepler moved to the third step in his argument. Not only do humans naturally speak of the appearances of nature according to human sensory experience, and not only do biblical descriptions of nature share in that human reality, but it is not, he insisted, the purpose of the Bible to teach natural philosophy. Should we not, Kepler asked, "regard the Holy Spirit as a divine messenger, and refrain from wantonly dragging Him into physics class?" Again, when considering "other passages usually cited in opposition to the earth's motion," should we not "likewise turn our eyes from physics to the aims of scripture?" Perhaps it was bold for an astronomer to be expostulating on the "aims of scripture," but in this case, our astronomer also had theological training. He argued that the physical descriptions of earth, sun, sea, wind, and rivers in Ecclesiastes chapter one do not constitute "physical dogma," but rather that "the message is a moral one."[21] That beautiful celebration of nature, Psalm 104, receives an elegant and extended Keplerian analysis, the upshot of which is Kepler's claim that "nothing could be farther from the psalmodist's intention than speculation about physical causes" and that "the whole thing is an exultation upon the greatness of God, who made all these things." Noting the structural parallels between this Psalm and the creation account in Genesis 1, Kepler wrote that as the psalmist considers the work of the fourth creation day (sun and moon), "it is clear that he is not writing as an astronomer here."[22]

Kepler's conclusions about the purpose and use of Scripture more or less parallel his conclusion about the overall purpose of Psalm 104: "At the end, in conclusion, he declares the general goodness of God in sustaining all things and creating new things." The purpose of the Bible is to teach moral lessons, guide spiritual growth, and, like nature itself, declare the glory of God. This last purpose rests very near to Kepler's heart. "I, too, implore my reader, when he departs from the temple and enters astronomical studies, not to forget the divine goodness conferred upon men. . . . I hope that, with me, he will praise and celebrate the Creator's wisdom and greatness."

20. Kepler, *New Astronomy,* 61. Keep in mind that in 1609 a robust understanding of inertia was decades away. Newton's "First Law," under which Kepler's explanation here would have indicated an unspeakable devastation upon the earth, first appeared in print in 1687.

21. Kepler, *New Astronomy,* 63.

22. Kepler, *New Astronomy,* 63-65.

Unable, however, to resist a couple of parting shots, in a section harshly labeled "Advice for idiots" Kepler somewhat dampens the doxological mood by suggesting that anyone who might be "too stupid to understand astronomical science or too weak to believe Copernicus without affecting his faith" should just "mind his own business and betake himself home to scratch in his own dirt patch."[23]

Finally, after writing off "the mob of literalists," Kepler concluded: "so much for the authority of holy scripture . . . in theology, it is authority that carries the most weight, in philosophy it is reason." Even the most respected theological authorities, such as Lactantius, Augustine, the Inquisition, and many Doctors of the Church generally, have perpetuated serious errors in their understanding of physical nature, but "the truth is more pious still," and Johannes Kepler promises to guide his readers into a new understanding of physical truth.[24]

* * *

While Johannes Kepler continued to grow as an imaginative and technically brilliant astronomer, the technical nature of his work may have limited his audience somewhat. The *Astronomia Nova* proved to be daunting, even for experts, and the news of its genius spread steadily, but slowly. Meanwhile, at the University of Padua in the Venetian Republic, at the very time Kepler sat at his writing desk in Prague, Galileo Galilei (1564-1642) learned of an interesting novelty known as the "Dutch perspective glass," procured one for himself, and with his own significant understanding of optics, built his own modified version of the "eyeglass" or "spyglass" and began observing the heavens in a systematic way. The development of what would become known as the "telescope" and the publication of Galileo's astonishing findings (craters and other surface textured landforms on the moon, individual stars in the Milky Way, and the four famous moons of Jupiter, for starters) in his *Sidereal Messenger* (1610), introduced a permanent change into astronomy. Suddenly, cosmology became a much more widely discussed topic in Europe and Galileo himself was propelled to "all-star" status as a philosopher and man of letters.

Galileo's Copernican convictions remained rather quietly rooted in his personal reading and his studies at the University of Pisa long before the telescope disrupted his life (and that of all astronomy), but the amazing telescope emboldened Galileo's public Copernicanism at least as much as Kepler's discoveries had emboldened his. The sad tale of Galileo's confrontation with the philosophical and theological authorities of the Roman Church is well and often told, but the gist of the narrative is that Galileo believed that his findings convincingly proved the Copernican cosmology, and his detractors did not. Moreover, his detractors charged that Galileo's claims fell afoul of theological orthodoxy and sound bibli-

23. Kepler, *New Astronomy,* 65.
24. Kepler, *New Astronomy,* 66.

cal interpretation. Finally, since said detractors constituted ultimate authority in those parts at that time, Galileo was required to recant his Copernican views in 1633 and endure confinement at his own villa in Florence until his death in 1642.

Galileo's troubles were many, but fell largely into two major divisions: philosophical and theological. On the philosophical or scientific side, Galileo was beset by criticism about the accuracy and significance of his claims and findings. In addition, there were questions as to whether he had marshaled sufficient evidence to demonstrate the motion of the earth to the satisfaction of his patrons and scientific peers, especially the astronomers at the Jesuit Collegio Romano. He confidently addressed this challenge with bold claims, improved instruments, more observations, additional publications, enhanced arguments, and more frequent public appearances. His promise in *Sidereal Messenger* to "prove the earth has motion" and to do so with "countless arguments taken from natural phenomena" fairly represents his attitude throughout.[25]

On the theological side, Galileo began to understand that opposition was growing among theologians and officials in the church on the grounds that Copernicanism violated biblical teaching. Here he just as confidently waded into the engagement with a full-orbed exposition on what he deemed the appropriate use and role of the Holy Scriptures in matters of natural philosophy. It is this particular engagement that concerns us here.

Shortly after the publication of *The Sidereal Messenger* in 1610, Galileo secured his "dream job" — that of "Philosopher and Chief Mathematician" in the court of the young Grand Duke of Tuscany, Cosimo II de'Medici. The Grand Duke's mother (and widow of the late previous Grand Duke Ferdinando), Grand Duchess Christina of Lorraine, as the senior member of the court, would from time to time host social functions. In 1613, during a court luncheon at which Galileo's associate Benedetto Castelli was present, a concerned Grand Duchess enquired about the relationship between Copernicanism and accepted biblical interpretation. Upon hearing this, Galileo sketched a brief "Letter to Castelli" to equip his friend with arguments and material on this delicate subject. The 1613 "Letter to Castelli" was expanded into a fully developed treatise that became known as the "Letter to the Madame Christina of Lorraine, Grand Duchess of Tuscany, Concerning the Use of Biblical Quotation in Matters of Science," or simply "Letter to the Grand Duchess Christina." This manifesto appeared in 1615 as a hand-copied open letter both in Tuscany and in Rome, and besides presenting Galileo's most sophisticated expression of his understanding of the relations of Scripture with natural philosophy, its frank boldness certainly helped land Galileo in the chambers of the Inquisition. This open letter certainly stands as one of the very most important documents ever written on the topic, although

25. Galileo Galilei, "The Sidereal Messenger," ed. and trans. Maurice Finocchiaro, in *The Essential Galileo* (Indianapolis: Hackett, 2008), 63.

its wider influence experienced a delay, since it was not published until 1636, in far-off Strasbourg and under curious circumstances.[26]

After a detailed defense of the honor of Copernicus (including a reprise of Copernicus's own "triflers" passage, above), Galileo first affirmed in the "Letter" that "the Holy Scripture can never lie, as long as its true meaning has been grasped." That meaning, Galileo suggested, may frequently prove to be "very different from what appears to be the literal meaning of the words"; indeed, were someone "to limit himself always to the pure literal meaning . . . he could make Scripture appear to be full not only of contradictions and false propositions, but also of serious heresies and blasphemies," such as assigning to God actual human hands, feet, eyes, feelings, and frailties. But Scripture need not be understood so literally, Galileo argued: "[T]hese propositions dictated by the Holy Spirit were expressed by the sacred writers in such a way as to accommodate the capacities of the very unrefined and undisciplined masses." In addition to his claims that Scripture always speaks truth, should not always be interpreted literally, and is accommodated to common usage, Galileo also deeply believed in "the primary purpose of the Holy Writ, that is, to the worship of God and the salvation of souls."[27]

Having established these initial principles, Galileo then turned to a discussion of nature, Scripture, and human capacities. "The Holy Scripture and nature derive equally from the Godhead," Galileo wrote, "the former as the dictation of the Holy Spirit and the latter as the most obedient executrix of God's orders"; and further, "God reveals himself to us no less excellently in the effects of nature than in the sacred words of Scripture." Therefore, Galileo urged, "it seems that a natural phenomenon which is placed before our eyes by sense experience or proved by necessary demonstration should not be called into question, let alone condemned, on account of scriptural passages whose words appear to have a different meaning."[28] He concludes,

> I do not think that one has to believe that the same God who has given us senses, language, and intellect would want to set aside the use of these and give us by some other means the information we can acquire by them, so that we would deny our senses and reason even in the case of those physical conclusions which are placed before our eyes and intellect by sense experience or necessary demonstrations.[29]

26. In violation of the terms of his house arrest, Galileo likely improperly provided a copy of the "Letter" by courier to a Parisian contact, Elie Diodati (1576-1661), who arranged a diglot Latin-Italian edition. See Stephane Garcia, "Galileo's Relapse: On the Publication of the Letter to the Grand Duchess Christina (1636)," in *The Church and Galileo,* ed. Ernan McMullin (Notre Dame: University of Notre Dame Press, 2005), 265-78.

27. Galileo, "Letter to the Grand Duchess Christina," 114-15.

28. Galileo, "Letter to Grand Duchess Christina," 116-17.

29. Galileo, "Letter to Grand Duchess Christina," 117.

This strong endorsement of the human capacity to apprehend physical truth through human senses and intellect is buttressed with a lengthy quotation from Augustine's *De Genesi ad litteram,* after which Galileo concludes that "the Holy Spirit [i.e., through the inspired text] did not want to teach us whether heaven moves or stands still" or "other questions of the same kind," but is rather concerned with the theological issue of human salvation. In a very famous summation, Galileo quoted the Italian Cardinal Cesare Baronio (1569-1607) on this point: "[T]he intention of the Holy Spirit is to teach us how one goes to heaven and not how heaven goes."[30]

It may seem odd to think of the Roman Catholic Church as a bastion of biblical literalism, but here, one hundred painful years downstream from the posting of the Ninety-Five Theses, and in the wake of the provisions of the Council of Trent, the Church affirmed a new emphasis on the *sensus literalis,* the unanimous conclusions of the church fathers, and the authority of bishops and church councils in matters of biblical interpretation.[31] Unfazed, Galileo offered his prescription for those apparent contradictions between the findings of natural philosophy and theology: "because (as we said above) two truths cannot contradict one another, the task of a wise interpreter is to strive to fathom the true meaning of the sacred texts; this will undoubtedly agree with those physical conclusions of which we are already certain and sure through clear observations or necessary demonstrations."[32] Once the philosophers have established a particular physical phenomenon or proposition as actual truth, Galileo asserted, it becomes the duty of the theologians to interpret the Scripture in ways that do not contradict the previously established physical conclusion. Fortunately such occasions are very rare — the Bible speaks sparingly of natural phenomena, and usually in clear, non-controversial contexts. Unfortunately for Galileo, his status as a layman, his hubris as a would-be mentor to trained theologians, and in the end, ironically, his inability to provide the kind of proof or "necessary demonstration" of the motion of the earth that he himself would have demanded (accompanied by a healthy dose of his own undiplomatic behavior), conspired to bring all the good words and intentions of the "Letter to the Grand Duchess Christina" to naught. Galileo was muzzled in 1616 and muted in 1633 in two separate legal proceedings. Though this important document did not help its author in his hour of need, it did resonate elsewhere in Europe in the decades that followed, and it may offer us twenty-first-century

30. Galileo, "Letter to Grand Duchess Christina," 119.

31. Fourth Session, 8 April 1546, "Decree Concerning the Edition, and the Use, of the Sacred Books," in *The Canons and Decrees of the Sacred and Oecumenical Council of Trent, Celebrated under the Sovereign Pontiffs Paul III, Julius III, and Pius IV,* trans. J. Waterworth (London: C. Dolman, 1848), 19-21.

32. Galileo, "Letter to Grand Duchess Christina," 120.

sojourners just the kind of insights we need to navigate some of the ongoing "Bible-and-science" turbulence.[33]

* * *

An early defender of Galileo and the Copernican view in England was clergyman-philosopher John Wilkins (1614-1672). Wilkins became widely influential in academic, clerical, and political affairs during the socially turbulent decades of the Civil War and the Restoration. As a leader among the "Christian Virtuosi," he eventually led the effort to formalize the Royal Society of London in 1660. Having set the tone among the Fellows of the Royal Society that Christian religion and natural philosophy ought to be regarded as completely compatible (even if largely separate) pursuits, Wilkins repeatedly invoked biblical "accommodation" as a hermeneutical principle in his defense of Copernicanism.[34]

When the young Wilkins ventured in his anonymous 1638 *The Discovery of a World in the Moone* that the earth's moon bore so many similarities to the earth itself that it may be inhabited, he revealed a very heavy debt to Galileo's *Siderius Nuncius* (1610), and a working knowledge of Galileo's several telescopic discoveries about the heavens.[35] If his *Discovery of a New World* showed him acquainted with Galileo's telescopic discoveries, Wilkins's next volume, A *Discourse Concerning a New Planet* (1640), showed him thoroughly familiar with Galileo's *Dialogue on the Two Chief Systems of the World* and Galileo's *Letter to the Grand Duchess Christina.* (These treatises had been published for the first time in Latin — in 1635 and 1636 respectively — by a printer in Strasbourg, beyond the reach of the Congregation of the Index.[36]) With the images of Copernicus, Kepler, and Galileo adorning the frontispiece, Wilkins's *Discourse Concerning a New Planet* addressed the question of the interpretation of Scripture directly and early in this full-scale defense of Copernicanism (the earth itself being the "new planet"). "There is not," he argued in Proposition 2, "any place in Holy Scripture, from which (being rightly understood) we may infer the diurnal Motion of the Sun or Heavens." That is, if Scripture is understood correctly, even the historically longstanding geocentric model cannot be maintained from Scripture. And

33. Richard J. Blackwell, "Galileo Galilei," in *Science and Religion,* ed. Gary B. Ferngren (Baltimore: Johns Hopkins University Press, 2002), 110. Galileo, "Letter to Grand Duchess Christina," 126.

34. Barbara J. Shapiro, *Probability and Certainty in Seventeenth-Century England* (Princeton: Princeton University Press, 1983), 111-18.

35. John Wilkins, *The Discovery of a World in the Moone or, A Discourse Tending to Prove that 'tis probable there may be another habitable World in that Planet* (London: Michael Sparke & Edward Forrest, 1638), *passim,* esp. 85-94.

36. Garcia, "Galileo's Relapse," 265-78; Stillman Drake, *Discoveries and Opinions of Galileo* (New York: Anchor Books, 1957), 171.

in a passage deeply reminiscent of a key section in Galileo's *Letter to the Grand Duchess,* Wilkins yearned:

> It were happy for us, if we could exempt Scripture from Philosophical Controversies; if we could be content to let it be perfect for that end unto which it was intended, for a Rule of our Faith and Obedience; and not stretch it also to be a Judg of such natural Truths, as are to be found out by our own industry and experience. Though the Holy Ghost would easily have given us a full resolution of all such particulars; *yet he hath left this travel to the Sons of Men to be exercised therewith.*

In a Calvinesque statement of divine revelation as accommodated to the everyday experience of ordinary people, Wilkins suggested even more plainly that "the Holy Ghost, in many places of Scripture, does plainly conform his Expressions, unto the Errors [i.e., shortcomings] of our Conceits; and does not speak of divers things as they are in themselves, but as they appear to us," and further, that "divers Men have fallen into great Absurdities, whilst they have looked for the Grounds of Philosophy, from the words of Scripture; and therefore it may be dangerous, in this Point also, to adhere so closely unto the Letter of the Text." Wilkins added a note from John Calvin himself (Calvin's commentary on Ps. 148:4) who warned that "Such Men too servilely tie themselves unto the Letter of the Text."[37]

* * *

Meanwhile at mid-century the pamphlet *Letter of a Certain Anonymous Author Concerning the Motion of the Earth*[38] (1651) appeared in the Netherlands, arguing

37. John Wilkins, *A Discourse Concerning a New Planet, Tending to prove That 'tis probable our Earth is one of the Planets,* 4th edition (London: John Gellibrand, 1684), 21, 34-35, 39, 56. Barbara J. Shapiro, *John Wilkins, 1614-1672: An Intellectual Biography* (Berkeley and Los Angeles: University of California Press, 1969), 30-60, 191-250. R. Hooykaas, *Religion and the Rise of Modern Science* (Grand Rapids: Eerdmans, 1972), 126-30. See also Jean Dietz Moss, *Novelties in the Heavens: Rhetoric and Science in the Copernican Controversy* (Chicago: University of Chicago Press, 1993), 301-29. For a full rhetorical analysis of Wilkins, see Marko Oja, "Contesting Authorities: John Wilkins' Use of and Attitude towards the Bible, the Classics and Contemporary Science in *The Discovery of a World in the Moone* (1638)," in *Opening Windows on Texts and Discourses of the Past,* ed. Janne Skaffari et al. (Philadelphia: John Benjamins, 2005), 109-22. Oja argues that "Wilkins refers to the Bible mainly when discussing the fact that it is not to be used as a source. Thus it is possible to say that the Bible was not a source for Wilkins with respect to his theory, but he cited it because others had done so, and he wished to show the error in doing that" (121).

38. *Cujusdam Anonymi, Epistola, De Terrae Motu* [*Letter of a Certain Anonymous Author Concerning the Motion of the Earth*] (Utrecht: Johannis à Waesberge, 1651).

plainly that "when there is mention in the sacred writings of the things of nature, it is clear that the Holy Spirit does not want to speak of them in the manner of Philosophers." Rather, the anonymous pamphleteer wrote, "He keeps in view the main purpose of the Scripture" that is, that followers of Christ "might have always before our eyes what He wishes us to do, and how through the promised Seed He was to put away His wrath against us and receive us into His grace. That is what the Holy Spirit desired to reveal through the Word, and this is the purpose of Holy Scripture." Drawing heavily from Augustine's *De Genesi ad litteram* (ca. 395 C.E.), the writer reminded readers that "Scripture has deliberately forgone an exact description of the nature of things" since "the Spirit of God did not wish to teach men things which would not be an aid to anybody's salvation." Indeed, he asked further, "who would maintain that knowledge of physics is necessary for salvation?" In addition to relieving Scripture of the duty of teaching natural philosophy with scientific exactness, the writer (again after Augustine) noted that often when it does speak of nature, "Scripture borrows a style of discourse, an idiom of speech or a method of teaching from popular usage, *so that it may also fully accommodate itself to the people's understanding, and not to the wisdom of this world.*" Thus, "texts of Scripture dealing with natural things receive different interpretations" from those "on which our salvation depends."[39]

Though the circulation and influence of this *"Epistola de Terrae Motu"* remained as limited as its modest length, its themes resonated with the writings of other concerned mid-seventeenth-century Christian natural philosophers eager to delimit the Bible's role in the interpretation of physical nature while preserving and extending its theological authority — contemporary, yet curiously reminiscent of the *sixteenth* century. In fact, the unnamed author turned out to be Georg Joachim Rheticus (1514-1574), the very person who arranged for the publication of Copernicus's *De Revolutionibus Orbium Coelestium* over one hundred years before, and author of the *Narratio Prima* (1540) that prepared readers for the coming of the Copernican treatise. The *Epistola* was written about the same time, likely intended to serve as a companion piece to the *Narratio Prima.* Like Copernicus, Rheticus anticipated that Scripture-related objections to heliocentrism might appear, and this treatise was to serve as a preemptive argument to answer them — but it did not appear in print.[40]

How *Epistola de Terrae Motu* was lost (or withdrawn?) before publication and how it was found in the next century remains to be discovered, as well as whether the publisher Johannes van Waesberge ever knew the identity of the

39. *Letter of a Certain Anonymous Author Concerning the Motion of the Earth,* in R. Hooykaas, *G. H. Rheticus' Treatise on Holy Scripture and the Motion of the Earth* (Amsterdam: North-Holland Publishing Co., 1984), 66-69. Emphasis by the original publisher.

40. Dennis Danielson, *The First Copernican: Georg Joachim Rheticus and the Rise of the Copernican Revolution* (New York: Walker & Co., 2006), 108.

original author, who could hardly have been the least bit controversial by then. The publication seemed to come too late to influence much more change in the university (the publisher's intent), because the hermeneutical views of Kepler in Germany, Galileo in Italy, and Wilkins in England were already known and increasingly adopted among natural philosophers. And this, ironically enough, seems to have been due to the century-plus-old influence of John Calvin's "accommodation" view with respect to scriptural passages that described natural phenomena. Calvin had characterized astronomy in particular as "pleasant," "very useful," and that it "unfolds the admirable wisdom of God." Further, he had famously argued regarding the creation of the celestial bodies that "Moses wrote in a popular style things which, without instruction, all ordinary persons, endued with common sense are able to understand," even if it required his "descending to this grosser method of instruction."[41] This Augustinian-Calvinistic interpretative tool of "accommodation" had certainly found a home in Reformed Holland.[42]

* * *

Meanwhile back in England, the earlier statements by Galileo and Johannes Kepler on the status and role of the Bible appeared in print in English for the first time in 1661, just after the Restoration of the monarchy. Little is known about the translator, Thomas Salusbury (1625?-1665), but his *Mathematical Collections and Translations* (1661) certainly reveal his great interest in promoting a view of Scripture that would allow both natural philosophy and Christian faith to flourish in one another's presence. Among others, Salusbury's selections included Kepler's introduction to his *New Astronomy* (1609), Galileo's *Dialogue on the Two Chief Systems of the World* (1632) and *Letter to the Grand Duchess Christina* (1615; published 1636), excerpts from the *Commentary on Job* (1591) by Spanish friar Diego de Zúñiga (1536-1598), and the *Letter on the Pythagorean and Copernican Opinion of the Earth's Motion and the Sun's Rest* (1615) by Italian Carmelite Paolo Antonio Foscarini (1580-1616). Salusbury's choices are telling: all of the selections share the theme and objective of reconciling Copernicanism with Scripture, and all but the Kepler piece were condemned or suppressed by the Roman Church earlier in the century. Salusbury's intent was to "attempt to reconcile such persons to this Hypothesis [Copernicanism] as devout esteem for Holy Scripture, and dutifull Respect to Canonical Injunctions hath made to stand off from this Opinion" by

41. John Calvin, *Commentaries on the First Book of Moses called Genesis* (1554), trans. John King (1847) (Grand Rapids: Eerdmans, 1948), 86-87. For a modern historical debate regarding "accommodation" as a seventeenth-century hermeneutical tool, see Jack B. Rogers and Donald K. McKim, *The Authority and Interpretation of the Bible: An Historical Approach* (San Francisco: Harper & Row, 1979), 165-71; and a lively response in John D. Woodbridge, *Biblical Authority: A Critique of the Rogers/McKim Proposal* (Grand Rapids: Zondervan, 1982), 90-115.

42. Hooykaas, *G. J. Rheticus' Treatise,* 167-84; and the subject of this volume.

including relevant authorities and thereby "hoping that the ingenious and impartial Reader will meet with full satisfaction" on these questions. To comfort skittish or Roman Catholic readers, Salusbury even included an official imprimatur for the printing of these previously banished books.[43]

Salusbury's purposes can also be clearly seen in the editorializing fashion in which he rendered the titles and subtitles as he brought these works into English. For example, Galileo's *Letter to the Grand Duchess Christina* became "The Ancient and Modern Doctrine of Holy Fathers and Judicious Divines, concerning the rash citation of the Testimony of Sacred Scripture, in conclusions meerly Natural, and that may be proved by Sensible Experiments, and Necessary Demonstrations." The Kepler abstract was labeled as "His Reconcilings of Texts of Sacred Scripture that seem to oppose the Doctrine of the Earth's Mobility." The excerpt from de Zúñiga's *Job* was called "His Reconcilings of the said Doctrine with the Texts of Sacred Scripture" and to the long title of Foscarini's *Letter Concerning the Copernican Opinion* Salusbury appended "in which he reconcileth the Texts of Sacred Scripture, and Assertions of Divines, commonly alledged against this Opinion." In addition, every opening in this eighty-page stretch of Salusbury's book bore the header "The Authority of Scripture [left side] . . . in philosophical Controversies [right side]." (By "philosophical" here, Salusbury clearly means to signify "pertaining to natural philosophy.") Salusbury desired his readers to have the primary source material they might need to embrace the Copernican cosmology and remain theologically confident in the Scriptures. To achieve this, he chose authors who, in his view, had convincingly established the plausibility of the Copernican system and at the same time successfully delineated the role of Scripture as more specifically theological — that Scripture's references to nature do not constitute natural philosophy in the technical sense. Thus the "ancient and modern doctrine" found in these translations proved to be none other than this notion of the principled distinguishing of natural philosophy from theology, and that the "authority of Scripture in philosophical controversies" should remain nearly nil.[44]

The extent of the influence of Salusbury's translations is difficult to measure, as most of the key thinkers of the age could have read all of these works in their respective original languages. On the other hand, the mere presence of more copies of the books enhanced availability of the ideas. Young Isaac Newton (1642-1727) definitely used a diagram from one of Salusbury's translations of Galileo's *Dialogue* in 1665, when it was still at least warm off the press. Newton, a famously ravenous student of the Bible (mostly for the purposes of working

43. Thomas Salusbury, trans., *Mathematical Collections and Translations, the First Tome in Two Parts* (London: William Leybourn, 1661), 9-10, 504.

44. Salusbury, *Mathematical Collections,* 13, 425; headers, 425-503. See also Moss, *Novelties in the Heavens,* 301-3.

out his prophetical-historical timelines, his Arian theology, and his interests in numerology and symbolism), was also aware of the hermeneutical notion of "accommodation." In a well-known letter to colleague Thomas Burnet (1635-1715), who was preparing his *Sacred Theory of the Earth* (1681), Newton spelled it out clearly: in the creation account in Genesis "Moses, accommodating his words to the gross conceptions of the vulgar, describes things much after the manner as one of the vulgar would have been inclined to do had he lived and seen the whole series of what Moses describes."[45] Nevertheless, Newton and Burnet both participated in a lively "scientific" discussion on how to interpret the various passages of Genesis concerning the Creation and the Flood. Burnet inaugurated here what would become a decades-long trend known as "theory of the earth" or "physico-theological" writing, in which the latest in natural philosophy was brought to bear in the interpretation of Scripture.[46]

The enormously influential English natural philosopher Robert Boyle (1627-1691), whose thoughtful theological reflections interested him as much as his enthusiastic experimental work (gas pressure law; vacuum pump), considered that for the "Christian Virtuoso" (natural philosopher) the scientific study of nature ("the book of the creatures") was conducive and essential for the study of theology and "the book of the scripture." Too much fussing over the relative ranking of these two profound divine revelations was to "split a hair between them." Regarding Genesis, Boyle wrote in 1674 that on the one hand, there was no warrant to "deduce particular theorems of natural philosophy from this or that expression in a book that seems rather designed to instruct us about spiritual than corporeal things"; on the other hand, there was no reason to "turn the first two chapters of Genesis into an allegory." Since the Bible is "mainly designed to teach us nobler and better truths than those of philosophy," its "very considerable hints" as to the origins of physical nature should be taken "not unwarily, or alone."[47]

John Ray (1627-1705), an older associate of Newton's and Fellow of Trinity College Cambridge and of the Royal Society, published his *The Wisdom of*

45. Newton to Burnet, January 1680/81. In H. W. Turnbull, ed., *Correspondence of Isaac Newton*, vol. 2 (Cambridge: Cambridge University Press, 1960). Online at: http://www.newtonproject.sussex.ac.uk/view/texts/normalized/THEM00014. Richard S. Westfall, *Never at Rest: A Biography of Isaac Newton* (Cambridge: Cambridge University Press, 1980), 390-91.

46. Early examples of this genre included: Thomas Burnet's *Sacred Theory of the Earth* (1681), John Woodward's *Essay toward a Natural History of the Earth* (1695), William Whiston's *A New Theory of the Earth* (1696), and John Ray's *Three Physico-Theological Discourses* (1713). The point was to use the latest natural philosophy to explain biblical narratives.

47. Robert Boyle, "The Excellency of Theology" (1674), in *The Excellencies of Robert Boyle*, ed. J. J. MacIntosh (Peterborough, ON: Broadview Press, 2008), 105-6, 120-22. Reijer Hooykaas, *Robert Boyle: A Study in Science and Christian Belief* (Lanham, MD: University Press of America, 1997), 112-13. On Wilkins and Boyle, see Richard S. Westfall, *Science and Religion in Seventeenth-Century England* (Ann Arbor: University of Michigan Press, 1973), 162-92.

God Manifested in the Works of the Creation in 1691. This little book consists of a number of arguments from virtually every department of the natural world identified at that time (in the style that would later be called "natural theology") to show that the order, beauty, artifice, wonder, complexity, and genius of the creation bespeak a wise Creator. The book makes numerous references to the classic scriptural exclamations about nature (Psalm 104 launches the narrative), but exclusively and uniformly in a doxological fashion, as nowhere is Scripture cited to make a point of physical science. Ray embraced the "new astronomy," acknowledged the contributions of the telescope, and ridiculed the complications of geocentrism. He even considered the possibility of life elsewhere in the universe, because even the telescope might not be able to comprehend the unspeakable vastness of the heavens. His volume concludes with an exposition of the anatomy of the human body and draws scriptural life lessons for the reader for each key part: the eye, the hand, the feet, and so on. So John Ray's very high regard for Scripture in the waning years of the seventeenth century did not include a role for Scripture for explicating the physical workings of created nature, but he did go to great lengths to illustrate how the natural philosophy of his day spoke clearly of the same Creator testified to in Scripture.[48]

Ray's next contribution, the detailed *Three Physico-Theological Discourses* (1692, 1713) maintained a similar very high regard for the Scriptures but upheld the general principle that Scripture does not teach natural philosophy how nature physically works. Ray addressed three major topics in this volume — "The Primitive Chaos, and Creation of the World," "The General Deluge, Its Causes and Effects," and "The Dissolution of the World and Future Conflagration" — with a slightly different twist. Taking these two past and one future events described in Scripture as unquestionably authentic, Ray brought the considerable and growing resources of seventeenth-century natural philosophy to bear (especially Newtonian physics) to explain in "scientific" terms how these mighty events could have occurred, or yet will. In other words, "science" here served to help interpret passages of the Bible that referred to nature, but Ray made no effort to apply Scripture to the interpretation of natural philosophy.[49]

By the end of the seventeenth century it seemed that, although the Bible was not regarded as an appropriate source of technical information for the philosophical interpretation of nature, natural philosophy — now burgeoning with the vast promise of Newtonian physics — offered abundant resources that could make the interpretation of the Scriptures more precise, accurate, and meaning-

48. John Ray, *The Wisdom of God Manifested in the Works of the Creation* (London: Samuel Smith, 1691) [facsimile; Hildesheim, Germany: Georg Olms Verlag, 1974], *passim.*

49. John Ray, *Three Physico-Theological Discourses,* 3rd edition (London: William Innys, 1713) [facsimile; New York: Arno Press, 1978], *passim.* First published as *Miscellaneous discourses concerning the dissolution and changes of the world* (London: Samuel Smith, 1692).

ful. Although it is clear that these sentiments have some roots reaching back to Augustine, the modern origins of this more or less one-way arrangement can be traced to the writings of Sir Francis Bacon (1561-1626), which exerted great influence over the shaping of scientific attitudes and the scientific enterprise in the seventeenth century, especially in Britain. Bacon's vision of a new, more rigorous, more objective empirical and experimental method, practiced in the context of an organized, dedicated, and generously supported community, helped furnish the inspiration for the founding of the Royal Society of London in 1662. Besides encouraging a vision of science that serves society with wise and practical benefits, Bacon promoted the traditional "two books" approach. In his *On the Advancement and Proficience of Learning* (Oxford, 1605), Bacon wrote that no one "can search too far or be too well studied in the book of God's word, or in the book of God's works; divinity or philosophy." Therefore, he urged, "let men endeavour an endless progress or proficience in both." However, to make progress and increase proficiency in each, Bacon added quickly, an important condition must always be remembered: philosophers must make sure "that they do not unwisely mingle or confound these learnings together."[50]

Unwisely mingle or confound, Bacon had said. By century's end, a chorus of philosophers urged that natural philosophy play a role in interpreting Scripture (wise), but not the reverse (unwise). Aptly named by historian James Moore the "Baconian compromise," this approach would continue to influence the respective cultures of science and Christian faith in Britain into the nineteenth century.[51] (Charles Darwin inscribed parts of this very passage from Bacon opposite the title page of his 1859 classic *On the Origin of Species.* By inference, Darwin was reminding readers that the *separation* of natural learning from biblical learning and the principle of non-interference dated back 250 years in Britain.)[52]

* * *

Though the scope of this study has been necessarily limited, it has proved broad enough to reflect the state of affairs within the wider community of natural philosophers of the seventeenth century. Their writings would bear this out. Whether anatomist, geologist, microscopist, astronomer, "chymist," botanist, physician, or zoologist, most in the great growing company of natural philosophers would not have looked to the Bible for philosophical ("scientific") information or expla-

50. Francis Bacon, *The Advancement of Learning* (Oxford: Clarendon, 1873), 10.

51. James R. Moore, "Geologists and Interpreters of Genesis in the Nineteenth Century," in *God and Nature: Historical Essays on the Encounter between Christianity and Science,* ed. David C. Lindberg and Ronald L. Numbers (Berkeley: University of California Press, 1986), 322-50, on 323-24.

52. Charles Darwin, *On the Origin of Species by Means of Natural Selection* (London: John Murray, 1859; London: Penguin, 2009), 2.

nations of their areas of study. All this, even though earth, sun, moon, stars, fire, water, mountains, rivers, oceans, plants, fish, birds, land animals, and numerous aspects of the human body are all mentioned in the Bible. However, these same philosophers would increasingly have urged natural philosophy as a valuable resource for Scripture interpretation.[53]

Three hundred and fifty years after Galileo sparked the discussions presented here, on another continent, and with a new topic (geology instead of astronomy), Baptist theologian Bernard Ramm (1916-1992) published his landmark *The Christian View of Science and Scripture* (1955). This volume raised even more the temperature of an already-heated discussion about science and Scripture but remarkably, after all this time, one thing had not changed — the grand question: How is one to interpret Scripture, when Scripture speaks of nature? It is significant that Ramm identified many of the same problems our seventeenth-century characters encountered, most especially (as summed up in a section heading), "The Language of the Bible with Reference to Natural Things." Ramm argued that biblical language is "popular, not scientific"; it is "phenomenal" (relating to appearances); it is "pre-scientific" and "not anti-scientific"; and it is "non-postulational," that is, "it does not theorize as to the actual nature of things." Ramm seemed unknowingly to be echoing, with great precision, the prescriptions of the seventeenth century, and yet he cited or mentioned not even one of the natural philosophers we have examined here.[54] If there are lessons here for twenty-first-century readers of Scripture, perhaps among them is how imperative it is to know the intellectual history of the faith and how easy it is not to.

53. The case of the Genesis Flood merits a study of its own for the simple fact that according to Scripture it constituted a historical event with human eyewitnesses. (No human eyewitnesses beheld the Creation.) And yet, although always regarded as a "historical" event, the Deluge was not really regarded as a "geological" event until geology as a branch of natural philosophy came into being during the seventeenth century. After all, geological expressions such as "fossil," "sediment," "stratum," "superposition," or "petrification" are not found in Genesis, yet in the seventeenth century all of these philosophical concepts were developed and then brought to bear on the question of the Flood. On seventeenth-century geology, see, for example, Alan Cutler, *The Seashell on the Mountaintop* (New York: Plume, 2003).

54. Bernard Ramm, *The Christian View of Science and Scripture* (Grand Rapids: Eerdmans, 1955), 65-102.

FIVE

German Pietism and Scriptural Authority: The Question of Biblical Inerrancy

John D. Woodbridge

Philipp Jakob Spener (1635-1705), a German Lutheran pastor, helped launch "Pietism" — initially a self-proclaimed spiritual reform movement within the German Lutheran churches.[1] The emphasis of Pietism that "born again" Christians should experience a heartfelt "living faith in Christ" evidenced in personal holiness, became a staple belief of the Pietist-Methodist-Holiness-Pentecostal tradition. Today, churches from this tradition constitute a large component of worldwide evangelical Christianity.

Spener believed he wrote as a faithful disciple of Martin Luther (a "blessed instrument of God," "our dear Luther"). As noted historian James Stein suggests, Spener not only grounded his movement in Luther but "continued Luther's Reformation."[2] Like Luther, Spener made it clear that any reform of contemporary Christianity should be based on a faithful appropriation and application of Holy Scripture, the Word of God. He observed:

> This much is certain: the diligent use of the Word of God, which consists not only of listening to sermons but also of reading, meditating, and discussing (Ps. 1:2) must be the chief means for reforming something. . . . The Word of God remains the seed from which all that is good in us must grow. If we suc-

1. For general background on Pietism, see Dale W. Brown, *Understanding Pietism* (Nappanee, IN: Evangelical Publishing House, 1966); Kurt Aland, ed., *Pietismus und Bibel* (Duisberg: Luther Verlag, 1970); Martin Greschet, ed., *Orthodoxie und Pietismus* (Stuttgart: Kohlhammer, 1982); Peter C. Erb, ed., *Pietists: Selected Writings* (New York City: Paulist Press, 1983); Frederick Herzog, *European Pietism Reviewed* (San Jose: Pickwick, 2003); Carter Lindberg, ed., *The Pietist Theologians* (Malden, MA: Blackwell, 2005); Ulrich Groetsch, "Pietism," in *New Dictionary of the History of Ideas,* ed. Maryanne Cline Horowitz (New York : Charles Scribner's Sons, 2005).

2. For Spener's biography, see K. James Stein, "Philipp Jakob Spener (1635-1705)," in Lindberg, ed., *The Pietist Theologians,* 84-99; Stein, *Philipp Jakob Spener* (Chicago: Covenant Press, 1986).

> ceed in getting the people to seek eagerly and diligently in the book of life for their joy, their spiritual life will be wonderfully strengthened and they become altogether a different people.[3]

Students of the history of Pietism concur that Spener placed a high premium upon the "diligent use" of the Bible, the Word of God, as the source for a "living faith." The advocacy of this "use" constituted an essential premise of his "reform program." They have not reached a consensus, however, regarding Spener's views of biblical authority nor for the views of churches belonging to the Pietist-Methodist-Holiness-Pentecostal tradition. Some scholars have argued Spener believed in biblical inerrancy. Others have categorically denied this. By biblical inerrancy disputants often mean that the Bible is infallible for faith and practice as well as history and science.

A similar debate has rippled through churches and organizations belonging to the Pietist-Methodist-Holiness-Pentecostal tradition. Until 1969, the Wesleyan Theological Society (U.S.A.), for example, upheld a commitment to biblical inerrancy: "We believe that both Old and New Testaments constituted the divinely inspired Word of God, inerrant in the originals, and the final authority for life and truth." But in that year, the *Wesleyan Theological Journal* published a revised statement about scriptural authority: "We believe in the plenary-dynamic and unique inspiration of the Bible as the divine Word of God, the only infallible (i.e.), sufficient and authoritative rule of faith and practice."[4] Some proponents of the change have claimed it reflects more accurately the beliefs of Jakob Spener and other early German Pietists.

The central purpose of the present chapter is to assess the historical validity

3. Spener, *Pia Desideria or Heartfelt Desire for a God-pleasing Reform of the True Evangelical Church . . . ,* trans. and ed. Theodore Tappert (Philadelphia: Fortress Press, 1964), 91.

4. For a discussion of the debate regarding inerrancy in Wesleyan/Holiness circles, see Gareth Lee Cockerill, "After Inerrancy, What? *The Wesleyan Theological Journal,* 1978-2005" (Evangelical Theological Society, November 19, 2008). In the Discipline (1955) of the Wesleyan Church biblical inerrancy was affirmed: "These Scriptures we do hold to be the inspired and infallibly written Word of God, fully inerrant in their original manuscripts and superior to all human authority" (Cockerill, 1). Grant Wacker notes the commitment of early Pentecostals in the United States to a doctrine of Scripture tantamount to biblical inerrancy: "This assumption . . . fostered an abiding conviction that the Bible had been preserved from errors of any sort — historical, scientific, or theological. Granted, the earliest statements of faith normally spoke of Scripture's reliability as the 'all sufficient rule for faith and practice,' not factual accuracy. The crucial question therefore is what the absence of explicit discussion about the Bible's perfection really meant. Did it mean that early Pentecostals harbored doubts about the Bible's plenary accuracy? Or did it mean that they presupposed it so completely it never occurred to them to raise the question? The evidence taken in context, strongly suggests the latter explanation" (Wacker, *Heaven Below: Early Pentecostals and American Culture* [Cambridge, MA: Harvard University Press, 2003], 73).

of the thesis that Spener and other self-identified early German Pietists rejected the doctrine of biblical inerrancy but instead affirmed a doctrine of biblical authority that limited Scripture's infallibility only to matters of faith and practice. In a first segment we will review the determinative role that Scripture, the Word of Life, played as an authoritative source for early German Pietists' programs for spiritual reform. In a second segment we will assess the historical accuracy of arguments Donald Dayton has proposed to support his claim that German Pietists (especially Spener) and Pietists in general limited the Bible's infallibility to matters of faith and practice. In a third segment, we will provide evidence that many early German Pietists did in fact affirm a belief in biblical inerrancy. The views of these early German "church" Pietists are especially significant. Scholars often assume they constitute the "standard" beliefs for the Pietist movement in general. The perspectives of separating "radical German Pietists" over biblical authority will not figure in our study — influential as some of these views were.

The Word of Life as the "Seed" of a Living Faith (with Special Reference to Jakob Spener)

Jakob Spener's own spiritual life was nourished by studying and meditating upon Holy Scripture. For him, Scripture, God's written revelation, possessed supreme authority. It was the Word of Life, the seed of a living faith. Spener's understanding of spirituality was also informed by his readings in the church fathers, the "Mystical" classics by Tauler, Kempis, Gerson, and the author of *The German Theology.* He especially appreciated Martin Luther's writings. Moreover, he reflected deeply on the works of the English Puritans Emanuel Sontham, Richard Baxter, and Lewis Bayly among others.

One of Spener's favorite books was *True Christianity* (1606-1610) from the pen of the Lutheran pastor Johann Arndt (1555-1621).[5] Arndt was a persuasive advocate of "practical piety." He accented the teaching of regeneration. He believed the Christian's "New Birth" should result in a changed life: "Everything that is born of God is truly no shadowy work, but a true life work. God does not bring forth a dead fruit, a lifeless and powerless work, but a new man must be born from the living God." An authentic sign of a true Christian conversion was a changed life "rooted in love": "True love loves God and neighbor and nothing

5. For a biographical article on Arndt, see Johannes Wallmann, "Johann Arndt (1555-1621)," in Lindberg, ed., *The Pietist Theologians,* 21-37. Wallmann writes: "In the history of Protestantism there is no book apart from the Bible that has had such a circulation as Johann Arndt's *Bücher vom wahren Christentum (True Christianity)*" (21). Between 1605 and 1740, there were ninety-five editions of this book in German and twenty-six editions in other languages. Arndt's *True Christianity* exceeded Spener's *Pia Desideria* in terms of the number of copies circulating in Europe.

else. He who does not have this love is a hypocrite and God's word is useless to him. Self-honor makes everything an abomination before God."

Spener also esteemed Jean Labadie's *The Reformation of the Church by the Pastorate* (1667). Labadie claimed that Christians in his day had "lapsed" and lost their "pristine fervor." He indicated a great need existed for "a reformation in the entire Christian world."

In 1675, Spener published *Pia Desideria or Heartfelt Desire for a God-pleasing Reform of the True Evangelical Church. Together with Several Simple Christian Proposals Looking toward This End,* as a preface to Arndt's *True Christianity.*[6] The book became a reform manifesto of sorts for the Pietist movement.

Spener drew up a litany of complaints regarding the "wretched conditions" (31) of the contemporary religious scene. From his point of view the list rendered the pressing need for "reform" obvious. He decried the "sins and debauchery" at the courts of the Christian German princes (43). He bemoaned the drunkenness of some laity (58) and their litigious cupidity (59). He criticized prideful theologians who attempted to showcase their literary skills in arid tomes so unlike the spiritually nourishing works of Martin Luther. With sadness he took note of self-serving unconverted pastors who chased after ecclesiastical promotions from parish to parish (45). He disapproved of tippling divinity students who engaged in unseemly carousing and brawling.

In a word, Spener feared the Lutheran church of his day suffered from a perilously weakened spiritual state despite its formal orthodoxy. He wrote: "Although our Evangelical Lutheran Church is a true church and is pure in its teaching, it is in such a condition, unfortunately, that we behold its outward form with sorrowful eyes" (67). Spener worried that church people failed to discern that their adherence to formal theological orthodoxy (as important as this is) was not a substitute for experiencing a spiritual New Birth issuing in a "living faith" and the heartfelt pursuit of holiness.

Spener believed in justification by faith alone. He wrote: "We gladly acknowledge that we must be saved only and alone through faith and that our works or godly life contribute neither much nor little to our salvation, for as a fruit of our faith our works are connected with the gratitude which we owe to God, who has already given us who believe the gift of righteousness and salvation. Far be it from us to depart even a finger's breadth from this teaching, for we would rather give up our life and the whole world than yield the smallest part of it" (63).

At the same time, Spener referred to individuals who lived a "manifestly unchristian life" but possessed a "fleshly illusion of faith." They affirmed they believed in the orthodox doctrine of justification by faith alone. At the same time, they indicated they had "no intention of mending their ways in the future" and yet

6. Spener, *Pia Desideria.* In the remainder of this section, page references to this work are given in parentheses in the text.

were "convinced that they will be saved in spite of all this"! After all, it was not by how a person lives but by affirming faith in Christ that one will be saved. Spener was appalled by this kind of logic: "This is a delusion of the devil as terrible as any error ever has been or can be, to ascribe salvation to such a fancy of secure man" (64). This concept of faith, he wrote, was so different from how "our dear Luther" speaks of faith. Spener believed that the "New Birth" *(Wiedergeburt)* came though baptismal regeneration ("washing of regeneration and renewal in the Holy Spirit") by the power of the Word, not through the water. The "New Birth" was due to "a pure unmixed grace." It was not based upon any "righteous" good work accomplished by a sinner. The "New Birth" was accompanied by spiritual renewal *(Erneurung)*. If baptized people lived according to the "Old Man," and did not experience renewal as evidenced by a life of piety and discipleship, then they were not living in accord with the "New Birth."

By no means did Spener despair that Christians of his day were doomed to remain in a "hot-and-cold condition" (84). He believed that "God promised his church here on earth a better state" (76) than the one Lutheran churches of Germany were experiencing. He pointed out that the same Holy Spirit who had empowered the spiritually exemplary early church was available to contemporary Christians: "It is the same Holy Spirit who is bestowed on us by God who once effected all things in the early Christians, and he is neither less able nor less active today to accomplish the work of sanctification in us" (85). A postmillennialist, he envisioned that Jews might be won to Christ if they could see a "remarkable change and improvement in our church" (77). In a day when vitriolic theological controversies sometimes ate away at the spiritual vitality of church life, he reminded his readers that orthodoxy was preserved more by repentance and humility than by Christians displaying arrogance and staking everything on winning theological disputations (101). He indicated that seminaries should become "workshops of the Holy Spirit." He enjoined seminary professors to provide winsome models of humility and charity. Students after all would learn more by professors' examples of Christian humility than through pompous exhibitions of theological erudition. He referenced Gregory Nazianzen's panegyric that Basil's "speech was like thunder because his life was like lightning" (104).

A number of orthodox Lutheran theologians such as Abraham Calovius (1612-1686) warmly greeted Spener's teachings. Others reacted strongly against both his critical analysis of Lutheran church life and aspects of his reform program. As early as 1677, an opponent of Spener used the expression "Pietist" (apparently first minted in 1674) as a term of derision to designate anyone who embraced Spener's six-point reform program. Struggles ensued between Pietists and some Orthodox Lutherans. The latter were particularly troubled by the way Pietists described the necessity of a Christian manifesting a "living faith." To some Orthodox Lutherans, German Pietists appeared to neglect the importance of the sacraments, to downplay the authority of the Symbolical Books, and to undercut the doctrines of "forensic" justification by faith alone and imputed righteousness. Pietists were suspected of advocating works-righteousness and even the possibility of perfectionism. Orthodox Lutherans were especially critical of "separatist" Pietists (later called "Radicals") and their emphasis upon the Holy Spirit's illumination.[7] Not only did these "separatists" busy themselves in sorting out "true" from "false believers," but they also targeted supposedly worldly "church" Pietists and Orthodox Lutherans alike. A number of "separatist" Pietists sought ecstatic religious experiences and were enamored of eschatological predictions.

After 1689, conflicts between the Orthodox Lutherans and Pietists intensified. Denunciations of Pietists from the pulpit increased, outbreaks of persecution multiplied, and pamphlet warfare heated up. In 1690, the Elector of Saxony ordered Hermann Francke, Spener's close associate, into exile. In the early 1690s, the "radical" separatist Johann Konrad Dippel (1673-1734), apparently angered by the attacks of the Orthodox and emboldened by chiliastic expectations, ramped up his criticisms of the Orthodox. Dippel envisioned the year 1699 as one of crisis and decision and the year 1700 as one of deliverance.[8]

According to "church" Pietists, their emphasis upon the "New Birth" accompanied necessarily by "Renewal" (sanctification) merely echoed Luther's counsel. Had not the Reformer in his *Sermon on Good Works* (1520) reminded Christians of Jesus' words? "Good works proceed logically from a godly and good person. It is as Christ said: 'An evil tree bears no good fruit, a good tree bears no evil fruit.'" Luther also observed: "All good things come to us from Christ, who has received us into His own life as if He had been what we are. From us they should flow to those who are in need of them. . . . From all the foregoing, the conclusion follows that a Christian lives not in himself, but in Christ and his neighbor; in Christ by faith and in his neighbor by love."

As observed earlier, Spener made it clear that any reform of contemporary Christianity should be based on a faithful appropriation and "diligent use" of Holy Scripture, the Word of God. He called upon Lutheran pastors to rely more intentionally upon the laity in their ministries (the priesthood of all believers). He urged them to create "conventicles" (known as *Collegia pietatis,* ca. 1670), or small "pious" groups in which men and women could talk over sermons and read and meditate upon Scripture. Beginning in 1670, Spener regularly held such a group meeting in his home. He also sought to "encourage people to read the Bible privately." He remarked that "the more at home the Word of God is among us the more we shall bring about faith and its fruits" (87).

In 1689, a German professor of rhetoric named Joachim Fehler (1628-1691),

7. See Hans Schneider, *German Radical Pietism* (Lanham, MD: Scarecrow Press, 2007). Some of the "Radicals" were much influenced by the writings of Jakob Böhme (1575-1624) such as *The Way to Christ.*

8. Schneider, *German Radical Pietism,* 35-37.

in a eulogy pronounced at a theological student's funeral, highlighted the importance of Scripture for Pietist self-identity:

> The name of the Pietists is now known all over town.
> Who is a Pietist? He who studies the Word of God
> And accordingly leads a holy life.
> This is well done, good for every Christian
> For this amounts to nothing if after the manner of rhetoricians
> And disputants one puts on airs in the pulpit
> And does not live holy as one ought according to the teaching.
> Piety above all must rest in the heart.[9]

From Fehler's perspective, two traits characterized Pietists: (1) they studied God's Word; (2) from their hearts they desired to pursue a "holy life" according to God's Word.

In 1694, Spener published "The Necessary and Useful Reading of the Holy Scriptures." He wrote: "From the heavenly Father through Jesus Christ, his only begotten Son, I wish for the Christian reader the Spirit of wisdom and enlightened eyes of understanding to see the depths of the saving truth, given us by the gift of his Word so that he may walk with that Word and reach the Father by means of proper Bible reading." He cited Luther's advice on how to read Scripture: "In the first place, you are to know that the Holy Scripture is the type of book which makes all other books of wisdom foolishness because none of them teach of eternal life aside from it. As a result, you are not to reject its thought and understanding for without them you will never reach eternal life but are to kneel down in your inner closet and pray in proper humility and earnestness before God so that by his dear son he will give you his Holy Spirit who will enlighten you, lead you, and give you understanding."[10]

Like Spener, Johann Albrecht Bengel (1687-1752), a renowned German Pietist textual critic from the Duchy of Württemberg, also indicated that the spiritual health of the church depended upon Scripture: "Scripture is the life of the church: The church is the guardian of Scripture. When the church is strong, Scripture shines abroad, when the church is sick, Scripture is imprisoned."[11] Bengel believed it necessary that a biblical interpreter should be a Christian. He gave

9. Cited in Brown, *Understanding Pietism*, 13. The second verse of the eulogy reads: "The Pietists of our day, / Are Christians given wholly / To kindness, love, and truth; and they / Are striving to be holy. / I will confess that I embrace / Their doctrine of salvation / Without restraint or any trace / Of shame and hesitation" (14).

10. Erb, *Pietists: Selected Writings*, 71.

11. Erb, *Pietists: Selected Writings*, 256, from Bengel's *Gnomon of the New Testament* (1742). See also Beate Köster, "Evangelienharmonien im frühen Pietismus," *Zeitschrift für Kirchengeschichte* 103 (1993): 195-237.

this counsel: "Pray, place the Holy Scripture before you on the desk of your heart and acquaint yourself with the matter before you come to a decision."

In 1691, Spener's principal disciple, August Hermann Francke (1663-1727), began teaching as Professor of Greek and Oriental Languages at the University of Halle.[12] A brilliant biblical exegete and gifted organizer, Francke helped establish an orphanage for boys and girls (1695); charity schools; the *Collegium Orientale Theologicum* where divinity students could study Aramaic, Arabic, Ethiopian, Chaldean, Syriac, and Hebrew and work on translating and publishing a Hebrew Bible; the Canstein Bible Institute (1711); a printing press that published thousands of Bibles and pieces of Christian literature; and other educational, vocational, charitable, and missionary initiatives. Francke believed that the reform of the church would take place as Christians with the Holy Spirit's illumination heeded God's Word, properly interpreted and applied to daily living.

In 1707, a series of pamphlets constituting "a report card" of sorts on German Pietism appeared. They were published under Francke's aegis. The editor of the pamphlets rejoiced that many of the concerns Spener had raised in *Pia Desideria* (1675) about the weakened spiritual condition of "the Lutheran Church in Germany" had been partially remedied. Article 18 of the "Appendix" to these pamphlets reads: "The article of justification, and its coherence with true sanctification or holiness of life, has been set in a clearer light than before." Article 29 reads: "The practice of spiritual priesthood, a duty almost lost among Christians, has been revived in some degree in these years." Article 42 reads: "The brightness of the Gospel of Christ begins to shine forth in most distant countries. The voice of the turtledove is heard in foreign parts." Article 45 reads: "The great points of the Christian religion, that is, of a living faith in Christ, likewise of regeneration, mortification, contrition, resignation, self-denial, imitation of Christ and others of that nature, too slightly handled thereto, have begun to appear again and to be known among Christians."[13]

The German Pietist movement spread from centers such as Halle, Zinzendorf's *Herrenhut,* and Württemberg to various countries of Europe and to North America. The German Pietist emphasis that those who profess to be Christians

12. For a biographical article on Francke, see Markus Matthias, "August Hermann Francke (1663-1727)," in Lindberg, ed., *The Pietist Theologians,* 100-114. Cotton Mather in British America was thrilled that the "world begins to feel a warmth from the fire of God, which . . . flames in the heart of Germany." He greatly esteemed the ministry of Francke: "Dr. Francke is a person truly wonderful for his vast erudition, but much more so for his . . . shining piety; and yet more so for his . . . peerless industry; and most of all for the astonishing blessings of God upon his undertakings to advance His Kingdom in the world" (Lindberg, ed., *The Pietist Theologians,* 116).

13. Cited in Herzog, *European Pietism Reviewed,* 96-102 (drawn from "An Appendix Containing Some of the Most Significant Aspects of the Work of Reformation, Carried On in the Lutheran Church in Germany Since the Year 1688. Gathered by Some Strict Observers of the Signs of the Present Time").

should not only uphold "right doctrine" but have experienced a spiritual "New Birth" issuing in holy "right living," became a staple of the Methodist movement of the eighteenth century, the Holiness movement of the nineteenth century, and the Pentecostal movement of the twentieth century.

The English Evangelist John Wesley (1703-1791), for example, especially appreciated several Pietist emphases he had personally discerned among German Pietists. In preparing his *Explanatory Notes on the New Testament,* Wesley relied on the *Gnomen* of Johann Albrecht Bengel, the Pietist textual critic. Like Jakob Spener, Wesley wanted his followers to read Scripture, the source of "heavenly wisdom," and to obey biblical teachings in daily life. Wesley portrayed himself as "a man of one book" — the Bible. He observed: "The Scripture, therefore, of the Old and New Testament is a most solid and precious system of divine truth. Every part thereof is worthy of God: and all together are one entire body, wherein is no defect, no excess. It is the fountain of heavenly wisdom, which they who are able to taste prefer to all writings of men, however wise or learned or holy."[14] Wesley defined a "Methodist" as "one that lives according to the method laid down in the Bible."

Wesley was greatly troubled when he read a passage from Soame Jenyns's *View of the Internal Evidences of the Christian Religion.* Adopting a Socinian definition of accommodation, Jenyns proposed that the biblical authors had recounted stories "accommodated to the ignorance and superstition of the times and countries in which they had written." He observed further: "In the sciences of history, geography, astronomy and philosophy, they appear to have been no better instructed than others, and therefore were not less liable to be mis-led by the errors and prejudices of the times and countries in which they lived." Wesley countered:

> He [Jenyns] is undoubtedly a fine writer; but whether he is a Christian, Deist, or Atheist I cannot tell. If he is a Christian, he betrays his own cause by averring, that "all Scripture is given by inspiration of God; but the writers of it were sometimes left to themselves, and consequently made some mistakes." Nay, if there be any mistakes in the Bible, there may be as well a thousand. If there be one falsehood in that book, it did not come from the God of Truth.[15]

In the early twentieth century the Pentecostal movement emerged from Pietist-Methodist-Holiness streams of spirituality. And the Pentecostals also

14. John Wesley, *Explanatory Notes on the New Testament,* "Preface," Paragraph 10 (1754). See also Duncan S. Ferguson, "John Wesley on Scripture: The Hermeneutics of Pietism," *Methodist History* 22, no. 4 (July 1984): 234-45.

15. Soame Jenyns, *View of the Internal Evidences of the Christian Religion,* The Evangelical Family Library 14 (New York: The American Tract Society, n.d.). For the response of Wesley, see John Wesley, *The Works of John Wesley* (Grand Rapids: Zondervan, n.d.), 4:82 (journal entry August 24, 1776).

loved their Bibles. The African American William J. Seymour, one of the chief figures in the Azusa Street Revival in Los Angeles (1906), declared: "[Stay] within the lids of God's word."[16] The central purpose of the first organizing meeting of the Assemblies of God in 1914 was "to recognize Scriptural methods and order for worship, unity, fellowship, work and business for God, and to disapprove of all unscriptural methods, doctrines and conduct."[17] Until the 1950s, many American Pentecostal "Holy Ghost" schools or Bible Institutes were proud of the fact that the Bible was their only textbook.[18] Like the Pietist Fehler and the Methodist Wesley, early Pentecostals honored the Bible's authority and believed its teachings should direct a Christian's daily life.

Donald Dayton's Proposal That Pietists Rejected Biblical Inerrancy

Little doubt exists that Jakob Spener and early German Pietists upheld a high view of the Bible's authority as the Word of Life. But did they include the doctrine of biblical inerrancy as a component of their "high view" of biblical authority? This is a contested issue.

Donald Dayton, a distinguished historian of Methodism and the Pentecostal movement, stands out as a committed apologist for the thesis that inerrancy constitutes a doctrine foreign to the Pietist-Methodist-Holiness-Pentecostal tradition. His interpretation of the history of biblical authority for this tradition has gained considerable acceptance.

One of Dayton's most forthright efforts to uncouple "Pietism's theology" from biblical inerrancy once and for all is found in an article with the simple but telling title, "The Pietist Critique of Biblical Inerrancy." It was published in *Evangelicals, Scripture Tradition, Authority and Hermeneutics* (2004).[19] The article deserves a careful assessment owing to its significance.

Our own evaluation of Dayton's proposal will be admittedly provisional. His writings on Scripture's authority are vast. For his views to receive an ample and fair hearing, all of his writings devoted to biblical authority should be evaluated. Moreover, our evaluation will be provisional because one essential element of his proposal is not presently susceptible to assessment. Dayton does not inform us where in the corpus of Spener's writings the German Pietist "polemicized"

16. Wacker, *Heaven Below,* 71.

17. Wacker, *Heaven Below,* 70.

18. Wacker, *Heaven Below,* 71. The preferred Bible at the "Holy Ghost" schools was the King James (Authorized) Version.

19. Donald W. Dayton, "The Pietist Theological Critique of Biblical Inerrancy," in *Evangelicals, Scripture Tradition, Authority and Hermeneutics,* ed. Vincent Bacote, Laura C. Miguélez, and Dennis Okholm (Downers Grove, IL: InterVarsity, 2004), 76-89. In the remainder of this section, page references to this work are given in parentheses in the text.

against the doctrine of biblical inerrancy. Rather, as we shall see, he cites the writings of other authors who proposed that Spener did just that. But ironically enough, Dayton does not tell us in which writings of these secondary authors they say that Spener criticized the doctrine of inerrancy. Spener possibly did "polemicize" against the doctrine. The textual evidence he did this, however, is lacking in Dayton's article. Nor is it present in the writings of the authors he mentions as authorities. For this reason, the findings of our own study remain somewhat provisional.

If we have any contribution to make to the continuing discussion about Pietists' views of biblical authority, it will probably stem from our sustained research over the years focusing on the origins of French, Dutch, and German "higher criticism."[20] Specifically, this research suggests that Dayton's historical reconstruction of the German Pietist movement's views of biblical authority in the late seventeenth century and first half of the eighteenth century stands in need of serious revision. The struggles over the Bible's authority in this timeframe constitute a meaningful context into which to place statements made by early German Pietists about the Bible's authority. It also offers a prerequisite perspective from which to assess the significant argument of Gottfried Hornig to the effect that Johann S. Semler's higher criticism finds its essential roots in Pietism and the writings of Martin Luther.

Dayton makes four salient claims among others in his influential essay:

Claim One: The Pietist movement rejected the doctrine of biblical inerrancy and even polemicized against it.

Dayton writes: "Protestant orthodoxy, at least in the Lutheran context precipitated a reaction in the Pietist movement that included a self-conscious rejection of the inerrancy articulation of the authority of Scripture" (80). Dayton indicates that "Fred Holmgren of North Park Theological Seminary and Jim Stein have argued that Pietism polemicized against the inerrancy formulation, and that the Pietist Philipp Jakob Spener advised his followers not to defend it, especially with regard to concerns such as history, science and geography" (80).

Claim Two: The Pietists' rejection of biblical inerrancy challenged B. B. Warfield's assertion that the doctrine is a central teaching of the Christian churches.

Dayton indicates that this rejection by Pietists "constitutes a direct challenge to Warfield's claim about the church doctrine. In fact, it is quite striking that the debates about whether inerrancy is the church doctrine make no reference to Pietism" (80).

Dayton also asserts that the timing of the 1881 "Inspiration" article in which A. A. Hodge and B. B. Warfield defended the "inerrancy in the original auto-

20. See, for example, Henning Graf Reventlow, Walter Sparn, and John Woodbridge, eds., *Historische Kritik und biblischer Kanon in der deutschen Aufklärung* (Wiesbaden: Otto Harassowitz, 1988).

graphs" was "striking": "It appeared about the same time as the Catholic declaration of papal infallibility appeared, and it represents a classic declaration of a Protestant counterpart of biblical infallibility in opposition to church and papal infallibility, both over against the relativity of modern thought and the "acids of modernity" (77).

Claim Three: Pietists embraced "early forms of biblical criticism," especially textual criticism, and they were "pioneers of biblical criticism" (82).

Claim Four: Pietist and Enlightenment scholars at some points were "allied against orthodoxy" (82).

Dayton's proposal, which encompasses at least these four claims, creates in aggregate a serious historical interpretation. His extensive research in the history of the Pietist/Methodist/Holiness/Pentecostal tradition undergirds it. The interpretation deserves respectful consideration.

Compelling reasons exist for scholars to reconsider the interpretation's overall validity. The first reason is this: elements of Dayton's proposal do not easily comport with a number of reputable historiographies bearing on its arguments.

Historiographies Related to the Identity of Pietists

Dayton uses the term "Pietist" as if the movement constituted a unified whole. By no means is he alone in making this assumption. Many other Pietist scholars have written similarly about the views of "Pietismus" or of "Pietism." But the existence of differing schools of interpretation regarding the identity of Pietists raises serious questions about the adequacy and value of this approach.

Should only those Christians who self-identified as Pietists be deemed such? Scholars with this optic have tended to identify the Pietists with the Germans Spener, Francke, and their followers who embraced the term as a self-descriptor. The historian Johannes Waldmann argued strenuously for the validity of this "strict constructionist" view. By contrast, a number of scholars like Martin Brecht noticed apparent similarities of spiritual emphases between German Pietists, English Puritans, and other Christians.[21] They used the term "Pietist" to describe German Pietists *and* these other believers.

Ernst Stoeffler, the respected author of *The Rise of Evangelical Pietism* and *German Pietism during the Eighteenth Century,* sided with those who espoused a more expansive definition of Pietists. Alert to the existence of disputes regarding

21. Lindberg, ed., *The Pietist Theologians,* 2-3. Johannes Wallmann reviews the debates regarding the definition of Pietism in his "Philipp Jakob Spener — Begründer des Pietismus? . . .," in *Pietismus Herrnhutertum Erweckungsbewegung Festschrift für Erich Beyreuther,* ed. Dietrich Meyer (Cologne: Rheinland-Verlag GmbH, 1982), 22-38. Some scholars propose that Arndt was in reality the founder of Pietism.

the definition of Pietism, Stoeffler observed: "To give a universally satisfactory definition of Pietism would be quite impossible at this time (1976)." Stoeffler then proceeded to offer a "working concept of Pietism" that expanded the list of its adherents to groups of Christians beyond German Pietists. His "working concept of Pietism" is instructive:

> It is an historical movement within Protestantism which has its major roots in the Zwingli-Butzer-Calvin axis of the Reformation, which began to show its first characteristic evidences within English Puritanism and the Reformed churches of the seventeenth century, which influenced Lutheranism through Arndt, Spener, Francke, Bengel, and their followers, was radicalized by men like Gottfried Arnold and Konrad Dippel, romanticized by Lavater, Jung-Stilling and others, and perpetuated within and without the major communions of Continental Protestantism for an indefinite period of time. Through the Wesleys it helped to shape the evangelicalism of Great Britain.

Pietism's ethos was "experiential, biblical, perfectionistic, and oppositive."[22] For Stoeffler, Pietism constituted a reforming movement within Protestantism.

In *The Pietist Theologians* (2005), Carter Lindberg enlarged the contours of Pietist identity beyond Protestants to encompass even a Roman Catholic. His list of Pietists includes Arndt, Spener, and Francke; the Lutheran poet and hymn writer, Paul Gerhardt (1607-1676); the English Puritans William Perkins (1558-1602), Richard Baxter (1615-1691), and Lewis Bayley (d. 1631); the English spiritualist Jane Ward Leade (1624-1704); Johanna Eleonora Petersen (1644-1724); the "Radical Pietist" Gottfried Arnold (1666-1714); Gerhard Tersteegen (1697-1714); Nicholas Ludwig von Zinzendorf (1700-1760); the Protestant mystic Friedrich Christoph Oetinger (1702-1782); the Methodist John Wesley (1703-1791); the North American Cotton Mather (1663-1728); and the French Catholic mystic, Jeanne-Marie de La Motte Guyon (1648-1717).[23] Still other scholars have created more elastic definitions of Pietism that stretch to include Catholic Jansenism and Quietism and even Hasidism in Judaism as variant forms of Pietism.

In the Introduction to his work Lindberg observed that ongoing research regarding the relationship between "Protestant Orthodoxy" and "Pietism" has revealed that older dichotomous presentations juxtaposing the two movements as antagonistic to each other sheltered misconceptions. For example, the older

22. F. Ernest Stoeffler, ed., *Continental Pietism and Early American Christianity* (Grand Rapids: Eerdmans, 1976), introduction. See also Stoeffler, *The Rise of Evangelical Pietism* (Leiden: Brill, 1965).

23. For Madame Guyon's influence on German Pietists, see Jean-Marc Heuberger, "Les commentaires bibliques de Madame Guyon dans la *Bible de Berleburg*," *Revue de Théologie et de Philosophie* 133 (2001): 303-23.

interpretation that Protestant Orthodoxy lacked a commitment to "piety" and only emphasized "right belief" needs to be rethought: "But the assumption that Orthodoxy separated theology and piety in an obsessive drive to right belief distorts the picture. It may well be that struggles over confessional claims created a tough skin, but beneath it there pulsed a rich and heartfelt spiritual life. The period of Orthodoxy is the classical period of devotional literature."[24]

Hans Schneider's *German Radical Pietism* (2007) added further complexity to the Pietism definition puzzle.[25] His careful research put in bold relief the careers of Pietist "radicals" — individuals who initially accepted Spener's form of Pietism (reform within the church) and then opted to separate from the Lutheran and Reformed churches. They proffered mystical, spiritualist readings of Scripture and sometimes launched aggressive criticisms of established churches, whether Pietist or Orthodox Lutheran. On occasion, they ended up as heterodox loners. Perhaps foremost among them was Gottfried Arnold (1666-1704), author of *Impartial History of Church and Heretics* (1699-1700). He posited the controversial thesis that sometimes Orthodox Protestant Christians constituted the heretics in the history of the church and heretics were sometimes in reality the true followers of Christ.[26]

Many Orthodox Lutherans became quite infuriated by the contents of Arnold's book. One critic of Arnold wanted the following epitaph placed on his grave: "Here lies Gottfried Arnold, not so much a theologian, as the bitterest enemy of orthodox theologians; the persistent defender of heretics, the stupid representative of mystical theology — perhaps the first of all distorters of church history."

Specialists, then, continue to wrestle with complex issues related to defining Pietism and identifying a Pietist. Consequently Dayton's use of the expression, "the Pietist Critique of Biblical Inerrancy," has the trait of "false concreteness." The expression implies that Pietists constituted a unitary movement when much contemporary scholarship is not prepared to say this. Nor are these concerns about how to establish Pietist self-identity simply carping debaters' points. In certain histories figures appear who did not self-identify as Pietists, nor held theological views in conformity with those of Spener and Francke. They are nonetheless designated as Pietists.

The import of this matter for our study is significant. For example, in the mid-eighteenth century Johann S. Semler (1725-1791) began teaching at Halle Univer-

24. Lindberg, ed., *The Pietist Theologians,* 6. For the views of Scripture of "Orthodox Lutherans," see Robert Preus, *The Inspiration of Scripture: A Study of the Theology of the 17th Century Lutheran Dogmaticians* (Edinburgh: Oliver & Boyd, 1957). The "Orthodox" professor, John Conrad Dannhauer (1603-1666), influenced Spener.

25. Schneider, *German Radical Pietism.* Some of the "Radicals" were very much influenced by the writings of Jakob Böhme.

26. Schneider, *German Radical Pietism,* 29-35.

sity, a German Pietist citadel. Semler is often described as the father of German higher criticism. Because Semler taught at a Pietist university, does this mean his teaching should be viewed automatically as a normative expression of Pietist views of biblical authority? Some historians apparently think this is the case.

Fred Holmgren, an authority upon whom Dayton relies, placed Semler in the same Pietist tradition as Spener and Bengel despite Semler's commitment to higher criticism — something neither Spener nor Bengel advocated. Holmgren wrote that Semler "carried on the tradition of Spener and Bengel in opposing the view that the Bible was 'dictated' by the Holy Spirit. . . . In agreement with Martin Luther, Semler declared that it was more correct to confess (in light of our knowledge concerning the growth and content of the Bible) that the Bible contains the Word of God."[27] Holmgren added that within "the Covenant pietistic tradition there have been those also who have approached the Bible in the tradition of Spener, Francke, Bengel, and Semler. In company with these German pietists, they have combined a devout life and a love for the scriptures with a scholarly investigation of the text of the Bible."[28] Were Semler's writings regarding higher criticism in fact compatible with the beliefs of Martin Luther and earlier German Pietists? Did Luther affirm that Scripture contains the Word of God or did he more generally indicate Scripture is the Word of God? As we shall see, Semler in his personal diary named the French Roman Catholic priest Richard Simon and the Dutch Remonstrant Jean Le Clerc as the two persons who in particular stimulated him to develop his own ideas about what we call higher criticism. In this passage, he did not cite Luther or Spener as the sources of his inspiration.

Historiographies Regarding the "Enlightenment" and Pietism

Dayton uses the expression "Enlightenment" as if he and his readers will share a common understanding of its meaning. Some may. He embraces the older historiography that so-called Enlightenment partisans and Pietists entered into common cause in criticizing Orthodox Lutherans and Calvinists. Undoubtedly, a number of Pietists and Enlightenment figures did just that. What Dayton does not mention is the fact that on important theological matters such as the authority of Scripture Pietists and Enlightenment figures on occasion sharply disagreed. Historian Ulrich Groetsch observes:

> Yet the substance of the program of both the Enlightenment and Pietism with regard to religion could not have been more different. Whereas the rationalism

27. Fredrick Holmgren, "The Pietistic Tradition and Biblical Criticism," *Covenant Quarterly* 28 (1970): 55-56.

28. Holmgren, "The Pietistic Tradition and Biblical Criticism," 55-56.

of the Enlightenment sought to demystify religion, Pietism emphasized the inward spirituality of a "religion of the heart" as well as the centrality of Scripture. The historical-critical method of biblical criticism undertaken by proponents of the Enlightenment undermined scriptural authority completely, whereas for the Pietists the Bible practically served as the main source of guidance and knowledge.[29]

Dayton appears to believe that a so-called secular "Age of Enlightenment" dominated the eighteenth century in a paradigmatic fashion. A good number of historians, however, have abandoned this historiography. Historian Jeremy Black, for example, writes: "The concept of a de-christianized and enlightened Europe is increasingly questioned. It is not simply that the Enlightenment can be seen to have had a dark side, such as the preoccupation with the occult, but rather that the culture of the elite was still generally Christian." New "reception histories" are revealing the great residual power of the Christian faith in affecting the social, political, and cultural life of eighteenth-century Europe.[30]

The *philosophe* Voltaire acknowledged that he lived in both a *Siècle des lumières* (Age of Lights) and an "Age of Superstition" peopled in the main by Christians. In 1769, Diderot, the editor of the *Encyclopédie,* lamented in a letter to David Hume that Christians were more than holding their own in thwarting the advance of "philosophy": "Ah, my dear philosopher! Let us weep and wail over the lot of philosophy. We preach wisdom to the deaf, and we are still far indeed from the age of reason." In the 1770s, Voltaire complained that the influence of the "philosophic" movement had receded. Owing to the spiritual vitality of the Methodists and the apologetic efforts of Christian writers, the Deistic movement in England was largely quashed by the 1750s. The famous English historian Edward Gibbon lamented the fact that the "majority of English readers were so fondly attached even to the name and shadow of Christianity." What's more, historians of the book, Yvon Belaval and Dominique Bourel, surprised many scholars by describing the eighteenth century as an "Age of the Bible": "Whereas the production of religious books crumbled during the eighteenth century, never were more Bibles printed; it was the most read, the most edited, the most sought after [book]. Never since Luther were there so many translations and commentaries."[31]

29. Groetsch, "Pietism." For discussions of early "radical" partisans of the German *Aufklärung,* see the works of Martin Mulsow and Walter Grossmann. A number of these figures, such as Johann Christian Edelmann, had associated with Pietist circles. At the University of Halle Christian Wolff's emphasis on "reason's" authority played a key role in shaping Baumgarten's transitional theology and the thinking of Semler.

30. See in particular the works of Dale Van Kley devoted to the role of Jansenism in European cultural life. Van Kley has helped many historians to understand better the importance of religion as a major force in eighteenth-century French politics.

31. Yvon Belaval and Dominique Bourel, eds., *Le siècle de Lumières et la Bible, Bible de tous*

In brief, older paradigmatic portraits of the eighteenth century as an age largely secularized and dominated by the *philosophes* are losing some of their appeal. Presently, scholars like Dale Van Kley are searching for new ways to recount European history that take into account the surprising staying power or persistence of the Christian religion in Western European culture. Even Jonathan Israel, who extols the virtues of a so-called atheistic "Radical Enlightenment," acknowledges it did not dominate the eighteenth century. A "Moderate Enlightenment" existed as well. Its members like John Locke still upheld certain Christian values. Then again there were anti-*philosophe* Christian apologists who opposed the "Radical Enlightenment."[32]

Dayton's Claim Four, that Pietist and Enlightenment scholars at some points were "allied against orthodoxy," needs at the very least significant clarifications.

Historiographies Regarding the Augustinian Church Doctrine of Biblical Inerrancy

Dayton appears determined to uncouple Pietism from the doctrine of biblical inerrancy. His perspective appears to mirror the thrust of a "Neo-orthodox" historiography that portrays biblical inerrancy as a doctrinal innovation that departs from the central teachings of the Christian church and from the Bible's self-attestation about its own authority. This neo-orthodox historiography created in part by Ernst Bizer, an associate of Karl Barth, held sway among many historians until the 1980s. It proposed that Orthodox Protestant Scholastics of the seventeenth century betrayed the existential insights and christological focus of their forbears, the Protestant Reformers, regarding Scripture. Succumbing to the influence of Aristotelian "School" philosophies, the Orthodox Protestants allegedly created the doctrine of biblical inerrancy. Whereas the Reformers had associated the truth of Scripture with what it taught about Christ, the Scholastics extended the "truth" of Scripture beyond Christ, and matters of faith and practice to facts about history and science.

In 1984, Jill Raitt edited an important book, *Shapers of Religious Tradition in Germany, Switzerland, and Poland, 1560-1600* in which notable scholars directly challenged Ernst Bizer's historiography.[33] They argued that a general continuity

les temps (Paris: Beauchesne, 1986), 7:13. The editors begin their massive study by quoting in their introduction Voltaire's observation: "The Jews are the enemies of Christians, the Christians are divided into an infinity of sects, however all recognize the divinity of Scripture, all use it" (1756).

32. See, for example, Albert Monod, *De Pascal à Chateaubriand: Les défenseurs français du Christianisme de 1670 à 1802* (New York: Burt Franklin, 1971 [1916]).

33. Jill Raitt, ed., *Shapers of Religious Traditions in Germany, Switzerland, and Poland, 1560-1600* (New Haven: Yale University Press, 1981). Ernst Bizer argued that Lambert Daneau was the first Reformed theologian who broke with Calvin's approach to doing theology and included

of theological beliefs existed between the Reformers and Protestant Reformed theologians post-1560. They dismissed the idea that a radical disjunction in theological thought occurred between the Reformers and the Scholastics. In impressive studies devoted to the history of Protestant Scholasticism, Richard Muller has made a similar judgment.[34] In *Engaging with Barth: Contemporary Evangelical Critiques* (2009) edited by David Gibson and Daniel Strange, several authors have offered additional criticisms of the Barthian historiography.[35]

The doctrine of biblical inerrancy [the Bible is infallible not only for matters of faith and practice but also for history and "science"] was not a seventeenth-century Protestant scholastic doctrinal innovation. Contra Dayton's implied assessment, substantial evidence exists that B. B. Warfield was correct when he claimed that biblical inerrancy had been the church doctrine of the Western churches since the patristic era. St. Augustine's articulation of biblical inerrancy, especially in his letter to Faustus the Manichean (405 C.E.), helped shape the thinking and commitments of both Roman Catholics and Protestants in this regard. St. Augustine wrote:

> I confess to your Charity that I have learned to yield this respect and honor only to the canonical books of Scripture: of these alone do I most firmly believe that the authors were completely free from error. And if in these writings I am perplexed by anything which appears to me opposed to truth, I do not hesitate to suppose that either the manuscript is faulty, or the translator has not caught the meaning of what was said, or I myself have failed to understand.[36]

From St. Augustine's perspective, if you thought you found an error in Scripture, it was because the manuscript was "faulty," or the passage was incorrectly translated or you simply misunderstood the passage. Hans Küng noted the import of St. Augustine's teaching in the history of the Western churches: "St Augustine's influence in regard to inspiration and inerrancy prevailed throughout the Middle Ages and right into the modern time."[37]

Evidence of Saint Augustine's continuing influence emerged in an exchange

---

the natural world under the purview of Scripture's authority. See Ernst Bizer, "Frühorthodoxie und Rationalismus," *Theologische Studien* 71 (1963).

Olivier Fatio, one of the distinguished authors in Raitt's volume, observed: "Why, then, do scholars [e.g., Bizer] criticize the rational framework to which he [Daneau] resorted as a corruption of the existential discoveries of the Reform?" (111).

34. Richard Muller, *Post-Reformation Reformed Dogmatics: The Rise and Development of Reformed Orthodoxy, ca. 1520 to ca. 1725*, 2nd edition (Grand Rapids: Baker, 2003), 2:101.

35. David Gibson and Daniel Strange, eds., *Engaging with Barth: Contemporary Evangelical Critiques* (Nottingham: Apollos, 2008).

36. Augustine, *Letters of St. Augustine* 82:3.

37. Hans Küng, *Infallible? An Enquiry* (London: Collins, 1972), 174.

(1518) between the Roman Catholics Johannes Eck and Erasmus on the eve of the Protestant Reformation. Eck suspected that Erasmus had affirmed an error existed in Matthew 2, one word incorrectly substituted for another. Eck thoroughly rejected the possibility that such an error actually existed. He cited St. Augustine's authority as his warrant:

> First of all then, to begin at this point, many people are offended at your having written in your notes on the second chapter of Matthew the words, "or because the evangelists themselves did not draw evidence of this kind from books, but trusted as men will to memory and made a mistake." For in these words you seem to suggest that the evangelists wrote like ordinary men, in that they wrote this in reliance on their memories and failed to inspect the sources, and so for this reason made a mistake.[38]

Eck was not about to let Erasmus's opinion stand: "Listen, dear Erasmus: do you suppose any Christian will patiently endure to be told that the evangelists in their Gospel made mistakes?" Eck could not imagine "any Christian" believed in anything other than biblical inerrancy. He referred to St. Augustine in building his case: "If the authority of Holy Scripture at this point is shaky, can any other passage be free from the suspicion of error? A conclusion drawn by St. Augustine from an elegant chain of reasoning."[39]

Like Eck, Martin Luther also upheld the doctrine of biblical inerrancy. In his *A Sure Ground on Which to Stand: The Relation of Authority and Interpretive Method in Luther's Approach to Scripture* (2006 [2004]), Mark Thompson demonstrates Luther believed in an equivalent position to biblical inerrancy.[40] Moreover, Luther identified Scripture with the Word of God.

Richard Muller accents the point that the Protestant Scholastics of the Seventeenth Century were not the inventors of the doctrine of the Bible's full infallibility:

> In a similar vein, the frequently heard characterization of the orthodox view of Scripture that Protestantism rejected an infallible Roman Pope only to replace him with an infallible "paper pope" is, at best, a catchily worded misunderstanding of the history of the doctrine of Scripture. On the one hand, it ignores the continuity of Christian doctrine on the point: catholic teaching before the

38. Letter 769 from Johann Maier von Eck, 2 February 1518 (*The Correspondence of Erasmus* [Toronto: University of Toronto Press, 1979], 5:289).

39. Letter 769 from Johann Maier von Eck, 2 February 1518, 5:289-90.

40. Mark Thompson, *A Sure Ground on Which to Stand: The Relation of Authority and Interpretive Method in Luther's Approach to Scripture* (Eugene, OR: Wipf & Stock, 2006 [2004]); Thompson, "Witness to the Word: On Barth's Doctrine of Scripture," in Gibson and Strange, eds., *Engaging with Barth*, 168-69.

> Reformation assumed the infallibility of Scripture as did the Reformers — the Protestant orthodox did not invent the concept.[41]

Dayton presents a Pietist like Spener as strongly reacting against Lutheran Orthodoxy's commitment to biblical inerrancy. He claims that "Protestant orthodoxy, at least in the Lutheran context, precipitated a reaction in the Pietist movement that included a self-conscious rejection of the inerrancy articulation of the authority." But it should be remembered that Spener identified the contemporary Evangelical Lutheran Church of his day as a "true church" and "pure in its teaching" (this would include Scripture). What concerned Spener was not so much the orthodox theology of the Lutheran Church but the failure of its members to live out their faith in a pious and godly manner. Spener wrote: "Although our Evangelical Lutheran Church is a true church and is pure in its teaching, it is in such a condition, unfortunately, that we hold its outward form with sorrowful eyes." As for Dayton's claim that the Pietists rejected the doctrine of biblical inerrancy, as we shall see, many at Halle, a Pietist center, not only upheld the infallibility of their "vulgar Bibles," but they also affirmed the infallibility of the Masoretic pointing of the Hebrew text.

Historiographies Regarding the Old School Princetonians and Biblical Authority

In Claim 2 Dayton indicates B. B. Warfield's assertion that biblical inerrancy constituted the church doctrine of Christian churches is countermanded by the example of Pietists who did not uphold that doctrine. But as will be demonstrated, many Pietists affirmed the doctrine. Dayton's further observation that the Princetonians' articulation of biblical inerrancy "represents a classic declaration of a Protestant counterpart of biblical infallibility in opposition to church and papal infallibility, both over against the relativity of modern thought and the 'acids of modernity,'" as if the Princetonians intended to offset the Catholic definition of papal infallibility at Vatican I (1870-1871) by creating the doctrine of biblical infallibility [in an inerrancy construal], is not at all convincing. In fact, A. A. Hodge and B. B. Warfield had no need to create a new doctrine of biblical inerrancy "in opposition to church and papal infallibility." The Roman Catholic Church already upheld an Augustinian doctrine of biblical inerrancy and reaffirmed this doctrine at Vatican I.

In November 1893, Pope Leo XIII published *Providentissimus Deus, Encyclical of Pope Leo XIII on the Study of Holy Scripture* in which he reiterated the Roman Catholic Church's commitment to the Augustinian church doctrine of

41. Muller, *Post-Reformation Reformed Dogmatics*, 2:289-90.

biblical inerrancy. He indicated the Roman Catholic Church affirmed that Holy Scripture is without error not only for matters of faith and practice but also for matters of history and science (inerrancy). He specifically criticized those who limited the inerrancy of Scripture to matters of faith and morals:

> But it is absolutely wrong and forbidden, either to narrow inspiration to certain parts only of Holy Scripture, or to admit that the sacred writer has erred. For the system of those who, in order to rid themselves of these difficulties, do not hesitate to concede that divine inspiration regards the things of faith and morals, and nothing beyond, because (as they wrongly think) in a question of the truth or falsehood of a passage, we should consider not so much what God has said as the reason and purpose which he had in mind in saying it — this system cannot be tolerated.[42]

In summarizing Catholic teaching about biblical inerrancy, Pope Leo XIII referenced the passage from St. Augustine we have already considered as the warrant for this church doctrine:

> It follows that those who maintain that an error is possible in any genuine passage of the sacred writings, either pervert the Catholic notion of inspiration, or make God the author of such error. And so emphatically were all the Fathers and Doctors agreed that the divine writings, as left by the hagiographers, are free from all error, that they laboured earnestly, with no less skill than reverence, to reconcile with each other those numerous passages which seem at variance — the very passages which in great measure have been taken up by the higher criticism. . . . The words of St. Augustine to St. Jerome may sum up what they taught: "On my part I confess to your charity that it is only to those Books of Scripture which are now called canonical that I have learned to pay such honor and reverence as to believe most firmly that none of their writers has fallen into any error. And if in these Books I meet anything which seems contrary to truth, I shall not hesitate to conclude either that the text is faulty, or that the translator has not expressed the meaning of the passage, or that I myself do not understand."[43]

B. B. Warfield and A. A. Hodge appear much less the lonesome figures in their defense of the church doctrine of biblical inerrancy when it is understood that Pope Leo XIII taught essentially the same doctrine.

In *Divino afflante Spiritu on Promoting Biblical Studies Commemorating the*

42. Pope Leo XIII, *Providentissimus Deus, On the Study of Holy Scripture,* Encyclical of Pope Leo XIII, November 18, 1893, section 18.

43. Pope Leo XIII, *Providentissimus Deus,* section 21.

Fiftieth Anniversary of Providentissimus Deus (1943), Pope Pius XII reaffirmed the Roman Catholic Church's commitment to the doctrine of biblical inerrancy: "Finally, it is absolutely wrong and forbidden either to narrow inspiration to certain passages of Holy Scripture, or to admit that the sacred writer has erred, since the divine inspiration not only is essentially incompatible with error but excludes and rejects it absolutely and necessarily as it is impossible that God Himself, the Supreme Truth, can utter that which is not true." He then made an important declaration: "This is the ancient and constant faith of the Church (Section 3)."

Reconsidering the Relationship between German Pietism and the Origins of Higher Criticism

Few historians doubt that the German Jacob Spener qualifies as a significant Pietist. Understandably, his views on biblical authority should count for something in determining what a standard German Pietist view of biblical authority involves. In Claim One Dayton indicated that Pietism manifested "a self-conscious rejection of the inerrancy articulation of the authority of Scripture." He indicated that Fred Holmgren and Jim Stein argued that Pietism "polemicized against the inerrancy formulation, and Pietist Philipp Jakob Spener advised his followers not to defend it, especially with regard to concerns such as history, science, and geography."[44]

But did Spener and Pietism as a movement in fact reject biblical inerrancy and polemicize against it? An excursus regarding the origins of higher criticism as juxtaposed to early Pietism's history reveals such is unlikely.

Spener published *Pia Desideria* (1675) in the years between the appearance of two epochal controversial works related to biblical authority: Baruch Spinoza's *Tractatus Theologico-Politicus* (1670) and Richard Simon's *Critical History of the Old Testament* (1678).[45] In these works Spinoza and Simon actually did "polemicize" against the infallibility of Scripture. But they were severely chastised for doing so. By contrast there is no hint in *Pia Desideria* that Spener intended to reject biblical inerrancy. Nor did he "polemicize" against the doctrine in that hallmark Pietist work.

Spinoza made a sharp distinction between Holy Scripture and Word of God.[46] He denied that Moses wrote all of the Pentateuch — a denial that infuriated many

44. Bacote et al., *Evangelicals, Scripture Tradition,* 80.

45. Benedict de Spinoza, *A Theologico-Political Treatise* (New York: Dover, 1951).

46. Spinoza indicated that he "pays homage to the Books of the Bible, rather than to the Word of God. I show that the Word of God has not been revealed as a certain number of books, but was displayed to the prophets as a simple idea of the Divine mind, namely, obedience to God in singleness of heart, and in the practice of justice and charity" (*A Theologico-Political Treatise,* 9).

Christian scholars. Had not Christ himself indicated that Moses was the author of the Pentateuch? Was Spinoza's real goal to throw aspersions upon Christ? Spinoza's *Tractatus* smuggled into France under the cover of frontispiece pages disguised with false titles (such as "The Key to the Sanctuary") and false attributions of authorship, converted Spinoza into a pariah — a dangerous enemy for both orthodox Christians and Jews. Hardly any theologians wanted to identify their own views of the Bible with those of Spinoza, who earlier in his life had been excommunicated by a synagogue in Amsterdam. Spener certainly did not do so.

In one sense, Simon constituted an even more troubling personage for Christians than Spinoza. Why? Simon wrote as an "insider" — a Roman Catholic in priest's garb.[47] In his *Critical History of the Old Testament* (1678) Simon developed the famous "public scribes" hypothesis. Simon professed that this hypothesis constituted a responsible answer to parry Spinoza's arguments that Moses did not write all of the Pentateuch.[48] And with this theory Simon took a momentous step in the direction of what we call today higher criticism.

Simon indicated that so-called public scribes kept the archives of the republic of Israel. These public scribes emended the writings of Moses, adding references such as those in which the Patriarch was spoken of as "he," the third-person singular pronoun. In this way, Simon proposed that Moses was indeed the principal author of the Pentateuch even if unknown public scribes (also inspired by the Holy Spirit) had also added elements to its final form.

Bossuet, the Bishop of Meaux and tutor for Louis XIV's son, happened to read a brief section of Simon's *Histoire critique du Vieux Testament* in which the priest claimed that Moses did not write all the Pentateuch. Greatly alarmed, Bossuet urged the government of Louis XIV to condemn the volume. In 1678, the white and yellow flames of a governmental bonfire consumed nearly the entirety of the 1,300 copies of the first edition. Members of the Oratorian house in Paris expelled Simon from their order the same year.

Simon is sometimes touted as the father of biblical higher criticism. Not shy to tout his own "accomplishments," Simon claimed he was the first scholar

47. See Paul Auvray, *Richard Simon 1638-1712 Études bio-bibliographiques* (Paris: Presses Universitaires de France, 1974); August Bernus, *Richard Simon et son Histoire critique du Vieux Testament* (Geneva: Slatkine Reprints, 1969 [1869]); Jacques Le Brun and John D. Woodbridge, eds., *Richard Simon: Additions curieuses sur la diversité des langues et religions d'Edward Brerewood* (Paris: Presses Universitaires de France, 1983); Henri Margival, *Essai sur Richard Simon et la critique biblique au XVIIe siècle* (Paris: Maillet, 1900); Jean Steinmann, *Richard Simon et les origines de l'éxègese biblique* (Paris: Desclée de Brouwer, 1960); Jacques Le Brun, "Richard Simon," in *Supplement au Dictionnaire de la Bible* (Paris: Letouzey & Ané, 1996), 12:1354-83.

48. Concerning Richard Simon's assessment of Spinoza's views of Scripture, see Woodbridge, "Richard Simon's Reaction to Spinoza's Tractatus Theologico-Politicus," in *Spinoza in der Frühzeit seiner religiösen Wirkung*, ed. Karlfried Gründer and Wilhelm Schmidt-Biggemann (Heidelberg: Lambert Schneider, 1984), 201-26.

to employ the French word *critique* in referring to the study of the Bible. Amazingly enough, he even asserted that he was the first scholar ever to understand the way the Bible should be translated and commented upon. Had not earlier commentators tried to bolster the doctrinal stances of their own churches in the translations and notes of their works? For his part, Simon indicated he embraced another approach. He translated and added notes with a "perfect neutrality," that is, without partisanship for any particular church's theology.[49] Moreover, he would offer a number of meanings for Hebrew and Greek words if their sense appeared equivocal.

In the very first paragraph of the *Critical History of the Old Testament,* Simon acknowledged both the commitment of St. Augustine and that of most of his contemporaries in the 1670s (when Spener wrote) to the full infallibility of Scripture:

> One is not able to doubt that the truths contained in Holy Scripture are infallible and of a divine authority, since they come immediately from God, who in doing this used the ministry of men as his interpreters. Is there anyone, either Jew or Christian, who does not recognize that this Scripture being the pure Word of God, is at the same time the first principle and the foundation of Religion? But in that men have been the depositories of Sacred Books, as well as all other books, and that the first Originals [*les premiers Originaux*] had been lost; it was in some measure possible that a number of changes occurred, due as much to the length of time passing, as to the negligence of copyists. It is for this reason St. Augustine recommends before all things to those who wish to study Scripture to apply themselves to the Criticism of the Bible and to correct the mistakes [*fautes*] of their copies. *Codicibus emendandis primitus debet invigilare solertiae eorum, qui Scripturas Divinas nosse desiderant* [Augustine, Book 2 of Christian Doctrine].[50]

Simon therefore recognized that Saint Augustine had pursued a program of "lower criticism," that is, the attempt to correct scribal errors in the copies of Scripture with the goal of restoring as faithfully as possible the "lost originals," or the infallible original texts of Scripture. But then the priest catapulted over St. Augustine's program of "lower criticism" to define criticism in another fashion. Because allegedly unknown authors, so-called public scribes, contributed to the writing of the biblical books, the biblical scholar should no longer busy himself in the elusive task of determining who made up the full roster of Scripture's authors. Simon added that the public scribes only chose certain sample histories

49. See Woodbridge, "Richard Simon and the Charenton Bible Project: The Quest for 'Perfect Neutrality' in Interpreting Scripture," in *Knowledge of Religion as Profanation,* ed. Martin Mulsow, International Archives of the History of Ideas (New York: Springer, forthcoming).

50. Richard Simon, *Histoire Critique du Vieux Testament* (Rotterdam: Reinier Leers, 1685), 1.

from the many that existed in Israel's archives to include in Holy Scripture. For this reason, Simon asserted that Scripture should not be esteemed as presenting an infallible chronological history, setting forth the full history of Israel: "One will not be able to establish on the authority of these same Books, a certain and infallible Chronology, because things were not always reported according to the times they happened; but (the scribes) were rather often content to join together several happenings by abridging them."[51] Simon had little use for the writings of the "chronologists" who labored so intensively to establish the dating of the events recorded in Scripture.[52]

Between the years 1685 and 1687 Richard Simon and Jean Le Clerc entered into a five-book battle royal over the authority of Scripture. Both attacked the infallibility of Scripture. In *Sentimens des quelques théologiens d'Hollande . . .* (*Sentiments of Several Theologians of Holland*) the young Le Clerc, a professor at the Remonstrant seminary in Amsterdam, accused Simon of fancifully making up his public scribes hypothesis and of being a poor student of Hebrew to boot. Under the guise of one of the theologians of Holland, Le Clerc proposed an even more radical hypothesis than Simon in terms of the authorship of the Pentateuch: "All of these traits come together in the person of the Israelite *sacrificateur* who was sent from Babylon in order to instruct the new inhabitants of Palestine concerning how they should serve God, as the author of the books of Kings recounts it in Chapter 17 of the second book."[53] Moreover, Le Clerc conjectured that the Scriptures were not divinely inspired (except the prophetical writings and Christ's own teachings). All the biblical writings had to be was historically accurate for them to be worthy purveyors of the Christian religion. Le Clerc did acknowledge that most Christians of his day believed in the infallibility of the Scriptures.

According to his own witness, Simon, an irascible soul, became infuriated upon reading Le Clerc's book (it took him some time to identify Le Clerc as the author). Simon plopped down on the floor and bolstered by pillows wrote nonstop during a number of days and nights a lengthy rejoinder to Le Clerc's book (Simon's *Response to Sentiments of Several Theologians of Holland . . .*). The priest stuffed himself with chocolate to keep awake during the herculean writing stint. He complained later that the ingestion of so much chocolate had caused his face to break out and he had to go on a fish diet in consequence. Not a bit amused by Simon's stinging rejoinder, Le Clerc wrote a response and Simon in turn wrote a response to Le Clerc's response.

51. Simon, *Histoire Critique du Vieux Testament,* "Preface de l'Auteur," 5.

52. In his lecture "Biblical Chronology: Legend or Science?," James Barr indicated that Martin Luther, Joseph Justus Scaliger, James Ussher, and Isaac Newton, all of whom drew up biblical chronologies, believed that Scripture was "divinely inspired and equally infallible in matters of normal human history, as well as in theological matters" (4).

53. Jean Le Clerc, *Sentimens de quelques théologiens d'Hollande,* 129.

The debate between Simon and Le Clerc constituted one of the most important battles for the Bible in European history. It took place during Paul Hazard's celebrated "Crisis of the European Mind" (1680-1715).[54] Many leading intellectuals of Europe like John Locke, Isaac Newton, Pierre Bayle, and others followed the twists and turns of the debate very closely. Normally, a sensitive theological debate of this import was carried on in Latin so as not to offend the religious sensitivities of the general public. But Simon and Le Clerc chose French as their language of battle. This linguistic move spiked greatly the size of their audience. Pierre Bayle wrote to Le Clerc and warned him that his work could only sow doubts about the Bible's authority in the minds of thousands.[55] The biblical scholar Jean Astruc (1684-1766) looked back on the controversy as a turning point in the history of scriptural authority. So did a number of French *philosophes.* Voltaire hailed the "savant Le Clerc" as the scholar in the Republic of Letters who had provided persuasive proofs that Moses could not have written the book of Genesis.

For their part, many English, French, German, and Dutch theologians of the late seventeenth and early eighteenth centuries weighed in and excoriated Simon and Le Clerc as dangerous and damnable heretics. Germany was one of the areas of Europe where Simon's works were widely reviewed:

> German theologians between Leibniz and Semler reacted to the works of Richard Simon with varying degrees of animosity and appreciation. By the mid-1680s the portrait of Richard Simon as a suspect critic who had denied the Mosaic authorship of the Pentateuch, who had shucked traditional views of biblical inspiration, and treated the Scriptures like any other work of man-made literature was emerging. A battery of authors stepped forward who promptly relegated the priest into the feared ranks of "anti-Christians" like Hobbes, Spinoza, and Le Clerc and deemed him a "tool of Satan."[56]

Among critics of Simon was the prominent German Pietist scholar Johann Jakob Rambach (1693-1735). His *Institutiones Hermeneuticae Sacrae* (1723) served as one of the standard Pietist textbooks on hermeneutics and biblical authority.[57] It passed through eight editions. In the volume Rambach placed Simon in the suspect company of Isaac de la Peyrère, Thomas Hobbes, and Spinoza, all of whom he deemed dangerous heretics. Rambach believed that Simon's public

54. Paul Hazard, *The European Mind: The Critical Years 1680-1715* (New York: Fordham University Press, 1990 [1935]).

55. Bayle lamented: "All your Treatise on the inspiration of the prophets and of the Apostles can do is sow a thousand doubts and a thousand seeds of atheism in people's minds" (University of Amsterdam K3b, Bayle to Le Clerc, July 18 [1685?], my translation).

56. Woodbridge, "German Responses to the Biblical Critic Richard Simon: from Leibniz to J. S. Semler," in Reventlow et al., eds., *Historische Kritik und biblischer Kanon,* 80.

57. Rambach, *Institutiones Hermeneuticae Sacrae,* 2nd edition (Jena: Hartung, 1725).

scribes hypothesis constituted a direct challenge to the Mosaic authorship of the Pentateuch and subverted biblical authority.[58] Rambach believed in the Bible's infallibility.

That Rambach, a Pietist, would take a strong stance against Simon is not at all surprising. Contrary to Dayton's key claim to the effect that Pietists rejected biblical inerrancy and polemicized against it, many of the teachers and clergy in Halle were in fact noteworthy defenders of the doctrine, at least during the first four decades of the eighteenth century.

In the *Allgemeine Bibliothek,* a literary publication, the famous biblical critic Johann Gottfried Eichorn (1752-1827) who was a great admirer of Johann David Michaelis (1717-1791) but certainly no friend of the doctrine of biblical infallibility, provided a retrospective history of the beliefs of the Pietist faculty and clergy at Halle in the first four decades of the eighteenth century. He indicated that these clerics and professors upheld the absolute infallibility of Holy Scripture and that Michaelis even defended the Masoretic pointing of the Hebrew text early in his career.

Eichorn's historical account is revelatory. It directly countermands the validity of Dayton's claim that early German Pietists rejected the doctrine of biblical inerrancy. Eichorn wrote:

> A Bible with various readings had been printed at Halle in the year 1720, and notwithstanding the use of the whole noble apparatus, they [clergy/professors] adhered still pertinaciously to the infallibility of the vulgar text.... They had discovered upon investigation, and exposed to view in this edition of the Bible, the contradictions of the Masora — the most satisfactory evidence of their fallibility: and yet they had sworn, in as solemn a manner, to the absolute infallibility of the same, as they had sworn to their symbolical articles. Michaelis, on his first appearance as a public teacher, was full, to overflowing, of this faith of his fathers. In the year 1739, he decked out, after his fashion, in a dissertation on "the antiquity of the Hebrew points." . . . In the year 1740, he came forward in the disputation concerning Psalm 22 as an advocate of the infallibility of the entire text.[59]

From Eichorn's point of view, not only did some of the clergy in Halle in the first decades of the eighteenth century believe in the infallibility of the vulgar text, but others affirmed the infallibility of the Masoretic Text — including Johann David Michaelis as late as 1739.[60] It is difficult to imagine that the clergy at Halle of

58. Rambach, *Institutiones Hermeneuticae Sacrae,* 44.

59. "An Account of the Life and Writings of John David Michaelis from Eichorn's *Allgemeine Bibliothek,*" in *Biblical Repertory* (1826), 2:261.

60. "An Account of the Life and Writings of John David Michaelis," 2:261.

the 1720s held positions on the infallibility of Scripture out of line with the teachings of Spener, notwithstanding Dayton's claim that the Pietist "polemicized" against the doctrine. Further research devoted to the views of the clergy in Halle (1720s) regarding the infallibility of the Masoretic pointing of the Hebrew text is needed. Interestingly enough, in Geneva street-fighting apparently broke out between partisans and foes of the infallibility of the Masoretic pointing.[61]

Dayton also argued that Pietists were more open to biblical criticism than orthodox Lutherans. Undoubtedly, some early German Pietists were experts in textual criticism. Bengel's *Gnomen* (1742), for example, constitutes a benchmark study of textual criticism. Bengel used textual criticism in part as a means to defend his very high view of biblical authority. He wrote: "The Scriptures of the Old and New Testaments form a most reliable and precious system of divine testimonies. For not only are the various writings, when considered separately, worthy of God, but they together exhibit one complete and harmonious body, unimpaired by excess or defects." He approved an "Augustinian" doctrine of accommodation: "Certainly the wisdom of God employs a style worthy of God, even when through his instruments he accommodates himself to our grossness. And that which is worthy of God, it is not our part arrogantly to define, but humbly to believe." He continued: "The holy men of God, in both the Old and New Testaments, exhibit, not only an exact knowledge of the truth, but also a systematic arrangement of the subject, a precise expression of their meaning, and genuine strength of feeling."[62] Bengel defended the infallibility of the "autographs" of Scripture.[63]

The respected German historian Gottfried Hornig proposed that Johann S. Semler built his program of higher criticism upon theological premises stemming from Martin Luther and earlier Pietists.[64] But the founders of German higher criticism, Johann S. Semler, Johann David Michaelis, and others with Pietist backgrounds, looked more to the writings of Richard Simon, Jean Le Clerc, and

61. Barthélemy Barnaud, *Mémoires pour server à l'histoire de troubles arrivés en Suisse à l'occasion du Consensus* (Amsterdam: J. Frédéric Barnard, 1727).

62. Bengel, *"Gnomen,"* in Erb, ed., *Pietists: Selected Writings,* 258-59. Confronted by the 30,000 variant readings in John Mill's 1707 edition of the Greek New Testament, Bengel reduced the number drastically through careful scholarship. He indicated he "found rest in the sure conviction that the hand of God's providence must have protected the words of eternal life which the hand of His Grace had written."

63. Alan Thompson, "Pietist Critique of Inerrancy? J. A. Bengel's *Gnomen* as a Test Case," *JETS* 47 (2004): 71-88. Thompson answers convincingly the arguments of Professors Dayton, Stein, and others to the effect that Bengel did not uphold a belief in biblical inerrancy. Bengel allegedly believed the authors of Scripture were inspired, less so the text; Pietists affirmed "the ongoing process of inspiration in the church" vs. "the once-for-all givenness and absoluteness of the process of biblical inspiration"; Bengel noted that the quality of the Greek varied between biblical authors (74-87).

64. Gottfried Hornig, *Die Anfänge der historisch-kritischen Theologie Semlers Schriftverständnisse und seine Stellung zu Luther* (Göttingen: Vandenhoeck & Ruprecht, 1961).

English biblical critics for inspiration than to Luther's writings or to those of Spener, Francke, Rambach, Bengel, and other Pietists.

By the 1750s, scattered signs in Germany signaled that the study of biblical criticism was entering a new stage, especially regarding the New Testament. Johann David Michaelis observed: "The learned world since 1750 has made new and important contributions to the criticism of the New Testament which has given the Discipline a different *Gestalt*."[65] A number of contemporary scholars attributed this "different *Gestalt*" to the growing acceptance of Richard Simon's writings on higher criticism. Several German Protestant scholars had begun to shrug off the priest's negative reputation for being too much the Roman Catholic or too much the blatantly anti-Christian scholar. Rather they openly acknowledged and embraced in Simon's writings pathbreaking innovations regarding the emerging discipline of higher criticism.

Whereas in earlier decades German theologians had castigated the French Roman Catholic priest as a "tool of Satan," now a chorus of German biblical scholars anointed him as the "Father" of the new biblical criticism. In his *Introduction to the Divine Writings of the New Covenant* (second edition), Johann David Michaelis, formerly a traditional Pietist who had earlier defended the infallibility of the Masoretic text, now praised Simon's works: "One finds in them a wide-ranging learning and a sound judgment in his critical history which is also easy to read; and due to it, one can name him [Simon], the father of the newer criticism."[66] Herder would later echo Michaelis's sentiment by designating Simon as the "father" of the newer criticism: "Richard Simon is the Father of Criticism for the Old and New Testaments in recent times."[67]

Even the University of Halle professor Johann S. Semler, often singled out as the father of German higher criticism, recognized that this honor duly belonged to the Frenchman Simon. That Semler should have become fascinated by the writings of Richard Simon was not too surprising given the fact Jacob Baumgarten, his mentor at the University of Halle, had reviewed Simon's writings and appreciated several scholarly contributions of the French priest. Moreover, in his youth Semler surmised that few German theologians had reflected sufficiently well about matters of criticism. He concluded that only by reading Simon, Le Clerc, and others could he learn about the history of biblical texts. In his diary, he made a very significant comment about the influence Simon and Le Clerc had in stimulating his thought about biblical criticism: "Should I be unwilling to reflect about Richard Simon and Le Clerc as was the custom of German theologians

65. Johann David Michaelis, *Einleitung in die göttlichen Schriften des Neuen Bund* (Göttingen: Verlag de Witwe Vandenhoeck, 1765), 1:x.

66. Michaelis, *Einleitung in die göttlichen Schriften,* 1:668.

67. J. Herder, *Das Studium der Theologie* (1780), in *Herder, Sammtliche Werke,* ed. Bernard Suphan (Berlin: Weidmannsche Buchhandlung, 1879), 10:11.

earlier in Germany?"[68] In time, Semler translated a number of Simon's major works into German.

Gottfried Hornig indicated that Semler viewed Simon's work to be a confirmation of his program of higher criticism but his principal stimuli were the writings of Luther.[69] On occasion Semler did seek to justify his program of higher criticism by suggesting Luther would have approved its pursuit. At the same time, it will be recalled that Semler acknowledged that the Roman Catholic priest Richard Simon was the founder of the newer criticism he was in fact pursuing. The premise of Dayton, that inherent within Pietism were elements naturally conducive to an openness to the pursuit of higher criticism, does not receive much support if the career of Johann S. Semler is used as a test case.

More pertinent in explaining Semler's openness to higher criticism was his adoption of a "Socinian" definition of "accommodation" according to which the biblical authors accommodated their writings to the cosmologies and superstitions of their contemporaries.[70] In consequence, they incorporated errors of fact into the biblical text. Semler recommended the "free" investigation of the Bible to establish a canon within a canon of "authentic" Scripture, that is, to separate out "authentic" Scripture from the cultural, uninspired dross with which it was mixed. He indicated that Holy Scripture and Word of God "must certainly be differentiated." Semler repudiated the doctrine of biblical infallibility and distanced himself from certain "orthodox" doctrines he thought were based not on "authentic Scripture" but upon mythological and non-inspired biblical passages.[71]

Semler, therefore, did not uphold an Augustinian doctrine of accommodation as had a Reformer like John Calvin.[72] According to an Augustinian definition, God accommodated Scripture to the weakness of our understanding. As a result, what we read in Scripture is truthful but is communicated to us in the language of appearance and everyday language. The Augustinian definition of biblical accommodation comported well with a doctrine of biblical inerrancy. Scripture described things simply but truthfully.

68. Semler, *Lebensbeschreibung von ihm selbst abgefasst* (Halle, 1781), 258.

69. Hornig, *Die Anfänge der historisch-kritischen Theologie . . .*, 187 ("Semler hat Simons Forschungen als eine Bestätigung seines eigenen Schriftverständnisse empfundet").

70. See Richard A. Muller, "Accommodatio," in *Dictionary of Latin and Theological Terms: Drawn Principally from Protestant Scholastic Theology* (Grand Rapids: Baker, 1996), 19; Stephen D. Benin, *The Footprints of God: Divine Accommodation in Jewish and Christian Thought* (Albany: State University of New York Press, 1993), 94-112.

71. For example, Semler did not believe in the reality of demons, heaven, or hell, but staunchly affirmed the reality of Christ's resurrection.

72. See Glenn Sunshine, "Accommodation in Calvin and Socinus: A Study in Contrasts" (M.A. thesis, Trinity Evangelical Divinity School, 1985); Zbigniew Ogonowski, "Faustus Socinus 1539-1604," in Raitt, ed., *Shapers of Religious Traditions*, 195-209. See also multiple studies devoted to Calvin's Augustinian concept of divine accommodation.

By contrast, the Socinian definition of accommodation did possess the premise that Scripture erred. This premise constituted a working assumption of Semler's program of higher criticism. Charles Hodge complained later that it was Semler's writings linked to a Socinian definition of accommodation that had dangerously undermined Protestant orthodox theology in Germany on the eve of the nineteenth century:

> It will be perceived that the historical method of interpretation here reprobated, is the application of the doctrine of accommodation which has been mentioned on the 20th page of the preceding article, to the interpretation of the N.T. Perhaps few causes have operated more extensively and effectually, in promoting erroneous opinions than the prevalence of this doctrine. Its most active and successful promoter was J. S. Semler, professor of Theology, at Halle.[73]

Even though Semler taught at what had been a Pietist citadel, the University of Halle, it should not be supposed his views of biblical authority replicate the beliefs of Jakob Spener and other early German Pietists. When Semler began teaching in the 1750s, there was a greater openness to higher criticism than in the days when Spener and Francke wrote. Nonetheless, a number of traditional German Pietists and Lutheran Orthodox roundly criticized Semler's writings regarding biblical authority and his criticism of biblical infallibility. Semler complained that relatively few theologians initially accepted his program of biblical criticism.

The Elusive Provenance of the "Spener Polemized against Biblical Inerrancy" Claim

One of Dayton's benchmark claims is that Pietism and Spener not only denied the doctrine of biblical inerrancy, but actually "polemicized" against it. To support this assertion, Dayton referred to the writings of Holmgren and Stein. Dayton wrote: "Fred Holmgren of North Park Theological Seminary and Jim Stein have argued that Pietism polemicized against the inerrancy formulation, and Pietist Philipp Jakob Spener advised his followers not to defend it, especially with regard to concerns such as history, science, and geography."[74] But Dayton did not cite the specific works in which Holmgren and Stein made this claim.

73. Charles Hodge, "Introduction to Charles Christian Tittmann on Historical Interpretation," *Biblical Repertory* 1 (1825): 125-27. See also Mark Rogers, "Charles Hodge and the Doctrine of Accommodation," *Trinity Journal* 32 (2010): 225-42. Between 1763 and 1817, at least thirty-one volumes treating the subject of biblical accommodation appeared in Germany. Many of these works apparently promoted a Socinian doctrine of accommodation.

74. Dayton, "The Pietist Theological Critique of Biblical Inerrancy," 80. In the remainder of this section, page references to this work are given in parentheses in the text.

Dayton's source regarding Stein appears to be the latter's *Philipp Jakob Spener.* Surprisingly, Stein does not cite an actual statement from Spener but rather refers to Holmgren's writings to justify the claim that Spener polemicized against biblical inerrancy: "Fred Holmgren notes that Spener actually counseled preachers not to proclaim the inerrancy of the Scriptures in such areas as history, geography and chronology."[75]

As a bibliographical warrant, Stein cites Fredrick Holmgren, "The Pietistic Tradition and Biblical Criticism." Surprisingly, in this article, Holmgren also does not cite a statement from Spener but rather indicates the claim finds its warrant in the writings of a "number of scholars": "Because, for Spener, the authority of the Bible was a 'spiritual' one, that is, one that related to a man's Christian life, he did not emphasize the inerrancy of the Bible. In fact, according to a number of scholars, Spener actually counseled preachers *not* to proclaim the inerrancy of the Scripture in such areas as history, geography, and chronology."[76]

As a bibliographical warrant, Holmgren cites Erich Beyreuther's *Der geschichtliche Auftrag der Pietismus in der Gegenwart* as the source for his charge. Surprisingly, in this book, Beyreuther also does not cite a primary source statement from Spener but simply affirms without any documentation that "Philipp Jakob Spener had warned preachers no more to uphold the infallibility of Scripture in its historical, geographical, chronological and scientific statements."[77]

What's more, Beyreuther surprisingly postulated that the writings of the Oratorian priest, Richard Simon, particularly his public scribes hypothesis, had created the new intellectual environment that prompted Spener to give the counsel to preachers he allegedly offered.[78]

The evidence supporting Dayton's claim that Spener in particular "polemicized" against the doctrine of biblical inerrancy recedes and disappears into a bibliographical netherworld. The claim turns out to be much less robust than his readers would suppose. In fact, none of the scholars in the provenance lineage of the important claim cite primary source statements from Jakob Spener himself.

Now it is possible Jakob Spener made the assertion Beyreuther attributes to him. But students of German Pietism need to be afforded this primary source statement so they can assess its actual wording, context, and import. Moreover, Beyreuther's thesis that Richard Simon's writings prompted Spener to make the statement appears less than persuasive. We know that other early German Pietists including Rambach were sharply critical of Simon's writings. That they would be of this disposition while Spener was supposedly prompted to develop his new view of

75. Stein, *Philipp Jakob Spener,* 151.

76. Holmgren, "The Pietistic Tradition and Biblical Criticism," 53 (cited in note 27 above).

77. Erich Beyreuther, *Der geschichtliche Auftrag der Pietismus in der Gegenwart* (Stuttgart: Calwer Verlag, 1963), 19.

78. Beyreuther, *Der geschichtliche Auftrag der Pietismus,* 18-19.

biblical authority owing to the priest's influence seems quite problematic, at least upon the face of it. Once again, more research is needed regarding these matters.

Concluding Comments

Though provisional, our study provides substantial evidence that early German Pietists at the University of Halle not only upheld the infallibility of their Vulgar texts of Scripture but even the infallibility of the Masoretic pointing of the Old Testament. Eichorn clearly said as much. This viewpoint appeared to dominate the teaching at the University of Halle, at least until the 1730s. It will be recalled that the young Johann David Michaelis defended a thesis that upheld the Masoretic pointing as late as 1739. Then Michaelis and later Semler turned their backs on this view of Scripture and advocated higher criticism and the *errancy* of Scripture. Michaelis and Herder hailed the Roman Catholic priest Richard Simon as the father of the new discipline. Semler himself declared: "It remains true that Richard Simon began a new field in theological learning."

Dayton's central claim that Pietism and Spener "polemicized against the doctrine of biblical inerrancy" turned out to have no cited, primary source confirmation in the writings of the historiography (Stein, Holmgren, Beyreuther) we reviewed.

Contra the interpretation of Holmgren, Semler's advocacy of higher criticism was not fully aligned theologically and methodologically with the teachings of earlier German Pietists like Rambach. One telltale sign of this incompatibility of perspectives becomes manifest by comparing Rambach's attitude towards Richard Simon's writings and Semler's estimate. Rambach criticized Simon sharply, whereas Semler touted him as a guide for the kind of new higher criticism he wanted to pursue. Semler's perspectives should not be identified as tantamount to those of early German Pietists.

Should further research demonstrate that Jakob Spener gave the "anti-inerrancy" counsel attributed to him, this would mean at the most some early German Pietists (albeit an important one, Spener) did not uphold the doctrine of biblical inerrancy. At the same time, we remember Eichorn's testimony that many early German Pietists at the University of Halle upheld the infallibility of the Bible including the Masoretic text.

In a word, Donald Dayton's principal claim that biblical inerrancy was foreign to the beliefs of Pietists is not well founded — at least as it bears upon the self-identified German Pietists of our interest. In fact biblical inerrancy constituted an esteemed doctrine for many of them. Until the 1960s, most evangelicals in the Pietist-Methodist-Holiness-Pentecostal tradition still upheld the belief.[79]

79. Various churches and organizations of this tradition joined the National Association

Today's Christians in the Pietist/Methodist/Holiness/Pentecostal tradition who desire to witness spiritual reform within their churches have a marvelous repertory of books and tracts from which to seek instruction and inspiration — a bequest from their spiritual forbears the early German Pietists. Jakob Spener's *Pious Desires* (1675), for example, possesses a pertinent, contemporary "reform" message for today. Spener reminds us that the "diligent" use of the Word of God should be the chief means we employ in seeking the reform of the church:

> This much is certain, the diligent use of the Word of God, which consists not only of listening to sermons but also of reading, meditating, and discussing (Ps 1:2) must be the chief means for reforming something. . . . The Word of God remains the seed from which all that is good in us must grow. If we succeed in getting the people to seek eagerly and diligently in the book of life for their joy, their spiritual life will be wonderfully strengthened and they become altogether a different people.[80]

This would be wise counsel for us to appropriate as evangelicals both within and without the Pietist/Methodist/Holiness/Pentecostal tradition as we seek and pray for spiritual renewal both individually and collectively in our churches. Jakob Spener also reminds us, as he did Christians in his own day, we should not despair if we desire spiritual reform and renewal. Our "pious desires" are not illusory ones. They are not vain. The Holy Spirit who worked so powerfully in the early church is available to us to enliven our own spiritual lives and our churches today. Spener points out that it is this same Holy Spirit "who is bestowed on us by God who once effected all things in the early Christians, and he is neither less able nor less active today to accomplish the work of sanctification in us."[81] Now *that* is an encouraging word for us to remember each day.

---

of Evangelicals founded in 1943. NAE upheld the doctrine of biblical inerrancy. Dayton proposes that many of the Holiness, Methodists, and Pentecostals who affirmed the doctrine of biblical inerrancy in the first half of the Twentieth Century had succumbed to the influence of American Fundamentalists who advocated the belief. But as we have seen, the doctrine actually constituted an essential belief of many Christians of the Pietist-Methodist-Holiness-Pentecostal tradition since the earliest days of the Pietistic movement — in the far-distant past.

80. Spener, *Pia Desideria,* 91.

81. Spener, *Pia Desideria,* 85.

SIX

Wesleyan Theology and the Authority of Scripture: Historic Affirmations and Some Contemporary Issues

Thomas H. McCall

Throughout much of the history of the Christian church, Christians have held that "the books of both the Old and New Testaments in their entirety, with all their parts, are sacred and canonical because written under the inspiration of the Holy Spirit, they have God as their author and have been handed on as such to the Church herself . . . [and] since everything asserted by the inspired authors or sacred writers must be asserted by the Holy Spirit, it follows that the books of Scripture must be acknowledged as teaching solidly, faithfully, and without error that truth which God wanted put into sacred writings."[1] The Bible *is* God's Word, and as such it carries God's authority. Given by inspiration of the Holy Spirit, the Bible is absolutely trustworthy and utterly reliable (thus "infallible" or "inerrant"). Despite their disagreements among themselves on many matters, Christians of various ecclesial and theological commitments consistently have held this view or something close to it. In fact, I take this to be settled enough that I shall henceforth refer to it as the "classical" account of Scripture.

The relation of Wesleyan theology to this classical view has become the source of some controversy. A particular narrative has become dominant, and several distinctively "Wesleyan" objections to the doctrine are sometimes adduced as latter-day reasons to reject the classical view. In what follows, I challenge what has become the standard narrative; here I show that the story is much more complicated than is sometimes assumed. I also address several of the more prominent of the "Wesleyan" objections to the classical account, and I argue that none

1. *Dei Verbum: Dogmatic Constitution on Divine Revelation, Solemnly Promulgated by His Holiness, Pope Paul VI on November 18, 1965* (Boston: Pauline Books and Media, 1965), 9.

I am grateful to many friends and colleagues (most notably A. Philip Brown, Gareth Cockerill, James R. Gordon, Matthew D. Johnson, Ronald E. Smith, Douglas A. Sweeney, M. William Ury, Kevin J. Vanhoozer, and John D. Woodbridge) for helpful discussion of these matters. All remaining errors are, of course, their fault entirely.

of these offer compelling reasons to reject it or to replace it with an alternative. Finally, I conclude with the suggestion that Wesleyan Christians — *qua* Wesleyans — have good reason for adhering to the classical account.

Historic Wesleyan Views of Scripture: A Brief Tour of the Gallery

Due to the fact that various narratives compete for dominance, it is not always easy to discern the relation of the Wesleyan theological tradition to the classical account.

Two Tales Told

According to what has become the dominant story (at least in many quarters), the Wesleyan theological tradition never endorsed nor cared much about defending the classical view. Wesleyans (along with other Pietists) were mostly concerned about evangelism, spiritual formation, and social justice, and they considered the endless debates over the nature, origin, and authority of Scripture to be misbegotten at best and misleading — perhaps even dangerously so — at worst. Wesleyans, so the story goes, initially cared about the gospel and its implications; they were not obsessed with the defense of traditional orthodoxy (regarding the Bible or cardinal doctrines). It is not as though they *attacked* the classical doctrine of Scripture — they just did not see the need to defend it. To attack the classical account would be to lose focus from the transforming and life-giving power of the Holy Spirit (who works in and through the Bible) — but to be side-tracked into defending it from various attacks would be to miss the meaning of Christianity entirely. Instead of being drawn into the debates about the inspiration and authority of the Bible, so the story goes, Wesleyans acted in good Pietist fashion by allowing that higher-critical biblical studies might have a legitimate place and indeed might undermine the classical view — and then cheerily going on with the ministry to which God had called them without even caring very much about the classical view. So the story goes. When faced with the inconvenient facts that some prominent Wesleyan theologians and confessional statements actually *embrace* the classical view, the standard response is that this (unfortunate) alignment with the classical view was only the result of keeping bad company: Wesleyan theologians (and formal confessional statements) only endorsed the classical account *after they had lost their genuinely Wesleyan moorings,* and only after they had been unduly influenced by either *fundamentalists* or *Calvinists.*[2] This story itself has gained something like

2. Donald W. Dayton has been very influential, e.g., *Discovering an Evangelical Heritage* (New York: Harper & Row, 1976). Paul M. Bassett's insightful article ("The Fundamentalist Leavening of the Holiness Movement, 1914-1940: The Church of the Nazarene: A Case Study,"

the status of infallibility in some quarters of the Wesleyan movement, but it is not above scrutiny. Indeed, a closer look at the data suggests that far from being a later innovation, the classical view is the dominant view among the early Wesleyans. Additionally, we shall see that it is not at all likely that this commitment to it is the result of undue influence by Reformed theology, for many of the most dedicated defenders of the classical account were also some of the most polemical antagonists *against* Calvinism in America.

Exhibits in the Gallery

The views of John Wesley himself are fairly well known. By his own admission, he was *homo unius libri.*[3] He often pointed to the biblical affirmation that "all Scripture is given by inspiration of God," and he held that God is the source of all Scripture.[4] As Randy L. Maddox puts it, Wesley "sees Scripture itself as being directly from God. His most typical way of expressing this is to describe Scripture as the direct words or teaching of God."[5] Wesley argues for the divine inspiration of Holy Scripture both inductively and deductively. Inductive evidence for the divine origin of the Bible is seen in the fact that it is accompanied by divine power, wisdom, goodness, and holiness.[6] In his deductive argument, Wesley first argues that the Bible must come from either good human persons, angels, evil human persons, demons, or God. He then makes a case that there are good reasons to deny that it came from either human persons, angels, or demons, and he concludes that the only reasonable alternative is to conclude that it comes from God. Scott J. Jones puts it succinctly: for Wesley, "the words of the Bible are God's words."[7]

Wesleyan Theological Journal 13 [1978]: 65-91) focuses upon the early twentieth century, but does not deal with the significant "back-story."

3. Wesley, *Letters of the Rev. John Wesley, M.A.*, ed. John Telford (London: Epworth Press), 4:299. See the helpful discussion of Thomas C. Oden, *John Wesley's Scriptural Christianity: A Plain Exposition of His Teaching on Christian Doctrine* (Grand Rapids: Zondervan, 1994), 56.

4. In this paragraph and the next two I am deeply indebted to the fine (but, alas, routinely ignored) work of Daryl McCarthy, "Early Wesleyan Views of Scripture," *Wesleyan Theological Journal* 16, no. 2 (1981): 95-105.

5. Randy L. Maddox, *Responsible Grace: John Wesley's Practical Theology* (Nashville: Abingdon, 1994), 31.

6. John Wesley, "A Clear and Concise Demonstration of the Divine Inspiration of the Holy Scriptures," in *The Works of the Rev. John Wesley, M.A.* (Oxford: Clarendon, 1975-83), 11:484. See the helpful discussions offered by Oden, *John Wesley's Scriptural Christianity,* 60-62, and Donald A. D. Thorsen, *The Wesleyan Quadrilateral: Scripture, Tradition, Reason, and Experience as a Model of Evangelical Theology* (Grand Rapids: Zondervan, 1990), 131-33.

7. Scott J. Jones, "The Rule of Scripture," in W. Stephen Gunter, Scott J. Jones, Ted A. Campbell, Rebekah L. Miles, and Randy L. Maddox, *Wesley and the Quadrilateral: Renewing the Conversation* (Nashville: Abingdon, 1997), 50.

Wesley draws a direct connection between Scripture's source, reliability, and authority. Because Scripture comes from the inspiration of God, we can be assured that it is "true and right concerning all things."[8] Jones states that, given Wesley's view of inspiration, "it is inevitable that the words of Scripture are infallible."[9] In his comments on a Mr. Jenyn's essay *The Internal Evidence of the Christian Faith,* Wesley protests that the author's own theological convictions are obscure: "If he is a Christian, he betrays his own cause by averring that 'all Scripture is not given by inspiration of God, but the writers of it were sometimes left to themselves, and consequently made some mistakes.' "[10] Wesley's own response leaves no question about this own convictions: "Nay, if there be any mistakes in the Bible, there may as well be a thousand. If there be one falsehood in that book, it did not come from the God of truth."[11] Since " 'all Scripture is given by inspiration of God,' consequently, all Scripture is infallibly true."[12] As Jones puts it, "God's authorship thus provides a negative guarantee that the Scripture is free from error. It also provides a positive guarantee that Scripture is unquestionably true, perfect, and consistent."[13] It seems plain enough, on a straightforward reading, that Wesley held to the classical view.[14]

Richard Watson, the first and very influential systematic theologian of the Methodist movement, took pointed interest in the humanity of the biblical authors: "the verbiage, style, and manner of each was not so much displaced, as elevated, enriched, and employed by the Holy Spirit."[15] And yet while resisting any sort of mechanical dictation theory, he does insist upon the plenary inspiration of Scripture.[16] It is, therefore, an "infallible authority."[17]

Thomas Ralston's *Elements of Divinity* contains an extended and spirited discussion of the inspiration and authority of Scripture. He is convinced that the theologians of early Christianity uniformly embraced the plenary inspiration

8. Wesley, *Works,* 8:45-46.

9. Jones, "The Rule of Scripture," 51.

10. John Wesley, *The Journal of the Rev. John Wesley, M.A.* (London: Epworth Press), 6:117. See the discussion by McCarthy, "Early Wesleyan Views," 97.

11. John Wesley, *Journal,* 6:117. Maddox notes that "Wesley explicitly denied that there were any errors in the Bible on at least three occasions." *Responsible Grace,* 269 n. 96. Maddox also notes that Wesley's approach differs from those of some modern "inerrantists" in various ways.

12. Wesley, *Works,* 5:193.

13. Jones, "The Rule of Scripture," 52. Jones also thinks that Wesley's own position is untenable today (e.g., 59), but he is faithful to explicate Wesley's understanding.

14. Some critics aver that Wesley's comments on the genealogies of Jesus show that he had found error in Scripture, but to this see McCarthy, "Early Wesleyan Views," 97-98.

15. Richard Watson, *The Works of Rev. Richard Watson,* 12 vols. (London: John Mason, 1834-35), 6:13.

16. For discussion see McCarthy, "Early Wesleyan Views," 102.

17. Richard Watson, *Theological Institutes: Or, a View of the Evidences, Doctrines, Morals, and Institutions of Christianity,* 2 vols. (New York: N. Bangs and J. Emory, 1826), 1:248.

and full authority of the Bible, noting that the Socinians were notable for their rejection of plenary inspiration and for their assertions that Scripture was "liable to error."[18] He refers to modern German scholarship as "a hot-bed of infidelity in this insidious guise," and he rejects the approaches of Coleridge, Schleiermacher, and others (596). Because of the inspiration of the biblical authors — Ralston calls them the "amanuenses" of God — by the Holy Spirit, the Bible is "really God's writing — God's book — God's word" (597). The inspiration of Scripture extends to the parts and even the very words as well as the whole; the result is clearly a view of plenary and verbal inspiration: "the Bible is inspired, not as to *ideas* only, but as to *words* also" (598). This does not mean that only one manner of inspiration was operative, nor surely does it mean that inspiration destroyed the individuality of the biblical authors (598-99). Ralston is convinced that something absolutely crucial is lost if plenary and verbal inspiration is denied: "Abstract the idea of an inspiring Spirit guiding the pen of the sacred writer in every sentence, word, and letter, from the Holy Gospels, and the heavenly unction — the divine power — of the book is gone. It is no longer the record of Heaven we trace — no longer the voice of God we hear" (600). This view of inspiration leads Ralston to his conviction that Holy Scripture is absolutely truthful and trustworthy. Although infallibility extends only to the writings of Scripture rather than to the authors (when working beyond their "official capacity"), it is nonetheless clear for Ralston that Scripture is without any error at all. "What the Bible says, God says; what the Bible declares to be true, is true; what it declares to be right, is right; what it declares wrong, is wrong. What it teaches is to be believed" (598). Thus he concludes that "Moses, John, and all the rest of Heaven's chosen amanuenses, in every sentence of the sacred canon which they penned, were aided, not only by the inspiration of 'superintendence,' freeing them from the possibility of mistake or error, but by the inspiration of 'elevation' and 'suggestion,' lifting their thoughts infinitely higher than nature's pinions can soar . . . [thus] the Bible, from Genesis to Revelation, is the infallible word of God" (603).

Samuel Wakefield held to a similar position, as is clear in his *A Complete System of Christian Theology.*[19] He defines the inspiration of Holy Scripture as "that extraordinary influence of the Holy Spirit upon the human mind by which men are qualified to communicate to others religious knowledge without error or mistake" (71). He argues that inspiration is possible, and he further argues that it

18. Thomas N. Ralston, *Elements of Divinity: A Concise and Comprehensive View of Bible Theology; Comprising the Doctrines, Evidences, Morals, and Institutions of Christianity; with Appropriate Questions Appended to Each Chapter* (New York: Abingdon), 596. In the remainder of this paragraph, page references to this work are given in parentheses in the text.

19. Samuel Wakefield, *A Complete System of Christian Theology: Or, A Concise, Comprehensive, and Systematic View of the Evidences, Doctrines, Morals, and Institutions of Christianity* (Cincinnati: Walden & Stowe, 1869). In the next two paragraphs, page references to this work are given in parentheses in the text.

is reasonable. Indeed, he says, given the magnitude and importance of the issues at stake, we might expect God to inspire the human authors of the Bible. For "the more important the communication is, the more it is calculated to preserve men from error, to stimulate them to holiness, and to guide them to happiness, the more reasonable it is to expect that God should make the communication free from every admixture of error" (72). Moreover, Wakefield extends this argument to make the case that inspiration is *necessary* — "how, for instance, could Moses have given a correct history of the creation of the world, and of antediluvian times, if he had not been divinely inspired?" (72).

Wakefield rejects a dictation theory of inspiration (at least for most of the Bible), and he allows that the Holy Spirit may have worked in various ways in this process, for "the same degree of Divine assistance was not necessary in every part" (78). But he insists upon plenary inspiration. This leads him to conclude that the Scriptures, "taken as a whole, may be called the *Word of God*" (81). We "give them this denomination," he says, "because they were written by persons who were moved, directed, and assisted by the Holy Spirit, and who were, therefore, infallibly preserved from error. Hence we are authorized to consider all the doctrines, precepts, promises, and threatenings which they contain, as true, righteous, and faithful; and to believe also that the events which are said to have happened did so happen, and that the words which are said to have been spoken were so spoken" (81).

In his *Systematic Theology,* Miner Raymond contends for the classical view; he concludes that "what the Bible says God says."[20] Similarly, the British Methodist William Burt Pope holds that the doctrine of the inspiration of Scripture by the Holy Spirit leads us to the conclusion that "we pay also a certain homage to the Scriptures as [the Spirit's] finished work," and that we do so without danger of "bibliolatry."[21] He recognizes that there is more than one manner of inspiration attested to in the Bible; while sometimes the Spirit uses the human authors "almost mechanically," in many cases the Spirit works in other ways (171). But however the process(es) work, Pope is sure that the result is "plenary inspiration" (174). This means that Holy Scripture is "the absolute and final authority, all-sufficient as the supreme Standard of Faith, Directory of Morals, and Charter of Privileges to the Church" (174). The fact that it is *divine* revelation means that "of course" the Bible "cannot contain anything untrue" but is instead "infallible" (174). And while Pope recognizes that Scripture is not written as if it were intended to be a textbook of natural science — it is "comparatively silent as to human science"

20. Miner Raymond, *Systematic Theology* (New York: Eaton and Mains, 1877), 1:100.

21. William Burt Pope, *A Compendium of Christian Theology, Being Analytical Outlines of a Course of Theological Study, Biblical, Dogmatic, Historical,* vol. 1, 2nd edition, revised and enlarged (New York: Hunt & Eaton, 1889), 170. In the remainder of this paragraph, page references to this work are given in parentheses in the text.

(174) — he is also so "strong in [his] conviction that this book . . . is the record of that Providential government for the sake of which the world exists, we may be sure that it will not be contradicted in fundamental points by anything that the records of nature, or the authentic annals of history, will disclose" (190). Pope engages those who employ the Christological analogy (i.e., Scripture is analogous to the person of Christ in being both divine and human), and here he seems to be more concerned with Nestorianism (separating the divine from the human elements) than he is with "Eutychianism" (making the human element so passive that it virtually disappears) (183). To those who favor the Christological analogy, however, Pope has an important reminder: "it ought not to be forgotten that the human nature of our Lord was sinless and incapable of sin. If its upholders allow that the human element in the Bible is unsusceptible of real error, however affected by infirmity, their doctrine may be made safe, and, if safe, it is deeply interesting and instructive" (184-85).

Thomas O. Summers lands at a similar place; for him a sober confession of the authority of Scripture means that "even in all subordinate and collateral matters of history, chronology, ethnography, topography, sociology and the like, the Scriptures are perfectly consistent with themselves, with all other trustworthy records, and with all phenomena and facts which are now patent to our observation."[22]

Randolph S. Foster's *Evidences of Christianity: The Supernatural Book* takes and defends a similar position.[23] He recognizes that "the claim set up by all evangelical Christians, of whatever phase of faith, is, that the Scriptures of the Old and New Testament either directly or indirectly contain [Christ's] teachings; and that, in substance, they are of divine authority and are to be received as such; in other words, that the Bible is a divinely inspired book, and that he was a divinely sent teacher, and that the substance of what is found in the Bible is a revelation from God, and as such is to be accepted as final authority on all matters of which it makes deliverances" (1-2). It is *this* account that he works to defend from its critics. He recognizes that the level of immediacy in the process of inspiration by the Holy Spirit varies, and he admits that there indeed are errors in the extant manuscripts (e.g., 3-4, 6-7). Yet he makes clear his convictions about the nature of Holy Scripture:

> [T]he claim set up is not simply that the Bible is in the main true; nor yet that its teachings are in the main flawlessly correct; nor that Jesus was a flawless

22. Thomas O. Summers, *Systematic Theology: A Complete Body of Wesleyan-Arminian Divinity Consisting of Lectures on the Twenty-Five Articles of Religion,* vol. 1 (Nashville: Publishing House of the Methodist Episcopal Church, South, 1888), 436.

23. Randolph S. Foster, *Studies in Theology: Evidences of Christianity, The Supernatural Book* (New York: Hunt & Eaton, 1889). In the remainder of this paragraph, page references to this work are given in parentheses in the text.

> character and a teacher of pre-eminent worthiness; nor that the holy books contain even a flawlessly sound ethical system. The claim is all this, but it is also more: namely, that the teachings are the teachings of divinely commissioned men, and of a divine incarnation sent into the world to deliver them, and that they are therefore of supreme, universal, and perpetual authority. (4-5)

Foster's view of inspiration leads him to conclude that the human authors of the Bible were "chosen amanuenses of God" (33). And he closely relates the doctrine of God to the doctrine of Scripture, concluding that the trustworthiness of the former entails the trustworthiness of the latter. Foster takes this trustworthiness to extend to all that Scripture addresses: "[I]f a divine deliverance, its historical statements must be veracious, its doctrinal contents sound, and its ethical teachings correct. Falsity in any part will be fatal to the whole, or so far vitiate its claim as to destroy its authority" (38). Foster's view, like those of the other theologians canvassed, is clear: he takes the classical account to be essential to Christianity.

Nor is this commitment to the classical account only evident in formal treatises in systematic theology. For instance, Milton Terry's venerable *Biblical Hermeneutics* defends the classical view against modern historical-critical biblical scholarship.[24] This widespread commitment to the classical account can also be seen in the periodicals that were influential in nineteenth-century Methodism such as the *Methodist Review.*[25]

A critical defender of the narrative so widely accepted in contemporary Wesleyan circles (that Wesleyan theology only endorsed the classical view when it was unduly influenced by fundamentalists and/or Calvinists) might protest that I have offered a selective and prejudiced reading of the Wesleyan tradition, one that privileges statements that would appear to endorse a "high view" of the Bible and thus skews the evidence. But this is not merely my reading of the evidence; various theologians have observed (and sometimes applauded) the later Wesleyan *rejection* of its former commitment to the classical view. In his observations published in 1906, Henry C. Sheldon states that his "investigation of American Methodism" reveals that "many changes have occurred in relation to a few of the themes of theology, and that tentative efforts are being made for more or less revision of the traditional views in connection with some other themes . . . the themes to which we shall have occasion to refer are the conception of the Bible, original sin, the person and work of Christ, the conception of personal salvation, and eschatology" (32).

24. Milton Terry, *Biblical Hermeneutics: A Treatise on the Interpretation of the Old and New Testaments* (New York: Hunt & Eaton, 1891), 52-57.

25. This is noted by Henry C. Sheldon, "Changes in Theology among American Methodists," *American Journal of Theology* 10 (1906): 34. In the next three paragraphs, page references to this work are given in parentheses in the text.

Sheldon details what he means by the changes in the "conception of the Bible":

> For several decades Methodists, in common with other American Christians, have been aware of a conflict between two contrasted theories of the Bible. On the one hand is the high technical theory, which at the acme insists upon complete verbal inspiration of every part of Scripture, and in any case maintains the inerrancy or detailed infallibility of the Bible as originally written. On the other hand is the broader theory, which indeed cordially grants that the Bible contains the materials of a complete ethical and religious system, but renounces the notion of a detailed infallibility or inerrancy of every part, and places the stress upon the trend and outcome of the biblical teaching. (32)

Sheldon makes plain his reading of Methodism: "[T]he evidence indicates that American Methodism began substantially upon the basis of the high technical theory, so far as that theory affirms inerrancy" (32). He bases this conclusion on the explicit statements of major theologians (noting that even John Miley "was noncommittal in this relation, and the most that can be said on the basis of his printed writings is that he took very little account of the possibility of errors in Scripture"), the more popular writings of American Methodists, and the fact that a book "written in advocacy of strict verbal inspiration" was required for some years in the conference course (33-34).

Sheldon notes, however, that while "the high technical theory had not spent its energy in the Methodist body by the middle of the nineteenth century, and, indeed, that it was not without self-assertive vigor up to the last quarter of the century," by the end of the nineteenth century significant changes were underway (34). At the turn of the century, Sheldon seems delighted to see that "with little, if any, exception, Methodist exegetes of any considerable experience and rank, who have written in recent years, have given evidence of their preference for the broader, as opposed to the high technical, theory of the Bible" (35). Sheldon attributes this to retreat before higher-critical biblical studies, and he concludes that "it is undeniable that the critical views in question have been winning much territory in every prominent branch of Methodism. . . . The evidence seems, therefore, to enforce the conclusion that an effective movement toward a modified conception of the Bible is in progress within the domain of American Methodism." It must, therefore, "in all sobriety be regarded as the theory which is favored with the promise of the future" (35-36).

One need not be convinced that every road taken by the nineteenth-century Methodist defenders of the classical view was the right one, nor that all who took the better routes made it all the way to the desired destination. But, even on a casual reading of this literature, one cannot help but be struck both by the facts that the major theologians in the (nineteenth century) Methodist tradition were committed to the classical view *and* that they were very energetic in their defense of it. In conclusion, while we should admit that the story of the movement *away from* the classical account is complex (and a full exploration of it would take us far beyond the parameters of this essay), what is reasonably clear are these facts: first, that the early Wesleyans held to a high view of the inspiration and authority of the Bible and only much later began to distance themselves from it, and second, that it is deeply mistaken to claim that either "fundamentalism" or "Calvinism" was in any way responsible for basic Wesleyan commitments to the traditional doctrine of Scripture. These early Wesleyan proponents of the classical view predate the "fundamentalist controversy" by decades, and the view they held deserves the label "fundamentalist" if and only if the official position of the Roman Catholic Church does as well. Moreover, many of these same proponents are also the most strident and pugnacious of the polemicists against Calvinism. Thus John Wesley claims that if determinism is true (and Jonathan Edwards's defense of it in particular), then "we can no longer maintain that 'all Scripture was given by inspiration of God,' since it is impossible that the God of truth should be the author of palpable falsehoods."[26] Similarly, Thomas Summers (following the lead of Richard Watson) argues that Thomas Paine's rejection of Christianity was at least in large part motivated by his confusion of Christianity with "Calvinism," and in his apology against Paine he admits that it is "very obvious that if this doctrine [the Calvinist doctrine of predestination] be identified with Christianity, Christianity cannot stand in an *age of reason*."[27] But the apologist for the Christian faith need not capitulate here, for "there is no more Calvinism in the Bible than there is popery."[28] Wesleyan defenses of the classical view were hardly the result of influence by "Calvinism" — they are sometimes given by the most pugnacious of Calvinism's critics. In point of fact, in some cases the criticisms of Calvinism and the defense of the classical doctrine of Scripture are interwoven.

A "Wesleyan Quadrilateral"?

These affirmations bring us to a place from which we can make some observations about the authority of Scripture in ongoing discussions of the "Wesleyan Quadrilateral." Although the term was neither coined nor approved by Wesley himself (or any of the other early Methodists — it came from Albert Outler),

26. E.g., John Wesley, "Thoughts upon Necessity," in *Works of John Wesley* (Grand Rapids: Zondervan, n.d.), 10:466-67. See also Randolph Sinks Foster, *Objections to Calvinism as It Is* (Salem, OH: Schmul, 1998), and Thomas N. Ralston, *Elements of Divinity*, 193-327.

27. Thomas O. Summers, "The Theological Works of Thomas Paine," *Quarterly Review of the Methodist Episcopal Church, South* 8 (1854): 485.

28. Summers, "The Theological Works of Thomas Paine," 485.

the "Wesleyan Quadrilateral" is sometimes used to refer to Scripture, Tradition, Reason, and Experience as sources and/or norms of theology.[29] This is not the place to enter into the debates about the future of the notion,[30] but one point should be clear indeed: in any remotely "Wesleyan" sense of a "quadrilateral," the Bible is supreme over all other "sources" or "norms" of theology. Reason is the "candle of the Lord" given to us "to help us appropriate revelation," and Wesley himself never forgot or denigrated the lessons he had learned as an instructor of logic at Oxford, but in no way was it ever understood by Wesley to be equal in authority to the Bible.[31] The broad Christian tradition is an important resource (and even a cursory reading of, say, "An Address to the Clergy" makes plain Wesley's own appreciation of Christian antiquity),[32] but Wesley saw its proper role as the clarification of "those aspects of Scripture that were ambiguous" and the provision of "specific implications of Scripture's general principles."[33] Likewise, he thought that experience (by which he often meant what Maddox refers to as "an external, long-term, communal reality") could confirm or disconfirm an *interpretation* of Scripture, and he wholeheartedly celebrated "experimental religion," but in no way did religious experience ever function as an independent authority alongside Scripture. To the contrary, as Maddox puts it, "its subordination to Scripture was clear."[34] In summary, then, the place of reason, tradition, and experience is "*never* to subordinate or replace Scripture."[35] Maddox is right when he states forthrightly that "Wesley's so-called 'quadrilateral' of theological authorities could more adequately be described as a unilateral *rule* of Scripture within a trilateral *hermeneutic* of reason, tradition, and experience."[36]

29. Outler recognizes that much misunderstanding has come with the employment of this term (and concept), and he has publicly expressed regret that he ever coined the term itself. Albert C. Outler, "The Wesleyan Quadrilateral in John Wesley," *Wesleyan Theological Journal* 20, no. 1 (1985): 16.

30. William J. Abraham is among the strongest critics of the notion of a "Quadrilateral," e.g., *Waking from Doctrinal Amnesia: The Healing of Doctrine in the United Methodist Church* (Nashville: Abingdon, 1995), 56-65.

31. See the discussion by Maddox, *Responsible Grace,* 41, 271. Maddox does not note the Lockean echoes. See further Nicholas Wolterstorff, "John Locke's Epistemological Piety: Reason Is the Candle of the Lord," *Faith and Philosophy* 11 (1994): 572-91.

32. John Wesley, "Address to the Clergy," in *Works of John Wesley,* 10:484, cf. 492.

33. Maddox, *Responsible Grace,* 43.

34. Maddox, *Responsible Grace,* 46.

35. Gunter et al., *Wesley and the Quadrilateral,* 132, emphasis original.

36. Maddox, *Responsible Grace,* p. 46, emphasis original. See also Gunter et al., *Wesley and the Quadrilateral,* 142: "We believe that the Quadrilateral, when defined as 'the rule of Scripture within the trilateral hermeneutic of tradition, reason, and experience,' is a viable way of theologizing for United Methodism." Jones points to a "leader of the United Methodist Church who was quoted in a newspaper article as saying, 'I ran the issue of homosexuality through the

"Wesleyan" Objections to the Classical View: An Engagement

Many of Wesley's theological progeny now reject — and sometimes even vehemently repudiate — the classical account of the nature and authority of the Bible. They do so for many different reasons: some reject the classical account (or important parts thereof) for the same reasons that other Christians do — they say that the classical doctrine is no longer tenable to "modern" people who enjoy the benefits of scientific and historical scholarship, or they strike a "prophetic" stance and claim that "postmodern" concerns unmask the classical view as not only false but also as *dangerously* false.[37] Other Christians in the Wesleyan tradition, however, criticize and reject elements of the classical view because of concerns that are motivated (or at least intensified) by their broadly Wesleyan theological commitments. Thus it is not at all hard to find theologians in various sectors of the Wesleyan theological tradition who say things like "but I'm a Wesleyan, so I'm not committed to *that* view of the Bible" (often being sure to include such adjectives as "wooden," "modern," "fundamentalist," or "naïve" to describe the view being rejected).[38] In this section I take up several of such concerns. Dealing with what I take to be the most common of these criticisms, I argue that in each case these are either based upon misunderstandings or that significant theological resources are available to deal with the problems.

The Dayton Objection (Again)

We may start with what may simply be called "the Dayton Objection." Donald W. Dayton argues that the "Pietist" understanding of the nature of Scripture is very different from — and even at odds with — the "orthodox" or "scholastic" doc-

quadrilateral, and Scripture lost, three to one.'" Jones says that this is nothing less than "an abuse of Wesley's legacy." Jones, "The Rule of Scripture," 42.

37. The rejection of the classical view by other theologians can only charitably be understood as based upon a near-total and disastrous misunderstanding of it, e.g., J. Kenneth Grider, *A Wesleyan Holiness Theology* (Kansas City, MO: Beacon Hill Press, 1995), 63-100. Grider holds to inerrancy in matters of "doctrine and practice," while also inveighing against "total inerrancy." A significant part of his case against "total inerrancy" rests upon the fact that Hebrew and Greek are languages without sufficient precision for inerrancy. He seems not to notice that all human languages have imprecision, nor that it may be his notions of "precision" and accuracy that need reexamination. Moreover, he seems not to notice that if the fact that Greek and Hebrew are not precise enough for inerrancy regarding "non-faith" matters, then neither are they precise enough for "faith and practice." At any rate, how the observation that God used human languages might amount to an objection is far from obvious.

38. The meaning of "wooden" is never defined; reading between the lines, I take it that *woodenness* — whatever it is — is an unpleasant, undesired, and perhaps dangerous quality.

trine, and he insists that the Pietist model is the legitimate but suppressed source for Christians in the Wesleyan traditions (and in evangelicalism more broadly).[39]

At first glance his argument appears to be a strictly historical one. But first appearances can deceive, and on closer inspection Dayton's project cannot reasonably be understood as the result of purely historical research. For he cannot plausibly be arguing that the early Wesleyans understood things as he does — as I have shown, we have ample evidence that they (or at least many of them) wholeheartedly adopted and defended the classical view. What he must be arguing, then, is not that this *is* the historic Wesleyan understanding; rather it is that Wesleyans *should have* seen and *should* see things this way.[40] As I understand him, his basic contention comes to this: since Methodist, holiness, and other Wesleyan-Arminian movements come from Pietism rather than Scholasticism, and since Pietism never endorsed — or even cared much about — the classical accounts of inspiration and authority, contemporary Wesleyans should reject those doctrines as well. His argument may be summarized thusly:

(1) If Wesleyan-Arminian theology comes from Pietism rather than Scholasticism, then contemporary Wesleyan-Arminian theology should affirm only what derives from Pietism and should reject what is characteristic of Scholasticism.
(2) The classical account of biblical inspiration and authority does not derive from Pietism but is characteristic of Scholasticism.
(3) Therefore, contemporary Wesleyan-Arminian theology should reject the classical account of biblical inspiration and authority.

Unfortunately, this argument suffers from two problems, both of them devastating: it has no fewer than two flawed premises. There are good reasons to think that (2) is simply false; John D. Woodbridge has argued that Dayton's interpretation rests upon a misreading of Pietism, and I will not here rehearse his arguments.[41] Instead, let us focus on (1), which is problematic for several reasons. First, it assumes a radical dichotomy between "Pietism" and "Scholasticism." It is problematic because it presupposes that a theological heritage could only derive from *either* Pietism *or* Scholasticism, and it assumes further that Wesleyan-Arminian theology derives from Pietism *rather than* Scholasticism. All of these presuppositions are as important as they are massive.

But none of these assumptions is safe. To the contrary, all are open to

39. E.g., Donald W. Dayton, "The Pietist Theological Critique of Biblical Inerrancy," in *Evangelicals and Scripture: Tradition, Authority, and Hermeneutics,* ed. Vincent Bacote, Laura C. Miguelez, and Dennis L. Ockholm (Downers Grove, IL: InterVarsity, 2004), 76-89.

40. Dayton, "The Pietist Theological Critique of Biblical Inerrancy," 89.

41. See John Woodbridge's contribution to this volume.

question. While I do not deny that the distinctions drawn by historians between "Pietism" and "scholasticism" (or "orthodoxy") are in some ways legitimate and may have some heuristic value, these categories may just as easily mislead if they are taken to be mutually exclusive (or perhaps even "wooden"). The stubborn fact is that there are too many exceptions to such overly tidy categorizations. These exceptions are found on both "sides" of the divide: there are "scholastics" who care deeply about what are allegedly only the concern of the "Pietists" (some of these scholastics predate "Pietism" as a movement) while there are plenty of "Pietists" who show appreciation for and indeed employ the methods of "scholasticism." Examples abound: in the former category we could place the proponents of the Dutch *nadere reformatie;* they are consumed with the desire for personal faith and holiness while also working to produce massive theological treatises that focus upon the Christian life even while exhibiting the "scholastic method." Much the same could be said of many Puritan theologians; John Owen, for example, stands out as an example of someone who was concerned with both precision and piety. On the other "side," it is not at all hard to find theologians who hold to "Wesleyan-Arminian" theology who can only rightly be interpreted as scholastic theologians. Assuming that Arminius might qualify as an Arminian theologian, one need look no further than his discussion of the divine attributes — and his endorsement of the doctrine of *scientia media* in particular — to see that he is a quintessential Protestant scholastic.[42] The same is true of some of the very adherents of Pietism that Dayton views as important: John Wesley himself seems not at all hostile to everything "scholastic,"[43] while some of the major theologians of early Methodism endorse theological proposals drawn from (or at least characteristic of) the dreaded "Schoolmen."[44]

At base, the fundamental and serious problem is this: Dayton takes (1) to be self-evident. But it is not self-evident at all, and he offers no reasons to think that it should be accepted. Instead, he commits something like the mirror image of the genetic fallacy. But if (1) were true (and could be generalized), then we could expect no cross-fertilization between theological traditions, nor could we account for any real development of doctrine that crosses the lines of theological traditions. But I cannot see how this is even plausible — cross-fertilization between religious traditions is very common, as is genuine doctrinal development. To the contrary, Stanley J. Grenz is right when he says that both "Pietism" and

42. On this see Richard A. Muller, *God, Creation, and Providence in the Thought of Jacob Arminius: Sources and Directions of Scholastic Protestantism in the Era of Early Orthodoxy* (Grand Rapids: Baker, 1991).

43. This is strikingly evident in his "Address to the Clergy," in Wesley, *Works of John Wesley,* 10:480-500.

44. See, for example, John Miley's discussion of "middle knowledge," *Systematic Theology,* vol. 1 (New York: The Methodist Book Concern, 1892), 180-93.

"scholasticism" are part of the evangelical heritage. As he puts it, "Being indebted to both trajectories, I find myself unwilling to choose one view of the Bible at the loss of the other. I would contend that the concern with viewing Scripture as the source both of spiritual sustenance and of sound doctrine is not misguided as such, for the purpose of the Bible is to nurture the soul *and* to inform the mind. In fact, the latter is a crucial aspect of the former."[45] At any rate, I think it is safe to conclude that the Dayton Objection (despite Dayton's well-deserved status as a fine historian) has little to commend it as a historical argument — and it has even less going for it as an argument for a constructive theological proposal. It provides no reason whatsoever to reject the classical view.

The Agency Objection

Much more serious for many Wesleyans is what I shall refer to as the "Agency Objection." Here the basic concern is this: the classical doctrine of Scripture fails to do justice to genuine human agency in the authorship of Scripture, and without an adequate account of free human agency there is no place for moral responsibility. At one level, the main motivation seems to be protection of access to the Free Will Defense (FWD). Thus David and Randall Basinger argue that on the assumption that the "dictation theory" of inspiration is false, belief in the verbal, plenary inspiration of an inerrant Bible is impossible for the person who holds to libertarian freedom. As they say in the conclusion of their initial argument, "any person wishing to *both* use the free will defense in his theodicy *and,* at the same time, defend inerrancy against dictation is attempting the impossible."[46] And, of course, since the FWD is not to be surrendered, so much the worse for belief in the verbal, plenary inspiration of an inerrant Bible.[47]

Summarizing their argument well, William Lane Craig states that "the defender of the classical doctrine of inspiration must argue along the following lines:

(4) The words of the Bible are the product of free human activity.
(5) Human activities (such as penning a book) can be totally controlled by God without violating human freedom.
(6) God totally controlled what human authors did in fact write.
(7) Therefore, the words of the Bible are God's utterances.

45. Stanley J. Grenz, "Nurturing the Soul, Informing the Mind: The Genesis of the Evangelical Scripture Principle," in Bacote et al., eds., *Evangelicals and Scripture: Tradition, Authority, and Hermeneutics,* 39.

46. Randall Basinger and David Basinger, "Inerrancy, Dictation and the Free Will Defense," *The Evangelical Quarterly* (1983): 179, emphasis original.

47. Their argument as it stands is directed against *inerrancy,* but by my lights it applies just as much to the doctrine of verbal, plenary inspiration.

(8) Whatever God utters is errorless.
(9) Therefore, the words of the Bible are errorless.[48]

What is wrong with this argument? Why do the Basingers reject the conclusion? The basic concern of the Basingers seems to be that (5) can be true only if we accept compatibilism. But since any affirmation of compatibilism would block access to the FWD, the Christian who holds to the FWD should reject (5) — and with (5) goes the classical doctrine of biblical inspiration and authority.[49] As they conclude, "[T]hose who believe God infallibly guaranteed an inerrant Scripture written freely by humans cannot also utilize the FWD to absolve God of responsibility for evil. They must instead affirm some form of best-of-all-possible-worlds theodicy."[50] Their claim that the proponent of the classical view "must instead affirm some form of best-of-all-possible-worlds theodicy" is unsupported, and I can see no reason to think it might be true (someone who holds to the classical view might adopt yet another theodicy or none at all). But this need not detain us here, for the central point pressed by the Basingers is that the defender of the classical account cannot also hold to the FWD.

I must confess to a great deal of sympathy for the concerns registered by the Basingers. I too think that the FWD is an important aspect of any appropriate theological response to the problems of evil; while it is not all that the Christian can or should say, it is surely part of what the Christian can say about evil. While there is of course a great deal more to say about these complex matters (more than can be said here), even these brief reflections show that the Basingers have raised some important concerns. If theological compatibilism is the only way to account for the classical account of biblical inspiration and authority, then we are faced with a daunting problem. The choice seems clear for those who accept the foregoing account of the divine authorship of the Bible: either abandon the classical account, or embrace theological compatibilism and be prepared to give up any denials that God is the author of sin. But neither option looks attractive.

Fortunately, however, we need not take either way. Craig helpfully observes that, as stated, (5) contains a critical ambiguity. It may be understood as either existentially quantified, thus giving us

(5*) Some human activities (such as penning a book) can be totally controlled by God without violating human freedom

48. William Lane Craig, "'Men Moved by the Holy Spirit Spoke from God' (2 Peter 1:21): A Middle Knowledge Perspective on Biblical Inspiration," *Philosophia Christi* (1999): 64. I have changed the numbers of the premises to follow on from our arguments (1) to (3) above.

49. Again, this is on the assumption that the dictation theory of biblical inspiration is false (an assumption that they take to be a safe one).

50. David Basinger and Randall Basinger, "Inerrancy and Free Will: Some Further Thoughts," *The Evangelical Quarterly* (1986): 354.

or as universally quantified, thus giving us

(5**) All human activities (such as penning a book) can be totally controlled by God without violating human freedom.[51]

As Craig points out, "[T]he Basingers require (5**) for their argument to be sound. But one could maintain that while it was within God's power to control the writing of Scripture without violating human freedom, that does not imply that God can so control human activity in general that no one ever freely does evil." Craig then makes this important point: "[I]n order for the classical doctrine of inspiration to be incompatible with the Free Will Defense, (5) must be taken as universally quantified rather than as existentially quantified. But now a familiar move in the Free Will Defense may be turned against Basinger and Basinger: (5), so understood, is neither necessary or essential to Christian theism nor a logical consequence of propositions that are."[52] His conclusion is appropriate: once we see both that their objection hinges on the adoption of the universal-quantification interpretation and that only the existential-quantification interpretation is needed, we can see that "no incompatibility has been demonstrated between the classical doctrine of inspiration and the Free Will Defense."[53]

To say this much does not, of course, offer much guidance as to how to think about the *process* of inspiration.[54] There are current proposals available to the indeterminist proponent of the classical account: one might adopt Craig's own "middle knowledge" account and thus conclude that "because God knew the relevant counterfactuals of creaturely freedom, He was able to decree a world containing just those circumstances and persons such that the authors of Scripture would freely compose their respective writings, which God intended to be his gracious Word to us."[55] Alternatively, the indeterminist proponent of the classical view could endorse something like the (indeterminist) Thomism offered by Alexander R. Pruss.[56] Both of these approaches require theological (and metaphysical) commitments that are inherently controversial. But neither has, by my lights, been shown to be impossible (or even implausible). And if either way is open, then it is possible to affirm the classical account of the inspiration and authority of Scripture without being forced to embrace theological compatibilism.

51. Craig, "Men Moved by the Holy Spirit," 67.

52. Craig, "Men Moved by the Holy Spirit," 67-68.

53. Craig, "Men Moved by the Holy Spirit," 68.

54. I judge this to be consistent with earlier Wesleyan treatments of the matter.

55. Craig, "Men Moved by the Holy Spirit," 82.

56. Alexander R. Pruss, "Prophecy without Middle Knowledge," *Faith and Philosophy* (2007): 433-47.

The "Formation vs. Information" Objection

Some Christians from the broadly Wesleyan tradition raise concerns from another quarter. The central complaint comes in different packages, but the basic concern seems to be this: Christians should — and Wesleyan Christians generally have — understood Scripture as being concerned with spiritual formation or transformation rather than as a vehicle of information. They protest that we err when we think of Scripture as something that is a repository of information — no matter how "divinely inspired" it might be. We should not, they say, read the Bible to add to our storehouse of "facts" about God and religion; instead we should read the Bible for personal transformation and ecclesial formation.

The work of William J. Abraham stands at the forefront of this protest.[57] Abraham is convinced that the "fundamental problems which arise in treatments of authority in the Christian faith stem from a long-standing misinterpretation of ecclesial canons as epistemic criteria."[58] By "ecclesial canons" he means whatever "comprise[s] materials, persons, and practices officially or semi-officially identified and set apart as a means of grace and salvation by the Christian community. They are represented by such entities as creed, Scripture, liturgy, iconography, the Fathers, and sacraments" (1). Epistemic criteria, on the other hand, "are constituted by norms of justification, rationality, and knowledge. They are represented by such entities as reason, experience, memory, intuition, and inference" (1). Ecclesial canons are "means of grace," and as such they are "akin to medicine designed to heal and restore human flourishing; they are akin to various exercises appointed to reorient the whole of human existence to its proper goal" (1; cf. 27). But epistemic criteria "belong to a very different arena," one where "norms or criteria generally arise out of puzzlement about gaining rationality, justified beliefs, and knowledge" (1). Epistemic norms are not a means of grace; they are better understood as "means of demarcating truth from falsehood, reality from illusion, rationality from irrationality, knowledge from opinion" (1-2). The natural home of ecclesial canons is the church, the community of faith. But the natural home of the epistemic criteria is the philosopher's study or seminar room.

Abraham is convinced that both ecclesial canon and epistemic criteria are important, but he decries the confusion of the two categories. As he tells the story,

> [O]ver a long period of time and due to a great variety of pressures, ecclesial canons, which once served in very diverse ways to initiate one into the life of

57. To be sure, there is a lot more going on in Abraham's work than these issues.

58. William J. Abraham, *Canon and Criterion in Christian Theology: From the Fathers to Feminism* (Oxford: Oxford University Press, 1998), 1. In this section, page references to this work are given in parentheses in the text.

> God, were transformed into epistemological categories . . . canon ceased to be seen as a list of concrete items, such as a list of books to be read in worship, and came to be seen as a criterion of justification in theology. More broadly, Scripture and the tradition of the Church were interpreted as sources of authority. (2)

Abraham is convinced that this migration of the canon to "criterion" produced "devastating consequences for both sets of concepts," for as the materials of which the canon was composed "were transformed into norms of epistemology, they were forced into moulds which warped their original use and purpose." Similarly, discussions of epistemology "were forced into channels which pictured the justification of theological claims in terms of offering sure and certain foundations upon which everything else could be constructed" (2). The effects of this, as Abraham sees things, have been nothing less than lethal for the robust life of the church. Abraham tells a long story about the movement from "canon" to criterion; he laments the fallout of the division between Eastern and Western Christianity, the rise of "theological foundationalism," the disastrous results that came with claims of "sola scriptura," and the noble but flawed attempt at forging an "Anglican *via media*." He argues that the powerful efforts of Enlightenment rationalism and modern liberalism as well as those of the "Princetonians," "Barthians," and revisionists were similarly doomed to failure — not because of lack of ingenuity or effort, but because the entire project was ill-begotten and fundamentally flawed from the outset.

The story as he tells it is interesting and in places very enlightening and provocative. Fortunately, many of the details need not detain us at this point. What is important for our purposes is his central contention that Scripture should be understood and embraced as (on his account, *part of*) the ecclesial canon *rather than* as an epistemic norm, that Scripture serves to initiate people into the life of the community of faith — and thus to transform persons and communities — *rather than* serve to provide information. As he summarizes his project, his aim is "to recover a way of thinking about canon which is soteriological rather than epistemological in outlook, and to pave the way for a fresh approach to the epistemology of theology" (466).

To evaluate Abraham's proposal, we need to disambiguate what he says about "epistemology" and "epistemic criteria." He says that epistemology is concerned with issues of rationality, the justification of belief, and knowledge (e.g., 1). He also says that epistemic criteria are "means of demarcating truth from falsehood, reality from illusion, rationality from irrationality, knowledge from opinion" (1-2). Abraham's analysis and proposal can be — and sometimes are — taken in different ways, and we need to proceed carefully. Perhaps we can usefully distinguish between assertions made as truth claims (which sometimes seem to fall under what he calls "epistemology") and epistemology per se (or "epistemology in the strict philosophical sense"), which is concerned with higher-level reflection and with the more technical discussions that are to be found in philosophical textbooks and classrooms.[59] When we say "the cat is on the mat," we are not offering an epistemological proposal (in the philosophical sense), but we indeed are (or, depending of course on the context, very well *could be*) making truth claims. In other words, statements such as "the cat is on the mat" come nowhere close to epistemology per se, but *they do make claims to "demarcate truth from falsehood [and] reality from illusion."*[60]

Abraham's work is open to various interpretations. Sometimes the focus is on assertions made as truth claims, while in other places the focus is on genuine epistemology. This complicates matters considerably, and makes engagement with his analysis and proposal a bit more challenging. Suppose that we start with the first option (which I think is a possible though much less likely interpretation), and accordingly understand Abraham as being deeply concerned with mere truth claims. If so, then we are to understand that Abraham is exercised to combat the migration of the text of Scripture from an "ecclesial canon" to something "epistemological." In other words, he would be opposed to the very idea that Christians should understand Scripture as a set of truth claims; instead, on this reading of Abraham's proposal, Christians should take Scripture in an exclusively "ecclesial" or formational sense.

But such a story is simply mistaken. The Christian church has always understood itself to be reading Scripture as a set of claims about reality — a set of claims to be the sober truth. The notion that the church began to read Scripture as if it were making claims to truth only with (or after) the Great Schism is hard even to take seriously. If the debates over, say, Arianism show anything, they show that the participants in these debates took with utter seriousness the notion that they were dealing with Scripture as a means of "demarcating truth from falsehood, reality from illusion . . . knowledge from opinion" (2). To think that the participants in these debates were willing to risk persecution and exile for anything less is preposterous. And commitment to the complete authority of the truth claims made in Scripture was so widespread and deep-seated that those on all sides of these debates took it as basic. R. P. C. Hanson even says that both the neo-Arians and their pro-Nicene opponents alike held to the "inerrancy" of the Bible.[61] Surely this is not the proper interpretation of Abraham's proposal.

59. Perhaps the former is not worthy of the honorific title "epistemology," but I use it here because it seems to be operative in some of what Abraham says.

60. The example was offered by Abraham at the Wesleyan Theological Society, 6 March 2010.

61. R. P. C. Hanson, *The Search for the Christian Doctrine of God: The Arian Controversy, 318-381 AD* (Edinburgh: T. & T. Clark, 1988), 825-26. John Chrysostom speaks of the "unerring truth of Scripture" in "Homilies on St. John, LXVIII," *Nicene and Post-Nicene Fathers* (Grand Rapids: Eerdmans), 14:252 (thanks to Alex Pruss for the reference to Chrysostom).

On another reading, Abraham means only to inveigh against reception of Scripture as epistemology per se. If so, then what he is primarily concerned about is the temptation to read the Bible as if it were a treatise on epistemology. If this is Abraham's target, then it surely is — or would be — a worthy one. For to do so would be to set ourselves up for failure in epistemological endeavors, because the Bible as such simply is not concerned with the familiar problems of perception, warrant, justification, and the like. Much worse, we would easily miss the importance of the content of Scripture if we were to read it this way.[62] To trawl through the Gospels looking for arguments for the right view of epistemic justification, or to read the Prophets to find the right account of perception, would not only be a dead end — it could also easily cause us to miss the *Sache* of Scripture. Again, if this is Abraham's target, then it surely is — or *would be* — a worthy one.

Would be? Unfortunately, however, there is a bit less here than meets the eye. This is not how Christians have traditionally read Scripture. More modestly, at least, Abraham's long and fascinating narrative fails to demonstrate that any of the major traditions under his microscope have done this. He does not, so far as I can see, succeed in showing that Christians were unsuccessful in attempting such an appropriation of Scripture. I agree with Abraham that such attempts would have been doomed to failure, but I don't see that he has shown that we have evidence of such failure. Why not? Because he does not present us with evidence that any of these major movements actually *tried* to do so. The various movements that feature in his narrative (at least many of them) surely are concerned with claims to the *truth* of the Christian faith, and Abraham is right to point out both that the strategies for ascertaining and defending this truth vary widely and in many cases must be judged finally to have failed. But he has not shown that any of them in fact *were* concerned with understanding the Bible as a handbook of epistemology. This would not be beating a dead horse — it would be flailing away at one that shares ontological status with *The Black Stallion, Smoky the Cow Horse,* and other fictive creatures of equine lore.

But surely there is a better way to understand Abraham. He says that his "aim" is "to recover a way of thinking about canon which is soteriological rather than epistemological."[63] Fortunately, however, he goes on to say that he wants to "pave the way for a fresh approach to the epistemology of theology."[64] I do not think that he means "rather than" in any kind of strict sense. He is happy to point out that "the canonical material itself clearly raised epistemological questions,"

62. This point is brought home forcefully by Nicholas Wolterstorff, "True Words," in *But Is It True? The Bible and the Question of Truth,* ed. Alan G. Padgett and Patrick R. Keifert (Grand Rapids: Eerdmans, 2006), 34-43.

63. Abraham, *Canon and Criterion,* 466.

64. Abraham, *Canon and Criterion,* 466. He issues a "promissory note" on p. 35; I take his *Crossing the Threshold of Divine Revelation* (Grand Rapids: Eerdmans, 2006) as an extension of the mortgage.

and he goes on to say that "the canonical material itself clearly contains epistemological suggestions and proposals."[65] I agree; indeed I think that the canonical material itself raises such questions and offers such suggestions in actual epistemology by staking such truth claims. In other words, the canonical materials (understood either more traditionally as the canon of Scripture or in Abraham's broader sense of canon) raise concerns and invite reflection on epistemological matters precisely by making truth claims.

If I am correct in understanding Abraham to mean that Scripture is primarily formational rather than informational, if he intends to say that Scripture is given for soteriological purposes rather than to give us a storehouse of facts about God and creatures or to inform us about theories of how we might have knowledge of God and creatures, then he is expressing a concern that should resonate deeply within the hearts of Wesleyan Christians (as well, of course, as others). In this case he is, in my judgment, exactly right. But this in no way entails that if we would only recover the view of the early church (on Abraham's account, before the "Great Schism") we would reject the notion that Scripture is concerned with epistemological issues (in the broad sense). For the early Christians themselves, there is no other legitimate way to read Scripture than as a set of truth claims. Scripture is given to make us "wise unto salvation" (2 Tim. 3:15) — and not to satisfy our curiosity — but it does so by claiming to be the truth about that of which it speaks. To borrow the language of speech-act theory, God may perform *many* actions by revelatory communication; he may command, invite, implore, warn, chasten, curse, forgive, bless, and cleanse (and much more) as well as inform. But this amazing and gracious surplus of speech-activity in no way implies that God does *not* inform through Scripture. As David K. Clark points out, "the informational and the transformational functions of Scripture reinforce each other: Reading the Bible is the occasion for transformation as the spiritual power of the Triune God flows into the lives of individual people, spiritual communities, and whole cultures. Scripture as information opens a window to the reality of the Triune God, who acts transformationally."[66] There simply is no good reason to think that it must be information *rather than* transformation, or that "ecclesial canons" are "means of grace" *rather than* claims to truth.

Recall Abraham's analogy for "ecclesial canons" as "means of grace": "they are akin to medicine designed to heal and restore human flourishing; they are akin to various exercises appointed to reorient the whole of human existence to its proper goal."[67] I think that this is a helpful analogy. But consider it further:

65. Abraham, *Canon and Criterion,* 469.

66. David K. Clark, "Beyond Inerrancy: Speech Acts and an Evangelical View of Scripture," in *For Faith and Clarity: Philosophical Contributions to Christian Theology,* ed. James K. Beilby (Grand Rapids: Baker Academic, 2006), 126.

67. Abraham, *Canon and Criterion,* 1.

physicians make unmistakable truth claims whenever they prescribe such medications in good faith, and patients make unavoidable epistemological judgments when they trust the knowledge and good will of the attending physician. The physicians — at least not all of them — need not be schooled in formal study in epistemology. In point of fact, it seems that it generally will be better for a patient if the physician cares more about the patient's health than about her own interests in, say, puzzles about perception or theories of epistemic justification. But make no mistake: the physicians *are* making truth claims. And they — as well as their patients — know that these claims *matter.* The physicians as well as the patients trust that the prescribed medicine will heal the diseased and bring comfort to the miserable. They do so because they trust the prescription — and they do so ultimately because they place trust in the author of it.

The Christian who receives and trusts the canonical truth claims of Scripture is in a similar position. Such a Christian need not — and indeed should not — read the Bible as if it were intended as a textbook of epistemology. Instead, she should receive it as a gift offered "so that we might believe, and believing have eternal life" (John 20:31). But she cannot believe *this* unless she believes that *this* is true — and she will ultimately place her trust in such truth claims because she believes that the author of those claims is trustworthy.

In conclusion, we can see that Abraham's thesis, despite the fact that it is open to several unfortunate (mis)interpretations, raises some legitimate and important concerns. In this respect it is similar to the concerns raised by the Basingers. But in this case — as well as that of the Basingers — such concerns provide no compelling reason to abandon the classical view.

Conclusion

To this point I have argued that early Wesleyan theologians held close to what I've termed the "classical" account of the authority of Scripture. I have also addressed several distinctly "Wesleyan" objections to that account, and here I have made a case that while there are some legitimate concerns in the neighborhood (of some of those objections), they do not provide Wesleyans with good reasons for abandoning the classical view.

In conclusion, however, I wish to suggest that Wesleyans — of all Christians — have good theological reason to endorse the classical account. Wesleyan Christians place special emphasis upon God's goodness: God is supremely benevolent and all-loving, God is pure and holy, God is simply *good.* God does not desire that any of his human creatures be lost, and God does not intend to mislead or misdirect when he communicates with his creatures. This means that God is utterly trustworthy and ultimately reliable. Thus it is, for Wesleyan Christians as well as many others, simply unthinkable that God would mislead those creatures made in his image and made to share in the glory of his own triune life. Furthermore, Wesleyan Christians have placed special emphasis (too much emphasis, critics would contend) upon God's ability radically to transform the human will so that it is in genuine and complete accord with God's own. Given God's utter goodness and truthfulness, to suggest that God *would not* or *could not* communicate truthfully is wildly and radically implausible for Wesleyan Christians. And to suggest that God *would not* or *could not* so transform the human person so as to conform the human will to the divine is again to deny the radical optimism about grace that has always characterized the Wesleyan theological tradition. As Paul Merritt Bassett puts it, the "center of holiness theological logic" is this: "not the enlightenment of the saints but the love of the Holy One."[68] Perhaps what is needed most for a recovery of the classical *Wesleyan* account of Scripture is not endless wrangling over the *process* of inspiration but instead is a recovery of an adequate doctrine of sanctification: *the Holy triune God giving Holy Scripture as a means of grace whereby the Holy Spirit transforms sinners into truly holy persons by uniting them to the incarnate Son.*

68. Paul Merritt Bassett, "The Theological Identity of the North American Holiness Movement: Its Understanding of the Nature and Role of the Bible," in *The Variety of American Evangelicalism,* ed. Donald W. Dayton and Robert K. Johnston (Downers Grove, IL: InterVarsity, 1991), 95.

SEVEN

The "Old Princetonians" on Biblical Authority

Bradley N. Seeman

In 1815, Harvard sent Edward Everett, its young, newly minted Professor of Greek Literature, off to Germany to study with the renowned biblical critic Johann Gottfried Eichhorn. Everett (1794-1865) grew up among the Unitarian "Boston Brahmins" of the early decades of the American republic, and the precocious youth had attracted the attention of some powerful people on his way to graduating at the head of the class of 1811. Harvard's president, John Thornton Kirkland, soon began encouraging Everett to enter the ministry, and invited him to live in the president's house. The president's high opinion of Everett was shared by the Reverend Joseph Stevens Buckminster, who had been appointed Dexter Lecturer in the wake of the Unitarian takeover of Harvard in 1805.[1] Together, Reverend Buckminster and President Kirkland urged the promising young man to complete his studies in Germany, where he could imbibe the latest German biblical scholarship. There, it was hoped, Everett would learn to use tools that could be employed "both destructively, as a means of purging religion of the distorted metaphysical theology of the Calvinists, and constructively, as a means of re-establishing the pure and reasonable Christianity of the Gospels."[2]

Everett became the first American to earn a German doctorate, and many followed his path.[3] But upon returning from Germany in 1820, he was not quite

1. See Daniel Walker Howe, *The Unitarian Conscience: Harvard Moral Philosophy, 1805-1861* (Cambridge, MA: Harvard University Press, 1970), 4-12. Howe also details the strong influence of Common Sense Realism on Unitarian thought.

2. Jerry Wayne Brown, *The Rise of Biblical Criticism in America, 1800-1870: The New England Scholars* (Middletown, CT: Wesleyan University Press, 1969), 41. The picture of Everett in this paragraph draws heavily from Brown's account. Also helpful was Paul A. Varg, *Edward Everett: The Intellectual in the Turmoil of Politics* (Selinsgrove, PA: Susquehanna University Press, 1992).

3. Beginning with Everett down to 1920, almost 9,000 students from the United States studied in Germany. See Jürgen Herbst, *The German Historical School in American Scholarship* (Ithaca, NY: Cornell University Press, 1965) as quoted in Brown, *The Rise of Biblical Criticism*

what the gentlemen of Harvard were hoping for. The acids of German scholarship that were to dissolve orthodoxy also ate away Everett's Unitarian liberalism. As he put it in a letter to his brother:

> If I am let alone, I shall trouble nobody's faith or peace, but if I am not, I will do what has never yet been done, — exhibit those views of the subject of Christianity, which the modern historical and critical enquiries fully establish, stripped of the palavar with which the Professors here avail themselves, to appease the public clamour, and also unincumbered with the scandals of the French Philosophers. A sort of work, against which I can imagine no defence, except the very suspicious one of denying the premises.[4]

Everett decided to trouble nobody's faith (though he made a strong impression on the young Ralph Waldo Emerson before leaving Harvard in 1825), and pursued a career in politics.[5]

A short time later, in October 1826, the young Charles Hodge (1797-1878) of Princeton Seminary left his wife and two young children and boarded a ship for Germany, where he would interact with leading German scholars, including Friedrich Schleiermacher. Like Everett, Hodge went because the successful discharge of his duties as a professor required "access to those richly furnished libraries and those eminently skilled and profound masters of Oriental Literature of whose assistance he cannot avail himself in his present situation."[6] Also like Everett, Hodge had attracted the attention of some well-placed people, including Archibald Alexander (1772-1851), the professor around whom the recently estab-

---

in America, 38. Mark A. Noll, *America's God: From Jonathan Edwards to Abraham Lincoln* (New York: Oxford University Press, 2002), 255, also notes this rising German influence on theologians in the United States.

4. Edward Everett to Alexander H. Everett, 5 January 1816; from the Everett Papers in the Massachusetts Historical Society Library, with portions on microfilm in the Princeton University Library. Cited in Brown, *The Rise of Biblical Criticism in America,* 41. The punctuation and spellings of the words are left as cited in Brown. In his journal from his time in Europe, Everett expressed sentiments about the Bible that would have departed from aspects of Harvard's polite Unitarian rationalism: "[I]t is the last book that ought to be used, as an instrument of improving Barbarian natives" (microfilm edition of the Everett Papers, Michigan State University, Reel 30, Folder 132); quoted in Varg, *Edward Everett,* 22.

5. Everett not only influenced Emerson as his minister and, later, as his professor at Harvard, he also edited the *North American Review* from 1820 to 1824, contributing sixty-one pieces during that time. Noted historian of American literature Harry Hayden Clark observes that Emerson "could have found practically all of his early transcendental and romantic ideas in the pages of the *Review*" ("Literary Criticism in the *North American Review,*" *Wisconsin Academy of Sciences, Arts, and Letters* 31 [1939]: 299-300; quoted in Varg, *Edward Everett,* 27).

6. Letter to the Board of Directors of Princeton, 25 September 1826; cited in Alexander A. Hodge, *The Life of Charles Hodge* (New York: Arno Press & The New York Times, 1969), 102.

lished Princeton Seminary was being built. But a crucial difference set Hodge apart from Everett, one that emerges clearly in Hodge's correspondence. Thus we find Dr. Alexander writing to Hodge in Germany:

> My Dear Sir: — . . . I hope while you are separated from your earthly friends, you will take care to keep the communication open! Remember that you breathe a poisoned atmosphere. If you lose the lively and deep impression of divine truth — if you fall into skepticism or even into coldness, you will lose more than you gain from all the German professors and libraries. May the Lord preserve you from error and from all evil. You may depend upon any aid which my feeble prayers can afford. Write as often as you can. Do not be afraid of troubling me. Affectionately, yours.[7]

While those at Harvard sent Everett hoping he would find a sharp instrument for destroying a reviled orthodox Christianity, those who sent Hodge followed him with prayers that he would return both deepened in his warm evangelical faith and equipped to sift through the new German scholarship, learn from it, and respond wherever it threatened to overturn something that had always been dear to Christians: the ability to receive the Bible as God's written Word. When Hodge returned to Princeton September 18th, 1828, he set out on a remarkably energetic and productive career of responding to the new intellectual and spiritual challenges facing the church — challenges that were deeply influenced by the recent developments in German philosophy and biblical criticism.

Hodge and Everett were caught up in a tumultuous time that shaped American religion and education. As American scholarship was reawakening and looking eagerly again to Europe after the upheaval of the Revolutionary War and the political ferment that followed, the theologians and biblical scholars of the rapidly growing seminary movement were all aware that something both new and momentous was going on in German biblical scholarship.[8] Unitarians almost instinctively sensed a potential ally in their attempts to throw off Trinitarian and Calvinist theological accretions that obscured a pure, rational religion they hoped to salvage from Scripture.[9] Here was a revolution that could be pressed into ser-

7. Letter from Archibald Alexander to Charles Hodge, 24 March 1827; cited in Alexander A. Hodge, *The Life of Charles Hodge,* 102.

8. On the prominent place of seminaries in the rapid development of American education, see Noll, *America's God,* 254.

9. It should be noted that Unitarians varied in the credence they gave German biblical criticism and theology. Andrews Norton, for example, was somewhat tepid in his reception of German scholarship, at least with respect to the Gospels (Brown, *The Rise of Biblical Criticism in America,* 81-93). Norton warmed more to criticism of the Old Testament, which he regarded as "imbedded in myth, worthless liturgy, and inauthentic history" (Brown, *The Rise of Biblical Criticism in America,* 93). At the same time Norton caught flack for not going far

vice for their ongoing theological battles. Orthodox Christians also understood that in their day a new and vigorous challenge to the church's faith was being forged: the humanity and historical genesis of the Bible were being emphasized to the point where they jeopardized the church's normative receptivity to God in the words of Scripture.

Today we continue to swim in some of the same currents in which these older scholars swam. There are those who instinctively jump into the same broad stream of scholarship Everett and Hodge jumped into with the hopes that it will prove useful in undermining things they would like to see undermined. Thus Gary Dorrien, in an aggressively apologetic book, issues a warning to evangelical Christians:

> If evangelicalism is to become something more than fundamentalism with good manners, however, it must become clearly distinguished from fundamentalism in its approach to core theological issues, especially concerning the nature and authority of scripture. Without a clear difference of kind with regard to theological authority, there is no such thing as evangelicalism. Evangelicalism cannot seek merely to repristinate the theologies of Luther or Calvin, but no such thing as evangelicalism can exist if evangelicals do not make a clean break with scholasticist and fundamentalist notions about what it means to affirm "the Reformation doctrine of the final authority of scripture."[10]

Other scholars, no less aware of and versed in the kind of scholarship that impresses Dorrien, seek to learn from that scholarship and then reaffirm in a new context the integrity of what the church of Jesus Christ understood from the earliest times.

> In reading the Bible as a unified canon, however, we are not only engaging Scripture and its human authors; we are engaging — and being engaged by — God. God is ultimately the one responsible for the way in which the various books of the Bible cohere. The canon is a *divine command performance;* stated differently, *God is the ultimate agent of canonical discourse.*[11]

---

enough with his critical views. For a fascinating look at the criticism Norton received for defending Jesus' miracles and for remarks critical of Spinoza and Schleiermacher, see Charles Hodge, "The Latest Form of Infidelity," *The Biblical Repertory and Princeton Review* 12, no. 1 (January 1840): 39ff.

10. Gary Dorrien, *The Remaking of Evangelical Theology* (Louisville: Westminster John Knox, 1998), 9; grammar and wording as in the original.

11. Kevin J. Vanhoozer, *The Drama of Doctrine: A Canonical-Linguistic Approach to Christian Theology* (Louisville: Westminster John Knox, 2005), 178; emphasis in original.

Moreover, as in Hodge's day, a host of variations play out around the two basic tendencies, each seeking a loosening or a reaffirmation of classical Christian teachings and practices in various ways and at different points.

In the last forty years or so, an increasing number of scholars at different points along the theological spectrum have found it useful to argue that when Charles Hodge and other "Old Princetonians" sought to defend what they understood to be classic Christian teaching about the authority of Scripture, they ended up being theological innovators who unwittingly birthed a novel doctrine called "inerrancy" that substantially modified the church's historic understanding of biblical authority. Stanley Grenz puts the charge this way: "In holding to their understanding of the nature of inspiration and biblical authority, the Princeton theologians claimed the legacy of Reformation theology. Nevertheless, their articulation of the doctrine marked a significant innovation from that of many of the seventeenth century scholastics."[12] Against this recent argument — call it the

12. Stanley J. Grenz, *Renewing the Center: Evangelical Theology in a Post-Theological Era* (Grand Rapids: Baker, 2000), 75. Some lines of the historiography trace back at least as far as Charles A. Briggs, *Whither? A Theological Question for the Times* (New York: Charles Scribner's Sons, 1889), and substantial impetus was given by neo-orthodox scholars, including Sydney Ahlstrom, "The Scottish Philosophy and American Theology," *Church History* 24, no. 3 (September 1955): 257-72; and J. K. S. Reid, *The Authority of Scripture: A Study of the Reformation and Post-Reformation Understanding of the Bible* (London: Methuen, 1957). Ernest Sandeen also contributed substantially to the contemporary prominence of the historiography. See Ernest R. Sandeen, "The Princeton Theology: One Source of Biblical Literalism in American Protestantism," *Church History* 31, no. 3 (September 1962): 307-21. Among the most aggressive formulations of this kind of argument are Jack Rogers and Donald McKim, *The Authority and Interpretation of the Bible: An Historical Approach* (New York: Harper & Row, 1979), and Dorrien, *Remaking Evangelical Theology.* Stanley Grenz has also leaned heavily on a slightly chastened version of the argument, in Stanley J. Grenz, *Renewing the Center;* Grenz, *Revisioning Evangelical Theology: A Fresh Agenda for the 21st Century* (Downers Grove, IL: InterVarsity, 1993); and Grenz and John R. Franke, *Beyond Foundationalism: Shaping Theology in a Postmodern Context* (Louisville: Westminster John Knox, 2001). This pattern of argumentation also appears in Nancey Murphy, *Anglo-American Postmodernity: Philosophical Perspectives on Science, Religion, and Ethics* (Boulder, CO: Westview, 1997); Murphy, *Beyond Liberalism and Fundamentalism: How Modern and Postmodern Philosophy Set the Theological Agenda* (Harrisburg, PA: Trinity Press International, 1996); A. T. B. McGowan, *The Divine Authenticity of Scripture: Retrieving an Evangelical Heritage* (Downers Grove, IL: InterVarsity, 2007); Carl Raschke, *The Next Reformation: Why Evangelicals Must Embrace Postmodernity* (Grand Rapids: Baker Academic, 2004); and many of the contributors to John W. Stewart and James H. Moorhead, eds., *Charles Hodge Revisited: A Critical Appraisal of His Life and Work* (Grand Rapids: Eerdmans, 2002). In *America's God,* Mark Noll advances the argument in a more moderate form than is found in his earlier work. See also George M. Marsden, *Fundamentalism and American Culture: The Shaping of Twentieth Century Evangelicalism, 1870-1925* (New York: Oxford University Press, 1980); Marsden's work strongly influences various popular works, such as Karen Armstrong, *The Battle for God* (New York: Alfred A. Knopf, 2000).

"Innovation Argument" — it will be argued here that Hodge and the other "Old Princetonians" were doing substantially what they understood themselves to be doing, namely, reaffirming a classically Christian understanding of the authority of Scripture in the face of a new and vigorous intellectual challenge.

The burden of the current argument does not involve defending every point of the theological method of the Old Princetonians, nor does it involve arguing that the Princetonians remained untouched by the philosophical and scientific currents of their day, such as Scottish common sense realism and a "Baconian" view of induction. To be clear: the theological method of the Princetonians had flaws, and they were influenced to some degree by the vocabulary of the intellectual movements of their day. "The surprise," notes Mark Noll, speaking of Charles Hodge, "is not that an ambitious individual who wanted his ideas to count used that vocabulary, but that in using it Hodge maintained as well as he did the integrity of pre-Revolutionary Calvinism."[13] This integrity included the vigorous reaffirmation of the church's historic recognition that "all Scripture is God-breathed" (2 Tim. 3:16) through a process in which "men spoke from God as they were carried along by the Holy Spirit" (2 Pet. 1:21) so that Scripture is without error in whatever it truly affirms.[14] The vocabulary the Princetonians used in reaffirming this historic teaching can grate on us today, and it may have led to misapplications of that historic understanding of biblical authority and perhaps to underestimates of the hermeneutical challenges attending the various literary genres in Scripture. In this they faced the same challenges and temptations every age of the church has faced — including, notably, our own. But the vocabulary of the day did not lead the Princetonians to substantial departures from the church's understanding of the authority of Scripture. Instead we see remarkable fidelity to historic church teaching, and a vibrant, careful reaffirmation of that teaching called out by the first sustained, formidable challenge to what the church had always held. Given the nature of the challenge they faced, their clarification and formulation of the doctrine was — unsurprisingly — more crisp and nuanced than it had been in earlier eras where the doctrine had not been challenged. How could it be otherwise, given the nature of the challenge? But the Princeton teaching on biblical authority spoke in one accord with the teaching of the orthodox church from the patristics, through the Reformation (and the Roman Catholic Church they sought to reform), down to their own day.

The case against the Innovation Argument will be advanced in the first two sections of this essay by briefly canvassing the challenge of the new biblical criticism that attained its mature voice during Hodge's lifetime, and then giving a

13. Mark A. Noll, "Charles Hodge as an Expositor of the Spiritual Life," in Stewart and Moorhead, eds., *Charles Hodge Revisited,* 215.

14. See especially the essays by Hill, Helm, Jensen, Cole, Blocher, and Vanhoozer in this collection.

bibliographically heavy reminder of the degree to which this was a challenge to the classic Christian understanding of biblical authority. With these reminders in place, the third and central portion of the paper will consider what the Princetonians actually wrote on the topic, focusing especially on the many articles they wrote for the *Princeton Review* that Charles Hodge edited from 1825 to 1871. Some scholars who advance the Innovation Argument recycle one or two tired passages from Hodge's "Introduction" to his *Systematic Theology* and then attach a QED to the passages. But Hodge was only the most prominent member of a tight-knit community of highly competent Christian scholars, and the *Systematic Theology* was only an impressive work near the conclusion of a life of vibrant scholarly engagement. Moreover, as Mark Noll has noted,

> the most impressive Reformed theology in nineteenth-century America — a theology pithy and profound on the cardinal tenets of the faith, expanding provocatively to encompass both recondite academic discussions and the practical problems of the church, manifesting a consistent synthesis of learning charged with piety and piety infused with learning — was not Charles Hodge's *Systematic Theology* of 1872/3. It was rather the "systematic theology" that Charles Hodge scattered serially, with profligate Christian brilliance, in the pages of the *Princeton Review.* But because of its form, that more compelling "systematics" remains unread, while those who know Hodge at all read him in the sturdy, edifying, thoughtful, but still somewhat paler pages of his formal *Systematic Theology.*[15]

The pages of the *Princeton Review* will thus feature prominently in what follows, displaying a more finely grained picture of the challenges to which the Princetonians were responding and their ways of reaffirming, clarifying, and sharpening historic orthodox understandings of the nature of biblical authority. The method-

15. Mark A. Noll, "The Princeton Review," *Westminster Theological Journal* 50 (1988): 302; see also Noll, "Charles Hodge as an Expositor of the Spiritual Life," 207-8. John Stewart notes that the *Princeton Review* "is unquestionably the best source for contemporary scholars to measure the depth and range of Hodge's thought and influence" ("Introducing Charles Hodge to Postmoderns," in Stewart and Moorhead, eds., *Charles Hodge Revisited,* 6). Neglect of the *Princeton Review* significantly weakens much of the secondary literature, which, for example, frequently passes over what Stewart called Hodge's "most complete argument" (21) on the question of biblical authority, namely his essay "Inspiration" (*The Biblical Repertory and Princeton Review* 29, no. 4 [October 1857]: 660-98). Among the prominent exceptions to this neglect of the *Princeton Review* are Mark Noll's work and the essays in *Charles Hodge Revisited,* along with the work of scholars like Andrew Hoffecker, *Piety and the Princeton Theologians* (Grand Rapids: Baker, 1981) and Paul Kjoss Helseth, *"Right Reason" and the Princeton Mind: An Unorthodox Proposal* (Phillipsburg, NJ: P&R, 2010). Electronic reproductions of the *Princeton Review* are available at http://moa.umdl.umich.edu/moa_browse.html.

ology here will be (1) to display how the challenges facing the Princetonians were *departures* from classical Christian teachings, and (2) to show how the Princetonians responded by *reaffirming and sharpening* how the church understood its central moment of receptivity to God in his Holy Scriptures, giving special attention to assertions to the contrary advanced by contemporary advocates of the Innovation Argument, where appropriate. It should also be noted that the essay will focus mostly on the earlier Princetonians, bringing in important later scholars like Archibald Alexander Hodge and Benjamin Breckinridge Warfield only to show the continuity of their thought with those who preceded them. Most of the weight of the Innovation Argument falls on Archibald Alexander and, particularly, Charles Hodge and his generation, so we must attend to their work most closely. It is also worth noting that in his 1888 inaugural lecture at Princeton, B. B. Warfield avowed his continuity with Hodge: "though the power of Charles Hodge may not be upon me, the theology of Charles Hodge is within me."[16] After making the argument that the Princetonians were not theological innovators in their reaffirmation of the classic understanding of biblical authority, the conclusion considers some issues raised by contemporary use of the Innovation Argument.

As the argument of the following pages unfolds, it will be important to bear in mind the whole point of the doctrine of the authority of Holy Scripture. Perhaps it is best to put the point in terms of a "dramatic" understanding of doctrine that reminds us of how all of this meets up with life.[17] Some worry that the Princetonians advanced a view of biblical authority that "actually undermines the authority of the Scriptures" by making them into congeries of propositions for the theologian to "arrange and exhibit," leaving us with "something cold and clinical, which *we* possess and which *we* manipulate."[18] This is an understandable worry; we certainly don't want bloodless systematic theologies usurping the place that belongs to Scripture. Mere human constructions don't deserve that place. But of course *any* understanding of Scripture will be a human construct involving propositions. So, perhaps the understanding that Scripture is without error in whatever it truly affirms serves precisely as a *safeguard* against our tendency to seek a knowledge of God that we can manipulate. *These words are from God,* and whatever understanding of them we come up with must continually check itself against them, and *whatever propositions we (inevitably) affirm must answer to those words.* None of them can be set aside as being mistaken or in error; these

16. Benjamin Breckinridge Warfield, *The Idea of Systematic Theology Considered as a Science* (New York: Anson Randolph & Co., 1888), 5-6. It is interesting to note that several proponents of the Innovation Argument use this passage to link Warfield to Hodge. See Dorrien, *The Remaking of Evangelical Theology,* 26; and Rogers and McKim, *The Authority and Interpretation of the Bible,* 326.

17. For helpful explication of a dramatic understanding of doctrine, see Vanhoozer, *The Drama of Doctrine.*

18. McGowan, *The Divine Authenticity of Scripture,* 116-17.

words are "breathed out" by God, and faithful, painstaking exegesis of them is the lifeblood of theology. Speaking thus of the authority of the Holy Scripture reminds us that Scripture is our central and normative point of *receptivity* to God, and once all the serious hermeneutic and exegetical work has been done as well and as prayerfully as we can, we understand that *these words are God's words,* breathed out by him and without error in whatever they affirm; they are intended by him as he inspired and took up the words of the human authors such that in Scripture *God himself gives* us the world we are to inhabit. We cease caviling and seek the Spirit's abundant and loving redemptive grace to bring our lives into line with all that Scripture teaches. We rejoice in the promises; we seek to submit to all God's commands even where they call us to difficult things about our time, money, sexuality, our ways of being with others, and the sins we cherish; we carefully and lovingly investigate the implications for every area of life. In short, the church has recognized a central moment of *canonical receptivity* that gives hope that a *human spontaneity* deeply marred by sin and prone to idolatry of all sorts may yet hear God and respond to him when quickened by his Spirit.[19]

It is the historic understanding of *canonical receptivity* expressed in the church's understanding of *biblical authority* that the Princeton teaching on inerrancy reaffirmed in the face of challenges that threatened to hollow out that moment of receptivity, leaving sinful *human spontaneity* in its place. This elevation of human spontaneity over canonical receptivity comes to fruition in myriad variations of an idea stated by Wilfred Cantwell Smith: "Scripture has been . . . a human activity: it has been also a human propensity, a potentiality. There is no ontology of scripture"; rather, Scripture and other human activities "are subsections of the ontology of our being persons."[20] With only the noxious air of human constructions to breathe, theology withers. Like the church today, the Princetonians had to "resist the subordination of Holy Scripture to cultural poetics."[21] Or, as Charles Hodge put it, in the vocabulary of his own day, it was "subversive of the authority of the Scriptures" to hold that since its teachings "are really the product of the human mind, more or less under the influence of personal or national prejudices, we may receive or reject the teachings of the Bible, according as they agree

19. The language of receptivity and spontaneity goes back at least as far as a fundamental tension running through the work of Kant. See Immanuel Kant, *The Critique of Pure Reason,* trans. Paul Guyer and Allen W. Wood (New York: Cambridge University Press, 1998), A51/B75 (p. 193). This language helpfully captures a central philosophical tension facing Kant, and has been taken up by Vanhoozer, *The Drama of Doctrine,* and John Webster, "The Human Person," in *The Cambridge Companion to Postmodern Theology,* ed. Kevin J. Vanhoozer (Cambridge: Cambridge University Press, 2003).

20. Wilfred Cantwell Smith, *What Is Scripture? A Comparative Approach* (London: SCM, 1993), 237; quoted in John Webster, *Holy Scripture: A Dogmatic Sketch* (Cambridge: Cambridge University Press, 2003), 7.

21. Webster, *Holy Scripture,* 2.

or disagree with the teachings of our own inward life."[22] The Princetonians thus undertook to reaffirm the church's historic understanding of canonical receptivity against determined attempts to install human spontaneity at the heart of religion. It is small wonder that they met with determined opposition.

The Challenge to Canonical Receptivity

When Charles Hodge entered into the German academic scene in 1826, he encountered a world where much that he understood about the Bible already faced well-developed academic challenges. 1826 was also the year Ferdinand Christian Baur (1792-1860) assumed the chair of Church History and Dogmatics at Tübingen, a chair from which he would initiate what would come to be known as the "Tübingen School" of biblical criticism — perhaps the most influential critical voice in the nineteenth century. Nearly twenty years earlier, Wilhelm Martin Leberecht de Wette (1780-1849), styled by some as "the founder of modern critical Old Testament scholarship," had published his groundbreaking *Contributions to Old Testament Introduction* (1806-7).[23] Indeed, Thomas Hobbes's (1588-1679) *Leviathan* of 1651, Baruch Spinoza's (1632-1677) *Tractatus theologico-politicus* of 1670, Richard Simon's (1638-1712) *A Critical History of the Old Testament* of 1677, Johann Salomo Semler's (1725-1791) *Free Research on the Canon* of 1771-75, and the works of many other scholars had long since begun to establish a line of inquiry.[24] But in the late eighteenth and early nineteenth centuries the line of in-

22. Charles Hodge, "Inspiration," *The Biblical Repertory and Princeton Review* 29, no. 4 (October 1857): 698.

23. Gerald Bray, *Biblical Interpretation: Past and Present* (Downers Grove, IL: InterVarsity, 1996), 276. Bray is reporting what others have said, not advancing a thesis. Indeed, advancing candidates for *the* "father of biblical criticism" is a difficult and perhaps fruitless endeavor, for there are many important developments along the way, going back at least as far as Baruch Spinoza's *Tractatus theologico-politicus* of 1670. Indeed, in John Barton, *The Nature of Biblical Criticism* (Louisville: Westminster John Knox, 2007), chapter 5, an argument is advanced that "biblical criticism as we now know it genuinely does go back to the remote past" (132), extending past the Reformation and Renaissance back to Jerome and to Julius Africanus's letter to Origen. However, arguing that Jerome, for example, had any sense of "biblical criticism as we now know it" involves stretching biblical criticism "as we know it" well past the breaking point. But the point is made: There is probably no clear line to be drawn.

24. For helpful sketches of some of the earliest work that began initiating biblical criticism, see Bray, *Biblical Interpretation,* chapter 6, "The Beginning of the Historical-Critical Method." For a helpful consideration of the influence of the French biblical critic, Richard Simon, on early German biblical criticism, see John D. Woodbridge, "German Responses to the Biblical Critic Richard Simon: From Leibniz to J. S. Semler," in *Historische Kritik und biblischer Kanon in der deutschen Aufklärung,* ed. Henning Graf Reventlow, Walter Sparn, and John Woodbridge (Wiesbaden: Otto Harrassowitz, 1988).

quiry initiated earlier was beginning to be consolidated in Germany in particular. Before this time the critical impulse lacked well-developed philosophical underpinnings, and the work was more occasional in nature, motivated by apologetic aims of various sorts. Simon, for example, at least ostensibly sought to vindicate a need for papal authority by destabilizing Protestant understandings of Scripture, Hobbes sought to undermine a possible ground of political rebellion, and various English deists sought to advance their rationalized religion on a kind of Lockean grounds. But in late-eighteenth-century Germany biblical criticism rapidly gained powerful philosophical grounding in the work of Immanuel Kant (1724-1804), Friedrich Schelling (1775-1854), and Gottfried Wilhelm Friedrich Hegel (1770-1831).

Kant was at the fountainhead of this movement. Put schematically, Kant opened what he would later call a "chasm" between the "sensible" and the "supersensible." On the one hand, through sensible *understanding* we are *receptive* to objects in the phenomenal world of our experiences of the everyday world — the world accessible to natural science. On the other hand, in the noumenal realm of the supersensible, *reasoning* constructs *spontaneously* those things needed for its own possibility of thought and action. Religion fit into the latter, while the former was hermetically sealed against anything breaking with a seamless lawfulness of cause and effect. Crucially, this made religion into a matter that lay outside of human *receptivity* and cognition. In short, religion became a human construct, governed by the laws arising spontaneously from human reason — laws Kant identified with consistency and (therefore) morality.[25]

Already in Kant's day there were attempts to unify what Kant had put asunder, but on a higher plane that would not disrupt what were taken to be his most crucial insights. Many of these attempts took their cues from Kant's *Critique of Judgment* (1790), in which he identified the problem of bridging the chasm between phenomena and noumena. Kant had looked to the aesthetic realm to bridge the chasm, and in this he would again influence the direction of later thought. Thus Schelling gave the "notion of the aesthetic as the locus of recovered unity between freedom and nature . . . an ontological foundation."[26] This ontology is found in the fact that "nature and consciousness have ultimately the

25. Kant, *The Critique of Pure Reason;* Immanuel Kant, *Religion within the Boundaries of Mere Reason,* trans. Allen W. Wood and George Di Giovanni (Cambridge: Cambridge University Press, 1998). Kant interpretation is a notoriously hazardous endeavor. One important contribution to the field is Henry E. Allison, *Kant's Transcendental Idealism: An Interpretation and Defense* (New Haven: Yale University Press, 1983). For Kant's views on religion, see Allen W. Wood, *Kant's Moral Religion* (Ithaca, NY: Cornell University Press, 1970); Nicholas Wolterstorff, "Is It Possible and Desirable for Theologians to Recover from Kant?" *Modern Theology* 14, no. 1 (January 1998): 1-18; and Anthony C. Sciglitano, "Prometheus and Kant: Neutralizing Theological Discourse and Doxology," *Modern Theology* 25 (2009): 387-414.

26. Charles M. Taylor, *Hegel* (New York: Cambridge University Press, 1975), 42.

same source, subjectivity."[27] If the things Kant bifurcated had a deeper source in an all-encompassing subject, it would turn out that they were unified after all. Schelling initially stated these views, and Hegel worked them into a system of breathtaking scope and power. In Hegel's hands, all of history was the movement of *Geist* (Spirit, or Mind) since humanity "is the vehicle whereby the cosmic spirit brings to completion a self-expression," and *Geist* "is a spirit who lives as spirit only through men."[28] In Hegel's hands human beings become "the vehicles, and the indispensable vehicles, of his spiritual existence, as consciousness, rationality, will."[29] Continual overcoming of opposition drives history: "our attempt to grasp things in knowledge first negates them as particulars; then, negating this negation, we recover them by grasping them through meditated conceptual consciousness."[30] The key to the connection with biblical criticism is Hegel's notion that "representations" are early intimations of the conceptual outworking of *Geist*.[31]

A rough and ready example may clarify things a bit. Under the influence of Hegel, a scholar would expect that the history of Jewish people would itself be a rough, highly suggestive outworking of the deeper realities that could be more clearly worked out through philosophical insight and the progress of human culture itself. The Semitic cult of *Yahweh* would be subsumed in the great monotheism of the Hebrew prophets, which would itself be subsumed in the religion of Jesus, and so on. In the particular events of history, a universal Subjectivity was realizing itself. As with Kant, religious language was not making *cognitive* claims such as might be made in physics; but with Hegel it could be thought that it did something that was, in some ways, even more important. Religious language gave aesthetic insight into the most basic unity. Moreover, it could be taken to install religion (and therefore academic religious scholars) very close to the heart of that which unified all knowledge and integrated living. This was pretty heady stuff.[32]

27. Taylor, *Hegel,* 42.

28. Taylor, *Hegel,* 44, 45.

29. Taylor, *Hegel,* 45.

30. Taylor, *Hegel,* 145; see also 76-78.

31. An excellent summary of the relation of Hegel's thought to religion generally and biblical criticism specifically may be found in Alister E. McGrath, *The Making of Modern German Christology, 1750-1990,* 2nd edition (Grand Rapids: Zondervan, 1994), chapter 3, "The Hegelian School: From Strauss to Feuerbach": "Religion initially comprises *Vorstellungen* [representations] of God [*Geist*] which, although speculatively deficient, in that they combine 'finite' and 'infinite' elements, are capable of being resolved into the *Begriff* [concept] of God. It is therefore necessary to progress from the sensuously mediated images and experiences of *Vorstellung* to the *Begriff* of God. . . . Hegel emphasizes that in the *ordo essendi* (that is, the way in which things are in reality), the *Begriff* is prior to the *Vorstellungen* which embody it. For Hegel, the incarnation is the supreme religious *Vorstellung* from which theological and philosophical speculation may begin" (53).

32. It should be noted that even after Hegel's philosophy was no longer regnant, many of the patterns and assumptions that were set during this fundamental period in biblical criticism

To get a sense of how the German philosophical machinery began to shape biblical criticism, it will be helpful to return to the prominent Old Testament critic, W. M. L. de Wette. In 1799, the young de Wette began studying at Jena in the school where Schelling, Hegel, and Johann Fichte were all plying their philosophical trade, and J. J. Griesbach and H. E. G. Paulus were holding forth on religion. While imbibing Paulus's rationalist readings of Scripture, de Wette attended lectures on Kantian philosophy. As his biographer put it, at Jena de Wette "learned how to translate the key terms of the faith of his youth — conversion, putting on the new man, grace, the love of God and Christ — into Kantian philosophical language. These ideas now seemed to him to be more meaningful, and they made the lectures of Paulus even more exciting."[33] In his semi-autobiographical novel, *Theodor,* de Wette described his own experience:

> [H]e felt himself especially uplifted and satisfied when his biblical teacher presented Christ as a Kantian sage, who taught, in pictures and ideas appropriate to his time, what the present age could deduce clearly and purely from reason.[34]

And yet this Kantian moralistic rationalism in religion left him emotionally barren. Again, de Wette ties his own experience to the character of Theodor: "The Kantian doctrine of God . . . fell like a damp squib into his soul, extinguishing the holy fire of devotion and leaving in its place a dismal darkness."[35] As de Wette's biographer notes, this Kantian teaching

> seemed to deny the idea that God exists, and that we come from him and belong to him. It implied that human reason exists, and that God exists only at reason's behest. De Wette (Theodor) found himself asking: "Is this a real and living God, and not rather a projection of our own thoughts? Is this the God who spoke to the patriarchs and prophets, and who revealed himself in mighty deeds? . . ." The answer to these questions appeared to be no, and de Wette suddenly found himself alone in the world.[36]

---

by scholars beholden to Kant and Hegel continued to hold sway in myriad different ways. This continues down to the present.

33. John W. Rogerson, *W. M. L. de Wette: Founder of Modern Biblical Criticism* (Sheffield: Sheffield Academic Press, 1992), 31. The way the quotations from de Wette are woven together below follows Rogerson very closely.

34. W. M. L. de Wette, *Theodor oder des Zweiflers Weihe: Bildungsgeschichte eines evangelischen Geistlichen,* vol. 1 (Berlin, 1822), 21; quoted in Rogerson, *W. M. L. de Wette,* 31 (Rogerson is unclear on the page number of this quotation from de Wette). Rogerson argues convincingly that de Wette is referring to his own experiences here.

35. De Wette, *Theodor,* 1:24; quoted in Rogerson, *W. M. L. de Wette,* 31.

36. Rogerson, *W. M. L. de Wette,* 31-32; Rogerson is quoting de Wette, *Theodor,* 1:24-25. Rogerson (p. 98) has a very nice summary of the fundamentally Kantian pattern of thinking

De Wette had accepted Kant's philosophical strictures and all their implications, and they had stripped his religion down to only what could be countenanced by Kantian moral rationalism.

De Wette moved forward from the blanched rationalism of Kant and Paulus by appropriating the insights of his other teachers at Jena. German idealism lit the way; and the way was fundamentally aesthetic and mythic. In this vein we find de Wette lifting his voice in rapture:

> O holy art, you alone can open up to me the sense of the divine, and teach of the divine, and teach to the heart better, nobler feelings. In your magical creations, as in a clear, beautiful mirror, you present to limited vision the beauty and harmony that is not to be perceived in the infinite universe. You bring down to us from heaven the divine in earthly form, and bringing it into our view you move the cold and narrow heart to accept feelings that are divine and mediate harmony.[37]

In the end, de Wette held that "religion could only be consciously grasped by religious symbols."[38] In this he showed how deeply patterns of thought derived from contemporary German philosophy marked his approach to the biblical text.[39] One was not receptive to God in the canonical text in a directly cognitive way, but only as those texts mediated an aesthetic experience. In place of canonical receptivity, de Wette elevated a spontaneous aesthetic experience moving the heart to "accept feelings that are divine and mediate harmony."

The same philosophical assumptions that pointed de Wette away from the church's historic position of canonical receptivity were inscribed on the thought of German scholars throughout the nineteenth century — explicitly at first, and then as the assumed background of their work as it took new forms. From there, the assumptions of this theological departure were exported to England and the United States, and the movement was dubbed — fittingly enough — "neology."[40] It was because he was aware of this challenge that Archibald Alexander wrote to Charles Hodge on 27 July 1827, "I pray God to keep you from the poison of *Neology!* I wish you to come home enriched with Biblical learning, but abhorring

---

that continued to set the pattern of de Wette's Old Testament scholarship throughout his career.

37. W. M. L. de Wette, *"Eine Idee über das Studium der Theologie,"* 20; quoted in Rogerson, *W. M. L. de Wette,* 38.

38. Rogerson, *W. M. L. de Wette,* 129.

39. It is interesting to note that Rogerson identifies de Wette's fundamental weakness as his overreliance on another philosopher, J. F. Fries, in trying to make his way out of the Kantian impasse. See Rogerson, *W. M. L. de Wette,* 266-67.

40. Strictly speaking, "neology" refers to the early Kantian rationalism of scholars like H. E. G. Paulus.

German philosophy and theology."[41] Dr. Alexander clearly understood that what was going on in German biblical scholarship was a significant and powerful departure from the church's historical position of canonical receptivity. He was praying that his protégé would return equipped to help the church reaffirm a critically important teaching in the face of this theological departure.

Classic Christian Orthodoxy on the Authority of Holy Scripture: A Reminder

If many within the German theological scene were departing from the church's historical understanding of Scripture, what was it they were leaving behind? A brief sketch will have to suffice here, more as a reminder and a bibliographic starting point than as a full exposition.[42]

Beginning with the church in the first century, we find Clement of Rome writing in his *First Letter to the Church at Corinth:* "You have studied Scripture [the Old Testament] which contains the truth and is inspired by the Holy Spirit. You realize that there is nothing wrong or misleading in it."[43] And again, in Justin Martyr's second-century *Dialogue with Trypho,* he declares that,

> if a Scripture which appears to be of such a kind be brought forward, and if there be a pretext (for saying) that it is contrary (to some other), since I am entirely convinced that no Scripture contradicts another, I shall admit rather that I do not understand what is recorded, and shall strive to persuade those who imagine that the Scriptures are contradictory, to be rather of the same opinion as myself.[44]

41. Letter from Archibald Alexander to Charles Hodge, 27 July 1827; quoted in Archibald Alexander Hodge, *The Life of Charles Hodge,* 161. Alexander continues on to say, "I have been paying some attention to Kant's philosophy, but it confounds and astonishes me." This is a familiar feeling to anyone who has made a serious attempt to work through *The Critique of Pure Reason.*

42. This section is the briefest of sketches, serving only to remind readers what is amply shown elsewhere by careful attention to the primary source documents from the church fathers down to the Princetonians' own day. For fuller treatment of these issues, please refer to other essays in this collection — notably those by Hill, Woodbridge, McCall, and Lane — as well as the bibliographic sources in the notes below.

In what follows, I happily acknowledge my debt to John D. Woodbridge, *Biblical Authority: A Critique of the Rogers/McKim Proposal* (Grand Rapids: Zondervan, 1982). Woodbridge's painstaking examination of the primary source documents from the church fathers onward points out severe difficulties for the Innovation Argument.

43. 1 Clement 45, in *Early Christian Fathers,* ed. Cyril Richardson (New York: Macmillan, 1970), 64; quoted in Woodbridge, *Biblical Authority,* 32.

44. Justin Martyr, *Dialogue with Trypho,* in *The Ante-Nicene Fathers,* ed. Alexander Roberts

Or again, consider Augustine, who states flatly that "everything written in Scripture must be believed absolutely," and affirms his view of the authority of Scripture quite clearly:

> I have learned to yield this respect and honor only to the canonical books of Scripture: of these alone do I most firmly believe that the authors were completely free from error. And if in these writings I am perplexed by anything which appears to me opposed to truth, I do not hesitate to suppose that either the MS. [manuscript] is faulty, or the translator has not caught the meaning of what was said, or I myself have failed to understand it.[45]

The church fathers clearly taught that Scripture had nothing wrong in it, did not contradict itself, and was without error, and Augustine clearly drew the sensible distinction between the original autographs and the copies. Add to this that they innocently spoke of Scripture as "true utterances of the Holy Spirit" (Clement of Rome), "the oracles of the Lord" (Polycarp), "God's voice spoken by the apostles . . . and prophets" (Justin Martyr), and "the Lord's Scriptures" (Irenaeus), in an age before there were serious challenges to biblical authority, and it appears that the early church simply started from Scriptures that were taken to be without error because they were from God.[46] Indeed, if anything, the early church occasionally needed to be reminded that the human authors were more than flutes in the mouth of God. In any case, they had a very robust understanding of Scripture's authority.

We now glance briefly at medieval Christianity and then move to the Reformation. Thomas Aquinas says that "the author of Holy Scripture is God," and that "it is plain that nothing false can ever underlie the literal sense of Holy Scripture."[47] That Aquinas's view was for centuries the Roman Catholic understanding of Scripture (down to the twentieth century, when Rome began adopting some of the conclusions of biblical criticism), appears clearly from the fact that John

---

(Grand Rapids: Eerdmans, 1973), 1:230; quoted in Woodbridge, *Biblical Authority,* 32. Compare A. T. B. McGowan's observation that when faced with apparent contradictions, inerrantists frequently reply by arguing "that this is only an antinomy, an apparent but not a real contradiction" (*The Divine Authenticity of Scripture,* 112). It is worth noting that Justin clearly shares this inerrantist concern.

45. Augustine, "Letter 82.3, to Jerome," in *Nicene and Post-Nicene Fathers,* First Series, vol. 1, *The Confessions and Letters of St. Augustine,* ed. Philip Schaff (Peabody, MA: Hendrickson, 2004), 350. See Woodbridge, *Biblical Authority,* 43-45 for helpful commentary.

46. J. Barton Payne, "The Biblical Interpretation of Irenaeus," in *Inspiration and Interpretation,* ed. John F. Walvoord (Grand Rapids: Eerdmans, 1957), 15, 17.

47. Thomas Aquinas, *Summa Theologica,* I, i, 10, in *Introduction to Thomas Aquinas: The Essence of the Summa Theologica and the Summa Contra Gentiles,* ed. Anton C. Pegis (New York: Random House, 1945), 18, 19.

Eck, one of Luther's fiercest opponents, scolded Erasmus regarding the possibility of error in Matthew's Gospel: "Listen, dear Erasmus: do you suppose any Christian will patiently endure to be told that the evangelists in their Gospels made mistakes? If the authority of Holy Scripture at this point is shaky, can any other passage be free from the suspicion of error?"[48] Indeed, while Roman Catholic *hermeneutics* and *exegesis* were clearly problematic in Catholic resistance to Galileo, it's clear that they were seeking to maintain a high view of *scriptural authority.* A Scripture without errors in whatever it affirmed was simply a widely assumed part of the medieval background.

Whatever their disagreements, Roman Catholics shared a high view of Scripture with the first-generation reformers, Luther and Calvin.[49] Characteristically, Luther puts things bluntly: "It is impossible that Scripture should contradict itself; it only appears so to senseless and obstinate hypocrites."[50] Elsewhere he draws a hard line between the Holy Scriptures and the writings of the church fathers: "But everyone, indeed, knows that at times they [the fathers] have erred as men will; therefore I am ready to trust them only when they prove their opinions from Scripture, which has never erred."[51] Yet again, in connection with how communion is to be understood, Luther emphasizes the importance of the *words* of Scripture. Emphasizing the words of Matthew 26:26ff., John 6:63, and Ephesians 1:20, Luther states that "we must remain content with them, and cling to them as the perfectly clear, certain, sure words of God which can never deceive us or allow us to err."[52] Likewise, Calvin refused to mince words. Indeed, he was even clearer on the question than Luther: "[W]e see that the Spirit is not less diligent in narrating burials

48. John Eck, in Desiderius Erasmus, *Collected Works of Erasmus,* trans. R. A. B. Mynors and D. F. S. Thomson, vol. 5, *The Correspondence of Erasmus* (Toronto: University of Toronto Press, 1976), 289-90; quoted in John D. Woodbridge, "A Neoorthodox Historiography under Siege," *Bibliotheca Sacra* 142 (1985): 12.

49. There is a wealth of solid scholarship showing how Luther and Calvin viewed Scripture. See especially the essay by Kolb in this collection. It is interesting to note that even in his attempts to claim Luther and Calvin for neo-orthodoxy, J. K. S. Reid is forced to acknowledge difficulties in his reading. Thus he admits that "one cannot deny that out of the available material a formidable case for holding Calvin to be a literalist can be constructed"; and, regarding Luther: "The distinction between Scripture and the Word of God, which Luther maintained, but so often by his own utterances imperiled, is now lost, and the two are regarded as identical" (Reid, *The Authority of Scripture,* 35, 83).

50. Martin Luther, *Sämmtliche Schriften,* 2nd edition, ed. Joh. Georg Walch (St. Louis: Concordia, 1881-1930), 9, 356; quoted in Woodbridge, *Biblical Authority,* 53.

51. Martin Luther, *Luther's Works,* 55 vols., ed. Jaroslav Pelikan and Helmut T. Lehman, vol. 32, *Career of the Reformer II,* ed. George W. Forell (Philadelphia: Fortress Press, 1961), 11; quoted in Woodbridge, *Biblical Authority,* 53.

52. Martin Luther, *Luther's Works,* vol. 37, *Word and Sacrament,* ed. Robert H. Fischer (Philadelphia: Fortress Press, 1958), 308; quoted in Woodbridge, *Biblical Authority,* 53.

than the principal mysteries of the faith."[53] And again: we "ought to embrace with mild docility, and without any exception, whatever is delivered in the Holy Scriptures."[54] Indeed, Calvin's painstaking attempts to show that apparent discrepancies were merely *apparent* discrepancies also testify to his view of the authority of Holy Scripture. Throughout the writings of the Reformers we find a view that Scriptures are without error in everything that they teach. They hold this view naturally and simply, without taking pains to defend it against challenges that did not yet exist.

That these views continued through the teachings of immediate heirs of the Reformers is hardly a surprise.[55] Nor is it difficult to see this line of classic orthodoxy running through John Wesley ("Every part thereof is worthy of God; and all together are one entire body, wherein is no defect, no excess"), and picked up widely through the fledgling republic.[56] Orthodox Christians — Baptists, Methodists, and Lutherans no less than the Calvinists at Princeton — knew full well what Vanhoozer summarizes: "[I]t was a virtually unanimous assumption in the early church that the Holy Spirit was the author of Scripture and that its meaning, even where it was multiple, was determinate. *Church tradition accorded supreme authority to Scripture.* Doctrine was to be accepted primarily *because it was biblical.*"[57] While hermeneutic approaches varied, the church's understanding of the authority of Scripture did not: "all Scripture is God-breathed" (2 Tim. 3:16) through a process in which "men spoke from God as they were carried along by the Holy Spirit" (2 Pet. 1:21) so that Scripture is without error in everything it affirms.

The "Old Princetonians" on Biblical Authority

Already in the 1826 volume of *The Biblical Repertory and Princeton Review* (at the time it was titled *Biblical Repertory*), Charles Hodge translated an essay by a

53. John Calvin, *Institutes of the Christian Religion,* trans. Henry Beveridge, 3 vols. (Edinburgh: Calvin Translation Society, 1845), 3.25.8; quoted in Woodbridge, *Biblical Authority,* 63.

54. John Calvin, *Institutes of the Christian Religion,* 1.18.4; quoted in Woodbridge, *Biblical Authority,* 63.

55. Richard A. Muller, *Post-Reformation Dogmatics,* vol. 2 (Grand Rapids: Baker, 1987), 86-96.

56. John Wesley, "Preface," in *Explanatory Notes upon the New Testament,* vol. 1, *Matthew to Acts* (Grand Rapids: Baker, 1986), paragraph 10; quoted in George A. Turner, "John Wesley as an Interpreter of Scripture," in John Walvoord, ed., *Inspiration and Interpretation* (Grand Rapids: Eerdmans, 1957), 160. The widespread agreement on inerrancy in the early days of the American Republic is made abundantly clear in John D. Woodbridge and Randall H. Balmer, "The Princetonians and Biblical Authority: An Assessment of the Ernest Sandeen Proposal," in *Scripture and Truth,* ed. D. A. Carson and John D. Woodbridge (Grand Rapids: Zondervan, 1983), especially 271-76.

57. Vanhoozer, *The Drama of Doctrine,* 164-65.

Professor Stapfer from the French.[58] It was titled "The Life of Kant," and in his introduction to the essay Hodge says of Kant's philosophy, that "the influence which the system has had upon religious opinion in Germany, is so obvious, that it forms even for the Theologian one of the most necessary and interesting chapters in the history of the last half century."[59] From the outset, Charles Hodge and the pages of the *Princeton Review* took up an examination of the German theological scene and the influence of Kantian (and, later, Hegelian) philosophy on the emerging scholarship. Throughout Hodge's editorship, the *Princeton Review* consistently displayed a high level of engagement with the leading edge of scholarship and the pressing questions of the day. The overwhelming sense upon reading through the pages of the journal is that of engaging with very bright scholars who are doing their level best to think through their entire world in light of a vibrant, thoughtful, personally relevant Christian faith — all in worship of their Lord Jesus Christ, who laid rightful claim to all creation.[60]

"A Sound and Wholesome Doctrine": Archibald Alexander within the Wider Church

One of the brightest of the scholars to labor alongside Hodge in the pages of the *Princeton Review* was his mentor, Archibald Alexander. In 1830, in the section of the journal titled "Notices of New Publications," Dr. Alexander penned a short

58. The first part of Hodge's stay in Europe involved study of Arabic and Persian in Paris.

59. Professor Stapfer, "The Life of Kant," *Biblical Repertory* 2, no. 4 (1826): 299; punctuation as in original. The translation is unsigned, but states that it is "by the editor." Archibald Alexander Hodge attributes the translation to Charles Hodge (*The Life of Charles Hodge,* 99), but misidentifies the year as 1828.

60. Hodge himself was a polymath who read and intelligently interacted with an astonishing array of scholarly work, as well as commenting astutely and widely on the culture of his day. Among his contemporaries, Hodge was among the leading English-speaking scholars in terms of his familiarity with German scholarship: "[H]e had studied, and studied seriously, in Germany, the great fatherland of erudition; even in the next generation, probably only the Swiss-born and German-educated Philip Schaff could boast equivalent exposure" (James Turner, "Charles Hodge in the Intellectual Weather of the Nineteenth Century," in Stewart and Moorhead, eds., *Charles Hodge Revisited,* 42). Indeed, B. A. Gerrish marvels at the extent of Hodge's engagement with the German scholarship of the time: "It is astonishing in a work of systematic theology" ("Charles Hodge and the Europeans," in Stewart and Moorhead, eds., *Charles Hodge Revisited,* 139).

The other Princetonians were no less remarkable. Archibald Alexander's son Joseph Addison Alexander, for example, mastered twenty-seven languages and also wrote insightfully on an incredible variety of topics. It is all the more remarkable, then, when even some who were averse to the Old Princeton theology judge that Benjamin Breckinridge Warfield was the brightest of those who taught at Princeton.

review titled "Wilson's Evidences of Christianity." Daniel Wilson was a popular preacher in a large church outside of London, and his book *The Evidences of Christianity* received favorable notice from Dr. Alexander. Alexander lingers over Wilson's treatment of inspiration, saying that Wilson

> maintains a sound and wholesome doctrine; teaching that the sacred writers, in all cases, possessed such a degree of inspiration as was necessary to render them infallible in what they wrote. Less would have been insufficient to render the scriptures a safe foundation for our faith, in all that they inculcate; for what if their slips and errors should only affect matters of small importance, who shall tell us what those things are which belong to this class? But how easy was it for that Spirit which guided them in great matters to superintend their pens also in things of apparently small moment? . . . This is a point on which, if we begin to yield, there is no place afterward where we can obtain firm footing. The ideas of a partial or imperfect inspiration is in itself so unreasonable, that he who adopts this opinion will for consistency soon reject the inspiration of the writers altogether.[61]

On reading this passage, one notices the obvious continuity with classic Christian teaching.[62] From the outset it is clear that any charges of "innovation" leveled against Charles Hodge and the other Princetonians will have to be broadened to encompass British theology prior to 1830 as well. In light of the historical sketch above, one begins to suspect this is because the view was no innovation, but the common heritage of the church.[63] Additionally, whatever one thinks about the line Dr. Alexander draws on the proper way of handling the epistemological problems raised by "partial theories" of inspiration (How will it be decided which parts of Scripture need to be cut out in order to isolate God's word as it is "contained" in the Bible?), Alexander clearly believes that the entirety of Scripture is inspired and without error.

Alexander also made the same fairly sensible point about the original autographs we have seen that Augustine made centuries earlier. As Alexander put it,

61. Archibald Alexander, "Wilson's Evidences of Christianity &c.," *The Biblical Repertory and Theological Review* 2 (1830): 149.

62. As Augustine wrote: "[I]t seems to me that the most disastrous consequences must follow upon our believing that anything false is found in the sacred books. . . . For if you once admit into such a high sanctuary of authority one false statement, as made in the way of duty, there will not be left a single sentence of these books which, if appearing to any one difficult in practice or hard to believe, may not by the same fatal rule be explained away, as a statement in which, intentionally, and under a sense of duty, the author declared what was not true" (Augustine, "Letter 28.3, to Jerome," in *The Confessions and Letters of St. Augustine,* p. 252; quoted in Woodbridge, *Biblical Authority,* 37).

63. Again, see Woodbridge and Balmer, "The Princetonians and Biblical Authority," 271-76.

"[W]e should consider the circumstances under which these books have been transmitted to us, and the almost absolute certainty, that in so many ages, and in the process of such numerous transcriptions, mistakes must necessarily have occurred, and may have passed into all the copies extant."[64] When God inspired the authors of the books of Scripture, he inspired what they actually wrote. Speaking of a later Princeton scholar who defended "the inerrancy of the original autographs," Stanley Grenz notes that "A. A. Hodge claimed, not without cause, that this was the position of the church throughout its history."[65] The point about the original autographs can be overstated, so that we drive too great a wedge between the autographs and our best reconstructions of them. It is only a slight overstatement to say that the original autographs "might very well look just like our existing manuscripts, including all of the difficulties, synoptic issues, discrepancies and apparent contradictions, because that was what God intended."[66] Or, in the words of Princeton's B. B. Warfield, "We already have practically the autographic text in the New Testament in nine hundred and ninety-nine words out of every thousand."[67] Warfield's position was sensible and balanced:

> That some of the difficulties and apparent discrepancies in current texts disappear on the restoration of the true text of Scripture is undoubtedly true. That all the difficulties and apparent discrepancies in current texts of Scripture are matters of textual corruption, and not, rather often of historical or other ignorance on our part, no sane man ever asserted. . . . The Church . . . does not assert that the genuine text of Scripture is free from those apparent discrepancies and other difficulties, on the ground of which, imperfectly investigated, the errancy of the Bible is usually affirmed.[68]

64. Archibald Alexander, "Review of Dr. Woods on Inspiration," *The Biblical Repertory and Princeton Review* 3 (1831): 10. It is worth noting in passing that Leonard Woods defines inspiration as "a supernatural guidance or assistance afforded to the sacred writers, that divine guidance having been such as entirely to guard them against error, and to lead them to write just what God saw to be suited to accomplish the ends of revelation" (Leonard Woods, *Lectures on the Inspiration of the Scriptures* [Andover, MA: Flagg & Gould, 1829], fifth lecture; quoted in Alexander, "Review of Dr. Woods on Inspiration," 18). Note also that here is *another* scholar outside of Princeton defending a view of biblical authority in accord with the common view of the church.

65. Grenz, *Renewing the Center,* 76. Grenz acknowledges the work of Woodbridge, *Biblical Authority,* in this connection.

66. McGowan, *The Divine Authenticity of Scripture,* 119. One might wonder about the "just like" here, but the point still stands: it is a mistake to posit a gulf between the *autographa* and our current text of the Bible.

67. Benjamin Breckinridge Warfield, "The Westminster Confession and the Original Autographs," in *Selected Shorter Writings of Benjamin B. Warfield,* vol. 2, ed. John E. Meeter (Phillipsburg, NJ: P&R, 1973), 589. I owe my awareness of this passage to Fred G. Zaspel, *The Theology of B. B. Warfield: A Systematic Summary* (Wheaton, IL: Crossway, 2010), 171.

68. Benjamin Breckinridge Warfield, "The Inerrancy of the Original Autographs," 582-

When the Princetonians from Alexander through Warfield drew the distinction between the autographs and the extant manuscripts they made a sensible and important point — one clearly drawn through the ages of the church.[69]

"The Only Safe Method": James Waddel Alexander's Critique of Baconian Extremes

Archibald Alexander's son, James W. Alexander, also contributed extensively to the pages of the *Princeton Review,* covering a breathtaking range of topics.[70] In 1832, James Alexander turned his attention to an important topic: "On the Use and Abuse of Systematic Theology." This essay takes up questions of "Baconian" methodology in theology, and thus bears on one of the charges frequently leveled against the Princetonians on biblical authority: Having followed the "Protestant scholastics" in imbibing the assumptions of Modernism, the Princetonians wedded a need for theological certainty with a naïve "Baconian" methodology that led them to a view of the Bible as an inerrant foundation for their Enlightenment project. The Princetonians sought ahistorical rational demonstration where they should have relied on the testimony of the Holy Spirit. The charge usually features a quote like the following from the pages of Charles Hodge's "Introduction" to his *Systematic Theology:*

> The Bible is to the theologian what nature is to the man of science. It is his store-house of facts, and his method of ascertaining what the Bible teaches is the same as that which the natural philosopher adopts to ascertain what nature teaches.[71]

For example, in casting Hodge as exemplary of one of two "ideal types" of modernism in theology, Nancey Murphy features the passage above as the centerpiece of a highly selective, ellipsis-filled one-page quote of *six pages* from Hodge's "Introduction."[72] Interestingly, Murphy's selection not only elides all the details that flesh out Hodge's central point and exhibit his philosophical competence, but

---

83. This passage was initially brought to my attention by Paul Helm, "B. B. Warfield's Path to Inerrancy: An Attempt to Correct Some Serious Misunderstandings," *Westminster Theological Journal* 72 (2010): 34-35.

69. See, for example, the essays by Hill, Dempster, and Williams in this collection.

70. See Noll, "The Princeton Review," 292-93 for an overview of how Archibald Alexander's sons were involved with the *Princeton Review.* According to Noll, James W. Alexander "was a polymath" who wrote on "everything . . . everyone . . . and nearly every place."

71. Charles Hodge, *Systematic Theology,* 3 vols. (New York: Charles Scribner's Sons, 1871-73; reprint, Peabody, MA: Hendrickson, 2008), 1:10.

72. Murphy, *Beyond Liberalism and Fundamentalism,* 33-34.

also ends just prior to some important context Hodge provides when he notes that what he has said is consistent with "the controlling power over our beliefs exercised by the inward teachings of the Holy Spirit," and that "the question is not first and mainly, What is true to the understanding, but what is true to the renewed heart?"[73] Also missing are Hodge's numerous statements in the *Princeton Review:* "We believe the external evidence of the Bible to be perfectly conclusive; we believe its internal evidence, (that is, its majesty, its purity, its consistency, its manifold perfections) to be no less satisfactory; but we believe also, that the ultimate foundation of the Christian's faith, is the testimony of the Holy Spirit, by and with the truth in our hearts."[74] The *Holy Spirit* is the ultimate foundation, according to Hodge. All the same, Murphy tells us that Hodge adhered to "the special foundational status of Scripture" wedded to a "Baconian" methodology.[75]

Other scholars pick up the same thread of thought, and the Princetonians are pilloried as "foundationalists" who "routinely approach theological reflection in a somewhat piecemeal manner, indicative of an understanding of knowledge that sees it as the compiling of correct conclusions from a sure foundation."[76] The Princetonians, we are informed, had a naïve theological methodology in which facts simply presented themselves to the theologian to be arranged as needed. The resulting theologies "often give the appearance of being elaborate collections of loosely related facts deriving from the Bible, which is understood as a 'store-house of facts.'" Accordingly, "once a theologian has set forth the proper foundation (which for the conservative modernist is often focused on an inerrant Bible, whereas for the liberal it is based on religious experience), he or she is free to construct the house of theological knowledge in any order."[77] As children of the Enlightenment, their "quest for scientific theology required an unassailable foundation," and so they "set forth an invulnerable foundation for theology in an error-free Bible, viewed as the storehouse for divine revelation. Above all, this agenda, characteristic of the theology inaugurated by Archibald Alexander, dominated Princeton Seminary throughout the nineteenth and early twentieth centuries."[78] All this misguided pining for certainty arose because the Princetonians "had drunk deeply at the well of Enlightenment foundationalist rationalism" and thus "sought an intellectually unassailable bedrock upon which to construct their theological house."[79] According to adherents of the Innovation Argument, then, both the Princetonians and the biblical critics to which they were responding were modernists, and we need not get caught up in their disputes today. The

73. Hodge, *Systematic Theology,* 1:15, 16.

74. Hodge, "The Latest Form of Infidelity," 39.

75. Murphy, *Beyond Liberalism and Fundamentalism,* 16.

76. Grenz and Franke, *Beyond Foundationalism,* 50.

77. Grenz and Franke, *Beyond Foundationalism,* 50.

78. Grenz, *Renewing the Center,* 72, 70.

79. Grenz, *Renewing the Center,* 70.

anxious search for theological foundations may be abandoned, thus relieving us of any need for inerrant Scriptures.

In approaching this common charge, it's helpful to recall that the challenge the Princetonians were facing had to do with the basic theological moment of canonical receptivity. At what point is the church *receptive* to God? Kant and Hegel and the biblical criticism inhabiting their philosophies seriously jeopardized the very possibility of such receptivity, or countenanced it only in purely rationalist terms or in terms of a non-cognitivist aesthetics added to the rationalism — that is, in ways that can look suspiciously like mere human spontaneity dressed up for church.[80] In their day, the Princetonians faced a determined, philosophically sophisticated movement that threatened to dissipate canonical receptivity in the human spontaneity of the canon's authors, leaving theology at the mercy of *contemporary* expressions of human spontaneity, *which stand on the same ground* as those of the apostles and prophets. As Hodge observed of the theology of his day,

> It has a source of knowledge higher than the scriptures. The life of God in the soul is assumed to be as informing now as in the case of the apostles. The scriptures, therefore, are not needed, and they are not regarded, as either the ground or rule of faith. . . . By this neglect of scripture the door is opened for all sorts of vagaries to usurp the place of truth.[81]

Thus in 1843, Ludwig Feuerbach, a "left-Hegelian" standing at the end point of the Kantian-Hegelian trajectory of German biblical criticism, declared that "Theology is anthropology."[82] Does human spontaneity reign in religion? And, if so, whose spontaneity? Which anthropology? This question transcends modernism and postmodernism. One cannot simply make the question go away by labeling it a vestige of modernism; nor is it a question of certainty. Nor do we make any headway toward theological receptivity if Feuerbach is modified: "Theology is cultural anthropology."[83] For, again, we must ask: which culture? Receptivity to God dis-

80. Some of these structures of human spontaneity may come in the form of one or another "historical *a priori*" dominating modernity or, let it be said, "postmodernity." On the notion of the historical *a priori,* see Michel Foucault, *The Order of Things: An Archaeology of the Human Sciences* (New York: Vintage Books, 1994), xxii, xxiv, 157-60. The Christian must finally depart from Foucault's analysis at a number of points, if for no other reason than that sin gives direction to any particular historical *a priori* such that it is never *merely* historical.

81. Charles Hodge, "Bushnell's Discourses," *The Biblical Repertory and Princeton Review* 21 (1849): 275.

82. Ludwig Feuerbach, *The Essence of Christianity* (Amherst, NY: Prometheus Books, 1989), xvii. As early as 1846, Hodge addresses Feuerbach's thought. See Charles Hodge, "The Religious State of Germany," *The Biblical Repertory and Princeton Review* 18, no. 1 (January 1846): 527-28.

83. Compare Vanhoozer, *The Drama of Doctrine,* 175.

sipates in competing cultural structures of human spontaneity. In their defense of biblical authority, the Princetonians were not caught up in an ephemeral concern of a now-transcended modernism. They were standing squarely at the center of a key, perennial theological question — the question of genuine receptivity to God — and defending the answer the church had always given: the normative ground of receptivity to God is the Scriptures God inspired. To cite Augustine again, the normative authority for the church's thought about and relationship with God resides in "canonical books of Scripture" given to the church by the activity of God so that the inspired "authors were completely free from error."[84]

None of this is to say that there are not hard questions to be asked of the Princetonians at this point, though they should be addressed more to their hermeneutics than their understanding of the authority of Holy Scripture.[85] But the Princetonians were not naïve; nor was their theological approach as unthinkingly inductive as it is sometimes made out to be. To see this, we can return to James Alexander's essay "On the Use and Abuse of Systematic Theology." While it is true that when the Princetonians sought to defend canonical receptivity they looked for models in the natural science of their day — a practice that valorized Bacon, Locke, and Newton — they did not adopt those models wholesale or without significant departures. In looking to this model, they sought to preserve a robust canonical receptivity; but their interaction with the scientific practice of their day was not naïve, as will be noticed in the following passage where Alexander urges caution with inductivism. After arguing "that exegesis answers to experiment or observation in the natural world, and consequently that the theologian is to consider exegetical results as the basis of all his reasonings," Alexander continues:

> We avow our belief that the theologian should proceed in his investigation precisely as the chemist or the botanist proceeds. "The botanist does not shape his facts," says a late ingenious writer. Granted, provided that you mean that the botanist does not *wrest* his facts, to a forced correspondence with a hypothesis.

84. Augustine, "Letter 82.3, to Jerome," in *The Letters of St. Augustine,* 350.

85. At the same time, the Princetonians were certainly not naïve in this regard. See, for example, Hodge's close associate, William Henry Green, "Theology of the Old Testament," *The Biblical Repertory and Princeton Review* 25, no. 1 (January 1853): 102-20. After warning against the problematic approaches to the Old Testament driven by the philosophies of Kant and Hegel, he cautions believers not to overreact in ways that "reduce the entire Scriptures to one uniform homogeneous mass, from the whole of which thus blended, the system of truth is drawn. The Old Testament and the New are ranged precisely upon a level, and proof-texts are taken indifferently from one or from the other" (116). Hodge is also sensitive to the fact that not everything in the "storehouse" of Scripture is like everything else, as may be clearly seen in Hodge, "Inspiration." It is an "orchestra," and the different literary characters of the authors clearly emerge in their writings, and thus the different books need to be weighted differently (683-84, 680, *passim*). Not all the books are of the same value, though they are all equally inspired.

> Neither does the genuine theologian "shape his texts," nor *constrain* them to an agreement with his system. But both the botanist and the theologian do, in this sense, "shape their facts," that they classify and arrange the fruits of their observation, and gather from them new proofs of that general system which has previously commended itself to their faith.[86]

Alexander applies the inductivist model in order to emphasize the crucial importance of *exegesis* of the biblical text. What is being emphasized is that, as John Webster (certainly no naïve modernist) puts it, Christian theology "is a positive science. That is, it works both from and towards a *positum,* a given. That given we have already characterized as the communicative presence of God, Father, Son, and Spirit."[87] Therefore, "Holy reason is not a *poetic* but a *receptive* enterprise," and thus "the fundamental theological responsibility is exegesis."[88] If theology is to avoid the idolatry stemming from an unfettered human spontaneity that naturally runs after sin, a sanctified spontaneity must give itself to the receptivity to God in exegesis — a receptivity God himself gives to his church. Such *exegetical answerability* of the theologian to the norm of canonical Scripture drives Alexander's appeal to the "analogy" of a scientific model: "exegesis is the true instrument of discovery, and the test of all pretended results."[89] The point of the *analogy* was to preserve canonical receptivity.

But although Alexander calls this the method of Bacon and Newton, he did not take part in the era's "infatuation with Baconian science," if by that one means that he thought "theological method could and should be disinterested."[90] Instead, as Alexander insists, the theologian unavoidably "shapes" this exegetical moment. Indeed, a previous system is brought by faith to exegesis, but this "shaping" does not "wrest" or "constrain" the exegesis of the Scriptures. It is still responsive to the texts. Alexander makes this clear:

> The impartiality of the mind is in no degree secured by the banishment of all previous hypotheses. There is a partiality of ignorance, a partiality of self-will

86. James W. Alexander, "On the Use and Abuse of Systematic Theology," *The Biblical Repertory and Theological Review* 4, no. 2 (April 1832): 184.

87. John Webster, *Holiness* (Grand Rapids: Eerdmans, 2003), 16.

88. Webster, *Holiness,* 16, 18; emphasis in original.

89. Alexander, "On the Use and Abuse of Systematic Theology," 186.

90. Noll, "Charles Hodge as an Expositor of the Spiritual Life," 107. Noll argues that Hodge succumbs to such Baconian assumptions. The central book driving this part of the received historiography on the Princetonians is Theodore Dwight Bozeman, *Protestants in an Age of Science: The Baconian Ideal and Antebellum American Religious Thought* (Chapel Hill: University of North Carolina Press, 1977). For a critical examination of this historiography, see Bradley N. Seeman, "The Development of a Common Sense Realism Historiography in American Church History from 1955 to 1994" (M. A. Thesis, Trinity Evangelical Divinity School, 1995).

> and intellectual pride, a partiality of innovation, no less dangerous than the predilections of system. Or, to bring the whole matter to a speedier issue, the condition of mind *in equilibrio,* which it is proposed to secure, is utterly impossible — the merest *ens rationis* — which was never realized, and never can be realized by any one in a Christian country. It is like the chimerical skepticism of the Cartesians, the creature of an overheated imagination. For when you have carefully withheld all orthodox systems of theology from your pupil, he comes to the study of the Scriptures, emptied indeed of all coherent hypotheses, but teeming with the crude and erroneous views which spring up like weeds in the unregulated mind. . . . Everyone who commences the study of Scripture does so with some system, true or false, symmetrical or crude, written or conceived.[91]

These are not the words of a naïve Baconian inductivist who thinks inerrant exegetical facts just present themselves for classification, nor of one who — as the Innovation Argument would have it — "assumed that there was no going behind the quest for certainty introduced by Descartes."[92] Alexander recognizes that human spontaneity will always work itself out in the theological project, whether for good or ill: "[I]t is manifestly impossible for anyone to come to the study of the Word of God without entertaining some general scheme of divine truth as substantially correct."[93] Once again, Alexander is apparently in happy agreement with Webster. Theology requires a *sanctified spontaneity:* "Christian theology is not a moment of intellectual detachment, a point at which the theologian steps aside from the presence of revelation and the practice of faith and adopts a different — more abstract or critical — stance towards the Christian confession."[94] The facts of the inerrant Holy Scriptures will be of no avail in theology apart from a Spirit-sanctified human spontaneity that is conditioned to the subject matter of theology itself: the Holy Triune God, the cross, and the empty tomb. If, as George Marsden asserts, Baconian influences led theologians to take Scripture simply as a "compendium of facts" and then proceed to a theological systematization that "needed only to classify the facts, and follow wherever they might lead," then Alexander was no Baconian.[95] Indeed, it is interesting to note that in his essay, Alexander is *answering* the charge that the Princetonians are *not being sufficiently Baconian* in their theological method. *"The only safe method,"* Alexander's *opponents* asserted, "is to reject all the hypotheses of the divines, to come to the examination divested

91. Alexander, "On the Use and Abuse of Systematic Theology," 187.

92. Grenz and Franke, *Beyond Foundationalism,* 33. Grenz and Franke assert that the Princetonians are of a piece with liberals here in holding that "there was no return to a seemingly irrational appeal to external religious authority."

93. Alexander, "On the Use and Abuse of Systematic Theology," 187.

94. Webster, *Holiness,* 14.

95. Marsden, *Fundamentalism and American Culture,* 56.

of all preconceived opinions, to consider the scattered revelations of Scripture as so many phenomena, and to classify, generalize, and deduce from these phenomena."[96] This is an exemplary statement of "Baconianism," and Alexander's concern is to represent the Princeton stance by arguing *against* it.

A reading of the text will always be a "shaped" reading, then, according to Alexander. In this he stood opposed to the biblical critics of his day and ours, who commonly hold that the biblical text should be read like any other. This one way of reading a text sets aside ("brackets") "prior convictions about the text's meaning, drawn from an interpretative tradition."[97] The reading performed by the biblical critic is "noncommittal."[98] This stands in contrast to other readings of Scripture, for "those who think everything in the Bible is true (in some sense) usually have an idea already of what the truth is and believe that the Bible will turn out to conform to it."[99] Of course there is a point here. There is a danger of letting a culturally shaped human spontaneity overwhelm any genuine receptivity to a text, but this is a danger on all sides. One might squint right back at the biblical critics' "noncommittal" reading of the text and wonder if they "usually have an idea already of what the truth is and believe that the Bible will turn out to conform to it." Alexander is keenly aware of the point. Not without a little flavor in his prose, he notes that "the very persons whose delicate susceptibilities lead them to shrink from the contact of an orthodox system or exposition, lest they should receive some undue bias, are at the same time under no apprehensions from the contagion of German neology."[100] For Alexander the question is not whether historical forces *will* shape one's reading of Scripture, but *which ones should rightly exercise that influence.* Just as Alexander notes that his historic orthodoxy shapes his own approach to the scriptural text, he is alive to the way other readings are shaped by what they bring to the text. The commitments of many "noncommittal" readings of Scripture turn in deep eddies beneath them. Alexander, in harmony with the other Princetonians, insisted on the vital importance of reading Scripture from *within* the history of the church.

Questions about Charles Hodge's "Store-house of Facts"

Before leaving behind the matter of whether inerrancy owed materially to naïve Baconian foundationalism on the part of the Princetonians, the question of how

96. Alexander, "On the Use and Abuse of Systematic Theology," 183; emphasis added. To be sure, some of Alexander's terminology grates on our ears today, but we should not let that obscure the substance of his argument.

97. Barton, *The Nature of Biblical Criticism,* 124.

98. Barton, *The Nature of Biblical Criticism,* 124.

99. Barton, *The Nature of Biblical Criticism,* 124.

100. Alexander, "On the Use and Abuse of Systematic Theology," 188.

much Charles Hodge fell into this must be considered. After all, even if Alexander was innocent, Hodge was more influential than Alexander. But on a careful reading of Hodge, it is clear that he carefully worked out a thoughtful, vibrant theology, even if his language sometimes exhibits a debt to his times. Like Alexander, Hodge's purpose in making a rhetorical tie to the model of science in his day is to emphasize receptivity in the face of a spontaneity threatening to swallow theology whole. "It is important that the theologian know his place. He is not master of the situation. He can no more construct a system of theology to suit his fancy than the astronomer can adjust the mechanism of the heavens according to his own good pleasure."[101] Who God is and what he has done stands independently of us. There is a given in theology to which we must be receptive; exegesis of Scripture must drive theology. Hodge thus deplores the impulse to give the theological imagination sway in matters relating to God, urging us to see that it is "a hopeless and useless task," for " 'No man knows the things of God but the Spirit of God.' We must *humbly receive* what he has revealed, or remain in darkness."[102] As with Alexander, Hodge uses the analogy with science to emphasize the *exegetical answerability* of the theologian to the words *of God.*[103]

Also like Alexander, Hodge's rhetorical use of the language of science does not enforce a completely ahistorical understanding of theology. Hodge put the point quite clearly:

> We are, indeed, not separated from the past in our religious, any more than we are in our social and civil life. The political state of a nation in one age is in a great measure determined by its previous history. And so, too, the condition of the church in one age is largely influenced by ages which have gone before.[104]

Hodge knew quite well that human understanding of theology did not float lightly above history, untouched by the assumptions of the culture, the proclivities of the

101. Hodge, *Systematic Theology,* 1:34.

102. Charles Hodge, "Bushnell on Vicarious Sacrifice," *The Biblical Repertory and Princeton Review* 38, no. 2 (April 1866): 185-86; emphasis added. Thus, in opposition to the impulse exemplified by Horace Bushnell, Hodge emphasizes the receptivity of science. The scientist "cannot invent facts . . . cannot ignore them . . . cannot undervalue them" (185). In short, the chemist should not simply make up results in a lab; she must see how things turn out. So also theologians should ground their work in painstaking exegetical work. Hodge sees this question of humble receptivity as opposed to unfettered spontaneity as being at the heart of his critique of Horace Bushnell's theologizing. Bushnell is identified as the father of American liberal theology by Gary Dorrien, *The Making of American Liberal Theology: Imagining Progressive Religion, 1805-1900* (Louisville: Westminster John Knox, 2001), 111.

103. See the essays by Jensen and Doriani in this collection.

104. Charles Hodge, "Dr. Schaff's Apostolic Church," *The Biblical Repertory and Princeton Review* 26, no. 1 (January 1854): 164.

individual, and the shape of one's training and education — not to mention the way sin twists humanity in and through all of this. Care needs to be taken, therefore, when making assertions that a "radically atemporal character of knowledge followed from Hodge's adherence to the common sense realism of the Scottish Enlightenment, especially as formulated by Thomas Reid."[105] Certainly Hodge held that there were God-given structures to the human mind that had to be relied on by all people if knowledge was to be possible at all. But Hodge was alive to the historical influences on human endeavors to know God. And whether it is true to say that Hodge "did not consider knowledge itself in any *fundamental* way *conditioned* by historical context" depends on what one means by *fundamental* and *conditioned.*[106] For while Hodge recognized that one's history did shape or condition one's theology, he also definitely held that the words of the Holy Scriptures rightly portrayed a reality that did not change with the vagaries of human history, and that because of this the "Church is always equally near to Christ and to the Holy Scriptures as the source of life."[107] As always, Hodge insisted on genuine receptivity to God in the canon, enabled by the Spirit of God. Thus there could be — and in fact had been — real progress through history in the church's understanding of God and his actions. The Trinity was a case in point for Hodge. A *sanctified spontaneity* owing to the work of the Spirit through the Scriptures and the history of the church was critically important for relating rightly to God. The Spirit progressively eliminated from the believer's life historically conditioned influences that obscured right relationship to God, weaving the believer into a new history that enabled the believer to understand Scripture aright and live rightly in relationship with him — the history of the church.

None of this is to deny that Hodge sometimes extends his rhetorical connection to his own day's understanding of science farther than he should have, as when he talks about "the truths which the theologian has to reduce to a science," or when he states that theology has "the facts of Scripture for its subject."[108] The subject of theology is the triune God, known best in the incarnation, and a *reduction* of theology to a science risks devising a flat, lifeless theology. Hodge is on safer ground in the *Princeton Review:*

> Finally, God has revealed Himself to us in the person of His Son. No man knoweth the Father, but the Son, and he to whom the Son shall reveal Him. Jesus Christ is the true God. The revelation which He made of Himself while on earth, was the manifestation of God in the flesh. He and the Father are one.

105. Turner, "Charles Hodge in the Intellectual Weather of the Nineteenth Century," 58.

106. Turner, "Charles Hodge in the Intellectual Weather of the Nineteenth Century," 58; emphasis added to the word "fundamental."

107. Hodge, "Dr. Schaff's Apostolic Church," 163.

108. Hodge, *Systematic Theology,* 1:11, 32.

> The words of Christ were the words of God. The works of Christ were the works of God. The love, mercy, tenderness, and forgiving grace, as well as the holiness, severity, and power manifested by Christ, were manifestations of the nature of God. We see, therefore, as with our eyes what God is. We know that, although infinite and absolute, He can think, act, and will; that He can love and hate; that He can hear prayer and forgive sin; that we can have fellowship with Him as one person can commune with another. Philosophy must veil her face and seal her lips in the presence of God thus manifest in the flesh, and not pretend to declare that He is not, or is not known to be, what He has just revealed himself as being.[109]

Hodge knows this well, and when he talks about "the facts of Scripture" he means to refer to the Trinity and the incarnation, among other realities. But his concern to make rhetorical connections to his culture occasionally betrays his best insights.[110] Hodge has taken a beating for his comments about a reduction of theology to a science and his ill-advised "store-house of facts" remark. As Mark Noll has written, "It is doubtful whether a major American thinker ever published anything that so seriously damaged his intellectual reputation as these pages on method in the *Systematic Theology*."[111] And yet, as Noll also notes, "most of Hodge's earlier theological exposition — as well as much of what followed in the *Systematic Theology* — proceeded in blithe disregard of these methodological counsels."[112] While Hodge's theological practice largely rose above the rhetorical connections in the opening pages of the *Systematic Theology*, it is likely that some American Christians outside of Princeton emphasized some aspects of Hodge's methodological comments without sufficient attention to the care and rigor that marked his theology as a whole.

And yet Hodge's flaws as a theologian can be, and often are, overemphasized.

109. Charles Hodge, "Can God Be Known?" *The Biblical Repertory and Princeton Review* 36, no. 1 (January 1864): 152 (variations in capitalization of pronouns in the original).

110. There are other points where it is difficult to know how to read Hodge. For example, in speaking of "Scriptural facts," Hodge states that "they arrange themselves in a certain order by an inward law, just as certainly and as clearly as the particles of matter in the process of crystallization or in the organic unity of the body of an animal" (*Systematic Theology*, 2:315). Read epistemologically, this is a problem. The results of the most painstaking exegetical labors do not fall out neatly in all matters — though they do in the central outlines of the gospel and in much else. Read ontologically, which may be the preferable reading, Hodge is of course correct. There is some theological state of affairs that actually is what it is, and the facts of that situation are arranged however they are arranged independently of us. Even Richard Rorty, *Contingency, Irony, and Solidarity* (New York: Cambridge University Press, 1989), admits that "the world is out there" (5) — though he seems to think it is an epistemological cipher. One wishes Hodge would have been a bit clearer in drawing epistemological and ontological distinctions at times.

111. Noll, "Charles Hodge as an Expositor of the Spiritual Life," 106.

112. Noll, "Charles Hodge as an Expositor of the Spiritual Life," 106.

Even in the much-maligned "Introduction" to Hodge's *Systematic Theology* we find important methodological insights regarding the exegetical answerability of theologians. This appears clearly in a section titled "The theologian to be guided by the same rules as the man of science." While the terminology may grate on us today, Hodge's point, again, is to emphasize responsible canonical receptivity in the face of the rapidly growing impulse to look to human spontaneity as the theological authority. In emphasizing the "collection of facts," Hodge means to emphasize that the theologian's exegetical work is to be thorough and painstaking. "This collection must be made with diligence and care. It is not an easy work. There is great liability to error." Thus when Hodge refers to a scientist who performed an experiment a thousand times before being confident in the results, he is urging theologians to show painstaking care and rigor in their exegesis. Moreover, exegesis must seek results that are "comprehensive, and if possible, exhaustive."[113] Theologians must strive to let the text stand over against their own preferences and proclivities, and Hodge rightly insists that exegetical results we do not like "must not be willfully denied or carelessly overlooked, or unfairly appreciated. We must be honest here, as the true student of nature is honest in his induction."[114] Only an uncharitable reading could miss the point of Hodge's use of the science analogy here: Theologians should be as thorough, painstaking, and scrupulously fair as they can manage in their exegesis. If we can set aside the outdated vocabulary, we find Hodge making many vital points about theological method — points still worth emphasizing.

Not only did Hodge emphasize the theologian's exegetical answerability, he also developed a thoughtful theological method. Surprisingly, given the press he has received, Hodge has a theological epistemology that is nuanced and quite amenable to contemporary concerns. Hodge holds that "men need not be told or taught that the things thus *perceived* [by direct intuition] are true. These *immediate perceptions* are called intuitions, primary truths, laws of belief. . . . [T]he mind is so constituted that it perceives certain things to be true without proof and without instruction."[115] Moreover, the theologian "must take for granted that he can perceive, compare, combine, remember, and infer; and that he can safely *rely* upon these mental faculties in their *legitimate* exercise." With regard to sanctified human spontaneity, Hodge holds that "believers have an unction from the Holy One: they know the truth. This inward teaching produces a conviction that no sophistries can obscure and no arguments can shake."[116] The argument is even more direct in the *Princeton Review:* "We believe the existence of the infinite God to be known by such a perception. We could arrive at it by the conscious

113. Hodge, *Systematic Theology,* 1:11.

114. Hodge, *Systematic Theology,* 1:12.

115. Hodge, *Systematic Theology,* 1:191; emphasis added.

116. Hodge, *Systematic Theology,* 1:9, emphasis added; 1:15.

exercise of reason; but it seems we *instinctively perceive* it in the marks of design in nature, and in providence."[117] Hodge's language calls to mind recent work on the warrant for Christian belief and the "basic beliefs" emphasized by Reformed epistemologists. Philosophers have recently come to realize the importance of Thomas Reid's insights in these and other matters. Nor is it clear among contemporary epistemologists that Quine or Wittgenstein (or Derrida or Žižek) offer better paths than Reid.[118]

Though no claim is being made here that Hodge had worked out a full-fledged Reformed epistemology along the lines of Alvin Plantinga or Nicholas Wolterstorff, it is clear that Hodge is no wooden epistemological foundationalist in the vein of René Descartes or W. K. Clifford. Nor does Hodge make the Bible hostage to a demand for certainty. "It is a monstrous idea, that the thousands of illiterate saints who have entered eternity in the full assurance of hope, had no better foundation for the faith than the testimony of the learned to the truth of the Bible."[119] Hodge states that the historic teaching on biblical authority is

> perfectly consistent with the admission that there are many intellectual difficulties connected with the doctrine, that the Scriptures are the word of

117. Charles Hodge and Francis A. Marsh, "Sir William Hamilton's Philosophy of the Conditioned," *The Biblical Repertory and Princeton Review* 32, no. 3 (July 1860): 503; emphasis added. On the following page, the authors emphasize the connection with morality and refer to Romans 1:19-20. Hodge's writings on William Hamilton and Henry Longueville Mansel are particularly fascinating. B. A. Gerrish comments that in dealing with Mansel and Hamilton in *Systematic Theology,* "Hodge's acute criticisms show him at his argumentative best" ("Charles Hodge and the Europeans," 137). Also of interest are the tight arguments of Hodge, "Can God Be Known?" 122-52. For background, see Bernard V. Lightman, *The Origins of Agnosticism: Victorian Unbelief and the Limits of Knowledge* (Baltimore: Johns Hopkins University Press, 1987), chapter 2, "Mansel and the Kantian Tradition." Some of Hodge's arguments regarding Mansel's notion of knowledge of God as merely "regulative" could be modified and helpfully applied to the positions in George Lindbeck, *The Nature of Doctrine: Religion and Theology in a Postliberal Age* (Philadelphia: Westminster Press, 1984) and some of the "postconservatives" who follow him (see, for example, Murphy, *Beyond Liberalism and Fundamentalism,* 127-31; Grenz and Franke, *Beyond Foundationalism,* 48-49). Hodge (140) also prefigures some of the objections to John Hick's Religious Pluralism made in Alvin Plantinga, *Warranted Christian Belief* (Oxford: Oxford University Press, 2000).

118. See Nicholas Wolterstorff, *Thomas Reid and the Story of Epistemology* (Cambridge: Cambridge University Press, 2001); Keith Lehrer, *Thomas Reid* (New York: Routledge, 1989); and *The Cambridge Companion to Thomas Reid,* ed. Terence Cuneo and René van Woudenberg (Cambridge: Cambridge University Press, 2004).

119. Hodge, "The Latest Form of Infidelity," 36. Like Hodge, Warfield denies that "a man must be a learned apologist before he can become a Christian. . . . There are other evidences of the truth of the Christian religion besides the philosophical and historical ones" (Benjamin Breckinridge Warfield, "A Review of *De Zekerheid des Geloofs,*" in *Selected Shorter Writings of Benjamin B. Warfield,* 2:113).

> God. It is our duty to endeavour to solve these difficulties; to disperse these clouds; to bring the understanding into harmony with our spiritual convictions. *But our faith is in no degree dependent on the success of these endeavours.* There are difficulties connected with the being of God and his relation to the world, which no human intellect can solve, and yet our belief that God is, and that he is the creator, preserver, and governor of the world, is none the less assured.[120]

Or again, speaking of the various objections that might be raised against the Scriptures, Hodge states that "we can even afford to acknowledge our incompetence to meet them in argument, or to answer their objections; and yet our faith remain unshaken and rational."[121] These are not the words of someone who needs some sort of Cartesian certainty or external, scientific evidences before believing, nor of one who "searched for a foundation for theology that could stand firm when subjected to the canons of a supposedly universal human reason," as adherents of the Innovation Argument would have it.[122] The Princetonian reaffirmation and defense of the church's teaching on biblical authority is not beholden to an indefensible epistemological stance.[123]

120. Hodge, "Inspiration," 662-63; emphasis added.

121. Hodge, "Inspiration," 662. Hodge continues: "Comparatively few men are able to meet or refute the arguments of a skillful idealist, and yet comparatively few are the least shaken in their convictions of the reality of the external world." This is not entirely unlike what might be said for the existence of other minds by some contemporary epistemologists.

122. Grenz and Franke, *Beyond Foundationalism,* 34.

123. It is worth noting in passing that Hodge was in many ways very leery of the use of "common sense" reasoning. In his important debate with Edwards Amasa Park, a theologian who applied common sense reasoning very freely, Hodge poses a dilemma: "If this 'higher nature' of man, which thus accords with the spirit of the Bible, is his renewed nature — his nature purified and enlightened by the Holy Spirit — then we have a solemn truth disguised and dandified to curry favour with the world. But if this 'higher nature' be the nature of man, in any of its aspects, as it exists before regeneration, then is the language of Professor Park a treasonable betrayal of the scriptural truth. The doctrines of depravity, and of the necessity of divine influence, are virtually denied" ("The Latest Form of Infidelity," 37). Compare Dorrien's assertion that Hodge was so thoroughly enamored of Scottish "common sense" philosophy that the "incongruity between this trust in the reliability of common sense and the Reformed doctrine of universal depravity gave him little pause" (*The Remaking of Evangelical Theology,* 25). Along with some other advocates of the Innovation Argument, Dorrien's real issue with "Common Sense Realism" is not so much the "common sense" but the *realism,* especially in any sort of *theological* application. In any case, Hodge was not nearly as sanguine about the Scottish enlightenment as advocates of the Innovation Argument often make him out to be.

Some have also alleged that Hodge borrowed an ontologically conceived faculty psychology from Scottish common sense realism. This charge has been given a thorough, well-argued reply in Helseth, *"Right Reason" and the Princeton Mind.*

"Put the Shoes from Off Your Feet": Devoted Theology at Old Princeton

If Hodge's reaffirmation of inerrancy did not emerge from a faulty epistemology, neither did it spring from an arid and narrow rationalism. Yet many who advance the Innovation Argument paint Hodge as a rationalist. For example, after intimating that there are "unsettling similarities" between Hodge and a "modern gnostic heresy," Carl Raschke informs us that "the 'heart,' which Luther and Wesley regarded as the seat of spiritual discernment, is of little bearing. It is the mind that counts" for Hodge.[124] In a similar vein, Stanley Grenz acknowledges "a pietistic strand, evident in [Hodge's] alleged warning to his students to 'beware of a strong head and a cold heart.' Nevertheless, his focus on propositions led him to view the Bible as above all the source for religious teachings, with faith being primarily assent to truth."[125] This claim is supported with a quotation from Hodge's critique of Andover theologian Edwards Amasa Park: "Revelation is the communication of truth by God to the understandings of men. It makes known doctrines. For example, it makes known that God is . . . that Christ is the Son of God; that he assumed our nature; that he died for our sins, etc. These are logical propositions."[126] On this reading, Hodge emerges as a partisan of an overly intellectualized religion that emphasizes doctrine to the detriment of piety and soteriology — with the Bible warped and twisted until it fit this Enlightenment

124. Raschke, *The Next Reformation,* 128. On pp. 120-34, Raschke makes quite a number of assertions about Hodge and other evangelical Christians that need more argumentation than is given. For example, Raschke informs his readers that "Hodge first enunciated what we now call the inerrantist claim in 1866 in a sermon" (123). There is no citation, so it is difficult to tell which sermon Raschke has in mind. In any case, any number of essays by Hodge (or the Alexanders, William Henry Green, Lyman Atwater, or others) prior to 1866 would cause difficulties for Raschke's claim, including Hodge's meticulously argued "Inspiration" of 1857. The historical sketch above, other essays in this volume, and John Woodbridge's painstaking work in his *Biblical Authority* create even deeper difficulties for assertions like Raschke's.

125. Grenz, *Renewing the Center,* 72. Compare Charles Hodge, "Suggestions to Theological Students, on Some of Those Traits of Character, Which the Spirit of the Age Renders Peculiarly Important in the Ministers of the Gospel," *The Biblical Repertory and Theological Review* 5, no. 1 (January 1833): 110-11: "Impress deeply upon your mind that morality is a great part of religion, a great and essential part of the service which we owe to God. Habituate yourselves always to look at the moral character of everything you are called upon to do. Determine always to do what is right, regardless of consequences. Never trifle with your moral feelings; it is trifling with God." For more on Hodge's warm concern for the condition of the heart, see Hoffecker, *Piety and the Princeton Theologians.*

126. Charles Hodge, "The Theology of the Intellect and That of the Feelings, Article II," in *Essays and Reviews* (New York: Robert Carter and Bros., 1857), 609-10; cited in Grenz, *Renewing the Center,* 72, and in Grenz and Franke, *Beyond Foundationalism,* 62; the ellipses are Grenz's. The quote comes from Charles Hodge, "Professor Park's Remarks on the *Princeton Review,*" *The Biblical Repertory and Princeton Review* 23, no. 2 (April 1851): 345.

epistemological project. "Hodge," Raschke tells us, "was prepared to transform what throughout history has been primarily a soteriological perspective into a straightforward *epistemological* claim."[127] Or, as Gary Dorrien asserts, for Hodge and "his tradition," "scripture should be understood primarily as the answer to an epistemological question."[128] Such charges are legion among advocates of the Innovation Argument. These scholars tell us that, for the Old Princetonians, epistemology pushed soteriology and devotion to the margins — and that a novel stance on biblical authority was of a piece with this rationalism.

Hodge certainly thought the inspired words of the Bible frequently conveyed propositions, but he stressed this primarily because the life of the church is tied to the reality to which those propositions reach out. Take one of the propositions Hodge mentions, the proposition that Christ "assumed our nature" — the reality of the incarnation. What happens to the life of the church without that reality? Surely the devotion of the church through the ages is not indifferent to whether that happened or not. "The Word became flesh and made his dwelling among us. We have seen his glory, the glory of the One and Only, who came from the Father full of grace and truth" (John 1:14). These are words — inspired words of God. They are not *merely* a proposition reaching out to a reality: that "Christ assumed our nature." But they are not *less* than that.[129]

Such points required restatement and reemphasis in the theological context of Hodge's day, inspired, as it was, by Kant and Hegel. As we have seen, Kantian and Hegelian patterns of thought (sometimes mediated through popularizers like Samuel Taylor Coleridge and Ralph Waldo Emerson) increasingly held sway among American theologians, such as Horace Bushnell and Edwards Amasa Park. Bushnell could thus speak of a "chemistry of thought" that could be applied to doctrinal statements, such that he felt ready "to accept as great a number as fell in my way . . . one seldom need have any difficulty in accepting as many as are offered him."[130] Never mind that the doctrines may contradict one another, for doctrines like the Incarnation and the Trinity "offer God, not so much to the

127. Raschke, *The Next Reformation,* 123.

128. Dorrien, *The Remaking of Evangelical Theology,* 25.

129. Nor, I want to be clear, do I think Grenz finally thought they *were* less than that, though some adherents of the Innovation Argument do. Vanhoozer, *The Drama of Doctrine,* gives a very helpful account of how the propositions dovetail with the "more" that the various words of the Holy Scriptures are doing. Vanhoozer labels his theology "postconservative," but there seems to be an important difference between Vanhoozer and other theologians like Nancey Murphy who take up the "postconservative" label. On the "postconservative" label, see Richard Mouw, "How Should Evangelicals Do Theology? Delete the Post from Postconservative," *Books & Culture* 7, no. 3 (May/June 2001): 21-22. See also the essay by Padilla in this volume.

130. Horace Bushnell, *God in Christ: Three Discourses, Delivered at New Haven, Cambridge, and Andover, with a Preliminary Dissertation on Language* (Hartford, CT: Brown & Parsons, 1849), 82. Hodge critiques this statement in Hodge, "Bushnell's Discourses," 266.

reason, or logical understanding, as to the imagination, and the perceptive or esthetic apprehension of faith."[131] If one will simply *sing* the doctrine that offends the understanding, the problem disappears: "veiled in flesh the Godhead see, hail th'incarnate Deity." While not literally true, the offending doctrine may yet elevate the *feelings*.[132] Though Park certainly remained more in line with the historic teaching of the church than Bushnell, Hodge worried that Park's defense of a "theology of the feelings" separate from a "theology of the intellect" ended up giving away the farm.[133] Thus, a few sentences after the passage Grenz quoted in support of the Innovation Argument, Hodge says that Park's theory "makes revelation to be the awakening and elevating [of] the religious feelings, which, when thus roused, have higher intuitions of spiritual things than were possible before."[134] The Princetonians were not advancing a project of Enlightenment certainty; they were resisting a Modernist epistemology that threatened not only the historic teaching of the church, but the church herself. "Christ commissioned his disciples to teach. The church was made the teacher of the nations; she has ever regarded herself as the witness and guardian of the truth. Heresy she has repudiated, not as an insult to her authority, but as destructive of her life."[135] The Princetonians did emphasize the cognitive content of the faith over against a challenge that denigrated it, but they did this to *safeguard* the salvation and the devotional life of the church.

Hodge repeatedly and warmly emphasized a vibrant love of God as of the essence of the church's life. For example, in his essay "Suggestions to Theological Students," Hodge enjoined "a spirit of elevated piety, as a requisite for the ministry": "when temptations, dangers, and difficulties are multiplied on every hand; when men need so much teaching and so much guidance, which can only come from the indwelling of the Holy Ghost, then it is we look around for those who are deeply and sincerely pious; who live near to God and the cross, as the hope and stay, under Jesus Christ, of the Church."[136] Far from downplaying devotion and soteriology, Hodge emphasized it strongly. In Hodge's most thorough exposition of the inspiration of Scripture, the importance of the renewed heart is made very clear at the outset. "Faith . . . in Christ involves faith in the Scriptures," and this faith "rests in the demonstration of the Spirit. This demonstration is internal. . . .

131. Bushnell, *God in Christ,* 111. See Hodge, "Bushnell's Discourses," 268.

132. Such hoary approaches have great currency today. For example, see Thomas A. Carlson, "Postmetaphysical Theology," in Vanhoozer, ed., *The Cambridge Companion to Postmodern Theology,* 67, 72.

133. See D. G. Hart, "The Critical Period for Protestant Thought in America," in *Reckoning with the Past,* ed. D. G. Hart (Grand Rapids: Baker, 1995).

134. Hodge, "Professor Park's Remarks on the *Princeton Review,*" 345.

135. Hodge, "Professor Park's Remarks on the *Princeton Review,*" 343. It is worth noting that Hodge speaks extensively about the indispensable place of the feelings in this essay.

136. Hodge, "Suggestions to Theological Students," 112-13.

It is no mere intellectual cognition, cold as a northern light, but it is a power, controlling at once the convictions, the affections, and the conscience."[137] Yet given the place of "feeling" in German biblical scholarship, Hodge carefully clarifies the place of this testimony. The testimony did not function in any way as it did for W. M. L. de Wette in his paean to a "holy art" that could "bring down to us from heaven the divine in earthly form, and bringing it into our view . . . move the cold and narrow heart to accept feelings that are divine and mediate harmony."[138] Rather, the testimony bears witness to a communication from a God who stoops down to us in the Scriptures to make himself known, and this communication has cognitive content. "Christianity," Hodge observes, "always has had a creed. A man who believes certain doctrines is a Christian. If his faith is mere assent, he is a speculative Christian; if it is cordial and appreciating, he is a *true* Christian."[139] One could not *truly* be a Christian without a warm faith in the Lord Jesus Christ as an objective reality — that is, a really existing Person who became incarnate and who rose from the grave, conquering sin and death — and who, as such, is adored and followed. Hodge roundly and regularly affirms "the necessity of truth to piety," and he urges Christians to "let the soul always be so full of the Holy Ghost, that it shall always be preoccupied; and let the determination be graven on both tablets of the heart, always to do what is right in the sight of God, not what is politic, nor what a party wishes."[140] The reason for affirming inerrancy is that "it is one of the fundamental principles of the Bible, that truth is as essential to holiness as light is to vision."[141] When Hodge emphasized the intellectual dimensions of God's revelation, it was not because he denigrated warm devotion to the Lord Jesus Christ — but because the church's ability to receive knowledge of the One we love was being assailed by the intellectuals of his day.

Hodge passed down his warm emphasis on devotion to the Lord to his most capable student: B. B. Warfield. Just as Hodge displayed deep pastoral concern in writing "Suggestions to Theological Students," Warfield showed the same warm pastoral heart when he delivered an address titled "The Religious Life of Theological Students" to the students at Princeton Seminary — an address on "the most important subject which can engage your thought."[142] Warfield exhorted the students to recall that they could not flourish unless knit into the worshiping community of the church.

137. Charles Hodge, "Inspiration," 661.

138. De Wette, *"Eine Idee über das Studium der Theologie,"* 20; quoted in Rogerson, *W. M. L. de Wette,* 38.

139. Hodge, "Inspiration," 693; emphasis added.

140. Hodge, "Suggestions to Theological Students," 106, 110.

141. Hodge, "Inspiration," 693.

142. Benjamin Breckinridge Warfield, "The Religious Life of Theological Students," in *Selected Shorter Writings of Benjamin B. Warfield,* vol. 1, ed. John E. Meeter (Nutley, NJ: Presbyterian and Reformed, 1970), 411.

> No man can withdraw himself from the stated religious services of the community of which he is a member, without serious injury to his personal religious life. . . . Who are these people, who are so vastly strong, so supremely holy, that they do not need the assistance of the common worship for themselves; and who, being so strong and holy, will not give their assistance to the common worship?[143]

Warfield continued on to remind the students of their need to be "giving organic expression to their religious life as a community in frequent stated diets of common worship. Nothing can take the place of this common organic worship of the community as a community, at its stated seasons, and as a regular function of the corporate life of the community."[144] Warfield also echoed Hodge in insisting that theologians never isolate their theology from this warm devotion to the Lord:

> Make all your theological studies "religious exercises." This is the great rule for a rich and wholesome religious life in a theological student. Put your heart into your studies; do not merely occupy your mind with them, but put your heart into them. They bring you daily and hourly into the very presence of God; his ways, his dealing with men, the infinite majesty of his Being form their very subject-matter. *Put the shoes from off your feet in this holy presence.*[145]

Like the rest of the Princetonians before him, Warfield saw no disjunction between mind and heart, devotion and intellect.

The unity of heart and mind in Warfield's theology creates problems for the way some scholars have read Warfield. Some have portrayed Warfield as having "unbounded confidence in the apologetic power of the rational appeal to people of common sense."[146] Given Warfield's "opinion of the power of unaided reason in demonstrating the truth of Christianity, it was essential to Warfield's position to maintain that intellectually the believer and the non-believer stood on common ground."[147] Such rationalism eliminated "a venerable line of explanation for

143. Warfield, "The Religious Life of Theological Students," 418.

144. Warfield, "The Religious Life of Theological Students," 418-19.

145. Warfield, "The Religious Life of Theological Students," 416; emphasis added.

146. Marsden, *Fundamentalism and American Culture,* 115.

147. Marsden, *Fundamentalism and American Culture,* 115. Marsden supports his contention by citing a passage that has since frequently been cited by others: "It is solely by reason that [Christianity] has come thus far on its way to kingship. And it is solely by reasoning that it will put all its enemies under its feet." Benjamin Breckinridge Warfield, "Introduction to Francis R. Beattie's Apologetics," in *Selected Shorter Writings of Benjamin B. Warfield,* vol. 2, 100. A nearly identical passage appears within Warfield, "A Review of *De Zekerheid des Geloofs,*" 120-21. Within the Innovation Argument, this passage has come to play the same role with respect to Warfield that the "store-house of facts" passage plays with respect to Hodge. See, for example,

the failures of reason." As far back as Augustine, "the Fall was often regarded as having so blinded the human intellect that natural knowledge of God has been suppressed and therefore no one could have true understanding without receiving the eyes of faith."[148] Warfield's rationalism, we are told, leads to a fairly major departure from classic Christian teaching about sin. But such judgments need to be qualified, in light of Warfield's emphasis on the *unity* of authority, intellect, and heart. Thus the authority of God devolves onto the Scriptures he "breathed out." The Scriptures "cannot be fully understood by the intellect, acting alone. The natural man cannot receive the things of the Spirit of God. They must first convert the soul before they are fully comprehended by the intellect. Only as they are lived are they understood. Hence the phrase, 'Believe that you may understand,' has its fullest validity."[149] Only a "holy heart" and a "sanctified intellect" could rightly receive the things of God from the Scriptures.[150] Warfield's theology tightly bound together authority, intellect, and heart, insisting that only as the work of the Holy Spirit suffused each could any of them function rightly in theology's task to "beget in us a living religion," a vital devotion to the Lord.[151]

Warfield's concern that theology be of one piece with devotion to the Lord drove his emphasis on biblical authority. The Scriptures, far from being congeries of barren propositions at the foundation of a system, revealed the reality of a personal God and what he has done — and such realities "do not terminate on the intellect. . . . They terminate on the heart."[152] Because of this, theology "does not exist when only the intellect is busied with the apprehension of logical propositions about God, but can come into existence only in beings that possess religious

---

Karen Armstrong, *The Battle for God,* 142, which follows Marsden's reading of Warfield closely. But Marsden's reading neglects crucial context for Warfield's statements about reason: "We are not absurdly arguing that Apologetics has in itself the power to make a man a Christian or to conquer the world to Christ. Only the Spirit of Life can communicate life to a dead soul, or can convict the world in respect of sin and of righteousness, and of judgment" (Warfield, "Introduction to Francis R. Beattie's Apologetics," 99). Or again: faith "can result only from a radical change in the relation of the sinner to God, brought home to the sinner by that creative act of the Holy Ghost which we call the *testimonium Spiritus Sancti*" ("A Review of *De Zekerheid des Geloofs*," 116). For important correctives to Marsden's reading of Warfield, see particularly Helseth, *"Right Reason" and the Princeton Mind.* Also quite helpful are David P. Smith, "B. B. Warfield's Scientifically Constructive Theological Scholarship" (Ph.D. Diss., Trinity Evangelical Divinity School, 2008); Zaspel, *The Theology of B. B. Warfield,* and Paul Helm, "B. B. Warfield's Path to Inerrancy." All of this said, Warfield's statement about reason is incautious and invites a reading that neglects his more measured statements in the same essays and elsewhere.

148. Marsden, *Fundamentalism and American Culture,* 115.

149. Benjamin Breckinridge Warfield, "Authority, Intellect, Heart," in *Selected Shorter Writings of Benjamin B. Warfield,* vol. 2, 671.

150. Warfield, "Authority, Intellect, Heart," 671.

151. Warfield, "Authority, Intellect, Heart," 671.

152. Warfield, "Authority, Intellect, Heart," 671.

natures and through the actions of the religious faculty. The knowledge of God, accordingly, which it is the end of Theology to produce, is that vital knowledge of God which engages the whole man; it can terminate only in distinctively religious knowledge."[153] And so, when Warfield spoke of theology as a "science," he in no way denigrated the devotional or practical dimensions of theology. Like Hodge before him, Warfield knew and clearly affirmed that theology "not only may remain a science while yet 'practical' in aim; it cannot even exist without this 'practical' aim."[154] In the face of Hegelian-inspired theologies that menaced theology's practical aim by emphasizing human spontaneity in the genesis of Scripture, Warfield called theology a "science" to emphasize its character as a kind of receptive knowing, answerable to God. For theology could only be "practical" as it humbly *received* revelation of the realities to which people would fitly respond in devotion. Warfield thus reaffirmed the church's historic understanding of biblical authority because people "are continually striving to be rid of the effects which are ascribed to inspiration in the Scriptures and the formularies of the church; their plea is that inspiration is not to be so conceived as to require these effects."[155] When theology conceives of its normative authority in ways that invite the substitution of personal and cultural forms of human spontaneity for theological receptivity, it imperils its practical aim — it imperils devotion to God and opens the door wider to idolatry.

Conclusion

Mark Noll has candidly cautioned scholars regarding "loose talk about Hodge as a 'scholastic'" and "simplistic, unqualified judgments, of which I have myself been guilty, that Hodge was dominated by the Scottish philosophy of common sense."[156] To be sure, Hodge and his Princeton colleagues were human and made missteps in their theology, and at times their theological vocabulary echoes assumptions of their culture in ways that can grate on us today. But too frequently these faults are magnified by scholars who want to advance the Innovation Argument, resulting in loose talk that doesn't stand up well when viewed in light of what the Princetonians actually wrote — especially as one moves beyond the opening pages of

153. Benjamin Breckinridge Warfield, "Theology a Science," in *Selected Shorter Writings of Benjamin B. Warfield,* 2:210. It is worth noting in passing that Warfield is not holding to an outmoded "faculty psychology." See Helseth, *"Right Reason" and the Princeton Mind* for a consideration of such issues.

154. Warfield, "Theology a Science," 212.

155. Benjamin Breckinridge Warfield, "The Divine and Human in the Bible," in Benjamin Breckinridge Warfield, *Evolution, Scripture, and Science: Selected Writings,* ed. Mark A. Noll and David N. Livingstone (Grand Rapids: Baker, 2000), 52.

156. Noll, "Charles Hodge as an Expositor of the Spiritual Life," 207.

Hodge's *Systematic Theology*. In the pages of the *Princeton Review*, an exceedingly well-informed, nuanced theology enters into lively conversation with a breathtaking array of questions. Many of these questions were of perennial concern to the church, and new answers were being pressed with great philosophical sophistication — answers that urged departures from the church's historic understanding. B. B. Warfield cut to the heart of the matter: "The issue in short — Is Christianity given of God, or made by man?"[157]

Nowhere was the challenge to the church's genuine receptivity to God more important or more insistent than with the biblical criticism that coalesced around the powerful influences of Kant and Hegel. The Old Princetonians were part of the first generation of Christians who faced the challenge of a philosophically sophisticated, modern biblical criticism, and they answered in accord with the church's historic understanding of biblical authority. The Princetonians rightly saw that the life of the church required the church to uphold canonical receptivity in the strongest viable form. They saw no need to abandon the classic Christian belief in this connection. "Greeks, Romans, and Protestants all agree in saying, that everything in the Bible . . . is to be received with the same faith and submission, as though spoken directly by the lips of God himself."[158] Charles Hodge and the other Princetonians marshaled ideas extending back past Augustine and the earlier church fathers to the Scriptures, clarifying them in the face of criticisms earlier ages of the church had not faced. Standing within this history, the Princetonians undertook a reaffirmation and defense of the classic understanding of canonical receptivity as of first importance to the faithful devotion of the church to her Lord. For as Hodge noted, if the doctrines of Scripture "are really the product of the human mind, more or less under the influence of personal or national prejudices, we may receive or reject the teachings of the Bible, according as they agree or disagree with the teachings of our own inward life."[159] If human spontaneity produces the Scriptures — either as personal prejudice ("theology is anthropology") or cultural prejudice ("theology is cultural anthropology") — then what we receive there is insufficient to hem in the personal and cultural forces at play in us as they meet up with our own sinful nature. Theology is bankrupt without canonical receptivity, dissipating across a field of competing spontaneities. Hodge thus set out to defend the whole point of a canon: "The end to be accomplished is the communication or the record of truth. That communication or record is made in human language; unless the language is determined by the Spirit, the communication after all is human, and not divine."[160]

157. Benjamin B. Warfield, "How to Get Rid of Christianity," in *Selected Shorter Writings of Benjamin B. Warfield,* 1:60.

158. Hodge, "Inspiration," 664.

159. Hodge, "Inspiration," 698.

160. Hodge, "Inspiration," 675.

Hodge thus pointed to the pressing problem that dogs alternatives to the church's historic understanding of biblical authority. Admixtures of spontaneity threaten to substitute *our* words for *God's* words. *At precisely those places where the alternative model of authority departs from the church's historic understanding of biblical authority,* "the Bible would be a mere human production. It would lose its supernatural character and divine authority, and one part would differ from another, in its title to our deference and submission, just as the writers were more or less enlightened in their subjective feelings and conceptions."[161] Given this understanding, wherever readers identify points where the Bible is of merely human manufacture, they are free to substitute ideas they prefer. In disagreeing with Scripture, one's own ideas are not pitted against God's, but only against those of other human beings in their historical context. If that is the situation, why shouldn't our own ideas carry at least equal or greater weight? There is no principled reason why they shouldn't, and at just these points it is very easy for our own voices — shaped as they are by individual and cultural proclivities — to be the practical authority in religion. Charles Hodge brings the lived question to a point: "They receive just what pleases them and reject what they dislike, or what conflicts with their critical or philosophical principles."[162] It is already all too easy for us to give rein to our sinful spontaneity in our exegesis. Rejecting the church's historic understanding of biblical authority greatly extends and deepens the areas where our spontaneity undercuts the receptivity to God that is the church's very life. Talk of "the Spirit" can easily be a shill for our own preferences.

Inerrancy serves as a safeguard against human spontaneity usurping the normative authority of Scripture in the life of the church. It is an imperfect safeguard, to be sure. There remain numerous ways in which our spontaneity can elide the moment of normative, canonical receptivity to God, and Cartesian certainty is not available to us in any case. Yet for all that, the recognition that "all Scripture is God-breathed" and errs in nothing it affirms is a critically important safeguard against substituting *our* words for *God's* words — one that the church has instinctively and wisely recognized from the start as indispensable for her continued faithfulness and vitality. In reaffirming and defending this in the face of challenges that gained full voice in their day, the Old Princetonians stood in line with the church of all ages.

161. Hodge, "Inspiration," 668.
162. Hodge, "Inspiration," 696.

EIGHT

Accommodation Historically Considered

Glenn S. Sunshine

Throughout history, Christian theologians have used the concept of accommodation to defend the authority of Scripture against challenges to its teaching. For example, in the patristic period, accommodation was used to explain why the unchanging God changes his demands on us between the Old and New Testaments; in the early modern period, it was used to reconcile contemporary understandings of science and law with Scripture; today, it is used to address ethical and scientific concerns raised by the Old Testament. The basic principle of accommodation is simple to understand: for an infinite, perfect, and holy God to interact with finite, fallible, and fallen humanity, he must accommodate himself to our ability to understand him, coming down to our level so that we can grasp what he says and does. Although this idea is implied in the Latin terms *accommodare* and *attemperare,* the terms most often used for accommodation, it is conveyed more clearly by the favored Greek term for the principle, *synkatabasis,* which translates literally to condescension in its original, non-pejorative sense of coming down from a high place to a lower one to be with someone. This means, among other things, that God's interactions with us are adjusted to historical customs, mores, and concepts about the world, as well as our finite human capacity to understand an infinite God and to obey him. Over time, accommodation grew beyond a tool for apologetics to provide a framework for understanding all of God's dealings with humanity. For example, in the *Institutes,* Calvin uses accommodation far more often with respect to the sacraments and to election than to Scripture.[1]

But precisely what does accommodation imply? Does God's accommodation to a fallible and sinful humanity involve him in error? To what extent does accommodation to people in a particular historical and cultural setting mean that false ideas and norms in the culture must be adopted in order to communicate

1. Glenn S. Sunshine, *Accommodation in Calvin and Socinus: A Study in Contrasts* (M.A. thesis, Deerfield, IL: Trinity Evangelical Divinity School, 1985), 43.

effectively? Answers to these and related questions have profound implications for scriptural authority and interpretation.

Accommodation in the Patristic Era

During the patristic era, accommodation was used widely in biblical interpretation, particularly for addressing the question of the relationship between the two Testaments. In dealing with Jews and with Gnostics who claimed that the orthodox did not understand the deeper meanings of Scripture, and in developing theological concepts such as the divinity of the Holy Spirit, the early church fathers were forced to develop the fundamental outlines of a theory of accommodation that would remain largely intact until the eighteenth century.[2]

Accommodation was first deployed by the church fathers to explain why the Laws that God commanded in the Old Testament no longer applied under the New Testament. This was a fundamental issue that continued to be discussed for several centuries. If God had wanted sacrifices and other ordinances in the Law, why did Christians abandon them? And if he did not want them, why did he command them? Justin Martyr (103-165) was the first Christian writer to deal with this question. In his *Dialogue with Trypho,* Justin explained that God's intention for humanity was encapsulated in the Ten Commandments; all of the other aspects of the Mosaic Law were added after the Israelites worshiped the golden calf. In essence, they were punishment for Israel's inordinate desire for idolatry. The New Testament, then, restored God's original purposes and so God's design for humanity remained constant.[3]

The Gnostics would take this argument one step further, saying that the Apostles and even Jesus hypocritically accommodated the truth to their audience; the Gnostics, however, had the full truth and thus understood the true Gospel better than the orthodox, and thus they held the key to God's purpose for humanity. In response, Irenaeus of Lyons argued that Scripture came to us in the

2. The most complete study of accommodation in this period and in Judaism is Stephen D. Benin, *The Footprints of God: Divine Accommodation in Jewish and Christian Thought,* SUNY Series in Judaica: Hermeneutics, Mysticism, and Religion, ed. Michael Fishbane, Robert Goldenberg, and Arthur Green (Albany: State University of New York Press, 1993). Arnold Huijgen, *Divine Accommodation in John Calvin's Theology: Analysis and Assessment,* Reformed Historical Theology 16, ed. Herman J. Selderhuis (Göttingen: Vandenhoeck & Ruprecht, 2011), also has a very good survey of the history of accommodation in the church fathers that includes several figures not covered by Benin.

3. *Ante-Nicene Fathers,* vol. 1, *The Apostolic Fathers, Justin Martyr, Irenaeus,* ed. Alexander Roberts and James Donaldson (1885), accessed through the Christian Classics Ethereal Library, http://www.ccel.org/ccel/schaff/anf01. The discussion begins in chapter 16, page 202, and continues for most of the rest of the book.

form of progressive revelation, with the message uniquely adapted to the ability of the people to understand it in the time in which it was given. His focus was on the process by which God revealed himself to his people: the Israelites lived long ago and thus they were new to God's ways, and as a result, God had to adapt his message to their level. He uses the analogy of a mother feeding an infant:

> For as it certainly is in the power of a mother to give strong food to her infant [but she does not do so], as the child is not yet able to receive more substantial nourishment; so also it was possible for God Himself to have made man perfect from the first, but man could not receive this [perfection], being as yet an infant. And for this cause our Lord in these last times, when He had summed up all things into Himself, came to us, not as He might have come, but as we were capable of beholding Him. He might easily have come to us in His immortal glory, but in that case we could never have endured the greatness of the glory; and therefore it was that He, who was the perfect bread of the Father, offered Himself to us as milk, [because we were] as infants. He did this when He appeared as a man, that we, being nourished, as it were, from the breast of His flesh, and having, by such a course of milk nourishment, become accustomed to eat and drink the Word of God, may be able also to contain in ourselves the Bread of immortality, which is the Spirit of the Father.[4]

Irenaeus further argued that the gospel as taught by Jesus and the Apostles was not like the Old Covenant, but was the simple truth unaccommodated to the false beliefs or sin of the people. It may have come to us in simple form, but it was the simple, unvarnished truth. In making this argument, Irenaeus created a durable metaphor to explain the concept of accommodation and progressive revelation. He described God as a physician who prescribed medicine that was particularly suitable to the patient. Not everyone with a particular disease can be treated the same way, since medicines appropriate to a strong person might kill someone who is weak; the medicines must thus be adjusted to the person receiving them. In the same way, God gave to people exactly what they needed in their circumstances. In Moses' day, the Jews needed the Law to lead them ultimately to Christ. With Jesus, we now have the fullness of the gospel, and we can receive it because we have been made ready for it by the earlier medicine of the Law, and thus we can count on it as the truth. The medical metaphor for scriptural accommodation would continue to be used well into the early modern period.[5]

Irenaeus's use of a concept of progressive revelation led him to focus on the literal meaning of the biblical text, understanding it as accommodated to its era. The Alexandrine school of exegesis, influenced by Philo and neo-Platonism, was

4. *Against Heresies* 4.38 (http://www.ccel.org/ccel/schaff/anf01.ix.vi.xxxix.html).
5. *Against Heresies* 3.5 (http://www.ccel.org/ccel/schaff/anf01.ix.iv.vi.html).

much more open to the idea of deeper meanings hidden within Scripture than Irenaeus. Origen's *On First Principles* argues that just as human beings are composed of body, soul, and spirit, so Scripture has three layers of meaning embedded within its simple language.[6] In another metaphor that would be used extensively to explain accommodation, Origen compared this to baby talk:

> Just as when we are talking to very small children we do not assume as the object of our instruction any strong understanding in them, but say what we have to say accommodating it to the small understanding of those whom we have before us, and even do what seems to us useful for the education and upbringing of children, realizing that they are children: so the Word of God seems to have disposed the things which were written, adapting the suitable parts of his message to the capacity of his hearers and to their ultimate profit.[7]

At the same time, this baby talk contains deeper meanings that are hidden from the uneducated and can only be ferreted out with study. In this case, the biblical text is accommodated to the capacity of the reader, so that different readers will see different things that God has placed in the text:

> For there are different appearances, as it were, of the Word, according as He shows Himself to each one of those who come to His doctrine; and this in a manner corresponding to the condition of him who is just becoming a disciple, or of him who has made a little progress, or of him who has advanced further, or of him who has already nearly attained to virtue, or who has even already attained it.[8]

In other words, the text itself was not accommodated simply to the culture in which it was first given, but rather is accommodated in a dynamic fashion to each reader according to his ability.

In addition to defending Christianity against Jews and Gnostics, accommodation played an important role in developing orthodox theology. Thus Origen argued that the incarnation was an even greater accommodation to humanity than Scripture: it is the ultimate example of God coming down (*synkatabainein,* to condescend) to our level.[9] Accommodation was linked with biblical exegesis in Athanasius's defense of the deity of Christ against the Arians.[10] Similarly, the

6. Benin, *The Footprints of God,* 10.

7. *Contra Celsum* 5.16; 4.71, quoted in Benin, *The Footprints of God,* 12.

8. *Contra Celsum* 4.16, quoted in Huijgen, *Divine Accommodation in John Calvin's Theology,* 65-66.

9. Huijgen, *Divine Accommodation in John Calvin's Theology,* 63-64.

10. For a summary, see Huijgen, *Divine Accommodation in John Calvin's Theology,* 69-72.

Cappodocian Fathers would use accommodation both as a rhetorical and exegetical tool in defending the deity of the Holy Spirit.

The Cappodocians were particularly important for advancing the church's understanding of accommodation and the relationship between the Old and New Testaments, developing the idea that the Old Testament should be understood as shadows and types of the New. The Cappodocians continued to use the imagery of medicines and baby talk in discussing accommodation, but in keeping with the general trends of the Antiochene School of biblical exegesis, these metaphors are set in the context of the changing historical circumstances from Adam through the New Testament era. John Chrysostom, arguably the most important of the Antiochene Fathers, made accommodation a centerpiece of his teaching, both as a theological principle and as a rhetorical device for adapting his preaching to the needs of the audience. To Chrysostom, accommodation explained the changing dispensations of Scripture, each of which was perfect for its own time but could then be superseded by another as historical conditions changed; it explained anthropomorphisms and visible manifestations of God in Scripture; it explained why Paul could give different instructions concerning dietary laws in Romans and in Colossians (the two churches needed different remedies because the Colossians were stronger in the faith than the Romans); it explained how Christ could be fully God and yet become fully human in the Incarnation.[11] This last is particularly important to Chrysostom. In Christ, God came down to our level to such an extent that we are able to see him face to face, and yet was not diminished in any way by doing so. He further accommodated himself to our capacity when he spoke to people as suited their needs and abilities rather than according to his own knowledge, power, and glory. This is the very substance of our salvation, a great mystery before which we should respond with awe and worship.[12] Chrysostom's understanding of the incarnation as divine condescension is particularly significant: the fact that Christ could be fully human yet without lessening his divinity demonstrates that for Chrysostom, divine accommodation does not necessitate involvement in human fallibility and error.

In the Latin West, Augustine's use of accommodation made it a fixture in biblical exegesis for well over a thousand years. Augustine's view of accommodation was complex, involving his understanding of the relationship of immutable divine purpose in changing historical and cultural contexts, as well as his theories of signs and of language.[13]

11. Benin, *The Footprints of God,* 63-65, 69; Huijgen, *Divine Accommodation in John Calvin's Theology,* 75-84.

12. Benin, *The Footprints of God,* 69-71.

13. Huijgen notes that Augustine does not use the term *accommodare,* but the principle is used in his discussion of the language of the Bible and in God's dealings with people; it is thus hermeneutical and pedagogical in focus (*Divine Accommodation in John Calvin's Theology,* 84).

As was true of many of the other fathers, Augustine's primary focus in his discussion of accommodation had to do with the relationship of the Old Testament and the New Testament. If God was unchanging, why did he demand sacrifices he did not want from the Jews, and then drop them in favor of other rituals for Christians? Augustine's answer was that there was continuity at the heart of all of God's relations with humanity, but that since human cultures and historical circumstances differed, the expression of God's law would necessarily vary across time and space. In other words, God and the religion he mandates are unchanging, but since human societies vary across time and culture, immutable religion must take mutable forms to be expressed properly in differing historical and cultural contexts. Christianity is thus the continuation of Israel's religion in a new era *(dispensatio).* The sacrifices of the Old Testament were an adaptation of pagan practices to a people who expected them to be a normal part of religion, but were properly redirected from idols solely to the one true God.[14] At the same time, they functioned as signs or figures *(figurae)* pointing ahead to the death of Christ on the cross via their likeness *(similitudinem)* to Christ's final sacrifice. The sacrificial system was thus the appropriate expression of true religion before Christ *(ante Christum);* in Christ's passion *(in Christo)* the heart of true religion is revealed; and in the sacraments of the church we have the expression of that same religion after Christ *(post Christum).*[15] Augustine explained the need for these changes by recourse to the familiar metaphor of a physician who prescribes different remedies to different patients according to their ability to tolerate the medicines. Both the Old Testament sacrifices and the New Testament sacraments are signs that point beyond themselves to spiritual realities. For Augustine, signs form the connection between the recipient of the sign and the thing that is signified; both the Jewish sacrificial system in its time and place and the Christian sacraments connect the believer to the substitutionary sacrifice of Christ.

But sacraments are not the only type of sign that is important for religion. For a trained rhetorician like Augustine, words function as signs that point to reality beyond themselves; they are in fact the primary form of human communication, in no small part because they can explain other signs, but not the other way around. The words of Scripture, then, are the critical means by which divine truth is communicated to us. As Benin puts it,

> For [Augustine], Scripture had become "the face of God," and one was required to study, to peruse, to contemplate, and to ponder the words of Scripture in order to fathom and drink deeply from its nourishing and refreshing depths. Scripture bridged the gulf between the human and the divine, and its imagery

14. Benin, *The Footprints of God,* 93-97.
15. Benin, *The Footprints of God,* 103-7.

> needed interpretation. Augustine understood that Scripture also employed signs, and signs in general were needed as a result of humanity's diminished capacities after the Fall. . . . Augustine provided an allegorical method to interpret signs and scripture, a method that developed into a new *"doctrina christiana,"* in which language played a featured role.[16]

As a rhetorician, Augustine was well aware that in order to communicate to different groups, language needed to be accommodated to the audience; this in part accounted for the differences between the Old and New Testament. His allegorical method of reading particular Old Testament texts smoothed out many of these differences. But human fallibility means that our interpretations are subject to error even if the text itself is not. Augustine discussed this in detail in *On the Literal Meaning of Genesis.* The section is worth quoting in its entirety because it shows Augustine's attitude toward the complete truthfulness of the Bible when properly interpreted, but also the many ways we can fall into improper interpretations of the text:

> 38. Let us suppose that in explaining the words, "And God said, 'Let there be light,' and light was made," one man thinks that it was material light that was made, and another that it was spiritual. As to the actual existence of "spiritual light" in a spiritual creature, our faith leaves no doubt; as to the existence of material light, celestial or supercelestial, even existing before the heavens, a light which could have been followed by night, there will be nothing in such a supposition contrary to the faith until unerring truth gives the lie to it. And if that should happen, this teaching was never in Holy Scripture but was an opinion proposed by man in his ignorance. On the other hand, if reason should prove that this opinion is unquestionably true, it will still be uncertain whether this sense was intended by the sacred writer when he used the words quoted above, or whether he meant something else no less true. And if the general drift of the passage shows that the sacred writer did not intend this teaching, the other, which he did intend, will not thereby be false; indeed, it will be true and more worth knowing. On the other hand, if the tenor of the words of Scripture does not militate against our taking this teaching as the mind of the writer, we shall still have to enquire whether he could not have meant something else besides. And if we find that he could have meant something else also, it will not be clear which of the two meanings he intended. And there is no difficulty if he is thought to have wished both interpretations if both are supported by clear indications in the context.[17]

16. Benin, *The Footprints of God,* 95.

17. *St. Augustine, the Literal Meaning of Genesis,* vol. 1, Ancient Christian Writers, trans. and annotated by John Hammond Taylor, S.J. (New York: Paulist Press, 1982), 64-65.

The goal of exegesis is thus determining authorial intent, a process that can be quite difficult and demanding. It involves careful study of the words of Scripture in context, the overall teaching of Scripture, and the use of human reason. The last is critically important in some circumstances, because when Christians insist on an interpretation of Scripture that violates human reason and knowledge of the natural world, it can bring the entire gospel into disrepute among informed pagans:

> 39. Usually, even a non-Christian knows something about the earth, the heavens, and the other elements of this world, about the motion and orbit of the stars and even their size and relative positions, about the predictable eclipses of the sun and moon, the cycles of the years and the seasons, about the kinds of animals, shrubs, stones, and so forth, and this knowledge he holds to as being certain from reason and experience. Now, it is a disgraceful and dangerous thing for an infidel to hear a Christian, presumably giving the meaning of Holy Scripture, talking non-sense on these topics; and we should take all means to prevent such an embarrassing situation, in which people show up vast ignorance in a Christian and laugh it to scorn. The shame is not so much that an ignorant individual is derided, but that people outside the household of the faith think our sacred writers held such opinions, and, to the great loss of those for whose salvation we toil, the writers of our Scripture are criticized and rejected as unlearned men. If they find a Christian mistaken in a field which they themselves know well and hear him maintaining his foolish opinions about our books, how are they going to believe those books in matters concerning the resurrection of the dead, the hope of eternal life, and the kingdom of heaven, when they think their pages are full of falsehoods on facts which they themselves have learnt from experience and the light of reason? Reckless and incompetent expounders of holy Scripture bring untold trouble and sorrow on their wiser brethren when they are caught in one of their mischievous false opinions and are taken to task by those who are not bound by the authority of our sacred books. For then, to defend their utterly foolish and obviously untrue statements, they will try to call upon Holy Scripture for proof and even recite from memory many passages which they think support their position, although "they understand neither what they say nor the things about which they make assertion."[18]

Significantly, Augustine does not rely on accommodation directly to deal with the question of the relationship of Scripture to human reason. For him, the information the text contains about the natural world is not accommodated to the beliefs of the people of the day. Rather, the text is true if we interpret it correctly, and any reading that contradicts human reason is likely wrong. In short, he focuses less on the "scientific" implications of the text and instead focuses on

18. *St. Augustine, the Literal Meaning of Genesis,* 66.

its theological meaning, which is to be understood as an adaptation of eternal truth to temporal circumstances.

In summary, Augustine argued that Scripture is inerrant (though accommodated to the unlearned and written in common language), but our interpretations are not. We must therefore be very careful in our exegesis, taking into account God's accommodation to the historical and cultural circumstances at the time the texts were written, the intent of the author, and the full revelation of God in Christ (hence his allegorizing of Old Testament passages).

Augustine's comments in *On the Literal Meaning of Genesis* are among the first to address the typical modern question of the relationship between the Bible and science. He and most church fathers were far more concerned with the broader question of how the infinite, eternal God could reveal himself to finite, temporal people, and in particular, why the immutable God would change the way he deals with human beings. This question was also of vital concern to the Jewish community. They needed to reconcile the sacrificial system God commanded in Scripture with the destruction of the Temple, the only place where those sacrifices could be made.

Accommodation in Judaism

Following the principle that "Torah speaks in human language," Rabbinic Judaism saw God's interactions with Israel as accommodated to the capacity of the people of Israel, both individually and collectively. Thus manna tasted different to each individual, and the divine revelation at Sinai was perceived differently by each person there. But God also accommodated his self-revelation according to what the people as a whole needed at the time — a warrior at the Red Sea, a teacher at Sinai, an elder in the book of Daniel, a young man in Solomon's day, etc. In particular, the sacrificial system was an accommodation to people who were used to Egyptian religion and thus looked to God to require sacrifice; God allowed it, but intended it as a means to wean Israel away from idolatry.[19] In the centuries following the rabbinic period, Jewish thinkers used accommodation to respond to Christian and Muslim challenges to Judaism. Because Judaism maintains the chasm between the divine and the created order that is bridged in Christianity by the incarnation, Jewish thinkers used accommodation to deal with the physical and psychological anthropomorphisms in Scripture, again relying on the maxim that "Torah speaks in human language" and using accommodation to mediate between reason (i.e., what the people of the time were capable of understanding) and revelation.[20]

Maimonides, the greatest Jewish thinker of the Middle Ages, used accom-

19. Benin, *The Footprints of God,* 127-32.
20. Benin, *The Footprints of God,* 142-45.

modation extensively in all his writings and provided a comprehensive, if controversial, account of the reasons for the end of the sacrificial system. In response to Christian and Muslim claims that the Law was a burden, Maimonides argued that it was paganism that placed meaningless burdens on people and that the Law relieved people of these burdens. Unlike pagan practices, all of God's commands were given for a reason, though we may not always understand what it is. The sacrificial system thus had a purpose: in keeping with rabbinical thought, Maimonides argued that the sacrificial laws were intended to lead the people away from idolatry. The pagan Egyptians practiced sacrifice, and in their time in Egypt Israel had begun to see this as an essential element in worship. God accommodated this belief, not because it was necessary, but as a means to get Israel to abandon their tendency toward idolatry. To do this, God allowed them to continue to sacrifice, but began to put restrictions on the practice: all sacrifices were to be made to him alone; they had to be conducted in certain times and places, and could only be performed by specific people; eventually, they could only be offered at the Temple; the Temple was removed because the people had outgrown idolatry, and so the pedagogical purpose of the sacrificial laws had been fulfilled. The entire sacrificial system was thus a "divine ruse" intended to move people to monotheism by an indirect, subtle route accommodated specifically to the growing capacity of the people of Israel over time to leave polytheism and idolatry behind.[21] Of course, this interpretation was challenged by other Jewish scholars, who, for example, pointed out that Noah offered sacrifices after the Flood.[22] They were particularly troubled by the implication that some parts of the Law had fulfilled their historical purpose and thus were no longer relevant.[23] Nonetheless, Maimonides continued to influence Jewish thought, not only in the specifics of his approach to sacrifice but more generally in his highly sophisticated and systematic use of accommodation. On the latter point, he would even influence Christian scholastic theologians in the thirteenth century.

Accommodation in Scholastic Theology

Given the methodology of medieval scholasticism, it is no surprise that the scholastic theologians worked to integrate as many sources as they could into their approach to accommodation.[24] In terms of scriptural interpretation, medieval

21. Benin, *The Footprints of God,* 151-62.

22. Benin, *The Footprints of God,* 163.

23. Benin, *The Footprints of God,* 178.

24. Scholasticism as a method involved six steps: (1) ask a question, ideally in yes/no form; (2) list authorities that support each side of the question; (3) analyze the authorities to try to resolve the differences between them as much as possible; (4) present the solution to the question; (5) anticipate objections; and (6) refute the objections raised in part 5. As a

fourfold exegesis developed out of Origen's view of Scripture having multiple, hidden meanings that could be discovered through diligent study. The approach was summarized in the Latin verse:

> *Lettera gesta docet,*
> *quid credas allegoria,*
> *moralia quid agas,*
> *quo tendas, anagogia.*[25]

For medieval exegetes, finding these interpretations was a matter of precedent, standardized symbolism, and personal ingenuity. As scholars, the theologians were expected to be able to uncover the deeper meanings of the text that were hidden from the common people, following again Origen's understanding of the accommodated nature of the biblical text. As time went on, however, many increasingly emphasized the various layers of figurative interpretation at the expense of the literal, a point lamented by one of the greatest medieval exegetes, Nicholas of Lyra (1270-1349).

Not every medieval theologian followed the fourfold exegetical approach, of course. William of Auvergne (1180/90-1249), professor of theology and later bishop of Paris, had a very different method of exegesis. Although still very tied to an Augustinian approach to Scripture, William was a key figure in the adoption of Aristotelian methods in theology and was heavily influenced by Maimonides as well, particularly with regard to his use of accommodation. His focus once again was on historical change. Like Maimonides and citing his *Guide,* William argued that the Old Testament laws were all given for a reason, and that reason was principally to wean the people away from idolatry. The multitude of detailed commandments was necessary because, like children, the Israelites did not understand generalities. An apple has to be cut up into small bites for a child to eat it; in the same way the principles of God had to be "cut up" into small, specific commandments so the people could follow them.[26] William relied very heavily on the idea of progressive revelation: the prophets were superior to the Law, because the people were further along on the road away from idolatry; the New Testament brings the complete and clear teaching of God to the world, unaccommodated to the ignorance of the people — similar to the argument of Irenaeus of Lyons.[27]

William's approach to accommodation was thus very closely tied to changing

---

result, the scholastics necessarily incorporated as many patristic and early medieval sources as possible in their analyses.

25. "The literal teaches history, the allegorical, what you should believe, the moral, (i.e., tropological), what you should do, the anagogical, where you are going" (http://www.uvm.edu/~wstephan/dante/typessay.htm).

26. Benin, *The Footprints of God,* 179-80.

27. Benin, *The Footprints of God,* 181.

historical eras following the example of Augustine, though William applied this idea very differently than the great Latin father did. In particular, despite his argument for progressive revelation, William saw little direct connection between the Old and New Testament. Thus Old Testament sacrifices did not forgive sin; they were pious acts that were pleasing to God in their era. They have now been superseded by the church's sacraments, not because the former prefigured the latter but because the sacraments are more perfect and thus more pleasing to God. Similarly, the biblical text is accommodated to our capacity to understand it, and thus the elites of Israel were able to penetrate to deeper truths than the common people; nonetheless, William does not seem to think that these deeper truths included the Incarnation, the Trinity, the atoning work of Christ, and other Christian doctrines that other theologians saw in the Old Testament through their figurative readings of the text.[28] To put it differently, William had some similarities with modern dispensationalists, who likewise tend to emphasize the disjunction between the two testaments and to take a more literal, less figurative approach to exegesis.

William was far from the mainstream in medieval biblical exegesis; he represents a rather surprising anti-figurative pole in the spectrum of medieval theologians, many of whom went to the opposite extreme and focused on figurative meanings and largely ignored the literal.[29] Perhaps the most successful theologian to bridge the gap between the two extremes was Thomas Aquinas.

Following earlier precedents, Aquinas argued that the religion of the Old and New Testament were one and the same; the differences came from accommodating the precepts of true religion to the capacity of people in different eras. Aquinas distinguished between the Old Testament ceremonial and judicial laws: "the ceremonial precepts are determinations of the moral precepts whereby man is directed to God, just as the judicial precepts are determinations of the moral precepts whereby he is directed to his neighbor."[30] Further, the ceremonial and the judicial law each in its own way had both literal and figurative significance. The ceremonial law was intended to regulate Israel's relationship with God in ways that were appropriate to their time. They had literal functions in that era, "whether they refer to the shunning of idolatry; or recall certain Divine benefits; or remind men of the Divine excellence; or point out the disposition of mind which was then required in those who worshipped God."[31] At this point, Aquinas echoes themes from Maimonides and William of Auvergne, but he does not stop

28. Benin, *The Footprints of God,* 182.

29. John of La Rochelle is a prime example of the figurative interpretation of Scripture. See Beryl Smalley, "William of Auvergne, John of La Rochelle, and St. Thomas Aquinas on the Old Law," in *St. Thomas Aquinas Commemorative Studies* (Toronto, 1974), 1:47-51.

30. *Summa Theologica,* II, q. 101, art. 1 (http://www.newadvent.org/summa/2101.htm).

31. *Summa Theologica,* II, q. 102, art. 2 (http://www.newadvent.org/summa/2102.htm #article2).

there: he also argues (contrary to William) that the ceremonial law foreshadows the work of Christ, "whether they be taken from Christ himself and the Church, which pertains to the allegorical sense; or to the morals of the Christian people, which pertains to the moral sense; or to the state of future glory, in as much as we are brought thereto by Christ, which refers to the anagogical sense."[32] The reason for these figurative meanings is that we are unable "to gaze on the Divine Truth in Itself," and so it must be hidden behind figures. Our eternal end is still shrouded in figures as well, though Christ is now revealed and thus in the New Testament we can see him and the New Law clearly and literally, not symbolically.[33] Aquinas's argument here parallels Irenaeus's argument that the gospel is the simple truth, unaccommodated to human error and ignorance.

To Aquinas, the judicial law also is simultaneously literal and figurative. The literal significance of the judicial law is obvious, but Aquinas argues that the law also can be interpreted in both the allegorical and moral senses.[34] Of course, these laws are figurative in a different way than the ceremonial laws, which by their very nature point beyond themselves. The judicial law has as its focus the regulation of interpersonal relationships, but is nonetheless figurative by virtue of the fact that it was given by God to Israel:

> [the judicial laws] did foreshadow something consequently: since, to wit, the entire state of that people, who were directed by these precepts, was figurative, according to 1 Corinthians 10:11: "All . . . things happened to them in figure." . . . The Jewish people were chosen by God that Christ might be born of them. Consequently the entire state of that people had to be prophetic and figurative, as Augustine states (Contra Faust. xxii, 24). For this reason even the judicial precepts that were given to this people were more figurative than those which were given to other nations. Thus, too, the wars and deeds of this people are expounded in the mystical sense: but not the wars and deeds of the Assyrians or Romans, although the latter are more famous in the eyes of men.[35]

For Aquinas, both the literal and figurative interpretations of the Law were accommodations to the people. In the literal sense, they were the appropriate laws to regulate worship and behavior to lead the Israelites toward godliness; in the figurative sense, they revealed to the Israelites as much as they were ready to understand at that time, while revealing much more to us today who have the

32. *Summa Theologica,* II, q. 102, art. 2 (http://www.newadvent.org/summa/2102.htm#article2).

33. *Summa Theologica,* II, q. 101, art. 2 (http://www.newadvent.org/summa/2101.htm#article2).

34. *Summa Theologica,* II, q. 104, art. 2 (http://www.newadvent.org/summa/2104.htm).

35. *Summa Theologica,* II, q. 104, art. 2 (http://www.newadvent.org/summa/2104.htm).

New Testament and the ultimate revelation of God in Jesus Christ, to whom the Law and the Prophets testified. While other scholars in succeeding centuries would sometimes swing to either the literal or figurative poles, Aquinas maintained a balance, bringing together the ancient traditions of the church which principally saw accommodation as the means to explain the differences between the Old and New Testament, the multiple senses of Scripture inherited from Alexandrine exegesis, and even the work of Maimonides, whom Aquinas himself cited.[36]

Accommodation in the Reformation

In the early modern period, the ground shifted considerably with respect to accommodation. In the patristic and medieval periods, accommodation was used principally to explain why the unchanging God would change his Laws between the Old and New Testaments, and to note that God's dealings with humanity are accommodated to our capacity corporately and individually; thus those who are ready for "meat" rather than "milk" would see the deeper, figurative meanings of Scripture according to their abilities. Some Renaissance thinkers, notably Erasmus, continued to discuss these issues, though with a different focus. For Erasmus, the key principle was *similia similibus* (like to like). Thus for God to reach us, he had to accommodate himself to us, both in the Scripture and especially in the incarnation. Within Scripture, spirit and letter exist in dialectical tension. The spirit must come to us in the letter *(similia similibus)* for us to understand it. But just as Jesus came to raise us up to God, so the letter is given to lead us to the spirit. The fourfold sense of Scripture therefore functions as a ladder to raise us from the literal to the spiritual/allegorical meaning of the text, and we should seek that allegorical meaning as soon as possible. (At the same time, medieval theologians tried to force-fit their interpretations into the fourfold sense. Erasmus rejected this, however: the deeper meanings had to be drawn from the text itself.[37]) For Erasmus, accommodation is thus a two-way process: God accommodates the spirit to our capacity by presenting it in the letter, and we for our part need to accommodate ourselves to the spirit as we seek out the allegorical meaning of the text and change to conform to it. This is another application of *similia similibus:* just as God accommodates himself to us in the incarnation and the spirit to the letter in Scripture, so the intent of that accommodation is to raise us up to the spirit and to God, so that we can be like them. Accommodation is first

36. E.g. *Summa Theologica,* II, q. 101, art. 1, obj. 4 (http://www.newadvent.org/summa/2101.htm).

37. Manfred Hoffman, *Rhetoric and Theology: The Hermeneutics of Erasmus* (Toronto: University of Toronto Press, 1994), 101.

down to our level, with the goal of then raising us to the higher level of the spirit as we accommodate ourselves to the written and Incarnate Word revealed to us.[38]

Other Renaissance and Reformation thinkers did not ignore the changes in the Testaments or figurative readings of Scripture, but changed the terms of the discussion considerably. While the relationship of the Old and New Testaments remained a subject of contention, particularly between the so-called Magisterials and Radicals, it was no longer focused on explaining why God's rules changed with the New Testament, but rather on whether the Old Testament model of sacral community and the accompanying connection between government and religion had any relevance at all for the church era. And while accommodation continued to be seen as the fundamental principle governing all of God's relations with humanity, many scholars influenced by humanist methodologies rejected the concept of multiple senses of Scripture. For scholars such as Lefevre d'Étaples, the sole meaning of Scripture tended to be figurative, especially in the Old Testament; for Martin Luther (especially early in his career as a Reformer), it was whichever sense pointed to a Christological interpretation, typically the literal in the New Testament and the figurative in the Old Testament. At the same time, new issues also began to emerge during this period. In particular, the sixteenth century saw the beginnings of an apologetic application of accommodation to biblical passages that came under fire from the growing scientific knowledge of the physical world.

All of these trends come together in the work of John Calvin, the theologian of the Reformation most closely associated with accommodation. Calvin's reliance on accommodation as a general theological principle grew out of his deep sense of the gap between God and humanity, a gap that played a greater role in his theology than it did for most other theologians. If an infinite and holy God is to interact with finite and sinful humanity, he must come down and reach us at our level as an act of grace, because we cannot lift ourselves up to reach him. As a result, like Chrysostom, Calvin saw all of God's interactions with humanity as necessarily accommodated to our capacity and thus the principle played a central role in his theology.

God's principal accommodation to us is the person of Jesus Christ, the Mediator between God and humanity. He is the ground, source, and content of all of God's revelation to us:

> how could [those to whom the Son chooses to reveal the Father] either have comprehended God's mysteries with the mind, or have uttered them, except by the teaching of him to whom alone the secrets of the Father are revealed. Therefore the holy men of old knew God only by beholding him in his Son as in a mirror (cf. II Cor. 3:18). When I say this, I mean that God has never man-

38. Hoffman, *Rhetoric and Theology,* 106-12; Huijgen, *Divine Accommodation in John Calvin's Theology,* 93-103.

> ifested himself to men in any other way than through the Son, that is, his sole wisdom, light, and truth.[39]

This knowledge becomes effective in us through faith, yet that itself only comes to us through the mediator, as Calvin notes in his commentary on 1 Peter 1:20: "It is evident . . . that we cannot believe in God except through Christ, in whom God in a manner makes Himself little, in order to accommodate Himself to our comprehension."[40]

Not surprisingly, accommodation extends to the means of grace. Prayer influences divine sovereignty through a process of accommodation: "[God] so tempers the outcome of events according to his incomprehensible plan that the prayers of the saints, which are a mixture of faith and error, are not nullified."[41] In the case of discipline, Calvin used the ancient medical metaphor to explain how God accommodates his treatment of us to our individual needs, noting that God disciplines us "in accordance with what is healthful for each man. For not all of us suffer in equal degree from the same diseases or, on that account, need the same harsh cure."[42] Preaching is an accommodation to our needs as well. In sermons, God "provides for our weakness in that he prefers to address us in human fashion through interpreters in order to draw us to himself rather than to thunder at us and drive us away. Indeed, from the dread with which God's majesty justly overwhelms them, all the pious truly feel how much this familiar sort of teaching is needed."[43]

In the *Institutes,* Calvin uses accommodation more with respect to the sacraments than any other topic. Two quotations, both explaining why God gave us the sacraments, reveal the overall tenor of his discussion:

> as our faith is slight and feeble unless it is propped up on all sides and sustained by every means, it trembles, wavers, totters, and at last gives way. Here our merciful Lord, according to his infinite kindness, so tempers himself to our capacity that, since we are creatures who always creep on the ground, cleave to the flesh, and, do not think about or even conceive of anything spiritual, he condescends to lead us to himself even by these earthly elements, and to set before us in the flesh a mirror of spiritual blessings.

He later adds:

39. *Institutes* 4.8.5.

40. *Calvin's New Testament Commentaries: A New Translation,* vol. 12, *Hebrews and I and II Peter,* trans. W. B. Johnston, ed. David W. Torrance and Thomas F. Torrance (Grand Rapids: Eerdmans, 1963), 250.

41. *Institutes* 3.20.15.

42. *Institutes* 3.8.5.

43. *Institutes* 4.1.5.

> And because we are of flesh, [God's promises] are shown to us under things of flesh, to instruct us according to our dull capacity, and to lead us by the hand as tutors lead children. . . . For by them he manifests himself to us . . . as far as our dullness is given to perceive, and attests his good will and love toward us more expressly than by word.[44]

All of this illustrates the broad range of subjects for which Calvin made use of the principle of accommodation. In the long run, the role of accommodation in his exegesis would become the most important aspect of his use of the principle. Calvin's basic premise is that when God communicates with us, he does it in simple language that all can understand. This applies both to general revelation[45] and to Scripture, about which he commented, "Scripture, having regard for men's rude and stupid wit, customarily speaks in the manner of the common folk."[46] Speaking in this manner includes using various literary genres to communicate with people more effectively[47] and accommodating the content of Scripture to the ability and needs of the audience. So, for example, Calvin noted with respect to anthropomorphisms, "who even of slight intelligence does not understand that, as nurses commonly do with infants, God is wont in a measure to 'lisp' in speaking to us? Thus such forms of speaking do not so much express clearly what God is like as accommodate the knowledge of him to our slight capacity."[48] Beyond accommodating expressions to our slight capacity as finite creatures, Calvin also said that Jesus accommodated his teachings to the specific needs and expectations of the people, for example in connection with manna.[49]

Calvin also resorted to accommodation to address conflicts between scriptural passages dealing with the natural world and the science of his day. Calvin generally resolved these by arguing that Scripture was written in the language of appearance, in other words, that the words of Scripture describe the world as we see it, not "with philosophical acuteness,"[50] so as not to confuse the uneducated. One example of this approach is Calvin's response to the question of how

44. *Institutes* 4.14.3.

45. "But upon his individual works [in Creation] he has engraved unmistakable marks of his glory, so clear and so prominent that even unlettered and stupid folk cannot plead the excuse of ignorance." *Institutes* 1.5.1, cf. 1.5.2.

46. *Institutes* 1.11.1.

47. As discussed below, the division of accommodation into two categories, "manner" and "matter" (or form and content), was fundamental to scholarly discussions of accommodation at least as far back as the nineteenth century, and provides a helpful lens for viewing Calvin's exegetical practice.

48. *Institutes* 1.13.1. See also 1.17.13 concerning the repentance of God.

49. *Institutes* 4.14.25, cf. 2.10.6.

50. *Calvin's Commentaries,* vol. 1, *Genesis,* trans. Rev. John King, Calvin Translation Society (reprint Grand Rapids: Baker, 2005), Gen. 1:14, 84.

the moon can be described as one of the two great lights that govern the heavens when, first, Saturn is larger than the moon, and, second, the moon is a reflector of light rather than a source of light in its own right. Calvin replied:

> Moses wrote in a popular style of things which, without instruction, all ordinary persons, endued with common sense, are able to understand. . . . [B]ecause he was ordained a teacher as well of the unlearned and rude as of the learned, he could not otherwise fulfill his office than by descending to this grosser method of instruction. Had he spoken of things generally unknown, the uneducated might have pleaded in excuse that such subjects were beyond their capacity. . . . [S]ince the Spirit of God here opens a common school for all, it is not surprising that he should chiefly choose those subjects which would be intelligible to all. If the astronomer inquires respecting the actual dimensions of the stars, he will find the moon to be less than Saturn; but this is something abstruse, for to the sight it appears differently. Moses, therefore, adapts his discourse to common usage. . . . Moses . . . only proposes things which lie open before our eyes.[51]

In other words, Saturn may be larger, but in terms of our daily experience, the moon's appearance is larger; understood in terms of the language of appearance, the passage is true.

Concerning the moon as a source of light, Calvin's comments are similar:

> it is not here philosophically discussed, how great the sun is in the heaven, and how great, or how little is the moon; but how much light comes to us from them. For Moses here addresses himself to our senses, that the knowledge of the gifts of God which we enjoy may not glide away. Therefore, in order to apprehend the meaning of Moses, it is to no purpose to soar above the heavens, let us only open our eyes to behold this light which God enkindles for us in the earth. . . . For as it became a theologian, [Moses] had respect to *us* rather than the *stars*. Nor, in truth, was he ignorant of the fact, that the moon had not sufficient brightness to enlighten the earth, unless it borrowed from the sun; but he deemed it enough to declare what we all may plainly perceive, that the moon is a dispenser of light to us.[52]

In addition to illustrating the use of the language of appearance to eliminate a conflict between science and Scripture, this passage is very significant for what it says about Moses' knowledge of the natural world. Statements such as this are sometimes misread as saying that the Genesis account is simply a mythic

51. *Calvin's Commentaries,* Gen. 1:16, 87.

52. *Calvin's Commentaries,* Gen. 1:15, 85-86.

retelling of the origin of the universe accommodated by God to the pre-scientific mentality of the age, but that is clearly not what Calvin is arguing here. He says that Moses knew the scientific facts about which he wrote, but that he (not God) accommodated the text to the ignorance of the people to teach the "rude and ignorant" about God and his works without confusing them with extraneous information.

Calvin's reliance on the language of appearance resembles Augustine's argument in *On the Literal Meaning of Genesis* that we should avoid insisting on one specific, highly literal interpretation of Scripture when there are other options available, if by so doing it will bring the gospel into disrepute. While Calvin generally interpreted biblical texts literally, when a conflict arose with contemporary science, he resolved it using accommodation to maintain the truthfulness of Scripture properly interpreted (i.e., as accommodated to the common people who received it) while recognizing that science did teach us about the natural world. Like Galileo, who said that the Bible was given to teach us how to go to heaven, not how the heavens go, Calvin said we should not get our science from Scripture: "He who would learn astronomy, and other recondite arts, let him go elsewhere."[53]

David F. Wright has identified another, more unusual aspect of accommodation in Calvin's commentaries. Calvin found repugnant the commands that God gave to the people of Israel concerning slavery (Lev. 25:42), particularly separating wives from husbands (Exod. 21:1-6) and selling one's children to be slaves (Exod. 21:7-11). As a lawyer, he saw this as a violation of equity and natural law, and thus as something that God could not have wanted in an absolute sense. Rather, God accommodated his commands in this case to the barbarity of the people of Israel in much the same way that the sacrificial system was an accommodation to their primitive and barbaric culture.[54] This parallels the earlier discussions of why God commanded sacrifices that he tells us he did not actually want. Just as the sacrificial system was seen as an accommodation to residual paganism by some thinkers, the laws concerning slavery were an accommodation to their barbarous culture.[55]

Calvin's use of accommodation in his theology and exegesis is thus anchored

53. *Calvin's Commentaries,* Gen. 1:6, 79.

54. David F. Wright, "Calvin's Accommodating God," in *Calvin Sincerioris Religionis Vindex: Calvin as Protector of the Purer Religion,* ed. Wilhelm H. Neuser and Brian G. Armstrong, Sixteenth Century Essays and Studies 36 (Kirksville, MO: Sixteenth Century Journal Publishers, 1997), 10-13.

55. Another potential parallel is Jesus' comment that God permitted divorce in the Law because of the hardness of the recipients' hearts (Matt. 19:8): that Law does not express God's perfect will or character, but it is a concession to their inability to live by his standards. Calvin does not interpret this passage in this way in his commentary, however; rather, he sees it as a means of vindicating women in the face of abuse by men.

in Christian tradition dating back to the church fathers, but is at the same time adapted to the newer questions emerging from the early phases of the scientific revolution as well as from legal concepts of equity and natural law. Calvin used accommodation to demonstrate that apparent conflicts between biblical texts or between the Bible and natural philosophy were just that: apparent. The necessarily accommodated nature of Scripture permits an approach to interpretation that allows technical inaccuracies in Scripture (e.g., the moon as a great light) to be resolved in a way that maintains the truthfulness of the text. The ethical issues raised by certain Old Testament Laws were seen as concessions to the primitive state of their society. Just as the earlier theologians argued that God adapted his unchanging will to changing times, so Calvin saw these laws as an imperfect expression of God's justice that would be corrected with additional revelation and cultural change. Calvin thus used accommodation in an effort to maintain biblical authority and truthfulness even in the face of scientific and ethical difficulties. This approach would be challenged by other, more rationalistic sixteenth- and seventeenth-century thinkers who would begin to push biblical interpretation and accommodation in a very different direction, however.

Accommodation in Rationalist Theologians

The Italian theologian Faustus Socinus (Fausto Sozzini, 1539-1604) was one of the first to change the way accommodation was used in biblical exegesis. Socinus was an anti-Trinitarian rationalist. Although he argued for biblical authority in his 1570 treatise *De Auctoritate Sacrae Scripturae,* reason was even more fundamental to his theological methodology than the text of the Bible. In essence, he argued that properly interpreted, the Bible never contradicts human reason. This is why Socinus was an anti-Trinitarian: the Trinity defies human logic. Further, for Socinus, there was a canon in the canon: the "doctrine" of Scripture, its essential saving message, which consists of "the Holy precepts it prescribes, and those most admirable Promises, worthy of God, contain'd therein,"[56] is infallible; the rest may contain errors in matters of "light weight." The term "doctrine" is confusing here since Socinus did not include many topics that other theologians would consider doctrinal issues. For example, although he personally believed in the virgin birth, he was willing to allow the Josephites — a group that believed that Joseph was Jesus' father — into the Polish Brethren because the virgin birth was not "doctrine" since one could "live piously and die for Christ" without believing it. Further, the Josephites believed that the biblical text had been changed

56. *An Argument for the Authority of Holy Scripture; from the Latin of Socinus, after the Steinfurt Copy. To which Is Prefixed a Short Account of His Life,* trans. Edward Combe (London: W. Meadows, 1731), 77.

and therefore accepted the authority of everything that they accepted as part of the Scripture.[57]

Socinus does not rely heavily on accommodation in most of his works; it never appears in *De Auctoritate,* for example. There is one very telling instance, however, in which he used accommodation to deal with a problem in Scripture. Socinus did not believe in Hell or in conscious existence after death until the final resurrection, and even then only the righteous would be raised while the rest would remain dead. But at the same time, he did not think that this should be generally taught. He explained his position as follows:

> One should deal cautiously with [the state of the dead before the Last Day], just even as Christ himself and the Apostles accommodated themselves to the level of the people as the parable of Lazarus [Luke 16:20ff.] and the rich man teaches. This was not the time to perturb the Jews, as even now is not the time, although Jesus sometimes speaks thus in order that it be sufficiently clear that he will resuscitate only the faithful, John 6[:38f., 40, 54]. And Paul [Phil. 3:10f.] most clearly proclaims that he labors in order that he "may, if possible, attain the resurrection." Thus, in the meantime, certain things may be said that even indicate this thing [General Resurrection] to men, until at length the age matures and men are able to accustom themselves to these ways of talking [about the state and destiny of the righteous dead].[58]

This paragraph introduces a new and highly influential approach to using accommodation in interpreting Scripture. Since Socinus did not find what Jesus said in the parable reasonable, that is, it did not fit his beliefs about the state and destiny of the dead, he simply dismisses it as false, an accommodation to the incorrect beliefs of the Jews of Jesus' day. To be sure, Socinus does cite other Scriptures to support his view, but rather than working to reconcile them with the parable,[59] he argues that Jesus knowingly affirmed the false beliefs of people of the day. This represents a major change in the function of accommodation as a tool for biblical exegesis. Up to this point, accommodation had been used to eliminate apparent errors in the text, in essence arguing that the text is true because it was accommodated to the people's needs. With Socinus, we see the opposite: the text is false because it was accommodated to the people's erroneous beliefs.

57. "Epitome of a Colloquium Held in Racow in the Year 1601," in *The Polish Brethren: Documentation of the History and Thought of Unitarianism in the Polish-Lithuanian Commonwealth and in the Diaspora, 1601-1685,* ed. and trans. George Huntston Williams (Missoula, MT: Scholars Press, 1980), 90, 92.

58. "Epitome of a Colloquium Held in Racow in the Year 1601," 121-22.

59. He could, for example, have argued that as a parable it was not intended to be taken literally.

Socinus's approach to accommodation was a response to his faith in human reason, which he saw as unfallen since "it . . . is not plausible that in any way one sin should have such force that it obscures the minds of men."[60] Socinus was thus at the leading edge of a growing rationalism in European culture that gradually replaced Augustine's maxim, "Seek not to understand that you may believe, but believe that you may understand,"[61] with the idea that reason is superior to faith. This idea was taken one step further by Baruch Spinoza, who used accommodation as a way of undermining biblical authority altogether. In his *Tractatus Theologicus Politicus,* Spinoza used the Reformed principle of *sola scriptura* and the idea that Scripture should interpret Scripture to argue that the Bible was in essence a closed system, that it could only be interpreted in terms of itself, and thus that it was completely independent of philosophy and should not be used in conjunction with philosophical discussion. The fact that all of Scripture is accommodated ultimately means it tells us nothing objective, but it becomes the duty of each person to accommodate the biblical text to his own beliefs and reason.[62] While Socinus attempted to maintain some form of biblical authority, even if secondary to reason, Spinoza represents those who would jettison the Bible altogether in favor of reason alone.

The development of rationalism and its impact on attitudes toward the Bible and biblical interpretation was a very complex phenomenon, involving new discoveries in science, the recovery of the writings of Sextus Empiricus and Pyrrhonical skepticism, literary studies, and anthropological and historical issues raised by the discovery of human civilizations and new species of animals in the Americas. Some of these, such as the Galileo affair or Cartesianism, are obvious and well known (though rarely well understood). Others, such as Spinoza's *Tractatus Theologicus Politicus* or the Simon-Leclerc debates, are typically known only to specialists. For present purposes, the critical point is that all of these trends, along with the fragmentation of Christendom in the Reformation and the devastation caused by the Wars of Religion, led to a highly critical attitude toward ecclesiastical institutions, biblical authority, and the exclusive claims of Christianity among important segments of the intellectual elite in Europe.

Although some Enlightenment figures followed Spinoza in rejecting biblical authority altogether, liberal theologians in the eighteenth century typically followed Socinus's lead by trying to maintain some form of biblical authority while accepting more critical and rationalistic approaches to the text. One way to do this was to modify the doctrine of inspiration by emphasizing the role of accommodation in the production of Scripture. For example, Zachariä's *Erklärung*

60. "Epitome of a Colloquium Held in Racow in the Year 1601," 109. Note that the implication is that reason is self-authenticating: reason says that reason cannot be impaired by sin.

61. Cf. Anselm, *credo ut intelligam* and *fides quaerens intellectum.*

62. Huijgen, *Divine Accommodation in John Calvin's Theology,* 31-33.

der Herablassung Gottes zu den Menschen (Schwerin, 1762) shifted the focus of accommodation away from the human authors of Scripture to God himself. As we have seen, Calvin argued that Moses understood science correctly but accommodated the text to the level of common people so as not to confuse them; Socinus argued that Jesus accommodated his parables to the false views of his hearers. In contrast, Zachariä argued that "the revelations of God in the Old Testament, the establishment of the old and new covenants, the incarnation of Christ — in other words, the facts of revelation in general — were only set forth as an 'accommodation' of God to men."[63] While this has obvious resonances with the views of Chrysostom and Calvin that all of God's interactions with humanity were necessarily accommodated, Zachariä took Socinus's argument about Jesus accommodating to contemporary religious beliefs and extended it to all aspects of divine revelation: he argued that a significant percentage of Scripture was simply God cloaking his message in the superstitious beliefs of the people of the day. This idea had radical implications for biblical authority and reliability, but was highly influential among eighteenth-century German rationalist theologians, who spent a great deal of effort trying to reconcile their reason with Scripture by identifying which passages in Scripture were concessions to prevailing beliefs. For example, Johannes Semler argued that Jesus deliberately misapplied to himself Old Testament prophecies that were not actually messianic in order to accommodate his teachings to the misunderstandings of the Jewish people of his day. Under the influence of the *Aufklärung,* a movement which emphasized human reason and potential and rejected the supernatural, much of the New Testament was dismissed as concessions to primitive superstition, including its statements about angels, demons, and even the atonement.[64]

In response to these developments, conservative theologians in the nineteenth century subjected the concept of accommodation to a much more rigorous analysis than it had been given in earlier centuries. The basic issue was framed in terms of pedagogy: since it is impossible to remove all misconceptions and ignorance from students instantly, particularly when dealing with difficult, controversial, or complex subjects, it is inevitable and necessary to adapt one's teaching to the students' capacity. Scholars drew two distinctions to provide a framework for understanding this process.[65] The first distinguished between accommodation

63. Rudolf Hofmann, "Accommodation," in *The New Schaff-Herzog Encyclopedia of Religious Knowledge,* vol. 1, *Aachen-Basilians,* ed. Samuel Macauley Jackson (Grand Rapids: Baker, 1951).

64. Hofmann, "Accommodation"; cf. "Accommodation," *Oxford Dictionary of the Christian Church,* 2nd edition, revised, ed. F. L. Cross and E. A. Livingstone (New York: Oxford University Press, 1983).

65. See, e.g., the articles on accommodation in *A Religious Encyclopedia,* ed. Philip Schaff (1891), *A Dictionary of Doctrinal and Historical Theology,* ed. John Henry Blunt (1892), and *A Concise Cyclopedia of Religious Knowledge,* ed. Elias Benjamin Sanford (1904).

of manner and of matter. Accommodation of manner dealt with rhetorical issues such as the use of parables, proverbs, poetry, literary devices, the language of appearance, etc. Questions of truthfulness or accuracy are irrelevant to this class of accommodation because it only deals with how ideas are expressed, not with the ideas themselves. Accommodation of matter, on the other hand, deals with content, and thus potentially could affect the truthfulness of the text.

This leads to the second distinction, between positive accommodation *(simulatio)* and negative accommodation *(dissimulatio),* both of which involve accommodation of matter. According to Rudolf Hofmann, this distinction dates back to ancient Greek ethical theorists who grappled with the issue of dealing with wrong ideas held by students.[66] In positive accommodation, the teacher knowingly affirms a false belief that students hold in order to teach them a different lesson. This is the sort of accommodation that Socinus argued for in his discussion of the parable of the Rich Man and Lazarus, and that the eighteenth-century liberal German theologians saw in Jesus' affirmations of Mosaic authorship of the Pentateuch or of the messianic intent of passages in the Old Testament. According to Greek ethicists, however, this was tantamount to lying to the student and thus was not ethical. The alternative is negative accommodation, in which the teacher tacitly permits a student's false beliefs to stand for a time without affirming them, with the intention of correcting them later. Greek ethicists argued that this type of accommodation was legitimate and even necessary in practical terms. Since pedagogy is the process of leading people from ignorance and misconceptions to greater and more accurate knowledge, as long as the teacher does not lie to the students by affirming falsehood, it is ethical to allow students to hold false ideas temporarily without immediately correcting them.

The scholars who developed this analysis of accommodation intended to preserve biblical authority and inspiration by demonstrating that biblical accommodation only involved either accommodation of manner or negative accommodation and thus was ethically appropriate. Critical scholars largely ignored this approach, however, preferring instead to focus on the psychology and anthropology of inspiration. Even Clarence Augustine Beckwith's addendum to Hofmann's article on accommodation tried to steer the article away from Hofmann's analytical approach to the subject. Beckwith, "who is clearly embarrassed by the whole question,"[67] argued that:

> The theory of theological accommodation, so far as it is drawn from the New Testament, grows out of a particular conception of the knowledge of Christ and the scope of inspiration. If one holds that Christ possessed complete knowl-

66. Hofmann, "Accommodation."

67. Peter Richardson and Paul W. Gooch, "Accommodation Ethics," *Tyndale Bulletin* 29 (1978): 91.

> edge of all matters relating to the natural world, the Old Testament, the events of his own time, and the future of the kingdom of God on earth, he may affirm either that all of Christ's teaching on these subjects is authoritative and final, or else that in many instances he fitted his teaching to the immediate needs of his hearers; in the latter case, one could not be sure as to the precise nature of the objective fact. If, how ever [*sic*], it be alleged that Jesus's intelligence followed the laws of human growth, that he shared the common scientific, historical, and critical beliefs of his day, and that for us his knowledge is restricted to the spiritual content of revelation, then his allusions to the natural world, to persons, events, books, and authors of the Old Testament, to demons, and the like are to be interpreted according to universal laws of human intelligence; thus the principle of accommodation drops away. In like manner, inspiration may be conceived of either as equipping the sacred writers with an accurate knowledge concerning all things to which they refer, and yet leading them to fit their communications to the temporary prejudice or ignorance of their readers, or as quickening their consciousness concerning spiritual truth, while they were left unillumined about matters which belong to literary, historical, or scientific inquiry. It is thus evident that the question of theological accommodation in the New Testament turns in part on a solution of two previous questions — the content of our Lord's knowledge, and the scope of inspiration in the authors of the various books.[68]

Beckwith's preference, judging from his other writings, was for the rationalist approach to accommodation updated to include ideas about the history of religions drawn from nineteenth-century comparative religion. As he pointed out in the quotation above, this approach effectively eliminates the need for accommodation altogether.

Changing approaches to critical scholarship, including the widespread acceptance of higher criticism and an evolutionary view of Judaism and Christianity derived from studies of comparative religion, meant that accommodation no longer played a central role in biblical studies for most of the twentieth century. It reappeared late in the century because of two separate developments. First, the emergence of contemporary versions of creationism led to a backlash against what was seen as a too-literal reading of the Bible. This included a rediscovery of accommodation as a historical principle that allowed for a non-literal reading of Scripture. In some cases, such as the writings of Bruce Vawter, the version of accommodation had more in common with eighteenth-century German liberal theology than with the earlier tradition. For example, he argues that biblical religion "treats the Bible for what it is, a record of religious experience, a fairly narrow experience, it must be admitted, in view of the far wider dimensions of

68. Hofmann, "Accommodation."

human experience throughout the millennia, but nevertheless an experience that is entirely respectable and deserving of acknowledgement."[69] At the same time, Vawter recognizes that this is not the older, traditional understanding of accommodation. Thus he notes that Chrysostom argued that the authors of Scripture condescended with God in producing the Bible, though today we have advanced in our understanding of the "psychology of inspiration" beyond Chrysostom, so that we no longer need to assume that the human authors of Scripture knew the philosophical (and scientific) truths behind what they wrote.[70] The debate on creationism was quickly extended to discussions of inerrancy, with parallel arguments utilizing accommodation to argue that historically the church had always held to an errant Bible.[71] These discussions showed no evidence of an awareness of the sophisticated analysis of accommodation developed by nineteenth-century theologians, but they typically used accommodation simply to show that past theologians recognized that the text was not always literal, thereby confusing literalism with inerrancy.

Second, at about the same time as the discussions of creationism and inerrancy, scholars in Calvin studies rediscovered his use of accommodation. Ford Lewis Battles led the way with his article "God Was Accommodating Himself to Human Capacity."[72] Battles argued that accommodation was primarily a rhetorical principle for Calvin, a view that has largely prevailed in Calvin studies.[73] The main dissenter to this view has been David Wright, who in a series of articles questioned the rhetorical sources for Calvin's use of accommodation and instead demonstrated that it was more of a theological than a rhetorical principle to Calvin.[74] In particular, as noted above, Wright highlighted the passages in Calvin's

69. "Creationism: Creative Misuse of the Bible," in *Is God a Creationist? The Case against Creation Science,* ed. Roland Mushat Frye (New York: Charles Scribner's Sons, 1983), 75.

70. *Biblical Inspiration* (Philadelphia: Westminster Press, 1972), 41.

71. See, for example, Jack Bartlett Rogers and Donald K. McKim, *The Authority and Interpretation of the Bible: An Historical Approach* (San Francisco: Harper & Row, 1979).

72. *Interpretation* 31 (1977): 19-38.

73. A thorough survey of the growth of accommodation in Calvin studies can be found in Jon Balserak, "The God of Love and Weakness: Calvin's Understanding of God's Accommodating Relationship with His People," *Westminster Theological Journal* 62 (2000): 178-95, n. 5. One reason for the popularity of accommodation in Calvin studies may be the influence of Karl Barth. Battles's view of accommodation as divine rhetoric seems particularly well suited to Barth's idea that through Scripture, we can have an authoritative encounter with God — in other words, that in Scripture God meets us at our capacity.

74. See, for example, "Calvin's Pentateuchal Criticism: Equity, Hardness of Heart, and Divine Accommodation in the Mosaic Harmony Commentary," *Calvin Theological Journal* 21 (1986): 33-50; "Calvin's 'Accommodation' Revisited," in *Calvin as Exegete: Papers and Responses Presented at the Ninth Colloquium on Calvin and Calvin Studies,* ed. Peter De Klerk (Grand Rapids: Calvin Studies Society, 1995), 171-90, and "Calvin's Accommodating God." For an example of Wright's influence, see Jon Balserak, "God of Love and Weakness."

commentaries where he sees provisions of the Torah as violating principles of equity and natural law, which Calvin then attributes to the accommodation of the Law by God to the barbarity of the Israelites. Other scholars, such as Jon Balserak and Arnold Huijgen, have used Wright's work as a starting point for further explorations of the topic.[75]

The work of scholars such as David Wright and Stephen Benin, who have done extensive comparative studies of accommodation throughout Christian and Jewish history,[76] has led to a growing recognition of the role of accommodation as a theological principle throughout church (and Jewish) history. Although in the wake of Battles accommodation had generally been viewed as a rhetorical or exegetical category, recent studies make it clear that it is far broader in scope. At its heart, accommodation addresses a number of very important issues: How does an infinite and holy God interact with finite and sinful humanity, and how does he adapt that interaction across time and culture? It thus includes an explanation of the changes in covenants within the Old Testament and to the New Testament, as well as providing a framework for understanding inspiration and the role and limitations of the human authors of Scripture, and even Jesus' *kenosis.*

In terms of biblical authority, the consensus of the church until the rise of early modern rationalism was that accommodation was a means for resolving apparent errors in Scripture by showing that properly understood, they were not errors at all but were written in language adapted to the capacity of the common people. Chrysostom's discussion of the Incarnation is suggestive here: in Jesus, God accommodated himself to human nature yet without in any way losing any of his divine nature. In the same way, Scripture is written by humans in human language accommodated to us and to our capacity and needs, as well to the various time periods and cultures in which it was written, without in any way compromising its faithfulness to divine truth. It does not necessarily always perfectly reflect the will of God: God never truly desired sacrifice, for example, and some of his laws were concessions to barbarism, but these were accommodations to the era in which Scripture was given and would be corrected with further revelation. Only with the rise of post-Reformation rationalism was this consensus about accommodation broken, along with belief in the reliability of Scripture, the

75. Jon Balserak, *Divinity Compromised: A Study of Divine Accommodation in the Thought of John Calvin,* Studies in Early Modern Religious Reform 5 (Dordrecht: Springer, 2006), tries to explain some of the problems raised by Wright through the nominalist distinction between *potentia absoluta* and *potentia ordinata,* though given Calvin's explicit rejection of that distinction Balserak's argument remains problematic. Huijgen's *Divine Accommodation in John Calvin's Theology* is to date the most extensive discussion of the topic and presents a compelling argument that Calvin's thinking on accommodation was drawn from the church fathers, especially Chrysostom; that his terminology came from Erasmus; and that his use of accommodation falls into two categories, divine pedagogy and divine revelation.

76. See, for example, *The Footprints of God.*

incarnation, supernatural events, the atonement, etc. In approaching accommodation in the aftermath of the rationalists, the kind of detailed analysis of types of accommodation promoted among nineteenth-century conservative scholars can be very helpful in sorting out exactly what past theologians meant when they appealed to accommodation, and in particular, for understanding its implications for the reliability and authority of the biblical text.

NINE

The Answering Speech of Men: Karl Barth on Holy Scripture

David Gibson

Although it is probably too early to tell, it may be that the topic of Scripture in Barth studies stands at a crossroads. On the one hand, ongoing debates over Barth's doctrine of election could have the effect of relegating what Barth says about the Bible to the sidelines of his theology. Intentionally or not, the significance of his contribution in this area will arguably be marginalized. Such an approach is exemplified in the work of Bruce McCormack, one of the leading theologians in the hotly contested domain of Barth's doctrine of election. McCormack suggests that evangelical engagement with Barth should move "from a quibbling with matters which stand on the periphery of Barth's concerns to matters that stand, for him, at the very center." The issues of errancy and inerrancy within Barth's doctrine of Scripture and also his alleged universalism are peripheral, while his exposition of election, Trinity, and Christology in actualistic terms is central.[1]

On the other hand, recent work that reads the *Church Dogmatics* more along the lines of a unified exposition of a consistent argument has seen in Barth's treatment of Scripture both a far-reaching theological strategy and a compre-

1. B. L. McCormack, "The Being of Holy Scripture Is in Becoming," in *Evangelicals and Scripture,* ed. V. Bacote, L. C. Miguélez, and D. L. Okholm (Downers Grove, IL: InterVarsity, 2004), 55-75 (75). Elsewhere McCormack says, "When the history of theology in the twentieth century is written from the vantage point of, let us say, one hundred years from now, I am confident that the greatest contribution of Karl Barth to the development of doctrine will be located in his doctrine of election"; cf. "Grace and Being," in *The Cambridge Companion to Karl Barth,* ed. J. Webster (Cambridge: Cambridge University Press, 2000), 92-110. The reason for McCormack's confidence is his belief about the radical nature of Barth's doctrine of election. But not all Barth interpreters agree. The most recent challenge to his reading is George Hunsinger, *Reading Barth with Charity* (Grand Rapids: Baker Academic, 2015).

I am very grateful to Henri Blocher, Jonathan Gibson, Rob Price, Justin Stratis, John Webster, Martin Westerholm, and Don Wood for their comments on a previous version of this chapter.

hensive hermeneutic that should not be passed over too quickly in any reading of his corpus. Don Wood reads Barth's dogmatic project as forging a new path between the alternatives of liberal Protestantism and Roman Catholicism by offering "an extended restatement of the Protestant scripture principle," which in turn required "a broad dogmatic context involving an extended development of a trinitarian doctrine of revelation."[2] In this way, Barth's doctrine of Scripture is not a topic that can be considered separate from or in any way peripheral to his doctrine of the Trinity. Rather, Scripture functions as part of his exposition of the Trinity precisely because both Trinity and Scripture are part of his doctrine of revelation. While McCormack's reading tends to foreground election in Barth's theology, Wood's reading foregrounds not particular *loci* but a coherent argument driving the *loci*.

Only hindsight will reveal whether there is a major difference here that will impact the fate of Barth's doctrine of Scripture in studies of his theology. Nevertheless, in this chapter I wish to suggest that fruitful evangelical engagement with Barth does not entail moving *away* from his doctrine of Scripture to other topics in his corpus (as important as they are) but rather, at the very least, consists of moving *deeper* into his presentation of Scripture, understood as a contextual restatement of the Reformed scripture principle. This is not to suggest that, where evangelicals once thought there were problems, there are in fact none to be found. On the contrary, my argument will be that Barth's treatment of Scripture as part of a *church* dogmatics puts forward a deeply theological account of biblical interpretation that is full of promise even as it contains a problematic rendering of the ontology of Scripture. A close analysis of the problems in Barth's account can be just as fruitful for constructive theological thinking as glad and humble reflection on its riches. This focus on interpretation and ontology prohibits a comprehensive overview of Barth on the Bible. Nor will I attempt a broad critical engagement with the wide range of presuppositions and decisions in his doctrine of Scripture.[3] Rather, in pursuing depth, my intention is to take up some of the issues in McCormack's essay by offering a detailed treatment of Barth's understanding of the inspiration of Scripture.

The chapter will unfold in four main parts. First, outlining Barth's understanding of the nature of Scripture will show that McCormack has grounds for his assertion that evangelicals should not be too quick to raise the problem of subjectivity in Barth's language of the Bible "becoming" the Word of God. Barth's concept of the Bible as a "witness" to revelation contains neglected hermeneu-

2. D. Wood, *Barth's Theology of Interpretation* (Aldershot, UK: Ashgate, 2007), xiii.

3. This has been ably attempted elsewhere; cf. M. D. Thompson, "Witness to the Word: On Barth's Doctrine of Scripture," 168-97, and M. S. Horton, "A Stony Jar: The Legacy of Karl Barth for Evangelical Theology," 346-81, in *Engaging with Barth: Contemporary Evangelical Critiques*, ed. D. Gibson and D. Strange (New York: T. & T. Clark, 2009).

tical depths capable of educating us in how to handle this language with care. But, moving from the outline to the details of inspiration, I will suggest that the idea of "dynamic infallibilism" (a phrase that McCormack coins and that he suggests is compatible with an evangelical view of the Bible) in fact turns out to be the heart of the problem in Barth's doctrine of Scripture. I will seek to show this in part two of the chapter by sketching ways forward for historical and exegetical analysis of biblical inspiration in Barth's account (here Calvin will come into view as a dialogue partner). Part three will provide theological engagement. Then, in the final section, I will suggest that the problems in Barth's material point towards a redeployment of his category of mystery for our thinking about Scripture. Mystery, it will be argued, is not a convenient escape route through a thorny maze, but a conceptually disciplined way of indicating the Spirit's agency in the production of the Bible.

I

In 1935 Karl Barth returned to the parish of Safenwil in the Aargau region of Switzerland and to the church that he had pastored from 1911 to 1921. The visit afforded him the occasion for a reflection on how much he had changed in the intervening years. On the First Sunday of Advent Barth addressed his old congregation:

> I can see now that I did not preach the gospel clearly enough to you during the time when I was your pastor. Since then I have often thought with some trepidation of those who were perhaps led astray or scandalized by what I said at that time, or of the dead who have passed on and did not hear, at any rate from me, what by human reckoning they ought to have heard.[4]

It is a poignant and revealing statement. By this time, of course, Barth's move out of the theological liberalism of his early years was behind him and he had already embarked on his *Church Dogmatics.* But these words from the Safenwil pulpit are clearly not just a comment on his theological development. Urgent, and attentive to pastoral realities, they point to Barth's radically altered conception of what the church ought to hear from a preacher. A year earlier had Barth described his renewed understanding of preaching in this way:

> I reach and "interest" my hearers most when I least rely on possible and already existing analogies to God's Word, when I least rely on being "able" to proclaim this Word, when I am least confident in my skill in reaching people by means

4. K. Barth, *Theologische Existenz heute* 37, pp. 29-30; cited in E. Busch, *Karl Barth: His Life from Letters and Autobiographical Texts,* trans. J. Bowden (Grand Rapids: Eerdmans, 1994), 64.

> of my rhetoric, and when instead I allow my language to be turned and shaped as much as possible by what the text seems to want to say to me.[5]

Barth's personification of the Bible here indicates what had become, by this stage, one of his most important conceptions of the nature and interpretation of the Bible: it is a witness pointing to a particular object, and so the task of the interpreter is to perceive what it is that the sign is signifying. The consistent thread running from Barth's "Die neue Welt" lecture of 1917 right through his mature treatment of Scripture in the *Church Dogmatics* is that the Bible is to be understood in irreducibly active terms. By speaking of *God,* it confronts the humans who read its pages in much the same way that God confronts humanity in the stories and events of its pages. The text and its interpreter are identified theologically. More than a species of natural history, the text is *holy* Scripture; the interpreter is not a value-neutral reader, but a rebel called to lay down arms.[6] The object to which the text points its readers is the revelation of God, what Barth came to elaborate at length as being "the lordship of the triune God in the incarnate Word by the Holy Spirit."[7] This means that, as John Webster says, when Barth sets out his "extended and architectonic understanding" of both Scripture and its readers, "the claim from which everything else radiates concerns the relation between Scripture and revelation."[8] For Barth, this relation, this pointing — essentially a mode of participation and mediation — is best explained by describing the Bible as a "witness" to revelation.

Don Wood is entirely right to say that while the designation "witness" identifies Scripture ontologically in Barth, this is not its only purpose. "The formula also has the function, sometimes overlooked, of structuring a theological account of the church's interpretative responsibilities and freedoms."[9] I think we can go beyond this and say that the concept is, in fact, essentially hermeneutical. Webster suggests that Barth's chapter "Holy Scripture" in *Church Dogmatics* I/2 views the Bible from two perspectives: first, from God's use of Scripture and, second, from the church's use of Scripture. Webster follows this suggestion, however, with a crucial observation: "Handling these two issues together, Barth is in effect suggesting that our perception of the nature and authority of Scripture is bound up with being a certain type of reader."[10] This neatly captures the fact that, because

5. Barth, "Nein!," *Theologische Existenz heute* 14, p. 62; cited in Busch, *Karl Barth,* 270.

6. The best account of the continuity and development of this theme is Wood, *Barth's Theology of Interpretation;* cf. also H. Kirschstein, *Der Souveräne Gott und die Heilige Schrift: Einführung in die Biblische Hermeneutik Karl Barths* (Aachen: Shaker Verlag, 1998).

7. Barth, *Church Dogmatics,* ed. G. W. Bromiley and T. F. Torrance (Edinburgh: T. & T. Clark, 1956-75), I/2, 457 (hereafter *CD*).

8. J. Webster, *Barth* (London/New York: Continuum, 2000), 65.

9. Wood, *Barth's Theology of Interpretation,* 137.

10. Webster, *Barth,* 65.

Barth is assuming the church as the proper location for dogmatic reflection, he is not trying to account for the Bible as a fact in the world so much as he is trying to explore what may be said about the Bible as a confession of faith by the church. And this necessarily involves a certain kind of stance on the part of the one doing the exploring: prayerful faith. In this way ontology and hermeneutics are inseparably connected in Barth's doctrine of Scripture. It is my suggestion that, because "witness" is at the heart of what Barth is doing here, some of his striking language about the Bible "becoming" the Word of God, though unconventional, need not be seen as overly problematic in itself.

Bruce McCormack believes that evangelical criticism of Barth "has ultimately foundered on this one point, namely, the claim that the Bible *becomes* God's Word."[11] He understands the evangelical complaint as being that this opens the door to subjectivism in theology: if the Bible is not God's Word in itself but is only so in the context of a spiritual experience, then a perilous divide opens up between what the Bible is objectively and what it becomes subjectively. Now McCormack's way forward is to look at the issue through the lens of a strong account of Barth's actualism in the context of his theological ontology. There is much to commend this approach and it could well be one of the most fruitful ways of reading Barth.[12] But might the concept of "witness" (a designation not treated by McCormack) allow us to speak of a "hermeneutical actualism" in a way that also makes sense of the "becoming" terminology?

Barth's bifurcation of the Bible as both a human text that *is* the Word of God and a human text that *becomes* the Word of God is certainly a puzzling aspect of his treatment of Scripture. Taken on their own, these claims are each coherent propositions; the puzzle arises in Barth's case because he affirms that both are true. In *CD* I/1 he says that "in the statement that the Bible is God's Word the little word 'is' refers to its being in this becoming."[13] In *CD* I/2 he says that "Holy Scripture as the original and legitimate witness of divine revelation is itself the Word of God."[14] Both propositions in Barth need to be taken seriously. It is not the

11. McCormack, "The Being of Holy Scripture," 55-56. McCormack gives no examples of evangelical falterings, but perhaps he means something like the following. Geoffrey Bromiley responds to some of Barth's exegesis by saying "surely the act of the Spirit in the authors cannot be suspended on the response of the hearers or readers"; cf. G. W. Bromiley, "Karl Barth's Doctrine of Inspiration," *Journal of the Transactions of the Victoria Institute* 87 (1955): 66-80 (74). I will try to show that expressing divine action as "suspended" on human action in Barth's account is infelicitous.

12. McCormack's reading is followed very closely by J. D. Morrison, "Barth, Barthians and Evangelicals: Reassessing the Question of the Relation of Holy Scripture and the Word of God," *Trinity Journal* 25 (2004): 187-213. Morrison suggests that regardless of how Barth is read here, problems remain in his account of inspiration, although he does not explore this further.

13. *CD* I/1, 109.

14. *CD* I/2, 502.

case that Barth thinks the Bible *is a witness* to the Word of God and only *becomes the Word* in the miraculous event-moment of revelation. For he can just as easily say that the Bible has to become a witness: "If it is to be a witness at all, and to be apprehended as such, the biblical witness must itself be attested by what it attests."[15] So what it is going on here?

We need first of all to recognize the way in which Barth says that the Bible is the Word of God. In *The Göttingen Dogmatics,* where Barth states quite freely that "the Bible cannot come to be God's Word if it is not this already,"[16] he discusses the possibility of any talk about God. In the context of human inability — "the prophets and apostles could no more talk about God than we can" — the fact that the Bible exists at all is due to revelation, and so the Bible is in a sense the result of revelation. Scripture is the "permission and command to speak about God."[17] Ordinary human speech thus enabled may be called the Word of God. "Revelation gives rise to scripture and itself speaks in it. This is what makes scripture God's Word without ceasing to be historically no more than the words of the prophets and apostles."[18]

A similar idea appears later when Barth refers to the Bible as "a reflection or echo or historical mediation" of revelation. True to the principle that God makes himself known only by God, Barth suggests that even if in the Bible God is known "only relatively in the form of indication or historical mediation, we can hardly avoid seeing in this mediation God's own Word."[19] Always for Barth this mediation is indirect, but it is nevertheless a form of speaking that in some way really does participate in God's Word. The Bible is God's Word not "in the form of God's direct speaking, but only indirectly in the form of human speaking about God in the face of God's own speaking, in the form of a 'Thus saith the Lord' whose content will then be human, earthly, historical words."[20] In an essay from 1948, Barth explains the participation in this way:

> None of the biblical writers claimed that he came to speak of revelation by virtue of some special faculty or aptitude: on the contrary, they all testify that the revelation of God came to them with a supreme authoritativeness of its own. . . . But — and this is the all-important point — they *answered* something

15. *CD* I/2, 469.

16. Barth, *The Göttingen Dogmatics: Instruction in the Christian Religion,* vol. 1, ed. H. Reiffen, trans. G. Bromiley (Grand Rapids: Eerdmans, 1991), 219 (hereafter *GD*).

17. *GD,* 56. Webster argues that for Barth "there is no point of contact between God's revelation and the recipient of revelation other than that which revelation establishes by its occurrence" (*Barth,* 54).

18. *GD,* 57.

19. *GD,* 212. For more on the Bible as an "echo" of revelation, see Barth, *Evangelical Theology: An Introduction,* trans. G. Foley (Edinburgh: T. & T. Clark, 1963), 15-36.

20. *GD,* 212.

> that came *to* them, not from them. "They spoke," the Bible says, "in the power and truth of the Holy Spirit." By the Holy Spirit the Bible means a reality that comes to man.[21]

The significance of these statements is that for all Barth's stress on the humanness of the biblical writings and their historical particularity he never intends to say that the Bible is *merely* human. What men wrote they wrote as an answer to what they had first seen and heard. Divine action caused the Bible to be.[22] There are two important implications here. First, Webster is right to point out that one of the problems in using "witness" language to describe the Bible is that it can "suggest a somewhat accidental relation between the text and revelation . . . the text is considered a complete and purely natural entity taken up into the self-communication of God."[23] We can see, however, that Barth's understanding of witness manages to navigate this danger precisely because he does not see the text as "a purely natural entity." Second, what I have traced in outline here is what takes shape as Barth's "unity-in-differentiation" thesis, whereby the Bible (and preaching) are both united to the Word of God and also distinguished from it.[24] As Barth famously explains in *CD* I/1, the one Word of God is given in threefold form: "It is one and the same whether we understand it as revelation, Bible, or proclamation. There is no distinction of degree or value between these forms."[25] In *CD* I/2 we discover that this language of distinction ("we distinguish the Bible as such from revelation") and unity ("in this limitation the Bible is not distinguished from revelation") is now further elaborated in the specific context of the Bible as a witness.[26] It is when we see the Bible as a witness that we are able to see how it both is the Word of God and how it becomes the Word of God.

Barth explains this in §19.1 by analyzing the way language works. All human words point to an object: "[W]e do not speak for the sake of speaking, but for the

21. Barth, "The Christian Understanding of Revelation," in *Against the Stream: Shorter Post-War Writings 1946-52,* ed. R. G. Smith, trans. S. Godman (London: SCM, 1954), 203-40 (224).

22. Barth can also speak of revelation being "found in the Bible" or even being "contained in the Bible" because of the *content* of the Bible, the object that it witnesses to: "the Covenant of God which is fulfilled in the appearance of Jesus Christ"; cf. "Christian Understanding of Revelation," 218. Barth intends this language in a relative, not absolute, sense. It is simply because the Bible *exists,* and it is because it says *what* it says, that it shares in the Word of God. Cf. *CD* 1/2, 491, where Barth states that the authors of Scripture, as witnesses to revelation, were "empowered."

23. J. Webster, *Holy Scripture: A Dogmatic Sketch* (Cambridge: Cambridge University Press, 2003), 24.

24. McCormack rightly points out that this is simply a pared-down version of the same ideas that had been expressed in Barth's Göttingen prolegomena ("The Being of Holy Scripture," 59). Wood refers to this as "differentiated identity" (*Barth's Theology of Interpretation,* viii).

25. *CD* I/1, 121.

26. *CD* I/2, 463.

sake of the indication which is to be made by our speaking."[27] Barth goes as far as saying that we can only meaningfully hear a human utterance when it is clear to us "in its function of indicating something that is described or intended by the word, and also when this function has become an event confronting us, when therefore by means of the human word we ourselves in some degree perceive the thing described."[28] It is obvious that this language of general hermeneutics mirrors Barth's more theologically freighted language of "becoming," "event," and "object," and in fact Barth is at pains to say that his general hermeneutic of how language works actually comes from his special hermeneutic of how the Bible works. Barth's stress on the humanity of the biblical writers is always with a view to arguing that the words of these writers, like all human words, witness to *something* and that there is no true understanding where that *something* is not perceived:

> When their word is heard, and in the hearing attention is paid to what is signified and intended in this word, and there is an understanding of the full meaning and scope of their humanity in the light of this object of their word, then a proper exposition of their word can take account of their humanity in all its scope and meaning — not, however, *in abstracto,* but in its connection with the object revealed in their word as it is heard and understood.[29]

So here is what I think is happening: although he is certainly doing more, in designating the Bible as a witness Barth is not doing less than saying that the Bible becomes what it already is when it is read as it is meant to be read, when it is heard as it is meant to be heard, and when understanding does not simply stop at the witness itself but perceives the divine object witnessed, so that this object is seen and understood and believed.

As outlined above, Barth's expression here of the humanity of the biblical word does not mean he sees it as *purely* human; he cannot, for he regards revelation as the "basis, object and content of this word."[30] So when Barth speaks of the event of the Bible becoming the Word of God, he does not mean it changes into something it is not but that it is seen for what it is: "If we have really listened to the biblical words in all their humanity, if we have accepted them as witness, we have obviously not only heard of the lordship of the triune God, but by this means it has become for us an actual presence and event."[31] Just as ordinary human speech is meant to "become" something, intends to lay hold of us to reveal

27. *CD* I/2, 464.
28. *CD* I/2, 464-65.
29. *CD* I/2, 467.
30. *CD* I/2, 463.
31. *CD* I/2, 463.

something, so also "God's revelation in the human word of Holy Scripture not only wants but can make itself heard. It can become for us real subject-matter, and it can force us to treat it objectively."[32]

To illustrate, perhaps Barth is saying something like this. In the context of a particularly significant event a father may say to his son, "Today you have become a man." Now in one sense the young man was always a man, and yet, in another sense, because of the event that has taken place, he has "become" what he already is.[33] Although there are more layers to Barth's account than are present in this simple analogy, it may express something close to what Barth means when he thinks of both the difference that exists between the words of the Bible and the Word of God and also of the unity that exists between them. The Bible does not become something it never was; it simply becomes something it already is when the Spirit so enables a reader to encounter its object. The particular words of the text are there to witness to a certain object and reality; they are a sign indicating the thing signified. We have no access to the signified apart from the signifiers; they really are, in a sense, part of what they signify, but they are not the sum total of the thing itself.

If this understanding is valid, then it is worth pausing to reflect briefly on the significance of what Barth is doing here. By speaking of Scripture as a "witness," Barth is ordering the task of interpretation to be contingent upon the creature's relation to the Creator more than upon a general account of how readers derive meaning from texts. In Mark Bowald's words, it is the claim that "[w]e read Holy Scripture against a thicker theological horizon of divine agency *or we do not read it at all.*"[34] At every turn, Barth is attempting to privilege an account of interpretation bound up not simply with textual poetics and background historical knowledge, but also with spiritual graces as they are born out of encounter with the divine object witnessed to by the Bible.

> The universal rule of interpretation is that a text can be read and understood and expounded only in reference to and in the light of its theme. But if this is the case, then in the light of the theme — not *a priori,* but from the text itself — the relationship between theme and text must be accepted as essential and indissoluble.[35]

Barth is instructive here in a number of ways. First, he is offering a thoroughgoing revision of the concept of "objective, historical" study of the biblical text.

32. *CD* I/2, 471.

33. I owe the illustration to Michael Rea.

34. M. A. Bowald, "Rendering Mute the Word: Overcoming Deistic Tendencies in Modern Hermeneutics; Kevin Vanhoozer as a Test Case," *Westminster Theological Journal* 69 (2007): 367-81 (373, emphasis added).

35. *CD* I/2, 493.

Instead of an interpretation that focuses solely on the particular time, circumstances, personality, and piety of the biblical writers, Barth urges penetration to the *Sache,* the subject-matter of the text: God himself.[36] Only when we read in this way do we truly read historically, for only in this way do we truly see what it is that the historically specific text is indicating. The spare description of the Bible's theme at this point in the *Church Dogmatics* will receive fuller description in Barth's claim that the Bible says only one thing: "the name Jesus Christ, concealed under the name Israel in the Old Testament, revealed under his own name in the New Testament."[37] What is at stake here is the relationship between exegesis and theology in the reading of Scripture, and Barth suggests that exegesis only really happens when theology is accorded primacy.[38] Instead of positing a naïve impartiality on the part of the interpreter, Barth claims that the nature of the text specifies the nature of its appropriate interpretation. The Bible remains dark to us if we read it and see any other relation between God and man than the one determined once for all by Jesus Christ.[39] This is the witness of the text and if we do not see it as we read, we do not read at all. Barth is probing the question of what exegesis actually is.

But more than this, Barth's account has at its heart the idea that the interpreter should not see the relation between God and man in Jesus as relevant to another person, a statement about what is true in general, without seeing it as a statement about *this* reader in particular. I cannot read the Bible properly if I have not let the Bible read me properly. My grasp of what it says is dependent on its grasp of me, or better, for Barth, it depends on the extent to which I have

36. For a detailed treatment of these ideas in the early Barth, cf. R. E. Burnett, *Karl Barth's Theological Exegesis: The Hermeneutical Principles of the Römerbrief Period* (Grand Rapids: Eerdmans, 2004). On the influence of Calvin in Barth's formation in this regard, see J. Webster, "'In the Shadow of Biblical Work': Barth and Bonhoeffer on Reading the Bible," *Toronto Journal of Theology* 17 (2001): 75-91.

37. *CD* I/2, 720. Elsewhere I have attempted to explore in greater detail than is possible here what Barth intends by this language and, crucially, what it means for his theology of interpretation and his exegetical practice; cf. my *Reading the Decree: Exegesis, Election and Christology in Calvin and Barth* (London/New York: T. & T. Clark, 2009), chapter 4. In my opinion there are significant gains and serious problems in Barth's version of "christocentric" exegesis; cf. my "The Day of God's Mercy: Romans 9–11 in Barth's Doctrine of Election," in Gibson and Strange, eds., *Engaging with Barth,* 136-67.

38. For example, in his comments on Augustine's tractates on John's Gospel, Barth says: "If we want to be truly objective readers and expositors of John's Gospel . . . we will not want to free ourselves from the fact that we are baptized, that for us, then, John's Gospel is part of the canonical Scripture of the Christian church." Cf. *Witness to the Word: A Commentary on John 1,* trans. G. W. Bromiley (Grand Rapids: Eerdmans, 1986), 4. These things, for Barth, are not presuppositions that we have to "suspend or repress" for the sake of "scientific investigation" of the biblical text (5).

39. *CD* I/2, 720.

been searched and shattered by the Word, made new by its justifying grace and continually renewed by its sanctifying power. In this way, speaking of Scripture as a witness is, first, the simple "recognition of a reality that precedes us,"[40] but it is then, second, a repentant acknowledgment that as we read "we are infinitely invested in securing ourselves from the gracious judgment that scripture wishes us to hear and understand."[41]

This is why, when Barth describes the act of interpretation — detailing in a rich way what it means to subordinate all our concepts, ideas, and convictions to the biblical witness — he casts it as something that is *always* a self-referential descriptor of sinful finitude and incapacity and *always* a God-ward descriptor of grace and enabling.[42] It is only the gospel that tells me who I am as man; therefore it is the gospel that tells me what I should be like as reader. For Barth, "the primary thing to be said about the interpretation of scripture is that it is dependent wholly upon a logically and indeed materially prior hearing that, being coincident with the forgiveness of sins, is to be explicated in soteriological rather than abstractly hermeneutical terms."[43] Despite the differences that were to remain between them on scriptural ontology, everywhere Barth maintained what he had learned from Calvin: wherever "it is a matter of acting *with* God and *for* God, knowledge *of* God has to come first."[44]

But let us return to the main issue. I suggest that the category of "witness" can help us to see that the problem in Barth's account is not in his "becoming" language *per se*. It is certainly not an invitation to subjective accounts of the nature of the Bible.[45] It could be argued that in the traditional inspiration-illumination distinction there is a sense in which the Bible "becomes" what it is already is, as God illumines the heart of the reader in a given instance to properly perceive and receive what he has spoken. Barth's formulations gesture in this direction, despite the clear differences in his account. By an alternative route we have arrived at a similar conclusion to McCormack: "[W]hen Barth says that 'the Bible

40. Wood, *Barth's Theology of Interpretation,* 137.

41. Wood, *Barth's Theology of Interpretation,* 171.

42. See *CD* I/2, 710-40, esp. 720.

43. Wood, *Barth's Theology of Interpretation,* 173.

44. Barth, *The Theology of John Calvin,* trans. G. W. Bromiley (Grand Rapids: Eerdmans, 1995), 388. Cf. P. D. Molnar, "'Thy Word Is Truth': The Role of Faith in Reading Scripture Theologically with Karl Barth," in *Thy Word Is Truth: Barth on Scripture,* ed. G. Hunsinger (Grand Rapids: Eerdmans, 2012), 151-72. In many respects Barth's theology of interpretation opens out to the elegant contemporary treatment of scriptural reading and theological education offered by Webster in *Holy Scripture,* chapters 3 and 4.

45. Klaas Runia stresses that although for Barth saying "The Bible is God's Word" is a statement of faith, in Barth's account faith has a receptive, not creative, function: cf. *Karl Barth's Doctrine of Holy Scripture* (Grand Rapids: Eerdmans, 1962), 124-30. For instances in Barth that rule out subjectivism, cf. *CD* I/2, 534.

becomes the Word of God,' he is not speaking of what the Bible is so much as he is making a statement with respect to particular interpreters of it in a definite place and time."[46]

Unlike McCormack, however, I do not think this is sufficient to alleviate Barth's account of significant weaknesses. The problem with the Bible becoming what it already is lies precisely in Barth's conception of *what* the Bible already is: the difficulty is with its being, not with the idea of its becoming. The questions to be faced revolve around whether the senses in which Barth holds that the Bible "is" the Word of God are deep enough, exegetically and theologically, to sustain a truly satisfying conception of what it means for the Bible to "become" the Word of God. Is Barth's ontology of the answering speech of men a sufficient coordination of the agency of the Spirit with the activity of the authors? Is his ontology drawn from a comprehensive reading of the relevant biblical texts, and is it one that, as he claims, enjoys support in the tradition? Is it one that allows him to achieve the kind of dogmatic purchase he requires, not just for what he says about God in the light of the text's inspiration but also for what he says about hermeneutics in light of inspiration?

II

At the heart of Barth's conception of the Bible's becoming is a particular account of the Spirit's role in the Bible's being. His aim is to draw a parallel between the Spirit's activity in the writing of the Bible and the Spirit's activity in the reading of the Bible, the striking feature of which is that he designates both acts of the Spirit as one act of inspiration. At every point he is *against* a concept of "inspiredness" inhering in the biblical text, and *for* a concept of inspiration as something that happened then but also has to happen now. McCormack expresses it like this: "Inspiration is the experience of the prophets and apostles; it is not something that perdures beyond the immediate experience, becoming a permanent attribute of the texts they write."[47] It may be better to follow Richard Burnett's description: inspiration "has to do with God's *promise* which goes with the words of the Bible."[48] It is possible to hear the biblical writer and yet not hear him; the difference is the presence or absence of inspiration. For Barth, what they received in writing we have to receive in reading. If we say that the Bible "has" divine authority, or "is" the Word of God, then we actually need to look back at something that has already taken place and look forward to something that will

46. McCormack, "The Being of Holy Scripture," 71-72.
47. McCormack, "The Being of Holy Scripture," 69-70.
48. Burnett, *Karl Barth's Theological Exegesis,* 99 n. 18.

take place.[49] According to Barth, we recollect that in the Bible we encountered God; we expect to encounter God in the Bible in the future. In view of these two things, in the center, in the present, "imprisoned in thankfulness and hope,"[50] as we read the text so the promise of the inspiration of the Spirit may be fulfilled and the Word of God may again become what it is. We bind ourselves to these particular words in this particular text in the anticipation that "we may be freed by God himself to and for God himself."[51]

These three points of the Spirit's activity — recollection of the past; present reality; expectation for the future — constitute Barth's circle of inspiration that he seeks to defend exegetically and historically in two small-print sections of his argument.[52] Given that some of these issues are explored in more detail elsewhere in this collection I do not intend an exhaustive analysis. Rather, because it is important to Barth that his position is closely aligned with Luther and Calvin, I will take Calvin as a test-case to see how close their views actually are at this point. The purpose of this brief comparison is not to use Calvin as the measure of orthodoxy, but to examine Barth's own claim that his insertion of his views into the tradition is continuous with it at one important point.[53]

Taking the exegetical and historical excurses together, then, one of the striking features of both is their unusual construction. The shape of the historical material is unavoidably dated. Apart from a passing reference to Thomas, Barth's division of material into early church, Reformation, and post-Reformation inevitably presents a truncated analysis by offering nothing on medieval precedents and continuities. This is significant because in Barth's hands Luther and Calvin become innovative on the doctrine of Scripture. With the Reformation's restoration of biblical authority to the church "there now grew up a new doctrine of Scripture, and especially of the inspiration of Scripture, according to Scripture

49. *CD* I/2, 502.

50. *CD* I/2, 533.

51. Barth, *Witness to the Word,* 7.

52. *CD* I/2, 503-6, 514-26.

53. On Barth's retrieval of the Reformed tradition, see especially R. Glomsrud, "Karl Barth between Pietism and Orthodoxy: A Post-Enlightenment *Ressourcement* of Classical Protestantism" (unpublished D.Phil. dissertation; University of Oxford, 2009); Glomsrud, "Karl Barth and Modern Protestantism: The Radical Impulse," in *Always Reformed: Essays in Honor of W. Robert Godfrey,* ed. R. S. Clark and J. E. Kim (Westminster Seminary California, 2010), 92-114. Cf. also C. R. Trueman, "Calvin, Barth, and Reformed Theology: Historical Prolegomena," in *Calvin, Barth, and Reformed Theology,* ed. N. B. MacDonald and C. R. Trueman (Milton Keynes: Paternoster Press, 2008), 3-26. For discussion of problems in Barth's reading of Luther on Scripture, cf. R. A. Muller, *Post-Reformation Reformed Dogmatics: The Rise and Development of Reformed Orthodoxy, ca. 1520 to ca. 1725,* vol. 2, *Holy Scripture: The Cognitive Foundation of Theology,* 2nd edition (Grand Rapids: Baker Academic, 2003), 67; M. D. Thompson, *A Sure Ground on Which to Stand: The Relation of Authority and Interpretive Method in Luther's Approach to Scripture* (Carlisle: Paternoster, 2004), 70-90; Thompson, "Witness to the Word," 182.

itself."[54] Quite to the contrary, Richard Muller has shown that the early Reformation view of Scripture "stands in strong continuity with the issues raised in theological debates of the fourteenth and fifteenth centuries," and that inspiration receives relatively little treatment in the Reformation period because it was not a matter of debate among the Reformers and their adversaries.[55]

In the early church doctrine of inspiration Barth sees a recurring weakness, namely, a focus on the spoken or written biblical word as the dominant point in the circle of Scripture's inspiration. Where this happens we move from verbal inspiration to problematic verbal inspired-ness, with "dictation" misleadingly tied to divine authorship of the Bible. "Where there is this idea of a 'dictation' of Holy Scripture through Christ or the Holy Spirit, is not the doctrine of inspiration slipping into Docetism?"[56] Despite his unease with the word, Barth is happy to accept that the Reformers used it too, even recognizing that Calvin's use of "dictation" in his sermon on 2 Timothy 3:16 echoes the most disturbing uses of the term in Augustine and Gregory the Great. But, for Barth, Calvin's insistence that God himself speaks in Scripture in such a way that he dictates its words is "innocuous," and Calvin does not have a "manto-mechanical or docetic conception of biblical inspiration." It seems that for Barth this language is harmless because Calvin never intended it to be understood apart from a future act of inspiration in the reader, but it is very hard not to read his analysis as special pleading.

It is true that Calvin can speak of the Bible's dictation in close connection with the Spirit's work of illumination.[57] But careful consideration of Calvin's corpus shows that "dictation" is a dominant motif in his description of how the Spirit speaks by and in the mouths of the prophets and apostles, and one that he is capable of employing apart from any connection to the further work of the Spirit. For Calvin, the Evangelists were the Spirit's "clerks," such that "with the most perfect agreement but in different ways" they each wrote "freely and honestly what the Holy Spirit dictated."[58] Whereas Barth accepts a carefully qualified version of verbal inspiration and correspondingly rejects manto-mechanical dictation, Calvin's own conception is not identical to the position Barth accepts nor to the one he rejects.[59] Barth is certainly happy to say that God is the author

54. *CD* I/2, 519.

55. Muller, *Holy Scripture,* 63, 231; cf. also B. Gerrish, "Biblical Authority and the Continental Reformation," *Scottish Journal of Theology* 10 (1957): 337-60.

56. *CD* I/2, 518.

57. Calvin, *Comm. 2 Timothy, Calvin's New Testament Commentaries,* ed. D. W. Torrance and T. F. Torrance, 12 vols. (Grand Rapids: Eerdmans, 1959-72), 10:329-30 (hereafter *CNTC*).

58. Calvin, *Harmony of the Evangelists,* vol. 1, Matt. 2:1 (Edinburgh: Calvin Translation Society), 127.

59. Muller discusses the difference between verbal and mechanical inspiration in Calvin's use of the dictation analogy. The former assumes dictation; the latter moves beyond it in a way that denies the humanity of the writers; cf. *Holy Scripture,* pp. 234-39. For a detailed presenta-

of the Bible, but he never intends this in the more direct sense implied by Calvin's use of dictation. For Barth, "Even the old formula, 'Thus saith the Lord . . .' was not intended to imply that the prophet was about to utter words he had received from God verbatim, but rather that he was commanded to speak these words by God."[60] By contrast, to give one example, Calvin can say, "[T]he words which God dictated to his servant were called the words of Jeremiah; yet, properly speaking, they were not the words of man, for they did not proceed from a mortal man, but only from God."[61]

It is clear that what leads Barth to read the tradition in this way is his own theological concern to explain inspiration in a way that safeguards both the unity of the Holy Spirit and the Bible and "the fact that this unity is a free act of the grace of God, and therefore its content for us is always promise."[62] This is what he believes he has discovered in the Bible itself. He treats four biblical passages — 2 Timothy 3:16; 2 Peter 1:19-21; 2 Corinthians 3:14-18; 1 Corinthians 2:6-16 — taking the first two passages as containing "brief data" and the latter two passages as a commentary on the first.[63] A fair reading of Barth's exegesis here will find more problems in what he claims the passages deny than in what he claims they affirm.

Barth denies that the texts have any place for a concept of inspired-ness. This is the key issue for Barth. Inspiration of the Bible is past, present, and future in 2 Timothy 3:16 and 2 Peter 1:21. Barth sees all three aspects present in the text. In the case of Timothy, as Paul admonishes him about the Scriptures, Paul reminds Timothy that the Scriptures have "already given the proof of what they claim to be" and assures him that they will do so again in the future.

> In the middle of these two statements, throwing light both backwards and forwards, there stands the sentence: *pasa graphē theopneustos,* all, that is the whole Scripture is — literally: "of the Spirit of God," i.e., given and filled and ruled by the Spirit of God and actively outbreathing and spreading abroad and making known the Spirit of God.[64]

Here, for Barth, we are in the presence of mystery. The Spirit is "present and active before and above and in the Bible." In his exegesis of 2 Peter 1:19-21 Barth likewise finds past and future dimensions, but his understanding of the present dimension is altogether closer to Calvin. Barth understands "carried along by the Holy Spirit" as indicating that the Spirit is the true author of Scripture, while the

tion, see K. S. Kantzer, "Calvin and the Holy Scriptures," in *Inspiration and Interpretation,* ed. J. Walvoord (Grand Rapids: Eerdmans, 1957), 115-55.

60. Barth, "Christian Understanding of Revelation," 217.

61. Calvin, *Comm. Jeremiah,* Jer. 36:8 (Edinburgh: Calvin Translation Society, IV), 334.

62. *CD* I/2, 514.

63. *CD* I/2, 516-17.

64. *CD* I/2, 504.

human writers, as *auctores secundarii,* are nevertheless genuine authors. Their *theopneustia* involved their human action being placed under the "*auctoritas primaria,* the lordship of God," and being surrounded, controlled, and impelled by the Holy Spirit.[65] When Barth comes to 2 Corinthians 3 and 1 Corinthians 2, his aim is to show more clearly how the Spirit's work in connection with Scripture is always dynamic, not tied to a fixed textual state. He considers how in 2 Corinthians 3 Paul contrasts the Old Testament witness with his own apostolic ministry, "the spiritual ministry of the new covenant."[66] Barth contends that if Paul "affirmed a special inspiration of Scripture by God, it was obviously only in connection with his view of the present attestation of the same God by the work of the Holy Spirit."[67] In 1 Corinthians 2 Barth sees a fundamental contrast between the *psychikos anthropos* and the *pneumatikos,* and the difference is the work of the Spirit in the latter and not the former. Barth's argument from both of these passages is that the inspiration of the word of the prophets and apostles is what takes place when the same Spirit who created the Bible bears witness to its truth in those who hear and read it.[68]

It seems to me that response to this exegesis must focus on a number of questions. While Barth is right to point out past, present, and future language in the text, and certainly right to say that such language is bound up with the experience of the text, is it helpful effectively to conceptualize all of these various dimensions simply as forms of inspiration? This is not the language the biblical writers use to express the role of the Spirit in each instance.

Furthermore, is Barth warranted in seeing both active and passive senses in the *theopneustos* of 2 Timothy 3:16, so as to deny a fixed, past-tense rendering of the text's nature in the light of the Spirit's activity? Barth's construction renders the Scripture as outbreathing the Spirit when in fact the text says that it is God who has outbreathed the Scripture. A significant feature of this passage is that the God-breathed nature of Scripture is something that we may say about the *text* rather than something we may say about the experience of prophets and apostles or the present-day for the hearers. Runia objects to the construction Barth has placed on 2 Timothy 3:16 and 2 Peter 1:21: "[T]here is no indication whatsoever that we have to read the center from these two acts of recollection and expectation. The texts in no way state that the center, as it were, hangs dialectically between them so that it becomes reality only when recollection and expectation flow together in the act of revelation."[69] At every turn Barth posits a dynamic, free concept of inspiration

65. *CD* I/2, 505.

66. *CD* I/2, 514-15.

67. *CD* I/2, 515.

68. *CD* I/2, 516.

69. Runia, *Doctrine of Holy Scripture,* 135. The classic text on this issue remains B. B. Warfield, *The Inspiration and Authority of the Bible* (Philadelphia: P&R, 1948), and his detailed treatment of θεόπνευστος is more compelling. For a helpful discussion, see T. Ward, *Word*

as opposed to one that is static, fixed, and inert. But his efforts place him at odds with those he wishes to identify with. On 2 Corinthians 3, for instance, whereas Barth sees the text as fundamentally contrasting Old Testament Scripture with the work of the Spirit (albeit in a way that does not denigrate the former), Calvin says that "there is no doubt that by the *letter* [Paul] means the Old Testament and by the *Spirit* the gospel."[70] For Calvin the issue is a qualitative difference between law and gospel so that in the latter the "veil" is no longer in place. Although he does see connections to the enlightening work of the Spirit, the passage is not at all concerned with "inspiration" of the text in either dispensation.[71]

The real problem is Barth's contention that we may affirm past inspiration *only* in connection with the present attestation of the same act of God. Why *only* instead of *as well as*? For while Calvin famously places great emphasis on the ongoing work of the Spirit in the illumination of the reader, it is foreign to his mindset to see in illumination a corresponding rejection of an inspired text. Inspiration was in the past. It created a God-breathed text in which "the living words of God" were spoken so that now, in the present, the Spirit seals in our hearts the "utter certainty (just as if we were gazing upon the majesty of God himself) that [Scripture] has flowed to us from the very mouth of God by the ministry of men."[72] Considerations such as these point toward the suggestion that Barth's inspiration thesis is exegetically unproven and historically novel.

III

So far I have queried whether Barth's view of the Bible as the answering speech of men is an adequate conceptual paraphrase for the *apo theou* description of the Spirit's agency in inspiration (2 Peter 1:21). While in Barth's account the Bible does not become something it never was, he appears to locate divine action a step further from the production of the text than the text itself suggests and the

---

and Supplement: Speech Acts, Biblical Texts, and the Sufficiency of Scripture (Oxford: Oxford University Press, 2002), 263-88.

70. Calvin, *Comm. 2 Corinthians* (*CNTC,* vol. 10), 41.

71. Similarly on 1 Corinthians 2, Barth sees the language as relevant to biblical inspiration but this is not in view for Calvin; the matter is rather Paul's preaching. Cf. *Comm. 1 Corinthians* (*CNTC,* vol. 9), 60-64.

72. Calvin, *Institutes of the Christian Religion,* 2 vols., ed. J. T. McNeill, trans. F. L. Battles (Philadelphia: Westminster, 1960), 1.7.1; 1.7.5. On the relationship between inspiration and illumination in Calvin, cf. R. A. Muller, "The Foundation of Calvin's Theology: Scripture as Revealing God's Word," *Duke Divinity School Review* 44 (1979): 14-23. Barth also contends that for Luther and Calvin inspiration rests on the content of the Bible, on its witness to Christ (*CD* I/2, 520). My own suggestion is that Calvin's conception of the Bible witnessing to Christ relies on a different doctrine of revelation than Barth; cf. *Reading the Decree,* esp. 174-78.

tradition seems to affirm. More significant problems emerge when we consider the theological weight Barth places on his view of inspiration.

Barth follows his consideration of inspiration with a rhetorically powerful set of propositions contending that the Bible is the Word of God. His aim is to express the divine nature of the Bible in the closest possible proximity to its human nature. For Barth, to say "the Word of God" is to say "the miracle of God."[73] By this he means: "in speaking of the act of God in Jesus Christ, [the Bible] does itself speak of the grace of God as a reality that cannot be deduced or conceived in the context of human existence that we know, a reality that posits the end of all other events and opens up a new series of events."[74] It is important to see that this miracle of the Bible is not a compromise of its humanity in any way; rather, the miracle is "that the lame walk, that the blind see, that the dead are raised, that sinful and erring men as such speak the Word of God: that is the miracle of which we speak when we say that the Bible is the Word of God."[75] Up to this point, instead of talking about the "errors" of the biblical writers, Barth has deliberately preferred to speak only of their "capacity for errors."[76] But now, in heightened prose stressing the humanity of the prophets and apostles, Barth asserts that the prophets and apostles "even in the act of writing down their witness, they were real historical men as we are, and therefore sinful in their action and capable and actually guilty of error in their spoken and written word." Not only may the prophets and apostles have been at fault in *some* of their writing, Barth makes the "even bolder assertion" that they can have been at fault in *every* word. Yet, "being justified and sanctified by grace alone, they have still spoken the Word of God in their fallible and erring human word."[77] We are thus absolved from trying to differentiate fallible from infallible portions of the Bible. If God himself was not ashamed of Scripture's fallibility, historical and scientific inaccuracies, and theological contradictions, then neither should we be when God "wills to renew it to us in all its fallibility as witness."[78]

It is language like this that probably lies at the heart of McCormack's term "dynamic infallibilism."[79] Although McCormack offers no explanation of his own phrase, it seems to capture very well the sense of Barth's text. The traditional concept of inerrancy comes from the identification of God's words and human words

73. *CD* I/2, 528.

74. *CD* I/2, 508.

75. *CD* I/2, 529.

76. *CD* I/2, 508.

77. *CD* I/2, 529-30.

78. *CD* I/2, 531; the notion of "contradictions" in Scripture surfaces often. "In many things they said — and in some important propositions — they contradicted each other"; cf. Barth, "The Authority and Significance of the Bible: Twelve Theses," in *God Here and Now,* trans. P. M. van Buren (Routledge: London, 1964), 55-74 (59).

79. McCormack, "The Being of Holy Scripture," 73-74.

in the text. For Barth, however, the way in which human words participate in the divine Word means that in the miraculous event of revelation we may affirm that "God himself now says what this text says."[80] That is to say, dynamic infallibilism refers not to a property inherent in the text but to the way in which the text is used by God in the given moment of his choosing. "Verbal inspiration does not mean the infallibility of the biblical word in its linguistic, historical, and theological character as a human word. It means that the fallible and faulty human word is as such used by God and has to be received and heard in spite of its human fallibility."[81]

The problem with this construction lies less in a loose notion of errant and fallible words being somehow "used" by God and rather in the specific claim that "God himself now says what the text says." Such language is rare in Barth because his perception is that *Deus dixit* and *Paulus dixit* are not identical. Nevertheless, he does want to account for verbal inspiration and the fact that "if God speaks to man, he really speaks the language of this concrete human word of man."[82] Perhaps it is the underlying influence of the "older Protestantism" that leads him to say this here; perhaps it is the attempt to bring his argument to a crescendo; it may just be the consistent outworking of his simple desire to affirm that God speaks in the Bible. Whatever gives rise to it, such "dynamic infallibilism" is unstable because it suggests that at certain points — or even at every point — what God *says* is errant, inaccurate, and contradictory.

This is the heart of the problem in Barth's conception of "the Bible is the Word of God." I have argued that we have to take Barth seriously in his claim that the Bible cannot come to be the Word of God if it is not this already. But it is now obvious how far his meaning differs in principle and effect from the classical understanding of the same words. Traditionally, to say "the Bible is the Word of God" identifies the Bible with divine revelation without recourse to supplementary "becoming" terminology. For Barth, to say "the Bible is the Word of God" simply identifies the Word of God in the sign of the word of man, and the conceptuality of "becoming" is necessary to identify the Bible with revelation. Barth necessarily places fallible human words at the center of the definition of "the Bible" so that when the Bible "becomes" what it already is, fallibility is inextricably linked to the event-moment. It is not that the Bible "becomes" infallible; rather, the Bible becomes again the miracle of the grace of God to sinners just as it was at every point of its inscripturation.[83] The impulse to safeguard and elevate God's

80. *CD* I/2, 532 (translation altered).

81. *CD* I/2, 533.

82. *CD* I/2, 532.

83. This point is made with Barth's reference to God's acting on the waters of Pool of Bethesda as similar in kind to how God acts in and with the Bible: "A genuine, fallible human word is at this center the Word of God: not in virtue of its own superiority, of its replacement by a Word of God veiled as a word of man, *still less of any kind of miraculous transformation,* but, of course, in virtue of the privilege that here and now it is taken and used by God himself, like

grace reveals once again that soteriology is fundamental to Barth's bibliology. But in the process God's Word becomes less than it actually is, because the "becoming" is predicated of a "being" that is less than it actually is. That is to say, Barth's construal of God's speech is vastly underdrawn, for the biblical portrayal surely involves us in recognizing that the word of God carries the character of God. If God is trustworthy, then his word is trustworthy (Heb. 6:13-20).[84]

As we have already seen, of course, it is possible that Barth does not intend "God says what this text says" to be a verbatim "saying." Perhaps, more loosely, the phrase simply denotes responsibility for what is said in general terms, a divine endorsement of the substance of the witness. If this is what Barth intends, the difficulty is that because he also wants to reject any court of human opinion deciding which parts are "pregnant with revelation" and which parts "must be denied this honour,"[85] Barth needs to annex divine speech as closely and extensively as possible to the human witness. It is not clear how one could determine that certain parts of the Bible are not actually what God says. Yet this is what a looser understanding of his words demands if error is not to be attributed to divine speech. Even having to wrestle with questions like these makes it clear how far we have traveled from Calvin's way of putting things.[86]

Although it is often difficult to adjudicate between Barth's rhetoric and what he intends as the substance of his position, perhaps the fairest reading is one that sees his "errors and contradictions" language as part of his rhetoric and his "better to speak only of capacity for error" language as more substantive. The latter is certainly much more prevalent than the former. But the fact remains that he says both. Furthermore, although Barth has little interest in locating particular errors, it is vital to see that in many ways their presence is important to his position because this enables him to place the stress on the miracle of inspiration and revelation as being that which takes place here and now for the reader. Space is created for this kind of claim about the Bible: historical errors can be welcomed and doctrinal

---

the water in the Pool of Bethesda" (*CD* I/2, 530, emphasis added). The miracle of the becoming-event does not lie in the transforming of the human word into the divine Word, but in the divine humility using the human word as a means of divine grace and encounter.

84. Cf. P. Helm, "The Perfect Trustworthiness of God," in *The Trustworthiness of God: Perspectives on the Nature of Scripture,* ed. P. Helm and C. R. Trueman (Leicester: Apollos, 2002), 237-52.

85. Barth, "Christian Understanding of Revelation," 217. Here Barth rejects any concept of the Bible as "a more or less thick husk enclosing a sweet kernel." It is not "up to us to decide . . . where the revelation is to be found."

86. McCormack's assertion that although inerrancy and dynamic infallibilism are not identical they are compatible does not seem tenable ("The Being of Holy Scripture," 73). McCormack is certainly correct to say that Barth shares a very high view of biblical authority with the evangelical doctrine of Scripture. But his reading is much more generous in the direction of evangelical concerns than that which Barth himself provides. Barth derides inerrancy, so much so it is hard to see how he would have regarded his position as compatible with it.

errors should be accepted "as chastening reminders of our need for gracious redemption."[87] This is Barth's way of safeguarding the supernatural character of the Bible and not rendering God as a "secular postulate."[88] In sum, it is hard to disagree with Bromiley that in parts Barth's thesis is a "*tour de force* of self-contradictory disjunctions, which are unlikely to command substantial or lasting assent."[89]

But it would, I think, be unfair to Barth to leave the matter there. Bromiley suggested in 1955 that were Barth to write this part of the *Church Dogmatics* again he would surely have wanted to offer a more stable account of the Spirit's work.[90] This is debatable, not least in light of the trajectory of thought that Barth maintained consistently.[91] It may be more constructive to suggest that Barth's view of Scripture, which he seems to have held consistently, contains within itself a conceptual domain that could be employed for different ends than Barth himself proposed, and that might orient the doctrine towards a firmer exegetical and theological footing.[92]

IV

Barth's doctrine of Scripture is replete with the language of mystery. His dominant conception is of "the mystery of the sovereign freedom of the substance" of the Bible.[93] The mystery of the Bible is that in the peculiarity and secularity of the biblical word we are confronted with its divine subject-matter. Again, for

87. K. Sonderegger, "The Doctrine of Inspiration and the Reliability of Scripture," in Hunsinger, ed., *Thy Word Is Truth,* 20-28 (23).

88. *CD* I/2, 525.

89. G. W. Bromiley, "The Authority of Scripture in Karl Barth," in *Hermeneutics, Authority, and Canon,* ed. D. A. Carson and J. D. Woodbridge (Grand Rapids: Zondervan, 1986), 275-94 (294).

90. Bromiley, "Karl Barth's Doctrine of Inspiration," 80.

91. In 1955 Barth said, "For me the Word of God is a happening, not a thing. Therefore the Bible must become the Word of God, and it does this through the work of the Spirit"; cf. J. D. Godsey, ed., *Karl Barth's Table Talk* (Edinburgh: Oliver & Boyd, 1963), 26. Cf. also *Evangelical Theology,* 15-36.

92. Kevin Vanhoozer is optimistic about a rapprochement between Barth and evangelicals if both were to sign a speech-act peace treaty; cf. "A Person of the Book? Barth on Biblical Authority and Interpretation," in *Karl Barth and Evangelical Theology: Convergences and Divergences,* ed. S. W. Chung (Milton Keynes, UK: Paternoster, 2006), 26-59. I myself doubt that Barth would have agreed to this, given how scornful he often is of the idea of an "inspired" text. Elsewhere Vanhoozer's own constructive position is more satisfying; cf. "Triune Discourse: Theological Reflections on the Claim That God Speaks," in *Trinitarian Theology for the Church: Scripture, Community, Worship,* ed. D. J. Treier and D. Lauber (Downers Grove, IL: InterVarsity; Nottingham: Apollos, 2009), 25-78.

93. *CD* I/2, 470; cf. also *CD* I/1 §5.4, 162-86.

Barth this is the case with all human speaking — the mystery of speech is the true apprehension of that to which the speech refers. In the case of the Bible, "it is because what is said in the biblical word of man is divine revelation, and as such the *analogia fidei,* that everything which is said by human word is drawn into the darkness and light of its mystery."[94] The subject-matter of the Bible, the object to which the words of the Bible witness, is the Word of God in all its transcendent freedom and power. So the mystery is the event-moment in which the word "becomes" the Word, becomes what it is: "[I]n the mystery of God it takes place that here and now this text acquires this determination."[95] Undoubtedly for Barth the language of mystery applies to each of the past, present, and future senses of inspiration, because at every part in the circle of revelation we are dealing with how God uses created means for divine ends, fallible and erring words to speak the Word of God. Although Barth's use of mystery is more pronounced when describing the Bible's becoming, the text's inception as much as its reception is initiated by divine impulse, and so both are mysterious. It seems to me Barth is exactly right to use the term "mystery,"[96] but in so doing has overlooked some of the resources it offers to a wider exegesis of Scripture's ontology.

While Barth affirms that the human word of the prophets and apostles is the Word of God, nowhere does he intimate that their written words are the *words* of God. For Barth, God takes and uses human words so that they really do participate in the divine Word, but he does not acknowledge that the Bible identifies these words as "the words of God" (for example, Exod. 24:4; 34:27; Jer. 37:2; Rom. 3:2). Barth is right to want to coordinate the slender data of 2 Timothy 3:16 and 2 Peter 1:19-21 with other texts. Just so, it is legitimate to ask whether we should see any relation between the activity of the Spirit in these two passages and Scripture's own broader descriptions of what the written text actually *is.* The absence of this construction in Barth's presentation is another indication of dogmatic construction a step removed from the kind of full-orbed exegetical treatment that is required to offer a truly comprehensive picture. If there is a sense in which we can say the human words of the Bible are God's own words, this may point us toward a deeper and greater mystery than is present in Barth's understanding precisely because the spotlight now falls on a more intense coordination of human and divine in Scripture. Although there is only space for the barest of outlines, the mystery of divine words in human form might discipline our thinking in three areas.

94. *CD* I/2, 471.

95. *CD* I/2, 532.

96. Following Gabriel Marcel and Jacques Maritain, Thomas Weinandy offers a distinction between *problem* and *mystery* in the way a field of inquiry can be approached. He suggests that "the true goal of theological inquiry is not the resolution of theological *problems* but the discernment of what the *mystery* of faith is." What this amounts to in dogmatic terms is the recognition that "the intellect has to penetrate more and more deeply the *same* object"; cf. *Does God Suffer?* (Edinburgh: T. & T. Clark, 2000), 30-39.

First, this approach helps us to probe some of Barth's concerns about inspired-ness rendering the Bible "a bit of higher nature" and no longer dependent on the gracious activity of the Spirit.[97] Similar worries appear in John Webster's dogmatic sketch. Warning against "objectifying" the divine act of inspiration, Webster stresses that "inspiration is a mode of the Spirit's freedom, not its inhibition by the letter."[98] Inspiration should not be identified with "textual properties," nor in any way "make the text itself a divine agent."[99] Here it seems that inspired-ness is equated with a divine *thing,* something that is not God but that possesses a divine nature, a tangible artifact that is available "independent of the Word and work of God." The claim is that to speak of divine properties in the text spells "the end of the mystery of God."[100] But this objection only works when the proper focus on divine words is replaced — subtly, but significantly — with a concept of a divine text. Unless the latter is very carefully specified, the impression is given of a divine artifact of print and paper and binding in some way imbued with unspecified divine properties. But if by "text" we are simply using a shorthand designation for the sum total of the words, if these words are breathed out by God, then may not "divine properties" be circumspectly delineated as having reference to divine *character*? The Bible is not a divine object that it should be worshiped. But it does contain divine words so that how we respond to them is the measure of how we respond to the God who spoke them.[101]

This manner of indicating how God speaks in the Bible calls, secondly, for a degree of caution. This is particularly important in light of an idea that appears to be gaining in popularity, namely, that a Christological or incarnational analogy may be used to describe the relation of the human and divine in Scripture.[102] Barth himself makes use of it, albeit in a fairly loose way and without aiming to make the analogy work too hard dogmatically. For him, just as there can be no transmutation or admixture of the human and divine in the Bible, so too in the person of Christ the identity between God and man is an assumed and indirect

97. *CD* I/2, 518.

98. Webster, *Holy Scripture,* 33.

99. Webster, *Holy Scripture,* 39.

100. Webster, *Holy Scripture,* 33.

101. As Timothy Ward points out, Christians do not generally regard it as blasphemous to drop a Bible on the floor or allow it to become dog-eared because it is the words that are divine and not any given textual embodiment of the words; cf. "The Incarnation and Scripture," in *The Word Became Flesh: Evangelicals and the Incarnation,* ed. D. Peterson (Carlisle: Paternoster Press, 2003), 152-84.

102. T. Work's use is fairly unrestrained; cf. *Living and Active: Scripture in the Economy of Salvation* (Grand Rapids: Eerdmans, 2002). More cautious are L. Ayres and S. E. Fowl, "(Mis) reading the Face of God: The Interpretation of the Bible in the Church," *Theological Studies* 60 (1999): 513-28. Particularly careful is L. G. Tipton, "Incarnation, Inspiration, and Pneumatology: A Reformed Incarnational Analogy," *Ordained Servant* 17 (2008): 85-90.

identity, one that rests in "a decision and act of God to man."[103] But such language is not without its difficulties. Here the indirect identity depends on the hypostatic union, an essential concept in Christology for which (as Barth recognizes) there can be no corresponding term in bibliology.

Numerous problems lurk beneath the surface. Most contemporary deployments of the Christological analogy do not sufficiently explore exactly what is involved in using the term "analogy." As Paul Wells has shown, the role of analogy in the formulation of hypotheses is to note how previous knowledge can be applied to new settings. But "there is a mystery about the union of the two natures of Christ in the one person, which if it is confessed by faith, hardly enters into the field of that which is explicable to us." If hypostasis is absent in the case of the Bible the "mystery is not of the same sort as the mystery of Christ," and so the very use of analogy appears circular and self-defeating.[104] The crux of the issue is that by forcing bibliology to think in terms of the union of human and divine, the real question about Scripture has been placed on one side. For with the Bible the issue is not the *union* of human words with divine words but rather how we may speak of human words *as* divine words, and vice versa. This is the mystery: Scripture *is* the Word of God.[105]

Furthermore, instability inheres in the analogy given both the range of qualifications that are required to be introduced into it and that its usage depends on prior doctrinal commitments in Christology that vary greatly between proponents. This is illustrated, for instance, when the Logos taking a fallen or unfallen human nature is used to drive perceptions of the text's fallibility or impeccability. Underlying McCormack's use of the analogy — what he terms a "sacramental" rather than a hypostatic union — is the belief (shared with Barth) that "human language has no capacity in itself for bearing adequate witness to the Word of God." For McCormack this is simply what we learn from Reformed Christology. Christ's human nature is not divinized in the personal union, so neither are "the human words of the prophets and apostles divinized through the sacramental union by which God joins them to the Word of God."[106] It is very far from clear,

103. *CD* I/2, 499. Developing Barth's construction, Paul Dafydd Jones suggests that the indirect identity of divinity and humanity in Scripture is derivative of the hypostatic union definitive of Christ's person. This prevents the bibliolatry of inerrancy, which simply repeats the error of Docetism by collapsing the distinction between divine and human. This is no more helpful, however, than claiming that Barth's position gives new life to Nestorianism or adoptionism. Cf. "The Heart of the Matter: Karl Barth's Christological Exegesis," in Hunsinger, ed., *Thy Word Is Truth,* 173-95 (177).

104. P. R. Wells, *James Barr and the Bible: Critique of a New Liberalism* (Phillipsburg, NJ: P&R, 1980), 340.

105. See the careful discussion in G. C. Berkouwer, *Holy Scripture,* trans. J. B. Rogers (Grand Rapids: Eerdmans, 1975), 160, 195-212.

106. McCormack, "The Being of Holy Scripture," 70.

however, that Reformed Christology demands this understanding of creaturely capacities. Michael Horton suggests that such a construal ignores a vital distinction in Reformed orthodoxy between humanity's *moral* capacity and *natural* capacity for God.[107] If McCormack's point may be disputed, so too may the contention that the Bible cannot permanently bear the words of God. The analogy between the human nature not being divinized in the hypostatic union and the human words not being divinized in the union with the Word of God depends on the prior assumption that in the Bible we have to do with two entities (sacramentally) joined as one. The classical tradition, I would argue, sees two agents as having (mysteriously) produced one reality. The argument here is that *concursus,* not union, is the language for inscripturation that emerges most naturally from the biblical data.

Finally, taking a different line from Barth on the nature and adequacy of human language leads us to query Barth's refusal to see the words of the Bible as revelatory in a direct sense. In distinguishing the Bible from revelation, Barth is concerned to show that a witness is not absolutely identical with that to which it witnesses. This is exactly what we say of the Bible's human words written in human speech that speak of the lordship of the triune God.[108] If, however, there is a sense in which the human words are not simply answering the divine Word but are themselves, somehow, *also* divine words addressing the human hearer, their proximity to revelation should be drawn more closely than Barth suggests. Personal presence is conveyed in words; it does not seem possible ever to address another in speech without revelation taking place.[109] Webster is right to say that, rather than being a theory of theological knowledge that serves as a warrant for Christian belief, "revelation is in Barth's hands simply the doctrine of God in its cognitive effects."[110] And the concrete form that this takes for Barth, of course, elides any distinction between the content of revelation and the ends of revelation: "revelation is reconciliation."[111] What emerges in the biblical texts, however, and

107. Cf. Horton, "A Stony Jar," 354. Similarly, Wells: "it is sinfulness, not finitude, which separates the creature from the Creator"; cf. *James Barr and the Bible,* 355. Wells provides a fine treatment of the relation of human and divine in Scripture, one that outlines a biblical theology of communion with God and which points to the covenantal nature of the Bible (340-79). I have attempted to explore these issues in relation to divine freedom in "The God of Promise: Christian Scripture as Covenantal Revelation," *Themelios* 29, no. 3 (2004): 27-36.

108. *CD* I/2, 463.

109. Cf. K. J. Vanhoozer, "God's Mighty Speech Acts: The Doctrine of Scripture Today," in *First Theology: God, Scripture, and Hermeneutics* (Downers Grove, IL: InterVarsity; Nottingham: Apollos, 2002), 127-58. Runia seems justified in objecting that alongside Barth's mention of texts like Luke 10:16 ("He who listens to you, listens to me"), where he wants to stress the unity of the witness with revelation, Barth offers no exegetical evidence for his distinction between the text and revelation; cf. *Karl Barth's Doctrine of Scripture,* 33-39.

110. Webster, *Barth,* 58.

111. See Barth, "Revelation," in *God in Action,* trans. E. G. Homrighausen and K. J. Ernst (Edinburgh: T. & T. Clark, 1936), 3-19.

strikingly so in some instances where the "words of God" are referred to, is that human hearers are capable of remaining implacably hardened to the Lord *even as he speaks* (Jer. 13:10; 19:15; cf. Isa. 6:9-10). The great benefit of being a Jew and so "entrusted with the words of God" does not ensure that all have faith (Rom. 3:2). In the context of divine speech heeded by the nations but rejected by his own people, God says: "All day long I have held out my hands to an obstinate people" (Isa. 65:1-2). It is not obvious how in these instances God is not truly revealing his own self, even though as he does so "human opposition, alienation and pride" are not overcome and replaced "by knowledge, love and fear of God."[112] This is the mystery of revelation: it can reconcile *and* alienate. Perhaps we are closer to the biblical presentation if we suggest that revelation is the publication of the divine identity, regardless of its effects, even as God remains Lord of the effects.[113]

What might these brief attempts to move beyond Barth by thinking with Barth mean for an assessment of his theology of Holy Scripture? Francis Watson has suggested that the *Church Dogmatics* succeeds if it trains its readers "to read the Bible *differently.*" Conversely, by its own standards, it is a pretentious and presumptuous failure if it "does not persuade its readers to reread the Bible."[114] Herein lie the challenge and the problem of Barth's theology. The challenge is that from first to last Barth's conception of the work of the theologian is "in demonstrable and unassuming attention to the sign of Holy Scripture around which the church gathers and continually becomes the church." This makes a theologian — and "nothing else."[115] Considered in these terms, Barth has no modern peers as an exegetical dogmatician. Craig Bartholomew observes that as Barth's "conceptual framework takes hold, he does more and not less exegesis. It is as though the doctrinal framework stimulates rather than — as in too many contemporary theologies — suppresses exegesis."[116] It is obtuse to read Barth and not receive an invitation to reread the Bible. And yet precisely here lies the problem: Barth is not always persuasive in constructing a different reading of the Bible. Sometimes the difficulties lie in exegetical particulars; sometimes they exhibit themselves at the point where his particular doctrinal or historical framework has taken hold most deeply. In such instances — and Barth on Scripture is a case in point — it is hard to avoid the conclusion that some of the material he considers is commandeered too quickly toward his own dogmatic ends.

112. Webster, *Holy Scripture,* 15-16.

113. For further interaction with Barth, cf. S. Rehnman, "A Realist Conception of Revelation," in Helm and Trueman, eds., *The Trustworthiness of God,* 253-74.

114. F. Watson, "The Bible," in Webster, ed., *Cambridge Companion to Karl Barth,* 66.

115. *CD* I/1, 283-84.

116. C. G. Bartholomew, "Calvin, Barth, and Theological Interpretation," in MacDonald and Trueman, eds., *Calvin, Barth, and Reformed Theology,* 171.

TEN

Roman Catholic Views of Biblical Authority from the Late Nineteenth Century to the Present

Anthony N. S. Lane

The topic of this volume is the authority of Scripture. In examining Roman Catholic teaching we will naturally focus especially on the inspiration and truthfulness of Scripture, but to stop there would be to present a misleading picture. For Roman Catholicism, tradition also has an authority comparable to that of Scripture. Furthermore, it is the teaching authority of the church, the Magisterium, that decides how these may be interpreted. RC[1] teaching on the character of Scripture needs to be seen in this wider context.

We must also note the *manner* in which RC teaching develops over time. An example will illustrate this. For over a millennium the clear teaching has been "no salvation outside the church." That still is the official line, but Vatican II interprets this to mean that sincere Buddhists and even atheists can be saved.[2] Previous to Vatican II, in 1949 Father Feeney, a fiery Roman Catholic preacher in Boston, insisted on the traditional interpretation that only Roman Catholics are saved. After some years of controversy, Feeney was excommunicated by Rome

1. I shall refer to "Roman Catholicism" and "Roman Catholic" (= RC), rather than simply Catholic(ism). Rome's claim to exclusive identity with the Catholic Church is controversial. All quotations from councils are taken from Norman P. Tanner, ed., *Decrees of the Ecumenical Councils,* vol. 2 (London: Sheed & Ward; Washington, DC: Georgetown University Press, 1990), hereafter DEC. This contains both the Latin and an English translation, the pagination being the same for both. It refers consistently to the "holy Spirit" but I have capitalized the "H." All quotations from papal encyclicals are taken from the Vatican website www.vatican.va. These are not necessarily the best but have been chosen as they are widely accessible. In the translation of *Divino afflante Spiritu* (below) the word "times" consistently appears as "Times New Roman," which may or may not be an indication of corporate sponsorship!

2. E.g., *Lumen Gentium* 2.16 (DEC 861).

I am very grateful to Fathers Nicholas King, S.J., Philip Endean, S.J., and Henry Wansbrough, O.S.B., for reading this chapter and making helpful comments. They are not, of course, responsible for the remaining defects.

as an obstinate rigorist. Rome stated that "no salvation outside the Church" remains part of unchanging Catholic doctrine, but that it is not open to private interpretation.[3] Thus the church excommunicated a priest for holding to a traditional doctrine while all along insisting that Catholic doctrine is *semper eadem (always the same).* This shows how superficial it is simply to state that Rome reaffirms its past doctrines and acknowledges no changes. That is precisely the Roman way of introducing change! So, for example, historians of the Reformation may be surprised to learn that "the [RC] Church has never failed in taking due measures to bring the Scriptures within reach of her children" and that in such matters "she has never required, nor does she now require, any stimulation from without."[4]

The bulk of the chapter is devoted to surveying a range of official documents, starting with decrees from the Council of Trent and the First Vatican Council. We then turn to three papal encyclicals: *Providentissimus Deus, Spiritus Paraclitus,* and *Divino afflante Spiritu.* Most significant is the Dogmatic Constitution *Dei verbum* from the Second Vatican Council, and the *Catechism of the Catholic Church* will be reviewed for any light that it may shed on this. The survey concludes with an important document, on *The Interpretation of the Bible in the Church,* published by the Pontifical Biblical Commission on the centenary of *Providentissimus Deus.* Finally there will be a very brief examination of the effects of this upon RC biblical scholarship.

Council of Trent (1546)

Before turning to the nineteenth century we need to pause briefly at the Council of Trent, which was of course the Roman Catholic response to the Protestant Reformation. The first major decrees of the council, both from 8 April 1546, concerned the canon of Scripture and its relation to apostolic traditions, the status of the Latin Vulgate translation and the way to interpret Scripture. The canon of Scripture is the same as for Protestants, with the addition of the Old Testament "Apocrypha."[5] In a passage that was much disputed at the Second Vatican Council and the years preceding it, it is stated that the gospel is "the source of the whole truth of salvation and rule of conduct." "This truth and rule are contained in written books and in unwritten traditions which were received from the apostles from the mouth of Christ himself, or else have come down to us, handed on as it were

3. Heinrich Denzinger/Adolf Schönmetzer, *Enchiridion Symbolorum* (Freiburg: Herder, 1967 [34th edition]), *3866-73. Gerrit C. Berkouwer, *The Church* (Grand Rapids: Eerdmans, 1976), 144-48 discusses Feeney and the earlier teaching of Pius IX.

4. Leo XIII, *Providentissimus Deus* §8.

5. DEC 663-64.

from the apostles themselves at the inspiration of the Holy Spirit *(a Spiritu sancto dictatas).*" Both of these, Scripture and traditions, "the council accepts and venerates with a like feeling of piety and reverence."[6] The council also stipulated the retention of the Vulgate edition "as the authentic text in public readings, debates, sermons and explanations." It is the task of holy mother church "to pass judgment on the true meaning and interpretation of the sacred scriptures" so when it comes to Christian doctrine no one should rely on his "personal judgment" to twist their meaning contrary to the mind of the church.[7]

Shortly after the council, thanks especially to the catechetical work of Peter Canisius, Trent was perceived to have taught that Scripture and tradition were the two sources of revelation, tradition supplementing Scripture as the source for Roman Catholic teaching not found in Scripture. This interpretation was first questioned in the nineteenth century and then more seriously with the publication of an article by J. R. Geiselmann in 1956.[8] The publication of the Acts of the council debates at the beginning of the last century cast a new light on the significance of Trent. The first draft of the decree on Scripture and tradition stated that the gospel is "the rule of all saving truth and moral discipline" and that this truth is contained "partly in written books, partly in unwritten traditions." After some debate, the final version replaced the "partly . . . partly" with a simple "and."

The awareness that the draft had been changed gave birth to vigorous debate concerning its significance. The statement that the truth of the gospel is found in Scripture *and* tradition leaves open, in a way that the "partly . . . partly" formula does not, the possibility that the entire truth of the gospel is found in Scripture — that is, that Scripture is materially sufficient. This claim was vigorously contested, but it can hardly be denied that the wording of the decree is compatible with a belief in the material sufficiency of Scripture — though whether that was intended by the council fathers is another matter. The interpretation of the Tridentine decree was the subject of vigorous debate in the decade following Geiselmann's article. It was of more than academic interest because this was the time of the Second Vatican Council, when the dogmatic constitution *Dei verbum* was being written.

6. DEC 663.

7. DEC 664.

8. The debate was initiated by Josef R. Geiselmann, "Das Mißverständnis über das Verhältnis von Schrift und Tradition und seine Überwindung in der katholischen Theologie," *Una Sancta* 11 (1956): 131-50. For the interpretation of Trent in the intervening years, see Josef R. Geiselmann, "Das Konzil von Trient über das Verhältnis der Heiligen Schrift und der nicht geschriebenen Traditionen," in *Die mündliche Überlieferung,* ed. Michael Schmaus (Munich, 1957), 194-206.

First Vatican Council (1870)[9]

In the sixteenth century, Roman Catholic and Protestant alike accepted the inspiration, infallibility, and authority of Scripture; it was the interpretation of Scripture and the authority of the church that was the point of controversy. By the time of the First Vatican Council in 1870 this had changed. Liberal Protestants accepted neither the inspiration, nor the infallibility, nor the authority of Scripture, and such ideas were beginning to creep into the RC Church. The *Dogmatic Constitution on the Catholic Faith* sought to address them in its second chapter, "On Revelation."[10] The function of revelation is to make clear matters (such as the existence of God) that are accessible to human reason and, more importantly, to make known things (such as the Trinity) that utterly surpass human understanding. The teaching of Trent (as just expounded) is reaffirmed, and it is also stated of the scriptural canon that

> These books the church holds to be sacred and canonical not because she subsequently approved them by her authority after they had been composed by unaided human skill, nor simply because they contain revelation without error, but because, being written under the inspiration of the Holy Spirit, they have God as their author, and were as such committed to the church.[11]

Leo XIII, *Providentissimus Deus* (1893)[12]

Nearly a quarter of a century later Pope Leo XIII issued an encyclical *On the Study of Holy Scripture,* known as *Providentissimus Deus.*[13] This aims to encourage the correct use of the Bible in the RC Church, most especially in the areas of scholarship and the training of priests, but Leo also had to respond to the rise of modernism within the RC Church. The church, he states, now faces a new threat. The Protestant Reformers set Scripture above tradition and set their own private interpretation of Scripture against that of "the teaching office of the Church." For them the Scriptures were "the one source of revelation and the final appeal

9. On Vatican I, see Bruce Vawter, *Biblical Inspiration* (London: Hutchinson; Philadelphia: Westminster, 1972), 70-72.

10. DEC 806.

11. DEC 806. Vawter, *Biblical Inspiration,* 70, notes that this was "the first assertion of a general Council touching on the nature of scriptural inspiration." For the ideas being rejected, see 63-70.

12. On *Providentissimus Deus,* see Vawter, *Biblical Inspiration,* 72-75.

13. As with all official RC documents, while *On the Study of Holy Scripture* is the title, it is more often known by the opening words of the Latin text, *Providentissimus Deus.*

in matters of Faith." Now the church is confronted with "the Rationalists, true children and inheritors of the older heretics" who "have rejected even the scraps and remnants of Christian belief which had been handed down to them." They deny the very fact of revelation, inspiration, and Holy Scripture, seeing instead "only the forgeries and falsehoods of men" (§10). They bring with them various challenges. "Higher criticism" is an inept methodology that "pretends to judge of the origin, integrity and authority of each Book from internal indications alone," but "resolve[s] itself into the reflection of the bias and prejudice of the critics." In particular, it leads to "the elimination from the sacred writings of all prophecy and miracle, and of everything else that is outside the natural order" (§17). Modern science is also used to undermine the truth of Scripture. "There can never, indeed, be any real discrepancy between the theologian and the physicist, as long as each confines himself within his own lines." This involves the recognition that, in talking of scientific matters, the biblical authors "described and dealt with things in more or less figurative language, or in terms which were commonly used at the time" (§18).

Against these errors Leo reaffirms the teaching of Vatican I of the Scriptures that, "being written under the inspiration of the Holy Ghost, they have God for their author and as such have been delivered to the Church." He claims that "this belief has been perpetually held and professed by the Church" (§1), and for once the claim is plausible. The truthfulness of Scripture follows from its divine authorship. All of the canonical books

> are written wholly and entirely, with all their parts, at the dictation of the Holy Ghost; and so far is it from being possible that any error can co-exist with inspiration, that inspiration not only is essentially incompatible with error, but excludes and rejects it as absolutely and necessarily as it is impossible that God Himself, the supreme Truth, can utter that which is not true. (§20)

In particular, "it is absolutely wrong and forbidden, either to narrow inspiration to certain parts only of Holy Scripture, or to admit that the sacred writer has erred." Inspiration must not be limited to matters of "faith and morals." The idea that "in a question of the truth or falsehood of a passage, we should consider not so much what God has said as the reason and purpose which He had in mind in saying it — this system cannot be tolerated" (§20). Leo clearly argues for the inerrancy of Scripture. "Those who maintain that an error is possible in any genuine passage of the sacred writings, either pervert the Catholic notion of inspiration, or make God the author of such error." Against such a view Leo sets the teaching of the church fathers, especially Augustine (§21). Because God is the author of Scripture, we cannot accept that any truth of science or archaeology contradicts it, because "truth cannot contradict truth." We must seek the resolution of apparent contradictions and where no such resolution can be found be prepared to "suspend judgement for the time being" (§23). The divine authorship, inspiration, and truthfulness of Scripture are well summarized in one passage:

> Hence, because the Holy Ghost employed men as His instruments, we cannot therefore say that it was these inspired instruments who, perchance, have fallen into error, and not the primary author. For, by supernatural power, He so moved and impelled them to write — He was so present to them — that the things which He ordered, and those only, they, first, rightly understood, then willed faithfully to write down, and finally expressed in apt words and with infallible truth. Otherwise, it could not be said that He was the Author of the entire Scripture. (§20)

Leo also states that Scripture is "dictated by the Holy Ghost" (§5). So what about the human authors? Leo cannot altogether be absolved of the charge of reducing them to scribes.[14] They are the "instruments" of the Holy Spirit, who "moved and impelled them to write" so that "they wrote the things which He showed and uttered to them." Leo cites with approval the words of Gregory the Great: "Most superfluous it is to inquire who wrote these things — we loyally believe the Holy Ghost to be the Author of the book. He wrote it Who dictated it for writing; He wrote it Who inspired its execution" (§20). Calvin also states that the Holy Spirit dictated Scripture, but his attitude to the human authors is strikingly different. Vawter aptly notes of the tradition, "theoretically, the humanness that belonged to the Bible had never been denied, the rare exception noted. But practically it had often been submerged."[15]

Leo clearly has a high view of Scripture. He also reaffirms the teaching of Vatican I that "supernatural revelation . . . is contained both in unwritten Tradition and in written Books" (§1). Again, following Trent and Vatican I, he reaffirms that the true meaning of Scripture is that "which has been held and is held by our Holy Mother the Church," to whom has been entrusted the authoritative interpretation of Scripture. It is, therefore, illegitimate "to interpret Holy Scripture against such sense or also against the unanimous agreement of the Fathers." Where the Magisterium has declared the interpretation of a passage, it is the duty of RC exegetes to follow this. Elsewhere they should follow "the analogy of faith" — that is, not interpret any passage contrary to established RC doctrine (§14).[16] Teachers are to work from the Vulgate text, but they should not neglect the original Hebrew and Greek (§13).

14. On this, cf. Vawter, *Biblical Inspiration,* 73-75.

15. Vawter, *Biblical Inspiration,* 126.

16. "The sense of Holy Scripture can nowhere be found incorrupt outside of the Church, and cannot be expected to be found in writers who, being without the true faith, only gnaw the bark of the Sacred Scripture, and never attain its pith" (§15).

Finally, to end on a positive note, a recurring theme throughout *Providentissimus Deus* is the importance and usefulness of the study of Scripture (§§1-5). He quotes Jerome's statement that "to be ignorant of the Scripture is not to know Christ" (§3). It is desirable that "the whole teaching of Theology should be pervaded and animated by the use of the divine Word of God" (§16). This makes a refreshing contrast to the position that I have come across with some Roman Catholics that the church doesn't need the Bible and could function perfectly well without it.

Following on from *Providentissimus Deus,* Leo also in 1901/2 set up the Pontifical Biblical Commission, a committee of cardinals assisted by consulters. This had the role of laying down the law on issues of biblical scholarship like the authorship of the Pentateuch or the Synoptic problem. Its earlier decrees required biblical scholars to maintain that Matthew's Gospel was written in Hebrew or Aramaic before the other canonical Gospels (1911) and that Hebrews was genuinely Pauline, though possibly later modified by others (1914).[17]

Benedict XV, *Spiritus Paraclitus* (1920)

Again about a quarter of a century later, in 1920, Pope Benedict XV issued an encyclical commemorating the fifteenth centenary of the death of Jerome, with the aim of promoting "assiduous and reverent study of the Bible." As with *Providentissimus Deus,* Benedict affirms that God is the author of Scripture. He affirms, with Jerome, that "the Books of the Bible were composed at the inspiration, or suggestion, or even at the dictation of the Holy Spirit; even that they were written and edited by Him" (§8). Yet the human authors have an important role. They each "worked in full freedom under the Divine afflatus, each of them in accordance with his individual nature and character." While "God is the principal cause of all that Scripture means and says," Jerome also paid careful attention to the individuality of the different human authors — their language, style, and mode of expression, their "individual character, almost their very features." Having conceded that, however, Benedict rather spoils it by proceeding to compare them to the instruments used by a workman to produce a work, an illustration that appears to reduce their role to a passive one (§8). He continues with this tension, stating that "God, the principal cause, . . . through his grace illumines the writer's mind regarding the particular truth" that he is to teach and that God "moves the writer's will — nay, even impels it — to write" (§9).

The result of divine inspiration is "the divine dignity and absolute truth of

17. Thomas Aquinas Collins and Raymond E. Brown, "Church Pronouncements," in *The Jerome Bible Commentary,* ed. Raymond E. Brown, Joseph A. Fitzmyer, and Roland E. Murphy (London and Dublin: Geoffrey Chapman, 1969), 2:630.

Scripture" (§8), its "immunity from error or deception" (§13), its "absolute immunity . . . from error" (§16). Benedict commends Jerome's approach, shared with Augustine, toward "apparent discrepancies in the Sacred Books." He would persevere in seeking to resolve the issue, and where his attempts were not crowned with success "he would never accuse the sacred writers of the slightest mistake" (§15).

This exposition of Jerome should not be mistaken for an exercise in antiquarianism. Leo XIII had allowed for the fact that in scientific matters the Bible uses the language of the time (§18), and some had seized on this to justify the limitation of the Bible's "absolute truth and immunity from error" to the "primary or religious" as opposed to the "secondary or profane element in the Bible" (§19). Benedict firmly rejects such an approach and the attempt to justify it from *Providentissimus Deus,* which throughout insists that "the sacred narrative is absolutely free from error" (§§20-22).

Finally, Benedict, like Leo before him, seeks to encourage the reading of Scripture. He commends the Society of St. Jerome, which set out to distribute copies of the Gospels and Acts and other similar efforts by Roman Catholics (§44). Like Leo (§3), but less accurately, he quotes Jerome's statement that "ignorance of the Bible means ignorance of Christ" (§63).

Fifty Years On: Pius XII, *Divino afflante Spiritu* (1943)

In 1943, to commemorate the Golden Jubilee of *Providentissimus Deus,* Pope Pius XII issued the encyclical *Divino afflante Spiritu.* Here we find small, but significant, changes.

In *Providentissimus Deus* the exegete is expected to take the Vulgate as his text, making use of the Hebrew and Greek "wherever there may be ambiguity or want of clearness" in the Latin text. Now Pius XII taught the duty of the exegete to work from the original texts (§15). "The original text . . . having been written by the inspired author himself, has more authority and greater weight than even the very best translation, whether ancient or modern" (§16). This is not contrary to the status given to the Vulgate at Trent since that "applies only to the Latin Church and to the public use of the same Scriptures." The Vulgate is "free from any error whatsoever in matters of faith and morals" and so can be safely used for teaching and preaching. But when it comes to establishing the correct text of Scripture it is the original Hebrew and Greek that is normative. Indeed, it is permissible to translate the Scriptures into the vernacular "even [!] directly from the original texts themselves" (§§20-22).

Benedict XV in *Spiritus Paraclitus* spoke disparagingly of scholars who took refuge in ideas such as "kinds of literature" *(genera quaedam litterarum)* (§26), though he recognized that the biblical writers used the "forms of speech" *(loquendi rationes, norma loquendi)* that were in ordinary use in their times (§24).

Pius XII took a small but important step in the direction of sanctioning modern biblical studies. Discerning the literal sense of a passage from the ancient world is not as simple as for works written today. The interpreter needs to "go back wholly in spirit to those remote centuries" and determine what modes of writing *(litteraria genera)* were being used (§35). These may be very different from those in use today (§36). "Of the modes of expression *(loquendi rationes)* which, among ancient peoples, and especially those of the East, human language used to express its thought, none is excluded from the Sacred Books, provided the way of speaking *(dicendi genus)* adopted in no wise contradicts the holiness and truth of God" (§37).

Divino afflante Spiritu reaffirms the inerrancy of Scripture, though less emphatically than its two predecessor encyclicals. Just "as the substantial Word of God became like to men in all things, except sin," so the words of God, expressed in human language, "are made like to human speech in every respect, except error" (§37). Those who sought to "restrict the truth of Sacred Scripture solely to matters of faith and morals, and to regard other matters, whether in the domain of physical science or history, as 'obiter dicta'" were rightly condemned by *Providentissimus Deus* (§1).[18] But the significance of the encyclical lies in its greater openness to biblical scholarship, whether textual criticism (§§12-22) or, more tentatively, other forms of criticism (§§31-42). Twenty-five years later the editors of the *Jerome Bible Commentary* noted the revolution that had taken place in RC biblical studies, "a revolution encouraged by authority, for its Magna Carta was the encyclical *Divino afflante Spiritu* (1943) of Pope Pius XII."[19] The phrase is echoed in his foreword by Cardinal Bea, who has been seen as the influence behind the progressive material in the encyclical.[20] These statements must be seen against the background of the earlier decrees of the Pontifical Biblical Commission.[21] In 1955 the Pontifical Biblical Commission announced that biblical scholars could work with full liberty *(plena libertate)*, provided they respected the teaching authority of the church.[22]

18. "Obiter dicta" is a reference to the teaching of John Henry Newman (J. Crehan, "The Bible in the Roman Catholic Church from Trent to the Present Day," in *The Cambridge History of the Bible*, vol. 3, ed. Stanley L. Greenslade [Cambridge: Cambridge University Press, 1963], 228-30). For a recent study, see Henry Wansbrough, "Newman on Scripture," *Scripture Bulletin* 40 (2010): 53-62.

19. Brown, Fitzmyer, and Murphy, eds., *Jerome Bible Commentary*, 1:xvii, referring particularly to the acceptance and application of literary and historical criticism.

20. Brown, Fitzmyer, and Murphy, eds., *Jerome Bible Commentary*, 1:vii. Cf. Vawter, *Biblical Inspiration*, 125. By contrast, Pope John Paul II, in his *Address on the Interpretation of the Bible in the Church*, argues that *Providentissimus Deus* and *Divino afflante Spiritu* "are in complete agreement at the deepest level" (§§3-5).

21. See, e.g., at n. 17, above.

22. Collins and Brown, "Church Pronouncements," 629.

Second Vatican Council, *Dei verbum* (1965)

Where *Divino afflante Spiritu* opened the door a crack, Vatican II pushed it open. This is true for a huge range of subjects. For our present topic the key text is the *Dogmatic Constitution on Divine Revelation,* known as *Dei verbum* from its opening words.[23] This is a document that cannot be properly understood without a knowledge of the way in which it evolved. Whereas we had to wait three and a half centuries to discover this for the documents of the Council of Trent,[24] no such secrecy surrounded Vatican II. There is a thorough five-volume *Commentary on the Documents of Vatican II,* which includes a full account of *Dei verbum,* mostly written by one of the younger progressive theologians at the council, a certain Joseph Ratzinger.[25] He sees it as a "re-reading" of the earlier texts from Trent and Vatican I, "in which what was written then is interpreted in terms of the present, thus giving a new rendering of both its essentials and its insufficiencies."[26]

The teaching of *Dei verbum* forms the basis of the teaching on revelation, Scripture, and tradition in the highly authoritative 1994 *Catechism of the Catholic Church.*[27] This will be noted at the points where it has something to add to the Constitution, not where (as most of the time) it simply repeats it.

The History of the Document

This document was unusual in that it went through no fewer than five drafts.

The first draft presented to the council was entitled *De fontibus revelationis (The Sources of Revelation),* which was itself highly controversial. The draft was

23. Most of the documents produced by the council are declarations or decrees. The two dogmatic constitutions, on the church and on divine revelation, are the most authoritative documents from the council.

24. Until the publication of *Concilium Tridentinum. Diariorum, Actorum, Epistularum, Tractatuum Nova Collectio,* edidit Societas Goerresiana (Freiburg: Herder, 1901-76).

25. Herbert Vorgrimler, ed., *Commentary on the Documents of Vatican II,* vol. 3 (London: Burns & Oates; New York: Herder & Herder, 1968), a translation of the 1967 German original (hereafter, CDV). Pp. 155-272 cover *Dei verbum.* As well as this work, I have also used Gregory Baum, "Vatican II's Constitution on Revelation: History and Interpretation," *Theological Studies* 28 (1967): 51-75; George H. Tavard, *The Dogmatic Constitution on Divine Revelation of Vatican Council II: Commentary and Translation* (London: Darton, Longman & Todd, 1966); Peter van Leeuwen, "The Genesis of the Constitution on Divine Revelation," *Concilium* 3, no. 1 (January 1967): 4-10.

26. CDV 169.

27. The Catechism was published in French in 1994. Three years later the Latin text was promulgated and this became the definitive text. Earlier translations (including the English) needed minor amendments at this point and these revised versions are known as "second editions." The same English translation is found on various websites, such as http://www.vatican.va/archive/ENG0015/__P2.HTM.

seen as ultraconservative and scholastic, contrary to the pastoral and ecumenical aims of the council. It was debated from 14 to 20 November 1962, and when it was put to the vote on the last of these days some 60 percent of the council fathers voted for its outright rejection. For such a motion to pass required a two-thirds majority, but because of this decisive rejection Pope John stepped in and referred the text to a new body for substantial revision. There were five particular points that had aroused opposition:

(1) Revelation as consisting primarily and almost exclusively of revealed doctrines.
(2) Tradition and Scripture as two sources of revelation: "Holy Mother Church has always believed and believes that the fullness of revelation is not contained exclusively in Scripture, but in Scripture and tradition as a double source, though in different ways."
(3) Tradition as adding to Scripture: "Tradition, indeed, and this alone, is the way by which the Church can clearly know a number of revealed truths, particularly those that refer to the inspiration, canonicity and integrity of all books together and each book in particular." This statement was considered unacceptable because it condemned those like Geiselmann who understood Trent differently.[28]
(4) Inspiration as involving "absolute immunity of the entire sacred Scripture from error." It is recognized that the biblical writers used contemporary concepts and terminology, but (unlike *Providentissimus Deus*) there was no mention of literary genre *(litteraria genera).*
(5) The supreme task of theology as harmonizing Scripture with the teaching of the church.

The following March a corrected version of the first draft was produced, with most of the objectionable material removed. This was titled *De divina revelatione (Divine Revelation)* and in April was sent to the bishops for comment. This draft spoke of the gospel as the one source, in line with Trent, as we have seen, and spoke of the one deposit of faith, the Word of God written and passed on *(traditum).* God is the author of Scripture, and the human writers are also true authors. Through inspiration the Bible is "free from all error."

The second draft was not debated at the council but, in the light of the bishops' comments, a radically new draft was produced in April 1964. This draft is substantially the final version, further changes being only minor. It was debated from 30 September to 6 October 1964, meeting with general approval together with criticism of details.

28. "The best conciliar tradition [is] that the Church's teaching office should not decide academic controversies at a council" (CDV 160).

The fourth draft took account of the debate, and this revised version was itself debated in September 1965. Following this debate, and a series of votes from 20 to 24 September, it was further revised and put to the vote (chapter by chapter) on 29 October. There was a final vote on the entire text on 18 November 1965, when it was accepted by 2,344 votes to 6, an impressive endorsement of such a controversial document. Pope Paul VI solemnly proclaimed it on the same day.

All the drafts concluded with chapters on the Old Testament, on the New Testament, and on Scripture in the church. The first draft had a chapter titled "The Inspiration, Inerrancy and Literary Form of Scripture," which thereafter became "The Divine Inspiration and the Interpretation of Scripture." The opening chapter(s) were more fluid: "The Double Source of Revelation" (draft 1) became "The Revealed Word of God" (draft 2). In the third and subsequent drafts a further chapter was added, so the first two chapters became "Revelation Itself" and "The Transmission of Divine Revelation."

The Text of the Document

We will focus on some key issues raised by the text, noting especially the changes made in the various drafts and the extent to which the final text is a revision of previous teaching.[29]

The Nature of Revelation

> It has pleased God, in his goodness and wisdom, to reveal himself and to make known the secret purpose of his will. . . . By thus revealing himself God, who is invisible, in his great love speaks to humankind as friends and enters into their life, so as to invite and receive them into relationship with himself. The pattern of this revelation unfolds through deeds and words bound together by an inner dynamism, in such a way that God's works, effected during the course of the history of salvation, show forth and confirm the doctrine and realities signified by the words, while the words in turn proclaim the works and throw light on the meaning hidden in them. (1.2)

The first draft portrayed revelation in terms of revealed doctrines, a common scholastic view. Twentieth-century theology questioned this with rival theories of revelation as history and revelation as personal encounter. *Dei verbum* em-

29. Quotations from *Dei verbum* are taken from DEC 971-81. I have removed the biblical references.

braces all of these. Revelation is essentially personal, God revealing himself and his will, but this is not a contentless existential experience. It is worked out in history in God's deeds in the history of salvation. We are not left to our own devices in interpreting these deeds but God also speaks to proclaim and interpret the deeds. These deeds and words are "bound together by an inner dynamism." Many twentieth-century theologians taught a reductionist doctrine of revelation, reducing it purely to personal encounter or to God's mighty acts or to words. *Dei verbum* is to be commended for presenting a fully rounded picture that embraces all three. That does not guarantee, of course, that those who have interpreted it have not emphasized one and marginalized the others.

Tradition

Trent referred to *traditions* (plural), and this term referred especially to customs and practices, such as infant baptism or the sign of the cross.[30] *Dei verbum,* in keeping with more recent developments,[31] works with an all-embracing concept of tradition: "the church, in its teaching, life and worship, perpetuates and hands on to every generation all that it is and all that it believes" (2.8). The third draft referred rather to "all that the Church is, all that she has, all that she believes." Some of the bishops objected to this on the grounds that this too easily identified tradition with the church and ignored the fact that there can be a distorting tradition that needs to be reformed. The final text omits the phrase "all that she has" but still errs in the direction of identifying apostolic tradition too closely with the life of the church and failing to give criteria for the reform of tradition. Ratzinger agrees with this charge, regarding it as an unfortunate omission that there was no mention of the role of Scripture as critical of tradition. What is "perhaps the real crux of the *ecclesia semper reformanda* . . . has been overlooked."[32] *Unitatis*

30. Maurice Bévenot argues, in two important articles, that *mores* at Trent has a meaning broader than "morals" and includes the issue of discipline ("'Faith and Morals' in the Councils of Trent and Vatican I," *Heythrop Journal* 3 [1962]: 15-30) and that *traditiones* meant "observances" rather than conceptual additions to Scripture ("*Traditiones* in the Council of Trent," *Heythrop Journal* 4 [1963]: 333-47). If he is right, the decree has little, but *not* nothing, to say concerning the material doctrinal sufficiency of Scripture. In fact his view is questioned by Joseph Ratzinger, "On the Interpretation of the Tridentine Decree on Tradition," in Karl Rahner and Joseph Ratzinger, *Revelation and Tradition* (London: Burns & Oates, 1966), 50-68.

31. As, for example, in the report on *Scripture, Tradition and Traditions* from the 1963 Montreal meeting of the World Council of Churches: Patrick C. Rodger and Lukas Vischer, eds., *The Fourth World Conference on Faith and Order* (London: SCM, 1964), 50-61. For a comparison between that document and *Dei verbum,* see Avery Dulles, "Revelation, Scripture, and Tradition," in *Your Word Is Truth,* ed. Charles Colson and Richard J. Neuhaus (Grand Rapids: Eerdmans, 2002), 53-56.

32. CDV 193.

redintegratio, the *Decree on Ecumenism*, also touches on this theme, talking of the need for reform to extend even to "the way that church teaching has been formulated — to be carefully distinguished from the deposit of faith itself" (2.6), though without mentioning Scripture.[33] The Catechism distinguishes more sharply between Apostolic Tradition and ecclesial traditions, i.e. "the various theological, disciplinary, liturgical or devotional traditions, born in the local churches over time," these being "the particular forms, adapted to different places and times, in which the great Tradition is expressed." It goes on to refer to the reform of church traditions, but in the light of Apostolic Tradition and "under the guidance of the Church's Magisterium" (§83). Ratzinger's statement about the need to reform tradition is taken up, but Scripture is not mentioned except insofar as it forms part of Apostolic Tradition.

This section of *Dei verbum* also expresses the idea of growth or development of doctrine: "[A]s the centuries advance, the church constantly holds its course towards the fullness of God's truth, until the day when the words of God reach their fulfillment in the Church" (2.8). The idea of Roman Catholic theology as *semper eadem* has given way to an eschatological concept of truth, to which the Church is progressing.[34] This was opposed by conservatives with a static concept of tradition as unchanging and also by others who feared that this statement threatened the uniqueness of the once-for-all revelation and cut the church loose from its dependence upon the unchanging Word of God. Against this must be noted the earlier statement that "no new public revelation is to be expected before the glorious manifestation of our lord Jesus Christ" (1.4). The church advances in her grasp of the revelation given in Christ; she does not receive new revelation.[35] In the Catechism this is qualified with the statement that "even if Revelation is already complete, it has not been made completely explicit; it remains for Christian faith gradually to grasp its full significance over the course of the centuries" (§66).[36]

Another issue that caused extensive debate was the sufficiency of Scripture. The assumption that Trent, in its *Decree Concerning the Canonical Scriptures*,[37] portrayed tradition as a supplement to Scripture was questioned by Josef Geisel-

33. DEC 913.

34. This idea receives some support from the Declaration *Mysterium Ecclesiae* of the Sacred Congregation for the Doctrine of the Faith (24 June 1973), which warns, though, against the relativism of "truth being like a goal that is constantly being sought by means of . . . approximations" (http://www.saint-mike.org/library/curia/congregations/faith/mysterium_ecclesiae.html).

35. Protestants will not, of course, accept that Marian doctrines like the Immaculate Conception and the Assumption are part of the revelation given in Christ, but the issue here is not the *correctness* of these doctrines but the *grounds* on which they are held.

36. The Catechism also explains what is meant by "private" revelations as opposed to "public" revelation (§67).

37. Quoted at n. 6, above.

mann in 1956. What began as a more academic debate rapidly acquired an immediate relevance as the text of *Dei verbum* was forged. The first draft had spoken of the sources (plural) of revelation and had clearly regarded tradition as supplementing Scripture. After much controversy, the final version remained neutral on the question of the material sufficiency of Scripture, an implicit recognition that Trent had not settled the issue. "Sacred tradition and scripture are bound together in a close and reciprocal relationship. They both flow from the same divine wellspring, merge together to some extent, and are on course towards the same end" (2.9).

Having granted this, the final draft is not quite as neutral as is usually argued. The first draft stated that "tradition, indeed, and this alone, is the way by which the Church can clearly know a number of revealed truths, particularly those that refer to the inspiration, canonicity and integrity of all books together and each book in particular." The final draft states that "by this tradition comes the church's knowledge of the full canon of biblical books" (2.8). Here would appear to be at least one area where tradition supplements Scripture. As someone once commented, the one page of the Bible that is not inspired is the Contents page!

At the last stage Pope Paul insisted on the insertion of a sentence that negates the *sola scriptura* formula, though without actually denying the material sufficiency of Scripture: "[T]he church's certainty about all that is revealed is not drawn from holy scripture alone" (2.9).[38]

There are some who argue for a Catholic *sola scriptura,*[39] but by this they mean something very different from the Protestant concept.[40] Take a dogma like the Assumption of the Virgin Mary. It is not that Roman Catholic exegetes have suddenly increased in their confidence of being able to prove such a doctrine from Scripture. It is more the case that historical studies have shown that the earliest tradition offers no more support for the doctrine than does Scripture. If the doctrine is to be seen as part of the apostolic deposit of faith, neither Scripture nor tradition suffices. The supplementary view of tradition has lost its appeal because tradition fails to "supplement" where it is needed.[41] Thus the emphasis moves to

38. DEC 975. The significance of this statement will become clear when we consider RC biblical scholarship.

39. E.g., Karl Rahner, *Theological Investigations,* vol. 6 (London: Darton, Longman & Todd, 1974), 107-12. For a more recent approach, in the context of dialogue with evangelicals, see Thomas G. Guarino, "Catholic Reflections on Discerning the Truth of Sacred Scripture," in Colson and Neuhaus, eds., *Your Word Is Truth,* 79-101. Ratzinger discusses the implications of *Dei verbum* 2.9 for a Catholic idea of *sola scriptura* in CDV 191-92.

40. For the Protestant concept, see Anthony N. S. Lane, "*Sola scriptura*? Making Sense of a Post-Reformation Slogan," in *A Pathway into the Holy Scripture,* ed. Philip E. Satterthwaite and David F. Wright (Grand Rapids: Eerdmans, 1994), 297-327.

41. This is frankly acknowledged by Rahner, *Theological Investigations,* 6:91-93, 105-6, 109-10. Also in *Theological Investigations,* vol. 4 (London: Darton, Longman & Todd, 1966), 143-47.

the development of doctrine. The Marian dogmas, for example, are "implicit" in Scripture and early tradition, becoming explicit only after centuries of development. Thus affirmation of the material sufficiency of Scripture is compatible with Roman Catholicism in general and the Marian dogmas in particular. Clearly this is not the meaning of the Reformation *sola scriptura* since it proves to be compatible with that which the latter was designed to exclude.

Magisterium

> The task of authentically interpreting the word of God, whether in its written form or in that of tradition, has been entrusted only to those charged with the church's ongoing teaching function, whose authority is exercised in the name of Jesus Christ. This teaching function is not above the word of God but stands at its service, teaching nothing but what is handed down, according as it devotedly listens, reverently preserves and faithfully transmits the word of God, by divine command and with the help of the Holy Spirit. (2.10)

One of the fundamental Protestant charges against Roman Catholicism has been that the infallible teaching office stands above Scripture rather than being subject to it. *Dei verbum* denies this.[42] Later it is stated that "all the church's preaching . . . ought to be nourished and ruled by holy scripture" (6.21). As Ratzinger puts it, "[F]or the first time a text of the teaching office expressly points out the subordination of the teaching office to the word, i.e. its function as a servant."[43] There is no doubt that Vatican II and its aftermath represents a change from what went before. The idea, set out in the first draft, that the task of theology is to harmonize Scripture with the teaching of the church is manifestly not a description of the course of Roman Catholic theology at or since the council. Yet at the same time the fundamental issue has been muted, not eliminated. A doctrine like the Immaculate Conception of the Virgin Mary, "infallibly" defined by Pope Pius IX in 1854, is not open to reform in the light of Scripture, tradition, or any other factors.

Authorship and Truth of Scripture[44]

> By the faith handed down from the apostles, holy mother church accepts as sacred and canonical all the books of both the old Testament and the new, in

42. It should be noted, though, that "word of God" here embraces tradition as well as Scripture.

43. CDV 197.

44. On the crucial issue, see Aloys Grillmeier in CDV 199-218, 228-37.

> their entirety and with all their parts, in the conviction that they were written under the inspiration of the Holy Spirit and therefore have God as their originator *(auctorem):* on this basis they were handed on to the church. In the process of composition of the sacred books God chose and employed human agents, using their own powers and faculties, in such a way that they wrote as authors in the true sense, and yet God acted in and through them, directing the content entirely and solely as he willed. It follows that we should hold that whatever the inspired authors or "sacred writers" affirm is affirmed by the Holy Spirit; we must acknowledge that the books of scripture teach firmly, faithfully and without error such truth as God, for the sake of our salvation, wished the biblical text to contain. (3.11)

There are three points to note here. First, the divine authorship of Scripture. The earlier documents taught that Scripture was inspired by the Holy Spirit and so has God as its author. The first and second drafts of *Dei verbum* declared that God was the only "primary author" of Scripture; the final text simply affirms that he is the author of Scripture. Scripture is described as inspired *(inspirare)* rather than (as in some of the earlier documents from Vatican I to *Divino afflante Spiritu*) dictated *(dictare)* by the Spirit. Furthermore, "whatever the inspired authors or 'sacred writers' affirm is affirmed by the Holy Spirit." This is very similar to Warfield's famous "what the Scripture says, God says." The divine authorship of Scripture is clearly affirmed.

What about the human authors? The earlier documents that we have reviewed were sometimes weak on the human authorship of Scripture.[45] In the first and second drafts of *Dei verbum* the human authors are described as "instruments." The final text is stronger on human authorship, affirming that the biblical writers "wrote as authors in the true sense." But this does not undermine the divine authorship, since "God acted in and through them, directing the content entirely and solely as he willed." There is a careful balancing of the divine and human authorship.

The most hotly disputed area concerned the truth of Scripture, the question of inerrancy. The earlier documents from Vatican I to *Divino afflante Spiritu* all affirm that Scripture is without error and also describe this as an "absolute immunity," not restricted to matters of faith and morals, theology and ethics. The first draft stands in this tradition, affirming the "absolute immunity of the entire sacred Scripture from error" and allowing no error whatever in any field, religious or secular. The second draft still contained the phrase "utterly immune from all error." In the third draft this was stated more positively in asserting that all Scripture teaches truth without error.

45. Ratzinger notes that at Vatican II the traditionalist view of inspiration "involved an untenable view of the negligible human contribution in the transmission of revelation" (CDV 158).

The turning point came in a speech by Cardinal König on 2 October 1964 in which he argued that there were historical inconsistencies in Scripture. This came at the beginning of a five-day debate on this topic in which the overwhelming majority of speakers sided with König. It was held that the divine authorship of Scripture need not imply that God is responsible for a mistake made by the human author. Some argued that the infallibility of Scripture, like that of the pope, extends only to questions of faith and morals. In the light of this debate the following draft restricted the inerrancy of Scripture to all "saving truth," but this looked rather like the limitation of inerrancy to sacred as opposed to profane matters that had been rejected in the encyclicals that we have reviewed. The pope urged the revisers to reconsider this phrase, and so the final text restricts inerrancy to "such truth as God, for the sake of our salvation, wished the biblical text to contain." This was meant to exclude any division of Scripture into inspired (inerrant) and uninspired (errant) parts. The whole of Scripture is inspired and has God as its author, but not in such a way as to remove human limitations.[46]

It is clear that the final text is a compromise worked out between rival interests. Ratzinger concedes this, but he also claims that the outcome is "a synthesis of great importance," combining "fidelity to Church tradition with an affirmation of critical scholarship."[47] Much hangs on how one interprets the restriction of inerrancy to "such truth as God, for the sake of our salvation, wished the biblical text to contain." Clearly it implies a limited inerrancy, contrary to the teaching of the encyclicals from *Providentissimus Deus* to *Divino afflante Spiritu,* but it need not imply the specific positions that were there condemned.

Literary Forms

The first draft recognized that the biblical writers used contemporary concepts and terminology, but (unlike *Providentissimus Deus*) made no mention of literary genre *(litteraria genera). Dei verbum,* by contrast, begins its account of interpretation with the statement that "in order to get at what the biblical writers intended, attention should be paid (among other things) to *literary genres (genera litteraria)*" (3.12). This is followed by a paragraph explaining the importance of interpreting the text according to the historical, cultural, and literary context of the particular author and bearing in mind "the social conventions of the period" (3.12). If this is a green light to biblical scholarship, it is immediately followed by a yellow light. When interpreting individual passages, the exegete should equally

46. The Catechism (§107) quotes the final text of 3.11, but in its later brief summary states that the Scriptures "teach without error [God's] saving truth" (§136).

47. CDV 164.

pay attention to "the content and coherence of scripture as a whole, taking into account the whole church's living tradition and the sense of perspective given by faith *(analogiae fidei)*." The goal of exegesis is that "the church's judgment may mature," but the interpretation of Scripture "is ultimately subject to the judgment of the church, to which God has entrusted the commission and ministry of preserving and interpreting the word of God" (3.12).

A significant change is that while in *Divino afflante Spiritu* and the first two drafts of *Dei verbum* the emphasis is on resolving apparent errors in Scripture, in the final text the emphasis is simply upon discerning what Scripture is teaching.[48]

Divino afflante Spiritu states that just as the Word became flesh, so also, by God's condescension, his words are expressed in human language. This happens in a way that is consistent with God's holiness and truth, and God's words "are made like to human speech in every respect, except error" (§37). This is all repeated in *Dei verbum,* but without the reference to inerrancy (3.13).[49] Where the analogy of the incarnation was earlier used to support the idea of an unlimited inerrancy, now the divine condescension is used as a justification for the limitations of the human authors.[50]

A significant further green light for biblical scholarship is found in the chapter on the New Testament. The historicity of the Gospels is affirmed, but the inspired writers composed them "by various processes."

> They selected some things from the abundant material already handed down, orally or in writing. Other things they synthesised, or explained with a view to the needs of the churches. They preserved the preaching style, but worked throughout so as to communicate to us a true and sincere account of Jesus. (5.19)

This can be seen as a cautious endorsement of the methods of form criticism.[51]

Access to Scripture

The final chapter, on "Holy Scripture in the Life of the Church," contains many positive statements.

48. CDV 221, 224, 237. It is not, however, fair to *Divino afflante Spiritu* to say that "all hermeneutics was conceived exclusively in terms of the solution to the problems of scriptural inerrancy, as they were understood at the time" (CDV 237).

49. Pope John Paul II, in his *Address on the Interpretation of the Bible in the Church,* notes how the statement was "repeated almost literally," but glosses over the significant change (§6).

50. CDV 227.

51. 5.19 is heavily dependent on the instruction *Sancta Mater Ecclesia* issued by the Pontifical Biblical Commission on 21 April 1964.

- The church "keeps the scriptures, together with tradition, as the supreme rule of its faith." Since the Bible is "inspired by God and committed to writing once for all," it "communicates the word of God in an unalterable form." Therefore, all preaching "ought to be nourished and ruled by holy scripture" (6.21).[52]
- The Vulgate is listed as one of a number of ancient translations to be held in honor. Vernacular translations should be made from the original texts, and these may be produced "in collaboration with Christians of other denominations" (6.22).[53] This last phrase would imply that the RC Church is just another denomination, but the original Latin refers rather to separated brethren *(communi etiam cum fratribus seiunctis).*
- "The holy scriptures contain the word of God and, since they are inspired, really *are* the word of God; therefore the study of the 'sacred page' ought to be the very soul of theology" (6.24).[54]
- There is the, by now obligatory, quotation of Jerome's "ignorance of the scriptures is ignorance of Christ." Not just the clergy but also the laity are urged to engage in "serious bible study" (6.25). Ratzinger frankly acknowledges that in previous Roman Catholicism, "private reading of Scripture played no important role and even for meditation and for preaching was not considered of prime importance. . . . It is fair to say that Catholic piety has still largely to discover the Bible properly."[55] The call to study the Bible is not new, being found in *Providentissimus Deus* and *Spiritus Paraclitus,* but the difference is that Vatican II has without question led to a far greater openness to the Bible among Roman Catholics at every level.

The Interpretation of the Bible in the Church (1993)

Perhaps the most wide-ranging of the thirty-six documents produced by the Pontifical Biblical Commission since 1905 is that on *The Interpretation of the Bible in the Church,*[56] which deliberately commemorates the centenary of *Providentissimus Deus* and the fiftieth anniversary of *Divino afflante Spiritu.* It was presented by Cardinal Ratzinger to Pope John Paul II, who responded with an address.

52. 6.21 is based on the draft of a decree *De Verbo Dei (The Word of God),* which never materialized.

53. As Ratzinger puts it, "here Trent is indeed left far behind" (CDV 266).

54. Ratzinger brings out the "almost revolutionary" implications of this by showing how it is applied in the *Decree on Priestly Formation* (CDV 269).

55. CDV 270.

56. This was written in French. Those seeking a Swahili translation (or German, Italian, or Portuguese) may turn to the Vatican website. An English translation can be found at http://catholic-resources.org/ChurchDocs/PBC_Interp.htm.

This document examines a wide range of hermeneutical approaches to the Bible. These are assessed from the perspective of the Bible as the divine Word of God written by genuine human authors.

> The word of God finds expression in the work of human authors. The thought and the words belong at one and the same time both to God and to human beings, in such a way that the whole Bible comes at once from God and from the inspired human author. This does not mean, however, that God has given the historical conditioning of the message a value which is absolute. (III.D.2)

While different methods and approaches for interpretation are being discussed (I), the emphasis lies on the genuine human authorship. This point is made emphatically in the critique of fundamentalism (I.F). "Fundamentalist interpretation starts from the principle that the Bible, being the word of God, inspired and free from error, should be read and interpreted literally in all its details." It rejects the historical-critical and any other scientific method of interpreting Scripture. Fundamentalism (as thus portrayed) has a positive side. It "is right to insist on the divine inspiration of the Bible, the inerrancy of the word of God and other biblical truths." The trouble is that it reads the Bible in a way that is hostile to "all questioning and any kind of critical research." The reason is that it denies or ignores two things: "the historical character of biblical revelation" and "that the inspired word of God has been expressed in human language and that this word has been expressed, under divine inspiration, by human authors possessed of limited capacities and resources." In short, fundamentalism is commended for holding to the divine authorship of Scripture, but chided for failing to give due weight to its human authorship.

The result of this failure is that fundamentalism "pays no attention to the literary forms and to the human ways of thinking to be found in the biblical texts" and "places undue stress upon the inerrancy of certain details in the biblical texts, especially in what concerns historical events or supposedly scientific truth." So, for example, with the Gospels it "naively confuses the final stage of this tradition (what the evangelists have written) with the initial (the words and deeds of the historical Jesus)." This whole approach is dangerous because it offers an illusory certainty based on intellectual suicide.

Belief in the Bible as God's Word comes out more clearly in the later sections, on hermeneutical questions (II) and Catholic interpretation (III). The literal sense of Scripture is that expressed by the human author. "Since it is the fruit of inspiration, this sense is also intended by God, as principal author" (II.B.1). While Catholic exegetes must take heed to "the *historical character* of biblical revelation," they must "never forget that what they are interpreting is the *Word of God*" and that their ultimate goal is to explain "the meaning of the biblical text as God's word for today" (III.C.1).

The key to understanding *The Interpretation of the Bible in the Church* lies in the tension between the Bible as God's Word and the full acceptance of its human authorship *with human limitations.*

Roman Catholic Biblical Scholarship

It is impossible to do justice to such a vast theme in a few pages, so we will confine ourselves to making three basic points, illustrating these from Raymond E. Brown especially, with a few other random examples.[57]

Critical Study of the Bible

One feature of Roman Catholic biblical scholarship in the last fifty years has been its increasing openness to critical methods and conclusions, spurred on initially by *Divino afflante Spiritu*[58] and then by *Dei verbum.* RC biblical scholars will not necessarily reach conservative conclusions where the authorship, dating, or unity of books is concerned. Nor will they necessarily opt for the historicity of all that is taught in the Bible, such as the coming of the Magi.[59] As Raymond Brown expresses it concerning the virginal conception, critics "can no longer simply state with Jerome that they believe because they read it, since they now know the complexities of the scriptural accounts in which they read it."[60]

Key to this is the increasing recognition given to the genuine human authorship of Scripture, some implications of which are spelled out in *The Interpretation of the Bible in the Church.* A book that spells them out explicitly and at length is Jean Levie's *The Bible, Word of God in the Words of Men,* which appeared even before Vatican II, though after the 1955 declaration of the Pontifical Biblical Commission.[61] This has a chapter devoted to "Holy Scripture as the Word of Men: The Human Traits in the Inspired Work," which sets out implications under seven heads, all of them worth listing, with the key statements in italics as in the original:

57. I am very grateful to those who have advised me on this, especially Don Carson and Steve Walton. They are not, of course, to be held responsible for any shortcomings.

58. See at nn. 19-20, above.

59. Raymond E. Brown, *Biblical Exegesis and Church Doctrine* (London: Geoffrey Chapman, 1986), 10-16.

60. Raymond E. Brown, *The Virginal Conception and Bodily Resurrection of Jesus* (London: Geoffrey Chapman, 1974), 37.

61. Jean Levie, *The Bible, Word of God in the Words of Men* (London: Geoffrey Chapman, 1961), being the translation of a 1958 French original. See at n. 22, above.

1. *"Sacred Scripture can exhibit the various shades of meaning and the varying strength of human affirmation."* The author's "intention determines the scope of his assertions" and some teaching is temporary and contingent, most obviously passages like 1 Corinthians 11:2-16.[62]
2. *"Sacred Scripture, like human language in general, only asserts, according to sound logic, the judgement it makes and not the concepts it uses to form these judgements."* This applies especially to cosmological statements like Genesis 1:6-7.[63]
3. *"Sacred Scripture may admit the various methods of writing used in human documents."* Thus the gathering of material into the "Sermon on the Mount" is simply a literary device.[64]
4. *"Explicit or implicit quotations or, to use more up-to-date terminology, the way sources are used and reproduced"* are not in accord with modern expectations. This validates the use of the documentary hypothesis in investigating the origins of the Pentateuch.[65]
5. "*Holy Scripture contains different literary forms* to be interpreted according to the norms of the period in which these books appeared and not according to *a priori* norms drawn from our own times." This opens the question of the historicity of Jonah, for example, and of the patriarchal narratives in Genesis.[66]
6. "*Holy Scripture may and does include pseudepigrapha* and this without prejudice to inspiration, provided however that the pseudepigraphic procedure is not a dishonest trick to deceive the community of the faithful." This would cover Ecclesiastes and, more controversially, 2 Peter, but not Gnostic texts.[67]
7. "From the point of view of inspiration and inerrancy, there is the particularly grave problem of *moral difficulties raised by certain narratives and judgements in the Old Testament.*" Many examples of this are given, such as polygamy and the infamous prayer of Psalm 137:7-9. The key to understanding these is the progressive character of Old Testament revelation, which should be seen as paving the way for Christ.[68]

Independence of Exegetical Results

Roman Catholic exegetes have become much more independent of church dogma in their interpretation of individual texts. Probably the classic example is Jesus'

62. Levie, *The Bible, Word of God in the Words of Men,* 215-16.
63. Levie, *The Bible, Word of God in the Words of Men,* 216-17.
64. Levie, *The Bible, Word of God in the Words of Men,* 217-18.
65. Levie, *The Bible, Word of God in the Words of Men,* 218-22.
66. Levie, *The Bible, Word of God in the Words of Men,* 222-30.
67. Levie, *The Bible, Word of God in the Words of Men,* 230-31.
68. Levie, *The Bible, Word of God in the Words of Men,* 231-46.

words to Peter in Matthew 16:17-19, traditionally seen as a key foundation of the papacy. In his commentary Ulrich Luz, writing in the 1980s, notes the change that had taken place over about thirty years in Roman Catholic research. No longer is it true that "one's confessional standing determines the results of one's research."[69] Brown comments that an ecumenical study on this topic was facilitated by the fact that the RC participants neither sought to read the developed doctrine back into the New Testament nor claimed that it was an inevitable development from it.[70]

Another example is Raymond Brown's treatment of the virginal conception, which he repeatedly discusses.[71] He consistently sees the New Testament evidence as insufficient to demonstrate a literal historical virginal conception, though he sees it as favorable to such a belief. His own view is that the church has infallibly determined that the doctrine should be understood literally, but he recognizes that this could be disputed and that it remains an open question. The scientifically controllable evidence is ambiguous enough for the literal historicity of the doctrine to be a legitimate topic for enquiry. Such uncertainty would be destabilizing for an evangelical scholar, for whom doctrine is meant to be built upon Scripture. Brown, however, points out that RC dogma is taught by the church on the basis of both Scripture and tradition.[72] As noted above, *Dei verbum* teaches that "the church's certainty about all that is revealed is not drawn from holy scripture alone" (2.9). This means that the RC biblical critic can question the scriptural basis for a dogma without necessarily questioning the dogma itself. Brown also defends the doctrine of Mary's perpetual virginity, acknowledging that the natural reading of the New Testament points in a contrary direction.[73] The same applies to the dogmas of the Immaculate Conception and the Assumption, "and there is no evidence that any NT author thought" of them.[74]

69. Ulrich Luz, *Matthew 8–20: A Commentary* (Minneapolis: Fortress, 2001), 357.

70. Brown, *Biblical Exegesis and Church Doctrine,* 39-40. This is spelled out more fully in Raymond E. Brown, *Biblical Reflections on Crises Facing the Church* (London: Darton, Longman & Todd, 1975), 63-83. The study was between Lutherans and Roman Catholics and gave birth to Paul C. Empie and T. Austin Murphy, eds., *Papal Primacy and the Universal Church* (Minneapolis: Augsburg, 1974). There was a related biblical study: Raymond E. Brown, Karl P. Donfried, and John Reumann, eds., *Peter in the New Testament: A Collaborative Assessment by Protestant and Roman Catholic Scholars* (Minneapolis: Augsburg; New York: Paulist, 1973), of which note especially 83-101.

71. *The Virginal Conception and Bodily Resurrection of Jesus* (London: Geoffrey Chapman, 1974); *The Birth of the Messiah: A Commentary on the Infancy Narratives in the Gospels of Matthew and Luke* (London: Geoffrey Chapman, 1977); in an updated edition (1993) the appendix on the virginal conception from the original edition (517-33) is supplemented (697-712); *Biblical Exegesis and Church Doctrine* (London: Geoffrey Chapman, 1986), 35-37.

72. Brown, *Biblical Exegesis and Church Doctrine,* 17, 49-53.

73. Brown, *Biblical Exegesis and Church Doctrine,* 40-43. See also Brown, *The Birth of the Messiah* (London: Geoffrey Chapman, 1993), 605-7.

74. Brown, *Biblical Exegesis and Church Doctrine,* 43-45.

Loyalty to Roman Catholic Dogma

Since 1955 RC biblical scholars have been allowed to work with full liberty, provided they respect the teaching authority of the church.[75] By and large they have done so, though with some exceptions.[76]

An interesting exception is John Meier's consideration of the question of Jesus' "brothers." After a long discussion he concludes that "if — prescinding from faith and later Church teaching — the historian or exegete is asked to render a judgment on the NT and patristic texts we have examined, viewed simply as historical sources, the most probable opinion is that the brothers and sisters of Jesus were true siblings."[77] This is, "from a purely philological and historical point of view" the most probable opinion.[78] However, Meier takes care not to commit himself to this view: "It cannot be stressed too often that, for reasons of method, this book *prescinds* from faith and Church teaching as sources of knowledge, but by no means *denies* them."[79]

Less reserved is Rudolf Pesch, another RC exegete who argues that unbiased exegesis only allows the conclusion that Mark 6:3 refers to Jesus' blood brothers and sisters.[80] He cites Ratzinger for support in his claim that there is no dogmatic need to state otherwise. Ratzinger's words concern not the perpetual virginity of Mary but the virginal conception, which (he states) was not *necessary* for the incarnation to take place.[81] Pesch is both more radical than Meier and less so. He questions not just the perpetual virginity of Mary but also (implicitly) the virgin birth — but his statement merely concerns the implications of Mark 6:3.

As we have seen, *Dei verbum* states that the task of interpreting God's word has been entrusted to the Magisterium, but also spoke of the Magisterium as standing at the service of the Word of God (2.10) and the Catechism refers to reform (§83). Modern biblical studies and ecumenical debates have led to some shifts in doctrine (in the manner described at the beginning of this chapter), one

75. See at n. 22, above.

76. Raymond Brown notes that such dissent is exceptional (*Biblical Exegesis and Church Doctrine,* 18; see also 54-85).

77. John P. Meier, *A Marginal Jew: Rethinking the Historical Jesus,* vol. 1 (New York: Doubleday, 1991), 318-32, quotation at 331. He wrongly claims (319) that Calvin held to Mary's perpetual virginity (he remained agnostic), as also does Brown, *Biblical Exegesis and Church Doctrine,* 41.

78. Meier, *A Marginal Jew,* 1:332.

79. Meier, *A Marginal Jew,* 1:354 n. 15.

80. Rudolf Pesch, *Das Markusevangelium,* vol. 1 (Freiburg: Herder, 1976), 322-24: "leiblichen Brüdern . . . leiblichen Schwestern."

81. Joseph Cardinal Ratzinger, *Introduction to Christianity* (San Francisco: Ignatius, 2000), 274-75.

of the most significant concerning justification, in the *Joint Declaration on the Doctrine of Justification* (1999).[82]

Conclusion

The Roman Catholic view of biblical authority has shifted substantially in the period since Vatican I and, especially, the acknowledgment of the human authorship of Scripture has moved from being largely formal to increasingly significant. In particular, it now provides the basis for biblical criticism and qualified affirmations of biblical inerrancy. The effects of this are seen in RC biblical scholarship — in the acceptance of critical conclusions concerning the authorship, dating, and unity of books and concerning the historicity of biblical narratives. For evangelical biblical scholars such an acceptance would likely have doctrinal implications, but the situation is different for RC biblical scholarship because the ultimate doctrinal authority is the teaching of the church. At the same time as the weakening of formal statements about Scripture and the adoption of biblical criticism, there has been a massive increase in engagement with the text and openness to its results, and this has led to some doctrinal modifications in a biblical direction.

82. For an assessment of which, see Anthony N. S. Lane, *Justification by Faith in Catholic-Protestant Dialogue: An Evangelical Assessment* (London and New York: T. & T. Clark [Continuum], 2002).

Biblical and Theological Topics

ELEVEN

The Old Testament Canon, Josephus, and Cognitive Environment

Stephen G. Dempster

"Elephants in the Room" and Historiography

"The elephant in the room" is a popular saying for an inconvenient truth obvious to all but unspoken, avoided, dodged, or explained away in order to maintain a stance toward reality that has not taken into consideration the presence of this unwelcome creature.[1] In common everyday life situations, such elephants refer to uncomfortable truths such as sex in the Victorian age and death in ours. On university campuses in the United States one common elephant is the non-matriculation of student athletes.[2] The children's story of the emperor's new clothes is a classic illustration of a young boy pointing out an uncomfortable truth that everyone can see but no one has the courage to name. In worldview studies and in philosophical discourse, "elephants in the room" are often the difficult parts of reality that are either avoided or explained away. One thinks of the popular legendary story of the priest who refused to look through Galileo's proffered telescope. In historical studies, such elephants are major pieces of evidence that resist being compressed into tidy historiographical explanations. In academic study, such evidence cannot often be ignored, but it has to be made to fit into a particular theory.[3]

In the dominant understanding of the canon of the Old Testament in contemporary scholarship, there is one particular "elephant in the room" that is often dodged, evaded, maneuvered around, or finally explained away. It is a common criticism to argue that the terminology of canon should be avoided to describe the

1. Eviatar Zerubavel, *The Elephant in the Room: Silence and Denial in Everyday Life* (New York: Oxford University Press, 2007).

2. Zerubavel, *The Elephant in the Room*, 3.

3. If the fact becomes so distorted or it is totally dismissed, one can virtually label the theory Procrustean. Procrustes was a figure in Greek mythology who provided a bed for every traveler. If the travelers would not fit, they would be made to fit. Limbs that were too large would be cut to size, and ones that were too small would be stretched to size.

Bible since it could impose on to the early biblical evidence the later understanding of a fixed, closed list of divinely authoritative books. Historical anachronism should be avoided at all cost.[4] One must ruthlessly jettison "the tyranny of canonical assumptions."[5] Such claims in principle are clearly valid. The first thing that scholars need to do is to explain the evidence, not explain it away. Nevertheless, it is possible to become slaves to the tyranny of non-canonical assumptions and seek to avoid, maneuver around, or explain away evidence that clearly points in a certain direction, and challenges our previously formulated views.

The Contemporary Canon Debate

In studies of the history of the Old Testament formation of canon, it is difficult to point to an exact process that led to the formation of the current canons of the Old Testament.[6] There is so much that is not known. The external evidence is capable of various interpretations.[7] Currently there are two main and differing opinions about the meaning of this evidence, one that is more dominant than the other. The first is that of minimalism, which essentially argues that the canon of the Hebrew Bible was not completed in Judaism until the late second century C.E. and even then was occupied with questions about its exact boundaries until the third and fourth centuries.[8] The Law and the Prophets were essentially fixed

4. Eugene Ulrich, "The Notion and Definition of Canon," in *The Canon Debate,* ed. Lee M. McDonald and James A. Sanders (Peabody, MA: Hendrickson, 2002), 21-30; Robert Kraft, "Para-mania: Beside, Before and Beyond Bible Studies," *Journal of Biblical Literature* 126 (2007): 3-27.

5. Kraft, "Para-mania." The phraseology is that of Kraft.

6. There are three main ones: Protestant (based on the Hebrew Bible), Roman Catholic, and Orthodox. To be sure, the Protestant forms the irreducible core for the other two, to which are added deutero-canonical books. There are seven more books in the wider canon of Roman Catholicism: 1 Maccabees, 2 Maccabees, Ecclesiasticus, Judith, Tobit, Wisdom of Solomon, Baruch. There are also additions to the book of Esther, and a prayer of the three martyrs in the fiery furnace in Daniel. The Orthodox canon adds 1 Esdras and 3 Maccabees.

7. Stephen G. Dempster, "Canons on the Left and Canons on the Right: Finding a Resolution in the Canon Debate," *Journal of the Evangelical Theological Society* 52 (2009).

8. J. Barton, *Oracles of God: Perceptions of Ancient Prophecy in Israel after the Exile* (Oxford: Oxford University Press, 1985); P. Ackroyd, "The Open Canon," in *Studies in the Religious Tradition of the Old Testament* (London: SCM, 1987), 209-24; J. Sanders, "Canon: Hebrew Bible," *Anchor Bible Dictionary* 1:837-52; L. McDonald, *The Formation of the Christian Biblical Canon,* 2nd edition (Peabody, MA: Hendrickson, 1995); L. McDonald, *The Biblical Canon* (Peabody: Hendrickson, 2007); D. Carr, "Canon in the Context of Community: An Outline of the Formation of the Tanakh and the Christian Bible," in *A Gift of God in Due Season: Essays on Scripture and Community in Honor of James A. Sanders,* ed. R. D. Weis and D. M. Carr, JSOTSS 225 (Sheffield: Sheffield Academic Press, 1996), 22-65; James VanderKam, *From*

before the Common Era, and an emerging third section that became known as the Writings was probably closed sometime in the late second century C.E. or thereafter.[9] In the church, the situation was not as neat, as a wider canon — the so-called Septuagintal plus — was adopted amid much controversy. The primary evidence was provided by the great Greek codices of the fourth and fifth centuries C.E. that plainly show that "extra-biblical" books were mixed with so-called biblical ones without any attempt to distinguish them.[10] The maximalists, however, understand the evidence differently, arguing that the Hebrew Bible was essentially completed in its final form by the second century B.C.E.[11] Consequently the Christian church was born with a "narrow" canon in its hands. Decisions made by rabbis later about their canon did not so much decide which books were included or excluded but simply ratified an existing corpus. The evidence of the Christian church suggests

---

Revelation to Canon: Studies in the Hebrew Bible and Second Temple Judaism, Journal for the Study of Judaism Supplement 62 (Leiden: Brill, 2000); E. Ulrich, *The Dead Sea Scrolls and the Origins of the Bible,* Studies in the Dead Sea Scrolls and Related Literature (Grand Rapids: Eerdmans, 1999).

9. This view essentially modifies the standard theory that dominated the field of canonical studies for the last century. This theory was essentially based on the tripartite signature of the Hebrew Bible and argued that the canon evolved gradually in three separate stages. The Torah was closed in the postexilic period (400 B.C.E.), the Prophets about two centuries later (200 B.C.E.), and the Writings at a so-called rabbinic council of Jabneh (90 C.E.). But the evidence that was used to support this theory has been called into question, particularly the council of Jabneh. However, the same basic framework is modified by minimalists, usually by projecting the closure of the third division a century or so into the future. For the standard theory see Herbert Edward Ryle, *The Canon of the Old Testament: An Essay on the Gradual Growth and Formation of the Hebrew Canon of Scripture,* 2nd edition (London: Macmillan, 1904).

10. Vaticanus: + 6 = Wisdom of Solomon, Ecclesiasticus, Judith, Tobit, Baruch, Epistle of Jeremiah;
Sinaiticus: + 6 = Tobit, Judith, 1-2 Maccabees, Wisdom of Solomon, Ecclesiasticus;
Alexandrinus: + 11 = Baruch, Epistle of Jeremiah, Tobit, Judith, 1-4 Maccabees, Wisdom of Solomon, Ecclesiasticus, Psalms of Solomon.

This fact, of course, was not lost on authorities within the church, as is attested, for instance, by Athanasius in his Easter Letter (367 C.E.), in which there is the first evidence of the word "canon" used as a fixed list: "Inasmuch as some have taken in hand to draw up for themselves an arrangement of the so-called apocryphal books, and *to intersperse them with divinely inspired scripture . . . it has seemed good to me also to set forth in order the books which are included in the canon* and have been delivered to us with accreditation that they are divine" (emphasis added).

11. S. Leimann, *The Canonization of the Hebrew Scripture: The Talmudic and Midrashic Evidence* (Hamden, UK: Archon, 1976); R. Beckwith, *The Old Testament Canon of the New Testament Church* (Grand Rapids: Eerdmans, 1985); E. Ellis, *The Old Testament in Early Christianity: Canon and Interpretation in the Light of Modern Research* (Grand Rapids: Baker, 1992); P. Davies, *Scribes and Schools: The Canonization of the Hebrew Scriptures* (Louisville: Westminster John Knox, 1998); A. Steinmann, *Oracles of God: The Old Testament Canon* (Saint Louis: Concordia, 1999). There are different nuances in this position, but essentially the nascent church inherits an authoritative collection of sacred literature.

that as the church grew away from its roots in Judaism, its knowledge of the exact contents of the canon grew commensurately uncertain. Various church leaders tried to return it to its original canonical roots.

A number of quotes from the various positions amply demonstrate the two perspectives. The chief representative for the minimalist perspective is Lee McDonald, whose popular book on the biblical canon has become a standard textbook in many seminaries and colleges.[12] McDonald remarks,

> The relative silence about a well-defined collection of Scripture among the Pharisees, Essenes, and Sadducees in the first century strongly suggests an absence of concern with the idea of a closed biblical canon before the second century CE. . . . We would be well served again to heed [Jacob] Neusner's dictum: "What we cannot show, we now do know."

Of course, Neusner said the opposite, "What we cannot show, we do *not* know." The author or editor made a transcribing mistake in copying Neusner's well-known dictum for understanding the past.[13] But in fact, Lee McDonald has just provided an example of the *mistaken* citation: this relative *silence* of a well-defined collection among the Pharisees, Essenes, and Sadducees in the first century C.E. speaks for him loudly of the absence of a fixed canon of the Hebrew Bible before the second century C.E. He concludes,

> If there was a clearly defined biblical canon in the third century BCE or earlier, one would think that at least one statement saying so from that period would have survived. Perhaps the listing of such books in the late second century CE comes at that time because only then was there a special concern over the precise limits of Scripture in rabbinic Judaism. If a biblical canon existed before then, how could it have been lost or blurred in both Judaism and the early church? How could the two primary surviving religious sects of Judaism, Pharisaism (the forerunner of rabbinic Judaism) and early Christianity — both of which appealed to its sacred literature for support of the foundation of its life and ministries and all that it held sacred — have lost the contents of their sacred writings that at one time were clearly known and passed on in these communities . . . ? How could such a presumed collection be passed on generation after generation with no one specifying its contents — and only later have to be written down because the contents had been forgotten? No early traditions are appealed to by the rabbinic sages or the early church fathers

12. Lee Martin McDonald, *The Biblical Canon: Its Origin, Transmission, and Authority,* 3rd edition (Peabody, MA: Hendrickson, 2007), 170.

13. We all make "howlers," and of course when I mentioned this one to Lee, he pointed out a few more in a good-natured way.

> when they listed the contents of the sacred collections in the second century CE and later.[14]

McDonald also quotes P. Stuhlmacher: "Nowhere in the New Testament writings can any special interest in the canonical delimitation and fixing of scriptures be detected." McDonald concludes: "Instead of assuming that the early Christians paid little attention to what had been settled earlier, it is better to conclude that no such final decisions had been made in the church at this point."[15]

Thus the conclusion is virtually absolute. Absence of evidence leads to evidence of absence. What we cannot show becomes what we do now know.

This is the problem that confronts scholars and students of the Old Testament. It is easy to reach different conclusions from the same evidence since because of its paucity it is capable of different interpretations. For example, the relative silence about a well-defined collection of Scripture among the Pharisees, Essenes, and Sadducees in the first century C.E. (as well as the early Christian movement) strongly suggests an absence of concern with the idea of a closed biblical canon before the second century C.E., perhaps because the extent and scope of the canon was never really an issue. It was an assumed fact. The real issue was the interpretation of the canon. So for example, Earle Ellis remarks,

> as already in the late second century B.C. and probably two generations earlier, certain sacred books had a canonical status. That is, they constituted a definite and identifiable collection with a continuing, normative authority distinguished from that of other religious writings. . . . It is possible that, since the individual books are not named, those in the canon of one writer were not identical with those of the others. However, they are designated by very similar expressions and are apparently well-known works requiring no enumeration. . . . Only in the second century A.D. when uncertainty existed about their number and order, are the books of the Old Testament listed by name.[16]

Thus from exactly the same evidence possessed by McDonald, Ellis reaches the opposite conclusion.

These views are represented as the polar opposite positions in the contemporary canon debate in the Old Testament, and the former one is dominant in the field.[17] But are we condemned to historical and canonical solipsism because

14. McDonald, *The Biblical Canon,* 188-89.

15. McDonald, *The Biblical Canon,* 194, 214.

16. E. Earle Ellis, *The Old Testament in Early Christianity: Canon and Interpretation in the Light of Modern Research* (Eugene, OR: Wipf & Stock, 2003), 9-10.

17. Dempster, "Canons on the Left."

of the paucity and ambiguity of the evidence? I certainly do not think so, and I have weighed the pros and cons of the various positions in a recent study.[18]

Josephus: "The Elephant in the Room" in the Canon Debate

If there ever was a hefty "elephant in the room" in the contemporary canon debate for the regnant theory, it would be Josephus. His disappearance would be convenient. But unfortunately he will not disappear. His "inconvenient" evidence dates from the late first century C.E. (ca. 90-95) and is found in a ringing apology for Judaism — *Against Apion.* Apion (20 B.C.E.–50 C.E.) was a Greek grammarian born in Alexandria, who hated the Jews and publicized anti-Semitic propaganda. Josephus sought to defend his people. Since *Against Apion* succeeds *The Antiquities,* which was not received very well, Josephus sought to compensate by responding to the slanders of Apion, who had influenced the Romans against the Jews. Josephus thus is seeking to defend Judaism from such infamy, and also to show the antiquity and consequently the superiority of the Jewish culture, and win the admiration of a Roman audience.[19] As a historian he may not write contemporary objective history, but it should be borne in mind that anyone could verify his statements by simply checking with Jewish audiences in first-century Palestine. As he develops his argument, he compares the ancient records and books of other cultures with Jewish records and books:

> Naturally, then, or rather necessarily — seeing that it is not open to anyone to write of their own accord, nor is there any disagreement present in what is written, but the prophets alone learned, by inspiration from God, what had happened in the distant and most ancient past and recorded plainly in their own time just as they occurred — among us there are not thousands of books in disagreement and conflict with each other, but only twenty-two books, containing the record of all time, which are rightly trusted. Five of these are the books of Moses, which contain both the laws and the tradition from the birth of humanity up to his death; this is a period of a little less than 3,000 years. From the death of Moses until Artaxerxes, king of the Persians after Xerxes, the prophets after Moses wrote the history of what took place in their own times in thirteen books; the remaining four books contain hymns to God and instruction for people on life. From Artaxerxes up to our own time every event

18. Dempster, "Canons on the Left."

19. John M. G. Barclay, "Josephus v. Apion: Analysis of an Argument," in *Understanding Josephus: Seven Perspectives,* ed. Steve Mason, JSPSS 32 (Sheffield: Sheffield Academic Press, 1999), 194-221; see also Sid Z. Leimann, "Josephus and the Canon of the Bible," in *Josephus, the Bible, and History,* ed. Louis H. Feldman and Gōhei Hata (Leiden: Brill, 1989), 50-58.

> has been recorded but this is not judged worthy of the same trust, since the exact line of succession of the prophets did not continue. It is clear in practice how we approach our own writings. Although such a long time has now passed, no-one has dared to add, to take away, or to alter anything; and it is innate in every Judean right from birth, to regard them as decrees of God, to remain faithful to them and, if necessary, to die on their behalf. Thus, to date many have been seen, on many occasions, as prisoners of war suffering torture and all kinds of death in theaters for not letting slip a single word in contraventions of the laws and records associated with them.[20]

There are a number of salient points about Josephus's argument that are extremely important for knowledge of the canon of the Hebrew Bible. To begin with, this is the first explicit external witness for a closed canon of the Hebrew Bible. There is a specific *canonical list* that defines a limited number of books — twenty-two to be precise. Second, they belong to a *canonical epoch,* a limited time, which traces the history of the world from its beginning until the Persian period, which closes this epoch because prophetic inspiration has ceased. Third, there is a *canonical organization* as the books are enumerated into three divisions: (1) the five books of Moses; (2) thirteen prophets after Moses probably arranged chronologically; (3) remaining hymns to God and precepts for human life. This "tripartite signature" can also be subsumed under a "bipartite signature" later in the text as "laws and records." Fourth, there is a *canonical consensus* among the Jewish population about these books that leads to ultimate allegiance ("and it is innate in every Judean right from birth, to regard them as decrees of God, to remain faithful to them and, if necessary, to die on their behalf") precisely because they are sharply distinguished from other literary works as the "decrees of God." Finally for Josephus, this means that there is a *canonical text,* to which nothing can be added or subtracted from the works that have been enumerated.

Even if the term "canon" in the strict, formal sense, meaning "a fixed, closed list of books" to which no others can be added, does not occur until the fourth century C.E., the concept is clearly here in Josephus; and if he can be trusted, it can be extended to at least the first century B.C.E. if not before. Indeed, David Carr makes the point that

> Josephus appears to think he can make credible claims for the antiquity of this alphabetically defined body of scriptures, claims that would disqualify other points of view he makes in his arguments against Apion if they could be disproven easily. Therefore, we should not assume that this twenty-two or twenty-

20. *Against Apion* 8.37-43. For the translation see John M. G. Barclay, *Flavius Josephus: Translation and Commentary* (Leiden: Brill, 2006), 28-32.

four book body of Scripture first emerged in the late first century, although it is most clearly attested then.[21]

"Explaining" Josephus

But how do scholars, particularly minimalists, seek to reconcile this clear and coherent doctrine of "canon" with their views that such a canon did not exist at the time? There are a number of explanations provided below:

Rudolf Meyer: "A Marginal Jew"[22]

Meyer admits openly the apparent force of Josephus's *Kanontheorie* and articulates some of its points very clearly: definite number of books, specific bygone age, and textual standardization.[23] But he claims that the discoveries at Qumran as well as other considerations point to the fact that Josephus's views were only marginal at best, referring to an inner coterie of Pharisees that triumphed in the second century C.E. and whose views in no way reflected historical reality before then. First, he points out that the limited corpus of twenty-two volumes could not have preceded the destruction of the temple in 70 C.E. because the Qumran community attested to a large number of extra-biblical books, including Ecclesiasticus, which with its non-Pharisaic theology could not have been distinguished from the book of Proverbs. Citing a text from the *Tosefta* (190 C.E.), reflecting Pharisaic concerns, Meyer concludes that Ecclesiasticus is now excluded from the canon. This is regarded as "proof" for the artificial construction of Josephus. Second, as for the dogma *von der prophetischen Idealzeit,* Meyer argues that Josephus contradicts his own scheme by using the sources of 1 and 2 Maccabees to provide reliable history for the Jews even though these books postdate the prophetic era of inspiration. Josephus also describes "prophetic" individuals who postdate the prophetic age (e.g., John Hyrcanus). Moreover, Ben Sira seems to include the high priest Simon with his cast of biblical characters with no separation of a biblical and post-biblical age. Finally, the texts of Qumran prove that before the

21. David M. Carr, *Writing on the Tablet of the Heart: Origins of Scripture and Literature* (New York: Oxford University Press, 2005), 249.

22. R. Meyer, "Bemerkungen zur literargeschichtlichen Hintergrund der Kanontheorie des Josephus," in *Josephus-Studien: Untersuchungen zu Josephus. Die Antiken Judentum und Die Neuen Testament,* ed. O. Betz, K. Haacker, and M. Hengel (Göttingen: Vandenhoeck & Ruprecht, 1974), 285-99.

23. Meyer, "Bemerkungen zur literargeschichtlichen Hintergrund der Kanontheorie des Josephus," 286.

destruction of the temple there existed a textually fluid "Bible" reflected in the Samaritan Pentateuch, the Vorlage of the LXX, and the proto-MT.

Steve Mason has answered Meyer in an excellent essay.[24] I will summarize his response and add a few reflections. First, the number of extra-biblical books including Ecclesiasticus that were found at Qumran may point to a wider canon, but then again they may not. It is extremely hazardous to extrapolate the identity of canonical books from the presence of books in a library. And while there were debates about Ecclesiasticus later in the history of Judaism, the simple fact that it is not much different from Proverbs, does not mean that it should have been regarded as canonical. Second, if Josephus wanted to write a history of the Jews up to his present time, he had no choice but to include 1 and 2 Maccabees. He is not necessarily implying that these Maccabean writings are just as reliable as the previous prophetic writings, but the simple fact of the matter is that they are virtually all that he has as sources for the history of this period. Moreover, that the charism of a prophet definitely existed after Artaxerxes and was shown in sporadic form in no way contradicts Josephus's claim regarding a specific canonical epoch in which there was a fixed sequence of prophets in the distant past whose succession was broken. The end of an age of authoritative written revelation did not exclude the occasional appearance of a person with a prophetic charism. Finally, the presence of a more fluid textual situation before 70 C.E. does not invalidate a parallel movement toward textual quality control for which definite evidence exists. Some of these concerns will receive more consideration below.

Was Josephus simply reflecting the gradual emergence of a small circle of Pharisees, which decided the canon for all Jews in the second century C.E.? It needs to be borne in mind that if Josephus is simply delivering the propaganda of a small party-line in Judea, he forfeits his credibility as a historian. To jettison historical credibility while trying to win respect for one's people and culture is an odd combination for a historian.

John Barton: "Out of Step with His Contemporaries"

After discussing Rudolf Meyer's views about Josephus's understanding of canon, Barton states,

> Meyer's point that other authorities are less concerned than Josephus to fix limits to the "canon" is undoubtedly correct, and supports the present argument, but I am not sure that even Josephus should be read with later ideas of a

24. Steve Mason, "Josephus and His Twenty-Two Book Canon," in McDonald and Sanders, eds., *The Canon Debate,* 110-27.

> strictly delimited canon in mind. He may have indeed wanted to exclude from Scripture some books that other Jews accepted — the passage in *Against Apion* could be read that way; but it should be remembered that he is not writing for a Jewish readership, but rather to commend Judaism to people familiar with Greek literature. His argument that the Jews have only twenty-two sacred books is part of a polemic against what he chooses to see as the multitude of mutually inconsistent books believed in by Greeks. In maintaining the small compass of Jewish Scripture he does not, as a matter of fact, say that no other book could conceivably be found that would meet the criterion of prophetic authorship; only that no more than twenty-two have until now been found to do so. Even if we feel it is more natural to follow Meyer's reading of Josephus, however, we should certainly note as he does that in setting limits to the canon at all Josephus is out of step with his contemporaries.[25]

It is difficult to understand how Barton comes to this understanding of Josephus. It is hard not to agree with Mason that Barton's interpretation "strains Josephus's words beyond tolerance."[26] If one should not read Josephus with later ideas of strictly delimited canon in mind, then surely those ideas originate here — and even further back if Josephus can be trusted. Josephus obviously limits the canon to twenty-two volumes, and, for him as well as his Jewish contemporaries, it is closed. He certainly does not envision any book being added because of the failure of the exact succession of the prophets. The number twenty-two probably also indicates finality because it is the total number of letters of the Hebrew alphabet. At the same time, Barton does admit that Josephus is "out of step" with his contemporaries. But is this conclusion reached by a reconstruction of the evidence that excludes Josephus from being a major stakeholder in the debate? While Barton may be "in step" with his own contemporaries, his views might well be considered "out of step" with those of Josephus.

Lee McDonald: "Ahead of His Time"

> How reliable are Josephus's comments about the scope of the Jewish biblical canon at the end of the first century C.E.? Since he claims that the exact succession of the prophets ceased with Artaxerxes son of Xerxes, whom he elsewhere identifies as Ahasuerus from the book of Esther (*Ant.* 11.184), it is understandable why he concludes his biblical canon as early as he did, namely in the time of Artaxerxes. Does Josephus's accounting of these matters reflect what was

25. John Barton, *Oracles of God: Perceptions of Ancient Prophecy in Israel after the Exile* (New York: Oxford University Press, 2007), 58-59.

26. Mason, "Josephus and His Twenty-Two Book Canon," 126.

> believed among most Jews at the end of the first century or an emerging view that had not yet gained acceptance among the Jews?[27]

After suggesting that Josephus postulates a view that was then emerging as opposed to established fact, the idea that anyone could have verified whether Josephus was right by asking the nearest Jews about their sacred books is answered in the following way: "This test of veracity sounds plausible enough, but it assumes that the 'nearest Jew' would know the contents of the biblical canon and that all Jews would agree on the matter. What evidence exists that all Jews accepted the same books in their collection of sacred Scriptures?"[28] McDonald asserts his own view of the evidence — there is no consensus among Jews regarding a fixed canon — as a way to eliminate the force of the test of veracity. Such a test could not work because in McDonald's view there was no consensus of a fixed canon in Judaism. But that is the point that McDonald must prove from the evidence. The "nearest Jew" could provide any Roman citizen with information that could disprove Josephus — a fact that certainly would not have been lost on Josephus.

McDonald then supports this point by moving nearly a century later to Melito of Sardis, who traveled to the East to find out the exact nature of the content of the Old Testament, even though there was a large synagogue in Sardis. Presumably he would not have needed to do this, since he could have "crossed the street and asked the 'nearest Jew.'"[29] While there is a certain logic to this reasoning, it may be that the Jews in Sardis were not certain about the canon in Jerusalem either and Melito wanted to go to the "horse's mouth" in Jerusalem — "to the very place where the things in question were preached and took place."[30]

McDonald then concludes,

> It is clear that Josephus is out of step with other Jewish open-ended or fluid canons of the first century, for example, those at Qumran, which made no distinction between writers before and writers after Artaxerxes (i.e. the Ezra tradition), and of early Christianity. The freedom of the Jews to add or subtract from the biblical text suggests that there was no universally accepted closed biblical canon in the first century CE. Further, Mason suggests that Josephus's collection was "an inner-Pharisaic view that could have gradually come to prominence with the emergence of the rabbinic coalition after 70 [CE]; it cannot reflect a common first century view . . . Josephus appears to be ahead of his time."[31]

27. McDonald, *The Biblical Canon,* 154.
28. McDonald, *The Biblical Canon,* 155.
29. McDonald, *The Biblical Canon,* 155-56.
30. Eusebius, *Ecclesiastical History* 4.26.
31. McDonald, *The Biblical Canon,* 156.

McDonald proceeds to argue that Josephus's canon reflects a Babylonian origin, which was not popular in Palestine. It can be dated between 70 and 90 C.E. The problem, however, with his citation of Mason is that Mason himself cites Rudolf Meyer to refute the latter's position![32]

> The problem with this view will now be obvious for all the problems that Meyer finds in other sources are much more clearly and fully present in Josephus' own use of the Scriptures in *Antiquities* . . . if we lacked the *Against Apion,* Josephus would offer a clear case for an open canon. But we do have the *Against Apion,* in which the same Josephus, emphatically but matter-of-factly, insists that Judaean records have long since been completed in twenty-two volumes.[33]

R. Timothy McLay: "What's So Great about Josephus?"

In a chapter devoted to the Septuagint in Lee McDonald's textbook, Tim McLay deals with the question of the relevance of Josephus to the question of the Hebrew canon. He rightly points out,

> The major problem with determining the value of these testimonies for historical construction is that these witnesses either do not specifically name the books to which they refer or do so only in part. In the case of Josephus, for example, scholars are driven to fanciful reconstructions of what Josephus meant. Thus, Beckwith suggests that Josephus's five books of Moses refer to the Pentateuch; that thirteen volumes of the prophet are Joshua, Judges, Samuel, Kings, Isaiah, Jeremiah-Lamentations, Ezekiel, Minor Prophets, Daniel, Esther, Ezra-Nehemiah, Job and Chronicles; and that the final "four" are Psalms, Proverbs, Song of Songs and Ecclesiastes.

McLay proceeds to criticize this reconstruction of the evidence at a number of points since the content of Josephus's list is not absolutely clear. Then, he completely discounts Josephus with these words:

> The concept of a canon that defines a particular list of books that constitute sacred Scripture for a believing community cannot be dated prior to the fourth century CE. . . . Imagine living in the first century in Alexandria. Given the time needed for travel and communication in those days, plus the errors that

32. This is another one of those "howlers." I am indebted to Tim Stone for reminding me of it in his insightful review of McDonald's work: Timothy J. Stone, "The Biblical Canon According to Lee McDonald: An Evaluation," *European Journal of Theology* 18 (2009): 55-64.

33. Mason, "Josephus and His Twenty-Two Book Canon," 126.

> occurred in the copying of texts and the expense involved in copying them, how likely is it that all the Jews in the various communities had equal access to the same scrolls of Scripture? Is it probable that everybody had the same access to Scriptures and shared exactly the same notion of Scripture? Did all individuals even within a given community hold a common understanding of Scripture? Why should one individual, such as Josephus, be considered the spokesperson for all Jews? Given the evidence of alternative views of Scripture at Qumran, the texts preserved in the LXX, and the historical context, does not the hypothesis that all Jews shared a common canon — the one referred to by Josephus — strike one as a little too neat and tidy? Not only does this hypothesis seem untenable given the historical data, it does not reflect human nature. Is there any one individual upon whom all could agree to represent a doctrinal consensus today?

While it is true that the books included in Josephus's canon cannot be identified with exactitude, McLay seems to lose sight of the larger point. Josephus can be written off as idiosyncratic because one individual just *could not be* the spokesperson for all Jews, since his view is too neat and tidy and we know that such unanimity does not exist even today. One might add that certainly Josephus was aware of what it was like to live back then and, in spite of all the problems McLay perceives, he presents a claim that "his positions are held by all Judeans — women, children, prisoners of war — and he would presumably be vulnerable to refutation if he were making this up or presenting idiosyncratic views."[34] It is interesting that a pervading assumption in the missionary activity of the early church, which first proceeds to local synagogues, in its evangelistic practices is the presence of a collection of scriptures that each synagogue — though separated by considerable distances — seems to share in common with others.[35] Never once was there a debate over the extent of this collection.[36]

Josephus's Explanation: The "Cognitive Environment" of Canon

The above "explanations" in which Josephus is viewed as a stranger or intruder to his historical and cultural context result from a reading of that context which

34. Mason, "Josephus and His Twenty-Two Book Canon," 125.

35. "When they had passed through Amphipolis and Apollonia, they came to Thessalonica, where there was a Jewish synagogue. *As his custom was,* Paul went into the synagogue, and on three Sabbath days he reasoned with them *from the Scriptures*" (Acts 17:2). These same Scriptures are called variously "the Law and the Prophets" (Acts 13:15), "the word of the Lord" (Acts 13:44), "the Law of Moses and the Prophets" (Acts 28:23), the reading of "Moses" (Acts 15:21).

36. Even today, despite the incredible variety and diversity in Christendom, it would be only a fool who would say that no canon in the sense of a closed list of the Old Testament exists.

is fundamentally at odds with Josephus's owns views. But the "elephant in the room" just will not go away. Is it possible that Josephus is not a contextual misfit? In a recent book, John Walton seeks to shed light on the ancient Israelite worldview by trying to understand the cognitive environment of its world, that network of ideas, beliefs, and cultural assumptions that it shared with its Ancient Near Eastern neighbors.

> When we compare the literature of the ancient near east with the Bible, we are ultimately trying to recover aspects of the ancient cognitive environment that may help us understand the Israelite perspective a bit better. By catching a glimpse of how they thought about themselves and their world, we sometimes discover ways that the Israelites would have thought that differ totally from how we think.[37]

Is it just possible that Josephus lives and breathes in a "cognitive environment of canon" in which he is fundamentally at home rather than lives as an unwelcome intruder? Josephus himself believes that he shares a common understanding of "canon" with his fellow Jews of various theological stripes in sharp contrast with their Gentile neighbors. What are the various components of this canon consciousness and how widely was it shared in his Jewish cultural context? Perhaps it is possible to reconstruct the lost world of such a consciousness in Judaism.[38]

Canonical List

The first point that Josephus makes is that the Jews, in striking contrast to the myriads of Greek books, have a tightly restricted, extremely limited, number of books: "among us there are not thousands of books in disagreement and conflict with each other, but only twenty-two books, containing the record of all time, which are rightly trusted." Josephus is certainly aware of other Jewish books, but they do not belong to this fixed grouping. Was there anything in the cognitive environment of Josephus's Jewish world that would support his "outlandish" claims?

From the first century (10-80 C.E.), a careful study of Rabbinic evidence would point to a restricted corpus of books "which defiled the hands."[39] The term "render the hands unclean" is the ancient Jewish equivalent to "canonical" or "inspired Holy Scripture." The origin of the term is shrouded in mystery and it

37. John H. Walton, *Ancient Near Eastern Thought and the Old Testament* (Grand Rapids: Baker Academic, 2006), 22. My use of the term is borrowed from Walton.

38. Cf. J. Walton, *The Lost World of Genesis One: Ancient Cosmology and the Origins Debate* (Downers Grove, IL: InterVarsity, 2009).

39. *Eduyyoth* 5:3; *Yadayim* 3:5.

is not immediately clear why holy writings would contaminate the hands.[40] There seem to be disputes between different schools of rabbis regarding a few books that belonged to this group, but the fact of the matter is that a limited corpus existed, distinguished from all other works. Books that defiled the hands were different from books that did not.

At approximately the same time as *Against Apion* was written, an apocalyptic Jewish work was written, 4 Ezra, which presents in one of its chapters (chapter 14) an apologetic for a larger group of writings, in fact ninety-four books that have been written by Ezra after the return from the exile. The book explains that all ninety-four texts are inspired, but that twenty-four of them can only be read in public while the remaining seventy can be read in private for the wise among the people. The writer is probably trying to extend canonical legitimacy to many other Jewish books (seventy), but at the same time in doing this he acknowledges a restricted group of twenty-four that are in "the public domain."[41] Such works imply liturgical use, and most scholars agree that this is a reference to a canon. This evidence is extremely important because while arguing for a more inclusive canon it proves the existence of an exclusive one in the public domain. The writer "doth protest too much" in favor of the larger canon, revealing the strength of the "default" attitude he is trying to overcome.[42] The twenty-four-member list of

40. For further study see Beckwith, *The Old Testament Canon,* 278-83. McDonald, *The Biblical Canon,* 58-63. As McDonald points out, the expression was probably first used in a debate that Rabbi Johannan ben Zakkai (50 C.E.) had with the Sadducees about texts that defiled the hands. Evidently the Sadducees thought it was ironical to impute contamination to sacred texts. They wondered how it could be that the scriptures defiled the hands while the writings of Homer did not. They were answered, "As is our love for them so is their uncleanness — that no man make spoons from the bones of his father or mother" in contrast to the bones of an ass, because the bones of an ass are clean but the bones of a parent are unclean and thus in a completely different "untouchably reverent" category (*Mishna Yadaim* 4:6). Note also: "And why did the Rabbis impose uncleanness upon a Book? Said R. Mesharsheya: Because originally food of *terumah* was stored near the Scroll of the Law, with the argument, This is holy and that is holy [it was therefore appropriate since the food and the scriptures were holy]. But when it was seen that they [the Sacred Books] came to harm [i.e., they would be eaten by rodents attracted by the food], the Rabbis imposed uncleanness upon them." *Babylonian Talmud: Shabbat* XIV a.

41. As Beckwith notes, scholars frequently think that this passage in Ezra speaks against a canon of twenty-four books since it is the desire of the writer to enlarge the canon. "But really the writer's desire to do this makes his involuntary evidence all the stronger. If the canon had actually been open . . . there would have been no need for the writer to make this grudging admission that 24 of the inspired books are in a special position, 'only published for the worthy and unworthy to read'. . . . He is thus clearly striving for the recognition of his pseudepigrapha against a public opinion which recognizes only the 24 canonical books." See R. T. Beckwith, "A Modern Theory of the Old Testament Canon," *Vetus Testamentum* 41 (1991): 392. Beckwith is specifically dealing with Barton's book, *Oracles of God,* 64-66. See also McDonald, *The Biblical Canon,* 163.

42. Timothy J. Stone, *The Compilational History of the Megilloth: Canon, Contoured Intertextuality and Meaning in the Writings* (Ph.D. thesis: University of St. Andrews, 2010), 57.

4 Ezra is a slightly different number than Josephus's twenty-two member grouping, but it is extremely telling since it is known in the early church (beginning in the third century C.E.) that the Jews had two enumerations of the same canon: twenty-two and twenty-four.[43]

Within a generation of Josephus and the author of 4 Ezra, the author of a Christian apocryphal work, *The Gospel of Thomas,* writes about Jesus as being the goal of Israelite prophecy: "Twenty-four prophets spoke in Israel, and they all spoke concerning you."[44] Shortly thereafter, two strands of evidence, one Jewish and one Christian, explicitly identify the contents of this number. First, in a *baraita* in the Babylonian Talmud, or citation that dates from Mishnaic times but was not included in the Mishna (ca. 150 C.E.), there is a specific number of books that are enumerated.[45] The number is twenty-four.[46] Second, from about 170 C.E., Bishop Melito records a list that he claims was derived from Jewish sources in the East. The number is twenty-five. Notably it excludes the book of Esther, but this may be an accidental omission. So we have two lists, both slightly longer. About fifty years later, Origen provides knowledge that in Judaism there was a list of twenty-two based on the Hebrew alphabet, and it was arrived at by combining Ruth with Judges and Lamentations with Jeremiah.[47] A century and a half later Jerome mentions that the Jews have two ways of organizing their canon, one with the number twenty-two and one with the number twenty-four.[48] The first number represents a list modeled on the alphabet to stress its symbolic value. It does not take a large logical leap to connect the historical dots here and reach the conclusion that the two numbers reflected in Josephus and 4 Ezra are alternate arrangements of the same books, and not significantly different from the later lists that have been just mentioned.

As mentioned in the introduction to this essay, the charge is often made that maximalists use anachronistic terms to describe historical realities, the term "canon" being the parade example of this practice. Since the term "canon" used in a formal sense to refer to a closed, fixed list of books was not used until the fourth century C.E. at the earliest, some scholars suggest that it would be inappropriate to use the term to describe collections of sacred writings earlier. Some even claim that Judaism "would not have accepted the idea of 'canon' at all if it had not been that Christians insisted in later times on talking in such terms."[49] But it is clear

43. E.g., Jerome, *Prologus Galeatus.*

44. *Gospel of Thomas* 52.

45. *Baba Bathra* 14b.

46. It is interesting that in the Shepherd of Hermas there is mention of the thirty-five prophets of God and his ministers (92.4). *Perhaps* this is a reference to a twenty-four-book canon. This number is achieved by counting the Minor Prophets as twelve. I am indebted for these references to Simon Gathercole (personal communication, June 20, 2010).

47. Origen in Eusebius, *Ecclesiastical History* 6.25.

48. Jerome, *Prologus Galeatus.*

49. Barton, *Oracles of God,* 63.

that Josephus's cognitive environment implies the acceptance of a fixed grouping of books to which no others can be added. He was not a "cognitive alien" to the Jewish culture but a "cognitive citizen" of that culture. While he did not use the word "canon," the conception is the same. While Shaye Cohen does not agree with Josephus regarding his views, he forthrightly states: "Although Josephus does not use the word canon, he clearly is describing a collection of books that we (and the church fathers of the fourth century) would call 'canonical.'"[50] Even more telling is Frank Cross's understatement that "thinly concealed behind Josephus's Greek apologetics is a clear and coherent theological doctrine of canon."[51]

Canonical Title/Organization

Canons of sacred literature are defined, and usually they are organized and given labels, particularly if they are well known. Widespread use of the literature leads to nomenclature for practical reasons of identification.[52] Not only are the individual books within the collection titled, but the books are organized into divisions with distinct labels. In Josephus's statement the canon is much like a list or a library and is not named specifically in his text on canon, but it is significantly organized into three divisions to accentuate history, as virtually all scholars recognize: the five books of Moses, from the beginning of time until Moses' death; thirteen prophets who record history from the death of Moses until the reign of Artaxerxes, the king during the time of Esther; and four remaining ahistorical books containing hymns and precepts. This three-part organization — Moses (Law), Prophets, and the Rest — can be called later simply "the laws and the records associated with them."[53] Is there anything similar in Judaism's cognitive environment of nomenclature reflecting a tripartite or bipartite signature? The earliest possible reference is one in which Ben Sira praises the scribe: "But he

50. Shaye J. D. Cohen, *From the Maccabees to the Mishnah* (Louisville: Westminster John Knox, 1989), 188. Note the remark by Bruce: "[Josephus's] language can scarcely signify anything other than a closed canon." See F. F. Bruce, *The Canon of Scripture* (Downers Grove, IL: InterVarsity, 1988), 23.

51. F. M. Cross, "The Text behind the Text of the Hebrew Bible," in *Understanding the Dead Sea Scrolls,* ed. H. Shanks (New York: Vintage, 1993), 139-55, esp. 152.

52. "[T]he canon had become a sufficiently unified body of material to attract to itself certain comprehensive titles and descriptions, some of which passed into general use." See Roger T. Beckwith, *The Old Testament Canon of the New Testament Church, and Its Background in Early Judaism* (Grand Rapids: Eerdmans, 1984), 105. Beckwith notes some twenty-eight titles in his discussion, and his point about nomenclature is valid.

53. Mason seems to be a voice crying in the wilderness against the significance of this tripartite structure as a possible means of indicating divisions within a canonical library, but the natural reading of the text indicates the presence of three divisions. See Mason, "Josephus and His Twenty-Two Book Canon." Cf. Barclay, *Flavius Josephus.*

gives his mind to and meditates on the *law of the Most High;* he will seek out *the wisdom of all the ancients;* and will occupy himself in *prophecies.*"[54] Here there is possibly a tripartite organization, but one slightly different from that of Josephus: Law, Prophecies, Wisdom. Two generations later, Ben Sira's grandson refers three times to a tripartite division of sacred books that his grandfather wrote about: the books are always referred to with a tripartite division; although the third division seems like a more general category, yet it is grammatically defined each time it appears: (1) "*the* law and *the* prophets and *the* books which followed after them"; (2) "*the* law and *the* prophets and *the* other books of our fathers"; (3) "*the* law and *the* prophecies and *the* rest of the books."

The similarity of this threefold arrangement to Josephus's canon is striking. Throughout the cognitive environment of Judaism, the sacred literature of the Jews is often referred to with the use of a bipartite formula: the Law and the Prophets (or a variant). It occurs in the Maccabean writings (e.g., 2 Macc. 15:9; 4 Macc. 18:10), Qumran (e.g., CD 7:15-17; 1QS 1:1ff.; 8:15-17), and is the common designation of the scriptures in the New Testament. Scholars often conclude that this formula indicates that a third division had not yet emerged. But this is hardly necessary since one might expect a shorter form to be used regularly in place of a longer form.

There are some other possible usages of a tripartite organization in Josephus's world that may help elucidate his statement about canonical divisions. In Qumran (ca. 125 B.C.E.), alongside a reference to a bipartite designation, there may be a tripartite designation, although the text is fragmentary. The relevant text, a halachic letter, states that if a Jewish leader considers that the scriptures are being fulfilled, he will be able to "understand the Book of Moses [and] the Book[s of the P]rophets and Da[vid]" (4QMMT). In 2 Maccabees (ca. 100 B.C.E.), there is a reconstruction after the catastrophe of the desecration of the temple, and there is a reflection on *the law* that was given to the exiles, and the gathering of the "*acts of kings and prophets* and *the things of David*" (2 Macc. 2:1-15). This functions as a precedent for Judas Maccabeus's activity in gathering together lost holy books. In the first quarter of the first century C.E. Philo describes a group of ascetic individuals, named the Therapeutae, who practiced their faith by entering closet sanctuaries, not bringing any food, drink, or physical comfort. What they brought with them were documents described as "laws and oracles delivered through the mouths of prophets, as well as hymns and anything else that fosters perfection, knowledge and piety."[55] A natural way of understanding this text is to see it as a description of laws — the Torah, oracles from the Prophets, and psalms

54. Ecclesiasticus 39:1-2. For a more in-depth interpretation see Stephen G. Dempster, "Torah, Torah, Torah: The Emergence of the Tripartite Canon," in *Exploring the Origins of the Bible: Canon Formation in Historical, Theological, and Literary Perspective,* ed. Emanuel Tov and Craig A. Evans, Acadia Studies in Bible and Theology (Grand Rapids: Baker Academic, 2008), 110-12.

55. *De vita contemplativa* 25.

representing a third division. The "anything else" could also refer to a further description of a third division, a possible fourth division, or simply other literature that the sect used.[56] The fact that all of the units are connected by a similar conjunction complicates matters, but allows for each of these possibilities.[57] This may again be evidence of a canon with a tripartite signature, as the "law, prophets, and hymns" is remarkably similar to Josephus's divisions.

Finally, alongside the many references to describing the scriptures as the Law and the Prophets or Moses and the Prophets in the New Testament,[58] there is the following reference in Luke, in the resurrected Jesus' words to his dull disciples on the Emmaus Road: "These are my words which I spoke to you while I was yet with you, that it is necessary that all things be fulfilled which have been written in the law of Moses and in the prophets *and in the psalms* concerning me" (Luke 24:44). Luke then describes Jesus in the following manner: "Then he opened their minds to understand the scriptures" (v. 45). Again, there is a conspicuous similarity to Josephus's structure of the canon with the terms "Law, Prophets, and Psalms."

The table on page 340 shows the remarkable correspondence to Josephus's library of canonical books in the Jewish cognitive environment of canon. The rabbinic organization of twenty-four books into three categories dates from the middle of the second century C.E.: the Law, the Prophets, the Writings.[59] This reflects a similar tripartite organization, but the arrangement of the individual books is clearly different since the rabbinic organization divides the canonical list into groups of five, eight, and eleven instead of five, thirteen, and four. Since these canons probably arrange the same canonical books differently, it is apparent that the list found in Josephus is based on the principle of genre and that of the rabbis on theology and literary artistry. In Josephus's arrangement all the historical books from the rabbinic third section are transferred to the second division of the Prophets, and certain books are combined based on context such as Ruth with Judges and Lamentations with Jeremiah in order to achieve the number of twenty-two. As to the question of which arrangement was older, that is not an unimportant question, but it is interesting that the tripartite order is found in both, and Josephus's arrangement with its concern for genre divisions, even though it

56. Such as the writings of the sect itself. See T. N. Swanson, *The Closing of the Collection of Holy Scriptures: A Study in the History of Canonization of the Old Testament* (Ann Arbor: University Microfilms, 1970), 248-50.

57. See A. Sundberg, review of R. Beckwith, "The Old Testament Canon in the New Testament Church," *Interpretation* 42 (1988): 82. McDonald (*Formation,* 39) observes that "the law and oracles delivered by the prophets" suggest one unit and not two. C. Evans ("Scripture of Jesus and His Earliest Followers," in McDonald and Sanders, eds., *Canon Debate,* 188), however, points out that Moses — the giver of the law — was regarded as a prophet and thus this text could be understood as a reference at least to two collections by this designation.

58. There are fourteen references in all (e.g., Matt. 5:17; Luke 16:16; 24:27; Rom. 3:21).

59. *Baba Bathra* 14*b*.

Date	Source	1	2	3
180-65 B.C.E.	Ben Sira	Law	Prophecies	Wisdom of Ancients
130 B.C.E.	Grandson 130 B.C.E.	Law	Prophets	The other books that followed after
		Law	Prophets	The other books of our fathers
		Law	Prophecies	The rest of the books
150-25 B.C.E.	Qumran -4QMMT	Moses	Prophets	[Da]vid
100 B.C.E.	2 Maccabees	Law	Acts of Kings and Prophets	The things of David
30-40 C.E.	Therapeutae	Laws	Oracles of Prophets	Hymns and anything else
80 C.E.	Luke 24	Moses	Prophets	Psalms
95 C.E.	Josephus	Moses	The Prophets	The remaining books of hymns

is unique, is reflected in the later Christian lists of the Septuagint[60] — or at least with its concern for the principle of genre is the precursor of such lists — while the rabbinic order dominates in later Judaism. The two lists can be compared by observing the chart on page 341.

It is probably the case that Josephus's arrangement was not idiosyncratic, as it would probably damage his credibility as a historian.[61] Thus there are two traditions of early arrangements of canonical books, one based on the alphabet and principle of genre and probably morphing into some of the arrangements evidenced in the LXX, while the other was more theological and artistic, and reflected a specific canonical view. Perhaps the canonical tradition behind Josephus's understanding — the twenty-two-letter alphabet — was done for heuristic reasons as a way to inculcate the abc's at the macro-level of canon in the same way an acrostic psalm teaches its message at the micro-level.[62]

60. Steinmann, *The Oracles of God,* 194-95. See also M. Haran, *The Biblical Collection* (Jerusalem: Magnes Press, 1996). Probably the first to make this argument, although he argued for the historical priority of Josephus's canon, was Peter Katz, "The Old Testament Canon in Palestine and Alexandria," *Zeitschrift für die neutestamentliche Wissenschaft* 47 (1956): 191-217.

61. Cf. Beckwith, *The Old Testament Canon,* 125; Albert C. Sundberg, *The Old Testament of the Early Church* (Cambridge, MA: Harvard University Press, 1964), 71.

62. "The alphabet was the water in which the student swam, throughout his education in

Josephus*	**Rabbis†**
Genesis	Genesis
Exodus	Exodus
Leviticus	Leviticus
Numbers	Numbers
Deuteronomy	Deuteronomy
Joshua	Joshua
Judges-Ruth	Judges
Samuel	Samuel
Kings	Kings
Isaiah	Jeremiah
Jeremiah-Lamentations	Ezekiel
Ezekiel	Isaiah
Daniel	Twelve
Twelve	
Job	
Chronicles	
Ezra-Nehemiah (= Esdras)	
Esther	
Psalms	Ruth
Proverbs	Psalms
Ecclesiastes	Job
Song of Solomon	Proverbs
	Ecclesiastes
	Song of Solomon
	Lamentations
	Daniel
	Esther
	Ezra-Nehemiah
	Chronicles

*For a slightly different arrangement of the books see among others Barclay, *Flavius Josephus,* 30.

†*Baba Bathra* 14*b.*

---

both Greek and Hebrew systems. Within this context the creation of a collection of Hebrew Scriptures, with a numbering corresponding to the letters of the alphabet, would have been an ultimate manifestation of a more broadly attested alphabetical principle." See Carr, *Writing on the Tablet of the Heart,* 271.

"Canonical Epoch"[63]

Josephus writes of the twenty-two books being written by prophets who prophesied in exact succession, and when that succession came to an end, so did the books: "To a fixed number of canonical books, therefore, there corresponds a canonical epoch, one which is brought to a close by the failure of the prophetic succession *(diadoche)*."[64] Pious books written after this time, even though they were highly esteemed, did not make the "canonical cut": "From Artaxerxes up to our own time every event has been recorded but this is not judged worthy of the same trust, *since the exact line of succession of the prophets did not continue.*" Thus, the twenty-two were confined to a limited period, from Moses to Artaxerxes.

It has become common in modern scholarship to criticize this view as a late and artificial theological construction of the rabbis, which served to justify their study of the canonical texts and to suppress new revelation from charismatic enthusiasts, who claimed prophetic inspiration. The evidence is interpreted to mean that the rabbis constructed a "theological deliberation aimed at restricting the rise of legitimate prophecy to an ideal canonical period in the past."[65] In fact it is often pointed out that Josephus contradicted his own views, as he decidedly did not relegate prophecy in his writings to any canonical epoch.[66] John Hyrcanus was viewed as a prophet (*War* 1.69), prophecy occurred among the Essenes (6.288), and Josephus also portrayed himself in a similar manner (4.626). Clearly also prophecy was viewed as occurring during the New Testament period. How is this evidence to be explained? Does theological theory contradict practical reality?

It is probably the case that prophecy succeeding Artaxerxes was viewed as sporadic and not as part of the *succession* of prophets that marked the canonical epoch. This prophecy is more intermittent but does not bear the antiquity and hence the authority of the prophecy in the "golden age" of revelation. Rebecca Gray, following John Barton, argues that this view of prophetic restriction to a canonical epoch was "one expression of a vague nostalgia that idealized the past

63. The phrase is Joseph Blenkinsopp's. See next note.

64. Joseph Blenkinsopp, "'We Pay No Heed to Heavenly Voices': The 'End of Prophecy' and the Formation of the Canon," in *Biblical and Humane: A Festschrift for John F. Priest,* ed. Linda Bennett Elder, David L. Barr, and Elizabeth Struthers Malbon (Atlanta: Scholars Press, 1996), 21.

65. R. Meyer, "προφήτης," in *Theological Dictionary of the New Testament,* 6:816. Similarly, "There never was in Israel a prophetic age in the sense of a fixed historical period" (6:816). See also David E. Aune, *Prophecy in Early Christianity and the Ancient Mediterranean World* (Grand Rapids: Eerdmans, 1983), 103-4; F. Greenspahn, "Why Prophecy Ceased," *Journal of Biblical Literature* 108 (1989): 37-49; Per Bilde, "Josephus and Jewish Apocalypticism," in *Understanding Josephus: Seven Perspectives,* ed. Steve Mason, JSPSS 32 (Sheffield: Sheffield Academic Press, 1998), 45-48.

66. Meyer, "Bemerkungen zur literargeschichtlichen Hintergrund der Kanontheorie des Josephus."

as a time when people were, in some indescribable way, closer to God and holier than in the present."[67] But for Josephus, as Mason has shown, prophecy *after the succession was broken* is not canonical.[68] "[Josephus] is simply denying that the same degree of prophetic historiographical reliability was in operation after Artaxerxes as before, thus emphasizing the uniquely authoritative status of the closed canon."[69]

But what about the question of such a canonical epoch in the cognitive environment of Josephus? Three texts in 1 Maccabees make the point that prophecy had probably ceased:

> So they tore down the altar and stored the stones in a convenient place on the temple hill until there should come a prophet to tell what to do with them. (4:45b-46)

> Thus there was great distress in Israel, such as had not been since the time the prophets ceased to appear among them. (9:27)

> And the Jews and their priests decided that Simon should be their leader and high priest forever, until a trustworthy prophet should arise. (14:41)

It is perhaps possible to understand these statements in a way that does not reflect the absence of the activity of prophecy, but it is certainly not a natural reading of these texts.[70] The first and the last express a hope in a coming age of prophecy — also reflected in the later texts in the Old Testament (e.g., Joel 3:1) — while the second indicates the absence of such an age in the present in an almost matter-of-fact manner.[71] "For our author, it was an article of faith that prophecy had ceased after Haggai, Zechariah, Malachi, and had not reappeared during the event covered by his history. The return of prophecy would come shortly before God's ultimate victory."[72]

67. Rebecca Gray, *Prophetic Figures in Late Second Temple Jewish Palestine: The Evidence from Josephus* (Oxford: Oxford University Press, 1993), 34.

68. Mason, "Josephus and His Twenty-Two Book Canon," 115-19. Mason also shows that the linguistic terminology for prophecy is virtually restricted to the biblical figures. See also Best's study in which he shows that Josephus limits the phrase *theion pneuma* to the biblical period: E. Best, "The Use and Non-Use of Pneuma by Josephus," *Novum Testamentum* 3 (1959): 218-25.

69. Barclay, *Flavius Josephus*, 31.

70. Aune, *Prophecy in Early Christianity and the Ancient Mediterranean World*, 103-4.

71. "Respect is shown to the idea of prophecy, whose day is past (9:27), though there is a lively hope that a true prophet will appear" (4:46; 14:41). See J. R. Bartlett, *The First and Second Books of the Maccabees* (Cambridge: Cambridge University Press, 1973), 15.

72. Jonathan A. Goldstein, *I Maccabees*, Anchor Bible 41 (Garden City: Doubleday, 1976), 12-13.

A natural reading of the New Testament in which there is the outbreak of prophecy at the beginning of the period in the appearance of John the Baptist is that the beginning of an eschatological age of prophecy has occurred (Matt. 3:1-12). The continuation of prophecy in the person of Jesus, who is regarded as the ultimate Prophet (Matt. 17:1-5; Acts 3:12-26), and in the life of the early church (Acts 2:14-21), suggests that this is something radically new, after a long period of relative silence. But even within the early church it was envisioned that such new revelation constituted not so much an addition to the canon as a new understanding of the canon.

The twenty-four-book canon described in 4 Ezra restricts the composition of the twenty-four canonical books and the seventy books that it desires for canonical inclusion to the writings of Ezra. Why? It is probable that books written after the Persian period do not pass the canonical test.

Signs of this belief can be seen among the rabbis of the Mishna, where the prophets are regarded as preceding the rabbis.[73] A reference in the Tosefta makes explicit this understanding: "When the latter prophets died, that is, Haggai, Zechariah, and Malachi, then the Holy Spirit came to an end in Israel. But even then they made them hear through an echo."[74] Other examples from rabbinic sources describe the cessation of a prophetic age: "Until then, the prophets prophesied by means of the holy spirit. From then on, give ear and listen to the words of the sages."[75] The Rabbinic age that emphasized the study of texts is the new reality.

Another clear indication of the prevalence of a belief in the end of a prophetic epoch is the proliferation of pseudepigrapha. A myriad of books were written under pseudonyms: Apocalypse of Adam, Apocalypse of Abraham, Apocalypse of Elijah, 1-3 Enoch, Testament of Moses, 4 Ezra, Joseph and Aseneth, Testaments of the Twelve Patriarchs, etc.[76] While there may be many reasons for the use of pseudonyms, the most reasonable explanation is to secure "canonical authority" for the literature, by dating it to a period during the exact succession of the prophets.[77] The book of Daniel presents a real problem here since modern scholarship believes that it is certainly pseudonymous, as it attempts to show the fulfillment of a detailed prophecy of the future right down to the very details of the Maccabean age. According to this view, the details are so precisely described until the death

73. *Aboth* 1:1; cf. *Peah* 2:6.

74. *Sotah* 13:3 A, B. The translation is that of Neusner. The echo refers to the *bat qol,* which is to be distinguished from the direct voice of prophecy.

75. *Seder Olam Rabbah* 30. Cf. 2 Baruch 85:3; *Babylonian Talmud Sotah* 48*b; Sanhedrin* 11*a.*

76. James H. Charlesworth, *The Old Testament Pseudepigrapha,* vol. 1, *Apocalyptic Literature and Testaments,* 1st edition (New York: Doubleday, 1983).

77. Aune surveys the various reasons and argues in a qualified way that the most likely explanation is that "[p]seudonymity was used to secure the acceptance of an apocalypse during a period when the canon was virtually closed and prophetic inspiration had ended." Aune, *Prophecy in Early Christianity and the Ancient Mediterranean World,* 109-10.

of Antiochus that it must necessarily be an example of prophecy after the fact. The only difficulty with this interpretation is that one must conclude that, unlike all the other pseudonymous works that claimed an ancient, canonical pedigree, the book of Daniel "fooled" everyone and made it into the canon! John Van Seters states this candidly:

> All the works within a "canon" must be attributed to an author who bears the appropriate authority, and for Scripture this could only be satisfied by divine inspiration from the age of revelation that ended with Ezra. The closest parallel to this is, of course, the establishment of the Greek classics, especially Homer, the rival of Moses. Notions of authorship in the case of the Hebrew Scriptures seem to have been directly influenced by the conceptions of the Hellenistic world. At the very time the limits of Scriptures were being debated, the ancient world knew a lot about pseudepigraphy and the attribution of false authors to texts in order to gain authority for the views expressed in those writings. The book of Daniel is a rather blatant example of an instance in which a pseudepigraphy succeeded in deceiving the rabbinic "canonizers."[78]

Needless to say, one finds this lone example of blatant deception problematic. Were the "canonizers" that dense?[79]

But this idea of a long-lost prophetic age is also shown by important, devout works that were not written under pseudonyms but nonetheless lacked the important qualification. A statement in the Tosefta reads, "The books of Ben Sira and all books written thenceforward do not impart uncleanness to hands."[80]

Finally, there is evidence of a wisdom redaction in the Hebrew Bible that suggests the fading out of prophecy and the emerging prominence of the sage and interpreter of revelation.[81] All of this evidence points to a cognitive environment in Judaism that suggests the awareness of a bygone age to which canonical authority was assigned.

78. John Van Seters, *The Edited Bible: The Curious History of the "Editor" in Biblical Criticism* (Winona Lake, IN: Eisenbrauns, 2006), 373.

79. It should be noted that even the Qumran community was "fooled," as Daniel was acknowledged as canonical there: 4Q174 2:3.

80. *Yadayim* 2:13 B.

81. Gerald T. Sheppard, *Wisdom as a Hermeneutical Construct: A Study in the Sapientializing of the Old Testament,* BZAW 151 (Berlin: Walter de Gruyter, 1980); Raymond Van Leeuwen, "Scribal Wisdom and Theodicy in the Book of the Twelve," in *In Search of Wisdom: Essays in Memory of John G. Gammie,* ed. Leo G. Purdue, Bernard B. Scott, and William Johnstone (Louisville: John Knox Press, 1993), 31-49; Stephen G. Dempster, "From Many Texts to One: The Formation of the Hebrew Bible," in *The World of the Aramaeans I: Biblical Studies in Honour of Paul-Eugene Dion,* ed. P. Michèle Daviau, John William Wevers, and Michael Weigl (Sheffield: Sheffield Academic Press, 2001), 19-56; Dempster, "Canons on the Left."

Canonical Consensus

In the Jewish culture of the first century C.E., scholars have shown that there was a remarkable pluralism. A criticism of older scholarship was that it often read first-century Judaism through the lens of a later monolithic Pharisaism, which triumphed after the destruction of the second temple and the collapse of apocalyptic hopes. Given such pluralism in the cognitive environment, the apocalyptic and eschatological groups (Qumran, Christianity) versus the traditionalists (Pharisees), the revolutionaries (Zealots) versus the establishmentarians (Sadducees), one could legitimately ask if the same pluralism extended to the canon, a claim that Josephus denies. Josephus's own words are as follows: "but it is innate in every Judean right from birth, to regard [these books] as decrees of God, to remain faithful to them and, if necessary, to die on their behalf."[82]

While there is a virtual multitude of literature circulating during the period from the second century B.C.E. to the second century C.E., it is remarkable how little of it functioned authoritatively across a wide spectrum of groups. For example, when Ben Sira wishes to give parade examples of heroes, he cites them from the biblical canon in remarkable canonical order, which shows that the whole of this text is one long meditation on the scriptures from Adam to Nehemiah before Simon the high priest is praised.[83] This is largely the complete biblical storyline as found in the later Hebrew Bible, which begins with Adam and ends with Nehemiah. But significantly the heroes in Ben Sira's parade do not need a formal introduction; they are *household names* to his audience. Noted in this text is a clear separation between the first five books of the Torah and the Prophets, with Joshua considered to be a prophet.[84] There is particular mention of the Minor Prophets as a booked entity — and not as individuals, so that one scholar can say, "The main thing that strikes one in these chapters is that Ben Sira while following the chronological order of these persons (down to Nehemiah though with Adam to close the series) seems to rely on the Bible as an established canon.

82. The consensus described here is not absolute. No such absolute consensus ever existed in the history of Judaism and Christianity. What is meant is "general agreement, both among the leaders of the community and in the body of the faithful." See R. Beckwith, "Formation of the Hebrew Bible," in *Mikra: Text, Translation, Reading and Interpretation of the Hebrew Bible in Ancient Judaism and Early Christianity,* ed. Martin Jan Mulder (Minneapolis: Fortress Press, 1990), 59.

83. *Ecclesiasticus* 44–49.

84. *Ecclesiasticus* 46:1: "the successor in prophecies." Note P. Bentjees's comment: "The description of Joshua in Sir 46:1 is strong evidence that in Ben Sira's time the later terminology of reckoning the books of Joshua, Judges, Samuel, and Kings to the 'Former Prophets' was already in the air." Bentjees, "Canon and Scripture in the Book of Ben Sira," in M. Saebo et al., *Hebrew Bible/Old Testament,* vol. 1, part 2, *From the Beginnings to the Middle Ages (until 1300)* (Göttingen: Vandenhoeck & Ruprecht, 2000), 594.

Thus the twelve prophets are mentioned in 49:10."[85] Moreover there seems to be a use of Scripture in Ben Sira that presupposes an intimate knowledge of written texts as shown in the use made of citations, inverted quotations, and unique word combinations.[86] In an important recent study, L. Grabbe shows the indispensable dependence on the Bible not just for the heroes mentioned in this list but also for the actual wording of their exploits. Clearly there was a biblical text that Ben Sira had before him that was similar to what was later viewed as canonical in Judaism.[87]

In a study on the use of Scripture in the Apocrypha and Pseudepigrapha, Devorah Diamant has shown there are nineteen examples of explicit quotations, thirteen from the Torah, three each from the Prophets and the Writings. These are all "biblical phrases of at least three words, more or less accurately reproduced, and introduced by special terms and explicit references to the source."[88] It is telling that there are no examples of a text cited outside this corpus introduced by a special term, which indicates its sacred authority.[89]

At Qumran, it is often argued that the presence of many books in the community besides the ones that are later found to be included in the Jewish Bible provide evidence of a wider canon, especially if these books claim divine inspiration: "Again we must underscore that at Qumran nonbiblical texts were discovered right beside the biblical books with no discernible way to distinguish them."[90]

85. M. Gilbert, "Wisdom Literature," in *Jewish Writings of the Second Temple Period,* ed. M. Stone (Assen: Van Gorcum, 1984), 283-329, esp. 297. See also J. Koole, "Die Bibel des Ben Sira," *OTS* 14 (1965): 374-96; Alon Goshen-Gottstein, "Ben Sira's Praise of the Fathers: A Canon-Conscious Reading," in *Ben Sira's God: Proceedings of the International Ben Sira Conference, Durham — Upshaw College 2001,* ed. Renate Egger-Wenzel, BZAW 321 (Berlin: De Gruyter, 2002), 235-67. Goshen-Gottstein argues forcefully for a reading of the Torah and the Prophets with the Prophets being clearly separated between 45:26 and 46:1.

86. Bentjees, "Canon and Scripture," 596ff.

87. See "The Law, the Prophets and the Rest: The State of the Bible in Pre-Maccabean Times," *Dead Sea Discoveries* 13 (2006): 319-38, esp. 324-26. Grabbe believes the Bible is essentially the same as the later biblical canon in Judaism with the exception of Daniel and Ezra-Nehemiah.

88. Devorah Dimant, "Mikra in the Apocrypha and Pseudepigrapha," in Mulder, ed., *Mikra,* 385.

89. Ken Penner in an unpublished paper makes mention of three texts in the *Testament of the Twelve Patriarchs* that seem to cite the book of Enoch authoritatively, but the text is not explicitly quoted in a direct manner. "For I have seen in a copy of the book of Enoch that your sons will be ruined by promiscuity" (T.Simeon 5:4); "I know from the writings of Enoch that in the end-time you will act impiously against the Lord" (T.Levi 14:1); "At that time I put an end to the sons of Hamor, as is written in the tablets of the fathers" (T.Levi 5:4). See Penner, "Citation Formulae as Indices to Canonicity in Early Jewish and Christian Literature." I would like to thank Ken for a copy of this paper. It is uncertain where these texts occur exactly in Enoch, but they do suggest the authority of this book in some circles.

90. McDonald, *The Biblical Canon,* 132. See also James C. VanderKam, *From Revelation to Canon: Studies in the Hebrew Bible and Second Temple Literature* (Leiden: Brill, 2002), 25-27.

In fact, there is some evidence for the presence of every book of the Bible with the exception of Esther.[91] But again, as anyone with a library knows, it would be hazardous to make historical conclusions about "canonical" books from the volumes displayed on the shelf. Nevertheless, it is a different matter when texts are cited authoritatively in the books of the Qumran library. Thus, a discernible way to distinguish canonical from non-canonical books lies ready at hand. Of the forty-two explicit citations found in the Qumran literature, there is possibly only one from an extra-biblical book.[92] There are twenty-two citations from the Torah, twenty-one from the Prophets, and one from the Writings.[93] Similarly, when there is a commentary on any book, it is a book from the later biblical canon.[94] The lack of citations from the Writings probably reflects the eschatological interest in the Qumran sect.

Philo's canon of authoritative books is virtually limited to the Torah, but this may be because much of his work deals with this section of the Bible.[95] His discussion of other books outside the Torah is used to expound the Torah.[96] Philo displays a Torah-centric authority in his writing, expounding Torah texts and using other biblical texts to provide illustration and example. These texts do not include Ruth, Esther, Ecclesiastes, Songs, Lamentations, Ezekiel, and Daniel. But Ruth may have been part of Judges and Lamentations part of Jeremiah. Philo also never cites books from the Apocrypha and Pseudepigrapha.

In the New Testament there is only one clear example of a text from a non-canonical work that is cited authoritatively, the book of Enoch, cited in the book of Jude (Jude 14-15; cf. 1 Enoch 1:9). It is interesting that this particular text was the cause of difficulties for Jude's inclusion in the New Testament canon.[97] But it

91. There is also no reference for Nehemiah, but it was probably attached to the book of Ezra, for which there is some evidence.

92. See the list of VanderKam in Eugene Ulrich, "Qumran and the Canon of the Old Testament," in *The Biblical Canons,* ed. J. M. Auwers and H. de Jonge (Leuven: Leuven University Press, 2003), 80. VanderKam himself places a question mark beside this reference from Jubilees to indicate possible doubt. J. Lust does not regard this text as a citation. See J. Lust, "Quotation Formulae and Canon in Qumran," in *Canonization and Decanonization,* ed. A. van der Kooij and K. van der Toorn, Studies in the History of Religions 82 (Leiden: Brill, 1998), 67-77. The text in question is CD 16:2-4, and it is unclear where in Jubilees is found the source for the information that Israel would be blind to the regulations in the law of Moses.

93. Joseph A. Fitzmyer, "The Use of Explicit Old Testament Quotations in Qumran Literature and in the New Testament," in *Essays on the Semitic Background of the New Testament* (Grand Rapids: Eerdmans, 1997), 3-58.

94. There are no commentaries on the Torah, twelve on the Prophets (Isa. 5; Hos. 2; Zeph. 2; Mic. 1; Nah. 1; Hab. 1), and one on the Writings (Psalms).

95. Herbert Edward Ryle, *Philo and Holy Scripture: Or, the Quotations of Philo from the Books of the Old Testament, with Introduction and Notes* (New York: Macmillan, 1895).

96. Barton, *Oracles of God,* 159-60.

97. "Jude the brother of James, left a short epistle which is reckoned among the seven

is remarkable given the hundreds of citations from the Old Testament (Torah 123, Prophets 107, Writings 87) that only one may be a source from a book that was not part of the Jewish canon. It may be that the book from which the citation comes is not considered canonical, but the citation is regarded as inspired.[98]

As for the Mishna, which codifies the rabbinic opinion of the Tannaim (70 C.E. to 200 C.E.), there is a difference of opinion as to the role that Scripture plays in this important text that was finally reduced to writing around 200 C.E. On one side is the view that this oral Torah is simply an exposition of the scriptures. On the other is the understanding that the Mishna is largely autonomous from the Bible, with the biblical texts being supplied as later proof-texts that justified the earlier decisions. There are other scholars who take a mediating position between these two views. But that being the case, no one can deny in the present Mishna the importance of biblical citation. The simple formula used by the authorities recorded in the Mishna, "As it is said," is a lightning rod, "explicitly alerting the reader to their reliance on a prior discourse to advance their own."[99] There are 397 references to the Torah, 74 citations from the Prophets, and 40 from the Writings, all cited authoritatively so that there is no sign of levels of authority among the various canonical divisions.[100] All books are explicitly cited with the exception of Daniel, and this may simply be because of chance. It is clear that Daniel is canonical.[101]

One clear contradiction to Josephus's consensus might be the Sadducees, who, as Josephus, the New Testament, and Rabbinic sources all affirm, were a well-established though limited group within first-century C.E. Judaism.[102] Since some have claimed that the Sadducees believed that only the Torah was canonical, this would seem to present a major challenge to Josephus's claim of canonical

---

catholic epistles, and because in it he quotes from the apocryphal book of Enoch it is rejected by many. Nevertheless by age and use it has gained authority and is reckoned among the Holy Scriptures." See Jerome, *De Viris Illustribus* 4. Cf. also Eusebius, *Ecclesiastical History* 2.23.25.

98. "While this word [Enoch prophesied] indicates that Jude regards the prophecies of 1 Enoch as inspired by God, it need not imply that he regarded the book as canonical scripture." See Richard J. Bauckham, *2 Peter, Jude,* Word Biblical Commentary 50 (Waco: Word, 1983), 96. But see the comments of J. VanderKam, Review of R. T. Beckwith, *The Old Testament Canon of the New Testament Church, Journal for the Study of the Pseudepigrapha* 2 (1989): 121. Note also T. McLay's sober comments about this text, "Use of the Septuagint," in McDonald, *Biblical Canon,* 231.

99. Peter Acker Pettit, *Shene'emar: The Place of Scripture Citation in the Mishna* (Ph.D. dissertation, Claremont Graduate School, 1993), 1. See also Bruce M. Metzger, "The Formulas Introducing Quotations of Scripture in the NT and the Mishnah," *Journal of Biblical Literature* 70 (1951): 297-307.

100. Pettit, *Shene'emar.*

101. *Yadaim* 5:5.

102. Anthony J. J. Saldarini and James C. C. VanderKam, *Pharisees, Scribes and Sadducees in Palestinian Society* (Grand Rapid: Eerdmans, 2001), 302.

consensus. The Sadducees would thus hold to the same views of scriptural authority as the heretical Samaritans. It is also sometimes argued that their failure to accept the doctrines of resurrection and angelology confirms their rejection of the Prophets and the Writings since these doctrines are explicitly taught in these canonical divisions (e.g., Ezekiel 37; Isaiah 25–26; Daniel 12). But it is just as clear that there are examples of angels in the Torah (Gen. 28:12; 32:1), and one could easily interpret the references to resurrection metaphorically outside the Torah. Josephus indicates that the Sadducees did not "accept any observance apart from the Laws," but this probably meant that they did not accept the oral Torah, the rabbinic traditions of interpretation (*Antiquities* 18.16). They believed in *Sola Scriptura.* Josephus is conspicuously silent on the question of a separate Sadducean canon, a fact that would not be lost on his readers.[103] Similarly silent is the New Testament, as are the early Rabbinic Writings. Later references in the church fathers to the Sadducees only accepting the canonical Torah probably results from their confusion with the Samaritans.[104]

While one cannot be certain about the exact boundaries of the authoritative collections of sacred books in the various groups of first-century Judaism, there is a remarkable consensus in practical terms that borders on canonical. In disagreements there are never arguments over the extent of the authoritative collection(s) but only over its meaning.[105]

It is certainly true that there were disputes among the rabbis regarding the appropriateness of certain books as canonical, and some rabbis seem to extend canonicity to Ben Sira, but it would be a mistake to conclude from these examples that there was never an overall consensus for the large majority of early Judaism. Disputes probably arose *because of the prior inclusion* of books in the canon. How could, for example, Ecclesiastes, Esther, and Songs be in the canon when there is no mention of the divine name? How could Ezekiel be included when its plans for the temple contradict Exodus? How could Proverbs be canonical when it contains

103. David Carr feels the force of this criticism but nevertheless concludes: "Josephus's silence on the Sadducees' canon is important, but is not decisive evidence against a Sadducean Torah-only canon." Enough said. See his "Canonization in the Context of Community: An Outline in the Formation of the Tanakh and the Christian Bible," in *A Gift of God in Due Season: Essays in Scripture and Community in Honor of James A. Sanders,* ed. Richard D. Weis and David M. Carr, JSOTSS 225 (Sheffield: Sheffield Academic Press, 1996), 36.

104. Origen (*Against Celsus* 1.49); Jerome (*Commentary on Matthew* 22.31). See the strong, concise treatment of this issue by Stephen B. Chapman, *The Law and the Prophets: A Study in Old Testament Canon Formation,* FAT 27 (Tübingen: Mohr Siebeck, 2000), 266-68.

105. E.g., "When in debate with Jewish theologians, Jesus and the apostles appealed to the scriptures; they appealed to an authority which was equally acknowledged by their opponents." See Bruce, *Canon,* 41. Similar comments could be made about the Qumran community in its debates with other sects.

contradictions?[106] Esther is not mentioned in some Christian lists as well. But apropos is Beckwith's statement: "If [a closed canon] means a situation where such unanimity about the identity of the canonical books has been achieved that no individual ever again questions the right of any of them to its place in the Bible, the canon of neither Testament has ever been closed, either among Jews or among Christians."[107]

Canonical Text

Josephus claims for his authoritative list that it is completely closed and that there has been nothing added or subtracted from the list and text "for long ages." "This statement makes sense only if in Josephus' time (late first century C.E.) the Biblical text had been fixed and universally recognized for at least several generations."[108] One of the implications of this statement is that the sacred characteristic of the scriptures has led to a concern for quality control, so that textual additions and subtractions do not occur whether on the larger level, in terms of the addition or subtraction of a new book, or on the lesser level, the addition or subtraction of a portion of text within a book. This suggests that canonization has led to a standardization of the text. Sooner or later one cannot take the reproduction of valuable texts for granted, and their sanctity needs to be guarded by careful textual transmission. In the biblical period there is evidence suggesting that sacred texts were stored in the temple and their transmission would have been supervised by a group of expert scribes. There were many texts produced during the course of biblical times, but only certain ones have survived, probably because of their sacred status.[109]

This question of text was not that important before the discovery of the Qumran scrolls. Before that time, the evidence suggested a strong presumption for the Masoretic Text as the basic text from which all texts diverged. Text-critical scholars consulted the Septuagint, but usually its readings were not taken as seriously as those of the MT or were seen as due to translation. Similarly the text reflected in the Samaritan Pentateuch was regarded as inferior because of its obvious theological *Tendenz*. But with the discovery of the Scrolls around the Dead Sea, there are now not only Hebrew precursors for MT (Proto-MT) but

106. See, e.g., Mishna *Yadayim* 3:5 (Ecclesiastes, Songs), Babylonian Talmud, *Shabbat* 30b (Proverbs); *Shabbat* 13*b* (Ezekiel); *Megillah* 7*a* (Esther); *Baba Qamma* 92b (Ben Sira).

107. Beckwith, "Formation of the Hebrew Bible," 59.

108. Robert Gordis, *The Biblical Text in the Making: A Study of the Kethib-Qere* (Jerusalem: Ktav, 1971), xxxiii.

109. There are twenty-four "extra-biblical" books mentioned in the Hebrew Bible, books such as the Book of Jashar (Josh. 10:13; 2 Sam. 1:18), the Book of the Wars of the Lord (Num. 21:14), and the Book of the Acts of Solomon (1 Kgs. 11:41).

also for the Septuagint and the Samaritan Pentateuch.[110] In addition, there are many Hebrew texts that are not aligned with any textual tradition. The picture does not seem to be as neat and tidy as it once was. For example, Emanuel Tov describes the diversity as follows under five different categories: Qumran Practice 20 percent, Proto-Masoretic 35 percent, Pre-Samaritan 5 percent, Close to LXX 5 percent, Non-Aligned Texts 35 percent.[111]

If this textual pluriformity at Qumran provides a window into the wider Jewish world, it seems to suggest that Josephus's view of the canonical text is totally out of touch with reality, as there seems to be no standardization, and no assumption of a privileged, canonical text. To be sure, after the destruction of the temple in 70 C.E., the proto-MT text type alone survives, which suggests a more uniform, standardized tradition.[112] But some scholars would suggest that this later situation is not a systematic attempt at textual uniformity but rather a historical accident in which the MT text type is simply a textual survivor of the destruction of Jerusalem.[113] Thus the reality in the first century was not a uniform text but a pluriform one.

But this may be something of a hard intellectual pill to swallow, given the importance of sacred literature to temple authorities and given the number and quality of the proto-Masoretic manuscripts at Qumran. These may have emanated from temple circles, meaning that there was "a basically uniform tradition beside a pluriform tradition in Palestine Judaism in the last centuries B.C."[114]

> Since 𝔐 contains a carefully transmitted text, which is well documented in a large number of copies, and since it is reflected in the rabbinic literature as well as in the Targumim and many of the Greek versions of G, it may be surmised that it originated in the spiritual and authoritative center of Judaism (later to be known as that of the Pharisees), possibly in the temple circles. . . . The fact that all the texts left by the Zealots at Masada (dating until 73 CE) reflect 𝔐 is also important.[115]

110. F. M. Cross, *Qumran and the History of the Biblical Text* (Cambridge, MA: Harvard University Press, 1975).

111. E. Tov, *Textual Criticism of the Hebrew Bible,* 2nd edition (Minneapolis: Fortress, 2001), 115. In the first edition of Tov's book (1992) the proto-Masoretic text mss. accounted for 60 percent of the mss. A third edition of the book has further revisions: the Qumran practice category has been eliminated, which has increased the Proto-MT and nonaligned groupings.

112. The texts left behind by the zealots at Masada (ca. 73 C.E.) all reflect the MT text type, as do the texts at Wadi Muraba'at and Nahal Hever (ca. 132-135 C.E.).

113. B. Albrektson, "Reflections on the Emergence of a Standard Text of the Hebrew Bible," *VT* 29 (1978): 49-65.

114. A. van der Woude, "Pluriformity and Uniformity: Reflections on the Transmission of the Text of the Old Testament," in *Sacred Texts and Sacred History,* ed. J. F. Bremmer and F. García Martínez (Kampen: Kok Pharos, 1992), 161.

115. Tov, *Textual Criticism,* 28. Al Wolters makes a similar argument using Tov to buttress his point: A. Wolters, "The Text of the Old Testament," in *The Face of Old Testament Studies:*

One of the clear inferences to be drawn from such textual uniformity would have been a previous compilation of authoritative texts.[116] It is also not without significance that Greek translations were being revised toward this particular textual tradition.[117] Recent studies have made it clear that certain Greek translations in the first century B.C.E. were in fact recensions that revised the Old Greek to proto-MT. One only has to think of the Minor Prophets Scroll, from Nahal Hever (the so-called *kaige* text), Papyrus Fouad from Egypt, and a Qumran manuscript (4QLXXNum). All represent pre-Christian Greek recensions toward proto-MT. This clearly shows the privileged position of such a Hebrew text form. As Brevard Childs has remarked, "[T]he text of a book would not have been corrected and stabilized if the book had not already received some sort of canonical status."[118]

There is some other important evidence that supports the idea of textual quality control happening in the context of the temple. Within the Old Testament

A Survey of Contemporary Approaches, ed. D. Baker and B. Arnold (Grand Rapids: Baker Academic, 2001), 28-31. It may seem that Tov has changed his mind when he later argues that "a unified tradition before the turn of the eras never existed" ("The Status of the Masoretic Text in Modern Text Editions of the Hebrew Bible," in McDonald and Sanders, eds., *Canon Debate,* 239). But he qualifies this by stating that "while most groups did not insist upon a single textual tradition, temple circles and later the Pharisees, embraced a single textual tradition (proto-MT)." So he acknowledges that within this particular tradition there may have been considerable diversity before the third century B.C.E.

116. Van Seters finds Tov's position very problematic (*The Edited Bible,* 77, 325) because it implies a standardization that Van Seters argues did not really exist, based on comparative evidence among the classical Greek works. Thus the evidence for the dominance of MT after 70 C.E. becomes either the triumph of the "winners" among the many different sects of Judaism (the Pharisees) or simply an accident of history since the Pharisees "were the only group that survived the destruction of the Second Temple" and their texts (MT) survived with them.

117. For a lucid description of this process see J. Sanders, "The Issue of Closure in the Canonical Process" in McDonald and Sanders, eds., *Canon Debate,* 254-56.

118. Brevard S. Childs, *Biblical Theology of the Old and New Testaments: Theological Reflections on the Christian Bible* (Minneapolis: Augsburg Fortress, 1993), 60. Again, Van Seters (*The Edited Bible,* 340-46) argues that revisions toward the Hebrew do not need to imply recensional activity; they may imply unconscious revision based on the work of bilingual scribes who knew the original text extremely well. But the real question is, Why is there a concern for revision to the Hebrew? This suggests the authority of the original text, the so-called "Hebrew truth." On when "canonization" took place, see Cross, "The Text behind the Text," 153-54; E. Tov, *The Greek Minor Prophets Scroll from Nahal Hever,* DJD 8 (Oxford: Clarendon Press, 1990), 9-10, 99-158; R. Hanhart, "Problems in the History of the LXX Text from Its Beginning to Origen," introduction to Martin Hengel, *The Septuagint as Christian Scripture: Its Prehistory and the Problem of Its Canon* (London: T. & T. Clark, 2002), 1-17. See also Tov, *The Septuagint Translation of Jeremiah and Baruch: A Discussion of an Early Revision of the LXX of Jeremiah 29–52 and Baruch 1:1–3:8,* HSM 8 (Missoula, MT: Scholars Press, 1976), 169. For Tov's recent position on this see Emanuel Tov, "The Many Forms of Hebrew Scripture," in *From Qumran to Aleppo,* ed. Armin Lange, Matthias Weigold, and Jószef Zsengellér, FRLANT 230 (Göttingen: Vandenhoeck & Ruprecht, 2009), 24-25.

itself, sacred texts are linked to the temple. From the earliest times, a copy of the Ten Words was stored in the Ark of the Covenant (Exod. 25:16; Deut. 10:2); this was followed by a copy of the Torah being placed near the ark (Deut. 31:26), and copies of other books being placed near the tabernacle (Josh. 24:26). The king was also commanded to make a copy of the Torah under the supervision of the Levites (Deut. 17:18). The "Book of the Covenant" was found in the temple during Josiah's time (2 Kgs. 22:8), and from later tradition there is evidence that a Hebrew copy of the Torah was provided by the high priest in Jerusalem to Ptolemy of Egypt in order to provide the basis for the translation of the Septuagint: "In the presence of all the people I selected six elders from each tribe, good men and true, and I have sent them to you with a copy of our law."[119] This was done because of the poor quality of Hebrew manuscripts in Egypt and because they "do not represent the original text as I am informed by those who know."[120] The quality manuscripts, of course, would be in the care of the high priest in the temple in Jerusalem. Josephus, in a number of places, writes about holy books being stored in the temple.[121] From the Talmud there is a text that recalls three texts from the temple archive, each of which is known for its idiosyncrasies.[122] The texts that are chosen to be the superior texts are the ones that agree with each other the most, a sort of majority text type. The suggestion has been made that these may have been examples of a superior text type that was used for copying biblical texts. There is similar evidence that testifies to correctors *(maggihîm)* "that received their fees from the temple funds." It was important also to teach from a corrected text *(sēper muggah)*. There is also evidence of scribal corrections that date to early times.[123] While it is always dangerous to make conclusions drawn from later evidence, it is worthwhile noting that these particular traditions claim to antedate the destruction of the temple and are linked with the temple and they cohere with the textual evidence already mentioned, that of a uniform tradition *alongside* one that is pluriform, and the eventual triumph of the uniform tradition. This would suggest that Josephus's claim that nothing had been added or subtracted from the biblical texts was not hyperbole within the dominant uniform tradition. He

119. *Letter of Aristeas* 46.

120. *Letter of Aristeas* 31.

121. *Antiquities* 3.1.7.38; 4.8.44.303; 5.1.17.61.

122. Jerusalem Talmud, *Ta'anit* 4.68*a*. For the marshaled evidence see Emanuel Tov, *Textual Criticism of the Hebrew Bible,* rev. edition (Minneapolis: Augsburg Fortress, 2001), 32-33. See also Armin Lange, "'They Confirmed the Reading' (*y. Ta'an* 4.68*a*): The Textual Standardization of the Jewish Scriptures in the Second Temple Period," in *From Qumran to Aleppo: A Discussion with Emanuel Tov about the Textual History of Jewish Scriptures in Honor of His 65th Birthday,* ed. Armin Lange, Matthias Weigold, and József Zsengellér, FRLANT 230 (Göttingen: Vandenhoeck & Ruprecht, 2009), 29-80. Lange's entire article on standardization is oriented around this text.

123. See, e.g., Gordis, *The Biblical Text in the Making.*

would have been writing at a time when that tradition had been the only one for the previous three decades, and had a long pedigree.[124]

A new study suggests that from the Second Temple period the temple became the locus for the production of biblical texts, and from this new organization a scribal culture developed. Internal, external, and comparative evidence are all gathered to reach this conclusion. For example, in different Ancient Near Eastern societies scribes

> were recruited from the social upper class, [and they] went through years of training before they exercised their profession. Those who followed an advanced training became the scholars of antiquity. They were responsible for the creation, preservation and interpretation of the classic texts of their time. Their professional center, materially as well as spiritually, was the workshop of the temple. . . . [This] connects the scribes responsible for the Bible with the temple, and indicates a specialization within the priesthood focusing on writing and scholarship. The flourishing of scribal culture that produced this Hebrew Bible occurred in Judah in the Second Temple period. . . . There was an intimate link between the scribal profession as it took shape in the Persian era and the application and interpretation of the written Law. . . . The Jewish scribes developed into the scholars of the nation and the guardians of its literary heritage.[125]

The destruction of the temple might also explain why for the first time concern about the number of books and their order starts to appear, as Andrew Steinmann has cogently argued: "The clear implication of the evidence is that

124. Ian Young presents excellent arguments for a trajectory of textual quality control starting around 164 B.C.E. with the Hasmonean triumph. There is a concern for the collection of the biblical books within the context of the temple. If the Qumran evidence is dated to the middle of the first century B.C.E., its diversity reflects the beginning of the quality control. By the time of 70 C.E. that diversity has vanished. This of course depends on the dating of the Qumran evidence. See Ian Young, "The Stabilization of the Biblical Text in the Light of Qumran and Masada: A Challenge for the Conventional Qumran Chronology?" *Dead Sea Discoveries* 9 (2002): 364-90. Armin Lange argues that a uniform tradition cannot be pushed back further than the first century B.C.E., but plurality within Judaism, even outside Qumran, does not necessitate the elimination of a uniform tradition. It seems to me that the *Letter of Aristeas* from an earlier period assumes both uniformity and plurality (31-32). Up until 70 C.E. one dominant tradition exists with others, and after 70 C.E. that one tradition *curiously* remains alone. See Lange, " 'They Confirmed the Reading.' "

125. Karel van der Toorn, *Scribal Culture and the Making of the Hebrew Bible* (Cambridge, MA: Harvard University Press, 2009), 6. It is certainly true that there was a locus outside of the temple for writing attested in other cultures, such as the court (e.g., Prov. 25:1; 2 Sam. 8:17; Ps. 45:1; 2 Chron. 24:11). For some important qualifications of van der Toorn's thesis, see W. M. Schniedewind, "Review of Karel van der Toorn, *Scribal Culture and the Making of the Hebrew Bible*," *Journal of Hebrew Studies* 10 (2010), http://www.arts.ualberta.ca/JHS/reviews/reviews_new/review455.htm.

before the fall of Jerusalem in AD 70 canonicity was determined by a book's admission to the archives of the Scripture in the Temple, not by being part of a list of accepted books as in later times."[126] The simple reason for no interest in this before was that the question never arose. If one wanted to know the number and order of the books, one could simply visit the temple, where one could instantly gain access to the material. It was common knowledge. But after the destruction of the temple, the knowledge of the official list(s) was clearly in jeopardy and it had to be specifically enumerated and organized. It may be that the shorter list was from Palestine (Josephus) and the longer one was from Babylon.[127]

One of the main criticisms of Josephus is that he is regarded as someone who breaks his own rules and frequently adds to the "canonical" text in his own expositions. Examples are legion. But the question needs to be asked, Was Josephus engaged in anything like textual transmission or Bible translation? Or was not much of his work to be understood in the category of midrash? Feldman argues that perhaps Josephus understands himself as preserving the Jewish tradition in general, which includes the oral tradition later embodied in the midrashim.[128] If so, there would be no problem. If not, the practice would be inconsistent with his orthodox beliefs. One of the points that is made by Mason should make every historian pause before reaching judgments based on circumstantial evidence alone: "[I]f we did not have Josephus's statement about canon, we could easily be misled about his practice and conclude that his work showed clear evidence for an open canon."[129] This shows that practice cannot always be used to make certain conclusions about doctrinal beliefs. If many modern preachers were judged on this basis, one could certainly reach the conclusion that Marcion's canon has been revived.

The Cognitive Environment of Canon and the Resurrected Christ

All of the above factors suggest that, far from being a marginal point of view, a viewpoint out of step with contemporaries or ahead of its time, Josephus's understanding formed an essential part of the cognitive environment of canon in the first century of the Common Era. And it was also the conceptual water in which the early church swam. The story of the resurrected Christ's appearance to two of his disciples on the road to Emmaus (Luke 24:13-53) can help provide a further illustration of the importance of this cognitive environment to early

126. Steinmann, *The Oracles of God,* 113; cf. 192-94.

127. It specifically mentions that Ezra was responsible for writing out the twenty-four books to be read in public (4 Ezra 14).

128. Louis H. Feldman, *Studies in Josephus' Rewritten Bible,* SJSJ 58 (Atlanta: Society of Biblical Literature, 2005), 542.

129. Mason, "Josephus and His Twenty-Two Book Canon."

Christianity. In this text the risen Lord patiently listens to and then teaches his beleaguered and blind students *about himself* from a fixed body of sacred literature. Throughout the text correlative terms for this corpus are used: "all that the prophets have spoken" (v. 25); "Moses and all the prophets" (v. 27); "in all the Scriptures" (v. 27); "the Scriptures" (vv. 32, 45); "the law of Moses, the prophets, and the psalms" (v. 44). The word "all" is used three times in this short span, suggesting a complete corpus of sacred writings. It is probably not an accident that this text in the New Testament provides the only unambiguous reference to a tripartite canon. The resurrected Christ is establishing the *comprehensive* nature of the witness to his life and death and resurrection. *All* the scriptures — a defined body of text — testify to him. Period. This brings together *canonical list* (all the scriptures), *canonical organization* (the law, prophets, and psalms), and *canonical epoch* (all that the prophets have spoken). Presumably there is also a *canonical consensus* since there is no debate about the extent of the canon (and there never was in the New Testament).[130] The disciples are neither blind nor confused about the extent of the canon, but they are blind and confused about its meaning. They find that meaning when the resurrected Christ "opened their minds to understand the Scriptures" (v. 45). As for *canonical text,* one clearly gets the sense that these scriptures are inviolable, that is, they are complete. As a completed revelation they bear witness in their totality to Jesus Christ, who is the goal and end of revelation. Indeed, as Richard Hays remarks, "The whole story of Israel builds to its narrative climax in Jesus, the Messiah, who had to suffer before entering into his glory. That is what Jesus tries to teach them on the Road."[131]

Thus the church is born not just with a canon in its hands, but with a christological canon in its hands. But it was not just that the early church was born with a canon in its hands; the canon in a sense gave birth to Christ, who gave birth to the church. The canon of the Old Testament and Christ are inseparable: the one is the story, and the other is the point of the story.

Finding a *Sitz im Leben* for Canon

The above evidence points to two possible historical situations antecedent to Josephus that would qualify for a time in which the canon was closed. There would

130. "The NT often refers to the Scriptures in the plural which seems to indicate that there is some kind of collection; it is hard to believe that passages like Matthew 5:17-20; Luke 24:25, 44-45; 1 Corinthians 15:1-8; and 2 Timothy 3:14-16 are compatible with an open category of Scriptures without definite bounds." See Timothy Stone, *The Compilational History of the Megilloth: Canon, Contoured Intertextuality and Meaning in the Writings* (Ph.D. thesis, University of St. Andrews, 2010), 48.

131. Richard B. Hays, "Reading Scripture in the Light of the Resurrection," in *The Art of Reading Scripture,* ed. Ellen F. Davis and Richard B. Hays (Grand Rapids: Eerdmans, 2003), 229.

have to be enough time for such a tradition to have developed in which a defined list with a specific organization was produced in a definite epoch with a consensus, and was produced by an authoritative center in Judaism, namely the temple. The time of the Maccabean crisis is clearly one of those times, when there was a reconstitution of Judaism under the Hasmoneans after the rededication of the temple. The Hellenistic crisis that had led to the revolt of the Maccabees resulted in the destruction of many copies of scriptural books (cf. 1 Macc. 1:56-57). After the successful revolt it is noted in 2 Maccabees that Judas sought to gather writings for the temple in much the same way Nehemiah had a few centuries earlier:

> The same things also were reported in the writings and commentaries of Nehemiah; and how he founding a library gathered together the acts of the kings, and the prophets, and of David, and the epistles of the kings concerning the holy gifts. In like manner also Judas gathered together all those things that were lost by reason of the war we had, and they remain with us. (2:13-14)

Judas's action in collecting books lost in the war is a textual enterprise like that of his predecessor years before. This is one possibility, that canon closure occurred here.[132] But it is equally possible that the reference to Nehemiah can provide the *Sitz im Leben.* This would cohere best with Josephus's statement and with the evidence listed above, particularly the cessation of prophecy. When scholars speak of the beginning of canonization in Israelite history they often point to Ezra as providing the impetus for this with the canonization of the Torah (Neh. 8:1-18). It is clear that there seems to be a symbolic elevation of the scriptures during this period, but perhaps this activity with Ezra and Nehemiah represents a consolidation of the scriptures and the authoritative promulgation of the sacred documents. The fact that this period is the *terminus ante quem* for the production of the vast majority of biblical books is not incidental.[133] In the earliest explicit canonical list of the Hebrew Bible, the Bible ranges from Adam to Nehemiah, with the book of Chronicles providing a summary of the entire narrative. Both Chronicles and Nehemiah date to the Persian period. Josephus also dates the end of the biblical period with the reign of Artaxerxes. The temple would have provided the source for quality manuscripts for the biblical books — in effect standardization. In my judgment, given the nature of the documents, later Greek influences would not have been necessary to stress the importance of

132. See, e.g., M. Segal, "The Promulgation of the Authoritative Text of the Hebrew Bible," *Journal of Biblical Literature* 53 (1953): 35-47. Cf. also Beckwith, *The Old Testament Canon of the New Testament Church.* Beckwith argues that canonization is completed during this time as well. See also Sid Z. Leiman, *The Canonization of Hebrew Scripture: The Talmudic and Midrashic Evidence,* 2nd edition (New Haven: Connecticut Academy of Arts & Sciences, 1991).

133. Of course, Daniel is an exception, as it "fooled" everybody.

accuracy in transmission.[134] The temple would have ensured quality control; but at the same time, the popularity of the documents would have led by necessity to plurality. But the two should not be confused.

Some recent studies have tried to take Josephus's statement about the preservation of the original text of the canonical books seriously. Armin Lange has taken the process back to the first century B.C.E., where there is clear evidence of standardization.[135] Young has sought to trace it back to the reconstitution of Judaism under the Maccabees.[136] But Adrian van der Woude has pushed it back to the time of Ezra, and thus has taken Josephus most seriously. A number of other recent studies concur that the Persian period provides a fitting conclusion to the biblical period.[137] Prophecy has expired and now a text must bear the complete burden of authority. In my judgment it is more likely that the revival of Judaism under the Maccabees is just that — a restoration of what existed before. Perhaps after this period there was more of a concerted effort at standardization, given the nature of the previous crisis.

The Canons of the Christian Church

From the preceding study it is clear that while the word "canon" is a word that is coined to describe a closed body of sacred writings at a rather late period in the history of the church, the concept certainly was not absent from an earlier period. But how does one explain the "wider canon" of the early church in the fourth and fifth centuries C.E.? The view that the church had inherited a wider canon from the Alexandrian Jewish community, to which the Septuagint had been bequeathed, is no longer tenable, as Sundberg has convincingly demonstrated.[138] But neither can it be shown that a wider Palestinian canon existed in the first century C.E., and was inherited by Christians when they left the synagogues, while the Jews later narrowed it at Jabneh.[139] The claim that the "uncertainty in the church about the extent of the Old Testament could not have arisen if the extent of the Old Testament had already been fixed in the time of Jesus and the

134. See Lange and the literature cited there: " 'They Confirmed the Reading,' " 75-78.

135. Lange, " 'They Confirmed the Reading.' "

136. Young, "The Stabilization of the Biblical Text."

137. Hendrik J. Koorevaar, "Die Chronik als intendierter Abschluss des alttestamentlichen Kanons," *Jahrbuch für evangelikale Theologie* 11 (1997): 42-76; Julius Steinberg, *Die Ketuvim — ihr Aufbau und ihre Botschaft,* Bonner Biblische Beiträge 152 (Hamburg: Philo, 2006), 186-92.

138. Albert C. Sundberg, *The Old Testament of the Early Church* (Cambridge, MA: Harvard University Press, 1964).

139. A. C. Sundberg, " 'The Old Testament': A Christian Canon," *Catholic Biblical Quarterly* 30 (1968): 143-55; G. M. Hahneman, *The Muratorian Fragment and the Development of the Canon,* Oxford Theological Monographs 12 (Oxford: Oxford University Press, 1992), 1:77.

primitive church"[140] is one possible conclusion from the evidence, but it really has to dodge a particularly large "elephant in the room."

A more plausible alternative would suggest that confusion about the boundaries of the canon entered into the church because of its separation from Judaism and also because of the massive influx of Greek-speaking Gentiles into its confines. The Septuagint thus became the "default" Bible of the church, further removing it intellectually and culturally from its Hebrew roots. Consequently Melito, Bishop of Sardis, was compelled to go to the East ("where these things were preached and done") to gain certain knowledge of the scriptures of the Old Covenant around 170 C.E. His list contains twenty-five books with Esther missing.[141] This is the first Christian list, and it is arranged more like the later Greek codices, with the Wisdom literature in a middle section after the History books, and the Prophets at the end. The number and the tweaking of the generic divisions suggest that it is a mutation of Josephus's list. The next list (i.e., Origen's) specifically states that the Jews have a canon of twenty-two books, and Origen enumerates twenty-one, which suggests that he has forgotten to list the Twelve (minor prophets).[142] It is interesting that Origen specifically separates the first two books of Maccabees from his list by placing them at the end with a qualification. From Origen's correspondence it is clear that he acknowledges that the church's practice has included a wider canon, which he believes has been inspired by God, but in arguments with the Jews he will not use it.[143] Other Eastern lists are all based on the twenty-two-book list of Josephus, and *at the end of the lists* there are often added extra-canonical books for ecclesiastical edification.[144] Some church fathers desire more clarity to be brought into the canonical confusion.

In the West, since the church has moved further from Jerusalem, the picture is not so orderly, as in many lists there is an interspersing of putative non-canonical books among canonical ones. At the same time, Jerome states that there are two Jewish canonical orders, one that uses the number twenty-two and one that uses the number twenty-four.[145] It is also clear from Jerome's writings that he is aware of writings that have been added to the Hebrew canon, and he wishes to return to the "Hebrew truth." The clash between Jerome and Augustine is famous, with the latter arguing that the Holy Spirit inspired the books of the wider canon

140. Sundberg, *The Old Testament of the Early Church,* 130.

141. Eusebius, *Ecclesiastical History* 4.13.26.

142. Or perhaps the omission is Eusebius's fault in both instances (The Twelve in Origen and Esther in Melito). See Eusebius, *Ecclesiastical History* 6.25.

143. See, e.g., in his letter to Africanus.

144. See, e.g., Athanasius, Cyril of Jerusalem, Epiphanius *(haer.; de mens. et pond. 4),* Pseudo-Athanasius, John of Damascus. For a convenient compilation of the lists see Henry Barclay Swete, *An Introduction to the Old Testament in Greek: With an Appendix Containing the Letter of Aristeas,* 1st edition (Cambridge: Cambridge University Press, 1902), 203ff.

145. *Prologus Galeatus.*

that have been used by the church,[146] and Jerome coming back again and again to the Hebrew truth.[147]

The great Greek codices of the early church, Vaticanus and Sinaiticus of the fourth century C.E. and Alexandrinus of the fifth century, show orders based on genre. But in Vaticanus the order is Torah, History, Wisdom, and Prophets, and in Sinaiticus and Alexandrinus the order is Torah, History, Prophecy, and Wisdom. In all the books there are "extra-canonical" books generally placed with their generic counterparts.

While Jerome himself wished to retrieve the Hebrew text and use that for his Old Testament, the earliest Vulgate copies suggest that the wider canon prevailed. With the division of the Orthodox Church the canon was enlarged again. It was not until the Reformation that the Protestant church returned to the early Jewish roots of the church with the canon that was first placed into its hands. The Protestant arrangement is a curious hybrid in which it reflects the generic order of early Christian arrangements and the narrow canon of Judaism. The Catholic Church later affirmed the wider canon of the early church at the Council of Trent, and in 1566 Sixtus of Siena, a Christian convert from Judaism, made the distinction between proto-canonical books (narrow canon) and deutero-canonical books (wider canon). Such a distinction implies no inferiority for the deutero-canonical writings.

Christianity has always been in danger of abandoning its Jewish roots. Which canon of the Old Testament to follow is thus a crucial theological question. This is an integral part of what has been called the problem of the Christian Bible.[148] Shall the church by dint of tradition add to the canon of ancient Israel like Augustine, or should it return to the Hebrew truth like Jerome? Perhaps there is a place for both, which is seen in the early attempt of the church to read some books for edification, and the others solely for doctrine. David de Silva has pointed out that if it were not for Augustine, many books would have been lost to the church; if it were not for Jerome many books would not have been distinguished.[149] But this study has sought to show that it is the latter group of books that the church first received, and then pointed to its crucified and risen Lord. Thus it is this group of books from which the church receives its life, for these books are in fact "the decrees of God."[150]

146. Augustine, *On Christian Doctrine* 2.15.

147. Adam Kamesar, *Jerome, Greek Scholarship, and the Hebrew Bible,* 2nd printing (Oxford: Clarendon Press, 1993), 41-48.

148. Brevard S. Childs, *Biblical Theology of the Old and New Testaments: Theological Reflection on the Christian Bible* (Minneapolis: Augsburg Fortress, 1993), 60-68.

149. D. DeSilva, *An Introduction to the Apocrypha* (Grand Rapids: Baker, 2004), 27.

150. Josephus, *Against Apion* 1.42. A recent book on the canon that I was not able to interact with here is by Timothy H. Lim, *The Formation of the Jewish Canon* (New Haven: Yale University Press, 2013). While Lim gives Josephus credit for his view of canon as a "credible generalization" of the state of affairs at the end of the first century C.E., it is only for that time and it is a "generalization." See my forthcoming review in *Journal of Hebrew Studies.*

TWELVE

"Competing Histories, Competing Theologies?" Reflections on the Unity and Diversity of the Old Testament('s Readers)

V. Philips Long

Although the title above might suggest an interest in the well-worn topic of the unity and diversity of the Old Testament's own histories and theologies,[1] my actual concern in what follows is with the unity and diversity of the Old Testament's readers. In particular, I want to explore how the "competing theologies" embraced by those writing histories of Israel these days influence the "competing histories" they produce. The pertinence of this topic in the present volumes on Scripture is at least twofold. First, history matters. By any objective measure, Judeo-Christian faith is dependent — to a degree unparalleled in any other religious system — on the actual occurrence "in history" of certain core events. Should the historical truth claims of Scripture — assuming that these have been rightly discerned — prove false, then the faith founded upon them is likewise proved false. This point is nowhere made more clearly or authoritatively, nor in respect to an event more central to Christian faith, than in 1 Corinthians 15:14's famous "if Christ has not been raised, then our proclamation has been in vain and your faith has been in vain."[2] Second, and following from the first point, history is the arena in which the Bible is most open to external control and hence to challenge and potential falsification. If the Bible's historical truth claims should be disproven — again assuming that they have been rightly discerned — then why should anyone have confidence in its other truth claims, theological, ethical, or whatever?

So, history matters a great deal to students of the Bible — or at least it should. As I have already intimated, in what follows we shall take the current state of

1. One thinks, for instance, of the distinctive theological perspectives exhibited in the so-called Primary History of Genesis-Kings as compared with the Secondary History of 1-2 Chronicles; for a case study and a brief discussion of how the distinctive histories may complement one another, see V. P. Long, *The Art of Biblical History* (Grand Rapids: Zondervan, 1994), 76-86 (hereafter Long, *ABH*).

2. Unless otherwise indicated, Scripture citations are from the NRSV.

history-of-Israel studies as our test case, though much of what we discover will apply equally well to other areas of biblical studies. The focus will be on what unites and especially what divides scholars currently writing histories of Israel, or writing about writing such histories. My twofold thesis is (1) that, with all that unites well-informed scholars, their disagreements often begin at a deep and often undiscussed level and (2) that mutual understanding and profitable discussion could be greatly enhanced by acknowledging *and occasionally discussing* this deep-level diversity. My plan, after a few paragraphs sketching the current state of discourse on Israel's ancient history, is to consider (1) how "control beliefs, comfortable theories, and objectivity" interrelate; (2) how the "historical-critical method" is generally understood and how it might be revised and expanded; (3) how, if at all, scholars embracing very different control beliefs might still find it possible to engage in profitable conversation; and (4) why this all seems to matter so much to so many people.

As a preliminary, then, a few comments on the current state of affairs in history-of-Israel studies are in order. Those conversant in the field will know that recent decades have witnessed a lively interest in the history of ancient Israel, an interest so lively in fact that the rhetoric has at times become heated. This invites two questions: Why the interest? and Why the heat? One contributing factor is the rise in popularity (beginning at least in the latter quarter of the twentieth century) of synchronic literary approaches to the Old Testament, which seemed to threaten the hegemony of more traditional historical-critical approaches and elicited a variety of reactions. Some scholars resisted the newer literary approaches; I recall overhearing in the early 1980s a couple of lecturers in a prestigious British university speaking dismissively of "all this literary rubbish." Others (including the present author) welcomed the newer literary approaches (not least because they sometimes offered helpful alternatives to unconvincing source-critical theories) but nevertheless retained a keen interest in historical questions. Still others embraced the newer approaches but took them in *ahistorical* directions, seeming almost to assume that the more "literary" a text proved to be, the less "history" it was likely to contain. The wrongheadedness of this literature-versus-history assumption became most apparent to me one day, again in the early 1980s, when it dawned on me that my occasional occupation as a portrait painter required that I marshal *artistry* in the interest of *history*. Why should the same not be true of the Bible's narrative tradition? Might not literary art be employed in the service of historical subject matter?[3] The answer, I would suggest, is "Of course."

But this raises other questions. On what grounds do we assume in the first place that certain biblical narratives constitute a kind of history-writing? For one

3. For full discussion of the similarities between portraiture (visual representational art) and historiography (verbal representational art), see Long, *ABH*, 58-87.

thing, whatever their literary traits, many biblical narratives certainly *seem* to show an interest in recounting and interpreting events of the past. R. Alter writes:

> In all biblical narrative and in a good deal of biblical poetry as well, the domain in which literary invention and religious imagination are joined is history, for all these narratives, with the exception of Job and possibly Jonah, purport to be true accounts of things that have occurred in historical time.[4]

Most scholars are likely to agree with Alter and to share R. Smend's opinion that the biblical narrators "wrote generally in good faith that the events which they were narrating had actually happened."[5] Most, but not all. Some insist, to the contrary, that the OT is a very late postexilic creation, at best a repository of "cultural memory" but hardly a viable source of much historical information about earlier periods.[6] Not surprisingly, such divergent views have sparked debate about both methods and outcomes. But methodological discussion alone will never achieve true mutual understanding. To begin to understand how and why we disagree, we must add to our discussions of method, as important as these are, more explicit explorations of the reality models we each embrace and the ways in which these models influence the decisions we make. Such explorations will take us into unfamiliar territory — forbidden territory, some might say. But unless we muster the courage to travel beyond the borders of the familiar and the comfortable, our debates will remain superficial and continue generating more heat than light. Stated more positively, as we gain greater clarity on just why and how we disagree with one another — that is, at *what level* we disagree — we shall be in a position to engage in more enlightened (and less heated) discussion. At the very least, we may achieve higher-quality disagreements. Taking then the "competing histories" of ancient Israel as our test case, a good place to begin our exploration is to . . .

4. R. Alter, "Introduction to the Old Testament," in *The Literary Guide to the Bible,* ed. R. Alter and F. Kermode (Cambridge, MA: Belknap Press of Harvard University Press, 1987), 11-35, on 17.

5. "Tradition and History: A Complex Relation," in *Tradition and Theology in the Old Testament,* ed. D. Knight (Philadelphia: Fortress, 1977), 49-68, on 54; cf. B. Halpern, *The First Historians: The Hebrew Bible and History* (San Francisco: Harper & Row, 1988).

6. See, e.g., P. R. Davies, *Memories of Ancient Israel: An Introduction to Biblical History — Ancient and Modern* (Louisville: Westminster John Knox, 2008), esp. 105-23 on "cultural memory." The concept of cultural memory may, after due consideration and proper nuancing, prove useful in understanding aspects of biblical historiography. But one must be careful (more careful than Davies appears to be) to avoid divorcing the *memory* from its precipitating historical *event.* As R. Rodriguez rightly notes in a thorough and helpful discussion of cultural, or "collective," memory, "The demonstration of a narrative's links to the concerns of the present *does not* constitute evidence of any quality that that narrative is unrepresentative of the past *as the past.*" *Structuring Early Christian Memory: Jesus in Tradition, Performance, and Text* (London: T. & T. Clark, 2010), 53.

"Look Who's Talking": On Control Beliefs, Comfortable Theories, and the Ideal of Objectivity

Not surprisingly, biblical scholars, as academics, are quite good at keeping things, well, "academic." Occasionally, however, a comment bubbles to the surface of academic discourse that betrays something large lurking below the surface. A telling example, which I have cited before,[7] is the brief, sharp exchange some years ago between the late Norman Whybray and Philip Davies in the pages of *Expository Times.*[8] In his short essay, Whybray, dismayed by Davies's dim view of the value of the OT for reconstructing Israel's history, wonders aloud about Davies's "extreme radicalism" and whether it might not be motivated by "a touch of iconoclastic zeal." In reply, Davies wonders whether Whybray's more positive appraisal of the OT's usefulness to the historian might not be "driven by reactionary conservatism or religious attachment to Christian scripture." These revealing comments no sooner bubble to the surface than they are submerged again, Davies worrying that to "debate on this level" could "bring scholarship as a whole into disrepute."

Now this is a curious thing. Both Whybray and Davies intuitively sense that the other's scholarship is not entirely disinterested. Both suspect that "other issues" are involved, that something large lies below the academic surface. And yet neither sees fit to investigate (or, better, to divulge) what this large thing might be. This is common scholarly practice, at least among biblical scholars and historians (perhaps less so in other fields?). But is it good practice? If, as V. A. Harvey has famously noted, "all our judgments and inferences . . . are but the visible part of an iceberg lying deep below the surface,"[9] might not an occasional deep dive prove bracingly refreshing? My sense is that the occasional subsurface exploration could accomplish at least two things: (1) by improving mutual understanding among scholars, it might enable greater clarity and civility in debate; and (2) it might help to explain why, in instances where the evidence is limited or inconclusive, some scholars tilt this way and others that. Where "definitive and certain data" are lacking, it is often "a leaning toward one of the dominant views within scholarship" that makes the difference. And of course these views themselves are often "influenced by ideological, theological or other tendencies." In other words, the position one takes in ambiguous cases is often prompted "by such factors as fashion, predisposition or belief."[10] Only sub-

7. Cf. V. P. Long, "Renewing Conversations: Doing Scholarship in an Age of Skepticism, Accommodation, and Specialization," *Bulletin for Biblical Research* 13 (2003): 227-49, on 241-42.

8. The 1996 essays by Whybray and Davies are reprinted in V. P. Long, ed., *Israel's Past in Present Research: Essays on Ancient Israelite Historiography,* Sources for Biblical and Theological Study 7 (Winona Lake, IN: Eisenbrauns, 1999), 181-91.

9. *The Historian and the Believer: The Morality of Historical Knowledge and Christian Belief* (New York: Macmillan, 1966, 1996), 115.

10. So Y. Amit, *The Book of Judges: The Art of Editing* (Leiden: Brill, 1999), 367-68, commenting on the dating of the book of Judges.

surface exploration will discover such influences as these. We wouldn't want to stay too deep for too long; the pressure might kill us. But to float forever on the surface, *never* peering beneath to discover the true shape of the hidden nine-tenths of the "iceberg," leaves us seriously ignorant of what underlies and undergirds scholarly judgments and inferences, and tempts only to speculation.

To remark on the importance of what lies below the surface of interpretive practice is nothing new. Attention is regularly drawn to the importance of assumptions, presuppositions, background beliefs, worldview, and the like. But seldom, in Old Testament studies at least (again, it may be different in other fields), does one take the time to explore just *how* the subsurface portion of the iceberg affects what happens on the surface. So that's what we want to do (especially in the next major section). But first, it is worth considering why, if the occasional deep-dive could be so helpful, there is such reticence to take the plunge. I have noticed at least three reasons (and there may be more). The three involve (1) fear of certain levels of debate, (2) failure to distinguish bias from background beliefs, and (3) flight to "method" as an assumed safe haven. Let us look at each in turn, spending most time on the second.

Fear of Debating at a Disreputable Level

Davies's concern, noted above, that debating at a certain level might bring scholarship as a whole into disrepute has some force. It seems a fair observation, however, that the problem is not so much the *level* of debate as its *manner.* Speculatively characterizing or even caricaturing one's opponent is inappropriate and unhelpful. Guessing at another's motivations is seldom accurate, necessary, or good. But confessing one's own motives and beliefs (offering a glimpse of one's own "iceberg," if you will) is a very different matter — good for the soul perhaps, and certainly clarifying in debate. After all, as is widely acknowledged these days, no one, neither Bible reader nor biblical scholar, approaches the task of Bible reading as a completely disinterested observer. "Other issues" are always present. Most scholars today recognize this. But some mistakenly assume that these "other issues" are simply a matter of *bias,* the solution to which is to expunge the bias and try to be more "objective." This brings us to the second reason deep-level exploration is rare among Old Testament scholars.

Failure to Distinguish Bias from Background Beliefs

M. B. Moore begins her helpful treatise on *Philosophy and Practice in Writing a History of Ancient Israel* by lamenting the fact that, although "historians of ancient Israel and Judah, like all other historians, come to their work with certain presuppositions and goals in mind," very rarely do we "find a historian who sets forth his or her philosophy of history in writing."[11] Not only does Moore encourage more explicit discussion of the assumptions underlying attempts to write histories of ancient Israel,[12] but she also commends a way forward in the study of the history of Israel and Judah — viz., the way of "objectivity."[13] Setting objectivity in opposition to *subjectivity,* and specifically *bias,* Moore contends that the goal of the objective researcher should be to "abandon all biases and to apprehend and present information in a value-free manner."[14] Following C. B. McCullagh,[15] she suggests that bias is best known by its fruits, which are (1) misrepresentation of evidence; (2) omission of evidence; (3) implication of facts "known to be false"; and (4) failure to mention "all important causes of events in an explanation."[16] To be "objective," then, is to eschew bias and its fruits and instead — if I may summarize what seems to me to be the gist of Moore's discussion — to be *fair, thorough, and balanced.* To McCullagh's warnings against bias, Moore adds two further guidelines for would-be "objective" historians. These two, I suggest, have little if anything to do with bias (at least in its negative connotations). "First, objective historians must be clear about which historical statements correspond closely to evidence and which are interpretations."[17] Moore seems to have in mind here the necessary distinction between *descriptions of the data* (which, depending on how bare these descriptions are, can tend toward objectivity) and *interpretations of the data* (which invariably involve a subjective dimension).[18] Second, Moore insists that

> inferences, interpretations, or explanations that arise from the historian's own experiences or conjectures about the evidence should be determined as far as possible and acknowledged as such, and any social-scientific or other theory that enters into historical reconstruction should be acknowledged and explained.[19]

11. M. B. Moore, *Philosophy and Practice in Writing a History of Ancient Israel,* Library of Hebrew Bible/Old Testament Studies 435 (New York/London: T. & T. Clark, 2006), 1.

12. A sentiment with which I entirely agree, as my own past writings demonstrate; see, e.g., V. P. Long, *ABH,* 120-22, 131-34, 171-76, and *passim.*

13. Moore, *Philosophy and Practice,* 5, 8-11, 79-83, 112-13, 138-44.

14. Moore, *Philosophy and Practice,* 8.

15. C. B. McCullagh, "Bias in Historical Description, Interpretation, and Explanation," *History and Theory* 39 (2000): 39-66, 40.

16. Moore, *Philosophy and Practice,* 10; cf. 139.

17. Moore, *Philosophy and Practice,* 139.

18. On the question whether data, such as archeological data, can ever be presented without at least some measure of interpretation, see F. Brandfon, "The Limits of Evidence: Archaeology and Objectivity," *Maarav* 4 (1987): 5-43, and the brief discussions in Long, *ABH,* 144-47.

19. Moore, *Philosophy and Practice,* 139-40.

This second guideline moves in the direction of a distinction that needs to be made much more clearly — viz., the very real difference between bias and background beliefs. Bias is to be recognized and as far as possible expunged. Simply to admit one's biases is not to excuse them. Bias is bad. Its fruits are neither fair, thorough, nor balanced. *But background beliefs are a very different matter.* Having background beliefs, or a worldview, a model of reality, is an inevitable aspect of sentient human existence. Background beliefs have staying power, which is not to say that one's background beliefs can never grow, change, or even experience a Kuhnian paradigm shift.[20] Both individuals and societies may experience growth, transformation, or even collapse of worldviews.[21] The point is simply that no one lives without a worldview. Sweeping the house clean of one set of background beliefs will only invite the entry of another. This is not to suggest, of course, that all background beliefs, any more than beliefs in general, are of equal value or validity. Some may be unsupported by evidence or experience. Some may be delusional and even harmful. But the fact that background beliefs, unlike bias, cannot and should not simply be expunged means that they *should be disclosed and made discussable.* As F. Deist insists:

> the perspective from which a historian selects and combines, interrelates and connects events, that is, the perspective from which s/he assigns meaning to the whole should be explicated. This allows fellow historians as well as the "average intelligent person" to evaluate the argument from the correct perspective, and to criticize the perspective itself. The integrity of historical narration has very much to do with the question whether the perspective giving explanations for series of events of the past is stated in such a way that it can be discussed and criticized by those for whom (and/or about whom!) the history has been written.[22]

Background beliefs affect interpretive judgments. This seems beyond serious dispute. But what exactly are background beliefs?

20. The allusion is, of course, to Thomas Kuhn's *The Structure of Scientific Revolutions,* 3rd edition (Chicago: University of Chicago Press, 1996; orig. 1962).

21. Of societies, for instance, Z. Zevit (*The Religions of Ancient Israel: A Synthesis of Parallactic Approaches* [London: Continuum, 2001], 21) remarks that although "religion and worldview" are sometimes treated as terms "referring to static situations, it is a truism that societies change." Zevit cites as an ancient example the destruction of the Jerusalem temple in 586 B.C.E., "which necessitated changes in the worldview of groups believing in the inviolability of Jerusalem and the permanent nature of a covenant between YHWH and Judah." As in ancient times, so also in the present, "alterations in various parts of a worldview . . . are possible because worldviews are neither rigidly logical philosophical constructs nor closed systems."

22. F. E. Deist, "Contingency, Continuity and Integrity in Historical Understanding: An Old Testament Perspective," *Scriptura* S11 (1993): 99-115, on 112.

By background beliefs I have in mind what N. Wolterstorff describes as "control beliefs." These are not simply presuppositions, or assumptions. Rather, control beliefs are *convictions* that together constitute a worldview. They are deep-level convictions about life, about what it means to be human, about whether human life has meaning, whether history has meaning, whether there is a God, whether this God can be known, and so forth. "Not simply one belief among many," control beliefs "function as a control over many other beliefs. They will affect the selection of the theories one believes in, the questions one asks and one's behavior."[23] In other words, as I have argued elsewhere,[24] one's *model of reality* (one's control beliefs) influences what *methods* and *theories* one prefers. As Wolterstorff explains,

> in weighing a theory one always brings along the whole complex of one's beliefs. One does not strip away all but those beliefs functioning as data relative to the theory being weighed. On the contrary, one remains cloaked in belief — aware of some strands, unaware of most.[25]

Specifically, Wolterstorff distinguishes three types of belief: *data beliefs, data-background beliefs,* and *control beliefs.* W. Brewbaker succinctly explains these three categories of beliefs in an essay on Christian legal scholarship:[26]

> These correspond respectively (and very roughly) to (1) beliefs about what the facts are, (2) beliefs about how we know what the facts are, and (3) fundamental assumptions about human identity and the meaning and purpose of life that are shaped not only by our religious commitments but also by our cultural background, life experience, and other factors. Wolterstorff's account of the place of control beliefs is both descriptive and normative: descriptive in that he argues that we all do have a web of beliefs that control which theories of the world we are likely to accept; and normative in that for Christians, our "authentic Christian commitment" should function in this manner.

As a law professor and a Christian, Brewbaker contends that

> Christian control beliefs, then, while not dictating full-orbed theoretical accounts of legal or political controversies will tend to place Christians in pre-

23. D. K. McKim, *Westminster Dictionary of Theological Terms* (Louisville: Westminster John Knox, 1996), 61.

24. Long, *ABH,* 120-21.

25. N. Wolterstorff, *Reason within the Bounds of Religion,* 2nd edition (Grand Rapids: Eerdmans, 1984), 66-67.

26. W. S. Brewbaker III, "Theory, Identity, Vocation: Three Models of Christian Legal Scholarship," *Seton Hall Law Review* 39, no. 17 (2009): 17-61, on 56.

dictable places with respect to certain theories. We might expect Christians, for example, to question legal theories that rely exclusively on behavioristic accounts of the human person or those that posit that the ultimate goal of law ought to be the maximization of a society's material wealth, or that law or political processes are sufficient to respond to a society's deepest questions of meaning and purpose.

Similarly, to return to our present concern with history-of-Israel studies, *control beliefs* — whether they be Christian or some other — will tend to place those who hold them in "predictable places," even while stopping short of dictating "full-orbed" historical accounts. Control beliefs wield their influence on all people, not just religious people. For it is not only religious beliefs that count as control beliefs, but also "secular worldviews that occupy the same conceptual space."[27] Non-theists are just as likely as theists to be drawn by their control beliefs to certain "predictable places." P. R. Davies, for instance, candidly admits that he takes exception to what he describes as "precisely a biblical belief" — that is, "belief in a single transcendental being who can comprehend, indeed controls, all history" — and in so doing embraces "a world-view incompatible with that of the biblical writings." Davies's contra-biblical worldview in turn leads him to discount the possibility of "objective history," by which he seems to mean "the past" not simply as "a temporal unity but a metaphysical one." To his credit, he goes on to acknowledge that "a certain kind of religious belief *might* well dictate a certain definition of 'history.'"[28] Indeed so, as his own case illustrates. His non-theistic worldview leads him to one view of "history," while a theistic worldview would lead to a very different view of "history," to a "competing history," if you will.

The inevitable presence of control beliefs (whether we are conscious of them or not) means that all of us find various theories more or less attractive, depending on the extent to which they are "consistent with our control beliefs. Or, to put it more stringently, we want theories that comport as well as possible with those beliefs."[29] There is a link, in other words, between "control beliefs" and what Samuel Sandmel calls "comfortable theories."[30] "A comfortable theory," according to Sandmel, "is one which satisfies the needs of the interpreter, whether theological or only personal, when the evidence can seem to point in one of two opposite directions." Sandmel maintains that "all of us gravitate to comfortable theories" — not just those of us who embrace more traditional views: "modernists

27. Brewbaker, "Theory, Identity, Vocation," 19.

28. P. R. Davies, "Whose History? Whose Israel? Whose Bible? Biblical Histories, Ancient and Modern," in *Can a "History of Israel" Be Written,* ed. L. L. Grabbe, JSOTSS 245 (Sheffield: Sheffield Academic Press, 1997), 104-22, on 116-17.

29. Wolterstorff, *Reason within the Bounds of Religion,* 67-68.

30. S. Sandmel, "Palestinian and Hellenistic Judaism and Christianity: The Question of the Comfortable Theory," *HUCA* 50 (1979): 137-48.

and iconoclasts alike have their comfortable theories; untraditionalism breeds just as many comfortable theories as does traditionalism."[31]

L. Grabbe rightly draws attention to the relevance of Sandmel's concept of the "comfortable theory" for history-of-Israel debates.[32] But in offering his own "interpretation of Sandmel's thesis," Grabbe seems to distort its original sense slightly but significantly. A comfortable theory, according to Grabbe, "is not a disinterested search for the 'facts,' the 'truth' or whatever term one wishes to use, but a means of maintaining our position with the least amount of effort."[33] What Grabbe describes, it seems to me, is closer to *bias,* or prejudice, than to what Sandmel seems to have in mind. Moreover, Grabbe's phrase "disinterested search for the 'facts'" shows little awareness or appreciation of the presence of control beliefs. Given the inevitable presence of control beliefs, however, some theories will at first blush be more satisfying, more "congenial" (as Sandmel puts it) to this or that scholar precisely because they are more or less concordant with these deep-level convictions. This, I would argue, is as it should be.

Having said that, however, I must hasten to add that *we cannot stop there*! Lest the legitimate sway of background beliefs give rise to the distortions of bias, *the "comfortable" theory must be tested rigorously against the known data.* Every effort must be made to conduct a methodical appraisal of all available evidence — and not just of the evidence thought to support the comfortable theory. Then, if the comfortable theory still stands, the scholar can embrace it without guilt.[34] Lest I be misunderstood, let me stress that I am not at all suggesting a kind of relativism whereby any theory is as good as another so long as it aligns comfortably with one's background beliefs. My point is simply that background beliefs do play a role in determining what theories one prefers, and sometimes our debates should be engaged at the deeper level of background beliefs. When someday the full story is told, some background beliefs will prove true and others false, just as some theories will prove true and others false.

31. Sandmel, "Palestinian and Hellenistic Judaism and Christianity," 139.

32. L. L. Grabbe, *Ancient Israel: What Do We Know and How Do We Know It?* (London/ New York: T. & T. Clark, 2007), 21-22.

33. Grabbe, *Ancient Israel,* 22.

34. Sometimes it is initial discomfort with a particular theory that piques interest and leads to careful reappraisal of the evidence purportedly supporting the theory: for an example of an uncomfortable theory prompting a more thorough investigation, see V. P. Long, "How Reliable Are Biblical Reports? Repeating Lester Grabbe's Comparative Experiment," *VT* 52 (2002): 367-84. Grabbe's response to my essay seems to miss or misconstrue the point of the original exercise ("'How Reliable Are Biblical Reports?' A Response to V. Philips Long," in *Historie Og Konstruktion. Festskrift Til Niels Peter Lemche I Anledning Af 60 Års Fødselsdagen Den 6. September 2005,* ed. M. Møller and T. L. Thompson, Forum for Bibelsk Eksegese 14 [Copenhagen: Museum Tusculanums Forlag, 2005], 153-60). Further discussion, if deemed useful, must await another occasion.

Mention in the preceding paragraph of a "methodical appraisal" leads to a third reason that the subsurface portion of the scholarly "iceberg" is frequently ignored. In addition to the two already discussed — viz., fear of debating at a disreputable level and failure to distinguish bias from background beliefs — the third reason is . . .

Flight to Method as a Safe Haven

With few nowadays willing to deny that "all historians work from some philosophical or theological base, whether consciously or not,"[35] the appeal to careful method as a means of eliminating bias seems fair enough at first glance. But further reflection reveals that it is not just historians but historical methods themselves that assume a "philosophical or theological base." Methods are neither neutral nor self-evident. Rather than assuming, therefore, that "method" provides a value-free zone where bias is quashed and background beliefs can be safely ignored, interpreters must instead recognize that scholarly methods themselves, no less than those employing them, are undergirded by "control beliefs." Indeed, control beliefs, or worldviews, are involved at every level of scholarly engagement. This means, as I wrote some years ago, that

> not only must I, as an interpreter, seek to gain a more conscious awareness of my own worldview, but I must also seek to discover the worldview embodied in the text I am studying, the worldview undergirding the method I am applying, and the worldviews held by other interpreters whose writings I may consult. Where there are differences at the fundamental level of worldview, tensions and disagreements on the levels of interpretation and/or application are inevitable. If the interpreter's model of reality is distinctly different from that embodied in the text, there will be tension. If a method is applied to a text whose fundamental assumptions about the world and reality run counter to the assumptions underlying the method, there will be tensions. If interpreters approaching a given text disagree fundamentally on how they view reality, they will likely also disagree on how to interpret the text, or at least on whether the text, once interpreted, is to be believed and obeyed.[36]

It should by now be clear that the "competing histories" characteristic of history-of-Israel studies these days reflect to some degree — perhaps to a large

35. J. M. Miller, "Reflections on the Study of Israelite History," in *What Has Archaeology to Do with Faith?* ed. J. H. Charlesworth and W. P. Weaver (Philadelphia: Trinity Press International, 1992), 60-74, on 65.

36. Long, *ABH,* 172.

degree — the "competing theologies" held by the historians themselves and/or underlying the methods they employ. I would argue, moreover, that differing control beliefs *should* call forth differing historical methods. But how would this look? Having considered the importance of (and three hindrances to) looking below the surface to discover how individual scholars are influenced by their control beliefs, we are now in a position to look below the surface of the methods themselves. So, when we speak for instance of the *historical-critical method, . . .*

"What Are We Talking About?": On What We Mean by the Historical-Critical Method

A good case could be made that there is no such thing as *the* historical-critical method.[37] Still, whenever historical method is discussed, certain key principles tend to be mentioned. Chief among these are the so-called three canons of historical criticism put forward by Ernst Troeltsch (1865-1923): criticism, analogy, and correlation.[38] For present purposes, these principles can serve as a basis for exploring how different control beliefs can legitimately dictate different formulations of the three principles. These principles are discussed thoroughly elsewhere, seminally by W. J. Abraham[39] and subsequently by Long[40] and others. A brief

37. One need only consult recent histories of Israel to discover how very differently they describe the historical method, if indeed they talk of method at all. An astute analysis of differing methodological approaches is available in Z. Zevit, *The Religions of Ancient Israel: A Synthesis of Parallactic Approaches* (London: Continuum, 2001), esp. 30-80. Zevit presents and evaluates the chief tenets of four "paradigms," which may be very roughly described (using my terms) as modern positivist, modern non-positivist, postmodern minimalist, or deconstructionist (though some included under this heading [e.g., Sternberg] seem ill-suited to this category), and new historicist-cultural, the latter category still emerging. Zevit describes his own approach as a "reconstructed version of the second paradigm" with just a hint of the "amorphous fourth" (75). For a description of the hermeneutics of the historical method preferred by the present writer, see Part One (= 3-104) of I. Provan, V. P. Long, and T. Longman III, *A Biblical History of Israel* (Louisville: Westminster John Knox, 2003) (hereafter Provan, Long, Longman, *BHI*); cf. also the earlier treatment in Long, *ABH,* esp. 169-200.

38. Troeltsch's own articulation of his historical method is found in "Über historische und dogmatische Methode in der Theologie," now available in E. Troeltsch, *Gesammelte Schriften,* vol. 2, *Zur religiösen Lage, Religionsphilosophie und Ethik,* 2nd edition (Aalen: Scientia Verlag, 1962 reprint; orig. 1922), 729-53. English readers may consult Troeltsch's essay titled "Historiography," in *Encyclopaedia of Religion and Ethics,* 13 vols., ed. J. Hastings (Edinburgh: T. & T. Clark, 1914), 4:716-23.

39. W. J. Abraham, *Divine Revelation and the Limits of Historical Criticism* (Oxford: Oxford University Press, 1982), ch. 5 (= 91-115).

40. Long, *ABH,* 123-35.

summary can suffice here. The key points to note in the brief descriptions below are (1) that each of the canons of the historical-critical method can be construed in more than one way and (2) that a given scholar's preference for a particular construal will (or at least should) reflect that scholar's control beliefs.[41]

The *principle of criticism* can be defined in at least two rather different ways: (1) as entailing *systematic doubt*[42] or (2) as implying a *careful and dispassionate appraisal* of one's sources and a readiness to revise one's understandings in the light of valid criticisms or new evidence. Whether a scholar tends toward the first or the second definition of what it means to be "critical" will depend to some degree on what the scholar thinks of a source's character. When the source is the Bible, background beliefs (theology, if you will) make some difference. In some respects of course the Bible should be treated like any other ancient source — carefully and competently analyzed to see what it might have to offer — but not in every respect. For instance, a Christian or Jewish scholar for whom the Hebrew Bible/ Old Testament is regarded as sacred scripture will not approach this source in *exactly* the same way that a non-theistic scholar might. A non-theist, to be logically consistent, will have to assume that whatever the biblical source has to say about God or his actions cannot count as true in any meaningful sense (at least not in any ontological or historical sense), because God finds no place in a non-theist's worldview, except perhaps as the "imaginary friend" of the credulous.[43] A Christian scholar, by contrast, will want to acknowledge the God presented in scripture as more than a mere "literary icon." Whatever uncertainties may remain in regards to the interpretation of this or that biblical passage, the reality (ontological and historical, if you will) of the God of scripture will count as a given. We see, then, that while it may be appropriate, or at least logically valid, for a non-theist to construe the principle of criticism as enjoining systematic doubt of the Bible's metaphysical assertions, for the theist this may be "the most inappropriate procedure imaginable for dealing with the Bible."[44] The theist will want to construe the principle of criticism in the milder sense of careful and dispassionate appraisal.

The second canon of the Troeltschian historical-critical method is the *principle of analogy*. The gist of this principle as commonly understood and applied is that present experience provides the criterion for making probability judgments

41. In practice, scholars are often inconsistent in assuring consistency between control beliefs and methodological practices (more on this presently).

42. Cf., e.g., Van A. Harvey, *The Historian and the Believer: The Morality of Historical Knowledge and Christian Belief* (New York: Macmillan, 1966), 111; G. W. Ramsey, *The Quest for the Historical Israel: Reconstructing Israel's Early History* (London: SCM, 1982), 7.

43. The non-theist must, nevertheless, at the very least acknowledge as a historical datum the fact of the theistic belief and its potential to influence the course of history.

44. So G. Maier, *Biblical Hermeneutics*, trans. R. W. Yarbrough (Wheaton, IL: Crossway, 1994), 25; cited in Long, *ABH*, 178, which see for fuller discussion.

about what may or may not have occurred in the past. Only that which is in keeping with normal or habitual human experience can qualify as a "historical" occurrence. The principle of analogy's motto is "the present is the key to the past." There is some force in this principle, of course, but differing control beliefs will lead to differing understandings of how the principle of analogy is construed. In its common, *narrow* formulation, the principle of analogy can lead to an unnecessarily reductionistic approach to what can count as "historical." For instance, in his quest for the historical King David, S. McKenzie begins with J. M. Miller's assumption that the past is "basically analogous to the present and to what is known of similar societies and circumstances" and then expands this principle of analogy to suggest that "people of all time have the same basic ambitions and instincts."[45] While these generalities may be true enough *as generalities,* to apply the principle of analogy narrowly in such a way that exceptions *cannot* occur, or at least cannot count as "historical," is reductionistic. Surely, "it is simply a matter of logic that what is generally the case about human reality (to the extent that this can be established) need not always be the case, whether in the present or the past."[46]

Having adopted a narrow definition of the principle of analogy, McKenzie finds it "simply beyond belief," for instance, "that the crown prince [Jonathan] would surrender his right to the throne in deference to David"; and on this basis he concludes that Jonathan's abdication cannot be historical.[47] A less mechanistic worldview, to say nothing of a fully theistic worldview in which *religious impulses also count as historical data,* can yield a very different, wider understanding of the principle of analogy and, in turn, of Jonathan's behavior. The present may indeed be the key to the past — though I would also argue conversely that our beliefs about the past are key to our understanding of the present — but not everyone's experience of the present or beliefs about the past are the same. Jonathan's deference to David, remarkable as it appears, may have been prompted — if we take our cues from the text of 1 Samuel — by a sense that God's hand was no longer on the house of Saul but on another (cf. 1 Sam. 15:28). Reference to "God's hand" will resonate with some people because it is concordant with their theistic control beliefs and their present experience, but it will make little sense to those for whom God does not exist.

To offer another example, if Christian interpreters experience what they believe to be answers to prayer *in the present,* they will find it no great hurdle to believe that answers to prayer, such as God's answers to Elijah's prayer in 1 Kings 18:36-37 or to Elisha's in 2 Kings 6:17-18, may have occurred in the past. For such interpreters, accounts of answered prayer might pass the principle-of-analogy

45. S. L. McKenzie, *King David: A Biography* (Oxford: Oxford University Press, 2000), 44.

46. Provan, Long, Longman, *BHI,* 100.

47. McKenzie, *King David,* 84-85.

test and thus count as "historical" in a broad sense, *depending always of course on whether genre-sensitive reading leads to the conclusion that a historical truth claim has been made in the first place.*

Whether accounts of answered prayer become part of a history one is writing depends on the kind of history one is attempting and the kind of audience to be addressed. For non-theistic interpreters, "answered prayers" may count as psychological or even psychic experiences but will have no further reality. For theistic interpreters, a far greater, interpersonal (indeed, divine-human) "event" may be understood. Theistic historians may not always speak overtly of such things in the histories they write, but they will at least leave a place in their histories for including such elements when the audience and occasion are appropriate. What they must avoid is succumbing to "some alternative view or blend of views that happens to be in fashion." They must beware of growing "accustomed to the current assumptions of the academic world, positivist, historicist, Marxist or whatever."[48]

The third canon of Troeltschian historical criticism is the *principle of correlation.* This principle states that historical events are bound up in a nexus of causation. Events do not simply happen as bolts out of the blue, unconnected with prior causative factors. Historical events are precipitated, and they, in turn, precipitate other events. As commonly construed, the principle of correlation allows only two kinds of causation in history: human agency and natural forces (or a combination of the two). The absence of *divine* agency in this formulation creates severe strain with the biblical texts where "divine involvement in human affairs" is frequently assumed and on occasion "depicted as direct and overt."[49] How this tension is negotiated will depend, again, on the control beliefs embraced by this or that interpreter. Abraham helpfully distinguishes between a *material* principle of correlation and a *formal* one. According to the *material* definition, the driving forces in history are human agency and natural forces (as noted above). But according to the *formal* definition, which speaks of *personal* (not just *human*) agency, divine agency may also find its place. Understandably, the formal definition of the principle of correlation will appeal to theists.[50]

The point in all this is that "the historical-critical method" is not as straightforward as some seem to assume when appeal is made to method as providing an objective arena where scholars can simply lay aside their control beliefs and play by agreed-upon "rules of the game." The minute we take up a method, we effec-

48. D. W. Bebbington, *Patterns in History: A Christian View* (Downers Grove, IL: InterVarsity Press, 1979), 186. For further discussion of the principle of analogy, see especially Abraham, *Divine Revelation,* 100-105; followed by Long, *ABH,* 129-31; and most recently and thoroughly, Provan, Long, Longman, *BHI,* 70-73.

49. J. M. Miller, *The Old Testament and the Historian* (Philadelphia: Fortress, 1976), 17.

50. See Abraham, *Divine Revelation,* 105-9.

tively, even if unconsciously, allow ourselves to be guided by the control beliefs underlying that method, whether or not we agree with these control beliefs or are even aware of them. Where this fact is not recognized — and it often enough appears not to be — interpreters can find themselves using methods that assume control beliefs quite contrary to their own. For instance, Christians employing a historical method whose principle of *criticism* enjoins principled doubt of the Bible, whose principle of *analogy* sweeps every purported unique or unpredictable occurrence from the stage of history, and whose principle of *correlation* excludes all but human agency and natural forces as drivers of history, will find themselves submitting (even if only for the sake of method) to control beliefs out of accord with the Bible's own view of things and thus subversive to Christian faith.

Instances of (schizophrenic?) methodological practice leading ultimately to a crisis of faith and, in some cases, to loss of faith are all too common. Plainly stated, the competing theology underlying the most commonly practiced version of the historical-critical method can over time undermine and even overwhelm one's personal theology as derived from Scripture. But this need not, and should not, happen. Theistic and, more specifically, Christian thinkers should make certain that the historical method they employ is robust enough to take into account a full set of Christian background beliefs, including for instance belief in God as history's "master semiotician,"[51] belief in the Bible as revelatory of the divine character and divine activity, and so forth. This advocacy of a specifically theistic (even Christian) historical-critical method is not meant to obscure the fact — noted already above — that Christian historians must *in certain respects* approach the Bible as they would any other ancient text. Linguistic and literary features, historical background, date and place of writing and editing (where these can be known), and so forth, all need to be considered. Texts need to be read with as much "ancient literary competence" as possible, including genre sensitivity, alertness to differing standards of citation and historical reportage, etc.[52] But the Christian historian will want to work to a method such as described above, where *criticism* implies careful and thoughtful appraisal, where *analogy* assumes not a narrow but a wide definition (in which unique or unexpected events are not excluded), and where *correlation* regards even an event as unprecedented as the Incarnation not as a bolt out of the blue but as the subtly presaged fulfillment of the grand narrative of the First Testament.

In short, Christian biblical historians should not do their work as if their

51. M. Sternberg, *The Poetics of Biblical Narrative: Ideological Literature and the Drama of Reading* (Bloomington: Indiana University Press, 1985), 118.

52. On what is meant by "ancient literary competence," see, e.g., R. Alter, *The Art of Biblical Narrative* (London: Allen & Unwin; New York: Basic Books, 1981), 185, 188; J. Barton, *Reading the Old Testament: Method in Biblical Study* (London: Darton, Longman & Todd, 1984), 26-29; Long, *ABH,* 33-34, 42-43.

Christian commitments made no difference. A second thing they should not do is stand on the sidelines of historical scholarship only to arrive late in the day to point out what is amiss in the work the "real historians" have been doing. As Wolterstorff insists in an essay on "Public Theology or Christian Learning," what we *don't* need is Christian theology that simply

> takes the results of the various academic disciplines, and then performs on those results such activities as setting those results within a larger theological context, pointing out similarities between reality as seen within some nontheological discipline and reality as seen within theology, and so forth.[53]

What we need, according to Wolterstorff, is theologically faithful academicians. To criticize is not enough. Indeed, when theologians now and then "criticize certain results" and describe their criticisms as "prophetic critique," those actually practicing the discipline are likely to perceive the criticisms simply as complaint:

> The theologian is a complainer. Those who work within the discipline have been laboring in the hot midday sun. Now, as cool breezes begin to blow, the theologian turns up and complains about what has been accomplished. Why wasn't he working in the field when economics [for instance] was being developed? Why does he only turn up when the workers rest?[54]

What is needed according to Wolterstorff is not, for instance, "a theology of economics but theologically faithful economics."[55] With respect to histories of Israel, what is needed is not a theology of history but theologically faithful histories. Every discipline needs Christians who are fully engaged *as full-bodied Christians.*

For all that unifies good scholars — thoroughness, command of the data, logic of deduction, etc. — the diversity of their "competing theologies" will lead them, if they are consistent, to similar diversity of method, which in turn will result in "competing histories." Both the "eyes of faith" and the "eyes of unfaith" affect how we see things and what we do with what we see.[56] This leads us to a further question:

53. N. Wolterstorff, "Public Theology or Christian Learning?" in *A Passion for God's Reign: Theology, Christian Learning, and the Christian Self,* ed. M. Volf (Grand Rapids: Eerdmans, 1998), 65-87, on 76.

54. Wolterstorff, "Public Theology or Christian Learning?" 77.

55. Wolterstorff, "Public Theology or Christian Learning?" 77.

56. The recent work of J. B. Kofoed, and particularly his description of the "path-dependent" character of biblical historical scholarship, is very helpful in elucidating this basic point; see, e.g., J. B. Kofoed, *Text and History: Historiography and the Study of the Biblical Text* (Winona Lake, IN: Eisenbrauns, 2005); "The Role of Faith in Historical Research: A Rejoinder,"

"Can We Still Talk?": On Inter-Faith Dialogue

I am, of course, not using "inter-faith dialogue" in its normal sense. But in view of all that has been discussed so far regarding the character and content of control beliefs lying below the visible surface of academic discussion, to speak of "inter-faith dialogue" is not far off the mark. The work of biblical scholars and historians (and indeed of all who are interested in either Bible or history) takes place in the context of belief, or faith. P. R. Davies, for instance, characterizes himself as a "nonreligious believer,"[57] by which he must mean a non-believer in religion; but the expression he uses is apt in any case, as it recognizes that he, like everyone else, is a believer in something, even if it is the non-existence of something. Davies's non-theistic faith comes to expression in various ways in his scholarship. In a discussion of historical explanation, for instance, he remarks that "history without a god is a more 'economical' explanation (in Occam's sense)."[58] This claim is perfectly consistent with *Davies's* faith stance, but not with everyone's. That other people, including the present writer and a host of theistic scholars, should see things differently is also equally consistent with *their* faith positions. Faith and learning are inextricably tied, and it is encouraging that increasing numbers of scholars are at least implicitly acknowledging this fact by offering occasional autobiographical glimpses, with an eye to conveying something of how their own control beliefs have been shaped.[59]

SJOT 21, no. 2 (2007): 275-98, esp. 291-92; the rejoinder is to T. L. Thompson, "The Role of Faith in Biblical Research," *SJOT* 19 (2005): 111-34.

57. P. R. Davies, *Memories of Ancient Israel: An Introduction to Biblical History — Ancient and Modern* (Louisville: Westminster John Knox, 2008), 177.

58. P. R. Davies, "Biblical Israel in the Ninth Century?" in *Understanding the History of Ancient Israel,* ed. H. G. M. Williamson (Oxford: Oxford University Press, 2007), 49-56.

59. To cite just a few examples: J. W. Rogerson, in his recent *A Theology of the Old Testament: Cultural Memory, Communication, and Being Human* (London: SPCK, 2009), describes himself as an "Anglican priest whose faith in its present form owes much to modern Lutheran German theology," who also is "a humanist and a socialist," and who sets the agenda of his book by his own "perception of the human condition in today's world(s)" (11); W. G. Dever, in *What Did the Biblical Writers Know and When Did They Know It? What Archaeology Can Tell Us about the Reality of Ancient Israel* (Grand Rapids: Eerdmans, 2001), details over a few pages his journey from Christian fundamentalist upbringing to liberal Protestantism to his eventual conversion to non-theistic Judaism (ix-xi); Davies, as we have seen, is quite open in a number of places about his atheism; and more examples could be mentioned, space permitting. Occasionally one encounters witting bifurcation, as in K. L. Noll's parenthetical comment, "for the record, I am theistic off the job and professionally agnostic" ("The Ethics of Being a Theologian," *The Chronicle of Higher Education,* http://chronicle.com/article/The-Ethics-of-Being-a/47442/ [accessed March 26, 2010]). For a description of how theological commitments inform (not determine) my own work and that of some of my colleagues, see chapter 5 of Provan, Long, Longman, *BHI* (especially 101-4); cf. also Long, *ABH,* 175.

If scholars operate, then, under very different control beliefs, the question is whether fruitful dialogue is still possible among them. Can we still talk?[60] Is history-of-Israel scholarship destined to continue generating as much heat as light? Or is the "rational, considerate and informed" dialogue to which H. G. M. Williamson's recent edited volume, *Understanding the History of Ancient Israel,* aspires a possibility?[61] Might we, despite our differences, learn to get along and even to benefit from one another? Perhaps we could derive most benefit *precisely in the areas of our disagreements,* by pressing one another for *argument* and not mere *assertion* or *assumption.* I believe that we can do better, better even than was accomplished in parts of the Williamson volume.[62] But to do better, we must consider carefully how we frame our discussions and how we conduct them. Perhaps a good way to begin framing our discussions is to recognize three categories of scholars currently involved in the study of ancient Israel. The first is what we may call . . .

Metaphysical and Methodological Theists

These scholars are characterized by a consistency of metaphysic and method, of faith and academic practice. In keeping with the Bible's own view, they tend to believe that God not only exists but that he is active in history in both event and word. They are likely to concur with G. Maier that the OT simply "cannot speak of God without telling of the history brought about by him, nor can it speak of history, without bringing it into relation with God."[63] They are not content with the a- or anti-theological approaches to history that have evolved since the Enlightenment.[64] They tend to share the biblical prophets' view of history as God's

60. N. P. Lemche, "Conservative Scholarship-Critical Scholarship: Or How Did We Get Caught by This Bogus Discussion?" *The Bible and Interpretation,* http://www.bibleinterp.com/articles/Conservative_Scholarship.shtml (accessed May 28, 2010), has wistfully suggested that we can't (or shouldn't be allowed to), but see my response (V. P. Long, "Conservative Scholarship–Critical Scholarship: Can We Talk?" *The Bible and Interpretation,* http://www.bibleinterp.com/articles/Long_Conservate_Critical_Scholarship.shtml [accessed May 28, 2010]).

61. See Williamson, ed., *Understanding the History of Ancient Israel,* xiv.

62. See V. P. Long, "Review of *Understanding the History of Ancient Israel,* ed. H. G. M. Williamson (Proceedings of the British Academy; Oxford: Oxford University Press, 2007)," *Themelios* 34 (2009): 94-96.

63. "Wahrheit und Wirklichkeit im Geschichtsverständnis des Alten Testaments," in *Israel in Geschichte und Gegenwart,* ed. Gerhard Maier (Wuppertal and Giessen: R. Brockhaus Verlag; Basel: Brunnen Verlag, 1996), 9-23; quote from 20 (my translation). Full English translation now available in Long, *Israel's Past in Present Research,* 192-206.

64. For discussion of the "anti-theological tendencies in some historical critical approaches," see the section by that name in Long, *ABH,* 123-35.

conversation with his people.[65] Indeed, they believe that God is central to history, and that it is impossible rightly to understand the *meaning* of history if God is marginalized or denied. In holding such views, these scholars sense a closer affinity to believers of ancient times than to secularists of today. As consistent metaphysical and methodological theists, they will resist the charge that their rejection of hard-core Enlightenment rationalism and naturalism is a collapse into irrationalism and will insist, rather, that this would be the case only if their theism were in fact mistaken. Even then, their approach would not be irrational, just mistaken.

A second approach, the opposite of the first, is that of . . .

Metaphysical and Methodological Non-Theists

P. R. Davies, cited above, represents this category of scholar. Unlike those in the first category, scholars of this second type will experience considerable tension with the biblical text, especially as regards its belief in God and in God's involvement in history. Theirs is "a world-view incompatible with that of the biblical writings." With their rejection of the biblical notion of God as that "transcendental being who can comprehend, indeed controls, all history," they lose also the possibility of meaning in history that supersedes the limited vision of the knowing human subject(s).[66] Such scholars, like the first category, are characterized by a consistency of worldview and method. Their approach is not irrational, just mistaken from the vantage point of theists. There is also a third category, a kind of hybrid of the first two. It comprises . . .

Metaphysical Theists and Methodological Non-Theists

These scholars believe that God exists (and they may even acknowledge him in some way), but they embrace a method deriving from a view of historical science that excludes "God-talk." Thus, they too, like their non-theistic colleagues, experience considerable tension in doing history from the biblical text, where God's presence is pervasive. This species of metaphysical theist but methodological non-theist is quite common in the academy, though some may be quite unaware of their hybrid nature and thus also unaware of why they feel the tensions they do when seeking to do biblical history. This category of scholars is typified by

65. Cf. H. W. Wolff, "The Understanding of History in the Old Testament Prophets," in *Essays on Old Testament Interpretation,* ed. C. Westermann (London: SCM, 1963 [German 1960]), 336-55; reprinted in Long, *Israel's Past in Present Research,* 535-51.

66. Davies, "Whose History?" 116-17.

an incongruency between the methods they employ and the model of reality they embrace.[67] There is a sense in which this approach, unlike the first two, is irrational. But perhaps it can be defended as a necessary compromise, a kind of middle way that makes fruitful dialogue possible between scholars otherwise fundamentally divided.

One of the best recent descriptions of this "middle way," though he doesn't *explicitly* commit himself to it, is presented by R. L. Webb in the introductory essay to an important collaborative study of the historical Jesus.[68] In a section entitled "Historical Explanation, Worldview, and the 'Supernatural,'"[69] Webb asks whether — and if so, how — fruitful conversation may be possible between those whose respective worldviews are in tension, either among themselves or with the object of their study. Webb wants to know how scholars whose "views of reality" differ markedly can agree to a common historical method. Working with a broad brush, Webb distinguishes two types of scholars: "ontological naturalists" and "critical theists" (which equate, respectively, to what we have been terming "non-theists" and "theists"). He then proposes three possible approaches to doing history, as indicated in his chart reproduced on page 383.

The two top approaches correspond to our categories two and one, respectively. Ontological naturalists believe in a closed universe. Nothing exists beyond the natural (material) world. And they write their histories accordingly. Critical theists believe in an open universe. Not just the natural world but the supernatural (spiritual) world also exists. And they, too, write their histories accordingly. It is possible for both ontological naturalists and critical theists to be entirely self-consistent in the historical method they adopt and in the history they write. The former will rule out as impossible all but the immanent, terrestrial drivers of history, while the latter will remain open to the possibility of transcendent agency. As an example of a contemporary scholar who operates as a critical theist, Webb cites N. T. Wright. The problem with these first two approaches, as Webb sees it, is that ontological naturalists and critical theists can find little common ground for conversation. Their respective worldviews are mutually contradictory. "Is there a way forward," Webb asks, "or must this ontological difference lead to a methodological impasse?"[70]

Webb's third approach, that of "methodological naturalistic history," is de-

67. A reverse variety of this hybrid class may also exist — viz., metaphysical non-theists and methodological theists. Davies ("Whose History?" 117 n. 19), for instance, faults W. G. Dever and B. Halpern, both agnostics or atheists by Davies's account, for inconsistently espousing a "view of history that is theistic."

68. R. L. Webb, "The Historical Enterprise and Historical Jesus Research," in *Key Events in the Life of the Historical Jesus: A Collaborative Exploration of Context and Coherence,* ed. D. L. Bock and R. L. Webb (Tübingen: Mohr Siebeck, 2009; Grand Rapids: Eerdmans, 2010), 9-93.

69. Webb, "Historical Enterprise," 39-54.

70. Webb, "Historical Enterprise," 41.

Diagram: Historical Method and Views of Reality

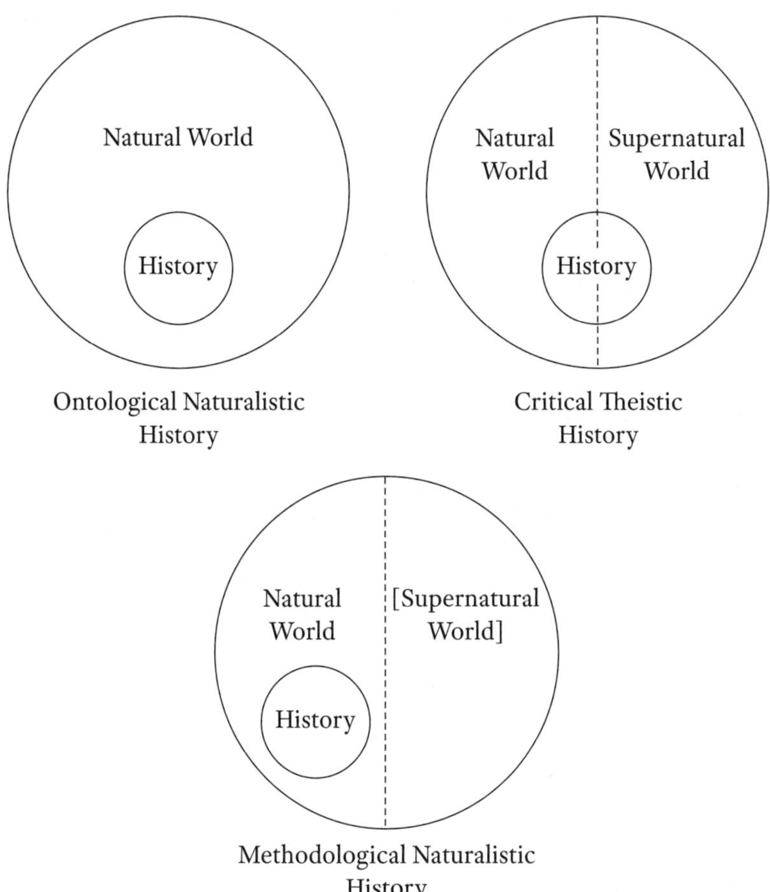

signed to establish "common ground between these two poles."[71] Practitioners of this approach may believe in an open or a closed universe, they may or may not discount the supernatural, but they mutually agree, as a point of *method,* to exclude all but the immanent, terrestrial drivers of history.

To return to the question we posed earlier, is this middle approach irrational? It is difficult to give a simple answer. Willingly to assume a mismatch of metaphysic and method is in one sense irrational. Still, as I myself have suggested,

> At times . . . for the sake of dialogue with those who do not share the same background beliefs, theistic historians may legitimately adopt a qualified ma-

71. Webb, "Historical Enterprise," 41.

terial conception of correlation — but this only as a temporary methodological constraint. In other words, theistic historians may choose not to talk about all they believe in order to talk profitably, even if on a minimalist level, with those who believe less.[72]

In the same context, however, I note two dangers inherent in the methodological naturalist histories (what I call lowest-common-denominator histories):

> First, whenever talk of divine agency is methodologically excluded, there can be a real temptation to seek an exclusively natural explanation for each and every occurrence in the past, even for those occurrences that the Bible presents as involving direct divine action.[73]

This is not to suggest that divine action (even divine "wonders") and natural explanations are necessarily mutually exclusive. One need only think of verses like Exodus 14:21 ("Then Moses stretched out his hand over the sea. The LORD drove the sea back by a strong east wind all night, and turned the sea into dry land; and the waters were divided") or Joshua 3:16 ("the waters flowing from above stood still, rising up in a single heap far off at Adam") to realize that divine interventions can and often do include aspects of natural causation.[74] But theists will at least want to resist the temptation to allow a natural explanation to exclude *any* notion of divine causation, even if they choose not to bring the latter explicitly into historical discussion in certain contexts.

A second danger when adopting the minimal "methodological naturalist" approach

> is that biblical historians may unwittingly allow the minimalist method, adopted for the sake of dialogue, to begin to infect their model of reality. Methodological procedure can all too easily slide into metaphysical profession.[75]

When this happens, one has allowed limited and limiting methods to *determine* one's model of reality, whereas it should be one's model of reality (one's control beliefs) that determines which methods are appropriate. This is not to deny, of course, that true knowledge gained through appropriately deployed methods can lead to refinements (or even more sweeping alterations) of one's

72. Long, *ABH,* 132-33.

73. Long, *ABH,* 133.

74. On Exodus 14:21, see the interesting speculations of Cambridge physicist C. J. Humphreys (*The Miracles of Exodus: A Scientist's Discovery of Extraordinary Natural Causes of the Biblical Stories* [San Francisco: HarperSanFrancisco, 2003]); and on Joshua 3:16, see Provan, Long, Longman, *BHI,* 174 and literature cited there.

75. Long, *ABH,* 133-34.

control beliefs. The point, rather, is that one should take care lest a given method (especially a lowest-common-denominator method) unwittingly become confused with one's fuller model of reality. When this happens, one becomes like

> the fisherman who is convinced that his fishing hole contains no fish smaller than five centimetres in length, simply because he has never caught any. When a bystander points out that the fisherman's net has a mesh too large to catch fish smaller than five centimetres, the fisherman insists, mistakenly, that what his net (method) cannot catch does not exist (model of reality).[76]

Webb does not seem to be particularly concerned about this danger, but I suspect that this is because he assumes a narrow, technical definition of what constitutes "history." He defines the term " 'history' *not* in the sense of past event" but in the sense of a "narrative account" of "*human* events, actions, and responses" (my emphasis). By this narrow definition, many an event of the past does not count *technically* as "a *historical* event."[77] "[T]he concern of history per se is not the totality of reality even in the natural sphere of the physical, space-time universe."[78] Geological events, meteorological events, and so forth may count as *past* events, but unless they impinge directly on human activity — Webb cites as an example Hurricane Katrina[79] — they are by definition not to be regarded as *historical* events. This technical definition of "history," a definition shared by many historians, will seem to some historians and non-historians alike as too narrow and limiting. It might seem to exclude, for instance, " 'middle-range explanations' — what we today would call sociological, economical, geographical, climatic considerations"[80] or even to effect an unhealthy division between theology and history. But Webb responds:

> This is not a bifurcation and separation of history and theology; rather, the point is that history has narrow and specific limits, and that history can operate in this way without imposing an ontological judgment on the existence of a supernatural realm. The methodological naturalistic view allows historians who have differing worldviews to participate together in the historical enterprise in spite of their differing worldviews — much in the same man-

76. Long, *ABH,* 134; see also Hans Peter Dürr's parable of the ichthyologist and the metaphysician, as described by J. Spieß, "Die Geschichtlichkeit der Heiligen Schrift," *Jahrbuch für Evangelikale Theologie* 4 (1990): 117.

77. Webb, "Historical Enterprise," 17.

78. Webb, "Historical Enterprise," 42.

79. Webb, "Historical Enterprise," 17.

80. J. H. Hayes, "The History of the Study of Israelite and Judaean History," in *Israelite and Judaean History,* ed. J. H. Hayes and J. M. Miller (London: SCM, 1977), 1-69, on 39.

ner as scientists can participate in the scientific enterprise yet have differing worldviews.[81]

Webb makes about as good a case for the methodological naturalist position as can be made, I think. And provided that everyone is and remains crystal clear — which, it must be said, many aren't and don't — about the historical method *not* describing the totality of past reality, and provided that everyone is and remains alert to the twin dangers noted above — namely, (1) wrongly filling in the blanks with purely natural explanations when God-talk is excluded from history and (2) unwittingly allowing methodological convention to slide over into metaphysical conviction — then the methodological naturalist approach, the middle way, may provide a means for fruitful conversation between theists and non-theists. It will, by definition, be a "minimalist" conversation, but so long as the cautions just issued are observed, this approach is neither incoherent nor irrational.

In practice, of course, the theist might choose to toggle back and forth between the critical theist approach (very appropriate when conversing with fellow theists) and the methodological naturalist approach (when conversing with non-theists). More often than not, however, the default position in the academy is in the direction of naturalism, whereby much of what the Bible seems to say *about the past* simply can't be discussed. An alternative methodological approach that might commend itself in "mixed groups" would be for all participants, theists and non-theists alike, to suspend disbelief for the time being and assume the control beliefs *of the text* as a "reading strategy." The advantage of this approach would be that fruitful conversations could develop between theists and non-theists regarding what the *theists* of the biblical texts actually believed about their own history.[82] In such a discussion, some would simply be "acting as if" they were theists for the sake of discussion, just as in the methodological naturalistic approach some are asked to "act as if" they are non-theists for the sake of discussion. I believe that there may be a time and place for both conversations to take place. Rather than our "competing theologies" and their resultant "competing histories" forever causing discord and even discourtesy, perhaps mixed groups could decide in advance of each discussion whether they wish to take on theistic or non-theistic guise. At the end of the day, of course, theists will likely remain theists, and non-theists non-theists, though careful and courteous conversation might well open eyes on both sides of the divide to things they had not yet seen. In any case, this kind of approach would regularly remind participants in debate of the subsurface portion of their respective icebergs and thus enable them to ascertain at what level their disagreements actually lie.

81. Webb, "Historical Enterprise," 47.

82. See Long, *Israel's Past in Present Research*, 580-92, for a brief description of what this might look like.

So, "can we still talk?" I believe we can. But we must think clearly not only about how we *frame* our discussions but also about how we *conduct* ourselves in discussion. Recent writings in history-of-Israel studies are not lacking in admonitions to do better in how we converse, to avoid ad hominem arguments, to cease dismissing people because of their supposed motivations, and to deal instead with their arguments. But, regrettably, admonition often surpasses performance. While it is tempting to cite specific examples here, and no doubt it might be entertaining (except perhaps to the exemplars), for me to do so would risk breaching the very principles I wish to commend. And so, I shall just leave it there for now.

As we bring this essay to a conclusion, we may ask one final question.

"Why All the Fuss?": Concluding Reflections

Why should people care so much about the history of ancient Israel? Why is the competition between those writing the histories so fierce at times? The answers to these questions are likely to be as diverse as the competing theologies (or, more dispassionately, the diverse control beliefs) of those engaged in the discussion. For many, of course, political agendas are in play; how deep are the "native roots" of those currently occupying (or not) the land that once was called Canaan? For others, it may simply be about the thrill of academic victory or the agony of academic defeat. For very many biblical scholars, it has to do with intellectual integrity and, perhaps more importantly still, with a desire to continue to improve our understanding of the Bible, reading it as best we can on its own terms and doing justice as best we can to all its varied speech-acts and truth claims, including its apparently historical truth claims.[83] As I. Finkelstein once remarked with respect to a particular period in Israel's ancient history, "Apart from the specific issue of the rise of Early Israel, it has become a debate over the historicity of the biblical text and the value of archaeology in historical research."[84]

But why such concern for the "historicity of the biblical text"? An answer to this question was adumbrated already in the first paragraph of this essay, and to attempt a fully satisfying answer would take us well beyond the scope of this

83. I say "apparently historical," because grasping the truth claims of the "foreign literature" of Scripture is always the prior and ongoing task. After all, "it is no good defending a text with respect to claims that it never makes" (Long, *ABH,* 96). As we learn to read texts better, in keeping with their ancient conventions, our understanding of their historical import also improves. Discussions of orality and cultural memory, for instance, may add nuance to our understanding of what we mean when we speak of the Bible's historical truth claims.

84. I. Finkelstein, "The Rise of Early Israel: Archaeology and Long-Term History," in *The Origin of Early Israel — Current Debate: Biblical, Historical and Archaeological Perspectives,* ed. S. Aḥituv and E. D. Oren, Beer-Sheva 12 (Jerusalem: Ben-Gurion University of the Negeb Press, 1998), 7-39, on 7.

essay. Suffice it to say, then, that for many Christian scholars, and indeed for Christians generally, it has to do with something lying very close to the heart of their "control beliefs." With all that must be insisted upon in terms of proper interpretation and the provisional nature of our understandings of biblical texts, the importance of *history* in the "history of redemption" seems inescapable. To return to the Pauline pronouncement cited at the start of this essay: "If Christ has not been raised, then our proclamation has been in vain and your faith has been in vain" (1 Cor. 15:14). And if Christ did not die, he could not have been raised. And if Christ did not live, he could not have died. So did Christ live, historically? The very heart of Christian faith rushes quickly to historical questions. And these historical questions give rise to others, pressing backward into the lives of the forebears of this greater Son of David, and forward into the lives of his followers, some of whom are still alive today.

THIRTEEN

Ehrman's Equivocation and the Inerrancy of the Original Text

Peter J. Williams

The idea of an inerrant or even an infallible original text of Scripture has been a matter of wide controversy. In part such controversy has merely reflected fundamental divisions over the nature of Scripture, its historical reliability, and the extent and essence of its authority. However, it is the contention here that the controversy has partly been complicated by the multivalence of key terms being used by advocates of inerrancy. This means that, while advocates of inerrancy are carefully presenting nuanced arguments that are exegetically well grounded and logically compelling, there are stumbling blocks to their message other than the sheer offensiveness of a doctrine of inerrancy. Advocates of inerrancy need to adopt clearer terminology to ensure that the doctrine is correctly understood at the popular level. In addition, this essay argues that the burden of proof should be on those who distrust the basic integrity of the New Testament text. The work of Bart D. Ehrman is used to illustrate the problems that can arise through terminological confusion and when the burden of proof is wrongly shifted onto those who maintain the basic integrity of the New Testament text.

Bart Ehrman and the Inerrancy of the Originals

The story of Bart Ehrman has become well known through his autobiographical Introduction to his best-selling book *Misquoting Jesus.*[1] After a conversion expe-

1. Bart D. Ehrman, *Misquoting Jesus: The Story Behind Who Changed the Bible and Why* (New York: HarperSanFrancisco, 2005), 1-15; UK edition: *Whose Word Is It? The Story Behind Who Changed the New Testament and Why* (London: Continuum, 2006). Ehrman also puts a personal testimony of his deconversion at the beginning of his other popular titles: *God's Problem: How the Bible Fails to Answer Our Most Important Question — Why We Suffer* (New York: HarperOne, 2008), 1-15; *Jesus, Interrupted: Revealing the Hidden Contradictions in the Bible (and Why We Don't Know about Them)* (New York: HarperOne, 2009), ix-xi, 15-18; and

rience in his teens, Ehrman studied at two well-known institutions committed to biblical inerrancy: Moody Bible Institute and Wheaton College. Through his studies, especially subsequently at Princeton Theological Seminary, Ehrman abandoned belief in biblical inerrancy and developed a prominent and successful career as a textual critic. As a leading textual critic and ex-inerrantist he has critiqued the idea of biblical inspiration on many occasions, not least on the ground that it is meaningless to attribute the property of having being inspired to a document (the original) that is now lost.[2]

From observing the reception of Ehrman's writing and speaking it is clear that in mounting this critique he is touching what for many people is a raw nerve. His message can be summarized as follows: many Christians hold to the absolute authority of the original text of the Bible, but this is lost and they are therefore left with no absolute authority. Or to put it more succinctly: Christians follow something they do not have. This message is clearly attractive to many skeptical of Christianity, and worrying to many adherents of the faith. It appears that not only does Ehrman think that he has correctly represented Christian belief, but also that many Christians believe he has done so too.

I will maintain that in several ways Ehrman's case gains force through the logical fallacy of equivocation, namely the confusing of two separate meanings of the same terms. The key problem seems to be that central terms used in discussing a doctrine of Scripture — terms such as "Bible," "text," and "original" — can have both physical and non-physical meanings.[3] The focus of Ehrman's critique can often shift indiscriminately between valid but doctrinally irrelevant assertions that we do not have certain physical documents and doctrinally relevant but historically questionable assertions that we do not have the wording of the New Testament, which is of course non-physical. We consider key terms that may facilitate this confusion.

In addition, Ehrman's case gains force by unwarranted shifting of the burden of proof onto those who wish to maintain the integrity of an ancient text and by focusing on small areas of uncertainty while ignoring large and increasing areas of certainty.[4]

Forged: Writing in the Name of God — Why the Bible's Authors Are Not Who We Think They Are (New York: HarperOne, 2011), 1-5. There is at least as much tension between these different narratives as there is between the different synoptic portrayals of Jesus.

2. Ehrman, *Misquoting Jesus,* 211.

3. The seeds of some of these thoughts are expressed in an online review of *Misquoting Jesus* located at http://evangelicaltextualcriticism.blogspot.com/2005/12/review-of-bart-ehrman-misquoting-jesus_31.htm and in various postings on http://evangelicaltextualcriticism.blogspot.com.

4. Evidently during Ehrman's evangelical days he believed that "objective proofs" for the faith must exist, and he seems to have understood the term "proof" in a hard sense (Ehrman, *Forged,* 4). Thus Ehrman has probably ascribed an unwarranted burden of proof to Christianity

Equivocations Examined

The Term "Bible"

"Bible" is a multivalent term and a relative newcomer among theological terminology, arguably existing for only about half of church history, and in one of its senses for just over a third. There have been considerable shifts over time in the terms Christians have used for their sacred writings. In English only a few centuries ago "holy writ" and "holy Scripture," or "the Scriptures,"[5] were more common. However, the English term "Bible" (variously spelled) has also been used for the best part of a millennium and since at least the fourteenth century has carried two different meanings: the one referring to the collection of books that constitute holy Scripture, the other referring to a physical copy of these books. It is in this latter sense that the secondary plural developed, so that one may talk of a collection of *Bibles.* The *Oxford English Dictionary* (s.v.) thus gives the first definition as "The Scriptures of the Old and New Testament" and the second as "A copy of the Scriptures." The term is, of course, derived ultimately from Greek mediated via the Latin plural *biblia,* which changed into a singular in various Western European languages, facilitated by the fact that Latin *biblia* could be reanalyzed as a feminine singular and there was no corresponding singular **biblium* to prevent this.[6] It was only after it had been a singular for some time that a secondary plural developed.

The importance of this is that proponents of biblical inerrancy believe in the inerrancy of the Bible in only one of the two senses of the word "Bible," namely when it refers to the collection of books or Scriptures, not to a physical document containing those books.

Consider the following hypothetical exchange:

ENQUIRER: Do you believe the Bible is without error?

INERRANTIST: Yes.

ENQUIRER (holds up a particular Bible translation): Is this the Bible?

INERRANTIST: Yes.

ENQUIRER: So you believe that there are no errors in this Bible . . .

---

since before his deconversion. There is no evidence in Ehrman's writings that while being an adherent he ever properly understood either (a) evangelical doctrines of Scripture, or (b) classic evangelical epistemologies.

5. Capitalization, though there have been some significant shifts in usage over the centuries, is ignored here.

6. Max Pfister, *Lessico Etimologico Italiano* (Wiesbaden: Reichert Verlag, 1984-), 5:1467-68, knows of just one occurrence of the singular *biblium.*

INERRANTIST: Well, actually there may be errors because it is only a translation of the Bible.

This highlights the awkwardness with which at the popular level it may seem necessary to qualify an initial statement of the inerrancy of Scripture. The exchange has, however, only been possible because of a level of multivalence in the word "Bible." If the exchange were adapted with the word "Scriptures" substituted for "Bible" it is likely that less awkwardness would be felt because the term more obviously puts the focus of discussion on the books as writings rather than on any particular copy or translation, and the enquirer would have had to ask "Is this *a copy of* the Scriptures?" It would be obvious therefore that one could not dismiss the inerrancy of the Scriptures simply by reference to a physical copy of them. Some people may be put off by the term "inerrancy" through what they perceive as backtracking: the proponent of inerrancy initially makes a bold statement — "the Bible is inerrant" — and then proceeds to list numerous qualifications. This procedure may be necessary, but we should at least consider whether there are alternatives.

There seems to have been a shift over time toward use of the term "Bible," particularly in popular parlance, and this results in a mismatch between the terms used in doctrinal definition and those used in common Christian parlance. As an example of technical discourse we may take the Chicago Statement on Biblical Inerrancy.[7] This statement uses the term "Scripture" fifty-seven times and the term "Scriptures" fourteen times (four times each qualified as "holy"). By contrast it uses the term "Bible" a mere sixteen times, "biblical" seven times, and "biblically" once. However, in the culture at large the proportions are rather different, and when large corpora of English are searched we see that the term "Bible" clearly now predominates over "Scripture" or "Scriptures":[8]

7. The problem with the name of this statement and of the International Council on Biblical Inerrancy is not one of content, but of branding. If "Bible" has two meanings then "biblical" is capable of relating to both of these meanings and as said earlier it is only in one of these two meanings that "Bible" may properly be said to be inerrant. A related issue is the definite article: "the Bible" is more generally used synonymously with "the Scriptures" whereas "a Bible" almost always designates a copy of the scriptures, which may contain some errors. Of course, we may defend the use of the term "biblical" by claiming that it generally relates to the Bible as a work, not to a Bible as a document.

8. Based on searches on 7 May 2010 of the British National Corpus, www.natcorp.ox.ac.uk, containing about 100 million words, and the Corpus of Contemporary American English, www.americancorpus.org, containing over 400 million words. I discuss the term "Bible" further in "The Bible, the Septuagint, and the Apocrypha: A Consideration of Their Singularity," in *Studies on the Text and Versions of the Hebrew Bible,* ed. G. A. Khan and Diana Lipton (Leiden: Brill, 2012).

Occurrences in large corpora

	American English		*British English*	
	sg.	pl.	sg.	pl.
Bible	11009	572	1941	106
Scripture	2399	1005	390	290

To illustrate the growth of the term "Bible" through time we may note that articles of faith dealing with Scripture in historic Reformed confessions entirely lack the word "Bible."[9] However, more recent evangelical statements of faith show a tendency to include this word. An example of this shift can be seen in the widely used doctrinal basis of the Universities and Colleges Christian Fellowship (UCCF; formerly Inter-Varsity Fellowship) in the UK. The article on Scripture had originally read:

> The divine inspiration and infallibility of Holy Scripture as originally given, and its supreme authority in all matters of faith and conduct.[10]

But when the article was revised for the sake of modernization it was replaced with the following:

> The Bible, as originally given, is the inspired and infallible Word of God. It is the supreme authority in all matters of belief and behaviour.[11]

"Scripture" was replaced by "Bible," which is obviously intended in the sense of the *OED*'s first meaning — the "Scriptures of the Old and New Testament." The change of wording therefore involves no shift in primary referent, but it does at least facilitate a shift of focus, since the new term introduced, namely "Bible," is multivalent and allows a focus on the physical object rather than on the words of the books themselves.

Although this shift does not by itself cause Ehrman's arguments to work, it does allow them to gain rhetorical force. After all, his contention appears to be that Christians adhere to a holy book they do not have, and the proof that they do not have it is the lack of a physical copy of the book. If Christians more widely spoke of the "inerrancy of the Scriptures" or the "inerrancy of Scripture" I imagine that Ehrman might find the target at least a little harder to hit.

9. Joel R. Beeke and Sinclair B. Ferguson, eds., *Reformed Confessions Harmonized: With an Annotated Bibliography of Reformed Doctrinal Works* (Grand Rapids: Baker, 1999), 10-19.

10. http://www.ciccu.org.uk/docbasis.php, accessed 15 June 2010. The Cambridge Inter-Collegiate Christian Union preserves the earlier form and calls it the doctrinal basis of the UCCF, without showing awareness that UCCF has officially adopted revised wording.

11. http://www.uccf.org.uk/about-us/doctrinal-basis.htm, accessed 15 June 2010.

The Term "Original"

A further term that provides ammunition for Ehrman is the word "original."[12] Of course, in the time of John Owen or Matthew Henry, "original" could mean simply "origin," especially in the phrase "divine original," but it is no longer used in this way. However, when the word "original" is used in an unqualified way adjectivally we must ask what noun is implied. Are we to understand it as original *language* (or *tongue*), original *text,* or original *manuscript?* Whatever noun we supply it is clear that earlier writers wrote about the original as something they possessed. For instance, commenting on 1 Corinthians 16:11 Matthew Henry says

> *Conduct him forth in peace, that he may come to me, for I look for him with the brethren* (*v.* 11); or *I with the brethren look for him* (the original will bear either), ἐκδέχομαι γὰρ αὐτὸν μετὰ τῶν ἀδελφῶν.[13]

Clearly Henry knew that he did not have the original manuscript (autograph), so we can eliminate that as a possible meaning for what he said. It seems that for him, as for many earlier writers, "original" was defined by contrast with what was translated. "Original" was not an absolute term; it could be made absolute by speaking of the *first original.*[14]

12. The field of textual criticism has been widely influenced by Eldon J. Epp's article "The Multivalence of the Term 'Original Text' in New Testament Textual Criticism," *HTR* 92 (1999): 245-81, so that the term "original text" is now generally avoided. Many of Epp's objections to the term, based on the works of Helmut Koester, Bart D. Ehrman, and William L. Petersen, are unconvincing if one is not already convinced of the models of early Christianity proposed by those scholars. For instance, part of the evidence cited from Koester (Epp, "Multivalence," 256) is that his comparisons of the *Secret Gospel of Mark* and canonical Mark help him to discern an earlier form of Mark behind canonical Mark. But if the *Secret Gospel of Mark* is in some way inauthentic then this is hardly a firm foundation on which to question the notion that there was an original text. My objection to the term "original text" is not the conviction that there was no original text, but that the expression itself is unclear.

13. Matthew Henry, *An Exposition of the New Testament,* vol. 8 (London: William MacKenzie, n.d.), 156. Cf. also the statement in the KJV preface: "The translation of the Seuentie dissenteth from the Originall in many places."

14. For instance, Matthew Poole, *Annotations on the Holy Bible* (1685; repr. as *Commentary on the Holy Bible* [Edinburgh: Banner of Truth Trust, 1962]), commenting on Genesis 6:15 and arguing that all the creatures would have been able to fit on Noah's ark, says "That the differing kinds of beasts and birds, which unlearned men fancy to be innumerable, are observed by the learned, who have particularly searched into them, and written of them, to be little above three hundred, whereof the far greatest part are but small; and many of these which now are thought to differ in kind, in their *first original* were but of one sort, though now they be so greatly altered in their shape and qualities, which might easily arise from the diversity of their climate and food, and other circumstances, and from the promiscuous conjunctions of those lawless creatures" (emphasis added).

By contrast with Henry who saw the original as something he possessed, we have Ehrman who takes it to be something lost. In writing of his own struggle with inerrancy he says:

> I kept reverting to my basic question: how does it help us to say that the Bible is the inerrant word of God if in fact we don't have the words that God inerrantly inspired, but only the words copied by the scribes — sometimes correctly but sometimes (many times!) incorrectly? What good is it to say that the autographs (i.e., the originals) were inspired? We don't *have* the originals! We have only error-ridden copies, and the vast majority of these are centuries removed from the originals and different from them, evidently, in thousands of ways.[15]

This is a fairly confused section. Ehrman claims that we do not have the words God inspired, but he has not demonstrated that to be the case. If John the Evangelist or his amanuensis wrote the letter sequence εναρχηηνολογος (John 1:1) then we *have* the words he wrote, whether we have the words in our minds or in a modern printed edition. One thing that Ehrman never seems to do is to attempt to show that we do not have (either in our minds or in manuscripts) all of the words that the authors wrote. In fact, the situation for the New Testament text is that there are no words that are known or even widely believed by textual critics to be missing from the New Testament text.[16]

Though Ehrman does show what is widely known, namely that there are variants in the manuscripts, this does not amount to a demonstration that we do not have the words God inspired. To do this he would have at least to demonstrate that some words that were alleged to be inspired have been lost, and at most to demonstrate that all words that were alleged to be inspired have been lost.

Then when he glosses the word "autographs" with the explanation "originals" it is clear that he is using the word "original" in a different sense from Henry. Clearly he means a physical entity — an actual manuscript. The problem here is that it is to misrepresent Christian belief to suggest that a physical manuscript was somehow inspired by God. Rather it was the words on the manuscript that, according to Christian belief, were inspired. Most importantly, when the sequence of words found on the autograph is copied onto another manuscript it does not become less inspired through being copied or written out a second time

15. Ehrman, *Misquoting Jesus,* 7.

16. The situation for the New Testament is somewhat different than for the Old, where it is widely held that wording is missing from a text such as 1 Samuel 13:1. For those who want to argue that some wording has been lost from the New Testament, the suggestion that an earlier ending of Mark's Gospel was once located after 16:8 surely provides a showcase. However, even in this case many scholars are convinced that the Gospel ended at 16:8 and there are no patristic sources that are clearly quoting lost wording. So while one cannot prove that nothing has been lost, equally one cannot prove that something has been.

(Exod. 34:1; Jer. 36:28) and Scripture even allows for Scripture to be lost for a time (2 Kgs. 22:8). In other words, Ehrman has simply mistaken what a Christian doctrine implies.[17]

A further difference between Henry and Ehrman is probably one of the burden of proof. Given that Ehrman does not distinguish clearly between the first manuscript and the wording on the first manuscript, we have to reconstruct his view. However, he frequently states that we have only "copies of the copies of the copies of the originals."[18] This implies a contrast between "original" and "copy," which probably would not make sense of what Henry says. Moreover, it seems that whereas Henry assumes that the words transmitted to him are those of the autograph unless shown otherwise, Ehrman takes the view that the words of a copy cannot be supposed to be those of the autograph under any circumstance. We will return to this below.

The Term "Text"

Aside from its recently acquired meaning of "text message," the word "text" is used in popular parlance both of a physical entity, an artifact with writing on it, and of the non-physical entity of writing abstracted from its physical context. In strict technical parlance it normally means the non-physical entity alone.[19]

Ehrman uses Galatians as a prime example of the problem of the idea of an original text. He says:

> Even at the point of the original penning of the letter, we have numerous difficulties to consider, which may well make us sympathetic with those who want to give up on the notion of knowing what the "original" text was. Galatia was not a single town with a single church; it was a region in Asia Minor (mod-

17. In addition to the problems noted here the word "original" has seemed to some less appropriate for the Old Testament, where it has not appeared adequately to allow for even minor editorial activity after composition (see Michael A. Grisanti, "Inspiration, Inerrancy, and the OT Canon: The Place of Textual Updating in an Inerrant View of Scripture," *JETS* 44 [2001]: 577-98). The problem can in part be reduced by remembering that *original* earlier was used in opposition to a translation and by recognizing that both *final* and *original* can refer to the same stage of a text.

18. Ehrman, *Misquoting Jesus,* 10.

19. Dictionaries, e.g. *OED, Collins Dictionary of the English Language* (2nd edition) appear understandably reluctant to admit this physical meaning. However, one can find numerous examples on the Internet where text is used to denote a physical object, e.g., "he held a text in his hand" (Catherine McGregor, "Bring It to Life: Youth Performing Socio-Politically in a Northern Urban Environment" [Ph.D. dissertation, Simon Fraser University, 2007], 358 [http://ir.lib.sfu.ca/bitstream/1892/4202/1/etd2800.pdf, accessed 18 June 2010]), or "the text weighed over ten pounds" (http://en.wikipedia.org/wiki/Hendrik_Christian_Andersen; accessed 18 June 2010).

> ern Turkey) in which Paul had established churches. When he writes to the Galatians, is he writing to one of the churches or to all of them? Presumably, since he doesn't single out any particular town, he means for the letter to go to all of them. Does that mean that he made multiple copies of the same letter, or that he wanted the letter to circulate to all the churches of the region? We don't know.[20]

Ehrman's example may not be well chosen, since Paul's call to recognize his extra-large handwriting (Gal. 6:11) most likely points to a single physical document being taken round the churches. But Ehrman's point is this: for some works it is likely that there was more than one "original text" and that in any case we cannot now have the original text or know what it was. Since Ehrman connects any conception of inerrancy with the idea of an original text (as he understands it) the non-existence of the original text makes inerrancy untenable.

From a rather different angle A. T. B. McGowan complains about the emphasis on the autographa, which we do not possess, in Warfield's doctrine of Scripture. He says,

> The second argument against inerrancy concerns the emphasis placed on the *autographa* by those in the Warfield tradition. If textual inerrancy is so vital to the doctrine of Scripture, why did God not preserve the *autographa* or precise copies of the same? Indeed, if inerrancy only applies to the *autographa* (which we do not possess), then surely it is a somewhat pointless affirmation? Everyone accepts that there are errors in the extant manuscripts and translations. What is the point of insisting that there once existed (very briefly) perfect versions of these texts, if we no longer possess them? Those who emphasize the inerrancy of the *autographa* are thus faced with a difficult question: "What was the point of God acting supernaturally to provide an inerrant text providentially if it ceased to be inerrant as soon as the first or second copy was made?"[21]

Though Ehrman and McGowan have very different perspectives on the scriptures they have in common a perception that supporters of inerrancy attribute inerrancy to something we do not have, namely the original text or autograph. Since Ehrman never engages with formal statements of evangelical doctrine, we may surmise that he is responding to evangelical doctrine as he perceived it during his youthful days as an evangelical. In the case of McGowan he is specifically responding to "those in the Warfield tradition." In this latter case it might at least be worth raising an initial query as to whether the question of the autographs

20. Ehrman, *Misquoting Jesus,* 58.

21. A. T. B. McGowan, *The Divine Spiration of Scripture: Challenging Evangelical Perspectives* (Nottingham: Apollos, 2007), 109.

is really so prominent within the Warfield tradition. At least in the case of Warfield himself the core ideas to which he returns are *revelation* and *inspiration,* not the original text, and it would be quite wrong to say that he holds, in McGowan's words, that "inerrancy only applies to the *autographa.*"

When Warfield did come to define a text in his *Textual Criticism of the New Testament* it is clear that he held to the immaterial definition of text. In fact he chose to open his book, remarkable for its lack of explicit theology, with a definition of "text" that runs for more or less four pages. The book begins:

> The word "text" properly denotes a literary work, conceived of as a mere thing, as a texture woven of words instead of threads. It designates neither, on the one side, the book which contains the text, nor, on the other side, the sense which the text conveys. It is not the matter of the discourse, nor the manner of it, whether logical, rhetorical, or grammatical. It is simply the web of words itself. It is with this understanding that the text of any work is concisely defined as the *ipsissima verba* of that work.[22]

After explaining the origins of the word "text" Warfield goes on to say:

> There is an important distinction, however, which we should grasp at the outset, between the text of a document and the text of a work.[23]

> The text of a document is the words on that document; the text of a work is "what ought to be the *ipsissima verba* of all the documents or copies that profess to represent it, — it is the original, or, better still, the intended *ipsissima verba* of the author. It may not lie in the document before us, or in any document. All existing documents, taken collectively, may fail to contain it. It may never have lain, perfect and pure, in any document. But if an element of ideality thus attaches to it, it is none the less a very real thing and a very legitimate object of search.[24]

Shortly later he says:

> Such are the limitations of human powers in reproducing writings, that apparently no lengthy writing can be duplicated without error. Nay, such are the

22. B. B. Warfield, *Textual Criticism of the New Testament* (London: Hodder & Stoughton, 1889), 1.

23. Warfield, *Textual Criticism,* 2.

24. Warfield, *Textual Criticism,* 3-4. Similarly, John M. Frame, *The Doctrine of the Word of God* (Phillipsburg, NJ: P&R, 2010), 243, says "what is at issue is not primarily the autographic document, but the autographic *text.* The *text* is a linguistic object that can be found in any number of physical media."

> limitations of human powers of attention, that probably few manuscripts of any extent are written exactly correctly at first hand. The author himself fails to put correctly on paper the words that lie in his mind.[25]

What is striking here is that Warfield shows full awareness of all of the arguments that over a century later Ehrman would use as objections to inerrancy. However, it is important not to mistake what Warfield believes. In the penultimate quotation he uses the word "original" and then states his preference for the synonymous phrase "the intended *ipsissima verba* of the author." Warfield makes it clear that this phrase was "better still" than "original." Thus it would hardly go against the flow of Warfield's thought to dispense with the word "original" entirely. Moreover, since Warfield states so clearly that these intended *ipsissima verba* of a work may never have existed in a physical copy, this opens the question as to whether a follower of Warfield would need to believe that the intended words of divine Scripture ever needed to have existed in their perfect and exact form in an actual document at the time of the human author in order for the necessary conditions of the making of Scripture to have been fulfilled.

If so, then McGowan's suggestion that followers of Warfield put emphasis on the autographa is not relevant for Warfield himself. An autograph is a physical entity. The text of an autograph is not only immaterial, but is also the text of a document. By Warfield's definition, the text of a document should not necessarily be equated with the text of a work of literature.

Here Warfield, though not mentioning the doctrine of Scripture, or even the text of the New Testament, shows full awareness of the view that to speak thus of the text of an author may seem idealistic. Yet his emphasis on the text as an immaterial entity that need not have a physical manifestation is hardly just an example of Platonism in theology (not that having echoes of Plato necessarily means that a view is wrong!). There are a number of biblical texts suggesting the primacy of the immaterial word over its physical copy. The Ten Words (Ten Commandments) were given orally first, and then in written form. When the only physical copy of the Ten Words was destroyed by Moses (Exod. 32:19), this did not make the words cease to exist or become uninspired; they were simply given again (Exod. 34:27-28). When Joshua spoke (to others or himself) the text of the book of the law, then the book was said to be in his mouth (Josh. 1:8). The book was wherever it was spoken, even though a physical copy might be absent. Similarly God's words to Jeremiah were clearly inspired before being written down (Jer. 36:18), and could not be destroyed even if one eliminated all physical copies of them (Jer. 36:28). In a rather different way John 1:1 and 1:14 stress the existence of word prior to physical form. In other words, Ehrman's insistence that inspiration is not a meaningful belief unless one can produce to him a perfect physical copy

25. Warfield, *Textual Criticism,* 7.

of a text not only fails to recognize that Christian doctrines are not focused on physical copies, but also makes a rather arbitrary insistence on the necessity of a physical copy of God's words in Ehrman's own vicinity.

The focus on the immaterial nature of God's words also accords with modern studies of orality in the ancient world including the Old Testament. Ancient reading was generally out loud,[26] and our tendency to see the written in opposition to the oral is not therefore appropriate. Oral communication may exist without writing, but written communication did not generally exist without oral communication. So while writing is important to spread and transmit God's words, there is no sense in which God's words become more inspired by virtue of being written down.

All this means that Warfield with his stress on the significance of the intended wording of the author is a very long way from stressing the significance of a physical lost document as he has sometimes been understood to have emphasized.

Resultant Ambiguity

We have seen so far that three of the key terms used in discussion of the inerrancy of Scripture, namely "Bible," "original," and "text," suffer from multivalence, and that there is a danger in each case that friend or foe of inerrancy alike may understand inerrancy to apply to one of these terms in a meaning that is not appropriate. One of the results of this discussion is that we can see that any emphasis that attributes inerrancy to a document (physical entity), rather than to the text of a document, is misguided. However, even the text on a document needs to be distinguished from the text of a work. It is to the text of the work, not of the document, that inerrancy applies. Therefore it is wrong to see inerrancy as having an emphasis on a physical entity that we no longer have.

The Burden of Proof: Do We Have the Wording or Not?

Having established that it is the wording, not the physical autographa, that matters, we need to consider whether or not we can have confidence that we have the wording of Scripture. This is partly a question of epistemology and of the burden of proof. Between the time of Matthew Henry and Bart Ehrman there clearly has been a significant shift from emphasizing what we have to what we do not have. For Ehrman it appears that one does not have the authorial wording until a

26. For classical references see Annette Weissenrieder and Robert B. Coote, *The Interface of Orality and Writing: Speaking, Seeing, Writing in the Shaping of New Genres,* WUNT 260 (Tübingen: Mohr Siebeck, 2010), x.

proof is produced that one does have it. One also wonders whether there could ever be a proof that would demonstrate to Ehrman's satisfaction that we had the authorial wording. On the other hand, Henry seems to hold to the position that what is brought to him by the testimony of manuscript witnesses *is* the authoritative wording. To dissuade Henry of this position we may imagine it would be necessary to adduce actual manuscript testimony.

Although the position of believing that what you have received is the intended wording of the author may appear more credulous than not believing it to be so, we may at least notice one difference between these approaches. Those who actively refuse to believe the wording to be that of the author and prefer to remain agnostic, are in an epistemically invulnerable position. This may seem to be its strength, but it is also a weakness since it means that no amount of textual evidence could ever move one from agnosticism to active belief. Their approach thus allows little room for falsification.

A further disadvantage with the skeptical position is that it has no (or little) forfeit if it is wrong. In most areas of life, such as investments or medicine, there are consequences both to right and wrong beliefs. However, in the discipline of history as now conceived skepticism is not penalized, but actively encouraged. Thus whereas there is a potential benefit or loss for an investor involved with adopting both the belief that the market will go up and the belief that it will go down,[27] for the historian there is a quite disproportionate loss of reputation for affirming something to be true when some doubt remains and no loss of reputation for disbelieving something when there is some limited evidence for its truth.

In addition we may note that Ehrman is unreasonably demanding proof concerning a negative if he asks others to demonstrate that the text has not changed, and in this case the negative is not possible to prove. When we work from the manuscript evidence we actually have, we observe the point made by both Warfield and Ehrman (among many others) that when a document of any significant length is made by copying, it is likely that errors are introduced. However, when we take the history of transmission we also see that the rate of introduction of errors, even in the earliest centuries, is not such that it creates a situation in which any part of the wording of the work is more likely to have been changed through transmission than preserved. Whether we work from late-fifteenth-century manuscripts of the New Testament and measure the rate of change from earlier documents, or consider the range of difference among the very earliest papyri and versions, we see that change in the wording through transmission is generally rarer than stasis.

In general, then, the presumption that we have the authorial wording until

27. I am aware that for hedge fund managers the forfeits do not depend on the rises or falls in the market, but the point still holds that there are consequences, including forfeits, for unwise choices.

evidence arises to the contrary seems a more reasonable position than to refuse to believe that we have the authorial wording until an impossibly high level of proof be obtained that we do. The rational status of belief in the correctness of the text is that of a *disprovable presumption.*

However, one can put the case for textual reliability much more strongly than this. Here we simply outline a number of different lines of argumentation that can be used to establish a high degree of confidence in our knowledge of the authorial wording of the New Testament.

1. It is possible to use many forms of *a fortiori* argumentation based on high levels of scholarly confidence of the wording of other ancient or classical works. In an overwhelming number of cases witnesses for the books of the New Testament outstrip other ancient works in number, geographical diversity, and age. The New Testament text also shows up in a great variety of material forms: papyrus, parchment, paper, stone, pottery; codex and scroll; majuscule and minuscule; continuous text, lectionary, and extract.
2. The New Testament writings are also almost invariably attested in a greater variety of languages than other ancient writings. For instance, John's Gospel existed in eight different dialectal versions of Coptic,[28] and in two pre-Jerome Latin versions,[29] the Vulgate, and in the Old Syriac and Peshitta versions, to mention early versions in just three languages. In the case of other ancient writings any one of these versions would, on its own, be taken to give scholars a reasonable level of confidence as to the content of a work.
3. In addition to manuscripts and translations (versions) we have extensive quotation of the New Testament by church fathers.
4. Any one of the three main categories of witness (Greek manuscript, versions, church fathers) on its own would be sufficient to be able to have detailed discussions of matters such as the grammatical style of the authors. Taken together these provide a mass of data allowing us to reach rational conclusions about how texts were transmitted. When we consider how we *know* texts were transmitted based on actual evidence, and extrapolate the same processes back into the short period before our earliest witnesses, we do not reach radical uncertainty about the wording of the books of the New Testament.
5. We are able to make a number of genealogical observations about the interrelationship of witnesses and thereby trace the occurrence of errors in manuscripts and discount them from the editions that we make.

28. C. H. Askeland, *John's Gospel: The Coptic Translations of Its Greek Text* (Berlin: de Gruyter, 2012).

29. Philip Burton, *The Old Latin Gospels: A Study of Their Texts and Language* (Oxford: Oxford University Press, 2000), 74.

6. The existence of manuscripts such as P52 and P90, containing parts of John 18 dating from the second century and coming from Egypt, suggests that large numbers of copies of parts of the New Testament were made in a short time. It would be logistically almost impossible for anyone to enter systematic changes into the text of any book once a significant multiplicity of copies was spread over a wide area.
7. For those who express confidence in their ability to reconstruct sources of the Old or New Testaments (e.g., Q as a Gospel source), an *a fortiori* case can be made for confidence in our knowledge of the text of the New Testament.
8. The history of the study of the wording of the New Testament gives us a high degree of confidence in that wording. The printed wording of the first Greek New Testament of Erasmus, based on seven manuscripts from the twelfth century or later, and on no more than four in any one instance, is relatively speaking reasonably close to the wording of modern critical editions. This means that the text that would be produced if we disposed of nearly five centuries of discovery would still be relatively similar to the modern text. In broad terms, if one were to dispose of our earliest 5,000 or so witnesses and then to make a critical text based on what remains, the difference between the text thus produced and critical editions such as the Nestle-Aland 28th edition would probably be less than the difference between the Textus Receptus of Erasmus and the Nestle-Aland edition.
9. The text of the New Testament does not depend on any single witness. We could ignore a favorite witness such as Codex Sinaiticus from the fourth century. How much would this change our text? The answer can be found by considering the edition that Tregelles made of Matthew and Mark, which differs relatively little from the Nestle-Aland edition. In fact, the editions of Tregelles, Tischendorf, and Eberhard Nestle were made without knowledge of the papyri that are now important for the text of the New Testament. Nevertheless, their editions do not differ greatly from those in the later twentieth century (Nestle-Aland 26th edition), which are made using knowledge of such papyri. Thus we can say that even the discovery of quite important witnesses makes only a small impact on the shape of the New Testament text in contemporary editions.
10. If one had grounds for rational confidence in the text in the sixteenth century, when the gap between the earliest available manuscripts and the time of composition of the New Testament was over one millennium, *a fortiori* one may have confidence now that the gap is a mere 250 years at most for any part of the New Testament and usually much less.
11. The history of textual criticism also gives us confidence because the discovery of significantly earlier evidence has not added new large points of uncertainty in the New Testament text. This being the case, the assumption

that yet further evidence would not reveal new uncertainties about the New Testament is justified. Doubts about Mark 16:9-20 and John 7:53–8:11 have been known in parts of the church since patristic times. The same applies to many smaller disputed passages. The vast increase in number and age of manuscripts over the last four centuries has not added more passages of uncertainty.[30] This leads naturally to the prediction that, based on the evidence we have already collected, we do not anticipate that new discoveries are likely to throw up previously unknown uncertainties about passages of significant length.

12. Ehrman's own text-critical and exegetical work often depends on his being able to establish one form of the text as prior to the others. In fact the text that Ehrman affirms differs relatively little from that found in modern editions of the Greek New Testament.
13. Although Ehrman's soundbite the "Orthodox Corruption of Scripture" has been widely received, he has in fact demonstrated how little deliberate corruption went on. The number of examples of deliberate corruption that he alleges is rather limited, and we must remember that Ehrman brings these examples together from *all* manuscripts. Without even allowing for the fact that many of his examples may in fact be wrong,[31] it is amazing to find so few cases even of possible deliberate corruption when searching across so many manuscripts. Thus Ehrman's own research shows how overwhelmingly scribes did not seek deliberately to change the text.
14. When we are dealing with our uncertainties as to the identity of the original text, we are dealing with known unknowns.

The Possibility of Translation

It is often suggested that the need for translation is a significant objection to any doctrine of the inspiration of the original wording. As Ehrman says,

30. Gesa Schenke, "Das Erscheinen Jesu vor den Jüngern und der Ungläubigc Thomas: Johannes 20,19-31," in *Coptica — Gnostica — Manichaica: Mélanges offerts à Wolf-Peter Funk,* ed. Louis Painchaud and Paul-Hubert Poirier (Louvain: Peeters, 2006), esp. 902, argues that a Coptic manuscript (Ms Copt e150p from the Bodleian Library in Oxford) might possibly be a witness to a Greek text of John's Gospel without John chapter 21. However, an unpublished critical analysis of the manuscript has suggested that this is most unlikely: Christian Askeland, "Was There a Coptic Translation of John's Gospel without Chapter 21?," paper presented at the Society of Biblical Literature annual meeting, Christianity in Egypt: Scripture, Tradition, and Reception section (21 November 2009).

31. For instance, I argue that his claim that *orgistheis* was deliberately corrupted into *splanchnistheis* in Mark 1:41 is unwarranted in "An Examination of Ehrman's Case for *orgistheis* in Mark 1:41," *NovT* 54 (2012): 1-12.

> If he [God] wanted his people to have his words, surely he would have given them to them (and possibly even given them the words in a language they could understand, rather than Greek and Hebrew).[32]

Behind this seems to be the suggestion that something significant is lost in translation, but even Christians may wonder what is the use of believing in an inerrant autographic wording if most believers are not able to read that wording. Are advocates of inerrancy putting undue emphasis on a purely theoretical entity that has no bearing on most believers?

The strange thing behind Ehrman's suggestion above is that Christians believe that God has given people words in languages they can understand because God has allowed his word to be translated. God's word (singular) does not cease to be his word in translation, though one cannot speak of his words (plural) in translation in the same way. As for the suggestion that God might give words in multiple modern languages so that people would understand them, this would run foul of Ehrman's objection that a doctrine of inspiration is meaningless unless there's a single fixed wording. Thus Ehrman's objections do not appear to be internally consistent.

In response to this contemporary *Angst* about the possibility of translating the scriptures we may say the following:

1. Since at least the third century B.C.E., there has been belief in the value of translating Old Testament scripture. New Testament authors quote in Greek Old Testament scriptures originally written in Hebrew as having direct application to their Greek-speaking hearers (e.g., 1 Cor. 9:9-10).
2. Many translations such as the *kaige* revision of parts of the Old Testament, Aquila, the Targumim, the Harclean Syriac have involved both the conviction of the value of translation and simultaneously a strong affirmation of the value of the wording of the original language. Thus affirming translation does not involve denying the authority of the original.
3. There seems to be no comparable contemporary *Angst* about the value of translating other texts, as if books and films lose their purpose or effect in translation.
4. Uncertainty in one area of translation does not spill over into all areas of translation. We regularly appreciate films or literature or follow instructions even though, for whatever reason, we have missed part of the information given. We recognize that the significance of what we have missed is limited.
5. When we are dealing with unresolved questions of translation we are dealing with known unknowns.

32. Ehrman, *Misquoting Jesus,* 11.

Proposals

The sorts of criticisms that Ehrman has made of inspiration are significant and require response. However, the fact that the critique has resulted in part from misunderstanding should also goad inerrantists to check that their own formulations have been as clear as they can be. The contention here is that they have not, and that we need to engage in debate as to what terms might serve well at both the popular and the scholarly level in the future. These are my initial proposals:

1. Where possible we should seek to make the older terms "Scripture" and "Scriptures" more current rather than the term "Bible" when speaking of the doctrines of inspiration and revelation since Scripture and Scriptures have a narrower focus and avoid physical associations.
2. We should avoid the term "text." This can be replaced by "wording" since, again, "wording" avoids the physical focus. It is easier for someone to deny that we have the original text (which might mean original document) than it is for them to deny that we have the original wording.
3. However, even the word "original" has its ambiguities, having earlier been used in opposition to a translation. In some instances it may be possible to replace this by the word "authorial," so that we might speak of "authorial wording" rather than "original text."
4. We should not speak of text of the autographa, but of wording *on* the autographa, or use other similar formulations that distinguish clearly between the message and the physical carrier of the message.

The purpose of all of these proposals is not merely to use precise language for doctrinal formulation among theologians, but also to introduce a shift of emphasis in common Christian parlance away from formulae that suggest or emphasize that we believe in the inerrancy of something nonexistent. The Word of God does not die or age when it is copied, nor is it less powerful when it is spoken without reference to a physical copy. It is not made less certain by our uncertainty as to its identity, nor is there a compelling reason why our own uncertainty as to the identity of one part of it should make us uncertain as to the identity of another part.

FOURTEEN

E pluribus unum? Apostolic Unity and Early Christian Literature

Simon Gathercole

In 1934, Walter Bauer felt able to describe the scholarly *status quaestionis,* which he was to attack so forcefully, as follows: "If my impression is correct, even today the overwhelmingly dominant view still is that for the period of Christian origins, ecclesiastical doctrine . . . always represents what is primary, while heresies, on the other hand, somehow are a deviation from the genuine."[1] In no small measure because of Bauer himself, no one could utter such a view today without blushing. There is a large and vocal body of scholarship now that regards the "Bauer thesis" as, in its essentials if not in all its details, correct. The purpose of the present essay on the other hand is to show that Bauer's argument is in its essentials wrong, even if the view that he is opposing cannot be sustained in all its details.

Out of a review of some of the authors most influential in the current discussion of the first and second centuries C.E., three particularly salient points emerge. First, there is general agreement that there was no core of earliest Christian belief at the beginning, but rather a many-hued "polydoxy" after which the more monochrome profile of orthodox belief prevailed only later. Second, and relatedly, the literature of the New Testament is taken to represent only fragments of the literature of earliest Christianity, and, crucially, its claims to apostolicity cannot be regarded as any more secure than the claims of other, non-canonical or "heretical," works. Third, the evidence from the early second century does nothing to dent the theory of the chaotic diversity of earliest Christianity, and none

1. W. Bauer, *Orthodoxy and Heresy in Earliest Christianity* (Philadelphia: Fortress Press, 1971 [1934]), xxiv.

In addition to the comments from other participants in this book (of whom Prof. Charles Hill made some very helpful observations at an early stage), I am particularly grateful to Prof. Richard Bauckham and Dr. James Carleton Paget for their careful reading and acute comments on a version of this essay.

of the literature from that time should be judged especially in continuity with (or discontinuity with) the apostles. These three contentions will be opposed in the respective parts of the present essay.

Prolegomena: The *Status Quo*

Walter Bauer: The Simultaneity of Heterodoxy and Orthodoxy

Much of the current literature on the diversity of early Christianity looks to W. Bauer's *Orthodoxy and Heresy in Earliest Christianity* (first published in 1934) as foundational in dismantling a naïvely Eusebian approach to Christian origins.[2] Although reviews criticized various aspects of the book, a number conceded that Bauer's basic point, namely that in a number of geographical locations what later became heresy had predominated and was only later displaced by Roman orthodoxy, had been made.[3] Throughout the book, Bauer is concerned with showing that it was the heretics who were chronologically prior, or had the upper hand numerically or in terms of wealth.[4] He is also particularly interested in debunking apostolic successions, sneering at Irenaeus's and Clement's claims to be only one stage removed from the apostles — only possible after a "darkening of historical memory"[5] — while noting the equally plausible (and perhaps equally implausible) claims of Basilides, Valentinus, and Ptolemy.[6] The appeals made by Egypt to successions of bishops going back to the apostolic age are very late, and quite fictitious, retrojections.[7] Similarly, Edessa's fancy that she had a direct connection with Jesus through Abgar's correspondence with him is the result of a fourth-century trick.[8]

A number of criticisms of Bauer's methods and conclusions could certainly be voiced. Of the first reviewers of the book, no less than six rebuke Bauer for overreliance on arguments from silence,[9] a criticism renewed more recently by

2. W. Bauer, *Rechtgläubigkeit und Ketzerei im ältesten Christentum* (Tübingen: Mohr, 1934). The second edition appeared in 1964, expanded in part by Georg Strecker, and it is this edition that is the Vorlage of the English *Orthodoxy and Heresy.*

3. G. Strecker, "Appendix 2," in Bauer, *Orthodoxy and Heresy,* 286-316.

4. Bauer, *Orthodoxy and Heresy,* 21, 31-32 (in Edessa, noting the impecunious and small band of Palutians), 62 (in Antioch), 72-73 (in Smyrna).

5. Bauer, *Orthodoxy and Heresy,* 119.

6. Bauer, *Orthodoxy and Heresy,* 119-20.

7. See Bauer, *Orthodoxy and Heresy,* 45, on Egypt.

8. Bauer, *Orthodoxy and Heresy,* 35-39 and elsewhere in the chapter.

9. Strathman, de Zwaan (misprinted as de Zwann), Dibelius, Völker, Simonin, Lebreton (Strecker, "Appendix 2," 290-94, 295).

Altendorf,[10] and even Bart Ehrman.[11] A further criticism noted by initial reviewers as well as by subsequent critics is, in contrast to his eking out whole constructions out of silences, "the ruthless treatment of such evidence as fails to support his case."[12] Moreover, probably the main difficulty from the point of view of this present discussion (as will be seen below) is his neglect of the NT. Bauer's focus of attention is explicitly on the second century, rather than on the first. For his view to work, however, he should really demonstrate that there is no unity *at the beginning,* that is, in the apostolic generation. This is a period that he really sidesteps, however, as both one initial reviewer and subsequent scholarship have recognized.[13]

The organization of the book is certainly eccentric. Why begin a book on early Christianity with a chapter on Edessa, about which we know practically nothing in the first two centuries? As Bauer admits toward the end: "I have already had to assume much more than I would like, but unfortunately, in this area, there is very little that one can know for sure."[14] The situation does not improve: chapter 2 is on Egypt predominantly in the first and second centuries, about which Bauer thought we could know very little, and modern scholarship even less.[15] Roger Bagnall, for example, has recently commented on Bauer's observation of the near absence of "orthodox" literature with the point that there is not

10. ". . . [eine] mit dem argumentum ex silentio spielende konstruktive Phantasie." H. D. Altendorf, "Zum Stichwort: Rechtgläubigkeit und Ketzerei im ältesten Christentum," *ZKG* 80 (1969): 61-74, on 64, quoted in C. Markschies, *Kaiserzeitliche christliche Theologie und ihre Institutionen: Prolegomena zu einer Geschichte der antiken christlichen Theologie* (Tübingen: Mohr, 2007), 360.

11. B. D. Ehrman, *Lost Christianities: The Battle for Scripture and the Faiths We Never Knew* (Oxford: Oxford University Press, 2003), 273 n. 20, also notes the point and gives a particularly egregious example.

12. H. E. W. Turner, *The Pattern of Christian Truth: A Study in the Relations between Orthodoxy and Heresy in the Early Church* (London: Mowbray, 1954), 79, identifying this, along with "the persistent tendency to over-simplify problems," as Bauer's "fatal weakness." Strecker identifies Moffatt, Völker, and Simonin as critical of this tendency ("Appendix 2," 295), Moffatt commenting that Bauer "tends to take the position of the barrister rather than of the judge" (quoted in Strecker, "Appendix 2," 292): there is an allusion here to the first page of Bauer's book (xxi) in which he casts himself in the role of judge.

13. C. Martin, Review in *Nouvelle revue théologique* 62 (1935): 750-51, referred to in Strecker, "Appendix 2," 293-94; H. Koester, "GNOMAI DIAPHOROI: The Origin and Nature of Diversification in the History of Early Christianity," in J. M. Robinson and H. Koester, *Trajectories through Early Christianity* (Philadelphia: Fortress, 1971), 114-57 (119). The title of Marshall's article about Bauer is good in this respect! See I. H. Marshall, "Orthodoxy and Heresy in Earlier Christianity," *Themelios* 2, no. 1 (September 1976): 5-14. This article deserves to have received more attention than it has.

14. Bauer, *Orthodoxy and Heresy,* 42.

15. See, e.g., Roger S. Bagnall, *Early Christian Books in Egypt* (Princeton: Princeton University Press, 2009).

really much material evidence of unorthodoxy which can reliably be dated early either.[16] Moving to Asia Minor, the third chapter begins by reproaching Ignatius for being "less concerned with depicting the actual situation than with portraying the ideal" — but as a man on his way to execution, Ignatius hardly had the leisure for *wissenschaftliche* description.[17] In the same chapter, Polycarp is also portrayed as beleaguered, but one astute critic draws attention to Polycarp's response to a request from Ignatius to send an envoy to Syria: "I will do this if I have a convenient opportunity, either myself or the one whom I am sending representing you and me" (Polyc. *Phil.* 13.1). Norris appends the comment: "Those are not the words of a man who saw the survival of the Antiochene church endangered or one who was so worried about the state of things in Smyrna that he could not leave that city."[18] This is not to say that everything is rosy in Antioch and Smyrna, but rather that the different emotional levels of Ignatius and Polycarp make it very difficult to "mirror-read" the situation, as Bauer does so confidently. One of the most substantial responses to Bauer, that of Thomas A. Robinson, argues that *Orthodoxy and Heresy* is deeply flawed because it is wrong in the only area in which it can be tested, that is, Asia Minor.[19] Nevertheless, for all its flaws, the book has wielded considerable influence.

Robinson/Koester: Multiple Trajectories

One instance of this influence is *Trajectories through Early Christianity* by Helmut Koester and James Robinson. This volume is a collection of eight essays, some of which were previously published as early as 1965.[20] Although, as Robinson's opening remarks put it, the volume represents the "indigenization of the Bultmann tradition on American soil" (1), it is also heavily indebted to Bauer, especially in the chapters written by Koester. Robinson's concern with the philosophy of history in chapter 1, with Q (chapter 3), and with John's Gospel (chapter 7) is perhaps less relevant for our purposes than Koester's more Bauerian stress upon diversity in earliest Christianity. Already in the introduction, however, Robinson identifies the line of continuity between Bauer and *Trajectories,* noting that

16. Bagnall, *Early Christian Books,* 10; cf. also C. H. Turner, *Manuscript, Society and Belief in Early Christian Egypt* (London: British Academy, 1979), 51-52, on the absence of material evidence for Gnosticism in Egypt in the second century.

17. Bauer, *Orthodoxy and Heresy,* 61.

18. F. W. Norris, "Ignatius, Polycarp, and I Clement: Walter Bauer Reconsidered," *VC* 30 (1976): 23-44 (28).

19. T. A. Robinson, *The Bauer Thesis Examined: The Geography of Heresy in the Early Christian Church* (Lewiston, NY: Edwin Mellen, 1988).

20. See Robinson and Koester, *Trajectories,* ix, for details of initial publications. Subsequent page references from this book are given in parentheses in the text.

Orthodoxy and Heresy "drew attention to a bifurcating trajectory: out of a fluid, amorphous primitive Christianity there gradually emerged a polarized antithesis between secondary developments, known to us as orthodoxy and heresy" (16).

Koester begins by wholeheartedly endorsing Bauer's conclusions: the latter "demonstrated convincingly in a brilliant monograph in 1934 that Christian groups later labelled heretical actually predominated in the first two or three centuries, both geographically and theologically" (114). This is confirmed by the Nag Hammadi discoveries, made use of in Koester's extensive discussion of the *Gospel of Thomas.* All Christian groups, orthodox and heretical alike, claimed apostolic credentials, and so it is useless to try to argue that one really is apostolic in contrast to the others (115). In compensation for Bauer's neglect of the NT, Koester aims to supplement Bauer's analysis by extending it back into the earliest period. Koester, then, traces the pluriformity and disunity noted by Bauer in the second century back into the first. "From the beginning, there was no uniformity in beliefs and institutions; disagreements must have led to debates and controversies very early" (119). Koester then proceeds, in the manner of Bauer, geographically.

The shadow of the Tübingen school hangs heavy over Koester's discussion of Jerusalem. He asserts that the principal line of division is between the law-observant Gospel of the Peter-James circle in contrast to the liberal Stephen and — even more sharply — the mission of Paul (120-21). In Antioch, in contrast to Bauer, Koester sees more continuity between Pauline theology and Ignatius. (Bauer argued both for a lacuna between the two, occupied by heresy, and for Ignatius's troubled situation attesting to a minority position on his part.) Koester takes it that Pauline Christianity "continued to play a significant role in Antioch" with the presence there ca. 100 C.E. of Ignatius (122). His question is principally that of whether the continuity between Paul and Ignatius is really as strong as is often thought. Moving to Edessa and the Osrhoëne, Koester aims to correct Bauer's conclusion that the earliest Christians there were Marcionites; in fact they were Thomas Christians, given that our earliest Christian literature from Edessa is the *Gospel of Thomas* (127).

The Gospels provide further evidence of differing strands within early Christianity. Mark is Pauline in its conception of the passion and the kerygma, but its portrait of Jesus is the same as that of Paul's opponents in 2 Corinthians (152). The view common among Bultmann's other students (e.g., Conzelmann, Käsemann) that Luke relativizes the cross appears. Since Luke's Gospel reduces the significance of the passion to a mere "appendix to the gospel" (153), it attests to the victory of these super-apostles: Jesus " 'performs' the fulfillment of the true essence of the religion of the Old Testament" (153). This fulfillment is accomplished in Jesus' ministry of powerful teaching and healing, but not through his passion and death (153). The focus is on Jesus as "divine man." "Without doubt, Luke, in all his admiration of the great Apostle to the gentiles, was really a student of Paul's opponents rather than of Paul himself" (153). Luke's Gospel is thus really a "sacrifice of the Pauline gospel" (156). This discussion of diversity of outlook in the Gospels is expanded in another essay, where images of Jesus in the Gospels as "divine man" and "wisdom's envoy" are taken to be quite at odds with one another (216-19; 219-23). Finally, like Luke, the Pastorals are "a sellout of Pauline theology," on the grounds of the disappearance of the eschatological tension and the appearance of theological norms as tests of heresy (156).

This all comports with statements elsewhere in the volume, such as the opening sentence of chapter 6: "Christianity did not begin with a particular belief, dogma or creed; nor can one understand the heretical diversifications of early Christianity as aberrations from one original true and orthodox formulation of faith" (205). As had Bauer, though, Koester reminds us that his own reconstructions "must remain both hypothetical and fragmentary" (119).

This is certainly at variance with the confident tone one finds elsewhere in Koester's conclusions, however. In particular, Koester makes rather sweeping remarks about features of the Gospels that he sees as problematically contradictory. Unlike Mark and John, who recast their miracle sources within the framework of the death of Jesus,[21] Luke's more straightforward characterization of Jesus as a *theios anēr* is a cardinal sin.[22] Or again, wisdom Christologies such as one finds in Matthew are found to be incompatible with real humanity: "It is not easy to see how wisdom mythologies could find a point of connection or reference in the *earthly Jesus.*"[23] On one level, it is simply a rather plodding criticism to say that the miracle-working, Spirit-empowered Jesus of the Gospels is contrary to the kenotic Christ of Paul: differing emphases, themselves held together in the Gospel narratives, do not entail contradiction.

Koester also repeats some of the methodological problems associated with Bauer's reconstructions based on oversimplistic "mirror-reading" of the conflicts in which some of the Apostolic Fathers are engaged.[24] Or to change the metaphor from "mirror-reading," texts are often treated as "transparent," such that the modern scholar can simply peer through to see the underlying situation.[25] The problem appears again in Koester's identification of Luke's "divine-man" Christology with that of the "super-apostles" in 2 Corinthians, where we allegedly

21. Koester, "GNOMAI DIAPHOROI," 152; "One Jesus and Four Primitive Gospels," in *Trajectories,* 158-204, on 189, 190-91.

22. Koester, "One Jesus and Four Primitive Gospels," 191.

23. Koester, "The Structure and Criteria of Early Christian Beliefs," in *Trajectories,* 205-31, on 220.

24. One would do well to apply to Bauer's reconstructions the careful method found in J. M. G. Barclay, "Mirror-Reading a Polemical Letter: Galatians as a Test Case," *JSNT* 31 (1987): 73-93.

25. This image is used by U. Luz, *The Theology of the Gospel of Matthew* (Cambridge: Cambridge University Press, 1995), 68, 82.

find "persuasive evidence" of the Corinthian opponents' view of Jesus.[26] In reality, however, it is quite impossible to deduce such a Christology from 2 Corinthians, which does not give us even indirect or implicit evidence for such a thing.[27]

Elaine Pagels: Joint Emergence of Orthodoxy and Gnosticism

A few years after the publication of this book, Koester's student Elaine Pagels established her reputation as a leading scholar of Gnosticism with the publication of her dissertation on Heracleon (1973) and a second monograph on the Gnostic reception of Paul (1975).[28] Her most celebrated book, *The Gnostic Gospels,* is more wide-ranging in scope, and has had a very considerable influence both on scholarship and in the popular realm.[29] The introduction reflects an excitement about the discovery and recent publication of the Nag Hammadi corpus, such that now the heretics can speak for themselves despite the orthodox attempts to destroy such books in antiquity.[30] The overall burden of the book is that doctrinal differences between the orthodox and the Gnostics (very broadly conceived: including almost all non-orthodox) cannot merely be explained in religious and philosophical terms; rather, doctrine is on both sides political or institutional at the same time. The resurrection is the first case in point. A once-for-all resurrection, where after forty days Jesus withdraws his physical presence, ensures that for the orthodox, the truth about Jesus can only be accessible through an apostolic succession; by contrast, the gnostic who can have his or her own vision of the risen Jesus is not limited by such strictures. Since for Pagels NT references to resurrection can lend themselves to physical and spiritual interpretations, we should not be surprised by the variety of beliefs. Similarly, the unity of God in orthodox thought ensured both monepiscopacy and the exclusivity of a clearly defined church. In fact, these are all mutually reinforcing. On the other side, the view that the orthodox were

26. Koester, "The Structure and Criteria of Early Christian Beliefs," 218.

27. Similarly Ehrman, *Lost Christianities,* 95, who wonders whether the Corinthian opponents here are forerunners of the Gnostics.

28. *The Johannine Gospel in Gnostic Exegesis: Heracleon's Commentary on John* (Nashville: Abingdon, 1973); *The Gnostic Paul: Gnostic Exegesis of the Pauline Letters* (Philadelphia: Fortress, 1975).

29. The Annual Meeting of the Society of Biblical Literature in New Orleans in 2009 featured a thirtieth-anniversary celebration of the book, at which the impact of the book on (at the time of its publication) young scholars was evident.

30. One point drawn to my attention by Prof. James Hamilton is that non-canonical orthodox works from the second century (e.g., apostolic fathers such as Papias) are not really attested any better than heterodox writings. As such, the fragmentary character of our evidence for heterodox literature from the second century is perhaps simply reflective of the lack of evidence of early Christian literature more widely.

worshiping the inferior demiurge freed gnostics from following episcopal instructions: indeed, the "redemption" ritual liberated the gnostics not only from the demiurge and his archons but also from the bishop and his presbyters.

It is perhaps striking, given the book's reputation in conservative circles, that probably the majority of the book is fairly straightforwardly historical in orientation, and — especially from today's perspective — uncontroversial. Indeed, Pagels's book is a good deal less speculative than those of Bauer and Koester/Robinson. However, there are clearly some historical judgments less defensible.

First, there is the occasional sleight of hand in chronology. In the context of mention of "the apostles' time," and questioning whether they "all believed the same teaching," Pagels states:

> But the discoveries at Nag Hammadi have upset this picture. If we admit that some of these fifty-two texts represent early forms of Christian teaching, we may have to recognize that early Christianity is far more diverse than nearly anyone expected before the Nag Hammadi discoveries.[31]

This is slightly disingenuous. If we merely take the last sentence above on its own, it is incontestably true. However, it appears in a context ("the apostles' time," mentioned in the previous paragraph) that makes it clear what Pagels means by "early Christianity." This is where the sleight of hand comes in. Yet the implication is that we are being dishonest if we do not accept her claim ("If we admit . . ."). Again, reference is made early on to "first- and second-century gnostic literature . . . like the 'Round Dance of the Cross' and the 'Thunder, Perfect Mind'" — highly dubious claims (19). Elsewhere, Pagels has more recently made it clear that John's Gospel, far from clearly pre-dating the *Gospel of Thomas,* is locked in controversy with it.[32] The labels of the apostles John and Thomas are appropriated to add authority to the documents used in the controversies. The discussion continues with talk of rivalry between "Peter Christians" and "Johannine Christians," where again apostolic patronage is claimed to justify superiority in the power struggles: indeed, they "involve more than power struggles: they involve the substance of Christian faith."[33] Pagels comments: "[W]e know virtually nothing about the persons who wrote the gospels we call Matthew, Mark, Luke, and

31. E. Pagels, *The Gnostic Gospels* (New York: Random House, 1979), xxii. Subsequent page references from this book are given in parentheses in the text.

32. E. Pagels, *Beyond Belief: The Secret Gospel of Thomas* (Basingstoke, UK: Macmillan, 2003).

33. The canonical gospels are taken to be engaged in controversy with one another: for example, in contradiction to John, "Luke says that Peter outran all the rest" (Pagels, *Beyond Belief,* 62). This is a clear mistake, however. Pagels comments that the Fourth Gospel always places Peter second to the Beloved Disciple, but C. K. Barrett, *The Gospel according to John,* 2nd edition (London: SPCK, 1978), 118-19, 587-88, rightly notes the importance of Peter in John 21:24.

John. We only know that these writings are attributed to apostles (Matthew and John) or followers of the apostles (Mark and Luke)" (17). The tendency to collapse the origins of the NT Gospels and of various works from Nag Hammadi into the same undifferentiated time-frame, however, is highly problematic.[34] Tuckett rightly observes that of course, as the Bauerians protest, the Christian apocrypha shed light on the history of early Christianity. "However, there is still the question of exactly how early is the 'early' Christianity they illuminate."[35]

Second, one of the main arguments that Pagels makes is that the political considerations are vitally important because a number of crucial questions could have gone either way: hence the political factor being decisive. In themselves, elements in the NT are not univocal and could lend themselves both to orthodox and to gnostic interpretations.

> So if some of the New Testament stories insist on a literal view of resurrection, others lend themselves to different interpretations. (6)

> Followers of Valentinus themselves demonstrated — convincingly — that many sayings and stories in John could lend themselves to such interpretation [sc. "one's inner capacity to find one's own direction"]. (120)

> If we go back to the earliest known sources of Christian tradition — the sayings of Jesus (although scholars disagree on the question of *which* sayings are genuinely authentic), we can see how both gnostic and orthodox forms of Christianity could emerge as variant interpretations of the teaching and significance of Christ. (148)

This recalls the point made above by Robinson, in his claim that an initially amorphous Christianity divided into more clearly defined, and opposing, trajectories. Similarly, Pagels takes it that the *tohu we-bohu* of the beginnings of Christianity only later split into orthodox and gnostic factions. Highly questionable, however, is her contention that both physical and non-physical interpretations of Jesus' suffering and resurrection might equally legitimately emerge from earliest tradition. One might mention here R. E. Brown's criticism of Bauer: "I do not think that he dealt sufficiently with a more important issue, namely whether what won out as orthodoxy was not truer than its opposite to the *implications* of what was held at the beginning."[36] Although some display reluctance to make such evaluations,

34. For further criticism of Ehrman and Pagels on this point, see S. J. Gathercole, *The Gospel of Judas: Rewriting Early Christianity* (Oxford: Oxford University Press, 2007), 143-47.

35. C. M. Tuckett, "The Gospel of Thomas: Evidence for Jesus?" *NTT* 52 (1998): 17-32, on 19.

36. R. E. Brown, *The Epistles of John,* AB (Garden City, NY: Doubleday, 1982), 55 n. 127.

it seems clear enough that non-physicalist interpretations of Jesus' death and resurrection are later departures rather than innate possibilities that might have developed naturally from the teaching of the apostles.

Bart Ehrman: Proto-Orthodox vs. Lost Christianities

Moving into the 1980s and up to the present day, Bart Ehrman can be identified as one of the most vocal of those advocating the Bauer hypothesis. Already in 1983, some of Ehrman's conclusions about diversity are couched in aggressively polemical rhetoric: "The conclusions mentioned above show the idea of a fixed canon in Alexandria during Athanasius's lifetime to be a fantasy."[37] After the publication of his doctorate (1986), Ehrman went on to write *The Orthodox Corruption of Scripture* (1996), according to which the very text of the New Testament became a tool in the legitimation of orthodoxy. The present study is not concerned with text-critical matters, but will discuss some of Ehrman's views of early Christian diversity more broadly. More recently, Ehrman's two books *Lost Scriptures* and *Lost Christianities* (both 2003) in particular are semi-popular works aiming to reach a student or lay audience. The former is an anthology of non-canonical works; the latter is more discursive, taking as its starting point the perspective of Pagels in *The Gnostic Gospels,* according to which the church in the first two centuries was actually more diverse than the church today.[38] It treats particular works in part I (the *Gospel of Peter,* the *Acts of Paul and Thecla,* the *Gospel of Thomas,* and the *Secret Gospel of Mark*), and Ehrman strongly relativizes the distinction between canonical and non-canonical Gospels in part through his emphasis on the original anonymity of the Gospels, and the late attachment of the attributions to Matthew, Mark, Luke and John.[39] Part II of *Lost Christianities* focuses on particular movements: the Ebionites, Marcionites, Gnostics, and finally, the "Proto-orthodox." Ehrman's work strongly emphasizes the "Proto-orthodox" as simply one of many groups, all laying claim to apostolic origins (177-78). Through a process of "vitriolic attacks" (161) in "its quest for dominance" (229) the Proto-orthodox won, and as the winners they "chose which records of the affair to keep and decided how to tell the history of the conflict" (161). Non-canonical books were "rejected, attacked, suppressed, and destroyed" (ix), or "rejected, scorned, maligned, attacked, burned" (4). As in

37. B. D. Ehrman, "The New Testament Canon of Didymus the Blind," *VC* 37 (1983): 1-21, on 18.

38. Ehrman, *Lost Christianities,* 1-2, picked up again at 135. Subsequent page references from this book are given in parentheses in the text.

39. B. D. Ehrman, "Christianity Turned on Its Head: The Alternative Vision of the Gospel of Judas," in *The Gospel of Judas,* ed. R. Kasser, M. Meyer, and G. Wurst, 1st edition (Washington, DC: National Geographic, 2006), 77-120, on 117-18.

the case of Pagels, we encounter the tendency to overplay the extent to which the four Gospels in the NT are essentially coeval with rival pictures (or if they are not, it is because some rival pictures have been destroyed). *Lost Christianities* is heavily indebted to Bauer,[40] and a number of the topics in the book are taken over from Bauer's *Orthodoxy and Heresy,*[41] but Ehrman is clearly the most sensationalist of all the authors in focus here.

Points of Departure

Three particular concerns arise out of this survey, which will together constitute the themes of the present essay.

The first is concerned with the idea, found throughout the authors discussed above, that there was no initial unity among Christian believers. This appears in different forms among the works noted in our survey: for Bauer, there is a stress on the historical priority, or at least supremacy, of heterodoxy in a number of important locations; Koester, Robinson, and Pagels highlight the amorphous character of Christian beginnings, so as to show a development from that to more clearly defined, and competing, "trajectories" or movements; Ehrman highlights the diversity from the beginning, out of which one group, the proto-orthodox, emerges dominant and quashes the rest. Despite these differing emphases, however, it should be evident what these authors share both in content and in their intentions.

The second is related to the first, and concerns the questions raised in some of the authors above about the figures who lie behind early Christian writings: our treatment will be for reasons of space confined to the Gospels. While he is trenchant in his criticisms of apostolic successions, Bauer is less interested in the origins of the Gospels than he is in their usage in the second century. He does, however, thereby develop an interest in attacking the external evidence for Johannine authorship of the Fourth Gospel.[42] Interestingly, Koester is more positive than many about the Gospels having names attached to them from the beginning, although, as we have seen, he considers claims to apostolicity to be worthless because of how widespread such claims are among orthodox and unorthodox alike.[43] In Pagels's work, the disciples are co-opted as authority figures in the competitive world of early Christian struggles for supremacy: the use of

40. Bauer is discussed in *Lost Christianities,* 172-79.

41. Cf. the titles of Bauer, *Orthodoxy and Heresy,* chapters 6-8 and of Ehrman, *Lost Christianities,* chapters 9-10.

42. Bauer, *Orthodoxy and Heresy,* 185-86.

43. H. Koester, *Ancient Christian Gospels: Their History and Development* (Harrisburg, PA: Trinity Press International, 1990); on names attached to the Gospels see 26-27; on claims to apostolicity see 115, also 131.

Matthew, John, and Thomas are all equally fictitious as far as their connections with their eponymous Gospels are concerned. Ehrman, as a textual critic, makes special use of the evidence of manuscripts as evidence for the anonymity of the Gospels. Again, then, in their different ways our authors in the survey above devote some considerable energy to decoupling the canonical Gospels from any apostolic connection.

Finally, the third part of this essay will discuss how the common apostolic deposit is followed in various early-second-century writings, as well as how some non-canonical gospels treat this apostolic tradition. The "proto-orthodox" are not merely one group among many, but rather have the strongest claim to be in continuity with the apostles.

The Apostolic Consensus about the Gospel

This section, then, will deal with the first issue raised by our sketch above, that earliest Christianity at its very beginnings was really an undifferentiated blur out of which clearly defined positions only appeared later. We will argue below, however, that there was a common understanding of the gospel among the apostles which can be taken to be the original core of earliest Christianity.[44]

The principal factor in any reckoning of early Christianity must be the orientation around the person of Jesus. This attachment to the person of Jesus, however, is accompanied in the gospel by some definition. This despite Koester's following comment:

44. No doubt other factors could be included that are not discussed here because of limitations of space, the identity of Jesus as Messiah and as future judge to name but two. Furthermore, it should also be noted that allied to the *content* of the Gospel is an accompanying mood, which was rooted in an expectation of the return of Jesus and thereafter an enjoyment of the presence of Christ unencumbered by sin or persecution or suffering of any kind. Furthermore, a common ethical core is also worthy of further consideration, though again there is not space to pursue this in depth here. Finally, in terms of the shape of the life of Christians, the person of Jesus was determinative: just as during his earthly ministry he called disciples to "follow" him, so subsequently *imitatio Christi* became a norm. It can also be summed up in the twofold definition of love of God and love of neighbor.

Related to this is the discussion by Markschies of the "identity in plurality" of the early church, in his response to Bauer in Markschies, *Kaiserzeitliche christliche Theologie,* 337-83. See also Markschies, *Between Two Worlds: Structures of Earliest Christianity* (London: SCM, 1999), on the unifying "structures" again here explicitly in connection with Bauer (ix-x). J. D. G. Dunn, *Unity and Diversity in the New Testament: An Inquiry into the Character of Earliest Christianity* (London: SCM, 1977), makes a number of important observations in response to Bauer. Although *Unity and Diversity* rather minimalistically confines the unity of the NT to "the unity between the historical Jesus and the exalted Christ" (369), it also sketches a number of other factors as very widespread in importance (e.g., 30, 370-71).

> Christianity did not begin with a particular belief, dogma or creed; nor can one understand the heretical diversifications of early Christianity as aberrations from one original true and orthodox formulation of faith. Rather, Christianity started with a particular historical person, his works and words, his life and death: Jesus of Nazareth.[45]

This is clearly a false antithesis. Of course the first Christians did not stand every Sunday to recite something as substantial as the Nicene creed, but there was a common understanding of the gospel that was central: it was not an uninterpreted, contentless Jesus who was proclaimed by the apostles. This can already be seen in our first documentary evidence of early Christianity, the Pauline epistles.

The Pauline Gospel as the Catholic Gospel

1 Corinthians 15:1-11

Paul frames his statements about the cross and resurrection in 1 Corinthians 15:3-4 with the introduction, "Allow me to remind you, brothers, of the gospel which I preached to you . . ." (15:1) — he is here going to sum up the gospel. It is this "through which you were saved" (15:2), and which is "first and foremost" (*en prōtois*, 15:3).[46] As captured in some translations (e.g., NRSV, NIV, ESV), it is "of first importance." Also emphasized strongly, indeed rhythmically stated twice in the course of this very compressed statement, is the phrase "according to the Scriptures." The point that emerges very clearly from the earliest testimony is that the Messiah Jesus' death and resurrection were central to the plan of God, constituted the focus of the OT scripture which they fulfilled, and brought salvation to the world through dealing with sins and bringing new life:

> For I passed on to you as of first importance what I also received: that Christ died for our sins according to the Scriptures, and that he was buried, and that he was raised on the third day according to the Scriptures. (1 Cor. 15:3-4)

45. Koester, "Structure and Criteria of Early Christian Beliefs," 205.

46. Douglas Campbell's *The Quest for Paul's Gospel* strangely has scarcely any discussion of the passage. Of the three references to 1 Cor. 15:3-4, one notes that the atoning death of Christ apparently occupies a "marginal role." D. A. Campbell, *The Quest for Paul's Gospel: A Suggested Strategy,* LNTS (London/New York: Continuum, 2005), 198. Perhaps the reason for this is Campbell's other comment — that Christ's death is "mentioned briefly" in the passage (183). But the reason it is mentioned briefly is that Paul is expressing the gospel in summary or shorthand form. The brevity of Paul's statements here does nothing to relativize their primary importance.

Various parties are listed as the recipients of the resurrection appearances: Peter and the rest of the disciples (15:5), the five hundred (15:6), James the brother of the Lord and all the apostles more broadly defined (15:7), and Paul himself (15:8). Paul in particular asserts that this gospel of the death and resurrection of Jesus the Christ as the basis of salvation from sin is something common to all the recipients of resurrection appearances: "Therefore whether it is I or they, this is what we have preached and this is what you have believed" (15:11).

Martin Hengel and Anna Maria Schwemer have probably done the most in recent times to draw attention to 1 Corinthians 15:11 as evidence for the harmony of early Christian beliefs about the gospel. Buried among the 1,500 footnotes of *Paul between Damascus and Antioch* are the assertions that 1 Corinthians 15:11 is "a text of which so far too little notice has been taken," but in fact "one of the most important theological statements made by the apostle!"[47] Elsewhere it is connected more directly with the debate in hand here:

> And finally I Cor 15:11, a text which scholars are persistently fond of suppressing, is a pillar for the — last — unit of the earliest Christian message at least during the first generation, i.e. the real "apostolic" age. . . . Precisely because Paul was such a contentious theologian, I Cor 15:11 is a tremendous statement to come from his pen, and we should reflect on it again today, when so much is being dissolved into vain subjectivity and confused pluralism (the two are connected).[48]

Leaving aside Hengel's application to contemporary culture, the point about Paul's somewhat "maverick" character does make the statement of concord in 1 Corinthians 15:11 more suggestive.[49] The gospel set out in 15:3-4 is that preached by all the apostles.

Galatians 1:23

In addition to 1 Corinthians 15:1-11, which has been copiously used, Jeff Peterson has recently drawn attention to Galatians 1:23 as expressive of a similar thought:

47. M. Hengel and A.-M. Schwemer, *Paul between Damascus and Antioch: The Unknown Years* (London: SCM, 1997), 335 n. 119, 408 n. 758.

48. Hengel and Schwemer, *Paul between Damascus and Antioch,* 290-91.

49. Hengel and Schwemer, *Paul between Damascus and Antioch,* 291. Hengel's wider argument, not of relevance here, is against the view that the account of the gospel in 1 Cor. 15:3-4 is a narrowly Antiochene concern, on which he makes the point that Paul is reporting here what he taught the Corinthians when he first planted the church there, in the company of the Jerusalem disciple Silas/Silvanus. The contrary view is essentially pure assertion, and is in any case seriously problematized by all the evidence assembled by Hengel for the connections between Paul and Jerusalem.

"I was personally unknown to the churches of Judea that are in Christ. They only heard the report: 'He who once persecuted us is now preaching the faith he once sought to destroy'" (Gal. 1:22-23).[50] It is important here that Paul claims to be quoting the actual report in the words of the Judean Christians, retaining the first-person plural ("persecuted *us*"). As Peterson remarks, "It is noteworthy that Paul presents this as the Judean churches' judgment, not his."[51] And in their judgment, they characterize Paul as one who preaches as the gospel the same faith that they, the Judean Christians, hold. This is further represented as coming from the very beginning of Paul's ministry — indeed, the report only makes sense as originating shortly after Paul's conversion. This reinforces the point that the harmony is not a late harmonization of Paul and Jerusalem such as the Baur school sees in the *Frühkatholizismus* of the Acts of the Apostles, but a fact of the beginning of the Pauline mission.

Further Connections between the Jerusalem Church and the Pauline Churches

But is this merely Paul's own rhetorical construction in denial of the facts on the ground? This is unlikely because of the extensive connections between the Pauline mission and the Jerusalem church, some of which were cultivated by Paul himself: "Paul has worked to bring both the Galatian and the Corinthian Christians into contact with Christians in Jerusalem. He has done this by organizing the collection for the poor of the saints there, enlisting both the Corinthians (1 Cor. 16:1-4; 2 Cor. 8–9) and the Galatians (1 Cor. 16:1; Gal. 2:10)."[52] Paul does not engender a connection through a gift to Jerusalem by a "bank transfer" undertaken by a third party; rather, he commands that members of the Corinthian church deliver the gift themselves (1 Cor. 16:3), with Paul's participation an option in special circumstances (16:4). He also implies that a similar procedure has already been followed by the Galatians (16:1). Peterson provides the instance of Paul's taking Titus to Jerusalem as a concrete example of Paul exposing his gentile co-workers to the situation in Jerusalem,[53] and one could adduce others, such as Paul taking Luke and Trophimus there (Acts 21:15, 17, 29).[54]

Numerous other points could be adduced. Paul himself spent time in Jeru-

50. J. Peterson, "The Extent of Christian Theological Diversity: Pauline Evidence," *RestQ* 47 (2005): 1-14, on 5, 7.

51. Peterson, "The Extent of Christian Theological Diversity," 7.

52. Peterson, "The Extent of Christian Theological Diversity," 10, citing L. W. Hurtado, *Lord Jesus Christ: Devotion to Jesus in Earliest Christianity* (Grand Rapids: Eerdmans, 2003), 159-60.

53. Peterson, "The Extent of Christian Theological Diversity," 10.

54. Here and in the rest of the essay I am assuming the basic reliability of Acts.

salem with Peter shortly after his conversion (Gal. 1:18). He was "head-hunted" by one of the founder-members of the Jerusalem church, Barnabas, to assist the work in Antioch. The connections between Antioch and Jerusalem were further cemented by Jerusalem-based prophets visiting Antioch (Acts 11:27-28), followed shortly by Barnabas and Paul journeying from Antioch to Jerusalem (Acts 11:29-30). The Jerusalem council is an obvious case of collaboration between the churches in these two cities. A further inference can be made from 1 Corinthians 16. The whole procedure of the collection relies on the good standing of Paul with the Jerusalem church because the procedure assumes that visitors to Jerusalem from Corinth can rely on letters of introduction from Paul being effective (1 Cor. 16:3).[55]

These strong links between Jerusalem and the Pauline mission mean that (a) it is extremely unlikely that there was significant tension between them, and (b) that Paul's comments in 1 Corinthians 15:1-11 about his agreement with the other apostles on the gospel should not be suspected as much as is commonly the case. The gospel of Christ's death for sins according to the scriptures and resurrection on the third day according to the scriptures cannot be relativized as a narrowly Pauline or Antiochene preserve.

The First Major Challenge and the First Official Document of "the Way": Gentile Converts, Circumcision, Commensality, and the Apostolic Decree

The first major controversy within early Christianity followed the beginning of gentiles coming into "the Way."[56] As F. F. Bruce memorably put it: "[M]en from Cyprus and Cyrene conceived the novel idea of trying the good news out on gentiles, to see how they would react to it," with the result that large numbers were converted.[57]

In both Acts and Galatians, two reactions to this are described. On one side, there is the position that these gentiles should be circumcised, but the other view, that they should not, prevailed. It can be noted that there is no straightforward dominical answer. Jesus tradition is not relevant here, because there is only one incidental reference to circumcision in the Gospels (John 7:22-23). *Gos. Thom.* 53, in which Jesus denies the value of physical circumcision, cannot be regarded as having any claim to authenticity. Is this then one of Ehrman's cases of the stronger party winning out *vi et armis*? He comments that the advocates of gentile

55. Peterson, "The Extent of Christian Theological Diversity," 10-11.

56. For further discussion of some of these matters, see R. J. Bauckham, "James, Peter, and the Gentiles," in *The Missions of James, Peter, and Paul: Tensions in Early Christianity,* ed. B. Chilton and C. A. Evans, NovTSup 115 (Leiden: Brill, 2005), 91-142.

57. F. F. Bruce, *The Pauline Circle* (Exeter, UK: Paternoster, 1985), 17, in reference to Acts 11:21.

circumcision are one group who had just as much of an apostolic claim as those who resisted it: various groups other than the proto-orthodox "may have claimed to represent views held by Jesus' own apostles, the original Christian views. One would think that the Judaizers in Galatia, at least, could make a pretty good case."[58] Koester also assumes that the Jerusalem church would naturally insist on the circumcision of gentile Christians: the Apostolic council arose "because the observance of the law was deemed essential by the Christians in Jerusalem, and probably also by other Christian groups."[59] Many such sentiments go back to F. C. Baur's contention that James and Peter were essentially on the side of the "teachers" in Galatians, even if in a slightly milder form: "[T]hey only consented not to oppose the Pauline Christianity, which with regard to their principles they were bound to oppose, and stipulated that they should be allowed to hold themselves passive towards it, or in one word to ignore it."[60]

In opposition to this, however, there is the unanimity of Paul and the Jerusalem apostles on the matter. Both the suspicious reading of Bauer and the more confrontational view of Koester are difficult to maintain in the light of the agreement between Paul on the one hand, and Simon Peter, James the brother of Jesus, and John son of Zebedee on the other (Gal. 2:1-10).[61] Paul for his part seems to take the position of the Jerusalem pillars very seriously in Galatians 2:2.[62] The pillars do not require Titus's circumcision, and so, as Vouga points out, the Jerusalem apostles have made no attempt to restrict the freedom of the Pauline gospel.[63] Does this mean that the pillars would have very much liked Titus to be circumcised, hoping that Paul would accept it, but reluctantly made a concession to Paul? Decisive here is the implication of Galatians 2:3: *all' oude Titos ho syn emoi, Hellēn ōn, ēnankasthē peritmēthēnai.* What does this statement imply about the Jerusalem pillars' attitude to gentile circumcision? This has been taken in three main ways:

58. Ehrman, *Lost Christianities,* 177-78.

59. Koester, "GNOMAI DIAPHOROI," 120. Quite apart from the speculative aside about the "other Christian groups," there are problems with Koester's characterization of the view of the Jerusalem Christians. Mention has just been made of the Jerusalem Hellenists like Stephen, whom Koester has just noted as examples of non-observance: "Peter and James remained within the realm of law observance and temple cult, whereas the Hellenists [here, those in Jerusalem] did not." There would, then, be a memory of the law-free diaspora-Jewish Christians in the church.

60. F. C. Baur, *Paul the Apostle of Jesus Christ: His Life and Works, His Epistles and Teachings* (Peabody, MA: Hendrickson, 2003), 1:131, though pp. 131-32 as a whole are important on this point.

61. See S. J. Gathercole, "The Pauline and Petrine *Sola Fide,*" in *Lutherische oder Neue Paulusperspektive?* ed. M. Bachmann, WUNT (Tübingen: Mohr, 2005), 309-27.

62. Gathercole, "The Pauline and Petrine *Sola Fide,*" 312-13, following Rohde, and to some extent Schlier.

63. F. Vouga, *An die Galater,* HNT (Tübingen: Mohr, 1998), 47.

(1) Titus was not *compelled* to be circumcised: that is, rather than the process taking place under duress, Titus was willing (cf. 1 Pet. 5:2: *mē anankastōs all' hekousiōs*) and was circumcised.
(2) Titus was *not compelled* to be circumcised: that is, the pillars would have very much liked Titus to be circumcised, hoping that Paul would accept the point, but they did not press him to do so.
(3) Titus was *not* compelled to be circumcised: that is, Paul might have wondered whether the Jerusalem pillars would require Titus's circumcision, but as it happens they did not.

The first option is not commonly entertained, though in the past it has had some distinguished adherents.[64] The second is Dunn's view: "The implication is that the pillar apostles did not agree with the 'false brothers' that Titus should be *compelled* to be circumcised, but they hoped Paul would agree to the proposition without compulsion."[65] The third option here has been criticized for not being as nuanced as the second, which has the merit of contrasting the pillars with the false brothers in Galatians 2:4-5 who would have required Titus's circumcision.[66] There is reason, however, to suspect that the third may be preferable to the first and second, because of Paul's placement of the *not.* The syntax, with *all' oude* at the beginning, suggests that Paul is saying: "I went up to Jerusalem to consult privately with the pillars in case I had run in vain: *but it was not the case* that Titus was compelled to be circumcised (and so I had clearly, *omnium consensu,* not been running in vain)."[67] If it was a matter of negating the *compulsion,* one would much more expect *alla Titos ho syn emoi, ouk ēnankasthē peritmēthēnai.* This is a key point, because it indicates that on the matter of whether gentiles need to be circumcised, Paul and the Jerusalem pillars stand together, in contrast to those whom Paul labels the "false-brothers," and to Acts 15's Judean visitors to Antioch, *tines tōn apo tēs haireseōs tōn Pharisaiōn pepisteukotes* (Acts 15:5; cf. 15:1). This still enables one to draw the contrast (rightly noted by Dunn) between

64. J. Weiss, *The History of Primitive Christianity,* vol. 1 (New York: Wilson-Erickson, 1937 [1914]), 272; F. C. Burkitt, *Christian Beginnings* (London: University of London Press, 1924), 118; the earliest reference I have found is F. W. Farrar, *Life and Work of Paul* (New York: Dutton, 1879), 416-19.

65. Dunn, "The Dialogue Progresses," in *Lutherische und Neue Paulusperspektive,* ed. M. Bachmann, WUNT 182 (Tübingen: Mohr [Siebeck], 2005), 418: this is not necessarily the implication at all, however, any more than it is the implication that Titus *was* circumcised, but willingly! Paul in the previous verse mentions the eventuality that *(per impossibile)* his gospel for the uncircumcised might not be compatible with the gospel of Jerusalem.

66. Dunn, "The Dialogue Progresses," 418, criticizing my view in Gathercole, "The Pauline and Petrine Sola Fide," 313.

67. This point is analogous to G. Alexander's criticism (NPNF first series, 13:14), on grounds of word order, of Farrar's argument for the first option.

the pillars and false-brothers of verses 4-5: these latter advocated circumcision, but the apostles did not.

The Spirit and Eschatology

For some scholars the assumption of a default position among the Jerusalem apostles that the gentiles should be circumcised is so strong that it is perhaps worth explaining *why* and *how* this might not be the case. According to Acts, part of the reason for the apostles' decision against circumcision is that they considered it the will of the Holy Spirit, under whose guidance they were led (Acts 15:28). Additionally, there is a pragmatic dimension: the apostles are concerned not to lay burdens beyond what is necessary (Acts 15:10, 19, 28).

But for all the appeal to the guidance of the Holy Spirit and the pragmatic dimensions to the decision, there are also two decisively theological rationales that can be articulated.

First, there is the contribution of Peter. A crucial guiding factor in the decision was the impression that the gentiles had already received the Holy Spirit: it is a small (and logical) step from this to the conclusion that thus circumcision was an irrelevance. Reference to the Holy Spirit in the statements about the influx of gentiles is certainly prominent. (1) In Acts 11:2-3, when Peter is criticized by the circumcised believers, he confirms to them that the gentiles had indeed received the Holy Spirit, a fact that reassures them (Acts 11:18). (2) Peter himself sees the coming of the Spirit as confirmation of what Jesus had promised about his baptism with the Holy Spirit (Acts 11:16; cf. Acts 1:5; Luke 3:16/Mark 1:8). (3) This pneumatological argument is repeated in Peter's speech at the Jerusalem council (Acts 15:8). (4) This idea is picked up by Paul, for whom the Spirit "trumps" circumcision in Romans 2:25-29 on the grounds that the Holy Spirit is the agent of the circumcision *of the heart*. The reasoning here is likely to be that it is irrational to impose circumcision, which is of course an *initiation* into the covenant, when the gentiles have already received the *eschatological filling* of the Spirit as promised by Jesus to those belonging to the Way.[68]

Second, there is the contribution of James, which seems to be less concerned with the event of the Spirit coming upon the gentiles (so crucial for Peter) and more concerned with exegesis. Bauckham's discussion of James's quotation from Amos 9:12 in Acts 15 is partly concerned to show that the argument does not rely on the wording of the LXX, but also notes that James applies to the gentiles the striking fact that God's name is invoked upon them.[69] The

68. Or, in the case of Rom. 2:25-29, experienced God's eschatological action.

69. R. J. Bauckham, "James and the Gentiles (Acts 15.13-21)," in *History, Literature, and*

phrase refers clearly to God's ownership, and indeed "in post-biblical Jewish literature it seems to have become . . . an expression of Israel's covenant status."[70] This is the eschatological viewpoint from which James views these gentiles as fulfilling Scripture. Thereafter, if the four requirements on the gentiles are drawn from Leviticus 17–18, as some think, it may be that James goes directly against the LXX. These requirements in Leviticus are cast in terms of what is enjoined upon "the alien who sojourns in your/their midst" (Lev. 17–18), whereas the view of the LXX translation according to which the "alien" is a "proselyte" is precisely the view that Acts 15 is trying to avoid.[71] Whatever the case with the four regulations, these gentiles are being seen *qua* gentiles in the midst of Jews (cf. LXX Jer. 12:16), rather than being incorporated *tout simple* into Israel by becoming Jews.

We are thus not merely dealing with the "quotidian" situation of gentiles converting to Judaism.[72] If we were in these realms of halakhic discussion, circumcision would almost certainly be a requirement.[73] Although there are various exceptional instances in which some considered circumcision unnecessary,[74] as Barclay puts it, "it is tolerably clear that male proselytes were required to get circumcised."[75] The closer analogy in pre-Christian Judaism if anything, however, is the circumstance perhaps envisaged in some early Jewish literature where, in the *eschatological* situation, gentiles are *included* in God's people without actually being *converted* or made Israelites by circumcision.[76] Both Peter and James see the eschatological scenario in which they find themselves as decisive.[77] What is

---

Society in the Book of Acts, ed. B. Witherington III (Cambridge: Cambridge University Press, 1996), 156-70.

70. Bauckham, "James and the Gentiles," 168, with a number of references. "Even the MT could easily have been understood by a Jewish Christian as predicting the extension of Israel's covenant status and privileges to the Gentile nations. The LXX merely makes this clearer" (169); "Amos 9.12 establishes that Gentiles may belong to the eschatological people of God precisely as Gentiles, without becoming Jews" (175). Interestingly, the Targum explicitly closes off this interpretation.

71. Bauckham, "James and the Gentiles," 177.

72. P. Fredriksen, "Judaism, the Circumcision of Gentiles, and Apocalyptic Hope," *JTS* 42 (1991): 532-64.

73. Peterson perhaps draws too clear a distinction between theology and halakah, which was certainly not a distinction Paul would have recognized.

74. N. J. McEleney, "Conversion, Circumcision and the Law," *NTS* 20 (1973): 319-41.

75. J. M. G. Barclay, *Jews in the Mediterranean Diaspora* (Edinburgh: T. & T. Clark, 1996), 439.

76. In addition to Fredriksen, "Judaism, the Circumcision of Gentiles," see T. L. Donaldson, *Judaism and the Gentiles: Jewish Patterns of Universalism (to 135 CE)* (Waco, TX: Baylor University Press, 2007), 501, 503-4, who sees Isa. 19:19-25 as a clear picture (cf. Isa. 25:6-10; Zech. 8:20-23), and, from the post-biblical period, *Pss. Sol.* 17 and *Sib. Or.* 5.493.

77. If the regulations in the Jerusalem Decree are drawn from Leviticus 17–18, the status of

probable in sum, is that because God had given gentiles the *eschatological* blessing of the Spirit, the *initiation* of circumcision is redundant. This is a quite reasonable deduction: Why insist on the traditional entry requirement if the gentiles are already in the house?[78] Put in this way, the insistence on circumcising gentile converts becomes the more illogical position.[79]

The Antioch Incident and Table-Fellowship

In addition to the question of circumcision, however, the question of Jew-Gentile commensality must be addressed. C. K. Barrett, for example, accepts that there was some recognition on the part of the Jerusalem disciples that gentile converts did not need to be circumcised, but considers the viewpoint of the pillars to be as follows: "We agreed that Gentiles might be evangelized, and that they might be converted and baptized; we allowed that they did not have to be circumcised, *but we never said that they might be permitted to share meals with Jews. They are Christians, but not Christians who can be allowed to share our Eucharist.*"[80] Dunn agrees.[81] Did Paul and the Jerusalem Christians disagree about table-fellowship, then? There are difficulties with this view as well.

Principally, it is clear that one pillar, Peter, had (with Barnabas) been eating regularly with gentiles according to Galatians 2:11-14 and 2:15: (a) Paul uses the imperfect tense *synēsthien* and thereby highlights Peter's ongoing habit of eating with the gentile Christians; (b) Paul implies that the same had been true to an even greater extent of Barnabas: that Paul says that "even he" (*kai Barnabas*) followed Peter suggests that Barnabas's habit of commensality was even more deeply rooted and longstanding; (c) Paul states that what was true of Peter and Barnabas was also true of the Jewish Christians in the church at Antioch, again implying that it had been their regular practice to share table-fellowship with the gentiles. The main point for our purposes here, however, is that (d) Paul can characterize Peter as having, up to the point of the arrival of those from James, acted *ethnikōs* in Antioch,[82]

---

the gentile believers is also analogous to that of resident aliens, though of course without any implication that they are of lower status than Jewish Christians.

78. A similar logic appears to lie behind not just Acts but also a good deal of Paul's reasoning. If God has already justified the gentiles, for example, why insist on the law observance which had that justification as its goal? Or again, if the gentiles already appear to be in reach of eschatological life, then, again, why insist on the law observance which had life in the age to come as its aim?

79. I am grateful to my colleague Dr. James Carleton Paget for extremely helpful conversations on this matter.

80. C. K. Barrett, *Freedom and Obligation* (London: SPCK, 1985), 12-13; emphasis mine.

81. Dunn, "The Dialogue Progresses," 420.

82. Gathercole, "The Pauline and Petrine *Sola Fide*," 321.

and (e) Peter shared with Paul the view that justification is by faith and not through works of Torah. That Peter had been acting *ethnikōs* shows that he had no objection in principle to sharing in table-fellowship with gentiles. In this sense, then, it is reasonably evident that Paul and Peter agreed on this theological point of the possibility, even necessity, of commensality. Dunn finds it impossible to consider that they agreed on the theological point because Peter and the others had deviated from the truth of the gospel: as such "Paul certainly thought the disagreement with Peter was theological in character and not merely a social nuisance or regrettable inconsistency. To exculpate Peter at this point is to diminish the theological weight of Gal 2:16."[83] Here, however, it should be recognized that Galatians 2:16 is defined precisely by Paul as what "we" (2:15: *hēmeis*, i.e., inclusive of both Paul and Peter) "know" (2:16: *eidotes*). And Paul's statement in verse 14 specifically addresses the *actions* (*orthpodousin*) of Peter and the others, rather than their theological convictions. Peter was apparently fearful that a report of his loose behavior would find its way back to Jerusalem, whether because it would stir up hostility from traditionalist Jewish believers, or because it would endanger mission to non-believers.[84] It is, nevertheless, precisely a matter of "regrettable inconsistency" (though Paul did not express it so mildly!) between Peter's theological convictions and his actions.

What about James, however? Does the Antioch incident reveal not only a rift between Paul and Peter but also tension between Peter and James? It is argued by a number that "those from James," accustomed to the conservative practices in Jerusalem, were sufficiently shocked by what was going on in Antioch that their disapproval provoked Peter to abandon the gentiles. It is certainly questionable, however, whether the disapproval of James is evident here. Certainly, Peter's instance of *akrasia* arose from his "fearing those of the circumcision." But this group, "those of the circumcision," can and should be distinguished from James and his envoys. One commentator has characterized this group as "a group whose self-identity was bound up with circumcision, that is, here at least, with maintaining the distinctive markers of Jewish identity which circumcision itself most clearly expressed. . . . Peter could well have shown some trepidation at confronting such zealous Jews, believers included."[85] Since the "false brothers" of Galatians 2:4 (as well as perhaps non-Christian Jews among whom Peter missionized) are more natural candidates for this profile, James is probably not included. Paul's syntax does not allow for easy overlap between "those from James" and "those of the circumcision," even though James may

83. Dunn, "The Dialogue Progresses," 422.

84. F. F. Bruce, *The Epistle to the Galatians: A Commentary on the Greek Texts,* NIGTC (Grand Rapids: Eerdmans, 1982), 130, implies that both these two possibilities are likely, commenting also (following Reicke) that the political troubles of the time would have exacerbated the anxieties in Jerusalem, with the growing anti-Roman fervor making Peter's commensality with gentiles doubly outrageous to many.

85. J. D. G. Dunn, *The Epistle to the Galatians* (Peabody, MA: Hendrickson, 1993), 123.

perhaps, if Galatians 2:1-14 pre-dates the Jerusalem council, have been more tolerant of the circumcision group than Paul. We have no evidence, however, that James disapproved of what was going on in Antioch. There is no evidence, outside of some scholarly interpretations of this passage, of any distance between James and Peter in these matters.

It is, then, a serious question as to whether Galatians 2:11-14 can really bear the weight of the Baur hypothesis either in its original form or in its repristinations by Barrett and Dunn. This is both because of what *can* be deduced (points a-e above), and also because very little else can be concluded with any confidence from a report so compressed that suspicious readings must rely more on conjecture than on solid evidence.[86]

The First Official Document of "the Way": The Apostolic Decree

One of the consequences of the two aspects of this controversy (i.e., both circumcision and table-fellowship) was the publication of the first official document of the early Christian movement.[87] Its primary author was perhaps James, although it was published under the auspices of the "apostles and elders" as a group. A number of copies of it were made, for it is sent to Antioch, Syria, and Cilicia. It is clear from Acts 16:4 that its audience is wider still, since Paul, Silas, and Timothy went to the towns around Derbe, Lystra, and Iconium instructing the churches "to keep the decrees (*dogmata*) considered by the apostles and elders who are in Jerusalem" (16:4). The purpose of the decree is presumably both to emphasize that gentiles are acceptable to God *qua* gentiles, and to ensure table-fellowship between Jewish and gentile believers, by exhorting gentiles not to organize meals along lines that would ride roughshod over long-held Jewish sensibilities.[88]

All in all, then, there is a good deal more unanimity on the apostolic gospel than the diversifiers allow. This is not to say that there were no differences of opinion. It may well have been, for example, that there were differing valuations of the temple. Some of the Jerusalem church who sided with the apostles clearly

86. Barclay, *Jews in the Mediterranean Diaspora,* 384, remarks on the Antioch incident that "the precise contours of that dispute are now obscure."

87. See C. K. Barrett, *The Acts of the Apostles,* ICC (Edinburgh: T. & T. Clark, 1998), 740 on source/redactional questions.

88. It may be that, as has been noted, these regulations are those applied to resident aliens in Leviticus, but additionally, the reasoning is probably that food offered to idols, strangled meat, and blood are so ingrained as abhorrent to Jews over centuries (15:21) that it is unreasonable to expect Jews simply to change their minds about the matter overnight. The reference to *porneia* is difficult on any explanation (why single out this particular moral item?), but would again be reassuring to Jews, given assumptions about Greek and Roman dining.

did not find commensality with gentiles as easy as Paul, as the Antioch incident shows. Nevertheless, there are clearly some scholarly assumptions, such as the idea that the Jerusalem apostles would naturally have required the circumcision of gentile converts, or that they disapproved of the Jew-gentile commensality in Antioch, which are in need of correction. As such, Ehrman's remark noted above that the Judaizers could make a good case for the authenticity of their views is an overstatement. Overall, the apostles held a unified core based on the scripturally rooted death of Jesus for our sins and resurrection, accompanied by a remarkable degree of agreement on how gentiles should be viewed.

Apostolic Connections to NT Literature (the Gospels and Acts)

If the basic argument of the first part of this essay is correct, then, do the literary remains (beyond the Apostolic Decree) of earliest Christianity in the NT have any real historical links to the apostles or their associates? Such connections are frequently assumed to be imaginary:

> The criterion "apostolic" is useless when Christian movements that were later condemned as heretical can claim genuine apostolic origin. It is certainly untenable that the orthodox church and only this orthodox church was the direct offspring of the teachings, doctrines and institutions of the apostles' times and that only this church was able to preserve the apostolic heritage uncontaminated by foreign influences.[89]

The matter was already treated to some extent, though in a different manner, by Bauer, who with his geographical focus had been particularly interested in debunking the claims of Edessa and Egypt to apostolic successions.[90] Pagels's treatment of this theme is perhaps slightly more of a problematic matter, since she cannot easily deal with the claims of the "gnostics" to apostolic tradition or succession, given her emphasis on how Gnostics did not feel restricted by historical connections to the apostles.[91] Most recently, the emphasis of Ehrman on the anonymity of the NT Gospels functions in the same way to stress the distance from the apostles.[92]

On the other hand, however, there is a good deal of evidence for strong historical connections between the apostles and a number of the NT books. For reasons of space we will limit the focus here to the apostolic connections of the

89. Koester, "GNOMAI DIAPHOROI," 115.
90. E.g., Bauer, *Orthodoxy and Heresy,* 9-10, 45.
91. E.g., Pagels, *Gnostic Gospels,* 25-26.
92. Ehrman, "Christianity Turned on Its Head," 117-18.

four NT Gospels, along with Acts. In each case we will treat the Gospels under the headings of "attribution" (dealing with the question of anonymity) and "apostolic credentials." We will begin with John, not trying surreptitiously to suggest Johannine priority, but because its evidence has implications for the attributions of the titles of the other Gospels.

John

Attribution

The manuscript evidence connecting John with the Fourth Gospel is the earliest for any of the Gospels:[93]

Superscript		**Subscript**	
P66 (c. 200)	*euangelion kata Iōannēn*		
P75 (early III)	*euangelion kata Iōanēn*		
ℵ (IV)	*kata Iōannēn*	ℵ (IV)	*euangelion kata Iōannēn*
A (V)	no superscript	A (V)	*euangelion kata Iōannēn*
B (IV)	*kata Iōanēn*	B (IV)	*kata Iōanēn*
C (V)	*euangelion kata Iōannēn*	C (V)	*euangelion kata Iōannēn*
D (V)	. . . *euangelion kata Iōannēn*	D (V)	*euangelion kata Iōanēn*
W (IV/V)	*euangelion kata Iōannēn*	W (IV/V)	*kata Iōannēn*

Clearly, then, there is some consistency here, the only difference being between the use of a longer and a shorter title. As we will see, this consistency is common to all the Gospels in the early uncials, and so, given the consistency of the titles with one another, it is likely that all four Gospels were called *euangelion kata . . .* in the manuscript tradition at the time of P66 around 200.

This is supported by several other pieces of evidence from the end of the second century:

93. For the textual data here, see S. J. Gathercole, "The Titles of the Gospels in the Earliest New Testament Manuscripts," *ZNW* 104 (2013): 33-76. NA[27] curiously does not mention subscript titles, except by giving mss. in brackets at the beginning. This is also misleading, as where a title appears at the beginning, NA[27] does not indicate whether it also appears at the end. This is a more widespread problem: editions of classical texts have also not always set out evidence for titles with the same completeness as for other textual variation. See, e.g., F. Susemihl, ed., *Aristotelis Quae Feruntur Magna Moralia* (Leipzig: Teubner, 1883). The datings of mss. below follow those provided in NA[27]. There are of course difficulties with dates being given with the precision (or indeed at the same time the vagueness) of, e.g., "ca. 200," but it is clearly far beyond the scope of this essay to engage in detailed discussion of dates of individual manuscripts.

- Irenaeus's use of the same "Gospel according to . . ." formula;[94]
- the reference to "according to Luke" in the Muratorian canon;[95]
- the use of the same "Gospel according to . . ." titles in Clement of Alexandria.[96]

This is interesting evidence for its geographical spread: we have three authors using the same formulaic gospel titles in Gaul, Rome, and Alexandria in the last quarter of the second century, and this in addition to what is also found in P66 and P75. Seriously under-researched in this connection are the old Gospel prologues, which are also worthy of consideration, though they may well be better dated after the second century.[97]

Perhaps some of the most underused evidence pointing in a similar direction is the fact that the same formula is attested in the titles of apocryphal Gospels composed in the second century, whose titles clearly pick up on the usage of the *euangelion kata* . . . formula connected with their first-century counterparts:

- the *Gospel according to the Egyptians* (attested in Clement and Hippolytus).[98]
- the *Gospel according to the Hebrews* (attested in Clement and Origen).[99]
- the *Gospel according to Peter* (attested in Serapion and Origen).[100]
- the *Gospel according to Thomas* (attested in Hippolytus and Origen)[101]
- the *Gospel according to Matthias* (attested in Origen)[102]
- the *Gospel according to Basilides (?)* (attested in Origen)[103]

There may of course be some assimilation of the titles to the more familiar formula, but this is unlikely in many cases: the fact that the title of the *Gospel according to Thomas* is also found in the colophon to the manuscript of that text; in the case of the *Gospel of Judas,* where the title is made up of the briefer "Gospel + genitive," the same is found in both Irenaeus's testimonium and in the manuscript of

94. Irenaeus, *AH* 1.26.2 (though this passage only survives in Latin; *AH* 3.12.12; fr. 29 (Harvey) = fr. 27 in *ANF* 1:573.

95. *Muratorian fragment,* line 2: *tertio evangelii librum secundo lucan.*

96. E.g., Clem. *Strom.* 1.21.147.5 (Matt.); *Quis div.* 5.1 (Mark); *Strom.* 1.21.145.2 (Luke); *Paed.* 1.6.38.2 (John).

97. For the texts, see R. G. Heard, "The Old Gospel Prologues," *JTS* 6 (1955): 1-16, who is opposed to an early date, in contrast to D. De Bruyne, "Les plus anciens prologues latins des Évangiles," *Revue Bénédictine* 40 (1928): 193-214, who in this first critical edition of the texts favored a second-century date (followed also by no less than A. von Harnack and F. C. Burkitt).

98. Clem. *Strom.* 3.9.63.1; Hippol. *Ref.* 5.7.9.

99. Clem. *Strom.* 2.9.45.5; Origen, *Comm. in Joh.* 2.12.87.

100. Serapion *apud* Eus. *HE* 6.12.2; Origen, *Comm. in Matt.* 10.17.

101. Hippol. *Ref.* 5.7.20; Origen, *Hom. in Luc.* 1.2 (Origen GCS 9:5, ll. 9-10).

102. Origen, *Hom. in Luc.* 1.2 (Origen GCS 9:5, l. 10).

103. Origen, *Hom. in Luc.* 1.2 (Origen GCS 9:5, l. 3).

that text. As such, it seems very likely that at least some of these second-century gospels took over an already-familiar formula for their titles.

Why then do such a large number of scholars consider the Gospels as anonymous compositions?[104] Some appeal to the uniformity of the titles as evidence of their lateness,[105] though for Hengel this is actually an argument in favor of their antiquity.[106] Hengel adds that anonymous or untitled composition is both rare, and problematic, given the absolute need for the organization of books in libraries. Even though the full "Gospel *according to* . . ." nomenclature may reflect the existence of a plurality of Gospels, this is no argument for anonymity, the case for which is in fact far weaker than is commonly assumed. A number of factors contribute to the impression that the attributions are very early. The evidence is not sufficient to say that they are original, but neither is it right to declare apodictically that the Gospels were anonymous. To say that they were is a classic logical fallacy: moving from "we do not know X" to "we know that not X."[107]

Apostolic Credentials

What of other evidence for connections specifically between the Fourth Gospel and an apostle? In the recent survey of the current state of Johannine scholarship, *What We Have Heard from the Beginning,* the index entry to "Cambridge University" has more page references than do the entries for "John Son of Zebedee, Apostle" and "John the Elder."[108] This is clearly reflective of the status of the historical John's connection to the Fourth Gospel in much twentieth-century scholarship. However, the past few years have also seen a renewed appreciation of the possibilities of Johannine authorship.

According to the majority of scholars, it is very unlikely that either John

104. "Most NT scholars agree that the gospels are anonymous and that the present titles probably were not added until sometime in the second century." E. D. Freed, *The New Testament: A Critical Introduction* (Belmont, CA: Wadsworth, 2000), 123.

105. Freed, *New Testament,* 123.

106. M. Hengel, *Die Evangelienüberschriften* (Sitzungsberichte der Heidelberger Akademie der Wissenschaften. Phil.-hist. Kl., 1984); repr. in Hengel, *Jesus und die Evangelien: Kleine Schriften V,* WUNT 211 (Tübingen: Mohr, 2007), 526-67. For a briefer exposition, see Hengel, *Studies in the Gospel of Mark,* and *The Four Gospels and the One Gospel of Jesus Christ* (London: SCM, 2000), 48-56. For a survey of some older English-language discussion, see N. Stonehouse, *The Origins of the Synoptic Gospels* (Grand Rapids: Eerdmans, 1963), 15-18.

107. Strauss is interesting to note on this point in another context: "[A]t all events the author of this work wishes especially to guard himself, in those places where he declares he knows not what happened, from the imputation of asserting that he knows that nothing happened." D. F. Strauss, *The Life of Jesus Critically Examined* (Ramsey, NJ: Sigler, 1994 [1835-36; ET 1846]).

108. T. Thatcher, ed., *What We Have Heard from the Beginning: The Past, Present, and Future of Johannine Studies* (Waco, TX: Baylor University Press, 2007).

the Son of Zebedee or a distinct Elder John composed the Gospel that bears his name. On the other hand, a great number of these scholars do consider there to be an indirect, even a *close indirect* relation. This includes the two most influential English-language commentaries of recent times. For Brown (or "early Brown," at least), the apostle John was "the source of the underlying historical tradition which had already undergone some development in his own preaching"; as such "we would posit *one principal disciple*" who shaped "the historical material received from John"; and so the gospel is "truly in the spirit of John."[109] Brown's "principal disciple" is not dissimilar from Barrett's pupil of John the apostle who composed John 1–20.[110] The same is true again of Schnackenburg, who considers that a Hellenistic disciple of John composed the gospel.[111] There are of course still a number, however, who conclude that the author is simply unknown,[112] or, as in the case of Bultmann, that there are various anonymous — and perhaps widely separated — authorial and redactional processes.[113]

There has, however, been a strong body of scholarship advocating that John son of Zebedee was the author. In particular, evangelical scholars such as Morris, Carson, and Blomberg have maintained this view. Carson has emphasized in particular some of the difficulties with the assumed obstacles to Johannine authorship. The problem of the apostle's age is no obstacle, Carson noting that C. H. Dodd published *Historical Tradition in the Fourth Gospel* when he was in his eighties![114] The apostle's age is also reinforced by the claim that Polycarp (died ca. 155 C.E.) had in his youth been acquainted with John (Irenaeus, *Letter to Florinus,* apud Eus. *HE* 5.20.6). Nor is great skill in a second language such a difficulty, according to Carson. Blomberg revives Westcott's arguments for Palestinian Jewish apostolic authorship, defending that view against its twentieth-century cultured despisers.[115]

Concurrent with these claims, however, have been cases made for a different author, who is yet also a disciple. In the 1970s, Cullmann took the author to be a real historical disciple of Jesus, not named in the Gospel, and not one of the twelve.[116] Currently, however, the best arguments in this category are for another

109. R. E. Brown, *The Gospel according to John I–XII* (Garden City, NY: Doubleday, 1966), c-cii.

110. Barrett, *John,* 133.

111. R. S. Schnackenburg, *The Gospel according to St John,* vol. 1, *Commentary on Chapters 1–4,* Herder's Theological Commentary on the New Testament (London: Burns & Oates, 1968), 102.

112. J. Marsh, *The Gospel of St John* (Harmondsworth, UK: Penguin [Pelican], 1968), 25.

113. R. Bultmann, *The Gospel of John: A Commentary* (Oxford: Blackwell, 1971), 11-12.

114. D. A. Carson, *The Gospel according to John,* PNTC (Grand Rapids: Eerdmans, 1991), 79.

115. C. Blomberg, *The Historical Reliability of John's Gospel* (Leicester: Apollos, 2001), 27-29.

116. O. Cullmann, *The Johannine Circle* (London: SCM, 1976), 75-76, on a disciple not one of the twelve, and 77, on a real historical figure.

John, another disciple, but *John the elder,* distinct from the apostle. The principal evidence for this is a passage in Papias, which distinguishes between John the apostle (son of Zebedee, brother of James) and John the elder:

> I will not hesitate in setting out for you, with interpretations, whatever I once learned well from the Elders and have well remembered, confirming their truth. For I did not rejoice, as many do, over those who talked a great deal, but rather over those who taught the truth; over those who remembered not strange (or: others') instructions (*tas allotrias entolas*), but those given reliably (*tēi pistei*)[117] from the Lord and coming from the truth itself. If it happened that someone who had also followed the Elders came, I enquired about these Elders' teachings, that is, what Andrew or what Peter said, or what Philip or what Thomas or what James or what John or what Matthew, or any other of the disciples of the Lord, including both Aristion and the elder John — those disciples of the Lord, said. For I did not think that material from scrolls would profit me as much as material from a living and abiding voice. (Eus. *HE* 3.39.3-4)

Hengel and Bauckham in particular find warrant in this passage for distinguishing between the apostle John, the son of Zebedee, and the other John, the elder. Hengel also presses the case for John the apostle having died relatively young, on the basis of a tradition that might go back to Papias. Bauckham appeals to a number of similar arguments, but in addition stresses that the earliest patristic evidence does not in fact support the identification of the evangelist with the son of Zebedee.[118] Such a Jerusalem-based disciple, perhaps with priestly connections, would be better equipped to compose such a "spiritual gospel," meeting the objection that it would be improbable for "a Galilean fisherman (admittedly a member of a 'family business') called, presumably for good reason, a 'son of thunder,' even being able to write or edit and publish, a work so profound and serene as the fourth gospel is."[119] Indeed, his personal acquaintance with Jesus also provides a rationale for the different perspective of John from that of the Synoptics: as an intimate of Jesus, John the elder felt uniquely qualified to *interpret* Jesus, rather than merely report.[120]

It is certainly true that the internal evidence of the Gospel presupposes an eyewitness author of at least the greatest part of the book. This is confirmed by the earliest patristic evidence of *a* John being the author. Certainly many of

117. Perhaps "to the faith" (thus Holmes).

118. M. Hengel, *The Johannine Question* (London: SCM, 1989); R. J. Bauckham, *Jesus and the Eyewitnesses: The Gospels as Eyewitness Testimony* (Grand Rapids: Eerdmans, 2006); Bauckham, *The Testimony of the Beloved Disciple: Narrative, History, and Theology in the Gospel of John* (Grand Rapids: Baker, 2007).

119. Marsh, *The Gospel of St John,* 25.

120. Bauckham, *Jesus and the Eyewitnesses,* 410-11.

the standard objections assumed in twentieth-century scholarship should be regarded now with a good deal of suspicion. If one opts for an author called John, however, one is still left with the difficulty of deciding between the two Johannine candidates.

In favor of the apostle is the fact that it is only the Papias reference that distinguishes between the two figures, and even there suspicions have been raised about the transmission of the Papias quotation.[121] Some of Bauckham's contentions about the second-century evidence are open to question, such as whether Polycrates really makes an exegetical identification of John the elder and John the priest of Acts 4:6,[122] and whether Irenaeus so clearly distinguishes between John the apostle and John the disciple of the Lord.[123] The evidence assembled by Hengel that John the apostle was martyred earlier in the first century is based on a number of pieces of data, but they are all fairly late. On the other hand, Papias's distinction between John the apostle and John the elder is on the surface fairly clear, and it does circumvent perhaps the most awkward of the objections to authorship by a fisherman and "son of thunder," that of the theological depth of the Gospel.

We cannot decide the question here: it would take far too much space to evaluate, for example, the attestation in Philip of Side, Gregorius Monachus, the *Martyr Calendar of Carthage* et al. of the Papias tradition about the death of John. It can simply be concluded that the evidence for authorship either by the apostle or the elder is perfectly reasonable to conclude. Even of those who have rejected the idea of authorship by an eyewitness, however, many have taken the Gospel to have been written by a disciple of the apostle. Barrett, Brown, and Schnackenburg thus all see the apostolic connection to be structurally the same as that which Papias asserts for the Gospel of Mark in its connection to Peter, to which we now turn.

Mark

Attribution

Although not stretching back as far as in the case of John, the early Markan manuscript tradition shows remarkable agreement in the titles prefacing, and appended to, the Gospel:

121. Eusebius perhaps tampering with it, according to some, as part of his anti-Chiliast agenda.

122. Bauckham, *Jesus and the Eyewitnesses,* 451. Even granting that second-century authors engaged in such exegetical strategies (can what Bauckham regards as methodical be distinguished from mere confusion?), would Polycrates make an identification of an evangelist with an opponent of the good news (Ac. 4.16-22)?

123. Bauckham, *Jesus and the Eyewitnesses,* 452-68.

Superscripts		**Subscripts**	
ℵ (IV)	*kata Markon*	ℵ (IV)	*euangelion kata Markon*
A (V)	*euangelion kata Markon*	A (V)	*euangelion kata Markon*
B (IV)	*kata Markon*	B (IV)	*kata Markon*
		C (V)	*euangelion kata Markon*
D (V)	*euangelion kata Markon*	D^sup124 (V?)	*euangelion kata Markon*
W (IV/V)	*euangelion kata Markon*	W (IV/V)	*euangelion kata Markon . . .*

In addition to the considerations discussed under the heading of John above, the attribution to Mark gains additional support when one considers the *testimonium* in Papias from the early second century, even though a title is not supplied there. If we are concerned here primarily with the attribution to Mark (i.e., authorship), rather than with the title *euangelion,* or the difficulties associated with the *kata,* there is no clear reason to doubt the antiquity, indeed the originality of the attribution.

Apostolic Credentials

Our earliest evidence for an apostle lying behind Mark's Gospel comes from Papias:

> And the Elder said this: "Mark was Peter's interpreter: whatever he remembered, he accurately wrote down what was said or done by the Lord, but not in order. For he neither heard nor followed the Lord, but, as I said, latterly followed Peter, who prepared his teachings according to necessity and did not prepare any kind of orderly arrangement of the Lord's words. So Mark made no mistake writing down various things as he remembered them. For he made it his single purpose not to omit anything of the things that he heard or to be untruthful about anything of them." (Papias *apud* Eus. *HE* 3.39.15)

Among the many details here, Papias's principal claim is that Mark wrote down the memoirs of Peter. Moreover, Papias says that his knowledge of this comes from a source, *ho presbyteros*; as such, we would need reason to think that Papias invented the idea.

Unlike the Hebrew Matthew theory (on which more later), there is other external evidence connecting Peter and Mark.[125] 1 Peter already has Mark as much more than Peter's interpreter: he is *ho huios mou* (1 Pet. 5:13). In Acts 12 Peter is

124. The title here comes from a later hand in D.

125. Cf. Marcus: "[W]ere it not for Papias, one would never suspect that the Second Gospel were particularly Petrine." J. Marcus, *Mark 1–8,* AB 27 (New York: Doubleday, 1999), 24.

presented as knowing and staying in the house of Mary, John Mark's mother.[126] It may well be, as F. F. Bruce has suggested, that Peter actually belonged to (and presumably led) the section of the Jerusalem church that met in Mary's house.[127] The size of Mary's house (it has a courtyard and a gate) speaks in favor of the possibility that it functioned as a "place of worship,"[128] and this is strongly implied by the statement in Acts 12:12 that a considerable number of people had gathered there and were praying. According to Acts, Peter's prominence and familiarity to the household means that his voice is quite naturally recognized by Rhoda, Mary's servant girl (Acts 12:14). John Mark is a member of the Jerusalem church, where Peter is one of the pillars. He retreated there when something occurred to make him leave the company of Paul and Barnabas in Acts 13. He presumably stayed there until the *paroxysmos* in Acts 15 when he went to Cyprus with Barnabas. Colossians refers to Mark as cousin (*anepsios*) of Barnabas (Col. 4:10), who had apparently been a member of the Jerusalem church with Peter from or nearly from its beginnings (Acts 4:36-37).

While Joel Marcus provides some acute criticisms of the view that Mark was a gentile, his arguments against the John Mark hypothesis do not convince. (Adela Yarbro Collins's recent commentary is much more open to the possibility of composition by John Mark.[129]) The possibility that Papias's claim on Mark's behalf is a counter to Basilides' claim to be a spiritual grandson of Peter is unlikely on chronological grounds:[130] if there is competing polemic, the reverse is far more likely.[131] Similarly, the objection that Mark does not appear closer to

126. John Mark is almost certainly the well-known Mark.

127. Bruce, *The Pauline Circle,* 74, citing Acts 12:12. Was James's section of the Jerusalem church elsewhere, as suggested when, *chez* Mary, Peter gives instructions for the story of his escape to be passed on to James and the brothers? Or does it mean that the brothers regularly met elsewhere?

128. R. J. Bauckham, "James and the Jerusalem Community," in *Jewish Believers in Jesus: The Early Centuries,* ed. O. Skarsaune and R. Hvalvik (Peabody, MA: Hendrickson, 2007), 55-95, on 87.

129. A. Yarbro Collins, *Mark: A Commentary,* Hermeneia (Minneapolis: Fortress, 2007), 5-6.

130. Marcus, *Mark,* 22-23.

131. A number of scholars place Papias's writing ca. 110 CE: see W. Schoedel, "Papias," *ABD* 5:140, noting Bartlet, Schoedel himself, and Körtner. The most important reasons for dating Papias's *floruit* to the late first/early second century are assembled (with criticisms of the mid-second-century date) in R. Yarbrough, "The Date of Papias: A Reassessment," *JETS* 26 (1983): 181-91. These reasons include the fragment of Irenaeus (*EH* 3.39.1; cf. *AH* 5.33.4) calling him an *archaios anēr* (cf. Manaen in Acts as an *archaios mathētēs*), and Eusebius himself, at the highpoint of his criticism of Papias, referring to his *archaiotēs* (*HE* 3.39.13), and fixing him firmly in the early part of Trajan's principate (*HE* 3.36); Yarbrough also adduces the evidence of Eusebius's *Chronicon* ("Date of Papias," 186). Papias belongs with "those who first succeeded the apostles" (*HE* 3.37.4), and is clumped with Clement, Ignatius, and Polycarp (*HE* 3.36 and

the events than Matthew and Luke is a rather vague and subjective judgment, which has in any case been contested.[132] Marcus may well be right that Papias is defending Mark against charges of being inaccurate or higgledy-piggledy, but this is no incentive to distrust him.[133] The objection that if Mark were the Petrine Gospel par excellence, one would expect Peter to be more prominent than in the other Gospels,[134] is illogical: in such matters, Mark cannot be evaluated by the standards of *later* works, and in any case, of the disciples Peter's name *does* have the greatest frequency in Mark (among the Synoptics) when the relative lengths of the Gospels are taken into account.[135]

This last objection from Marcus has been answered at further length by Bauckham. Peter being the first- and last-mentioned disciple might not form an inclusio of eyewitness testimony in Mark, as Bauckham argues,[136] but it is quite clear that in the first reference to the disciples and at the very end of the Gospel there are otherwise almost redundant (and therefore probably emphatic) references to Peter (1:16; 16:7).[137] It also possible, as Bauckham argues, that "the plural-to-singular narrative device" in Mark aligns the reader with "the perspective of Peter and those closest to him."[138]

Also widely neglected (as in, e.g., Marcus's commentary) is the evidence of Justin. In the *Dialogue,* there is a reference to Peter as a disciple whose name is changed by Jesus, and then immediately afterwards mention of the *apomnēmoneumata autou*:

3.38.5). Moreover, if Papias's claim that he has this tradition from John the elder is true (*touth' ho presbyteros elegen*), the acquisition of this particular piece of source material must be dated very early, that is, in the 90s or earlier. Basilides' activity is to be located in the principate of Hadrian (117-138 C.E.). See Turner, *Manuscript, Society and Belief,* 50; W. Löhr, *Basilides und seine Schule: Eine Studie zur Theologie- und Kirchengeschichte* (Tübingen: Mohr, 1995), 325.

132. Marcus, *Mark 1–8,* 23. On might contrast, e.g., Turner, who writes that in Mark, "we have before us the experience of a disciple and apostle. . . . Matthew and Luke are Christian historians who stand away from the events, and concentrate their narrative on the central figure." C. H. Turner, "Markan Usage: Notes Critical and Exegetical, on the Second Gospel V. The Movements of Jesus and His Disciples and the Crowd," *JTS* 26 (1925): 225-40, on 225, cited in Bauckham, *Jesus and the Eyewitnesses,* 156.

133. Marcus, *Mark 1–8,* 22-23. Marcus's tone is extraordinarily skeptical at one point: "[P]eople *sometimes* tell the truth when they are defending themselves or something they hold dear" (23)! In the copy of Marcus's commentary in the Divinity Library in Cambridge, a student has written in the margin, "How magnanimous!"

134. Cf. Marcus, *Mark 1–8,* 24.

135. Bauckham, *Jesus and the Eyewitnesses,* 125-26. John has a rather higher density than any of the Synoptics.

136. Bauckham, *Jesus and the Eyewitnesses,* 124-25.

137. Further, there is a redundant reference to the occupation of Simon and Andrew in Mark 1:16.

138. Bauckham, *Jesus and the Eyewitnesses,* 164, and 155-82 *in toto.*

> There is a statement that he renamed one of the apostles "Peter," and it is written in his memoirs (*en tois apomnēmoneumasin autou*) that this happened, and this is alongside the naming of another two apostles, the sons of Zebedee, with the name "Boanerges", i.e. "Sons of Thunder." (*Dial.* 106.3)

This has been thought variously to be (a) textually corrupt, (b) a reference by way of an objective genitive to *Jesus* ("memoirs *about* him"), or (c) a reference to the memoirs of *Peter,* and therefore Mark's Gospel.[139] Stanton's note of the reference in the same sentence to the sons of Zebedee having their names changed to Boanerges is important, however, given that James and John have this moniker in Mark, but not in Matthew or Luke (or John for that matter). For Stanton, and more recently Skarsaune, this is an argument in favor of Justin's knowledge of Mark, but it should also be taken into account as early evidence for the possible association of Peter's memoirs with Mark's Gospel.[140] It is perhaps especially striking that Justin's language here overlaps with that of Papias, who says that Mark wrote *hōs apemnēmoneusen.*[141]

Matthew

Attribution

Mark's authority is already assumed in its incorporation into Matthew and Luke,[142] which have sometimes been described as "second editions" of Mark.[143] On the

139. Foster has recently dismantled the theory advanced by a few scholars of connections between Justin and the *Gospel of Peter.* See his "The Relationship between Justin Martyr and the So-called Gospel of Peter," in *Justin Martyr and His Worlds,* ed. S. Parvis and P. Foster (Minneapolis: Fortress, 2007), 104-12.

140. G. N. Stanton, *Jesus and Gospel* (Cambridge: Cambridge University Press, 2004), 101; O. Skarsaune, "Justin and His Bible," in Parvis and Foster, eds., *Justin Martyr and His Worlds,* 53-76, on 72.

141. This point should not be pressed, however, as it would lose some of its force if Mark is the subject of the verb *apemnēmoneusen.* If Peter is the subject, however (for which see Bauckham, *Jesus and the Eyewitnesses,* 235), then it is striking indeed. Perhaps, however, Justin knows Papias's ambiguous statement and is interpreting it to mean that Peter is the subject of the verb, on which view the value of Justin's testimony as independent would be diminished.

142. I am aware of criticisms of this view, namely that Matthew and Luke rework Mark precisely because Mark was regarded not as sacrosanct but inadequate. Their extensive, often verbatim, adoption of Markan material tells against this, however. Moreover, Papias's *testimonium* provides an example of how Mark's Gospel can be regarded as quite acceptable on its own terms ("Mark made no mistake . . ."), but as requiring in a different context reorganization and expansion.

143. Despite the overlap, this is not particularly accurate, although second editions can

origins of Matthew, we do not have much in the earliest patristic testimony beyond the mere assertion that Matthew was the author. Papias's fuller claim that Matthew's Gospel was originally written in a Semitic language is certainly open to question. Davies and Allison are almost certainly right, however, that it is unlikely that Papias concocted the idea of Matthew's authorship of the Gospel "out of thin air."[144] Thereafter, Papias may be our only independent authority for this patristic attribution, however, since the numerous other references (e.g., Irenaeus, *AH* 3.1.1) appear either to repeat or to build on Papias.

The attribution in the manuscript tradition is comparable to what we find in the case of Mark, with the important exception of the much-neglected "fly-leaf" to Matthew accompanying P4:[145]

Superscript		**Subscript**	
P4 (early III)	*euangelion kata Maththaion*		
ℵ (IV)	*kata Maththaion*	A (V)	*euangelion kata Matthaion*
B (IV)	*kata Maththaion*	B* (IV)	*euangelion kata Maththaion*
C (V)	*euangelion kata Matthaion*		
		D (V)	*euangelion kata Maththaion*
W (IV/V)	*euangelion kata Maththaion*	W (IV/V)	*kata Mattheon*

The general considerations discussed above pertain to Matthew as well.

A further piece of external evidence can also be mustered. This comes in *Gos. Thom.* 13, a dialogue in which Jesus asks the disciples a version of the "Who do you say that I am?" question. The two interlocutors who initially supply wrong answers to the question are Matthew and Peter. (Thomas then gives a more accurate answer.) Peter is a natural choice in a work that seeks to undercut apostolic authority. Matthew is a strange disciple to include, however, unless of course he is known as the author of the Gospel most influential of the time (early-mid second century). Some have also raised the possibility of the wrong answer given

---

sometimes be, in the words commonly used in new editions of German books, *"völlig neu bearbeitet und stark erweitert"* (completely reworked and greatly expanded)!

144. W. D. Davies and D. C. Allison, *A Critical and Exegetical Commentary on the Gospel according to St. Matthew,* ICC (Edinburgh: T. & T. Clark, 1988), 1:17.

145. P4 is usually treated merely as a set of fragments of Luke 1–6, but accompanying it (in the stuffing of a third-century Philo codex) is a single sheet with the title of Matthew written in a different hand. This is usually taken to be later than the Luke fragments (which are usually dated late second or early third century), but of course must pre-date the Philo codex into which it was inserted. For discussion of this leaf, see now S. J. Gathercole, "The Earliest Manuscript Title of Matthew's Gospel (BnF Suppl. gr. 1120 ii 3 / 𝔓4)," *NovT* 54 (2012): 209-35. There is some important evidence for earlier use of the hook or apostrophe between double consonants in P. Comfort, *Encountering the Manuscripts: An Introduction to New Testament Paleography and Textual Criticism* (Nashville: Broadman & Holman, 2005), 108-9.

by Matthew ("you are like a wise philosopher") recalling the concentration of Jesus' *teaching* in Matthew.[146] Be that as it may, this exchange between Jesus and Matthew appears in a saying in *Gos. Thom.* which itself betrays Matthean influence: Matthew alone includes in the Caesarea Philippi dialogue Jesus' confirming Peter as the rock who is a foundation for the church.[147] As such, a reference to Matthew as the author of a gospel here is likely.[148]

Apostolic Credentials

Three small pieces of evidence internal to Matthew's Gospel can probably also be taken into account: (a) the alteration of Mark's account of the call of Levi (reproduced in Luke) to a call of Matthew is interesting (Matt. 9:9; cf. Mark 2:14; Luke 5:29), as is (b) the reference to "Matthew *the tax collector*" in the list of disciples (Matt. 10:3; cf. "Matthew" *tout simple* in Mark 3:18; Luke 6:15). Additionally, (c) Mark's version of the call story talks about Jesus reclining at *his* (Levi's) home, whereas in Matthew this simply becomes "in the house" or possibly just "at home" in Matthew (Mark 2:15/Matt. 9:10): the removal of the *third-person* possessive might be suggestive. The scribe instructed about the kingdom (Matt. 13:52) cannot be assigned any real weight.

There are numerous arguments against apostolic and specifically Matthean authorship, though few of them have any great weight.[149] The likelihood of Matthew as an eyewitness taking over so much of Mark with relatively little change, however, is questionable, especially when this is applied to his own call from Jesus (Matt. 9:9-13). Perhaps the most likely explanation is that of Bauckham, viz. that Matthew's early association with the Gospel arose from a knowledge that he was a principal source for it, rather than necessarily its primary author. On this view, the relationship between Matthew and Matthew's Gospel would be analogous to that between Peter and Mark's Gospel. It is also possible that Matthew's Greek Gospel is a translation, in the very loose sense that Josephus's *Antiquities* are a "translation" of the Old Testament (*Ant.* 10.218), which incorporated sections of Mark in the parallel material.[150] A further possibility is that Matthew himself

146. This suggestion is also made in Pagels, *Beyond Belief,* 47.

147. See discussion in R. Uro, *Thomas: Seeking the Historical Context of the Gospel of Thomas* (New York/London: T. & T. Clark, 2003), 88-89.

148. On Matthew in *Gos. Thom.* 13 as signifying the Gospel of Matthew, see S. J. Gathercole, *The Composition of the Gospel of Thomas: Original Language and Sources* (Cambridge: Cambridge University Press, 2012), chapter 7.

149. See discussions in, e.g., Stonehouse, *Origins of the Synoptic Gospels,* 19-47, and D. A. Carson, *Matthew 1–12,* Expositor's Bible Commentary (Grand Rapids: Zondervan, 1995), 17-19.

150. See Bauckham, *Jesus and the Eyewitnesses,* 209, for the analogy of Josephus with Papias's description of Matthew, though not for this theory of the origins of Matthew.

was the source for Mark's account of the call, which would explain why there are only very minor changes by Matthew to the Markan account.[151] But these last two theories must remain within the realms of speculative possibility.

Luke (and Acts)

Attribution

The evidence from the manuscripts can be set out as follows:

Superscript		**Subscript**	
		P75 (III)	*euangelion kata Loukan*
א (IV)	*kata Loukan*	א (IV)	*euangelion kata Loukan*
A (V)	*euangelion kata Loukan*	A (V)	*euangelion kata Loukan*
B (IV)	*kata Loukan*	B (IV)	*kata Loukan*
C (V)	*euangelion kata Loukan*	C (V)	*euangelion kata Loukan*
D (V)	*euangelion kata Loukan*	D (V)	*euangelion kata Loukan*
W (IV/V)	*euangelion kata Loukan*	W (IV/V)	*euangelion kata Loukan*

The situation here is thus rather better than with the other Synoptics because, as with John, we have the evidence of P75 from the third century. Again, the considerations discussed in connection with John above apply here as well.

It is in any case with Luke that real anonymity of the Gospel is most unlikely. Here it is necessary to clarify the meaning of "anonymity." If by anonymity we mean that the author's name is not included in the main body of the work itself, then a huge number of works from antiquity are anonymous — this would clearly be an absurd definition. If we mean that a work entered circulation without anyone ever knowing who wrote it, then it can be regarded as a truly anonymous composition. If, however, we mean that the work was not labeled with an author but whose authorship was nevertheless known by its earliest readers, then it is not really anonymous. (Indeed, on the theory of Gospel communities, such community Gospels cannot really be regarded as anonymous.) Another possibility is that a work might be anonymous in the sense that the name of its author is lost to us, but that would be an unusual use of the word. In any case, it is far from clear what most scholars mean when they say that the Gospels are anonymous.

This is particularly relevant to Luke because we are told who the immediate recipient, probably Luke's literary patron, is. It is highly likely that Theophilus is a real person, especially given the fact that his identity is — far from being a generic "lover/beloved of God" — given considerable specificity by the semi-titular *kratiste*.

151. It is hard to imagine that Mark had no other sources besides Peter.

It seems highly improbable that Theophilus opened his post one morning to find a big unsolicited scroll about Jesus, followed by another later about the early church. As such, it is clear that the identity of the third Gospel's author was known to its first recipient(s), thus making any real anonymity in a strong sense impossible.

Apostolic Credentials

A good deal can be said of Luke's apostolic connections. While he is not himself an apostle, with Luke we have most clearly an association with Paul. The author-narrator begins at Troas in Acts 16 to write in the first person plural, including himself as an eyewitness of the salvation-historical expansion of the gospel.[152] Some have argued that the author is employing this "we" as a literary device, but attempts to argue for this being a recognizable convention have failed.[153] Alternatively, Barrett's view that Luke has incorporated a travel diary source wholesale without editing the pronouns and verbs seems an even less likely hypothesis to entertain.[154] The most natural reading of the "we"-passages is thus surely correct. In these passages, Acts 16:10-18; 20:5–21:18; 27:1–28:16,[155] we see Luke to be a co-worker of Paul, though not such a close associate as some others: the narrator frequently disappears and reappears and so is perhaps not strictly a "follower" of Paul as Irenaeus asserts.[156] Luke does appear with Paul in Philemon, however, as well as in Colossians and 2 Timothy.[157]

This association with Paul does not just have implications for our understanding the author's knowledge of the events in which he accompanies Paul. These passages also indicate the wide acquaintance of Luke with apostolic circles. Early on in the "we"-passages, Luke keeps some relatively undistinguished company: Lydia (Acts 16:14), Sopater, Secundus, Gaius, Timothy, Tychicus, and Trophimus (20:4), Aristarchus (20:4; 27:2), Eutychus (20:9), and Julius (27:3) are named as those whom Luke encountered on mission. However, Luke makes perhaps more significant acquaintances when arriving with Paul at Jerusalem. Immediately prior to getting there, Luke and Paul stay with Philip the Evangelist, one of

152. So, rightly, C.-J. Thornton, *Der Zeuge des Zeugen* (Tübingen: Mohr, 1991).

153. See, e.g., V. K. Robbins, "By Land and by Sea: The We-Passages and Ancient Sea Voyages," in *Perspectives on Luke-Acts,* ed. C. H. Talbert (Macon, GA: Mercer University Press, 1978), 215-42. I am grateful to my colleague Dr. Michael Thompson for pointing out several criticisms of Robbins's theory. See, e.g., S. M. Praeder, "The Problem of First Person Narration in Acts," *NovT* 29 (1987): 193-218, on 210-14.

154. C. K. Barrett, *The Acts of the Apostles,* vol. 2 (Edinburgh: T. & T. Clark, 1998), xxix.

155. The precise extent of the "we-passages" is disputed: this enumeration is that of F. F. Bruce, *The Book of the Acts* (London: Marshall, Morgan & Scott, 1965), 19 n. 12.

156. Irenaeus, *AH* 3.1.1 (in Greek in Eus. *HE* 5.8.3).

157. Philem. 24; Col. 4:14; 2 Tim. 4:11.

the seven (21:8), staying there "a number of days" and meeting the early disciple Agabus as well (21:10; cf. 11:27-28). Arriving in Jerusalem, or possibly on the way, they stay with another early disciple, Mnason (21:16: *Mnasōni tini Kypriōi archaiōi mathētēi*).[158] They apparently first meet the "lay" members ("the brothers") in the congregation in Jerusalem (21:17), and then on the next day see James and all the elders (21:18). This perhaps enables the author to make the wide acquaintance of the "eye-witnesses from the beginning" and "servants of the word" that is implied in Luke 1. As well as James and others being obvious candidates, the reference to Mnason as an *archaios mathētēs* would certainly fit well with the description of Luke's sources as including *hoi ap'archēs autoptai.*

Alternative Claims to Apostolicity

What of Koester's claim, however, that it is not just that the orthodox party is wrong to claim a link to the apostles, but especially that *it alone* has such a claim? What of the other apostolic claims? Koester certainly cannot provide any evidence for historical links between apostles and non-canonical gospels, apparently to his disappointment:

> To be sure, we know from reliable sources that Peter had in fact been in Antioch, and that Paul was in fact a missionary in Asia Minor. In the case of Thomas, unfortunately, we do not have any direct historical evidence comparable to that for Peter in Antioch and Paul in Asia Minor, to confirm the assumption that Judas, the twin (brother of Jesus), actually was the apostle of Edessa. This must remain a mere conjecture.[159]

In this case, then, he reluctantly concedes ("unfortunately") — as every scholar also assumes — that there is no real historical connection between Judas Thomas and the *Gospel of Thomas.* Similarly, there have been no claims that have won any kind of scholarly acceptance for real connections between Mary and the *Gospel of Mary,* Philip and the *Gospel of Philip,* or Judas and the *Gospel of Judas.*[160] In the cases of the gospels of *Thomas, Judas,* and — to a lesser extent — *Mary,* suspicion

158. On the location of Mnason's home and the antiquity of his membership in the Way see the discussion in Bauckham, "James and the Jerusalem Community," 87-88.

159. Koester, "GNOMAI DIAPHOROI," 133.

160. Hardly any scholars even raise the question. To my knowledge no other scholars have followed de Boer's suggestion that the *Gospel of Mary* was probably written by a disciple of Mary Magdalene: see E. de Boer, *The Mary Magdalene Cover-Up: The Sources behind the Myth* (London/New York: T. & T. Clark, 2007), 65; C. A. Evans, *Fabricating Jesus: How Modern Scholars Distort the Gospels* (Downers Grove, IL: InterVarsity, 2006), 244-45, considers the possibility that the *Gospel of Judas* may preserve a memory of a private exchange between Jesus and Judas.

is naturally aroused by the claim that this is teaching that is delivered *secretly* by Jesus during his ministry.

What of the alternative claims to an apostolic tradition attributed to "heresiarchs"? One instance of this is the claim made by Basilides or his school that Basilides could trace his intellectual genealogy back to Peter: "just as Basilides also claims Glaucias, the interpreter of Peter, as a teacher, or so they boast" (*kathaper ho Basileidēs, kai Glaukian epigraphētai didaskalon, hōs auchousin autoi, ton Petrou hermēnea*).[161] It may well be, however, that the similarity to Papias's claim for Mark, also called a *hermēneutēs* of Peter, means that the Basilidean claim is taken over from Papias as a way of establishing Basilides' authority: as we have seen, the reverse order is improbable.

More plausible is the Valentinian claim that Valentinus was a student of one Theodas/Theudas who in turn was a disciple of Paul.[162] There is no obvious reason to doubt this. The only difficulty is that we only have the single reference from Clement (ca. C.E. 200), and we know nothing further at all about this Theodas.[163] (In contrast, for example, we have seen that we can know a good deal about Luke, also a companion of Paul.) What is especially unclear is any idea that Theodas was the recipient of any *secret* teaching of Paul, as Pagels claims.[164] Certainly in contrast to the general tenor of Pagels's treatment, sections of the Valentinian movement were interested in claiming apostolic legitimacy for their teaching: the *Epistle of Ptolemy to Flora* not only quotes John and Paul as authorities but also talks of "the apostolic tradition which we too have received by succession" (*tēs apostolikēs paradoseōs, hēn ek diadochēs kai hēmeis parelēiphamen*).[165] Presumably this is the succession to be traced back to Paul via Theodas.

We have noted the suspicion that may attach to claims to secret revelation. Similar clandestine apostolic successions appear in two places. The first is the claim of the Naassenes, a Gnostic group, to secret revelation that James the Lord's brother passed on to Mariamme.[166] Some have connected this to the *Gospel of Thomas,* also known to the Naassenes, in which James is a source of authority of some kind (*Gos. Thom.* 12), but the link does not help much: James is an unlikely source for Gnostic revelation.

161. Clem. *Strom.* 7.17.106.

162. Clem. *Strom.* 7.17.106.4: *hōsautōs de kai Oualentinon Theoda diakēkoenai pherousin· gnōrimos d' houtos gegonei Paulou.*

163. For discussion of Theodas, see C. Markschies, *Valentinus Gnosticus: Untersuchungen zur valentinianischen Gnosis mit einem Kommentar zu den Fragmenten Valentins* (Tübingen: Mohr, 1992), 298-302, and E. Thomassen, *The Spiritual Seed: The Church of the "Valentinians"* (Leiden: Brill, 2006), 418-19. While generally neutral about the matter, Thomassen does call the information "questionable" (419).

164. Pagels, *Gnostic Gospels,* 15, 36.

165. *Ep. Ptol. Fl. apud* Epiphanius, *Panar.* 33.7.9.

166. Hippolytus, *Ref.* 5.7.1; 10.9.3, where the spelling "Mariamne" may be read.

The most elaborate example of such a succession comes in a long section of the *First Apocalypse of James,* both in the Nag Hammadi and Codex Tchacos texts. Here Jesus instructs James about what he is to say in the so-called "redemption ritual" where the soul is questioned by archons guarding passage to salvation.[167] Later, however, it becomes clear that this revelation is going to be known more widely, in a kind of apostolic succession: James will reveal it to Addai/Addaios when he dies, that is, presumably when he is on his deathbed (23.13-15); Addai will write the words down ten years later, at which point they are taken from Addai and given to Manael/Masphel (23.19–24.1). Manael leaves them to his son, Levi, who marries a woman from Jerusalem, and has two sons: the elder is ignorant, but the younger will "grow up with" the words, and reveal them when he is seventeen years old (21.1-26). Many are saved by the words of this unnamed figure, though many also despise it (25.5-13). This is all set in a historical framework: James's death is followed immediately by war in the land (23.15-17); there is war again in the time of Levi (24.10-11) and again after Manael's son's seventeenth birthday (25.1-2). While a good case can be made for the historical existence of Addai, this account is clearly difficult to accept as historical.[168]

To these examples of apostolic successions can be added a number of examples of works (especially from Nag Hammadi) that claim authority directly from apostles, such as the *Apocryphon of John,* to give just one from among many examples. This device is also employed, though less frequently, by the orthodox in the second century, as in the case of the *Epistula Apostolorum.* Scholars have scarcely ever regarded these claims to apostolic connections as having any basis in fact, however.

We have seen, then, the tendencies of Koester and Ehrman to distance the Gospels from any apostolic connections. We have seen that the case for anonymity cannot really be made, even if the originality of the attributions to Matthew, Mark, Luke, and John cannot be definitively proven either. There is little reason to adopt a highly skeptical attitude to the attributions contained in the titles and other references, however. Additionally, in all four of the NT Gospels strong cases can be made for real links to disciples of Jesus. On the other hand, in the case of attributions of the apocryphal literature, no scholarly claims have even really been seriously entertained, let alone found a quorum of scholars to contend for them.

167. CT 19.24–22.23 // NH V 33.13–35.20. Subsequent citations are from the Codex Tchacos text.

168. See Bauckham, "James and the Jerusalem Community," 81, on the historicity of Addai, and S. J. Gathercole, "Quis et Unde? Heavenly Obstacles in Gos. Thom. 50 and Related Literature," in *Paradise in Antiquity: Jewish and Christian Views,* ed. M. Bockmuehl and G. G. Stroumsa (Cambridge: Cambridge University Press, 2010), 82-99, on 86-88, regarding this particular passage.

Some Illustrative Retrospects from the First Half of the Second Century

Finally, we conclude with some retrospective reflections on the apostolic Gospels that were the focus of the first part of this essay. They are included merely as illustrations, since it would require another extremely long discussion to take in the whole of the second century, but they reflect a reasonable spread of material from the composition of *1 Clement* at the very end of the first century to the middle of the second century (roughly up to, but not including, Justin). We can see here that there is a line of tradition consisting of works that can be seen to be in continuity with the apostles, whereas other works depart from them.[169]

Three "Apostolic Fathers": 1 Clement, *Ignatius, and Polycarp*

1 Clement

For Clement, there is already a canon of tradition, "the glorious and sacred rule of our tradition" (*ton eukleē kai semnon tēs paradoseōs hēmōn kanona*) (7.2). This comes to Clement because God sent Jesus, and Jesus passed the gospel to the apostles, and they passed it on to "us" (42.1). This tradition is centered on "the blood of Christ" (7.4).[170] Jesus is "the way" identified with salvation (36.1): the reference here also to Jesus as "high-priest" comes in a context that strongly evokes Hebrews more widely and so is suggestive of atonement. The letter quotes the entirety of Isaiah 53, as evidence that Jesus did not come in a display of his majesty, though he could have (16.1-17). The other OT passage cited at greatest length in the letter is Psalm 51:1-17, like Isaiah 53 concerned with forgiveness and atonement: these are the two principal (though by no means the only) "Scriptures" to which the gospel corresponds.

Resurrection also occupies three chapters (24-26). According to Clement, God "makes clear to us constantly" (*epideiknytai diēnekōs hēmin*) the fact of the resurrection in nature, through the cycle of the seasons (24), and most of all in the peculiar tale of the phoenix (25)! The focus is on the general resurrection in these chapters, but — as is conventional, and as we might expect in a letter heavily dependent upon 1 Corinthians — Jesus is highlighted as the first-fruits (24.1).

169. This is not to say that there is no gray area in between; the cases discussed here constitute important markers, however. Other works more difficult to classify could perhaps be plotted on a spectrum between, say, *1 Clement* and the *Gospel of Judas*.

170. Similar language appears in 21.6: "Let us honour the Lord Jesus Christ, whose blood was given for us."

As such, we have for this author an apostolic tradition based on the death and resurrection of Christ according to the Scriptures.

Ignatius

Ignatius commonly states that the death of Christ is the means of salvation, as in his reference to the new life "through the blood of God" (*Eph.* 1.1), and "the cross, which is a stumbling-block to unbelievers, but for us, salvation and eternal life" (*Eph.* 18.1). Despite his sense of his own significance, Ignatius is careful to distinguish himself from the apostles (*Trall.* 3.3; *Rom.* 4.3). The Ephesians are commended for being of one mind with the apostles (*Eph.* 11.2), and more specifically "fellow 'initiates' with Paul" (*Eph.* 12.2). Ignatius's conscious debt to the apostle(s) extends even to the manner of his letter-writing, as when he remarks that he greets the Trallians "in the apostolic manner" (*Trall.* 1.1, *en apostolikōi charaktēri*). In sum, Christians are to study diligently the teaching of Jesus and the apostles (a hendiadys?) as the sure guide in everything: "Be eager, therefore, to be established in the doctrines of the Lord and the apostles (*en tois dogmasin tou kyriou kai tōn apostolōn*), so that whatever at all you do may prosper both in the flesh and spirit" (*Magn.* 13.1).[171]

Ignatius's gospel is summarized in several places, of which two examples will suffice. The letter to the Trallians warns:

> Be deaf, therefore, when someone speaks to you without reference to Jesus Christ, who was descended from David, who was born from Mary; who was truly begotten, and ate and drank. He was truly persecuted under Pontius Pilate, truly was crucified and died, with those in heaven and on earth and under the earth looking on. He was also truly raised from the dead, his Father raising him. (*Trall.* 9.1-2)

Another instance, in which Ignatius is explicit about summarizing his message, comes in the dispute with the "archivist" about the gospel's contents. In response to his interlocutor's famous remark, "If I do not find it in the archives, I do not believe [it] in the gospel," Ignatius proclaims: "For me the 'archives' are Jesus Christ, the inviolable archives his cross and death and his resurrection, and the faith which comes through him. By these I want, through your prayers, to be justified" (*Phld.* 8.2). This is no declaration of some sort of Marcionite position, as Ignatius goes on to talk of the scriptural testimony to Jesus (*Phld.* 9.2: *hoi gar agapētoi prophētai katēngeilan eis auton*).

171. Cf. *Trall.* 7.1: "the ordinances of the apostles" (*tōn diatagmatōn tōn apostolōn*).

Polycarp

In brief, Polycarp's *Letter to the Philippians* has two particularly clear instances of quasi-creedal statements encapsulating the apostolic gospel of Christ's death and resurrection. In the introductory greeting, Polycarp refers in *Phil.* 1.2 to the fruit that the Philippians are bearing "for our Lord Jesus Christ, who endured for our sins facing even death, whom God raised up, having loosed the pangs of Hades." This appears to be a combination of the Pauline "for our sins" formula (1 Cor. 15:3; Gal. 1:4) with Acts 2:24 D ("loosing the pangs of Hades").[172] Other informal confessional statements appear later: for example, Ignatius, Zosimus, and Rufus are commended along with the apostles in *Phil.* 9.2 for not loving this age, but rather "the one who died for us and was raised by God on our account."[173] As is the case with *1 Clement* and Ignatius, the gospel is "in accordance with the scriptures" as well as with the apostles: "Let us then serve him in fear, and with all reverence, just as he has commanded us and as did the apostles who preached the Gospel to us and the prophets who proclaimed beforehand the coming of our Lord" (*Phil.* 6.3).

The Ascension of Isaiah

To supply an example from a different kind of text altogether, we can observe a kind of apostolic creed similar to that summarized by Paul and the apostolic fathers in the second-century *Ascension of Isaiah.*[174] Isaiah's first mention of Christ (usually referred to as "the Beloved one") comes in *Asc. Isa.* 3.13-18:

> It was through him [sc. Isaiah] that the going forth of the Beloved from the seventh heaven had been made known, and his transformation, and his descent to earth, and the likeness into which he would be transformed (that is the likeness of a man), and the persecution to which he would be subjected, and the torments which the sons of Israel would inflict on him, and that before the Sabbath he would be crucified on the tree, and that he would be crucified with wicked men, and that he would be buried in the tomb, and the twelve who had been with him would have their faith shaken, and the guards who would

172. The Western text probably replaces "the pangs of death" in Acts 2:24 with "the pangs of Hades," having derived the latter from Ps. 17:6 (Heb. 18:5).

173. Cf. also Pol. *Phil.* 8.1.

174. *Asc. Isa.* is usually taken to have been put into something like its present form in the second century. See, e.g., J. M. T. Barton, "The Ascension of Isaiah," in *The Apocryphal Old Testament,* ed. H. F. D. Sparks (Oxford: Clarendon, 1984), 775-812, on 780-81; J. Knight, *Disciples of the Beloved One: The Christology, Social Setting and Theological Context of the Ascension of Isaiah,* JSPSS (Sheffield: Sheffield Academic Press, 1996), 11.

guard the tomb, and the descent of the angel of the Christian church which is in the heavens (whom he will summon in the last days) and that <Gabriel>, the angel of the Holy Spirit, and Michael, the prince of the holy angels, would on the third day open the tomb, and the Beloved himself, sitting upon their shoulders, would come forth and send out his twelve disciples. *And they will teach all nations and every language about the resurrection of the Beloved; and those who believe in his cross and in his ascension to the seventh heaven (where he came from) will be saved.*

We have here, then, a summary of the ministry of Jesus, which culminates in the commissioning of the twelve disciples. Their message is summarized as teaching about "the resurrection of the Beloved," which is then glossed with the statement that the necessary *credenda* for salvation are the cross (cf. 9.31) and the ascension. Essential here are Christ's death, resurrection, and ascension — the latter receiving greater prominence than usual in part (a) for its own sake (cf. e.g., 1 Tim. 3:16), (b) because of the apocalyptic genre of *Asc. Isa.*, and (c) to highlight the fact that the seventh heaven was Jesus' place of origin.

Two Gnostic Gospels: The Gospel of Judas *and the* Gospel of the Egyptians

We find a similar kind of retrospect, *mutatis mutandis,* in two Gospels from a fundamentally opposing viewpoint, that of (Sethian) Gnosticism.[175]

The *Gospel of Judas* is generally dated to the mid-second century, since it must pre-date Irenaeus's reference to it in *Adversus Haereses* 1.31.[176] This work, like the "apostolic fathers," begins by construing an apostolic college. In the preface there is a rather strangely conventional reference to Jesus' call of the twelve disciples (33.10-14). Thereafter, however, the tone is set for the rest of the work in a section in which Jesus laughs at the disciples' celebration of their eucharist/thanksgiving (*eucharistia*: 34.5). The disciples are later characterized in a gruesome temple-vision (38.1–39.17) as wickedly celebrating this apparently murderous eucharist. Jesus unequivocally condemns this concern with sacrifice (39.18–40.26), probably concluding (the text is somewhat lacunose): "Stop sacrificing!" (41.1-2). After the revelatory discourse that constitutes the heart of the

175. Edwards has made clear that those often called *Sethian* Gnostics (usually in contrast to Valentinian Gnostics) are just what both the fathers and the school of Plotinus alike called Gnostics. The Valentinians differ quite radically from these. See esp. M. J. Edwards, "Gnostics and Valentinians in the Church Fathers," *JTS* 40 (1989): 26-47, and "Neglected Texts in the Study of Gnosticism," *JTS* 41 (1990): 26-50.

176. On the *testimonium* see Gathercole, *Gospel of Judas,* 114-31.

work, the *Gospel of Judas* concludes with the events leading up to and including Good Friday. The work ends with Judas handing Jesus over to the scribes (58.24-26). In Jesus' previous revelation, however, he declares that when he dies, he will not really be affected because his human body is a mere carrier for his real spiritual person.[177] The death of Jesus is not narrated, though it is forecast as a torment (56.7-8). In some ways much of the *Gospel of Judas* is taken up with ridiculing the position of apostolic Christianity in its concern with the celebration of Jesus' death in the eucharist. In sum, then, in the *Gospel of Judas* we have in a similar manner to what is evident in *1 Clement* a body of apostles who are characterized as celebrating the sacrificial death of Jesus in their eucharist. The only difference is that this is radically subverted by the *Gospel of Judas,* rather than being continued as it is by the aforementioned apostolic fathers. They all, from two very different perspectives, highlight an apostolic identification of the death of Jesus as "of first importance."

The *Gospel of the Egyptians* is very similar to *G. Jud.* in its theological outlook. Rather than setting up its criticism at the outset, as does *G. Jud.,* it rather reserves until its conclusion the fact that "since the days of the prophets and the apostles and the preachers, the name has not at all risen upon their hearts, nor is it possible. And their ear has not heard it" (NH III, 68.5-9). Thus the implicit criticism is not only of the apostles but of all between the primordial hiding of the book by "the great Seth" and the revelation of his seed, the Gnostics (68.10–69.5) — as such it cannot be a gospel "according to the Scriptures." The alternative gospel set out in the *Gospel of the Egyptians* sums up the work of the great Seth (who in revealed form is "Jesus the living one," in 64.1-3). The traditional message of crucifixion is actually reversed: it is used as a metaphor in which Seth "nailed the powers of the thirteen aeons" (64.3-4). Positively, he establishes his seed with knowledge (64.5-9).

These two works illustrate, then, not only a concern for a different message. They also have a strategy for subverting or undermining the conventional picture according to which Jesus commits his message to the twelve, who are then the means by which the gospel is spread. Judas is almost certainly chosen as a way of bypassing the twelve. Jesus states there that he will separate Judas from the twelve, and that — as in the canonical portrait in Acts — another will take his place. He is thus an alternative channel of revelation. The same is true in the *Gospel of the Egyptians,* where the great Seth is the means of revelation. He trumps the apostles not only by his antiquity, but by actually being identifiable with Jesus himself. As has been noted, Hippolytus's account of the Gnostic group

177. See, e.g., *Gos. Jud.* 56.19-21, where Jesus says to Judas, "You will sacrifice the man who carries me about." There is also a new fragment of p. 56, in which Jesus states that when that which carries him is tormented, no man will really be sinning against him or doing him harm. For the new fragments, see H. Krosney, M. Meyer, and G. Wurst, "Preliminary Report on New Fragments of Codex Tchacos," *Early Christianity* 2 (2010): 282-94.

the Naassenes describes them as similarly pursuing an alternative route back to Jesus, because James the brother of Lord passed their doctrines down through Mariamme.[178]

The Gospel of Thomas *and the* Gospel of Mary

These two works are not so starkly antithetical to the apostolic tradition as are the gospels *of Judas* and *of the Egyptians,* though they still have subversive elements. They are not Gnostic, but neither do they presuppose or advocate anything close to a gospel of Christ's death and resurrection, though in the case of the *Gospel of Mary* we must be wary of pronouncing anything (especially a negative) with any confidence because of the fragmentary nature of the text.

The *Gospel of Thomas* is complete, however, and we can see some of its attitude — albeit through a glass darkly — to the Old Testament, the apostles, and the conventional gospel message. On the first of these, *Thomas* is fairly explicit, first, in its apparent suspicion of anything that might be "according to the scriptures." *Gos. Thom.* 52 has Jesus announcing that the twenty-four prophets are "dead." This is reference to the Old Testament as a whole, with twenty-four a conventional way of numbering the books of the OT.[179] And it is not merely a statement of the obvious fact that the OT authors or the prophets in particular have passed away; "dead" is an epithet in *Thomas* denoting membership in the transient corpse-like realm of this world, in contrast with Jesus, named as "the living one" in this same saying. The twelve do not come off much better; there is certainly no nostalgia for the apostles as in *1 Clement* and Ignatius. There are no really positive references to them, and they are described as having "become like the Jews" in their ignorance (*Gos. Thom.* 43).[180] In particular, Matthew — as noted above, known to *Thomas* as the writer of a foundational gospel document — and Peter, as the figurehead of apostolic Christianity, are dismissed as providing inadequate accounts of who Jesus is (*Gos. Thom.* 13). With these devaluations of the *magna ecclesia* in place, a very different message based on revelation and knowledge (e.g., *Gos. Thom.* 1-3; 17) takes center stage, with the death of Jesus mentioned only in passing (*Gos. Thom.* 55) and the resurrection of Jesus perhaps transformed from an event into a kind of timeless reality.[181]

As has been noted, the *Gospel of Mary* is hard to classify because of the poor state of its preservation. It seems to have a negative valuation of the "lawgiver"

178. Hippol., *Ref.* 5.7.1.

179. *4 Ezra* 14.44-47; *Numbers Rabbah* 18:21; Victorinus, *In Apoc.* 4.5.

180. *Gos. Thom.* 12, however, may be taken as envisaging a role for them.

181. There is no mention of any resurrection, although Jesus is referred to as the "living one" in *Gos. Thom.* prologue, 52, and probably 59 and 111.

(8.22–9.4), though it may be that this is not too distant from that of, say, Paul or Hebrews. There is also more of a rapprochement between the secret revelation that has been entrusted to Mary, and the teaching of the disciples. Even though Peter and Andrew are initially hostile to Mary's revelations (despite Peter having solicited them), they eventually appear to be won over. At risk of mirror-reading too much, one might surmise here that this reflects both the tension that some feel between the "conventional" message and the additional truth revealed by Mary. Both the rhetorical construction of Mary's revelation as supplementary and the way in which the work incorporates standard gospel language such as "Peace be with you" (8.14) suggest that this gospel at least may be envisaged by its author as compatible with existing Christian teaching.[182] Because of its more uncompromising stance toward the disciples, the same is less likely to be true of *Thomas.*

Second-Century Retrospects: Summary

The apostolic fathers, the *Ascension of Isaiah,* and the gospels of *Judas* and the *Egyptians* display, in their very different ways, a knowledge of a primitive "orthodoxy" associated with the apostles: the difference is that the *Gospel of Judas* and the *Gospel of the Egyptians* repudiate any connection between the apostles and the real truth. The *Gospel of Judas* specifically repudiates the theology of the cross and the eucharist, whereas the *Gospel of the Egyptians* recasts it such that the only crucifixion which takes place is that of the powers by Jesus (in stark contrast to 1 Cor. 2:8). They repudiate not only the apostolic testimony, but also the scriptural witness clearly maintained by the apostolic fathers and strikingly illustrated by the *Ascension of Isaiah,* in which Isaiah has very precise knowledge of the work of Jesus. In contrast to all of these, the *Gospel of Thomas* provides an example of a work that, rather than proclaiming or repudiating the gospel of the death and resurrection of Christ, effectively sidesteps it. The same is true for the *Gospel of Mary,* as far as our knowledge of the text goes, though it must be remembered that that is not very far.

Conclusion

No doubt in some respects this essay has been overly wide-ranging and has left a number of hostages to fortune. Nevertheless, it is contended here that the central

182. Cf. E. Pagels, "Gospel Truth," *New York Times,* 8 April 2006: "Many regarded these secret Gospels not as radical alternatives to the New Testament Gospels, but as advanced-level teaching for those who had already received Jesus' basic message." The *Gospel of Mary* is probably not typical in this respect, however.

planks are well founded. The emphases of the "diversifiers" sketched in the Prolegomena above must again and again be regarded with some suspicion for various reasons, some of which lie at the level of method, others of which have more to do with more discrete interpretations of data. In the first place, we have above pressed the point that irrespective of what diversity one might find in the first and second centuries among all the various groups that may lay claim to the name Christian, there is a well-founded unity among the earliest apostles. Since these are the figures closest to Jesus, they have a claim not only to greatest antiquity but also to be closest in relationship to the founder. This apostolic unity is based on Jesus' death for sins and resurrection, both of which are seen as "in accordance with the Scriptures." Second, we have traced the connections between the apostles and the NT Gospels. In contrast to apocryphal Gospels, their canonical counterparts can be argued to have real historical links to apostles. Neither were the attributions of the Gospels to apostles or apostolic companions merely much later accretions; rather they have a claim to considerable antiquity. Third, we have showed that there was literature that continued the apostolic agenda: the "proto-orthodox" authors, as Ehrman calls them, are not just one part of the diversity, but rather those who carry on in the vein of the apostles.

As we noted at the beginning, a number of scholars initially responded to Bauer by identifying numerous problems, but considering Bauer's overall contribution as extremely valuable. When such a great number of criticisms are amassed, however, there must come a moment when the theory approaches breaking point. Although for many this is thinking the unthinkable, perhaps twenty-first-century scholarship will in light of the contrary evidence that Bauer so ruthlessly dispatched from view embark on a healthy reaction against his thesis.

FIFTEEN

Why a Book? Why This Book? Why the Particular Order within This Book? Some Theological Reflections on the Canon

Graham A. Cole

Expectations regarding the study of the canon need careful management. Two of the reasons for this are well expressed by Walter C. Kaiser Jr. et al.:

> The canon of Scripture is both an emotional issue and a theological problem. It is a problem because the New Testament never speaks of such a canon (which is natural because while it was being written it was only in the process of becoming a canon). It is an emotional issue because, as the only authoritative document of the Christian faith (in Protestant eyes), anything that might add to or detract from Scripture is highly threatening.[1]

How then do we proceed?

A time-honored method in theology is that of the *via negativa* ("the negative way"). Classically, the *via negativa* aims to state what isn't the case concerning the divine nature (e.g., God is not finite). So at the outset I want to adopt the *via negativa* and state what isn't the burden of this study regarding the canon. In this chapter I am not dealing with the idea of canon as a criterion to test theological proposals. When Paul preached the gospel to the Bereans, they searched their Scriptures to see if he was right about the Messiah (Acts 17:11).[2] In this case scriptural warrant acted as the criterion. Rather, in this study "canon" refers to an authoritative body of sacred literature. In that light this exploration is not another attempt to retrieve the history of how the Christian canon of Scripture was formed.[3] There are many

1. Walter C. Kaiser Jr. et al., "Revelation 22:18-19 Protecting the Canon?" in *Hard Sayings of the Bible,* The Essential IVP Reference Collection (Leicester: InterVarsity Press, 2001, CD-ROM version).

2. I owe this example to D. B. Knox, in *D. Broughton Knox: Selected Works,* vol. 1, *The Doctrine of God,* ed. Tony Payne (Kingsford, NSW: Matthias Media, 2000), 319.

3. John Webster explains this notion of canon in these terms: "The term 'canon,' originally meaning a measuring rod or rule, and then a catalog or set of standards, has from the fourth century been in general Christian theological usage as a technical term for the list of sacred

such studies.[4] Nor is it an attempt to justify the list of books that constitute the Protestant canon.[5] There are many such apologies.[6] So much then for saying what this study is not about.

Theology is not to be done in merely negative mode. Positively put, this study is a quest for conceptual clarity. Put in classical terms, the positive approach is that of the *via positiva* ("the positive way"). With regard to theological clarity the following questions suggest themselves: Why the need of a canon? And if a written one, then why this volume we call the "Holy Bible"?[7] And when it comes to the various books that make up this canonical volume, just who sequenced them, and does sequencing confer authority?

Let's start our exploration where all good theology begins and as does the canon, that is to say, with God (Gen. 1:1).

The God Who Speaks

In Genesis 1, the reader is introduced to a speaking God.[8] God is a communicative being. He speaks and creatures come to be (e.g., light in Gen. 1:3). Indeed

---

writings deemed normative for Christian belief and practice" ("Canon," in *The Dictionary of the Theological Interpretation of Scripture,* ed. K. J. Vanhoozer [London: SPCK; Grand Rapids: Baker Academic, 2005], 97). D. A. Carson and Douglas J. Moo would question Webster's etymology. They correctly maintain that "canon" was originally a Semitic loan word meaning "reed" that later came to mean "measuring rod" or "rule" (*An Introduction to the New Testament,* 2nd edition [Grand Rapids: Zondervan, 2005], 726). Also see George Aichelle, "Toward a Semiotics of Canon," *Australasian Pentecostal Studies* 2, no. 3 (March 2000): 105-6.

4. For example, Lee Martin McDonald, *The Biblical Canon: Its Origin, Transmission, and Authority* (Peabody, MA: Hendrickson, 2007), especially the bibliography, 475-521. The general view is that it took centuries for a New Testament as we have it to appear. However, this view has recently been challenged. See David Trobisch, *The First Edition of the New Testament* (New York: Oxford University Press, 2000). Trobisch argues that the twenty-seven books of the New Testament were published as one volume during the second century.

5. For the different lists see Jaroslav Pelikan, *Whose Bible Is It? A Short History of the Scriptures* (London: Penguin, 2006), 253-54.

6. For example, R. C. Sproul, *Scripture Alone: The Evangelical Doctrine* (Phillipsburg, NJ: P&R, 2005), esp. 39-62.

7. This is an external question. Questions about how the canon came together and what books ought to be in it are internal questions that accept the propriety of a canon understood as a closed list of sacred texts understood to be normative for a particular community of readers. See George Aichelle, "Toward a Semiotics of Canon," *Australasian Pentecostal Studies* 2, no. 3 (March 2000): 105. For an argument that the idea of a closed list was "inherent in the Christian movement from the very outset given the uniqueness of the Christ event," see Charles H. H. Scobie, *The Ways of Our God: An Approach to Biblical Theology* (Grand Rapids/Cambridge: Eerdmans, 2003), 57.

8. Jaroslav Pelikan rightly begins his history of the Bible on the same note. His first chapter is titled "The God Who Speaks," in *Whose Bible Is It?* 7.

as Jaroslav Pelikan points out: "Eleven times the opening chapter of the Torah uses the verb 'to say' in reference to God, in addition to related verbs 'to call' and 'to bless.'"[9] There is even arguably intradeical speech: "Let us make man in our image, in our likeness" (Gen. 1:26). The very next chapter presents this imaging creature as God's conversation partner: "And the Lord God commanded the man" (Gen. 2:16). There is then extradeical speech, too. Special revelation is a pre-fall phenomenon. In fact, from Genesis to Revelation, Scripture exhibits a communicative God in communicative action.[10] This God of biblical testimony is no celestial mime artist. A. J. Heschel rightly suggests: "This seems to be part of our pagan heritage: to say that the Supreme Being is a total mystery; and even having accepted the biblical God of creation, we still cling to the assumption: He who has the power to create a world is never able to utter a word. Yet why should we assume that the endless is forever imprisoned in silence?"[11] The Bible writers never make that assumption.

In every division of the Hebrew Bible we find that God is depicted as a speaker. In the Torah, God speaks extradeically when he addresses the patriarchs in Genesis (e.g., Gen. 12:1). Abraham, Isaac, and Jacob are God's conversation partners. Famously he utters the Ten Commandments in Exodus 20:1-17. In the Prophets he speaks (e.g., the throne scene in Isa. 6:9-10). In the Writings he speaks (e.g., the psalm on the Word celebrates "all the laws that come from [his] mouth," Ps. 119:13). The New Testament is all of a piece with the older one. At Jesus' baptism there is the voice from heaven: "This is my Son" (Matt. 3:17). Hebrews begins with this summary statement: "In the past God spoke to our fathers by the prophets at many times and in various ways, but in these last days he has spoken to us by his Son" (Heb. 1:1-2). Later in the same letter Psalm 95 is described as the speech of the Holy Spirit: "So, as the Holy Spirit says" (Heb. 3:7). Intradeical communication is also on view in the New Testament. In John 17 it is the Logos, who was with God in the beginning and is God but now *ensarkos,* who says "glorify me in your presence with the glory I had with you before the world began" (cf. John 1:1-2 and John 17:5). The last things (eschatology traditionally conceived) comport with the first things (protology). The end-time scene depicts the Holy City, the New Jerusalem descending from heaven and with it the divine voice resounds from the throne: "I am making everything new!" (Rev. 21:5). Both at the beginning and at the ending of the Scriptures, God speaks.

9. Pelikan, "The God Who Speaks," 9.

10. Well brought out by Kevin J. Vanhoozer, *The Drama of Doctrine: A Canonical Linguistic Approach to Christian Theology* (Louisville: Westminster John Knox, 2005).

11. Abraham Joshua Heschel, "A Preface to Understanding Revelation," in *Moral Grandeur and Spiritual Audacity: Essays, Abraham Joshua Heschel,* ed. Susannah Heschel (New York: Farrar, Straus & Giroux, 1997), 190.

In sum, God is rendered in the canon as a speech agent who promises (Gen. 12:1-3), permits (e.g., Gen. 2:16), warns (Gen. 2:17), informs (Exod. 3:14), and questions (e.g., 1 Kgs. 19:9). This list is not exhaustive, but indicative. The formal point having been made that God is a communicative being, the material question arises. What is the burden of divine speech-acts?

The God Who Reveals His Name

Even a cursory examination of the content of divine speech in the scriptural testimony soon reveals that divine discourse is not a matter of trivial pursuit. Scripture does not present a divine prattler who rambles on. God has a project and his discourse comports with it. Against the backdrop of human defection, the *missio Dei* involves nothing less than the reclamation of the created order and the restoration of true worship. Interestingly, in literary perspective, the canon of Scripture presents a divine comedy. The *Dictionary of Biblical Imagery* makes the point well:

> The overall plot of the Bible is a U-shaped comic plot. The action begins with a perfect world inhabited by perfect people. It descends into the misery of fallen history and ends with a new world of total happiness and the conquest of evil. The book of Revelation is the story of the happy ending par excellence, as a conquering hero defeats evil, marries a bride and lives happily ever after in a palace glittering with jewels.[12]

From Genesis to Revelation we observe the U-shaped structure working itself out: from the creational harmony of Genesis 1–2 (the unity of heaven and earth) through the disharmony of Genesis 3 caused by the Fall (the disunity of heaven and earth) through to Revelation 20 with creational harmony restored — albeit of the higher kind as seen in Revelation 21–22. The garden of God has become the city of God set within a new heavens and a new earth.

Crucial to the project is the identification of the God who not only speaks and acts, but who also desires our worship. Indeed, there is no greater privilege than the worship of the true God. Jesus said that the Father is seeking worshipers who will do so in spirit and in truth (John 4:23). Moreover, the book of Revelation commands, "Worship him who made the heavens, the earth, the sea and the springs of water" (Rev. 14:7). How we understand God's character is of crucial importance. The psalmist says of the worship of idols: "Those who make them

12. L. Ryken, J. C. Wilhoit, and J. C. Longman III, "Comedy as Plot Motif," in *Dictionary of Biblical Imagery,* The Essential IVP Reference Collection (Leicester: InterVarsity Press, 2001; CD-ROM version).

will be like them, and so will all who trust in them" (Ps. 115:8). We become like that to which we give our allegiance. As mentioned above, one way of construing the divine project is to consider it as God's plan to restore true worship throughout the created order.

The biblical way to present the identity of the God we are to worship is to speak of the revelation of the divine name and the high point of that revelation in the Old Testament era occurs on Sinai. Exodus provides the key account. In Exodus 33 Moses meets with God outside the camp in the tent of meeting. The Lord had in effect withdrawn his presence from his people because of the golden calf incident and declared that he would not go with Israel to the land flowing with milk and honey. Indeed, YHWH will work only with Moses (Exod. 33:14). However, Moses successfully argues the case for the Lord's persevering with Israel (Exod. 33:15-17). Moses then expresses his desire to know more deeply the God who had first revealed his name to him at the burning bush (cf. Exod. 3 and 33:13). In Exodus 3, the Lord had identified himself there as "I am Who I am" or "I will be what I will be" (Exod. 3:14). According to Brevard S. Childs, God is saying that the subsequent events of history will pour content into the name. He maintains: "The content of his name is filled by what he does (Exod. 3:14), and Israel experiences God's identity through revelation and not by clever discovery."[13] Daniel L. Migliore observes with reference to God: "[O]ur knowledge of persons requires *attention to persistent patterns* in their actions that manifest, as we might say, who they really are, what is in their heart, what their true character is" (original emphasis).[14] Incidentally, *ex hypothesi,* to see a pattern might require more than one book and one snapshot in time, but many books were produced over a length of time. Now having journeyed to Sinai, Moses wanted to know more. Moses Maimonides (1135-1204) suggests: "The phrasing 'Shew me now thy ways and I shall know thee' indicates that God is known by His attributes: if one knows the WAYS one knows Him."[15] Moses asks the Lord to show him his glory

13. Brevard S. Childs, *Biblical Theology of the Old and New Testaments: Theological Reflections on the Christian Bible* (Minneapolis: Fortress Press, 1993), 355. Childs's treatment of the canon is highly suggestive, especially "2. Search for a New Approach."

14. Daniel L. Migliore, *Faith Seeking Understanding: An Introduction to Christian Theology,* 2nd edition (Grand Rapids/Cambridge: Eerdmans, 2004), 36.

15. Moses Maimonides, *Maimonides, The Guide for the Perplexed,* trans. Chaim Rabin (Indianapolis: Hackett, 1995), 72; original emphasis. This verse (Exod. 33:13) contains an important epistemic principle. To know a person one needs to be exposed to their ways: that is to say, the characteristic behaviors of a person. This usually takes some time or exposure to stories that narrate those behaviors. It is not enough merely to know that God exists. One needs to know the moral disposition of the God who exists. Herein lies the genius of the "storied" nature of biblical revelation. See my article, "Exodus 34, the Middoth and the Doctrine of God: The Importance of Biblical Theology to Evangelical Systematic Theology," *The Southern Baptist Journal of Theology* 12, no. 3 (Fall 2008): 24-36. I am indebted in this section to this article at a number of points. Used with kind permission.

(Exod. 33:18). The divine response is instructive: "And he said, 'I will make all my goodness pass before you and will proclaim before you my name "The Lord." And I will be gracious to whom I will be gracious, and will show mercy on whom I will show mercy'" (Exod. 33:19).

Moses wanted to see the divine glory. He wanted to see the majesty of God displayed. But God gave him a declaration of divine goodness instead. God's glory lies not in his might, but in his goodness expressed in sovereign grace and mercy.

Next, in response to the Lord's command, Moses chisels out two stone tablets. YHWH will write afresh the Ten Commandments on them. Moses returns to the top of Sinai. The theophany that then takes place is described:

> The Lord descended in the cloud and stood with him there, and proclaimed the name of the Lord. The Lord passed before him and proclaimed, "The Lord, the Lord, a God merciful and gracious, slow to anger, and abounding in steadfast love and faithfulness, keeping steadfast love for thousands, forgiving iniquity and transgression and sin, but who will by no means clear the guilty, visiting the iniquity of the fathers on the children and the children's children, to the third and the fourth generation." (Exod. 34:5-7)

There is only one fitting response to the unveiling of the divine nature: "And Moses quickly bowed his head toward the earth and worshiped" (Exod. 34:8).

A. J. Heschel rightly says: "The God of Israel is a name, not a notion. There is a difference between a 'name' and a 'notion.' . . . A notion applies to all objects of similar properties. A name applies to an individual. The name 'God of Israel' applies to the one and only God of all men. A notion describes, defines, a name evokes. A notion you can conceive; a name you call."[16] The subsequent story of Israel in the wilderness provides evidence for Heschel's claim. Israel sins yet again and faces the divine displeasure (Num. 14:1-4). The Lord states that his dealings with Israel are at an end. They will be destroyed but Moses and his clan will alone become the bearers of the promise (Num. 14:11-12). Once more Moses intercedes for Israel. He does so by rehearsing the divine character as revealed on Sinai in the revelation of the name:

> Now may the Lord's strength be displayed, just as you have declared: "The Lord is slow to anger, abounding in love and forgiving sin and rebellion. Yet he does not leave the guilty unpunished; he punishes the children for the sin of the fathers to the third and fourth generation." In accordance with your great love, forgive the sin of these people, just as you have pardoned them from the time they left Egypt until now. (Num. 14:17-19)

16. Heschel, *Moral Grandeur*, 162.

The LORD responds, "I have forgiven them, as you asked" (Num. 14:20).

In New Testament terms, the locus of the revelation of the divine name is found in a person. John's Gospel claims that none have ever seen God at any time but the unique Son has made him known (John 1:18). The Prologue of this Gospel makes plain that this person is Jesus Christ, the logos enfleshed (John 1:14). Later in the Gospel Jesus goes on to argue in response to Philip's question that the person who sees him sees the Father (John 14:9). As A. M. Ramsey expressed it: "He [the Father] is Christlike and in him is no unChristlikeness at all."[17] In fact, Jesus sums up his ministry in terms of his revealing the divine name (John 17:6). In Pauline idiom: "the knowledge of the glory of God [is to be found] in the face of Christ" (2 Cor. 4:6).

A name in Scripture, then, can be much more than a mere designation. It can be freighted with content of enormous significance. Peter's address to the rulers and elders in Jerusalem in the early chapters of Acts underlines that significance. He is under criticism for healing a cripple. To which he replies: "It is by the name of Jesus Christ of Nazareth, whom you crucified but whom God raised from the dead, that this man stands before you healed" (Acts 4:10). He elaborates forcefully: "Salvation is found in no one else, for there is no other name under heaven given to men by which we must be saved" (Acts 4:12). Uniqueness attaches to this name and its story.

The logic of a canon is beginning to emerge. We have a canon because we have a God who has a name and with that name comes a story, and central to that story is the singular identity of the chief actor within it. Moreover the central character has desires for the creature made in the divine image. Those desires are expressed in his Word. And what are the divine desires? One already explored — albeit briefly — is that we be worshipers. Another divine desideratum — at least in part — is that we image his character. Or to use a more biblical idiom — God desires his people to walk in his ways. But even more fundamental than that desire is this one. Outside of Eden this side of the great rupture God desires — to use Paul's language — "all to be saved and come to a knowledge of the truth [knowledge that is of the gospel of Jesus Christ in the context]" (1 Tim. 2:4). We turn to this latter desideratum next.

The God Who Desires Us to Be Saved

The common title of Scripture is "Holy Bible." Is the adjective justified? I attended a wedding years ago that was performed in a very different tradition than my own. No one could touch the Bible with their bare hands. Special silk cloth was

17. Quoted by J. Munsey Turner, "Trinity Sunday: God's Three Ways of Being God," *The Expository Times* 85, no. 8 (1974): 243.

used as a barrier. Is this the holiness in view? I would argue not. So why then the adjective "holy"? The adjective is justified when two New Testament texts are brought into play. Romans 1:1-4 is the Pauline gospel *in nuce.* The apostle describes himself as set apart for the work of the gospel (Rom. 1:1). The gospel is God's message (Rom 1:1). It was promised in the prophets in the Holy Scriptures (*graphais hagiais,* Rom. 1:2). Paul then writes of Christ, his descent from David, and his resurrection from the dead (Rom. 1:2-4). The parallel between the apostle being set apart for the gospel task and the Scriptures being set apart for the gospel task is patent. Second Timothy 3:14-17 tells a similar story. Paul reminds Timothy of how Timothy had been acquainted with Scripture from his infancy (2 Tim. 3:15). He describes the Scriptures as "holy Scriptures" *(ta hiera grammata).* Paul elaborates: "which [Scriptures] are able to make you wise for salvation through faith in Jesus Christ" (2 Tim. 3:15). Again the idea of a body of writing set apart for the gospel task fits the context.[18]

Kenneth Kantzer reminds us that in the first instance Christianity does not offer a philosophy. Rather, "it is a religion of redemption."[19] A redemptive religion recognizes the reality of the fall. We humans have defected from our rightful Lord. But the God against whom we have rebelled has done for us what he need not have done. He has graciously provided a way back. The gospel is the message of that way back and that message is found in the Scriptures and is heard whenever those Scriptures are faithfully expounded. This sets Scripture apart from any other book. The title "Holy Bible" on the cover of the NIV translation that I am using as I write has biblical grounding.

The Scriptures are set apart to provide the gospel that we are to trust.[20] In this, more of the logic of a canon is merging. However, the God who desires our trust also desires our obedience. To that desideratum we now turn.

The God Who Desires Us to Walk in His Ways

The divine desire that we walk in his ways is a biblical theme first found right at the start of the biblical storyline, even before the Fall. As Abraham Joshua

18. What I have written is no brief for limited inspiration or limited inerrancy. Paul goes on in 2 Timothy 3:16-17 to specify how Scripture is vital to Christian maturity, encompassing as it does divine teaching, rebuking, correcting, and training in righteousness.

19. Kenneth Kantzer, foreword to Warren C. Young, *A Christian Approach to Philosophy* (Grand Rapids: Baker, 1977), 8. Kantzer does argue that the Bible contains a philosophy even though philosophy is not the burden of Scripture. I would prefer to argue that Scripture implies a worldview that may be philosophically articulated. See my "Do Christians Have a Worldview?" http://thegospelcoalition.org/pdf/cole/pdf (December 2007).

20. For the importance of the gospel in relation to Scripture see Peter F. Jensen's essay in the present volume.

Heschel observes: "The Bible is an answer to the supreme question: What does God demand of us?"[21]

Genesis presents the picture of the Creator creating a creature in the divine image (Gen. 1:27): "So God created man in his own image, in the image of God he created him; male and female he created them." Theologians differ as to what that image exactly is. The reason for the debate is simple. Scripture nowhere defines the expression. Even so, J. I. Packer usefully contributes to our understanding of the image:

> The statement at the start of the Bible (Gen. 1:26-27, echoed in 5:1; 9:6; 1 Cor. 11:7; James 3:9) that God made man in his own image, so that humans are like God as no other earthly creatures are, tells us that the special dignity of being human is *that, as humans, we may reflect and reproduce at our own creaturely level the holy ways of God,* and thus act as his direct representatives on earth. This is what humans are made to do, and in one sense we are human only to the extent that we are doing it.[22]

Packer is right to draw attention to the ways of God because walking in God's ways is a consistent biblical theme.

The biblical narrative makes it plain that God's son Adam failed to image God as he should have done (Genesis 3). The primeval pair is expelled from Eden. But God has not abandoned his project to have a creature that images his character in the world. Abraham is called into covenant with God and becomes a pivotal character in the divine plan to restore the creation order (Gen. 12:1-3; 15:1-21).[23] It is no surprise then that later in the Torah's unfolding story we find that God's corporate son Israel — composed of the children of Abraham — is rescued from Egyptian bondage to become a "a display-people, a showcase to the world of how being in covenant with Yahweh changes a people."[24] Imaging God involves walking in God's ways (Deut. 28:9-10): "The LORD will establish you as his holy people, as he promised you on oath, if you keep the commands of the LORD your God and *walk in his ways.* Then all the peoples on earth will see that you are called by the name of the LORD, and they will fear you"[25] (my emphasis). Leviticus 19:2

21. Heschel, *Moral Grandeur,* 186.

22. J. I. Packer, *Concise Theology: A Guide to Historic Christian Beliefs* (Wheaton, IL: Tyndale House, 1993), 71; my emphasis.

23. In the patriarchal period there is no evidence that the covenant needed written expression. In other words, a written form is not intrinsic to a covenantal relation. It is only deeper into the Pentateuch that we read of "the book of the covenant" (Exod. 24:7).

24. J. I. Durham, *Exodus,* Word Biblical Commentary 3 (Dallas: Word, 2002), comment on Exodus 19:6. CD-ROM version.

25. Walking in God's revealed ways is frequently accented in Deuteronomy (e.g., Deut. 5:33; 8:6; 10:12; 11:22; 19:9; 26:17; 30:16).

gives greater specificity as to what walking in God's ways looks like. In general terms Israel is to "[b]e holy because I, the Lord your God, am holy." More specifically Israel is to be morally different from the nations around about: different from the Egypt Israel left behind at the exodus (Lev. 18:1-5) and different from the nations to which they were headed (Lev. 20:22-23). Israel is to be set apart from the nations (Lev. 20:24).

In the New Testament both the corporate imaging of God and the walking in God's ways continue as accents. With regard to the former, 1 Peter 2:9 reaffirms the "display-people" motif of Exodus 19:5-6: "a chosen people, a royal priesthood, a holy nation, a people belonging to God." In relation to walking in God's ways, *imitatio Dei* becomes *imitatio Christi.* God's people are counseled: "Whoever claims to live in him must walk as Jesus did" (1 John 2:6).[26] John 13 provides an abiding example of what walking in his ways looks like. This famous story set in the upper room during the Passion Week presents Jesus as the servant who takes the humble role in another person-centered way. He provides the hospitality to others that should have been accorded to him. He draws the moral (John 13:13-17):

> You call me "Teacher" and "Lord," and rightly so, for that is what I am. Now that I, your Lord and Teacher, have washed your feet, you also should wash one another's feet. I have set you an example that you should do as I have done for you. I tell you the truth, no servant is greater than his master, nor is a messenger greater than the one who sent him. Now that you know these things, you will be blessed if you do them.

John 13 presents the imitable. Arguably having more than one gospel text gives the reader a better grasp of what the pattern of the ways of Christ is like. Even so, Jesus as the mediator between God and us is a unique vocation: "For there is one God and one mediator between God and men, the man Christ Jesus, who gave himself as a ransom for all men — the testimony given in its proper time" (1 Tim. 2:5-6). We need to note that not all of Jesus' actions are imitable.

But how are God's people to walk in God's ways if they do not know what they are? God needs to make them known.

The God Who Provides an Inspired Word

The apostle Paul offers a key insight into God's causal relation to Scripture. He describes Scripture as *theopneustos* ("God-breathed") in a locus classicus on

26. The NIV translation here is more a faithful paraphrase than a translation (lit. "The one claiming to abide in him [Jesus] ought to walk as that one walked").

Scripture (2 Tim. 3:14-17). Although "inspiration" is the standard descriptor for this relationship, Paul's accent is on expiration. An objective reality is in view. This literature has origins in God like no other. God as the creator sustains the canon of Shakespeare's works in existence, but the text of Hamlet is not *theopneustos.* By way of contrast, Scripture is not only sustained in existence by the divine will, but additionally is breathed out by God. A Petrine text adds to the picture in another classic text on Scripture. In 2 Peter 1:21 he refers to those moved by the Spirit to write.[27] Hebrews 3–4 provides a concrete example of this concursus or double-agency in its exposition of Psalm 95.[28] Contextually speaking, Psalm 95 is what the Holy Spirit is saying in Hebrews 3:7 and what the Holy Spirit is saying through David in Hebrews 4:7. It is a living word (Heb. 4:12). The Holy Spirit is speaking through the psalm to the readers of the letter. This is no dead word of the past. However, a caveat is in order. Scripture is non-postulational.[29] No theory of what this dual authorship looks like metaphysically or psychologically is on offer.

What we have observed in Hebrews 3–4 is highly suggestive for our purposes. If *theopneustos* in 2 Timothy says something about the unique origins of Scripture, Hebrews powerfully points to Scripture as a continuing vehicle of divine address. Jesus makes a similar claim in Matthew 22:31 in his debate with the Sadducees concerning the resurrection. He quotes Exodus 3:6 as a contemporary word: "[H]ave you not read what God *said to you* . . . ?" (Matt. 22:31, my emphasis).[30] Paul likewise has a view that Scripture is no antiquarian body of literature but in the good purposes of God has future audiences in mind such as Paul's own readers. Referring to God's judgment on Israel in the wilderness he informs the Corinthians: "These things happened to them as examples and were written down

27. I much admire Brevard S. Childs's contribution to the discipline of biblical theology and theological reflection on canonization. However, the paucity of references in his major work on biblical theology to the role of the Holy Spirit in the production of Scripture is a singular weakness and leaves a *diastasis* ("separation") between the text of Scripture and the Word of God. 2 Timothy 3:16 hardly figures in his work and 2 Peter 1:21 not at all according to his index of biblical references: Childs, *Biblical Theology,* 744-45.

28. The term "concursus" belongs in the doctrine of providence along with *conservatio* ("preservation") and *gubernatio* ("government"). The doctrine of Scripture, I would argue, may usefully be located within the doctrine of special providence. It is a crucial element in God's provision for his people, their preservation and government.

29. By "non-postulational" — following Bernard Ramm — I mean Scripture does not offer theories about the essences of things. Bernard L. Ramm, *The Christian View of Science and Scripture* (Grand Rapids: Eerdmans, 1954), 76.

30. Brevard S. Childs argues in more than one place that Scripture is "the area in which God's word is heard" and that this hearing takes place particularly in the context of prayer and worship: e.g., *Biblical Theology,* 721-22. However, as we have seen according to Matthew's account, Jesus believed God's Word can be read (Matt. 22:31). Hearing and reading are not antithetical.

[in the Old Testament Scriptures] as warnings *for us,* on whom the fulfillment of the ages has come" (1 Cor. 10:11, my emphasis).

The Epistle to the Hebrews — or should it more accurately be labeled "The Exhortation to the Hebrews"? — opens, as we have seen, with these words: "In the past God spoke to our forefathers through the prophets at many times and in various ways, but in these last days he has spoken to us by his Son" (Heb. 1:1-2).[31] Ex hypothesis, if God has spoken, then there are an authority and a value that attach to divine speech that place such discourse in another category to that of merely creaturely speech. Bernard Ramm rightly argues: "The concept of the Word of God determines the concept of canon."[32] Arguably then, canon is a corollary of special revelation and a written canon a corollary of divine inspiration.[33] D. Broughton Knox correctly maintains:

> The canon then is a very simple concept. It is putting into one classification or pigeon-hole those writings of which God is the Author, and putting into the other pigeon-hole all other writings which people have written — with a greater or lesser degree of truth — but which were not written by the direct inspiration of the Holy Spirit to convey God's mind and Word to the reader, and are consequently not authoritative over the conscience.[34]

He then adds with considerable understatement: "The canon is a simple concept, although the exact extent of it may be a cause for investigation and reflection."[35]

Given divine inspiration, the Christian canon is not reducible merely to an anthology of ancient Israelite texts and early church texts, as some have argued (e.g., H. Koester).[36] The so-called naturalization of the canon needs to be challenged by any who hold a robust doctrine of special revelation, divine inspiration, and a belief in God's providence (*gubernatio* in particular).[37] Like so many

31. "Exhortation" is appropriate given Hebrews 13:22 where the writer describes his work: "the word of exhortation" *(tou logou tēs paraklēseōs).*

32. Bernard L. Ramm et al., *Hermeneutics* (Grand Rapids: Baker, 1974), 14.

33. I am not using "corollary" in a technical mathematical or logical sense but in the looser sense of "a natural consequence." Also see Peter F. Jensen, *The Revelation of God* (Downers Grove, IL: InterVarsity Press, 2002), 185: "But if there is no inspiration, strictly speaking there can be no Bible."

34. Payne, ed., *D. Broughton Knox: Selected Works,* 47.

35. Payne, ed., *D. Broughton Knox: Selected Works,* 47.

36. Used as an example by Carson and Moo, *An Introduction to the New Testament,* 740. Also see Peter F. Jensen, *Revelation,* 185: "Without inspiration, it would be better to have two looser categories, 'literature of Israel' and 'literature of the early church.'" Jensen actually affirms divine inspiration.

37. The "naturalization" thesis is succinctly described by John Webster, "Canon," in *The Dictionary of the Theological Interpretation of Scripture,* ed. K. J. Vanhoozer (London: SPCK; Grand Rapids: Baker Academic, 2005), 98: "[T]he canon . . . comes to be regarded as an ar-

other areas of human inquiry, canon studies exhibit the great divide between naturalistic and supernaturalistic worldviews. Philosopher William H. Halverson describes the divide in his own field as follows: "It may be helpful to bear in mind from the beginning, however, that one theme underlines nearly all philosophical discussion is the perpetual conflict between naturalistic and nonnaturalistic worldviews."[38] The idea of divine providence at work in the formation of the canon is absurd to the naturalistic mindset, but not to the believer. Kevin J. Vanhoozer rightly comments: "Canonization, we might say, is 'the providence of God put into writing.'"[39]

The Reformers of the sixteenth century were not constrained by a naturalistic worldview. For them the idea of *sola scriptura* ("Scripture alone") is predicated on the uniqueness of special revelation now crystallized as God's Word written. Recently some have argued that the idea of the canonical should be expanded to include teachings, liturgies, sacraments, persons, and icons (e.g., William J. Abraham).[40] This thesis correctly recognizes that authorities other than Scripture de facto operate in church life. The Reformers knew this. Such authorities are *norma normata* ("ruled norms"). However, there is a norm of norms, a touchstone against which such putative authorities and their theological proposal are to be tested. The norm of norms is God's Word written (*norma normans* or "ruling norm"). Of course, *Sola scriptura* ought not to be misunderstood as proposing that only one authority operates in Christian life (i.e., *nuda scriptura*). Rather it is a claim about the finality, supremacy, and sufficiency of Scripture.[41]

But Why a Written Word?

Nothing argued thus far — a speaking God, the revelation of the name, provision of a word for God's people, walking in God's ways — demands a written word. That it could have been otherwise has long been recognized by theologians. For example, Amandus Polan (1561-1610) maintained: "God might have

bitrary or accidental feature of the Christian religion, to be explained, not transcendentally, but simply in terms of the immanent processes of religious history." Also see Childs, *Biblical Theology,* 98, where he argues that Scripture should be viewed as a "witness" to "a divine reality" and not reduced to a mere "source" of ancient religious ideas. What is missing from Childs's account is a robust sense of Scripture as norm.

38. William H. Halverson, *A Concise Introduction to Philosophy,* 4th edition (Boston: McGraw-Hill, 1981), 9.

39. Vanhoozer, *The Drama of Doctrine,* 230.

40. William J. Abraham, *Canon and Criterion in Christian Theology: From the Fathers to Feminism* (Oxford: Oxford University Press, 2006).

41. See my "*Sola Scriptura:* Some Historical and Contemporary Perspectives," *Churchman* 104 (1990): 20-34.

taught and maintained the Church, had he so willed, even without Scripture."[42] Likewise, Johan Heinrich Heidegger (1633-1698) argued: "God might have preserved the Church without Scripture: with God all things are possible."[43] Even so, according to these theologians, there is a necessity that attends Scripture but not of an absolute kind as though God could not have provided for his people another way. Rather, God provides a written Word by way of the so-called *necessitas ex hypothesi dispositionis* ("necessity on account of a hypothesis of disposition").[44]

In what then does the "necessity" lie? Francis Turretin (1623-1687) offers three reasons for such a necessity. First, a written word protects against "the infirmity of memory." Second, a written Word can be "more easily defended from the deceits and corruptions of Satan." Lastly, a written Word "might more conveniently be spread and transmitted."[45] B. B. Warfield (1851-1921) also addresses the question of the need for a written Word:

> I am far from contending that without such an inspiration [of the Bible] there could be no Christianity. Without any inspiration we could have had Christianity; yea, and men could still have heard the truth, and through it been awakened, and justified, and sanctified and glorified. The verities of our faith would remain historically proven true to us . . . even had we no Bible; and through those verities, salvation.[46]

Then comes his answer to our question:

> But to what uncertainties and doubts would we be prey! — to what errors, constantly begetting worse errors, exposed! — to what refuges, all of them refuges of lies, driven! Look but at those who have lost the knowledge of this infallible guide: see them evincing man's most pressing need by inventing for themselves an infallible church, or an infallible Pope. Revelation is but half

42. Quoted in Heinrich Heppe, *Reformed Dogmatics: Set Out and Illustrated from the Sources,* trans. G. T. Thomson (Grand Rapids: Baker, 1950), 32.

43. Quoted in Heppe, *Reformed Dogmatics,* 32.

44. Muller explains the *necessitas ex hypothesi dispositionis* in these terms: "a necessity brought about or conditioned by a previous contingent act or event so that the necessity itself arises out of contingent circumstances; thus, conditional necessity" (Richard A. Muller, *Dictionary of Latin and Greek Theological Terms: Drawn Principally from Protestant Scholastic Theology* [Grand Rapids: Baker, 1986], 200). That is to say, having decided to inspire a Word, God of necessity provides for its preservation, which as a consequence requires writing and a canon.

45. Francis Turretin, quoted in Heppe, *Reformed Dogmatics,* 31.

46. Warfield was well aware that the truth of Christianity was independent of whether there was a divinely given Scripture or not, as was A. A. Hodge. See Archibald A. Hodge and Benjamin B. Warfield, *Inspiration* (Grand Rapids: Baker, 1979), 8-9.

> revelation unless infallibly communicated; it is but half communicated; but it is half communicated; unless it be infallibly recorded.[47]

According to Warfield the need for a preserved written Word of God is epistemic.[48]

The Church That Discerns and Orders the Word of God Written

Following Cyprian, Calvin opens Book Four of his seminal *Institutes* in these terms:

> I shall start, then, with the church, into whose bosom God is pleased to gather his sons, not only that they may be nourished by her help and ministry as long as they are infants and children, but also that they may be guided by her motherly care until they mature and at last reach the goal of faith. "For what God has joined together, it is not lawful to put asunder," so that, for those to whom he is Father *the church may also be Mother.*[49]

With regard to playing a part in Christian maturation, Calvin gave the church a much higher value and role than many a present-day evangelical does. Epistemologically speaking, Calvin's claim also has another merit. Calvin in the *Institutes* recognizes the authority of the church but not its supreme authority. That authority belongs to Scripture alone. Even so, without the church, for example, I would not have the copy of the Scriptures used for this chapter. The authority question can be misconstrued, however. C. S. Lewis wisely warned:

> Beware of the argument "the church gave the Bible (and therefore the Bible can never give us ground for criticizing the church)." It is perfectly possible to

47. B. B. Warfield, *The Inspiration and Authority of the Bible* (Philadelphia: P&R, 1970), 441-42. If Warfield is right, epistemologically speaking, a Bible is not of the *esse* ("being") of Christianity, that is to say not necessary for the existence of Christianity. However, the Bible would be essential for either Christianity's *bene esse* ("well-being") or *plene esse* ("fullness of being"). For further explanation of these terms see Don S. Armentrout and Robert Boak Slocum, eds., *An Episcopal Dictionary of the Church: A User-Friendly Reference for Episcopalians* (New York: Church Publishing, 2000), 189: "Terms for characterizing the significance of a doctrine or practice for the church."

48. Warfield's soaring rhetoric begs the question as to why the establishment of the canon has not kept the church error free. We have an infallible guide provided (Scripture), but clearly we do not possess an infallible hermeneutic so as to interpret it perfectly on every occasion.

49. John Calvin, *Institutes of the Christian Religion,* 4.1.1, cited from *The Comprehensive John Calvin Collection,* ed. John T. McNeill, trans. Ford Lewis Battles (Rio, WI: Ages Software, 2002), CD-ROM version (my emphasis).

> accept B on the authority of A and yet regard B as a higher authority than A. It happens when I recommend a book to a pupil. I first sent him to the book, but, having gone to it, he knows (for *I've* told him) that the author knows more about the subject than I.[50]

Lewis was worried that the church might trump Scripture for some, and his warning raises the need for a careful distinction between "authorization" and "assent." John Webster puts it this way: "Canonization is thus to be understood as assent rather than authorization, as an act of reception and submission, and as a pledge to be governed by the textual norm given to the church."[51] Andrie B. Du Toit concurs: "The decisions of the church were in reality the acknowledgement of the intrinsic authority and power of these writings."[52]

One historic church that, some argue, has failed to make the distinction is the Roman Catholic Church.[53] However, the Roman Catholic position on canonization is a carefully qualified one. Vatican I (1869-70) was emphatic: "These books are held by the Church as sacred and canonical, not as having been composed by merely human labour and afterwards approved by her authority, nor merely because they contain revelation without error, but because, written under the inspiration of the Holy Ghost, they have God for their author, and have been transmitted to the Church as such."[54] More recently the *Catechism of the Catholic Church* (1994) affirms: "It was by the apostolic Tradition that the Church [the Roman Catholic Church] *discerned* which writings are to be included in the list of the sacred books. This complete list is called the canon of Scripture." Again, "The Church *accepts and venerates as inspired* the 46 books of the Old Testament and the 27 books of the New."[55] The fact that Protestants discern that only thirty-nine books belong in the Old Testament and the Roman Catholic Church forty-six books raises important epistemological questions that are beyond the brief of this study. Even so, despite material differences between Protestants and Roman Catholics, from a formal point of view the idea of discernment is a sound one and an apostolic desideratum (e.g., 1 Thess. 5:19-21). However, the Roman Catholic position becomes particularly problematic when her apologists sub-

50. C. S. Lewis, *The Collected Letters of C. S. Lewis,* vol. 3, *Narnia, Cambridge and Joy, 1950-1963,* ed. Walter Hooper (New York: HarperCollins, 2007), 1307-8; original emphasis.

51. Webster, "Canon," 99.

52. Andrie B. Du Toit, "Canon: New Testament," in *Oxford Guide to the Bible,* ed. Bruce M. Metzger and Michael D. Coogan (Oxford: Oxford University Press, 1993), 104.

53. So argues Michael Horton, "Sufficient for Faith and Practice: Covenant and Canon," *Modern Reformation* 19, no. 3 (May/June 2010): 13.

54. Vatican I, Dogmatic Constitution on the Catholic Faith, quoted in Alfred Duran, "Inspiration of the Bible, in *Catholic Encyclopedia, New Advent: Featuring the Catholic Encyclopedia,* 2nd edition (Pennsauken, NJ: Disc Makers, 2007), CD-ROM version.

55. *Catechism of the Catholic Church,* para. 120 and 138; my emphasis.

tly shift the language of discernment to the language of definition as does Peter Kreeft: "It is also a historical fact that the Church [the Roman Catholic Church] 'canonized' the Bible (defined which books belong to it)."[56] There is a claim to authority for the Roman Catholic Church in this assertion that Protestants find extremely difficult.[57]

The church's need to discern what is the scriptural canon historically has been driven by a very practical liturgical need that we need to note. The God revealed in Scripture gathers his people around his Word. Sinai is a case in point (Exodus 19). Subsequently the Ten Words deposited in the Ark of the Covenant in the tabernacle were at the center of Israel's life as it moved through the wilderness (Num. 10:11-36). The Book of the Law was rediscovered in the temple in Josiah's day (2 Kgs. 22). Ezra had the scribes read the Law to the assembled returnees (Nehemiah 8). Jesus read from the prophet Isaiah in the synagogue (Luke 4:16-20). Paul instructed Timothy to give attention to the public reading of Scripture (1 Tim. 4:13). According to Jesus, God desires worship in spirit and truth (John 4:24). The early church wanted to know what was to be read in the assembly and what was not to be read in the assembly but could be read privately or what was not to be read at all. Discerning the canon, then, was an urgent need relevant to the worshiping life of the church as can be seen in documents as diverse as the Muratorian Fragment of the second century and Article 39 of the North African Council of Carthage at the end of the fourth century.[58]

Imagining a Different Canonical Order[59]

Brevard S. Childs makes an interesting point with regard to the ordering of the canon: "[I]t is historically inaccurate to assume that the present printed form of the Hebrew and the Christian Bible represent ancient and completely fixed tra-

56. Peter J. Kreeft, *Catholic Christianity: A Complete Catechism of Catholic Beliefs Based on the Catechism of the Catholic Church* (San Francisco: Ignatius Press, 2001), 100. Surprisingly, some Protestants write similarly: "The church has defined the boundaries of Scripture as canonical and thus as having a position of decisive authority within the entire ongoing tradition" (Lesslie Newbigin, *Proper Confidence: Faith, Doubt, and Certainty in Christian Discipleship* [Grand Rapids: Eerdmans, 1995], 90).

57. See the discussion in R. C. Sproul, *Scripture Alone: The Evangelical Doctrine* (Phillipsburg, NJ: P&R, 2005), 41-42.

58. See the very useful treatment in Luke Timothy Johnson, *The Writings of the New Testament: An Interpretation,* rev. edition (Minneapolis: Fortress Press, 1999), 600-603.

59. Alternative orderings of the biblical books continue to attract scholarly interest. See the thoughtful article from Greg Goswell, "The Order of the Books of the New Testament," *Journal of the Evangelical Theological Society* 53 (2010): 225-41.

ditions. Actually the present stability regarding the ordering of the books is to a great extent dependent on modern printing techniques and carries no significant theological weight."[60] If the church does not confer authority on Scripture but has in fact sequenced or created the order of the books, one can imagine a different order of the books making up the canon.[61] For example, in the present order Matthew begins the New Testament, then Mark, followed by Luke and John. However, Luke and Acts are split by John, even though Luke-Acts constitute two volumes from the one writer. Matthew as the first book has the strength of explicitly connecting the New Testament with the Old Testament, beginning as it does with a genealogy going back to Abraham (Matt. 1:2-17).

A modest alternative structuring would start with the Gospel of John, which begins the Jesus story in eternity as it were with the Logos (John 1:1-2) but importantly does not subsequently unfold the story to the neglect of the claim that Jesus is Israel's promised Messiah/King (cf. John 1:41, 49; 20:31). Matthew, Mark, and Luke-Acts, Romans, etc. would follow.[62] One value of such an order is that it keeps Luke-Acts together. Indeed, Luke-Acts viewed as one work in two volumes constitutes over a quarter of the New Testament. Ideally, the two volumes ought to be read together, and this alternative view may help this practice. Moreover, this reordering keeps the present genre sequence: Gospels, Acts, Letters, Revelation.

A Radical Proposal Considered: Canonical Heritage

A very different approach to thinking about the canon is that of William J. Abraham. This alternative approach deserves consideration before this discussion is drawn to a close. William J. Abraham begins his preface to the 2006 paperback edition of his provocative *Canon and Criterion in Christian Theology: From the Fathers to Feminism* — originally published in 1998 — in these words:

> Revisiting the central thesis of this book can be as unsettling as when I first formulated it. Thus it remains no small task to ask theologians to rework two longstanding convictions. The first conviction is that the term "canon" means essentially a criterion; and the second is that the term "canon" applies only to

60. Childs, *Biblical Theology,* 74.

61. In fact in the early church period lists of both Old Testament and New Testament books differed in both content and order. In the present volume, see the essays by both C. E. Hill and Stephen G. Dempster. Also see Goswell, "The Order of the Books of the New Testament," 225-41.

62. With regard to the messianic motif in the Gospel of John see the useful discussion in Walter C. Kaiser Jr., *The Promise-Plan of God: A Biblical Theology of the Old and New Testaments* (Grand Rapids: Zondervan, 2008), 373-76.

> the bible. On my *revisionist* analysis "canon" is a much more modest notion, meaning essentially a "list"; and "canon" applies not just to the biblical canon, but to the canon of saints, the canon of doctrine, the canon of Fathers, and the like, adopted over time in the Church of the first millennium. Beyond these two crucial suggestions, I have proposed that we redescribe and reidentify canon in such a way that we think in terms of a canonical heritage; and that we envision that heritage as a network of *means of grace* intended for use in spiritual direction in the Church.[63]

Abraham clearly identifies his proposal as revisionist and gives his theology of the canon, or, better, canonical heritage a very broad definition.[64] That canonical heritage he sums up in the work itself as "constituted by materials [e.g., Bible and creeds], practices [e.g., rites of initiation], and persons [e.g., saints]."[65] This heritage consists of two types of canon.[66] One is the ecclesial one: creed, Scripture, liturgy, iconography, the Fathers, and sacraments. The other is epistemic: reason, experience, memory, intuition, and inference. Theologically construed, the canonical heritage in its ecclesial expression is to be viewed as "means of grace."[67] The heritage's value is pastoral rather than epistemological. It serves the church's task of spiritual direction.

In the preface Abraham enlists the support of the eminent Roman Catholic scholar Yves Congar. Congar argued that it was Aquinas who narrowed the church's understanding of "Scripture" to the Bible: "On the one hand, he reserved, with increasing precision, the words *revelare, revelatio, inspiratio* to biblical revelation and to scriptural inspiration; on the other hand, he distinguished clearly, though without opposing or separating them, the *auctoritas* of Scripture from that which is due to the Fathers and doctors."[68] However, on closer inspection there is an irony in Abraham's use of Congar as a witness. In an earlier quotation, one that Abraham uses, Congar argues:

63. Abraham, *Canon and Criterion,* vii; my emphases.

64. Lee Martin McDonald's conclusions to his study of the formation of the canon are consistent with Abraham's canonical heritage thesis. If I understand the thrust of his argument aright McDonald has problems with the notion of "a closed canon." See Lee Martin McDonald, *The Biblical Canon,* 126-429. In his view, "the true canon of faith for the church [is] our Lord Jesus Christ" (429). It is important to note that McDonald also argues: "[There is] a lot of work to do before we can draw final and responsible conclusions on the viability of changing our current biblical canon" (xxx).

65. Abraham, *Canon and Criterion,* 31 n. 3.

66. Abraham, *Canon and Criterion,* 1.

67. According to Abraham, over the centuries ecclesial canons such as Scripture were turned into epistemic ones that distorted their true purpose as a means of grace (*Canon and Criterion,* 2).

68. Quoted in *Canon and Criterion,* ix-x.

> The canonical Scriptures, the bible, were the *Scriptura sacra* and *divina pagina* par excellence; but the influence of the Holy Spirit had been felt in the patristic texts, and those of the councils, popes, and theologians, which in any case, *were only produced as an explanation of Scripture. In the simplicity and force of its Catholic faith, the Middle Ages never thought of them as anything else.*[69]

There may have been a vagueness in theologizing in the Middle Ages prior to Aquinas on matters of canon, but what appears to be clear, if Congar is right, is that other putative authorities had authority insofar as they were faithful in explaining the Scriptures. Significantly this is the one part of the lengthy Congar quote that Abraham leaves untouched by way of explication.

More recently, Abraham with others has proposed the notion of "canonical theism" in *Canonical Theism: A Proposal for Theology and the Church.* In one of his contributions to the volume, Abraham offers thirty theses. In Thesis I he explains the term: "*Canonical theism* is a term invented to capture the robust form of theism manifested, lived, and expressed in the canonical heritage of the church."[70] He amplifies "canonical heritage" in Thesis IX:

> Canonical theism is intimately tied to the notion of the canonical heritage of the church. The church possesses not just a canon of books in its Bible but also a canon of doctrine, a canon of saints, a canon of church fathers, a canon of theologians, a canon of liturgy, a canon of bishops, a canon of councils, a canon of ecclesial regulations, a canon of icons, and the like. In short, the church possesses a canonical heritage of persons, practices, and materials.[71]

None of the thirty theses privileges the Bible in any way. Rather, each of these canons has its own job to do in the divine economy: "Each has its own function in the healing and restoration of the human soul."[72] It seems to me that when a term like "canon" can be predicated of so many diverse realities it loses its meaningfulness. I contend that Abraham's proposal would benefit from a firm distinction between the canon of Scripture *(norma normans)* and "canonicals" like a creed *(norma normata).* That way we may speak of canonical heritage in a way that does not mask the special causal relation between Scripture and the Holy Spirit. Indeed, Abraham gives no inkling that the Holy Spirit may relate to his various canons in qualitatively different ways. He contends in Thesis X: "The canonical heritage of the church came into existence through the inspiration of

69. Quoted in *Canon and Criterion,* ix; my emphases.

70. William J. Abraham, Jason E. Vickers, and Natalie B. Van Kirk, eds., *Canonical Theism: A Proposal for Theology and the Church* (Grand Rapids: Eerdmans, 2008), 1.

71. Abraham, Vickers, and Van Kirk, eds., *Canonical Theism,* 2.

72. Abraham, Vickers, and Van Kirk, eds., *Canonical Theism,* 3, Thesis XV.

the Holy Spirit. The Holy Spirit was active in motivating, energizing, guiding, directing, and overseeing their original production in the church."[73] His claim makes the Pauline idea of *theopneustos* with regard to Scripture problematical in the extreme (2 Tim. 3:14-17). If Abraham is right we may ask, Is every element in the canonical heritage *theopneustos*?

Conclusion

The body of writing known to us as the Holy Bible reveals a God who desires to be in relationship with us. This is no anonymous deity. This God has made known his name. He can do so because he is the God who speaks. In fact, communicative action has always been a reality within the life of the essential Trinity. By grace creation is also addressed by the God who speaks. Indeed as Irenaeus suggested so long ago, this God relates to us with his two hands: Word and Spirit. The divine word spoken and the divine word written constitute special revelation. The existence of a canon is a corollary of inspired special revelation. It is fitting rather than a logical necessity, an expression of divine wisdom. Every word is precious, deserving of hearing, reading, and understanding. God has provided special revelation against the backdrop of human rebellion against him. God's Word written is the crystallization of crucial special revelation with its redemptive burden centered on the Christ. Hence, Christians have a book. Moreover, God the Spirit is causally related to Scripture's production in a way that is unique to it. Scripture is *theopneustos.* Hence, Christians have this book and not some other one. Again, as suggested previously but it bears repetition, the existence of a canon is a corollary of such inspiration. The church historically recognized the unique status of Scripture in forming a canon. It was a process of discerning the authority of these writings rather than conferring authority on these writings. The church needs to know both what is to be read and what is not to be read publicly in the gathering of God's people as it seeks to worship God in spirit and in truth. Now it is true that Roman Catholic and Eastern Orthodox have more books in the Old Testament part of their canon than Protestants. Even so, Protestants, Roman Catholics, and Eastern Orthodox all recognize the authority of the sixty-six books shared in common.[74] Lastly, it is patent that the church is responsible for the present order of the books making up the canon. Hence the particular ordering we find in this book. But ordering the canon and recognizing the authority of its makeup are separate matters and need to be kept distinct lest ordering becomes synonymous with the conferral of authority on Scripture by the church.

73. Abraham, Vickers, and Van Kirk, eds., *Canonical Theism,* 2.

74. A point well made by Vanhoozer, *The Drama of Doctrine,* 43.

SIXTEEN

God and the Bible

Peter F. Jensen

God and His Word

William Tyndale shaped a civilization by translating the Bible into English. He was determined that his countrymen should read the Scriptures for themselves and sealed that determination in a bloody martyrdom. What drove him on was his conviction that Scripture was the very word of God. To have the Scripture was to have the truth; to believe it was to embrace the truth, and so to embrace God himself. He spoke of it as a measure by which all religious and theological claims need to be tested, even those of Jesus: "Christ commandeth to search the scriptures John v. Though that miracles bare record unto his doctrine, yet desired he no faith to be given either to his doctrine, or to his miracles, without record of the scriptures."[1] He believed that as ordinary men and women read the Scriptures in their literal sense, they would find God's law which would expose their sins and God's promises through which forgiveness and eternal life would come. In short they would embrace the gospel and become the saved and obedient servants of the Lord.

Even those who profess the highest esteem for Scripture may treat it in a frigid or detached manner. For Tyndale, Scripture is more than a measuring line of doctrine, a court of appeal. The very words of Scripture, being the words of God, are integral to the intimate trust relationship between God and the believer. He says boldly,

> God is nothing but his law and his promises; that is to say, that which he biddeth thee to do, and that which he biddeth thee believe and hope. God is but his word, as Christ saith, John viii. "I am that I say unto you"; that is to say, That which I preach am I; my words are spirit and life. God is that only which

1. William Tyndale, *The Obedience of a Christian Man,* in *Doctrinal Treatises,* ed. Henry Walter (Cambridge: The Parker Society, 1848), 146-47.

> he testifieth of himself; and to imagine any other thing of God than that is damnable idolatry.[2]

Of course Tyndale did not believe that God was merely words ontologically. His real contention was twofold. First, that although we may distinguish words from other aspects of a person, we cannot separate them. In human relationships words have an indispensable role in revealing and bonding. When we trust another person, we trust what they say; when we obey another person, we obey what they say. It is both incoherent and insulting to say that we trust a person though we do not trust their words, or to say that we will submit to a person though not to their commands. Second, in dealing with God we are dealing with one whose words are absolutely true and trustworthy. As we may say even of another human, "That man is as good as his word," so we must say that in God's case his word cannot be separated, in Tyndale's view, from his person. When you trust the word of God, you are trusting God himself; when you keep the word of God, you are obeying God himself. You do not need to search behind or beyond the word for the real God. He is as good as his word.

Thus, when it comes to the human relationship with God, the Scriptures constitute not only a sufficient revelation of God's mind and purposes, but a unique instrument of our relationship with him. God alone is the Lord. The human instinct for idolatry can only be dealt with when we allow the Scriptures alone, as the word of God, to shape our thinking and our reactions. Its words are the words on which we must concentrate if we are to know God and serve him. Only thus can we live before him in faith and obedience, can we worship him in spirit and in truth. To subvert the Bible as God's direct word is to destroy our relationship with God — indeed it is an assault on God himself, since God is as good as his word. God rules over us through his word.

Relocating God's Word

In a powerful way, Tyndale brings out the spiritual heart of the classic "Scripture principle," that the Lordship of God is expressed in his inspired, inscripturated word.[3] In their survey of Scripture and tradition, Edward Farley and Peter Hodgson agree that the Scripture principle (with variations) has been the undivided confession of the Christian churches from the beginning of the gospel to the

2. Tyndale, *Obedience,* 160. Tyndale's reference arises from a very close reading of John 8:25, which he translates, "Then sayde they unto him who are thou? And Jesus sayde unto them: Even ye very same thinge yt I saye unto you."

3. "'Authority of Scripture' Is a Shorthand for God's Authority Exercised *Through* Scripture" (N. T Wright, *Scripture and the Authority of God* [London: SPCK, 2005], 17).

Enlightenment. But, in their view, the Enlightenment has changed everything. For them, and for those in the liberal tradition, it is no longer possible to make the simple identification that the Bible is the word of God. Historical criticism renders it impossible; but so too does theology itself. We must develop new and better understandings of the function of Scripture and the nature of revelation. In their vividly expressed judgment, "The house of authority has collapsed, despite the fact that many people still try to live in it. Some retain title to it actually without living there; others are antiquarians or renovators, attempting in one way or another to salvage it; still others have abandoned it for new quarters or no quarters at all."[4]

In the minds of many, the collapse of the house of authority is not considered a disaster. It is an opportunity for a proper theological reassessment of the place of Scripture, of the nature of revelation and of the relationship between God and his people. It offers the possibility of an improved way of describing God's revelation and his authority. The reconstructions of the doctrine of revelation are manifold, but four widely shared characteristics should be noted: negatively, they are driven by perceived theological and anthropological problems with the classic view, and, positively they call on Christological and pneumatological resources to offer a new way forward.

First, there is a theological problem: the classic tradition, with its strong doctrine of inspiration, identifies God too closely with the manifestly human elements of the biblical text. In the trenchant words of C. H. Dodd, "The old dogmatic view of the Bible therefore is not only open to attack from the standpoint of science and historical criticism, but if taken seriously it becomes a danger to religion and public morals."[5] If we insist on a strong doctrine of inspiration, we have tainted the character of God himself.

Second, there is an anthropological problem: the classic tradition compromises the necessary freedom of the human subject. "Many people inside and outside the church equate the idea of the authority of the Bible with coercion rather than liberty, with terror rather than joy."[6] The effect of true revelation is to liberate; it is to equip the human receiver with the capacity for critical reflection on what has allegedly been revealed. This is especially important with relation to the Bible. If the Bible is called the word of God in an absolute sense there is a danger of adopting patriarchal, sexist, or other oppressive stances. We are placed in the position of being slaves of God rather than partners with him.

4. Edward Farley and P. C. Hodgson, "Scripture and Tradition," in *Christian Theology,* ed. P. C. Hodgson and R. H. King, 2nd edition (London: SPCK, 2008), 76.

5. C. H. Dodd, *The Authority of the Bible* (London: Fontana, 1960), 24.

6. Daniel L. Migliore, *Faith Seeking Understanding,* 2nd edition (Grand Rapids: Eerdmans, 2004), 44. Cf. Paul Avis, "Divine Revelation in Modern Protestant Theology," in *Divine Revelation,* ed. Paul Avis (Grand Rapids: Eerdmans, 1997), 45-46, for the Enlightenment roots of the rejection of "heteronomous authority," and Hodgson and King, *Christian Theology,* 61-62.

Third, in order to reconstruct the doctrine of revelation, there is an appeal to Christology: our fellowship with God is through a personal Word, his Son, Jesus Christ. The danger is that the inspired words of the Bible will take the place of Christ as the focus of revelation and salvation. Our faith is in Christ, not the Bible, in a Person, not in words. "The spoken word," writes Emil Brunner, "is an indirect revelation when it bears witness to the real revelation: Jesus Christ, the personal self-manifestation of God, Emmanuel."[7]

Fourth, there is an appeal to pneumatology: the doctrine of revelation is complete only when it includes the human response to the work of the Holy Spirit. Revelation is an event. Thus John Macquarrie writes, "But we may remind ourselves that the scripture itself is not revelation, but testifies to the revelation in Christ; and that it is in the living context of the Church, as the community of the Spirit, that scripture comes alive as it were, so that in the human word of scripture, as read and preached, the word of God addresses us."[8] The inclusion to the Christian experience of the Spirit also opens the way to possible ongoing revelations by the Spirit.

Great energy and erudition have gone into such reconstructions. They represent a move from Scripture to revelation, from inspired words to the personal Word, from statement to event. Avery Dulles sums them up in these words: "Revelation is God's free action whereby he communicates saving truth to created minds, especially through Jesus Christ as accepted by the apostolic Church and attested by the Bible and by the continuing community of believers."[9]

The Key Issue

In order to meet the challenge of this reconstruction, I intend to address a more fundamental issue: What is integral to the Christian faith's own well-being and existence? Is the classical position necessary to the gospel? Or, can a contemporary approach, accepting the Christological and pneumatological correctives outlined above, save the gospel in a modern form?

Evangelical Christians have long and rightly observed that liberal views of Scripture are often at odds with the attitude of Jesus and his apostles.[10] For them, that is enough to make them reject contemporary reconstructions. A somewhat tendentious response could be that Jesus and his apostles merely reproduced the

7. Emil Brunner, *The Christian Doctrine of God* (Philadelphia: Westminster, 1950), 25.

8. John Macquarrie, *Principles of Christian Theology* (London: SCM, 1977), 454.

9. Avery Dulles, *Models of Revelation* (Dublin: Gill & Macmillan, 1983), 117.

10. E.g., Wayne Grudem, "Scripture's Self-Attestation and the Problem of Formulating a Doctrine of Scripture," in *Scripture and Truth,* ed. D. A. Carson and John D. Woodbridge (Leicester: IVP, 1983), 19-64.

inherited culture of their time and place and that their attitude to Scripture is a theological incidental. My argument is that the attitude of Jesus and the apostles is integral to Christianity, to the very nature of the gospel. Another way of putting the point is to say that the Jewish cradle of Christianity is essential, not incidental, to its being. Any reconstruction that moves away from the classical view fails theologically. It is not in accord with the inner necessity of the revelation that comes to us through Jesus Christ, the very revelation to which appeal continues to be made. You cannot both accept the revelation that is in Jesus Christ and also regard the Scriptures as other than the inspired word of God. To uncouple the word of God from Scripture is to undercut the very gospel itself. It is self-defeating. The theological and anthropological problems that drive such reconstructions must be addressed; but they must be addressed in a way that sustains the direct identification of Scripture with the word of God.

The Gospel-Heart of Revelation

The apostles preached the gospel of Jesus Christ. Often they called the gospel itself "the word of God."[11] According to the specific claim of Paul, it was not an invented gospel or a constructed gospel: it is a revealed gospel, a revelation (Gal. 1:11, 12; Eph. 3:1-6).[12] Acceptance of the gospel is what marks out the Christian. We hear the gospel preached and through this we believe and so are saved (Rom. 10:17). It is crucial therefore that the beliefs we develop as a consequence of becoming Christian are in line with the gospel we have received (Col. 2:6). We cannot begin in one way and end in another if we wish to preserve the integrity of what has been our salvation in the first place. This is what is at stake in current disagreements about the nature and function of Scripture.

Basic to the truth of the New Testament gospel are three presuppositions concerning Scripture. To abandon any of these presuppositions is to prejudice the gospel itself and so endanger our salvation and the whole Christian enterprise. The gospel presupposes, first, that Scripture is the word of God; second, that this inscripturated word is indispensable for true faith; and third, that this inscripturated word is indispensable for true obedience. Such abandonment is the key problem with any theology that distinguishes itself so seriously from the sort of tradition represented by Tyndale. It has also uncoupled itself from the New Testament gospel.[13] I will discuss each of these in turn.

11. E.g., 1 Peter 1:25.

12. Revealed specifically to him, but tested through consultation with those who preceded him (Gal. 2:2).

13. See J. Gresham Machen's classic *Christianity and Liberalism* (Grand Rapids: Eerdmans, 2009 [orig. 1923]).

The Gospel Presupposes That Scripture Is the Word of God

A pointer to the serious decay in Christian theology is the ready acquiescence, even in places of rich Christian learning, to the description of the Old Testament as "Hebrew Scriptures."[14] It already concedes what is foundational — that the fundamental reason for believing the gospel is that it is a fulfillment of the existing Scriptures. The truth of the gospel is demonstrated by an appeal to Scripture viewed as the word of God. The route by which Jesus came to be known as Lord was via the confession that he is "the Christ," that is, the promised Messiah: "And Paul went in, as was his custom, and on three Sabbath days he reasoned with them from the Scriptures, explaining and proving that it was necessary for the Christ to suffer and to rise from the dead, and saying 'This Jesus, whom I proclaim to you, is the Christ'" (Acts 17:2-3).

Wherever we can study the first preaching of the gospel, whether via the four Gospels, the Acts of the Apostles, or the Epistles we see the same pattern, namely an appeal to the words of the Old Testament as a demonstration of the truth of the gospel.[15] Thus Jesus speaks to his disciples: "everything written about me in the Law of Moses and the Prophets and the Psalms must be fulfilled" (Luke 24:44); thus in John he testifies: "If you believed Moses, you would believe me; for he wrote of me. But if you do not believe his writings, how will you believe my words?" (John 5:46-47); thus Peter preaches, "To him all the prophets bear witness" (Acts 10:43); thus Paul writes: "Paul, a servant of Jesus Christ, called to be an Apostle, set apart for the gospel of God, which he promised beforehand through his prophets in the holy Scriptures, concerning his Son . . ." (Rom. 1:1-3).

When the gospel is preached it comes as a word from God. But its claim to be a word from God, and thus the word of God, is verified by its deep inner coherence with the existing word of God, namely the Old Testament. Speaking of Paul, Professor James Dunn observes that "Scripture formed 'the substructure of his theology,'" having a status "as divinely authorized statements or oracles in writing" which he simply took for granted.[16] From one point of view, virtually the entire New Testament can be seen as an appendix to the Old, an extended discussion of the way in which Jesus is the fulfillment of the Old. This means that the Old Testament's testimony to Christ is indispensable for explaining the meaning of his person and work.[17] But it also verifies that he is the promised one.

14. Cf. Francis Watson, *Text and Truth: Redefining Biblical Theology* (Grand Rapids: Eerdmans, 1997), 5, 219.

15. Even the sermon to Gentiles as reported in Acts 17 was shaped by the Scriptures. In any case, however, gentile Christians were soon inducted into a world of scriptural authority (e.g., 1 Cor. 10:11).

16. J. Dunn, *The Theology of Paul the Apostle* (Grand Rapids: Eerdmans, 1998), 170.

17. R. W. L. Moberly, *The Bible, Theology, and Faith* (Cambridge: Cambridge University Press, 2000): "[T]here is no knowledge available from a realm beyond this life which is more

The ground for this is laid in the Old Testament itself, in two ways. First, there are the tests of prophecy enunciated in Deuteronomy 13 and 18, the tests of coherence and of fulfillment. The genuineness of a prophet can be tested by whether his prophecies come to pass or not. Even if he is able to do signs and wonders, he must also not teach against the existing word of God and so lead the people to worship other gods. In this way the prophet is only mirroring the way God vindicates himself, for it is when God promises and then brings to pass that Israel and the world know that he is indeed God, as opposed to the false idols who either cannot speak or whose word turns out to be false (see, e.g., Isa. 41:21-29; 46:8-13). That is why the Bible offers no deductive proof for the existence of God; rather God demonstrates his own reality in word and deed, in particular saying what he plans to do and then doing it: "And you shall know that I am the Lord," as Ezekiel says again and again (e.g., Ezek. 13:23). God is his own best witness.

Second, on a grander scale there is the covenantal structure of the Bible, a structure that makes it appropriate to think of promise and fulfillment as being proper categories to use in a description of the relationship of the Testaments.[18] Thus although the demonstration that Jesus is indeed the fulfillment of the prophetic expectation involves references to the details of the prophetic writings from his birth in Bethlehem (Mic. 5:2) to the agony of his death (Isa. 53) to the necessity of his resurrection (Ps. 16), there is a far deeper sense in which he completes what God began and is the demonstration that God keeps his covenantal promises. After all, his birth in Bethlehem is not merely notable because Micah foretold the city — it is the significance that his birth was in the city of David that counts. In other words, the indisputably eschatological nature of the gospel depends entirely on the existence of scriptural promises now fulfilled in the coming of the kingdom of God in Christ.

It is this to which Paul refers when he describes the mission of Jesus in these terms: "For I tell you that Christ became a servant to the circumcised to show God's truthfulness, in order to confirm the promises given to the patriarchs, and in order that the Gentiles might glorify God for his mercy. As it is written . . ." (Rom. 15:8-9). The apostle puts the work of Christ into the structure of the divine promises. He does not come only to save, but specifically to show God's truthfulness and confirm the promises. Indeed, in Romans and elsewhere much of the

---

significant or helpful for understanding Jesus and life with God than the moral and spiritual content of already existing scripture. Secondly, the implication is not that the story of Jesus does not have intrinsic significance, but that it needs to be set in a context beyond itself for that significance to be understood; that is, existing scripture provides the necessary context for understanding Jesus" (51).

18. Cf. C. F. D. Moule, *The Birth of the New Testament* (London: A&C Black, 1962), 57 n. 1: "[T]he note of *fulfilment* seems to be peculiar to the New Testament."

appeal to the Old Testament centers around the mystery that God had promised to call the Gentiles through the disobedience of the Jews, and on equal terms.

It is no accident therefore that Romans begins and ends with the same point: that God has kept his promises and that his faithfulness is demonstrated by the inclusion of all the nations in the gospel blessings. In the opening of the Epistle, it is the gospel that has been promised by God "through his prophets in the holy Scriptures," which has now meant that Paul has received "grace and apostleship to bring about the obedience of faith for the sake of his name among all nations including you who are called to belong to Jesus Christ" (Rom. 1:5-6). At the close of the Epistle we have the same theme, where he refers to "the revelation of the mystery that was kept secret for long ages but has now been disclosed and through the prophetic writings has been made known to all nations, according to the command of the eternal God, to bring about the obedience of faith" (16:25-26).

That God should include the Gentiles along with the Jews on the principle of faith in Jesus was clearly astonishing. That is why Paul labors to demonstrate that this was always intended and that the prophetic writings contained the mystery that is now disclosed. For the vindication of God involves a reciprocal relation between promise and fulfillment: the fact of fulfillment in such a massive and detailed way through Jesus demonstrates that we are dealing with the true God; but also the fulfillment explains the nature of the promises. It is not as though someone with the Old Testament in their hand could write a biography of Jesus in advance; but once Jesus had come, the Old Testament comes alive with meaning. Peter hints at the longing of the prophets to see the reality of what they had themselves predicted, and Hebrews is a sustained exposition of the way in which the law and the prophets foreshadowed Christ, explained Christ, and then in their turn were explained by Christ.

The significance of all this for our present understanding is plain. The very nature of the gospel was shaped in the crucible of the encounter between Jews and Gentiles. To put the matter simply: Christians were those who, having studied the Scriptures, came to see that Jesus was the one in whom all the promises of God find their yes and amen. Those who remained Jews only, were those who denied that Christ was the end of the law, the fulfillment of the covenants, the hope of Israel. This remains the case. But the Christian view, the Christian gospel, cannot begin to be sustained in any other terms. It is either the fulfillment of the Old Testament promises of God, or it is a fraud. And for that discussion even to commence we have to acknowledge that there are promises of God, that there is a word of God, that the word is written, and that it corresponds to the Old Testament as we have it. That is precisely the way in which Paul put the matter in Romans and Jesus himself put the matter as recorded in Luke. The Christian gospel itself depends upon the Old Testament scriptures ("the oracles of God" as Paul calls them) being the very words of God. Nothing else makes sense.

This Inscripturated Word Is Indispensable for True Faith

We receive God's revelation by faith. What happens to faith when God's revelation is thought of as a Word, to which humans bear witness in fallible words?

One response has been to say that faith is "trust" as opposed "assent," and to emphasize the "event" nature of revelation, rather than the static and public nature of the Bible thought of as revelation. We are to trust a Person, not believe in propositions: "What is offered to man's apprehension in any specific revelation is not truth concerning God but the living God Himself."[19]

But this is to divide the indivisible. Faith (or trust) relates us to God, but as Paul says, "faith comes from hearing, and hearing from the word of Christ" (Rom. 10:17). The activity of the first preachers was to "preach Christ," and those who responded positively to their word became "believers" by means of these words which they regarded as true and divinely given because they fulfilled words that themselves were true and divinely given. It was the gospel message that Jesus is Lord, the promised Christ of God, which by the Spirit created faith.

The severance of the Word from words relies on the misuse of the language of John 1, in which the Logos becomes a master concept for the whole theology of revelation.[20] This does not do justice to the Gospel of John, let alone the rest of the New Testament, for the Word himself speaks many words and invites trust in him through his words. When Paul refers to "the word of Christ" he does not mean a single word, "Christ," or even a name, "Jesus Christ." His message is a propositional assertion that Jesus *is* the Christ, vindicated at length by an appeal to an existing word of God, namely the Law, the prophets, and the writings. Elsewhere he says that "Jesus Christ is Lord" (2 Cor. 4:5) and that Christ's Lordship involves of necessity assenting to and trusting in his resurrection from the dead: "If you confess with your mouth that Jesus is Lord and believe in your heart that God raised him from the dead, you will be saved" (Rom. 10:9).

Faith in Christ by means of the word of Christ so preached is crucial to salvation. This is the testimony of the entire New Testament. But faith is only of use when it is based on the truth (Heb. 11:1; 1 Pet. 1:22). What does the denial of the classic doctrine of Scripture do to faith? Emil Brunner tried to distinguish faith in Christ from faith in the words about Christ:

> Faith in Jesus Christ is not based on a previous faith in the Bible, but is based solely on the work of the Holy Spirit; this witness, however, does not come to us save through the witness of the Apostles — that apostolic testimony to

19. William Temple, quoted in John Baillie, *The Idea of Revelation in Recent Thought* (New York: Columbia University Press, 1964), 33.

20. A point made in relation to Karl Barth by Wolfhart Pannenberg, *Systematic Theology,* vol. 1 (Edinburgh: T. & T. Clark, 1991), 235.

> which our relation is one of freedom, and, although it is true, it is fundamental for us, it is in no way dogmatically binding, in the sense of the theory of Verbal Inspiration. The Scripture . . . is a "word" inspired by the Spirit of God; yet at the same time it is a human message; its "human character" means that it is colored by the frailty and imperfection of all that is human.[21]

Brunner calls the apostolic witness the "means of faith," but not the "basis and object of faith."[22] This is surely an astonishing conclusion to reach. How can we arrive at the object of faith, without faith in the means? He describes the apostolic witness as a bridge to Christ, but what if the bridge "is colored by the frailty and imperfection of all that is human"? Do we not have to trust the bridge, and would not the God of the gospel of grace provide a bridge that is entirely trustworthy? For this is the point at issue. Has God "spoken" in a Word that does not speak, and left us with merely human means of attaining fellowship with him? Is this grace? The appeal to the Holy Spirit to overcome the abyss caused by this theology separates word from Spirit (note Eph. 6:17) and opens the way for the human spirit to be master of revelation. It corrupts saving faith.

In contrast to Brunner, Calvin says, "We enjoy Christ only as we embrace Christ clad in his own promises."[23] This exactly expresses the inescapable presupposition of the gospel, that God approaches us with words that are his own, so that we may be captive to the Word through faith. Our trust in the Lord is through words from the Lord; Tyndale was right that words and person cannot be divided. As R. P. Martin observes, speaking of 2 Corinthians 5:20, "It is not only that Paul voices God's word as his mouthpiece and messenger; the sentence is turned around to claim that God is present in Paul's words. Not that Paul is acting and speaking for God, but that God himself is the chief actor, working and speaking through Paul."[24] This is the theology of Tyndale. This is the basis of faith. This is the grace of God.

The gospel-revelation of God is inescapably verbal. His grace requires that he speak to us in his own words which are ours; our saving faith requires such words, so that we may trust our Lord. His verbal revelation of himself suits our nature as human beings. In particular, his words alone convey the promissory nature of his revelation. Only words from him create our true response of repentant faith. Saving faith is created by a revelation that is both fitting and promissory.

21. Brunner, *The Christian Doctrine of God,* 33-34.

22. Brunner, *The Christian Doctrine of God,* 33.

23. *Institutes* 2.9.4.

24. In Peter Bolt and Mark Thompson, eds., *The Gospel to the Nations* (Leicester: Apollos, 2000), 79.

A Fitting Revelation

John Frame's judgment is absolutely correct: "The idea that God communicates with human beings in personal words pervades all of Scripture and is central to every doctrine of Scripture."[25] It is true not only as a judgment about Scripture but as a judgment about persons. A gospel that, through faith, overcomes alienation and restores fellowship between God and humanity, requires God's speech in human language to accomplish divine self-disclosure and faith. That is the nature of persons. Even between humans, language is the supreme instrument of human relationship. It is not the only means. We overcome the physical distance between us in a number of ways: we see each other; we observe, touch, and smell each other. We use signs and symbols to communicate, often at a very profound level indeed. But, in the end, it is the language we share which is the indispensable and peerless vehicle of disclosure, of invitation, of relationship, of faith. That is why some of the most elevated of human experiences are related to poetry, oratory, and song. That is why the capacity to read is such an enriching part of being human, and why letters between friends are so cherished.

The good flourishing of a relationship needs the refreshment of many words, especially when there is distance between the parties. We misunderstand each other easily; we forget; we become engrossed with other things. We know each other best when there is opportunity for correction, for clarifying matters, for clothing our different experiences and behaviors in different forms of words: words that narrate, encapsulate, celebrate, elevate. A single personality wishing to disclose and invite must put language to variegated uses for the sake of a relationship in depth. The greater opportunity that exists for a relationship over time, the more exists the possibility for understanding and trust to grow, as long as words are possible.

Our encounter with the Lord, our personal encounter with him, is through the medium of words, words that themselves come in sentences, assertions, propositions, promises, exclamations, interrogations. The Bible is not ashamed of human language; it does not share our doubts that it can be the vehicle for the truthful God to speak infallibly (Exod. 4:11). Our inability to speak accurately to each other is a result of judgment on us at Babel, just as our continued habit of lying arises from the corrupt nature we have inherited from Adam. But God has made the mouth; he is the inventor and master of language; he can use human words to convey divine meanings. The fact that he speaks is what marks him out from the dumb idols. The richness of the whole of the Scriptures testifies to the many-sidedness of our faith-relationship with the Lord. Its supreme and unifying message is captured in the One Word in whom all the promises of God find their Yes (2 Cor. 1:20).[26]

25. John M. Frame, *The Doctrine of the Word of God* (Phillipsburg, NJ: P&R, 2010), 6.

26. Hence the vital importance of the contention of Graeme L. Goldsworthy, *Gospel-*

A Promissory Revelation

The gospel is promissory, because it is the gospel of the new covenant.[27] Basic to profound faith-relationships are promises. A promise is always verbal; it always points to the future; it is always apprehended by faith — indeed it creates and sustains faith, as long as it still stands in good faith. While it does, it serves to unite the person who makes and the person who receives the promise. When a promise is made formally — when it is sealed with an oath, for example, or when it takes the form of a covenant — it becomes especially an instrument of unity, inviting faith.

A promise is a means of overcoming time and space. First, it needs to be remembered: it stands in the past, able to be referred to by those who remember it. That is why solemn promises are often accompanied by a sign, or are written. They are a matter of record to creatures whose clutch on time is only the fleeting moment that they occupy. Second, because they always point forward, they turn faith into hope, or rather, they bring out the hopeful element of all faith. Third, promises are effective even when the parties are absent from each other; indeed they virtually presuppose absence. We trust when we cannot supervise, when we cannot observe. We have faith in what we cannot see.

And it is via the words of the gospel that we enter a faith relationship with Jesus Christ. A fallible report from someone else that he has made promises to us does not create the faith relationship which is the fruit of the gospel.[28] Nor can we bypass his words, as if to go directly to him. That is to act as though the Ascension never occurred or as though the age to come has already arrived in fullness. As we trust his words, so we trust him.

The promises of mere mortals are always at risk, through sin or inability. However, even men and women can make promises that are faithfully kept lifelong. The promises of God are true and unbreakable. Our limitations are not his. It is not surprising that he overcomes the distance between himself and us by making promises. His promises disclose and invite. Like all promises they stand ready to be inspected; they need to be remembered if they are to have present power. In the case of his promise never to destroy the earth by a flood, he has given us the bow in the clouds as a sign. But the sign would be without meaning if we did not have in the written record the promise of which it is a sign. And,

---

Centred Hermeneutics (Nottingham: Apollos, 2006), 58: "[T]he person and work of Christ are at the heart of hermeneutics."

27. Cf. Paul R. Williamson, *Sealed with an Oath* (Nottingham: Apollos, 2007), 43: "a solemn commitment, guaranteeing promises or obligations undertaken by one or both parties, sealed with an oath."

28. The classic doctrine of inspiration allows for human intermediaries to speak, but their speech must be more direct than merely a report of speech (2 Pet. 1:21). The word of the prophet *is* the word of God.

the promise, although valuable, would have little meaning if we did not have the narrative of the flood to explain to us why such a promise should be made.

The biblical gospel is founded on existing promises and is itself promissory in form: it is rightly called the new covenant. It stands as a record of the promises of God, to be reexamined whenever necessary for correction and for hope. We see this in the Pauline summary at the beginning of 1 Corinthians 15, for example:

> Now I would remind you brothers, of the gospel I preached to you, which you received, in which you stand, and by which you are being saved, if you hold fast to the word I preached to you — unless you believed in vain. For I delivered to you as of first importance what I also received: that Christ died for our sins in accordance with the Scriptures, that he was buried, that he was raised on the third day in accordance with the Scriptures, and that he appeared to Cephas, and then to the twelve. (15:1-5)

Paul's formulation is necessarily verbal: it was preached, which is how you deliver a gospel of promise. It is on the record and so could be readily referred to and remembered. Indeed, Paul's exposition itself reached back into a record that was even closer to the events than he was himself, for he received what he passed on to them. It reached from the past into the present and the future — it was that in which his hearers continued to stand and if so to be saved. They received this gospel by faith — which is how you receive a gospel of promise. It created extra Scripture because it arose from the promises of God in the existing Scriptures. It promised forgiveness of sins and resurrection of the body through the events of the death and resurrection of Jesus Christ. Its faith was unequivocally hopeful, for by this gospel God conquers the limitations imposed by time and space and death and sin. Its verbal nature is an indispensable concomitant of the space and time in which we now find ourselves — or, as Paul says elsewhere, "We know that while we are at home in the body we are away from the Lord, for we walk by faith, not by sight" (2 Cor. 5:6-7). His faith was based on words: the promises of the gospel, which cannot be separated from the one who speaks them.

In sum, the second presupposition of the gospel is the inscripturated word that is indispensable for true faith.

This Inscripturated Word Is Indispensable for True Obedience

The heart of the gospel is the kingdom of God, expressed through the lordship of Jesus Christ. This means that faith and repentance are not accidental corollaries of the gospel, but necessary consequences of it. They are foundational to the Christian life. If Christ is Lord, the only appropriate worship of him is to trust ourselves to him entirely, that is, to submit to him in an obedient faith that relies upon and takes its shape from words that come from the Lord. That is why in the same passage Paul speaks of the gospel not only as the word of Christ but also as "the word of faith which we proclaim" (Rom. 10:8). It is a word that engenders faith; it is a word that is proclaimed; it is a word that is explained in words; it is a word that is not far off and unobtainable, but one that "is near you, in your mouth and in your heart" (10:8); it is a word that invites obedience.[29]

As Tyndale stressed, another fact of human existence that makes language the especially appropriate medium of our relationship with God is our tendency to idolatry. In the post-Fall world, where the knowledge of God is suppressed, human beings remain as worshipers. That is the way in which we have been designed. But our ignorance and willfulness mean that we refuse to acknowledge the true God. Rather, we take up the created world, to create idols made in accordance with the desires of our hearts. In Paul's acute analysis, "Claiming to be wise, they became fools, and exchanged the glory of the immortal God for images resembling mortal man and birds and animals and reptiles" (Rom. 1:22-23). Thus from the earliest days of the biblical revelation, there is an unrelenting war against idolatry, the taking of part of creation and worshiping it in place of the true God.

The pressure on Israel to conform to the religions around them was immense. The plastic representation of the gods was so much more satisfactory than the invisible God whom they worshiped. It is very instructive to see where the contrast was according to Deuteronomy:

> Then the Lord spoke to you out of the midst of the fire. You heard the sound of words but saw no form: there was only a voice. And he declared to you his covenant, which he commanded you to perform, that is the Ten Commandments [lit. "words"] and he wrote them on two tablets of stone. And the Lord commanded me at that time to teach you statutes or rules, that you might do them in the land that you are going over to possess. (Deut. 4:12-14)
>
> Did any people ever hear the voice of a god speaking out of the midst of the fire, as you have heard and still live? (4:33)

In short, where Israel differed was not merely in the forbidding of images; it was through the voice of God giving the words of God transcribed into a permanent written record and taught by Moses and then by teachers and parents, which constituted the revelation of God and the continued reference point for the future. The supreme corrective to idolatry is inscripturated words from God.

What was so, remains so. Through the gospel we are enabled to be restored to

29. See Rom. 1:5; 2:8. The singular "word" is not intended to distinguish the heart of the message from the words that convey the gospel, but only to point to the unity of the message, as illustrated by Deut. 30:14.

the creatures we are meant to be, namely those who worship the true and living God. The very structure of creation is not removed, it is restored. Just as Adam and Eve were placed in the garden under the explicit command of God and were expected to order their lives by its rule if they wished to be in fellowship with God, so we too, in our restoration, are placed under the Lordship of the Son of God with the aim and purpose of pleasing him by obeying his specific word. In short, the heart of Christian piety is not self-maturation, any more than it is self-salvation. It is obedience to the word of God.[30]

That obedience to the word of God is fundamental to true godliness is pervasive in the Bible: It is the explicit teaching of Scripture at great and memorable moments. "Behold, to obey is better than sacrifice, and to listen than the fat of lambs," says Samuel to Saul when Saul forfeits the kingdom (1 Sam. 15:22); "This Book of the Law shall not depart from your mouth, but you shall meditate on it day and night, so that you may be careful to do according to all that is written in it," says the Lord to Joshua on the verge of entering the Promised Land (Josh. 1:8); "you have abandoned the commandments of the Lord and followed the Baals," says Elijah in his stern charge against a disobedient Ahab (1 Kgs. 18:18); "since . . . you have not kept my covenant and my statutes that I have commanded you, I will surely tear the kingdom from you," says the Lord even to the great Solomon at the end of his life (1 Kgs. 11:11); "Why is the land ruined . . . 'Because they have forsaken my law which I set before them and have not obeyed my voice,' " says the Lord through Jeremiah in the crisis of Exile (Jer. 9:12-13).

It is the explicit teaching of the Scripture in the wisdom literature and the Psalms: "Fear God and keep his commandments, for this is the whole duty of man" (Eccles. 12:13); "My son, if you receive my words and treasure up my commandments with you . . . then you will understand the fear of the Lord. . . . For the Lord gives wisdom; from his mouth come knowledge and understanding" (Prov. 2:1, 5-6); "Blessed is the man who walks not in the counsel of the wicked, nor stands in the way of sinners, nor sits in the seat of scoffers; but his delight is in the law of the Lord, and on his law he meditates day and night" (Ps. 1:1-2); "And the king stood in his place and made a covenant before the Lord, to walk after the Lord and to keep his testimonies and his statutes with all his heart and soul, to perform the words of the covenant that were written in this book" (2 Chron. 34:31).

It is the explicit teaching of Scripture through the Law, the Prophets, the apostles, and the Lord himself: "And now, O Israel, listen to the statutes and the rules that I am teaching you, and do them . . . you shall not add to the word that

30. Both Hebrew and Greek terms for obedience suggest listening: "attentive and hearty compliance with the directives of someone with acknowledged authority" (J. I. Packer, "Obedience," in *New Dictionary of Biblical Theology,* ed. T. D. Alexander et al. [Leicester: IVP, 2000], 680).

I command you, nor take from it, that you may keep the commandments of the Lord your God that I command you" (Deut. 4:1-2); "To the teaching and to the testimony! If they will not speak according to this word, it is because they have no dawn" (Isa. 8:20). "By this we know that we love the children of God, when we love God and keep his commandments" (1 John 5:2); "But be doers of the word, and not hearers only, deceiving yourselves" (James 1:22); "You should remember the predictions of the holy prophets and the commandment of the Lord and Savior through your apostles" (2 Pet. 3:2); "But thanks be to God, that you who were once slaves to sin have become obedient from the heart to the standard of teaching to which you were committed" (Rom. 6:17); "And everyone who hears these words of mine and does not do them will be like a foolish man who built his house upon the sand" (Matt. 7:26).

Some would argue that the coming of the new covenant rendered the appeal to the written word of God obsolete.[31] Has the written code not passed away? "But now we are released from the law, having died to that which held us captive, so that we serve not under the old written code but in the new life of the Spirit" (Rom. 7:6). Likewise, God "has made us competent to be ministers of a new covenant, not of the letter but of the Spirit. For the letter kills, but the Spirit gives life" (2 Cor. 3:6). Indeed, in the very passage where Jesus is most clearly identified as the Word of God, it says, "For the law was given through Moses; grace and truth came through Jesus Christ" (John 1:17).

This argument is, however, untenable. There is indeed what we may call both a pneumatological and a Christological revolution through the gospel, one that, as we read the Old Testament, results in a gospel hermeneutic.[32] But neither cancels the way of God in making himself known in and by the words of Scripture. Otherwise it would be impossible to explain the respect accorded to the Scriptures by the apostolic writers.[33] The coming of the Spirit changes the hearts of human beings so that the law is no longer the letter that kills. It does not mean that the law is anything but "holy and righteous and good" (Rom. 7:12), and indeed the moral law still provides the fundamental structure of the demand of God on human life. Where the law is no longer directly relevant, it is because Christ is the fulfillment of the law, and yet, as Hebrews demonstrates, without the law we would not be able to comprehend the work of Christ. We may no longer sacrifice animals, but without the law of sacrifice detailed in the Old Testament we should have a deficient understanding of the cross. As the apostle remarks concerning events recorded in the Torah, "Now these things happened to them as an example, but they were written down for our instruction, on whom the end of the ages has come" (1 Cor. 10:11), and, "For whatever was written in former

31. E.g., Brunner, *The Christian Doctrine of God,* 23.

32. Goldsworthy, *Gospel-Centred Hermeneutics.*

33. This includes the NT Scriptures as they came to be known (2 Pet. 3:16).

days was written for our instruction, that through endurance and through the encouragement of the scriptures we might have hope" (Rom. 15:4).

In sum, wherever you investigate the Scriptures, whether in the Old or New Testament, the basic pattern of piety is exactly the same: it is a love of the Lord expressed in obedience to his words spoken and then written. The words of God are clear; they must be taught to children (Deut. 6:6-9). They are utterly reliable; "the sum of your word is truth," says the psalmist (Ps. 119:160). They are sufficient to bring us to Christ and to instruct us in every good work that we need to do (2 Tim. 3:15-17). Since the Christian life begins with faith, and faith demands a trust in Christ through the words of the gospel, it is absolutely consistent that it also proceeds with exactly the same faith. It is only by trust in God that we can be persuaded to obey his words for the right reasons (Heb. 3–4). When theologians drive a wedge between God and his word written, they are not only cutting off the gospel by which we become Christians; they are presenting a novel and untenable version of the Christian life, one that is peculiarly susceptible to the vagaries of modern culture, not least the confusion between the human spirit and the Holy Spirit.

Of course a piety of obedience clashes deeply with the desire of our Western contemporaries to promote human autonomy as the highest aspiration. What was once a demand for political independence and freedom of thought has devolved into the demand that each individual be accorded moral and legal rights that will, it is thought, achieve an equal and hence just society. David Bentley Hart locates the seat of authority in the individual will: "the modern notion of freedom is essentially 'nihilistic': that is, the tendency of modern thought is to see the locus of liberty as situated primarily in an individual subject's spontaneous power of choice, rather than in the ends that the subject might actually choose. Freedom thus understood, consists solely in the power of choosing as such."[34]

As Hart describes the modern spirit, "At a rather ordinary level of public discourse, it obviously leads to a degradation of the very notion of freedom, its reduction in the cultural imagination to a fairly banal kind of liberty, no more — though no less — significant than a consumer's freedom to choose among different kinds of bread, shoes, televisions, political parties, or religions."[35] The quest for freedom has now washed up on the shore of infinite choice, the capacity of the individual to choose whatever he or she wants by way of lifestyle. But, like faith, freedom is never an absolute; it takes whatever virtue it has from that which we decide for, what we use freedom to accomplish.

From such powerful forces, Christians are not exempt. As the understanding of the Bible has changed, so the function of the Bible has changed. In liberal theological thought, the Bible's unity is marginal, since it does not derive from

34. David Bentley Hart, *Atheist Delusions* (New Haven: Yale University Press, 2009), 226.
35. Hart, *Atheist Delusions,* 224.

the inspiration of the Spirit or reflect the unity of the gospel. For many, it is no longer a unity, delivering a gospel, but a selection of texts from which wisdom may be drawn at will. Furthermore, since it is a witness to the Word rather than the word itself, we can and must stand in judgment over the tendencies of the Bible to endorse such culturally unfashionable causes as those that are labeled by such words as "patriarchy," "sexism," and "homophobia." The pneumatological "correction" to the doctrine of revelation is readily pressed into service to free Christians from obedience to what is seen to be the untenable letter of Scripture. By suppressing the scriptural testimony to its own plenary inspiration, the Spirit is claimed as the author of unscriptural teachings, especially of an ethical nature. In this case, it becomes a duty to disobey Scripture rather than obey it.[36]

The crisis of confidence in Scripture as the word of God has profound consequences for theological education and hence for the quality of church life. Thus the ready acceptance of the word "spirituality" among Protestant Christians is suggestive of unbiblical ways of thinking about the Christian life. In an earlier age, "godliness" was preferred and obedience was the aim.[37] It is not surprising that in a world that makes so much of personal development, teaching on the Christian life has become obsessively self-centered. The model of personal growth is most frequently favored, and the difficulties to be overcome are less sins than alleged personality defects and weaknesses, such as lack of confidence or self-esteem. Spirituality becomes the cultivation of the self, with the aim of arriving at a balanced personality. In Christian circles this is often given a religious or biblical flavor by references to "being like Jesus." But such an aim in itself is easily open to idolatrous manipulation as the actual content of Jesus' teaching is supplanted by idealized and selective imaginary portraits based on whatever stories fulfill the paradigm of love as understood in the twenty-first century.[38]

As Colin Gunton observes, "salient aspects of modern culture are predicated on the denial of the Christian gospel."[39] From the point of view of theological analysis the fundamental problem, whether in the broader community or within the Christian movement, is a misjudgment of human nature. For example, it is not surprising that John Stuart Mill's philosophy "reflects an extraordinary optimism

36. Cf. Frame, *Doctrine,* 20: "The adoption of intellectual autonomy as a theological principle was certainly at least as important as the church's adoption of the Nicene doctrine of the Trinity in 381, or the doctrine of the two natures of Christ in 451." It is one of the ironies of modern theology that the appeal to tradition is still made by many liberal theologians in support of doctrines such as the Trinity, while their attitude to Scripture thoroughly subverts the basis of the tradition that could lead to such doctrines.

37. I owe this observation to Professor G. A. Cole.

38. See the various writings of David Wells, e.g., *No Place for Truth* (Grand Rapids: Eerdmans, 1993).

39. Colin Gunton, *The One, the Three and the Many* (Cambridge: Cambridge University Press, 1993), 1.

about human nature,"[40] for only thus could his profoundly influential ideas about human freedom be thought to work. The utopianism of current culture and its commitment to human autonomy rests upon the repudiation of the doctrine of original sin.[41] It is thought that we can enter into our freedom as those who will use our liberty wisely since we are fundamentally trustworthy. We can afford to dismantle structures, to transgress boundaries, to rely on instinct rather than law because on the whole we will do the right thing.

The biblical view of human freedom begins with the recognition that, as creatures, we have been designed by God for our place in his world. By declaring that we are created in his image and likeness, he not only ennobles his human creatures, he underscores the fact of our dependent and servant status. Indeed, we are created to worship, and when we abandon the worship of the true God we do not cease to worship, but we find alternatives. True happiness, blessedness, or fulfillment comes not by fighting against this reality but by recognizing it and conforming to it. The fact of original sin and its malign effects in the human heart, so that even our desires may be evil, constitutes our human slavery. The gospel offers a new and loving Lord, one who forgives us because of the atoning sacrifice of the cross, one who gives us his Spirit that we may struggle against sin, and one who promises the liberation of the children of God at the end of history. Freedom is not defined by the absence of external direction in order to make unfettered choice, but in freedom from condemnation and in glad submission to the will of God. A human life lived without the rule of God is like a game of tennis without a net.[42]

In short, there is a fatal disjunction between what modern theologians propose theologically and what the New Testament itself sees as being the connection between the Word and the word of God. Tyndale was closer to the truth than the moderns. And this is no minor matter, for the gospel itself, root and branch, faith and obedience, depends on the identification of the word of God and the Scriptures and hence the authority of God and the Bible.

Conclusion: The Word and the Words of God

One of the virtues of David Kelsey's seminal work on the function of Scripture is that he takes the classic view as illustrated by B. B. Warfield seriously and understands the implications of abandoning it. Thus he accepts that there is a nexus between Warfield's commitment to full inspiration and his capacity to teach doctrine from the text of Scripture:

40. Gertrude Himmelfarb, *On Looking into the Abyss* (New York: Knopf, 1994), 84.
41. Chris Hedges, *I Don't Believe in Atheists* (London: Continuum, 2008), 14.
42. With apologies to Robert Frost!

> [F]or example when the *discrimen,* i.e., the mode of God's presence, is construed as a reality in the ideational mode, it follows that scripture will be taken with the force of "teaching" the doctrines or "commending" the concepts that comprise it. Hence, what is authoritative about scripture will be said to be the system of doctrine it teaches or the coherent set of concepts it commends.[43]

Likewise he sees that Warfield's position is necessary to his piety:

> And one basic reason for a Christian's holding the Bible to be authoritative scripture is simply that it does as a matter of fact function in his life as a holy object. Biblical texts construed as containing a system of doctrine, strike with numinous power so that one's initial responses, as Warfield reports it, are awe, trembling, and submission. He takes them as "scripture."[44]

The critique of the classic view of Scripture can and should be addressed. The key point, however, is that typical reconstructions fail at the fundamental theological point of not being in accord with the nature of the revelation that comes to us through Jesus Christ and his apostles. I would further argue this: that the chief point at issue is anthropological. In keeping with the culture of our times, it is the human quest to be free, to be regarded as the junior partner of God, which empowers the critique. Once more, then, we are confronted by the human tendency to idolatry and our determination to be free of the God whose own freedom has been put at the service of our salvation.

William Tyndale did not think that he was translating a book about God or a mere fallible witness to God, but the very word of God itself and a word so closely and rightly identified with God that by the Spirit it conveys the Word of God to the soul. In so doing he was not merely betraying a sort of premodern magical view of the text; he was being true to the text itself in its own self-understanding, and indeed to the gospel itself. Scripture is the word of the living God — as we treat it, so we treat the God whose word it is.

43. David H. Kelsey, *The Uses of Scripture in Recent Theology* (London: SCM, 1975), 24.

44. Kelsey, *The Uses of Scripture in Recent Theology,* 167.

SEVENTEEN

God and the Scripture Writers: The Question of Double Authorship

Henri A. G. Blocher

> I will take my stand to watch,
> and station myself on the tower,
> and look forth to see what he will say to me,
> and what I will answer concerning my complaint. (Hab. 2:1)

Our "pluralistic" age relishes diversity — contemporary theologians relish biblical diversity. "Bible" is truly a *plural* word: *Biblia* looked like feminine singular in Latin, but it was a Greek neuter plural form, *ta biblia,* "the books."

Even more than the collection of many writings from various pens and dates, late modern scholars have stressed the diversity of *genres,* literary and more than literary. After World War II, it became a major interest of Roman Catholic exegetes and theologians, encouraged by Pius XII's Encyclical *Divino afflante Spiritu,*[1] wishing to introduce more flexibility within the dogmatic framework.

In an important article, the French Protestant philosopher Paul Ricoeur endeavored to draw from the genres (also characterized as "speech-acts," *actes de discours*) the various features of the biblical experience of temporality — the message about time arising from the medium, or from the interplay of the media, rather than any conceptual content.[2] He was wont to highlight the import of generic

1. September 30, St. Jerome's feast, 1943; see especially §§35-38.

2. Paul Ricoeur, "Temps biblique," *Archivio di Filosofia* 53 (1985): 23-35. Ricoeur states his method by mentioning speech-acts and intertextuality — through inscripturation, a *Sitz-im-Wort* replaces the *Sitz-im-Leben* (26); he rejects a merely narrative theology and concludes, "[T]he biblical model of time rests on the polarity of narration and hymn, and on the mediation between 'telling the story' and 'praising' effected by the law and its temporal precedence, by prophecy and its eschatological time, and by Wisdom and its immemorial time" (35). English version: "Biblical Time," in *Figuring the Sacred: Religion, Narrative and Imagination,* ed. Mark I. Wallace, trans. David Pellauer (Minneapolis: Fortress, 1995), 167-80. I have used the French original (unless otherwise indicated, I am responsible for translating quotations from non-English sources).

diversity, selecting five "major forms": narratives, laws, prophecies, hymns, and wisdom writings.[3] On one occasion, at least, he mediated the threefold distribution of the Hebrew Canon: the Torah, the Prophets, and the (Other) Writings.[4]

Anthony C. Thiselton highlights the biblical use of more subtle language-games, such as riddles and jokes, parallel accounts of events, and polyphonic multivalence (in Job and Ecclesiastes).[5] Kevin J. Vanhoozer, an expert on Ricoeur, has also focused on the manifold variety of biblical genres, which "has been somewhat overshadowed by the paradigm of God as author": "The diverse literary forms, far from being a weakness of Scripture, ensure a rich communication and are actually one of Scripture's perfections."[6] He has grown more interested in kinds of speech-acts than in *literary* genres, though one can hardly separate them:

> Every text is a kind of something, a particular kind of communicative act, and the genre of the text is often the best indication of the kind of point the author is making.[7]

> Literary texts are thus best viewed as communicative actions performed on a variety of levels for the reader's contemplation.[8]

> It is vital to see the various literary genres in Scripture as diverse kinds of illocutionary acts.[9]

This perspective has proved most helpful and fruitful, though one is wise to heed warnings about abuses of speech-act analysis — *abusus non tollit usum.*[10]

3. Paul Ricoeur, "Herméneutique. Les finalités de l'exégèse biblique," in Paul Ricoeur, Henri Blocher, and Roger Parmentier, *Herméneutique de la Bible, prédication de la Bible, actualisation de la Bible* (Paris: L'Harmattan, 2005), 24; cf. his 25 n. 11 for references to other works in which he develops this further.

4. Paul Ricoeur, "L'Enchevêtrement de la voix et de l'écrit dans le discours biblique," *Lectures 3: Aux frontières de la philosophie* (Paris: Seuil, 1994), esp. 312-21.

5. Anthony C. Thiselton, "'Behind' and 'In Front Of' the Text: Language, Reference and Indeterminacy," in *After Pentecost: Language and Biblical Interpretation,* ed. Craig Bartholomew, Colin Greene, and Karl Möller, Scripture and Hermeneutics Series 2 (Grand Rapids: Zondervan, 2001), 114.

6. Kevin J. Vanhoozer, "The Semantics of Biblical Literature," in *Hermeneutics, Authority, and Canon,* ed. D. A. Carson and John D. Woodbridge (Grand Rapids: Zondervan, 1986), 79; the whole essay elaborates and establishes the claim (49-104).

7. Kevin J. Vanhoozer, "Exegesis and Hermeneutics," in *New Dictionary of Biblical Theology,* ed. T. Desmond Alexander et al. (Downers Grove, IL: InterVarsity, 2000), 59.

8. Vanhoozer, "Exegesis and Hermeneutics," 58.

9. Kevin J. Vanhoozer, "God's Mighty Speech Acts: The Doctrine of Scripture Today," in *First Theology: God, Scripture and Hermeneutics* (Downers Grove, IL: InterVarsity, 2002), 151.

10. Vern S. Poythress, "Canon and Speech Act: Limitations in Speech-Act Theory with

One more scholar, from another quarter, may be mentioned among apologists of diversity: John Goldingay. In his search for "models," Goldingay is more interested in theological than literary categories, but the differences he finds between "witnessing tradition," "authoritative canon," "inspired word," and "experienced revelation" are the main tools of his strategy. He thus resists universally ascribing to the whole Bible attributes he finds in only one part or kind.[11]

Such thinkers have been interested chiefly in *hermeneutics.* The import of Scripture's diversity for *systematic* bibliology has not drawn the same amount of attention. Abraham Kuyper made a brilliant start by claiming that biblical inspiration bears "another character in Lyrics, another in Prophecy, still another in *Chokma* ['Wisdom'], in Christ and with the apostles, so that each of these kinds of inspiration must be dealt with separately,"[12] and he offered a pioneering example.[13]

Gerrit C. Berkouwer, using the same word "character," suggested a few decades ago that, as literary genres vary, "truth continually assumes another character."[14] He claimed Bavinck's support for the thesis that the *truth* of Scripture is "absolutely not in all its components of the same [kind]."[15] David L. Bartlett, at some distance from orthodox bibliology, partially considered the effect on biblical *authority.*[16]

Conditions seem to be ripe for deeper, or at least complementary, inquiries. This essay explores whether and, if so, how generic and illocutionary diversity affect the core affirmations of the doctrine of Scripture with reference to the "double agency" of its composition, or, better, its "double authorship," which avoids awkwardly labeling God an "agent" (though the Spirit is the Agent of Father and Son) — or, in other terms, its "divine inspiration."

Double agency or authorship is a traditional *theologoumenon,* but it may be

---

Implications for a Putative Theory of Canonical Speech Acts," *WTJ* 70 (2008): 337-54, reprinted (with slight changes) as Appendix H in his book *In the Beginning Was the Word: Language — A God-Centered Approach* (Wheaton, IL: Crossway, 2009), 353-69. Poythress warns against oversimplifying and too zealously searching for clarity and rigor, but on most points he acknowledges that John R. Searle sounded the warning himself (344, 349 n. 40, 354 with n. 58 on Austin). Poythress in his own way, using the Trinitarian model, emphatically preaches plurality.

11. John Goldingay, *Models for Scripture* (Grand Rapids: Eerdmans, 1994), 18, and *Models for Interpretation of Scripture* (Grand Rapids: Eerdmans, 1995).

12. Abraham Kuyper, *Encyclopaedie de Heilige Godgeleerdheid* (Amsterdam: J. A. Wormser, 1894), 2:454 (§48).

13. Kuyper, *Encyclopaedie de Heilige Godgeleerdheid,* 2:468-92.

14. Gerrit C. Berkouwer, *Holy Scripture,* trans. Jack B. Rogers (Grand Rapids: Eerdmans, 1975), 131.

15. Berkouwer, *Holy Scripture,* 126. The English translation unfortunately hardens the choice of words in the Dutch original, *dezelfde aard* ("kind," in Berkouwer, *De Heilige Schrift,* 1:179), and here: "of the same nature." To get Berkouwer's exact expression of his views, one should go back to the Dutch original.

16. David L. Bartlett, *The Shape of Scriptural Authority* (Philadelphia: Fortress, 1983), ix-x.

worth revisiting. It is implied by God's being the *first* author *(auctor primarius)* of Scripture. As a conceptual tool, it serves the truth of St. Augustine's statement, *Deus per hominem more homino loquitur* ("God speaks in a human manner through a human being" [in the Scriptures]).[17]

Inspiration *(theopneustia)*[18] is the work that joins the two authors or agents.[19] Scholars who have not become alienated from the continuity of Christian faith and therefore confess that the human words of the Bible are, in some fashion, God's Word make room for a form of "double authorship." Emphasizing genres and illocutions prompts one to ask whether theologians have adequately appreciated human agency and perceived the diverse parts it plays.

Though the diversity of speech-acts is not his dominant concern, the Yale philosopher Nicolas Wolterstorff is an obvious partner as we start investigating the matter since he has given double agency a central place in his ambitious bibliological construction.[20] He broke the spell of "dialectical theology" and its idea of the Word as pure "event," a divine event that human hands cannot grasp and retain, a paradoxical event in which the Word takes on a form that contradicts itself,[21] or an ineffable "encounter." Wolterstorff recovered the ordinary biblical meaning of the Word of God as *divine discourse:* a significant advantage.[22]

17. Augustine, *De Civitate Dei* 17.6. Previously, St. Augustine had written, "God has spoken first by the prophets, then by himself, and then by the apostles, as he considered sufficient, and established the Scripture which we call canonical, of the highest authority" (11.3).

18. From *theopneustos* in 2 Tim. 3:16, "breathed-out." Benjamin B. Warfield's argument on the *passive* significance of *theopneustos* should not be disputed. Scholars of various stripes have recognized its strength (e.g., Timothy Ward, "Scripture, Sufficiency of," in *Dictionary for Theological Interpretation of the Bible,* ed. Kevin J. Vanhoozer [Grand Rapids: Baker, 2005], 730). It has the support of the supreme philologist of the twentieth century, Ceslas Spicq, *Les Epîtres pastorals,* 4th edition, Etudes Bibliques (Paris: Lecoffre-Gabalda, 1969), 2:793, and follows practically all the Greek fathers and commentators. We may note that Berkouwer (*Holy Scripture,* 139-41), affirms the meaning of the term, though he adds some ambiguous remarks.

19. We are using "inspiration" in a special theological sense, not the vague sense of literary or poetic inspiration.

20. Nicolas Wolterstorff, *Divine Discourse: Philosophical Reflections on the Claim That God Speaks,* Wilde Lectures 1993 (Cambridge: Cambridge University Press, 1995).

21. I am referring especially to Karl Barth's statements in the *Kirchliche Dogmatik* I/1, 5th edition (Zollikon-Zurich: Evangelischer Verlag, 1947), esp. 161-63 (§5.4), which underline that God's free Act of revelation uses a form that *contradicts* the content: the Word is to be understood *para tēn doxan,* in a way opposed to what appears (*Erscheinung,* 161). Barth's paradoxical nimbleness, however, allows him also to affirm that the Word, in the Event and as Event, is a divine speech *(Rede)* that takes on an intellectual character (*Geistigkeit,* 129), "a rational and not an irrational Event" (130).

22. A glimpse of my memories: as a young theologian I participated in a theological students conference on Scripture in French-speaking Switzerland (Crêt-Bérard), the other speakers being my father (Jacques A. Blocher), my former professor Roger R. Nicole, and Henry Bruston, who had held a chair in the Faculté Libre de Théologie Protestante of Aix-en-Provence

Thinkers like James Barr, Paul Ricoeur, Kevin Vanhoozer, and Anthony Thiselton have complained that the traditional doctrine has granted undue prominence to *one* biblical genre or kind of communicative action: the *prophetic* one.[23] It eclipsed the others. This mistreatment flattened out scriptural diversity. As a result, human agency has not received its share. Despite some words to the contrary, John Goldingay does not wish to universalize the prophetic paradigm: "The essence of the canon is not inspired word; its roots do not lie in prophecy."[24]

Our inquiry, therefore, deals first with the notion of prophecy and its relevance for the whole Bible. Since the data support the main tenets of the traditional doctrine, the second section addresses the reverse side — the *limits* of the prophetic model of biblical inspiration — and then considers *other models.* This focuses on the "articulation" of divine and human agency, the configuration of the relationship, the position assigned to the human writer, and the "stance" he (or she) is to adopt before God (or maybe, in all reverence, on the "stance" God himself adopts in theopneustic processes). We will then tentatively reflect on how we may interpret, integrate, "digest," and even deepen the findings.[25]

An admonition to self may be in order: since conformist pressures are high in the academic microcosm, we are tempted to use the greater flexibility of a diversity model to accommodate current majority opinions (especially in critical matters). But our entire loyalty should be to the evidence, wherever it leads us.

Scripture Prophetic: Defending the Validity of the Prophetic Model

Many people think that the "prophetic model" of biblical inspiration means the prophet is "God's mouth," a mere passive instrument; he or she does not really count, for the words uttered are only God's words. The orthodox tradition has

(Evangelical Reformed) and was at that time a leading theologian in the French Protestant Federation. Bruston's motto, which he kept hammering down as an axiom elevated far above any need of proving, was: "When God speaks, he makes no discourse."

23. Vanhoozer, "The Semantics of Biblical Literature," 81. Thiselton concurs (Thiselton, "'Behind' and 'In Front Of' the Text," 110): "Paul Ricoeur is utterly right to complain that too often we give privilege to the *prophetic* model of communication that is, after all, only *one* of five or more he identifies." Bartlett (*The Shape of Scriptural Authority,* 7) had criticized "treating the Bible as if it were all of one literary type"; "the implicit assumption of defenders of biblical authority is that as God gave oracles to the prophets, so God delivered oracles by dictation to the evangelists, the authors of the Hebrew Bible narratives (e.g., of Abraham, Moses, Saul, David), the composers of the Psalms, and the writer of the Book of Job."

24. Goldingay, *Models for Scripture,* 116. As will appear below, there are problems with his construal of "prophecy."

25. I leave aside the classical analysis of the *concursus* of the divine Spirit and the human mind under inspiration (usually prompted by 1 Pet. 1:21), *not* because I reject it, but because I see nothing original to add, and I wish to investigate areas that have received fewer visitors.

extended this basic scheme to the entire Scripture and has ruled the dogmatic locus *de Biblia:* Scripture is God's Word because of inspiration. This extension is legitimate and sound to supporters, but critics see it as an unfortunate move that betrays the variegated character of the divine communication and empties the writers' humanity of its significance, reducing them to the status of pens or puppets. How should we measure the truth of the account and evaluate the use of the model?

The Prophetic Office

The metaphor of the Lord's *mouth* is biblical indeed for the prophet's role and the source of his message.[26] The prophet is the spokesperson, in agreement with the etymology of the Greek word *prophētēs (prophēmi)*[27] and of the Hebrew *nābîʾ*, whether the derivation of the latter is found on the active side (proclaimer) or on the passive side (called by the Deity). The prophet is to God what Aaron was to Moses (Exod. 4:15-16; 7:1-2). The key element of the prophetic office is that the Lord puts his words into the prophet's mouth (Deut. 18:18). He does this when he calls young Jeremiah (Jer. 1:9), while in Ezekiel's case the words are represented in written form — a scroll to eat (Ezek. 2:8–3:3). The cardinal sin of the false prophets amounts to bringing words that are not the Lord's (Deut. 18:20), issuing oracles they did not receive from him (Jer. 23:18-32), speaking "out of their own hearts" and following their own "spirit" (Ezek. 13:1-2). Habakkuk, as he waits as a sentinel on his watchtower for the Lord's answer to the complaint the prophet has "filed" in his first chapter, clearly shows that the prophetic word does not originate with the prophet (Hab. 2:1). The prophet's position and stance is that of the royal *herald:* the typical *kô ʾāmar YHWH* "Thus says the LORD" borrows the messenger's introductory formula "Thus says the king . . ." (1 Kgs. 2:30; 20:2, 5; 2 Kgs. 18:19), with little if any emphasis on the herald's own personality.

The emphasis on the divine origin of prophecy is prominent in Judaism and the New Testament. It was a favorite theme of Philo's: "For a prophet utters nothing that is his own, but everything he utters belongs to another, since another is prompting him."[28] The famous passage in 2 Peter stresses that no prophecy originated in the human will (2 Pet. 1:21), and Bauckham's magnificent treatment

26. Isa. 1:20; 58:16; and 34:16, with a remarkable reference to the "Lord's book," presumably a scroll containing prophecies; Jer. 15:19, which shows the metaphor applies to the prophet himself.

27. This is not disputed; I mention as a historical curiosity that St. Thomas Aquinas, *Summa theologica* IIa-IIae, q. 171, art. 1, derives it, after Isidorus of Sevilla (*Etymologiae* 8.8), from *pro/porro* and *phanos.*

28. *Quis rerum divinarum heres sit,* 259, as quoted by Richard J. Bauckham, *Jude, 2 Peter,* WBC 50 (Waco, TX: Word, 1983), 229. Bauckham offers many other quotations.

of the preceding verse is quite convincing: that no prophecy "happens" (*ginetai,* a verbal choice a bit surprising in any reading) *idias epilyseōs* does not rule out the "private interpretation" of which prophecies would be the object,[29] but probably refers to origination.[30] Since "in a series of Hellenistic Jewish and early Christian statements which deny the human *origin* of prophecy, [*idios*] seems to have been virtually a technical term,"[31] the thought that is being rejected is that a true prophecy should have arisen from its own (merely human) interpretation of the vision or the sign or the event shown the prophet.[32] The Agent is the Holy Spirit. The Old Testament sometimes explicitly indicates his agency.[33] Judaism held that belief, and the New Testament concurs (2 Pet. 1:21; Acts 21:11). The NT implies the same both for old prophecy recalled and new prophecy introduced (Luke 1:67; 1 Cor. 12:10-11; 1 Pet. 1:10-11; Rev. 22:6).

A significant difference, however, must be observed. Philo goes beyond his affirmation that "no pronouncement of a prophet is ever his own; he is an interpreter prompted by another in all his utterances." He continues, "when knowing not what he does he is filled with inspiration, as the reason withdraws and surrenders the citadel of the soul to a new visitor and tenant, the Divine Spirit which plays upon the vocal organism and dictates words which clearly express its prophetic message."[34] The withdrawal of reason corresponds not only to the common fascination of the extraordinary but also to the Platonic desire *(erōs)* of the supra-rational, ineffable, First Principle.[35] Josephus, though more restrained,

29. This concern is not present in the immediate context. It surfaces only at the end of the Epistle (2 Pet. 3:16), and *idios* ("own") usually refers to what belongs, reflexively, to the subject.

30. Bauckham, *Jude, 2 Peter,* 229-33.

31. Bauckham, *Jude, 2 Peter,* 229.

32. Bauckham, *Jude, 2 Peter,* 232. Some have argued against this reading that v. 21 would repeat only v. 20, but Bauckham counters, "But this is not the case. The reason why scriptural prophecy is not simply a product of human interpretation is that its authors did not speak of their own volition but under the inspiration of God" (232). Samuel Bénétreau, *La Deuxième Epître de Pierre, l'Epître de Jude,* Commentaire Evangélique de la Bible (Vaux-sur-Seine: Edifac, 1994), 125-29, not entirely persuaded by Bauckham, prefers to understand that no prophecy possesses its own interpretation of itself: the Holy Spirit is needed. While I agree with the thought, of course, I cannot follow the exegesis. He argues that v. 19 is a preparation as it speaks of "the illumination of prophecy" (by the Spirit) in order that Christ may be discovered (129); but in v. 19, prophecy is not the object to be illumined but the lamp that shines in darkness! I also differ from Calvin, whom Bénétreau summarizes (126 n. 2).

33. Num. 11:25, 29 with an echo in Joel 2:28-29 [Hebrew 3:1-2]; Hos. 9:7; Mic. 3:8; Isa. 61:1; Ezek. 2:2. One should not sharply divide between "prophets of the Word" and "prophets of the Spirit." Cf. the strange episode in 1 Kings 22:18-28.

34. Philo, *De specialibus legibus* 4.49, as quoted by Jerome H. Neyrey, *2 Peter, Jude: A New Translation with Introduction and Commentary,* AB (New York: Doubleday, 1993), 182.

35. Already in Plato, the Idea of the Good is elevated "beyond the essence" (*epekeina tēs ousias,* in the *Republic* 6.509). Neo-Platonism enlarges on the theme.

puts on Balaam's lips (admittedly, Balaam is a special case) the confession that when the Spirit seizes upon prophets they are not even conscious of what they are saying.[36] Bauckham aptly summarizes,

> In Hellenistic Jewish writers . . . such language is often associated with a basically pagan understanding of the psychology of prophetic inspiration, as irrational ecstasy in which the prophet is a purely passive instrument of the divine Spirit, unconscious of the words the Spirit utters through him.[37]

Bauckham adds in the next sentence, "But the language of 2 Peter does not in itself require such a depreciation of the human role in prophecy." Nowhere does Scripture extol ecstasy as a superior degree of inspiration. Ecstasy was not absent,[38] but Scripture never suggests that it indicates a stronger intervention on God's part. When discussing the church's *charisma* of prophecy, Paul reminds his readers that prophets are in control (1 Cor. 14:32) and argues that prophecy is superior to tongues because intelligence *(nous)* is active, not "fruitless" (*akarpos,* v. 14).[39] Major prophets show no sign of having their intelligence or consciousness suspended as they carry on the duties of their office and shape their messages. Isaiah received his mandate in a vision (Isa. 6) but refers to no other. John the Baptist was hailed by our Lord himself as "a prophet and more than a prophet" (Matt. 11:9), and no ecstatic trait appears. Moses, as *the* Old Testament prophet, stands above all others because God does not communicate with him through visions and dreams but in the simplicity of transparent fellowship (Num. 12:6-8). The disqualification of human faculties is no essential part of the biblical idea of prophecy.

Further, emphasizing God's control and the divine origin of prophecy does not deprive the human service of its weight and significance. As the Lord's heralds, prophets take upon themselves fearful responsibilities (Ezek. 3:16-21; 33:1-9). They often wrestle with God, as they try to escape the calling (Jer. 1:6-7; cf. Exod. 3:11; 4:10-16). They receive honor from God (Isa. 49:5, the Servant speaking as a prophet). They are actively involved: Habakkuk is looking for the *Lord's* answer,

36. Josephus, *Ant.* 4.6.5.

37. Bauckham, *Jude, 2 Peter,* 234.

38. The "bands" of prophets in Samuel's time probably prophesied in a kind of frenzy; Ezekiel underwent strange (ESP?) experiences; and visions were ordinary as a means of divine communication. Popular piety was probably impressed with such phenomena.

39. Drawing on D. E. Aune's work, Neyrey (*2 Peter, Jude,* 180-81) reminds us that Greeks would distinguish the *mantis* who received the oracle (such as the Pythia in Delphi from Apollo) and the *prophētēs.* The oracle the *mantis* would utter was very often obscure, riddle-like: the *prophet* would exercise inspired intelligence to interpret it for inquirers and worshipers. The LXX translators used *mantis* for pagan soothsayers or diviners and chose *prophētēs* for *nābî'*.

which the Lord will make known "in" him or "through" him,[40] but it will be an answer to *Habakkuk's* complaint, which is also included in the book, in the prophecy (chapter 1)! Prophetic inspiration works through dialogue.

Abraham Kuyper goes so far as to characterize "prophetic inspiration" by the *duality of subjects:* he uses the words "dualistic" and "antithetical."[41] Though he uses the analogy of the musical instruments (the sound is not the same, even with the same player),[42] he is at pains to show that the prophet's humanity is fully involved; he highlights the anthropological basis of prophecy, even — somewhat dubiously — in parapsychic powers, hypnosis, telepathy.[43] The concept of "instrument" or "organ" (the two words are etymologically equivalent) may be misleading inasmuch as it suggests less than active, responsible, service: in this, we concur with Berkouwer.[44] Paul's ascribing boldness to Isaiah (Rom. 10:20) provides us with another powerful testimony. Though it would be foolish to imagine some symmetry between God and humans, prophecy does imply *double* agency.

Identical Meaning?

Does double authorship result in two meanings or one? If God speaks *through* his herald, does his illocutionary act coincide with the human person's?

For centuries, the divine inspiration of Scripture gave permission to the search for (and invention of) many meanings beyond the prophet's own. The sixteenth-century Reformation, a grand monotheistic purification, insisted that keeping to the one, "natural" sense of the text is the only way to honor the sovereign rule of the divine Word.[45] "Modern" treatments also rejected multiple meanings, but the (fatal) difference is that they no longer considered the human author — whose intention was the goal of the quest — to be "inspired," namely, someone God had raised, enabled, illumined, guided, and guarded to fulfill the prophetic task. In 1962, Kendrick Grobel could write of "[t]he now obvious answer [to the question 'How many meanings?'] that a passage of scripture, as of any other literature, has just one meaning," adding that it had to be won through a

40. *bî* may be translated either way, "in me" or "by me."

41. Kuyper, *Encyclopaedie,* 2:476. He writes: "In Jeremiah's struggle (Jer 20:7ff) this antithesis reaches its paroxysm."

42. Kuyper, *Encyclopaedie,* 2:477.

43. Kuyper, *Encyclopaedie,* 2:478-79 (cf. 432). I see three possible factors: (1) a high level of interest in parapsychical phenomena in Kuyper's intellectual environment; (2) Kuyper's sustained effort to link the work of creation and redemption; and (3) his tendency to bind the essence of prophecy to extraordinary modes (480) — to a degree I think unwarranted.

44. Berkouwer, *Holy Scripture,* 153-54.

45. See John Calvin in his *Commentary* on Gal. 4:22.

struggle caused by "a misunderstanding of the divine authority of the Bible, complicated by various theories of verbal inspiration."[46] Since that time, academia has taken a U-turn.[47] Academia values plurality, the ally of freedom and tolerance: maintaining only one sense signals deeply suspicious tendencies.

Even evangelicals disagree among themselves. Walter C. Kaiser has been strenuously fighting for the oneness of textual meaning, identifying God's meaning with the prophet's.[48] Alvin Plantinga, on the other hand, denies that "what the Lord intends to teach us is identical with what the human author had in mind; the latter may not so much as have thought of what is in fact the teaching of the passage in question."[49] Vern S. Poythress blazes a middle trail, attempting to persuade "one meaning" champions to accept flexibility and some plurality — he refrains from a straightforward advocacy of several *meanings:* "However, for most purposes I myself would prefer to avoid calling these three results three 'meanings.'"[50]

A Broad Concept of Meaning

Much depends on "the meaning of meaning." Even if we resist surrendering meaning to the creative imagination of reading communities, we may define meaning (or sense, taking the two words to be practically synonymous) in broader or narrower ways. If we call meaning everything that is in the speaker's mind, it will be more than difficult to ascribe the same meaning to both God and the prophet. For Poythress, "there is no need to insist that Luke understood all the ramifica-

46. Kendrick Grobel, "Interpretation, History and Principles of," in *The Interpreter's Dictionary of the Bible,* ed. George A. Buttrick (Nashville: Abingdon, 1962), 2:719.

47. It is symptomatic that in the *Supplementary Volume* of the same dictionary, ed. Keith Crim (Nashville: Abingdon, 1976), Leander E. Keck's and Gene M. Tucker's "Exegesis" (296-303) commends multiple approaches, emphasizing complexity, legitimate variations, etc.

48. Walter C. Kaiser Jr., *Toward an Exegetical Theology: Biblical Exegesis for Preaching and Teaching* (Grand Rapids: Baker, 1981) and several other works. He draws philosophically on the contribution of E. D. Hirsch Jr.

49. Alvin Plantinga, "Two (or More) Kinds of Scripture Scholarship," in *Behind the Text: History and Biblical Interpretation,* ed. Craig Bartholomew, C. Stephen Evans, Mary Healey, and Murray Rae, Scripture and Hermeneutics Series 4 (Grand Rapids: Zondervan, 2003), 26.

50. Vern S. Poythress, "Divine Meaning in Scripture," *WTJ* 48 (1986): 269. This long article (241-79), or its main part, was also published under the title "What Does God Say through Human Authors?" in *Inerrancy and Hermeneutic,* ed. Harvie M. Conn (Grand Rapids: Baker, 1988), 81-99. He also writes, "All this is true without any need to postulate an extra, 'mystical' sense. That is, we do not postulate an extra meaning which requires some esoteric hermeneutical method to uncover" (275). Quite typical of his "mediating" efforts, he confesses to being close to Raymond Brown's definition of *sensus plenior,* with a concern that "shows affinities with the rejection of *sensus plenior* by John P. Weisengoff" (276).

tions of each of Jesus' parables."[51] Poythress argues that since "people always know more and imply more than what they are perfectly self-conscious of,[52] it is possible, with respect to his *human nature,* that Jesus Christ is not exhaustively self-conscious of all the ramifications, nuances, and implications of what he says."[53] Such guarded language raises no strong objection. But when Poythress takes into account the whole Bible and draws from the divine use of Malachi 3:10 to stimulate *our* giving that "then in an ordinary sense each valid application is part of God's meaning (= intention),"[54] he proceeds too quickly. Poythress widens what he calls *application:* "I count as 'applications' both effects in the cognitive field (e.g., concluding mentally . . .) and effects in the field of overt action. . . . 'Application' in this sense *includes* all inferences about the meaning of a biblical text."[55] If application is then included in meaning, who among mortals is sufficient for these things? The meaning, according to Poythress, cannot be the same for God and for the prophet — and this, in my eyes, is a matter for serious concern.

May we equate meaning and intention? Should there be a distinction between intention as embodied in the speech-act (in a happy and responsible use of language, I say what I intended to say), and intention(s) *about* the speech-act? Even if we entertain a more modest idea of "application," is its relation to meaning so easy to assess? Hans-Georg Gadamer has revived the Pietistic stress on application *(Anwendung, subtilitas applicandi)* as an essential part of understanding,[56] but it remains controversial.[57] How broad is application? If it amounts to integrating the author's promise, command, or insight into my perception of reality

51. Poythress, "Divine Meaning in Scripture," 260. Cf. Poythress, *In the Beginning Was the Word,* 166: "But the human author remains finite and does not plumb all the depths of the implications of what he says."

52. Cf. Wolterstorff, *Divine Discourse,* 201.

53. Poythress, "Divine Meaning in Scripture," 261-62; emphasis original. The clause "with respect to his *human nature*" agrees with Chalcedonian Christology, since consciousness (like will and knowledge, or lack of knowledge, in Mark 13:32) seems to belong to the nature, while acts are of the Person. There is one sentence (fortunately, a negative one), 262, in which Poythress makes himself vulnerable to a suspicion of Nestorianism, as he says "that we do not have two antithetical interpretations, one for the human nature speaking and one for the divine nature speaking": but natures *do not speak.*

54. Poythress, "Divine Meaning in Scripture," 246.

55. Poythress, "Divine Meaning in Scripture," 248.

56. Hans-Georg Gadamer, *Truth and Method,* trans. Garrett Barden and John Cumming (New York: Continuum, 1975), 274, based on the 2nd German edition (1965), or *Truth and Method,* trans. and ed. Joel Weinsheimer and Donald G. Marshall (New York: Crossroad, 1989), 307-8, based on the 5th German edition (1986).

57. John Goldingay, *Models for Interpretation,* 256-62, offers an interesting discussion; he leans on the side of inclusion (no access to meaning without application), but mainly for the sake of practical exhortation (and out of sympathy for Liberation Theology): biblical truth is truth for obedience.

and judgments, making room for it in my world, then yes, I do not understand unless I apply. But I can truly understand what someone meant by a command she gave in her situation and yet remain unable to tell how this command should apply in my (different) situation.

A Narrow Concept of Meaning

In dealing with the identity or non-identity of God's and the prophet's respective meanings, it is better to deploy a *narrow* concept of meaning. I call "meaning" the content of the illocutionary act, *what is said* — promised (and one can hold the speaker to his or her word), ordered, affirmed, or denied; only proximate and certain inferences are strictly part of the meaning.[58] Undoubtedly, lines are hard to draw. Meaning, like many things human, has fuzzy edges. It is woven into a web of intentions and implications. But relatedness does not cancel the truth of particular, discrete identities: these are not reducible to "folds" in relational fields. As Pierre Teilhard de Chardin expressed it, there is a *granular* constitution of reality in our universe[59] — atoms are grains of matter, cells, grains of life, human minds, grains of thought. Meaning is this "grain" of communication that can still be distinguished from implications and applications and other "ramifications."

In favor of identity of meaning (in the strict sense just defined) is the very role of a spokesperson: God put his words into the prophet's mouth, therefore what the prophet uttered was simply God's word; the prophet's "boldness" characterizes the divine sense of the text, and no difference appears (Rom. 10:20).

There are objections that sound considerable. One objection is easily solved: the Israelite writers did not perceive — or at least *clearly* perceive — a *typological* meaning that the New Testament brings out in its interpretation of the Old; that typological meaning could be labeled another, divine sense. St. Thomas Aquinas already discerned that the so-called "spiritual sense" was the sense of the *things* to which the words refer.[60] God erected "types" and attached to them his *heilsgeschichtlich* meaning, but this is something other than the speech-act he performed through the prophets.

58. Even E. D. Hirsch's notion may be broader. As summarized by Poythress ("Divine Meaning," 245), "'Meaning,' in Hirsch's view, is what the human authors expressed, including what is expressed tacitly, allusively, or indirectly. It includes what can legitimately be inferred." Indirect inference may lead us far afield.

59. Pierre Teilhard de Chardin, *Le Phénomène humain* (Paris: Seuil, 1955), 34-35, 53, 80, 82-83.

60. St. Thomas Aquinas, *Summa theologica*, I^{a}, qu.1, art.10. Wolterstorff, *Divine Discourse*, 313 n. 3, knows about the medieval distinction, and remains "skeptical"; I am not sure that he truly understands it.

A passage (a proof-text!) is often appealed to against identity: "The conviction expressed in 1 Peter 1:10-12," Goldingay writes, "that the prophets did not know what they were talking about" parallels the Qumran belief that "God's 'mysteries' or 'secrets' were revealed to the prophets, but their meaning was hidden from them."[61] One needs only to reread 1 Peter 1 to realize that the text does *not* say that the prophets were ignorant of the *meaning* of the words they uttered: rather the opposite! What they were searching for was the *time* — and what kind of time (*eis tina ē poion kairon*) — of fulfillment, and God granted them a partial answer: it would not be their own time (v. 12). The prophets were not aware of many divine intentions (how, when, etc.) *concerning* the things they announced, but it does not follow that the meaning of the words in their minds differed from God's.

Probably the most popular reference among critics of the "one meaning" tradition is *Caiaphas's case* (John 11:50-51). Goldingay does not fail to use it,[62] and it is already the decisive "authority" argument *(sed contra)* for St. Thomas Aquinas asking whether prophets always know what they say.[63] The divine meaning of the words uttered by the wicked high-priest was altogether different from the man's, despite a formal analogy of structure (one dying instead of many) — the sublime truth of Christ's substitutionary atonement versus political cynicism — and since Caiaphas thus *prophesied,* the duality is taken to be paradigmatic of prophecy as such. Kuyper commented, "The clause *eipen ouk aph' heautou* [he did not speak of himself] is, for inspiration, the strongest expression one can think of,"[64] though it conflicts with Kuyper's emphasis on the duality of agents.[65] This suits contemporary ideas of prophecy in the biblical world.[66] However, such ideas, as already noticed, have roots in conceptions alien to the New Testament. Taking Caiaphas's prophesying as a paradigm raises serious difficulties. Since the difference between meanings is radical, how can readers ascertain the divine meaning? The human text is available only to the reader! The answer that the rest of Scripture tells us is not satisfactory, for the principle applies to all inspired texts: if God's meaning can be different from the meaning of the human writers, we cannot be sure about

61. Goldingay, *Models for Interpretation,* 151. His earlier (146-47) references to 1 Pet. 1:10-12 are more carefully worded.

62. Goldingay, *Models for Interpretation,* 149.

63. St. Thomas Aquinas, *Summa theologica,* IIa-IIae, q. 173, art. 4. "Ergo omnis qui prophetat non cognoscit ea quae prophetat."

64. Kuyper, *Encyclopaedie,* 2:460.

65. Kuyper apparently thinks that the second agent does not count unless *antithesis* becomes a structural element of the model, which is hard to swallow.

66. Goldingay, *Models for Interpretation,* 151, seems to be right for Qumran (hence the total disregard for historical and literary context in Qumranic *pesher*). Craig S. Keener, *The Gospel of John: A Commentary* (Peabody, MA: Hendrickson, 2003), 2:857, offers many significant references.

God's meaning *anywhere*! If one seeks for a *via media* and pleads that the *separation* of meanings is unique in Caiaphas's case but that in ordinary prophecy the two are found in harmony (i.e., the divine meaning is simply wider, richer, and deeper than the human one, along the same line), then how is Caiaphas's case relevant anymore? Is the issue illumined or clouded? *Either* the "plus" involved is God's knowledge about the meaning of the prophetic word with the conditions of fulfillment he has designed and the implications he can unfold (it can be partially revealed in other Scriptures, but we better not call it another meaning) *or* the "plus" is something else. If the latter, *how* can we determine what it is? Caiaphas is called neither a prophet (he was not called to that office) nor inspired, so in his case, we should not even talk of "double authorship." Instead, there are two different authors accidentally joined or superposed, two separate speech-acts. God, in judgment, mockingly plays on the words Caiaphas utters; God uses the sounds of Caiaphas's lips and a merely formal similarity of structure, but he does not speak through the *man*. It would be unwise to make his case the model case for biblical prophecy.[67]

Positively, there are indications that biblical prophets understood what they were saying as they were "borne along" (*pheromenoi*, 2 Pet. 1:21) by the Spirit. Though they were called to *speak*, it is striking how often their privilege is described in terms of imparted *knowledge*. The true prophets have been introduced into God's "secret council" *(sôd)* and have heard first what they are to report (Jer. 23:16-22); the Lord "reveals his secret counsel [again *sôd*] to his servants the prophets" (Amos 3:7). When he calls young Jeremiah, the Lord takes care that he understand the signs (Jer. 1:11-14). Peter's reasoning in his Pentecost sermon is remarkable: to buttress his claim that David's *prophetic* utterance in Psalm 16 foretells Jesus' resurrection, Peter ascribes to David *foresight* of what was to come on the basis of the promise he had received in 2 Samuel 7 (Acts 2:30-31). Even the prophets' investigations about fulfillment (*exezētēsan kai exēraunēsan*, 1 Pet. 1:10-12) show them intellectually present in their task and able to ask intelligent questions.[68] One finds no solid ground for a disjunction between divine and human meaning in true prophecy.

67. Poythress does not fall into the trap: he does not refer to Caiaphas in his article (though he does in his book *In the Beginning Was the Word*, but in a restrained fashion [388]). The other prophet, next to Caiaphas, who is sometimes mentioned is the enigmatic Balaam, who illustrates *unwilling* prophesying. But Balaam seems to have known the meaning of the oracles he was constrained to render (hence his reluctance!). Aquinas, *Summa theologica*, IIa-IIae, q. 72, art. 6, takes it as obvious that his prophesying was demonic.

68. Kuyper's metaphor for Ezekiel is rather unfortunate: "[T]he human *pneuma* seems to be little more than a phonograph" (*Encyclopaedie*, 2:454). (Kuyper contrasts it with Paul.) Ezekiel's unique style shows that the prophet's inner personality is active and bears fruit even in ecstatic states (maybe through unconscious dimensions).

The Prophetic Model in Traditional Bibliology

The quickest survey of the doctrine of Scripture in the history of the churches is enough to reveal the predominance of the prophetic model. The liturgical "This is the Word of the Lord" echoes the prophets' "Thus says the Lord." God speaks through all the sacred writers as he did through the prophets. What the Bible says, God says. "What the writers mean, God means."[69] The inspiration of *theopneustos* Scripture is of the kind we just described.[70] Scripture is God's word as breathed out through the prophetic "mouth." The tendency is to highlight the divine origin and authority and to say little of the human "instrument."

Continuity shines through the succession of Christian generations. Irenaeus wrote that believers know most rightly [*rectissime*] that "the Scriptures are perfect, since they were given/dictated [*dictae*] by the Word of God and his Spirit."[71] St. Hippolytus testified, "Scripture utters absolutely [*holōs*] no falsehood, and the Holy Spirit does not mislead his servants the prophets, through whom he was pleased to announce God's counsel to human beings."[72] St. Gregory the Great called God the primary author.[73] It was standard language through the Middle Ages. St. Salvianus beautifully describes "the oracle of Holy Scripture [as] somehow the mind of God [*Dei mens est*]."[74]

For Luther, the Bible is "the Holy Spirit's own and particular book, writing and word"; it was "put in letters [*gebuchstabet*] by the Holy Spirit,"[75] and the prophet may be compared to God's "pen" *(calamus)*.[76] Calvin, who often speaks of the biblical writers as God's secretaries *(amanuenses)* and *notarii,* does not tone down the teaching of 2 Timothy 3:16:

69. Eckhard J. Schnabel, "Scripture," in Alexander et al., eds., *New Dictionary of Biblical Theology,* 40 (the whole article, 34-43, is remarkable).

70. The word itself recalls the vocabulary used for prophecy. For Josephus, *Contra Apionem* 1.7, the prophets who wrote the sacred books were taught by the inspiration *(kata tēn epipnoian)* coming from God.

71. St. Irenaeus, *Adversus haereses* 2.28.2.

72. St. Hippolytus, *In Danielem* 4:6.

73. St. Gregory the Great, "Inspiration et inerrance," *Supplément au Dictionnaire de la Bible,* ed. André Robert (Paris: Letouzey & Ané, 1949), 4:492.

74. St. Salvianus, *De Gubernatione Dei* 3, from the Latin quoted in Luis Alonso Schökel, *The Inspired Word: Scripture in the Light of Language and Literature,* trans. Francis Martin (New York: Herder & Herder, 1965), 345 (with n. 24).

75. Luther, WA 38.340; 48.31.

76. Luther, WA 3.256 (on Ps. 44; Heb. 45). David W. Lotz, "*Sola Scriptura:* Luther on Biblical Authority," *Interpretation* 35 (1981): 263, accurately summarizes: "Luther never hesitates to speak of Scripture as God's Word. . . . Scripture for Luther *is* God's Word since it has God the Holy Spirit as its ultimate author." See also my "Luther et la Bible," in *Dieu parle: Etudes sur la Bible et son interprétation,* ed. Paul Wells (Aix-en-Provence: Kerygma, 1984), 127-41.

> This principle discerns our religion from all others: we know that God spoke to us, and we have full certainty that the prophets did not speak of themselves [*de leur propre sens*], but as organs and instruments of the Holy Spirit: they announced only what they had received from above. . . . [Hence,] we owe Scripture such a reverence as we have for God, since it proceeds from God alone, having nothing from man mixed with itself.[77]

Quenstedt, as a major representative of Lutheran orthodoxy, asserts, "God alone, if we wish to speak accurately, is to be called the author of Holy Scripture; the prophets and the apostles, indeed, cannot be called authors, except by catachresis, since they were rather the pens [*calami*] of God the author."[78] We could add many more, but the Thomist theologian Yves (later Cardinal) Congar will serve as an epitome of the classical Christian conviction; he explains how God works when he calls the biblical authors to speak in his name:

> That they may do so, he causes [*suscite*] in their minds and in their powers of expression a valid formula of his own thought or of his design in sacred history. Thus, while he is not perfectly manifest to us as he has promised to reveal himself in the very openness of his self-knowledge [eschatologically], but beyond what we could surmise about him as the Creator of natural regularities, God makes himself known to us in a word in the proper sense, through *signs* which express thought-content. These signs, he causes [*suscite*] them in the powers of representation of those to whom he "speaks," or, if he finds them already constituted, he ensures that they conform to what he wishes to signify precisely, of himself and of his design. In any case, he takes the initiative and responsibility. It is thus that we have the *Word of God* in some human words. One is no longer faced by mere human assertions, but, in human form, by assertions *of God,* which convey the thought of God, which are true of that absolute truth which is the truth of the Prime, Uncreated, Truth, that which is true by itself.[79]

All this could be said of prophets as such.

The extension of the prophetic model to Scripture as a whole runs the same risk as the understanding of prophecy as a special office: the risk of imbalance, the risk of leaving in the shadows human participation; it is there, but one should not exaggerate the risk. I candidly confess: I cannot be satisfied with the metaphor of pens or of musical instruments (cf. Athenagoras's *Legatio [or Supplicatio]*

77. John Calvin, *Commentaires sur le Nouveau Testament* (Paris: Meyrueis, 1854), 4:300-301.

78. Quenstedt, *Hutterus redivivus oder Dogmatik des evangelisch-lutherischen Kirche,* 7th edition, ed. Karl Hase (Leipzig: Breitkopf & Hartel, 1848), 98 n. 2 (Latin).

79. Yves Congar, *Foi et théologie,* le Mystère chrétien (Tournai: Desclée, 1962), 5-6.

pro christianis, chapters 7 and 9) and with Quenstedt's refusal to acknowledge the true "authorship" of hagiographers. The intention, however, is to glorify the divine origin, *not* to deny humanity's part. As should be obvious to all, the use of the verb *dictare,* usually translated "dictate," has nothing to do with a "Dictaphone" mode of inspiration. Schökel, to choose just one scholarly witness, points to the semantic evolution of the *dictare* family, with the *Dichtung* (poetry) line and the *dictator* one, and reminds us, "'*Dictare*' in the medieval world implied real intellectual and even poetic activity."[80] When Calvin rules out any human mixture, he clearly means something that would not proceed from God *first.* Calvin is most sensitive to the human traits of Scripture, as his exegetical practice demonstrates. Metaphors should not be pressed in unsympathetic ways. Critics of traditional theologians often betray the same wooden literalism, the same mechanical rigidity, with which they charge orthodox bibliology! Paul Ricoeur caricatures orthodox bibliology in a way unworthy of the great thinker: "[T]he authors repeat a word that was whispered into their ears."[81] Albert (Marie-Joseph) Lagrange, who strives to remain within the bounds set by *Providentissimus Deus,* borrows a metaphor that strikes the orthodox balance: "The sacred writers' soul was no mere channel: it was a source, although not the primary source."[82]

The Use of the Model Warranted

Deference to tradition ought never to degenerate into blind submission. The question may not be eluded: Was classical theology *right* when it extended the prophetic model to the whole Bible? Though it calls for nuance in the light of scriptural diversity (see below), the answer must remain a resounding *yes.* It is correct to label Scripture as a whole "prophetic" and to draw doctrinal consequences from that character.

The testimony of Scripture itself is in line with this conclusion. One can hardly doubt that the referent of the phrase "prophetic word" in 2 Peter 1 is the entire collection of holy writings.

> All other known occurrences of the phrase refer to OT Scripture, except 2 *Clem.* 11:2, which refers to an apocryphon which the writer presumably re-

80. Luis Alonso Schökel, *The Inspired Word* (New York: Herder and Herder, 1965), 71.

81. E.g., Paul Ricoeur, "Herméneutique philosophique et herméneutique biblique," in *Exegesis: Problèmes de méthode et exercices de lecture,* ed. François Bovon and Grégoire Rouiller (Neuchâtel-Paris: Delachaux & Niestlé, 1975), 224. One finds this caricature elsewhere, though lapses of that kind are extremely rare in Ricoeur, who generally respects opposing views.

82. Albert (Marie-Joseph) Lagrange, "Inspiration des livres saints," *Revue Biblique* 5 (1896): 219. Lagrange quotes from Father Pègues, with the only reference: *Revue Thomiste* (1895): 108.

> garded as part of OT Scripture (cf. *1 Clem.* 23:3). . . . This equivalence [in Philo and Justin Martyr] came about because in the current Jewish understanding all inspired Scripture was prophecy.[83]

Theopneustos in 2 Timothy 3 suggests the prophetic model, and it is applied to "all/every Scripture," clearly identified as the "sacred writings" *(hiera grammata)* of Judaism. Jesus himself called Daniel "the prophet," though the book that bears his name is not found in the "Prophets" section of the Hebrew canon (Matt. 24:15). Moses is not only *a* prophet, but *the* Prophet, as Deuteronomy 18 solemnly proclaims; the eschatological Prophet that Jews and Samaritans were looking for was the New Moses, whose coming the same passage promises (cf. John 1:21; 4:25, the woman refers to the *tāhēb* ("Restorer," when she uses the title "Messiah," which would be more readily understood by a Jewish interlocutor). The *tôrâ,* therefore, is also prophetic — the word *tôrâ,* we remember, may also stand for a prophetic utterance (Isa. 8:16, 20). The words of Peter in Acts 1:16

> give clear expression to the widespread belief of the early church about the OT as a whole — the Holy Spirit was its ultimate source; the Holy Spirit was speaking through persons, such as David, so that what was contained in the OT was the word of God, the word of the Spirit of God (see also Acts 4:25; 28:25; Heb. 3:7: 9:8; 10:15; *1 Clem.* 13.1; 16.2; 22.1; 45.2; cf. 8.1; *Barn.* 9.2. 10.2, 9; 14.2).[84]

The Jews were entrusted with the "oracles" *(logia)* of God (Rom. 3:2), and the Spirit who searches the depths of deity taught Paul the very words he used to communicate (1 Cor. 2:10, 13).[85] The extension of the same categories from the *tôrâ,* Prophets, and Writings to the apostolic "deposit" raises no theological difficulty: Paul's phrase "the old covenant" for the Bible books (2 Cor. 3:14) suggests it since he writes as a minister of the new covenant. The new covenant no less than the old must be endowed by prophetic writings. The apostles are also prophets, according to the likely reading of Ephesians 2:20 and 3:5. David

83. Bauckham, *Jude, 2 Peter,* 224.

84. Gerald F. Hawthorne, "Holy Spirit," in *Dictionary of the Later New Testament and Its Developments,* ed. Ralph P. Martin and Peter H. Davids (Downers Grove, IL: InterVarsity, 1997), 497.

85. It is hard to believe that Goldingay can comment on this passage, *Models for Scripture,* 255, the way he does: "To judge from what he [Paul] himself says, he does not see his letters as inspired or as the word of God (though we may believe they are), yet he does see his witness as inspired." Paul, on the contrary, affirms the equivalence of oral and written form (2 Thess. 2:15; cf. 2:2), and the status of the rules he lays down for faith and practice: the Lord's command (1 Cor. 14:37). Presumably, Goldingay maintains that the "witness" is "inspired" because he entertains vague notions of both.

Bartlett finds in 1 Corinthians 1:21-25 an understanding of apostolic preaching "strikingly similar" to that of prophecy.[86] Our whole Bible may be considered prophecy.

Another consideration that supports the thesis is the constant exchanges and interlacing between the literary and "revelational" genres. There is no neat separation between "prophecy" in the stricter sense and other forms. Isaiah and Jeremiah include narrative sections. Despite Wolterstorff's reluctance and critique, Meir Sternberg is properly sensitive to the quality of historical books, whose writers were made into prophets by inspiration: "So every word is God's word. . . . The product is neither fiction nor historicized fiction nor fictionalized history, but historiography pure and uncompromising."[87] Besides laws, the Pentateuch contains stories, hymns, and oracles. Wisdom personified adopts a prophetic posture (Prov. 1:20-23, with the mention of her *Spirit, rûḥî* in v. 23), while prophets borrow techniques and themes from sages. After expounding the close interrelationships, David A. Hubbard warns, *"[W]e must not set up rigid categories when we consider the offices of Israel — prophet, priest, and wise man."*[88] Referring to recent scholarship, Daniel J. Treier notes, "Proverbs has affinities with a covenantal document such as Deuteronomy (e.g., in orienting wisdom to the 'fear of the Lord'), whereas the Genesis narratives of creation and fall have both sapiential and covenantal motifs."[89] Variegated as it appears, the inspiration of Scripture is homogeneous: of the one Spirit, "Lord and life-giving, . . . who spoke through the prophets" (Nicaea-Constantinople).

The classical (prophetic) model of inspiration fits the object: the consequences are drawn in Scripture itself. The first "corollary" is the conviction that "what Scripture says, God says" and "what Scripture means, God means" (as explained above). Warfield's demonstration still stands, with the remarkable phenomenon of "God" replacing "Scripture" when the latter word was expected (Matt. 19:5) and the reverse (Gal. 3:8) — quite "naturally." Quotations from all parts of the Old Testament are received as utterances from the Most High. Authority, which, in precepts, laws, or commands, is the right to demand obedi-

86. Bartlett, *The Shape of Scriptural Authority,* 27. Self-authenticating is valid, claims Bartlett, because "that strain of prophetic and apostolic proclamation . . . is so central to Scripture, the strain which declares, 'Hear the word of the Lord!'" (33).

87. Meir Sternberg, *The Poetics of Biblical Narrative* (Bloomington: Indiana University Press, 1985), 35, and 58-59 for inspiration, as quoted by Wolterstorff, *Divine Discourse,* 317 n. 7, and 247. Wolterstorff (248) is probably right on Sternberg's use of "the concept of implied narrator," which does not apply, but Sternberg has well perceived the meaning of scriptural inspiration.

88. David A. Hubbard, "The Wisdom Movement and Israel's Covenant Faith," *TynB* 17 (1966): 15; emphasis original.

89. Daniel J. Treier, "Wisdom," in Vanhoozer, ed., *Dictionary for Theological Interpretation of the Bible,* 845.

ence;[90] in statements of facts (past, present, or future), in assertive illocutionary acts, is a title to full acceptance (cf. 1 Tim. 1:15);[91] in promises, is the privilege of reliability recognized and a claim upon trust; such authority follows, as the authority of the speaker is exercised through that speaker's words. Since the word (now written) is God's, its authority is God's. So it is final. *Scriptura locuta est (Deus locutus est), causa finita.* Hence the use of the introductory formula "It is written" — even in confrontation with the Tempter. Second Peter 1:19-21 emphasizes the absolute certainty of Scripture compared with that of other words.[92] Second Timothy 3:16-17 defines the usefulness in the twin areas of doctrine and of behavior: Scripture, being *theopneustos,* exercises the authority of doctrinal correction (correcting errors) and of moral training in righteousness. The idea that anyone could correct Scripture is foreign to that perspective! New Testament writers do not appeal merely to the general tenor of the biblical "witness"; they base arguments on specific elements, some of which many would have deemed "details," whether historical (David and his men eating consecrated bread, Matt. 12:3-4), grammatical (the singular "seed" in the Abrahamic promise, Gal. 3:16[93]), or theological — if anything theological can be considered a detail (maybe the fact that Melchizedek is recognized as a priest of the true God without any mention of his genealogy and biographical parameters, in contrast with Aaron, Heb. 7:3). Our Lord and his apostles never wavered in their conviction of the absolute trustworthiness of Scripture; in this, they agreed with contemporary Judaism,[94] but as heated controversies on the meaning of Scrip-

90. Goldingay, *Models for Scripture,* 93, creates an opposition between requiring obedience and giving reasons for the actions expected. This is gratuitous and unbiblical. Commanding without giving reasons is *not* authoritarian, and giving reasons does not weaken the right to be obeyed. We are servants, even *douloi* (Luke 17:10), *and* friends (John 15:14-15).

91. I leave aside the debate about the word "propositional." Vanhoozer, "The Semantics of Biblical Literature," 56-67, has shown the ambiguities and intricacies in the use of the word. The article "Proposition/Phrase/Enoncé," by Marc Baratin et al., in *Vocabulaire européen de philosophie. Dictionnaire des intraduisibles,* ed. Barbara Cassin (Paris: Seuil/le Robert, 2004), 1031-47, elaborates on the differences between languages. Poythress uses the word in a wise, non-technical way ("Divine Meaning of Scripture," 253): "When I say that communication is 'propositional,' I do not of course mean that it must be a logical treatise. I mean only that communication conveys information about states of affairs in the world."

92. 2 Peter 1:19 uses a comparative form, *bebaioteron,* "more firm (sure)," and there is no unanimity: either it is the equivalent of a superlative (as happens); or it is a comparative: Scripture is more sure than the voice from heaven / than any other word (implicit) / than what we thought before (again implicit).

93. This is no arbitrary exegesis: the singular *is* significant, since Abraham had several distinct seeds or lines of descendants, cf. Gen. 17:18-21. Other suggestions have been offered as to the significance of the singular form, which sometimes has plural meaning. Nevertheless, Paul's respect for the authority of the word as written is impressive.

94. Charles Perrot (in a private meeting) once mentioned that he knew one text — one

ture and the authority of *tradition* (Matt. 15:1-6) show, the agreement cannot be explained away as "accommodation." Far from being merely a common opinion Jesus could tolerate or condone, it played a strategic role in his difference from the religious establishment of his nation. It was axiomatic and decisive for him: what Scripture says and means, God says and means.

Another consequence of the prophetic inspiration of Scripture is the need of the Holy Spirit for a right reading of the "Old Testament." The second-century church develops it by defending the "spiritual" interpretation that the Jews rejected (the *Epistle of Pseudo-Barnabas* is a primary witness). It is more implicit than explicit in the New Testament, and it is found in the actual practice of the apostles (and the *testimonia*) rather than formulated in doctrinal terms. Nevertheless, Paul associates the freedom of the Spirit with the lifting up of the veil (2 Cor. 3:14-17), and he compares the spirit of wisdom and revelation to the illumination of the heart (Eph. 1:17-18). The New Testament remains on its guard against purely subjective claims to spiritual illumination: the spirits must be tested against apostolic teaching (1 John 4:6), and prophecy must conform to the "analogy of faith" (Rom. 12:6).

A "Polemic" Tailpiece

The general validity of the prophetic model, adopted with the force of its biblical application, entails that some theological constructions must be seriously criticized. Two major attempts, which have not severed all ties with the evangelical heritage, weaken the basic equation of Scripture and the Word of God, and they are quite hospitable to views that were typical of theological "liberalism."

John Goldingay

John Goldingay's *Models for Scripture* mixes some excellent insights with woefully inadequate statements. Discarding evidence to the contrary, Goldingay claims, "The expression 'word of God' refers to particular divine promises, commands, or messages, oral or written, and in the Second Testament characteristically to the gospel message itself, but it is not a scriptural term for scripture itself."[95] He restricts prophetic inspiration to a "tumultuous, extraordinary, unpredictable, invisible activity of Yahweh," and he draws two consequences:

---

only — referring to Palestinian Jews holding other, more critical, beliefs: the Pseudo-Philonic *Book of Biblical Antiquities* 25.13.

95. Goldingay, *Models for Scripture,* 3. In the remainder of this section, page references from this book are given in parentheses in the text.

> [1] As the word of God, inspired speech compares with the nature of the Qur'an as it has traditionally been seen, as received verbatim in its Arabic language without the vehicles of its reception contributing at all to its nature. . . . [2] The prophets, however, are also capable of speaking their own words. (207)

The important trait is effectiveness; the prophet's utterance is not true "in the sense of factual correctness, since it is likely to be a statement that is not at present factually correct, but in the sense of its reliability and effectiveness" (212).[96] How reliable is a promise that fails to match *the facts correctly* in fulfillment? Goldingay is pretty sure that the author of Ecclesiastes would have denied that he had received a word of God (259), but commentators, already in Judaism, consider the significance of 12:11: the One Shepherd is the Lord as the giver of wisdom. "[D]ivine inspiration does not change the nature of narrative written by humans, which as such is subject to the ten percent rule [of error]" (281). Speaking of Paul's quotations from the Old Testament, Goldingay can borrow G. Shaw's phrase and write that "there is the occasional passage where 'in Paul's hands scripture becomes a ventriloquist's dummy' " (135). (Contrast this with the Lord's description of the worshiper in whom he is well pleased: "who *trembles* at my word" [Isa. 66:2].) A statement about God's commands is revealing: "They are effective and they speak beyond their day — sometimes in regrettable ways, as happened when biblical material affirming slavery delayed the abolition of slavery" (257). This is no slip of the pen: several times Goldingay shows that he feels he can disapprove of biblical teachings in the name of the values that are supreme to a twenty-first-century Western intellectual (equality of women, tolerance, etc.) (310, 344).[97] Though he does love the Bible, his attitude is worlds apart from that of Israel's *ḥăsidîm* and of Jesus' apostles.

96. Oddly, Goldingay repeats the cliché "They affect that to which they refer," showing that he misunderstands Austin's "performative" category (211). Typical of Goldingay's method, he mentions (209 n. 2) Anthony C. Thiselton's article "The Supposed Power of Words in the Biblical Writings," *Journal of Theological Studies* 25 (1974): 283-99, which explodes the cliché, and he goes on as if he had not read it. However, in *Models for Interpretation,* Goldingay can write, "The dynamic power of the word is the dynamic power of God; it has no dynamism of its own, and it is not irrevocable in the manner of the Medo-Persian law" (192). Unfortunately, this lucid proposition leads to this thesis: "Yahweh's words do not offer infallible accounts of how the future will turn out. It is the serpent in Genesis 3 who gives Adam and Eve the most accurate account of what will happen." Goldingay frequently shows himself aware of the arguments contrary to his views (in my estimate weighty, decisive ones), but he does not refute them at all; they seem to count for nothing. But sometimes he contributes precious insights!

97. Cf. Goldingay, *Models for Interpretation,* 176-77.

Nicholas Wolterstorff

The Yale philosopher Nicholas Wolterstorff deserves praise and gratitude for having championed in the microcosm of higher education, where "cultured despisers" still abound, the recognition of Scripture as "divine discourse." Though he sorely hardens and exaggerates the distinction from "revelation"[98] and, with worse consequences, from "inspiration,"[99] he rightly chooses the central description of Scripture as God's Word. His critique of Karl Barth's views is perceptive, and he rightly sees that one motivation was Barth's inability to disallow the "results of criticism" (63-74, quote 73). He valiantly fights Jacques Derrida's deconstruction, and it is wonderfully refreshing to read about the claim that "a language is nothing else than canonized differences": "But that's nonsense. There have to be 'nodes' of difference'" (or "*bearers* of these differences") (153-70, quote 158). He also helpfully criticizes Ricoeur "in defense of authorial-discourse interpretation" (130-52), including his denouncing Ricoeur's "simplistic understanding of prophetic discourse" and inspiration caricatured as whispering or dictating (62-63; cf. 76). But Wolterstorff's own view is far from adequate.

Wolterstorff starts with "double agency" and tries to clarify the issue by analyzing double agency as practiced among human speakers (38-45). Two elements come to the fore: *deputizing,* as the head of state deputizes the ambassador, or a boss the secretary, and *appropriation* (186-87). For instance, he writes: "However these books came about, the crucial fact is that God appropriates that discourse in such a way that those speaking now mediate God's speaking" (187).

One form of appropriation that plays a key role in Wolterstorff's doctrine is *presenting:* one's speech-act may be accomplished by presenting a text to someone (55). Is the Bible one book of God? "I suggest that the most natural way of understanding the claim is to understand it in terms of divinely appropriated human discourse" (53). Wolterstorff is reluctant to admit that the apostles were deputized (as, at least in part, the prophets could be): the New Testament "never speaks of them as commissioned to *speak in the name of God*" (51). (Strange myopia, I must cry, while such passages as 1 Cor. 14:37 and 2 Cor. 13:3 are ignored!) The divine Agent is only loosely related to the text: "So we attribute the main point to God [in Psalm 93], and discard the psalmist's particular way of making

98. Wolterstorff, *Divine Discourse,* 19-36. In the remainder of this section, page references from this book are given in parentheses in the text. Wolterstorff denies (32, 35) that commanding and promising reveal anything of the agent; this is not persuasive. Though it is not the primary function, commanding and promising do reveal something of the speaker (at least, generally).

99. "X inspiring Y to say such-and-such? X saying such-and-such" (283); "I may dictate words to you; but of whose discourse these words are the medium depends on which of us *authorizes* them" (283). The argument is typical of Wolterstorff's method: he builds on what is (rather) true of human communication and applies it to divine discourse without inquiring into the biblical understanding of the notions used.

the point as of purely human significance" (210).[100] Wolterstorff suggests (with a rhetorical "perhaps") that the Gospels offer "portraits" of Jesus that incorporate traits "going beyond and even against the available chronicle, not claiming that things did go thus and so" (259).[101]

> I don't myself find obvious that God should assert only what is true. Why should God not "accommodate" Godself to us by sometimes asserting what is helpful in our particular situation even though it is not strictly speaking true? Parents do this sort of thing all the time, and are praiseworthy for doing so. (314 n. 7)[102]

I have not been that kind of parent. Is God? There is not a shred of evidence that holy men and women of God in biblical times (and also in the history of the church) ever thought so.

Wolterstorff then develops his idea of God speaking by *presenting*. Building on the right insight that a speech-act may imply saying different things at once to different intended addressees or audiences, he suggests that God may be saying to us something "rather different" from what he said to Roman Christians by *presenting* us the Epistle (56). Wolterstorff often illustrates this with St. Antony: as Matthew 19:21 was being read in church ("Sell all your possessions"), Antony felt that God was calling him personally: "It doesn't really matter what Jesus meant by those words, nor what Matthew took Jesus as meaning. It was by way of that lector's *locutionary act* of uttering those words that God performed the *illocutionary act* of speaking to Antony" (189).[103] This seems to be Wolterstorff's chief explanation of the way the Bible can be for us "divine discourse." But it opens the door to an unlimited variety of illuministic "words of God" adding to and twisting Scripture. It inaccurately analyzes what takes place in Antony-like cases: *if* God truly spoke to Antony,[104] what God said to him constitutes *another* illocutionary

100. Cf. 211: "[T]hough the human writer has spoken *literally,* God, as it were, has spoken tropically."

101. This implies discrepancies between parallel stories (cf. 291). Wolterstorff similarly posits discrepancies in Old Testament historical books, contra Sternberg (253, 319n17).

102. Wolterstorff made a similar statement on parental policies in *Reason within the Bounds of Religion* (1976; repr. Grand Rapids: Eerdmans, 1993), 156 n. 38. On biblical truthfulness, he does not seem to have changed his views: in his more recent (2001) "The Promise of Speech-act Theory for Biblical Interpretation," in Bartholomew et al., eds., *After Pentecost,* 85, he maintains that "the fact that the human authors of Scripture express various false beliefs does not prevent God from nonetheless infallibly speaking by way of what they say."

103. Wolterstorff refers to Antony's experience, 7, 56, 182, 188.

104. One could also analyze what happened in terms of application: Antony applied or misapplied to his own case (without the clear consciousness that he was doing so) what Jesus had said to the young ruler, and he was mistaken when he thought that God had spoken to

act, not to be confused with God's initial illocutionary act(s) through Jesus and Matthew, which had at least two intended audiences (the rich young ruler and disciples in all ages, for analogies as appropriate). If God performed an additional speech-act telling Antony that he should take the words once directed to the young man in the Gospels for himself literally, this is no part of the Gospel or Bible, and it does not contribute to the Bible being God's word to us. This present divine speaking, not canonical, pertains practically to the category of fallible church prophecy, and it can use non-biblical words: Wolterstorff himself refers to the *Tolle, lege* of St. Augustine's conversion as a parallel case (189).

The distance between Wolterstorff's account of divine discourse and what biblical evidence compels us to accept is glaring. Attitudes entailed and ways of handling texts widely differ. He transfers God's speaking by what he finds in human exchanges, without first listening to Scripture in obedient faith. His sharp intelligence misses the concerns and certainties that are biblically paramount: that the prophets' words *originated* with God and were uttered in utter dependence on God's leading and protecting (from any extraneous interference) as they were borne along by the Holy Spirit. The idea of a later "appropriation" that includes falsity is woefully inadequate. In Kevin Vanhoozer's words, "As commissioned divine-human discourse, the Bible is not only authorized but, in providential fashion, *authored* by God."[105]

Superficial Objections

Objections that betray a superficial understanding (to use a mild phrase) of the issue, such as indignation at the idea of "mechanical dictation,"[106] may be left

---

him in a special and direct way. If the application was valid, because Antony's case was similar enough to the young ruler's, one could say that God (Christ) had *indirectly* spoken to Antony.

105. Kevin J. Vanhoozer, "Word of God," in Vanhoozer, ed., *Dictionary for Theological Interpretation of the Bible,* 853. Earlier attempts to "water down" divine authorship in terms of later approbation or appropriation were sharply criticized by Herman Bavinck, *Gereformeerde Dogmatiek,* 2nd edition (Kampen: Bos, 1906), 1:452-53.

106. This is the language of slogans, manipulative indeed. As already stated, *dictare* does not imply a particular modality; there is also something suspect in the *a priori* assurance that God *cannot* speak in a "mechanical" way, whatever that means (Bavinck notes that some writers use the word simply to reject any significant role ascribed to the Holy Spirit in the writing of biblical books [*Gereformeerde Dogmatiek,* 1:454]). Another objection hardly worth considering is the meaninglessness of absolute certainty (as befits what is truly God's own Word), with the cutting edge of inerrancy, since we only have errant copies. The sophistry consists in an equivocation on the status of a *copy.* The copy is not the text, but a tool in the transmission of the text: if it fails to be entirely trustworthy, this does not affect the status and quality of the text — whereas the issue of trustworthiness of the original text remains decisive for these. See the essay by P. J. Williams, chapter 13 in this collection.

aside: the objection that carries some weight relates to the tendency of the "prophetic model" to deplete the human role of any substantial significance. As was seen, this is not imaginary: some classical theologians chose words that minimize human instrumentality. Many critics feel that speakers and writers who only spoke and wrote at God's prompting and under his total control could not produce a discourse that is authentically *theirs.* Such critics may use the loaded "puppet" metaphor.[107] Here the basic theological convictions, and the framework they define, come into play.

Abraham Kuyper faced the issue. In contrast to Satanic inspiration, which always implies alienation and ultimately destruction, the inspiration of God's chosen spokespersons, which heightened their human powers and glorified their identity, presupposes *God's omnipresent immanence* in the sense of Acts 17:28: he is the fountain of all good, *in him* only do we live and move and are everything we are.[108] We are nothing apart from him: How could his working in us threaten our being?

The second presupposition is the creation of humans *in God's image.* Kuyper argues that it involves a creational capacity for inspiration *(Inspiration/Fähigkeit);* it is destined to be the Temple of God in the Spirit (455-56). The inspiring God possesses thought and will, against pantheistic conceptions, and human consciousness has a kinship *(affiniteit)* with him (457-58). Since human faculties do not develop in a vacuum, the preparation of the sacred writers by all the circumstances of their lives is also a condition of the proper human participation in their task: Kuyper stressed the *providential* guidance through experiences like Moses' in Pharaoh's court and David with his sheep (464). The Lord *Pantokratōr,* who "operates [*energountos*] everything according to the decision of his will" (Eph. 1:11), freely shapes his servants to fit his purposes. The "God who operates [*energōn*] in [believers] both the willing and the operating [*energein*]" (Phil. 2:13) can speak through them whenever he wills so to do.

The difficulty arises if one repudiates such a grand vision of God. When God is viewed as limited (should I write "god"?) and his action is imagined after the likeness of created causes of which it cannot be said that we live and move and are "in them," a total control is antagonistic to freedom — indeed, of plenary existence and fulfilled identity. A fatal rivalry obtains: the more divine, the less human. Such a scheme apparently influences Goldingay's and Wolterstorff's treatment of the subject. Goldingay affirms, "The idea of human freedom and power is limited by the idea of divine constraint, *the idea of divine determination by that of human initiative and autonomy.*"[109] He obviously dislikes the "monar-

107. Goldingay and Wolterstorff are responsible enough to refrain from using it.

108. Kuyper, *Encyclopaedie,* 2:455. In the remainder of this section, page references to this volume of Kuyper's *Encyclopaedie* are given in parentheses in the text.

109. Goldingay, *Models for Scripture,* 323; my emphasis.

chic metaphor" and the predominance of the title "Lord."[110] Wolterstorff is more technical: he envisages that "all the events generative of divine discourse" are part of an original plan of God, but he considers what he calls "determinism" to be "highly unlikely" in view of chance micro-events *and* the actions of free agents.[111] He clearly defines the Molinist option, but does not retain it.[112] His sense of divine Lordship is not acute enough to prevent titling a chapter "Could God Have and Acquire the Rights and Duties of a Speaker?" God or a god?

Muslim piety today and reverence of God's transcendence, *tanzîh,* is a timely reminder for our late modern Christendom. The paradox, however, is that the concept of prophetic experience in Islam (and of the "coming down" of the divine word, *tanzîl*), is dominated by the scheme *the more to God/the less to man.* The implication, in Kenneth Cragg's words, is "that the more an activity is divine the less it is human, that God's recruitment of personal powers requires an abeyance of their due exercise in reason, emotion and love."[113] Hence the emphasis on Muhammad's alleged illiteracy (he was *ummî*). This logically implies that God and the prophet are rivals; it associates them in the same causal field, and it is guilty of anthropomorphism, of "associationism," *shirk,* the supreme theological crime![114] Such is the natural myopia of the human mind!

Scripture Prophetic AND . . . : Complementing the Prophetic Model

Historic Christian theology — patristic, catholic, reformational — has rightly extended to the whole of canonical Scripture the "prophetic model": what Scripture says and means, God says and means. By extending it, however, one *ipso facto* risks disregarding the diversity. The rule of the prophetic model inevitably eclipses the possibility of other models, not necessarily rival models but complementary ones. "Prophecy" in the stricter sense implies one form of inspiration;

110. Goldingay, *Models for Scripture,* 328. His remark, 13, sounds as a confession: old models "seemed to be discredited when we no longer liked the answers they provided to those questions (and indeed, no longer liked the questions)." His article "The Ongoing Story of Biblical Interpretation," *Churchman* 112 (1998): 6-16, quite candidly confesses the tensions in his soul: he does not like a God who tells people what to do, he feels attracted by Process theology on divine sovereignty (there is little left!), but he does not wish to discard such a verse as Acts 4:28.

111. Wolterstorff, *Divine Discourse,* 119-21.

112. Wolterstorff, *Divine Discourse,* 122. He can speak of God "taking chances" (122-23).

113. Kenneth Cragg, *Muhammad and the Christian: A Question of Response* (Maryknoll, NY: Orbis, 1984), 84. On revelation and transcendence, see also Kenneth Cragg, *The Call of the Minaret* (New York: Oxford University Press, 1964), 47-49. Cragg is a respected author among Muslim intellectuals.

114. I tried to argue along those lines in my "L'Evangile et l'islam: Relever le défi théologique," *Fac-Réflexion* 28 (September 1994): 7-8, cf. 12, 16.

the possibility of broadening the notion and applying it to the whole Bible in order to embrace all forms is gain; but what is *specific* with other forms remains to be seen.

We should explore this with one form lying beyond the scope of our inquiry: *graphic* inspiration, as Kuyper called it. He defined it as that "guidance afforded to the spirit/mind [*geest*] of the writers, editors and redactors of Holy Scripture by the Spirit of God whereby these *hagiai graphai* received such a form as was foreordained by God for his Church, among the *media gratiae,* in the counsel of salvation."[115] Rigor is found on Kuyper's side: he finely argues that even in the case of a book like Galatians inspiration for writing is not totally identical with apostolic inspiration.[116] In 2 Timothy 3:16, *theopneustos* applies to what stands *written.* For our purposes, however, the difference between graphic inspiration and forms of inspiration corresponding to the chief genres of biblical diversity seems too difficult to investigate. Though I sorely regret not being able to study the "graphic" form any further, I must here put aside any attempt at a separate treatment.

The "Former" Prophets

We draw the "prophetic model" ("Thus says the Lord") with an eye on Amos, Isaiah, Jeremiah, and other men whom the early Jewish tradition, as embodied in the shape of the canon, labels "Later Prophets." But what about the "Former Prophets" (or "first," *riʾšônîm*), the Hebrew overall title for our "historical" books? Though some powerful figures emerge who reflect the prophetic model, above all Elijah and Elisha, the books themselves seem to have been authored by anonymous writers, whose inspiration is of another character. We could call them the "sons of the prophets," to use a phrase that recurs in the Elisha cycle. They appear to be preeminently *disciples,* sharing in the prophetic ministry less directly, at a short distance. They form a kind of faithful community around Isaiah, and they are entrusted with the preservation of the prophetic testimony (Isa. 8:16-18; it is possible to understand that the "children" are the spiritual children of the prophet, his disciples, cf. Heb. 2:13).[117]

In his zeal for an anthropological preparation for inspiration, Kuyper develops the analogy with *epic* poetry.[118] The "I" of the poet recedes into the background, and the role of invisible partners is unveiled. Above all, the aim is to bring out the meaning of events in their succession. The last trait, especially,

115. Kuyper, *Encyclopaedie,* 2:493.
116. Kuyper, *Encyclopaedie,* 2:494.
117. So Bartlett, *The Shape of Scriptural Authority,* 20.
118. Kuyper, *Encyclopaedie,* 2:480-82.

characterizes biblical prophecy, and when it is expressed through narrative, it takes the form of a "dioramatic"[119] representation of history that determines the true meaning of every human life.

How could we describe the position and stance, under inspiration, of the "former" prophet? As Sternberg maintains, he is a prophet, he tells the story, and he confirms the facts and discloses their meaning, as God's instrument, borne along by the Holy Spirit. He has in common with Jeremiah a real access to the divine *sôd* ("council"). But he is not much of a "herald." He stands (or is seated!) by the side of the herald-prophet. He has a share in the mighty herald's spirit (Spirit); he is given the ability to *elaborate* the insight into the counsel of the Sovereign Lord. His inspiration enables him to *digest* prophetic communication (we ought to remember the old meaning of "digest"). This is the way he is the son of a prophet and a prophet himself (I am using masculine pronouns because I see no evidence in the Old Testament historical books of women in that role).

If such a sketch correctly locates the specific inspiration of "former" prophets, authors of inspired narratives, it also lifts from comparative oblivion one dimension of the "later" prophets' inspiration. The herald is no mere "mouth." The herald-prophet is no mere herald. He already elaborates and "digests" what he has seen, heard, preached. Isaiah served as a historian of the kingdom (2 Chron. 26:22; cf. 32:32). It is likely that the major prophets effected a true literary work on the collections of their oracles. J. A. Motyer legitimately protests against unfounded assumptions: "The hesitancy of specialists and commentators to see the prophets as their own editors is very difficult to understand and, in the main, arises from overlooking the prophet's own presuppositions about himself and his work."[120] Since Isaiah believed himself to be verbally inspired, our duty is "to ask what a man who had this conviction would be likely to do with the resultant material. Would he leave it, partly written and mostly oral, to the changes and chances of history?"[121] The difference between "former" and "later" prophets is not, after all, so radical.

The Law-Giver and the Teachers

Before the "former" prophets, *the* Prophet, unsurpassed as far as the Old Testament is concerned (Deut. 34:10), is Moses. He owns the title, but Jews and Christians do not remember him as prophet but as the one who led the exodus, established the Covenant, and dispensed the *tôrâ.* Since *tôrâ,* as I transcribe the word, is from the root *yrh,* "to teach," Jews call Moses *môrēnû,* "our Teacher"

119. Kuyper, *Encyclopaedie,* 2:482.

120. J. A. Motyer, *The Prophecy of Isaiah* (Leicester: InterVarsity, 1993), 30-31.

121. Motyer, *The Prophecy of Isaiah,* 31.

(from the same root). It is worth exploring how his inspiration may have differed from that of ordinary prophets.

Deuteronomy 34:11-12 recalls Moses' part in the people's liberation from Egypt, with the awesome power he displayed. If other prophets performed miracles, Moses is in another category! Probably, this historical role goes over the limits of what may be called the inspiration of Scripture, with its diversity. But it reminds us of the intimate solidarity between God's *works* of salvation and the *words* that accompany the works and enable the faithful to receive the benefits. The structure of God's speech-activity espouses that of *Heilsgeschichte,* as Hebrews 1:1 suggests: hence the closure of the Canon, which signifies the finality of Jesus Christ,[122] and the need to maintain, at all costs, the ultimate referentiality of language.

Deuteronomy 34:10 mentions first, as the privilege of Moses compared to prophets, his speaking with the Lord "face to face." The clause summarizes the extraordinary statement in Numbers 12:6-8, which elevates Moses far above other Old Testament recipients of revelation. St. Thomas Aquinas believed that Moses (like Paul later) beheld "the very essence of God" *(vidit ipsam Dei essentiam).*[123] This cannot be sustained. The text specifies that Moses saw a *tĕmûnâ* of the Lord, YHWH; whatever the precise nuance of the word ("form," "representation"), it is the word used for images in Exodus 20:4, and it implies that some distance remained. Even if Moses' inspiration fell short of pure immediacy, it involved an intelligent penetration of God's secrets, a fullness of understanding with regard to God's character and plans that was unique before Christ. Above the "servants the prophets," Moses, the faithful administrator of God's House, is given, no less than Abraham, the status of a friend.[124]

I suggest that Moses' privilege of knowledge is organically one with his role as the Law-Giver, the dispenser of *tôrâ.* For the Law is "the Law of Moses." The relationship of the Teacher, Doctor, Instructor, *môreh* to the words the teacher is to bring is deeper than the simple prophet's; they are "brainchildren," a spiritual progeny (through "conception"), part of the person. If it is true in other forms of inspiration, it is conspicuous in this case. And the second difference from oracles (though they may be called *tôrôt*) is that the instruction is not so closely bound to historical actuality. Prophecy is for this time, *hic et nunc; tôrâ* is for all times.

122. Goldingay, *Models for Scripture,* 115, puts this finality in jeopardy as he doubts that the canon can be closed, on principle: "When a new salvation event occurred" the Second Testament was constituted. "One cannot exclude the possibility that this might happen again." Goldingay is (mis)led to taking this position by his scale of values: changes in social ethics (accepted by society), such as feminine equality, seem to interest him more than the atonement of human sin before God, once for all. This is an old liberal preference, of course.

123. St. Thomas Aquinas, *Summa Theologica,* IIa-IIae, q. 174, art. 4, *Respondeo.*

124. Exodus 33:11 uses the word *rēa',* which means companion, neighbor, friend. God would converse with Moses as a man with his companion.

Tôrâ provides landmarks and foundations (it is interesting to note that, twice, the verb *yārâ* is used for the laying of foundations, Gen. 31:51 and Job 38:6). This requires a deep knowledge of the eternal God.

The privilege of the Law-Giver and his leadership in redemption imply that his *person* is glorified in his mission. The people put their faith in the Lord (YHWH) *and in Moses* his servant (Exod. 14:31). He is no mere herald: he is the *Mediator* of the Covenant (Gal. 3:19). The weight of his intensified humanity is felt when he says what God says, God says what he says. Such are his position and stance under inspiration.

Moses was uniquely privileged, but there are other *teachers,* teachers of doctrinal foundations, of laws that remain valid from generation to generation. Can we extend to them what was said of Moses' inspiration? A cautious affirmative answer seems possible. In the Old Testament, teaching the law was the duty of the priests (Jer. 18:18; Mal. 2:7); in the New Testament, God has instituted teachers *(didaskaloi),* and some of them are among the sacred writers (e.g., the author of the Epistle to the Hebrews). They had to think through the message in deeper ways, and their work mediated God's Word to his people.

Actually, this could also be said of the prophetic office. Again, this is a dimension of prophecy that lay half-hidden and that we may perceive more clearly as it is intensified in teachers. One cannot draw a sharp dividing line between prophecy and teaching — one can only observe the polarity we tried to describe, with much overlap. Among Jews, the *tôrâ*-Wisdom of Ecclesiasticus pours out "teaching *(didaskalian)* as prophecy" (24:33). In the church, the gift of prophecy goes with the knowledge of mysteries and all science (1 Cor. 13:2), and prophecy is "sandwiched" between science and doctrine (1 Cor. 14:6). False prophets, who imitate true ones, teach false doctrines (Rev. 2:20; cf. 2 Pet. 2:1). After all, we introduced Moses as *the* Prophet!

The Apostles

The apostles, who were responsible for the New Testament, were also prophets, we said. But they were first of all *apostles*! Is there a specific form of inspiration at play when they fulfill their office?

Apostolic Inspiration

One may note the emphasis, which is easily overlooked, on their *teaching* role. The earliest church persevered in the *didachē* of the apostles (Acts 2:42), with which they were filling Jerusalem (Acts 5:28), as the Lord had commanded them (Matt. 28:20). Paul claimed the title "Doctor [*didaskalos*] of the Gentiles" (1 Tim. 2:7).

This shows the high price put on instruction and information in biblical perspective. It is strange that even orthodox apologists today sound quite defensive about revealed *information,* as if one could close one's eyes on the vital importance of having the right information in so many human pursuits![125] Speech-act theory itself had to move from initially separating "informative" and "performative" to realizing their deep solidarity. Although "the Bible is not merely a handbook of information and description," Thiselton applies these insights to Scripture:

> The point behind the so-called "propositional" view is even more important. . . . The dynamic and concrete authority of the Bible rests, in turn, on the truth of certain states of affairs in God's relation to the world. As J. L. Austin succinctly put it, for performative language to function effectively, "certain statements have *to be true.*"[126]

The "doctoral" component of the apostolic office also confirms the fluidity and porosity of the biblical categories: the various forms of inspiration penetrate and impregnate one another. However, and precisely because the doctoral or didactic dimension is found in many forms, it is not *specific* of the apostles' role, and we must seek other traits.

Kuyper suggests that the apostles' inspiration was "ordinary" *(ordinaire),* bound to their "office" as the prophets' was not, centered on "remembering," *anamnesis* (John 14:26), while the prophets fashioned poetic images: "[T]he contrast is that of *imaging* and *remembering,* poetry and memory."[127] Kuyper's search for an anthropological basis of inspiration probably (mis)led him into too easy an alliance of poetry and prophecy, which would not be valid for some passages and for the "former" prophets. He was too selective (as many other authors have been) in his attention to extraordinary phenomena, and one can argue that these were not *essential* to prophetic inspiration.[128]

125. E.g., regarding the malignancy of cells analyzed or the preparation of a terrorist plot, will anyone minimize the value of accurate information? And, of course, in the whole edifice of natural science and all the technical applications, everything would be ruined if scientists and engineers were debarred from factually reliable information.

126. Anthony C. Thiselton, *The Two Horizons: New Testament Hermeneutics and Philosophical Description with Special Reference to Heidegger, Bultmann, Gadamer, and Wittgenstein* (Exeter, UK: Paternoster, 1980), 437, referring to J. L. Austin, *How to Do Things with Words* (Cambridge, MA: Harvard University Press, 1962), 45. Kevin J. Vanhoozer echoes the thought (referring to an earlier statement by Thiselton), in his article "Word of God," in Vanhoozer, ed., *Dictionary for Theological Interpretation of the Bible,* 830: "[W]hile we may welcome the recent emphasis on the performative rather than merely informative aspect of language, certain things that authors do with words depend upon the truth value of their cognitive content." See also Thiselton, *New Horizons in Hermeneutics* (London: HarperCollins, 1992), 294.

127. Kuyper, *Encyclopaedie,* 2:490.

128. Kuyper, *Encyclopaedie,* 2:489-90. Kuyper relates the forms of prophetic inspiration

John the Baptist, the supreme prophet according to Jesus' own testimony (Matt. 11:9), does not fit Kuyper's description. Kuyper's remarks on the relationship of inspiration and *office,* however, does hit something of great interest. Prophecy, he proposes, was *itself* the office and, therefore, "most aphoristic and without a cosmic basis."[129] In the apostles' case, on the contrary, the office is first embedded in their lives, and inspiration comes only next.[130] Though this scheme may not render full justice to the "official" dimension of the Old Testament prophetic ministry,[131] it points to the unique feature of the apostolic office: its historical association with Jesus Christ himself precedes inspiration. The apostles are not only God's heralds: they are Christ's *ambassadors* (2 Cor. 5:20). Instead of "Thus says the Lord," they claim, "Christ speaks through me" (2 Cor. 13:3). Jesus declares, "You shall be my *witnesses*" (Acts 1:8). It is as such that they constitute the church's foundation, *Jesus Christ himself being the cornerstone* (Eph. 2:20).

This implies the service of memory, as Kuyper stressed, as they deliver traditions that originated with Christ (1 Cor. 11:23). They are *included* in the final divine speaking "in [the] Son" of Hebrews 1:2, "once for all," and this privilege makes them, to borrow another of Kuyper's phrases, the *prōto-didaskaloi pasēs tēs ekklēsias.*[132] This also implies a governmental authority in the churches (2 Cor. 10:9; 13:10; the promise, likely, of Matt. 19:28), and the full involvement of their persons: they were witnesses to the end — martyrs.

The status of "witness" secondarily implies subjective "investment": it rests first of all on historical, factual relation.[133] The apostles were those who had been

---

as he sees them to the regime of the Holy Spirit's presence in Israel: no *inhabitatio* before Pentecost, but "only irradiation and works as if from the outside." Dealing with his interesting proposals lies beyond the scope of this essay; on the Holy Spirit in the Old Testament, I recommend Sylvain Romerowski, *L'Œuvre du Saint-Esprit dans l'histoire du salut,* Théologie biblique (Cléon-d'Andran: Excelsis, 2005).

129. Kuyper, *Encyclopaedie,* 2:490.

130. Kuyper, *Encyclopaedie,* 2:490. Bavinck suggests that the inspiration of Old Testament prophets was "more or less transcendent," from above or from without, whereas that of the apostles was "immanent in their hearts" (*Gereformeerde Dogmatiek,* 1:462).

131. Of which a Josephus was keenly aware (*Contra Apionem* 1.8).

132. Kuyper, *Encyclopaedie,* 2:490-91.

133. This hardly comes out in Bartlett's chapter "The Authority of Witness" (*The Shape of Scriptural Authority,* 113-30), which stresses congruity with life (123). Bartlett explains, "[T]he personality of the testifier becomes part of his message" (115). John Goldingay, *Models for Scripture,* recognizes "witnessing tradition" as one of the main forms, and does not ignore the importance of eyewitness testimony (35); yet he tends to dilute witness into "narrative" (61-76) and to confuse witness with interpretation (49-60). This peculiar notion of "witness" agrees with his comments on Dan. 11:40–12:13, which scorn the idea "that scripture gives grounds for believing that the mere facts are accurate"; "When it speaks of the future, it has only the scriptural text, and it is providing an illustrative, possible embodiment of that text, which is not to be pressed to provide historical data but to provide a scriptural revelation of what the events to come will

with Jesus (Acts 4:13), who had followed him since the days of John's baptism and were eyewitnesses of his risen glory (Acts 1:22) — even Paul, the exceptional apostle who also had "seen" the Lord (1 Cor. 9:1).

The apostolic form of inspiration is uniquely bound to a *Christological* association. Yet what we have observed of biblical inner relationships prompts us to ask whether something of the kind could also be found in *prophecy.* And, indeed, the Spirit who moved the Old Testament prophets is identified as the Spirit *of Christ* (1 Pet. 1:11). This biblical *theologoumenon* gives more precision to the constant conviction that all the Scriptures witness to his person and work (Luke 24:25-27, 44-47; John 5:39), that the previous economy only foreshadowed and prepared his coming, maybe that he is the Word from whom all the divine words proceed.[134] If the prophets' inspiration was already Christological, what is true of the apostles in the strongest, most direct and manifest way is also true of the prophets in a more hidden and indirect way. Just as the justification of Old Testament believers was based *in advance* on the atonement accomplished on the Cross (Rom. 3:25-26; Heb. 9:15), the prophets' ability to speak the Word of God was not independent from the earthly mission of the Personal Word.

If such a structural relationship obtains between the prophetic and apostolic ministries, if the Christological association of the apostolate is *latent* in prophecy, and if the "ordination" of prophecy to Christ's mission is *patent* in its apostolic fulfillment, why not prefer the apostolic paradigm for the inspiration of Scripture? Though the prophetic one is valid (as we argued), the model of the apostles' inspiration will presumably prove richer, better-balanced, and more illuminating.[135]

Incarnation and Inspiration

At this point, one should broach a much-debated issue: How should we relate Christology and bibliology? Drawing a *parallel* between the Chalcedonian dogma of the Lord's two natures and the ascription to Scripture of both divinity and humanity has been rather popular. Such a distinguished biblical scholar as Luis Alonso Schökel feels no embarrassment when he quotes, among others, Rupertus of Deutz and Pope Pius XII.

---

mean" (296). Goldingay shows no interest in the apostolic *office:* Paul mediates the gospel: "The churches then share on equal terms with him in the gospel and in its authority" (95).

134. This theological insight may or may not have been present in John's conscious meditation.

135. I remember that Edmund P. Clowney suggested this at the 1965 Wenham Consultation on Scripture, chaired by Harold J. Ockenga. I was struck and helped by this insight, but the echo was rather faint. (I was, I think, the youngest of all the theologians invited.)

> Blessed Zion, before she did his flesh, gave birth to the same and one Christ, to the same and one Word of God, *through the mouth of the prophets.*[136]

> Just as the substantial (*substantiale* [maybe: hypostatic]) Word of God was made in the likeness of men in every respect 'except sin,' so also the words of God, as expressed in human languages, are in every respect assimilated to human discourse, except error. Such is the *sunkatabasis* or condescension of God in his providence which already St. John Chrysostom magnificently extolled and again and again affirmed to be present in the Sacred Books.[137]

Kuyper compares Christ and Scripture: "Both are the *Logos prophorikos,* but in the first case *sarx genomenos,* in the second case *eggraphos,* and these two overlap perfectly [*dekken elkander*]."[138] Bavinck develops the parallel presentation:

> The *Logos* became *sarx,* and the word became Scripture. . . . Christ became flesh, a servant, without seemliness or majesty, the one despised of men; He descended to the lower regions of the earth, and became obedient even to the death of the cross. And so also has the word, the divine revelation which has entered the creaturely realm, the life and history of human beings and peoples, in all the human forms of dreams and visions, of research and reflection, even down to human weakness, contempt and disrepute; the word became writing, and as a writing was subject to the lot of all writings.[139]

A common objection to the doctrine of biblical infallibility/inerrancy is that it amounts to docetism, but that presupposes the parallel. Otherwise the charge loses its point since docetism is a *Christological* heresy. On that basis, or within that framework, it is fairly easy to rebut the charge: "Just as what is human in Christ, though weak and lowly, remained free from sin, so also is Scripture *sine labe concepta* [conceived without any flaw]."[140] Its traditional standing surely warns us against despising the Christological analogy or parallel.

136. Schökel, *The Inspired Word,* 52, quoting from Rupertus's *Commentary on Isaiah* (Migne's *Patrologia latina* 167:1362; my translation and emphasis; the English translation unfortunately omits the last clause).

137. Schökel, *The Inspired Word,* 52, quoting from the Encyclical *Divino afflante Spiritu* (my translation).

138. Kuyper, *Encyclopaedie,* 2:425.

139. Bavinck, *Gereformeerde Dogmatiek,* 1:459-60. In the last sentence of our quote, Bavinck uses *schrift* as he has done in the first sentence; but in the first, he does with a capital S, hence my translation "Scripture," and not in the last one, hence my translation "writing."

140. Bavinck, *Gereformeerde Dogmatiek,* 1:460. That "flaws" would include errors is clear from Bavinck's discussions, his choice of quotations from orthodox divines through the cen-

The analogy, however, is open to serious criticism.[141] What is one on one side is two on the other, and conversely! Confessing Chalcedon, Christology deals with *one* Person and *two* natures classically conceived as *distinct substances.* If one is reluctant to use the category of "substance," Christ's deity and humanity must still be thought of as "realities" of which the first preexisted and the second implies "something" in common with humankind existing separately. Bibliology deals with the cooperation of *two* persons and *one act,* speech-act, with qualities one should not think of as substances! There is little warrant for representing the divine discourse as preexistent and *adding* a human expression, as a kind of second nature, in the event of inspiration. Rather, God speaks through his human "mouth": his speech-act is precisely what he causes the prophet or apostle, through the Spirit's assistance, to do in his name. This dispels the fantasy of two distinct "layers" in the text (the text embodies the illocutionary act): a deeper divine one and a merely human vehicle. Inasmuch as the Christological parallel may send the reader on the wrong track, it must be handled with care.

Shall one dare to show a more excellent way? More exact than parallelism, *articulation and extension* may characterize the relationship between Christology and bibliology. The apostles, whose office provides the better "model" of biblical inspiration, are Jesus Christ's associates, whom he sends after him as the Father had sent him (John 20:21). They are his witnesses who *remember* his own discourse, the words he uttered, and they *spread them on* to the ends of the earth. One core component of the apostles' *paradosis,* and therefore of the New Testament, is simply Jesus' own teaching. In his case, there is only one Person, and clearly one speech-act (for acts belong to the person), with qualities related to the two natures but not possessing two natures (for acts do not possess "natures"). When the person of the apostle is added, his inspiration enables him further to *extend* Jesus' ministry, but it does not change essentially the way the Discourse is both human and divine. Jesus Christ being foundationally the Faithful Witness (Rev. 3:14) and the Apostle of our confession (Heb. 3:1), the apostolic word may be considered *his* word — through his instruments, and friends (cf. John 15:15). Since the apostolic model may be applied to the whole Bible, Scripture as a whole may then count as the fruit of Jesus Christ's prophetic ministry — in his own Person, "in the days of his flesh," and through his chosen witnesses, before he came and at the time of fulfillment.[142]

---

turies (424-37), and his association of error *(dwaling)* with sin in Christ's case (472). The same thought is in Pius XII's Encyclical *Divino afflante Spiritu.*

141. One finds a nuanced discussion in Paul R. Wells, *James Barr and the Bible: Critique of a New Liberalism* (Phillipsburg, NJ: P&R, 1980), 7-41, referring mainly to Barr's and Barth's views.

142. On our topic and the relationship between prophetic and apostolic modes, cf. Bruce L. McCormack, "The Being of Holy Scripture Is in Becoming: Karl Barth in Conversation with American Evangelical Criticism," in *Evangelicals and Scripture: Tradition, Authority and Hermeneutics,* ed. Vincent Bacote, Laura C. Miguélez, and Dennis L. Okholm (Downers Grove, IL: InterVarsity, 2004), 55-75; I owe this recommendation to David Gibson.

The Christological perspective made possible by concentrating on the apostolic form of inspiration suits the structure of *Heilsgeschichte;* it offers a theological rationale for the role of *human* instruments: they are attached to Christ's *humanity* since he is speaking as the God-Man, and it helps us clarify the notion of *authority.* The *Lord* is speaking. Can one deny in good faith that the title "Lord," supreme in Christian confession, draws our attention to his authority? The authority of Scripture *is* the Lord's authority as he exercises it over us, and therefore it remains sovereign and prior to whatever effects the contents of the discourse may have on or in us.

This last point has not been appreciated as it ought to be. There has been, in recent decades, a distaste for what is labeled, unsympathetically, "formal" authority.[143] John Webster can write, "Scripture's authority is not exercised apart from the work performed upon the text by its readers; its authority is not a formal property, but an aspect of the inter-action between God's self-revelation and its hearers."[144] The first proposition can be accepted as a description of fact: yes, the *exercise* of authority always requires a receptive activity on the part of the addressees. But the second proposition obscures the issue. Authority, according to its concept, is a formal property. Authority, as distinct from mere power, is the *right* to be followed (to have one's testimony believed, conclusion embraced, orders obeyed). Typically, the authority of a word proceeds from the status or recognized quality of the person who issued the word. The authority of the command "Stop!" proceeds from the policeman's delegation; the authority of the scholar's pronouncement proceeds from his past achievements. Authority conditions the reception of content and is logically prior to the appropriation of content (and therefore "formal"). Even in the case when it is *grounded* on the excellency of content, it is still distinct from the mere effect of content. I am struck and enthused by the beauty and depth of a piece of writing; I thereupon form an estimate of the author's powers, lucidity, etc., and the author climbs several steps up my scale of reverence; when I reread the text, the note of authority is then added to my reception. Knowing the Lord Jesus Christ, knowing him as Lord, I bow in advance to whatever he is pleased to tell me. This is "formal," though it does not imply any ultimate separation between form and content: the Lord is my Savior,

143. Berkouwer was one of the writers who initiated that mood in "evangelical" circles (cf., e.g., *Holy Scripture,* 349-50).

144. John Webster, "Scripture, Authority of," in Vanhoozer, ed., *Dictionary for Theological Interpretation of the Bible,* 727. Webster's thesis remains complex. He affirms that "Its [Scripture's] authority does not lie within itself, the authority of Scripture is the authority of its content" but also that it is "that of a commissioned witness or herald" — and this is a matter of formal status — and "de jure," not "simply de facto" (726). His sentence: "That to which the church submits in its obedience to the authority of Scripture is not a contentless norm, a purely formal statute, but rather the commanding force of its truth-content" (726) is not incompatible with a more formal notion, owing to the ambiguity of qualifiers (contentless, purely).

he is the Way, the Truth, and the Life, and it would be foolish and ungodly to separate his Lordship from what it means in concrete terms.[145]

The Wise

The pursuit and practice of wisdom interlaces with many, if not all, biblical genres. It plays a major part in the didactic or doctoral form of ministry; but it occupies center-stage in the so-called "sapiential" books. With those wisdom books specially in mind, it is worth looking for characteristic features of their inspiration. We already insisted that the *wise* benefited from the prophetic gift in the widest sense (and ultimately "apostolic"). Lady Wisdom in Proverbs preaches on the streets, and she invites those who hear her to what amounts to conversion. As Bruce K. Waltke points out, at the end of the book "Agur and King Lemuel label their sayings as *maśśā'*, the term prophets use to designate their divine 'oracles,' and Agur defines his sayings more particularly as 'an inspired utterance' (*n*^{e}*'ûm;* 30:1; 31:1)."[146] May we then discern a specific position or stance?

Since scholarship does not agree in its portrayal of the wisdom phenomenon in Israel, it is appropriate that I draw a few traits to indicate which representation, in my estimate, best fits the evidence.[147] The sages, were, on the one hand, the bearers of popular wisdom, men *and women* (2 Sam. 14), masters of wit and rhetoric, who were able to distil the fruit of universal experience in common sense and shrewd perception. They were on the other hand *royal* counselors, and, hopefully, the kings themselves were to be wise, with Solomon as *the* reference-figure in our sapiential literature.[148] Training in wisdom was organized, and a third category of sages emerged: the scribes, who had more than a hand in the redaction of the biblical books.[149] Wisdom was practical indeed and interested in solving problems of everyday living, but was not restricted to counsels for life-management. It included "scientific" or "encyclopedic" ambitions (cf. Solomon's

145. This is akin to the old Socratic dilemma: Is the good good because God wills it so, or does God will the good because it is the good? The question must be rejected as deeply impious, implicit blasphemy. Both "horns" disfigure the true God. Raising the question presupposes that humans may elevate themselves to the level of deity and speculate on the good and on God's will in an autonomous fashion — the demonic lie.

146. Bruce K. Waltke, *An Old Testament Theology: An Exegetical, Canonical, and Thematic Approach* (Grand Rapids: Zondervan, 2007), 915.

147. I still abide by the arguments in my Tyndale Biblical Theology Lecture for 1977, "The Fear of the LORD as the 'Principle' of Wisdom."

148. E.g., *Wisdom of Solomon* dates to the first century B.C.E.

149. See the title of dom Hilaire Duesberg's pioneering work, *Les Scribes inspirés: Introduction aux livres sapientiaux,* 2 vols. (Paris: Desclée de Brouwer, 1938-39).

Onomastica, 1 Kgs. 4:33). It involved intellectual gymnastics, the acquiring of penetration and nimbleness through the invention of enigmas and riddles (Prov. 1:6), epigrams and parables (*m^e^šālîm*). It was not devoid of "theoretical" concerns, even speculative efforts at discovering the way the world is going (Prov. 3:13-20),[150] at examining the processes of rational thought and its pathology (Eccles. 7:25),[151] at plumbing the depths of "being" (*mâ-šehāyâ,* 7:24). This must not be overlooked, though the style is markedly different from the Greeks', with a leaning toward symbol and picture rather than formal analysis, and the recognition of human limits and need of revelation (the "fear of the Lord" instead of the Greek *hubris* of reason deemed divine).[152] The inspired sages know of both their *positive* and their *critical* task: this is the probable meaning of the metaphors of Ecclesiastes 12:11: the words of the wise, their collected sayings, are like *stakes* to fix the nomads' tents, to give enduring stability *maśm^e^rôt,* and *goads* to stimulate, to awaken from dogmatic slumbers *dorbonôt.*[153] This duality may correspond to that of Proverbs, on the one hand, and Job and Ecclesiastes on the other. Wisdom is not afraid to welcome non-Israelite contributions (it would be difficult to deny that Prov. 22:17–23:11 borrows from the Egyptian Wisdom of Amenemope),[154] but it is by no means a "foreign body" in the religion of YHWH. It truly follows from its "principle" *rē'šît:* the fear of the Lord.[155]

If such a sketch of wisdom's physiognomy be accepted, is it possible to spot specific features of its inspiration? Paul Beauchamp offers interesting insights on the difference between Law, Prophets, and Wisdom: the Law discloses what is true foundationally, the *archē* (a "beginning" that is first logically and ontologically); the Prophets what is true *now;* the Wise, what is true *always.*[156] However, the relevance for the form of inspiration is not obvious. Two main considerations

150. The advantages of wisdom are based on its creational role (Prov. 3:19-20).

151. It is probably significant that the root *ḥšb,* used for thinking and counting, is found three times in the passage (Eccles. 7:23-29) together with one instance of "counting" (7:28). The LXX translates the two slightly different words in vv. 27b and 29b by the same Greek word, *logismos.*

152. Kuyper highlights both traits (*Encyclopaedie,* 2:473-75).

153. Already the interpretation of Christian D. Ginsburg, *Songs of Songs and Cohelet* (1857; repr., Library of Biblical Studies; New York: Ktav, 1970), 474.

154. This trait is the key one for Paul Ricoeur (who is openly indebted to Paul Beauchamp), "L'Enchevêtrement de la voix et de l'écrit dans le discours biblique," in *Lectures 3: Aux frontières de la philosophie,* 321: "Through Wisdom, the singularity of Israel communicates with the universality of cultures."

155. I simply recall William F. Albright's strong statement: "While Proverbs may contain a very high proportion of matter originating outside Israel, it is saturated with Israelite theism and morality," in "Some Canaanite-Phoenician Sources of Hebrew Wisdom," in *Wisdom in Israel and in the Ancient Near East,* VTS 3 (Leiden: Brill, 1955), 13.

156. Paul Beauchamp, "L'analyse structurale et l'exégèse," in *Congress Volume Uppsala 1971,* VTS 22 (Leiden: Brill, 1971), 126-27.

may prove helpful: one based on the manner of the sages' work, the other on remarkable indications of Wisdom's mission.

The wise observe, examine, assess, ruminate; they raise questions; they scrutinize paradoxes; they seek to express their thoughts adequately, accurately, effectively, and pleasantly (Eccles. 12:9-10). In all this, they seem to stand, or sit, at a distance. Compared to the prophets, they do not directly transmit or "relay" the divine Word, but rather they "digest" its implications and explore how reality may be viewed in the light of that Word. They are receptors, hearers, before they are speakers. In this, their human faculties function in a more "autonomous" fashion, and at the same time, the fact that they do so under divine inspiration signifies that this relative autonomy depends radically on God: God is the Lord of hearing — and so demonstrates both how humans "desperately" need his grace (they need his grace just to hear) and how his pleasure is to *promote* a human appropriation of his gifts, personal, reflective, imaginative, critical.[157] The sages are not first heralds, but *pupils* of the Lord and his apprentices. Their aim as teachers is to *raise* others to higher levels. Sapiential inspiration raises men and women to the competence of observers and students who, sitting nearby, can appreciate what their Master is doing and draw the right consequences.

And wisdom, which the Lord's pupils acquire, is first of all his Wisdom, the Principle (*rēʾšît*) of his ways and the Firstborn of all creation, whom he begat in himself before the foundation of the world (Prov. 8:22-25). The thought is inevitable: the link between God and humankind is Wisdom! And the thought shines through the prosopopeia of Wisdom in Proverbs 8:22-31. As Paul Beauchamp discovered, the first word is YHWH, the Lord, the last *bᵉnê ʾādām,* "sons of Adam") and right in the middle of the poem (v. 27a), the "I" of Wisdom (*ʾănî*)! The last verses repeat the rare word "delight" (*šaʿăšuʿîm*). Wisdom was YHWH's delight, and the children of Adam were *her* delight. Wisdom clearly functions as *mediatrix,* and on the mode of delight. In other words, Wisdom institutes the bond of *fellowship* between God and his pupils. The human creature is enabled "to think God's thoughts after him," to grow and flourish as the earthly "image of God."

Along both lines, the specific trait of sapiential inspiration appears to be a blossoming of the human spirit. Even its location by the side or nearby provides the opportunity to highlight the fulfillment of humanity under inspiration — while the bond of dependence on God the Master becomes even more intrinsic to this fulfillment. The international openness of wisdom may be interpreted in that light: human nature as such is being promoted and freed from its self-destructive foolishness, while, as Kuyper stressed, his wayward children restored and purified recover Adam's original wisdom.[158]

157. The frequent uses of Hebrew *ḥokmâ* ("wisdom"; think of Bezalel) emphasize craft, expertise, and artistic mastery.

158. Kuyper, *Encyclopaedie,* 2:473-74.

A subcategory may be mentioned, which cannot be dealt with here: that of the *seers,* the apocalyptic writers. It is rather widely recognized that their genre is a kind of hybrid of prophecy and wisdom. Their object was God's design in history, as it was with the prophets, but within the larger, international, cosmic horizon of the wise and in their reflective mood. We may presume that the form of their inspiration combined prophetic and sapiential traits.

The Singers

The book of Psalms is so important that Bible societies often print as one small volume the New Testament *together with the Psalms.* Luke 24:44 uses its name for the whole third part of the Hebrew canon, the Writings. Is it possible to characterize the inspiration of the composers of the psalms and of kindred pieces of poetry elsewhere in Scripture? They may be called, more or less approximately, the "singers" or "worship leaders" or "praying poets," with David as the archetypal figure.[159] The New Testament, as we saw, underscores the prophetic import of the psalms, but this does not preclude our inquiring about specific features of psalmic or hymnic inspiration.

In his zeal for anthropological connections, Kuyper labels the form "lyrical inspiration" and stresses above all the expression of *feeling.*[160] Its smacks a little too much of ready-made categories, though we may indeed maintain that this form of inspiration attunes the worshiper's emotions and affections to God's own compassion and rejoicing. The chief paradox of the psalmic genre is that in most psalms, God is being addressed — the human speaker or writer says "I" and he speaks or sings *to* God. How can words said to God be also God's words to his people?

The usual answer is that God offers us models for our praise and our prayer. John Goldingay explains, "The way scripture itself most systematically goes about teaching people about praise and prayer is by offering models of praise and prayer, by praising God and by praying."[161] He testifies, "I have attempted to do this by taking a psalm section by section and talking to God out of my own experience in the light of the psalm, acknowledging to God the ways the psalmist's experience and mine resonate. . . ."[162] On the so-called "imprecatory" or "vindicatory" psalms — a notorious difficulty — Goldingay beautifully comments, "The Psalms' prayers for judgment on the wicked are prayers for God's justice to be at work in the world, and the cross is God's 'Yes' to the prayer for wickedness to be

159. However we interpret the superscription *lᵉdāwid* in individual cases.

160. Kuyper, *Encyclopaedie,* 2:469-72.

161. Goldingay, *Models for Interpretation of Scripture,* 263.

162. Goldingay, *Models for Interpretation of Scripture,* 264.

punished."[163] Schökel also comments, "Prayer written under the motion of the Holy Spirit is the word of God teaching us to pray."[164] This is literally true of the so-called "Lord's prayer" *(Pater noster),* and it may be accepted generally for the prayers of the Bible, though the teaching is implicit. We may add that "hearing" already implies some germinal "responding": if God is the Lord of our hearing, the communication of his word also embraces a human response.

What does this mean for the position and stance of the composer of psalms and other prayers? It indeed heightens the responsibility of the human speaker or writer! Not so much a "mouth," but rather a face turned toward the face of God: a face-to-face fellowship! The inspired composer who prays is no longer first a herald, nor a witness, nor even a pupil. What, then? I can think only of one title: a *child,* a son or a daughter — a child who, in the fear of God, is free to speak to the Father, and even sometimes to cry, "Awake, O Lord!" and even sometimes to murmur, "Abba! Dear Father." And this cannot be separated from the Christological dimension of all biblical inspiration.

The Spirit of Christ, by whom the inspired psalmists were borne along, helped them in their praying (Rom. 8:26a), but the testimony of Scripture goes even further: God the Holy Spirit *prays with them;* God prays to God (Rom. 8:26b-27). Revelation 22:17 confirms that the Spirit comes on our side: the Spirit and the Bride pray the same prayer together. This might be the secret of the paradox: words addressed to God are words of God; they are of the Spirit, *theopneustoi.*

The enrichment of the "prophetic model" that our consideration of other inspirational genres has provided, with the "apostolic model" gaining primacy, brings out the inadequacy of comparing the human writers to mere "pens." They are responsible heralds, ambassadors, and witnesses, well-trained pupils of God, and his sons and daughters. Who are the "authors"? Schökel points to the ambiguity of the term: in Greek, one can distinguish between *syngrapheus* and *archēgos;* in German, between *Verfasser* and *Urheber;* in English, between "writer" and "originator."[165] Of God inspiring, we cannot say that he is the author in the sense of writer, *Verfasser.* This belongs to the human inspired writers (traditionally called *scriptores, hagiographi*). Robert P. Gordon's preference for "general editor" or "series editor" to describe God's role falls woefully below the mark.[166] Schökel offers the inadequate suggestion that God's depiction of the biblical characters compares to Shakespeare's or Cervantes' creation of characters.[167] God is indeed

163. Goldingay, *Models for Interpretation of Scripture,* 354. This elicits some hope that Goldingay will retreat from his rejection of penal substitution.

164. Schökel, *The Inspired Word,* 145.

165. Schökel, *The Inspired Word,* 80.

166. Robert P. Gordon, "A Warranted Version of Historical Biblical Criticism? A Response to Alvin Plantinga," in Bartholomew et al., eds., *Behind the Text,* 84.

167. Schökel, *The Inspired Word,* 73-77. The comparison ignores the role of the *offices* of prophet, apostle, teacher (Schökel does not take them enough into account).

the author in the sense of originator *and* fully efficient guide, overseer, signatory. The speech-act of the text should be counted as unreservedly his, and he is himself present in his word. Only he speaks through a variety of genres, raising men and women in diverse positions and who adopt various stances, in more or less direct and indirect ways,[168] but always making them more fully human than they would be apart from inspiration. The Holy Ghost is no "ghost writer."

A Few Theological Reflections: Underlying Mysteries

Mysteries lie under the biblical data we have gathered.

Absolute Monotheism

The logic of the classical doctrine of Scripture, with the paradigmatic role the prophetic office is called to play, answers to the proclamation of biblical monotheism. Let the earth keep silent before the Sovereign Lord of the Universe: he speaks, and every creature trembles; he speaks, and nothing else can count — the thing is decided, *gegraptai.*

Biblical, that is also radical, monotheism, implies that creatures are totally open to his action. No metaphysical principle can check his intervention; no obstacle is in the way of him from whom, through whom, and for whom are all things. Catholic scholars speak of the creature's *potentia oboedentialis.* Hence, he can raise, guide, assist, and even control (an ugly word today!) his human instruments without violating their integrity. On the contrary, he fulfills their humanity.

This monotheism honors a God who, to borrow a jewel phrase from Abbé Jules Monchanin, is "wholly other — than another."[169] Mere otherness would entail a form of dualism, with the suicidal logic "the more to God, the less to man," but the One God is wholly other than another. The concept of *double* agency or, better, authorship, is itself valid only as an approximation: counting God and creature as "two" is problematic inasmuch as God transcends all categories in which he could be "counted." One could add that the Infinite, who sounds at first dualistically opposed to the Finite, actually embraces the Finite (otherwise, it would be limited!), but such a speculation, from which Scripture chastely refrains, is fraught with dangers. It is wiser to stick soberly to the *concrete* Creator/creature pattern.

168. I hesitate to say with the mighty Roman Catholic dogmatician Christian Pesch that God speaks to us "immediately" *(immediate),* as quoted by Schökel, *The Inspired Word,* 41 (with n. 20). Is not speaking a mediation?

169. Quoted (no reference) by Henri de Lubac, *Athéisme et sens de l'homme: Une double requête de* Gaudium et Spes, Foi vivante 67 (Paris: Cerf, 1968), 69 n. 114.

Unique Son and Incarnate

The advantages of the "apostolic model" of biblical inspiration draw attention to the centrality of the Incarnation for the divine speaking in history. Since the Fall, God communicates with fallen humankind on the basis of the Son's incarnation — through instruments who "extend" his human role. This incarnation itself, as orthodox theologians perceived, is grounded in God's eternal being on the distinction between God and his Word and Son: God *monogenēs* is the *alter ego* of the Father, the perfect expression of God in himself, and thus the principle of all revelation (John 1:18).[170] His incarnation manifests his *unique* (exclusively divine) ability to become what he was not without ceasing to be what he was, or rather who he is eternally. His union with created being in *one* person, the wonder of wonders, making closer the bond of creation, is *the closer than which none can be conceived* (to paraphrase St. Anselm). In the economy of redemptive grace, since the apostles and prophets are to be seen as joined to his humanity, the hypostatic union is the precise foundation of the union of God and human speakers or writers in the same speech-act.

Since the Unique Son (*unigenitus,* "only begotten," was the traditional rendering; it keeps the flavor of traditional faith) became a man, the consistency of human reality under divine inspiration is established beyond all question. In him human speech reaches its ordained end: mediating truth and life.

The Fellowship of the Holy Spirit

Fellowship through participation in wisdom, in God's own Wisdom, and intimate association of the Spirit's prayer with ours are themes that direct our thoughts toward the second divine "mission," the mission of the Holy Spirit. Since he is the Spirit of Christ, the fellowship he creates is none other than the union with Christ which we just recalled. The Son and the Spirit are, with the Father, one God, sharing the totality of the divine essence which exists only once — this must be maintained at all costs against the contemporary seduction of tritheistic schemes.[171] It follows that, in many respects, the second mission is one with

170. Attempting maximum precision: the Son and Logos as such is, in the Godhead, the ground of all revelation. He is so *asarkos,* not-yet-incarnate, from all eternity and, in the creational covenant, for the benefit of humankind before Adam's disobedience (as such the principle, *rē'šît, archē,* of creation, Prov. 8:22; Rev. 3:14; and the wisdom-image of God, according to the exegesis I find most convincing, in Col. 1:15, after Wisd. 7:26). He is *ensarkos,* incarnate, or *incarnandus* (by anticipation of his future incarnation) after the Fall inasmuch as revelation is then granted for the sake of redemption.

171. See my article, "La Trinité, une communauté an-archique?" *Théologie Evangélique* 1, no. 2 (2002): 3-20.

the first. The Spirit is the Breath in which the Word is uttered — eternally, and in God's historical communication: the Word in Person is conceived of Mary's flesh through the creative agency of the Holy Spirit, and the words of God are produced and preserved as God-breathed Scripture.

The second mission, however, is distinct, and it sheds light on the culmination of God's grace to humankind. In the psalmists' form of inspiration especially, it becomes clear that men and women are introduced into the very life of the Trinity. God prays to God, and human prayers go with that of the Spirit. It is through the ministry of the Spirit that the truth becomes conspicuous: God is wholly other than another. Brothers and sisters of the Word who became flesh share, through his Spirit, in Trinitarian life.

Though the reference to the Trinity should not be used as a key to unlock all doors, as a magical formula to solve all problems, theological reflection on the "double authorship" inspiration of Scripture leads us to discern that *Trinitarian* monotheism is the only radical, consistent monotheism. Since Unitarian monotheism locates the principle of plurality, the Multiple, *outside* of deity, it logically slides into dualism if it affirms the reality of multiplicity, or into monism/pantheism if it denies it. Trinitarian monotheism confesses both the fullness of God's being and the distinction of Creator and creature. This foundation is required for fully affirming the being of creatures, above all of the Image-creature made for fellowship with the Father of spirits, and for its gracious promotion or glorification. The One God — Father, Son/Word, and Holy Spirit — is able to "breathe out" the discourse of human authors as his own.

EIGHTEEN

Myth, History, and the Bible

Bruce K. Waltke

This chapter has four goals:

1. Define "myth" cogently for the theologian. We argue that myth is a story informed by pantheism and magic. Biblical narrative as literature could be labeled *historio-poesis* but not *mytho-poesis.*

2. Determine whether Israel's early religion evolved out of Canaanite myth or history.[1] It claims the latter, and we agree: Israel's prophetic faith is grounded in her exodus from Egypt. The Canaanite textual and artifactual evidence exists because Israel apostatized.

3. Decide the best explanation for the similarities between the stories in Genesis 1–11 and Mesopotamian myths. We suggest that Israel's narrator of the flood account retained a pure memory of this historical event and that the narrator of the cosmogony cast historical events in the form of a Mesopotamian cosmogony.

4. Decide the best explanation for the references to Canaanite myths in Hebrew poetry. We argue that Israel's poets borrowed Canaanite imagery but not theology.

Definition of Myth

Deciding an Accredited Method

An accredited method of defining a word includes three considerations:

1. In this chapter "Israel" refers to Abraham's offspring and the nation from his lineage that Moses founded. Occasionally, we distinguish between "nominal Israel" and "true Israel." The former refers to the nation bound together by their common blood and historical memory, but lacking Abraham's faith in the God who covenanted with Abraham to give him offspring that would be as numerous as the stars in the heavens, bless the earth, and inherit the land God swore to give him. "True Israel" refers more narrowly to those within Israel who have Abraham's faith and demonstrate that faith by keeping the covenant that God mediated with Israel through Moses.

1. *usus loquendi* ("use in speaking");
2. its relation to homologous words;
3. its denotation (an actual, primary, and specific meaning) and connotation (a suggested or implied additional meaning).

Usus Loquendi

Humpty Dumpty was wrong when he said in rather a scornful tone to Alice, "When I use a word . . . it means just what I choose it to mean — neither more nor less." If everyone defines terms according to their whim, meaningful conversation breaks down, confusion reigns, and prejudices alienate. Yet during the past century this has been the fate of the term "myth." Its *usus loquendi* has become a briar patch of polysemy. Michael Fishbane, professor of Jewish studies at the University of Chicago's Divinity School, complains, "Myth is that most elusive of cultural forms — forever avoiding the constraints of definition and analysis."[2] Nevertheless, "myth" is commonly used, and theologians would be wise to pin down a meaning to facilitate cogent discourse and not mislead the church.

A Theologian's Taxonomy

The method proposed here for pinning down the meaning of myth is similar to the Linnaean taxonomic hierarchy for biology.[3] We categorize the current uses of myth into an ordered hierarchical taxonomy by homologies and by a system of binomen to determine the most fitting and useful category of the term for theology.[4] Our homology should be broad enough to include the salient characteristics of myth and narrow enough to exclude it from a higher homology.

The field of biology is divided into several kingdoms: Kingdom Bacteria, Kingdom Plantae, and Kingdom Animalia. Those kingdoms are subdivided. Kingdom Anamalia is divided into about thirty-five phyla, including Phylum Chordata. Phylum Chordata includes Classes Osteichthyes (bony fish) and Mammalia (mammals). Within Class Mammalia are Order Primates (which includes *Homo sapiens* — humans) and Order Artiodactyla (which includes *Ovis aries* — domestic sheep). "Mammal" is too narrow a category to be used in place of Phylum

2. Michael Fishbane, *Biblical Myth and Rabbinic Mythmaking* (Oxford: Oxford University Press, 2003), 1.

3. Taxonomy is that branch of science focused on the classification of organisms into an ordered system. Swedish botanist and zoologist Carolus Linnaeus published *Systema Naturae per regna tria naturae, secundum classes, ordines differentiis, synonymus, locis* in 1735. The tenth revised edition (1758) introduced a binomial system for identifying animal species.

4. The method is loosely analogous to Aristotle's *Categories*.

Chordata since it excludes other animals with backbones such as the megamouth shark and parson's chameleon. On the other hand, Phylum Chordata is too broad a category to replace Class Osteichthyes, since the distinguishing feature of having a backbone is not limited only to bony fish. Thus, for a biological term to be helpful to a zoologist or botanist, a term must be neither too narrow nor broad.

Classification by a hierarchical taxonomy of homologies is relative to a discipline. Moreover, taxonomies may overlap. On the one hand, a theologian's taxonomy to define myth may place it under Kingdom: "God" or Kingdom: "Matter."

- Kingdom: "Matter" could include Phylum: "Origin of Matter" and Phylum: "Composition of Matter."
- Phylum: "Origin of Matter" could include Class: "Natural Origin" and Class: "Supernatural Origin."
- Class: "Supernatural Origin" could include Order: "Tradition" and Order: "Revelation."
- Order: "Tradition" could include Family "Archaic Society" and Family: "Ancient Near Eastern."
- Family: "Ancient Near Eastern" could include Genus: "Creation by *Chaoskampf* [see below] and Genus: "Creation by Word."
- Genus: *Chaoskampf* could include Specie: "Sumerian" and Specie "Canaanite."
- Order: "Revelation" could include Family: "Biblical Cosmogony" and Family: "Quranic Cosmogony."
- Family: "Biblical Cosmogony" could include Genus: *Chaoskampf* and Genus: "Word."
- Genus: *Chaoskampf* could include Specie: "Psalm 74" and Specie: "Job 38–41."
- Genus: "Word" could include Specie: "Genesis 1:1–2:3," Specie: "Psalm 104," and Specie: "John 1."

On the other hand:

- Kingdom: "God" could include Phylum: "Divine Nature" and Phylum: "Divine Activity."
- Phylum: "Divine Activity" could include Class: "Primordial Acts" (i.e., cosmogony) and Class: "Historical Acts."
- Class "Cosmogony" could include Order: "Tradition" and Order: "Revelation."
- The lower taxonomies would be the same as starting with Kingdom: "Matter."

In short, the issue is to critically appraise definitions and/or uses of myth to determine if they are defined and/or used too high in the taxonomic hierarchy and so miss important differences and/or too low and so minimize important similarities. I have tried to critically evaluate every current use of myth according to this proposed paradigm to determine the best denotation of myth.[5]

To categorize myth too specifically may not be useful. Narrowing "lamb" into Specie: "Blemished" and Specie: "Unblemished" may be useful to a child entering her pet lamb into a state fair but not for a child who just wants a pet. Narrowing Ancient Near Eastern cosmogonies into species of Sumerian, Akkadian, and Canaanite does not well serve the field of theology because it may distract from their salient homology and may be cumbersome for the humanities generally.

To use a higher order for a lower order may be misleading as well as confounding. If someone says of a mother, "she sent her animal to school," the Phylum: "animal" will be interpreted as an insult to the mother and/or her child. When Mary brought her lamb to school, it made the children laugh and play; a lamb cannot learn to read and write or calculate with numerals. The essence of being human is so different from an animal that in common usage we do not refer to humans as animals or mammals.

Denotation and Connotation

The definition of myth commonly both *denotes* phenomenal characteristics and *connotes* an evaluative judgment. The Oxford English Dictionary *(OED)* defines myth as "a purely fictitious narrative usually involving supernatural persons, actions, or events and embodying some popular idea concerning natural and historical phenomena."[6] "Narrative usually involving supernatural persons" denotes a phenomenon; "purely fictitious narrative" connotes an evaluation. In defining myth, we distinguish between the phenomenal and the evaluative.[7]

Denotation

In seeking the best denotation of myth let us slot and appraise current uses of myth into the suggested paradigm.

5. Regrettably, I learned of Kevin Vanhoozer's *Remythologizing Theology,* Cambridge Studies in Christian Doctrine (Cambridge: Cambridge University Press, 2010) too late to use it in this essay.

6. *Oxford English Dictionary* (Oxford: Clarendon, 1961), 6:818, s.v. "myth." Since the brothers Jacob Grimm (1785-1863) and Wilhelm Grimm (1786-1859) labeled a myth as a story about the gods (plural), "Their collection of myths was in the service of the increasingly regnant model that humanity's earliest literary productions began as myths" (Robert A. Oden Jr., *ABD,* 4:956, s.v. "Myth in the OT"). The alleged monotheism of Akhenaten (i.e., "the effective spirit of Aten," the solar disk, in contrast to Amun-Re, the sun), nevertheless, was a pantheistic and naturalistic religion.

7. Some define myth as denoting a cultural function and so avoid an evaluative connotation. See p. 547 below.

Worldly Imagery for the Otherworld

Rudolf Bultmann, late professor of New Testament at the University of Marburg, defines mythology as "the use of imagery to express the otherworldly in terms of this world and the divine in terms of human life, the other side to this side."[8] His definition restricts myth to the phenomenon "the otherworldly." In the proposed taxonomy, his definition belongs to Kingdom: "God" because — like *OED* — he categorizes all references to the divine realm as myth. This classification is not best for the theologian for three reasons: (1) it assumes without warrant that reason's facts are the only ontological reality; (2) it obscures essential differences in the lower homologies of the theologian's taxonomy of terms; (3) "to express the otherworldly in terms of this world" is banal, for the otherworldly, which is not experienced by the five human senses, must be expressed through analogy: by anthropomorphisms and anthropopathisms.

Parenthetically, Bultmann also confuses mythological and phenomenological language. He illustrates his understanding of myth by the worldview of the cosmos in biblical times as a "three-decker universe" — a flat earth canopied by an ocean and undergirded by water that breaks out from below.[9] Harry M. Buck, associate professor of Bible and religion at Wilson College, rightly comments, "Bultmann's well-known three story universe accompanied by divine intervention is not, strictly speaking, a mythology; it is a *Weltanschauung*."[10] The biblical writers' worldview of a three-tiered vision of the cosmos derives from observation, not solely from tradition and/or imagination. Modern man still invokes a vision of the stars as in the sky, of the sun as rising and setting, and the sky as blue. From a scientific perspective, this phenomenological language is incorrect, but from the perspective of common human experience, it is accurate. Biblical writers lived in a pre-scientific age and necessarily employed phenomenal language, just as they necessarily represented spiritual truth through the symbols of the Greek, Aramaic, and Hebrew languages. God accommodates his revelation to human constructs that are obtained through the senses and through processes involved in the sociology of knowledge.[11] There is no other way to communicate.

Accordingly, the Gospel writers, as interpreted by the Apostles' Creed, in their pre-Copernican world represent Jesus Christ as descending from heaven to earth, his death as his descent into Hades,[12] and his return to the Father as

8. Rudolf Bultmann, "New Testament and Mythology," in *Kerygma and Myth: A Theological Debate,* ed. Hans Werner Bartsche, trans. Reginald H. Fuller (London: SPCK, 1953), 10 n. 2.

9. Bultmann, "New Testament and Mythology," 1.

10. Harry M. Buck Jr., "From History to Myth: A Comparative Study," *JBR* 29 (1961): 219.

11. Cf. Peter L. Berger and Thomas Luckmann, *The Social Construction of Reality: A Treatise in the Sociology of Knowledge* (Garden City, NY: Anchor, 1966). See the essay by Glenn Sunshine in this volume, chapter 8.

12. We need not debate here whether the creedal statement is well founded exegetically.

his ascent to heaven. Their common human experience and their sociological conditioning give rise to these spatial metaphors.

Action of Divine Beings in Primordial Times

Myth, according to Fishbane, refers "to (sacred and authoritative) actions of the deeds and personalities of the gods and heroes during the formative events of primordial times, or during the subsequent historical interventions or actions of these figures which are constitutive for the founding a given culture and its rituals."[13] Fishbane's definition groups together Kingdom: God and Kingdom: Mankind (heroes) and Order: "Primordial Activity" and Order: "Historical Activity." For convenience, let us simplify his use of myth in the proposed taxonomy as follows:

- Kingdom: God/Heroes
- Phylum: "Supernatural"
- Class: "Divine Activity"
- Order: "Primordial, formative events"

This precision is better than Bultmann's imprecision, but his definition still obscures distinctions between Genus: Pagan Cosmogony and Genus: Biblical Cosmogony. Lumping together these diverse cosmogonies gives the biblical theologian indigestion.

Pantheism and Magic

James Barr (1924-2006), formerly professor of Hebrew at Oxford, assumes *OED*'s definition of myth but focuses on myths in the world of the Old Testament. Barr also thinks that Bultmann's definition is inadequate and misleading. He remedies Bultmann's use of myth in three ways:[14]

1. Myth strives for an integrated worldview: "Its goal is a totality of what is significant to man's needs, material, intellectual and religious." Myth "moulds and controls the minds of men and in another way equally is expressing them or being molded by them."
2. Myth is not a symbolic metaphor but "a direct expression of its subject mat-

13. Fishbane, *Biblical Myth,* 11.

14. James Barr, "Meaning of Mythology in Relation to the Old Testament," *VT* 9, no. 1 (1959): 3-6.

ter" (i.e., pantheism).[15] In Canaanite religion Baal is the thunderstorm; Baal does not represent it.

3. Myth, outside of the Bible, always "maintains a secret correspondence or hidden harmony of some kind between gods and man, god and nature, man and nature, the normative primeval and the actual present." This secret correspondence involves both the recitation of the myth and rituals that accompany it as an "essential instrument for the maintenance of actual human life in the world [i.e., magic]."[16] In contrast to pagan myths, Israel's faith is based on *historia* (factual events).

In short, Barr regards Bultmann's view of myth as misleading because it fails to distinguish "Israel's special position among the mythological cultures which surrounded it."[17]

Barr rightly notes that true Israelite thought is a totality, and we should add that, ironically, its totality — its center — repudiates the other two aspects of myth: pantheism and magic. Barr's equation of the essence of myth outside of Israel's worldview with pantheism and magic finds almost universal support among comparative religionists. So Barr shows the error of lumping biblical cosmogony and Ancient Near Eastern cosmogony into the same homology. Ancient Near Eastern cosmogony identifies the gods with nature, manipulates them through mimetic rituals, and is indifferent to *historia.* Israel's religion represents *I AM* as transcendent, conditions prosperity on ethics, and as one who reveals himself in word and pertains to *historia.*

John Oswalt, research professor of Old Testament at Wesley Biblical Seminary, without citing Barr, agrees with Barr's distinctions of Ancient Near Eastern cosmogony ("myth") and the biblical cosmogony. He unites the ideas of pantheism and magic with the abstraction of "continuity," namely, "the idea that all things that exist are part of each other. There are no fundamental distinctions between the three realms: humanity, nature, and the divine."[18] His abstraction has explanatory power, but is not an explicit phenomenal characteristic in the Ancient Near Eastern cosmogonies.

Barr's denotation of myth is best because it is broad enough to cover the Class: "Supernatural Origins" and narrow enough to distinguish between Genus:

15. Barr refers to this as "identity" (i.e., the identity of a god with a phenomenon of nature/matter).

16. Contra Lawrence Toombs, "The Formation of Myth Patterns in the Old Testament," *JBR* 29, no. 2 (1961): 109, who posits that through the cult the human community integrates itself with the world order; it does not bring about the repetition of a cycle that might otherwise not occur. We need not decide that issue here.

17. Barr, "Meaning of Mythology," 7.

18. John N. Oswalt, *Bible among Myths: Unique Revelation or Just Ancient Literature?* (Grand Rapids: Zondervan, 2009), 48.

Ancient Near Eastern Cosmogony (pantheism, magic, and *a-historia*) and Genus: Biblical Cosmogony (sovereign transcendence, ethics, and *historia*).

Chaoskampf

Chaoskampf is a species of Genus: Ancient Near Eastern Myths. The word is German for theomachy, a cosmogonic battle myth. Mary Wakeman, in her Brandeis University Ph.D. dissertation (1969), compares and analyzes twelve theomachies spanning Sumer, India, Anatolia, Mesopotamia, Greece, and Canaan — a culture that stretched from Gaza in the south to Ugarit in the north in the Late Bronze Age (ca. 1300-1100 B.C.E.).[19] For example, albeit simplified, in Sumer, Ninurta (god of release) defeats Asag (god of restraint); in India, Indra (release) vanquishes Vritra (restraint); and in Mesopotamia, Marduk (release) pierces Tiamat (restraint). In each of these, the defeat of chaos enables the victorious god to establish the cosmos (regulation). Wakeman concludes that in spite of their great variety, the theomachies of these diverse civilizations are about the same thing. Regardless of the particulars, she observes, their crucial action consists of three parts:

1. A repressive monster, often a serpent, restrains the earth mound and contains within itself the potential existence of all things.
2. A heroic god, born out of the restraining monster, vanquishes the monster and so releases from her the forces essential for life.
3. The hero god brings the forces under his control and organizes them into a cosmos.

With respect to *Chaoskampf*, the species of biblical cosmogonies present two views of creation. On the one hand, the biblical cosmogonies of Genesis 1:1–2:3; Proverbs 8:22-31; and Psalm 104:6-9 represent God as sovereignly controlling the dreaded sea, not as a *Chaoskampf*. In this cosmogony there is no hint that the primordial abyss and surd (i.e., what is senseless from the human viewpoint) resist his *rûaḥ* ("wind" or "spirit") and his word. In the cosmogony of Genesis 2:4–3:24, the struggle is between God's ethical will and the human insubordinate self-will, a struggle whereby God produces a social system of ethics and spiritual virtue. On the other hand, some biblical poets present God as battling the sea *in illo tempore* and the sea's surviving after the creation and the flood as hostile to God and a persistent threat to the cosmos. We argue in the last section of this essay that the biblical poets borrowed this imagery to glorify God.

19. Mary K. Wakeman, *God's Battle with the Monster: A Study in Biblical Imagery* (Leiden: E. J. Brill, 1973). We need not digress to discuss the connection of *Chaoskampf* with royal ideology.

A-historia

Barr contrasts the mythological mindset based almost exclusively on nature with the historical consciousness of the biblical writers: "It is thus perhaps possible to say that history in the Israelite mind was the greatest factor in enforcing the differences from the mythological environment."[20] George Ernest Wright contends that the basis of true Israel's faith was God's acts in history, not the action of the gods in nature: "The basis of the [biblical] literature was history, not nature," he writes, "because the God of Israel was first of all the Lord of history who used nature to accomplish his purpose in history."[21] Wright goes too far when he says that divine action in history is unique to Israel. Bertil Albrektson documents many instances in Ancient Near Eastern literature where a god acts in behalf of a client.[22] J. J. M. Roberts adds that Albrektson does not go far enough, documenting extended Ancient Near Eastern historiographies, including some that endeavor to grasp the theological significance of the past.[23]

Nevertheless, only the biblical writers present God as acting according to a consistent trajectory of salvation history *(Heilsgeschichte)* from the creation to the eschaton. That history is divided into segments by God's initiating covenants with Israel, and it climaxes in his new covenant that entails the life, death, and resurrection of Jesus Christ. Israel's comprehensive history is unique.

Eternal Return to the Primordial State

In "traditional religions," myth is commonly tied to "ritual" so that the two together, the verbal and the dramatic action, are central components of religious practice.[24] Mircea Eliade, in addition to promoting a symbolic meaning of myth (see below),[25] also promoted the influential theory of the Eternal Return.[26] This

20. Barr, "Meaning of Mythology," 8.

21. G. Ernest Wright, *The Old Testament against Its Environment* (London: SCM, 1950), 28. I disagree with Wright's view of revelation as history.

22. Bertil Albrektson, *History and the Gods* (Lund: Gleerup, 1967). For a critique of Albrektson, see W. G. Lambert's review in *Orientalia* 39 (1970): 170-77; "Destiny and Divine Intervention in Babylon and Israel," *OTS* 17 (1972): 65-72.

23. J. J. M. Roberts, "Myth Versus History," *CBQ* 38 (1976): 1-13.

24. I understand Eliade means by "traditional religions" those whose worldview is based on inherited traditions.

25. Robert Luyster, assistant professor of philosophy and religion at the University of Connecticut, notes that Eliade recognizes in myth "the phenomena of nature are transformed by the psyche in 'an autonomous act of creation' into symbols of the power and holiness they reveal to the beholder" ("The Study of Myth: Two Approaches," *JBR* 34, no. 3 [1966]: 235).

26. Mircea Eliade, *The Myth of the Eternal Return: or, Cosmos and History,* trans. Willard R. Trask (New York: Bollingen, 1954); *Patterns in Comparative Religion,* trans. Rosemary Sheed

theory holds that myths and rituals, though not necessarily coextensive, enable the client to participate in primordial events.

Eliade defines myth as follows: "[M]yth relates the *gesta* of supernatural Beings and manifestation of their sacred powers and so becomes the exemplary model for all significant human activities."[27] Myths in traditional societies are etiologies that always relate to creation. Since the cosmos is the masterpiece of the gods, the myths function as "exemplary models for all human rites and all significant human activities — diet or marriage, work or education, art or wisdom." As modern man considers himself to be constituted by history — "Man is explicable by nothing less than all his history" (Ralph Waldo Emerson) — the man of traditional societies regards himself as the direct result of primordial events recounted in the myth. Through the recitation of the handed-down myth and the performance of the ritual, the priest, who was often a king, magically manipulates something, a force of nature, to repeat itself according to the original creative event.[28]

Turning to Ancient Near Eastern cosmogonies (Egypt, Mesopotamia, and "Jews"), Eliade finds essential similarity with archaic societies: both feature the same eternal return.[29] He focuses on the Mesopotamia *Akitu* festival in which the renewal/beginning is connected organically with the end, the chaos that preceded it. According to Eliade, the religion of early Israel (before 850 B.C.E.) shared the characteristic of the Eternal Return with the Ancient Near Eastern cosmogonies. "One of the chief ideas of the [early] Jews [i.e., Israel] was the enthronement of Yahweh as king of the world, the symbolic representation of His victory over His enemies, both the forces of chaos and the historical enemies of Israel."[30] Eliade's inclusion of early Israel in this mythic thinking is based on the theory of the Myth and Ritual School and in particular on Mowinckel's theory of an Israelite Enthronement Festival.

Robert Oden rightly criticizes the Myth and Ritual School: "The very pe-

---

(New York: Sheed & Ward, 1958). Note Eliade's effect on how Brevard S. Childs defines myth in his influential study *Myth and Reality in the Old Testament* (London: SCM, 1960): "In the drama of the cult an actualization of the original cosmic events takes place in which that which once occurred is again realized *hic et nunc*" (19).

27. Mircea Eliade, *Myth and Reality,* trans. Willard R. Trask, World Perspectives 31 (New York: Harper & Row, 1963), 6.

28. Eliade, *Myth and Reality,* 8-11.

29. For handy summaries of cosmogonic myths in the Ancient Near East, see H. Cazelles, "Mythe et l'A.T.," in *Dictionnaire de la Bible,* Supplement 6 (Paris: Letouzey & Ané, 1960), 246-61; T. H. Gaster, "Myth, Mythology," in *Interpreter's Dictionary of the Bible,* ed. George A. Buttrick (New York: Abingdon, 1962), 3:481-87; Jack Finegan, *Myth and Mystery: An Introduction to the Pagan Religions of the Biblical World* (Grand Rapids: Baker, 1989).

30. Sigmund Mowinckel, *He That Cometh,* trans. G. W. Anderson (New York: Abingdon, 1956), 26; cited by Eliade, *Myth and Reality,* 48.

riod in which scholars such as Pedersen, Mowinckel, Hooke and Gaster were writing also saw the rise of an eventually devastating tide of criticism directed against the entire myth-ritual approach."[31] In other words, scholars dismantled the foundation on which the Biblical Myth and Ritual School hoped to rebuild Israel's early religion.

Sigmund Mowinckel, lecturer at the University of Oslo, is regarded by many as the most significant Psalms scholar. He is famous for his theory of Yahweh's Enthronement Festival. "Myth in essence," he explains, "relates, in epic form, the 'salvation' which is made present and experienced again in the religious cult."[32] He theorizes that some forty psalms reflect a vision of creation by myth and ritual as annually affected by the enthronement of Yahweh in Israel's fall festival. However, suffice it here to note the criticism of the Enthronement Festival theory by Erhard Gerstenberger, professor of Old Testament at Philipps-Universität: "The reconstructed background of the so-called cultic Psalms, be it called New Year/Enthronement Festival or Covenant Renewal Festival, at times looks like a specter or a bag of bubbles."[33] Although the Myth and Ritual School is quite dead, it survives.[34]

Conclusion

The Ancient Near Eastern cosmogony has five essential characteristics: (1) pantheism, (2) magic, (3) *Chaoskampf* (so most, not all), (4) eternal return, and (5) marginalization of *historia*. Any one of these characteristics differs from the essentials of biblical cosmogony.[35] Therefore, theologians should *conserve* myth to denote exclusively stories like those of Ancient Near Eastern cosmogonies. A "little" difference can be as great and decisive as the difference between water at 211 degrees Fahrenheit not being able to move a freight train and at 212 degrees Fahrenheit being able to move it. Likewise, any one of these five differences is so essential and decisive in shaping a culture that in theological discourse Genus:

31. Oden, "Myth in the OT," *ABD*, 4:958.

32. Sigmund Mowinckel, "Drama, religionsgeschichtliches," *Die Religion in Geschichte und Gegenwart*, 3rd edition, ed. Kurt Galling (Tübingen: Mohr Siebeck, 1960), 4:275, col. 1.

33. E. Gerstenberger, *Psalms in Old Testament Form Criticism*, ed. J. H. Hayes, Trinity University Monograph Series in Religion 2 (San Antonio: Trinity University Press, 1974), 197.

34. I say "quite dead" because I "Googled" "Ugarit and the Bible" and found someone representing the Quartz School of Theology like this: "As in the Ugaritic myths, the purpose of Yahweh's enthronement is to re-enact creation."

35. A biblical cosmogony affirms a transcendent and sovereign Creator of all matter (contra pantheism), in an ethical (contra magic) conflict with the human will (contra *Chaoskampf*) in a comprehensive scheme of salvation history from creation to the eschaton (contra an eternal return) involving *historia* (contra *a-historia*).

Pagan Cosmogony and Genus: Biblical Cosmogony should not be lumped together into an indigestible homology of Genus: "Myth."

For the hierarchy of homologous literary terms involving myth, I suggest the following nomenclature:

- Kingdom: *Weltanschauung* (God, Mankind, and Matter/Cosmos) including Phylum: "Origins" and Phylum: "Ontology"
- Phylum: "Origin" including Class: Cosmogony and Class: History
- Class: Cosmogony including Order: "Naturalism" and Order: "Supernaturalism"
- Order: "Naturalism" including Family: "Evolutionism" and Family: "Jungian Psychology"
- Order: "Supernaturalism" including Family: "Myth" (pantheism and magic) and Family: "Divinely Revealed" (transcendence and history)
- Family: "Myth" including Class: "Enlightenment Cosmogony"
- Both classes including Order: "Primordial Origins (cosmogony)" and Order: "Supernaturalism"
- Order: "Naturalism" including Genus: "Evolution" and Genus: "Jungian Psychology"
- Order: "Supernaturalism" including Family: "Myth" and "Divine Inspiration"; Family: "Myth" (pantheism and magic); and Family: "Divine Revelation"
- Family: "Myth" including Genus: "Ancient Near Eastern" and Genus: "Chinese"
- Family: "Divine Revelation" including Genus: "Prose" and Genus: "Poetry"
- Genus: "Ancient Near Eastern" including Specie: "Mesopotamia" and Specie: "Ugarit"
- Genus: "Prose" including Specie: "Genesis 1:1–2:3" and "Genesis 2:4–4:26"
- Genus: "Poetry" including Specie: "Job 38–41" and "Proverbs 8:22-31"

Here is a suggested schema:

- Kingdom: Worldview (God, Man, Cosmos)
- Phylum: Origins (versus Ontology)
- Class: Cosmogony (versus History)
- Order: Naturalism and Supernaturalism
- Family: Evolutionism,[36] Myth, and Historio-Poesis
- Genus: Ancient Near East Prose and Poetry
- Specie: Mesopotamia, Ugarit, Genesis 1:1–2:3, and Job 38–41

36. Evolutionism refers here to "Neo-Darwinism," the combination of Darwinian evolution with genetics. See Julian Huxley, *Evolution: The Modern Synthesis* (New York/London: Harper & Bros., 1942), cited by Christopher Southgate, *The Groaning of Creation: God, Evolution and the Problem of Evil* (Louisville: Westminster John Knox, 2008), 11.

Connotation

Before 1900, the scholarly community regarded myth as *in partem malo,* but at the turn of the twentieth century, against popular parlance, the academies of religious and biblical studies used the term *in partem bono.* Here we trace that history.

Contempt for Myth

The Enlightenment reinforced the historically entrenched connotation of myth as an untrue story.

Before the Enlightenment In popular parlance (see *OED*) myth connotes "purely fictitious narrative."[37] Raffaele Pettazoni notes that this contempt had its origin in classical antiquity.[38] Xenophanes (ca. 565-470 B.C.E.) hurled darts of derision against Homer and Hesiod for perpetuating the scandalous tales about the gods. (Was Greece in the sixth century impacted by the Jewish Diaspora?) Ensuing Greek philosophers contrasted myth, what cannot exist, with *logos* (reason) and *historia.*[39]

Philo inherited the Greek philosophers' understanding of myth. For him, the Old Testament differed from the Greek myths by dealing with history.[40] Myth has no place on biblical soil: "Have nothing to do with godless and silly myths" (1 Tim. 4:7; cf. 2 Tim. 4:4; Titus 1:14; 2 Pet. 1:16).[41] In modernity, D. F. Strauss renewed the potency of this common meaning when he defined myth in explicit contrast to history. Moreover, according to Strauss, the "purpose of myth is to provide a logical model capable of overcoming a contradiction," and the "kind of logic which is used by mythical thought is as rigorous as that of modern science."[42]

After the Enlightenment The Enlightenment exacerbated this negative attitude toward myth. Bultmann's innocuous definition of myth is deceptive. He clearly opposes myth to modern science, and for him modern science represents ontological reality. His use is rooted in C. G. Heyne, who, according to Brevard

37. Cf. Harold O. J. Brown, "The Bible and Mythology," *Christianity Today* 18, no. 25 (1974): 8.

38. Raffaele Pettazzoni, *Essays on the History of Religions,* Studies in the History of Religions: Supplements to Numen (Leiden: Brill, 1967).

39. Please forgive me for not involving myself in defining "fact" more philosophically as an "intellectually formulating event" (in the words of Susanne Langer, *Philosophy in a New Key* [Cambridge, MA: Harvard University Press, 1941], 269).

40. Cited by Brown, "The Bible and Mythology," 10.

41. Cf. Ethelbert Stauffer, "Mythos," in *TDNT* 4:793.

42. D. F Strauss, *Das Leben Jesu* (Tübingen: Fues, 1835).

Childs,[43] defined "myth as a necessary and universal form of expression within the early stage of man's intellectual development, in which unexplainable events were attributed to the gods." The Enlightenment gave rise to Darwin's cosmogony of evolution and the correlative *Zeitgeist* of evolutionary progress.[44] The so-called "mythical school" (Eichhorn, Gabler, G. L. Bauer) applied Heyne's evolutionary concept of the myth to the Old Testament, and D. F. Strauss (and, more recently, Bultmann) applied it to the New Testament.[45] Bultmann's historical-critical *Weltanschauung* cannot accommodate salvation-history.

Within the Cambridge school, the famous anthropologist Sir James George Frazer (encouraged by William Robertson Smith, who was linking the Old Testament with early Hebrew folklore) claimed that myth emerges out of ritual during the natural process of religious evolution. Frazer collected a vast assortment of data from cultures around the world and from a dispassionate unbelieving perspective sought to understand the worldwide process of religion, including that of Israel, as a common development from animism and belief in magic (ritual) through belief in polytheism (myth) to a belief in one or a common higher spirit to science.[46] Its thesis is that all religions originate from an ancient fertility cult that revolved around worshiping and periodically sacrificing to a sacred king. This king, it was believed, was the incarnation of a dying and reviving god, a solar deity, who underwent a mystic marriage to a goddess of the Earth, who died at the harvest, and was reincarnated in the spring.

Richard S. Hess succinctly surveys and critically appraises the influential thinkers who addressed the study of religion from the dispassionate perspective of the Enlightenment: Karl Marx (1818-1883), Friedrich Max Mueller (1823-1900), James George Frazer (1854-1941), William James (1842-1910), Sigmund Freud (1856-1939), Emile Durkheim (1858-1917), Rudolf Otto (1869-1937), and Mircea Eliade (1907-1986).[47] Hess applauds the work of E. E. Evans-Pritchard (1902-1973), professor of social anthropology at Oxford, because Evans-Pritchard thought the best means to understand a society and religion was to view it from within, not from a supposed disinterested position of unbelief,

43. Brevard S. Childs, *Myth and Reality in the Old Testament* (London: SCM, 1960), 13.

44. Earlier, Hegel's dialectical understanding of history influenced Vatke (1806-1882) in 1835 to argue for a three-stage development of the spirit of history based on, among other antitheses, myth versus history and magic/cult versus ethical. According to Vatke, the earliest stage was paganism comprised of nature religion with myth, magic, and cult. Prophetic religion, which climaxed in the writing prophets of the eighth century B.C.E., was marked by the spiritual and ethical. The third stage was marked by legalism as seen in the priestly and Deuteronomistic sources.

45. Childs, *Myth and Reality*, 13-14.

46. James George Frazer, *The Golden Bough*, 3 vols. (New York: Macmillan, 1922).

47. Richard S. Hess, *Israelite Religions: An Archaeological and Biblical Survey* (Grand Rapids: Baker, 2007), 35.

and to view religion in terms of a unique culture, not by abstracting a general theory of religion:

> His careful and thorough research from within the society led him to severely criticize many of the theorists of religion who had preceded him (1956). Their theories were abstracted from data collected from around the world. Had they studied just one culture in depth, as Evans-Pritchard did, they would have learned how inadequate their assumptions were about religion among tribal peoples.[48]

Hess also applauds the anthropologist Clifford Geertz (1926-2006) for attempting to understand culture and religion as distinctive in each society.[49]

When Gaster defines myth as "a story of the gods in which results of natural causes are accounted for supernaturally,"[50] he assumes, like Heyne and the Enlightenment, that all events have nothing but natural causes.[51] The assumptions of the Enlightenment diametrically oppose those of the Bible's understanding of an Ultimate Cause often working in conjunction with immediate causes. Darwin's cosmogony of evolution belongs to Kingdom: "Matter (not Kingdom God)"; Phylum: "Origin"; Class: "Natural"; Order: "Animal"; Family: "Enlightenment Cosmogony"; Genus: "Evolution." A species of "Evolution" could be "Punctuated Equilibrium."

Rehabilitation of Myth

Oswalt notes that the content of myth has not changed; rather, the contemporary worldview toward myth has changed.[52] Since the turn of the twentieth century, ethnologists, sociologists, and historians of religion have positively refurbished myth to connote a story that is "true," "sacred," "exemplary," or "significant." Paradoxically, for many scholars a myth is subjectively true but historically fictitious. Several factors have contributed to the changed attitude toward myth from *in partem malo* to *in partem bono:* (1) cultural relativism; (2) a psychological understanding of "truth"; (3) a sociological understanding of myth according to

48. Hess, *Israelite Religions,* 35.

49. Hess, *Israelite Religions,* 36-37.

50. Theodor Herzl Gaster, *Myth, Legend, and Custom in the Old Testament* (New York: Harper & Row, 1969).

51. The Enlightenment is an intellectual movement rooted in the scientific advances of the seventeenth century that expanded in the eighteenth century to advocate reason as the primary means of advancing knowledge. Reason was then applied to religious, literary, and socio-economic theories.

52. Oswalt, *Bible among the Myths,* esp. 1-18.

its function; and, commendably, (4) a dissatisfaction with a positivistic view of history and religion and an innate need for poetic imagination to symbolize truth.

Cultural Relativism The rehabilitation of myth occurred at about the same time that the academic community adopted cultural relativism as an axiomatic principle.[53] Ethnologists, anthropologists, and comparative religionists commonly evaluate myths in terms of their culture, not by an absolute standard. The hostility of anthropologists who seek to save pagan myths against missionary efforts to "save" souls is painfully true.

Psychological "Truth" Cardinal Avery Dulles notes that modern studies in fields such as depth psychology "stress chiefly the value of myth in the subjective order."[54] For the Swiss psychiatrist Carl J. Jung (1875-1961), myths afford new insights into the structure of the human psyche. Myths stem from what Jung labels "archetypes" that lie in the deepest levels from the primal inherited patterns of human thought and experience. Archetypes are somewhat like animal instincts. At birth the human mind, according to Jung, is not a *tabula rasa* but is endowed with a limited number of archetypes. This "collective unconscious" is the ancient and unconscious source of much of what humans think and do. The emotions that arise from one's unique conditioning of the archetype are transformed into pictures as attested in dreams and visions. Likewise, in Jung's view, the collective conscience gives rise to myths about the other world. The human responses to situations in the symbolic, picture-language of myth are said to be essentially the same in all cultures.

Jung's understanding of myth assumes, like evolutionism, that a world that is not accessible through the human senses is not *historia,* but fiction. As Martin Buber points out, Jung advocates a religion of "pure psychic immanence," for "he conceives of God not as a Being or a Reality to which a psychical content corresponds, but rather as this content itself."[55] Further, as Bernhard W. Anderson notes, "An analysis which eclectically lumps together the myths of the mother-goddess with distinctively biblical motifs fails to take account of one significant fact: [true] Israel's faith protested vehemently against certain ancient Near Eastern archetypes."[56] Finally, the God of the Bible is incomparable. His Name is

53. Culture relativism is the principle that an individual's beliefs and activities should be understood as true in terms of the individual's own culture, not in terms of an external, objective standard. See Franz Boas, "Museums of Ethnology and Their Classification," *Science* 9 (1887): 589.

54. Avery Dulles, S.J., "Symbol, Myth, and the Biblical Revelation," *Theological Studies* 27 (1966): 2-26.

55. Martin Buber, *The Eclipse of God* (New York: Harper & Brothers, 1952), 104-22, 171-76.

56. Bernhard W. Anderson, "Myth and the Biblical Tradition," *Theology Today* 27, no. 1 (1970): 55.

I AM WHO I AM; he is like none other. No human archetype naturally relates simultaneous transcendence and immanence, concurrent ubiquity and unique presence, absolute love with passionate moral indignation, and sovereignty and freewill, to name a few.

Culturally Formative Story Irving Hexham and Karla Poewe along with other anthropologists functionally define myth as "a story with culturally formative power that can shape the lives of individuals and even entire societies." They elaborate: "Once accepted, a myth can be used to ennoble the past, explain the present, and hold out hope for the future."[57] This functional definition includes the first of Barr's refinements of Bultmann's definition of myth but excludes Barr's other two caveats.

This definition of myth may usefully and appropriately help anthropologists understand what shapes a society in contrast to other factors, but it is not useful for theologians because it eclipses the whole taxonomy of concepts that bring order to theology. It bypasses Kingdom because it does not distinguish between God and Matter; it bypasses Phylum without distinguishing Phylum: Supernatural and Phylum: Natural; it bypasses Class: "Primordial" and Class: "Historical [or Legend]"; it bypasses Family: Enlightenment Cosmogony and Family: Tradition/Revelation Cosmogony; it bypasses Genus: Evolutionism and Genus: Biblical Cosmogony. Moreover, this functional denotation marginalizes *historia.*[58]

Nevertheless, Hexham and Poewe's definition highlights the importance of a society's cosmogony: it permeates a people's pattern of perception and thought.[59] If so, differentiating the essence of the biblical cosmogony from other cosmogony may be even more important than differentiating Mary and her lamb.

Dissatisfaction with Positivism Deriving from Enlightenment thinkers such as Henri de Saint-Simon (1760-1825) and Pierre-Simon Laplace (1749-1827), Auguste Comte (1798-1857) replaced metaphysics in the history of thought with the scientific method (i.e., the only authentic knowledge is based on sense experience and positive verification). Leopold von Ranke (1795-1896), the father of historicism, relied primarily on the "narratives of eye-witnesses and the most genuine immediate documents" and sought to write history without an informing vision of metaphysics. He considered that "the strict presentation of the facts, contingent and unattractive though they may be, is undoubtedly the supreme law." Von Ranke's method profoundly influenced Western thought, but it leaves the human spirit, which craves for meaning, without meaning. James B. Wiggins,

57. Irving Hexham and Karla Poewe, "Myths and Mythological Fragments," in *New Religions as Global Cultures: Making the Human* (Boulder, CO: Westview, 1997), 83-84.

58. It satisfies only the first of Barr's characterizations of myth (see p. 547 above).

59. For bibliography, see T. Stordalen, *Echoes of Eden* (Leuven: Peeters, 2000), 28 n. 36.

professor of religion at Syracuse University, rightly complains that the positivistic writing of history has produced "the utter barrenness, desolation, and ultimate meaningless of a view of reality constructed only of reason's facts."[60]

Perhaps the quest to satisfy this hunger of the human spirit for ultimate reality explains in part why ethnologists, sociologists, and historians of religion refurbished myth to connote a story that is "true," "sacred," "exemplary," or "significant" for a given culture. In fact, some define myth as "a narrative in which there is a deeply serious use of symbolism to convey profound realities."[61] According to that definition, the Bible is myth. Nicolas Wyatt calls myth "the narration of a religious story, or just reference to chosen words within it [which will evoke] the whole complex of ideas and above all feelings which are part of membership of the groups."[62] According to this definition, however, it does not matter whether the symbols and stories are *historia*. The symbols may represent subjective and/or existential "truth," although they do not represent *historia*. The symbolic homology, as used by Wyatt, marginalizes history and potentially robs the gospel of *historia*. The religion of Israel differs in part from pagan religions by being based on the *magnalia Dei* (God's mighty interventions in history), not on nature.

Conclusion

The term "myth" in theology should be reserved for stories informed by pantheism and magic. From the time of Xenophanes to the present, myth connotes historical fiction, not *historia*. Some wish to categorize myth broadly; others wish to use the term positively by redefining it functionally; and others evaluate myths as subjective truth. But the stubborn fact remains that in *usus loquendi* myth connotes fiction, not *historia*. Nicolas Wyatt, defining myth as symbolic language, writes, "Stories of the beginning and end of the world, and of the resurrection, ascension and second coming of Christ are not in any sense 'historical' narratives. . . . Couched in historiographical form, the narrative of biblical historiography bears the veneer of history."[63]

The sociological definition of myth — "culturally formative story" — revises this *usus loquendi*. Hexham and Poewe admit, "In common speech, to call a story a 'myth' is to say that it is untrue."[64] Nevertheless, they assert, "Contrary to many writers, we do not believe that a myth is necessarily unhistorical. In itself a story that becomes a myth can be true or false, historical or unhistorical,

60. James B. Wiggins, "The Release of History through Myth," *AThR* 59, no. 2 (1977): 151-61.

61. Oswalt, *The Bible among the Myths,* 38.

62. Nicolas Wyatt, "The Mythic Mind," *SJOT* 15 (2001): 44.

63. Wyatt, "The Mythic Mind," 42-43.

64. Hexham and Poewe, "Myths and Mythological Fragments," 80.

fact or fiction."[65] But this is so because of their unique definition of the myth for sociologists. The truth is that Humpty-Dumpty cannot overcome *usus loquendi.* The connotation of myth as an untrue story with reference to *historia* is too entrenched, so that a *sui generis* scholarly definition confounds and misleads. Would it not bring order to scholarly discourse to communicate according to common speech and to speak simply of a "symbolic story" or a "culturally formative story" instead of co-opting an entrenched term to invest it with new meaning? Like it or not, "myth" connotes a story that is historically not true.

To refer to the biblical cosmogony and the formative events in Israel's history as myth at the least marginalizes the importance of *historia,* confounds phenomenal essentials and misleads the innocent. Theologians who have a high view of inspiration should strive to conserve the historic meaning of myth as expressions of paganism to protect the gospel from being misrepresented or misunderstood.

Having said that, however, the rehabilitation of myth for its poetic, symbolic significance gives human voice to the bankruptcy of reducing ontological reality to reason's facts. To know reality humans need both reason that is based on physical realities and intuitive imagination, an illumination, which transcends these mundane realities and sees beyond them to the realm of the divine, of spirit, of ethics, of virtue. The biblical narrative satisfies both of these needs. The next section argues that *historio-poesis* is an appropriate literary label for biblical narrative.

Historio-poesis

The Bible saliently combines the value of mythopoesis (i.e., presenting through symbols what is true, sacred, exemplary, or significant) with *historia.*[66] Both myths and the Bible poetically present spiritual and psychological realities that cannot be subject to demonstration of the same kind as demanded by the hard sciences — *wie es eigentlich gewesen ist* ("what actually happened," von Ranke), but the Bible differs from myth by insisting on *historia.* Barr rightly contrasts the mythological mindset, which is based almost exclusively on nature, with the historical consciousness of the biblical writers.

The human spirit craves both reason's facts and an intuitive vision to interpret the facts. There is an ancient quarrel between philosophy (i.e., reason alone) and poetry (intuitive imagination).[67] This is so because humans tend to polarize

65. Hexham and Poewe, "Myths and Mythological Fragments," 81.

66. For recent defenses of the historical veracity of the Bible, see Iain Provan, V. Philips Long, and Tremper Longman III, *A Biblical History of Israel* (Louisville: Westminster John Knox, 2003); K. A. Kitchen, *On the Reliability of the Old Testament* (Grand Rapids: Eerdmans, 2003); Hess, *Israelite Religions.*

67. Stanley Rosen, *The Quarrel between Philosophy and Poetry: Studies in Ancient Thought* (New York: Routledge, 1988).

notions even when they need both; in their thirst for truth/reality, humans need and respond to both facts-based reason and poetic imagination that lifts them to spiritual heights that transcend "reason's facts." Warren Gage, professor of Old Testament at Knox Seminary, notes,

> Poetic writers like J. R. R. Tolkien and C. S. Lewis are continually imagining and setting before us cities and civilizations in imagery so powerful that they seem to participate in a kind of immortality of their own. These imaginary kingdoms and principates [*sic*] somehow have the power to summon us to a higher realm of human virtue and aspiration than we might have otherwise known within the limited horizons of the merely mundane.[68]

Though the writings of J. R. R. Tolkien and C. S. Lewis are fictitious, not historical, and though they are the product of their poetic nature and lively imagination, which lift their readers to spiritual heights, their literature should not be labeled mythopoetic. Unlike pagan myths, their vision is informed primarily by the historically minded biblical narrators, not primarily by nature.

Wiggins helpfully seeks to combine the rich symbolic power once enlivening mythic narratives with the historical critical practice, calling it *historiopoesis.* Any good historical writing is interpretive, not just reporting. "History writing is not a record of fact — of what 'really happened' — but a discourse that claims to be a record of fact."[69] It creatively represents "reality." The biblical narrators generate both a mood stance — reflection, exploration, edification, celebration (i.e., strengthening community bonds), cathartic cleansing, and/or sheer delight — and a plot. Biblical narrators plot the historical events within salvation history, a metanarrative that climaxes in the person and work of Jesus Christ.

Karl Barth (1886-1968) similarly interprets the biblical cosmogonies as consisting of both history and imagination and places them within his understanding of divine inspiration.[70] Barth represents the biblical cosmogonies as linking the historical with the supernatural, which is known spiritually or intuitively — what Reformed theologians call "illumination." Because myth in common parlance does not refer to *historia,* Barth rightly rejects the term for biblical cosmogonies: "the real *object* and *content* of myth are the essential principles of the general real-

68. Warren Austin Gage, *Theological Poetics: Typology, Symbol and the Christ* (Fort Lauderdale, FL: St. Andrews, 2010), 7.

69. Brevard S. Childs, *Myth and Reality in the Old Testament* (London: SCM, 1960), 72-82.

70. Unfortunately, Barth ties inspiration too closely with illumination, making the former inseparable from the latter. While recognizing that both are needed for sound theology, evangelicals should keep them distinct. "Inspiration" pertains to the role of the Holy Spirit to superintend the writing of Scripture to guarantee its truthfulness. "Illumination" pertains to the role of the Spirit to interpret the Scriptures.

ities and relationships of the natural and spiritual cosmos, not bound to particular times and places (in contrast to concrete history)."[71]

Barth, seeking a neutral genre between myth and history, labels the biblical cosmogony as *Sage* ("saga"). By *Sage* he means a story that refers both to *historia* (and thus subject to critical historiography) and an imaginative reality not visually observable. The resulting composite narrative, he rightly asserts, is the "true history." Unfortunately, the English equivalent of German *Sage,* "saga," does not work as a label for the biblical cosmogony. "Saga" in English denotes either "a prose narrative recorded in Iceland in the twelfth and thirteenth centuries of historic or legendary figures and events of the heroic age of Norway and Iceland" or "a modern heroic narrative resembling the Icelandic saga."[72] Moreover, "saga" connotes a story that is less than certain *historia.* Nevertheless, if I understand Barth correctly, by *Sage* he means what Wiggins means by *historio-poesis.*

Wiggins's literary category *historio-poesis* and Barth's *Sage* are appropriate terms for labeling the genre of biblical narrative from the perspective of the human author. By the spiritual gift of faith, however, the church "knows" the Holy Spirit inspires the writer's imagination to interpret reason's facts according to eternal truth. Allowing *"historio-"* to represent the biblical narrative's *historia* and *"poesis"* to represent the informing vision, *historio-poesis* comports well with B. B. Warfield's concursive theory of inspiration: fully human and fully divine. The analysis of biblical narrative as consisting of both historical facts and divinely inspired imagination also comports well with the distinction in modern literary criticism between story (the content, the event) and plot (the human author's representation of the event within a metanarrative). This analysis frees a theologian to subject the narrative to scientific investigation and yet demands faith in the biblical writer's vision. Israel's inspired salvation history is grounded in *historia,* the *magnalia Dei,* and in God's revelation which interprets that *historia* within an interpretative plot that climaxes in the life, death, resurrection, and ascension of Jesus Christ.

Myth and the Early Religion of Israel

For the past forty years scholars whose understanding of the religion of Israel is based on extra-biblical textual and artifactual evidence or who are greatly in-

71. In this presentation of Barth's reflections on the creation narratives, I lean heavily on Garrett Green, "Myth, History, and Imagination: The Creation Narratives in Bible and Theology," *HBT* 12, no. 2 (1990): 19-38.

72. *Merriam-Webster's Collegiate Dictionary,* 10th ed. (Springfield, MA: Merriam-Webster, 1997), 1030, s.v. "saga."

fluenced by them have also conceived of Israel's early religion as rooted in the ideology of Ancient Near Eastern myths — that is, in pantheism and magic.

Frank Moore Cross, in his influential collection of essays in *Canaanite Myth and Hebrew Epic: Essays in the History of the Religion of Israel* (1973), departed from his mentor, William Foxwell Albright, in marking the *point de départ* for studies in the history of Israel's religion. Albright, George Ernest Wright, Walter Kaufmann, and others radically contrasted the religion of Israel with its pagan neighbors. Cross, however, while recognizing an early appearance of the worship of *I AM* during the "the Tribal League" (traditionally "the time of the judges," 1250-1050 B.C.E.), regarded Israel's religion as having developed from previous forms and ideas in Ugaritic and Canaanite cult and myth. For examples of this new direction in understanding Israel's religion that prioritize extra-biblical sources over the Bible's own witness, see Hess's judicious survey of the material.[73] This essay tersely summarizes the studies of Mark Smith and William Dever.

Mark Smith and William Dever, each for his own reasons, also revise the Bible's own witness to the origin of Israel's religion. According to the Bible, Moses founded Israel's ethical monotheism in connection with *I AM*'s historical, dynamic intervention on behalf of Jacob's descendants at the time of the exodus and the conquest (ca. 1250 B.C.E.). According to the Myth and Ritual School and these revisionists, Israel's religion during the nation's formative period, 1250-850 B.C.E., was homologous to the immoral nature religions of her world.

Mark Smith, professor of Bible and Ancient Near Eastern studies at New York University, argues that biblical monotheistic religion evolved out of Canaanite polytheistic religion, but he does not deny a tradition of the exodus within Israel. He combs the biblical texts and the Ancient Near Eastern texts to make his case.[74] He writes, "The Baal cycle [of the Ugaritic texts] expresses the heart of the West Semitic religion from which the Israelite religion largely developed."[75] According to Smith, this West Semitic religion as found in the Bible and at Ugarit served a pantheon of deities within which Yahweh was at a secondary level, subordinate to El; only later did Yahweh become identified with El and achieve a first-level status.

73. Hess, *Israelite Religions,* 64-79.

74. Mark Smith, *The Early History of God* (San Francisco: Harper & Row, 1990); *The Origins of Biblical Monotheism: Israel's Polytheistic Background and the Ugaritic Texts* (Oxford: Oxford University Press, 2001); *The Memoirs of God: History, Memory, and the Experience of the Divine in Ancient Israel* (Minneapolis: Augsburg, 2004). Cf. Richard S. Hess, review of Mark S. Smith, *The Memoirs of God, Denver Journal* 8 (2005), http://www.denverseminary.edu/article/the-memoirs-of-god/ (accessed May 14, 2010).

75. Mark Smith, *The Ugaritic Baal Cycle* (Leiden: Brill, 1994), 1:xxvi. In other writing, Smith seemingly qualifies this statement by arguing that the tradition of a historic exodus from Egypt is unique to Israelite religion and not found elsewhere in West Semitic religion (*Early History of God,* 2nd edition [Grand Rapids: Eerdmans, 2002], 25).

William Dever privileges the archeology (i.e., material culture — not so much the ancient Egyptian and other written sources) over the biblical material as he thinks the latter is late and distorted by ideology ("elitist"). Paradoxically, he finds a kernel of truth for the exodus but denies the historicity of the Bible's witness to the exodus as the origin of its distinctive faith.[76] The scholarship of these revised histories is flawed in four respects: (1) the biblical text's date, (2) archeology, (3) historiography, and (4) Israel's poetic use of Ancient Near Eastern myths.

Text's Date Flawed

The reconstructions of early Israel's religion as homologous to the pagan religions normally assume the Wellhausian reconstruction of Israel's religion. According to Wellhausen, what the Bible attributes to Moses was formulated much later in Israel's history (ca. 625-450 B.C.E.). Dever argues that during the late divided monarchy an elite group of misogynistic priests and prophets emerged who objected to the heretofore pantheism and magic of Israel's religion and triumphed in purging the text of the earlier religion.[77] Having divorced Moses from the Deuteronomist's Book of the Law, the revisionists construct their paradigm of early Israelite religion from Israel's pagan neighbors, from Israel's poetry, and from archeology. Unfortunately, the space restraints of this paper prevent a critique of the Wellhausian synthesis.[78] Suffice it to note that although the date of extant texts may be exilic, it retains a credible historical memory.[79] Moreover, whereas the exodus provides a credible explanation for the origins of Israel's unique religion, the revisionists offer none.

Archeologically Flawed

Dever looks to Palestinian artifacts for his revisionist history.[80] For example, a collection of inscriptions from Kuntillet 'Ajrud (800 B.C.E.) are commonly understood as mentioning "Yahweh and his Asherah." If so, it is thought, Yahweh

76. William Dever, *What Did the Biblical Writers Know and When Did They Know It?* (Grand Rapids: Eerdmans, 2001); *Who Were the Early Israelites and Where Did They Come From?* (Grand Rapids: Eerdmans, 2003); *Did God Have a Wife? Archaeology and Folk Religion in Ancient Israel* (Grand Rapids: Eerdmans, 2005).

77. Dever, *Did God Have a Wife?*

78. For a recent critical appraisal of Wellhausen's documentary hypothesis, see Hess, *Israelite Religions.*

79. Cf. Provan, Long, and Longman, *A Biblical History of Israel,* 3-97.

80. Dever, *Who Were the Early Israelites?* For a rebuttal of the revisionist historians Dever and Smith, see Oswalt, *Bible among Myths,* 181-84.

is presented as a member of the pantheon of Iron Age Palestine. The artifacts, however, are better interpreted to support the prophets' accusation against Israel. The Bible makes nominal Israel's constant apostasy as clear as language can express (Exod. 32:1; Num. 25:1-9; Judg. 2:13; 1 Sam. 7:3; 1 Kgs. 11; 2 Kgs. 17; Ezek. 8–9).

The inability of archeology to shed light on Israel's religion during the early monarchy may be compared to its inability to shed light on the prophetic faith from the Elephantine papyri. The religion of the Elephantine Jews (400 B.C.E.), according to some, included a recital or representation of the annual marriage of Yahweh and Anat.[81] Money was given to such deities as Anatyah, Anatbethel, and others, and oaths were taken before them. No scholar, however, foolishly draws the conclusion that the literary prophets had not centuries earlier denounced this sort of syncretism. It is just as foolish to revise Israel's early history from ambiguous artifacts. In fact, it is almost impossible to confirm true Israel's faith by archeology, for that religion forbade the making of any image of the only God, *I AM WHO I AM.*

Historiography Flawed

The complaint against the Myth and Ritual School by Frank Moore Cross could equally apply to Smith and Dever. Cross complains, "There is a tacit assumption in this school that the development of the cult must move from the 'natural' to the 'historical.'" Worse yet, he accuses the School of sloppy scholarship: this school "*has not grappled with the problem* of 'earlier' historical elements, later mythological elements, in the cult." With his typical meticulous scholarship, Cross demonstrates that Israel's earliest poems, such as the Song of the Sea (Exodus 15) and the Song of Deborah (Judges 5), were composed before the monarchy. In short, the earliest documented Israelite literature, even before the monarchy, celebrates the *magnalia Dei,* not nature.[82]

81. Hess, *Israelite Religions,* 341-42, finds the evidence is weak for an association of Yahweh with Anat.

82. Frank Moore Cross, *Canaanite Myth and Hebrew Epic: Essays in the History of the Religion of Israel* (Cambridge, MA: Harvard University Press, 1973), 82-83; emphasis added. Cross's starting point is a rigid scientific-historical methodology based on assumptions of cultural relativism. Moreover, he thinks the Song of the Sea, which represents Pharaoh's army as drowned in the sea, is more accurate than the "legendary" prose account of Israel crossing the sea on dry land. However, matching Exodus 14–15 and Judges 4–5, the "Kadesh Battle Inscriptions of Ramses I" and "The Political Stele of Merneptah" present in stone, undoubtedly written at the same time, two major, differing accounts of the same campaign: "a prose report of a more or less factual nature and a poetic version abounding in hyperbole" (Miriam Lichtheim, *Ancient Egyptian Literature* [Berkeley and Los Angeles: University of California Press, 1976], 2:57).

Interpretation of Israel's Poetry Flawed

Israel's poets allude to Ancient Near Eastern cosmogony, but these allusions are better interpreted as borrowed imagery from broken Canaanite myths than evidence of Israel's religion evolving from it (see below). Israel's poets are so secure in their faith that they can cite the Canaanite literature, even as the English poets cite Greek and Roman mythology, without fear of being misunderstood. Smith's sort of evidence is similar to that of Ben Johnson's words to Celia: "But might I of Jove's nectar sip, I would not change for thine."[83] The Puritan John Milton drew heavily on Greek mythology to enrich his poetic imagery even in his picture of creation,[84] and the same could be noted of Dante Alighieri's *Divine Comedy.*[85] Perhaps two thousand years from now a scholar will suggest that a remnant of intellectuals during the times of the High Middle Ages, of Tudor England, and of the Romanticists retained a belief in the Roman god Jupiter!

Myth and Prose

The discovery and decoding of Ancient Near Eastern texts from Mesopotamia to Egypt and an interest in archeology in the nineteenth century led to an emphasis on comparing Ancient Near Eastern literature with that of the Bible.[86]

Similarities between Genesis 1–11 and ANE Texts

George Smith opened the floodgate of this scholarly endeavor by comparing the Genesis flood story with that found in the Mesopotamian Gilgamesh epic.[87] In both flood stories, (1) a hero builds a boat to preserve the human race through a

83. "To Celia" (1616).

84. W. F. Albright, *History, Archaeology and Christian Humanism* (London: Black, 1965).

85. I am indebted to Nathan Chambers for this observation.

86. See Richard S. Hess, "One Hundred Fifty Years of Comparative Studies on Genesis 1–11: An Overview," in *"I Studied Inscriptions from before the Flood": Ancient Near Eastern, Literary, and Linguistic Approaches to Genesis 1–11,* Sources for Biblical and Theological Study 4, ed. Richard S. Hess and David Toshio Tsumura (Winona Lake, IN: Eisenbrauns, 1994), 3-26.

87. There are three Mesopotamian flood myths: (1) the Sumerian account with the hero Ziuusdra ("Found Long Life," last king of the Sumerian king list before the flood), (2) the Old Akkadian account with the hero Atrahasis ("Extremely Wise"), and (3) the Old Babylonian account with the hero Utnapishtim ("He Found Life"). Scholars believe that the Gilgamesh epic originated as a series of Sumerian legends and poems about the mythological hero-king Gilgamesh, which were gathered into a longer Akkadian epic much later. The most complete version existing today is preserved on twelve clay tablets from Ashurbanipal's library collection of the seventh century B.C.E.

universal, devastating flood from which a new world emerged from the aquatic chaos; (2) the hero sends birds to survey the earth's new terrain after the flood; and (3) when the humans emerge from the boat, they offer sacrifices to the gods.

Similarly, the biblical account of the creation of the cosmos (Gen. 1:1–2:3) has similarities to the Mesopotamian *Enuma Elish* (called "the Babylonian Genesis").[88] The Babylonian and biblical accounts share striking similarities in form, content, and sequence of events. Both refer to (1) divine spirit and cosmic matter; (2) chaos: *Tiamat/tᵉhôm* (Heb. "abyss") enveloped in darkness; (3) light existing before creation of luminaries; (4) creation of the firmament; (5) creation of dry land; (6) creation of luminaries; (7) creation of man; (8) and G/god(s) resting.

Differences between Genesis 1–11 and ANE Texts

Before seeking to explain these similarities, the striking differences in these accounts should also be noted. The biblical flood narrative stands head and shoulders above the others in wisdom and theology, lifting the audience to heavenly heights of virtue and praise:

1. The dimensions of Noah's ark are those of modern ships, but the Babylonian ship, though pitched within and without, is an unstable cube.
2. Noah sensibly releases the raven, which braves the storm, can feed on carrion, and can remain in flight much longer than the dove. He then releases the gentle, timid, and low-flying dove. The hero in the Babylonian parallel, however, sends a dove, a sparrow, and then a raven.
3. The Bible invests the story with a covenant concept in a metanarrative of God developing a covenantal relationship with his chosen people. In the Mesopotamian accounts, overpopulation or humanity's noise interrupts the sleep of the gods and provokes their wrath, and the hero's wisdom and bravery save him. In the Bible humanity's wickedness arouses God's anger, and Noah's righteousness, not his wisdom and bravery, motivates God to save him. The biblical narrative is calculated to place all wisdom on God and promote human trust and obedience to him.
4. In the Mesopotamian account, the gods gather around the sacrifice like flies because they are hungry; in the biblical account, Noah's sacrifice assuages God's heart regarding sin.

88. The *Enuma Elish* exists in various copies from Babylon and Assyria. The version from Ashurbanipal's library dates to the seventh century B.C.E. Most scholars date the composition of the text to between the eighteenth to sixteenth centuries B.C.E., although some scholars favor a later date of ca. 1100 B.C.E.

The biblical account of the creation of the cosmos also differs radically from the *Enuma Elish* and other Ancient Near Eastern cosmogonies in both theology and texture. As for theology, all other Ancient Near Eastern cosmogonies are myths because they are informed by (1) pantheism, (2) magic, (3) *Chaoskampf,* (4) eternal return, and (5) marginalization of *historia* — that is so say, not participating in a metanarrative plot. To the discerning, the biblical theology is vastly superior. Israel's cosmogony differs in two ways: (1) it implies God's aseity, radically differentiating him from the impersonal matter he calls into existence, and (2) creation is a unique first act in salvation history. With regard to texture, the frivolity of the *Enuma Elish* contrasts sharply with the stately, dignified narrative of Genesis 1. Marduk probably is represented as breaking wind in Tiamat's face, and she opens her mouth wide to swallow the wind dispatched from his rear, whereupon he shoots arrows at her and deflates her.[89] In his classic work on comparing and contrasting Genesis with the Babylonian parallel, Alexander Heidel concludes, "In the light of the differences, the resemblances fade away almost like the stars before the sun."[90]

Explaining Similarities between Genesis 1–11 and ANE Texts

The stories in Genesis 1–11 are not myth, and they are vastly superior in theology and ethics to parallel Ancient Near Eastern texts. But how can we best explain these parallels with Ancient Near Eastern myths?

The best explanation for the flood stories is that both went back to a historical memory of a single great flood and that the Bible preserves the purest account of that historical event. This explanation finds support in native global flood stories that are documented as history or legend in almost every region on earth. Ancient civilizations such as China, Babylonia, Wales, Russia, India, America, Hawaii, Scandinavia, Sumatra, Peru, and Polynesia have their own versions of a giant flood. James George Frazer notes, "It has long been known that legends of a great flood, in which almost all men perished, are widely diffused over the world."[91] Moreover, these flood stories are frequently linked by common elements like those cited above. The biblical account commends itself as preserving the story of a single historical flood in its purest form.

What about the parallels between the Babylonian Genesis and the biblical

89. Victor Hurowitz, "The Genesis of Genesis: Is the Creation Story Babylonian?" *Bible Review* 21, no. 1 (2005): 38-48, 52, esp. 41.

90. Alexander Heidel, *The Babylonian Genesis: The Story of Creation,* 2 vols. (Chicago: University of Chicago Press, 1951), 1:139. Cf. A. R. Millard, "A New Babylonian 'Genesis' Story,'" *TynB* 18 (1967): 3-18.

91. James George Frazer, *Folk-Lore in the Old Testament* (London: Macmillan, 1919), 1:105.

Genesis? Since some think the Mesopotamian account originated circa 1100 B.C.E., we cannot rule out that the *Enuma Elish* is a bastardized version of the biblical account. More probably, however, the original text of the *Enuma Elish* antedates Moses. Biblical theologians commonly suggest the creation accounts in Genesis demythologize the Ancient Near Eastern mythic cosmogonies.[92] Barr says, "The old creation story is very thoroughly demythologized."[93] According to his understanding the biblical narrator recast the myth in a form compatible with Israel's distinctive religious convictions. The demonstrable evidence (see below) points in the opposite direction: the biblical writers recount *historia* in the form and motifs adopted from the Mesopotamian cosmogony.

It could be argued reasonably by analogy with the flood stories that Genesis retains a pure form of an original creation account and that the depraved Mesopotamian civilizations also bastardized this account. The creation story, however, unlike the flood story, depends upon an original revelation, not on human memory. If the biblical account preserves an original revelation before the time of Moses, one that Moses preserved by inspiration, why, in contrast to the flood stories, is there no comparable global evidence of such an original revelation beside the Babylonian Genesis?

The ancient cosmogonies plausibly influenced the highly literate biblical authors.[94] Israel was in Egypt four hundred years prior to Moses. More important, having been highly educated in Pharaoh's courts as the son of Pharaoh's daughter, Moses had unique access to the Ancient Near Eastern myths and almost certainly was acquainted with them, for the archeological evidence shows that they were widely circulated. Also, almost all other forms of biblical literature conform in form — emphatically not in their theology! — with corresponding forms of other ancient literatures of the biblical world. In outward form Israel's evolving cultures, history writing, and prophets fit nicely into the Ancient Near Eastern world. To the spiritually discerning, however, the theology and ethics of the biblical literature are vastly superior to their pagan counterparts. In fact, the theological and ethical contrast is so great it validates the conviction that the Holy Spirit inspired the biblical literature. The same can be said of the comparison between the Sumerian King List and the line of Seth. The longevity of the antediluvian kings in the Sumerian King list is preposterously long, making the longevity of the antediluvian line of Seth more plausible (Genesis 5). In sum, God inspired Moses to write an infallible account of the creation of the cosmos that wore the garb of the Mesopotamian cosmogony. If so, the biblical creation

92. To be sure, the mythical language of the ANE was demythicized to play a part in the common Hebrew language.

93. Barr, "Meaning of Mythology," 7.

94. Bruce K. Waltke, *An Old Testament Theology: An Exegetical, Canonical, and Thematic Approach* (Grand Rapids: Zondervan, 2007), 197-202.

account probably also functions as a polemic against Marduk, who by his victory over Tiamat, created the cosmos from her carcass.

This suggested explanation conforms to sound theology. Inspiration does not bypass the personality of the human author but utilizes his experiences, style, culture, and research. Inspiration includes direct revelation (1 Cor. 2:7-13; 11:23; Gal. 1:11-12), experience (Acts 17:28; Gal. 2:11-14), and historical investigation (Luke 1:1). "In the treatment of the doctrine of inspiration, the question is not: 'How did the holy writers obtain the truths which they wrote?' but rather, 'Did the Holy Ghost prompt the sacred writers to write down certain words and thoughts which God wanted men to know [cf. 2 Tim. 3:16; 2 Pet. 1:21]?'"[95]

But what shall we say of the extraordinary elements in the second biblical cosmogony (Gen. 2:4–3:24): visible trees whose fruit conveys spiritual life and ethical knowledge, a woman built from a rib, and a talking snake? These details of the cosmogony do not accord with normal experience. Nevertheless, the second cosmogony by the above definition of myth is not myth. God in this narrative is transcendent (not identified with nature); mankind is responsible (not manipulating God by magic); and the writer of Genesis intends *historia*. This can be deduced by his linking Adam, the first Adam, as the head of a continuous genealogy climaxing in the twelve sons of Jacob, and by his naming and locating the four rivers that flowed from the Garden, along with his geographical comment that the Pishon river "winds through the entire land of Havilah, where there is gold. (The gold of that land is good; aromatic resin and onyx are also there.)" At the least, the story appears to be *historia*.

But what about the extraordinary details of the story? Are they also literal? Or are they, as Origen argued, unhistorical details that point symbolically to spiritual meanings?[96] Perhaps — and this is only a suggestion — the extraordinary details are creative spiritual symbols added to *historia*. Meir Sternberg notes that the biblical narrator has three concerns: history, aesthetics, and ideology.[97] Correlatively, his narrative has two parts: story *(historia)* and plot (his creative representation of the story by aesthetics) to deliver his message. To speak of spiritual and ethical matters beyond the capability of the human senses, an author must be creative. Let us assume that an artist wants to represent the idea that a glass half full of water is in fact full: the upper half full of invisible gases (air) and bottom half full of visible liquid H_2O (water). She could get across her idea by putting the water on the top and the air on the bottom, hoping the fantastic picture may

95. John T. Mueller, *Christian Dogmatics* (St. Louis: Concordia, 1934), 110.

96. Origen thought both biblical cosmogonies were spiritually symbolic, not historical (*De Principiis* 4.1.6, translated by Marcus J. Borg in his *Reading the Bible Again for the First Time: Taking the Bible Seriously but Not Literally* [San Francisco: Harper, 2001], 71).

97. Meir Sternberg, *Poetics of Biblical Narrative: Ideological Literature and the Drama of Reading* (Bloomington: Indiana University Press, 1985), 44.

make her point. Now let us further suppose that our artist wants to represent the abstract truth that both the visible and invisible gases are essential to life. To get across that idea she could put a goldfish in the water of the upper half and a canary in air of the bottom half. The audience could not distinguish between the ostensive reality of the half glass of water and the creative additions, but the artist will have communicated her idea in connection with a factual reality.[98] Is the narrator of the early chapters of Genesis capturing our attention and communicating the theology of the *historia* by these extraordinary pictures? Whatever the case, we can know the historical reality and its spiritual significance only through the narrator's inspired picturesque narrative.

Myth and Poetry

As George Smith's decoding of the Gilgamesh epic marked a turning point in biblical studies by correlating the narrative of Genesis 1–11 with similar Ancient Near Eastern myths, so also the discovery of ancient of poetic myths at Ugarit (1929) and their later decoding and publishing (1940) marked a turning point in understanding Israel's religion and poetry.[99] The Canaanite myths about Baal and other "Canaanite" deities mentioned in the Bible date from the thirteenth century B.C.E.

Chaoskampf

About a dozen OT poetic texts refer to a *Chaoskampf* ("war with chaos") between *I AM* and the Sea, Leviathan, and the like.[100] Cyrus Gordon's study of Leviathan in both the Bible and Ugaritic texts shows beyond reasonable doubt that Leviathan is the repressive god in Canaanite mythology and that Baal, the Canaanite storm god, is the god who released its life forces by vanquishing her.[101] Ugaritic text 67.1.1 says of Baal, "When you smite Lotan [= Leviathan] the evil dragon / Even destroy the crooked dragon / The mighty one of the seven heads." Psalm 74:13-14 reads: "It was you who split open the sea by your power; you

98. See Waltke, *An Old Testament Theology,* 93-112.

99. The lost city of Ugarit (modern Ras Shamra) is located on the Syrian coast across from the feather-pointed tip of Cyprus.

100. For a collection of such passages, see J. L. McKenzie, "A Note on Psalm 73 (74): 13-15," *TS* 11, no. 2 (1950): 275-82. A standard introduction to this topic is John Day, *God's Conflict with the Dragon and the Sea: Echoes of a Canaanite Myth in the Old Testament* (Cambridge: Cambridge University Press, 1985).

101. Cyrus H. Gordon, "Leviathan: Symbol of Evil," in *Biblical Motifs: Origins and Transformations,* ed. Alexander Altmann (Cambridge, MA: Harvard University Press, 1966), 1-9.

broke the heads of the monster in the waters. It was you who crushed the heads of Leviathan and gave it as food to the creatures of the desert." This identification of Leviathan also clarifies Job's petition, "May those who curse days curse that day [of my birth], those who are ready to rouse Leviathan" (Job 3:8). Job is asking for the bouleversement of his birthday by the imagery of repressive Leviathan.

Israel's poets use the sea-monster imagery for at least three victories in salvation history:

1. God's creation in the primordial past. "God does not restrain his anger; even the cohorts of Rahab cowered at his feet" (Job 9:13; cf. 26:12-13). In Job 41 Leviathan symbolizes the ungovernable surd in the cosmos.
2. *I AM*'s historic victory over Pharaoh in the exodus, whereby he created Israel. "Awake, awake, arm of the LORD, clothe yourself with strength! Awake, as in days gone by, as in generations of old. Was it not you who cut Rahab to pieces, who pierced that monster through? Was it not you who dried up the sea, the waters of the great deep, who made a road in the depths of the sea so that the redeemed might cross over?" (Isa. 51:9-10; cf. Ps. 74:13-14).
3. God's ultimate triumph over hostile nations and ultimately Satan. "In that day, *I AM* will punish with his sword — his fierce, great and powerful sword — Leviathan the gliding serpent, Leviathan the coiling serpent; he will slay the monster of the sea" (Isa. 27:1; 30:7; Job 7:12; Ezek. 29:3-5; 32:2-6). Consider also: "Michael and his angels fought against the dragon, and the dragon and his angels fought back. . . . The great dragon was hurled down — that ancient serpent called the devil, or Satan, who leads the whole world astray" (Rev. 12:7-9).

The fuller contexts of these dozen poetic references demonstrate that the Israelite poets were orthodox with respect to the Mosaic covenant, and if so, they must have adopted and adapted Canaanite imagery, not its pantheistic, polytheistic, and magical theology.[102] Job protests his innocence by claiming his adherence to the theological purity of true Israel: "If I have looked at the sun when it shone, or the moon going in splendor; and my heart became secretly enticed . . . that too would have been an iniquity calling for judgment, for I would have denied God above" (Job 31:26-28). Isaiah confesses, "This is what the LORD says — Israel's King and Redeemer, the LORD Almighty: I am the first and I am the last; apart from me there is no God" (Isa. 44:6; cf. 45:6-7; passim). This is the fuller context

102. Ronald Barclay Allen, "The Leviathan-Rahab-Dragon Motif in the Old Testament" (ThM thesis, Dallas Theological Seminary, 1968). Some refer to this borrowing of mythic elements as "broken myths," but that sense must be distinguished from Tillich's use of the term to refer to myths that are rejected by critical thinking but still have a symbolic value.

of Psalm 74:13-14: "The day is yours, and yours also the night; you established the sun and moon. It was you who set all the boundaries of the earth" (vv. 16-17).

Borrowed Imagery, Not Theology

The Myth and Ritual School and others, such as Mark Smith, mistakenly interpret biblical poetic allusions to myth too woodenly. In their view Israel's poets reflect Canaanite theology, not borrowed Canaanite imagery.[103] Several lines of evidence dismantle their woodenly literalistic base and so deconstruct their revisionist history of Israel's religion.

1. The theological tenor of the Bible that incorporates these allusions deconstructs the revisionists. Kaufmann says, "Biblical religion is in essence non-mythological; the myth is demolished and suppressed, existing only in shredded remnants."[104] An author has final control of his literary composition and does not incorporate material that subverts his intention. When read holistically, not by *dicta probantia,* all biblical poets uphold the values of Israel's prosaic covenants, not those of myths.

2. Unlike the Canaanite texts, the aquatic chaos-monster in the hands of Israel's poets lacks a bibliography, is not a fully distinct divine personality, and occurs within non-mythic contexts. In the context of Israel's poems, the Canaanite myths are disarmed of pantheism and of magic.[105] They are "historicized and used metaphorically."[106] Nevertheless, Israel's poets do not turn myths into "cut flowers," in Paul Ricoeur's terms. Levenson rightly asserts that biblical cosmogonies use myth to represent creation as fragile and ever threatened by chaos.[107] *I AM*'s faithful covenant partners depend on God's oaths and majestic strength to assure the triumph of good over an ever present evil both in the cosmos and in history.

3. Israel's poets adopt mythic imagery selectively and discreetly. True Israel absorbs mythic imagery and rejects mythic theology. Anderson comments that Israel's drawing freely upon mythical imagery "was not a weak and spineless syncretism. Israel was highly selective in the way she appropriated mythical materials from the environment. Some images were appropriated by Israel; others were

103. E.g., Jon D. Levenson, *Creation and the Persistence of Evil* (Princeton: Princeton University Press, 1988), 5-13.

104. Yehezkel Kaufmann, "The Bible and Mythological Polytheism," *JBL* 70, no. 3 (1951): 182.

105. See Elmer B. Smick, "Mythology and the Book of Job," *JETS* 13, no. 2 (1970): 101-6; "Another Look at the Mythological Elements in the Book of Job," *WTJ* 40 (1978): 213-28; "Mythopoetic Language in the Psalms," *WTJ* 44 (1982): 88-98.

106. Gerhard von Rad, *Studies in Deuteronomy* (London: SCM, 1953), 74-91.

107. Levenson, *Creation and the Persistence of Evil.*

flatly rejected."[108] One of those images they adopted is *Chaoskampf,* a borrowed image that demands fuller exploration.

Function of Broken Myths

H. L. Ginsberg convincingly argues that Psalm 29 adopts a hymn once composed for the Canaanite storm god Baal and adapts it by substituting *YHWH* for Baal in every verse but the middle one (v. 6).[109] This adopted and adapted psalm of praise implicitly polemicizes against the Canaanite storm god.[110] This may also be the intention of referring to *I AM* as the "Rider of the Clouds" (Deut. 33:26; Pss. 68:33 [Hebrew 34]; 104:3), an epithet for Baal in the Ugaritic Texts (KTU I.3; II.46).

Israel's poems that preserve their most ancient forms use mythic elements to enhance the theological significance of historical events.[111] For example, the Canaanite god, Baal Zaphon, was associated with Mount Zaphon ten kilometers (6.2 miles) north of Ugarit. Mount Zaphon was the sacred mountain of the Canaanite storm god, Baal. Mount Zion, by contrast, was the city of *I AM;* from here he ruled heaven and earth. To pilgrims approaching Mount Zion from the valleys around Mount Zion or from the City of David to the south, where most of the residents of Jerusalem lived, the climb to the temple (387 ft.) may have seemed a great height, but in comparison to Mount Zaphon (5,607 ft.) it was a lowly mountain. To elevate the height of Mount Zion (2,460 ft.), Psalm 48:2 (Hebrew 48:3) compares it to the lofty and beautiful Mount Zaphon: "Beautiful in its loftiness, the joy of the whole earth, like the heights of Zaphon is Mount Zion,[112] the city of the Great King" (Ps. 48:2). The psalmist transforms a mythological motif by identifying Mount Zion with Mount Zaphon. His comparison

108. Bernhard W. Anderson, "Myth and the Biblical Tradition," *Theology Today* 27 (1970): 55.

109. H. L. Ginsberg, *tby 'wgryt* [Hebrew] (Jerusalem: The Bialik Foundation, 1936), 129ff.

110. Peter Machinist argues that the similarities between Solomon's temple and similar temple constructions in the Ancient Near East, such as an excavated temple at 'Ain Dara in northern Syria, functioned as a polemic that Yahweh had conquered the Canaanite deities ("Literature as Politics: The Tukulti-Ninurta Epic and the Bible," *CBQ* 38 [1976]: 455-82).

111. Michael Fox (*Proverbs 1–9,* AB [New York: Doubleday, 2000], 352; see esp. n. 227), speaking of Woman Wisdom in Proverbs, so defines myth: "I use the Greek form 'mythos' to recall Plato's use of the word, a narratival trope that serves as an explanatory paradigm in areas where literal discourse must be supplemented by poetic imagination." Since myth is a trope, it is not actual. Finegan (*Myth and Mystery,* 15) agrees: "Myth may be defined as a form of symbolic thought in which intellect, imagination, and emotion combine to communicate a perceived truth. A myth is not, then, in the first instance, a fanciful tale, but a symbolic or poetic expression of that which is incapable of direct statement." A symbol may (e.g., George Washington) or may not (e.g., Cinderella) be historical.

112. Lit., "Mount Zion the farthest reaches of Zaphon."

also functions to polemicize against Baal worship. In his world, Israel's God, *I AM,* is King — not Baal.

From his close analysis of Israel's earliest poems, Frank Moore Cross speaks of "the tendency to mythologize historical episodes to reveal their transcendent meaning."[113] Lawrence Toombs says, "The concepts and vocabulary of pagan mythology are drawn upon and used to illuminate historical events. They are, accordingly, taken from their original context, rearranged, readjusted to an historical beginning, and, in consequence radically transformed."[114] Stephen G. Dempster demonstrates that such is the case in the Song of Deborah.[115]

Conclusion

Theologians and possibly others in the humanities would be best served by returning to the *usus loquendi* standard and, further, defining myth more narrowly. Myth denotes a story that identifies the gods with conflicting forces of nature, as capable of being manipulated by a recounting of the primordial story, usually in connection with mimetic rituals to restore the primordial state of deified nature, and has no transcendent vision that in the end they will eliminate both physical and moral evil. All the literature of the Genus: *historio-poesis* differs from the species of the Genus: myth by being anchored in *historia.* Moreover, to the discerning, the species of biblical narrative, especially its cosmogonies, far surpasses myths in its theology and ethics. Israel's sovereign God created matter out of nothing, is transcendent in his rule over all of his creation, conflicts with cosmic and volitional evil to produce virtue and bring rightful praise to him, and created the cosmos as the first of his saving acts in a trajectory ending with his kingdom irrupting into the world through his *magnalia Dei* and word and an eternal state in which he finally eliminates all hostility. The radical difference between the inspired biblical cosmogony and other genera of cosmogony points to its supernatural origin, though ultimately the Spirit must illuminate that truth.

Theologians should be grateful that since the turn of the twentieth century ethnologists, sociologists, and historians of religion, in spite of their cultural relativism, have refurbished myth to connote a story that is "true," "sacred," "exemplary," or "significant." This is so because the positive refurbishing of myth points to the hunger of the human heart for a reality that exists beyond what can be known via positivism. The human spirit in its hunger for truth, for reality, requires the philosopher's reasoning and the poet's intuition. Literature that satisfies both

113. Cross, *Canaanite Myth,* 144.

114. Toombs, "Formation of Myth Patterns," 109.

115. Stephen G. Dempster, "Mythology and History in the Song of Deborah," *WTJ* 41 (1978): 33-53.

needs may well be labeled *historio-poesis.* That sort of literature stands in marked contrast to mythopoesis, the making of myths.

The parallels between Mesopotamian myths and Genesis 1–11 can be explained in two ways: (1) the Mesopotamian myths bastardize the historical reality, which the Bible preserves in pure form. This is probably the case of the flood accounts; (2) the Holy Spirit inspired the biblical narrator to transform pagan myths to recount *historia* in accord with God's values as revealed in his covenants with his chosen people. The parallel between the mythmakers of the Ugaritic texts and Israel's poets is best explained as the latter borrowing imagery, not theology, from the former.

Theologians should be grateful to the scholars of Ancient Near Eastern artifacts and texts because they help (1) to better interpret the literary allusions in the Bible, (2) to anchor the Bible more firmly in history, and (3) to profile for the spiritually discerning the vast superiority of the Bible's theology and ethics. The difference is so great that it points to the Bible's heavenly inspiration.

NINETEEN

Biblical Authority and Diverse Literary Genres

Barry G. Webb

Until comparatively recently discussions of biblical authority and biblical genres have taken place in quite distinct fields of study. Discussions regarding biblical authority have normally occurred in the church, in the context of systematic theology, and as an aspect of the doctrine of the word of God. In the universities, discussion of genres has normally occurred in the context of biblical criticism and as an aspect of biblical introduction. The separation of the two spheres of discussion reflects the fundamental distinction between the church as a confessional community, and the academy as a non-confessional environment. All agree that the Bible[1] contains a wide variety of genres, and that no study of it can ignore this. But for the most part genre study has functioned differently in the two settings. In the church it has generally been viewed as an aid to responsible exegesis, with a positive relationship to biblical authority. In the university it has mainly been concerned with what it can tell us about the oral pre-history of the literature, and the life settings in which the genres originally functioned, with inferences relating to biblical authority generally being negative. For example, genre study of the gospels has more often than not been accompanied by skepticism about their historical value. In the broad field of biblical interpretation and literary theory, a generally philosophical approach has dominated academic discussion, with little or no reference to biblical authority.[2]

1. In this essay the word "Bible" refers to the Christian Bible, containing the Old and New Testaments, but not the Apocrypha. Scripture quotations are from the NIV (1984) unless otherwise indicated.

2. See, for example, the collection of essays in David G. Firth and Jamie A. Grant, eds., *Words and the Word: Explorations in Biblical Interpretation and Literary Theory* (Nottingham: Apollos, 2008). There are exceptions, of course. The work of Kevin Vanhoozer, which we will come to shortly, is a particularly fine example.

Thinking Genre and Authority Together

A significant contribution towards bridging the gap between genre and authority came in 1979 with the publication of Brevard Childs's *Introduction to the Old Testament as Scripture.*[3] Childs's basic dissatisfaction with the kind of biblical criticism that had been practiced in the university environment for the last couple of centuries was that it had produced little of value to the church because it had not given sufficient attention to the genre of the literature it had been studying. The neo-orthodoxy of the 1930s, and the biblical theology movement that had flourished with it, had promised much, but by the 1970s had been largely discredited. Childs's concern was that in the wake of this collapse, biblical studies would again fragment into academic specialties with no desire or capacity to do the constructive work that theological study of the biblical material required. A new kind of biblical theology was needed that would reengage with the Bible as Scripture.[4] By Scripture Childs did not mean divinely inspired literature with absolute authority, but a body of literature (the canon) that was densely cross-referenced and fundamentally theological. This meant that no part could be studied satisfactorily without taking into consideration the contribution it made to the whole, and the way it was conditioned by the whole. In short, Childs brought the canon into focus as the primary context for biblical exegesis, and therefore biblical theology into focus as a proper and necessary aspect of biblical criticism. He described the approach he was advocating as follows:

> The approach which is being proposed is not to be confused with homiletics, but is descriptive in nature. It is not confessional in the sense of consciously assuming tenets of Christian theology, but rather it seeks to describe as objectively as possible the canonical literature of ancient Israel which is the heritage of both Jew and Christian. If at times the description becomes theological in its terminology, it is because the literature itself requires it. The frequent reference to the term "canonical" is not to suggest that a new exegetical technique is being developed. Rather, the term denotes a context from which the literature is being understood.[5]

In view of the radically different approach to the literature that this involves, the assertion that no new exegetical technique is involved is somewhat misleading. What is clear, though, is that Childs did not intend to disengage from the kind of critical study that was and remains basic to the academy. Study was still to be done

3. Brevard S. Childs, *Introduction to the Old Testament as Scripture* (London: SCM, 1979).

4. Brevard S. Childs, *Biblical Theology in Crisis* (Philadelphia: Westminster, 1970), esp. chapter 5.

5. Childs, *Introduction,* 14.

on the basis of evidence and reason alone, without recourse to the divine inspiration and authority of the text as controls on the process of exegesis. But the insistence on canon as context, and the acceptance of theology as a necessary and proper aspect of the study of biblical literature, were both major steps towards making the academic study of the Bible more likely to deliver results that are useful to the believing communities for whom the Bible is authoritative. Childs is a striking example of how the recognition of a particular genre (in this case "Scripture") can affect biblical criticism and bring confessional and non-confessional study of the Bible into positive connection with one another, without blurring the distinction between them.

It can also do more than this, however. Recognition of the text as Scripture can enable belief in its divine authority to be defended and/or clarified. A notable example from the same general period as Childs's *Introduction* is Meredith Kline's *The Structure of Biblical Authority*.[6] Kline was reacting to the then prevailing critical view that the Old Testament canon had developed over time from early oral material to later written material, and began to function as canon when an early form of it was published with royal authority in the seventh century B.C.E. in support of Josiah's reforms.[7] Building on his earlier work, *Treaty of the Great King*,[8] Kline argued that the book of Deuteronomy and the core of the book of Exodus had the form of treaty documents from the second millennium B.C.E., and therefore the Old Testament canon must have originated as such a document. It was written and of binding authority from the start, since that is the nature of a treaty document. The growth of the canon took place as Yahweh the Great King administered his covenant relationship with Israel by sending prophets as his spokesmen from time to time. In the revised edition, published in 1975, Kline extended his treatment to the New Testament, arguing that the gospel genre is not derived from secular first-century C.E. models, but is a continuation of the Old Testament treaty model, with special dependence on the book of Exodus. By implication the treaty model of canon could be extended from the gospels to the New Testament as a whole, just as it can be extended from the treaty documents of the Pentateuch to the Old Testament as a whole.

This way of thinking about canon has major implications for the relationship between Scripture and church:

> If the covenant is the product of the suzerain's unilateral decree of its terms and content and rests on a history of his own liberating action, then the vassal

6. Meredith C. Kline, *The Structure of Biblical Authority*, rev. edition (Grand Rapids: Eerdmans, 1975 [1972]).

7. E.g., Georg Fohrer, *Introduction to the Old Testament*, trans. D. Green (London: SPCK, 1970), 483-87.

8. Meredith C. Kline, *Treaty of the Great King: The Covenant Structure of Deuteronomy: Studies and Commentary* (Grand Rapids: Eerdmans, 1963).

> is on the receiving end. Ultimate authority always resides outside the self and even outside the church, as both are always *hearers* of the WORD and *receivers* of its judgment and justification.[9]

The main weakness in Kline's approach is the difficulty of accommodating *all* the materials of the canon within the treaty model. The radical wisdom literature such as Job and Ecclesiastes, for example, resists such accommodation. Nevertheless, Kline has shown how an observation about genre can be used to challenge prevailing views about the nature and authority of Scripture.

A study that likewise begins from a confessional standpoint but does more justice to the variety of biblical genres is Kevin Vanhoozer's "The Semantics of Biblical Literature" (1986).[10] He approaches the issue of the diversity of the biblical literature from the vantage point of speech-act theory,[11] and concludes, among other things, that

(1) In terms of speech-act theory, the biblical canon can be described as a collection of the inscribed speech-acts of God. (93)
(2) "Scripture does many things with words, and hence its authority is multifaceted." (94)
(3) "Infallibility means that the Scripture's diverse illocutionary forces [to assert, warn, command, etc.] will invariably achieve their respective purposes." (94)
(4) "Inerrancy [is] a *subset* of infallibility," and means that "on those occasions when Scripture does affirm something, the affirmation is true." (95)

This is a good example of a doctrine (the authority of Scripture) being clarified using tools developed in the academy rather than the church. Both the examples just given demonstrate the potential fruitfulness of bringing the discussion of genre and the discussion of authority together. In his more recent work Vanhoozer has developed his basic approach further, applying it to more extended forms of biblical discourse, and even to Scripture as a whole.[12] Vanhoozer's work

9. Michael S. Horton, "Theologies of Scripture in the Reformation and Counter-Reformation," in *Christian Theologies of Scripture: A Comparative Introduction,* ed. Justin S. Holcomb (New York: New York University Press, 2006), 88.

10. Kevin J. Vanhoozer, "The Semantics of Biblical Literature: Truth and Scripture's Diverse Literary Forms," in *Hermeneutics, Authority, and Canon,* ed. D. A. Carson and John D. Woodbridge (Grand Rapids: Zondervan, 1986), 53-104. Subsequent page references to this work are given in parentheses in the text.

11. For a good introduction see Richard S. Briggs, "Speech-Act Theory," in Firth and Grant, eds., *Words and the Word,* 75-110.

12. Kevin J. Vanhoozer, *Is There a Meaning in This Text? The Bible, the Reader, and the Morality of Literary Knowledge* (Downers Grove, IL: InterVarsity, 1998); *The Drama of Doctrine: A Canonical-Linguistic Approach to Christian Theology* (Louisville: Westminster John Knox,

is first class, and what follows is no substitute for it. What I propose, though, is to tackle the same broad issue of how the various biblical genres function as Scripture in the more bottom-up approach of an exegete and biblical theologian than the more top-down, philosophical approach of Vanhoozer.[13] Of course in an essay of this length only a few representative examples can be looked at. Issues related to history and myth will be covered elsewhere. But first, a matter of fundamental importance: Given that "genre" and "form" are related, how is the authority of Scripture related to its form more generally?

Authority and Translatability

The characterization of Scripture as the speech-acts of God implies that its authority is derived from God as its divine author, however many human agents may have been involved in its production. In other words, its authority follows from the activity of God in inspiring the human agents and using human language to address us. But is the particular *form* that this divine speech takes in Scripture fixed? Does inscripturation make it unalterable? Can its form be changed without compromising its authority?

In contrast to Islam, Judaism and Christianity have always believed in the translatability of Scripture, the most striking example being the Septuagint, which was produced within Judaism and functioned as Scripture in both Judaism and Christianity. The legitimacy of this is put beyond all doubt for Christians by the way the New Testament writers cite the LXX and other extant translations as Scripture. But the translation of Scripture from one language to another entails a very significant change in its form; indeed, change is of the essence of translation, and the need for it is the reason why translations are made. Translation always entails both gain and loss. What is gained is the accessibility of Scripture to a wider audience. What is lost is the precise form of the original, and with it

---

2005). For Vanhoozer's own distinctively theological and Christian version of speech-act theory see *Is There a Meaning?* 207-65.

13. Nor is it meant to be a critique of the many other fine books on biblical hermeneutics that have been published in the last two decades, e.g., John Goldingay, *Models for the Interpretation of Scripture* (Carlisle: Paternoster, 1995); Craig G. Bartholomew, C. Greene, and K. Moller, eds., *Renewing Biblical Interpretation* (Carlisle: Paternoster, 2000); Craig G. Bartholomew and Elaine Botha, *Out of Egypt: Biblical Theology and Biblical Interpretation* (Bletchley and Milton Keynes, UK: Paternoster; Grand Rapids: Zondervan, 2004); Firth and Grant, eds., *Words and the Word.* What I am attempting to do is logically prior to the task of interpretation, namely, understanding how the various genres function as Scripture in their canonical context. It is descriptive rather than method-oriented. I believe that such description is possible, despite claims to the contrary. My own description is of course open to correction and improvement by others engaged in the same task.

an inevitable loss of some aspects of its meaning and impact. In this respect it is noteworthy that the contrast between Islam on the one hand, and Judaism and Christianity on the other, is not absolute.

> Yes, Jews have permitted the translation of the Torah, but the date of the completion of the Septuagint was long observed as a fast because the translation was considered by some as a tragedy. . . . Orthodox Jews continue to insist on Torah readings and prayers being done in Hebrew, and there is a saying that reading the Torah in translation is like kissing your bride through a veil. Even reform Jews have to read Hebrew for their Bar Mitzvah. At the same time, there is increasing Islamic acceptance of translations of the Qur'an, although these are seen as interpretations and not [strictly speaking] as translations.[14]

And it is interesting how, in the context of doctrinal controversies between Judaism and Christianity, and within Christianity itself, there arose a recognition of the need to produce translations that adhered as closely as possible to the wording of the original. However, while this entailed a recognition of the loss entailed in translation, it never went so far as to stop translations being made and the resulting translations being regarded as Scripture. It is clear, therefore, that within the communities that preserved and transmitted the Bible to us, some change was regarded as possible without compromising the authority of Scripture. But within the permissible range of translation options, the original retained a privileged, normative status. A similar phenomenon appears in modern statements about the inerrancy of Scripture "as originally given" (or words to that effect).[15] In other words, the authority of Scripture is not a property of the words as separate entities, but of the words assembled in a particular way in order to communicate something and do something.[16] And it is this meaning-effect (what is *expressed* by the text) and rhetorical effect (its persuasiveness) that are translatable. It follows that Scripture as the speech-acts of God is translatable; it can exist in more than one form without its authority being compromised. But a prior question concerns the forms already present in the biblical literature itself. Are these literary forms, in all their particularity, compatible with Scripture being divine and not merely human speech? And are these forms/genres translatable? Can Scripture be Scripture without them?

14. Private communication from Ida Glaser.

15. F. F. Bruce, "As Originally Given," *The Theological Students Fellowship Terminal Letter* 14 (Spring 1956): 2-3.

16. For the significance of this distinction for translation and biblical interpretation respectively see Moises Silva, "Are Translators Traitors? Some Personal Reflections," in *The Challenge of Bible Translation: Communicating God's Word to the World; Essays in Honor of Ronald F. Youngblood,* ed. Mark L. Strauss, Glen G. Scorgie, and Stephen M. Voth (Grand Rapids: Zondervan, 2003), 37-50; and Firth and Grant, eds., *Words and the Word.*

Words of Men and Word of God

How can such genres as narratives, oracles, psalms, instructional wisdom (Proverbs), radical wisdom (Job, Ecclesiastes), laments, protests, and hymns, to name a few, function as divine speech-acts, when most of them are manifestly not so? The psalms, for example, are almost entirely words addressed to God, or spoken about God, rather than the speech of God himself. The proverbs, for the most part, are generalizations about the observed world, and take the form of a parent speaking to his child, or a teacher addressing his pupils rather than divine speech. In fact God as speaker is almost entirely absent from this literature. Similar problems exist for much of the rest of the Old Testament. Only prophetic oracles and Mosaic law are presented as the speech of God. The incarnation of God in Christ in the New Testament alters this situation significantly in the gospels, and this continues to some extent in the epistles, which in some respects parallel the oracular literature of the Old Testament. Even so, it is difficult to construe everything as divine speech, especially where the connection with the apostolic office is weak or unclear, or when Paul himself distinguishes between his own speech and that of Christ (as in 1 Cor. 7:8, 12, 25), implying that Paul's speech at those points is more advice than oracle.[17] So how can biblical literature as a whole be considered the inscribed speech-acts of God, or to use more traditional language, the words or word of God?

The answer most commonly given is that the Scriptures are inspired by God, and therefore *his* words in the sense that he is the primary author of them. Appeal is made to explicit statements about the divine origin of Scripture in such passages as 2 Peter 1:21 ("prophecy never had its origin in the will of man, but men spoke from God as they were carried along by the Holy Spirit"), 2 Timothy 3:16 ("All

17. But, one hastens to add, *apostolic* advice! Paul's distinction between what he gives as a command of Christ ("not I, but the Lord") and what he gives only as his own word ("I, not the Lord") cannot be taken as distinguishing between what has apostolic authority and what does not. He writes the entire epistle as "an apostle of Christ Jesus by the will of God" (1:1). The basic distinction seems to be between appealing to a specific teaching of Jesus, and speaking as an apostle without being able to appeal to any specific teaching of Jesus regarding the issue at hand. But in 2 Corinthians 8 Paul also uses the "command/advice" *(epitagē/gnōmē)* distinction between two ways he speaks as an apostle without reference to whether or not he is appealing to a specific teaching of Jesus. In other words, even as an apostle he leaves room for some freedom in the way what he says is received and applied. But as he says later in the present chapter, even when he is only giving "advice," he does so as one "who by the Lord's mercy is trustworthy" (7:25 NIV). Just as the Old Testament Scriptures contain "command" (law) and "advice" (wisdom teaching), so do the writings of the apostles; but all of it is Scripture. Compare Goldingay's comment on material in the Torah such as Deuteronomy 24:1-4, which allows divorce under certain conditions: "The material that makes allowance for human stubbornness still has Moses' authority. It is still part of scripture." *Theology and Canon,* 16. See also the discussion of 1 Corinthians 7:10, 12, and 25 in Roy E. Ciampa and Brian S. Rosner, *The First Letter to the Corinthians,* PNTC (Grand Rapids: Eerdmans, 2010).

Scripture is God-breathed and is useful for teaching"), and Hebrews 1:1 ("In the past God spoke to our forefathers through the prophets at many times and in various ways"). Effectively, this understands the words of Scripture to be God's words in the way the words of a novel (say) are the author's words, even though they are put in the mouths of many different characters, and accommodated to the personalities and circumstances of these characters.[18] Understandably, these classic passages have featured prominently in discussions about the inspiration and authority of Scripture. They testify to the fact that the Jewish belief that the literature of the Old Testament was the result of God speaking through prophets was carried over into early Christianity and formed the basis of the church's own eventual doctrine of Scripture. The catalyst for this continuity was Jesus' own frequent reference to "the Scriptures," which, as the gospels show, included the Law and the Psalms, as well as the Prophets (Luke 24:44). In fact there are good reasons for believing that the first included the entire Old Testament Hebrew canon, from Genesis to 2 Chronicles, with all its diverse genres.[19] Furthermore, the authority conferred on the apostles by Jesus paved the way for this understanding of the inspiration and authority of the Old Testament Scriptures to be extended in due course to the apostolic writings of the New Testament as well.

There is ample warrant, therefore, in the practice of Jesus and the apostles for regarding the words of men in Scripture as the word(s) of God. But this still leaves unaddressed the key questions we are concerned with in this essay: (1) Of what significance is it that the Scriptures of the Old and New Testaments are comprised of so many diverse genres? (2) How do these diverse genres function as the word of God? and (3) Is this variegated form of Scripture intrinsic to its authority, or incidental to it? Could the translatability of Scripture be extended to the genres, such that it could all be recast into, say, propositional form, without its authority being compromised?[20]

Narrative as Scripture's Master Genre

It hardly needs saying that the Bible is basically a story. In academic circles it is not fashionable to state the obvious; it lacks sophistication. But this can all too

18. This is only one possible model. Others include, for example, delegation and appropriation. For a detailed discussion of the various ways in which human speech can function as divine discourse see Nicholas Wolterstorff, *Divine Discourse: Philosophical Reflections on the Claim That God Speaks* (Cambridge: Cambridge University Press, 1995).

19. See Matthew 23:35, Luke 11:51, and the discussion in Roger T. Beckwith, *The Old Testament Canon of the New Testament Church and Its Background in Early Judaism* (London: SPCK, 1985), 110-15.

20. See the "hard questions" concerning propositional revelation posed by Vanhoozer in *The Drama of Doctrine*, 5.

easily lead to the obvious being lost sight of altogether, a mistake that can skew the whole project of biblical studies, especially the study of the Bible's theology.[21] The fact is that Bible begins with creation and ends with new creation, and that a narrative thread links all that is between the beginning and the end. Not only so, but this narrative thread is not just a chronicle, a list of uninterpreted events arranged in chronological order; it is much more than this. It exhibits all the elements of a classical plot: initial state of rest, disturbance, quest, climax, and denouement, including arrival at a final state of rest.[22] Furthermore, this holds true whether the books of the Old Testament follow the order of our English Bible, based on the Vulgate and the LXX (Pentateuch, historical books, poetical and ethical books, prophetical books) or the traditional order of the Hebrew canon (Law, Prophets, Writings). There are, after all, different ways of telling the same story! This narrative thread is in effect the spine of the biblical canon; it is not everything, but is basic to everything. Everything is linked to it in some way or other, and its contribution to the Bible's unity can hardly be overstated. We will call this narrative thread the Bible's *core narrative.*

The core narrative begins with God speaking the world into existence, and then continuing to speak, mainly through prophets and apostles. By speaking promises, especially to Abraham, he creates momentum and gives the core narrative (and therefore the Bible's theology) a basic promise-fulfillment structure. As the plot unfolds various things happen: covenants are made, laws are issued, songs are sung, wisdom teaching is given, buildings are erected, conflicts happen, praise and prayer are offered, hard questions are asked, and interactions of all kinds take place between people and people, and between people and God. In the process a wide range of discourse happens, and the core narrative is expanded in various ways. From time to time the core narrative slows down or comes to a complete stop while we are shown in great detail what happens at a particular time and place. These are *lateral expansions* of the core narrative in the sense that they emerge at right angles to the direction of its developing plot. A striking Old Testament example is the mass of legal and ritual material that is located during Israel's long stay at Mount Sinai (Exod. 19:2 — Num. 10:11-12). Other Old Testa-

21. See Hans W. Frei, *The Eclipse of Biblical Narrative: A Study in Eighteenth and Nineteenth Century Hermeneutics* (New Haven: Yale University Press, 1974).

22. This basic point is contested of course. For example, Seitz sees the basic structure of the Old Testament canon as the threefold division into Torah, Prophets, and Writings, and does "not find the generic term 'narrative' very illuminating." Christopher Seitz, "Canon, Narrative, and the Old Testament's Literal Sense: A Response to John Goldingay, 'Canon and Old Testament Theology,'" *TynB* 59, no. 1 (2008): 29. I would argue that a narrative is what the entire Bible is, and that this is therefore either more basic or more comprehensive than any of its subdivisions, including even the division into Old and New Testaments. This is not to deny that the traditional divisions that Seitz refers to are significant, but that their significance lies essentially in their contribution to the Bible's overarching, unifying narrative.

ment examples include the psalmic and sapiential material of the Psalter and the book of Proverbs respectively, which is linked through David and Solomon with the relatively short period of the united monarchy, and the mass of oracular material in the books of the Latter Prophets, which is linked through named prophets with particular moments in the eighth to sixth centuries B.C.E. New Testament examples include the apocalyptic material of the book of Revelation associated with the apostle John's exile on Patmos, and the so-called prison epistles of the apostle Paul. Lateral expansions like this are technically digressions, since they are departures from the narrative thread (the core narrative), do not materially advance the linear development of the plot, and are usually of a different genre. But functionally they are like zoom shots in a piece of photo journalism, points at which the journalist remains in one place for a time in order to show in more detail something that is particularly interesting or important, before resuming his journey. They are usually particularly rich theologically, and contribute content to the core narrative that it carries with it when it begins to move forward again. We will see several examples of this in what follows.

A second kind of enrichment of the core narrative is what we will call here *resumptive expansions.* These occur when the core narrative doubles back on itself and goes over the same ground again from a different perspective. Classic Old Testament examples include the two accounts of creation in Genesis 1–2, and the way 1-2 Chronicles revisits ground already covered in 1 Samuel 31 — 2 Kings 25. In the New Testament the parade example is the fourfold treatment of the life, death, and resurrection in the four gospels, especially the three synoptics. Unlike the lateral expansions, these resumptive expansions involve no change of genre, and no digression from the core narrative, but what results in all cases is a "thicker," richer coverage of the ground in question. Neither kind of expansion detracts from the significance of the core narrative, but enriches it, resulting in what we will call the Bible's *comprehensive* or *meta*narrative. This metanarrative is the given form of the Bible's theology and the carrier of all aspects of its message. It does not overwhelm and obliterate the other genres, but unifies and contextualizes them by making space within itself for each of them to be heard and make their distinctive contribution to the whole. The Bible's variegated theology, its interconnected themes, is progressively developed as this narrative unfolds. It is partly obscured by the traditional division of the Old Testament into Law, Prophets, and Writings, but is implicit in the biblical canon as a whole, from Genesis to Revelation, and is in fact coterminous with it. It is the Bible's master genre, and the literary setting of all its other genres. These are effectively subgenres of Scripture's one metanarrative, the narrative of God's acts as Creator and Redeemer to fulfill his promise to judge and save his world. It is the plenary form of Scripture's gospel.[23]

23. Cf. John Goldingay, *Old Testament Theology,* vol. 1, *Israel's Gospel* (Leicester/Downers Grove, IL: InterVarsity, 2003), 15-41.

Narrative as Scripture's Indispensable Genre

It follows from the conclusions reached in the previous section that there are limits to how much the form of Scripture can be changed without turning it into something else. It can be translated into other languages. This inevitably entails the gains and losses involved in the translation of any text, but does not fundamentally change the nature of Scripture. It is still recognizably the same metanarrative of God's acts as Savior and Redeemer; the same scriptural gospel. It can, however, be summarized in various ways. The core narrative can serve as a summary of the comprehensive metanarrative. This involves loss of the theologically rich expansions noted above, but again does not change the essence of Scripture or of the biblical gospel. It can be summarized more drastically as an account of the life, death, and resurrection of Jesus the Messiah, provided this is presented as the fulfillment of what has gone before, as in the New Testament Gospels with their frequent references and allusions to the Old Testament. It can be faithfully rendered in sermon form, as in the apostolic preaching of the book of Acts. It can even be summarized in two or three pithy sentences, as in Paul's summary of his "gospel" in 1 Corinthians 15:3-5: "that Christ died for our sins according to the Scriptures, that he was buried, that he was raised on the third day according to the Scriptures, and that he appeared to Peter, and then to the Twelve." Something rather different, though, begins to happen in the New Testament epistles, where aspects of the biblical gospel are expounded at length and used as the basis for ethical instruction. Here the implications of the biblical metanarrative for what Christians should believe and do begin to be spelled out, which begins a development that will lead eventually to the creeds of the first four centuries of the Christian church and beyond. The creeds are not so much summaries of the biblical metanarrative as summaries of what the church has come to believe about God, Father, Son, and Holy Spirit, as a result of *reading* this narrative. The trajectory from the apostolic letters to the historic Christian creeds is the development, on the one hand, from biblical narrative to biblical exposition to ethical instruction (the epistles), and from biblical theology to Christian doctrine (the creeds). We have entered the world of historical theology and doctrine that will lead eventually to Christian ethics of a more systematic and philosophical kind. These forms of Christian thought are no longer Scripture, since they are no longer either the scriptural metanarrative itself, or summaries of it, but extensions of it into the history of the church and Christian thought. They must always be distinguished from Scripture and subject to correction by it.

The earliest stages of these developments are found in Scripture itself, particularly the lateral and resumptive expansions we noted above. But because these expansions emerge from the core narrative as it runs its course from Genesis to Revelation, and feed back into it as we have seen, it is quite proper to understand them as part of the metanarrative that is coterminous with Scripture itself. In other words they are canonical expansions rather than extra-canonical ones. The task of the biblical exegete and theologian is to understand how these various parts of Scripture, with their various genres, function as parts of its metanarrative. To provide a comprehensive answer to this question is clearly beyond the scope of this paper. In what follows, however, I will show what an answer might look like by considering some representative examples of the biblical genres.

Old Testament Genres

Narrative Foundations: Genesis

Form criticism and related studies have shown that Genesis is comprised of a number of different genres.[24] My purpose here, however, is not to discuss whether or not chapters 1–11 are myth, or whether chapters 12–50 are saga, or whether either are authoritative in the historical sense. Rather, our focus will be on the book as a whole, and on what can be said about its genre and authority by considering its location and function in its biblical context.

Clearly Genesis is narrative in the sense that it is an ordered account of events from the creation of the world and humankind to the death of the last Israelite patriarch. It has some of the elements of classical plot structure: an opening stable situation, a disturbance, and a quest to redress the disturbance. The disturbance happens in chapter 3 and widens and deepens in chapters 4–11. The quest begins in chapter 12, and continues to the end of the book. This quest becomes something of a family obsession, dominating the lives of Abraham's descendants, saga-like, for several generations. But it is an unfinished quest. It breaks off without resolution at the end of the book, with the death of Joseph in Egypt. This plot structure gives the narrative a dramatic quality. Furthermore, although there is a focus on one family from chapter 12 onwards, the setting provided by the vast panorama of chapters 1–11, and the scope of the quest itself (blessing for all peoples of the earth), give the drama epic proportions. But the fact that it ends without resolution implies that its full significance lies beyond itself, in the eventual consummation or frustration of the quest that has begun here.

At the most general level Genesis is a narrative of beginnings: the beginning of the heavens and earth, the beginning of humankind and their environment, the beginning of human rebellion against God, the beginning of the worship of

24. Hermann Gunkel, *Genesis,* HAT 1 (Göttingen: Vandenhoeck & Ruprecht, 1901); *The Legends of Genesis: The Biblical Saga and History* (New York: Schocken, 1964); Hermann Gunkel and Mark E. Biddle, *Genesis,* Mercer Library of Biblical Studies (Macon, GA: Mercer University Press, 1997); Hermann Gunkel, John J. Scullion, and William R. Scott, *The Stories of Genesis* (Vallejo, CA: BIBAL Press, 1994).

God, the beginning of civilization, the beginning of Abraham's family, and the beginning of a quest (ultimately a divine quest) to bless all people. Genesis contributes to the overarching metanarrative of Scripture as a whole by establishing its agenda and setting it in motion. It is the seed from which the entire metanarrative emerges. It functions as "beginning" in a meaning-laden sense. It is a profoundly theological narrative. It begins with God and is driven forward by his speech and actions. It lays the groundwork for a theology of everything: God, the universe, humanity, good and evil. In more systematic terms it establishes the framework for a biblical theology, anthropology, and soteriology. But all these depend on whether or not there is a sequel to Genesis. Only continuation, and a resolution of some kind, can validate it. Which brings us to the issue of authority. As the quest is unresolved at the end of Genesis, so is the authority of the book. God features as the leading character, but not as the author. Abraham is a prophet (20:7), but utters no oracles. The narrator is anonymous, and so (if the two can be distinguished) is the author. Genesis itself provides no materials for constructing a case for its authority based on authorship.

However, the elements of such a case are provided indirectly through the continuation of the narrative into Exodus. This brings Genesis into connection with Moses, the exodus from Egypt, and the giving of the covenant law at Sinai. Law and covenant are authority-laden by nature, and prophecy as established under Moses is especially so. Meredith Kline's thesis about the formal elements of ancient treaty documents comes into play at this point, and catches Genesis up into something larger than itself. It is no longer simply a narrative of beginnings, but part of an extended prelude to the national covenant between Yahweh and Israel concluded at Sinai and committed to writing through Moses' mediatorial role as prophet. The connection with what has gone before is made particularly strongly by the way Exodus opens, rehearsing in summary fashion the descent of Jacob and his sons into Egypt. The name of each son is given, followed by a reminder that Joseph was already there (Exod. 1:1-5). The setting for what is to come is made by the note that a new king arose who did not know Joseph (v. 8), which leads into the account of Israel's oppression, the birth of Moses, and his transference to a position of power in Pharaoh's court (2:10). Finally, Israel's cry for deliverance is answered by God recalling his covenant "with Abraham, with Isaac, and with Jacob" (2:24). The connection with Genesis could not be more explicitly or strongly made. The patriarchal narratives of Genesis 12–50 become an indispensable prelude to the covenant-making at Sinai.

But the connections reach further back than this. The opening words of the Decalogue in Exodus 20 recall the exodus from Egypt, but the law itself as summarized in the Decalogue reaches right back to creation. Idolatry is forbidden since it wrongly deifies created things, whether in heaven above, or on the earth beneath, or in the waters below (v. 4). The Sabbath is to be observed because "in six days the Lord made the heavens and the earth, the sea, and all that is in them, but he rested on the seventh day" (v. 11). Here in Exodus, for the first time, writing becomes an indispensable part of covenant-making. The original two tablets of the law are written by God himself (31:18), but their replacements (after the golden calf incident of chapter 32) are written by Moses at God's command (34:27-28). Even before this there is mention of Moses writing down "everything the LORD had said" (24:4), resulting in a "book *(sēper)* of the covenant" (24:7). The detailed material concerning the making of the tabernacle in Exodus 25–40 is an elaboration of this basic document produced through the mediation of Moses as God's authorized spokesman (25:22). By analogy, Genesis functions as an elaboration of the core book of the covenant in the other direction, back through the patriarchs to creation. All of this adds up to an inner-biblical rationale for the acceptance of Genesis as covenant literature validated by its association with the Sinai covenant and Moses as Yahweh's prophet. The tradition of Mosaic authorship goes further than the biblical data, but is an expression of the same basic logic. For the Christian, the authority issue is clinched by Jesus' citation of Genesis as Scripture, to which the gospels bear witness.[25]

Psalms: The Psalter

The Psalms are an appropriate type of Old Testament literature for us to consider here for a couple of reasons. First, they present the problem of human-divine discourse in an acute form. They are almost entirely words of human beings addressed to God, so how can they be understood as God's word to human beings? Second, the Psalms are the part of the Old Testament most cited in the New Testament, so they are potentially a good case study, with possible applications to other genres. Of course the psalms are not a single genre, but many different genres, and the function of these genres in public worship and private devotion has been the subject of a great deal of scholarly literature.[26] But they are unified by their poetic form, and the way they have been collected and arranged to form the Psalter.[27] For our purposes it will suffice to consider the psalms together as a collection, and ask how this collection functions as word of God. While psalms that are not part of this collection, such as the Song of the Sea (Exodus 15) and the Song of Hannah (1 Samuel 2), may also be instructive, our focus here will be on the Psalter.

25. Matthew 19:4; Mark 10:6-7; John 7:22; cf. Luke 24:27.

26. Hermann Gunkel and Joachim Begrich, *Introduction to Psalms: The Genres of the Religious Lyric of Israel,* trans. J. D. Nogalski (Macon, GA: Mercer University Press, 1998); Sigmund Mowinckel, *The Psalms in Israel's Worship,* 2 vols., trans. D. R. Ap-Thomas (Oxford: Basil Blackwell, 1962).

27. Brevard S. Childs, *Introduction to the Old Testament as Scripture* (London: SCM, 1979), 511-25; J. Clinton McCann, *The Shape and Shaping of the Psalter,* JSOTSS 159 (Sheffield: JSOT Press, 1993); G. H. Wilson, "The Shape of the Book of Psalms," *Interpretation* 46 (1992): 129-44.

The existence of the Psalter in book form is the first and most obvious starting point. What began as liturgy for public worship and/or personal devotion has become a literary work, and the way it is introduced provides important clues to how it is to be read and how it functions as Scripture. The first two psalms form an introduction to the whole, and set before us at once the twin themes of God's Torah (Psalm 1) and God's Messiah (Psalm 2). That these psalms are meant to be read as a two-part introduction to what follows is suggested not only by their placement at the beginning, but by various ways in which their wording and content unite them. They are framed by the beatitude that opens Psalm 1, "Blessed is the man who does not walk in the counsel of the wicked," and the one that closes Psalm 2, "Blessed are all those who take refuge in him." Psalm 1 talks about meditating on the law; Psalm 2, using the same Hebrew verb, speaks of those who meditate on what is vain (rebellion against the LORD's anointed). Psalm 1 presents us with the blessed "man" (unspecified) who meditates on the law; Psalm 2 presents us with a particular man (God's king) whom he has installed on Zion his holy hill. In the background lies Deuteronomy 17:14-20, which speaks of the king as one who should write for himself a copy of the law, keep it with him, read it, and be careful to obey it all his life. Psalm 1 speaks of "the way *(derek)* of the wicked," which will perish (v. 6), and Psalm 2 of rebels being "destroyed in [their] way *(derek)*" (v. 12).

By directing us to God's law and God's king, these two psalms alert us at the outset to the covenantal foundation of the Psalter's theology, namely, the Sinai and Davidic covenants. They also raise the issue of the choice that faces human beings: to submit to the law of God and his messiah and be blessed, or to foolishly rebel against them and perish. They also touch on the issue of the afterlife by introducing the idea of judgment in an absolute sense, *the* (final) judgment, which gives profound urgency to the choice people must make between two fundamentally different ways of living. In all these ways, and more, the introduction provided by the opening two psalms orients us to the collection of psalms that follows.

In general terms, the Psalter as a whole reflects the shape of Israel's history: from the inauguration of the monarchy (Psalm 2), to the fall of Jerusalem and the apparent end of the Davidic line (Psalm 89), to the post-exile, post-monarchy period in which *divine* kingship becomes the primary focus and basis of hope, as in the enthronement psalms with their declaration, "the LORD [Yahweh] reigns" (Pss. 93:1; 96:10; 97:1; 99:1). But since all the psalms end up as the hymnbook of the second temple, there is a sense in which the whole Psalter becomes eschatological.[28] The psalms of David and Zion continue to be sung as an expression of the hope for a *new* David and a *new* Zion.

Given all this, the Hebrew term *tôrâ* in Psalm 1 takes on added significance. While the primary reference is almost certainly to the law of Moses, its use in the

28. Childs, *Introduction,* 517-18. But cf. Goldingay, "Old Testament Theology and the Canon," 17-21.

opening couple of verses of the Psalter suggests that it should also be taken here in the more general sense of "teaching," or "instruction" (a common meaning of the term in the wisdom literature), and that this is how we, as readers now rather than worshipers in the Old Testament sense of the term, should regard the whole of the Psalter. This is consonant with how the two-part introduction sets before us the "two ways" in a manner reminiscent of the wisdom literature, especially the book of Proverbs. So we appear to have a paradox: material that is fundamentally words addressed to God as prayer and praise, is presented to us as a form of divine instruction comparable to the *tôrâ* (law) of Moses.[29] But is it simply the way it is introduced that makes it so, or something intrinsic to the material itself? The answer lies in the centrality of the figure of David in the psalms, because David is not just anyone. Psalm 2 tells us, in one of the rare examples of direct, divine speech in the Psalter, that the king is the Son of God (v. 7), which is the bridge into the collection of Davidic psalms that follows. We are instructed by this to read these psalms, with their mixture of prayer and praise, not simply as the words of an anonymous human being, but as the prayers and praises of the Son of God, which in turn prepares the way for the New Testament's Christological use of the psalms. This is an extension of their meaning, but also something fully consonant with the meaning they already have in the Psalter itself. And if the king can be called the Son of God, his words can legitimately be taken as the word of God, as the New Testament does when it cites them as Scripture. It is also consonant with the New Testament's designation of David as a prophet (Acts 2:30), and with Jesus speaking the words of David as his own (Ps. 22:1; Matt. 27:46).

But what are we to make of the communal and non-Davidic psalms, which bulk large in the Psalter? The answer lies in the connection that is made between Yahweh's king and the people of God in the closing beatitude of Psalm 2 (and therefore in the last verse of the two-part introduction to the Psalter), namely, "Blessed are all those who take refuge in him." These "blessed" people stand in contrast to the rebels of Psalm 2 and the wicked of Psalm 1. In positive terms they are the righteous of Psalm 1. They take refuge in God's king in the sense that they submit to him and place themselves under his protection. They are his subjects and willing servants. In the Psalter as a whole, their prayers and praises are offered to God in conjunction with those of the Messiah. His prayers and praises are what authorize their own and guarantee that they are acceptable to God. By extension, we who now read the Psalms as Scripture identify with the Messiah and his people, whose prayers and praises function as *tôrâ* for us, providing guidance for our own lives of prayer and praise.[30]

29. The division of the Psalter into five books may be an intentional allusion to the Mosaic Torah (Genesis-Deuteronomy).

30. Cf. Graeme Goldsworthy, *Preaching the Whole Bible as Christian Scripture: The Application of Biblical Theology to Expository Preaching* (Grand Rapids: Eerdmans, 2000), 196-202.

To summarize, we have seen that the Psalter, as a lateral expansion of the core narrative of Scripture, is linked with it through the figure of David. It mirrors it in its own movement from messianic kingship, through the fall of the Davidic monarchy, to a final focus of divine kingship. As a collection of songs that continued to be sung by Israel in the postexilic period it ends up by being fundamentally eschatological, giving hymnic expression to the prophetic hope of a future messiah and the final establishment of the kingdom of God. As Scripture it continues to function this way in the life of the church.

Fundamentally, the psalmic material of the canon is related to the core narrative through the figure of David, as the legal material (law) is related to it through the figure of Moses. In the same way the wisdom of Proverbs is connected to the core narrative through the figure of Solomon. There is other material in the Old Testament, however, where the connection with the core narrative is less clear, and the relationship to the mainstream theology of the Old Testament is more tenuous. We shall take the book of Ecclesiastes as an example.

Radical Wisdom: Ecclesiastes[31]

In terms of genre, Ecclesiastes is an ironic royal testament about the *hebel* (vanity, emptiness, transitoriness, meaninglessness)[32] of human existence. It is spoken by one Qohelet (teacher, preacher) who bases his testimony on his own experience of life "under the sun." There are transparent allusions to Solomon, though he is never named (1:12), and there is an obvious tension between the generally negative tone of Ecclesiastes and the much more positive, confident tone of Proverbs. However, the negativity is countered to some extent by occasional exhortations to find satisfaction in food, drink, and work as God's gifts (2:24; 3:13; 5:18; cf. 11:9). The clash with Proverbs is also moderated by the voice of a frame narrator (the implied author of the book),[33] who speaks about Qohelet in the third person (1:1-2; 7:27; 12:8), and adds a substantial epilogue that makes the relationship between Qohelet's teaching and that of mainline wisdom clearer (12:9-14).

Ecclesiastes is an example of radical wisdom. The allusions to Solomon effectively pose the question: In view of the negative aspects of Solomon's life (his apostasy, and the consequent undoing of all that he achieved) what qualifications have to be made to the kind of confident wisdom that he represented at the height

31. See my treatment of Ecclesiastes in *Five Festal Garments: Christian Reflections on the Song of Songs, Ruth, Lamentations, Ecclesiastes and Esther,* NSBT 10 (Leicester/Downers Grove, IL: InterVarsity, 2000), 83-109.

32. The term *hebel* is ambiguous.

33. Michael V. Fox, "Frame-Narrative and Composition in the Book of Qoheleth," *HUCA* 48 (1977): 83-106.

of his career? The answer is threefold: first, that even the greatest achievements of the greatest of men are vanity in the sense that they are fleeting, and do not make one immune from the eventual loss of everything guaranteed by the inevitability of old age and death (2:1-16); second, that such joy as is possible in this world is not found in work as a means of achievement, but in work, and the small satisfactions it brings, as a gift of God (3:13; 5:19); and three, that in the end the only thing that can rescue us from a merely animal existence and enable us to be truly human is fearing God and keeping his commandments (12:13).

These summary observations by the frame narrator suggest that the connection between Ecclesiastes and mainstream wisdom may be stronger than first appears, and an examination of Qohelet's teaching in the body of the book bears this out. We have already noted the allusions to Solomon. There are also numerous connections with the creation and fall narratives of Genesis 1–3. God is the maker of all things (11:5), and "your Creator" (12:1). In particular, he "created mankind upright, but they have gone in search of many schemes" (7:29 NIV [2011]) — probably an allusion to the creation of human beings in the image of God (Genesis 1) and their subsequent fall (Genesis 3). This connection is made virtually certain by references to man being made from the dust and destined to return to it (3:20; 12:7). The wording here is so close to that of Genesis that direct dependence seems undeniable.

Furthermore, the view that God made everything "beautiful in its time" probably alludes to the six-day creation narrative of Genesis 1. The recognition that there is wisdom and knowledge that God has placed beyond human reach (3:11; 7:23) reflects the teaching about the forbidden tree of Genesis 2. Finally, the teaching of Ecclesiastes that there is a crookedness to the world that God has put there and human beings are powerless to remove (7:13), and that frustrating toil is a "heavy burden" that God has placed on humanity (1:13; 3:10) confirms, again, that the fall narrative of Genesis 3 is not far below the surface. As in Genesis, God is judge, and the one who determines the conditions of human existence on earth, precisely because he is first of all creator.

Qohelet does not simply repeat the teaching of Genesis, however, but works with it in his own distinctive way.[34] In Proverbs the inferences from creation are positive (the ordered world makes achievement possible); but in Ecclesiastes they are essentially deterministic and negative. The creator of the world has also made the "times," the bad as well as the good (7:14). But since he has set severe limits to human knowledge (3:11) his ways remain incomprehensible to human beings, who are therefore never in a position to secure guaranteed outcomes for particular kinds of behavior. There are good things to be enjoyed and commandments to be obeyed, but notions of success and profit are logically excluded. Human beings experience life in the world as *hebel.* Proverbs teaches these things

34. C. C. Forman, "Koheleth's Use of Genesis," *JSS* 5 (1956): 256-63.

too, but the special contribution of Ecclesiastes is to insist on *hebel* as a universal datum of human experience that must be acknowledged, and to rule out of court any kind of teaching that refuses to do this, even if its practitioners claim to be disciples of Solomon. The book of Job does the same for the uncomfortable reality of undeserved suffering. These kinds of books guard wisdom against the danger of unreality. As part of Scripture as a whole they guard Christian as well as Jew against the damaging effects of overrealized eschatology. We who have the Spirit still groan with the whole creation as we wait for a release that is still to come (Rom. 8:19-24).

In view of all this, books like Ecclesiastes are not as unorthodox as they seem. Far from undermining the authority of the core narrative they actually strengthen it. They allow the questions, pain, and struggle involved in living in a fallen world to be fully acknowledged, and the voices that stand in tension with the central ones to be heard.[35] They help the people of God to stay together as they wait for the coming of the kingdom of God, and to process their honest doubts and questions rather than deny them and give in to either despair or triumphalism.[36] The association with Solomon through the figure of Qohelet effectively functions as a claim for Ecclesiastes to be heard as Scripture in association with the proverbs of Solomon, as the psalms of Asaph and others are read as Scripture in association with the psalms of David. We need radical wisdom to live in the world as it is, as well as traditional wisdom.

Provisional Conclusions

Assuming that Genesis, Psalms, and Ecclesiastes can fairly be taken as test cases, we might expect further study to yield the following general conclusions about how the main Old Testament genres function as Scripture:

- **Narrative** functions as the basic structure of the Bible's theology, and the carrier of its developing themes. It serves as the framework for all the other genres.
- **Law/torah** functions by means of command, prohibition, promise, and warning, to lay down the parameters within which life in covenant with Yahweh is to be lived.

35. E.g., Philip Jenkins has noted how biblical laments, especially community laments, have given voice to suffering Christian minorities in the global south and elsewhere. *The New Faces of Christianity: Believing the Bible in the Global South* (Oxford: Oxford University Press, 2006), 77.

36. In referring to "staying together," I'm thinking of the challenges of the tension between contemporary Western Christianity and that of the global south of which we have become aware in recent decades.

- **Prophecy** functions by means of exhortation, warning, and prediction to interpret and shape Israel's history in response to its compliance or noncompliance with its covenant obligations.
- **Mainline psalmody** (prayer and praise) functions, by modeling, to give appropriate shape to the worship of God as creator and redeemer.
- **Radical psalmody** (lament and protest) functions, by modeling, to shape worship of God in the midst of disorder (evil, injustice, and suffering).
- **Mainline wisdom** such as Proverbs functions by means of generalization and advice to guide the exercise of human freedom (choice) in accordance with a general principle: the fear of Yahweh.
- **Radical wisdom** such as Job and Ecclesiastes functions to guide engagement with issues of disorder (evil, injustice, and suffering) in accordance with the same general principle: the fear of Yahweh.
- **Apocalyptic**, such as Daniel, serves to sustain hope and guide behavior in a hostile environment, in light of the final breaking in of God's kingdom.

If the study were extended to the New Testament we might expect conclusions of the same general type:

- **The gospels** document the earthly life, death, and resurrection of Jesus, and interpret its significance in the light of Old Testament prophecy and the teaching of Jesus himself.
- **The book of Acts** documents the history of the early church and interprets its significance in light of the post-resurrection preaching of the apostles.
- **The epistles** guide the beliefs and conduct of Christian persons and congregations in accordance with the post-resurrection preaching of the apostles.
- **The book of Revelation** sustains and guides the life of Christian congregations in the context of persecution, in light of the revelation of Jesus Christ given to the apostle John, and the eschatological teaching of Scripture as a whole.

This is fine as far as it goes, but of course it doesn't go nearly far enough. At best, all that these statements do is try to identify what is distinctive about the way each of the main biblical genres function. But the way they function is considerably more complex than these minimal statements capture. For example, the book of Acts does much more than document the history of the early church, and the epistles much more than guide the beliefs and practices of Christian persons, and both draw on the Old Testament every bit as much as the gospels do. And explicit statements of purpose such as the introductions to both parts of Luke-Acts need to be taken much more into account. More significantly still, the above statements do not take into account the massive change that happens when the New Testament is added to the Old. The way the Old Testament genres function as Christian Scripture must take account of how the Old Testament functions in relation to the New.

Old Testament Genres in the Context of the Whole Bible

While the statement that the law of Moses "lay[s] down the parameters within which life in covenant with Yahweh is to be lived" may be true of how it functioned in the life of Israel, it is not true of how it functions in the life of Christians. The Pauline statements about the law being a guardian *(paidagōgos)* to bring us to Christ (Gal. 3:24), about Christ being the end *(telos)* of the law (Rom. 10:4), and about Christians not being "under the law" (Gal. 5:18) require a radical restatement of how the law functions now as part of the whole Christian Bible, and not simply as part of the Old Testament. The same is true, in various ways, of all the Old Testament genres. But if the summary statements about them above are true as far as they go, the restatement required by the larger context should entail an extension, rather than fundamental contradiction, of how they functioned previously. And it should not entail a complete nullification of the authority exercised by the literature that still contains these various genres. The diverse Old Testament genres, with all their particularity, are just as much a part of the Christian Bible as they are of the Old Testament, and their continued authority is established by the way the New Testament writings are so densely referenced to them. There is difference in the way the Old Testament genres now function, but there is also continuity.

The Psalms provide a helpful starting point for understanding how this works in practice. In our earlier discussion we noted in passing how there is a development in the function of the individual psalms that is traceable in the text of the Psalter itself. The headings of the psalms of praise and lament testify to their original function in the life of David and/or the worship of Israel. Psalms that occur outside the Psalter, such as the Song of the Sea (Exod. 15:1-18) or the Song of Deborah and Barak (Judges 5) provide further evidence of the original function of at least some psalms in various settings. However, with the gathering of the psalms into collections, and the incorporation of these collections into the Psalter, new dimensions of meaning and function occur. The psalms recontextualized in this way now contribute in various ways to the themes and theology of the *book* of Psalms. Moreover, as we have seen, the use of the Psalter in the worship of postexilic Israel gives the psalms — especially the Davidic and Zion psalms — an essentially eschatological meaning; they come finally to express the hope of a new David and a new Jerusalem. Importantly, this extension and transformation of their meaning happens within the history of Israel itself, and is mirrored in the literature that this history gave rise to. Hence the New Testament use of the psalms can be seen, not as an imposition of something foreign on the psalms themselves, but as an extension of the meaning and function they already had in the Old Testament and in the history of Israel.

Although it would take further work to establish it, it is arguable that what is true of the psalms is true of the other forms of Old Testament literature as well. We argued above that all these are an expansion, in one way or another, of the core narrative that undergirds and unites the whole of Scripture. If this is so, it follows that all the genres, as expansions of this narrative, enrich and participate in various ways in the forward movement of this narrative towards its goal, which turns out to be reached only *beyond* the Old Testament. In other words the entire Old Testament is essentially eschatological, and all its genres play some part in this eschatology. With all this in mind we may restate the function of the various Old Testament genres as follows:

- **Narrative** functions as the basic structure of biblical theology and the carrier of its developing themes. It serves as the integrating framework for all the other genres, *and provides the forward momentum basic to biblical eschatology.*
- **Law/Torah** functions by means of command, prohibition, promise, and warning, to lay down the parameters within which life in covenant with Yahweh is to be lived *as the people of God hope and wait for a new covenant, and for all that has been promised to them to be fully realized.*
- **Prophecy** functions by means of exhortation, warning, and prediction to interpret and shape Israel's history in response to its compliance or non-compliance with its covenant obligations, *and to sustain the hope of salvation through and beyond judgment.*
- **Mainline** psalmody such as prayer and praise functions, by modeling, to give appropriate shape to the worship of God as creator and redeemer and *to express the hope of a new David and a New Jerusalem.*
- **Radical psalmody** such as lament and protest functions, by modeling, to shape the worship of God in the midst of disorder (evil, injustice, and suffering), *and to process pain and enable the worshiper to move beyond it to renewed hope in God.*
- **Mainline wisdom** such as Proverbs functions by means of generalization and advice to guide the exercise of human freedom (choice) in accordance with a general principle, the fear of Yahweh, *in view of the certainty of future judgment.*
- **Radical wisdom** such as Job and Ecclesiastes functions to guide engagement with issues of disorder (evil, injustice, and suffering) in accordance with the same general principle, the fear of Yahweh, *in view of the certainty of future judgment.*
- **Apocalyptic**, such as Daniel, serves to sustain hope and guide behavior in a hostile environment *in light of the final inbreaking of God's kingdom.*

With these revised statements about Old Testament genres in place we are in a position to review the provisional statements we made above about the function of New Testament genres. These were made on a purely hypothetical basis. The case studies that follow are intended to provide a basis for revising them to make them more adequate.

New Testament Genres

Gospel: Matthew

As a genre, "gospel" is a subset of "narrative." We begin this sampling of New Testament genres with Matthew's Gospel for two reasons: because of its traditional placement at the beginning of the New Testament, making it an introduction to all that follows,[37] and because it is so densely referenced to the Old Testament. Matthew contains fifty-nine citations of the Old Testament, compared with thirty-one for Mark, twenty-six for Luke, and sixteen for John. Matthew is the gospel that most strongly links the Old Testament genres we have just been considering with the New Testament ones we are about to consider.

Of all the gospels, Matthew is the one that most pointedly identifies the birth of Jesus as the continuation of the core narrative that anchors and integrates all the Old Testament genres. Jesus is introduced as "the son of David, the son of Abraham," and then the broad sweep of Old Testament history is reviewed in a stylized, three-part genealogy: from Abraham to David, from David to the exile, and from the return from exile to Jesus the Messiah (vv. 2-17). This strongly suggests that if the Old Testament core narrative is basically eschatological, pressing forward to a climax that lies beyond it, this climax is reached with the arrival of Jesus, Israel's Messiah.

This is confirmed in a host of ways in what follows: Jesus is the long-awaited Savior and new Joshua (1:21), the Immanuel (God with us) of Isaiah 9:6 (1:23), and the Bethlehem-born ruler of Micah 5:2[38] (Matt. 2:6). Then at once the worldwide implication of the birth of Israel's Messiah is marked by the Matthean passage about the coming of the Magi to worship him (2:1-12). This distinctive opening is nicely complemented by the way Matthew ends with the echo of "Immanuel" (God with us) in Jesus' promise to be "with" his followers as they obey his command to go and make disciples of "all nations" (28:18-20). This effectively expands the notion of "his people" (1:21) to include all who in the future will become Jesus'

37. Cf. Craig L. Blomberg, "Matthew," in *Commentary on the New Testament Use of the Old Testament,* ed. G. K. Beale and D. A. Carson (Grand Rapids: Baker Academic; Nottingham: Apollos, 2007), 2.

38. Micah 5:1 (Hebrew).

disciples through the worldwide proclamation of the gospel. In other words, Matthew forcefully presents Jesus as the *universal* Savior.

This central definition of Jesus is enriched by other Old Testament citations and allusions that identify him, among other things, as the new Moses who ascends a mountain and gives Israel his distinctive torah (Matthew 5–7), and the promised king and smitten shepherd of Zechariah 9–14 (Matt. 21:5; 26:31). And so we could go on. Matthew cites the Servant Songs of Isaiah 40–55 more extensively than any other gospel: there are three citations in Matthew, compared with only one in each of the other gospels.[39] The ground is well traversed and need not be detailed any further. The point is that a central concern of Matthew's Gospel is to establish Jesus' identity as the promised Messiah of Old Testament prophecy. This is typical of the gospel genre, but Matthew does it in an especially thorough way. Of particular interest to us here, however, is that Matthew's Gospel closes with Jesus making a breathtaking statement about his authority: "All authority *(exousia)* in heaven and on earth has been given to me." All the gospels are concerned with Jesus' authority as manifested directly in his claims about himself, his actions, and the manner in which he taught. Three things, however, make this statement in Matthew 28:18 of particular significance: its scope (*all* authority *in heaven and on earth*), its timing (after Jesus' resurrection), and its placement in the final paragraph of this gospel. In this position it identifies the resurrection as the vindication of all the other claims Jesus made about his authority. Prospectively, it justifies the worldwide, disciple-making mission of the disciples by showing that it is directly authorized by the Jesus whose claims to authority have been vindicated. But also, more subtly, it vindicates the claims that Matthew himself has made about Jesus in his gospel. For Matthew's Gospel itself, with its testimony to the identity of Jesus and the significance of his words and deeds, is a form of the very disciple-making that Jesus has authorized. The gospel genre is a literary extension of the oral "gospeling" of Jesus' disciples. The tradition that this particular gospel was written by Matthew, one of the twelve, expresses the church's conviction that it has the kind of apostolic authority that justifies its acceptance as Scripture. But the authority of Jesus himself is primary, not the authority of the church. *All* authority has been given to *him.* All other authority, including that of Scripture and the church, is secondary and derivative.

History: The Acts of the Apostles

Acts is the second part of the two-part work commonly referred to as Luke-Acts. The purpose of the entire work, according to the opening paragraph of Luke's Gospel, is "that you [Theophilus] may know the certainty of the things you have

39. There are two in Luke if Isaiah 61:1-2 is counted as part of a fifth Servant Song.

been taught" (1:4). The identity of Theophilus is not known, but his name (dear to God, friend of God) and the way he is addressed by Luke ("*most excellent* Theophilus"), suggest that he was a pious Greek of high standing in Roman society, perhaps of the equestrian order.[40] He had been "taught" certain things about the Christian faith, but was unsure of its "certainty" *(asphaleian).* Since this refers to the content of the teaching Theophilus has been given, the "certainty" on view here must be objective (truth, actuality) rather than merely subjective (inner conviction). So Luke goes about his task as a historian; having "investigated everything from the beginning," he sets out "to write an orderly *(kathexēs)* account" to assure Theophilus that the Christian faith he has been taught has a sound factual basis.[41] Given the author's intention and method, the result has a prima facie claim to be regarded as history. It is history-like (to use Frei's expression)[42] in that it locates what it describes in calendric, real time, rather than fictive time.[43] But it is not "pure" history, because no such thing exists. Like all history writing it is not the history itself — the stuff to which it refers — but a literary depiction of it. To what extent Acts in particular is accurate in its historical claims is a matter of ongoing debate that need not detain us here.[44] Suffice it to say that many of its particulars can be confirmed,[45] and all agree on its persuasive, apologetic character.[46]

It is also clear though, that with Acts we have arrived at something different from a gospel. The introduction to Acts indicates both continuity and discontinuity with what has gone before. It is sharply separated from the gospels, and Luke in particular, by the ascension of Jesus. The gospels are about what Jesus "*began* to do and teach" in his earthly life (Acts 1:1); Acts is about what he *continued* to do through his apostles after his ascension. The phase of his ministry that the gospels are primarily concerned with is initiated by Jesus' water-baptism in the Jordan (Luke 3:21-22). The phase that Acts deals with is inaugurated by the disciples' Spirit-baptism in Jerusalem on the day of Pentecost (Acts 1:5; 2:1-39). In view of

40. The lower of the two aristocratic classes, next only to the patricians. F. F. Bruce, "Theophilus," *NBD* 3:1180.

41. I am aware that *kathexēs* does not necessarily entail strict chronology. I mean only that, given the broad sweep of what follows, it must refer here to the *kind* of "orderliness" characteristic of historical rather than other kinds of writing. Cf. R. J. Dillon, "Previewing Luke's Project from His Prologue (Luke 1:1-4)," *CBQ* 43 (1981): 205-27.

42. Frei, *The Eclipse of Biblical Narrative,* 10.

43. Gerard Loughlin, "Postmodern Scripture," in *Christian Theologies of Scripture: A Comparative Introduction,* ed. Justin S. Holcomb (New York: New York University Press, 2006), 311-12. In Ricoeur's terms, it "owe[s] a debt to the past." Paul Ricoeur, *Time and Narrative,* 3 vols. (Chicago: University of Chicago Press, 1984-88), 3:143 (cited in Loughlin, 312).

44. But the issue of historicity is important. For a recent discussion see David G. Peterson, *The Acts of the Apostles,* PNTC (Nottingham: Apollos; Grand Rapids: Eerdmans, 2009), 23-25.

45. Colin J. Hemer, *The Book of Acts in the Setting of Hellenistic History,* ed. C. H. Gempf, WUNT 49 (Tübingen: J. C. B. Mohr, 1989; repr. Winona Lake, IN: Eisenbrauns, 1990).

46. Peterson, *Acts of the Apostles,* 19-23.

these differences it is best to see Luke as using two different genres to accomplish his overall purpose: the gospel genre for the first part of it, and another related genre for the second part.[47] Acts is difficult to classify precisely, but is probably best regarded as an apologetic history of the early church, or more precisely, an apologetic history of the progress of the gospel from Jerusalem to Rome. The specific issue we are concerned with here is the relationship between the genre of Acts, so defined, and its authority as Scripture. In this connection three matters deserve special comment: first, the prominence given to the apostles as reflected in the content and structure of Acts; second, the frequent reference to the Spirit (fifty-six references in all); and third, the frequent reference to the Old Testament (forty-two citations). All three are related in one way or another to the issue of authority.

The importance of the apostles in Acts is signaled at the outset by the reference to them as "the apostles he [Jesus] had chosen" (1:2), the forty days he spends with them after his resurrection (1:3), and the replacement of Judas by Matthias so as to restore their original number (1:12-26). Peter comes into prominence in this context (1:15), and the rest of Acts is largely structured around the ministries of Peter and Paul respectively. The primary focus is on Peter in chapters 1–5, and Paul in chapters 13–28, with chapters 6–12 acting as a bridge between the two. The gospel proclaimed by the apostles begins to break the boundary between Jew and Gentile with Philip's witness to the Ethiopian eunuch in chapter 8, and Peter's witness to the household of Cornelius in chapter 10. It is taken further in the missionary journeys of Paul beginning in chapter 13, and finally reaches Rome, the center of the Gentile world, in chapter 28. This movement is described as the word of God "growing" and "multiplying" in 12:24, and "growing mightily" and "prevailing" in 19:20.[48] So while the apostles feature prominently, Acts is not fundamentally about the progress of the apostles, as though the evangelization of the world is their achievement. They are agents of the word of God, which advances through them — especially through their preaching of that word. And since it is the word rather than the apostles that advances, it is possible that this advance may continue after the apostles themselves are no longer present. In the book of Acts itself, Stephen and Philip are instances of others being involved in the progress of the gospel.

Of particular significance for us here is the author's extensive reference to himself as a traveling companion of Paul by the use of the first-person plural pronouns "we" and "us," forty-six times in all between 16:10 and 28:16, twenty of them in the context of Paul's journey to Rome to be tried before Caesar. The tradition that this person was Luke, Paul's traveling companion and close associate,

47. Peterson, *Acts of the Apostles,* 15.

48. See Peter T. O'Brien, *Consumed by Passion: Paul and the Dynamic of the Gospel,* Moore College Lectures 1992 (Homebush West, NSW: Lancer Books, 1993).

if not proven, is certainly consistent with the references to him as being present with Paul in Rome in Colossians 4:14 ("our dear friend Luke"), 2 Timothy 4:11 ("only Luke is with me"), and Philemon 24 ("Mark, Aristarchus, and Luke, my fellow workers"). Given this, Luke-Acts, addressed to the Greek Theophilus, can properly be seen as an extension of Paul's gospel ministry to the Gentiles, and a further instance of the word of God continuing to grow, multiply, and prevail.

In view of the way Acts opens and closes, its theme, at the deepest level, is about the kingdom of God. It begins with the risen Jesus speaking to his disciples for forty days about the kingdom of God (1:3), and ends with Paul in Rome, boldly preaching the kingdom of God (28:31). In between, Paul sums up his two-year ministry of evangelism and church-planting in Ephesus as "going about preaching the kingdom" (20:25). In other words, the "*word* of God" that advances and prevails in Acts, is the message about the "*kingdom* of God," and is the means by which God exercises his kingly authority in the world. To summarize, Acts is an *apologetic* history in the sense that it aims to persuade the reader that the progress of the gospel from Jerusalem to Rome was a fact of history and a work of God. The tradition that Luke is its author expresses the church's conviction that it is fundamentally apostolic, and therefore has the authority of Christ himself.

The prominence given to the Holy Spirit is widely recognized as one of the distinctives of Luke-Acts, from the six references to the Spirit in the birth narratives of Luke 1–2, through to the final reference to the Spirit in Acts 28:25. There are fifty-six references to the Spirit in the book of Acts alone. The way the coming of the promised Holy Spirit at Pentecost dominates the first two chapters sets the agenda for all that follows.[49] The Spirit comes again in 8:14-17, 10:44-48, and 19:1-7, as the blessing of Pentecost is extended to Samaritans, the household of Cornelius, and the new disciples in Ephesus, as Spirit-empowered witnesses take the gospel further and further afield in fulfillment of the program of Acts 1:8.

The famous quotation from Joel 2 in Peter's sermon on the day of Pentecost identifies this new movement of the Holy Spirit as the fulfillment of the Old Testament promise of the pouring out of the Spirit in "the last days" (Acts 2:17). It is an epoch-marking event: a sign that the last stage of salvation history has begun. In Acts generally the earthly phenomena associated with this outpouring of the Spirit (prophecy, visions, dreams, and speaking in tongues) are all associated in one way or another with the proclamation of the gospel. The Spirit empowers those who proclaim the gospel (1:8; 2:4; 4:31), gives them direction at critical moments (13:2; 15:28; 16:6), and gives signs to mark the inclusion of new people groups or confirm the truth of the spoken message (5:32; 10:44-46). In short, as Turner, Peterson, and others have argued, all these activities of the Spirit belong to the broad category of "prophetism," and testify to the fact that forgiveness of

49. In much the same way as the birth narratives of Luke 1–2 set the agenda of Luke's Gospel.

sins, and the privilege of knowing God as Moses and the prophets knew him, has been extended to all those who believe the gospel message.[50] This outburst of prophetism is an important aspect of the restoration of Israel. Prophecy, which according to Jewish tradition had ceased in the time of Ezra, reappeared with the advent of first John the Baptist, and then Jesus the Messiah. Hence the emphasis on the Spirit and inspired utterance in the birth narratives of Luke 1 and 2. The prominence of the Spirit in the book of Acts testifies to the fact that prophecy did not cease when Jesus ascended to heaven, but continued, and even increased. It was no longer the preserve of the few but of the many, and happened not just in the places where Jesus himself had ministered, but wherever his Spirit-empowered witnesses now went.

Another, less obvious consequence of the coming of the Spirit is implied by the very existence of Luke-Acts itself, namely, that it made the production of Scripture possible again. Prophetism itself was democratized in the sense that the Spirit was poured out on all the followers of Christ, so that all were empowered to proclaim the gospel. Nevertheless, as Acts shows, this did not obliterate the distinction between the apostles and other believers. The sermons that are preserved in written form in Acts are all by the apostles, or people like Stephen and Philip who were closely associated with them. And as we'll see when we come to the epistles, especially 1 Corinthians, the same distinction is preserved there. All can prophesy, but only within the guidelines laid down by Paul as an apostle (1 Cor. 14:37). In the same way, the literature that eventually came into existence as a consequence of the restoration of prophecy in the last days was of two kinds: apostolic and non-apostolic, with only the former regarded as having authority equal to that of the apostles themselves. As we have seen above, it was because Luke-Acts was understood to be apostolic in this sense that it was recognized as Scripture. To summarize, it was the pouring out of the Spirit at Pentecost, and his continued presence with Jesus' followers after his ascension, that made it possible for Acts itself to be produced and recognized as Scripture. In terms of its purpose, Acts is *apologetic* history, intended to persuade the reader of the actuality of the gospel events it records. In terms of its authority, it is *apostolic* history, and its authority is traceable, ultimately, to the very outpouring of the Spirit to which it testifies.

Frequent reference to the Old Testament is hardly a distinctive of Acts, since it also occurs in the gospels and other New Testament writings. It is noteworthy, however, that of the total of forty-two such references in Acts, forty are in speeches made by either the apostles Peter and Paul, or men such as Stephen

50. As promised in Jeremiah 31:34, cf. Peterson, *The Acts of the Apostles,* 62-63; M. M. B. Turner, "The 'Spirit of Prophecy' as the Power of Israel's Restoration and Witness," in *Witness to the Gospel: The Theology of Acts,* ed. I. Howard Marshall and David G. Peterson (Grand Rapids: Eerdmans, 1998), 330-37.

and Philip who were directly appointed by them. The only exceptions are the quotation of Psalm 2:1-2 in the prayer of the believers in Jerusalem, with Peter and James among them (4:25-26), and the author's quotation of Isaiah 53:7-8 as the passage the Ethiopian eunuch was reading when Philip joined him (8:32-33). The effect is to substantiate the claim repeatedly made by the apostles that the events they refer to, including the pouring out of the Spirit at Pentecost and Paul's subsequent call and mission to the Gentiles, not only happened, but happened in fulfillment of what had been foretold in the Old Testament Scriptures. By the speeches in the book of Acts, Luke effectively claimed to be passing on the apostolic tradition to this effect, a claim that the church found persuasive as witnessed by its inclusion in the New Testament. In this way the many references to the Old Testament indirectly, but nonetheless powerfully, support the authority of Acts as Scripture.

Epistles: 1 Corinthians

The third New Testament genre we will consider is the epistles, with special reference to the one we know as Paul's first letter to the Corinthians. With the gospels and Acts we were dealing with works that are part of the core, unifying narrative of Scripture as a whole. With the epistles, as in the Psalms for example, we return to the expansions of this narrative rather than parts of it. None of the epistles is a narrative, but each presupposes one. Epistles are normally written because the author already has a relationship of some kind with the recipients. This implies a narrative that includes, among other things, his initial contact with them and events that have led to the present state of his relationship with them. In 1 Corinthians Paul explicitly refers to this narrative background in such passages as 2:1-5: "When I came to you, brothers, I did not come with eloquence or superior wisdom. . . . I resolved to know nothing while I was among you except Jesus Christ and him crucified. . . . I came to you in weakness . . . ," and so on. A fuller version of this narrative can be found in Acts 18:1-18. The epistle alludes to other, subsequent elements of this narrative, to which we have only indirect access, such as Paul hearing certain things about the church in Corinth (5:1), and receiving correspondence from them (7:1). Nevertheless, the epistle itself is not part of this narrative, but an expansion of it that allows us to see in some detail Paul's perception of the condition of the church in Corinth, and his own responsibility in relation to it.

The intensely personal nature of the epistles is normally acknowledged formally by an opening greeting that identifies the writer and the addressee(s) and gives some indication of the reason for the writing. The last of these is particularly clear in the introduction to Galatians: "I am astonished that you are so quickly deserting the one who called you by the grace of Christ and are turning to a different gospel" (1:6). More commonly, the reason for writing is withheld until after an opening thanksgiving, or prayer, or theological reflection of some kind — sometimes quite long, as in the opening two or three chapters of Ephesians and Colossians. This gives Paul's letters a particularly strong theological and didactic quality that moderates to some extent their occasional character. His letters typically have elements more characteristic of a theological essay than a letter, but personal and pastoral aspects are never lacking, and generally become more prominent as the letter runs its course. The point is that, even with these variations from the norm, Paul's correspondence does belong to the epistle genre, and it is the nature of epistles to be occasional and personal. So when we read Paul's letters to various churches we are overhearing him speaking to different addressees than ourselves. We are reading someone else's correspondence. This raises important issues concerning how such an epistle can be Scripture in the sense of God's word to us.

This problem is not unique to epistles, of course. We already encountered it in the book of Acts, which is addressed to Theophilus. It is also true in a more general sense of the entire Old Testament, which is the literary deposit of God's dealings with Israel rather than with us. Nevertheless, it is in the epistles that we meet the occasional and personal in a way that is inherent to the genre itself, and in which the issue of relevance to us requires a different kind of explanation than for other biblical genres. As we shall see, since in Paul's epistles this is closely connected with the issue of Paul's authority as an apostle, we cannot talk about the one without at the same time talking about the other.

First, we should note that 1 Corinthians is not addressed to an individual, but to a community: "the *church (ekklēsia)* of God in Corinth." Paul adds personal requests and greetings at the end (16:5-24), but the epistle itself is not addressed to these persons as individuals but to the community they belong to. So this epistle is not as particular, in terms of addressee, as letters in general are. It belongs to a subcategory of the epistle genre: communal epistles as distinct from personal epistles.

Second, while individual persons cannot be expanded to include more than the one addressed, communities *are* capable of extension of this kind. Furthermore, Paul seems to be aware, as he writes to this particular community, of a wider community, or class of communities, to which the Corinthian *ekklēsia* belongs, and refers to it in his opening greeting: "To the church of God in Corinth, to those sanctified in Christ Jesus and called to be holy, *together with all those everywhere who call on the name of our Lord Jesus Christ — their Lord and ours*" (1:2).

Third, Paul writes 1 Corinthians quite self-consciously as an apostle (1:1), and this has to be borne constantly in mind. It has relevance to all the particular issues he deals with. He refers to it explicitly with reference to his right to warn and discipline the Corinthians (4:14, 18; 9:1-2; cf. 5:4-5), his right to marry and receive financial support from them (9:3-12a), when he is instructing them on the proper exercise of spiritual gifts (12:28; cf. 14:37), and refuting the claim that there is no resurrection of the dead (15:7-8, cf. v. 12). Paul's relationship with the Corinthians has a personal dimension to it (9:2), but his authority as an apostle is not limited to them; it extends far beyond them. He is an apostle to the Gentiles (Rom. 11:13; 1 Tim. 2:7), but also of all Christians everywhere, and it is to this widest scope of his apostolic authority that he refers in his introduction to 1 Corinthians.

Finally, in writing 1 Corinthians, as in all his epistles, Paul makes frequent reference to the Old Testament Scriptures. There are seventeen references in all, spanning virtually the whole letter, eight of them introduced by the citation formula, "It is written."[51] Among other things, this illustrates a general principle: what was written to and for the people of God who lived in one period of salvation history, can and does speak to those who live in another, later period of salvation history. The *manner* in which it does so may be different because of significant developments that have taken place in the interim (especially the fulfillment that has come in Christ), but it nevertheless can continue to function as word of God to another, later generation than those to whom it was originally addressed. Furthermore, it is clear from 1 Corinthians, as other epistles, that the citing of Old Testament Scripture does not drive a wedge between Paul's own authority and that of preexistent Scripture, as though what Paul himself writes has a lesser authority. On the contrary, he insists that what he himself writes "is the Lord's command," and calls on those who might be inclined to do otherwise to acknowledge this fact (14:37). In other words, Paul is conscious that in writing as he does to the Corinthians, *even in an occasional epistle of this kind,* he is writing Scripture.

For all these reasons the Christian church is fully justified in recognizing Paul's epistles as Scripture, and is in fact bound to do so. Applying it to later generations requires careful attention to the differences in time and situation, but the task of doing this can be undertaken with assurance that it is right in principle to do so. The epistles contribute to the core narrative of Scripture by enriching it with apostolic teaching and exhortations that continue to have relevance beyond the particular time and place that they were given.

Apocalyptic: The Book of Revelation

Our final example is apocalyptic, with special reference to the book of Revelation. As a literary genre apocalyptic has proven to be notoriously difficult to define, but J. J. Collins's definition has commanded widest acceptance: "[Apocalyptic] is a genre of literature with a narrative framework, in which a revelation is mediated

51. 1 Corinthians 1:19, 31; 2:9; 3:19; 9:9; 10:7; 14:21; 15:45.

by an otherworldly being to a human recipient, disclosing a transcendent reality which is both temporal, insofar as it envisages eschatological salvation, and spatial insofar as it involves another, supernatural world."[52] This helpfully identifies some of the most distinctive features of apocalyptic, but has some limitations. It was developed with reference to Jewish apocalyptic in general, including mainly non-canonical intertestamental works, and tends to distinguish apocalyptic too sharply from other genres. This is particularly so with reference to *biblical* apocalyptic. The book of Revelation, from which the label "apocalyptic" is derived, is also referred to in the work itself as an epistle (1:19), and a prophecy (1:3; 22:18). Furthermore, in the apocalyptic discourse of Matthew 24, the saying about "the abomination that causes desolation" in Daniel 9:27 is referred to by Jesus as "spoken through the prophet Daniel" (v. 15). In view of this, it is preferable, especially with reference to biblical apocalyptic, to think of it as a particular kind of prophecy rather than a distinct genre. The importance of this for our present purpose will become apparent below.

Common to all apocalyptic is a sustained focus on the "end" in an absolute sense — the end of history, and of the world as we know it. It characteristically involves a radical foreshortening, so that the "now" of historical existence and the "then" of the end of it are brought into such close contact with one another that the "end" is seen and felt as already present. The pains already experienced are both the death throes of the present age and the birth pangs of the age to come. The "end" has come, so it, too, becomes "now," and apocalyptic is crisis literature of the most absolute kind. This is clearly seen in the book of Revelation, in which the *contingent* "now" of John's exile and the churches' struggles (1:19; 2:19) gives way to the *eternal* "now" of God's triumphant reign (12:10; 21:3) without any connecting narrative. The movement by which the "end" arrives is not horizontal but vertical, by John being caught up to heaven and by heaven coming down to earth (4:1-2; 21:1-2).

Nevertheless, the book does have some narrative elements. The account of John's vision and commissioning in 1:9-20 is a mini-narrative. Each set of judgments in chapters 4–20 has seven parts (seven seals, seven trumpets, seven plagues, etc.),[53] and within each set the seven elements follow one other in chronological order. There is also an overall progression from the situation at the beginning of the book to the situation at the end. For all the foreshortening, there remains a distinction between "what is now" and "what will take place later" (1:19). Nevertheless, the ordering of the material in the body of the book is not fundamentally chronological. The letters to the seven churches in chapters

52. John J. Collins, *The Apocalyptic Imagination: An Introduction to Jewish Apocalyptic Literature,* 2nd edition, Biblical Resource Series (Grand Rapids: Eerdmans, 1998), 5.

53. Graeme L. Goldsworthy, *The Gospel in Revelation: Gospel and Apocalypse,* Biblical Classics Library 6 (Carlisle: Paternoster, 1984; repr. 1994), 57.

2–3 are simply placed side by side. Each of them speaks of the present condition of the church in question and future reward for those who are faithful, but there is no chronological progression from one letter to the next. Likewise, the sets of judgments in chapters 4–20 all depict the same reality (final judgment) in a cyclical rather than a sequential pattern. The narrative, such as it is, keeps doubling back on itself until the theme of judgment is completed and gives way to peace in chapters 21–22.

The book of Revelation's relationship to the core narrative of Scripture is twofold. First, it is an expansion of it in the sense that one event or moment in it (God's final intervention to judge and save the world) is elaborated to the point of exhaustion. At the same time, Revelation is not a digression from the core narrative, but the completion of it. The predominance of vertical over horizontal movement slows the forward progression of the core narrative to a crawl, and then a complete stop. Hence its function in relation to the core narrative must be thought of not simply in terms of expansion, but of closure, a closure in which Jesus as the risen and coming judge plays an absolutely central role. It brings us to Christ, "the Alpha and the Omega, the First and the Last, the Beginning and the End" (22:13), the One in whom the whole history of salvation coheres and reaches its goal. Revelation is about arrival, and the end it brings us to is Christological, from the opening vision of Christ (1:9-20), to the final prayer for his coming (22:16-17).

In keeping with this theological agenda, the book of Revelation refers extensively to preexistent Scripture. "No other book of the New Testament is as permeated by the Old Testament as Revelation. Although the author seldom quotes the Old Testament directly, allusions and echoes are found in almost every verse."[54] Depending on the criteria used, the number of references ranges from 394 to 1,000. Particularly prominent are the creation narratives of Genesis, the book of Exodus, the Psalms, and the prophecies of Isaiah, Ezekiel, and Daniel.[55] It is as though the author ransacks the entire biblical corpus to make the point that the complex of events he is writing about in Revelation will leave no prophetic foreshadowing of the end unrealized.

A particularly striking instance of the way Revelation refers to the Old Testament is the solemn warning of 22:18-19:

> I warn everyone who hears the words of the prophecy of this book: If anyone adds anything to them, God will add to him the plagues described in this book. And if anyone takes words away from this book of prophecy, God will

54. G. K. Beale and Sean M. McDonough, "Revelation," in *Commentary on the New Testament Use of the Old Testament,* ed. G. K. Beale and D. A. Carson (Grand Rapids: Baker Academic; Nottingham: Apollos, 2007), 1081.

55. Beale and McDonough, "Revelation," 1082.

> take away from him his share in the tree of life and in the holy city which are described in this book.

The implication is that the account of the last things in the book of Revelation is comprehensive and final. The wording alludes transparently to Deuteronomy 4:1-2:

> Hear now, O Israel, the decrees and the laws I am about to teach you. . . . Do not add to what I command you and do not subtract from it, but keep the commands of the LORD your God that I give you.

This entails the further implication that the situation of the readers of John's prophecy is analogous to the situation of those addressed by Moses in Deuteronomy. Deuteronomy was the second version of the law, but it was also the last; not that laws could never again be made, but that there would be no more law with the same authority and foundational role in Israel's life as the *Mosaic* law. The force of the warning at the end of Revelation is that the prophecy contained in it is final in the same way; not that there could be no more prophecy,[56] but that there would be no more prophecy of the same character as that given in the book of Revelation. In other words, Revelation not only brings closure to both the core narrative and metanarrative of Scripture, it also brings closure to prophecy of the foundational, apostolic kind.

The traditional placement of Revelation at the very end of the biblical canon suggests that the warning of 22:18-19 was understood as having implications for Scripture as a whole. In the background is the well-documented Jewish understanding that prophecy and Scripture are intrinsically connected. With the cessation of prophecy in the time of Ezra the closure of the Old Testament canon became inevitable. Other writings could be produced, but none with the authority of Scripture.[57] The New Testament testifies to the resumption of prophecy with the arrival of John the Baptist (Matt. 11:7-10), and John the apostle signals the cessation of it by his warning at the end of Revelation. The implication is that there can be no more Scripture: the closure of prophecy entails the closure of the canon.

In view of all this we may discern in Revelation an authority structure that, in principle, applies to the canon as a whole. The author of Revelation is referred to in the opening verse as God's "servant" (1:1). He has an encounter with Christ and is directly commissioned by him to "write" (1:19), and what he writes is called "prophecy" (1:3; 22:18). If we can accept (as seems reasonable) the traditional

56. The continuation of prophecy in the life of the church is anticipated in Acts 2:17 and implied, for example, by Paul's teaching on the spiritual gifts in 1 Corinthians 12–14.

57. Josephus, *Against Apion* 1.41.

belief that the author is the apostle John, then apostleship features strongly in the issue of authority here, as in the other New Testament works we have surveyed. The authority of God, the supreme Creator, King, and Judge of chapter 4, is exercised for us through Christ, the risen and reigning Lamb of God (chapter 5), who personally commissions the apostle John (1:9-20), whose ministry leads to and authorizes the production of "prophecy," which has the finality of Scripture (22:18).

This concludes our sampling of New Testament genres and puts us in a position to fine-tune the summary statements of their several functions that we proposed earlier. The changes are in italics:

- **The gospels** *substantiate the claims Christianity makes about Jesus* by documenting his life, death, and resurrection, and interpreting its significance in the light of Old Testament prophecy and the teaching of Jesus himself.
- **The book of Acts** *substantiates the claim that the remarkable spread of Christianity was a fact of history and a work of God,* by documenting *the progress of the gospel from Jerusalem to Rome* and interpreting its significance in the light of *the outpouring of the Spirit in fulfillment of Old Testament prophecy,* and the post-resurrection preaching of the apostles.
- **The epistles** *establish emerging Christianity on the foundation of apostolic teaching, by giving instruction in sound doctrine and godly living.*
- **The book of Revelation** sustains and guides the life of Christian congregations in the context of persecution, in the light of the revelation of Jesus Christ given to the apostle John, and the eschatological teaching of Scripture as a whole.

Finally, it should be noted that the New Testament, like the Old, includes some contributions whose voices are in tension with the dominant ones, for example, James's insistence on the role of good works in justification ("a person is justified by what he does and not by faith alone," James 2:24), or the way John's Gospel differs from the synoptics. But these tensions occur *within* genres (epistle and gospel respectively), rather than *between* genres (as between the radical wisdom of Job and Ecclesiastes and the mainline wisdom of Proverbs). Nor is the issue complicated, as in the Old Testament, by the anonymity of the works concerned. In terms of their apostolic status, James and John have as much right, or more so, to be heard as Paul and Matthew, Mark, and Luke. The tensions in the New Testament are *within* the mainline, apostolic witness rather than between it and voices that have to establish their claim to be heard on other grounds. The fact is that such differences exist, and their presence within the New Testament canon is testimony to the fact that the principle of apostolic authority does not flatten the theological landscape by allowing only one voice to be heard. It allows the complexity of the issues to be acknowledged in a way that strengthens rather than weakens the authority of Scripture.

Conclusions and Theological Reflections

Scripture is not authoritative because it has a diversity of genres. For the Christian, the authority of Scripture is a corollary of the lordship of Jesus Christ.[58] The Old Testament is authorized as Scripture for Christians by the way Jesus regarded it and used it, and the basis for the New Testament to be regarded as Scripture is Jesus' appointment of apostles to be the founders of the church and the mediators of his teaching to it. Statements in Scripture itself that bear on the question of its authority refer to its divine origin (inspired by God), and to the instrumentality of prophets and apostles, but not to its diversity of genres.[59] However:

(1) Its diversity of genres is one of the distinctives of Christian Scripture, in contrast to the Qur'an, for example, and this has important theological implications (see below).

(2) Some of Scripture's genres are more closely related to its authority than others. The nature of the gospel, grounded in significant events and involving promise and fulfillment, privileges narrative and prophecy as two genres that are fundamental to the nature of Christian Scripture.[60] However, Scripture

58. For a philosophical response to the alleged circularity of this position see Paul Helm, "Faith, Evidence, and the Scriptures," in *Scripture and Truth,* ed. D. A. Carson and John D. Woodbridge (Grand Rapids: Zondervan, 1983), 314-19.

59. Two possible exceptions are Hebrews 1:1 and Numbers 12:1-8. Both link the status of a revelation with the manner in which it was given. Hebrews 1:1-2 states that in the past God spoke *polymerōs kai polytropōs,* "in fragmentary and varied fashion" (NEB), but has now spoken finally *en huiō,* "by his Son" (NIV). But it is unlikely that diverse genres as such are what is primarily on view, if they are on view at all, and in any case authority is not located in the ways God spoke, but in God himself, who used whatever means best suited his purpose. "The opening paragraph [of Hebrews] does not spell out how this revelation in Old Testament times was fragmentary and diverse, but it would presumably include God's address in mighty works of mercy and judgment, the meaning and purpose of which he made known through his prophets; his word in storm and thunder to Moses (Exod. 19:17-25; Deut. 5:22-27; to which allusion is made in Heb. 12:18-24); the still small voice to Elijah (1 Kings 19:12); along with his speaking through priest and prophet, sage and singer." Peter T. O'Brien, *The Letter to the Hebrews,* PNTC (Grand Rapids: Eerdmans, 1996), 49. Some genres, such as law, wisdom teaching, and prophecy, have a more natural or direct connection with authority than others, but this does not of itself give them their authority as Scripture. That depends on the inspiration and/or office of the one who uses these genres. Numbers 12:1-8 contrasts the way God revealed himself to the prophets (in visions, dreams, and riddles) with the way he revealed himself to Moses (face to face). The end result in both cases is divinely inspired Scripture. But the implication is that because of Moses' superior status and the greater immediacy and clarity of the revelation given through him, "if there is any tension in interpretation between Moses and the prophets, Moses has priority." Bruce K. Waltke with Charles Yu, *An Old Testament Theology: An Exegetical, Canonical, and Thematic Approach* (Grand Rapids: Zondervan, 2007), 48.

60. By extension, it is arguable that "gospel" is the appropriate genre term for Scripture as

is not authoritative simply because it is narrative or prophecy, but because *this particular* narrative, and the prophecy embedded in it, are endorsed as Scripture by Christ and his apostles.[61]

(3) In general, the diversity of genres exhibited by Scripture bears a *functional* relationship to its authority. It enables its authority to be brought to bear on and engage with the full range of the human personality (the mind, emotions, and will) and the diversity of human experience (order and disorder, alienation and inclusion).[62] It enables it to function as Scripture in ways that would be impossible without this diversity.[63]

But what are the implications of this diversity for the kind of authority the Bible exercises? It tells us that the authority of the Bible is the kind of authority that fully engages with our humanity. It speaks to us from within our humanity, and not just from outside it (as in creation, for example). It is not an authority of raw power, but one that fully recognizes and engages with our weakness, struggle, and sinfulness. In other words it is a gracious rather than coercive authority.

Furthermore, the difference between the Bible and the Qur'an reflects a fundamental difference between the God of Christianity and the God of Islam.[64] Unlike the God of the Qur'an, the God of the Bible is not so separate from humanity that he cannot participate in humanity without compromising his "God-ness." On the contrary he is a God who can and has fully embraced humanity, not just in

a whole, as in Goldingay, *Old Testament Theology,* vol. 1, *Israel's Gospel;* cf. Goldingay, *Theology and Canon,* 4: "The canon's being dominated by narrative signifies for Old Testament theology that Israel's faith is a gospel, a story declaring news about what God has done."

61. "Scripture is a narrative of God's kingdom, but is not *merely* that. It is God's own account of that kingdom, and it is that kingdom's written institution." John M. Frame, in *Antithesis and the Doctrine of Scripture,* inaugural lecture in 2006 into the J. D. Trimble Chair of Systematic Theology at Reformed Theological Seminary, Orlando, FL. URL: http://www.frame-poythress.org/frame_articles/2006Antithesis.htm. See note 58 above on the alleged circularity of this position.

62. It also enables the Bible to function as word of God for people and people groups of vastly different cultures, as in the division between Christians of the global north and the global south. Jenkins, *New Faces of Christianity,* 190-93.

63. Cf. Goldingay, *Theology and Canon,* 5: "The dominance of narrative in the Old Testament canon also makes it possible to discuss complex theological questions that are not open to being 'solved' in the form of the discursive, analytical statement that came to dominate theology." But Goldingay notes that "narrative is not everything," and that the inclusion of non-narrative material complements and further enriches the basic narrative. Cf. also John M. Frame, "The Spirit and the Scriptures," in Carson and Woodbridge, eds., *Hermeneutics, Authority and Canon,* 219.

64. I owe the theological insights of this paragraph to a private communication from Ida Glaser, author of "Qur'anic Challenges for the Bible Reader" (ch. 32 in this volume).

exercising his authority over us in such a gracious way, but by becoming incarnate in Jesus Christ — something that is absolutely unthinkable in Islam. In short, the form of the Bible has deep implications for the nature of God. He is the God who not only gave us a book and a prophet, but gave us himself.

TWENTY

The Generous Gift of a Gracious Father: Toward a Theological Account of the Clarity of Scripture

Mark D. Thompson

One of the most unfortunate developments in the history of the Christian doctrine of Scripture has been its separation and even isolation from the rest of the theological curriculum. Too often, apologetic concerns have seemingly necessitated a treatment of the nature and use of Scripture within a series of prolegomena, which provide the backdrop but are not subsequently related to — and certainly not integrated with — the primary theological task of giving an account of God and his work in creation and redemption. In some treatments, the Bible is simply discussed as one of the "sources" of theology, and the consequences are far reaching (even when it is identified as the most important of these sources).[1] When this happens, the discussion of Scripture tends to lose touch with its theological and, more specifically, *Christological* character.[2] Historical and hermeneutical questions become determinative and the whole enterprise begins to resemble Descartes's search for a solid and reliable foundation for knowledge.[3]

1. This continues to be the practice across the theological spectrum in the standard introductions to theology. Peter C. Hodgson, *Christian Faith: A Brief Introduction* (Louisville: Westminster John Knox, 2001); Daniel L. Migliore, *Faith Seeking Understanding: An Introduction to Christian Theology,* 2nd edition (Grand Rapids: Eerdmans, 2004); Alister E. McGrath, *Christian Theology: An Introduction,* 4th edition (Oxford: Blackwell, 2007), which unwittingly highlights the problem by discussing Scripture in "Part II: Sources and Methods" before turning to "Part III: Christian Theology."

2. An insistence that Scripture must be understood in relation to God as he is revealed to us in Jesus Christ is not, of course, novel in the history of Christian doctrine. Nor is it necessarily affirmed at the expense of genuine engagement with the humanity of these texts (i.e., they are the product of the conscious and creative involvement of the human authors). See Henri Blocher's contribution to this collection (chapter 17).

3. Similar observations have been made by John Webster with reference to the Christian doctrine of revelation more generally (*Holy Scripture: A Dogmatic Sketch* [Cambridge: Cambridge University Press, 2003], 11-13). See also Telford Work, *Living and Active: Scripture in the Economy of Salvation* (Grand Rapids: Eerdmans, 2002), 9.

Reflection upon the clarity of Scripture might seem vulnerable to a similarly distorting isolation.[4] If it is approached simply as the quality of a specific text or collection of texts, then are we not thrust immediately into the abyss of contemporary hermeneutical theory? Modern and postmodern concerns about the nature of texts and language itself begin to dominate the discussion, setting an agenda that resists the introduction of specifically theological factors.[5] Prominence is often given to the historical, cultural, and linguistic distance between the authors of these texts and their readers millennia later. The fragility of language as a vehicle of communication is exaggerated, heightened by contemporary awareness of the contribution of the interpreter or the interpreter's community to a construction of meaning. In such a context the social and political dimensions of reading — texts as locations of identity or a means of control — further isolate the discussion of these particular texts from their theological location in the gospel and hence in the character and purpose of God. The proper function of the doctrine within the wider theological corpus is hidden from view. What will we say about Scripture that is not true also of other pieces of written communication?[6]

The clarity of Scripture needs to be placed firmly in the context of the living God's involvement with the world he has made and the people he has redeemed. It needs explicit relation to the character of God and his saving activity, in particular his determination to be known by men and women in and through the person of Jesus Christ. On such terms an exposition of the clarity of Scripture becomes a confession of faith in the benevolence of our heavenly Father, a confession anchored in the redemptive work of the Son and made possible in the present by the operation of the Holy Spirit on sinful human hearts and otherwise suspicious human minds.[7]

Approaching the clarity of Scripture from such a determinedly theological perspective does not, as it turns out, involve a radical departure from classical accounts of the doctrine. Martin Luther asked Erasmus in 1525, "[I]f Scripture is

4. I have preferred the term "clarity" to the more traditional "perspicuity" or amplifications such as "accessibility and intelligibility."

5. For an extended treatment of the doctrine, one that engages at length with these modern and postmodern concerns, see my *A Clear and Present Word: The Clarity of Scripture* (Nottingham: InterVarsity, 2006), 17-47.

6. So early in his treatment of the subject James Callahan gives this definition: "Scripture's clarity is, simply put, how Christians account for the union of text, reader and reading." James Callahan, *The Clarity of Scripture: History, Theology and Contemporary Literary Studies* (Downers Grove, IL: InterVarsity, 2001), 19.

7. Here we are reminded of John Calvin's definition of faith as "a firm and certain knowledge of God's benevolence toward us, founded upon the truth of the freely given promise in Christ, both revealed to our minds and sealed upon our hearts through the Holy Spirit." *Institutes* 3.2.7.

obscure or ambiguous, what point is there in God giving it to us?"[8] Repeatedly, he made clear that God's character and purpose were at stake in Erasmus's rejection of the doctrine, not least because Scripture is *God's gift* to us.[9] Heinrich Bullinger introduced his treatment of the subject with a simple but richly theological statement: "God's will is to have his word understood of mankind."[10] Benedict Pictet, one of Calvin's successors at the Academy in Geneva, similarly suggested that "the scripture would have been given in vain, if it were obscure." Those who deny the clarity of Scripture are faced with an unenviable dilemma: "[E]ither God *could not* reveal himself more plainly to men, or he *would not.* No one will assert the former, and the latter is most absurd; for who could believe that God our heavenly Father has been unwilling to reveal his will to his children . . . ?"[11] Notwithstanding the polemical context in which such statements were made in the sixteenth and seventeenth centuries, it remains true that the expectation of scriptural clarity shared by these men arises from certain convictions about God's character and his benevolence toward us.

Nevertheless, it is true to say that the last decade has seen a fresh awareness of the proper theological cast of this doctrine. So John Webster insists, "Scripture is self-interpreting and perspicuous by virtue of its relation to God. . . . The clarity of Scripture is a function of its place in the divine self-demonstration."[12] In a later, fuller exposition of the doctrine he comments, "Holy Scripture is clear because God is light and therefore the one in whose light we see light."[13] Another contemporary definition reads, "The clarity of Scripture is that quality of Scripture which, arising from the fact that it is ultimately God's effective communicative

8. M. Luther, "The Bondage of the Will (1525)," WA 18, 655.25-26 = LW 33.93.

9. That is why he could describe such a denial as both "impudent and blasphemous." WA 18, 656.6 = LW 33.94. For a fuller account of the Erasmus-Luther debate on the issue see Thompson, *A Clear and Present Word,* 143-50.

10. Heinrich Bullinger, *Decades* (1587), trans. H. I., ed. T. Harding (Cambridge: Cambridge University Press, 1849), 71.

11. Benedict Pictet, *Christian Theology,* trans. F. Reyroux (Surrey: Seeley & Sons, 1833), 48; emphasis original.

12. Webster, *Holy Scripture,* 93.

13. J. Webster, "On the Clarity of Scripture," in *Confessing God: Essays in Christian Dogmatics II* (London: T. & T. Clark, 2005), 40. Webster's account of the clarity of Scripture strongly accents Scripture's instrumental character: "Scripture is clear as the instrument of the reconciling clarity of God whose light is radiantly present in Jesus Christ and the Holy Spirit" (42). While he is aware of the danger of undermining any sense in which the text itself is clear (47), a number of his own formulations sometimes raise similar concerns: "Holy Scripture is clear as the sanctified creaturely auxiliary of the communicative presence of God"(46); "Clarity does not mean ease or immediacy of access or absolute semantic transparency. [Has anyone ever suggested this?] It means this text is caught up in God's self-manifestation as the light of the world, and becomes the means through which the Spirit makes plain the gospel" (52).

act, ensures the meaning of each biblical text, when viewed in the context of the canonical whole, is accessible to all who come to it in faith and dependent upon the Holy Spirit."[14] Such definitions insist that we continue to speak of the clarity *of Scripture;* we have not left the text behind as we wonder afresh at God's goodness and radiant glory. Yet, just as the spoken word of God is inseparable from the one who speaks it, so the written word of God is inseparable from the Spirit who so moved the human authors in a variety of ways (2 Pet. 1:21) that the result is a collection of texts (*pasa graphē*) properly identified as God-breathed (*theopneustos,* 2 Tim. 3:16). In the end, the character of these texts cannot be considered in abstraction from God's being and in particular his determination to be known. To affirm the clarity of Scripture in this way need not compromise the genuine humanity of the biblical texts, since neither obscurity nor error is a necessary corollary of genuine humanity, even in a fallen world. However, this is an observation to which we will return.

To sharpen the focus just a little, the distinctively Christian character of this doctrine arises from the unavoidable center of God's self-disclosure in the person and work of the incarnate Son and Israel's Messiah, Jesus of Nazareth. He is the one who embodies the love of God for sinful men and women, a love that will not rest content with judgment (Rom. 5:8; 1 John 4:10). He is the gift given by the Father to the world (John 3:16). Old Testament promise and New Testament fulfillment come together in him (2 Cor. 1:10; Heb. 1:1-2). He stands uniquely as the guarantor of both: he identified the Old Testament as the word of God without qualification and sent the eleven and Paul on that mission which in time would generate the New Testament (Matt. 28:18-20; Acts 1:8; 9:15-16). Most importantly for our purposes, his own use of the scriptural texts in a variety of settings was laden with assumptions about the character of Scripture. There are, then, good theological reasons for beginning an exposition of this doctrine with an examination of Jesus' engagement with the extant Scripture of his day.

However, before concentrating our attention upon Jesus' use of the Old Testament in the course of his earthly ministry, a brief comment is in order about the apparent circularity of any argument from the content of Scripture in order to establish an aspect of the doctrine of Scripture. How secure is the case for Jesus' attitude toward Scripture when its only evidence comes from Scripture itself?

14. This is a development of the definition given in Thompson, *A Clear and Present Word,* 169-70. Of course, to say that the meaning is accessible to all who come to it in faith and dependent upon the Holy Spirit is not to say that all such people will necessarily embrace that meaning. As we will argue below, there are other factors involved. The point that needs to be emphasized in the present climate, however, is that disagreement over meaning need not, and in this case is not, the result of some defect in the text itself.

A Brief Excursus on Methodology

At first glance any appeal to Scripture to establish an aspect of the doctrine of Scripture seems muddleheaded. It appears to be an exercise in circular reasoning, with the conclusion presupposed in the premises of the argument.[15] Doesn't our appeal to Scripture assume the very clarity of Scripture that we are setting out to establish? Responses to this concern come from three directions: the eyewitness character of the Gospels and their testimony to Jesus; a long history of establishing doctrine, including the doctrine of Scripture, from the testimony of Scripture; and theological and philosophical considerations to do with the nature of arguments for final authority.

An appeal to the Gospels for an understanding of the pattern of Jesus' ministry relies in the first instance on the eyewitness character of the Gospels rather than any assumption about the clarity of Scripture. While confidence that we can access the meaning of these documents is not unimportant, the rationale for turning to them lies not in that accessibility and intelligibility in and of itself (after all, other texts share these qualities too) but in their self-presentation as the proclamation of Jesus Christ by those who in fact saw him and heard him. Richard Bauckham has explored the phenomenon of eyewitness testimony at length, probing it at both the conceptual level and at the level of describing these particular texts. By identifying the features of ancient eyewitness accounts and by careful analysis of the form, content and express purpose of the canonical Gospels themselves, he demonstrates that there are very good reasons to accept them as records of eyewitness testimony. He concludes,

> The Gospel writers, in their different ways, present their Gospels as based on and incorporating the testimony of eyewitnesses. The literary and theological strategies of these writers are not directed to superseding the testimony of eyewitnesses but to giving it a permanent literary vehicle.[16]

Bauckham does not stop there, however. He asks why we would ever accept knowledge based on the testimony of others at all. His answer hinges on the significance of "trust." He cites the work in this area by philosopher C. A. J. Coady,

15. Strictly speaking, this need not be the case. The present argument does not in fact include the proposition "Scripture is clear" as a premise. Nevertheless, there is a certain reliance upon the truth of the conclusion in defending the conclusion: it would seem that the argument from Jesus' own approach to Scripture assumes an accessibility of meaning in the Gospels sufficient to enable a reasonably accurate picture of what Jesus believed about the clarity of Scripture. (Thanks to Michael Rea for providing some methodological clarity at this point and others.)

16. Richard Bauckham, *Jesus and the Eyewitnesses: The Gospels as Eyewitness Testimony* (Grand Rapids: Eerdmans, 2006), 472.

who concludes "our trust in the word of others is fundamental to the very idea of serious cognitive activity."[17] Such trust need not be naïve and uncritical. Claims to eyewitness status are not simply taken at face value. Rather, wisdom suggests something like Paul Ricoeur's "prudential rule": "First, trust the word of others, then doubt if there are good reasons for doing so."[18] So even if we can be satisfied that the Gospels are eyewitness testimony, the obvious next question is: Can this testimony be trusted?

The historical reliability of the eyewitness testimony that shapes the Gospels has been a matter of extensive investigation and considerable debate. A fascinating contemporary instance is a series of exchanges between Marcus Borg of the Jesus Seminar and N. T. Wright. The skepticism of the Jesus Seminar is almost legendary and Wright has taken considerable care in explaining his persistence in relying on the historicity of the New Testament in general and the Gospels in particular.[19] Similarly, Paul Barnett has provided extended reflection upon the relation of history and theology in the Gospels and the essentially reliable historical underpinnings of the New Testament documents.[20] In this light, appeal to the New Testament to establish the attitude of Jesus, a critical component of a genuinely Christian doctrine of Scripture, does not seem viciously circular at all.

Second, such appeal to the text of Scripture to establish the doctrine of Scripture is hardly novel, though this way of framing the question of method bears all the marks of late-twentieth- and early-twenty-first-century reasoning. Arguments from Scripture about Scripture were a feature of early Christian apology

17. C. A. J. Coady, *Testimony: A Philosophical Study* (Oxford: Clarendon, 1992), vii. Considerable debate about the place of testimony as a basic source of knowledge has been a feature of epistemological discussion since the much-maligned Thomas Reid described it as one of the "social operations of mind" (Thomas Reid, *Essays on the Intellectual Powers of Man* [London: Richard Griffin, 1854], 34). Coady's debt to Reid is explicit: C. A. J. Coady, "Reid and the Social Operations of Mind," in *The Cambridge Companion to Thomas Reid*, ed. T. Cuneo and R. van Woudenberg (Cambridge: Cambridge University Press, 2004), 196. See also A. Plantinga, "Reason and Belief in God," in *Faith and Rationality: Reason and Belief in God* (Notre Dame: University of Notre Dame Press, 1983), 85.

18. Paul Ricoeur, *Memory, History, Forgetting*, trans. K. Blamey and D. Pellauer (Chicago: University of Chicago Press, 2004), 165, cited in Bauckham, *Eyewitnesses*, 479.

19. N. T. Wright, "Five Gospels but No Gospel: Jesus and the Seminar," in *Authenticating the Activities of Jesus*, ed. Bruce Chilton and Craig A. Evans (Leiden: Brill, 1999), 83-120; Marcus J. Borg and N. T. Wright, *The Meaning of Jesus: Two Visions* (San Francisco: Harper, 1999); Marcus J. Borg, "An Appreciative Disagreement," in *Jesus and the Restoration of Israel: A Critical Assessment of N. T. Wright's* Jesus and the Victory of God, ed. Carey C. Newman (Downers Grove, IL: InterVarsity, 1999), 227-43.

20. Paul W. Barnett, *Jesus and the Logic of History* (Grand Rapids: Eerdmans, 1997). See also his *Jesus and the Rise of Early Christianity: A History of New Testament Times* (Downers Grove, IL: InterVarsity, 1999).

and the earliest examples show some awareness of the methodological question.[21] Sustained reflection upon the issue can be found in the writing of Origen, Jerome, Augustine, and many others.[22] Medieval debates about the proper use of Scripture, while for the most part assuming the unique character of the text as God-breathed, reasoned extensively from Scripture itself in the discussion of appropriate interpretive practice.[23] At the time of the Reformation, the defense of *sola scriptura* relied heavily upon texts drawn from Scripture, and debates on the clarity of Scripture saw both sides appealing to Scripture as a basis for their arguments.[24] Similarly, discussions of Scripture and interpretation over the last two centuries — from right across the theological spectrum — appeal to Scripture in order to justify their conclusions.[25] Of course the simple fact that this appeal has a long pedigree does not constitute an argument that it is legitimate. However, it does demonstrate that this method of argument is much more than the eccentric practice of a marginal group of philosophically naïve conservative theologians in the nineteenth, twentieth, and twenty-first centuries, assuming what they ought to be proving in the first place.[26] Its appropriateness has been recognized by even the most methodologically aware over the past two thousand years.

Third, there are several other reasons why such an appeal to Scripture is unavoidable and even necessary as we discuss the clarity of Scripture. From a theological perspective, the discussion takes place in the context of the Christian church's confession of the final authority of Scripture. Whether it be Thomas Aquinas's insistence that "our faith rests on [*innititur*] the revelation made to the Prophets and Apostles who wrote the canonical books, not on a revelation, if such there be, made to any other teacher," or Thomas Cranmer's confession that "whatsoever is not read therein [in Holy Scripture], nor may be proved thereby,

21. Justin Martyr, *De Resurrectione* 1 (ANF 1:294); Clement of Alexandria, *Stromata* 4.1 and 7.16 (ANF 2:409, 551).

22. Origen, *De Principiis* 4.1 (ANF 4:349-50); Jerome, *Tractatus sive Homiliae in Psalmos* 57 (*FOC* 48:410); Augustine, *De Doctrina Christiana* (NPNF1 2:519-97); Gregory the Great, *In Hiezechihelem* 7-9.

23. B. Smalley, *The Study of the Bible in the Middle Ages,* 3rd edition (Oxford: Blackwell, 1983); G. R. Evans, *The Language and Logic of the Bible,* 2 vols. (Cambridge: Cambridge University Press, 1984-85).

24. See Thompson, *A Clear and Present Word,* 143-59.

25. Schleiermacher, *The Christian Faith,* §§128-35 (Edinburgh: T. & T. Clark, 1999), 591-619; B. B. Warfield, *The Inspiration and Authority of the Bible,* ed. S. G. Craig (Phillipsburg, NJ: P&R, 1948); J. I. Packer, *'Fundamentalism' and the Word of God* (London: Inter-Varsity, 1958); J. R. W. Stott, *Christ the Controversialist* (London: Inter-Varsity, 1970), 65-105; James Barr, *Escaping from Fundamentalism* (London: SCM, 1984); John S. Spong, *Rescuing the Bible from Fundamentalism: A Bishop Rethinks the Meaning of Scripture* (San Francisco: Harper, 1992).

26. I leave aside for the moment the question of whether it is the task of the theologian, in any event, to *prove* the doctrine he or she is expounding. See John Webster, "Theological Theology," in *Confessing God* (London: T. & T. Clark, 2005), 18-20.

is not to be required of any man, that it should be believed as an article of the faith, *or* be thought requisite or necessary to salvation," this testimony to the unique and final authority of Scripture in determining faithful Christian doctrine has been treated as axiomatic.[27] Philosophically speaking, many have observed that arguments about final authority in any sphere cannot avoid being formally circular if they are to be coherent. As Michael Kruger puts it, "To deny circularity when it comes to an ultimate authority is to subject oneself to an infinite regress of reasons."[28] So, for instance, an appeal to anything other than Scripture to demonstrate the final authority of Scripture runs the risk that this other source (an independent historical reconstruction, a "scientific" analysis of reality, a philosophical principle, the cumulative experience of Christians through the centuries, the magisterium of the church, etc.) is put in a position of authority alongside or even above the Scriptures. The effect would be to adopt a method of argument that undermines the argument being mounted. An argument for the clarity of Scripture that operates at a level of abstraction that excludes appeal to the text and its testimony to Christ's use of Scripture would similarly run the risk of being self-defeating.[29]

This philosophical consideration must be tempered by two others of a more theological nature. The circularity of the argument about Scripture from Scripture is only formal. Strictly speaking, an appeal to Scripture is in fact an appeal to God himself, precisely because Scripture commends itself as the written word of God.[30] Of course God cannot be reduced to the words on the page nor can

27. T. Aquinas, *Summa Theologiae* Ia. 1, 8; Article 6 of *The Thirty-nine Articles of Religion* (emphasis added).

28. Michael J. Kruger, "The Sufficiency of Scripture in Apologetics," *The Master's Seminary Journal* 12 (2001): 81 n. 31. See also J. Frame, *Apologetics to the Glory of God: An Introduction* (Phillipsburg, NJ: P&R, 1994), 10: "The point is that when one is arguing for an ultimate criterion . . . one must use criteria compatible with that conclusion."

29. An analogy might be drawn with the issue facing God himself as attested in Hebrews 6:13-14: "For when God made a promise to Abraham, since he had no one greater by whom to swear, he swore by himself, saying 'Surely I will bless you and multiply you.'" Perhaps the most celebrated witness to this principle in the Western theological tradition is John Calvin, who insisted that Scripture is "self-authenticated" (*autopiston*), exhibiting "fully as clear evidence of its truth as white and black things do of their color, or sweet and bitter things do of their taste" (*Institutes* 3.1.7; 3.1.2). Contemporary studies in epistemology make much the same point when they acknowledge a distinction between vicious and non-vicious circularity in argument. In certain circumstances (definitions, "customary doxastic practices," and arguments for final authority) self-attestation does not undermine the validity of the argument being mounted. If this is true, then a blanket dismissal of any argument that involves a measure of circularity is certainly unwarranted. See J. A. Burgess, "When Is Circularity in Definitions Benign?" *The Philosophical Quarterly* 58 (2008): 214-33; and William P. Alston, "Epistemic Circularity," *Philosophy and Phenomenological Research* 47 (1986): 1-30.

30. N. T. Wright, *Scripture and the Authority of God* (London: SPCK, 2005), 17.

his authority be circumscribed by the text in such a way that reference beyond itself is defeated. Nevertheless, this extraordinary connection between God and his word, in which, for example, the words of the prophets can be spoken of as words God spoke (Acts 3:21; Heb. 1:1), suggests care should be taken in suggesting either that the appeal to Scripture is circular or that the implicit appeal to God raises questions about the authority of the Scriptures themselves.

The Bible refuses to be domesticated as an endlessly self-referring set of linguistic symbols. No doubt it contains quite a deal of self-reference or intertextuality. Fulfillment is understood in the light of promise even as it goes beyond it. Biblical theology, the sense of an unfolding drama that unites the entire canon of Scripture as a testimony to the fulfillment of God's purposes in the Son — incarnate, crucified, risen and ascended — provides the proper context for approaching individual passages. Yet the Bible is constantly referring beyond itself to the God whose word it is.[31] Eternal life comes not simply from being able to rehearse the Scriptures but through the work of the Spirit drawing men and women to him about whom Scripture consistently testifies (John 5:39-40). The referent and the means of reference cannot be isolated from each other. They must be distinguished but not detached. It is impossible to take God seriously without taking seriously the word he has spoken and caused to be written "for our instruction" (Rom. 15:4). Conversely, a properly theological account of Scripture is not turned in on itself but turned outwards, toward the living God who addresses his people with human words and toward that moment in human history in which he has acted in a way that is decisive for genuine Christian faith (1 Cor. 15:12-19).

Further, any argument about God and his word, and so any human account of the doctrine of Scripture or any part of it, cannot escape our creaturely dependence upon a word from God if it is to correspond to reality. Basic to our experience of reality and our reasoning about it is our creatureliness. We simply cannot get behind created reality in order to describe that reality; we must always attempt our explanations from the inside. In terms of the Bible's own presentation, we were created to engage with our world in the light of the words God addresses to us and our perception is open to distortion whenever we adopt some other point of reference.[32] We cannot describe the process of God's address of human beings from the outside, since we always remain those to whom the word of God comes, commanding a hearing and our allegiance. Similarly, we

31. This could be further developed in terms of the Alethic realism of W. P. Alston (*A Realist Concept of Truth* [Ithaca, NY: Cornell University Press, 1996], 5-84) or the critical realism espoused by, among others, T. F. Torrance (*Reality and Evangelical Theology* [Philadelphia: Westminster, 1982]).

32. Genesis 1–2 gives an account of creation in which the man and the woman are to learn good and evil in fellowship with their Creator. The attempt to circumvent this fellowship in the pursuit of a direct and independent means of evaluating life in the world God has made is presented as the archetypal sin (Genesis 3).

never stand in a position of neutrality or absolute objectivity from which to make judgments about the nature of Scripture or the way it should properly be used. The contingent nature of human knowledge in general and of our knowledge of God and his purposes in particular is not just a product of the Fall. It is part of what it means to be a creature rather than the Creator.

Having reflected briefly on methodology, we now turn our attention to an exposition of the doctrine of Scripture's clarity that finds its center of gravity in the person, words, and work of Jesus Christ.

The Incarnate Son's Confidence in the Clarity of Scripture

The life and ministry of Jesus was characterized by deep engagement with the Hebrew Scriptures. This is hardly surprising given the place of the Hebrew Bible in the culture and religion of Israel throughout its history. Even under foreign occupation and oppression, its influence in public and personal life was pervasive. These holy writings were read in the synagogues, read and explained at the Temple, and were memorized by aspiring religious and civil leaders.[33] The annual cycle of Jewish life meant at least three pilgrimages to Jerusalem and the Temple, where priests read from the Scriptures to recount the mighty deeds of God on behalf of the nation. Jesus became familiar with the Scriptures from a very early age. The one incident from Jesus' childhood that is recounted for us in any detail in the canonical Gospels, the visit to Jerusalem when he was twelve, records the amazement of those in the temple at the extent of his understanding and his capacity to answer the questions put to him (Luke 2:41-52). By the time he reached adulthood it is evident that his familiarity with the "Old Testament," along with his determination to allow it to shape his self-understanding and his perspective on all that was going on around him, was extraordinary.

However, just as significant for our purposes is his expectation that his contemporaries were not only familiar with the Scriptures but understood their meaning. The entire Sermon on the Mount relies upon such a familiarity and understanding, as Jesus explains how he came, not to abolish the Law and the Prophets, but to fulfill them (Matt. 5:17). He certainly builds upon the acknowledged meaning of the texts he cites ("You have heard that it was said . . . but I say to you"), exposing that casuistic approach to the teaching of the Old Testament associated with the mere external righteousness of the scribes and Pharisees (v. 20). Yet this correction relies upon an at least formal willingness to allow behavior to be corrected by the Scriptures and an assumption that their meaning is not beyond those who read them or hear them read. Such an assumption un-

33. Leadership among the Jews could not, of course, be neatly divided between religious and civil categories. There was a very significant degree of overlap between them.

dergirds Jesus' regular appeal to the text of the Old Testament, whether by direct quotation or allusion, throughout his public ministry.

This expectation is even more pointed in Jesus' ongoing confrontation with the religious leaders of his day. Jesus regularly responded to their grumbling at his words and actions with the question, "Have you not read . . . ?" So, for instance, when the Pharisees challenge Jesus because his disciples picked some grain to eat on a Sabbath, Jesus asks, "Have you not read what David did when he was hungry?" (Matt. 12:1-8). When challenged about divorce, he responded, "Have you not read that he who created them from the beginning made them male and female . . . ?" (Matt. 19:3-9). When the Sadducees sought to ridicule the very idea of a resurrection, Jesus' reply included "Have you not read what was said to you by God: 'I am the God of Abraham, and the God of Isaac and the God of Jacob'?" (Matt. 22:31-32). In each case the question was meant as a stinging rebuke.[34] Of course the relevant texts had been read by them. The rabbis of Jesus' day prided themselves on an extensive and detailed knowledge of the Scriptures. Yet we are bound to ask how much of the sting would have been felt, how effective Jesus' question would have been in each instance, if reading the Old Testament could not reasonably be expected to result in understanding. In the end, it wasn't because the words were obscure that the Pharisees failed to obey the Scriptures or the Sadducees were without hope. There were other, moral failures involved. These words were familiar to Jesus' opponents but they had found ways of avoiding their import, either by overlaying the teaching of the Scriptures with their own traditions or by refusing to believe what had been written.

On other occasions Jesus' appeal to the Old Testament as the decisive element in his argument is prefixed by the words "it is written." The most obvious example is the temptation in the wilderness immediately following his baptism. Jesus was presented with three genuine temptations: to provide for himself, to prove his identity, and to pursue another road to glory. At each point he responded to the satan's suggestion by appealing to the teaching of the Scriptures, more specifically the second statement of the Law in Deuteronomy. This, he considered, settled the matter. Each citation begins "It is written" (Matt. 4:4, 7, 10), and at one point the satan himself uses these words in an archetypal battle of the texts (v. 6). The authority of the Scriptures to settle questions about Jesus' identity and mission is an important element of this encounter. However, once again such an appeal can only work on the assumption that the meaning of the text is clear. The same assumption is required by Jesus' use of this citation formula in other settings during his public ministry (Matt. 21:13; 26:31; Luke 24:46; John

34. The sharply polemical and deeply ironic character of these questions has long been recognized: cf. W. Daube, *The New Testament and Rabbinic Judaism* (London: Athlone Press, 1956), 433; W. D. Davies and D. C. Allison, *Matthew,* 3 vols., ICC (Edinburgh: T. & T. Clark, 1997), 3:10.

6:45; 8:17) and by the Gospel writers' use of it in the course of their narrative (Matt. 2:5; Mark 1:2; Luke 2:23; John 12:14). Any extension of meaning or fresh reference in the light of Jesus' person, words, and work, necessarily builds upon what is already there.[35]

Jesus' teaching about the sufficiency of Scripture — even prior to the inclusion of the New Testament documents — carries with it similar assumptions that the meaning of the text is intelligible to its readers. The most obvious example is his parable of the rich man and Lazarus (Luke 16:19-31). The point of the parable comes at the end, when the rich man asks Abraham to send Lazarus to his brothers because "if someone goes to them from the dead, they will repent" (v. 30). Abraham's reply is a rebuke to the rich man, to the Pharisees "who were lovers of money" (v. 14), and also to those readers of the Gospel inclined to put their trust in miracles to secure faith: "If they do not hear Moses and the Prophets, neither will they be convinced if someone should rise from the dead" (v. 31). The conclusion the hearer is meant to draw is that these five brothers have the warning they need to avoid the mistakes of the unnamed rich man. From Moses and the Prophets they should have learned not to trust in riches and to exercise compassion toward the poor. But how would these ancient texts be of any help if they were not clear? If the warning they are meant to convey was garbled somehow, would it be of any benefit at all? So, for this parable to work, here too an assumption is made that not only are these warnings available but they make sense. This does not require every question to be answered or all loose ends to be tied up. In isolation from other parts of the New Testament, questions would remain, for instance, about the relation of faith in Christ to the warning against a hard-hearted materialism that seems to be the main concern of the parable. Nevertheless, along the way this further point is insisted upon: Moses and the prophets are clear enough for the rich man's brothers to be accountable for the choices that they make.[36]

Jesus' appeal to the Old Testament was not simply a rhetorical device used in the midst of theological controversy. He repeatedly explained his own mission in terms of categories provided by the Hebrew Scriptures. Here, however, a slightly different dynamic was at work. While the Old Testament made sense on its own terms as a revelation of the living God and his character, anchored in the concrete realities of Israel's history — sometimes presented as history, at other times as a poetic response to God's mercy in that history, at others still as the prophetic

35. In this sense it is important to acknowledge a progressive revelation that culminates in the life, death, resurrection, and ascension of Jesus Christ. Jesus is himself the climax of God's self-revelation: "all the promises of God find their 'Yes' in him" (2 Cor. 1:20).

36. "Clear enough" here points again to the critical connection between the clarity of Scripture and the purposes for which Scripture is given. If the confession of Scripture's clarity is not to be distorted, then it must be held in close relation to other aspects of the doctrine of Scripture.

promise that God's purposes will not be overthrown even by Israel's rebellion — it always pointed forward to the deliverer to come. That he would come ought to have been clear. Understanding at that level was possible. Yet a new level of understanding would be possible when the bearer of these promises was at last identified.[37] Jesus' appeal to the Old Testament messianic titles, to redemptive and covenantal categories of thought and to significant events in Israel's history operates as such an identification. It stands alongside the prophetic testimony of John the Baptist, the voice from heaven at Jesus' baptism and the miracles that attended his proclamation of the kingdom of God. In the light of this cumulative testimony, refusal to come to Jesus was inexcusable. Jesus explicitly rebuked the Jews who challenged him following the healing at the Pool of Bethesda in these terms: "You search the Scriptures because you think that in them you have eternal life; and it is they that bear witness about me, yet you refuse to come to me that you may have life" (John 5:39-40). The sting in that rebuke comes from Jesus' assumption that they should have known. The promise that he now fulfills was not hidden from them in obscure words.

Jesus cited Old Testament texts as explanations of what he had come to do. Highly significant was his appeal to Isaiah 61 during his visit to the synagogue at Nazareth in the early weeks of his public ministry. It set the scene for all that was to follow. After reading from the scroll, Jesus simply remarked, "Today this Scripture is fulfilled in your hearing" (Luke 4:21). Further explanation may well have followed that arresting comment, though this is not even hinted at in the Gospel record. However, Jesus appears to assume that the essential meaning of the text is evident and that by taking up these words he will be directing the expectations of those who heard him.

Similarly, at the other end of Luke's Gospel, Jesus makes use of the Passover tradition, the new covenant promise of Jeremiah, and the song of the suffering servant of the Lord in the prophecy of Isaiah, to prepare his disciples for the events soon to unfold (Luke 22:7-37). Once again there appears to have been little explanation. What is more, there is no indication that the full import of these allusions was grasped by the disciples at the time. The role they had been given in the events of that night and beyond apparently necessitated a certain failure to comprehend Jesus' predictions about his imminent death — though these had been delivered in the plainest language. On this subject at least, the significance of what Jesus had told them repeatedly was concealed from them (Luke 9:45;

37. The point is neatly illustrated by the Ethiopian eunuch of Acts 8. He understood that the prophet Isaiah had spoken of the agent of God's purposes yet to come. However, he did not know the identity of this promised deliverer. Was it the prophet himself or was there another? So while at one level he had understood what was written, understanding on a whole new level awaited the identification of the one to whom the text referred. Philip's explanation of the good news about Jesus provided what was lacking for a fuller understanding of Isaiah's prophecy.

18:34), a reference not to a deficiency in Jesus' words but to the gracious activity of God in the lives of the apostles as the events of that night unfolded around them. However, on the other side of the resurrection, the Holy Spirit would bring back to their minds these predictions, presumably alongside the words spoken in the upper room and in the Garden of Gethsemane (John 14:26; cf. 7:37-39). Recalling these words, the apostles would be able to assure future generations of Christians that nothing happened to Jesus that was not planned from the beginning for their salvation.

Jesus' confident appeal to the Old Testament is an unmistakable characteristic of his public ministry. He persisted with such an appeal in the face of rejection by those who refused to listen to it (John 5:39-40), despite the propensity of the general populace to distort it in the direction of their own aspirations (John 6:15), and alongside a dullness on the part of the disciples that was divinely intended to serve the interests of the saving events of which they were a part. None of these were the result of failings in the text. Rather they were each illustrative of the relation between revelation and salvation.

Jesus' perspective on this relation is most evident in his explanation of why he taught in parables. The familiar images used in the parables suggest they are exercises in accommodation, aids to effective communication pure and simple. However, Jesus explains that in reality the parables have a double edge that cannot be understood apart from the discriminating purpose of God. These brief stories make sense in themselves but their significance is grasped only by those to whom it has been given:

> To you has been given the secret of the kingdom of God, but for those outside everything is in parables so that "they may indeed see but not perceive, and may indeed hear but not understand, lest they should turn and be forgiven." (Mark 4:11-12, quoting Isa. 6:9-10).

There are several indicators in this brief sentence that revelation and God's saving purpose are intimately connected. In the first place, Jesus contrasts "you" ("those around him with the twelve," Mark 4:10) and "those outside." In isolation we might conclude from this observation that, at least when it comes to the parables, the real issue lies with the hearers rather than the clarity or otherwise of the language Jesus is using.[38] Hearers, as postmodern theorists are keen to insist, are not mere passive recipients of information. The attitude that each brings to the act of hearing (or reading) has a significant impact on how, and indeed whether, the message is received. Furthermore, the appeal to Isaiah 6 suggests

38. "[T]he efficacy of the parables depends, not on the parables, but on the character of the hearers" (T. W. Manson, *The Teaching of Jesus* [Cambridge: Cambridge University Press, 1931], 77).

that "parables are prophetic instruments," which present a message some do not want to receive.[39] However, there is more to be said. We should notice the most controversial feature of this text, the *hina* in verse 11, which T. F. Torrance once identified as "a scandal."[40] The parables are *intended* to distinguish between two types of hearers. To some the mystery of the kingdom of God has been *given.* To others, those outside, the parables become a barrier to perception and understanding. They will not turn and they will not be forgiven. This is not because of some defect in the parable, some ambiguity or obscurity that places the meaning beyond reach to all but the most determined. Ultimately it is God who, in an act of sovereign mercy or equally sovereign and yet appropriate judgment, determines the nature of the hearing.[41] Jesus would later thank God for hiding "these things from the wise and understanding and revealing them to little children," recognizing that this was God's gracious will (Matt. 11:25-26).[42] Revelation in the fullest sense (i.e., including its reception) remains a sovereign act of God, inseparable from a saving relation to the Son (v. 27).

It is the incarnate Son who engages the Scripture extant at the time of his earthly life and public ministry in these ways. Yet is his confidence in the clarity of Scripture, its openness to being understood subject to the redemptive purposes of God, itself explained as an act of accommodation? Was Jesus merely echoing the conventional understanding of those around him, either as a result of his genuine incarnation as a Jewish man at the beginning of the first century, or in order to be understood by others who could not think otherwise? Did he treat Scripture as the authoritative word of God, as a decisive element in God's effective communication with men and women that must not be avoided, ignored or overturned, simply because to have treated it in any other way would not have made sense to his contemporaries?[43]

Such a suggestion may arise from a concern to take seriously the genuine

39. K. R. Snodgrass, *Stories with Intent: A Comprehensive Guide to the Parables of Jesus* (Grand Rapids: Eerdmans, 2008), 159.

40. T. F. Torrance, "A Study in New Testament Communication," *SJT* 3 (1950): 303.

41. Cf. Luke 19:41-44. In my opinion, Torrance jumps too quickly from Mark 4:12 to verse 22 and then verse 33, leading him to conclude, "In the parable, so to speak, the Kingdom of God comes into the midst and throws a man into the crisis of decision, and yet by its veiled form the Word of the Kingdom holds man at arm's length away in order to give him room and time for personal decision" (Torrance, "A Study in New Testament Communication," 304).

42. Jesus' prayer of thanks finds an echo in Paul's argument in 1 Corinthians 1, where God has made foolish the wisdom of the world. Paul Moser's suggestion that God hides himself to prevent the almost inevitable cognitive idolatry of human beings may be helpful here but it needs more substantial grounding in the teaching of the New Testament in particular. Paul K. Moser, "Cognitive Idolatry and Divine Hiding," in *Divine Hiddenness: New Essays,* ed. D. Howard-Snyder and P. K. Moser (Cambridge: Cambridge University Press, 2002), 120-48.

43. John Wenham has an extended discussion of these questions. *Christ and the Bible,* 2nd edition (Grand Rapids: Baker, 1984), 43-63.

humanity of the incarnate Son. By taking the form of a servant (Phil. 2:7), he accepted the limitations common to our creaturely existence and one of those is the historical and cultural location of all our thinking. Yet while it is true that the eternal Son was incarnate as a first-century Jewish man and "increased in wisdom" (Luke 2:52) in ways appropriate to that context, there is ample evidence that his understanding of God and his purposes had deeper roots. He willingly accepted limits to his understanding: he explained to his disciples that the timing of his return is known only to the Father (Matt. 24:36). Yet just as evidently his knowledge of creaturely realities far exceeded that of his contemporaries. He knew Nathaniel's character (John 1:48), the Samaritan woman's marital history (John 4:18), and Lazarus's medical condition (John 11:11). He knew that a shekel would be found in the mouth of the first fish Simon caught during one of his visits to Capernaum (Matt 17:27). Most significant of all, he knew the details of his own death and resurrection long before the event, extending to the identity of his betrayer and the number of times that Peter would deny him on the night of his arrest (Luke 9:21-22, 43-45; 18:31-34; 22:31-34; John 13:21-30). The wonder of the incarnation is that a genuine human nature is joined in one person to the divine nature of the Son without compromise to either and this must extend to his thinking as much as every other facet of his incarnate life. The assumption of scriptural clarity which is so pervasive in his ministry is not simply a result of his creaturely limitation or historical location.

Yet the suggestion might also arise from a recognition of divine accommodation as a consistent feature of God's dealings with human beings and in an important sense an explanation of the incarnation itself. God approaches us in ways accommodated to *our* limited understanding. Calvin famously spoke of God "wont in a measure to 'lisp' in speaking to us." He had in mind those anthropomorphisms used in Scripture to describe God and his action: "[S]uch forms of speaking do not so much express clearly what God is like as accommodate the knowledge of him to our slight capacity."[44] The image Calvin uses may be unfortunate, raising more questions than it answers and suggesting to some an impediment on God's part, but his conviction that God is concerned to address us in ways that we can understand is easily established from the testimony of Scripture.[45] From the be-

44. *Institutes* 1.13.1.

45. In the history of Christian doctrine there have been two distinct uses of the concept of accommodation with relation to Scripture. The predominant use of the concept follows that of Calvin: truth explained in terms and with images intelligible to finite human beings. However, Faustus Socinus spoke of a divine willingness to express himself within the erroneous worldviews of the human authors of Scripture and their contemporaries. Faustus Socinus et al., "Epitome of a Colloquium Held in Rakow in the Year 1601," in *The Polish Brethren: Documentation of the History of Unitarianism in the Polish-Lithuanian Commonwealth and in the Diaspora 1601-1685*, 2 vols., ed. George H. Williams (Missoula, MT: Scholars Press, 1980), 2:121-22. As John Woodbridge demonstrates in his contribution to this collection, such a view entered main-

ginning, it appears, God does not address men and women in a celestial language that needs to be translated in some way before it can be understood. Even in the Garden of Eden, God addresses his creatures with the same words they might use in other contexts. They are able to repeat those words when challenged by the serpent. Furthermore, the incarnation is itself the supreme act of accommodation — though we must immediately add it is much more than that — as the Word becomes flesh and dwells among us, embodying grace and truth and exegeting the Father for us (John 1:14, 18). Yet nowhere does such divine accommodation stretch to endorsing erroneous perspectives in the service of clear communication. Jesus repeatedly shows himself willing and able to challenge convention when it obscures gospel truth. He does not hold back from eating with tax collectors and sinners though this was very evidently not the convention among those who prided themselves on taking the Scriptures seriously (Matt. 9:10-13). His disciples did not fast (Matt. 9:14-17), ate with unwashed hands (Mark 7:1-8), and grazed on the harvest as they traveled (Matt. 12:1-8) — all, apparently, with his approval. Jesus himself healed on the Sabbath (Matt. 12:9-14) and humbled himself before his own disciples (John 13:1-20). He spoke to women outside of his family circle (John 4:1-30) and openly challenged the conventional practice of Corban (Mark 7:9-13). Jesus' appeal to Scripture and his implicit assumption of its clarity cannot be explained as mere acquiescence to prevailing convention. It was not simply a pedagogical device. It had far deeper roots than that.

However, is there not counter-evidence from Jesus' own teaching ministry? Were there not times when Jesus' own words were obscure, perhaps deliberately so? Didn't the disciples themselves need to seek an explanation of his words in private (Mark 4:10)? Was it not with some relief that they exclaimed, "now you are speaking plainly and not using figurative speech!" (John 16:29). The case of the parables has already been examined. However, Jesus' discussion of "eating his flesh and drinking his blood" in John 6:51-58 is another striking example. None of those listening that day in the synagogue at Capernaum understood what he was saying, and many faithful men and women have puzzled over these words ever since.

It may be helpful at this point to distinguish between the clarity of Jesus' teaching in its original setting (i.e., in the midst of his teaching ministry, before the cross and resurrection, the giving of the Spirit and the completion of the canon) and the clarity of Jesus' teaching in its canonical context (including the completed Gospel records and the apostolic proclamation). The canonical context includes other references to participation in the benefits of Jesus' atoning death using the imagery of eating and drinking (e.g., 1 Cor. 10:14-17; 11:26) and these place the reader of the New Testament in quite a different position to those

---

stream Christian thinking through Richard Simon, Jean Le Clerc, Hermann Samuel Reimarus, and Johann S. Semler.

who first heard Jesus on the topic in the Capernaum synagogue. Jesus did not always speak so enigmatically, even in public. However, during the course of his public ministry, there were times when he did not speak plainly for a variety of reasons, some of which we have already canvassed. Nevertheless, when these words are read as part of the Gospel narrative culminating in Jesus' death and resurrection, and in the light of the apostolic proclamation that followed the giving of the Spirit at Pentecost, their reference becomes clearer. We will return to the question of why debate continues about such texts shortly.

Our investigation of the concept of scriptural clarity has so far focused on Jesus' attitude to the Scriptures of his day. We now turn to an explanation of that confidence in terms of Jesus' understanding of the origin, nature, and function of Scripture.

The Father's Gift of the Clarity of Scripture

Undergirding Jesus' use of Scripture throughout his public ministry was his conviction that these texts can be identified as the word of God (Mark 7:13; John 10:35). Such an identification places the biblical text in the closest possible connection with God himself, underscoring its authority but also placing it in the context of God's gracious movement toward his creation with a view to the ultimate reconciliation of all things in Christ (Col. 1:20). The word of God is a source of both delight and trembling in those who are rightly related to God (Ps. 119; Isa. 66:2). It is the means by which he executes his purposes; and whether in creation, redemption, or judgment it will not fail to accomplish what he intends (Isa. 55:10-11). As the writer to the Hebrews would put it, "the word of God is living and active, sharper than any two-edged sword, piercing to the division of soul and of spirit, of joints and of marrow, and discerning the thoughts and intentions of the heart" (Heb. 4:12).

Jesus spoke of his own delight to do the Father's will and to make known the words that he had been given by his Father (John 4:34; 6:38; 17:8). The significance of the plural (*rhēmata*) in this last context should not be overlooked. Jesus was not speaking of some abstract principle, his teaching as a whole, or even the proclamation of the kingdom in more general terms.[46] He utters the words that have been given to him by his Father and by means of those words his disciples have "come to know in truth that I came from you." Words are the principal currency of relationships and that observation is given ontological depth by the place words have in the relationship of the Father and the Son.[47] Of course words

46. D. A. Carson, *The Gospel according to John,* PNTC (Leicester: Inter-Varsity; Grand Rapids: Eerdmans, 1991), 560.

47. See reflection on this passage (John 17) in Vern Poythress, *In the Beginning Was the*

may be hollow if they find no echo in the behavior of the one who utters them. However, in Jesus the incarnate Son there is much more than an echo. In his case there is a perfect consistency between words and action: "The words that I say to you I do not speak on my own authority, but the Father who dwells in me does his works" (John 14:10). The designation of Jesus Christ as the Word of God (John 1:1-14) is not arbitrary.

This relational intent of language — a perspective that enables us to appreciate both the personal and the propositional dimensions of revelation — is on display throughout the Old Testament and into the New. God addresses the man and the woman in the Garden with a word of blessing and a word of command (Gen. 1:28-30; 2:16-17). By so doing he both gives them information and binds them to himself (and it is this latter aspect that ensures their subsequent decision to embrace another word will have such devastating consequences). Yet God continues to address men and women after the Fall (Gen. 3:8-19; 4:6-7, 9-15; 6:13-21). Indeed the narrative momentum of the entire Old Testament is due in no small measure to the words God addresses to individuals and later to the nation. Of particular significance is the call of Abraham in Genesis 12, the foundation of a unique relationship between God and Abraham's descendants. So powerful is God's commitment to the promises he made to this man and his family that he will not abandon the nation that comes from them despite their habitual rebellion (Deut. 9:5-6). The pattern continues with the call of Moses (Exodus 3), the selection of David (1 Sam. 16:1-13), the prophetic summons into exile (Jer. 25:1-14), and the promise of a return (Isaiah 40), just to select a few landmark examples.

Speaking and words are central in the biblical portrait of the living God. God is most fundamentally one who speaks.[48] The first words recorded in Scripture are spoken by God (Gen. 1:3) and God speaks throughout and at the end (Rev. 21:5). Unlike the idols of the nations, who are mute and powerless "like scarecrows in a cucumber field" (Jer. 10:5), God addresses men and women with powerful words that define, rather than merely describe, reality.[49] Indeed, the distinctive character of Hebrew religion, with its prohibition on images and its focus on words as critical to the relationship between the believer and God, arises from the ineradicably verbal character of divine revelation: "Then the Lord spoke to you out of the midst of the fire. You heard the sound of words, but saw no form; there was only a voice" (Deut. 4:12). So, as one contemporary account puts it, "when God gave the gift of language to mankind, it included the intention that

---

Word: Language — A God-Centered Approach (Wheaton: Crossway, 2009), 19; also *God-Centered Biblical Interpretation* (Phillipsburg, NJ: P&R, 1999), 16-25.

48. See Peter Jensen's contribution to this volume.

49. The point being made here is simply that there is a difference between the way creatures relate to the reality they inhabit and the way the Creator relates to the reality he brings into being. God is not constrained by the world he has made, nor is he bound merely to describe it: "by the word of the Lord the heavens were made" (Ps. 33:6).

God would participate as a speaker of language."[50] Whatever else may happen along the way, words and language were designed as critical facilitators of the relationship between God and his people. The appropriateness of the incarnation *of the Word* is seen in a new light once this is recognized. So too the apostle Paul's observation, "faith comes *from hearing,* and hearing through the word of Christ" (Rom. 10:17).

Wonder at the privilege of being addressed by the living God is a conspicuous feature of Hebrew piety. Once again it was Moses who set the pattern: "Did any people ever hear the voice of a god speaking out of the midst of the fire, as you have heard, and still live?" (Deut. 4:33) Yet it is among the psalms that this delight in the words God has given, and the relationship they generate, is given fullest expression. Blessed is the one who delights in the law of the Lord and meditates on it day and night (Ps. 1:2). This gift of God revives the soul, makes wise the simple, and rejoices the heart (Ps. 19:7-11). The word of God provides guidance for life in the present (Ps. 119:105) and hope for the future (Ps. 119:81). It should hardly need saying that these sentiments are expressed about words that the psalmist knows principally in written form. However, this transition from spoken to written form presents no difficulty, since it is God himself who authorizes it (Exod. 24:12; 31:18; 34:1; Deut. 9:10). God gives his written word (once again without compromising the genuine, conscious, and creative contribution of human authors), not as an alternative to his personal presence but as a true and clear expression of the mind and purpose of one who promises to be present with his people (Josh. 1:8-9). This is the trajectory that would lead to Paul's critical statement: "All Scripture is breathed out by God . . ." (2 Tim. 3:16).

These considerations must temper any reservation about the clarity of Scripture based upon the observed frailty of human language. If words are from the beginning the means God provides to establish and nourish relationships, we must hesitate before suggesting that they are "an unsuitable medium for God's self-presentation."[51] We might not always be able to avoid demonstrating the capacity for miscommunication when words are abused, deliberately or otherwise. However, most of our human communication succeeds most of the time and God is certainly not subject to our propensity to confuse or deceive. When it is God who is using human language to speak of himself, his will, or its realization within the created order, there is no reason to consider that it will fail to deliver the revelation he intends. "We must be insistent," one significant study of the subject opines, "that human language is not ultimately a human invention, but God's gift, a gift reflective of his own capacities as the Giver. That recognition engenders confidence."[52]

50. Poythress, *Word,* 256.

51. Karl Barth, *Church Dogmatics* I/1, 166.

52. Richard Gaffin, "Speech and the Image of God: Biblical Reflections on Language and

The accessibility of the words that God gives to his people throughout the Old Testament arises in this context of God's determination to be known by those he has claimed as his own and God's gift of human language as critical to the process of making himself known. After all, even the incarnate Son did not simply appear or act without explanation. His was no mere mute presence among us. He came in the context of Old Testament prophecy and the Baptist's testimony, and he spoke the words his Father had given him (John 17:8). In such a context it becomes obvious that the clarity of Scripture plays an important role in the redemptive purpose of God. Throughout human history he addresses men and women with words that explain his powerful saving activity and elicit from them — though not without the operation of the Holy Spirit — the proper response of that wholehearted trust that transforms lives. So Moses insists,

> this commandment that I command you today is not too hard for you, neither is it far off. It is not in heaven, that you should say, "Who will ascend to heaven for us and bring it to us, that we may hear it and do it?" Neither is it beyond the sea, that you should say, "Who will go over the sea for us and bring it to us, that we may hear it and do it?" But the word is very near you. It is in your mouth and in your heart, so that you can do it. (Deut. 30:11-14; cf. Rom. 10:5-17)

This is the proper basis for the confidence that Jesus demonstrates in the effectiveness of God's communicative act in Scripture. Human words have featured in the relationship between God and human beings from the beginning. Such words given by God to his people have become Scripture without any loss in their effectiveness. This is not a text that God has "commandeered" despite its unsuitability. Scripture is properly understood as the generous gift of a gracious Father. God's undeniable capacity to accomplish his communicative purposes, coupled with his essential benevolence toward his people — repeatedly demonstrated in the history of Israel — undergirds Jesus' confidence that the meaning of Scripture is accessible.[53]

The Spirit's Enabling of the Clarity of Scripture

Jesus' understanding of the role of the Holy Spirit in the production of the biblical texts provides further grounds for confidence that Scripture is clear. In identifying a connection between word and Spirit Jesus was not being innovative. The

Its Uses," in *The Pattern of Sound Doctrine: Systematic Theology at the Westminster Seminaries; Essays in Honor of Robert B. Strimple* (Phillipsburg, NJ: P&R, 2004), 191.

53. We are brought again to the dilemma posed by the alternative to scriptural clarity as expounded by Benedict Pictet (see above, n. 11).

inseparability of word and Spirit is on view right through the Old Testament (and through the New Testament as well). The Spirit or breath of God is connected to the creative word of God at the very beginning (Gen. 1:2-3). Time and again, when the Spirit comes to rest upon human beings they speak, typically words of prophecy (Num. 11:25, 29; 1 Sam. 10:10; Joel 2:28). David spoke of how "the Spirit of the Lord speaks by me," anticipating the way the New Testament would cite Old Testament texts as the words of the Holy Spirit (Acts 1:16; 4:25; Heb. 3:7; 10:15-17). Zechariah could speak of the words of the prophets who had come before him as "the words that the Lord of hosts had sent by his Spirit through the former prophets" (Zech. 7:12).

Jesus echoed this testimony to the Spirit's involvement with the Old Testament when he cited Psalm 110 after attributing it to "David, in the Spirit" (Matt. 22:43). However, on the night of his arrest he spoke of a future ministry of the Spirit. The Helper, whom he promised the Father would send to the disciples in his name, the Spirit of truth, would teach them all things and bring to their remembrance "all that I have said to you" (John 14:26). He would guide them into all truth, not speaking on his own authority but speaking whatever he hears — taking what belongs to Jesus and declaring it to them (John 16:13-15). These are promises that are realized in the apostolic mission that generates the New Testament. When, on the Day of Pentecost, the Spirit is given to the assembled disciples, the first result was speaking. As the observers remarked, "we hear them telling in our own tongues the mighty works of God" (Acts 2:11). Years later, Peter would write of the way the prophetic word came, not simply as the result of a human decision, but rather as the result of those through whom it came being "carried along [*pheromenoi*] by the Holy Spirit" (2 Pet. 1:21). Previously, Peter appeared to have Jesus' promise in mind (and perhaps also its first moment of fulfillment on the Day of Pentecost) when he wrote of the things announced through those who preached the gospel "by the Holy Spirit sent from heaven" (1 Pet. 1:12).

A unique work of the Spirit in the lives of those who spoke and wrote produced what would ultimately be Scripture "breathed out by God" — the associations between breath and Spirit should not be overlooked in the critical passage in 2 Timothy either. This work does not overwhelm or obscure the human element in their writing. There remains the indelible indication of its anchor in the lives, personalities, background, and circumstances of the individual human authors. They were consciously and — properly understood — creatively involved. Yet this dual authorship does not make distortion inevitable. The final product (not the authors and not some primal word that they are responsible to convert into text) is described as "breathed out by God." In this way we can speak of the Spirit giving a particular character to these texts that distinguishes them from all others.[54]

54. This might be explored in terms of Colin Gunton's suggestion of a particularizing aspect of the Spirit's role as "the perfecting cause of the creation" (following Basil of Caesarea,

The Spirit's involvement extends beyond the production of the Scriptures to their reception. The apostle Paul would insist that "no one can say 'Jesus is Lord' except in the Holy Spirit" (1 Cor. 12:3). Earlier in that same epistle he spoke at some length of the role of the Spirit in enabling "the things freely given us by God" to be understood (1 Cor. 2:6-16). His emphasis is on an impediment to understanding in those who hear or read rather than on some deficiency in what has been given. Paul does not advocate a proto-Gnostic secret knowledge restricted to insiders and not available to others that somehow must be added to Scripture before it is intelligible. The "secret and hidden wisdom of God, which God decreed before the ages for our glory" (1 Cor. 2:7) has now been manifest in the cross of the Christ — "the power of God and the wisdom of God" (1 Cor. 1:24). Yet apart from the Spirit of God, all that is seen is folly and weakness: "The natural person does not accept the things of the Spirit of God, for they are folly to him and he is not able to understand them because they are spiritually discerned" (1 Cor. 2:14). Paul would return to this theme in his second letter to the Corinthians, where he attributes the Jewish resistance to what the Scriptures teach to a veil that lies over their hearts. "Only through Christ is it taken away," he declares, and "where the Spirit of the Lord is, there is freedom" (2 Cor. 3:14, 17).

In considering this aspect of how the Spirit enables the clarity of Scripture, we are not far from Luther's understanding of "the *internal* clarity of Scripture."[55] He described the Spirit's involvement in the production of the Scriptures, which amongst other things ensured the words make sense as they stand, as "the *external* clarity of Scripture." The Spirit has made it possible for anyone to read these words in the way other human words are read. They are not jumbled nonsense. However, without the Spirit at work at the other end of the phenomenon of reading as well, in the readers as well as with the text, the significance of what is being said will be lost on them. Both the external and internal clarity of Scripture are important and both are the work of the Spirit who carries God's word to its effective conclusion in the present just as he did in the beginning.[56]

The presence of the Spirit with believers, both as redeemed persons and as the gathered people of God, highlights an often-neglected aspect of Christian engagement with the Scriptures. In a way that is not necessary and almost always

---

On the Holy Spirit 15.36). C. E. Gunton, *The One, the Three and the Many: God, Creation and the Culture of Modernity* (Cambridge: Cambridge University Press, 1993), 182-83. However, there is a tendency in Gunton (and those who follow his lead) to develop this notion beyond all scriptural warrant. After all, the perfector of faith in the New Testament is the Son rather than the Spirit (Heb. 12:2).

55. M. Luther, "The Bondage of the Will (1525)," WA 18, 609.4-5 = LW 33.28.

56. For a more extensive and nuanced discussion of these ideas in Luther's writings, see my *A Sure Ground on Which to Stand: The Relation of Authority and Interpretive Method in Luther's Approach to Scripture* (Carlisle: Paternoster, 2003), 232-40.

not true of other texts, the Bible is never read in the absence of its primary author. Scripture is never read, never studied, never commented upon, behind God's back as it were. God has not abandoned his word to the vicissitudes of human literary criticism. A recognition of this fact has the potential to transform the act of reading. High-handed treatment of the text of Scripture should be more difficult, as a humble confidence that our heavenly Father wants his word to be understood, and has provided all that is necessary for that to happen, replaces the proud human tendency to stand over the word to "decide" its meaning and relevance. Perhaps above all, prayer will accompany reading, in recognition not only that Scripture is God's good gift, but that the same Spirit who caused it to be written is able to open our eyes to see and understand.

Explicit consideration of the role of the Spirit in the production and reception of Scripture, and in particular his role in ensuring the clarity of Scripture, comes after the resurrection and ascension of Jesus. It is part of the apostolic proclamation that Jesus himself commissioned. Yet it is entirely of a piece with Jesus' own recognition of an intrinsic connection of word and Spirit. The Spirit is involved, and remains involved, at each stage of the life of these texts — in the experience of those who wrote them, in the process of their inscripturation, and in their reception.

Against Erroneous Inferences

The exposition of the clarity of Scripture in such a Trinitarian fashion, yet with its center of gravity in the person, words, and work of Jesus Christ, enables a response to a number of false inferences that are sometimes drawn from a confession of the doctrine. First, the clarity of Scripture does not imply that all texts are equally and uniformly clear. We must take seriously the textured quality of the Scripture God has given us. Questions of genre, the personal style of each human author, the location of the text in the sweep of redemptive history, and the nature of what is being communicated at each point, all add to the richness of this texture. This has long been acknowledged in standard accounts, such as that in the Westminster Confession of Faith: "All things in Scripture are not alike plain in themselves, nor alike clear unto all."[57] At the heart of any confession of clarity are, to use the words of the Confession, "those things which are necessary to be known, believed and observed for salvation." Other doctrines and other texts may demand more of the reader. It is useful to remember that Peter did not suggest everything in Paul's letters is difficult to understand. Only "some things in them" require this extra effort (2 Pet. 3:15-16).

Confidence that even the "difficult" texts are not impenetrable is anchored

57. *Westminster Confession of Faith* (1647), 1.7.

in God's communicative intention and his benevolence, but it is also a function of the fact that their proper context is now the Christian canon. Too often the difficulty of such texts is magnified because they are treated in isolation from their context in the whole of Scripture. "Scripture is its own interpreter," the Reformers insisted.[58] As one text is compared with others, many of the difficulties are overcome. In this way the Reformers gave new meaning to the expression "the analogy of Scripture," insisting that Scripture be approached as an interconnected whole in which the more easily understood passages provide the proper framework for understanding the more difficult ones. The biblical canon may thus be seen as itself a critical resource for reading Scripture rightly and so for conveying its inherent clarity. This Reformation principle obviously involved a commitment to the unity of Scripture (a unity ultimately grounded in the one God whose word it is and in Scripture's focus upon his plan of redemption in Christ). It also meant insisting that it is illegitimate to "so expound one place of Scripture, that it be repugnant to another."[59] The proper assumption is consistency rather than contradiction. From this perspective, the textured nature of Scripture need not be taken as a barrier to a confession of the clarity of Scripture. In short, we have a clear Scripture because we have an entire Scripture.

Similarly, the clarity of Scripture does not imply transparency or even simplicity. A carefully detailed argument may ultimately aid clarity even though it is not simple. Difficulty might prove to be a divinely intended mechanism for enabling access to meaning, encouraging concentrated attention rather than allowing the reader to remain content with a superficial reading.[60] In the comment of Peter about some elements in Paul's letters, both Peter's recognition that Paul had written about the appropriate way to view the interim between Jesus' ascension and his return, and his encouragement to his own readers to avoid the way false teachers have "twisted" Paul's teaching, express confidence that such difficulties as we encounter are not insurmountable. It was possible to identify Paul's "untwisted" teaching. The writings of Paul, like the "other Scriptures" —

58. The expression is most usually attributed to Luther. "*Assertio omnium articulorum* (1520)," WA 7, 97.23-24. It was also an element of the official *protestatio* drawn up by a group of German princes at the Diet of Speyer in 1529. Hajo Holborn, *A History of Modern Germany: The Reformation* (New York: Knopf, 1961), 208.

59. The Thirty-nine Articles of Religion (1571), art. 20.

60. So George Steiner explained (with particular reference to poetic writing) that difficulty can in fact be productive of an ultimately clear communication of meaning: "Contingent difficulties aim to be looked up; modal difficulties challenge the inevitable parochialism of honest empathy; tactical difficulties endeavor to deepen our apprehension by dislocating and goading to new life the supine energies of word and grammar. Each of these three classes of difficulty is part of the contract of ultimate or preponderant intelligibility between poet and reader, between text and meaning." George Steiner, "On Difficulty," in *On Difficulty and Other Essays* (New York: Oxford University Press, 1978), 40. I am grateful to Kevin Vanhoozer for this reference.

and, as we've seen, to a certain extent because they are properly located alongside the other Scriptures — may be approached with confidence that they can be understood.

Augustine spoke of how the difficulties of Scripture are divinely intended:

> The Holy Spirit, therefore, has generously and advantageously planned Holy Scripture in such a way that in the easier passages *(locis apertioribus)* He relieves our hunger; in the more obscure *(obscurioribus)* He drives away our pride. Practically nothing is dug out from those obscure texts which is not discovered to be said very plainly in another place.[61]

Augustine's confidence that the benevolence of God extends to the nature of his communicative activity enables him to view even difficulties in a positive light. Gregory the Great could likewise speak of how Scripture "holds in the open that by which little ones may be nourished [and] keeps hidden that by which those of lofty intellect might stand in wonder."[62] So Tyndale's plowboy can approach the text with confidence while the scholar can return again and again in anticipation of discovering more that he or she has not seen before. There remains room to grow in our understanding of the word that God has given us (Eph. 3:14-21; 1 Tim. 4:11-16; 2 Pet. 3:18).

Nor ought we to infer, thirdly, that the clarity of Scripture renders teaching, commentary, and other scholarship unnecessary or irrelevant. The doctrine of the clarity of Scripture, as classically expounded, has never endorsed an individualistic piety that has no place for the research or insights of others or for the consensus of faithful Christian men and women in other times and other places. To suggest that the clarity of Scripture confers a "right private judgment" is mistaken.[63] All our reading must take seriously the determined note of corporate address in both the Old Testament and the New — we read as members of Christ's church. Furthermore, it is the risen and ascended Christ himself who gifts his church with teachers (Eph. 4:11).

It is certainly true that the clarity of Scripture has historically been an important part of the Reformation challenge to an ecclesiastical "magisterium" that insists on its right to determine the true meaning of Scripture for all.[64] Furthermore,

61. Augustine, *De doctrina Christiana* 2.6 (8) (*NPNF1*, 2:537 = *CCSL*, 32:36).

62. Gregory the Great, *Moralia in Job* ad. Leand. IV (*CCSL* 143:6). He goes on to say that Scripture is like a river that is both shallow and deep, "in which both the lamb may find a footing and the elephant swim."

63. Charles Hodge put "the perspicuity of Scripture" alongside "the right of private judgment" in his *Systematic Theology*, 3 vols. (London: Nelson, 1871-73), 1:183.

64. So the decree of the fourth session of the Council of Trent on 8 April 1546 against those who "presume to interpret the said sacred Scripture contrary to that sense which holy mother Church, — whose it is to judge of the true sense and interpretation of the holy Scrip-

it has always been possible for teachers and scholars — both inside and outside the churches — to assume a similar posture, necessitating fresh attention to this doctrine. Yet it is instructive that the Protestant reformers, among the most ardent supporters of the doctrine, made abundant reference to the writings of those who had expounded the Scriptures before them and wrote numerous biblical commentaries themselves. Indeed, they insisted that there must be good grounds for overturning the exegetical and theological tradition and these must include an appeal to the details of what the biblical text clearly says. It would never have occurred to them to read Scripture as autonomous individuals.[65] Furthermore, in the centuries since, historical and archaeological research has demonstrably aided a better understanding of what is in fact being taught in Scripture.[66]

Of course the text must stand over the history of conclusions about the meaning of the text. The consensus of the faithful may be mistaken for a variety of reasons (e.g., the mistranslation of Matt. 4:17 that undergirded the medieval penitential system). But Paul was willing to set his gospel before the apostles in Jerusalem, in order to ensure that he "was not running or had not run in vain" (Gal. 2:2). Similarly, Luther remained open to being shown from Scripture that his own conclusions were exegetically unfounded and contrary to the articles of faith. He understood he had a responsibility to subject his own thinking about the teaching of Scripture to the scrutiny of others. False teaching and distortions of biblical teaching in our own interests are only too possible. Yet the test of all readings, novel and traditional, individual and corporate, is the words of the text itself.

Perhaps the most persistent false inference, though, is that the clarity of Scripture, if it were true, would remove all disagreement on the meaning of any portion of Scripture. On the face of it, then, the long history of seemingly intractable exegetical and theological disagreement provides a powerful counterargument to the doctrine. It need hardly be said that such disagreement must be taken seriously rather than dismissed lightly or prematurely. Deeply held differences over the meaning of particular texts, on the part of men and women who give every indication of seeking to submit themselves to the teaching of Scripture in faith and prayerful dependence upon the Holy Spirit, have been a conspicuous feature of church history. This is a genuine pastoral and experiential problem that has led some to ask whether the doctrine of the clarity of Scripture has become meaningless.[67]

---

tures, — hath held and doth hold." *Creeds of Christendom,* ed. P. Schaff (repr. Grand Rapids: Baker, 1977), 2:83.

65. Moises Silva, *Has the Church Misread the Bible? The History of Interpretation in the Light of Current Issues* (Grand Rapids: Zondervan, 1987), 94-97.

66. It should be recognized, however, that the danger of such background factors becoming the foreground, and reconstructions built upon them subverting what the text in fact explicitly teaches, has not been entirely avoided over the years.

67. Silva, *Has the Church Misread the Bible?* 79.

However, such disagreement does not necessarily sound the death knell for a confession of Scripture's clarity. After all, disagreement arises from a variety of sources.[68] Readers are never entirely passive in the act of reading, bringing their own perspectives to the texts they are reading. Personal preferences, cultural blind spots and allegiance to the community of which the reader is a part — or to an interpretative tradition associated with that community — all have the potential for distorting our reading. We can all fall into the habit of unwittingly reading our convictions into the text of Scripture rather than letting Scripture challenge them. One immeasurable benefit of reading Scripture "in the company" of readers in other times and places is that *our* blind spots can be exposed and *our* convictions challenged. So, our postmodern aversion to the violence of Old Testament sacrificial imagery perhaps says more about us than about the biblical picture of the horrific nature of human sin and God's gracious provision of a means by which it might be dealt with until the day when he bears the cost himself in the person of his Son. Our Western preoccupation with individual rights may distort our exposition of biblical calls for unity and service.

Sometimes disagreement about Scripture's meaning arises from differing honest attempts to fill in details in a biblical text despite a lack of such explication in the text itself. For example, a detailed description of the nature and differentiation of the gifts given by the Spirit in 1 Corinthians 12 is not provided in the text. Yet Christians have divided as they have attempted to fill this lacuna. As a matter of fact, such descriptions are not necessary in order to understand what is being taught in 1 Corinthians 12 — "To each is given the manifestation of the Spirit for the common good" (v. 7). Perhaps the timing and mode of administering baptism may be another example where later readers have read their own practice into the biblical narratives despite the lack of specific instructions from Jesus or the apostles on how and when.

We must also reckon with the lamentable reality that deliberate human sinfulness can intrude on our reading of Scripture in ways that cause division. A clear message can be circumvented or labeled inconclusive in the interests of divergent thinking or behavior. Attempts to modify biblical prohibitions on all sexual activity outside of the covenant/kinship union of a man and woman in marriage are but the most obvious examples of this.

So disagreement, even persistent disagreement, need not be the result of a lack of clarity in Scripture itself. It may instead arise from one or many of a variety of causes outside of the biblical text. Where disagreement occurs, the appropriate response is to acknowledge our capacity for misunderstanding and return to read again, taking very seriously the questions raised by others. Such rereading need not, however, take place in an atmosphere of confusion, doubt, or even the sus-

68. We have already alluded to the difficulty that arises when texts are treated in isolation from their context, either their immediate context or the wider canonical context.

picion that we will never know the answer. Rather, an appreciation of the triune God's investment in effective communication engenders confidence that his word will again prove to be "a lamp to my feet and a light to my path" (Ps. 119:105).

Approaching Scripture with Confidence

The clarity of Scripture functions within the Christian doctrine of Scripture to encourage an attentive reading of the biblical texts by all Christian people. The Scriptures are not the private possession of an ecclesiastical or scholarly elite, with the rest of us dependent upon them to clarify a text we have no hope of understanding otherwise. They can be approached with confidence, following the example of Jesus himself, as the generous gift of a gracious heavenly Father. They come to us at our Father's initiative. They are most certainly human texts, constructed from human language. However, language is itself God's idea, a means he created to nourish the relationship he desires with men and women. Contemporary denials of the clarity of Scripture all too often exaggerate the fragility of human language and fail to appreciate God's determination to be known.

God knows how to communicate with men and women effectively. He has been doing it from the beginning. Jesus, the Word incarnate, expected confident engagement with the Scriptures to characterize God's redeemed people. The same Spirit who played such a decisive role in the production of the Scriptures has been given to us and is able to transform stubborn hearts and suspicious minds, dispelling our darkness with the light of God's word. The clarity of Scripture remains an element of the Christian doctrine *of Scripture* but its contours are deeply theological and its center of gravity is found in the example and teaching of Jesus Christ.

TWENTY-ONE

Postconservative Theologians and Scriptural Authority

Osvaldo Padilla

Ecclesia non est magistra, sed ministra scripturae;
non mater, sed filia;
non autor, sed custos, testis et interpres;
non iudex, sed index et vindex

The church is not master, but servant of Scripture;
not mother, but daughter;
not author, but keeper, witness and interpreter;
not judge, but pointer and defender.

D. Hollaz

One of the theological movements within broad evangelicalism that has gained momentum in the past decade is postconservatism.[1] The movement is by no means monolithic, and therefore a precise definition would be reductionist. There are, however, a number of philosophical and theological trajectories that are broadly shared by postconservatives. These include: a rejection of foundationalism,[2] an emphasis on the role of religious communities as seats of authority, and stress on the perspectival nature of all knowledge. There are of course numerous theologians who are on board with these trajectories and yet are not postconservatives. What sets the postconservatives apart is, I believe, their tone. This is seen in the provocative manner in which philosophical and theological proposals are asserted. The result is that postconservatives often emerge as dangerously close

1. On the origin of the term, see R. E. Olson, *Reformed and Always Reforming: The Postconservative Approach to Evangelical Theology* (Grand Rapids: Baker, 2007), 10-15, who himself takes credit for the manner in which the term is used today.

2. On foundationalism, see further below as well as the contributions by Rea and Beilby in this volume.

to elevating community over Scripture (or giving both equal authority) and to an extreme form of perspectivalism. The tone of postconservatives is heard not only in their relation to philosophy and doctrine, but also in their posture *vis-à-vis* traditional evangelical theologians. The tone is extremely critical, often to the point of caricature. We can therefore add tone as one of the traits of postconservatives. Some of the most influential postconservative theologians include: Roger E. Olson, Nancey Murphy, Stanley Grenz, and John R. Franke. For the purpose of this essay, I shall focus on Grenz and Franke, whom I believe can serve as representatives of the broader movement.

This essay is concerned with an examination of the place of Scripture in the developing theology of postconservative theologians. In order to accomplish this, it will be necessary to explore the philosophical and theological thought that lies behind postconservatism. Following this, we will look broadly at the theologies of Grenz and Franke and their view of Scripture in particular and offer evaluation. We will conclude with a number of comments that are offered as suggestive refinements for the postconservative movement.

Philosophical and Theological Strands behind Postconservatism

Like any theological movement, there are a number of influences that have shaped postconservative thought. In fact, it could perhaps be argued that what is "original" in postconservatism is simply a synthesis of postmodern thought and postliberal theological method with a certain type of evangelical influence. Whether this is a fair characterization or not, it is true that postconservatives draw from the following.

Rejection of Foundationalism

Postconservatives are unanimous in their sharp rejection of foundationalism. It is clear that whatever else they reject at the philosophical level, foundationalism is certainly out.[3] It is less clear just what they understand by the term.

Within the field of philosophy, foundationalism is part of epistemology. In epistemology we ask questions that have broadly to do with how we reach certain beliefs and how we can justify those beliefs.[4] Foundationalism is one account

3. The titles of books themselves show this: *Beyond Foundationalism: Shaping Theology in a Postmodern Context,* ed. S. Grenz and J. Franke (Louisville: Westminster John Knox, 2001); *Theology without Foundations: Religious Practice and the Future of Theological Truth,* ed. S. Hauerwas, N. Murphy, and M. Nation (Nashville: Abingdon, 1994).

4. For an accessible introduction, see W. J. Wood, *Epistemology: Becoming Intellectually Virtuous* (Downers Grove, IL: InterVarsity, 1998).

of how we order our beliefs in order to provide their justification. As the term indicates, foundationalism works with an architectural metaphor in which a set of *non-basic* beliefs is built upon the evidence of other *basic* propositions. Part of the focus is on "What are the *proper starting points* for belief formation?"[5] These "proper starting points" that must function as the foundation of my belief system are *basic;* and the foundation is basic "if and only if I don't accept it on the evidential basis of other propositions."[6] The next natural question is: What sort of a proposition is one that does not need the evidence of other propositions and is therefore basic? In the words of Plantinga: "A proposition is properly basic, for a person *S* if and only if it is *self-evident* for *S,* or *incorrigible* for *S,* or *evident to the senses* of *S.*"[7] Therefore, if the foundations of my belief system are not self-evident, incorrigible, or evident to the senses, then they are not proper and hence the legitimacy of my entire edifice of knowledge runs the risk of collapse. This is rightly called *classical foundationalism.* The vast majority of epistemologists today reject classical foundationalism.

There are, however, other types of foundationalisms that are not classical and are held by many current philosophers. Wood speaks of "modest" (others refer to it as "soft") foundationalism, as, for example, was held by Thomas Reid. In this case, there are no "claims about the invincible certainty of one's basic beliefs or about a need to be reflectively aware of which beliefs have the status of basic."[8] It is clear that for this modest or soft type of foundationalism the stringent demands of a Cartesian system have been relaxed. Foundationalisms of this softer type, in the words of Rea, "are thriving."[9]

One of the significant problems in many postconservatives' account of the rejection of modernist epistemology is a failure to grapple with the different types of foundationalisms. Grenz and Franke, for example, speak of "*philosophical* foundationalism" as "the desire to overcome the uncertainty generated by our human liability to error and the inevitable disagreements that follow. Foundationalists are convinced that the only way to solve this problem is to find some means of grounding the entire edifice of human knowledge on invincible certainty."[10] This is a description of *classical* foundationalism. To call this "philosophical" foundationalism is unhelpful and potentially misleading, as it gives the impression that there is only one type of foundationalism in philosophy. Although further on they do mention modest foundationalism, they quickly pass over it by suggesting that

5. R. Swinburne, *Faith and Reason,* 2nd edition (Oxford: Oxford University Press, 2005), 54; emphasis added.

6. A. Plantinga, *Warranted Christian Belief* (Oxford: Oxford University Press, 2000), 83.

7. Plantinga, *Warranted Christian Belief,* 84; emphasis added.

8. Wood, *Epistemology,* 98.

9. M. Rea, "Introduction," in *Analytic Theology: New Essays in the Philosophy of Theology,* ed. O. Crisp and M. C. Rea (Oxford: Oxford University Press, 2009), 12.

10. Grenz and Franke, *Beyond Foundationalism,* 30.

"most Enlightenment thinkers readily adopted Descartes's concern to establish some type of sure foundation for the human knowing project."[11] A similar superficial engagement with the different types of foundationalisms is found in the more recent work of Olson.[12] I shall come back to this important matter in my interaction with Franke.

Cultural-Linguistic Turn

This is the next significant theological approach that postconservatives have absorbed in their revisioning of evangelical theology. The pioneer of this approach was George A. Lindbeck in his massively influential *Nature of Doctrine,* originally published in 1984.[13] Lindbeck builds on the cultural anthropology of C. Geertz and the philosophy of language constructed by L. Wittgenstein. On the philosophy of language, the later Wittgenstein changed from an understanding of language as having meaning only in connection with the empirical world to language as having meaning in its use in a particular community. According to Wittgenstein, different communities have entirely different frameworks or grammars for understanding terms. Hence, two people can use the same word, but depending on the community in which they exist, the meaning of that word could be entirely different. Thus, meaning in language is a matter of use-in-a-specific-community-framework rather than correspondence with some external reality.[14]

Lindbeck appropriated these seminal ideas and employed them in his construal of doctrine. For him, the cultural-linguistic turn meant a way out of the impasse created by, on the one hand, the cognitive approach, and, on the other hand, the liberal approach.[15] In addition, he hoped that the cultural-linguistic method would open new avenues for ecumenical dialogue.[16] For Lindbeck doctrines function primarily as rules or as a grammar for specific communities. In a religious community, doctrines "are not primarily an array of beliefs about the true and the good (though it may involve these)." Instead, doctrine "is similar

11. Grenz and Franke, *Beyond Foundationalism,* 32.

12. Olson, *Reformed and Always Reforming,* 128-38.

13. G. Lindbeck, *The Nature of Doctrine: Religion and Theology in a Postliberal Age,* 25th Anniversary Edition (Louisville: Westminster John Knox, 2009).

14. L. Wittgenstein, *Philosophical Investigations,* The German Text, with an English translation by G. E. M. Anscombe, P. M. S. Hacker, and Joachim Schulte, 4th edition (Oxford: Blackwell, 2009), especially 30, 43, and 86.

15. Lindbeck, *The Nature of Doctrine,* 1-5. He calls the latter approach "experiential-expressive."

16. This cultural-linguistic, or as he also calls it, "regulative" approach, has the potential in ecumenical dialogue of "explaining the possibility of reconciliation without recapitulation" (*The Nature of Doctrine,* 4). See also 32-58.

to an idiom that makes possible the description of realities, the formulation of beliefs, and the experiencing of inner attitudes, feelings, and sentiments."[17] Doctrine, it may be said, is important because it articulates the practice of the community. Thus in Lindbeck's model doctrines are primarily meant to order the life of particular religious communities without attempting to make universal claims about their ontological status. As for Scripture and the community, what counts as authoritative in this model is the pronouncement of the community, even though, at least in principle, Scripture is supposed to act as the guide for the community.[18]

Naturally, this raises the question of the relationship between one religious community and another.[19] In the case of the Christian tradition, there has historically been an impulse to export its teachings on the conviction that, as a unique divine revelation, it provides the only means of redemption for the entire world. Thus Lindbeck has to tackle the question: What about the salvation of those who belong to other religious communities? According to Lindbeck, any claims for superiority or unsurpassability on the part of this or that religious community would ultimately "imperil dialogue."[20] At the end, Lindbeck embraces a proposal by Karl Rahner that he labels the "prospective theory."[21] Put roughly (but not, I believe, incorrectly), Lindbeck suggests that the prospect of salvation for both Christian and non-Christian occurs after death. The time of decision *for both* happens in the hereafter: "Thus it is possible to be hopeful and trusting about the ultimate salvation of non-Christians no less than Christians even if one does not think in terms of a primordial, prereflective experience of Christ's grace."[22] In this way Lindbeck can affirm the nature of doctrine as a communal pragmatism without having to provide justification for its ontological status.[23]

Postconservatives enthusiastically embrace many aspects of the cultural-linguistic turn in theology. This is due in part to the potential alternative to foundationalism provided by this approach. As will be seen below, the emphasis of

17. Lindbeck, *The Nature of Doctrine,* 19.

18. See the telling statement by H. Frei, "The literal meaning of the text is precisely that meaning which finds the greatest degree of agreement in the use of the text in the religious community. If there is agreement in that use, then take that to be the literal sense" (*Types of Christian Theology* [New Haven: Yale University Press, 1992], 15). I owe this quotation to K. J. Vanhoozer, *The Drama of Doctrine: A Canonical-Linguistic Approach to Christian Theology* (Louisville: Westminster John Knox, 2005), 11 n. 34.

19. Recall that Lindbeck's approach is strongly motivated by ecumenism.

20. Lindbeck, *The Nature of Doctrine,* 41.

21. Lindbeck, *The Nature of Doctrine,* 43.

22. Lindbeck, *The Nature of Doctrine,* 45.

23. See a similar ambivalence on the part of Lindbeck with respect to the status of Christianity *vis-à-vis* other religions in his dialogue with A. McGrath in *The Nature of Confession: Evangelicals and Postliberals in Conversation,* ed. T. R. Phillips and D. L. Okholm (Downers Grove, IL: InterVarsity, 1996), 252.

Lindbeck on religious communities as the authoritative filters of doctrine has had an effect on the matter of scriptural authority in many postconservatives. In addition, the conception of truth claims in the context of missions by postconservatives bears a resemblance to Lindbeck's, although they do not go as far as positing a prospective version of salvation.

Postliberalism

There is a sense in which a rejection of classical foundationalism and the adoption of the cultural-linguistic turn could both be placed under this heading. They are two of the constituent features of postliberalism. As true as this is, given the context of this essay, I have placed postliberalism separately because it is not a given that postconservatives have always taken their identity *solely* through the medium of postliberalism.

Much as is the case with postconservatism, it is likewise difficult to give a tidy description of postliberalism. While some simply label postliberalism as the "Yale school" of theology, this is too restrictive. For, as George Hunsinger shows, not all members of Yale's faculty can be called postliberals. In addition, even between the two principals of postliberalism, Lindbeck and Frei, there are significant theological and epistemological differences.[24] Hunsinger thus suggests that we broaden the camp of postliberalism to include figures like Karl Barth and Hans Urs von Balthasar. When Frei and Lindbeck are combined with these other theologians, Hunsinger believes that a much richer and sophisticated version of postliberalism emerges. In this version, the themes of truth, doctrine, and religion look different from what the traditional picture of postliberalism has been. In this scenario, truth would be determined by critical realism rather than pragmatist theory (Lindbeck).[25] Doctrine, rather than being dependent on this or that philosophical structure, would take God in his triune existence as justification for belief.[26] Lastly, religion would be Christocentric. That is, although one must act in an irenic spirit toward those outside the Christian church, the claim of *solus Christus* would remain as a non-negotiable.[27]

It must be admitted that this portrait of postliberalism as a coherent, existing version does not exist (except for Hunsinger, of course); it is an ideal. One of the reasons why Hunsinger would like to push postliberalism in this direction is that

24. G. Hunsinger, "Postliberal Theology," in *Postmodern Theology,* ed. K. J. Vanhoozer (Cambridge: Cambridge University Press, 2003), 42-45.

25. Hunsinger, "Postliberal Theology," 45-49.

26. Hunsinger, "Postliberal Theology," 50-53.

27. Hunsinger, "Postliberal Theology," 53-57. Note that Lindbeck himself holds strongly to this. Lindbeck does not contradict himself in holding *solus Christus* with his concept of prospective salvation: even after death salvation would come through Christ alone.

that form which has been shaped by Lindbeck has received severe criticism. This is the case particularly with the primacy of epistemic pragmatism of community over ontology.[28] To be noted briefly here is that for some influential postconservatives, postliberalism has primarily to do with this social approach to doctrinal epistemology, an approach that they themselves have followed to various degrees.[29] Therefore, some of the criticisms that are brought against postliberals can equally apply to postconservatives. We will come back to this matter in the final section of this essay.

Postconservatives and Scripture

Since postconservatives acknowledge postmodernism and postliberalism as providing a significant impulse to the configuring of their theology, it was necessary in the first section of this essay to provide, even if in broad strokes, a description of some of the aspects of these movements. In what follows I would like to investigate, in view of what has preceded, the place of Scripture in the thought of perhaps the most influential postconservative theologians. We will look at Stanley Grenz and John R. Franke.

Grenz: Scripture and Community (or Community and Scripture)

In various publications Grenz made creative attempts to move evangelical theology forward by appropriating some of the tenets of postmodernism and postliberalism. In particular, he took seriously the social angle of epistemology in his formulation of doctrine.[30] This can already be seen in his definition of theology in 1994: "Basically, systematic theology is the reflection on and the ordered articulation of faith."[31] Nine years later he offered a more detailed definition: "Theology is the determination, delineation, and articulation of the beliefs and values, as well as the meaning of the symbols, of a particular faith community"[32] The stress placed on community in this definition is clear.

With respect to the authority of the Scriptures, Grenz believes that the mat-

28. See the recent critique by A. Vidu, *Postliberal Theological Method: A Critical Study* (Carlisle: Paternoster, 2005).

29. See, e.g., John R. Franke, *The Character of Theology: An Introduction to Its Nature, Task, and Purpose* (Grand Rapids: Baker, 2005), 30, 40; Olson, *Reformed and Always Reforming*, 145, 166-69.

30. Stanley Grenz, *Revisioning Evangelical Theology* (Downers Grove, IL: InterVarsity, 1993); *Theology of the Community of God* (Nashville: Broadman & Holman, 1994).

31. Grenz, *Revisioning Evangelical Theology*, 1.

32. Grenz, "Ecclesiology," in *The Cambridge Companion to Postmodern Theology*, 252.

ter should be viewed from both the "external" (Scripture) and "internal" (the witness of the Holy Spirit) principles.[33] This serves as a base for further exploration into the relationship of the witness of the Spirit and Scripture.[34] This relationship is developed by invoking two of the classic doctrines of bibliology, namely inspiration and illumination. Grenz attempts a significant nuance by calling both of these "the *one* act of the Spirit" (emphasis added). The nuance in this is Grenz's attempt to move illumination, as it were, one step backwards. Whereas illumination has been traditionally understood as a work of the Spirit that is dependent on a scriptural canon, Grenz posits that illumination was already happening in the very formation of Scripture. In his words, inspiration and illumination are intertwined "in the historical process of Scripture formation itself."[35] How does Grenz seek to demonstrate this?

First, Grenz appeals to the canonical approach developed by Brevard Childs in an attempt to show that both inspiration and illumination took place in the context of the believing community. That is, the faith communities were involved in the very process of Scripture formation.[36] Following Childs, Scripture is not only the result of God transmitting an authoritative message to an individual (say, David or Jeremiah), but also the reception of that message by a Spirit-led community that acknowledges its divine status and expands it, thereby itself participating in Scripture-formation. Grenz therefore follows Childs in the belief that traditions and community were the core aspects in the forging of Scripture.

Second, Grenz attempts to provide scriptural footing to this suggestion by following the lead of Edward Goodrick. The latter states that the principal point of a text which has been traditionally understood as explaining the nature of inspiration, namely 2 Timothy 3:16, may after all be the function of the community in the process of inspiration.[37] Grenz thus takes this text to support the assertion that "The church, in short, came to confess the inspiration of Scripture because the early believers experienced the power and truth of the Spirit of God through these writings."[38]

It must be kept in mind, lest we fail to grasp the significance of Grenz's argument, that in the above statements he is not referring to the process of can-

33. Grenz, *Revisioning Evangelical Theology,* 380. He calls this the "classic" Reformed view.

34. It is not immediately clear what Grenz means by the "witness of the Spirit" in the dialectic of authority. Does it refer to the Spirit's action of inspiring Scripture? Or does it refer to the witness of the community as it is moved by the Spirit? It will become clear that Grenz refers to the latter scenario.

35. Grenz, *Revisioning Evangelical Theology,* 383.

36. See B. S. Childs, *Biblical Theology of the Old and New Testaments: Theological Reflection on the Christian Bible* (Minneapolis: Fortress Press, 1992).

37. Edward W. Goodrick, "Let's Put 2 Timothy 3:16 Back into the Bible," *JETS* 25 (1982): 479-87.

38. Grenz, *Revisioning Evangelical Theology,* 386.

onization. Instead, Grenz is indissolubly linking the very God-breathed nature of Scripture with the community's realization of its power (i.e., illumination). Inspiration is thus being understood to include both the biblical authors and/or the biblical texts as well as the ancient community that read the texts. Therefore, it would appear that Grenz is suggesting that the inspiration of the Bible includes its affirmation as such by the believing community. In short, it would appear that Grenz is saying that the inspiration of the Bible is closely tied to the life of the ancient community, perhaps going so far as to suggest that inspiration is a matter of the church's confession rather than of an intrinsic value of the scriptural texts (because they claim God's authority). But does not this run the risk of subjectivism, with the result that Grenz's view could be labeled just another form of neo-orthodoxy?

Grenz is aware of this danger. However, he does not believe that his formulation inevitably leads to this extreme. How is this risk to be averted? His answer: "We avoid subjectivism as we remember that our declaration of the inspiration of the Bible asserts that this book is objectively divine Scripture; the Bible is Scripture regardless of whether or not we subjectively acknowledge this status."[39]

By way of evaluation, the careful reader will note that, in his reconfiguration of Scripture and authority, Grenz is attempting to move away from classical foundationalism. He does not wish to operate doctrinally in such a manner that belief in an inerrant Bible would be the privileged base upon which the rest of theology would be constructed. Concluding his discussion on the potential of subjectivism opened by his view, he asserts: "Our attempt to avoid the danger of subjectivism ought not to blind us to the opposite danger. We cannot follow the lead of those theologians who set forth the inspiration of the Bible as the first thesis of the doctrine of Scripture."[40] Consequently, a doctrine of Scripture must also include the work of the Spirit in the community for the formation of the Bible. In this manner, classical foundationalism is overcome and replaced by a social epistemology (for which see above under the "Cultural-Linguistic Turn" heading). To the extent that Grenz attempts to move theological method beyond classical foundationalism, he is to be commended. However, we must ask the question: Has his move to the community devalued the authority of Scripture over the community?

The first part of Grenz's argument to fuse inspiration and illumination and thereby provide the community with scriptural formation-authority is based on the work of Childs. This is not the place to engage in concerted dialogue with Childs.[41] The following two points, however, may be noted. First, Childs himself

39. Grenz, *Revisioning Evangelical Theology,* 388.

40. Grenz, *Revisioning Evangelical Theology,* 388.

41. For this, see the important work of Paul R. Noble, *The Canonical Approach: A Critical Reconstruction of the Hermeneutics of Brevard S. Childs* (Leiden: Brill, 1995).

demurred from those critics who accused him of basing the canonical status of the Bible on the verdict of the faith community.[42] Second, Childs's concept of inspiration has remained fuzzy. Noble suggests that for Childs's approach to work it would be necessary for him to develop "a 'strong' doctrine of inspiration."[43] Yet Childs has not yet provided such a strong doctrine. All this is to say that building on Childs's work at the theoretical level (as Grenz does) still leaves a number of important questions unanswered. Grenz needs further substantiation to make his model more tenable. He tries to do this by suggesting a fresh understanding of 2 Timothy 3:16.

As was seen above, following Goodrick, Grenz takes this text to mean that the main reason the Scriptures were considered God-breathed was the community's experience of their power and truth. I would suggest that there are severe problems with this understanding of 2 Timothy 3:16. I sketch the salient points of the verse and its context in order to offer my critique.

1. Prior to the text-unit that contains verse 16 (3:10-17), Paul has spoken at length of the character of certain men who will rise in "the last days" (v. 1). Of course, a reading of Pauline theology shows that "the last days" have already dawned. Paul provides a catalogue of vices to describe these men (vv. 2-4). For our purposes, it should be noted that Paul highlights their attempt to oppose the truth (*houtoi anthistantai tē alētheia*), using as examples old foes who had opposed Moses.[44]

2. After reassuring Timothy that he has in fact followed Paul's teaching and conduct, Paul comes back to the men of the last days, stating that they both deceive and are being deceived (v. 13). How is Timothy himself to avoid being deceived by these men?

3. The answer is twofold, both dependent on the participle "knowing" of verse 14.[45] First, Timothy has learned from trustworthy people, namely his mother and grandmother (1:5) and above all, Paul. What they taught him is thus dependable. The second manner in which Timothy can avoid being deceived is his knowledge of the "holy Scriptures." These Scriptures, Paul says, have been known to Timothy since his childhood; furthermore, the Scriptures "can lead to salvation through faith which is in Christ Jesus."

4. Having spoken about the power of the Scriptures, Paul moves in verse 16 to

42. Brevard S. Childs, *Biblical Theology in Crisis* (Philadelphia: Westminster, 1970), 105. He stated that no community of faith "can ever make a book canonical." Cf. also Childs, *Biblical Theology of the Old and New Testaments,* 70.

43. Noble, *The Canonical Approach,* 206. By "strong" he means a concept that is equivalent to a more traditional, conservative view of biblical inspiration.

44. Although the names Jannes and Jambres do not actually appear in the Exodus account (cf. Exod. 7:11), in Jewish tradition these were the names given to the Egyptian magicians who opposed Moses. See I. H. Marshall, *The Pastoral Epistles* (London: T. & T. Clark, 1999), 778-79.

45. *eidōs* is more than likely causal: "*because* you know."

clarify the *nature* of the Scriptures. The implicit question may be: What is it about these Scriptures that can lead to salvation? The answer is that they are "God-breathed." That is, they find their source in God himself. That is why they are trustworthy to lead to salvation. Furthermore, *because*[46] they are God-breathed they can have important functions in the community. That is, they are valuable for the purpose of "teaching, reproof, correction, training in righteousness." All these terms carry doctrinal and behavioral overtones.[47]

I have attempted to trace the flow and logic of the passage in order to put us in a position to interact with Grenz's use of this text for support of his view.

First, in order to make his point, Grenz approves of Goodrick's statement that the text does not support "the pristine character of the autographs."[48] This is a case of a straw man argument. In the opinion of many serious evangelical scholars, the point of this passage is not to do with the support of the "pristine character of the autographs." While, to be sure, the assertion of the God-breathed nature of Scripture provides it with considerable trustworthiness, it is a caricature to say that the text is directly dealing with "the pristine character of the autographs."[49]

Second, Grenz engages in an either/or argument that is not sustainable. That is, in introducing Goodrick's statement, he states that "*rather* than supporting the 'pristine character of the autographs,' the text focuses on how valuable the Spirit-energized Scriptures are."[50] This is an unnecessary false dichotomy; the text supports *both* the inspired nature of Scripture (although the autographs are not in view) as well as its usefulness, the latter because of the former. And this leads to the third point.

It is simply a misreading of 2 Timothy 3:16 to state that its assertion of the God-breathed nature of Scripture is dependent for its efficacy on the community. This is to put matters in reverse order. As we saw above, the logic of the passage is that *because* all Scripture is God-breathed it is useful for teaching, reproof, and so forth. At the risk of simplification, it could be said that first comes the divine nature of the writings and then their usefulness. Or put negatively, if the Scriptures are not God-breathed, then they cannot be useful in the way that Paul is describing in this chapter. Thus, Grenz has put the cart before the horse in arguing that the texts are inspired because they are useful for the community. I am not at all here suggesting that there is not a sense in which believers come to confess the divine source of the Scripture based on the internal work of the Holy Spirit. This is traditional Reformed pneumatology. But this has been understood

46. The sense of *kai* in the second clause of v. 16.

47. See Marshall, *The Pastoral Epistles*, 795-96.

48. Goodrick, as quoted in Grenz, *Revisioning Evangelical Theology*, 386.

49. For example, two evangelical commentaries on the Pastoral Epistles, those of George Knight and Philip H. Towner, do not even mention the autographs.

50. Grenz, *Revisioning Evangelical Theology*, 386; emphasis added.

as the work of the illumination of the Spirit upon the canon. But if I understand Grenz correctly, he is suggesting that the illumination of the Spirit for the ancient communities is what turned authoritative traditions into Scripture.

Let me summarize Grenz. In the building of doctrine in general and the authority of Scripture in particular, he argues that evangelicals have taken an approach that necessitates an unquestionable, inerrant Bible as the necessary base if the rest of the structure is to be trustworthy. However, he believes that this is to operate with a foundationalist approach, which is rejected in today's postmodern world. He therefore attempts to move beyond foundationalism by positing a pragmatist epistemology. *In fact,* argues Grenz, based on his reading of the works of Childs and Goodrick, when we look at the way that the Scriptures came to be, we realize that the Old and New Testament communities (a rather fuzzy concept, one might add), illumined by the Spirit, were just as authoritative as the traditions that they received. These ancient communities, therefore, were not just a passive group that merely assented to the traditions. Rather, they were *active,* and, by the illumination of the Spirit, *formed* Scripture. Authority in the ancient communities was thus not only a matter of a static deposit (i.e., the traditions) but also of the living judgments of a community illumined by the Spirit. Grenz reasons that as it was in the ancient communities so it must be today; and in this way we can move beyond foundationalism. But, logically, one may ask, does it not follow that also *today* the Christian communities, illumined as they also are by the Spirit, can have as much authority as the ancient communities? And does this not leave the door ajar for an open canon or equal authority between Scripture and community? Grenz does not wish to go this far:

> Yet we must acknowledge one far-reaching difference. Israel and the ancient Christian community engaged in the interpretive task within the context of the process of the formation of the canon. We now enjoy the Spirit's illumination as he speaks to us through the completed Bible. They participated in the process of Scripture-formation; we do not.[51]

But why not? Given Grenz's account, there is no reason why a contemporary, Spirit-illumined community cannot have the same type of authority as the ancient, Scripture-forming community. Indeed, Grenz wants to attribute a considerable amount of authority to the contemporary, Christian community,[52] but not go as far as to say that its pronouncements are canonical. But again, is this not inconsistent with his understanding of illumination and inspiration? It appears to this writer that Grenz is inconsistent; the only way he can stop the encroachment of the community upon the canon is by an arbitrary argument that dogmatically

51. Grenz, *Revisioning Evangelical Theology,* 387.
52. See his essay on ecclesiology in *Postmodern Theology,* cited above.

pronounces that things are different today from Israel and the New Testament community. Grenz cannot have his cake and eat it too. Yet, it appears that his exclusive commitment to a particular type of Anglo-American postmodern epistemology has landed him in this quandary.[53] Grenz's revisioning of Scripture and community is both logically flawed and inconsistent with Scripture, particularly the seminal passage of 2 Timothy 3:16. It ultimately runs the risk of putting Scripture and community on the same level of authority.

Franke: Scripture and Truth Claims

Like Grenz, this author has engaged very closely with postmodern thought. Perhaps a more appropriate word is "embraced" postmodernity, since Franke's theological program is pluralistic in nature.[54] In order to situate his theological stance, Franke spends time providing a helpful account of postmodernity (13-28). He argues that the portrayal of postmodern thought by many theologians as inherently atheistic and nihilistic is reductionist. While, to be sure, thinkers such as Nietzsche and Derrida modeled the atheistic and nihilistic features that have come to be associated with postmodern philosophy, the movement as a whole should not be viewed as essentially hostile to Christian thought. In fact, argues Franke, what gives cohesion to postmodernism is not any kind of philosophy that is consciously anti-Christian; rather, what provides unity to the movement is its "rejection of the program of modernity." Franke continues: "This observation enables us to suggest a basic, minimalist understanding of postmodernism as referring primarily to the rejection of the central features of modernity, such as its quest for certain, objective, and universal knowledge, along with its dualism and its assumption of the inherent goodness of knowledge" (21). From this there emerge two features of the postmodern view of knowledge and reality that are of particular importance to Franke, namely the cultural-linguistic turn and the non-foundationalist turn.

As to the cultural-linguistic turn, Franke appears to be sympathetic to one of its principal insights, namely, that language is not a simple descriptor of reality. Building on the works of Ferdinand de Saussure, Ludwig Wittgenstein, and Peter Berger and Thomas Luckmann, Franke sees language as primarily a social construct that is dependent on particular settings and communities for

53. See also his *Renewing the Center: Evangelical Theology in a Post-Theological Era* (Grand Rapids: Baker, 2000) for similar inconsistencies due to an exclusive approach to postmodernism.

54. For this essay, I interact with what I consider to be Franke's determinative work thus far, *The Character of Theology: A Postconservative Evangelical Approach* (Grand Rapids: Baker, 2005), not with his latest, somewhat more popular exposition, *Manifold Witness: The Plurality of Truth* (Nashville: Abingdon, 2009). Subsequent page references from *The Character of Theology* will be given in parentheses in the text.

meaning. As such, Franke states (apparently sympathetically), "language does not represent reality as much as it constitutes reality" (26). With his sympathy for non-foundationalism, Franke resonates with the critiques of modern thought and its search for objective, universal, certain knowledge as well as its belief in the inherent goodness of that knowledge. He states that this thirst for universal knowledge, given humans' fallen nature, is nothing other than their "desire to seize control of the epistemic process in order to empower themselves and further their own ends, often at the expense of others" (28).[55]

Given his understanding of postmodernism as essentially a rejection of modernity, Franke is sympathetic to contemporary movements that attempt to fill the theological vacuum left by modernity. In particular, he acknowledges strong affinities with postliberalism. Franke summarizes his understanding of postliberalism as follows: "Postliberal theology takes as its starting point the shared language and practices of a particular religious community and understands its primary task as that of self-description rather than of correlation with universal human experience and reason" (32). However, despite his agreements with these basic convictions of postliberals, Franke prefers to be identified as a *postconservative.* The reason for this is that, while joining postliberals in their critique of modernism, postconservatives nevertheless maintain allegiance to what can be broadly called evangelicalism (37-40).

From this exploration of the contemporary theological landscape and his rejection and acceptance of its different engagements, Franke can state his definition of theology:

> Christian theology is an ongoing, second-order, contextual discipline that engages in the task of critical and constructive reflection on the beliefs and practices of the Christian church for the purpose of assisting the community of Christ's followers in their missional vocation to live as the people of God in the particular social-historical context in which they are situated. (44)

A central aspect of the "beliefs" of the Christian church is God in his triune identity. Therefore, the subject of theology is the Trinity (45-65). Since the triune existence is to be understood as social existence between the Father, Son, and Holy Spirit, the matter of mission emerges: God desires to bring humans into the relationship of love that is already shared by the members of the Trinity (65-72). As his missionary agents, believers are therefore to speak knowingly of God. But in order to do this, revelation from God is necessary. It is in this missional context that Franke develops his doctrine of Scripture. His goal is to be faithful

55. See also *The Character of Theology,* 18 and 81, for Franke's almost Levinesque view of knowledge and attempts at legitimation.

to orthodox Christianity while at the same time taking serious consideration of the postmodern situation.

The first thing to note about Franke's approach is that he seems to accept the radical strain of postmodernity's understanding of social and linguistic construction. I am referring to the notion that the world we inhabit is our own social and linguistic construction rather than an independent object that we can objectively examine, even if we do so without Cartesian clarity. This raises a significant challenge for a Christian view of revelation. Franke notes this: "If we are immersed and embedded in language, how can we speak of truth beyond our linguistic contexts?" (74; see also 194). He dismisses the thesis put forth by R. Scott Smith, namely, that "God breaks through language" to give us access to ultimate reality (74).[56] For Franke this would mean pulling humans out of their situatedness, thereby canceling out human finitude; this would contradict a basic postmodern premise which apparently has been accepted by Franke. According to Franke, rather than pulling us out of our contexts, God, as it were, *comes down* into our situatedness and "uses language in the act of revelation as a means of accommodation to the situation and situatedness of human beings" (75). At this point Franke appeals to Karl Barth's concept of "indirect identity" as well as his dialectic of veiling and unveiling. According to Barth (as Franke reads him), because God uses human creatures as his means of revelation without at the same time performing a divinization of those creatures (just as the humanity of Christ in the incarnation did not become divinized), the revelation remains indirect. Yet, the revelation, for all its indirectness, remains real, for God genuinely reveals himself. Thus, in the very process of unveiling himself, God veils himself because he is using a finite, situated medium. This implies that revelation cannot be grasped at by simple human will; God must give humans the eyes of faith in order to perceive the unveiled God through the veiled medium. Franke concludes: "In this conception, revelation has both an objective moment, when God reveals himself through the veil of a creaturely medium, and a subjective moment, when God gives human beings the faith to understand what is hidden in the veil" (76).

The second aspect of Franke's doctrine of Scripture is related to the first. If we are totally dependent on God to receive his revelation, it follows that any epistemology that encourages us somehow to achieve the knowledge of truth by human independence is incompatible with Christianity. Franke believes that foundationalism encourages this. Conservative evangelical theologians such as Wayne Grudem, Carl F. H. Henry, and Charles Hodge, all swayed by the program of modernity, are examples of this foundationalist approach to theology (88-89). By contrast, Franke's approach is non-foundationalist. By this he means a rejection of the "notion that among the many beliefs that make up a particular

56. See R. Scott Smith, "Postmodernism and the Priority of the Language-World Relation," in *Christianity and the Postmodern Turn,* ed. Myron Penner (Grand Rapids: Brazos, 2006).

theology there must be a single irrefutable foundation that is immune to criticism and provides the certain basis on which all other assertions are founded" (78). This non-foundationalist approach, while holding to strong convictions, is nevertheless open to criticisms and corrections. This leads us away from the aim of securing universal, incorrigible knowledge that may lead to exploitation of others. These attempts to seize epistemic control "are all too common throughout the history of the church and, no matter how well intentioned, inevitably lead to forms of oppression and conceptual idolatry" (81). Non-foundationalism attempts to avoid this by proposing a dialogue between partners rather than dependence on a single source of knowledge, "be it Scripture, tradition, reason or experience." The only source is God himself. Franke concludes: "Therefore, if we must speak of 'foundations' for the Christian faith and its theological enterprise, then we must speak only of the Triune God, who is disclosed in polyphonic fashion through Scripture, the church, and the world, albeit always in accordance with the normative witness to divine self-disclosure in Jesus Christ" (79).

Franke is to be admired for producing an account of bibliology that attempts to be faithful to orthodox faith and at the same time takes into account philosophical challenges of postmodernity. But has he succeeded?

First, Franke is of course entirely right in stressing, with postmodern epistemology, the situatedeness of human knowledge. We all see through our culture, language, gender, and so forth. On the other hand, it seems that Franke has ceded too much. If I read him correctly, he also accepts that radical strain of postmodernity that asserts that our linguistic situatedness negates *any* access to ultimate reality beyond our own constructions. It is one thing to say that, although we have access to ultimate reality, yet our humanness does not allow us to have access to an absolute understanding of reality; our knowledge goes beyond ourselves but is *limited.* It is quite another to affirm that "we live in a linguistically construed social-cultural world of our own creation" (74). Once this is accepted, Franke's task to present a doctrine of Scripture that is also orthodox becomes, in my opinion, impossible.[57] Franke, as we saw above, reaches out to Barth's notion of direct/indirect revelation in order to preserve the possibility of knowledge of God. I believe that this is what, depending on his reading of Barth, Franke is saying: "Reality is not simply 'out there' for humans to seize. Reality is, as it were, with God, and thus *he* chooses when to reveal it and when to hide it. We are in a position of complete epistemic dependence." But this solution does not really solve the postmodern problem. It still assumes that, for all our situatedness, we can still have access to ultimate reality (although we are presented here more as passive recipients). Franke raises the philosophical problem of radical postmod-

57. Note that Franke realizes that one response to radical postmodern epistemology would simply be that it is incompatible with Scripture, yet he rejects it (*The Character of Theology,* 74). This is a position taken, for example, by Plantinga, *Warranted Christian Belief,* 425.

ernism but then sidesteps it by saying (the rather obvious) that we must depend on God to receive the truth.

But perhaps this is not what Franke means. It may be that his point is simply that although we can, by God's grace, have access to ultimate reality, yet our grasp and understanding of it is not absolute and is also mediated through our cultural-linguistic situations. If this is what he means, it is entirely right; and I think few Christians would disagree with it. Maybe Franke is using provocative language to make the point that we are not autonomous beings who simply can seize the truth whenever we wish and use it to wield power over others. This is a more tenable position that, although not at all new, needs to be continually heard. In any case, we hope that in future publications Franke will provide clarification on the matter.

The second aspect of Franke's understanding of Scripture has to do with foundationalism. We have already spoken briefly on this matter, and others in this volume will provide more detailed accounts. Nevertheless, Franke's description of foundationalism is so severely flawed that at least two comments are necessary. First, someone who had little or no acquaintance with epistemology would come away from reading Franke with the conception that there exists only one version of foundationalism and that all philosophers today view it with disdain. But this is really a caricature. What Franke describes is classical foundationalism, which is indeed mostly rejected today. But there are numerous respectable philosophers today who accept a chastened version of foundationalism. William Alston, for example, speaks of a "modest" foundationalism.[58] In contrast to classical foundationalism, in which only infallible, incorrigible, and indubitable beliefs can serve as the legitimate foundations that can provide justification for indirect beliefs, modest foundationalism broadens the foundations. Hence, Alston speaks of experience as a foundation. These experiences can include: "bodily sensations, intuitions of self-evidence, senses of obligation or moral rightness, religious experiences, and so on."[59] Another possibility for foundations is a mixture of experience and other beliefs. Alston comments on "how a perceptual belief can be partly based on sensory experience (perceptual appearances) and partly on other beliefs."[60] Naturally, this is a less rigid foundationalism since the superstructure is itself contributing to the foundation. Alston even speaks of coherence as part of the mixture in a hybrid foundation.[61] In short, in modest foundationalism we can still speak of directly justified beliefs anchoring indirectly justified beliefs,

58. W. P. Alston, *Beyond "Justification": Dimensions of Epistemic Evaluation* (Ithaca, NY: Cornell University Press, 2005), 233. He also calls it "simple" or "minimal" foundationalism. See his *Epistemic Justification: Essays in the Theory of Knowledge* (Ithaca, NY: Cornell University Press, 1989), 19-38, 39-56.

59. Alston, *Beyond "Justification,"* 231.

60. Alston, *Beyond "Justification,"* 233-34. He calls these "hybrids."

61. Alston, *Beyond "Justification,"* 234-35.

but the foundations are not infallible, incorrigible, and indubitable. In addition, there is a modesty in explaining just how indirectly justified beliefs are anchored by directly justified beliefs.

There is none of this in Franke.[62] He speaks of foundationalism *simpliciter* without any mention of its range. But, as Alston notes, this lack of precision is not uncommon today:

> The term "foundationalism" has fallen on hard times, not only because the position is well nigh universally excoriated but also because the term itself is one of the most variously used, and abused, in epistemology. In the hands of one or another writer it is used to designate a commitment to absolute truths . . . an uncritical acceptance of dogmas, a realist metaphysics of some sort, etc., etc.[63]

When foundationalism is understood in this loose manner, it is used to swat aside with only a few words ("this is a foundationalist way of arguing") theological approaches that are not accepted by the interlocutor. For example, when tackling the very difficult problem of ecclesial authority, Franke refuses to approach the matter in the traditional way: "Which has priority, Scripture or the church? . . . However, posing the question in this manner is ultimately unhelpful in that it rests on a foundationalist understanding of the derivation of knowledge."[64] Is this really foundationalism? Franke errs in believing that the positing of a privileged starting point necessarily makes a method foundationalist.

The second problem with Franke's understanding of foundationalism is the false antithetical options that he implies. It seems that the only options available are classical foundationalism or non-foundationalism. But as we saw above, there are different forms of foundationalisms that are intellectually respectable. An example of a theological approach that is foundationalist in the modest version is Kevin Vanhoozer's canonical-linguistic method. Vanhoozer privileges the canon of Scripture as a starting point. Yet this is not classical foundationalism because his overall approach to theological knowledge "is neither immediate nor indubitable [as in classical foundationalism]; it is rather mediated via interpretative frameworks. No set of data is ever foundational because the data is always framework-filtered and theory-laden."[65] Thus, it is incorrect to label an approach as foundationalist just because there is a trusted basis.[66] It should be noted that

62. Or in Grenz, or in Olson, or in most postconservatives.

63. Alston, *Beyond "Justification,"* 230.

64. Franke, "Scripture, Tradition and Authority: Reconstructing the Evangelical Conception of *Sola Scriptura*," in *Evangelicals and Scripture: Tradition, Authority and Hermeneutics*, ed. V. Bacote, L. C. Miguélez, and D. L. Okholm (Downers Grove, IL: InterVarsity, 2004), 201.

65. Vanhoozer, *The Drama of Doctrine*, 292. Vanhoozer does not go on to espouse radical perspectivalism.

66. This is noted, if not in so many words, by Nancey Murphy, *Beyond Liberalism and*

I am not trying to imply that one must be a foundationalist in order to retain orthodoxy. Rather, I am merely pointing out that it is simplistic to present only two options — classical foundationalism or non-foundationalism — as accounts of justification.

We come to the third problem with Franke's account of bibliology. Since Franke believes that any theological method that posits a privileged starting point is foundational, and since he does not want to be a foundationalist thus understood, he offers the following non-foundationalist alternative with respect to authority. He indicates that a non-foundationalist approach "attempts to affirm that the ultimate authority in the church is not a particular source, be it Scripture, tradition, reason, or experience, but only the living God."[67] This is a rather platitudinous statement: of course we want the living God to be our ultimate authority. But the question is, where are we to encounter the living God? Franke has an answer: Scripture, the church, and the world.[68] Now we must recall that his rejection of foundationalism (again, as he understands it) prohibits Franke from privileging any of these sources. He thus envisions these three sources as dialoguing in the construction of a theology: "A nonfoundationalist conception envisions theology as an ongoing conversation between Scripture, tradition, and culture through which the Spirit speaks."[69]

I would suggest that there are some severe problems with this conception of theology. First, to say that the Spirit speaks through culture is shocking. Scripture clearly speaks of an enmity between the world and the Spirit: "The Spirit of truth. The world cannot accept him, because it neither sees him nor knows him."[70] Rather, the Spirit convicts the world: "When he comes, he will convict the world of guilt in regard to sin and righteousness and judgment."[71] Even R. Olson, who is otherwise very supportive of Franke, parts ways with him in this assertion.[72]

The second problem with this conception of theology is what I consider to be a rather romanticized notion of dialogue. Franke envisions theology as a conversation between Scripture, the church, and the world that apparently will be very smooth and non-contradictory. Paul Helm raises a legitimate concern:

> Human conversations are notoriously open-ended and unpredictable. Who knows where they may lead? . . . Suppose that during the conversation the

Fundamentalism: How Modern and Postmodern Philosophy Set the Theological Agenda (Valley Forge, PA: Trinity Press, 1996), 13.

67. Franke, *The Character of Theology*, 78.

68. Franke, *The Character of Theology*, 79.

69. Franke, *The Character of Theology*, 79.

70. John 14:17. The term *kosmos* includes culture in its range of meaning.

71. John 16:8. Cf. also 1 Corinthians 2:6-16.

72. Olson, *Reformed and Always Reforming*, 113-14. Olson believes that Franke thus opens the door to relativism but does not in fact walk through it.

> conversation partners are led to the conviction not that the glory of God is revealed supremely or exclusively in the face of Jesus Christ, but that (in John Hick's phrase) God has many faces. Then, on Franke's paradigm, that is the way things must go. We must follow our theological method wherever it leads, even if it leads in unforeseen directions.[73]

But perhaps Franke has a way to ensure that the conversation would not go in this direction. This leads to the third observation.

Franke's statement about the three-way conversation of theology is concluded with the following reassuring words: "*. . . albeit always in accordance with the normative witness to divine self-disclosure in Jesus Christ.*" Further, he repeats that this conversation is *"centered on Jesus Christ in a variety of local settings."*[74] And later, "This perspective seeks to nurture an open and flexible theology that is in keeping with the local and contextual character of human knowledge *while remaining thoroughly and distinctly Christian.*"[75] But can Franke be consistent in proposing that theology is a three-way conversation of equal partners (Scripture, church, and culture) which at the same time "is in accordance with the normative witness to divine self-disclosure in Jesus Christ"? One should not be labeled cynical if one asked: "*Which* Jesus Christ? The one presented in Scripture, the ecclesial one, or the cultural Jesus?" Church history shows that this is not at all an irrelevant or malicious question. It seems to me that Franke has two options: (1) to acknowledge an amount of inconsistency in his account (and therefore to attempt a reformulation); or (2) to privilege Scripture as the ultimate norm to adjudicate between true and false portraits of Christ. But if he does the latter, then Franke would be a foundationalist, a label that he seems to want to avoid even at a high price. For according to Franke, this is not only modernist and indefensible, but also "inevitably" leads to oppression. I would like to close my interaction with Franke's work by focusing on this last item.

Scripture presents a different paradigm, one that affirms the possibility of the Christian receiving ultimate truth, proclaiming that truth, and yet not "inevitably" leading to oppression of others. I would like to draw from an event of the life of Jesus, namely his trial before the Sanhedrin. I will focus on the Markan account (14:53-65), although all Synoptics present a very similar picture of the trial. I sketch below the salient elements of the account.

1. Mark is at pains to show that the charges[76] are false. He shows this in two

73. Paul Helm, "No Easy Task: John R. Franke and the Character of Theology," in *Reforming or Conforming? Post-Conservative Evangelicals and the Emerging Church,* ed. G. L. W. Johnson and R. N. Gleason (Wheaton: Crossway, 2008), 98.

74. Franke, *The Character of Theology,* 79; emphasis added.

75. Franke, *The Character of Theology,* 80; emphasis added.

76. More than likely, from the Roman perspective, the charge was that of *maiestas.* In Mark 14:61-64, the emphasis is on Jesus' apparent blasphemous statement *vis-à-vis* God, that is, he

ways: first, by stating that although the leadership was seeking testimony against Jesus, nevertheless they found none (v. 55). When some *were* found,[77] Mark states that their testimonies were contradictory (vv. 56-59). Second, by means of terminology and Old Testament echoes, the evangelist presents Jesus as the suffering Righteous One.[78]

2. When the High Priest sees that the use of eyewitnesses is not leading the "trial" in the direction he wishes, he himself intervenes and asks Jesus directly if he is the messiah.

3. Jesus' response (which has caused voluminous research),[79] although enigmatic to many of us, was quite clear to the High Priest and the Sanhedrin, as is shown by their reaction (vv. 62-64). In essence, Jesus affirmed that he was the messiah (*egō eimi*) and explained the concomitant results by a quotation from Psalm 110:1 and Daniel 7:13. These passages highlight Jesus' divinity as well as his capacity as eschatological judge. We may paraphrase Jesus' confession this way: "Yes, I am the messiah; and the next time we meet, I will be the one doing the judging."[80] Blunt, to be sure, but it explains the High Priest ripping his tunics and the subsequent beating: How dare this Galilean peasant claim divinity and the future right to judge the highest court in Israel? In essence, Jesus was turning the tables: "Although now *you* judge me," he tells the judges, "at my return *I* will be the one judging *you*."[81]

4. Despite these astounding statements, in the very next scene Jesus allows himself to be beaten and ridiculed (v. 65); in a few hours he will be shamefully

---

was claiming to sit at the right hand of God's throne. Had the Jerusalem leaders presented this as the charge before Pilate, the latter would probably have dismissed it as a matter of inter-Jewish religious argumentation, just as Gallio did with Paul and the Jews in Acts 18:12-17. The Jerusalem leaders, therefore, *interpret for Pilate the significance of Jesus' claim in relation to Roman rule.* To claim to be the Anointed One, the leaders knew very well, had significant repercussions for Gentile rule over the Jews (see, e.g., Ps. Sol. 17). R. Pesch, *Das Markusevangelium,* vol. 2, *Kommentar zu Kap. 8, 27-16, 20,* 4th edition (Freiburg: Herder, 1991), 457, reaches the same conclusion by focusing on Pilate's question in 15:2: "Die Frage . . . des Pilatus wiederholt in heidnischer Formulierung (interpretatio romana) die Frage des Hohenpriesters aus 14, 61." ("Pilate's question repeats in pagan formulation [interpretatio romana] the High Priest's question from 14:61.") On Jesus' trial, see D. L. Bock, "Blasphemy and the Jewish Examination of Jesus," in *Key Events in the Life of the Historical Jesus: A Collaborative Exploration of Context and Coherence,* ed. D. L. Bock and R. L. Webb (Tübingen: Mohr Siebeck, 2009), 589-667.

77. And Mark is clear that they were "bearing *false* witness against him" (v. 56).

78. See Pesch, *Das Markusevangelium,* 431-32, and passim. Pesch believes that this motif was already part of a pre-Markan tradition.

79. See Bock, "Blasphemy."

80. J. Marcus, *Mark 8–16: A New Translation with Introduction and Commentary* (New Haven: Yale University Press, 2009), 1016.

81. See N. T. Wright, *Jesus and the Victory of God* (Minneapolis: Fortress Press, 1996), 525-26.

crucified. Someone picking up the narrative at this point would have expected Jesus to use his messianic prerogative, seize control of Jerusalem, and violently expel the Romans. Of course, we know he had that chance but refused it (14:43-50); and in any case it was God's will that his body be broken (14:22).

Some may reject the applicability of this passage as a paradigm since, after all, it was Jesus who uttered these statements — and he is the Son of God! Jesus' attitude, however, is presented as paradigmatic both in the Gospel of Mark and in other texts of the New Testament.

In the first passage, we can see some striking similarities between Jesus' trial and his instruction to the disciples as found in the eschatological discourse of Mark (13:1-37). Particularly important is verse 9: "Watch out for yourselves. They will hand you over (*paradōsousin*) to the councils (*synedria*) and you will be beaten in their synagogues, and you will be made to stand before governors and kings because of me for testimony (*martyrion*) to them." The terminology used of the disciples' future trials and of Jesus' own trial are thus very similar.[82] Mark is here using *synkrisis* in order to highlight the continuation from Jesus to his disciples.[83]

Another very important aspect in the Markan account is the disciples' response when they are on trial because of their testimony for Jesus. The disciples are not to worry about what they should say, but they are to speak "whatever is given to you in that hour" (13:11); the reason for this is that "You will not be speaking but the Holy Spirit." This is a remarkable statement. It suggests that in their hour of trial, in a mysterious manner, God will intervene in a very unique manner to speak through them.[84]

A second passage showing the paradigmatic nature of Jesus' attitude in his trial is found in 1 Timothy 6:13. In the context of enemies "inside and outside the church,"[85] Timothy is commanded: "I exhort you before God who gives life to all things and Jesus Christ, who testified to the good confession before Pontius Pilate." The "good confession" can refer specifically to Jesus' messianic identity or more generally to Christian truth as a whole. Jesus' attitude in his trial is to serve as an example to Timothy.

Having looked at the Markan passages as well as 1 Timothy, I would suggest the following paradigm *vis-à-vis* the Christian's claim to the universal truth of the gospel: the making of gospel truth claims is not seen in Scripture as prideful and as inevitably leading to epistemic control and violence. The Bible envisions

82. On *paradidōmi*, see 15:1.

83. Thus also Marcus, *Mark 8–16*, 885; A. Y. Collins, *Mark: A Commentary* (Minneapolis: Fortress Press, 2007), 607.

84. As C. A. Evans, *Mark 8:27–16:20* (Nashville: Thomas Nelson, 2001), 311, indicates, the motif of God intervening to speak through one of his messengers is already present in the Old Testament.

85. Marshall, *The Pastoral Epistles*, 663.

Christians boldly proclaiming scriptural truth claims *followed by a willingness to be martyred for this truth rather than taking a violent approach to enforce this truth.* Here I find the words of Vanhoozer appropriate: "The vocation of the Christian theologian is to be an interpreter-martyr: a truth-teller, a truth-doer, a truth-sufferer. Truth requires evangelical passion, not postmodern passivity; personal appropriation, not calculation."[86]

Conclusions

In this essay I have focused on Grenz and Franke, not only because they are representatives of the broader postconservative movement, but also because, in my estimation, they are two of its most influential voices. This is not only so at the academic level, but also at the ecclesial one. One of the evangelical movements that has been growing in recent times is the emerging church. Probably the most authoritative voice in this movement has been Brian McLaren, who acknowledges Grenz and Franke as the theologians who have exerted the most sway in his vision of theology and the church. Of course, McLaren may not be adequately appropriating Grenz and Franke and it would thus be foolish to make them responsible for the intellectual thrust of the emerging church. Nevertheless, the fact remains that they are being read, and this (among other things) makes their work on Scripture an important source with which to interact.

In the previous pages my opinions on the works of Grenz and Franke have been mostly negative. Nevertheless, I would like here to acknowledge that there are many aspects of their work that can be of great benefit to the academy and church. I have read with appreciation their critiques of the individualism that plagues the church, particularly in North America. I have also resonated with their call to modesty and humility that should characterize theological dialogue inside and outside the church. Further, their emphasis on narrative provides a much more scriptural and rich account of our God than a focus exclusively on propositions. It is therefore with the hope of refinement that the concluding suggestive comments are offered.

First, postconservatives should consider structuring their theological account primarily with Scripture rather than philosophy (modern or postmodern). I find this to be one of the great ironies among postconservatives (particularly Grenz and Franke). They voice the complaint that traditional conservative theology (and liberalism) has been bound by modern accounts of epistemology, principally foundationalism. This dependence on philosophy, they claim, has distorted Christian theology. And yet, they go right ahead and exchange one

86. K. J. Vanhoozer, *First Theology: God, Scripture and Hermeneutics* (Downers Grove, IL: InterVarsity, 2002), 372-73.

philosophy for another, except that now it is not foundationalism, but pragmatism or Anglo-American postmodern epistemology or holism. N. Murphy, for example, after complaining that the philosophy of modernity (mainly foundationalism) is the primary reason for the split between liberal and conservative Protestantism, ends up exchanging it for a hybrid of holism and pragmatism. The goal seems to be to fit Christian doctrine with a philosophical model rather than allowing doctrine to be the thrust of the inquiry. This is not of course to suggest that our construction of doctrine is not linguistically and communally mediated, but rather that our ultimate allegiance is to a theology whose master is Scripture.

Second, postconservatives like Franke should further reflect whether their approach to theology does not in fact endanger *sola scriptura.* To be sure, Franke affirms *sola scriptura;* but the question is if his concept of revelation does not effectively relativize the place of Scripture. I believe that Franke's approach can be said to affirm *sola scriptura* only at the expense of being internally inconsistent. The same can be said for Grenz. His fusion of inspiration and illumination effectively raises the community to a place of equal authority with Scripture. Again, it is likely that Grenz would have formally denied this.[87] Yet, his formulation of the doctrine of Scripture, if not tacitly positing for equal authority, certainly opens the door in that direction. It should be noted that the upholding of *sola scriptura* is not a naïve belief that the interpretation of Scripture by the community is a simple affair; or that our collocation in a particular tradition does not profoundly affect how we read Scripture. Vanhoozer's words in this respect are very helpful: "If *sola scriptura* means 'the Bible alone apart from the church and tradition,' it has no future. But this is not what *sola scriptura* means. *Sola scriptura* is a protest not against tradition as such but against the presumption that church tradition (interpretation) and Scripture (text) necessarily coincide."[88] And so as evangelicals we relish in reading and interpreting Scripture in joyful community. But we recognize that even as a community enlivened by the Spirit our interpretations will not ineluctably agree with Scripture.

Lastly, as a maturing movement, postconservatives should adopt a more charitable attitude, especially toward their evangelical forebears. Sociologists tell us that rejection of a parent movement is often one way in which a new group forges its identity. And so it is. But criticisms of the forebears should be done with more charity. Postconservatives have not always operated this way. There is often caricaturing of views if not slander.[89] The whipping boys tend to be Grudem, Henry, and Hodge. Olson, for example, in commenting on Henry's strong tone

87. With respect to Scripture, Olson discloses that Grenz "to his dying day in March 2005 affirmed the supernatural inspiration and even inerrancy of Scripture" (Olson, *Reformed and Always Reforming,* 25). But this still misses the point.

88. K. Vanhoozer, "Scripture and Tradition," in Vanhoozer, ed., *Postmodern Theology,* 167.

89. An example of this is found in several pages of Olson, *Reformed and Always Reforming.*

against a rejection of inerrancy, states: "This is the spirit of conservative evangelicalism; it breathes the same air as fundamentalism even if it is not quite as toxic."[90] This type of labeling is not only tendentious but also impedes progress in dialogue. To be sure, Henry's doctrine of revelation leaned in the direction of propositionalism to the neglect of narrative. But a charitable reading would recognize that Henry was engaging with a denial of cognitive propositions that was abundant in the period in which he wrote.[91]

90. Olson, *Reformed and Always Reforming*, 18-19, n. 20.
91. See Vanhoozer, *The Drama of Doctrine*, 45.

TWENTY-TWO

Reflections on Jesus' View of the Old Testament

Craig L. Blomberg

Arguably the most influential twentieth-century studies in American evangelical scholarship on the topic of Scripture's inspiration were those gathered together in B. B. Warfield's *The Inspiration and Authority of Scripture.*[1] Here, the renowned professor of systematic theology at Princeton Seminary from 1887 to 1921 begins with the general trustworthiness of Scripture, which he takes to be established on historical grounds apart from explicitly presupposing Christian faith, and demonstrates the pervasiveness of the Bible's claims about itself. If even a small portion of these prove accurate, the God-breathed (*theopneustos*) nature of Scripture is upheld. Most of Warfield's volume proceeds to explicate the nature of this inspiration and to defend it against competing views.

On the European side of the Atlantic, during the second half of the twentieth century, no one was better known for championing the authority of the Bible than John Wenham, Greek lecturer and vice-principal of Tyndale Hall, Bristol, and then warden of Latimer House, Oxford. His *Christ and the Bible* employed a similar, largely evidentialist apologetic to contend that, even if only the broad contours of the canonical Gospels' teachings attributed to Jesus were authentic, Jesus' views of the Bible of his day, the Hebrew Scriptures, so permeate the accounts of Matthew, Mark, Luke, and John that anyone who acknowledges Jesus as Lord must accept the Gospel portraits of his views of what we call the Old Testament.[2] These views find Jesus ascribing the equivalent of what has come to

1. Benjamin B. Warfield, *The Inspiration and Authority of the Bible* (Philadelphia: P&R, 1948). The chapters were first individually published in a variety of sources dating from 1893 to 1915.

2. John W. Wenham, *Christ and the Bible* (London: Tyndale, 1972; Downers Grove, IL: InterVarsity, 1973). Wenham's views go back at least as far as his Tyndale New Testament lecture

I am grateful to my 2009-10 research assistant Clint Wilson for help in locating certain key works and synthesizing various important issues related to the topic of this paper.

be known as plenary, verbal inspiration to the Scriptures. That is to say, all parts of all books of the Hebrew canon, to the extent that we can reconstruct their autographs, uniquely originated from God, not apart from all of the standard processes of human composition of written documents, but in a fashion so as to guarantee the complete truthfulness, reliability, and authority of these works.[3]

Warfield's and Wenham's works ranged more widely and deeply than these brief summaries indicate. Both were characterized by meticulous attention to the details of both Testaments. Neither, however, actually defended the authenticity of any of the teachings of Jesus. They merely assumed it, or at least assumed that enough of his teachings about the Bible could be trusted that his general attitude toward it could be taken as established. Even in the last years of Warfield's life, Gospel form criticism had unleashed a broadside attack against this assumption;[4] by Wenham's day redaction criticism routinely called into question the authenticity of a large percentage of the sayings ascribed to the historical Jesus in the canonical texts.[5] The so-called third quest of the historical Jesus over the last thirty years has actually made it possible to mount a plausible case for the trustworthiness of the general contours of at least the Synoptic Gospels to a greater extent than in the heyday of either form or redaction criticism.[6] But more skeptical approaches receive greater press,[7] and scholarship that seeks to convince in the larger academic world will still use various "criteria of authenticity" in order to contend that specific texts or themes truly did originate from Jesus himself.[8]

---

for 1953, published as *Our Lord's View of the Old Testament* (London: Inter-Varsity Fellowship, 1953).

3. Another booklet containing a treasure trove of the basic data from the Gospels on these topics was R. V. G. Tasker, *Our Lord's Use of the Old Testament* (Glasgow: Pickering & Inglis, 1953).

4. Martin Dibelius, *Die Formgeschichte des Evangeliums* (Tübingen: Mohr, 1919); K. L. Schmidt, *Der Rahmen der Geschichte Jesu* (Berlin: Trowizsch, 1919).

5. See especially Günther Bornkamm, Gerhard Barth, and Heinz J. Held, *Tradition and Interpretation in Matthew* (London: SCM; Philadelphia: Westminster, 1963); Willi Marxsen, *Mark the Evangelist* (Nashville: Abingdon, 1969); and Hans Conzelmann, *The Theology of St. Luke* (New York: Harper & Row, 1960; London: Faber & Faber, 1961).

6. See especially James H. Charlesworth, *The Historical Jesus: An Essential Guide* (Nashville: Abingdon, 2008); and James H. Charlesworth and Petr Pokorný, eds., *Jesus Research: An International Perspective* (Grand Rapids and Cambridge: Eerdmans, 2009).

7. Most notably the various publications of the Jesus Seminar, supporters of the Gnostic Gospels, and the wide-ranging publications of Bart Ehrman. For discussions of and responses to all these and related trends, see especially Philip Jenkins, *Hidden Gospels: How the Search for Jesus Lost Its Way* (Oxford and New York: Oxford University Press, 2001); and Darrell L. Bock and Daniel B. Wallace, *Dethroning Jesus: Exposing Popular Culture's Quest to Unseat the Biblical Christ* (Nashville: Nelson, 2007).

8. By far the best singly authored example of this process is Craig S. Keener, *The Historical Jesus of the Gospels* (Grand Rapids and Cambridge: Eerdmans, 2009).

A model of this kind of careful argumentation is the recent volume from the Institute of Biblical Research's Historical Jesus Study Group, *Key Events in the Life of the Historical Jesus*.[9] Here appear compelling cases for the authenticity of Jesus' baptism by John, his exorcisms and kingdom teaching, the call and instruction of the Twelve, table fellowship with sinners, coming into conflict with various Jewish leadership groups especially over the Sabbath, Peter's declaration of Jesus' identity on the road to Caesarea Philippi, the royal entry into Jerusalem, the temple incident, the last supper, his conviction by the Sanhedrin for blasphemy, his trial and crucifixion under Pontius Pilate, and his empty tomb and resurrection appearances. From these studies, one of the book's editors, Darrell Bock, concludes,

> Understanding the historical Jesus requires appreciating the scope of the significance of his acts and the element of authority implicit in them. Those acts pointed to a new time and an appointed person. Jesus presented himself in his activity with both a demand and an invitation to participate in God's restorative rule. It was a rule that the historical Jesus' ministry in core events and activities sought to illustrate and to inaugurate.[10]

This summary alone moves us a long way toward the first step in Warfield's apologetic, giving us reason to accept Jesus as the authoritative teacher for Christian belief and practice. Absent, however, is any study of Jesus' view of Scripture, an absence that characterizes most recent historical Jesus research, even in evangelical circles.

Numerous studies over the past generation, of course, have examined the use of the Old Testament in individual Gospel passages, entire Gospels, and in the rest of the New Testament more generally. They have been captivated by consideration of the hermeneutics employed, by intertextual echoes and allusions in addition to explicit quotations, by the text-types utilized (Qumranic, Septuagintal, Masoretic, or distinctive), and by the theological positions staked out by Jesus and the Evangelists as a result.[11] Almost nothing, though, has addressed in any detail the question of the authenticity of the texts needed to establish

9. Darrell L. Bock and Robert L. Webb, eds., *Key Events in the Life of the Historical Jesus: A Collaborative Exploration of Context and Coherence* (Tübingen: Mohr Siebeck, 2009; Grand Rapids and Cambridge: Eerdmans, 2010).

10. Darrell L. Bock, "Key Events in the Life of the Historical Jesus: A Summary," in Bock and Webb, eds., *Key Events in the Life of the Historical Jesus*, 852.

11. The reference tool that interacts with and consolidates the greatest number of these studies and their findings is G. K. Beale and D. A. Carson, eds., *Commentary on the New Testament Use of the Old Testament* (Grand Rapids: Baker; Nottingham: Apollos, 2007). Elsewhere in the present volume, see especially Douglas J. Moo and Andrew D. Naselli, "The Problem of the New Testament's Use of the Old Testament" (chapter 23).

the historical Jesus' perspective on the inspiration or authority of the Bible of his world.[12] This chapter seeks to begin to fill this gap. It will then reflect on the resulting picture of Jesus' convictions and their significance for contemporary bibliological debates.

The Criteria of Authenticity and Jesus' View of the Old Testament

The standard criteria of authenticity are well known: multiple attestation, dissimilarity, coherence, Palestinian environment, necessary explanation, embarrassment, and the like. Products of the periods dubbed by some as "no quest" and the "new quest," they have also frequently been critiqued in this era of the "third quest."[13] Most notably, dissimilarity from Judaism stands in a certain tension with a Palestinian environment. Holding out even more potential is N. T. Wright's double similarity and dissimilarity criterion,[14] or what the German trio of Gerd Theissen, Annette Merz, and Dagmar Winter have dubbed *die Plausibilitätskriterium.*[15] This four-pronged criterion looks for that which is *both* plausible within a Jewish context in Israel during the first third of the first century, *yet* dissimilar enough from conventional Jewish thought or practice that the average ancient Jew (or Jewish-Christian) is not likely to have invented it, *and* plausible within the context of Jesus' first followers, *yet* dissimilar enough from subsequent early Christianity that the average ancient Jewish (or gentile) Christian probably didn't make it up. When elements in the Gospels reasonably well satisfy all four parts of this criterion, a powerful case can be made that the teaching or action in question goes back to the historical Jesus.

This is precisely what emerges when we examine Jesus' teaching and behavior with respect to the Hebrew Scriptures. On the one hand, Jesus appears to adopt the identical body of authoritative Scriptures as the Judaism of his day. He quotes from all three of their major subdivisions (the Law, the Prophets, and the Writings), and from all three kinds of law (as later Christianity would label

12. The closest one comes in a work of any length is R. T. France, *Jesus and the Old Testament: His Application of Old Testament Passages to Himself and His Mission* (London: Tyndale, 1971; Grand Rapids: Baker, 1982; Vancouver: Regent, repr. 1992). The subtitle, however, indicates the primary focus of the volume; and even then, it is now forty years old.

13. See especially Stanley E. Porter, *The Criteria for Authenticity in Historical-Jesus Research: Previous Discussion and New Proposals* (Sheffield: Sheffield Academic Press, 2000).

14. N. T. Wright, *Jesus and the Victory of God* (London: SPCK; Minneapolis: Fortress, 1996), 131-33.

15. Gerd Theissen and Annette Merz, *The Historical Jesus: A Comprehensive Guide* (London: SCM; Minneapolis: Fortress, 1998), 115-18; Gerd Theissen and Dagmar Winter, *The Quest for the Plausible Jesus: The Question of Criteria* (Louisville and London: Westminster John Knox, 2001), 172-225.

them — ritual, civil, and moral). He seems to view narrative texts as historical in nature. He attributes the Bible to God himself and considers Scripture's words as God's words. He consistently quotes, alludes to, or echoes this collection of holy writings because he believes it is authoritative for himself and for his listeners. In these respects he fits squarely into the Jewish milieu of Israel at the dawn of the Common Era.

On the other hand, Jesus repeatedly quotes Scripture against various Jewish leaders or groups of leaders. Sometimes he returns to what he understands to be a text's original purpose over against subsequent distortion, misinterpretation, or misapplication. Often he challenges his conversation partners by alleging that they have simply ignored or disobeyed the clear teaching of a sacred text. Frequently, he understands Scriptures to have been fulfilled in him and/or in the events surrounding his life and ministry. Occasionally, these involve direct predictions, the contents of which have now occurred. Far more commonly, they reflect typology — the recognition of patterns in historical events believed to be the work of the same sovereign God disclosing his recurring, characteristic activity with humanity, especially in events related to their salvation or judgment.[16] Often Jesus interprets Scripture Christologically, seeing both direct and typological predictions pointing to himself as the newly arrived messianic King. Even when his appeals to Scripture do not directly serve Christological ends, his sovereign authority over Scripture implicitly raises the question of his identity, or at least of who he *thought* he was.[17] This combination of very atypical approaches to Scripture clearly fits the prong of our criterion that looks for dissimilarity with ancient Judaism.

Early Christianity adopted Jesus' abiding respect for Scripture, his high view of its divine origin, its overarching authority, and the historical nature of its narratives. It agreed with and pushed even further his typological and, more specifically, Christological (and eventually Trinitarian) interpretations.[18] But it quickly broke from Jesus' convictions that all of Torah — civil, ritual, and moral

16. On which, see especially Leonhard Goppelt, *Typos: The Typological Interpretation of the Old Testament in the New* (Grand Rapids: Eerdmans, 1982; Eugene, OR: Wipf & Stock, 2002). Cf. also Darrell L. Bock, "Single Meaning, Multiple Contexts and Referents: The New Testament's Legitimate, Accurate, and Multifaceted Use of the Old," in *Three Views on the New Testament Use of the Old Testament,* ed. Kenneth Berding and Jonathan Lunde (Grand Rapids: Zondervan, 2007), especially 118-21.

17. Unlike the rabbis, he never cited previous authorities in his interpretations of Scripture. Unlike Qumran, he "used Scripture as a commentary on and means of expressing God's present activity in his ministry; he did not use the present circumstances of God's people or his followers to interpret Scripture" (Ben Witherington III, *The Christology of Jesus* [Minneapolis: Fortress, 1990], 185).

18. For an excellent introduction, see Christopher A. Hall, *Reading Scripture with the Church Fathers* (Downers Grove, IL: InterVarsity, 1998).

laws alike — were still in effect in his own day. Arguably, Jesus' own teaching paved the way for this rupture. Fledgling Christianity also quickly turned to different kinds of debates in which it invoked Torah. As early as in the Acts and the Epistles, the *primary* controversies were no longer about Sabbath-keeping, the role of the temple, fasting, or feasting with sinners. The more heavily gentile-laden the emerging Jesus movement became, the more the debates surrounded circumcision (Acts 15; Gal. 2; a topic surprisingly absent from the Gospels), idolatrous worship (1 Cor. 8–10), prophecy and speaking in tongues (1 Cor. 14), gender roles (1 Cor. 11:1-16; Eph. 5:21-33; and 1 Tim. 2:8-15), vegetarianism (Rom. 14), celibacy (1 Cor. 7), and numerous other topics that played little or no role in Jesus' ministry but loomed large in the interaction of Judaism and Hellenism in the first-century Greco-Roman milieu. It remains to pursue each of these four strands of comparison in more detail.

Continuity with Judaism

In resisting the devil's temptations in the wilderness, Christ three times quotes Scripture as authoritative in ways that presumably even Satan will recognize. At least it leads the devil to leave him alone (Matt. 4:1-11; Luke 4:1-13). A simple *gegraptai* ("it stands written"[19]) introduces each quotation. The temptation narrative stood near the beginning and served as a foundation for the early-Q source; the criterion of embarrassment (at having a Messiah thus tempted) supports authenticity.[20] Multiple attestation and coherence come into play as well. The principles Jesus cites are clearly timeless ethical ones: the need for spiritual in addition to physical nourishment, the prohibition against testing or tempting God, and the command to worship and serve only him (Deut. 8:3; 6:16; 6:13). No Jew at that time should have disagreed with the way Jesus applied these texts.[21]

19. Stanley E. Porter, *Verbal Aspect in the Greek of the New Testament, with Reference to Tense and Mood* (New York: Peter Lang, 1989), 269. Porter classes the New Testament uses of this perfect form under the "timeless" subcategory of stative aspect.

20. See, respectively, Luigi Schiavo, "The Temptation of Jesus: The Eschatological Battle and the New Ethic of the First Followers of Jesus in Q," *JSNT* 25 (2002): 141-64; and Charles A. Kimball, *Jesus' Exposition of the Old Testament in Luke's Gospel* (Sheffield: Sheffield Academic Press, 1994), 82-84.

21. Targ. Ps.-Jon. on Deut. 8:3 reads, "Not by bread alone does man live but by everything that is created by the Memra [word] of the Lord does man live." Targ. On. adds a verb to Deut. 6:13 so that people are called not just to fear God but worship him too. The later rabbinic literature repeatedly stresses ways one should not test God (Hermann L. Strack and Paul Billerbeck, *Kommentar zum Neuen Testament aus Talmud und Midrasch,* vol. 1 [Munich: Beck, 1922], 152-53). Craig A. Evans ("Exorcisms and the Kingdom: Inaugurating the Kingdom of God and Defeating the Kingdom of Satan," in Bock and Webb, eds., *Key Events in the Life of the Historical Jesus,* 167-68) argues for the authenticity of the Q-version of the temptation narrative because

The Golden Rule as a summary of the "Law and the Prophets" (Matt. 7:12) differs from Hillel's so-called silver rule by stating positively what Jesus' older contemporary put negatively (*b. Sabb.* 31a), but the significance of the difference between the two forms can easily be exaggerated. Both viewed how we would want to be treated or not treated as the key to how we deal with others.[22] So, too, Jesus' enunciation of the double love command as the most important of the Jewish commandments (Mark 12:28-34 pars.; cf. Deut. 6:5 and Lev. 19:18) would have garnered widespread approval among his contemporaries, as it did from the lawyer himself in the narrative at hand. Jesus simultaneously endorses both Jewish monotheism (Deut. 6:4) and the first of the Ten Commandments (Exod. 20:3), alongside the obligation to love one's neighbor. Philo even attests a pre-Christian Jewish combination of the twin commands on love:

> And there are, as we may say, two most especially important heads of all the innumerable particular lessons and doctrines: the regulating of one's conduct towards God by the rules of piety and holiness, and of one's conduct towards men by the rules of humanity and justice; each of which is subdivided into a great number of subordinate ideas, all praiseworthy. (*Spec. Laws* 2.15)

What was unique to Jesus, supporting authenticity, was the extent to which he universalized the definition of "neighbor" to include even one's enemy (Luke 6:27 par.; 10:30-35).[23]

A straightforward application of the fifth commandment to honor one's parents (Exod. 20:12) emerges in Jesus' criticism of the Pharisees' and scribes' abuse of the *korban* tradition (Mark 7:9-13 par.). What "Moses said" (v. 10) is equated with "the word of God" (v. 13).[24] The Jewish leaders may have been outraged at his challenge but they had no legitimate reason to reject his application of the law.[25] In the Mishnah and Talmud, such abuse of the Decalogue

---

the event "coheres with the kingdom versus Satan theme in such a way as to suggest its core authenticity and is an event finding itself stubbornly deposited in a largely sayings tradition, pointing to the event's roots reflecting an early tradition."

22. Gerd Theissen ("Die Goldene Regel [Matthäus 7:12//Lukas 6:31]: Über den Sitz im Leben ihrer positive und negative Form," *BI* 11 [2003]: 386-99) points out that it is usually the negative form of the "rule" that embraces almost everyone, just as Jesus' positive version does, *both* contra the typical limitations of the positive form in Jewish and pagan writings to particular social circumstances. On the right combination of similarity with and dissimilarity from Judaism for authenticity, see Geza Vermes, *The Authentic Gospel of Jesus* (London: Allen Lane, 2003; New York: Penguin, 2004), 98-100.

23. Cf. Reinhard Neudecker, "'And You Shall Love Your Neighbor as Yourself — I Am the Lord' (Lev. 19,18 in Jewish Interpretation)," *Bib* 73 (1992): 496-517.

24. All quotations from the Bible are taken from Today's New International Version.

25. Josephus (*Against Apion* 2.27) affirmed that honoring one's parents ranked next only to honoring God among the commandments. Philo (*Spec. Laws* 2.261) added more specifically,

would even be forbidden, but at this earlier date it was still at times tolerated.[26] The fifth commandment appears again, along with the sixth through the ninth (Exod. 20:13-16), plus the command not to defraud, as Jesus' initial reply to the rich young ruler's question about how to get eternal life (Mark 10:19; Matt. 19:19 substitutes neighbor love for not defrauding, while Luke 18:20 simply omits it). Thus far Christ echoes one existing strain in the Judaism of his day.[27] But by the end of the conversation, telling the rich man to sell his possessions and follow him, Jesus "upholds the Torah, only to place his person and authority above it,"[28] thus again creating the requisite similarity and dissimilarity to suggest authenticity.

The civil law or legal principle that a judicial matter must be established by at least two or three witnesses (Deut. 19:15) underlies Jesus' teaching on church discipline in Matthew 18:16.[29] Thus Jesus endorses not only broad moral principles from the Torah but specific legal prescriptions. He does, however, apply them more widely than in their original courtroom context.[30] The more theological (or doxological) pattern of small children praising God (Ps. 8:2) leads to Christ's rebuke of those who criticized the children who called out Hosannas in Jesus' presence (Matt. 21:16). They disputed his too close equation with deity, but his use of the scriptural text to justify the children's worship in and of itself was unobjectionable.[31] Here is one of several places in the Gospels in which Jesus

---

"Let not him who honors his parents dutifully seek for any further advantage, for if he considers the matter he will find his reward in his own conduct."

26. Jon N. Bailey, "Vowing Away the Fifth Commandment: Matthew 15:3-6 // Mark 7:9-13," *RestQ* 42 (2000): 193-209. The criterion of Palestinian environment thus comes especially into play. Cf. also Keener, *Historical Jesus of the Gospels,* 217-18.

27. Arseny Ermakov, "The Salvific Significance of the Torah in Mark 10.17-22 and 12.28-34," in *Torah in the New Testament: Papers Delivered at the Manchester-Lausanne Seminar of June 2008,* ed. Michael Tait and Peter Oakes (London and New York: T. & T. Clark, 2009), 21-31.

28. Rikki E. Watts, "Mark," in Beale and Carson, eds., *Commentary on the New Testament Use of the Old Testament,* 200. Cf. Morna Hooker, "Mark," in *It Is Written: Scripture Citing Scripture,* ed. D. A. Carson and H. G. M. Williamson (Cambridge: Cambridge University Press, 1988), 223.

29. Josephus endorses this principle (*Ant.* 4.219; *Life* 256), as does Philo (*Spec. Laws* 4.53-54). The Dead Sea Scrolls provide a particularly close parallel to the Matthean context by insisting that disputes should be resolved privately if at all possible. Then if a matter must be brought to the congregation, at least two witnesses are required (1QS V:25–VI:1; cf. also CD IX:22-23).

30. Cf. also John 8:17; 2 Cor. 13:1; and 1 Tim. 5:19. "Apparently, the rule enjoyed a certain popularity as a directive that was applicable to various situations." Maarten J. J. Menken, "Deuteronomy in Matthew's Gospel," in *Deuteronomy in the New Testament,* ed. Maarten J. J. Menken and Steve Moyise (London and New York: T. & T. Clark, 2007), 55.

31. Only the LXX of Psalm 8 explicitly includes the word "praise," perhaps borrowed from the tradition later reflected in *Mekilta on Exod.* 15:1 with its assumption that those who praised God at the Red Sea, as mentioned in Exodus 15:2, included children. See further W. D. Davies

introduces his quotation of Scripture with the polemical question, "Have you never (or 'not') read . . . ?" In each instance he assumes shared knowledge of the sacred text but denies that his opponents have understood it properly or paid attention to the right material (cf. also Mark 2:25-26 pars.; Mark 12:26 par.; Matt. 19:4; and Matt. 21:42).[32]

Each of the uses of this introductory formula occurs in the context of debates in which Jesus takes it for granted that he and his interlocutors shared a common, authoritative, written[33] document — the Hebrew Scriptures. Jesus' *interpretation* of the text may or may not appear novel, but his appeal to its *normative nature* certainly is not. In the parable of the wicked tenants (Matt. 21:33-46 pars.), Christ builds on Jewish precedent when he asks if the Jewish leaders have not read Psalm 118:22 and proceeds to give the "cornerstone" a messianic interpretation (see the Cairo Geniza *Songs of David* A 18 and Targ. Ps. 118).[34] That this is part of the original interaction following an authentic parable is suggested by the wordplay in Aramaic or Hebrew but not present in Greek between the "son" *(bēn)* who is killed (vv. 38-39) and the "stone" *(eben)* who is rejected.[35] In the accounts of the plucking of grain on the Sabbath (Mark 2:23-28 pars.) and the debate with the Sadducees over the resurrection (Mark 12:18-27 pars.), Jesus proves far more controversial. But the very reason he appeals to a seemingly odd text for affirming resurrection life (Exod. 3:6) is that the Sadducees derived binding doctrine only from the five books of Moses, which do not obviously articulate resurrection. So to preserve common ground by arguing from an agreed-on authority, his hermeneutic turns creative.[36] Tellingly, whereas the Sadducees allude only to what

---

and Dale C. Allison Jr., *A Critical and Exegetical Commentary on the Gospel according to St. Matthew,* vol. 3 (Edinburgh: T. & T. Clark, 1997), 142.

32. Cf. Michael P. Knowles, "Scripture, History, Messiah: Scriptural Fulfillment and the Fullness of Time in Matthew's Gospel," in *Hearing the Old Testament in the New Testament,* ed. Stanley E. Porter (Grand Rapids and Cambridge: Eerdmans, 2006), 64-66.

33. It is fashionable today to underestimate the amount of literacy that even Jewish *teachers* would have had, contra which Alan Millard (*Reading and Writing in the Time of Jesus* [Sheffield: Sheffield Academic Press, 2000], 158) stresses that this kind of language presumed that they read aloud written texts, even while language like that in the antitheses of the Sermon on the Mount showed that the crowds were used to listening (e.g., "you have heard that it was said . . ." [Matt. 5:21, 33, etc.]).

34. J. C. de Moor, "The Targumic Background of Mark 12:1-12: The Parable of the Wicked Tenants," *JSJ* 29 (1998): 77-78.

35. See especially Klyne Snodgrass, *Stories with Intent: A Comprehensive Guide to the Parables of Jesus* (Grand Rapids and Cambridge: Eerdmans, 2008), 290.

36. Even here, though, Jesus' argumentation resembles that of *b. Sanh.* 90b, deriving the resurrection from Num. 18:28 with its command to the Levites in perpetuity to tithe to "Aaron the priest" the tithes they receive from the people. God must, therefore, have foreseen Aaron's resurrection, so the logic proceeds. For Jesus' own approach, see especially Bradley R. Trick, "Death, Covenants, and the Proof of Resurrection in Mark 12:18-27," *NovT* 49 (2007): 232-56.

Moses said (Matt. 22:24 pars.), Jesus replies in terms of what *God* has declared through the Scriptures (v. 29 pars.).[37] Notice the same contrast in Matthew 19:6-7.

The Dead Sea Scrolls have made it clear that at least some Jews saw Isaiah 35:5-6 as messianic (see 4Q521).[38] Thus, when Jesus instructs John the Baptist's disciples to tell their master that the blind see, the deaf hear, the mute speak, and the lame walk (Matt. 11:5; Luke 7:22), as his answer to John's question about whether or not he is the Coming One, his listeners should have recognized the affirmative implications of his reply. They might not all have agreed with him, but Jesus' logic remains firmly rooted in existing Jewish thought. Yet because there was enough diversity of thought on the topic, the Gospels' description of Jesus' perspective is not likely to have been invented based on some pre-formed tradition or expectation.[39]

Only Matthew and John quote Zechariah 9:9 in the context of Christ's "triumphal entry" (Matt. 21:5; John 12:15), and not Jesus himself, but it is hard to see how his deliberate choice of a donkey and his acceptance of royal acclamation as he rode into Jerusalem the week before the Passover could have been anything except a conscious enactment of a scriptural prophecy in a decidedly messianic context.[40] As Craig Keener explains, "Clearly Jesus did enter Jerusalem during this week, and clearly he already had enjoyed the reputation of a prophet; *something* like the triumphal entry is therefore inevitable" (italics his).[41] But it was probably modest in scale, susceptible to a variety of interpretations, peaceful and thus, for the time being, permitted by the authorities. "The disciples, however, would have remembered the event in great detail, and what Jesus intended to convey to them through the symbolic act is more critical than the immediate understanding of other bystanders."[42]

Christ employs Micah 7:6 less straightforwardly and more typologically in Matthew 10:35-36 and parallel, predicting that Jesus' disciples may have their families torn apart by interreligious strife, just as in the prophet's day. Typology, how-

37. The implications are less explicit but still present in the Markan form. See James L. Mays, "Is This Not Why You Are Wrong? Exegetical Reflections on Mark 12:18-27," *Int* 60 (2006): 42.

38. On which, see especially Hans Kvalbein, "The Wonders of the End-Time: Metaphoric Language in 4Q521 and the Interpretation of Matthew 11.5 par.," *JSP* 18 (1998): 87-110.

39. Hans Kvalbein, "Die Wunder der Endzeit: Beobachtungen zu 4Q521 und Matth 11,5p," *ZNW* 88 (1997): 111-25.

40. Cf. especially Brent Kinman, "Jesus' Royal Entry into Jerusalem," in Bock and Webb, eds., *Key Events in the Life of the Historical Jesus,* 383-427. Even Marcus J. Borg and John Dominic Crossan (*The Last Week: A Day-by-Day Account of Jesus's Final Week in Jerusalem* [San Francisco: HarperSanFrancisco, 2006], 1-30) use Jesus' entry into Jerusalem as the (historically authentic) paradigm of the contrast between his kingdom and the Roman empire.

41. Keener, *Historical Jesus of the Gospels,* 259-60.

42. Keener, *Historical Jesus of the Gospels,* 260. Cf. especially Kim Huat Tan, *The Zion Traditions and the Aims of Jesus* (Cambridge: Cambridge University Press, 1997), 138-43.

ever, remains equally grounded in the Hebrew Scriptures,[43] so his followers were unlikely to have found this application of prophecy surprising. The same may be said of Jesus' appeal to Isaiah 6:9-10 as a precedent for lamenting the obduracy of his generation, leading to his need to speak in parables (Mark 4:11-12 pars.),[44] and of his citation of Isaiah 29:13 to explain the religious leaders' vain, hypocritical worship (Mark 7:6b-7 par.).[45] The "den of robbers" in Mark 11:17b and parallel similarly reapplies an Old Testament prophet's label for corrupt leaders in his day (Jer. 7:11) to an analogous situation in Jesus' time. In this instance, however, Jesus' quotation comes right after one from Isaiah 56:7 that already had appeared in a more eschatological context in the Tanakh. That the temple was to become a house of prayer for all nations (Mark 11:17a par.) was implicit in the presence of a "Court of the Gentiles" from the beginning, but it would take on added significance in the messianic age when the nations would stream to Jerusalem in unprecedented numbers to worship her God. Still, all of these appeals to a scriptural authority fell well within the range of what was acceptable in early-first-century Palestinian Judaism.[46]

The same is certainly true of Jesus' appeal to Psalm 110:1 to silence his critics during his final public appearance in the temple (Mark 12:35-37 pars.). Given their shared conviction that David authored the psalm, Jesus' logic proved irrefutable. Only one "Lord" above the king could be God, so who was this other one of whom David declared, "The Lord said to my lord . . ."? If one answered the Messiah ("David's son" — v. 35), then this "lord" could not be a merely human descendant of King David, the purely political and military ruler to overthrow the Romans for whom so many longed. He had to be more exalted still. Little wonder that the Matthean parallel adds at the end that "no one could say a word in reply, and from that day on no one dared to ask him any more questions" (Matt. 22:46)![47] Because Jesus' language was ambiguous enough, though, to make it possibly sound as if he

43. Particularly as the Exodus became a model for later prophecies, especially in Isaiah. See Rikki E. Watts, *Isaiah's New Exodus in Mark* (Tübingen: Mohr, 1997; Grand Rapids: Baker, 2000); and David W. Pao, *Acts and the Isaianic New Exodus* (Tübingen: Mohr Siebeck, 2000; Grand Rapids: Baker, 2002).

44. On which, see especially Craig A. Evans, *To See and Not Perceive: Isaiah 6.9-10 in Early Jewish and Christian Interpretation* (Sheffield: JSOT, 1989). Later attempts to tone down the perceived predestinarian emphasis of Mark's version support the authenticity of the quotation by the criterion of embarrassment.

45. The authenticity of this logion is supported by its consistency with intra-Jewish polemic of the time, more similar to the Targum on Isaiah than to the early church, yet reflecting a distinctive, controversial perspective on purity within Judaism. See Thomas R. Hatina, "Did Jesus Quote Isaiah 29:13 against the Pharisees? An Unpopular Appraisal," *BBR* 16 (2006): 79-94.

46. See especially Klyne R. Snodgrass, "The Temple Incident," in Bock and Webb, eds., *Key Events in the Life of the Historical Jesus,* 429-80. Cf. Barry D. Smith, "Objections to the Authenticity of Mark 11:17 Reconsidered," *WTJ* 54 (1992): 255-71.

47. On the use of Psalm 110 here and throughout the New Testament, see especially Martin Hengel, *Studies in Early Christology* (Edinburgh: T. & T. Clark, 1995), 119-225.

was questioning Davidic descent of the Messiah altogether, it is not likely that it was invented by an early Christian.[48]

Other uses of the Hebrew Scriptures by Jesus fully consistent with standard Jewish approaches of his day may be summarized more briefly. Frequently, he referred to narrative material and events in the life of key Old Testament characters to justify his teaching or his behavior. He obviously knew that he and his listeners shared the convictions that these things really happened and were recorded as authoritative illustrations of good and bad behavior for subsequent generations. Thus he speaks of those who in past eras persecuted the prophets (Matt. 5:12 par.). He refers to Tyre, Sidon, and Sodom as paradigms of evil cities of old (11:21-24 par.). He believes that Jonah survived the belly of the great fish and that Nineveh subsequently repented at Jonah's preaching, and he affirms that there was a Queen of Sheba who visited Solomon (12:40-42 par.). He highlights the days of Noah and later of Lot and the catastrophes that occurred during their lives (24:37-39 par.). He recalls the time of Elijah and Elisha and their experiences with the widow and with Naaman, respectively (Luke 4:25-27). He assumes that Moses indeed erected a bronze serpent in the desert (John 3:14) and that God provided manna for the Israelites during that same period of wilderness wanderings (6:32, 49, 58). Finally, in his sweeping pronouncement that his generation will bear the judgment for "all the righteous blood that has been shed on earth, from the blood of righteous Abel to the blood of Zechariah son of Berekiah" (Matt. 23:35; cf. Luke 11:50-51), he presupposes the historical veracity of a huge swath of Old Testament narratives, from beginning to end, either chronologically or canonically (depending on which Zechariah is in view[49]).

Wenham provides a full list of such references and then correctly observes that, while some of them could refer to characters, whether real or fictitious, in well-known literature, the contexts of many of the references require the historicity of the characters and the actions attributed to them.[50] To take just the final example, it would make no sense at all to condemn the Jewish leaders in Jesus' day as being in solidarity with those forefathers who had similarly martyred God's spokesmen unless those people had actually lived and been executed as the Old Testament narratives depict.[51]

48. Keener, *Historical Jesus of the Gospels,* 270.

49. For the full range of interpretive options, see Robert H. Gundry, *The Use of the Old Testament in St. Matthew's Gospel* (Leiden: Brill, 1967), 86-88.

50. Wenham, *Christ and the Bible,* 12-16.

51. The extent of Jesus' conflict with Jewish leaders has, of course, been debated, and Matthew 23 has often been seen as an unhistorical zenith of anti-Semitism on Matthew's part. But only those Jews who rejected Jesus come in for criticism, so this cannot be anti-Semitism in the normal sense of the expression as prejudice or hostility against an entire people group. For the authenticity of this material, see further Keener, *Historical Jesus of the Gospels,* 223-37, especially 235-36.

In still other instances, Jesus employs Scripture to convict his interlocutors of faulty theology or behavior in ways that might have incensed them, but again by means of an impeccable hermeneutic with which his critics could not have justifiably found fault. The clearest examples, in passages not yet discussed, appear in John 7–8 in Jesus' teaching in Jerusalem during Tabernacles. Here Christ begins from the common ground of the Mosaic, and therefore binding, origin of Torah to charge even the most pious of Jewish leaders with not entirely keeping it (7:19).[52] He appeals to a hierarchical ranking of Scripture's laws, already a common Jewish practice,[53] in this case to the custom of permitting circumcision on a Sabbath if it fell on the eighth day of the baby boy's life, in order to justify his own practice of healing on the Sabbath (7:23). He summarizes a key scriptural theme in 7:38 as "rivers of living water" flowing from the believer (or possibly from Jesus himself).[54] And he utilizes Deuteronomy 19:15 again to argue that both the Father and he provide the necessary two or three witnesses to testify to his identity (8:17-18).[55]

Finally, there are occasions on which Jesus takes still unfulfilled prophecy as a true, authoritative account of what must yet happen, just as his contemporaries would have. There will still come an "abomination that causes desolation standing where it does not belong" (Mark 13:14) — a sacrilege of the temple in Jerusalem (cf. Matt. 24:15; Luke 21:20) reenacting the horrors of Daniel 9:27, 11:31, and 12:11. He applies the apocalyptic language of Hosea 10:8 to that future day when people will cry out to the mountains to fall on them and kill them, ending their

52. For the authenticity of the various Johannine texts cited in this chapter, see the relevant sections of Craig L. Blomberg, *The Historical Reliability of John's Gospel: Issues and Commentary* (Leicester and Downers Grove, IL: InterVarsity, 2001), and the literature there cited. Further supporting their authenticity is the observation of Judith Lieu ("Narrative Analysis and Scripture in John," in *The Old Testament in the New Testament,* ed. Steve Moyise [Sheffield: Sheffield Academic Press, 2000], 160) that although John's portrait of Jesus highlights his roles in fulfilling Scriptures Christologically, the actual citations of Scripture attributed to Jesus in the Fourth Gospel do not highlight these roles. They are thus unlikely to be attributable to Johannine redaction. Or, as Johannes Beutler ("The Use of 'Scripture' in the Gospel of John," in *Exploring the Gospel of John,* ed. R. Alan Culpepper and C. Clifton Black [Louisville: Westminster John Knox, 1996], 158) summarizes, "[T]he author seems to be more interested in the fact of the witness of scripture to Jesus than in the details of it."

53. Craig S. Keener (*The Gospel of Matthew: A Socio-Rhetorical Commentary* [Grand Rapids and Cambridge: Eerdmans, 2009], 551) lists as examples m. Abot 2:1 and 4:2, Sifra V. D. Deho. par. 1.34.1.3 and par. 12.65.1.3, and ARN 1 and 8B.

54. Both the punctuation (and therefore the translation) and the Old Testament text or texts in view are disputed. See Andreas Köstenberger, *John* (Grand Rapids: Baker, 2004), 240-41 and nn. 56-58.

55. A law likewise appealed to in 11QT 61.6-7, 64:8; CD 9.3-4, 17-23; Jos. *Ant.* 4.219; and Test. Abr. 13:8A. See Craig S. Keener, *The Gospel of John: A Commentary,* vol. 1 (Peabody, MA: Hendrickson, 2003), 740 n. 356.

misery from the tribulation in this world (Luke 23:30). He exploits the imagery of Isaiah 13:10 and 34:4 to depict the cosmic upheavals accompanying his return (Mark 13:14 par.).[56] And he looks forward to a coming eschatological banquet for God's people from all of the nations (Matt. 8:11-12 par.; cf. Isa. 25:6-8).[57] In all these ways, then, Jesus of Nazareth's use of the Old Testament stood in clear continuity with the Judaism of his day.

Discontinuity with Judaism

More remembered in many Christian circles over the years, however, have been the ways in which Jesus differed from his religion's and culture's conventional attitudes toward Scripture. If much of the history of the church has overestimated these differences, often leading to various degrees of anti-Semitism, many scholarly circles today have underestimated them, even while rightly emphasizing that Jesus would have identified himself throughout his life as a Jew and that he scarcely intended to found an entirely new religion.

The programmatic passage for understanding Jesus' overall view of the Old Testament is Matthew 5:17-20. Correct exegesis of this thesis paragraph of the Sermon on the Mount proves crucial in capturing the balance between similarities and differences with other forms of Judaism among Jesus' contemporaries. On the one hand, Jesus begins by disabusing his listeners of any notion that he has come to do away with (*katalysai*) any part of the Hebrew Scriptures ("the Law or the Prophets" — v. 17a). He goes on to insist emphatically that before this current universe is dissolved not the smallest part of any letter of any word written in the Bible will disappear (v. 18), and that any of his followers who set aside (*lysē*) the least of Torah's commandments will be called least in God's reign (v. 19).[58]

All of this, nevertheless, stops well short of demonstrating that Jesus thought that the *implementation* of the Law remained unchanged by his coming. He pronounced the forgiveness of sins on individuals apart from their offering animal sacrifices in the temple (Mark 2:5 pars.; note the reaction elicited in vv. 6-7 pars.).[59] As we will see below, he set the precedent for understanding all foods to now

56. For the authenticity and probable reconstruction of Jesus' original Olivet Discourse, see David Wenham, *The Rediscovery of Jesus' Eschatological Discourse* (Sheffield: JSOT, 1984; Eugene, OR: Wipf & Stock, 2003).

57. Contra the view that any or all of these references refer merely to socio-political upheavals in the near future, see Dale C. Allison Jr., "Jesus and the Victory of Apocalyptic," in *Jesus and the Restoration of Israel,* ed. Carey C. Newman (Downers Grove, IL: InterVarsity; Carlisle: Paternoster, 1999), 126-41.

58. A reference probably to how God looks on them now in the already-realized portion of God's kingdom. See Herman N. Ridderbos, *Matthew* (Grand Rapids: Zondervan, 1987), 101.

59. Wright, *Jesus and the Victory of God,* 271-72.

be kosher. He announced the imminent arrival of an era in which the land of Israel would no longer be uniquely holy and thus the ideal place for worshiping God (John 4:21-23).[60] He challenged Sabbath laws in ways that went beyond just charging the religious leaders of his day with too stringent *halakah* (see below).[61] It is thereby significant that, after declaring he has not come to abolish Torah, Christ does not state that he has come to preserve it unchanged. Rather, he speaks of fulfilling it (v. 17b), the same verb already used six times in Matthew (*plēroō*; 1:22; 2:15, 17, 23; 3:15; 4:14) for the occurrence of an event to which Scripture, either literally or typologically, had pointed.[62] This meshes perfectly with the temporal clause in verse 18, "until everything is accomplished." Everything needed to atone fully for the sins of humanity was accomplished through Christ's cross-work, so that, while the sacrificial laws of Leviticus remain part of inspired Scripture for believers, they are not to be literally obeyed, even if an actual temple in Jerusalem were again erected.[63] The time for separating Israel off from the nations in a variety of ritual or ceremonial contexts has likewise passed; Jesus goes out of his way to welcome "sinners" of many kinds, including gentiles, into fellowship with him apart from Torah regulations (see, most dramatically, Matt. 8:5-13 par.).[64]

Clearly, if one did not accept Jesus' frequently implicit and occasionally explicit claims to divine messiahship, such "alterations" to the Law would have been outrageously unacceptable. Here, then, is where we see the most striking discontinuity between Jesus' views on the Old Testament and the rest of early

60. Joseph H. Hellerman, *Jesus and the People of God: Reconfiguring Ethnic Identity* (Sheffield: Sheffield Phoenix Press, 2007), 188-202.

61. Werner Kahl, "Ist es erlaubt, am Sabbat Leben zu retten oder zu toten? (Marc. 3.4): Lebensbewahrung am Sabbat im Kontext der Schriften vom Toten Meer und der Mischna," *NovT* 40 (1998): 313-35.

62. Cf. H. Hübner, "πληρόω, ἀναπληρόω," in *Exegetical Dictionary of the New Testament,* ed. Horst Balz and Gerhard Schneider, vol. 3 (Grand Rapids: Eerdmans, 1993), 108-10. Hübner's definitions are "fill completely, fulfill, bring to completion, realize" (108). Knowles ("Scripture, History, Messiah," 72) observes that Mark 14:49 precludes this language being attributable merely to Matthew or even Markan redaction that Matthew picked up.

63. Cf. especially D. A. Carson, "Matthew," in *Expositor's Bible Commentary,* rev. edition, ed. Tremper Longman III and David E. Garland, vol. 9 (Grand Rapids: Zondervan, 2010), 171-80.

64. A slightly different route to the same end point is found in Donald A. Hagner, *Matthew 1-13,* WBC (Dallas: Word, 1993), 108: "The law as interpreted by Jesus remains valid until all the events between the present and the full enjoyment of the eschatological era have occurred. This is fully in keeping with the Jewish and rabbinic view of Torah (see Str-B 1.245-6, and cf. Bar. 4:1; 4 Ezra 9:37). But again, as we have said, this is the law as understood in the context of the fulfillment of God's purposes announced by Jesus (hence the law *and* the prophets). For Jesus is the goal of the law and prophets, the bringer of the kingdom, and hence the final interpreter of the law's meaning. The law as *he* teaches it is valid for all time, and thus in effect the law is upheld."

first-century Judaism.[65] Not surprisingly, Matthew 5:17-20 is followed immediately by the famous "antitheses" — pronouncements of Jesus that contrast what his listeners have heard about Torah with what he declares to them about it (vv. 21-48). It has often been observed that the final antithesis begins with the one reference to Scripture out of the six that does not actually quote Torah but only a misunderstanding of it ("You have heard that it was said, 'Love your neighbor and hate your enemy'" — v. 43). As a result, commentators regularly conclude that Jesus never challenges the written law, only various (uninspired) oral interpretations of it.[66] In fact, Jesus' prohibitions of anger, lust, and divorce (vv. 22, 28, and 32) *intensify* the commands with which they are compared (murder, adultery, and providing a wife with a certificate to divorce her). Yet, whereas the Old Testament *commands* the fulfillment of vows and the *lex talionis,* Jesus forbids oaths and retaliation (vv. 33-42). Here he *is* changing prescriptive legislation from the written Torah itself. It is better, therefore, to recognize Jesus' role with Scripture as being its sovereign interpreter, rather than making sweeping generalizations about *either* his changing the Law *or* his leaving it unchanged. Each category or topic will have to be examined on a case-by-case basis.[67]

Luke 16:16-18 contains parallels to teachings of Jesus that appear in three separate contexts in Matthew and/or Mark. Verse 16 marks a similar shift from the age of "the Law and the Prophets" (including John the Baptist) to the time during which "the good news of the kingdom of God is being preached" (cf. Matt. 11:12-13).[68] Yet,

65. Ironically, it is not a point to which Messianic Jews should object, given their acceptance of Jesus as Messiah. Still, a growing number appear to be returning to the view that the Law still remains in force for Jewish believers, apart from Jesus' reinterpretations, and even as mediated by later rabbinic practice. See especially Mark S. Kinzer, *Post-Missionary Messianic Judaism: Redefining Christian Engagement with the Jewish People* (Grand Rapids: Brazos, 2005); contra which, see Craig L. Blomberg, "Freedom from the Law Only for Gentiles? A Non-Supersessionist Alternative to Mark Kinzer's 'Postmissionary Messianic Judaism,'" in *New Testament Theology in the Light of the Church's Mission: Essays in Honor of I. Howard Marshall,* ed. Grant R. Osborne, Ray van Neste, and Jon Laansma (Colorado Springs: Paternoster; Eugene, OR: Wipf & Stock, 2011), 41-56.

66. On Jesus' reputation as antinomian in his original context, see especially Michael F. Bird, "Jesus as Law-Breaker," in *Who Do My Opponents Say That I Am? An Investigation of the Accusations against Jesus,* ed. Scot McKnight and Joseph B. Modica (London and New York: T. & T. Clark, 2008), 3-26.

67. See especially Douglas J. Moo, "Jesus and the Authority of the Mosaic Law," *JSNT* 20 (1984): 3-49; cf. also Francois P. Viljoen, "Jesus' Teaching on the *Torah* in the Sermon on the Mount," *Neot* 40 (2006): 135-55; Donald A. Hagner, "Balancing the Old and the New: The Law of Moses in Matthew and Paul," *Int* 51 (1997): 20-30; and Samuel Byrskog, "Matthew 5:17-18 in the Argumentation of the Context," *RB* 104 (1997): 557-71.

68. D. A. Carson, "Do the Prophets and the Law Quit Prophesying Before John? A Note on Matthew 11.13," in *The Gospels and the Scriptures of Israel,* ed. Craig A. Evans and W. Richard Stegner (Sheffield: Sheffield Academic Press, 1994), 179-94.

lest people think that Christ is affirming no continuity between the ages, he again is adamant that it is easier for the universe to dissolve "than for the least stroke of a pen to drop out of the Law" (v. 17; cf. Matt. 5:18). The final verse in this triad is most puzzling of all in this context, as it reaffirms that those who wrongly divorce and remarry commit adultery (v. 18; cf. Mark 10:11 pars.). Is this commandment chosen to illustrate the point Jesus has just made about the permanence of the Law? Is it a short allegory likening someone who would abandon the Law altogether for something else to a man divorcing his wife and remarrying another woman? Or do these three Lukan verses actually introduce the subsequent parable of the rich man and Lazarus, which concludes with a reminder that the rich man who died and departed to Hades could have had a different fate had he listened to "Moses and the Prophets" (Luke 16:29)? Perhaps chapter 16 is more tightly connected than many realize, with both verses 16-18 and the parable that follows still jabbing at the Pharisees "who loved money" and had sneered at Jesus (v. 14) after he narrated the parable of the unjust steward (vv. 1-13). Perhaps *they* were the ones who had departed from the Law and the Prophets, allegorically divorcing that to which they should have been loyal.[69] In any case, Luke 16, including verses 16-18, discloses noticeably more discontinuity than continuity with the Jewish status quo.[70]

Christ's interaction with the leper he had just healed (Mark 1:44b pars.) has often been taken as an illustration of how he was concerned still to obey the ritual law: "Go, show yourself to the priest and offer the sacrifices that Moses commanded for your cleansing, as a testimony to them." But as a testimony to what? To Jesus' and/or the man's obedience to Torah? To the man's physical health? Or, as consistently elsewhere with Jesus' miracles, is the testimony Christological — letting the religious establishment see his power to make one ritually as well as physically whole apart from the divinely ordained priestly system? Every other use of *eis martyrion* plus the dative in the New Testament carries this Christological sense in context (Matt. 10:18, 24:14; Mark 13:9; Luke 21:13; Heb. 3:5), at times shading over even to a dative of disadvantage ("as a testimony *against*" someone — Mark 6:11; Luke 9:5; James 5:3). So perhaps that

69. For "parabolic" approaches, see John J. Kilgallen, "The Purpose of Luke's Divorce Text (16,18)," *Bib* 76 (1995): 229-38. The authenticity of these verses is seldom questioned, due both to multiple attestation and dissimilarity.

70. See Darrell L. Bock (*Luke 9:51–24:53,* BECNT [Grand Rapids: Baker, 1996], 1350-58) for the various options on each of these three verses (16:16-18). Bock rightly links them with verses 14-15 and concludes that Jesus "notes that the time of kingdom fulfillment has come with him. All that the law intended to accomplish in terms of God's plan will come to pass. He is the source of authority in terms of revealing the way to God, a major theme throughout Luke's journey section. Jesus' authoritative pronouncement prohibiting divorce is an illustration of that authority. It goes beyond the exception clause of Moses in its description of the perils of remarriage. It shows that righteousness hates divorce. Luke wishes the reader to see Jesus' identity as the authoritative messenger of God's kingdom" (1358-59).

is also the best understanding of this phrase in each of the Gospel accounts of this healing miracle.[71]

Only Matthew's Gospel adds Jesus' instruction, at the end of the passage on the call of Levi/Matthew, to "go and learn what this means: 'I desire mercy, not sacrifice'" (Matt. 9:13). As with the examples noted above in the section on continuity with Judaism, Jesus can take for granted that his critics share a high respect for Scripture. They will recognize the quotation and acknowledge its truthfulness and authority over them. But in this context, it functions more radically than in the Old Testament. Never in the Hebrew Scriptures did statements like these (Hos. 6:6; cf. 1 Sam. 15:22; Isa. 1:11) suggest that the sacrificial system had been superseded. "A, not B" meant "A much more than B."[72] Now, however, as Jesus accepts notorious sinners as followers (v. 9; cf. Mark 2:15b) without any hint of their undergoing the prescribed rituals that accompanied repentance, he is highlighting the discontinuity of his ministry with conventional Jewish thought and practice.[73]

Matthew distinctively adds the Hosea 6:6 excerpt again in his account of Jesus' disciples plucking heads of grain to eat on a certain Sabbath (Matt. 12:7).[74] Again, too, it is in the context of a disparaging statement about his critics' failure to understand Scripture's authoritative words ("if you had known what these words mean . . . you would not have condemned the innocent"). As in the Sermon on the Mount, Jesus goes well beyond just a new interpretation of the Scripture to view himself as Lord even over the Sabbath (v. 8). What he decides to do on this holy day can never be wrong because he speaks with a greater authority than the Law. Indeed, he is greater than the temple (v. 6), the officiants in which had Torah-given permission to break the Sabbath in order to work so that God's people could worship (v. 5). By *a fortiori* logic, Jesus has even more unequivocal permission to violate the Sabbath! Little wonder that a subsequent Sabbath-infringement (vv. 9-13) would lead to one of the Pharisaic plots to kill him (v. 14), especially after he announced that it was lawful to do any kind of good deed on

71. R. T. France, *The Gospel of Mark,* NIGTC (Carlisle: Paternoster; Grand Rapids: Eerdmans, 2002), 120. Cf. especially Edwin K. Broadhead, "Mk 1,44: The Witness of the Leper," *ZNW* 83 (1992): 257-65. For the authenticity of the core of the narrative, see Robert L. Webb, "Jesus Heals a Leper: Mark 1.40-45 and *Egerton Gospel* 35-47," *JSHJ* 4 (2006): 177-202.

72. Cf. Duane A. Garrett, *Hosea, Joel,* New American Commentary (Nashville: Broadman & Holman, 1997), 161; and David T. Tsumura, *The First Book of Samuel,* NICOT (Grand Rapids and Cambridge: Eerdmans, 2007), 401.

73. Evert-Jan Vledder (*Conflict in the Miracle Stories: A Socio-Exegetical Study of Matthew 8 and 9* [Sheffield: Sheffield Academic Press, 1997], 209) calls Matthew 9:13 the "strongest ideological legitimization of [Jesus'] position. . . . Jesus 'caught' [the Pharisees] out on their own value system" — i.e., "scripturally ordained mercy."

74. On the use of this verse in Matthew, see especially David Hill, "On the Use and Meaning of Hosea VI.6 in Matthew's Gospel," *NTS* 24 (1977-78): 107-19.

the Sabbath. Disagreements just about *halakah* would never have spawned so severe a response.[75] Even on the shorter, possibly earlier Markan parallel (Mark 3:1-6), R. T. France observes, "While few could object in theory to the notion that the Sabbath exists to benefit people (after all, it is repeatedly declared to be a day of joy) and is a time for 'doing good,' to make such broad principles the basis for the decision on what is and is not permissible is to threaten to overturn the whole halakhic process."[76]

A radical Jesus reappears with his typological application of the prophecy about Elijah as the forerunner of the Day of the Lord (Mal. 3:1; cf. 4:5) to John the Baptist (Matt. 11:10 par.). Apparently, the dominant view in Judaism was that Elijah would literally return from heaven, so that Jesus could expect objections to his application of the passage to anyone else. Thus he prefaces his identification with the condition, "if you are willing to accept it" (v. 14) and recognizes that only those with "ears" to "hear" will agree with him (v. 15).[77] The little parable of the householder in Matthew 13:52 seems to reflect the combination of old and new, of traditional and radical, which we have seen in these last several passages. The properly instructed Christian "scribe" resembles "the owner of a house who brings out of his storeroom new treasures as well as old." Most likely, the "old" is the Mosaic covenant, the Hebrew Scriptures and/or the "old age" as over against the good news of the kingdom and the new age and covenant that it ushers in, with respect to both their continuities and their discontinuities with the past.[78]

Sometimes those continuities can remain formally unchallenged, yet the Law is fulfilled and interpreted so unconventionally that the stress remains on the newness of the era Jesus is inaugurating. The delightful little account of the coin in the fish's mouth demonstrates that Jesus does indeed pay the temple tax, commanded in Exodus 30:13 (Matt. 17:24-27). But the method of acquiring the money to pay it shows that Jesus will not take funds from his normal sources of income. His comment that a king's children are exempt from taxation (v. 26), moreover,

75. On the authenticity and rationale of the Synoptic accounts of Jesus' conflicts with the Pharisees over the Sabbath, see especially Keener, *Historical Jesus of the Gospels*, 228-32.

76. France, *Mark*, 144. Cf. Mary A. Tolbert, "Is It Lawful on the Sabbath to Do Good or to Do Harm: Mark's Ethics of Religious Practice," *PRS* 23 (1996): 209: "[T]he conclusion of this story is quite radical. While it clearly endorses Jesus' ultimate authority over religious practice and law, it also asserts the priority of the exigencies of human existence over any religious ruler, even those of the Ten Commandments." Indeed, Jesus' interpretation on doing good "would threaten to undercut the entire legal system" (210).

77. Cf. further Craig L. Blomberg, "Elijah, Election, and the Use of Malachi in the New Testament," *CTR* 2 (1987): especially 102-5. On the authenticity of this conception of John the Baptist, see Keener, *Historical Jesus of the Gospels*, 170-71.

78. Cf. especially Ulrich Luz, *Matthew 8–20*, Hermeneia (Minneapolis: Fortress, 2001), 287-88. See also B. J. Syiemlieh, "Portrait of a Christian Scribe (Matthew 13:52)," *AJT* 20 (2006): 57-66.

suggests that God's children should not have to pay this levy, thus challenging head-on the abiding validity of a commandment from the written Torah.[79]

Sometimes the discontinuities can involve a return to the even more distant past. In his entry into Pharisaic frays about divorce, Jesus declares the Mosaic Law to have made temporary concessions to people's hard-heartedness (Mark 10:1-12 pars.). With the arrival of the kingdom age, however, this excuse for divorce may no longer be used. Christ's followers must return to first principles, to what have often been called creation ordinances — the way God established matters before the Fall: heterosexual monogamous marriage for life (v. 8; cf. Gen. 2:24).[80] For most Jews, however, the Law had become so immutable in their minds that even a change based on (earlier) Scripture itself could prove scandalous — even if logically irrefutable.[81]

Typological interpretations of Scripture, in some instances, can prove so "creative" that, even if the method itself is deeply rooted in Judaism, its specific application deserves to be listed under discontinuities rather than continuities. Perhaps no passage in the Gospels illustrates this better than Mark 14:27 and parallel ("I will strike the shepherd, and the sheep will be scattered"). Here Jesus more or less quotes Zechariah 13:7, which originally formed a command by God to "strike the shepherd, and the sheep will be scattered." In context, Zechariah was prophesying the destruction of the evil political and religious rulers of Israel in his day (note the plural in the LXX), so the change to a future indicative tense causes little surprise. But Jesus sees the pattern about to be reenacted in his own crucifixion and uses the quotation as an opportunity to once again affirm his subsequent resurrection (Mark 14:28). Those who put him to death obviously thought him to be wicked, too, while Jesus understood himself to be the messianic shepherd. But who else in his world would have made such an otherwise convoluted Christological application?[82] Perhaps it is the kind of hermeneutic

79. See Donald A. Hagner, *Matthew 14–28,* WBC (Dallas: Word, 1995), 512: "The disciples of Jesus are thus not obligated to pay taxes to their Father (cf., e.g., 5:16, 48; 6:1; 23:9). The implied conclusion is that they are free from the burden of the temple tax. Here again the surprising authority of Jesus over the commandment of Torah (Exod 20:13-14) is evident." Cf. further Rob Haskell, "Matthew 17:24-27: A Religio-Political Reading," *ERT* 32 (2008): 173-84.

80. See further Craig L. Blomberg, "Marriage, Divorce, Remarriage and Celibacy: An Exegesis of Matthew 19:3-12," *TrinJ* 11 (1990): 161-96.

81. Similarly A. E. Harvey, "Genesis versus Deuteronomy? Jesus on Marriage and Divorce," in Evans and Stegner, eds., *Gospels and the Scriptures of Israel,* 55-65. For authenticity, see Keener, *Historical Jesus of the Gospels,* 217.

82. Zechariah 13:7 appears in only one demonstrably pre-Christian source (CD-B 19:7-11), where it may be messianic or it may refer to the Teacher of Righteousness at Qumran. The post-Christian Targum to this verse interprets the figure as Davidic but as an enemy of God. Not until the Talmud does it appear in an unambiguously messianic context (b. Sukk. 52a). On the likelihood of Jesus having reflected scripturally on the meaning of his impending death and having uttered something like Mark 14:27, *ad hoc,* "in the press of the moment," see Craig A. Evans,

applied here that inspired the Evangelists, especially Matthew, to see similar fulfillments of Scripture in other unlikely circumstances of Christ's life and of the lives of those characters who intersected with him (see esp. Matt. 2:15, 18; 4:15-16; 8:17; 12:18-21; 13:35; 27:9-10; and John 12:38; 19:14, 28, 36-37).[83] The Fourth Gospel likewise contains texts in which such declarations about the fulfillment of Scripture are attributed to Jesus himself (John 13:18; 15:25; 17:12).[84]

A key passage, which on the one hand is regularly and rightly cited to prove Jesus' high view of the Old Testament in its entirety, on the other hand again involves some of his most creative exegesis. In John 10:34-35, Christ uses an *a fortiori* argument to ask the rhetorical question, if Scripture can call its human audience "gods" (Ps. 82:6, probably referring to the judges and rulers in Israel), why cannot he call himself God's Son, even in an exalted sense?[85] Tucked into this question is the aside, "and (the) Scripture cannot be broken" (John 10:35).[86] Translators since the appearance of the KJV seem locked into this rendering (so also HCSB, ESV, NASB, NET, NIV, NKJV, RSV), although it is hard to imagine what breaking Scripture in modern English could mean other than disobeying a commandment (or tearing a scroll?). Versions that read "set aside" (NAB, NJB, TNIV), "annulled" (NRSV), or "altered" (NLT) all seem preferable, but the Greek verb is *lyō*, the root of *katalyō*, often rendered "abolish" in Matthew 5:17.[87] The idea of doing away with Scripture so that it no longer has *any* application

"Zechariah in the Markan Passion Narrative," in *Biblical Interpretation in Early Christian Gospels,* vol. 1, ed. Thomas R. Hatina (London and New York: T. & T. Clark, 2006), 77-78.

83. Douglas J. Moo, *The Old Testament in the Gospel Passion Narratives* (Sheffield: Almond, 1983), 223-24, 275. See further Craig L. Blomberg, "Interpreting Old Testament Prophetic Literature in Matthew: Double Fulfillment," *TrinJ* 23 (2002): 17-33.

84. On which, see Fredrick C. Holmgren, *The Old Testament and the Significance of Jesus: Embracing Change — Maintaining Christian Identity* (Grand Rapids and Cambridge: Eerdmans, 1999), 45-46; and Herman N. Ridderbos, *The Gospel according to John: A Theological Commentary* (Grand Rapids: Eerdmans, 1997), 525.

85. For details, see especially D. A. Carson, *The Gospel according to John,* PNTC (Leicester: InterVarsity; Grand Rapids: Eerdmans, 1991), 397-99. Cf. also Carl Mosser, "The Earliest Patristic Interpretations of Psalm 82: Jewish Antecedents and the Origin of Christian Deification," *JTS* 56 (2005): 30-74.

86. Jaime Clark Soles (*Scripture Cannot Be Broken: The Social Function of the Use of Scripture in the Fourth Gospel* [Leiden and Boston: Brill, 2003], 260-61) argues that this is not an aside but the second protasis of the conditional sentence. Even if this should be the case, the first-class conditional force with which the sentence begins would presumably carry over to this second, elliptically introduced condition. Given the certainty with which Jesus would have viewed his affirmation of Psalm 82 calling its addressees "gods," we may safely assume that he was affirming with equal certainty that Scripture could not be broken.

87. Or, as E. Earle Ellis (*The Old Testament in Early Christianity: Canon and Interpretation in the Light of Modern Research* [Tübingen: Mohr, 1991; Grand Rapids: Baker, 1992], 129) puts it, linking these two texts as well, "the Scripture cannot be broken of its force."

likewise seems to be what the context in John 10 shows Jesus rejecting. But, again, that does not mean that the Old Testament applies in every instance in the *same* way in the new covenant that Jesus is enacting as it did during the period of the Mosaic covenant. What is often lost sight of in debates over bibliology is the remarkably creative and unprecedented use to which Jesus himself puts this Old Testament passage.[88]

The Christology of John 10:34-35 is indirect, as we have seen, via a "from the lesser to the greater" method of argumentation. In a variety of contexts, Jesus' Old Testament hermeneutic becomes more directly Christological. Programmatic for the full scope of his ministry is his inaugural sermon in the Nazareth synagogue (Luke 4:16-21). How directly or typologically one understands Jesus' claims to be fulfilling Isaiah 61:1-2a in his congregation's hearing depends on one's exegesis of Isaiah.[89] But in either event Jesus takes the text messianically and as being fulfilled in his ministry of "proclaiming good news to the poor . . . freedom for the prisoners, recovery of sight to the blind, [setting] the oppressed free, [and proclaiming] the year of the Lord's favor" (Luke 4:18-19). There is a Christological self-awareness in Jesus right from the outset of his public ministry.[90]

This approach culminates, after his death and resurrection, in Jesus' declaration in Luke 24:44 that "everything must be fulfilled that is written about me in the Law of Moses, the Prophets and the Psalms." Here is the one New Testament text that references all three parts of the Hebrew canon, with Psalms as a synecdoche for the Writings more generally.[91] Notice that Christ does not say that *all*

88. Or to state it conversely, Jesus argues that his very provocative self-identification is sanctioned by God's still-authoritative word. As A. T. Lincoln (*The Gospel according to Saint John* [London: Continuum; Peabody, MA: Hendrickson, 2005], 308) phrases it, "If the lesser can be called 'gods,' then not only is it baseless to dispute the validity of the greater calling himself Son of God but this would also be to dispute Scripture itself."

89. For good representatives of the contrasting perspectives, see John N. Oswalt, *The Book of Isaiah: Chapters 40–66,* NICOT (Grand Rapids and Cambridge: Eerdmans, 1998), 562-63 (in favor of an original messianic identity of the servant); and Brevard S. Childs, *Isaiah,* Old Testament Library (Louisville: Westminster John Knox, 2001), 504-5 (not seeing the link as present originally).

90. Cf. especially Wright, *Jesus and the Victory of God,* 535-36. For a rich unpacking of the possible details of a messianic reading of Luke 4:16-31, see Kenneth E. Bailey, *Jesus through Middle Eastern Eyes: Cultural Studies in the Gospels* (Downers Grove, IL: InterVarsity, 2008), 147-69. On authenticity, cf. Charles A. Kimball, "Jesus' Exposition of Scripture in Luke 4:16-30: An Inquiry in Light of Jewish Hermeneutics," *PRS* 21 (1994): 179-202; with Michael Prior, *Jesus the Liberator* (Sheffield: Sheffield Academic Press, 1995), 101-25. See also Stanley E. Porter, "Scripture Justifies Mission: The Use of the Old Testament in Luke-Acts," in his *Hearing the Old Testament in the New Testament,* 116-17.

91. So, cautiously, F. F. Bruce, *The Canon of Scripture* (Downers Grove, IL: InterVarsity, 1988), 31-32. More confident is Roger T. Beckwith, *The Old Testament Canon of the New Testament Church* (Grand Rapids: Eerdmans, 1985), 111-12. Perhaps Luke highlighted the Psalms

of the Scriptures point to him, as some throughout church history have claimed. There is no Christological meaning inherent in every verse of Genesis through Malachi. But he does assume that there are large enough numbers of texts that permeate each of the three main divisions of the Tanakh so that he can speak of all of the portions of these divisions *which were written about him.*[92] Indeed, already in Luke 24:27, Luke tells us that "beginning with Moses and the Prophets, he explained to them what was said in all the Scriptures concerning himself." If that was the beginning of his undertaking, he presumably moved on to include the Writings, and the prolonged conversation he had with the two disciples on the road to Emmaus suggests that he found quite a few passages to expound.[93]

The data that could be surveyed in this section have still not all been displayed. There are numerous events in Jesus' ministry that appear to carry Christological freight, deliberately enacted in ways intended to recall key Old Testament prophecies and narratives (e.g., the feeding miracles to show Jesus as a new Moses providing bread in the wilderness, the walking on the water as a theophany using language from Exodus 3:6, the resurrection of the widow's son of Nain recapitulating the similar miracle performed by Elisha for the Shunammite widow, etc.).[94] There are other references to Old Testament characters that not only seem to presuppose those people's historical existence in previous eras but are also so creatively utilized that they highlight Jesus' divergence from standard forms of Judaism (e.g., the enigmatic reference to Abiathar in Mark 2:26 or Jesus' claim that "before Abraham was, I AM" in John 8:58). There are innumerable probable allusions to Old Testament texts in Jesus' teaching, in passages that we cannot with confidence label as direct quotations, which further demonstrate his breaks from convention (e.g., Mark 14:7 pars., alluding to Deut. 15:11 on the poor always being with us, or Mark 15:34 par., alluding to Ps. 22:1 with its cry of dereliction). Further catalogues would merely belabor this point that by now has been adequately illustrated.[95]

---

because the Davidic Messiah represented in many of them was a key Christological category for him. See especially Peter Doble, "Luke 24.26, 44 — Songs of God's Servant: David and His Psalms in Luke-Acts," *JSNT* 28 (2006): 267-83.

92. For some history of the practice and reasonably balanced guidance for the present, see Sidney Greidanus, *Preaching Christ from the Old Testament* (Grand Rapids and Cambridge: Eerdmans, 1999).

93. "The disciples do not need to see how Jesus' death can be read out of the Scriptures, but how to understand the Scriptures in light of Jesus' suffering, death and resurrection as Messiah and the necessity for these events to which the Scriptures point" (Kenneth D. Litwak, *Echoes of Scripture in Luke-Acts: Telling the History of God's People Intertextually* (London and New York: T. & T. Clark, 2005), 121.

94. For several of these, see Craig L. Blomberg, "The Miracles as Parables," in *Gospel Perspectives,* vol. 6, *The Miracles of Jesus,* ed. David Wenham and Craig Blomberg (Sheffield: JSOT, 1986; Eugene, OR: Wipf & Stock, 2003), 127-59.

95. The fullest catalogue, including New Testament references, is *Citations and Allusions to*

Continuity with Early Christianity

Jesus' creative applications of the Hebrew Scriptures, especially by way of typology, characterize numerous other New Testament authors' approaches.[96] As the Jewish roots of Christianity were increasingly lost sight of, as early as the mid-second century, not just typological but overtly allegorical interpretations of Old Testament texts became increasingly common. The most frequent form of allegorizing, moreover, was Christologizing.[97] The high view of the Hebrew canon also endured, to such an extent that the debates that arose concerning what Jewish books should be treated as authoritative, with rare exceptions, were about the additional apocryphal writings composed largely between the testaments. In other words, early Christianity and, eventually, emerging Catholicism were much more inclined to *increase* the number of works they deemed inspired and therefore authoritative than to *decrease* the number from those already accepted in mainstream Judaism.[98] Indeed, what sometimes commended these intertestamental works to early Christians was their perceived value, if interpreted allegorically, as pointers to the coming of the Christ![99] Even within the rest of the New Testament outside the Gospels, the frequent citation of Old Testament texts as inspired and authoritative makes this strand of our four-part criterion the least controversial and the one on which we scarcely need dwell any further.

Discontinuity with Early Christianity

It is usually assumed that the ways in which Jesus' attitude to the Old Testament differed from the religion that emerged from his followers mirror at least some

---

Jewish Scripture in Early Christian and Jewish Writings through 180 C.E., by Bradley H. McLean (Lewiston, NY, and Lampeter, Wales: Edwin Mellen, 1992).

96. Of many excellent works that could be listed, cf. Carson and Williamson, eds., *It Is Written;* Craig A. Evans and James A. Sanders, eds., *Early Christian Interpretation of the Scripture of Israel* (Sheffield: Sheffield Academic Press, 1997); Steven Moyise, *The Old Testament in the New: An Introduction* (New York and London: Continuum, 2001); Craig A. Evans, ed., *From Prophecy to Testament: The Function of the Old Testament in the New* (Peabody, MA: Hendrickson, 2004); and Porter, ed., *Hearing the Old Testament in the New Testament.*

97. For an excellent introduction to this earliest period of Christian interpretation, replete with excerpts from the primary literature, see D. H. Williams, *Tradition, Scripture, and Interpretation: A Sourcebook of the Ancient Church* (Grand Rapids: Baker, 2006).

98. For the extant lists of proposed Old Testament canons from the earliest centuries of Christian history, see Lee M. McDonald, "Lists and Catalogues of Old Testament Collections," in *The Canon Debate,* ed. Lee M. McDonald and James A. Sanders (Peabody, MA: Hendrickson, 2002), 585-88.

99. For examples, see William W. Klein, Craig L. Blomberg, and Robert L. Hubbard Jr., *Introduction to Biblical Interpretation,* rev. edition (Nashville: Nelson, 2004), 105.

of the ways in which Jesus remained thoroughly a Jew of his time. Undoubtedly, this is true, especially with respect to his *practice.* He tells the scribes and Pharisees that they should continue to tithe, even while much more greatly prizing justice, mercy, and faithfulness (Matt. 23:23 par.), whereas after Pentecost there is no indication of Christians tithing. Instead they are to give proportionate to their income, generously and sacrificially (see esp. 1 Cor. 16:1-4 and 2 Cor. 8–9), commands that cannot be satisfied by everyone adhering to one unvarying percentage.[100] He assumes that his followers will fast, but insists that they do so joyfully without outward signs of their practice (Matt. 6:16-18). But the only references to fasting in Acts through Revelation appear twice in contexts of choosing church leaders (Acts 13:2-3; 14:23).[101] Jesus himself dutifully went to Jerusalem at festival times, especially Passover (as John's Gospel particularly highlights), and celebrated along with his disciples, but little appears after Jesus' death and resurrection to suggest that his followers, even Jewish ones, felt any obligation to continue the practice. Luke tells of one occasion when Paul, during his travels, was eager to get to Jerusalem by Pentecost (Acts 20:16), but whether this was directly related to his desire to celebrate the festival is undetermined. Obviously, his travels kept him from most such festivals year by year. And where Paul speaks of Passover, he follows Jesus' lead of interpreting it in typological fashion and of viewing Christ himself as believers' Passover lamb (1 Cor. 5:7).[102] In short, the idea that a decisive shift in the ages had begun with Jesus' death, resurrection, and sending of the Spirit at Pentecost emerged early and influentially in the evolution of the Jesus movement.

At the same time, and more importantly, Jesus promoted radical practices that his followers often seemed slow to adopt. We have already mentioned several of the "badges of national righteousness"[103] that his Jewish contemporaries highly valued, so that he came into sharp conflict with them when he challenged their permanence (circumcision, temple cult). But neither could Jesus' followers often maintain his perspective consistently. His view of the land has been described as one of "Christifying" it, so that there no longer is any uniquely holy space in which Christians must worship (John 4:21-24). His meek followers inherit the entire earth (Matt. 5:5), as Jesus reapplies the psalmist's promise that the faithful

100. Cf. especially David A. Croteau, *You Mean I Don't Have to Tithe? A Deconstruction of Tithing and a Reconstruction of Post-Tithe Giving* (Eugene, OR: Pickwick, 2010).

101. See further Joseph F. Wimmer, *Fasting in the New Testament: A Study in Biblical Theology* (New York: Paulist, 1982).

102. See further Hellerman, *Jesus and the People of God,* 145-66.

103. To use the term made famous by James D. G. Dunn in his contributions to the "new perspectives" on Paul and on ancient Judaism. An excellent overview and key selections of these appear in his *The New Perspective on Paul,* rev. edition (Grand Rapids and Cambridge: Eerdmans, 2008).

Jew will inherit the land of Israel (Ps. 37:11).[104] His radical approach to the Sabbath, already introduced above, is consistent in passages we have not treated as well (see esp. Luke 13:10-17 and 14:1-6; John 5 and 9).[105] Jesus' views of Sabbath-keeping to this day seem incredible to some conservative Christians, especially Messianic Jews, and Torah-centric alternatives are regularly offered instead. Still, Sunday is not the Christian Sabbath (a day of rest) but the day Jesus' followers adopted for *worshiping* the Risen Lord. But the idea that one of the foundational Ten Commandments was now fulfilled in Jesus' offer of rest through the easy yoke and light burden he offered people (Matt. 11:28-30), so that they need not cease work on some one-day-in-seven cycle, was not one that lasted long in the history of the church. Neither is it a development that is widely understood today.[106]

Most dramatically of all, in a passage we have deliberately not yet introduced, Jesus set the precedent for declaring all foods clean, an explicit change of the Levitical dietary laws. In Mark 7:14-15 and parallel, Jesus calls everyone in the crowd listening to him to understand that "nothing outside you can defile you by going into you. Rather, it is what comes out of you that defiles you." Even if we allow for the wide range of metaphorical discourse that ancient Judaism labeled parabolic,[107] this principle seems so straightforward and non-metaphorical that we are surprised when the disciples ask him later to explain "this parable" (v. 17). But apparently the literal meaning was too shocking to enable the Twelve to take Jesus at his word. They perhaps surmised that there must have been some hidden, allegorical meaning. Jesus, however, rebukes them for their dullness and basically just repeats the statement, adding that food in particular cannot defile a person because it remains only temporarily in one's body and then passes out of one's system (vv. 18-19a). Parenthetically, Mark adds, "in saying this, Jesus declared all foods clean" (v. 19b).

104. See, classically, W. D. Davies, *The Gospel and the Land: Early Christianity and Jewish Territorial Doctrine* (Berkeley: University of California Press, 1974; Sheffield: Sheffield Academic Press, 1994). Cf. especially Karen J. Wenell, *Jesus and Land: Sacred and Social Space in Second Temple Judaism* (London and New York: T. & T. Clark, 2007).

105. See further Donald A. Hagner, "Jesus and the Synoptic Sabbath Controversies," in Bock and Webb, eds., *Key Events in the Life of the Historical Jesus,* 251-92. For the case against treating Luke 13:10-17 and 14:1-6 as doublets, see John J. Kilgallen, "The Obligation to Heal (Luke 13,10-17)," *Bib* 82 (2001): 402-9. On the Johannine passages, see especially Steven M. Bryan, "Power in the Pool: The Healing of the Man of Bethesda and Jesus' Violation of the Sabbath (Jn 5:1-18)," *TynB* 54 (2003): 7-22; and Urban C. von Wahlde, "The Pool of Siloam: The Importance of the New Discoveries for Our Understanding of Ritual Immersion in Late Second Temple Judaism and the Gospel of John," in *John, Jesus, and History,* vol. 2, ed. Paul N. Anderson, Felix Just, and Tom Thatcher (Atlanta: SBL, 2009), 155-73.

106. See further Craig L. Blomberg, "The Sabbath as Fulfilled in Christ," in *Perspectives on the Sabbath: Four Views,* ed. Chris Donato (Nashville: Broadman & Holman, 2011), 305-58. Cf. especially D. A. Carson, ed., *From Sabbath to Lord's Day* (Grand Rapids: Zondervan, 1982).

107. See Joachim Jeremias, *The Parables of Jesus,* rev. edition (London: SCM; Philadelphia: Westminster, 1972), 20.

Audiences from conservative Messianic Jews to mainstream Jewish scholars to liberal biblical critics cannot believe this statement. Some try retranslating it, so that it says something quite different; others simply reject Mark's interpretation. Still others narrow the application to the immediate context.[108] All three kinds of readers protest that if Jesus really meant something so sweeping, then the disciples uniformly misunderstood him, or at least failed to live out the implications of his teaching, until Peter's vision of unclean food which prepared him for his encounter with Cornelius, over a decade later (Acts 10). Now had Mark attributed to *Jesus* the words, "I thus declare all foods clean," this protest would prove legitimate. But all he does is explain for *his* readers, probably no earlier than the 60s, the significance that Christ's followers had come to attach to his "parable" and its explanation, no doubt in light of Peter's vision. In essence, Mark is claiming that Jesus set the stage for the post-resurrection understanding that part of the inauguration of his new covenant would involve the rescinding of the kosher laws.[109] Or, better put, believers would obey the Levitical demands for *ritual* purity by means of behavior that reflected *moral* purity. Either way, it was now permitted to eat pork, shrimp, lobster, and bats, though no one *had* to do so. The very fact that it took so long, however, and required so dramatic an event as Peter's vision for the disciples to grasp the full significance of the historical Jesus' earlier teaching demonstrates how unlikely it would have been for anyone other than Jesus to have invented such instruction.[110]

Conclusion

Still other texts in the Gospels could have been cited to illustrate most of the points under each of these four subheadings. The upshot of even just this much is that Jesus' teaching and behavior *vis-à-vis* the Hebrew Scriptures satisfies the delicate balances of double similarity and dissimilarity with both the Judaism of his day and with the Christianity that quickly developed after him, so that we

108. See, respectively, John Fischer, "Messianic Congregations Should Exist and Should Be Very Jewish," in *How Jewish Is Christianity? Two Views on the Messianic Movement,* ed. Louis Goldberg (Grand Rapids: Zondervan, 2003), 133; Yair Furstenberg, "Defilement Penetrating the Body: A New Understanding of Contamination in Mark 7.15," *NTS* 54 (2008): 176-200; and James Crossley, "Mark 7.1-23: Revisiting the Question of 'All Foods Clean,'" in Tait and Oakes, eds., *Torah in the New Testament,* 8-20.

109. See especially Christian Stettler, "Purity of Heart in Jesus' Teaching: Mark 7:14-23 par. as an Expression of Jesus' Basileia Ethics," *JTS* 55 (2004): 467-502; cf. also James D. G. Dunn, "Jesus and Purity: An Ongoing Debate," *NTS* 48 (2002): 449-87.

110. Cf. David J. Rudolph, "Jesus and the Food Laws: A Reassessment of Mark 7:19b," *EvQ* 74 (2002): 291-311; Robert H. Stein, *Mark,* BECNT (Grand Rapids: Baker, 2008), 345-46; and Adela Y. Collins, *Mark,* Hermeneia (Minneapolis: Fortress, 2007), 356.

may rest confident that we are dealing with authentic, bedrock historical-Jesus material here.[111] We have not established the authenticity of every passage cited. Applying the older, individual criteria of authenticity text-by-text would have necessitated an entire book rather than one modest chapter within a large book, though we have frequently referenced scholarship that has already done this for individual texts. As in Wenham's work, we must concede that not every passage has as much going for it, historically speaking, as some others do. But, rather than just referring to a pervasive attitude on the part of Jesus in the Gospels (satisfying the older criterion of multiple attestation), we have compartmentalized much of the relevant data in ways that provide even stronger support for including Jesus' view of the Old Testament as part of the database of what we can know with reasonable probability about the historical Jesus. It remains, then, to assess the significance of these conclusions for current bibliological debates.

Contemporary Significance for a Doctrine of Scripture

When it comes to the inspiration, truthfulness, authority, and relevance of the Bible of his world, Jesus could scarcely have held to higher views. The central theological and moral truths of Scripture — monotheism, the double love-commandment, the frequent rebellion of humanity (including God's own people), the promises of eschatological judgment and blessing beginning with a Messianic age of God's beneficent reign on earth through that Messiah — all proved central to Jesus' own thinking as well. He acknowledged Scripture's divine origin as God's word and words. He quoted from the Bible extensively and intensively. He affirmed the inviolability of its contents down to the smallest details. To whatever degree the contents of the Hebrew canon had solidified by his day, Jesus affirmed their unity but also their tripartite division. He interpreted the historical narratives in ways that suggest he believed that at least most (and probably all) of the events narrated really happened. He saw the collection of scriptural writings as open-ended, however, pointing forward to a time when God would fulfill his complete salvation-historical purposes for the ages. He believed that such an era had been inaugurated with his ministry. As a result, he mined the Scriptures for predictions and patterns that so closely paralleled events in and surrounding his

111. William Loader (*Jesus' Attitude towards the Law: A Study of the Gospels* [Tübingen: Mohr, 1997; Grand Rapids and Cambridge: Eerdmans, 2002], 523-24) nicely captures this diversity of approaches, even just with respect to the Law, in his summary: "A reconstruction of Jesus' attitude towards the Law needs then to take into account diverse strands of tradition: the radically humane Jesus; the culturally conservative Jesus; the theologically strict Jesus in issues of morality; the Jesus who is like popular Hellenistic preachers, Jewish and non-Jewish; the Jesus who gives priority to ethical behaviours and attitudes above ritual and cultic law; the Jesus who shares John's eschatology, but claims its partial fulfillment."

life that the faithful Jew should have been able to see God's providential hand of guidance in them, fulfilling or filling full his word of old. Some did and became his followers, but others' hearts were closed to his claims.

Of course there are "fuzzy edges" surrounding many of these beliefs. We cannot demonstrate beyond a shadow of a doubt that Esther and Song of Solomon were widely accepted as part of the Hebrew canon, though a good case can be made that they were.[112] We cannot prove that Jesus did not think highly of one or more of the Apocrypha, though neither he nor any New Testament writer ever quotes them. On the other hand, Jesus *is* credited in the four Gospels with quoting from Deuteronomy twenty-two times; Psalms nineteen times; Exodus fourteen times; Isaiah eleven times; Leviticus seven times; Genesis six times; Daniel five times; Hosea three times; Numbers, Malachi, and Zechariah twice each; and Micah and Jonah once each.[113]

As already noted, not every reference to an Old Testament event necessarily implies that Jesus viewed the genres of all of the "historical books" of Scripture identically. Theoretically, when Jesus referred to Moses lifting up the serpent in the wilderness, he could have been referring to when the character Moses did so in the account in Numbers, irrespective of its actual historicity. But he could not have warned his generation about imminent punishment for the cumulative sins of their ancestors who killed God's faithful followers from Abel to Zechariah without believing that the sizable majority of "historical books" and their contents were in fact historical, at least according to the standards and conventions of what his contemporaries would have considered to be reliable history writing.[114] As already noted, too, more prophecies viewed as fulfilled were taken

112. Judicious surveys of the *status quaestionis* and compelling perspectives within the diversity of opinion may be found in Stephen G. Dempster, "Torah, Torah, Torah: The Emergence of the Tripartite Canon," in *Exploring the Origins of the Bible: Canon Formation in Historical, Literary, and Theological Perspective,* ed. Craig A. Evans and Emanuel Tov (Grand Rapids: Baker, 2008), 87-127; and "Canons on the Right and Canons on the Left: Finding a Resolution in the Canon Debate," *JETS* 52 (2009): 47-77.

113. Counting every text listed as a quotation in the UBSGNT, 4th ed., "Index of Quotations: New Testament Order," 888-89, which is attributed by the Gospel writer to Jesus, without reference to whether a given citation is listed more than once due to parallel occurrences in multiple Gospels. Multiple uses of the same OT text in different contexts may thus be seen as "skewing" the statistics, but our point here is merely heuristic.

114. For example, in Matthew 12:40-41 Christ compares his coming resurrection to Jonah's time in the belly of the large fish, and predicts that the people of Nineveh will condemn Jesus' unbelieving contemporaries on Judgment Day because they repented at Jonah's preaching and now one greater than Jonah has appeared. It is theoretically possible that Jesus is simply likening his death and resurrection to Jonah's being swallowed and vomited up, *as the story was recounted in the prophetic work that bore Jonah's name.* Jesus, nevertheless, could not have expected the Ninevites to condemn unbelieving Israel unless they really had repented at Jonah's preaching — in some ways, a greater "miracle" than surviving inside the fish! Most likely, Jesus saw the

typologically than predictively, but the logic was equally compelling in each case, given the faithful Jews' belief in a providentially ordered and guided world.[115]

What we do *not* see in Christ's teachings based on the Scriptures of his people is anything that would point to a canon within a canon — viewing only certain parts of the Bible as authoritative. To be sure, like other rabbis Jesus can recognize some books as more central than others and distinguish between the lighter and the heavier parts of Scripture (Matt. 23:23 par.). But all of the Bible remains inspired and all God's laws must be obeyed. We see nothing in the life of Christ to support various accommodationist views of Scripture that allow for full-fledged "error," by ancient standards (so long as such errors are restricted to what are deemed peripheral rather than central matters), nor that form of *Sachkritik* that rejects even central matters as credible or normative. We find nothing to suggest that Jesus distinguished between following the Bible on matters of faith and practice, or of doctrine and ethics, while allowing for mistakes in details of history that we can ignore.

Of course, it is very easy to become accustomed to dealing with prescriptive legal material or descriptive historical events and to forget that the inerrancy of the Bible means something quite different when we turn to very different genres such as psalms or proverbs. Every book of Scripture must be interpreted according to the best possible assessment of its literary genre, just as every individual passage must be understood according to its literary form or subgenre.[116] The truthfulness of a lament means something quite different than the reliability of a prophecy. But once we take these distinctions into account, there is nothing in Christ's use of the Old Testament to support denials of its inerrancy, once that doctrine is rightly understood as articulated in its most nuanced definitions, not just as it is sometimes promulgated in popular preaching.[117] Warfield's and Wen-

---

whole book as historical. On the other hand, when he refers to "three days and three nights" he is using a Semitic idiom that must be interpreted by the standards of his day, in which it was used to refer to any portion of three twenty-four-hour periods of time. See Robert H. Gundry, *Matthew: A Commentary on His Handbook for a Mixed Church under Persecution,* 2nd edition (Grand Rapids: Eerdmans, 1994), 244-45.

115. See also France, *Jesus and the Old Testament,* 39; quoting, in the last sentence, G. W. H. Lampe, *Essays on Typology* (London: SCM, 1957), 27: "[T]here is a consistency in God's dealings with men. Thus his acts in the Old Testament will present a pattern which can be seen to be repeated in the New Testament events; these may therefore be interpreted by reference to the pattern displayed in the Old Testament. New Testament typology is thus essentially the tracing of the constant principles of God's working in history, revealing 'a recurring rhythm in past history which is taken up more fully and perfectly in the Gospel events.'"

116. See especially Barry G. Webb, "Biblical Authority and Diverse Literary Genres," chapter 19 in this collection.

117. Still remarkably useful is Paul D. Feinberg, "The Meaning of Inerrancy," in *Inerrancy,* ed. Norman L. Geisler (Grand Rapids: Zondervan, 1980), 265-304. Many critics of inerrancy claim that the nuances offered in treatments of this kind make the doctrine "die the death of a

ham's syllogism still stands. If we are followers of Jesus, we will want to adopt his view of the Scriptures. He believed in their fully divine origin, reliability, and authority. Therefore, our view of the Old Testament should accept their complete God-given trustworthiness and claims on our lives as well. And just as nothing in the humanity of a person requires that a given writing of theirs contain errors, nothing in the humanity of Scripture logically compels us to find mistakes in it.[118]

If these conclusions about *trustworthiness* should make those holding non-evangelical (and even some liberal evangelical) bibliologies uncomfortable, a second cluster of observations should give more conservative evangelicals pause for reflection. Jesus' *hermeneutic* hardly matches what some Christian college or seminary professors have taught as the only proper way for believers to handle the Scriptures.[119] There is a pervasive typological, and occasionally Christological, interpretation of the Bible in the Gospels' portrait of Jesus' approach to the Old Testament that is hard to relegate solely to later redaction.[120] If the conservative religious leaders in Jesus' day were (wrongly) outraged by some of his applications of Scripture, especially to himself, then their successors among today's evangelical instructors had best beware of ever insisting that all forms of typological or Christological interpretations of the Bible that do not reflect the human authors' original intentions are misguided.[121]

To be sure, the reasons for caution are clear. Early Christianity did not stop with the New Testament's hermeneutics, but proceeded to move from legitimate typology to rampant, illegitimate allegory, though not always to the extent that

---

thousand qualifications," and so they prefer not to use the term. Curiously, though, there seem to be no more than a handful of significant qualifications, and certainly no more than are needed in the thoughtful systematic treatment of any other major doctrine, so one wonders if a straw man is being attacked. See also Paul Helm, "The Idea of Inerrancy," chapter 28 in this collection.

118. It is not merely divinely inspired documents that are (logically) inerrant. Many merely human compositions also lack factual mistakes (to be distinguished from typographical or scribal errors).

119. As, e.g., in the perspectives enunciated by Walter C. Kaiser Jr., "Single Meaning, Unified Referents: Accurate and Authoritative Citations of the Old Testament by the New Testament," in Berding and Lunde, eds., *Three Views on the New Testament Use of the Old Testament,* 45-89, at one end of a spectrum; and by Peter Enns, "Fuller Meaning, Single Goal: A Christotelic Approach to the New Testament Use of the Old in Its First-Century Interpretive Environment," in the same volume, 167-217, at the other end of that spectrum.

120. E.g., and despite claims to the contrary, the use of the suffering servant motif of Isaiah 52:13–53:12, used frequently in the New Testament to explain Jesus' identity, seems to have originated with Jesus himself. See especially France, *Jesus and the Old Testament,* 110-32. Jesus' own use of the Old Testament as the stimulus for the Gospel writers' uses is a recurring theme also in Emerson B. Powery, *Jesus Reads Scripture: The Function of Jesus' Use of Scripture in the Synoptic Gospels* (Leiden and Boston: Brill, 2003).

121. As especially for Walter C. Kaiser Jr., *The Uses of the Old Testament in the New* (Chicago: Moody, 1985; Eugene, OR: Wipf & Stock, 2001).

some introductory textbooks suggest.[122] The Lutheran wing of the Reformation spawned an approach to the Old Testament that overly dwelt on the inadequacies of the Law in order to make the gospel look that much more attractive by comparison. Covenant theology and dispensationalism debated perspectives that represented opposite ends of a spectrum ranging from an overemphasis on the continuities to an overemphasis on the discontinuities between the testaments, respectively.[123] Even Christians who fell into none of these camps too quickly forgot to interpret given Old Testament texts in their original contexts to begin with, before moving on to reflect on legitimate versus illegitimate ways of deriving Christian theology or contemporary applications from them.[124]

In short, grammatico-historical exegesis remains the appropriate foundation or starting point for interpreting the Old Testament.[125] But as one moves from original meaning to later significance, allows Scripture to interpret Scripture by means of the *regula fidei,* or tries to understand what Christians today are meant to do with texts in view of the speech-acts they create, we dare not overlook Jesus' central application of the inspired word to himself.[126] We must not take Richard Longenecker's approach, which he applies to the apostles' hermeneutic as well, and deem it irreproducible simply because we are not inspired.[127] Instead, we should study carefully just what kinds of "creative" uses of the Old Testament Jesus and the apostles employ, make sure we have understood as best as possible their reasoning, and then seek to duplicate those processes (but only those processes) as we turn to analogous Old Testament texts for which we have no New Testament appropriations.[128]

More disconcerting still for many in an age characterized by the "scandal of

122. The Ancient Christian Commentary on Scripture series (Downers Grove, IL: InterVarsity) demonstrates both of these points in massive detail.

123. Cf. the various contributions to Wayne G. Strickland, ed., *Five Views on Law and Gospel* (Grand Rapids: Zondervan, 1996). See further Robert Kolb, "The Bible in the Reformation and Protestant Orthodoxy," and Thomas H. McCall, "Wesleyan Theology and the Authority of Scripture: Historic Affirmations and Some Contemporary Issues," chapters 3 and 6, respectively, in this collection.

124. Thus necessitating, even today, discussions like those in Gary T. Meadors, ed., *Four Views on Moving Beyond the Bible to Theology* (Grand Rapids: Zondervan, 2009).

125. See further, Craig L. Blomberg, "The Historical-Critical/Grammatical Method," in *Biblical Hermeneutics: Five Views,* ed. Stanley E. Porter and Beth M. Stovell (Downers Grove, IL: InterVarsity, 2012), 27-47.

126. See the relevant sections of Henri Blocher, "God and the Scripture Writers: The Question of Double Authorship," chapter 17 in this collection.

127. Richard N. Longenecker, "Can We Reproduce the Exegesis of the New Testament?" *TynB* 21 (1970): 3-38.

128. See further Klein, Blomberg, and Hubbard, *Introduction to Biblical Interpretation,* 206-7, using Psalm 3, never quoted in the New Testament, as an example.

the evangelical conscience"[129] should be to see how often Jesus lambasted the Bible teachers and scholars of his day simply for their disobedience to Torah. The solution to the moral decadence of our day is not to return to a legalism from which freedom in Christ and reliance on the Spirit are absent, but rather to help others understand and to model for them balanced, creative, sensitive, contextualized, Spirit-filled applications of all parts of Scripture.[130] We must always preserve freedom in Christ, while never turning it into a license for sin or for leading others into sin (cf. 1 Corinthians 8–10). Still, as I have explored elsewhere, when one asks the question about with whom Jesus and the apostles got the most upset, the answer consistently was: not with the notoriously sinful in first-century societies, but with the well-educated and respected religious leaders who had turned what was intended to be a vibrant relationship with the living God into a long list of dos and don'ts far beyond anything God had ever intended. *Moreover, these were individuals who should have known better!* Conversely, the first Christians, like their Lord, were surprisingly solicitous and gracious when it came to extending God's love and forgiveness to the sinners and outcasts around them.[131] It is worth reflecting on how much the world can see of these patterns in contemporary evangelical engagement in the public square, particularly with the way we treat today's pariahs, be they women who have had abortions, individuals with homosexual orientations, illegal immigrants, those without adequate healthcare, and the like. Could it be that if Jesus walked on earth with us today, he would happily applaud this "Scripture project" but then ask why we were not at least three times more involved in projects of more overt mission and mercy at home and worldwide?[132]

129. Ronald J. Sider, *The Scandal of the Evangelical Conscience: Why Are Christians Living Just Like the Rest of the World?* (Grand Rapids: Baker, 2005).

130. The "Contemporary Significance" sections of the NIV Application Commentaries (Grand Rapids: Zondervan) go a long way toward these ends. See also Craig L. Blomberg with Jennifer F. Markley, *Handbook of New Testament Exegesis* (Grand Rapids: Baker, 2010), 239-68.

131. Craig L. Blomberg, "The New Testament Definition of Heresy (or When Do Jesus and the Apostles Really Get Mad?)," *JETS* 45 (2002): 59-72.

132. See further Craig L. Blomberg, *Neither Poverty nor Riches: A Biblical Theology of Possessions* (Leicester: Inter-Varsity; Grand Rapids: Eerdmans, 1999; Downers Grove, IL: InterVarsity, 2001); and *Contagious Holiness: Jesus' Meals with Sinners* (Leicester and Downers Grove, IL: InterVarsity, 2005), both in the NSBT, ed. D. A. Carson.

TWENTY-THREE

The Problem of the New Testament's Use of the Old Testament

Douglas J. Moo and Andrew David Naselli

Does the use of the OT in the NT argue against Scripture's inerrancy? Many scholars think it does. This essay explains why it does not.

Situating the Problem

The relationship of the two testaments that comprise the Christian Scriptures has been an enduring theological issue. The issue takes many different forms, ranging from very broad and fundamental theological and canonical concerns to very specific matters of textual comparison. Our focus in this essay is on the relationship between the meaning of OT texts in their own contexts and the meaning that NT authors ascribe to these texts. This particular issue has received considerable attention over the centuries, and the flood of literature relating to this matter shows no sign of abating.[1] Of particular interest to us are those as-

1. A good recent survey of the field is provided by Jonathan Lunde, "An Introduction to Central Questions in the New Testament Use of the Old Testament," in *Three Views on the New Testament Use of the Old Testament,* ed. Kenneth Berding and Jonathan Lunde, Counterpoints (Grand Rapids: Zondervan, 2008), 7-41. The most important monographs include the following: R. T. France, *Jesus and the Old Testament: His Application of Old Testament Passages to Himself and His Mission* (Downers Grove, IL: InterVarsity, 1971); D. A. Carson and H. G. M. Williamson, eds., *It Is Written: Scripture Citing Scripture; Essays in Honour of Barnabas Lindars, SSF* (Cambridge: Cambridge University Press, 1988); Martin Jan Mulder, ed., *Mikra: Text,*

This chapter is an updated version of Douglas J. Moo, "The Problem of Sensus Plenior," in *Hermeneutics, Authority, and Canon,* ed. D. A. Carson and John D. Woodbridge (Grand Rapids: Zondervan, 1986), 175-211, 397-405. Some material is also taken from Douglas J. Moo, "Paul's Universalizing Hermeneutics in Romans," *SBJT* 11 (Fall 2007): 62-90. We thank Jared Compton for his helpful critique. Unless otherwise noted, all Scripture citations are from *The New International Version* (NIV), © 2011.

pects of the problem that constitute a challenge to the doctrine of inerrancy. The essential problem, simply put, is the apparent occasional discrepancy between the meaning of OT texts in their original settings and the meaning that NT authors appear to give them. Paul Achtemeier's statement of the case is typical.[2] Attributing inerrancy to the Bible, he claims, ignores the NT authors' attitude towards the OT as demonstrated in their actual use of it. They habitually modify the OT text and read into that text meanings obviously not intended in the original, so they clearly do not regard the OT as an inerrant document, "the timeless formulation of unchanging truth."[3] Rather, Achtemeier argues, their use of the OT shows that the NT authors regarded the canonical books as part of a living tradition that could be freely modified in order to fit new situations. If we would be true to the NT itself, then, we will not impose on the Bible a static, oracular status such as the doctrine of inerrancy implies; we will view it and use it as the living, changing tradition that it is.

In formulating his argument, Achtemeier has two specific phenomena in mind: (1) places where the NT uses a text form of an OT passage that differs from the accepted Masoretic tradition and (2) places where the NT gives a meaning to an OT passage that does not appear to agree with the intention of the original. These issues are obviously intertwined because changing a text often gives a new meaning to an OT passage. However, since others have dealt competently with the textual side of the problem,[4] this essay addresses the second issue. To put the

---

Translation, Reading, and Interpretation of the Hebrew Bible in Ancient Judaism and Early Christianity, CRINT 2 (Minneapolis: Fortress, 1988); Richard B. Hays, *Echoes of Scripture in the Letters of Paul* (New Haven: Yale University Press, 1989); Hays, *The Conversion of the Imagination: Paul as Interpreter of Israel's Scripture* (Grand Rapids: Eerdmans, 2005); G. K. Beale, ed., *The Right Doctrine from the Wrong Texts? Essays on the Use of the Old Testament in the New* (Grand Rapids: Baker, 1994); Christopher D. Stanley, *Paul and the Language of Scripture: Citation Technique in the Pauline Epistles and Contemporary Literature,* SNTSMS 69 (Cambridge: Cambridge University Press, 1992); Stanley, *Arguing with Scripture: The Rhetoric of Quotations in the Letters of Paul* (New York: T. & T. Clark, 2004); Craig A. Evans and James A. Sanders, eds., *Early Christian Interpretation of the Scriptures of Israel: Investigations and Proposals,* JSNTSup 148 (Sheffield: Sheffield Academic Press, 1997); Richard N. Longenecker, *Biblical Exegesis in the Apostolic Period,* 2nd edition (Grand Rapids: Eerdmans, 1999); Francis Watson, *Paul and the Hermeneutics of Faith* (London: T. & T. Clark, 2004); Stanley E. Porter, ed., *Hearing the Old Testament in the New Testament,* McMaster New Testament Studies 8 (Grand Rapids: Eerdmans, 2006); G. K. Beale and D. A. Carson, eds., *Commentary on the New Testament Use of the Old Testament* (Grand Rapids: Baker, 2007); Berding and Lunde, eds., *Three Views on the NT Use of the OT.*

2. Paul J. Achtemeier, *Inspiration and Authority: Nature and Function of Christian Scripture,* 2nd edition (Peabody, MA: Hendrickson, 1999), 52-53, 73-81, 97-99, 115-16. Cf. the more negative assessment of S. Vernon McCasland, "Matthew Twists the Scripture," *JBL* 80 (1961): 143-48.

3. Achtemeier, *Inspiration and Authority,* 70.

4. E.g., Moisés Silva, "The New Testament Use of the Old Testament: Text Form and Authority," in *Scripture and Truth,* ed. D. A. Carson and John D. Woodbridge (Grand Rapids:

problem simply: How can we accord complete truthfulness to writings that appear to misunderstand and misapply those texts from which they claim to derive the authority and rationale for their most basic claims and teaching?

The apparently novel meaning that Jesus and the NT writers attribute to OT texts constitutes a potentially legitimate objection to Scripture's inerrancy. The NT writers do not casually appeal to the OT or argue merely by analogy. They repeatedly assert that we must believe and do certain things *because* of what is said in specific OT texts. The NT authors suggest that their teachings are grounded in the OT. The problem, then, becomes one of authority: Can we adopt as "true" NT claims based on "faulty" OT interpretation? Greg Beale titled his valuable collection of essays on the matter *The Right Doctrine from the Wrong Texts?* One might ask, however, if the doctrine can be "right" if the texts are "wrong." If the NT errs in drawing these causal relationships, then it has erred fundamentally, not just incidentally. The doctrine of inerrancy "requires that the meaning the New Testament author finds in the Old Testament and uses in the New is really in the Old Testament."[5]

This study investigates whether NT-specified meaning is "really in" the OT. On what basis does the NT so confidently apply OT texts? We begin by isolating the real nature of the problem. We then turn to proposed solutions to the problem and look at some examples of how the proposed approach might deal with some specific texts, and we conclude with some final reflections.

Correctly Defining the Problem

The modern insistence that the "historical" sense is a text's only legitimate meaning has to some extent created the "problem" we are dealing with in this essay. Before the modern period, Christian interpreters were quite happy to explain that

---

Zondervan, 1983), 147-65, 381-86. A broader issue, with serious canonical implications, has been raised recently by scholars working especially on Paul and Hebrews, whose quotations tend to follow the LXX quite closely. They suggest that this phenomenon reveals that for these authors (and perhaps for the NT generally) the "Scripture" is not the Hebrew text but the Greek text. See, for example, Radu Gheorghita, *The Role of the Septuagint in Hebrews: An Investigation of Its Influence with Special Consideration to the Use of Hab 2:3-4 in Heb 10:37-38,* WUNT 2.160 (Tübingen: Mohr Siebeck, 2003); J. Ross Wagner, "Greek Isaiah and the Septuagint as Christian Scripture," in *Scripture's Doctrine: Studies in the New Testament's Normativity for Christian Dogmatics,* ed. Markus Bockmuehl and Alan J. Torrance (Grand Rapids: Baker, 2008), 17-28; Francis Watson, "Mistranslation and the Death of Christ: Isaiah 53 LXX and Its Pauline Reception," in *Translating the New Testament: Text, Translation, Theology,* ed. Stanley E. Porter and Mark J. Boda, McMaster New Testament Studies (Grand Rapids: Eerdmans, 2009), 215-50.

5. S. Lewis Johnson, *The Old Testament in the New: An Argument for Biblical Inspiration* (Grand Rapids: Zondervan, 1980), 66.

the OT is compatible with the NT; their recourse was various forms of what we might call the "figural" sense. They extensively employed allegory and typology to show how the NT appropriates the OT to uncover the OT's true, "spiritual" meaning.[6] The assumption guiding such approaches was that the NT's use of the OT was valid and authoritative. The onset of higher criticism in the seventeenth and eighteenth centuries seriously challenged those assumptions and methods,[7] and a "hermeneutics of suspicion" replaced a "hermeneutics of consent."

The death knell for the traditional approach to the OT was insisting that the "grammatical-historical" meaning is the text's only legitimate meaning.[8] No longer did many theologians assume that the NT's interpretation of the OT is correct and the normative key to Scripture's unity. Convinced that the NT differs from the findings of modern, "scientific" historical exegesis, rationalist interpreters concluded that the NT errs and that its authors are guilty of arbitrary, illegitimate exegesis.

The response from "conservative" interpreters varied. Some of them proposed unlikely interpretations or forced harmonizations on texts to preserve doctrinal purity. But the majority of scholars, enamored with the "objectivity" that the "historical-grammatical" method illusorily promised, erred in the opposite direction by not approaching our problem with sufficient nuance. They illegitimately expanded the scope of the problem that the NT's use of the OT poses for inerrancy. They overstated the difficulties. We should remove some of these "phantom" difficulties before we analyze some of the most important proposed solutions to the problem.

The Nature of Inspiration

Some people wrongly assume that inerrancy necessarily involves a "dictation" theory of inspiration.[9] But the vast majority of inerrantists reject a mechanical-dictation view of inspiration. Most inerrantists view Scripture as the product of

6. We treat these briefly on pp. 725-30 below.

7. For the degree to which these kinds of problems were already being discussed before the popularity of the "grammatical-historical" method, see John D. Woodbridge, "Some Misconceptions of the Impact of the 'Enlightenment' on the Doctrine of Scripture," in *Hermeneutics, Authority, and Canon,* ed. D. A. Carson and John D. Woodbridge (Grand Rapids: Zondervan, 1986), 241-70, 410-21.

8. Peter Stuhlmacher, *Vom Verstehen des Neuen Testaments: Eine Hermeneutik,* GNT 6 (Göttingen: Vandenhoeck & Ruprecht, 1979), 124; G. W. H. Lampe and K. J. Woolcombe, *Essays on Typology,* SBT 22 (Naperville, IL: Allenson, 1957), 15.

9. E.g., Bruce Vawter, *Biblical Inspiration* (Philadelphia: Westminster, 1972), 16; William J. Abraham, *The Divine Inspiration of Holy Scripture* (New York: Oxford University Press, 1981), 105-7.

a "concursive" operation: human authors freely wrote what they wanted while the divine author simultaneously superintended and guided their writing. Since inerrantists do not hold a view of inspiration that entails an ahistorical, oracular process, they allow for flexibility in quotation and attention to historical context.[10]

The Nature and Purpose of References to the Old Testament

The NT appropriates the OT in many different ways: in quotations, allusions, and echoes; by using common themes; by presenting material in similar patterns; by direct references, etc. The OT provides much of the language and cultural context for the NT writers. They therefore often use its language and even quote it in a way that lends a certain air or connotation to what they are saying. For instance, if we warn our children about the consequences of an action by reminding them, "People reap what they sow" (Gal. 6:7), our applying Paul's words to a situation he never envisaged is valid. We are not saying exactly what Paul said or applying his words to the same situation. But we are, in a sense, implying that our warning carries some of the same seriousness that Paul's did. The Scripture language creates an "authoritative resonance."

When NT authors quote the OT to assert its "correct" meaning, their point is valid only if their interpretations of the OT are "correct." But other times to ask about a "valid" interpretation is to ask the wrong question of the text. NT authors do not always use OT language as authoritative proof. This is not surprising since the OT played a prominent role in their lives and cultural milieu. So when they appear to deduce a new meaning from the OT or when they apply it to a new situation, they are not necessarily misusing the text or treating it as errant. Three specific categories of the NT's use of the OT are not part of our problem.[11]

10. See, for instance, the discussion in B. B. Warfield and A. A. Hodge, "Inspiration," *Presbyterian Review* 2 (April 1881); reprinted in *Inspiration,* ed. Roger R. Nicole (Grand Rapids: Baker, 1979), 62-64.

11. Considerable attention has been given to the definitions of, and distinctions among, quotation, allusions, and echoes (see, e.g., Stanley E. Porter, "Allusions and Echoes," in *As It Is Written: Studying Paul's Use of Scripture,* ed. Stanley E. Porter and Christopher D. Stanley, Society of Biblical Literature Symposium 50 [Atlanta: Society of Biblical Literature, 2008], 29-40). For the purposes of this essay, these formal/literary distinctions can be ignored. For discussions of the function of quotations and allusions, see J. A. E. van Dodewaard, "La Force évocatrice de la citation," *Bib* 36 (1955): 482-91; Alfred Suhl, *Die Funktion der alttestamentlichen Zitate und Anspielungen im Markusevangelium* (Gütersloh: Mohn, 1965), 38-42; James Barr, *Old and New in Interpretation: A Study of the Two Testaments* (London: SCM, 1966), 115; and Martin Rese, *Alttestamentliche Motive in der Christologie des Lukas,* SNT 1 (Gütersloh: Mohn, 1969), 208-9. Silva mentions similar considerations ("NT Use of the OT," 156-59).

Using Old Testament Language as a Vehicle of Expression

The speech of a person raised on the classics is sprinkled with terms and idioms drawn from those texts. Similarly, the NT writers sometimes use OT language as a vehicle of expression without intending to provide a "correct" interpretation of the OT text they are quoting.

For example, Jesus laments in Gethsemane, "My soul is overwhelmed with sorrow to the point of death" (*perilypos estin hē psychē mou heōs thanatou*) (Mark 14:34/Matt. 26:38). This almost certainly alludes to the "refrain" of Psalms 42–43 (perhaps originally a single psalm) because *perilypos* is rare (only eight times in the LXX, never in Philo or Josephus, only twice in the NT), especially in combination with *psychē*.[12] But Jesus is not citing the psalm(s) as authoritatively prefiguring his sufferings in the Garden. He uses familiar biblical language simply to express his emotions. He may generally identify with the psalmist's plight (oppressed by enemies, seeking God's vindication and rescue), but even if there is no evidence that Psalms 42–43 predict Jesus' agony in Gethsemane, Jesus is not misusing the OT or reading new meaning into it.[13]

Romans 10:17 is another example of this phenomenon. Paul cites Psalm 19:4 to corroborate his claim that people have "heard": "their voice has gone out into all the earth, their words to the ends of the world." Paul appears to shift the application of Psalm 19:4, which extols God's revelation in nature.[14] Yet the implied object of the verb "heard" in Romans 10:17 must be "the word of Christ"; "their voice" and "their words" must then refer to the voices and words of Christian preachers (see Rom. 10:14-16). The simplest explanation for this application is that Paul is not really "quoting" Psalm 19:4. After all, we have here no introductory formula or quotation in contrast to the clear introductions when Paul quotes the OT in Romans 10:16, 19, 20, and 21. Paul may simply use the language of the psalm, with the "echoes" of God's revelation that it awakes, to assert the universal preaching of the gospel.[15]

The NT authors were more familiar with the OT than any other literature, so this phenomenon is normal and not germane to our problem.

12. Douglas J. Moo, *The Old Testament in the Gospel Passion Narratives* (Sheffield: Almond, 1983), 240-42.

13. Another example is Paul's use of Deut. 19:15 in 2 Cor. 13:1. See Silva, "NT Use of the OT," 157-58.

14. H. L. Ellison (*The Mystery of Israel: An Exposition of Romans 9–11* [Grand Rapids: Eerdmans, 1966], 69-71) unconvincingly denies such a shift. Paul's wording exactly follows the majority MSS tradition of the LXX, and the LXX accurately renders the MT.

15. See particularly Hays, *Echoes of Scripture,* 175. For this view, see many of the Greek fathers; Frederic Louis Godet, *Commentary on Romans* (reprint, Grand Rapids: Kregel, 1977), 388; Dunn, *Romans 9–16,* WBC (Waco, TX: Word, 1988), 624; J. Fitzmyer, *Romans: A New Translation with Introduction and Commentary,* AB (Garden City, NJ: Doubleday, 1993), 599.

Applying Old Testament Principles

A "willed type," explains E. D. Hirsch, extends or applies an author's language, particularly in legal texts. The author did not specifically, consciously intend that application, but his general meaning legitimately includes the application.[16] This phenomenon occurs when the NT applies an OT principle or law to a new situation.

For example, some criticize Paul for quoting Deuteronomy 25:4 ("Do not muzzle an ox while it is treading out the grain") to support giving money to Christian ministers (1 Cor. 9:9). Paul's use of the OT seems fanciful. What is the warrant for applying a law that protects the welfare of animals to Christian ministry? Moreover, Paul's next words appear to deny that the law had anything to do with animals: "Is it for oxen that God is concerned? Does he not speak entirely for our sake?" (1 Cor. 9:9-10, ESV). Paul appears to equate the "literal" sense with the "spiritual," Christian sense.

Explanations of Paul's use of Deuteronomy 25:4 include the following:

1. This is one of the few examples of allegory in Paul.[17]

2. Paul adopts a Hellenistic Jewish exegetical principle by which interpreters like Philo avoid the crassly literal sense of such laws by appealing to the "higher sense" God really intended.[18]

3. Paul's meaning depends strictly on the OT's original meaning, which in its context teaches masters and owners to care for their laborers — whether animal or human. Paul legitimately draws out the law's significance for the situation of churches and their "workers," and he rightly claims that the law is given for "us" human beings, not primarily for oxen.[19] Moreover, Paul is probably not saying that this is the only meaning of the law; the crucial word *pantōs* (1 Cor. 9:10) is best translated not "entirely" (as in the RSV and ESV) but "surely," "certainly," or "undoubtedly."[20]

4. It is, however, probably going too far to see Paul's interpretation as a

16. E. D. Hirsch Jr., *Validity in Interpretation* (New Haven: Yale University Press, 1967), 121-26.

17. Longenecker, *Biblical Exegesis,* 109-10.

18. Hans Conzelmann, *1 Corinthians: A Commentary on the First Epistle to the Corinthians,* ed. George W. MacRae, trans. James W. Leitch, Hermeneia (Philadelphia: Fortress, 1975), 154-55.

19. Walter C. Kaiser Jr., "The Current Crisis in Exegesis and the Apostolic Use of Deuteronomy 25:4 in 1 Corinthians 9:8-10," *JETS* 21 (1978): 3-18. Kaiser expands on Calvin's and Godet's approaches. And see now especially Hays, *Echoes of Scripture,* 165-66.

20. See Luke 4:23; Acts 18:21; 21:22; 28:4; and Anthony C. Thiselton, *The First Epistle to the Corinthians: A Commentary on the Greek Text,* NIGTC (Grand Rapids: Eerdmans, 2000), 686-87; cf. also David Instone-Brewer, "1 Corinthians 9:9-11: A Literal Interpretation of 'Do Not Muzzle the Ox,'" *NTS* 38 (1992): 225-43.

straightforward interpretation. Rather, we should view this as the application, in light of eschatological realities, of a principle found in Deuteronomy 25:4.[21] The phrase had become a popular proverb to express the idea that a worker deserves to be paid, so Paul's application does not have to match the application given the words in Deuteronomy. Paul implies that a principle expressed in one context can be applied to other contexts that share some kind of similarity.

Paul does not misuse the OT here. It is unfair to apply a rigid concept of meaning to his application of an OT law and then to charge him with misinterpreting the OT for going beyond what the OT specifically intends. A better test is whether the scope of the OT law legitimately includes Paul's application. Would the OT author acknowledge the validity of Paul's further application?

Representing Alternative Points of View

Some statements in 1 Corinthians are probably not Paul's own teaching but slogans of the Corinthians (e.g., "I have the right to do anything" [6:12; 10:23]; "It is good for a man not to have sexual relations with a woman" [7:1]; "We all possess knowledge" [8:1]). Similarly, the NT may quote the OT not to express the OT's teaching but to represent someone else's opinion or teaching.

This explains some of the quotations in Matthew 5 that are antithetical to Jesus' teaching. The clearest example is the addition of "hate your enemy" (Matt. 5:43) to the love commandment (Lev. 19:18). That expresses the teaching current among some Jews (perhaps Essenes).[22] Clear contextual indicators, however, are present here: additional language not in the OT (nor fairly representing OT teaching) and the introductory formula, "you have heard that it was said," which suggests a distance from the OT.

When contextual indicators like that are not present, we must use great caution before hypothesizing that the NT quotes the OT merely to represent the opinion of its listeners or opponents. For instance, some interpreters are uncomfortable with the way Paul appears to oppose one OT text to another in Romans 10:5-8 (which cites Lev. 18:5 and Deut. 30:10-14) and Galatians 3:11-12 (which cites Hab. 2:4 and Lev. 18:5), so they suggest that he may quote Leviticus 18:5 ("whoever does these things will live by them") according to the (false) meaning that

21. Gordon D. Fee, *The First Epistle to the Corinthians,* NICNT (Grand Rapids: Eerdmans, 1987), 408.

22. Although some scholars claim that the addition genuinely reflects OT teaching, such as is found in the "imprecatory psalms" (Robert H. Gundry, *Matthew: A Commentary on His Handbook for a Mixed Church under Persecution,* 2nd edition [Grand Rapids: Eerdmans, 1994], 96-97), this is almost certainly not the case. The most likely origin is the Qumran community, whose members were instructed to hate "the sons of disobedience."

his opponents were giving it.[23] But there is simply insufficient evidence that Paul's quotation represents a view different than his own. And there is good reason to think that Paul respects the original intention of Leviticus 18:5.[24]

Our point here, then, is that although it is valid in some cases to attempt to avoid the problem of the NT's use of the OT by disassociating the NT author from the meaning that others give the OT text, its help is very limited, and we must have compelling contextual evidence before adopting it.

The Meaning of Fulfillment Language

Some of the most textually and hermeneutically challenging uses of the OT in the NT are the ones Matthew precedes with fulfillment-formulas.[25] For example, Jesus and his family stayed in Egypt and subsequently returned to Palestine. According to Matthew 2:15, this "fulfills" Hosea's statement, "Out of Egypt I called my son" (Hos. 11:1b). This quotation is a virtual poster child for the NT's alleged misuse of the OT.[26] We do not want to minimize the genuine issues that the text creates, but it is important at the outset to eliminate one of the problems: Matthew claims that the Holy Family's departure from Egypt "fulfills" Hosea 11:1b.

If Jesus "fulfills" the OT only by doing what specific OT prophecies say the Messiah will do, then Matthew 2:15 is a problem because Hosea 11:1 simply states a fact (i.e., God called Israel out of Egypt) and does not prophesy that the Messiah will depart Egypt. But the meaning of "fulfill" (*plēroō*) is not so narrow. The NT authors use this word as a general way of describing the relationship of the OT to the NT. It describes how the new, climactic revelation of God in Christ "fills up," brings to its intended completion, the OT as a whole (the preparatory, incomplete revelation to and through Israel).[27] Thus, Mark summarizes Jesus' preaching

23. Cf. Silva, "NT Use of the OT," 159; Daniel P. Fuller, *Gospel and Law: Contrast or Continuum?* (Grand Rapids: Eerdmans, 1980), 98-99 (on Gal. 3:12).

24. See especially Preston M. Sprinkle, *Law and Life: The Interpretation of Leviticus 18:5 in Early Judaism and in Paul,* WUNT 2.241 (Tübingen: Mohr Siebeck, 2008). Contra, e.g., Vawter, *Biblical Inspiration,* 5; Achtemeier, *Inspiration and Authority,* 98-99.

25. See Krister Stendahl, *The School of St. Matthew and Its Use of the Old Testament,* ASNU 20 (Lund: Gleerup, 1954); Robert H. Gundry, *The Use of the Old Testament in St. Matthew's Gospel: With Special Reference to the Messianic Hope,* NovTSup 18 (Leiden: Brill, 1967); Wilhelm Rothfuchs, *Die Erfüllungszitate des Matthaüs-Evangeliums: Eine biblisch-theologische Untersuchung,* BWA[N]T 5.8 (Stuttgart: Kohlhammer, 1969).

26. E.g., Dewey M. Beegle, *Scripture, Tradition, and Infallibility* (Grand Rapids: Eerdmans, 1973), 237.

27. This is emphasized (perhaps too one-sidedly) by C. F. D. Moule, "Fulfillment-Words in the New Testament: Use and Abuse," *NTS* 14 (1967-68): 293-320. See also Bruce M. Metzger,

as announcing that time itself has been "filled up" and that the kingdom of God is at hand (1:15); Jesus claims that his teaching is the ultimate, climactic expression of God's will to which the OT law pointed (Matt. 5:17; cf. 11:13).[28] So when a NT author introduces an OT quotation with "fulfill," he does not necessarily regard the OT as a direct prophecy. Nor is he necessarily misusing the OT. Rather, he is making a claim about the way the testaments relate to one another, a claim that must be analyzed and verified on a broad theological basis. In the case of Matthew 2:15, then, the evangelist may suggest that Jesus, God's "greater son," brings to a climax ("fills up") the Exodus motif, a theme that had become eschatologically oriented even in the OT.[29]

Proposed Solutions to the Problem

We have reduced our problem's scope, but the problem remains. The force of the NT's argument often depends on the OT's proper, authoritative meaning (e.g., when it cites the OT to support theological conclusions or it explicitly says that the OT prophesies events it narrates), and sometimes the NT appears to give the OT meanings that we cannot demonstrate exegetically. What do we do with these texts? This section examines nine popular solutions: fideism, subjectivism, Jewish exegetical methods, dual authorship, theological exegesis, intertextuality, typology, *sensus plenior,* and a canonical approach. Several are inadequate, and others useful to various degrees.

Fideism

A fideistic approach argues that the modern view of exegetical procedure — not the NT — is at fault. The revelatory stance of the NT validates its inter-

---

"The Formulas Introducing Quotations of Scripture in the NT and the Mishnah," *JBL* 70 (1951): 297-307; Rothfuchs, *Erfüllungszitate,* 48-49; George Soares-Prabhu, *The Formula Quotations in the Infancy Narrative of Matthew: An Enquiry into the Tradition History of Mt 1–2,* AnBib 63 (Rome: Biblical Institute, 1976), 46-47; Gottlob Schrenk, in *TDNT,* 1:758-59.

28. For this interpretation of these key Matthean texts, see especially Robert J. Banks, *Jesus and the Law in the Synoptic Tradition,* SNTSMS 28 (Cambridge: Cambridge University Press, 1975), especially 207-12; John P. Meier, *Law and History in Matthew's Gospel: A Redactional Study of Mt. 5:17-48* (Rome: Biblical Institute, 1976), esp. 66-75; on Matthew 1–4 in particular, see Joel Kennedy, *The Recapitulation of Israel,* WUNT 2.257 (Tübingen: Mohr Siebeck, 2008).

29. D. A. Carson, "Matthew," in *Matthew-Mark,* 2nd edition, Expositor's Bible Commentary 9 (Grand Rapids: Zondervan, 2010), 118-20; cf. also G. K. Beale, "The Use of Hosea 11:1 in Matthew 2:15: One More Time," *JETS* 55 (2012): 697-715.

pretations, and when we cannot discover this meaning in the OT through our exegetical techniques, we should either abandon that method or else admit its inadequacy.[30]

This proposal makes a valid point. We are susceptible to "chronological snobbishness," the conviction that only we moderns have somehow transcended cultural bias and are uniquely able to understand things correctly. We must be careful not to think that "the authority and validity of apostolic interpretation . . . depend on its conformity to modern exegetical method."[31] In this, as in all other matters, Scripture itself must judge our understanding, not we it. Ultimately, it is impossible to "validate" the NT's use of the OT, in general or in detail, without a prior decision to accept what it says as true and authoritative.

While at one level this kind of response is adequate for the problem, it is less than satisfactory for three reasons:

1. In the last resort, it places Scripture in a realm above any real historical investigation or criticism. It is appropriate to a degree to dismiss these kinds of problems by appealing to the uncertainties and fallibility of all knowledge (the record of ancient history is far from complete, modern science could very well be wrong, etc.), but at some point the weight of unexplained discrepancies is too much for the doctrine to bear.

2. It places us in a rather vicious circle. We dismiss out of hand apparent discrepancies between our reading of the OT and the apostles' reading because our interpretation is fallible. But how can we know what the apostles' interpretation of the OT is except by using those same methods that we have rejected?

3. It leaves an issue fundamental to Christianity unresolved. The NT's appeal to the OT is too basic to the church's very identity to leave it in the realm of unexplained assertion. For all our legitimate emphasis on Christ as the center and fulfillment of revelation and as the "hermeneutical key" to the OT, we sacrifice too much by refusing to allow the OT to stand to some extent as an independent witness to the NT.[32] "All the while that we insist that nothing is exempt from the judgment of Christ — even our faith-understanding of the Old Testament — we must remember that the Old Testament was and, in some sense, is the criterion whereby Christ is Christ."[33] How can people validate the church's claim that it

30. The approach of Wilhelm Vischer (*The Witness of the Old Testament to Christ,* Lutterworth Library 33 [London: Lutterworth, 1949], 28-29) comes very close to this position. See also Anthony Tyrrell Hanson, *Studies in Paul's Technique and Theology* (Grand Rapids: Eerdmans, 1974), 226.

31. Silva, "NT Use of the OT," 163.

32. See, e.g., the concerns expressed by Christopher R. Seitz, "Christological Interpretation of Texts and Trinitarian Claims to Truth," *SJT* 52 (1999): 209-26.

33. James A. Sanders, "Habakkuk in Qumran, Paul, and the Old Testament," *JR* 39 (1959): 235. And see Francis Watson's extensive and detailed argument that the OT generated some of Paul's key theological ideas *(Paul and the Hermeneutics of Faith).*

(not Judaism) is the true "completion" of the OT if its (not Judaism's) use of the OT cannot demonstrably accord with the OT's meaning?

Subjectivism

A subjective approach eliminates the problem by arguing that all meaning and interpretation are inevitably subjective. For A. T. Hanson, for instance, a text does not have a "correct" meaning; rather, your presuppositions *(Vorverständnis)* decisively determine the meaning you arrive at.[34] And, of course, some forms of postmodernism, questioning the interpreter's ability to transcend his or her own context and determine a text's meaning, make a similar point with the aid of sophisticated philosophical and literary analysis.

Presuppositions certainly play a critical role in the way we read and apply the OT, and those presuppositions are due in part to faith rather than unaided reason. Yet it is ultimately both nonsensical and disastrous to the Christian faith to deny that interpreters can, humbly and always somewhat tentatively, come to conclusions about the "true" meaning of the biblical text.[35] Our presuppositions can and must be adjusted to "fit" the material under investigation: the "horizon" of the text and that of the interpreter can be "fused." Thus, without denying that interpretation is subjective, it is both reasonable and necessary that a text's "correct" interpretation exists and that we can find it.

Our ultimate decision about the validity of the NT's use of the OT depends considerably on whether we accept or reject the presuppositions of the NT authors. The NT authors based their detailed applications of specific OT texts on presuppositions that we must evaluate. One way to test them is to consider whether their acceptance leads to a more natural understanding of the OT than, say, the presuppositions at work in the Qumran community or among the rabbis. The process is inevitably circular, but the circle is not a closed one. Our goal is threefold: (1) "break into" the circle at the level of the actual use of the OT in the NT; (2) consider this use in light of fundamental theological and hermeneutical presuppositions; and (3) show that, granted these presuppositions, the NT's interpretations of the OT are not necessarily erroneous.

34. Anthony Tyrrell Hanson, *The New Testament Interpretation of Scripture* (London: SPCK, 1980), 13.

35. The issue is a huge one, treated elsewhere in this volume. For some useful suggestions along these lines, see N. T. Wright, *The New Testament and the People of God,* Christian Origins and the Question of God 1 (London: SPCK, 1992), 31-46; D. A. Carson, *The Gagging of God: Christianity Confronts Pluralism* (Grand Rapids: Zondervan, 1996); Kevin J. Vanhoozer, *Is There a Meaning in This Text? The Bible, the Reader, and the Morality of Literary Knowledge* (Grand Rapids: Zondervan, 1998).

Jewish Exegetical Methods

The NT authors appropriated Jewish methods of interpretation popular in their day, and today virtually all interpreters agree that this at least partially explains the NT's use of the OT. In this section, however, we examine the degree to which appealing to Jewish exegetical methods might solve our problem.

The similarities between exegetical methods in the NT and first-century Jewish sources are amply documented and undeniable. Both utilize similar citation techniques. For example, they combine verses on the basis of verbal resemblance (what the rabbis called *gezerah shawah;* cf. Pss. 110:1 and 16:8-11 in Acts 2:25-34); they argue from the lesser to the greater (*qal wahomer;* cf. John 7:23); they convey messages by subtly alluding to texts and themes (cf. the use of the "lament psalms" in the crucifixion narratives in the Synoptics); and they choose textual forms most conducive to their point (e.g., Acts 15:16-18). At another level, both the NT authors and their Jewish contemporaries are convinced that the OT ultimately speaks about their own community or situation.

So although modern readers may find the NT's use of the OT to be peculiar and unconvincing, a first-century audience familiar with such interpretive techniques and assumptions may have found them thoroughly convincing. We first need to understand just what the NT authors are doing with the OT vis-à-vis the OT and then evaluate the phenomenon's significance.

Evaluating Jewish Exegetical Methods Humbly

While rejecting a postmodern view that exegesis is completely relative and that our cultural context makes it impossible for us to find an ancient text's "correct" meaning, our own exegetical method requires humility. When we criticize Jewish exegetical methods, too often we assume that we, from our lofty twenty-first-century standpoint, have discovered *the* true method of interpretation against which all others must be compared. The relatively recent rediscovery of these useful ancient methods of interpretation soundly corrects such modern arrogance.[36] On the other hand, we should not entirely abandon a conviction about the general parameters of what constitutes "appropriate" interpretive methods. Therefore, our evaluation of Jewish exegetical methods found in the NT must combine careful analysis with a dose of humility.

36. The point is overstated by David Steinmetz, "The Superiority of Pre-critical Exegesis," *Theology Today* 37 (1980): 27-38.

Understanding Jewish Exegetical Methods

Jewish exegetical methods varied. While it has become popular to highlight examples that seem to modern interpreters to play fast and loose with the biblical text, there is evidence that the exegetical methods of the rabbis in the period before 70 C.E. were sober and careful.[37]

Another complicating factor is that people indiscriminately use terms such as "midrash" and "pesher" for Jewish exegetical procedures. "Midrash" often describes the interpretative approach of mainstream "Rabbinic" Judaism, while "pesher" describes the particular interpretive approach found in the Dead Sea Scrolls. Some interpreters think that simply describing NT exegesis as "midrashic" or "pesher" discredits its validity, but that conclusion depends on a particular definition of these terms. And there is no general consensus on how to define these terms.[38] Longenecker illustrates this problem by finding a considerable amount of "pesher" exegesis in the NT. That suggests to some people that the NT authors distort the text by following inappropriate exegetical practices, but for Longenecker, pesher includes the NT's "direct" application of the OT when proceeding from a revelatory basis.[39] So pesher, according to Longenecker's definition, does not necessarily invalidate the NT's exegetical conclusions.

This terminological uncertainty suggests that it is best simply not to use the terms "midrash" and "pesher" in our analysis. What is important is that we carefully compare the techniques we find in the NT with Jewish techniques. The NT authors' exegetical procedure undoubtedly resembles specific Jewish techniques,

37. David Instone-Brewer, *Techniques and Assumptions in Jewish Exegesis before 70 CE*, TSAJ 30 (Tübingen: Mohr Siebeck, 1992).

38. The bibliography on "midrash" and "pesher" in Jewish literature and the NT is enormous. Douglas J. Moo describes and categorizes some of these methods in *OT in the Gospel Passion Narratives*, 5-78. Useful surveys and discussions can be found in Joseph Bonsirven, *Exégèse rabbinique et Exégèse paulinienne*, Bibliothèque de théologie historique (Paris: Beauchesne et ses fils, 1939); R. Bloch, "Midrasch," in *DBSup* 5:1263-81; Otto Betz, *Offenbarung und Schriftforschung in der Qumransekte*, WUNT 6 (Tübingen: Mohr, 1960); F. F. Bruce, *Biblical Exegesis in the Qumran Texts* (Grand Rapids: Eerdmans, 1960); Joseph A. Fitzmyer, "The Use of Explicit Old Testament Quotations in Qumran Literature and in the New Testament," *NTS* 7 (1961): 297-333; Roger Le Déaut, "Apropos d'une définition du Midrash," *Bib* 50 (1969): 395-413 [ET in *Int* 25 (1971): 259-82]; E. Earle Ellis, "Midrash, Targum and New Testament Quotations," in *Neotestamentica et Semitica: Studies in Honour of Matthew Black*, ed. E. Earle Ellis and Max Wilcox (Edinburgh: T. & T. Clark, 1969), 61-69; Ellis, "How the New Testament Uses the Old," in *New Testament Interpretation: Essays on Principles and Methods*, ed. I. Howard Marshall, 2nd edition (Milton Keynes: Paternoster, 1979), 198-214; Merrill P. Miller, "Targum, Midrash and the Use of the Old Testament in the New Testament," *JSJ* 2 (1971): 29-82; R. T. France and David Wenham, eds., *Gospel Perspectives: Studies of History and Tradition in the Four Gospels*, Studies in Midrash and History 3 (Sheffield: JSOT, 1983); Longenecker, *Biblical Exegesis*, 18-30.

39. Longenecker, *Biblical Exegesis*, 54-57, 191-93.

but we must distinguish them in order to appreciate both their similarities and differences.

Comparing Jewish Exegetical Methods and NT Practices

Scholars often exaggerate the influence of Jewish exegetical methods on the NT. A vast gulf separates the often fantastic, purely verbal exegeses of the rabbis from the NT's sober, contextually oriented interpretations.[40] Indeed, the NT differs most from other Jewish literature when the latter strays furthest from what we would consider sound hermeneutics.

Distinguishing Appropriation Techniques and Hermeneutical Axioms

We may skew our analysis of the degree to which the NT is similar in its interpretational approach to ancient Judaism if we do not distinguish two levels of influence: what we might call "appropriation techniques" and "hermeneutical axioms."

Appropriation techniques are specific, "on the surface" methods that authors use to appropriate a text for a new situation. They may straightforwardly identify one situation or person with another, modify the text to suit the application, or associate several passages. It is at this level that the NT is often said to resemble the interpretive practices of its Jewish environment.

Hermeneutical axioms lie behind appropriation techniques and are ultimately crucial for how and where authors employ them. Hermeneutical axioms are a community's basic convictions about Scripture, its own identity, and God's movement in history.

For instance, the Qumran community directly applied the details of Habakkuk's prophecy to themselves and their enemies.[41] They utilized a variety of specific appropriation techniques to match the prophet's words with their own situation, but their hermeneutical axioms guided and validated (in their own minds) their appropriation: they were convinced that they were the people of God, that the last days had arrived, and that the prophets spoke in riddles about the last days. We find their exegesis strained and unconvincing because we are not convinced of their hermeneutical axioms, but it obviously made perfect sense to them.

Similarly, NT exegesis assumes the hermeneutical axioms that Jesus Christ is the culmination of God's plan and that "all the law and the prophets" ultimately point to him. Identifying Jesus with OT figures may lie behind NT "fulfillments" that appear merely to resemble OT texts. This does not mean that valid exegesis

40. See Moo, *OT in the Gospel Passion Narratives*, 388-92.

41. E.g., in 1QpHab, the pesher commentary on Habakkuk.

is entirely a product of arbitrary, unprovable hermeneutical axioms; some axioms and exegeses provide a much better "fit" with the material itself than others. Rather, the point is that at the level of appropriation technique the NT can closely resemble contemporary Jewish methods, but below the surface, basic theological connections between the Testaments provide the "validating" matrix for what may seem to be arbitrary exegesis.[42]

Solving the Problem?

If Jewish exegetical methods influenced the NT's appropriation of the OT as nuanced above, what does this imply for our problem?

Peter Enns argues that (1) the NT writers quite extensively accommodate their exegetical procedure to their hermeneutical environment and that (2) this similarity sheds light on how we should understand inerrancy.[43] Adopting what he calls an "incarnational" model of inspiration, Enns argues that determining whether the NT's appropriation of the OT is valid depends on the standards of their day, not ours. So we may defend inerrancy on the grounds that the NT interpretation is correct according to ancient standards, even if it is not according to modern standards. "What is 'proper' exegesis for Paul is determined by *his* time, not ours."[44] Enns has a point (as we suggest above): we too easily assume that we may objectively evaluate the interpretations of others from our lofty perch above the historical conditions of life. But Enns's approach goes much too far in the direction of subjectivity, finally providing no basis on which to decide the question of truth.[45] The doctrine of inerrancy, as generations of Christians have classically defined and held it, does not assert that a given teaching or conclusion is true only *for them* but that it is ultimately and timelessly true.

With respect to the issue before us, then, it is not enough to argue that the NT's use of the OT is "true" because it conforms to Jewish practices in place at

42. Moo, *OT in the Gospel Passion Narratives,* 75-78.

43. See Glenn Sunshine's essay in this collection, chapter 8: "Accommodation Historically Considered."

44. Peter Enns, "Fuller Meaning, Single Goal: A Christotelic Approach to the New Testament Use of the Old in Its First-Century Interpretive Environment," in Berding and Lunde, eds., *Three Views on the NT Use of the OT,* 185. See also Peter Enns, *Inspiration and Incarnation: Evangelicals and the Problem of the Old Testament,* 2nd ed. (Grand Rapids: Baker Academic, 2015), 121-49. For similar approaches to inspiration and inerrancy, see A. T. B. McGowan, *The Divine Spiration of Scripture: Challenging Evangelical Perspectives* (Nottingham: Apollos, 2007); Kenton L. Sparks, *God's Word in Human Words: An Evangelical Appropriation of Critical Biblical Scholarship* (Grand Rapids: Baker, 2008).

45. See especially the criticisms of G. K. Beale, *The Erosion of Inerrancy in Evangelicalism: Responding to New Challenges to Biblical Authority* (Wheaton, IL: Crossway, 2008).

that time. We must humbly evaluate the NT's use of the OT in light of what we would consider valid interpretational models. And recognizing that NT interpretational practices and Jewish techniques are similar does nothing to help us. Negatively, this similarity does not create any *prima facie* reason to question that the NT's interpretation is valid.[46] Positively, studying Jewish exegetical procedures may help (1) explain *what* the NT authors sometimes do with Scripture, (2) explain *why* they do it, and (3) show that Jesus and the NT authors often use methods that many of their contemporaries knew and accepted.

Some conservatives are content simply to note these similarities and then validate the NT authors' interpretations by appealing to their "charismatic" stance. They argue that the NT authors wrote inspired Scripture but that we cannot; therefore, we cannot replicate their non–historical-grammatical exegesis. Ellis explains Paul's procedure this way:

> His idea of a quotation was not a worshipping of the letter or "parroting" of the text; neither was it an eisegesis which arbitrarily imposed a foreign meaning upon the text. It was rather, in his eyes, a quotation-exposition, a *midrash pesher,* which drew from the text the meaning originally implanted there by the Holy Spirit and expressed that meaning in the most appropriate words and phrases known to him.[47]

We may assert on dogmatic grounds that the NT's exegesis of the OT finds the meaning that the Spirit intends, and it may be that our only alternative is a dilemma: (1) accept the NT's exegesis of the OT because of the NT's authority or (2) reject the NT's authority because it obviously misinterprets the OT. But it becomes clear at this point that appealing to Jewish exegetical techniques in the NT does not provide an answer to our fundamental problem: Is the meaning that these techniques discover "really in" the OT? Hays is correct:

> The more closely Paul's methods can be identified with recognized interpretive conventions of first-century Judaism, the less arbitrary and more historically understandable they appear; however, at the same time, such historical explanations of Paul's exegesis render it increasingly difficult to see how interpretations that employ such methods can bear any persuasive power or normative value for that mythical creature of whom Bultmann spoke with such conviction: modern man.[48]

46. Contra, e.g., Beegle (*Scripture,* 237-38 — on Matt. 2:15).

47. E. Earle Ellis, "Midrash Pesher in Pauline Hermeneutics," in *Prophecy and Hermeneutic in Early Christianity: New Testament Essays* (Grand Rapids: Eerdmans, 1978), 180. For a similar approach, see Longenecker, *Biblical Exegesis,* 191-92.

48. Hays, *Echoes of Scripture,* 8-9.

To employ the categories we introduce above, resemblance at the level of appropriation techniques does not get to the heart of the issue. Only when we consider hermeneutical axioms and the interpretations that they generate may we answer whether the interpretations are valid.

Do other proposals offer a better solution to our problem by demonstrating that the NT's exegesis is valid and coherent?

Dual Authorship

One time-honored solution to our problem (followed, e.g., by S. Lewis Johnson) is claiming that because NT authors wrote inspired Scripture, they could perceive meanings in the OT that the divine author intended but that the human authors neither expressed nor perceived. This approach correctly emphasizes that the NT authors claim to find the meaning that they give OT texts in the OT texts themselves, and, of course, we can agree that God was active in producing Scripture. But the theory of inspiration that it rests upon — positing that the divine and human authors did not mean the same thing — runs into severe difficulties with the traditional "concursive" view of how the divine and the human authors relate. Moreover, it is difficult for the view to explain why in passages such as Acts 2:29-35 the NT author directly refers to the human author of Scripture (in this case David, in Ps. 16:8-11) when claiming that the OT text is eschatologically significant.

Walter Kaiser's Theological Exegesis

Few people in our generation have given as much attention to the implications of the use of the OT in the NT for inerrancy as Walter C. Kaiser Jr.[49] His approach raises some of the most important questions involved in our problem.

Definition

From a doctrinal standpoint, Kaiser is convinced that it is illegitimate for a NT author to find more or different *meaning* in an OT text than the original human author himself intended. "The whole revelation of God as revelation hangs in

49. Many of the relevant articles are compiled and revised in Walter C. Kaiser Jr., *The Uses of the Old Testament in the New* (Chicago: Moody, 1985); and see, more recently, Kaiser, "Single Meaning, Unified Referents: Accurate and Authoritative Citations of the Old Testament by the New Testament," in Berding and Lunde, eds., *Three Views on the NT Use of the OT,* 45-89 (responses: 152-58, 218-25).

jeopardy if we, an apostle, or an angel from heaven try to add to, delete, rearrange, or reassign the sense or meaning that a prophet himself received."[50] NT authors may draw out some implications or applications from OT texts, but this involves *significance,* not meaning. Hermeneutically, Kaiser endorses an "intentionality" theory of meaning: a text's meaning is tied to what the author of that text intended to say.[51] This meaning is single, although it may embrace more than one concept or application. A text cannot have more than one meaning.

Kaiser goes beyond dogmatic assertion; he seeks to demonstrate his approach's validity by inductively tackling some of the NT's knottiest problem-quotations. For example, our section on "Applying Old Testament Principles" (pp. 708-9 above) summarizes how he interprets 1 Corinthians 9:9. His approach to the text illustrates his method: he carefully considers the OT context of the text cited, particularly the larger theological context that many exegetes ignore or fail to see. An illegitimately atomistic exegesis or a narrow, one-sided concern with form-critical questions frequently prevents exegetes from recognizing the "informing theology," the rich tapestry of unfolding theological themes and concepts within the OT that provide the crucial context for many OT texts that the NT cites.[52] If we sufficiently account for this theological context in both the OT and the NT, apparent discrepancies disappear between the meaning of OT texts and the meaning that the NT gives OT texts.

Strengths

Kaiser commendably highlights how serious this issue is, and much of his approach is right on target.

1. Kaiser exegetes theologically. Far too many OT exegetes focus exclusively on putative stages of tradition and rigidly interpret texts in terms of hypothetical *Sitze im Leben.* Or they are so concerned to find and defend the "original" meaning of the text that they simply ignore larger theological and canonical concerns. Such myopic exegesis entirely ignores or obscures the OT's theological significance. Because it does not interpret the OT naturally, contextually,

50. Walter C. Kaiser Jr., "Legitimate Hermeneutics," in *Inerrancy,* ed. Norman L. Geisler (Grand Rapids: Zondervan, 1980), 135.

51. Here Kaiser leans heavily on Hirsch, *Validity in Interpretation,* although there is some doubt as to whether Kaiser fully appreciates Hirsch's own refined perspective. See E. D. Hirsch Jr., "Meaning and Significance Reinterpreted," *Critical Inquiry* 11 (1984): 202-24; "Transhistorical Intentions and the Persistence of Allegory," *New Literary History* 25 (1994): 549-67. And see especially the restatement of an author-focused approach in Vanhoozer, *Is There a Meaning in This Text?*

52. Kaiser has been strongly influenced by Willis J. Beecher, *The Prophets and the Promise,* L. P. Stone Lectures (New York: Crowell, 1905).

or *theologically,* the alleged discrepancies it finds between the OT and NT are neither significant nor surprising since the NT authors read the OT as a single, thoroughly theological book.

2. Kaiser insists that a text has a single, determinative meaning. "Hermeneutical nihilism" plagues much modern literary criticism.

3. Kaiser successfully demonstrates that his theory explains several otherwise problematic NT applications of OT texts.

Weaknesses

Kaiser's proposal raises several questions. Some wrongly criticize him for committing the "intentional fallacy."[53] More serious is the criticism that he does not sufficiently allow for the intention of the divine author of Scripture or for the "added" meaning that a text takes on as a result of the ongoing canonical process. We deal with those issues in our sections addressing "Typology," *"Sensus Plenior,"* and "Canonical Approach" (pp. 725-36 below). Here we simply note that it is not so certain that meaning should be confined to the intention of the human author of Scripture.

1. While many OT exegetes miss or marginalize overarching theological constructs that undergird OT texts, Kaiser occasionally finds more theology than OT texts clearly support. For example, Kaiser argues that the key to the use of Hosea 11:1 in Matthew 2:15 is that Hosea "no doubt understood the technical nature of 'my son' along with its implications for corporate solidarity."[54] It is of course true that the OT uses "son" to describe Israel (e.g., Exod. 4:22). But what is the evidence that these other texts, or, more importantly, Hosea himself, used "son" in a corporate and individual sense? Ultimately, the crucial question is whether Kaiser's approach can solve every "problem text." Kaiser's approach succeeds only if the "informing theology" of the OT sufficiently undergirds the context of each OT text.

2. Kaiser's distinction between an OT text's meaning and significance does not always work. He argues that (1) the NT must apply an OT text's *meaning* in a way its OT author intended, but (2) the NT may apply an OT text's *significance* in a way its OT author did not consciously intend. For example, in the use of

53. See the criticism of Philip B. Payne, "The Fallacy of Equating Meaning with the Human Author's Intention," *JETS* 20 (1977): 243-52. See Walter C. Kaiser Jr. and Moisés Silva, *Introduction to Biblical Hermeneutics: The Search for Meaning,* 2nd edition (Grand Rapids: Zondervan, 2007), 29-30. The "intentional fallacy" describes the notion that one can appeal behind the text to the intention of the author. But Kaiser clearly insists that intention be tied to the evidence of the text. See also John Warwick Montgomery, "Biblical Inerrancy: What Is at Stake?" in *God's Inerrant Word: An International Symposium on the Trustworthiness of Scripture,* ed. John Warwick Montgomery (Minneapolis: Bethany Fellowship, 1974), 31.

54. Kaiser, *Uses of the OT in the New,* 47-53.

Deuteronomy 25:4 in 1 Corinthians 9:9, the OT text's *meaning* is the principle that workers (whether animal or human) deserve to be rewarded. Paul validly applies that principle to Christian ministers because he draws out the text's *significance.*

But that distinction is not so neat when NT authors appear to assign more or different "meaning" to an OT text than we can legitimately infer was part of the OT author's intention. This seems to be the case when the NT applies to Jesus OT texts describing God or Yahweh. Romans 10:13, for instance, applies to faith in Jesus the words of Joel 2:32: "Everyone who calls on the name of the LORD will be saved." There is no evidence from Joel or "antecedent theology" that the prophet intentionally refers to Christ. Of course, from what the NT reveals about Jesus, we understand that the NT legitimately applies OT passages about God to Jesus. Perhaps Kaiser regards this as an instance where an NT author perceives further significance in the Joel text, but this kind of procedure seems to go beyond drawing out the OT text's significance. Paul expands and more precisely defines the meaning of the word "Yahweh" (= LXX *kyrios*).[55]

Similarly, the NT applies to Jesus texts like Psalm 2:7 ("You are my son; today I have become your father") and 2 Samuel 7:14 ("I will be his father, and he will be my son"). The concept of the Davidic king and his descendants as the heirs to the promise is behind both texts, but the meaning of the word "son" is distinctly different when applied to David or Solomon than when applied to Jesus.

Partial Solution

Kaiser's theological exegesis partially solves our problem. We are extremely sympathetic to Kaiser's general approach and strongly support much of it, but it does not satisfactorily answer all the problems raised by the NT's use of the OT. Sometimes the NT attributes to OT texts more meaning than the OT author could have possibly known. That is fatal to inerrancy only if the meaning of OT texts must be confined to what we can prove their human authors intended. The next four proposed solutions look beyond the original human author.

Richard B. Hays's Intertextual Approach

One of the most innovative books on the use of the OT in the NT in recent decades is Richard B. Hays's *Echoes of Scripture in the Letters of Paul.* Hays argues for an intertextual approach to Paul's use of the OT, and his carefully worked out view is a good representative of this latest direction in interpretation.

55. However, see, for a different approach, C. K. Rowe, "Romans 10:13: What Is the Name of the Lord," *HBT* 22 (2000): 135-73.

Definition

Intertextuality, like so many recent developments in biblical exegesis, is indebted to insights from literary analysis. It focuses on how texts written at different times and places can resonate with one another, shedding new insight on both the old text and the new one. Intertextuality emphasizes that texts relate to one another at more fundamental levels than the explicit quotations we have focused on. Authors influenced by another text will express their dependence in a variety of ways, some of them subtle and discerned only by very careful reading.[56] We can clearly observe this process in the OT itself, and Hays sees Paul as continuing that pattern of intertextual interpretation that the Scripture itself appears to validate.

Hays focuses particularly on the literary convention of what he calls "allusive echo," *transumption,* or *metalepsis,* which he explains as follows: "When a literary echo links the text in which it occurs to an earlier text, the figurative effect of the echo can lie in the unstated or suppressed (transumed) points of resonance between the two texts."[57] In other words, an intertextual approach views allusions between texts in light of a broad interplay between those texts. Explicit quotations are the tip of an intertextual iceberg, representing only the surface level of far-ranging intertextual relationships.

Hays's insistence that Paul quotes OT texts with attention to their larger context is similar to C. H. Dodd's famous argument that NT writers quote from blocks of OT texts.[58] But Hays goes much further than Dodd in finding what he calls "echoes" that NT quotations and allusions awaken as the perceptive reader reflects on the rich and sometimes confusing interplay between NT fulfillment and OT context and narrative.

Example: Isaiah 52:5 in Romans 2:24

Hays's interpretation of Paul's quotation of Isaiah 52:5 in Romans 2:24 is a good example.[59] At the surface level, Paul seems to misquote the OT text. But when

56. The intertextual approach is usually traced especially to the work of Julia Kristeva. See the collection of her essays in *The Kristeva Reader,* ed. Toril Moi (New York: Columbia University Press, 1986). "Intertextuality," properly defined, carries with it assumptions about the way texts relate that would generally not be accepted among evangelicals. So it is important that evangelicals who do use this word use it knowledgably and clarify what they mean by it. See Richard J. Schultz, "Intertextuality, Canon and 'Undecidability': Understanding Isaiah's 'New Heavens and New Earth' (Isaiah 65:17-25)," *BBR* 20 (2010): 19-38.

57. Hays, *Echoes of Scripture,* 20.

58. C. H. Dodd, *According to the Scriptures: The Sub-Structure of New Testament Theology* (London: Nisbet, 1952), esp. 126-27.

59. Hays, *Echoes of Scripture,* 45-46.

we view the quotation in the light of the larger context of Isaiah 52 and of the direction of the argument in Romans, a different picture emerges. Isaiah 52 goes on to speak of God's eventual mercy to Israel, and Paul, of course, does the same thing as Romans progresses. Thus, Hays argues, once we have read to the end of Romans, we recognize that Paul's negative reading of Isaiah 52:5 is only provisional in light of the letter's larger argument.

Strengths

Hays's particular version of intertextuality has at least two strengths:

1. Against those who think that Paul quotes atomistically in proof-text fashion, Hays rightly insists that Paul often shows regard for the larger context from which he quotes.

2. Hays is also right, we think, to suggest that a rather linear and simplistic model of literary relationship has often constricted our approaches to the problem of the OT in the NT. Texts with which we are very familiar shape our thinking and writing in many different ways — some obvious, some very subtle. Hays rightly argues that we must approach Paul's interaction with the OT expecting that the OT will influence his writing in a variety of ways, some of them subtle and perhaps even unconscious to Paul himself.

Weaknesses

But we are not yet ready to jump on the intertextual bandwagon.

1. Our reaction to many interpretations indebted to a broadly intertextual approach is that they are too clever by half. Subtle relationships — sometimes too subtle for us to discern — become the central interpretive focus, often subordinating or even driving out what seem to be the text's explicit concerns. We are not so sure, for instance, that a reader of Romans, however perceptive, would note the word of promise that Hays finds in Paul's quotation of Isaiah 52:5.

2. But a more serious problem, particularly relevant to our own agenda, is the problem of validity. Hays's intertextual proposal offers little help at this point. He argues that Paul was not concerned about exegeting the OT's "original sense." Rather, under the influence of the Spirit, Paul read the OT in light of its culmination in Christ and uncovered latent meaning in the text of which the original authors themselves would often have been unaware.[60] Paul was himself convinced that his interpretations brought out the true, eschatological sense of the Scriptures, but the gap that we perceive between the original sense and the

60. Hays, *Echoes of Scripture,* 154-56.

NT application remains. Hays, we think, would argue that this gap — or at least the problem of the gap — is partly of our own making. It is only because we insist that the "historical-grammatical" method is the only way to uncover the "true" sense of the text that we have a problem at all. The gap we are talking about is created by our rather immodest insistence that the only true meaning is the meaning that *we* discover by *our* methods.

We have some sympathy with this response to the problem, but we need to look at this issue from a slightly broader perspective. We must proceed cautiously because we are moving onto ground that Hays himself does not cover. But we would at least tentatively suggest that postmodern views of meaning and interpretation influence Hays's intertextual approach (along with other similar intertextual methods). Hays seems to suggest that we can affirm that Paul's interpretation of the OT is valid only within the parameters of his hermeneutical assumptions about the fulfillment of the OT story in Christ. Further, Hays suggests that the OT may "echo" in Romans in ways of which Paul himself is not conscious. As Charles Cosgrove comments on Hays's proposal, "Paul becomes Paul-with-his canon, an intertextual field."[61] Lurking in the background seems to be the assumption that we have no "objective" perspective from which we can assess ultimate or absolute validity of interpretation. We have no metanarrative that enables us to evaluate and pronounce right or wrong the narrative of God's activity that Paul finds in the OT.

Postmodernism, to the degree that we understand it, poses both opportunities and challenges to evangelical Christianity. But surely its greatest challenge is the denial that we can discover absolute truth. And it is at this point that we are finally unsatisfied with Hays's proposal about Paul's interpretation of the OT. For all its strengths, it does not go quite far enough in dealing with the problem of validity.

Typology

For many scholars, typology is the key to understanding the NT's use of the OT.[62] Unfortunately, there is widespread disagreement about what it is.

61. Charles Cosgrove, *The Elusive Israel: The Puzzle of Election in Romans* (Philadelphia: Westminster John Knox, 1997), 56.

62. See, above all, Leonhard Goppelt, *Typos: The Typological Interpretation of the Old Testament in the New* (1939), trans. Donald H. Madvig (Grand Rapids: Eerdmans, 1982), 198: "Typology is the method of interpreting Scripture that is predominant in the NT and characteristic of it." See also Patrick Fairbairn, *The Typology of Scripture: Viewed in Connection with the Whole Series of the Divine Dispensations,* 2 vols. (Grand Rapids: Baker, 1975); Roger Nicole, "Patrick Fairbairn and Biblical Hermeneutics as Related to the Quotations of the Old Testament in the New," in *Hermeneutics, Inerrancy, and the Bible: Papers from ICBI Summit II,* ed. Earl D. Radmacher and Robert D. Preus (Grand Rapids: Zondervan, 1984), 767-76; S. Lewis Johnson,

Definition

Typology is not a method of exegesis; rather it is "an effort to hear the two-testament witness to God in Christ, taking seriously its plain sense, in conjunction with apostolic teaching."[63] More specifically, Baker's "working definitions" are helpful:

- A *type* is a biblical event, person or institution which serves as an example or pattern for other events, persons or institutions.
- *Typology* is the study of types and the historical and theological correspondences between them.
- The *basis* of typology is God's consistent activity in the history of his chosen people.[64]

This real correspondence between the OT and NT assumes that God acts similarly in both Testaments, and it is based on the narratives of God's activity in history. The NT antitype heightens the OT type with eschatological "fullness" or an advance *(Steigerung)*.[65] Typology is a specific form of the larger "promise-fulfillment" framework essential for understanding the OT and NT's relationship; it is a core component of the canonical approach (see pp. 734-36 below). This "salvation-historical" movement from OT to NT permeates the NT and ultimately validates its specific, extensive use of the OT.[66] Both the OT and NT

"A Response to Patrick Fairbairn and Biblical Hermeneutics as Related to the Quotations of the Old Testament in the New," in Radmacher and Preus, eds., *Hermeneutics, Inerrancy, and the Bible,* 794; Grant R. Osborne, "Type; Typology," in *ISBE,* 4:930-32; "Type, Typology," in *EDT,* 1222-23; John E. Alsup, "Typology," in *ABD,* 682-85; G. P. Hugenberger, "Introductory Notes on Typology," in Beale, ed., *The Right Doctrine from the Wrong Texts?* 331-41.

63. Christopher R. Seitz, *Figured Out: Typology and Providence in Christian Scripture* (Louisville: Westminster John Knox, 2001), 10. Seitz is referring especially to what is called "figural reading," but his definition appears to be appropriate to typology as a form of figural reading. Goppelt calls it "a spiritual approach that looks forward to the consummation of salvation and recognizes the individual types of that consummation in redemptive history" (*Typos,* 202).

64. David L. Baker, *Two Testaments, One Bible: The Theological Relationship between the Old and New Testaments,* 3rd edition (Downers Grove, IL: InterVarsity, 2010), 180.

65. Kurt Frör, *Biblische Hermeneutik: Zur Schriftauslegung in Predigt und Unterricht,* 3rd edition (Munich: Kaiser, 1967), 86-87: "In every typological reenactment, that which is coming is placed in comparison to the old. It is not a matter of a simple completed form of the old, or of a stage of development . . . but of an eschatological fullness. The relationship, then, is neither a repetition nor a comparison, but a unique end-time consummation" (translation by authors). See also Fairbairn, *Typology of Scripture,* 1:150; Goppelt, *Typos,* 17-18.

66. Oscar Cullmann, *Salvation in History,* trans. Sidney G. Sowers (New York: Harper & Row, 1967), is one of the more important statements of the position, but it is a widely recognized scheme. See also Herman N. Ridderbos, *Paul: An Outline of His Theology,* trans. John Richard

unfold God's character, purpose, and plan, but God's salvation through Christ fulfills OT history, law, and prophecy. That is why NT persons, events, and institutions sometimes fulfill OT persons, events, and institutions; they repeat the OT situation at a deeper, climactic level.

Scholars disagree, however, on whether types must always be *historical* figures, events, or institutions.[67] It seems likely, however, that the NT uses typology with at least the assumption that comparisons are being made with actual history.[68] Related to this issue is the question of the relationship between typology and allegory. Some think that any attempt to differentiate these two approaches is artificial.[69] However, it does seem appropriate to distinguish them, with allegory functioning at the level of the text and the symbolic world it creates (what Treier calls "symbolic mimesis") and typology at the level of history and narrative ("iconic mimesis," according to Treier).[70] Typology is strongly historical; a "real" correspondence must exist between type and antitype. But the real meaning of allegory depends on an extra-textual hermeneutical grid.

Scholars disagree whether typology may function both prospectively (i.e., the OT type has a genuinely predictive function) and retrospectively (i.e., typology is a way of looking back at the OT and drawing out resemblances).[71] Does

---

de Witt (Grand Rapids: Eerdmans, 1975), 44-90; and, for an evaluation of the movement, Robert W. Yarbrough, *The Salvation Historical Fallacy? Reassessing the History of New Testament Theology,* History of Biblical Interpretation Series 2 (Leiden: Deo, 2004).

67. Some claim that a historical basis for the type is unnecessary; all that is required is a "*salvation*-historical" basis. E.g., Gerhard von Rad, "Typological Interpretation of the Old Testament," in *Essays on Old Testament Hermeneutics,* ed. Claus Westermann (London: SCM, 1963), 20-38. However, Richard M. Davidson argues convincingly that the NT's use of typology depends for its validity on the historical reality of the type (*Typology in Scripture: A Study of Hermeneutical* Τύπος *Structures,* Andrews University Seminary Doctoral Dissertation Series 2 [Berrien Springs, MI: Andrews University Press, 1981], 398).

68. Davidson, *Typology,* 398. Jean Daniélou, "The Fathers and the Scriptures," *Theology* 57 (1954): 85: "Typology means not that there is a relation between things visible and invisible, but that there is a correspondence between historical realities at different stages of redemptive history." Typology is inextricably bound up with a salvation-historical scheme, while allegory is not. So Cullmann, *Salvation in History,* 132-33. Cf. Francis Foulkes, *The Acts of God: A Study of the Basis of Typology in the Old Testament,* Tyndale Old Testament Lecture (London: Tyndale, 1958), 35.

69. E.g., Mark Gignilliat, "Paul, Allegory, and the Plain Sense of Scripture: Galatians 4:21-31," *Journal of Theological Interpretation* 2 (2008): 137-41.

70. Daniel J. Treier, "Typology," in *Dictionary for the Theological Interpretation of the Bible,* ed. Kevin J. Vanhoozer (Grand Rapids: Baker, 2005), 825.

71. Davidson (*Typology,* 94) points out that typology has traditionally been viewed as having a predictive function, while many modern advocates see it as entirely retrospective. Thus, Fairbairn (*Typology of Scripture,* 1:46) requires that God design and ordain the type. See Goppelt, *Typos,* 17-18; Johnson, *OT in the New,* 56. On the other hand, others carefully distinguish typology from exegesis and claim that types need have no intrinsic prospective function. See Foulkes, *Acts*

the OT intend the NT's typological correspondence? We would answer "no" if "intend" means that the participants in the OT situation or the OT authors were always aware of the typological significance. On the other hand, we would answer "yes" if "intend" means that the OT has a "prophetic" function. In 1 Corinthians 10, Paul suggests that there is some kind of "prospective" element in typological events. He warns the Corinthians about presuming that the sacraments will shield them from God's judgment by pointing out that the Israelites also possessed a "baptism" and "spiritual food" but nevertheless experienced God's judgment. These events "occurred" to the Israelites "as examples" or types (*typoi* [1 Cor. 10:6]; *typikōs* [1 Cor. 10:11]), which implies that the events were typologically significant when they occurred.[72] While the OT participants and authors in these typological situations may have dimly perceived "anticipatory" elements, God ordered typological situations to function "prophetically."

Example: Psalm 22 in the Gospels

Psalm 22, usually categorized as an "individual lament," figures prominently in the narration of Jesus' crucifixion. Jesus uses its opening words to express his abandonment (Mark 15:34/Matt. 27:46); John 19:24 states that the dividing of Jesus' clothes "fulfilled" Psalm 22:18; and all four evangelists allude to Psalm 22 to depict the crucifixion. On what basis does the NT apply this psalm that does not appear to prophesy Jesus' passion? Five views are noteworthy:

1. There is no basis at all. Albert Vis argues that the early church arbitrarily and illegitimately applied the psalm to Christ for apologetic reasons.[73] But David, who wrote the psalm, is much more than an "individual" righteous sufferer. Many of his psalms are corporately and even eschatologically significant because he was Israel's king and because God made promises to him and his progeny.[74]

---

of God, 20-34; France, *Jesus and the OT,* 39-40; David L. Baker, "Typology and the Christian Use of the Old Testament," *SJT* 29 (1976): 149. For an example of typology that is primarily retrospective rather than prospective, see Andrew David Naselli, *From Typology to Doxology: Paul's Use of Isaiah and Job in Romans 11:34-35* (Eugene, OR: Pickwick, 2012).

72. See especially the careful exegesis of Davidson, *Typology,* 193-297.

73. Albert Vis, *The Messianic Psalm Quotations in the New Testament: A Critical Study on the Christian "Testimonies" in the Old Testament* (Amsterdam: Hertzberger, 1936), 38-40.

74. See Bruce K. Waltke, "A Canonical Approach to the Psalms," in *Tradition and Testament: Essays in Honor of Charles Lee Feinberg,* ed. John S. Feinberg and Paul D. Feinberg (Chicago: Moody, 1981), 11-14. Modern scholarship too often ignores this larger theological setting and significance. Cf. the critique of George Dahl, "The Messianic Expectation in the Psalter," *JBL* 57 (1938): 2: "There seems to be abroad a strangely perverted and sadistically exaggerated sense of honesty in estimating our sacred writings, according to which one ought always to choose the less worthy and less religious of two possible interpretations of any given passage. Whenever in the Psalms the word 'Messiah' appears, every nerve is strained, and every

2. Psalm 22 is a direct messianic prophecy. But the historical circumstances are too clear to accept this proposal.

3. Psalm 22 is part of a widespread "righteous sufferer" motif that the evangelists used to show the innocence of Jesus. This, of course, is true, but simply extends the problem to a larger series of passages.[75]

4. This is an instance of *sensus plenior* (see pp. 730-34 below).[76]

5. The NT applies Psalm 22 typologically.[77] This view is most persuasive. Jesus ultimately "fulfills" the experience and feelings that David undergoes in Psalm 22. David was not necessarily aware of his language's ultimate significance, but God so ordered David's experiences and psalm that they anticipate the sufferings of "David's greater son." Identifying Christ with David in a typological relationship — not chance verbal similarities — undergirds the NT's use of Psalm 22.

Partial Solution

Typology has a prospective element, but sometimes people can recognize it only retrospectively. The Israelites and OT authors certainly recognized the symbolic value of some of their history (e.g., the Exodus) and institutions (e.g., their cultus), but they did not recognize all of the OT types that God designed. Although the NT does not have to specifically designate an OT situation as a type for it to be a type,[78] (1) we would not know of some types if the NT did not reveal them to us, and (2) any types we may suggest lack Scripture's authority.

Typology obviously helps us with our problem. The NT may appear to apply

---

device of forced exegesis utilized, in order to make it refer merely to the secular king and his mundane affairs. Even where the whole context is saturated with the characteristic motifs of Israel's dynamic and intensely religious Messianic expectation, one must never admit that the Messiah is meant."

75. Eduard Schweizer, *Erniedrigung und Erhöhung bei Jesus und seinen Nachfolgern,* ATANT 28 (Zürich: Zwingli-Verlag, 1955), 22-24; Lothar Ruppert, *Jesus als der leidende Gerechte? Der Weg Jesu im Lichte eines alt- und zwischentestamentlichen Motivs,* SBS 59 (Stuttgart: Katholisches Bibelwerk, 1972). On the background of the concept, see Hans Werner Surkau, *Martyrien in jüdischer und frühchristlicher Zeit* (Göttingen: Vandenhoeck & Ruprecht, 1938), 7-29.

76. Pierre Grelot, *Sens chrétien de l'Ancien Testament: Esquisse d'un traité dogmatique,* 2nd edition, Bibliothèque de Théologie 1; Théologie Dogmatique 3 (Paris: Desclée, 1962), 463-64; Donald A. Hagner, "The Old Testament in the New Testament," in *Interpreting the Word of God: Festschrift in Honor of Steven Barabas,* ed. Samuel J. Schultz and Morris A. Inch (Chicago: Moody, 1976), 94-102.

77. Goppelt, *Typos,* 103; Moo, *OT in the Gospel Passion Narratives,* 289-300. For the Davidic connection, see John R. Donahue, "Temple, Trial and Royal Christology (Mk. 14:53-65)," in *The Passion in Mark: Studies on Mark 14–16,* ed. Werner H. Kelber (Philadelphia: Fortress, 1976), 75-77.

78. On this point, see the arguments of Fairbairn, *Typology of Scripture,* 1:21.

OT texts arbitrarily (e.g., based on mere verbal analogies), but these are often based on deeper, typological structures. Typology often explains how the NT's use of the OT is legitimate and coherent, although it is legitimate only if its foundational assumptions (i.e., hermeneutical axioms) are correct: God ordered OT history to prefigure and anticipate his climactic redemptive acts, and the NT is the God-breathed record of those redemptive acts.

But typology solves our problem only partially because it does not explain every problematic use of the OT in the NT. Many NT uses of the OT involve an apparently strained interpretation of specific words, and sometimes the element of correspondence is not clear.

Sensus Plenior

Definition

Sensus plenior means "fuller sense."[79] It is the idea that a scriptural text may have a "fuller sense" than what its human author consciously intended but what God, Scripture's ultimate author, did intend. When NT authors discern this fuller sense, they appear to find "new" meaning in OT texts. But this "new" meaning is part of the author's intention — the divine author but not necessarily the human author.

Raymond Brown, who wrote the most important statement and defense of *sensus plenior,* describes it as

> that additional deeper meaning, intended by God but not clearly intended by the human author, which is seen to exist in the words of a biblical text (or group of texts, or even a whole book) when they are studied in the light of further revelation or development in the understanding of revelation.[80]

79. Catholic scholars coined the term and thoroughly analyzed and debated the concept, but the term's concept (and often the term itself) is also popular among Protestants.

80. Raymond E. Brown, *The* Sensus Plenior *of Sacred Scripture* (Baltimore: St. Mary's University, 1955), 92. See also Brown's later article "The *Sensus Plenior* in the Last Ten Years," *CBQ* 25 (1963): 262-85; Raymond E. Brown and Sandra M. Schneiders, "Hermeneutics," in *New Jerome Biblical Commentary,* ed. Raymond E. Brown, Joseph A. Fitzmyer, and Roland E. Murphy, 2 vols. (Englewood Cliffs, NJ: Prentice Hall, 1990), 1146-65; Edward F. Sutcliffe, "The Plenary Sense as a Principle of Interpretation," *Bib* 34, no. 34 (1953): 333-43; Pierre Benoit, "La plénitude de Sens de Livres Saints," *RB* 67 (1960): 161-96; Grelot, *Sens chrétien,* 458-97; and the survey in Henning Graf Reventlow, *Hauptprobleme der Biblischen Theologie im 20. Jahrhundert,* Erträge der Forschung 203 (Darmstadt: Wissenschaftliche Buchgesellschaft, 1983), 39-49. Andrea Fernández apparently first used the phrase *sensus plenior* in this sense in 1927 (Brown, *The* Sensus Plenior, 88).

Brown's definition has five significant elements:

1. The human author could dimly but not fully perceive the fuller meaning. His awareness of the *sensus plenior* could range "from absolute ignorance to near clarity."[81] Generally, however, *sensus plenior* refers to a meaning that traditional grammatical-historical exegesis cannot demonstrate.

2. The literal sense that the human author intends must relate to the fuller sense that God intends.[82] Advocates of *sensus plenior* insist on this control lest people use the concept to excuse uncontrolled allegorizing.

3. The *sensus plenior* is different than typology. The former involves the deeper meaning of *words,* the latter the extended meaning of *things.*[83] The bronze serpent in the wilderness may be a "type" of Christ on the cross, but applying Psalm 2:7 ("You are my son") to Christ involves a "deeper sense" of the words themselves.

4. The *sensus plenior* is different than what Roman Catholic scholars call "accommodation," applying a biblical text to a situation that the text itself does not envisage.[84] The *sensus plenior* approach is necessary, argues Brown, because "accommodation" cannot adequately handle the data: "[The NT writers] certainly give no evidence that they are using the Scriptures in a sense not intended by God (accommodation); on the contrary, they make it clear that their spiritual meaning is precisely that meaning intended by God, but not realized by the Jews."[85]

5. We can deduce a valid *sensus plenior* only on the basis of "revelation" or "further development in revelation." For Brown and other Roman Catholics, this authority includes the church (the "magisterium") and the NT.[86] The *sensus plenior* is thus very important for Roman Catholics because it provides a way to scripturally justify Mariology and other poorly supported theological concepts. The *sensus plenior* approach is also very popular among Protestants, who confine that "further revelation" to the NT.[87]

81. Brown, *The* Sensus Plenior, 113. Grelot (*Sens chrétien,* 453-55) argues that the author of a given text would not have been aware of the *sensus plenior* in a "notional" way but may have been conscious of a fuller meaning in some other sense.

82. Brown, "The *Sensus Plenior,*" 277; Benoit, "La plénitude," 189.

83. Brown, *The* Sensus Plenior, 92. This distinction can be traced back at least as far as Aquinas.

84. "Accommodation" in this sense is different than "accommodation" as used with respect to God's adapting himself to human words in the process of revelation.

85. Brown, *The* Sensus Plenior, 70.

86. Benoit ("La plénitude," 184-86) wants to confine the *sensus plenior* to relationships between the Testaments.

87. John Wenham succinctly states a kind of *sensus plenior* approach: "The Holy Spirit knew beforehand the course of history with its consummation in Christ, and so in guiding the writers he intended a deeper meaning than they understood" (*Christ and the Bible,* 3rd edition [Grand Rapids: Baker, 1994], 107). Cf. Hagner, "OT in the NT," 91-92; Longenecker, *Biblical Exegesis,* xxxii-xxxiv.

Objections

People commonly object to *sensus plenior* for at least three reasons:

1. *Sensus plenior* lacks objective controls and is easily abused. On what basis does one decide what the Spirit's fuller meaning is through the text's words?[88] Some respond that we should accept only the "deeper meanings" that the NT specifically establishes. But whether we accept that restriction or not, this objection breaks a well-known logical principle: difficulties that a theory creates are never sufficient to falsify that theory if it is well-enough established on other grounds. If *sensus plenior* is a viable concept, we must simply live with the difficulties, much as we live with the difficulties inherent in a teleological view of world history.

2. *Sensus plenior* ruins the NT's apologetic value. The NT authors would not have appealed to a "hidden" meaning in the text because that would discredit their argument. Would skeptical Jews be likely to accept the early church's claims if they were based on unprovable assertions about what the OT "really" means? This objection has a point, but two considerations mitigate its force. (1) We must assess the "validity" of an interpretation in conjunction with the hermeneutical axioms that guide an interpretation. We would not expect, for instance, a Jewish rabbi to be immediately convinced by an NT interpretation of an OT text whose validity depends on the assumption that Jesus of Nazareth is the promised Messiah. (2) This objection assumes that the NT's audience was general and its purpose apologetic. But the design of much if not most of the NT's use of the OT is to assure or convince Christians who already assumed that the OT is relevant for the church.[89]

3. *Sensus plenior* is inconsistent with inspiration. This is the most serious objection. Since no biblical text clearly teaches *sensus plenior* and no biblical text clearly refutes it,[90] whether we accept or reject it finally depends on three factors:

88. John L. McKenzie, "Problems of Hermeneutics in Roman Catholic Exegesis," *JBL* 77 (1958): 202.

89. Cf. Hagner, "OT in the NT," 103 (though he overstates the case).

90. The text often cited with respect to this question is 1 Peter 1:10-12: "Concerning this salvation, the prophets, who spoke of the grace that was to come to you, searched intently and with the greatest care, trying to find out the time and circumstances [*tina ē poion kairon*] to which the Spirit of Christ in them was pointing when he predicted the sufferings of Christ and the glories that would follow. It was revealed to them that they were not serving themselves but you, when they spoke of the things that have now been told you by those who have preached the gospel to you by the Holy Spirit sent from heaven. Even angels long to look into these things." Kaiser argues that both indefinite pronouns in verse 10 refer to *kairon,* so that Peter is not saying that the prophets were uncertain about the person (see, e.g., "Current Crisis in Exegesis," 8). But it is perhaps more likely that the pronouns refer to two different matters: the person as well as the time (e.g., Wayne Grudem, *The First Epistle of Peter,* TNTC [Grand Rapids: Eerdmans, 1988], 74-75).

(1) Is it necessary to explain the phenomena? (2) Does it adequately explain the phenomena? (3) Does it cohere with an acceptable theory of inspiration?

Inspiration is how God breathed out his words through human authors, and the relationship between God and the human authors is "concursive." The final product is Scripture that is definitely and uniquely *God's* word and at the same time the culturally and historically conditioned words of those human authors. The argument against *sensus plenior* claims that if this is so, then *sensus plenior* is inconsistent with inspiration because God would be placing in Scripture meanings unknown to the human authors. This "fuller meaning" cannot be part of the *text* because the meaning of that text is limited to what the divine/human author intended.[91]

This objection has some validity. A view of inspiration that "divides" Scripture's divine and human authors may be as theologically suspect as a Christology that rigidly separates Jesus' divine and human natures.

But this objection is not decisive. Brown replies that Scripture's human authors were not God's "instruments" in a rigid, technical sense. As long as God uses that "instrument" (the human author) according to its "proper sphere" (i.e., cognition and intention) and the human author is always an instrument (in the sense that the "literal" sense is always present and the "fuller" sense does not exclude it), then it is neither impossible nor objectionable that God could "elevate that instrument to produce an additional effect outside the sphere of its proper activity." Brown quotes Manuel de Tuya: "From the fact that God is using an instrument which is capable of knowledge, it does not follow that God can use this intelligent instrument only in as much as he actually knows all that God wanted to express."[92] While not strictly parallel, since the production of inspired Scripture is not involved, the example of the "prophecy" of Caiaphas (John 11:49-52) is suggestive: as "high priest that year," he communicated a message from God that goes beyond anything he consciously intended.

Walter Kaiser objects, "Could God see or intend a sense in a particular text *separate* and *different* from that conceived and intended by his human instrument?"[93] But this erects a wider chasm between the "literal" and "fuller" senses than advocates of a *sensus plenior* conceive. Brown insists that the *sensus plenior* be "homogeneous" with the literal sense,[94] and J. I. Packer, defending a limited "fuller sense," insists that this further meaning "is simple extension, development,

91. Rudolf Bierberg, "Does Sacred Scripture Have a 'Sensus Plenior'?" *CBQ* 10 (1948): 195; John J. O'Rourke, "Marginal Notes on the 'Sensus Plenior,'" *CBQ* 21 (1959): 65-66; Vawter, *Biblical Inspiration,* 115-16; Kaiser, "Current Crisis in Exegesis," 8-9.

92. Brown, *The* Sensus Plenior, 133.

93. Walter C. Kaiser Jr., "Author's Intention: Response," in Radmacher and Preus, eds., *Hermeneutics, Inerrancy, and the Bible,* 444.

94. Brown, "The *Sensus Plenior,*" 277.

and application of what the writer was consciously expressing."[95] The question should rather be this: Can God intend a sense related to but more than what the human author intends? The doctrine of inspiration does not require that the answer be negative.

Partial Solution

The usual objections against the idea of a *sensus plenior* are not cogent, so there does not appear to be any compelling reason for rejecting the hypothesis. We think that a suitably nuanced *sensus plenior* describes at a fundamental level much of what is happening as the NT authors appropriate the OT. Jesus and the apostles discern a "deeper" or "fuller" meaning in the very words of the Old Testament. It is the basis on which we discern this deeper meaning that becomes a critical matter, and to that we turn in our next section.

Canonical Approach

Definition

Recent scholarship has seen a very welcome shift away from atomistic exegesis and being preoccupied with what is "behind" the text (source criticism, etc.) toward a renewed concern with the text's final form. Brevard Childs has put a "canonical approach" on the map of contemporary studies, and the somewhat amorphous and hard-to-define "theological interpretation" approach is also known for such a focus. While recognizing the considerable differences among Childs and the various proponents of theological interpretation, we might summarize the matter by saying that these approaches attempt to solve our problem by focusing on the ultimate canonical context of any single OT text as the basis on which to find a "fuller" sense in that text beyond what its human author consciously intends.

Many scholars who for various reasons do not accept the *sensus plenior* approach embrace this canonical approach. Norbert Lohfink, for example, argues that people think a *sensus plenior* is necessary because historical-grammatical exegesis imposes unnecessarily stringent restrictions on what the "literal sense" is. His solution is a " 'theological' literal sense," which "means nothing other than the meaning of the Scripture read as a whole and in the *analogia fidei*."[96]

95. J. I. Packer, "Infallible Scripture and the Role of Hermeneutics," in Carson and Woodbridge, eds., *Scripture and Truth*, 350.

96. Norbert Lohfink, *The Christian Meaning of the Old Testament* (Milwaukee: Bruce, 1968), 42-43.

Many other scholars advocate a similar proposal,[97] although they do not call it a " 'theological' literal sense" because that term is easily confused with the human author's conscious intention, which is often "theological." They argue that you can legitimately interpret any specific biblical text in light of its ultimate literary context — the whole canon — which receives its unity from its single divine author. The human authors may have had inklings that their words were pregnant with meanings that they did not yet understand, but they would not have been in a position to see the entire context of their words. Some biblical books written before them may not have been available to them, and they were unaware of subsequent revelation.

Strengths

The canonical approach has much to commend it.

1. The canonical approach builds on a salvation-historical framework. In this scripturally sound scheme, the OT as a whole points forward to, anticipates, and prefigures Christ and the church: "all the Prophets and the Law prophesied until John" (Matt. 11:13); "Christ is the culmination [*telos;* goal and end] of the law" (Rom. 10:4).[98] The NT views the OT as a collection of books that, in each of its parts and in its whole, was "incomplete" until Jesus "fulfilled" it by coming and inaugurating the era of salvation. Jesus "fills up" Israel's law (Matt. 5:17), history (Matt. 2:15), and prophecy (Acts 3:18). He also "fills up" the meaning of many specific OT texts.

2. The canonical approach has precedents within the OT itself because it gives deeper meaning to antecedent OT texts ("inner-canonical exegesis"). Outstanding events like the exodus become increasingly significant as they model God's future dealings with his people.[99] As the OT unfolds, Israel's Davidic king more clearly and specifically anticipates the messianic king. The "meaning" of the choice of David to be Israel's king deepens in light of further OT revelation; it goes beyond what David's contemporaries or even David himself recognized.

97. William Sanford LaSor, "Prophecy, Inspiration, and *Sensus Plenior,*" *TynBul* 29 (1978): 54-56; "The 'Sensus Plenior' and Biblical Interpretation," in *Scripture, Tradition, and Interpretation: Essays Presented to Everett F. Harrison by His Students and Colleagues in Honor of His Seventy-Fifth Birthday,* ed. W. Ward Gasque and William Sanford LaSor (Grand Rapids: Eerdmans, 1978), 273-75; Waltke, "Canonical Approach," 5-13; Packer, "Infallible Scripture," 350; Carson, "Matthew," 118-20. Cf. Longenecker, *Biblical Exegesis,* 60-61.

98. For this interpretation of this controversial text, see Douglas J. Moo, *The Epistle to the Romans,* NICNT (Grand Rapids: Eerdmans, 1996), 636-43.

99. Von Rad's salvation-historical approach particularly emphasized this phenomenon. See his *Old Testament Theology,* 2 vols. (Edinburgh: Oliver & Boyd, 1962). Cf. Walther Zimmerli, "Promise and Fulfillment," in Westermann, ed., *Essays on Old Testament Hermeneutics,* 112.

And this meaning reaches its deepest level when the greater son of David appears on the scene.

3. The canonical approach decreases and may eliminate the questionable division between the human and divine authors' intentions in a given text. This approach does not appeal to the divine author's meaning that is deliberately concealed from the human author in the process of inspiration (a *sensus occultus*); it appeals to the meaning of the text itself that takes on deeper significance as God's plan unfolds (a *sensus praegnans*). When God breathes out his words through human authors, he surely knows what the ultimate meaning of their words will be, but he has not created a *double entendre* or hidden a meaning in the words that we can uncover only through special revelation. The "added meaning" that the text takes on is the product of the ultimate canonical shape, although often we can clearly perceive it only if God reveals it.

4. The canonical approach's conclusions are verifiable to some degree. We can often verify the "fuller sense" that the NT discovers in the OT by reading OT texts as the NT authors do: as part of a completed, canonical whole.

Conclusions

As will have become clear, we are not convinced that any one of the approaches we have surveyed is adequate, by itself, to explain the multifaceted nature of the NT's use of the OT.[100] But we do think that three of these approaches, in particular, are important in providing a rationale for the NT's use of the OT. These approaches focus on slightly different aspects of the problem that we are considering.

1. The canonical approach provides the interpretive framework by answering the "why" question.
2. Typology describes one critical way in which the two testaments within the one canon can be seen to relate to each other — the "how."
3. And *sensus plenior* is the "what": the fuller, or deeper, sense that NT writers find in OT texts as they read canonically.[101] The NT authors discern a "fuller"

100. On the complicated relationship between NT and OT, analyzed in terms of the two key trajectories of "mystery" and "fulfillment," see D. A. Carson, "Mystery and Fulfillment: Toward a More Comprehensive Paradigm of Paul's Understanding of the Old and the New," in *Justification and Variegated Nomism*, vol. 2, *The Paradoxes of Paul*, ed. D. A. Carson, Peter T. O'Brien, and Mark A. Seifrid (Grand Rapids: Baker, 2004), 393-436.

101. For this kind of approach in general, see also, e.g., Waltke, "Canonical Approach"; Vern Sheridan Poythress, "Divine Meaning of Scripture," *WTJ* 48 (1986): 241-79; Douglas A. Oss, "Canon as Context: The Function of Sensus Plenior in Evangelical Hermeneutics," *Grace Theological Journal* 9 (1988): 105-27; Darrell L. Bock, "The Hermeneutics of Progressive Dispensationalism," in *Three Central Issues in Contemporary Dispensationalism: A Comparison of*

meaning in OT passages by placing those texts in a wider context than the original authors could have known.

The most basic of all NT "hermeneutical axioms," then, is the authors' conviction that the God who had spoken in the OT continued to speak to them and that it was this final divine context for all of Scripture that determines the meaning of any particular text.

A question often raised at this point is what Richard Longenecker famously asked in his 1969 Tyndale lecture: "Can We Reproduce the Exegesis of the New Testament?"[102] He and many after him have answered negatively. To be sure, our answer requires nuance. On the one hand, we do not have the same revelatory authority to reproduce the NT's specific applications. But on the other hand, we can usually see the theological structure and hermeneutical principles on which the NT's interpretation of the OT rests, and our interpretation can follow the NT by applying similar criteria.[103] The NT establishes a hermeneutical trajectory for future interpreters.

We can better appreciate this approach's nature and usefulness by applying it to some specific examples. In the following examples, the NT extends the OT's meaning, and the best explanation is that further revelation deepens the OT's meaning.

Psalm 8:6 in 1 Corinthians 15:27

In 1 Corinthians 15:27, Paul uses language from Psalm 8:6b to support his claim that all things would eventually be subjected to Christ: "he [probably God][104] 'has put everything under his feet' [*panta gar hypetaxen hypo tous podas autou*]."[105] The reference to this text illustrates the similarity at the level of appropriation tech-

---

Traditional and Progressive Views, ed. Herbert W. Bateman IV (Grand Rapids: Kregel, 1999), 85-101; Bock, "Single Meaning, Multiple Contexts and Referents: The New Testament's Legitimate, Accurate, and Multifaceted Use of the Old," in Berding and Lunde, eds., *Three Views on the NT Use of the OT,* 105-51 (responses: 90-95, 226-31), especially 116; Jared M. Compton, "Shared Intentions? Reflections on Inspiration and Interpretation in Light of Scripture's Dual Authorship," *Them* 33, no. 3 (2008): 23-33.

102. Richard Longenecker, "Can We Reproduce the Exegesis of the New Testament?" *TynB* 21 (1970): 3-38.

103. See Johnson, *OT in the New,* 73-83, 93-94; Silva, "NT Use of the OT," 162-64; Longenecker, *Biblical Exegesis,* 193-98; Beale, *Right Doctrine.*

104. See Fee, *First Corinthians,* 757-59.

105. Unlike both the MT and the LXX, Paul's citation uses the third-person singular verb rather than the second person, but this does not really affect the meaning; the change is necessary to fit the verse into Paul's context.

nique between Paul's use of Scripture and Jewish methods, for in 1 Corinthians 15:25, Paul alludes to the language of Psalm 110:1: "he [Christ] must reign until he has put all his enemies under his feet [*hypetaxen pantas tous echthrous hypo tous podas autou*]." Paul associates these texts on the basis of their similar wording, similar to the Jewish practice of *gezerah shewa.*

Hebrews 2:6-8, another NT text that quotes Psalm 8, is similar. The author of Hebrews apparently associates his quotation from Psalm 8 in Hebrews 2:6-8 with Psalm 110:1, which he quotes in Hebrews 1:13. However, whereas the Jewish technique of associating texts sometimes rested on no more than an incidental verbal similarity, associating Psalm 110:1 with Psalm 8:6 rests on a more substantive foundation. Psalm 8 praises God's majesty and expresses awe that he has given to insignificant humans such dignity and supremacy (with considerable dependence on Gen. 1:26-28); it has no ostensible "Messianic" meaning. What, then, is Paul's warrant for applying this language to Christ?

1. Paul does not really "quote" the psalm but simply borrows its language to make his point (cf. p. 707 above).[106] But although Paul does not introduce the quotation with a formula, he appears to cite the OT as evidence because his appeal is so significant in its context.

2. This is a case of the NT author finding in the OT a meaning unknown to the human author but revealed to the apostle. It is "an inspired exposition of its [the psalm's] hidden meaning."[107] We cannot exclude this possibility, but we should explore other options first.

3. A typological or even prophetic understanding of Psalm 8 validates how the NT applies it. An implicit "Son of Man" Christology lies behind the use of Psalm 8 in both 1 Corinthians 15 and Hebrews 2 because Psalm 8:4 uses the language "son of man."[108] This connection is possible, but it is not clear because neither Paul nor Hebrews has an explicit "Son of Man" Christology.

4. A canonical approach recognizes the theological significance of Paul's Adam-Christ comparison, specifically in 1 Corinthians 15. Paul sees Christ as the "second Adam," the "spiritual," "heavenly," eschatological Adam (1 Cor. 15:45-47).[109] Christ is both "like" Adam as a significant "representative head" and dif-

106. Jan Lambrecht, "Paul's Christological Use of Scripture in 1 Cor. 15:20-28," *NTS* 28 (1982): 510.

107. Charles Hodge, *An Exposition of the First Epistle to the Corinthians* (1857; repr., Grand Rapids: Baker, 1980), 332; Sutcliffe, "Plenary Sense," 333-34.

108. Joachim Jeremias, in *TDNT,* 1:143; Oscar Cullmann, *The Christology of the New Testament* (Philadelphia: Westminster, 1959), 188; George Wesley Buchanan, *The Epistle to the Hebrews,* AB 36 (New York: Doubleday, 1972), 38-51; Pauline Giles, "The Son of Man in the Epistle to the Hebrews," *ExpT* 86 (1975): 330-31. Francis J. Moloney has argued that the targum on the psalm may preserve an early semi-messianic interpretation that could have prepared for Paul's use ("The Reinterpretation of Psalm VIII and the Son of Man Debate," *NTS* 27 [1980]: 656-72).

109. See particularly the discussion in Ridderbos, *Paul,* 85.

ferent from Adam in his origin, nature, and impact on humanity (cf. also Rom. 5:12-21). Paul views Christ as the "perfect" human being — the ideal that Adam did not realize but that the "last Adam" now embodies. Granted Paul's viewpoint, we can see why he attributes language about the ideal human to Christ. The psalm itself does not indicate that it has in view anything other than human beings in their ideal, created state. But in light of NT revelation, we can see that only Christ fulfills the role of this ideal human. Paul does not appeal to a meaning that God deliberately hid in the OT text; he appeals to an extended or ultimate meaning of the text as it is seen in the light of Christ's significance.[110]

So Paul uses Psalm 8:6 in 1 Corinthians 15:27 by applying a NT hermeneutical axiom: Christ, the second human *(Adam),* is the ideal human being. Paul discerns in the psalm a "fuller sense" in light of the larger, canonical, context.

Habakkuk 2:4b in Romans 1:17 and Galatians 3:11

No OT text is more significant for Paul than Habakkuk 2:4b: "the righteous person will live by his faith." Paul quotes it in Romans 1:17 and Galatians 3:11 to substantiate his crucial doctrine of justification by faith. The MT of Habakkuk 2:4b is *w^eṣaddîq be'ĕmûnātô yiḥyeh:* "the righteous person will live by his faith/faithfulness." The LXX has two readings:

1. *ho de dikaios ek pisteōs mou zēsetai* (mss S, B, Q, V, and W*): "the righteous person will live by my faith/faithfulness"
2. *ho de dikaios mou ek pisteōs zēsetai* (mss A and C): "my righteous one will live by faith/faithfulness"[111]

In both his quotations, Paul departs from all known forms of the text by not using any pronoun. He has probably dropped the pronoun to aid his application

110. "As ever, the coming of Christ revealed a whole landscape on the horizon to which the Old Testament was pointing" (Derek Kidner, *Psalms 1–72: An Introduction and Commentary on Books I and II of the Psalms,* TOTC [London: Inter-Varsity, 1973], 68). Cf. Robertson and Plummer, *First Corinthians,* 357; Dodd, *According to the Scriptures,* 117-18; F. F. Bruce, *The Epistle to the Hebrews,* NICNT (Grand Rapids: Eerdmans, 1964), 36; Philip Edgcumbe Hughes, *A Commentary on the Epistle to the Hebrews* (Grand Rapids: Eerdmans, 1977), 83-87; Roy E. Ciampa and Brian S. Rosner, "1 Corinthians," in Beale and Carson, eds., *Commentary on the NT Use of the OT,* 742; Thiselton, *First Corinthians,* 1235.

111. Other Greek versions use the third-person qualifier (8 Hev XII gr, col. 12; Aquila) or the even more clear reflexive (Symmachus). On the textual situation, see Barnabas Lindars, *New Testament Apologetic: The Doctrinal Significance of Old Testament Quotations* (Philadelphia: Westminster, 1961), 231; Joseph A. Fitzmyer, *To Advance the Gospel: New Testament Studies* (New York: Crossroad, 1981), 240-42; D.-A. Koch, "Der Text von Hab 2 4b in des Septuaginta und im Neuen Testament," *ZNW* 76 (1985): 68-85.

of the text.[112] It is less clear that Paul has used this text because it had already become one of the early Christian "testimonies" to Christ in the OT.[113]

To understand how Paul is applying this verse, we must first set it in its context. Habakkuk 2:1 concludes the prophet's second complaint about the Lord's way with his people (1:12–2:1) with him taking his stand to await the Lord's answer, which comes in verses 2-4:

> 2Then the LORD replied: "Write down the revelation and make it plain on tablets so that a herald may run with it. 3For the revelation awaits an appointed time; it speaks of the end and will not prove false. Though it linger, wait for it; it will certainly come and will not delay. 4See, he is puffed up; his desires are not upright — but the righteous will live by their faithfulness — "

As the dashes around verse 4b in the NIV suggest, the reference to the "righteous person" interrupts a denunciation of the person whose soul is "puffed up" or "not upright" (v. 4a; the Heb. here is difficult). A few interpreters suggest that "the righteous" might refer to the Messiah,[114] but the implied contrast with the "puffed up" person along with Habakkuk's other uses of *ṣaddîq/dikaios* (1:4, 13) shows that he is referring to the person within the covenant community who remains loyal to Yahweh. This kind of person, Habakkuk proclaims, "will live by his faith/faithfulness." The identification of the antecedent of the pronominal suffix is unclear. The NIV, along with most English versions, assumes that the pronoun refers to "the righteous." But it could also refer to the Lord (this is the way the LXX reads it, whether as an inadvertent misreading or a deliberate interpretation) or to the "revelation."[115] Probably, however, Habakkuk 2:4b refers to the stance

112. See especially Lindars, *New Testament Apologetic,* 231; Dietrich-Alex Koch, *Die Schrift als Zeuge des Evangeliums: Untersuchungen zur Verwendung und zum Verständnis der Schrift bei Paulus,* Beiträge zur historischen Theologie 69 (Tübingen: Mohr Siebeck, 1986), 68-85; A. Feuillet, "La citation d'Habacuc II.4 et les Huit premiers chapîtres de L'Epitre aux Romains," *NTS* 6 (1958): 52-80; C. E. B. Cranfield, *A Critical and Exegetical Commentary on the Epistle to the Romans,* 2 vols., ICC (London: T. & T. Clark, 1975-79), 1:101-2.

113. As Dodd argues (*According to the Scriptures,* 49-51).

114. Richard Hays, " 'The Righteous One' as Eschatological Deliverer: A Case Study in Paul's Apocalyptic Hermeneutics," in *Apocalyptic and the New Testament: Essays in Honor of J. Louis Martyn,* ed. Joel Marcus and Marion L. Soards (Sheffield: Sheffield Academic Press, 1989), although Hays thinks the text also alludes to people who are righteous by the faith of the Messiah/their own faith; Douglas Campbell, *The Deliverance of God: An Apocalyptic Rereading of Justification in Paul* (Grand Rapids: Eerdmans, 2009), 683-84 (and 613-16 for more detail on Rom. 1:17); Desta Heliso, *Pistis and the Righteous One: A Study of Romans 1:17 against the Background of Scripture and Second Temple Jewish Literature,* WUNT 2.235 (Tübingen: Mohr Siebeck, 2007), who offers the fullest treatment and does not conclude in favor of a messianic interpretation but does argue that scholars should be open to the option.

115. J. Gerald Janzen, "Habakkuk 2:2-4 in the Light of Recent Philological Advances,"

of the righteous person, the interpretation found in both the Dead Sea Scrolls (faithfulness or loyalty to the Teacher of Righteousness [1QpHab 8:1-3]) and later rabbinic texts (Hab. 2:4b summarizes the entire Mosaic law [*b. Mak.* 24a]).

How has Paul appropriated this text? We may identify three "problems":

1. In both Romans and Galatians, "live" has the theological sense of ultimately attaining eternal life. But most scholars think that in Habakkuk "live" means "live out one's life," although the use of *ḥyh* in the Book of the Twelve gives some reason to suspect that the word may have a more theological sense. The verb occurs sixteen times, and apart from places where it refers simply to "living beings," most of the occurrences refer to "true life," "life before God," "blessing" (Hos. 6:2; 14:7; Amos 5:4, 6, 14; Zech. 10:9; the only other occurrence in Habakkuk refers to God's "reviving" his works [3:2]). To be sure, there is still a difference between Habakkuk and Paul, but it is the difference of a fuller conception of what life with the Lord consists in, not a shift from one concept to a completely foreign one.

2. In Habakkuk, "faith/faithfulness" modifies the verb, as the Masoretic punctuation suggests.[116] The situation is not so clear in Paul, who probably connects "by faith" with "righteous" in Romans 1:17.[117] In Galatians 3:11, the issue is much harder to determine; perhaps here Paul connects "by faith" with "live."[118] But even if Paul connects "by faith" with "righteous" in both passages, the difference from Habakkuk is again not great. "Righteous" in Habakkuk does not refer to a person who is morally righteous, but to one who is a faithful member of God's covenant people.

3. The word *'ĕmûnâ* has the sense of faithfulness (NIV), fidelity, or steadfastness.[119] In the OT, of course, people demonstrated this faithfulness to the Lord by obeying his law. Paul, however, appropriates the text to prove that people are in a right relationship with God based on "faith" apart from the law. Again, however,

---

HTR 73 (1980): 53-78; Francis I. Andersen, *Habakkuk: A New Translation with Introduction and Commentary,* AB 25 (New York: Doubleday, 2001), 213-14; Rikki E. Watts, "'For I Am Not Ashamed of the Gospel': Romans 1:16-17 and Habakkuk 2:4," in *Romans and the People of God: Essays in Honor of Gordon D. Fee on the Occasion of His 65th Birthday,* ed. Sven Soderlund and N. T. Wright (Grand Rapids: Eerdmans, 1999), 9-10.

116. We assume that "faith" in both texts refers to human believing rather than to the faith/faithfulness of Christ (contra, e.g., Frank J. Matera, *Galatians,* SP 9 [Collegeville: Liturgical, 1992], 119; Campbell, *Deliverance,* 863 [on Gal. 3:11]). I doubt that "faith" refers to Christ's faith/faithfulness anywhere in Paul. For a survey of the "faith of Christ" debate, see especially Michael F. Bird and Preston M. Sprinkle, eds., *The Faith of Jesus Christ: Exegetical, Biblical, and Theological Studies* (Peabody, MA: Hendrickson, 2009).

117. See especially Moo, *Romans,* 77-78.

118. See especially H. C. C. Cavallin, "'The Righteous Shall Live by Faith': A Decisive Argument for the Traditional Interpretation," *ST* 32 (1978): 33-43; Maureen W. Yeung, *Faith in Jesus and Paul: A Comparison with Special Reference to "Faith That Can Remove Mountains" and "Your Faith Has Healed/Saved You,"* WUNT 2.147 (Tübingen: Mohr Siebeck, 2002), 208-10.

119. A. Jepsen, *TDOT* 1:154-55.

while Habakkuk and Paul are not saying exactly the same thing, their meanings are not as far apart as they might first appear (or as many interpreters insist they are). In the OT *ʾĕmûnâ* refers to an underlying commitment to the Lord, to a "trust" in his person or promises, and in this context to "confident waiting on God to act."[120] In the old covenant era, this trust *resulted* in obeying God's law, but we should not equate it with obeying God's law. The sense of *ʾĕmûnâ* here is not so distant from Paul's concept of "faith," especially if the emphasis on faith in Habakkuk 2:4 depends on Genesis 15:6.[121] As Watson comments, " 'Faithfulness' speaks more adequately of the way of life that corresponds to the vision, whereas 'faith' speaks of the fundamental orientation towards the vision presupposed in this way of life; but each clearly entails the other."[122]

Paul, therefore, deepens the sense of some of the key words in Habakkuk while faithfully affirming what Habakkuk emphasizes: the person who is loyal to God will look for and wait for his vindication on the basis of a deep-seated trust in the Lord and his promises. Paul gives each term a specific nuance that the original does not have, but his interpretation preserves Habakkuk's essential thrust. This is far different from how Qumran documents and rabbinic texts apply Habakkuk 2:4 to law-keeping.[123]

Paul gives Habakkuk 2:4 more depth, new richness, and a more precise significance in the light of the revelation of the righteousness of God (Rom. 3:21).[124] God

120. F. F. Bruce, "Habakkuk," in *The Minor Prophets: An Exegetical and Expository Commentary,* ed. T. E. McComiskey (Grand Rapids: Baker, 1993), 2:861. Cf. Richard D. Patterson, *Nahum, Habakkuk, Zephaniah,* WEC (Chicago: Moody, 1991), 178-81; Charles H. H. Scobie, *The Ways of Our God: An Approach to Biblical Theology* (Grand Rapids: Eerdmans, 2003), 704-6.

121. Moisés Silva, "Galatians," in Beale and Carson, eds., *Commentary on the NT Use of the OT,* 802.

122. Watson, *Paul and the Hermeneutics of Faith,* 161; cf. his larger discussion on 157-63.

123. 1QpHab 7:17 quotes Hab. 2:4 and applies it to "all the doers of the law in the house of Judah" who will be delivered out of the house of judgment because of their sufferings and their faith in the teacher of righteousness (8:1-3a). Clearly, "faith in the teacher of righteousness," linked as it is to doing the law, means something far different from Paul's "faith in Jesus Christ." The rabbis set forth Hab. 2:4 as a key summary of God's demand, but it was related to keeping the law and monotheism (cf. b. Mak. 23b; Cranfield, *Romans,* 1:101).

124. Otto Michel, *Der Brief an die Römer,* 14th edition, KEK 4 (Göttingen: Vandenhoeck & Ruprecht, 1978), 90: "The OT and Jewish thought form has been expanded through the gospel" (translation by authors). Cf. Hermann Cremer, *Die paulinische Rechtfertigungslehre im Zusammenhange ihrer geschichtlichen Voraussetzungen,* 2nd edition (Gütersloh: Bertelsmann, 1900), 348-49; Ridderbos, *Paul,* 172. August Strobel ties Paul's use of this verse to a Jewish eschatological scheme based on Habakkuk 2:3 (*Untersuchungen zum eschatologischen Verzögerungsproblem: Auf Grund der spätjüdisch-urchristlichen Geschichte von Habakuk 2,2 ff,* NovTSup 2 [Leiden: Brill, 1961], 173-202), while Ellis suggests that Hab. 2:4 may function as part of a midrashic structure with Gen. 15:6 as its basis ("Midrash Pesher," 174-77). Neither suggestion has enough evidence to make it convincing.

obviously foresaw this added dimension to his words through the prophet, but there is no evidence that Paul cites the verse on the basis of a hidden meaning in it. God's further revelation is what gives Habakkuk's great principle its ultimate meaning.

Hosea 2:23 and 1:10 in Romans 9:25-26

Paul appropriates the OT a little differently in his mixed quotation from the prophet Hosea that defends his claim that God has "called" "objects of his mercy . . . not only from the Jews but also from the Gentiles" (Rom. 9:23-24). Paul applies Hosea with a striking "shift in application," what Ross Wagner calls "a radical rereading."[125] What might justify this?

Paul quotes freely from Hosea 2:23 (MT and LXX 2:25) in Romans 9:25 and then verbatim from the LXX version of Hosea 1:10a (MT and LXX 2:1b) in Romans 9:26. Paul changes the sequence of the verses, reverses the order of the two clauses he cites from 2:23, and uses wording different from both the LXX and MT:

> As he says in Hosea: "I will call them 'my people' who are not my people [Hos. 2:23c]; and I will call her 'my loved one' who is not my loved one" [Hos. 2:23b], and "In the very place where it was said to them, 'You are not my people,' they will be called 'children of the living God [Hos. 1:10].' " (Rom. 9:25-26)

These differences lead some to suggest that Paul has taken these quotations (perhaps with the others in Rom. 9:25-29) from a catena already in existence.[126] This is certainly possible, since 1 Peter 2:10 attests how popular this language from Hosea was in the early church.[127] Paul does modify the text in several ways, most notably by replacing the more generic verb "I will say" (in both the MT and LXX) with *kalesō,* "I will call." This is almost certainly Paul's own change since it matches exactly the point for which he quotes Hosea (cf. "call" in Rom. 9:24).[128] By reversing

125. J. Ross Wagner, *Heralds of the Good News: Isaiah and Paul "In Concert" in the Letter to the Romans,* NovTSup 101 (Leiden: Brill, 2002), 89.

126. E.g., O. Michel, *Der Brief an die Römer,* MeyerK (Göttingen: Vandenhoeck & Ruprecht, 1978), 316.

127. Others, however, doubt the existence of a pre-Pauline testimonium: Koch, *Schrift,* 104-5, 166-67; Stanley, *Paul and the Language of Scripture,* 109-13. For the use of Hosea in early Christianity, see Dodd, *According to the Scriptures,* 75.

128. Another difference between Paul's quotation and the majority LXX tradition is his use of the verb *agapaō* ("love") in Rom. 9:25b rather than *eleeō* ("have mercy"). It is possible that Paul found *agapaō* in his text (MS B has this verb). Lindars (*New Testament Apologetic,* 243), on the other hand, thinks that Paul independently translates the Hebrew. But it is more likely that Paul himself makes the change in order to compare it with Rom. 9:13: "Jacob I *loved,* but Esau I hated" (Mal. 1:3; emphasis added). See Wagner, *Heralds,* 81-82.

the order of the clauses in Hosea 2:23, Paul places *kalesō* at both the beginning and end of his composite quotation, which clearly indicates where his stress lies.[129]

But a potentially more serious instance of what seems to be arbitrary hermeneutics is how Paul applies these Hosea texts to the calling of Gentiles. Hosea predicts that God will renew his mercy toward the rebellious northern tribes of Israel (or perhaps toward Israel as a whole):[130] God again shows mercy and adopts as his people those whom he rejected and symbolically named (*Lo'-Ruḥāmâ;* "not pitied") and (*Lo'-'Ammî;* "not my people") (Hos. 1:6-9). Interpreters have sought to get around this difficulty by arguing that Hosea's prophecy includes the Gentiles.[131] But, however much one might want to justify this conclusion theologically, there is no exegetical evidence for it. Others avoid the difficulty by arguing that Paul applies these passages to the calling of the Jews rather than the Gentiles.[132] But the chiastic structure of the passage that we note above is against it, and the explicit mention of Israel in the introduction to the Isaiah quotations in Romans 9:27 implies a change of subject. Other apologists for the apostle's hermeneutics think that Paul may imply an analogy: God's calling of Gentiles operates on the same principle as God's promised renewal of the ten northern tribes.[133] But Paul requires more than an analogy to establish from Scripture that God calls Gentiles to be his people.

One of Paul's hermeneutical axioms helps to explain how he applies these Hosea prophecies to God's including Gentiles in Paul's day: the Christian church embodies the ultimate fulfillment of God's promise to Abraham. For Hosea's prophecy echoes the Abrahamic promise of Genesis.[134] The opening words of

129. Rom. 9:26 concludes, "they shall be called *(klēthēsontai)* sons of the living God."

130. Most commentators on Hosea think that Hos. 1:10 refers to the northern tribes only, but Douglas Stuart thinks that it refers to reunited Israel as a whole (*Hosea-Jonah,* WBC [Waco, TX: Word, 1987], 38).

131. See Theodore Ferdinand Karl Laetsch: "Very clearly God here prophesies the admission of the heathen into covenant relations with God" (*Bible Commentary: The Minor Prophets* [St. Louis: Concordia, 1956], 75).

132. John A. Battle Jr., "Paul's Use of the Old Testament in Romans 9:25-26," *Grace Theological Journal* 2 (1981): 115-29.

133. See, e.g., S. Lewis Johnson, "Evidence from Romans 9–11," in *A Case for Premillennialism: A New Consensus,* ed. Donald K. Campbell and Jeffrey Townsend (Chicago: Moody, 1992), 207-10; Jean Noël Aletti, *Comment Dieu est-il juste? Clefs pour interpréter l'épître aux Romains* (Rome: Editions du Seuil, 1991), 219-22; Jan Ridderbos, *Isaiah,* trans. John Vriend, Bible Students Commentary (Grand Rapids: Zondervan, 1985), 565-66. Scott J. Hafemann suggests that Paul's use of *hōs* ("as") in the introductory formula may signal the presence of such an analogy ("The Salvation of Israel in Romans 11:25-32: A Response to Krister Stendahl," *ExAud* 4 [1988]: 47).

134. Perhaps this is why some rabbis applied these Hosea texts to the conversion of proselytes (cf. *Pesiq. R.* 87b; H.-J. Schoeps, *Paul: The Theology of the Apostle in the Light of Jewish Religious History* [Philadelphia: Westminster, 1961], 240).

Hosea 1:10 (which Paul does not quote) predict, "Yet the Israelites will be like the sand on the seashore, which cannot be measured or counted." This theme of innumerable descendants is a constant refrain in the Abrahamic promise texts of Genesis, and the analogy with the "dust of the earth" or "the sand on the seashore" occurs four times.[135] Other OT texts use the language in the same way, and Paul quotes one of those texts in the very next verse (Isa. 10:22 in Rom. 9:27).[136] As Stuart reconstructs the logic, "Those who are in Christ constitute Abraham's seed, of whom this prediction of great growth was made."[137] So Paul does not apply Hosea arbitrarily. Rather, he reads the movement of salvation history in which he understands the "seed" of Abraham ultimately to encompass believers from all nations (Rom. 4). The legitimacy of Paul's interpretation of the OT rests on the movement of revelation. Only those who accept Paul's hermeneutical assumptions about the direction of this movement will see this application of Hosea's prophecy as legitimate.

A Final Note

At the end of the day, then, our conclusion to the problem of the OT in the NT is a limited one. We cannot *prove* that the NT's interpretation of the OT is correct at every point. What we can do, however, is to show how the NT's interpretation of the OT repeatedly rests on fundamental hermeneutical axioms that nearly all early Christians shared. In other words, we can demonstrate that their appropriation of the OT is internally consistent.

Perhaps we can shed some light on our approach by looking at some broader issues in contemporary interpretation. The traditional approach to validating the NT's use of the OT rests on what philosophers would call "foundationalism," the idea that we have a solid, unassailable foundation on which to construct and by which to assess our truth claims. Scholars would assume that modern historical-critical techniques would reveal *the* meaning of a particular OT text and that any deviation from that meaning in a NT quotation spells trouble for its validity. Postmodernism, of course, rejects any such foundation and, therefore, has the potential to throw us into a sea of relativism and chaos. But there is a middle position that both acknowledges the problems with foundationalism and yet rejects the relativity of postmodernism. Kevin Vanhoozer calls this "fallibilism," and he insists that the key issue is testability.[138] We may not be able to construct a truth

135. Gen. 13:16 and 28:14 use the Hebrew word *ʿāpār* ("dust") while Gen. 22:17 and 32:12 use the word *ḥôl* ("sand"). The LXX translates both with *ammos,* which also occurs in Hos. 2:1.

136. Wagner (*Heralds,* 89-92) emphasizes this point.

137. Stuart, *Hosea-Jonah,* 41.

138. Kevin J. Vanhoozer, "Christ and Concept: Doing Theology and the 'Ministry' of Phi-

claim from the ground up, each proposition following inevitably and rationally from the previous one and all resting on the unshakable foundation of agreed-upon propositions. But any truth claim must be able to survive the test of rationality and adequacy. Does it make sense? Does it explain the phenomena? If we apply this fallibilism to the problem we are addressing, then we should be asking, "Does the NT's interpretation of the OT make sense? Does it make better sense than the interpretation of the OT found at Qumran or in the rabbis?" We still may not be able to "prove" that the NT fulfills the OT.[139] But we can ask whether the overall framework of biblical truth established by the NT's interpretation of the OT validates their assumed unity.[140] Such a task goes far beyond the bounds of our present more modest study.

The phenomena of the OT in the NT, then, constitute a mixed picture for the doctrine of inerrancy. On the one hand, NT writers claim meanings for OT texts that cannot be demonstrated on the basis of the typical canons of modern grammatical-historical criticism. On the other hand, those canons are themselves no longer given the kind of objective and final weight in our interpretation of Scripture that they once were. In particular, as we have argued, meaning must be a product ultimately of the broader context in which we understand particular texts. Once we admit as vital to our interpretation of all of Scripture the reality of the developing canon, we can cogently argue that the NT's interpretation of the OT is reasonable.[141] Certainly, in our view, the issues do not constitute enough "inductive" data to overthrow the clear claims of Scripture for itself, claims that the Christian church through the centuries has recognized as significant to provide clear and enduring authority for the people of God.

---

losophy," in *Doing Theology in Today's World: Essays in Honor of Kenneth S. Kantzer* (Grand Rapids: Zondervan, 1991), 99-145, esp. 103.

139. See Peter Jensen's essay, "God and the Bible," chapter 16 in this collection.

140. The interplay of induction and deduction, noted by Watson, *Hermeneutics of Faith,* 190-91, is a similar approach to this issue. He explains, "The deductive approach keeps the inductive one from interpretative arbitrariness by insisting that it remains accountable to the texts; the inductive approach keeps the deductive one from abstraction by insisting that it remains accountable to the actuality of Christ."

141. For some examples, see especially Beale and Carson, eds., *Commentary on the NT Use of the OT.*

TWENTY-FOUR

May We Go Beyond What Is Written After All? The Pattern of Theological Authority and the Problem of Doctrinal Development

Kevin J. Vanhoozer

> And it is my prayer that your love may abound more and more, with knowledge and all discernment, so that you may approve what is excellent. (Phil. 1:9-10a)

Introduction: Mapping the Mystery, Walking the Way

> About that time there arose no little disturbance concerning the Way. (Acts 19:23)

Can Christians in the twenty-first century take their bearings from a document that originated in the first? How to remain faithful to the text while keeping biblical faith fresh in the present context is arguably one of the most important questions facing the church today, as it has been throughout the ages.

The Crux of Discipleship: Following the Way

"Mother, may I?" So begins the children's game in which players make various movement suggestions in an attempt to reach the Mother standing at the other end of the room. Every hop, skip, or step taken requires Mother's explicit permission.[1] The game originated in England sometime in the 1700s, about the same time as evangelicalism itself, and is an apt metaphor for the Christian life. For Christians belong to "the Way" (Acts 9:2; cf. 16:17; 18:25; 19:9, 23; 24:14, 22) and are thus followers of him who *is* the way, the truth, and the life (John 14:6). The evangelical variation on "Mother, may I?" is to inquire, "*Father,* may *we*?" and

1. For detailed instructions, see http://www.ehow.com/how_16079_play-mother-may.html.

to address this query to the Bible, the word of God written, in the power of the Spirit and the context of the church.

The Bible is the supreme authority for Christian faith and life. It is the written record of the revelation of the mystery that lies at the heart of the testimony of the prophets and apostles: the gospel of Jesus Christ — God *with* and *for* us, the ungodly. It is the map that charts God's way to us and guides us on our way back to the Father, through the Son, by the Spirit. Luther viewed the sacred page as "coming directly from God, about God, and for the pilgrim's journey to God."[2] Like Israel in the wilderness, God's pilgrim people need divine leading. Like Israel on the threshold of the promised land (cf. Josh. 18:1-4), we need maps — written descriptions of the terrain — if we are to advance and possess it, or rather *him:* the prize of fellowship in and with Christ.

"Mapping" the mystery and "walking" the way are metaphors for the authority of the Bible over Christian thought and life. It is important to follow the way of the biblical texts because there is no other way to salvation, no other gospel (Gal. 1:6-9), no other map to the mystery of God's will set forth in Christ (Eph. 1:9). But what does it mean to take up our book and walk? How can we be biblical when we encounter problems or issues about which the Bible is silent? Scripture says nothing explicit about nuclear warfare, global warming, Einstein's relativity theory, stem cells, or transsexuality.[3] Faced with such issues, do we not have to go "beyond" what is written?

"Not Beyond What Is Written" (1 Cor. 4:6): The Corinthian Principle

The apostle Paul apparently thinks not. He urges the Corinthians to "learn by us [i.e., Paul and Apollos] not to go beyond what is written" (1 Cor. 4:6). It is important to examine this passage in context, however, before making it a universal principle of theological method. Paul is addressing the problem of church divisions in Corinth, prompted in part by those who believe they have attained a superior state of spiritual wisdom, perhaps because they follow a particular teaching or teacher (1 Cor. 1:10-17). Paul views apostles not as rivals but as servants of Christ, "stewards [*oikonomous*] of the mysteries of God" (1 Cor. 4:1). Theologians, too, are stewards of these mysteries and are required to be trustworthy and faithful — to have an unswerving commitment to the substance of God's secret things,

2. Kenneth Hagen, "Luther, Martin (1483-1546)," in *Historical Handbook of Major Biblical Interpreters,* ed. Donald K. McKim (Downers Grove, IL: InterVarsity, 1998), 212-20, esp. 214, 219.

3. The latter forms a case study in my "A Drama-of-Redemption Model," in *Four Views on Moving beyond the Bible to Theology,* ed. Gary T. Meadors (Grand Rapids: Zondervan, 2009), 191-97.

which Paul has already identified as the power of God in the foolishness of the cross (1 Cor. 1:18-25; 2:2-8).

Commentators disagree as to the meaning of "not [to go] beyond what is written." Some translations take the neuter article *to* as a convention for introducing quoted material: "that you may learn . . . the meaning of the saying, 'Do not go beyond what is written'" (1 Cor. 4:6, NIV). What, however, does this maxim mean and, in particular, what does "what is written" refer to? Exegetes express considerable *Angst* over the interpretation of this passage; hence the following suggestion must remain somewhat tentative.[4]

It is likely that some at Corinth were trying to supplement the theology of the cross with a higher, second-stage "spiritual wisdom," a superior form of knowledge that led to boasting.[5] Paul's command not to go beyond what is written is best taken as referring to (1) the Old Testament in general; (2) what Paul has explicitly cited from the OT in 1:19, 31; 2:9, 16; 3:19, 20, about the importance of not boasting in worldly wisdom but rather in what the Lord has done; and (3) the "foolish" gospel message of the cross "in accordance with the Scriptures" (cf. 15:3-4). In context, then, to go beyond Scripture means "to boast in human wisdom supposing that we are, as it were, smarter than God."[6]

According to this "Corinthian principle," then, there is a sense in which Christians must never go beyond the "foolishness" of Christ crucified and the biblical texts that reveal it as God's wisdom and power of salvation. The definitive message of the cross implies a certain sufficiency of the gospel. Christians must not think that they have a superior knowledge of God or way of salvation if this conflicts with the God of the gospel or with the death and resurrection of Jesus Christ. To take leave of the gospel — call it the "bad beyond" (i.e., a move *against* the grain of the text) — is not an option. The question, however, is whether there is a "good beyond" (i.e., a move *along* the grain of the text) — a right and proper

4. Hans Conzelmann pronounces the phrase in question "unintelligible" (*1 Corinthians*, Hermeneia [Philadelphia: Fortress, 1975], 86), and even Gordon Fee ultimately pleads ignorance (*The First Epistle to the Corinthians*, NICNT [Grand Rapids: Eerdmans, 1987], 169). Anthony Thiselton (*The First Epistle to the Corinthians*, NICNT [Grand Rapids: Eerdmans, 2000], 352-55) examines seven interpretive possibilities and opts for a combination of the three most likely, a suggestion that I follow here as well.

5. So Morna Hooker, "Beyond the Things Which Are Written: An Examination of 1 Cor. iv.6," *NTS* 10 (1963): 127-32.

6. Richard B. Hays, *First Corinthians*, IBC (Louisville: John Knox, 1997), 69. Cf. Robert H. Gundry: "So to go beyond the things that are written would be to put a high estimate on worldly wisdom, in contradiction of Scripture, and thus be 'puffed up'" (*Commentary on the New Testament: Verse-by-Verse Explanations with a Literal Translation* [Peabody, MA: Hendrickson, 2010], 641). See also J. Ross Wagner, who argues that "what is written" refers specifically to what Paul cites in 1 Cor. 1:31 ("Let the one who boasts, boast in the Lord"), as this citation expresses a command that one can actually go beyond ("'Not Beyond the Things Which Are Written': A Call to Boast Only in the Lord (1 Cor. 4:6)," *NTS* 44 [1998]: 279-87).

way of building on and respecting the prophets and apostles that yields a *longer* obedience, and a *longer* understanding, in the same direction. Is there a way to go further than the Scriptures without ever leaving them behind? Stated differently: Can there be a *biblical* development of *biblical* doctrine?

The Protestant, Puritan, and Philippian Principles

The word of God is authoritative over Christian belief and action alike: it governs Mary and Martha, John and Peter.[7] In less figurative terms: the Bible governs both dogmatic and moral theology, both knowing and loving God. The Protestant principle, *sola scriptura,* asserts the Bible's right of final say-so as concerns all matters of truth and right, faith and practice, thought and life.[8]

Merely to give lip rather than life service to biblical authority is to make of the Protestant principle a paper tiger. It is also inadvisable to distinguish too strictly its authority over belief and behavior respectively. What we may term the Puritan principle is closer to the mark: biblical authority is a matter not simply of *knowing that* (this way mere theoretical knowledge lies) but of *knowing what* and *how* to say and do the kinds of things that Christian disciples ought to be saying and doing. The Puritans considered conscience the means through which God brings his word to bear on their daily lives.[9] J. I. Packer notes that the Puritans "agreed in conceiving of conscience as a rational faculty, a power of moral self-knowledge and judgment, dealing with questions of right and wrong, duty and desert, and dealing with them authoritatively, as God's voice."[10] William Ames is a good example.[11] He argues that conscience is cognitive power that issues in practical judgment: a deliberation on God's call and one's context that fixes on a particular course of action.

7. Augustine's thoughts on the relation of contemplation and action arise from his sermons on the biblical accounts of Mary and Martha and his reflections on Peter and John in his *Tractates on the Gospel of John.* It is noteworthy that, though he held contemplation to be superior to action ("Mary has chosen the better part" [Luke 10:42 NRSV]), in the *City of God* 19.19 he presents action (i.e., love) as the royal road to contemplation (i.e., truth).

8. Philip Schaff refers to the "formal" or "knowledge" principle of the Reformation in *The Principle of Protestantism* (Eugene, OR: Wipf & Stock, 2004; orig. pub. 1845), 98.

9. Of course, one can also appeal to the findings of conscience to counter or qualify what the Bible says, as was the wont of modern liberals. An Anabaptist appeal to the Spirit's speaking to individuals is but a variation on this theme. I shall argue below, however, that a biblically disciplined, Spirit-illumined, catholic conscience does indeed belong in the pattern of theological authority.

10. J. I. Packer, *A Quest for Godliness: The Puritan Vision of the Christian Life* (Wheaton, IL: Crossway, 1990), 109.

11. William Ames, *Conscience with the Power and Cases Thereof* (Norwood, NJ: Walter J. Johnson, 1975 [orig. pub. 1639]).

To walk the way of Jesus Christ in new situations, according to the Scriptures, requires allegiance to both the Protestant and the Puritan principles. One needs both the canon and conscience, both an objective foundation and frame of reference — "the foundation of the apostles and prophets" (Eph. 2:20) — and the subjective, Spirit-given ability rightly to understand it (1 Cor. 2:12-14). Both come together in what we could term the Philippian principle: "be thus minded" (Phil. 3:15, ASV). The apostle Paul exhorts those who are mature to "think this way" (i.e., his way, Christ's way) and, by implication, to "act this way" as well.

Paul employs the term *phroneō* ("to think, judge, or give one's mind to") and its cognates ten times in his letter to the Philippians (1:7; 2:2 [twice]; 2:5; 3:15 [twice]; 3:19; 4:2; 4:10 [twice]). *Phronēsis* refers to reason in its practical rather than theoretical mode, but it need not follow that it has nothing to do with systematic theology. The latter, insofar as it must deliberate on what to say and do to be faithful to the word of God in the face of intellectual and cultural problems, is a form of practical reasoning too.[12]

The present essay answers our lead question by reference to all three principles: Philippian, Puritan, and Protestant. For " 'Authority' is a term of practical reason,"[13] conscience too is "one part of practical reason,"[14] and Scripture is authoritative because it rules all forms of Christian reasoning. Discipleship means following the way of Jesus Christ. Such following involves both knowing and loving God. Disciples must understand who God is, what God has done, and what it means to live well to God's glory.

Knowing the truth is a necessary but not sufficient condition for followers of the Way: "You believe that God is one; you do well. Even the demons believe — and shudder!" (James 2:19). Technical correctness with regard to monotheism is not enough; the question for would-be disciples rather concerns how we respond to the one true God. We must believe, and *shuffle* — take at least baby-steps forward.

12. In saying this I am by no means reducing doctrinal truth to practice, only reminding us that truth is something that must be done — something to which we must conform and correspond if we would be wise. There are truths about the created order, for example, but it takes *phronēsis* to discern and fit in with it. Theology exists to help us discern and do the truth, to discover and desire to participate in the order of creation as it is being renewed in Christ. This is not to say that there is no place for eternal truths about God (there is!), though I would perhaps not go as far as Thomas Aquinas and call theology "a speculative science" (*Summa Theologiae* I, q. 1, art. 4). For an example of the importance of not going "beyond" the created order, see my treatment of cognitive enhancement technology in John Kilner, ed., *Why the Church Needs Bioethics: A Guide to Wise Engagement with Life's Challenges* (Grand Rapids: Zondervan, 2011), chapter 5.

13. Oliver O'Donovan, "The Reading Church: Scriptural Authority in Practice," http://www.fulcrum-anglican.org.uk/page.cfm?ID=422.

14. Thomas Goodwin, *Works of Thomas Goodwin,* vol. 6: *The Work of the Holy Spirit in Our Salvation* (Edinburgh: James Nichol, 1863), 272.

We must attend, with Paul, to Christian *phronēsis;* with the Puritans, to conscience; and with Protestants, to how Scripture rules both. Conscience is a compass that keeps disciples moving in the right direction, but only when calibrated by the canonical Scriptures that orient it to the magnetic north of God's living Word. To combine the Philippian, Puritan, and Protestant principles is to have one's conscience captive to the canon, one's inner compass oriented to the mind of Christ.

Paul depicts the disciple's life in terms of not only walking but racing: rapid movement in the right direction, toward the finish line. The Christian life is a steeplechase, a race in which runners take their bearings from church steeples as they run from one town to the next. The scenery has changed. We are no longer running through first-century Palestine. There are new challenges that complicate the course of discipleship (e.g., pluralism; postmodernity) — the intellectual and cultural equivalents of streams, stone walls, and ugly ditches.

May we ever go beyond what is written in our attempt to map the mystery and walk the way of Jesus Christ? The way forward through the storms of life is to fasten our hearts and minds to the mast of Scripture. We ought to say, with Luther, "My conscience is captive to the Word of God."[15] Yet which is the more reliable guide: canonical compass or church steeple? Scripture or tradition? Calvin devotes the longest of his four books in the *Institutes* to an examination of the external means "by which God invites us into the society of Christ and holds us therein," the chief of which is the holy catholic church, "our Mother."[16] Canon, conscience, church: Is it ever legitimate to appeal to the latter two in order to go "beyond" the first?[17] Mother, may we?

The Pattern of Theological Authority

Disciples need authoritative words to help them discern the truth of God and the way of Jesus Christ. Authority is the right or power to command people to walk this way rather than that: "Have *this* mind; do *this;* say *this.*" It should be obvious that the shape and substance of theological systems, both dogmatic and moral, have everything to do with their principles of authority. P. T. Forsyth rightly comments, "As soon as the problem of authority really lifts its head, all others fall to the rear . . . the principle of authority is ultimately the whole religious question."[18]

15. Diet of Worms, April 18, 1521.

16. *Institutes* 4.1.1. Calvin is here echoing Cyprian's thought: "One cannot have God for a Father who does not have the church for a Mother" (Cyprian, *De unitate ecclesiae* 6).

17. Note these three can be expanded into the more familiar Wesleyan quadrilateral: Scripture, reason and experience (both ingredients of conscience), and tradition (an aspect of "church").

18. P. T. Forsyth, *The Principle of Authority* (London: Hodder & Stoughton, 1913), 1, 3.

God, the unauthored Author of all, is the primal and final authority. While this is relatively undisputed, opinions diverge widely as to who speaks for God: "For there is no authority except from God, and those that exist have been instituted by God" (Rom. 13:1). As we have seen, canon, conscience, and church all clamor to be heard, and obeyed. The real challenge, then, is to specify not simply the principle of authority but also its *pattern* — the ordered way in which God expresses and executes his authority. I agree with Bernard Ramm: *"In Christianity the authority-principle is the Triune God in self-revelation."*[19] Elsewhere I have suggested that the triune God is our Scripture principle.[20] Stated differently: the Bible is the prime ingredient in the economy of communication by which the Father preaches the Son in the power of the Spirit. God the Father is the giver and revealer of Scripture; God the Son is the main theme; God the Spirit is the author and interpreter.[21] The Bible is God's word addressed to everyone, everywhere, at all times.

The triune God communicates his will — indeed, even himself (i.e., his light, life, and love) — through various media, with Scripture holding pride of place as the authoritative account of all his communicative activities. Note well: divine authority necessitates divine speaking, for without God's own verbal revelation we would never know what God was like or what God was up to. Word and deed are twin forms of communicative action. In the words of B. B. Warfield: "[I]t is easy to talk of revelation by deed. But how little is capable of being revealed by even the mightiest deed unaccompanied by the explanatory word."[22] Jesus Christ is God's corporeal discourse, to be sure, yet it is the canonical discourse that provides the normative specification of the Son's person and work.

The Bible, then, is triune discourse: something (content; testimony) someone (prophets; apostles; ultimately God) says about something (God; humanity; the world; the gospel) in some way (literary form; canon) for some purpose (revelation; redemption). The Scriptures have supreme authority. Yet the pattern of theological authority — the way in which we move from page to interpretation and practice — involves other ingredients as well. In particular, we need to account for the Spirit's leading the church (and often individuals) into all truth

19. Bernard Ramm, *The Pattern of Religious Authority* (Grand Rapids: Eerdmans, 1957), 21.

20. See my "Triune Discourse: Theological Reflections on the Claim That God Speaks," in *Trinitarian Theology for the Church: Scripture, Community, Worship,* ed. Daniel J. Treier and David Lauber (Downers Grove, IL: InterVarsity, 2009), 76.

21. N. T. Wright makes a similar claim: "The phrase 'authority of Scripture' can make Christian sense only if it is a shorthand for 'the authority of the triune God, exercised somehow *through* Scripture'" (*The Last Word: Beyond the Bible Wars to a New Understanding of the Authority of Scripture* [San Francisco: HarperSanFrancisco, 2005], 23), as does J. I. Packer (*God Has Spoken* [Grand Rapids: Baker, 1979], 97).

22. Benjamin B. Warfield, "Christian Supernaturalism," in his *Biblical and Theological Studies* (Phillipsburg, NJ: P&R, 1952), 17.

(John 16:13), a promise fulfilled in, with, and through the writings of the New Testament canon. The church, as Francis Turretin rightly observes, is Scripture's keeper, defender, and interpreter.[23] The church does not lord it over the Scriptures in unfolding the true sense of the text, however, for it exercises a ministerial rather than magisterial authority.

We can expand this thought to say that the pattern of theological authority is the triune God in communicative action, speaking magisterially in Scripture and ministerially through church tradition and conscience insofar as these accord with the word written. The newly minted statement of faith of the World Reformed Fellowship comes to a similar conclusion:

> Since the completion of the New Testament canon, the normative pattern has been for God to speak to us in and through the Holy Scriptures with the enlightenment of the Holy Spirit, who dwells in our hearts and reveals both the Father and the Son to us. Those who hear the Spirit's voice receive the inheritance promised to us in the Son, and with his help they do the will of the Father in their lives. It is to teach us what this means and to guide us as we seek to put God's will into practice that the Holy Spirit has given us written texts to inform, challenge and encourage us along the way.

Sola scriptura remains the evangelical watchword: Scripture alone is the authoritative script for right participation in the life and love of the triune God because it alone is the authorized text of the only true God. With regard to interpretation, however, Scripture is not alone but *above* other sources, the final but not the exclusive authority. These other sources (e.g., reason, experience, tradition) exercise in the Spirit's hands a ministerial role in interpreting the Bible, especially as concerns matters on which it speaks only indirectly: "For it has seemed good to the Holy Spirit and to us . . ." (Acts 15:28). Yet it remains vital that we ultimately assess Christian speech, thought, and action — the disciple's communicative action and practical reasoning — by divine communicative action, namely, Scripture, the oracles of God.

Doing theology should never be a matter of going beyond the word of God in the sense of leaving it behind or going against it, but rather of going beyond in the sense of *extending* it through patient interpretation, prayerful reflection, and "a long obedience in the same direction":[24] in a word, through ecclesial profession and practice in and for the contemporary context. The pattern of theological authority is thoroughly communicative: the privilege and responsibility of theol-

23. Turretin, *Institutes of Elenctic Theology,* vol. 1 (Phillipsburg, NJ: P&R, 1992) 2.16.1-26.

24. The phrase is Nietzsche's (from *Beyond Good and Evil*), but Eugene Peterson has coopted it to describe Christian discipleship in his *A Long Obedience in the Same Direction: Discipleship in an Instant Society,* 2nd edition (Downers Grove, IL: InterVarsity, 2000).

ogy is that of continuing the communicative activity initiated by the triune God, ministering the word of truth and life, and lighting the way of, and to, Jesus Christ.

The Argument in Outline

In one sense, our most important work is already done. We have set forth the Protestant principle and intimated the pattern of theological authority: the triune God in communicative activity, doing various things with biblical words that, in different ways, solicit our assent, trust, and obedience. It only remains to answer the question — May we go beyond what is written? — by setting forth the pattern of theological authority in greater detail. Accordingly, we begin by examining the genesis of doctrine. Are creeds and confessions examples of going "beyond" what is written? We then consider two strategies at opposite ends of the methodological spectrum: naïve biblicism and modern revisionism. Each in its own way proves inadequate to the task. The next section sets out some of the most popular ways in which evangelicals have sought to deal with our question.

A constructive proposal follows in which I attempt to hold fast to the best of prior attempts to maintain *sola scriptura* even as I set forth a new model with which to conceive its place in the pattern of theological authority. *Phronēsis* or practical reasoning here comes to the fore, together with the idea that the canon rules church and conscience alike. Setting forth a new vision for *sola scriptura* is only half the battle, however; we need concrete criteria as well if we are to put our doctrine of biblical authority into practice in real-world situations, and so make the vision visible. Accordingly, the final section tackles the criteriological question: How do we know we are going beyond the Bible rightly (i.e., along the grain) rather than wrongly (i.e., against the grain)? Disciples need to be able to tell when they are traveling rather than unraveling the pattern of theological authority.

The essay concludes with a plea to distinguish *critical* from naïve biblicism. The latter holds to a monistic principle of authority; the former affirms *sola scriptura* yet acknowledges the ministerial authorities of church tradition and conscience as ministries of the Holy Spirit's formation of people competent to counsel, and judge, canonically.

Where Do Doctrines Come From? The Problem Stated

> Not that I have already obtained this or am already perfect . . . (Phil. 3:12)

The law of the Lord is perfect (Ps. 19:7), systems of theology less so. Only when that which is perfect comes will our partial knowledge pass away (1 Cor. 13:10).

Until then, our theological formulations (i.e., doctrines) must be regarded as corrigible attempts to grasp the truth of God's word written (i.e., *sacra pagina*), together with its presuppositions, implications, and entailments. Theology done "according to the Scriptures" must be prepared to give an account of the manner in which the Bible generates and governs theology.[25]

The Problem: The Development of Doctrine

Let us call *sacra doctrina* (Greek *didaskalia*) the teaching of the Bible itself, and let us call "doctrine" what, on the basis of the Bible, the church believes, teaches, and confesses — both explicitly in its creeds and statements of faith and implicitly in its most characteristic practices.[26] While we may speak of progressive revelation *in* the Bible, evangelicals do not believe that divine revelation progresses *beyond* the Bible.[27] The canonical testimony of the prophets and apostles — twin choirs of inspired witnesses to the meaning and significance of the event of Jesus Christ — closes the book as it were on God's revealed word. *Sacra doctrina* is a fixed set: there is no room for further development of revelation or biblical teaching because Jesus Christ is God's final and definitive word, and he is "the same yesterday and today and forever" (Heb. 13:8). The same cannot be said, however, for Christian doctrine, that is, the church's attempt further to understand biblical revelation and to set forth this understanding in speech. The question, then, is how best to account for this difference — in vocabulary, concept, context, structure, purpose, etc. — between the teaching of the Bible itself and the church's doctrinal statements.

Alister McGrath's clever aphorism perfectly captures the difficulty of formulating doctrine on the basis of *sacra doctrina:* "The genesis of doctrine lies in the exodus from uncritical repetition of the narrative heritage of the past."[28] He

25. Cf. the related question posed to participants in a 2007 seminar at the University of St. Andrews — "To what extent, and on what grounds, does the New Testament shape and prescribe Christian theology?" — and the resultant text: Markus Bockmuehl and Alan J. Torrance, eds., *Scripture's Doctrine and Theology's Bible: How the New Testament Shapes Christian Dogmatics* (Grand Rapids: Baker, 2008).

26. See Jaroslav Pelikan, *The Christian Tradition: A History of the Development of Doctrine,* vol. 1, *The Emergence of the Catholic Tradition* (Chicago: University of Chicago Press, 1971), 1.

27. See Graeme Goldsworthy, *According to Plan: The Unfolding Revelation of God in the Bible* (Downers Grove, IL: InterVarsity, 2002). Note, however, that some scholars contend that there is doctrinal development within the thought of the human authors of the Bible as well. See, for example, E. P. Sanders, "Did Paul's Theology Develop?" in *The Word Leaps the Gap: Essays on Scripture and Theology in Honor of Richard B. Hays,* ed. J. Ross Wagner, C. Kavin Rowe, and A. Katherine Grieb (Grand Rapids: Eerdmans, 2008), 325-50.

28. Alister McGrath, *The Genesis of Doctrine: A Study in the Foundation of Doctrinal Criticism* (Oxford: Basil Blackwell, 1990), 7.

goes on to suggest that the biblical narrative generates doctrine, that doctrine "provides the conceptual framework by which the scriptural narrative is interpreted," and that the conceptual framework is "intimated (however provisionally) by scripture itself."[29] To take a concrete doctrinal example: Is the ontological framework employed in Trinitarian orthodoxy to describe the Son's equality with the Father *(homoousios)* suggested by Scripture itself, or did the fathers at the Council of Nicea go "beyond" what was written? Where does doctrine come from and how can we tell whether its development over time is indeed according to the Scriptures?

Maurice Wiles says that we need a new kind of "doctrinal criticism" that would examine the process of doctrinal development as "biblical criticism" examines the process of the biblical books' composition.[30] Wiles himself, a Protestant liberal, assumes that both processes are purely human, fallible, and contingent. For Wiles, the key criterion for formulating doctrine is not fidelity to past formulations so much as relevance in the present and respect for modern learning. He is therefore willing to "remake" certain doctrines, including, most notoriously, Chalcedonian Christology.[31]

By way of contrast, the Second Vatican Council claims in *Dei Verbum* 8 that the apostolic tradition "develops" in the church under the supervision of the Holy Spirit, for "there is a growth in the understanding of the realities of the words which have been handed down." Evangelicals can affirm this too, with certain qualifications, most notably the rider that all such development — all tradition — stands under the authority of Scripture.[32] Roman Catholics stake this claim as well, insisting that what the church teaches is simply an unpacking of the Bible's inner logic: "All of the councils of the church and all of the church's doctrinal statements are, for Catholicism, re-presentations of the same gospel of Jesus Christ."[33] Protestants object that certain Roman Catholic doctrines, such as

29. McGrath, *The Genesis of Doctrine,* 58-59.

30. Maurice F. Wiles, *Working Papers in Doctrine* (London: SCM, 1976), 160. Wiles borrows the idea from G. F. Woods, who coined the term "doctrinal criticism" to describe the task of subjecting doctrinal statements to the same kind of scrutiny that biblical critics bring to bear on the OT and NT. See Woods, "Doctrinal Criticism," in *Prospect for Theology: Essays in Honour of H. H. Farmer,* ed. F. G. Healey (London: J. Nisbet, 1966), 73-92. See also Wiles, *The Making of Christian Doctrine: A Study in the Principles of Early Doctrinal Development* (Cambridge: Cambridge University Press, 1967).

31. See his *The Remaking of Christian Doctrine* (London: SCM Press, 1974) and "Christianity without Incarnation?" in *The Myth of God Incarnate,* ed. John Hick (London: SCM, 1977), 1-11.

32. So Timothy George, "An Evangelical Reflection on Scripture and Tradition," in *Thy Word Is Truth: A Project of Evangelicals and Catholics Together,* ed. Charles Colson and Richard John Neuhaus (Grand Rapids: Eerdmans, 2002), 31.

33. Thomas G. Guarino, "Catholic Reflections on Discerning the Truth of Sacred Scripture," in Colson and Neuhaus, eds., *Thy Word Is Truth,* 99.

the Assumption of Mary and the infallibility of the pope, lack adequate biblical basis and may rather be seen as depositing new material into the account of faith.

Is the history of theology marked more by continuity or discontinuity? Does doctrine explain further what is already there in the Bible, at least in seminal form, such that development is a re-presentation of what is already implicitly present, perhaps in different terms?[34] Or is the history of theology the story of genuinely novel developments, such that theological conclusions emerge not only from biblical premises but from other sources as well? Both Protestants and Roman Catholics leveled the charge of novelty at one another: "Catholics had corrupted the ancient faith by addition, Protestants by departing from perennial belief and custom."[35]

John Henry Newman's famous *Essay on the Development of Christian Doctrine* (1845) argued that Roman Catholicism was neither a simple continuation nor a corruption of the ancient faith. Neither immutability nor entropy is a helpful model of doctrinal development. Newman proposed an organic model according to which Christianity's seminal "idea" grows as one ponders it. Doctrine is the mature plant that stems from apostolic seed.[36] One problem with Newman's account, however, is its failure sharply to distinguish the progressive revelation *within* Scripture from the progressive reflection upon Scripture from *without.*[37] Another, more significant, problem is that Newman's theory requires the Roman *magisterium* to serve as the final arbiter of doctrinal truth: the institutional church is our "informant and guide, and that an infallible one."[38]

The problem of doctrinal development ultimately concerns the place of Scripture in the larger pattern of theological authority. Protestants have tended to deal with this question under the rubric of hermeneutics.[39] Whether the rubric is

34. Malcolm B. Yarnell III calls this the "classical thesis" of doctrinal development and cites Vincent of Lérins as its chief proponent (*The Formation of Christian Doctrine* [Nashville: Broadman & Holman, 2007], 107-15).

35. Nicholas Lash, "Development, Doctrinal," in *A New Dictionary of Christian Theology,* ed. Alan Richardson and John Bowden (London: SCM, 1983), 156.

36. Yarnell correctly observes that Newman misapplies the metaphor of growth that he takes from Jesus' parables (e.g., Mark 4:26-29), for the parables concern the growth of the kingdom of God, not the development of doctrine (*Formation of Christian Doctrine,* 119).

37. "The development of doctrine from Pentecost to the Pauline epistles is on a par with Ignatius's doctrine of episcopacy and the later determination of the canon" (Yarnell, *Formation of Christian Doctrine,* 122). Cf. Owen Chadwick's pointed question: "In what meaningful sense may it be asserted that these new doctrines [e.g., the Immaculate Conception] are not 'new revelation'?" (*From Bossuet to Newman: The Idea of Doctrinal Development* [Cambridge: Cambridge University Press, 1957], 195).

38. Newman, *An Essay on the Development of Christian Doctrine* (London: Basil Montagu Pickering, 1878), 87-88.

39. So Peter Toon, "Development of Doctrine," in *New Dictionary of Theology,* ed. Sinclair Ferguson, David F. Wright, and J. I. Packer (Downers Grove, IL: InterVarsity, 1988), 196.

doctrinal development or hermeneutics, the crucial question with regard to going beyond Scripture is this: Who speaks for Scripture (i.e., interprets it correctly)? Another key issue, to which we shall return in due course, concerns "the nature of the Holy Spirit's ongoing activity in relation to Scripture,"[40] especially as this involves individual illumination and church tradition.

The Issue: The Sufficiency of Scripture

We have already acknowledged the importance of *sola scriptura* as the formal principle of the Reformation (the Protestant Principle): Scripture is the church's only infallible rule of faith and practice. To unpack the principle further: Scripture is both a necessary and a sufficient Rule. In the first place, Scripture is not only helpful but also *necessary* for coming to know and love God the Creator and covenant Lord. Calvin spoke of the Bible as the spectacles we must wear in order to see God's revelation in nature. As to the covenant, only divine speech could disambiguate divine behavior: we would not be able to know the terms of his covenant, much less the divine provisions for our failures in covenant keeping, without a divinely authored covenant document. Through Scripture, says Calvin, God has "rendered faith unambiguous forever, a faith that should be superior to all opinion."[41]

The question before us, however, concerns not the necessity but the sufficiency of the Bible as the locus of divine revelation and covenant constitution of the church. Yes, sinful human beings need the spectacles of Scripture in order to discern the one true God from idolatrous counterfeits, but do we see clearly enough the way forward? To change metaphors: Are the biblical "maps" reliable enough guides for the church as it enters new historical territory? Does the Bible provide sufficient direction or do we need new maps to supplement the canonical charts? That doctrine has developed in response to new challenges is taken as *prima facie* evidence by some that the church has indeed gone beyond what is written. Such a conclusion is peremptory because it begs the question: sufficient *for what*?

John Frame helpfully distinguishes between particular and general sufficiency.[42] Scripture is sufficient in particular for "making wise for salvation through faith in Jesus Christ" (2 Tim. 3:15). Article 6 of the Thirty-Nine Articles, on the

40. Timothy Ward, *Words of Life: Scripture as the Living and Active Word of God* (Downers Grove, IL: InterVarsity, 2009), 111.

41. Calvin, *Institutes* 1.6.2.

42. See John Frame, *The Doctrine of the Word of God* (Phillipsburg, NJ: P&R, 2010), chapter 32, 225-28. What Frame calls "particular" the tradition has usually termed "material" (see Ward, *Words of Life*, 108).

sufficiency of Scripture, states: "Holy Scripture containeth all things necessary to salvation." Of course, to achieve this purpose it must also suffice for everything that this purpose presupposes, entails, and implies. The Bible, then, is particularly sufficient in showing the way to life with God and godliness: for nurturing faith, hope, and love. The particular sufficiency of Scripture thus pertains to its ability "to form Christians and to guide them toward the destiny prepared for them by God and revealed to them through Christ."[43]

It is significant that both Old and New Testaments, the covenant charters of Israel and the church respectively, contain an inscriptional curse (Deut. 4:2; 12:32; Rev. 22:18-19) explicitly forbidding any addition to or subtraction from God's authoritative word. The Westminster Confession of Faith acknowledges this point: "unto which nothing at any time is to be added, whether by new revelations of the Spirit or the traditions of men." Hence our query: Does formulating doctrine "add" to what is written? As we shall see, one way of going "beyond" the Bible is simply to exposit it. The Westminster Confession says that everything necessary for faith and life "is either expressly set down in Scripture, or by good and necessary consequence may be deduced from Scripture" (1.6). However, there is still disagreement as to how to recognize that something is "necessary for salvation" rather than a matter of indifference, or liberty. The atonement is necessary for salvation, but is it also necessary to hold to a particular model of the atonement? The early church produced no creedal statements on the saving significance of the death of Christ. The atonement is a good example of a doctrine that, one way or another, "developed." The same could be said for others: everything from the Trinity and inerrancy to double predestination and six-day creationism. To what extent are all these "good and necessary consequences" of Scripture's particular sufficiency?

Scripture's "general" sufficiency, according to Frame, means that it contains "all the divine words needed for any aspect of human life."[44] Because we are to do all to the glory of God (1 Cor. 10:31), the Bible is sufficient even for plumbing, at least inasmuch as this concerns glorifying God. The point is that biblical revelation is sufficient at any point in redemptive history to enable disciples to carry out their responsibilities to God. Frame acknowledges that we will need extra-biblical information — the Bible does not tell us how to stop a faucet from leaking — but distinguishes this situational knowledge from the divine words that provide us with ultimate norms. The latter alone enable us to plumb to the glory of God: for example, by encouraging excellent and honest workmanship.

Some will think the above example of the Bible's sufficiency jejune, if not far-fetched. P. T. Forsyth no doubt speaks for many: "The Bible is there for the

43. Rowan Greer, *Anglican Approaches to Scripture: From the Reformation to the Present* (New York: Crossroad, 2006), xi.

44. Frame, *Doctrine of the Word of God,* 220.

Gospel, not for a system, not for scientific proof. . . . It is enough to make us see and taste Jesus. . . . That is the real seat and principle of authority in the Bible, the grace of God bringing salvation in Jesus Christ."[45] Yet Frame could rightly respond that the quest for godliness is not limited to "religion" but involves all that we say and do. In giving us true knowledge of God, the world, and ourselves, the Bible has something indirectly to say about everything.

That the Bible contains everything we need to know for salvation is its "material" sufficiency; that it serves as its own guide to its interpretation — that it sufficiently *constrains* readers — is its so-called "formal" sufficiency.[46] May we also affirm the *doctrinal* sufficiency of Scripture, by which I mean its adequacy as a foundation and framework for formulating doctrine? I agree with Athanasius: "[T]he sacred and divinely inspired Scriptures are sufficient for the exposition of the truth."[47] Scripture is the divinely appointed means by which God generates and governs the church's understanding of who he is and what he has done in the Son and Spirit for us and our salvation. Scripture is sufficient to serve as the church's covenant charter, constitution, and critical principle. It is sufficient to guide, and if necessary correct and reform, the community in the way of covenant faithfulness, even in the face of new intellectual, social, and cultural challenges in the strange new world of the twenty-first century.[48]

Two Inadequate Answers: Replication and Innovation

They all seek their own interests, not those of Jesus Christ. (Phil. 2:21)

May we develop doctrine beyond what is written? We can describe, and dispatch, two extreme responses to this question — an unqualified yes and no, respectively — rather briefly. The one exaggerates the discontinuity between the Bible and Christian doctrine, the other the continuity. Interestingly enough, both err in underestimating the Spirit's ability to illumine the church and her tradition.

45. Forsyth, "The Efficiency and Sufficiency of the Bible," *The Biblical Review* 2 (1917): 15, 27.

46. For a further elaboration of this distinction, see Timothy Ward, *Words of Life: Scripture as the Living and Active Word of God* (Downers Grove, IL: InterVarsity, 2009), 106-14.

47. Athanasius, *Contra Gentes and De Incarnatione,* ed. Robert W. Thomson, Oxford Early Christian Texts (Oxford: Oxford University Press, 1971), 3.

48. This is not to say that we can simply "read off" simple answers from Scripture to complex theological issues: "What the doctrine of the sufficiency of Scripture does recommend is the absolute necessity of careful, faithful, and subtle biblical exegesis as Christians try to listen for the divine voice on these [doctrinal and ethical] issues; the doctrine is however insufficient to determine the exegetical results in advance" (Timothy Ward, *Word and Supplement: Speech Acts, Biblical Texts, and the Sufficiency of Scripture* [Oxford: Oxford University Press, 2002], 299).

Biblicide: Innovating Authoritative Discourse

Theological revisionists happily go beyond what is written for the simple reason that they believe it is an insufficient answer to the pressing needs of the day. One of the hallmarks of modern liberal theology is the belief that the content of the Bible needs revising in the light of scientific learning (e.g., Darwinism) or social breakthroughs (e.g., feminism). This strategy is typical of modern thinkers wedded to an evolutionary view of history that subscribes to the myth of progress, and its presumption that humanity is changing for the better.

Conscience, rather than canon or church, here comes to the fore.[49] Kant's manifesto "What Is Enlightenment?" exhorts modern men and women to "Dare to use your own reason." An enlightened conscience here trumps canon. Of course, such "enlightenment" is every bit as culturally conditioned and relative as the older stories, traditions, and authorities that revisionists with their own rose-colored spectacles dismissed out of hand.

By "biblicide" I mean an approach to contemporizing theology that so revises biblical teaching, in order to make it intelligible and palatable to contemporary culture, as to change not only the form but also the substantive content of the message. Millard Erickson calls such theologians "transformers."[50] George Lindbeck describes them as "extra-textual," for they take something other than Scripture as their authoritative interpretive framework. I call them "innovators" — people who move beyond Scripture in ways that, far from continuing or preserving the past action, introduce new elements and make new initiatives that *break* with the past. Paul's words are apt: "I am astonished that you are so quickly deserting . . . and turning to a different gospel — not that there is another one" (Gal. 1:6-7).

(Naïve) Biblicism: Replicating Authoritative Discourse

David Bebbington's widely cited definition of evangelicalism lists "biblicism" — the belief "that all spiritual truth is to be found in [the Bible's] pages — as one of the four defining marks. To the extent that this definition expresses *sola scriptura,* it is unobjectionable."[51] More often than not, however, both scholars and laypeople use the term in a derogatory sense, when what they actually have in mind

49. I cannot say "into its own" because it does not. Conscience has integrity not when it becomes a self-standing principle but only when it takes its proper place in the pattern of theological authority.

50. Millard Erickson, *Christian Theology,* 2nd edition (Grand Rapids: Baker, 1998), 123-26. He takes as his example the "death of God" movement of the 1960s.

51. David Bebbington, *Evangelicalism in Modern Britain* (London: Routledge, 1989), 12.

comes closer to William Chillingworth's more radical manifesto: "The Bible, the whole Bible, *and nothing but the Bible,* is the religion of Protestants." Keith Mathison calls this "solo" *scriptura.*[52] While it contains an element of truth, Ramm rightly terms it the "abbreviated Protestant principle."[53] The unabridged Protestant principle involves both word and Spirit: both an external principle (i.e., the inspired Scriptures) and an internal principle (i.e., the illumined Scriptures).

Evangelical Protestants must work hard to distinguish *sola* from *solo scriptura.* What is ultimately at stake is not a vowel but rather the pattern of theological authority.[54] Today the term "biblicism" usually refers to an approach to biblical authority and theology characterized by one or more of the following features: (1) a failure to see the importance of extra-biblical knowledge; (2) a tendency to see the Bible as an authoritarian "textbook" that lords it over other textbooks in biology, history, philosophy, psychology, etc. too cavalierly;[55] (3) a lack of respect for creeds and confessions; and (4) an appeal to "proof-texts" taken out of historical and literary context.[56]

It is important not to throw out the Protestant baby *(sola)* with the biblicist bathwater *(solo).* On the one hand, "the genius of the Protestant position forbids any interpretation from possessing the same authority as the revelation itself."[57] On the other hand, "the Reformation made religion personal, but it did not make it individualistic."[58] Moreover: "He who would consistently banish creeds must silence all preaching and reduce the teaching of the church to the recital of the exact words of Holy Scripture without note or comment."[59] The Bible does not stand alone in splendid isolation. It exists in a symbiotic relationship with the community, the reading and listening community that harkens to it as the word

52. See Keith A. Mathison, *The Shape of Sola Scriptura* (Moscow, ID: Canon, 2001), 237-53.

53. Ramm, *Pattern of Religious Authority,* 29.

54. For an important critique of biblicism as a principle and practice of authority, see Christian Smith's *The Bible Made Impossible: Why Biblicism Is Not a Truly Evangelical Reading of Scripture* (Grand Rapids: Brazos, 2011).

55. While the Bible may not enable one to overturn empirical data yielded by the scientific method, it can put it into new light by questioning interpretative frameworks. On the metaphysical and presuppositional levels, then, the Bible can and must have a certain authority over not only theology, but all the other disciplines as well. See David Lyle Jeffrey and C. Stephen Evans, eds., *The Bible and the University,* Scripture and Hermeneutics Seminar 8 (Grand Rapids: Zondervan, 2007).

56. I am here following John Frame's description of the position, "In Defense of Something Close to Biblicism: Reflections on *Sola Scriptura* and History in Theological Method," *WTJ* 59 (1997): 269-318.

57. Ramm, *Pattern of Religious Authority,* 56.

58. Forsyth, *The Principle of Authority* (1952), 283.

59. R. L. Dabney, "The Doctrinal Contents of the Confession," in *Memorial Volume of the Westminster Assembly 1647-1897,* 2nd edition (Richmond, VA: Presbyterian Committee of Publication, 1897), 107.

above all earthly powers. To repeat: evangelicals subscribe to *sola,* not *solo scriptura.* Stated differently: the Bible is part of a larger pattern of theological authority, not an independent principle.

Of equal importance is the distinction between *naïve* and what I shall term below *critical* biblicism. Christian Smith mounts a sustained attack on naïve biblicism, a particular way of construing the Bible's theology that involves, among other things, a belief that the Bible contains everything God has to say to human beings, that it is comprehensive in the issues it covers, that any reasonable person can understand its plain sense without reliance on confessional schemes, that its teaching remains universally valid, and that it therefore serves as the Christian's authoritative handbook for all time and for all subjects, including science, politics, and philosophy.[60] The Achilles' heel of naïve biblicism, according to Smith, is the irreducible interpretive pluralism that pervades biblicist communities. How can the Bible provide definitive instruction and direction, asks Smith, if it gives rise to divergent interpretations among those who share the same biblicist beliefs? It is an excellent question. However, Smith himself fails to distinguish the naïve biblicism characteristic of *solo scriptura* from the critical biblicism that characterizes *sola scriptura.*

Excursus: Words and the Word

Despite their positions at opposite ends of the methodological spectrum, both revisionism and biblicism distort the pattern of theological authority in similar ways. Specifically, each neglects the formal and material centrality of Christ, the definitive revelation and living Word of God. Not so our next position.

One option that some, including evangelicals, presently find attractive is to see the words of Scripture as having an indirect authority, or as becoming authoritative when God graciously elects to use them to reveal Jesus Christ. Put differently: the Bible has authority to the degree that it "shows Christ." Christian Smith, for example, claims that a "truly evangelical" reading of Scripture means so focusing on Jesus Christ that the gospel becomes the spectacles through which we read Scripture and everything else. The pattern of theological authority on this view is thoroughly Christocentric and Christotelic. The relevant question on this view with regard to the development of doctrine is therefore not "Is it biblical?" but "Is it Christological?"

Bibliolatry is an effective bogey with which to scare young theologians. No one wants to be accused of elevating the Bible over Jesus Christ. It is therefore tempting for pietists and critics alike to say that one is going beyond (and often

60. See Smith, *The Bible Made Impossible,* chapter 1. Smith believes that naïve biblicism pervades the evangelical publishing market and a number of educational institutions.

against) what is written *in the name and for the sake of Jesus Christ.* For example, John Barton makes a rather facile appeal to "the gospel" as a message about God's love for the world and suggests that we use this as a sieve for filtering everything else in the text.[61] On this view, Jesus Christ *is* the gospel, and the Bible has authority *only* insofar as it bears witness to Christ.

What should we say in response? On the one hand, it is difficult to impeach an approach that acknowledges the centrality of the gospel of Jesus Christ. After all, the Son is the "exact imprint of God's very being" (Heb. 1:3, NRSV). At the same time, to make Christ the canon within the canon is to lose the frame from which the picture of Jesus Christ alone derives its sense. Is Christ divided? (1 Cor. 1:13). On the contrary: the person and work of Christ need a context in order to be meaningful, and to connote good news. Though Christ is present in the lives of individual Christians and in the church's preaching and sacraments, this is not to say that these constitute a normative specification (i.e., an authoritative answer) to the question "Who do you say that he is?"

Is it sacrilegious to say that the Bible norms the norm of Jesus Christ? It is not. The alternative is to posit Jesus Christ as a free-floating, or rather underdetermined, norm. Scripture alone is the ultimate touchstone, the normative specification of the prophetic and apostolic witness to Jesus Christ. Moreover, it was Jesus himself who acknowledged the words of Scripture as bearing the authority of God himself: "It is written" (Matt. 4:4).[62] If evangelicals hold to *sola scriptura,* then, it is in large part because they hold first and foremost to *solus Christus.*

Pilgrim's Process: Ways of Moving "Beyond"

> I press on toward the goal for the prize of the upward call of God in Christ Jesus. (Phil. 3:14)

Going Beyond: Preserving "Sameness" while Acknowledging "Difference"

If going "beyond" the Bible means an exodus from exact repetition (i.e., replication), then we all in some sense go beyond what is written. Each time we declare something in our present-day context "biblical" or "nonbiblical," we are doing more than repeating what has already been said. The challenge is to

61. Barton, *People of the Book? The Authority of the Bible in Christianity* (Louisville: Westminster John Knox, 1988), 89.

62. For more on Jesus' own appeal to the authority of what was written, see R. T. France, *Jesus and the Old Testament* (Vancouver: Regent College Publishing, 2000).

preserve the wine of Scripture in new cultural and conceptual wineskins. There are, of course, ways of going beyond the Bible that are beyond the evangelical pale: Bultmann's suggestion that descriptions of God's raising Jesus from the dead are not history but myth is but one example. Attempts to correct or revise the teaching of certain passages of the Bible by others are more difficult to adjudicate, not least because something similar appears to happen vis-à-vis the Old and New Testaments. On the other hand, the early church's insistence that Mary is *theotokos* ("God bearer"), while going beyond the explicit teaching of the New Testament, nevertheless yields a legitimate understanding of what the Bible implies.

I. Howard Marshall makes a compelling case for the need to go beyond grammatical-historical exegesis.[63] He commends evangelicals for excellence in studying "what it meant" in the original historical and cultural context, yet reminds them that the challenge is to know what to do with the original meaning today. He wants to avoid two extremes: first, dismissing what the biblical authors say as having antiquarian interest only; second, turning everything they say into transculturally relevant norms. The latter does not work, he notes, because the history of redemption within Scripture itself includes examples of doctrinal and ethical development.

What, then, counts as a good "beyond" — as going along rather than against the grain of the biblical text? The preposition ("beyond") is ambiguous: its meaning ranges from "outside the range of" to "more than." Obviously, all post-apostolic interpreters are beyond the Bible in a chronological sense. We live after it was written. The issue, however, is whether our doctrine is not merely "later" but also "out of [canonical] bounds."

Translation as Re-Textualization: Preserving Sameness

The desire to do theology "according to the Scriptures" has led some to adopt translation as a model for doing theology biblically.[64] The intent in translating is to reproduce in one language the propositional content of another. For example, Thomas Aquinas held that doctrine is both grounded and bounded by the literal sense of the apostolic writings, the depositories of revealed truth.[65] Translation is thus a fundamentally conservative exercise: the understanding that theology

63. I. Howard Marshall, *Beyond the Bible: Moving from Scripture to Theology* (Grand Rapids: Baker, 2004).

64. See, for example, Erickson, *Christian Theology,* 126-29.

65. See Christopher Kaczor, "Thomas Aquinas on the Development of Doctrine," *Theological Studies* 62 (2001): 283-302. Note, however, that Kaczor argues that Aquinas was open to doctrinal development on the grounds that God, the divine author, may have intended multiple meanings in his literal sense (298).

ministers is textual, a grasp of the way the words go (including their presuppositions, entailments, and implications). Theology on this view is simply an exercise in preserving the same (i.e., biblical content) across difference (i.e., linguistic form). To translate is to re-textualize.

Not everyone agrees. Translators sometimes have to come up with "dynamic equivalents" in order to communicate what the historically or culturally distant text means in terms of the receptor culture. For example, many translations locate deep feelings in the human "heart" or "breast" rather than "bowels," where the Hebrew locates them (cf. Ps. 22:14). David Kelsey argues that the "standard picture" of theology as a "translation" of the Bible is seriously flawed. When one actually examines the various ways in which theologians appeal to Scripture, he says, one finds not only diversity but also conceptual discontinuity: "The metaphorical use of 'translate' assumes a continuity of 'meaning' between theological proposal and scripture."[66] Note that Kelsey assumes that a translation's adequacy depends on "how far it has been able to preserve the same concepts."[67]

May we go beyond what is written? Clearly, one may not change the concepts if what results is "another gospel." However, Kelsey's notion of translation is too narrow. It is possible to convey the same meaning not only in different words but also with different concepts. Everything hinges, however, on what it means for two assertions to be "the same." I shall propose below that theology may move beyond the words and concepts of the Bible, but not beyond its underlying pattern of *judgments*. My main thesis will be that the same basic judgment can be preserved across a variety of languages, concepts, and contexts.[68]

Application as Contextualization: Acknowledging Difference

The challenge to walk the way of Jesus Christ, and hence to bring God's word to bear on new situations, is commensurate with the task of dogmatic and moral theology. We need theology in addition to the teaching of Scripture, says Frame, in order "to apply it to all areas of life."[69] Application is the operative concept, and it refers not to a single approach but to a spectrum of approaches for coping with "otherness" — with the fact that the cultural and intellectual worlds in which

66. David Kelsey, *Proving Doctrine: The Uses of Scripture in Recent Theology* (Harrisburg, PA: Trinity Press International, 1999), 186.

67. Kelsey, *Proving Doctrine,* 188.

68. On the distinction between "judgments" and the "conceptual terms" in which those judgments are rendered, see David S. Yeago, "The New Testament and the Nicene Dogma," in *The Theological Interpretation of Scripture: Classic and Contemporary Readings,* ed. Stephen E. Fowl (Oxford: Blackwell, 1997), 87-100.

69. Frame, *The Doctrine of the Word of God,* 276.

we live today are in many significant respects unlike the civilizations from which the Bible emerged.[70]

Naïve biblicism tends to downplay the difference between "then" and "now" in a sincere but ultimately misguided attempt to uphold biblical authority. The tendency is to assume universal relevance and to downplay otherness. In consequence, the "application" in many cases amounts to no more than piling up isolated biblical quotations and leads to the infamous "proof-text" (if such a thing — the pretext of a text without a context — exists!).[71] Such concordance theology (i.e., inductive biblical theologizing) errs in mistaking words for concepts, as James Barr devastatingly points out in *The Semantics of Biblical Language.*[72]

There are doubtless times when proverbial wisdom is appropriate, but as a theological method, application by quotation leaves much to be desired. No one makes this point more effectively than Edward Farley, in his *Ecclesial Reflection: An Anatomy of Theological Method,*[73] the most penetrating critique of the Scripture Principle of which I am aware. The book does what its subtitle promises: a close inspection of the bones and marrow of divinity. To switch metaphors: Farley does an archeological analysis of what he terms the "house of authority," looking in particular at the way in which the Bible serves as the foundation for theology. His basic complaint is that conservative theologians assume that it is enough to cite authoritative Scripture to establish one's claim, and that such argument by citation falls short of genuine inquiry. His main concern is that divine-human identity is thus claimed for the work of theology itself. Farley's own theological assumptions are highly questionable; yet, in my view, he has a point in calling attention to the tendency of naïve biblicism to elide the difference between text and interpretation.[74]

Evangelical theologians are generally aware that application involves more than proffering citations. Strictly speaking, interpretation goes beyond what is written every time one seeks to apply it to new contexts. Indeed, the history of the church and doctrine alike is the story of successive contextualizations. Church leaders have always had to use new language and concepts in order to deal with

70. To be sure, there is only one world (i.e., one reality). However, to appeal too quickly to this continuity risks overlooking important discontinuities. The approach commended here seeks to balance sameness and difference so that theology is simultaneously faithful to what is written in Scripture and relevant to what is being written today.

71. See Daniel J. Treier, "Proof Text," in *Dictionary for Theological Interpretation of the Bible,* ed. Kevin J. Vanhoozer (Grand Rapids: Baker, 2005), 622-24.

72. James Barr, *The Semantics of Biblical Language* (Oxford: Oxford University Press, 1961).

73. Edward Farley, *Ecclesial Reflection: An Anatomy of Theological Method* (Philadelphia: Fortress, 1982).

74. Cf. Geoffrey Wainwright's shrewd observation, in his review of Farley's book, that formal questioning of authorities does not usually begin until what they materially convey or propose has become problematic to the questioner (*Theology Today* 40 [1983]: 203).

the theological and ethical issues of particular places and times. "Contextualization" of the Bible is essentially a missiological concept and is necessary for two reasons: evangelicals want to minister God's word in new places (or in old places whose contexts have changed) and to bring it to bear on new problems (e.g., stem cell research, transgender issues). There are therefore good missiological and ethical reasons for wanting not merely to exposit but to *apply* the Bible.

It is common to think of application as the last step in an interpretative sequence: first determine the meaning; then apply it. This picture overlooks the fact that the interpreter too has a context (so does the biblical text, an instance of "culturally located divine discourse").[75] Stated differently: exegesis without presuppositions is not possible, for the simple reason that exegesis is a historically (and often theologically) situated practice too.[76] This applies to the authors of the New Testament as well.[77] It may therefore be more accurate to think of contextualization as the attempt "to hear Scripture's meaning speak in new contexts."[78] This is no reason to despair: Andrew Walls has shown that each cross-cultural contextualization of the gospel has resulted in a net conceptual gain, that is, an enriched understanding of the gospel and a surer grasp of its fullness.

Moving beyond what is written is inevitable: neither history nor culture stands still, and neither should the pilgrim church. The right way to move beyond what is written is to think biblically in whatever situation one happens to find oneself. The challenging complication for theology, however, is to know how to preserve the *same* gospel (i.e., textual meaning) in *different* settings (i.e., contexts). Opinions differ on how best to do this.[79]

Three Ways of Going "Beyond": A Representative Typology

The real dividing line today, however, is not simply *whether* one thinks the Bible authoritative but *how* the Bible's authority actually works. It is to highlight the latter question that we have featured Scripture's role in the *pattern* of divine authority. This is not the place to provide an encyclopedic catalogue of the ways in which theologians appeal to and apply biblical authority. I shall therefore limit

75. Jeannine Brown, *Scripture as Communication: Introducing Biblical Hermeneutics* (Grand Rapids: Baker, 2007), 256.

76. On the fluidity between exegesis and contextualization, see Brown, *Scripture as Communication,* chapter 11.

77. See Dean E. Flemming, *Contextualization in the New Testament: Patterns for Theology and Mission* (Downers Grove, IL: InterVarsity, 2005).

78. Brown, *Scripture as Communication,* 25.

79. See, *inter alia,* the many fine essays in Matthew Cook, ed., *Local Theology for the Global Church: Principles for an Evangelical Approach to Contextualization* (Pasadena, CA: William Carey Library, 2010).

myself to considering three ways in which evangelical theologians seek to preserve sameness of biblical meaning in other cultural contexts while nevertheless moving beyond grammatical-historical exegesis. Each is an *-ation,* an action or procedure for using the text to authorize theological conclusions: exemplification, extrapolation, and explication.[80]

Exemplification

Perhaps the most common way evangelicals go beyond those parts of what is written that are literally inapplicable is to "principlize": to extract universal principles from the culturally relative forms in which they are embedded in order to instantiate them in forms appropriate to one's own culture.[81] It is a matter of going up and down the "Ladder of Abstraction."[82] For example, Proverbs 20:2 warns that a king's anger is like a lion's growling, and he who provokes him risks losing his life. In this case, the underlying principle — "a succinct statement of a universal truth"[83] — concerns the respect one owes to one's government. Contextualization (i.e., moving beyond what is written) involves *exemplifying* this principle in the context of a representative democracy.

The great strength of this approach — exemplifying biblical principles in new contexts — is its pragmatism and simplicity. It provides a means with which to negotiate the tension between sameness and otherness (i.e., textual continuity and contextual discontinuity), and non-scholars readily understand it. Consider, for instance, the World Reformed Fellowship's new statement of faith:

> God's truth revealed in Scripture is universal, eternal and relevant for all cultures, ages and peoples. Nevertheless, there can be several and distinct applications of that truth. In contextualizing God's Word, the church should distinguish between biblical principles, which are the eternal and universal manifestations of God's truth, and the practical implications of those principles, which can vary in different contexts. It must always make sure that its applications are legitimate and proper extensions of the fundamental and unchanging principles.

Despite its strengths, exemplification (principlizing) also has some significant drawbacks: (1) it inadvertently treats the particularity of the Bible, includ-

80. See also Myk Habets, *The Spirit of Truth* (Eugene, OR: Wipf and Stock, 2010), 89-102, on "retroactivation."

81. For a spirited defense of principlizing, see Walter C. Kaiser, "A Principlizing Model," in Meadors, ed., *Four Views on Moving beyond the Bible to Theology,* 19-50.

82. Kaiser, "A Principlizing Model," 24.

83. Howard Hendricks and William Hendricks, *Living by the Book* (Chicago: Moody, 2007), 352.

ing its literary form, more as a problem to be solved than an exemplification of divine wisdom; (2) it risks making the principle rather than the actual text the higher authority; (3) it assumes that the interpreter is in a privileged position to discern what is and is not culturally relative, ignoring the cultural beam in his own eye: the principle abstracted from the text is often only one's culturally conditioned understanding; (4) it is in danger of becoming a proof-texting of a higher order.

A fifth and final objection is that principlizing often leads to moralizing: a way of reading the Bible that searches for principles to guide our behavior. While this is indeed part of discipleship, I wonder what help principlizing is for doctrinal theology. Principlizers are happy enough to speak of several applications of the same moral rule (i.e., "Thou shalt not steal"), but would they be as sanguine about the prospect of several *formulations* of biblical truth? How might this method of exemplification work with regard to doctrines such as the image of God, original sin, or the atonement? It is far from clear. Nevertheless, as David Clark notes, "Some kind of principlizing is necessary to evangelical theology."[84] As we shall see below, exemplification, too, gets a significant place in the pattern of theological authority.

Explication

The second way of going beyond has both an ancient and a modern pedigree. It is the way of deducing "good and necessary" consequences from Scripture. It is Anselm's way of "faith seeking understanding" through conceptual elaboration. Explication is a ministerial use of reason in which what is implied (*implicatus:* "folded in") by the text is made explicit (*explicatus:* "unfolded"). Strictly speaking, one moves "beyond" the text not by adding to but by further clarifying it.

Calvin is a staunch defender of this approach. In rebutting the objection that theology imposes "foreign terms" (e.g., *homoousios*) upon the biblical text, Calvin asks: "But what prevents us from explaining in clearer words those matters in Scripture which perplex and hinder our understanding?"[85] Theology is literally exegetical — a matter of leading the meaning out of the text. Foreign terms also serve to expose wrong interpretations, as Calvin notes in regard to Arius: "Say 'consubstantial' and you will tear off the mask of this turncoat, and yet you add nothing to Scripture."[86]

More recently, *analytic* theologians have breathed new life into this model

84. David K. Clark, *To Know and Love God* (Wheaton, IL: Crossway, 2010), 94. Clark argues for a "soft principlizing" that acknowledges the culturally conditioned nature of the interpreter's attempt to formulate biblical principles.

85. *Institutes* 1.13.3.

86. *Institutes* 1.13.5.

of going beyond.[87] Unlike those who seek to take theology captive to large-scale philosophical frameworks (e.g., existentialism, process), analytic theologians employ reason in ministerial fashion, an analytic handmaid to the biblical text. Specifically, reason is a tool for clarifying concepts (e.g., God), describing propositions (e.g., "Jesus does what only God can do"), and establishing the logical relationships between propositions (e.g., how Jesus, who is God's "son," can also be God). In brief: analytic theology is simply systematic theology "attuned to the deployment of the skills, resources, and virtues of analytic philosophy."[88] There is a particularly urgent need to clarify the implicit ontology that lurks behind biblical narratives about God's action in human history and the natural world.

In my view, there are more strengths than weaknesses in construing going beyond what is written in terms of analytic explication. Elsewhere I have advocated something similar, under the rubric of "biblical reasoning."[89] To reason biblically is, in brief, to think *with* rather than about the text. And this leads me to mention two caveats as concerns analytic theology. First, we must make sure to press beyond the concepts of the Bible to clarifying the larger pattern of judgments. Second, we must go beyond a focus on words and propositions in order to attend to what is happening at the larger (i.e., literary) level if we are indeed to think along the grain of the biblical text.

Extrapolation

A third approach puts more prepositional punch into the idea of going beyond, suggesting that interpreters must sometimes leave the Bible's teaching about certain things *behind*. Richard Longenecker, William Webb, and to some extent I. Howard Marshall have each explored the way in which certain "redemptive trajectories" that begin in Scripture yet ultimately point beyond the world of the text toward something higher.[90] For example, Paul urges Philemon to treat his runaway slave as a brother in Christ, yet nowhere in his epistle does he suggest abolishing the institution of slavery outright. However, proponents of this approach want readers to extrapolate from what Paul says to a conclusion that the

87. For a fuller description, see Oliver D. Crisp and Michael C. Rea, eds., *Analytic Theology: New Essays in the Philosophy of Theology* (Oxford: Oxford University Press, 2009), especially the introduction and chapters 1 and 2.

88. William J. Abraham, "Systematic Theology as Analytic Theology," in Crisp and Rea, eds., *Analytic Theology*, 54.

89. See my *Remythologizing Theology: Divine Action, Passion, and Authorship* (Cambridge: Cambridge University Press, 2010), 187-90.

90. Richard N. Longenecker, *New Testament Social Ethics for Today* (Grand Rapids: Eerdmans, 1984); William J. Webb, *Slaves, Women, and Homosexuals* (Downers Grove, IL: InterVarsity, 2001); Marshall, *Beyond the Bible*.

New Testament nowhere explicitly announces, namely, that slavery is always, everywhere, and for everyone wrong. To follow a redemptive trajectory is thus to plot its extra-canonical end-point — what Webb calls its "ultimate ethic."[91]

Webb is at pains to stress that he accepts the New Testament as God's final and definitive revelation. This does not mean, however, "that the NT contains the final *realization* of social ethics in all of its concrete particulars."[92] Webb and other proponents of the redemptive trajectory approach want us to trace the movement of the "redemptive spirit" behind the culture-bound letter. To be sure, one can plot certain trajectories along the course of redemptive history. However, these canonical trajectories find their end-point in Christ: either his first or second coming. By contrast, proponents of the redemptive trajectory approach posit an "omega point" (i.e., the realization of an ultimate ethic) that neither Christ not the canon instantiates. Marshall believes that even Jesus used imagery and forms current at his time to depict divine judgment. For example, Jesus concludes the parable of the unforgiving servant with the master throwing the servant into jail until his debts are paid. It is especially the postscript that troubles Marshall, however: "So also my heavenly Father will do to every one of you" (Matt. 18:35). This image recalls the violent God of the Old Testament who advocated the slaughter of Canaanites. Marshall's comment is telling: "It is incredible that God should so act."[93]

Marshall wants us to recognize the *accommodated* nature of these Old Testament stories and dominical teachings. Jesus addressed his audience in the only terms they could understand. From the standpoint of a redemptive trajectory hermeneutic, however, these images are sub-evangelical: "I suspect that the people of [Jesus'] day were not as aware of the unacceptability of such imagery as we, hopefully, are today."[94] It appears, then, that those who wish to extrapolate the redemptive spirit from the letter of the text are somewhat embarrassed by divine "accommodations": call it the scandal of *peculiarity.*[95]

91. Webb speaks of the "trajectory or logical extension of the Bible's (or passage's) redemptive spirit that carries Christians to an ultimate ethic" ("A Redemptive-Movement Model," in Meadors, ed., *Four Views on Moving beyond the Bible to Theology, 217).*

92. Webb, "A Redemptive-Movement Model," 246; emphasis his.

93. Marshall, *Beyond the Bible,* 66. For a critique of Marshall's suggestion that Jesus' view of God is defective due to its contextually conditioned nature, see my "Into the Great 'Beyond': A Theologian's Response to the Marshall Plan," in Marshall, *Beyond the Bible,* 85-86.

94. Marshall, *Beyond the Bible,* 67. I am tempted here to do theology by citation and respond: "But who are you, O man, to answer back to God?" (Rom. 9:20).

95. Kenton L. Sparks departs from Calvin's view of divine accommodation by insisting that God communicates to us in Scripture through human authors who are captive not only to their finite cultural categories but also to their fallenness (*God's Words in Human Words: An Evangelical Appropriation of Critical Biblical Scholarship* [Grand Rapids: Baker, 2008]). Such an assumption is crucial, Sparks thinks, for understanding the kind of passages that trouble Marshall, like those concerning genocide: God adopts fallen human authors and lets them

Identifying redemptive trajectories is as difficult as identifying universal principles. In each case, interpreters tend to underestimate their own historical, cultural, and socio-political locations. The task of identifying the *end-point* of a redemptive trajectory (its "ultimate ethic") is even more difficult. How do we know how far to extrapolate? Yes, slaves should be "equal" in dignity to their masters before God, in the eyes of the law, and in the church. But how far may one press equality? Should gays and transgendered have equal rights to minister in the church? Why or why not? This leads to my last concern: it is all too easy for those who use a redemptive trajectory approach to confuse what their own time finds ethically acceptable with the ultimate ethic. The presumption is simply that our culture is more "advanced" in its realization of the redemptive spirit of the text than that of the biblical authors. I worry that what begins as extrapolation ends in *correlation,* that is, with contemporary culture serving as the template for deciding what counts as progress.[96] Is it really the case that twenty-first-century North American culture is less violent than biblical times? Or have we merely refined (and institutionalized) certain forms of violence, so that we are now in greater danger from captive imaginations than from physical oppression?[97] David Bosch rightly notes that "Christians tend to sacralize 'the sociological forces of history that are dominant at any particular time, regarding them as inexorable works of providence and even of redemption.'"[98]

Professing the supreme authority of the Bible requires us to affirm "everything Scripture affirms, however unpalatable that may be to us today."[99] Despite the concerns expressed above, I believe that a limited degree of extrapolation belongs in the pattern of authority too. For there is movement in the Bible. The task that remains is to identify rightly what we must keep the same and what (as well as when, where, and how) we are allowed, or even obliged, to move beyond.

---

say the kinds of things that people who hate their enemies said in those days. See also Sparks, *Sacred Word, Broken Word: Redemption and the Theological Interpretation of Scripture* (Grand Rapids: Eerdmans, 2012), esp. chapter 5. The problem, of course, is that *all* of Scripture is divinely accommodated discourse, and it is not within the interpreter's purview to decide which parts to recognize as authoritative and which to declare superseded by modern values or learning.

96. Paul Tillich's famous method of correlation gives equal if not greater authority to the contemporary context by letting it pose questions to which the biblical text must give answer, thus letting the concerns of the present situation set the theological agenda. See his *Systematic Theology,* vol. 1 (Chicago: University of Chicago Press, 1951), 59-65.

97. Jesus' words are salutary: "Do not fear those who kill the body but cannot kill the soul" (Matt. 10:28).

98. David J. Bosch, *Transforming Mission: Paradigm Shifts in Theology of Mission* (Maryknoll, NY: Orbis, 1991), 439, quoting Stephen C. Knapp.

99. Al Wolters, in Meadors, ed., *Four Views on Moving beyond the Bible,* 309.

The "Uses of Scripture": Using or Being Used by God's Written Word?

At this point we need briefly to consider an objection to the very notion of "using" the Bible. Some critics complain that the three approaches we have just examined are examples of operations that readers *do to* or *perform on* the text. Each buys into a misleading picture of interpretation where one first determines the meaning and then, in a second step, its application. Dale Martin argues against the what-it-meant/means distinction that this two-step picture presupposes: "[S]tudents should be taught to think about what Scripture is in a Christian context *before* they are introduced to the practices of historical criticism."[100] If I understand the objection correctly, it has to do with not wanting to put the reader into the driver's seat of interpretation. On the contrary, being biblical means acknowledging its place in God's ongoing economy of redemption, in which it lives and moves and has its being. The point is that the word of God is a *subject* — "living and active" (Heb. 4:12) — not an inert object on which interpretive surgeons perform their operations.

Angus Paddison observes that books that speak of "using" Scripture end up focusing more on "methods" employed by the academy than on "membership" in the Spirit's school for reading the Bible rightly (e.g., church).[101] Any attempt to "use" the Bible "in abstraction from the people whose practices render them intelligible are bound to fail."[102] Richard Briggs makes a similar point, claiming that talk about "applying" the Bible is usually muddled, especially when this involves a race to find the "moral" or principle behind the biblical text.[103] Strictly speaking, the church neither "uses" nor "applies" Scripture but rather participates in the new world of the gospel. Being biblical here involves much more than information processing; it is rather a matter of being formed into God's covenant people by the book of the covenant.

William Abraham represents yet another way of expressing the same concern. His *Canon and Criterion* is an extended critique of theologians who use the Bible as an epistemic criterion and who thus (in his opinion) fail to recognize the canon as a means of grace.[104] What he shares with Paddison and Briggs is a desire to acknowledge Scripture for what it is: something that is first and foremost used by God rather than human beings. I believe that they are largely right in what they affirm but wrong in what they deny. They are right to call attention

100. Dale B. Martin, *Pedagogy of the Bible: An Analysis and Proposal* (Louisville: Westminster John Knox, 2008), 102.

101. Angus Paddison, *Scripture: A Very Theological Proposal* (London: T. & T. Clark, 2009), 38-45.

102. Paddison, *Scripture,* 39.

103. Richard Briggs, *Reading the Bible Wisely* (Grand Rapids: Baker, 2003), 83-95.

104. William J. Abraham, *Canon and Criterion in Christian Theology: From the Fathers to Feminism* (Oxford: Clarendon, 1998).

to the Bible's proper place in the church, but wrong to think that *sola scriptura* is to blame for skewing the pattern of theological authority. *Sola scriptura* is not a merely epistemic but a sapiential criterion: it is authoritative over the church's *lived* knowledge, the way it puts its knowledge of God into pious practice. It is the measure of the church's worship, witness, and wisdom alike.

The question whether it is interpreters who use or apply the Bible to speak of God or whether God uses Scripture to speak the church into existence is an interesting one. Perhaps we do not have to choose. To paraphrase Paul in Galatians 4:9: it is not simply a matter of coming to know/use Scripture, but also to be known/used by Scripture. Viewed in light of what it is — an element in the triune economy — we see that Scripture is not merely some "thing" that we subject to our methodological procedures but the word of the covenant Lord to whom we must be subject.

We need to change the picture. The problem is not knowing how to apply the text, as if Scripture were something external and remote to our everyday lives, but rather the reverse. The challenge is not simply to abstract universal principles from but *inhabit* the world of the text in the here and now. We should think less about transforming the Bible so that it fits into our world and more about our own and our world's conforming to Jesus Christ.[105] It is easier to do something to Scripture (i.e., subject it to this or that exegetical procedure) than to let Scripture do something to us (i.e., transform us by the renewing of our minds — Rom. 12:2). Biblical reasoning may well require not an operation that we perform *on* Scripture but rather our performance *of* Scripture. This, at least, is the gist of the dramatic proposal to follow: to think not merely about but with the text, to hear and to *do* the Scriptures.

Understanding Biblical Directions: A Dramatic Proposal for Following the Truth and Way of Jesus Christ

> What you have learned and received and heard and seen in me — practice these things. (Phil. 4:9)

Our model for rightly going beyond what is written must ultimately be Jesus Christ himself. Jesus went "beyond" the Law in such a way that he did not abolish but fulfilled it. His disciples may likewise go beyond what is written, but only in the same manner and for the same reason: to walk the way the words go further.

105. Cf. Oswald Bayer's comment: "A theologian is someone who is interpreted by the Holy Scripture, allows himself or herself to be interpreted by it, and as someone interpreted by it interprets it for others" (cited in Reinhard Hutter, *Suffering Divine Things: Theology as Church Practice* [Grand Rapids: Eerdmans, 2000], 72).

The goal is to make biblical judgments about what shape discipleship must take in a given situation, canonically normed judgments that display the mind of Christ. Stated differently: theology is about faith seeking and then demonstrating understanding, in word and deed, truth and obedience. To understand is to unfold — to explicate and exemplify — what has been implied ("infolded") in biblical discourse: "The unfolding of your words gives light; it imparts understanding to the simple" (Ps. 119:130).

We turn now to consider three interconnected ways of moving further along the grain of what is written: imitation, imagination, and improvisation. The three are not methodological operations as much as means of cultivating good habits of evangelical (i.e., biblical-theological) judgment. Going beyond what is written is ultimately a matter not simply of finding the right procedures but of becoming the right kind of persons: persons whose hearts, heads, and hands are intent on speaking, thinking, and acting according to the Scriptures and the "gospel of God" (Mark 1:14; Rom. 1:1; 1 Pet. 4:17). Theology's aim is to cultivate persons with holy wisdom: disciples who have the ability to articulate and advance the main action of the drama of redemption.

Imitation

A disciple is one who follows his master, walking "in his steps" (1 Pet. 2:21). Christians desire above all to conform to the example and the teaching of the Lord Jesus Christ. He is the definitive word of God, "the radiance of the glory of God and the exact imprint of his nature" (Heb. 1:3); it is to him that "all authority in heaven and on earth" has been given (Matt. 28:18). To have the mind of Christ is to conform to his "pattern *(typos)* of teaching" (Rom. 6:17 NET) and living. Following Christ is ultimately a matter of believing and doing what he said and what he continues to say via his designated spokesmen (the apostles). The last word the Matthean Jesus spoke was a command to make, baptize, and teach disciples (Matt. 28:18-20).[106] If discipleship means following the way the biblical words go, into new situations, then obeying Jesus' Great Commission obliges us to go beyond what is written for the sake of *prolonging* the pattern of what was written.[107]

The apostle Paul's "pattern of sound words" (2 Tim. 1:13; cf. 1 Tim. 1:10; Titus

106. According to Yarnell, Athanasius found the proper pattern of interpreting Scripture with which to counter the Arian misrepresentation of Christological passages in the Great Commission, specifically, in Christ's baptismal formula "in the name of the Father and of the Son and of the Holy Spirit" (*Formation of Christian Doctrine,* 187-91). There is a sense, then, in which the Nicene formula itself is a form of the imitation of Christ.

107. By "prolonging" I mean extending the reach of the word of the Lord in space and time. Cf. my earlier remarks about "a *longer* obedience, and a *longer* understanding, in the same direction."

1:9; 2:1) is integrally related to the pattern of Jesus' life, death, resurrection, and ascension. Note that the biblical words that serve as the supreme rule of faith and life are not simply the set of individual propositions (e.g., "He is risen") but the determinate pattern in which we discover these propositions, namely, the dramatic pattern summarized in Philippians 2:6-11 in which Christ humbles himself "by becoming obedient to the point of death, even death on a cross" (Phil. 2:8), and after which the Father exalts him.[108]

Paul urges the Philippians to be imitators both of him and of Jesus Christ. In 3:17 he employs a term found nowhere else in Greek literature: *summimetai* ("join in imitating me" or "be my fellow imitators [of Christ]"): "he 'educates' them into Christ by bringing them onstage with himself, as a fellow 'mime' of Christ."[109] They must not imitate those "who walk as enemies of the cross of Christ" (Phil. 3:18). Elsewhere he urges his readers to be imitators *(mimetai)* of him (1 Cor. 4:16) as he imitates Christ (1 Cor. 11:1).

Elizabeth Castelli criticizes the language and logic of imitation. Her reading of Foucault leads her to dismiss Paul's exhortation as part and parcel of a discourse of power that seeks to eliminate difference.[110] As Peter O'Brien rightly notes, however, "Imitating Paul was no formal copying of the apostle."[111] It is not simply a matter of "Micah see, Micah do." The kind of imitation Paul has in mind has nothing to do with mindless mimicking or mechanical duplication. Our imitations must not be literal replication. To think that one is imitating Christ by staging ritual crucifixions, for example, is actually to demonstrate one's *misunderstanding* of his work: his death on the cross for the salvation of the world is unrepeatable. We need to be more creative in our interpretation of what it means to "die daily."

Paul wants the Philippians to acquire the same underlying dispositions as Paul himself has learned from Christ: "Have *this* mind," the mind of Christ (2:5).[112] Disciples must adopt not so much an abstract principle as an attitude and disposition to behave in ways that display the same humility that Christ in his obedience dis-

108. Susan Eastman speaks of the "drama" imitation of Philippians 2:6-11 ("Imitating Christ Imitating Us: Paul's Educational Project in Philippians," in Wagner et al., eds., *The Word Leaps the Gap,* 427-51, esp. 429). On her view, Christ takes on our role (i.e., Adam after the Fall) and enacts the *phronēsis* that Paul replicates in his own life and commends to his readers as well.

109. Eastman, "Imitating Christ Imitating Us," 430.

110. Elizabeth Castelli, *Imitating Paul: A Discourse of Power* (Louisville: Westminster John Knox, 1991).

111. Peter T. O'Brien, *The Epistle to the Philippians,* NIGTC (Grand Rapids: Eerdmans, 1991), 446.

112. Wayne Meeks's paraphrase is worth pondering: "Base your practical reasoning on what you have seen in Christ Jesus" ("The Man from Heaven in Paul's Letter to the Philippians," in *The Future of Early Christianity: Essays in Honor of Helmut Koester,* ed. Birger Pearson [Minneapolis: Fortress, 1991], 265).

played to the Father. Those who are mature *(teleoi)* will think *(phronein)* the way Christ and Paul think (Phil. 3:15). Paul wants the Philippians to adopt the *phronēsis* of Jesus Christ: the style and substance of his practical reasoning.[113] In short: Paul wants his readers to adopt a specific pattern of thinking, feeling, and acting.[114]

That Paul's example should be as authoritative as his teaching should come as no surprise. The example one sets to others is the kind of indirect teaching whose lesson lasts longer than book learning. Indeed, new converts would not know how to embody commands like "die daily" without concrete exemplars. We can therefore adopt Wittgenstein's point about words ("look not to the meaning but to the use") to capture a key principle of Pauline pedagogy: look not only to trustworthy sayings but also to exemplary actions. Hans Urs von Balthasar observes that the saints are exemplars of practical wisdom whose lives embody biblical interpretations richer than any written commentary. The saints represent that "form of life" of the apostolic "language game" (Wittgenstein) that alone communicates the meaning/use. Put differently: the lives of the prophets, apostles, and saints display the use God's word makes of those in whom it richly dwells, teaching and training them in righteousness (2 Tim. 3:16).

As if to reinforce the point, Paul urges the Philippians to attend to "those who walk according to the example *(typon)* you have in us" (Phil. 3:17). O'Brien translates *typon* as "pattern." In Romans 6:17 Paul uses the term to indicate the "form of teaching" that is to serve as a standard or norm. Elsewhere (Acts 7:44; Heb. 8:5) it carries the more technical sense of a model or pattern. The point is that disciples are to order their lives and thoughts according to the pattern embodied by Jesus Christ and, by extension, the pattern of prophetic and apostolic judgment embodied in biblical discourse. For example: those who grow in Christian *phronēsis* will speak and act in ways that put others before themselves, in creative imitation of Christ's taking on the form of a slave.

Paul charges the church at Thessalonica with imitating the churches in Judea (1 Thess. 2:14). Again, to imitate is to adopt the underlying pattern of Christ-focused judgment: "Being 'a New Testament church' is not a matter of doing what the Corinthian or Thessalonian Christians did, but doing what they did in a manner appropriate to our context. This is the skill of living in time faithfully."[115]

113. I am using *phronēsis* not only in the sense of "deliberating about what to do in particular situations" but also as a term with which to bridge the theory/practice dichotomy. Practical reasoning involves both thinking *and* doing, beliefs *and* practices. In particular, it is about deliberating how to conform one's speech and action to reality — to the only reality that is, namely, the world as it has been created and renewed in, through, and for Jesus Christ (1 Cor. 8:6; Col. 1:16-20).

114. I am following Stephen Fowl's practice of translating the *phronein* terms in Philippians by phrases related to patterns of thinking, feeling, and acting (*Philippians,* Two Horizon New Testament Commentary [Grand Rapids: Eerdmans, 2005], 164).

115. Paddison, *Scripture,* 30.

Mature Christians exhibit in their individual and corporate lives the shape and *phronēsis* of discipleship: a pattern of judging that can be instantiated in a variety of cultures and conceptual schemes.

In summary: disciples may move beyond the letter of what is written only for the purpose of continuing the pattern of the dominical mind and extending the reach of apostolic discourse. When the church goes beyond in this way, it exemplifies covenant faithfulness and becomes a corporate translation, as it were, of the way of Jesus Christ in new cultural settings. To adopt the same pattern of thinking, feeling, and acting is thus to exemplify *sameness* in the midst of difference. Imitating Christ and Paul is a case study in navigating the tension between continuity and discontinuity with what is written. In walking its pilgrim way, the church today is not an exact replica of the first-century church but its *moving image.*

Imagination

"One of the primary tasks of practical reasoning is learning how to view things in the right way."[116] One way the Bible trains us in righteousness is by training us to discern meaningful patterns (e.g., typological relationships), especially as these pertain to what God has done, is doing, and will do to make all things new "in Christ." Discerning large-scale meaningful patterns, in biblical literature and history, involves more (but not less) than propositional knowledge. It requires a framework of understanding and a way of thinking parts under a greater whole. It requires, in a word, *imagination* — what C. S. Lewis calls the "organ of meaning."[117]

To imitate Jesus, Paul, and other Christians, we need to do more than answer the question "What am I to do?" According to Alasdair MacIntyre, we can only answer that question when we can answer a prior question: "Of what story do I find myself a part?" To this we must add an evangelical qualification: Of *whose* story do I find myself a part?

It is in Jesus' story that disciples live and move and have their being. Like Paul, we have been crucified and raised in Christ (Rom. 6:5-8; Gal. 2:20). Of course, the story of Jesus is the fulfillment of the broader covenantal history of Israel, and is unintelligible apart from it. I call this larger story that frames our Christian understanding of God, the world, and ourselves the "theodrama" of redemption, the primary substance of which is God's speech and action. We may move beyond what is written, though not the storied world it reveals, projects, and solicits. On the contrary, we extend that story into the present: "Today, if you

116. Fowl, *Philippians,* 107.

117. C. S. Lewis, "Bluspels and Flalansferes," in *Selected Literary Essays* (Cambridge: Cambridge University Press, 1969), 265.

hear his voice, do not harden your hearts as in the rebellion" (Heb. 3:7). To find our place in the theodrama, however, we need the imagination.

The imagination is, first, not merely a faculty for making pictures of absent things but, more importantly, a faculty for creating, and discerning, meaningful forms. In George MacDonald's words: "The imagination is that faculty which gives form to thought."[118] It is through the various literary forms of Scripture, including stories and histories, that the divine authorial imagination forms our view of God, the world, and ourselves. The pattern of sound doctrine — Jesus' filial obedience unto death on the cross — was the work of divine imagination before it was history.

The imagination, second, is a cognitive capacity — a faculty of the mind — that enables us to synthesize things. We need the imagination in order to perceive meaningful patterns. Analytic reason typically takes things apart; the synthetic imagination puts things together. Think of the imagination as a "formative" power: the ability to create or perceive meaningful wholes and coherent forms (including, as we shall see, *literary* forms). The imagination is thus a vital aid in discerning fittingness — the way parts "belong to" a whole.[119] The "whole" that Christians must discern and to which they must conform is not a system of ideas so much as it is a unified, already/not yet complete action: the drama of God's gospel.

Third, the imagination that enables us to "see" God and the kingdom of God at work in the world comes by *hearing,* and hearing from the word of Christ (Rom. 10:17). Scripture sets the evangelical imagination free to see, and more importantly to *inhabit,* the everyday world we live in *as* the world that was made through and for Christ. It takes eschatological imagination to see our world *as* the very world in which Jesus was born, for which he died, and to which he will return.

Finally, the imagination is not merely cognitive but engages the mind, will, and emotions alike. It is an integrative faculty that addresses human being in its entirety. It is precisely for this reason that some posit a connection between the imagination and what the Bible calls "heart" (Hebrew *lēb*).[120] The imagination is thus related to what Jonathan Edwards calls a "sense of the heart."

Several New Testament ethicists and theologians have recognized the imagination's role in responding to the Bible's authoritative claim upon our lives. Richard Hays believes that NT ethics involves not only the descriptive and synthetic tasks of examining the biblical material, but the hermeneutical and pragmatic

118. George MacDonald, "The Imagination: Its Functions and Its Culture," in *A Dish of Orts* (London: Sampson, Low, Maston & Co., 1895), 2.

119. C. S. Lewis viewed the imagination as an "organ of meaning" and reason as "an organ of truth" ("Bluspels and Flalansferes," 265).

120. For an extended discussion of this claim, see Alison Searle, *"The Eyes of Your Heart": Literary and Theological Trajectories of Imagining Biblically* (Milton Keynes and Colorado Springs: Paternoster, 2008), 33-40, and Garrett Green, *Imagining God: Theology and the Religious Imagination* (Grand Rapids: Eerdmans, 1989), 108-13.

tasks of relating the text to our situations in order to "live" its meaning. Oliver O'Donovan concurs: "The first discernment is *of* the text; the second discernment is *out of* the text, *of* our situation."[121] The latter tasks oblige us to go beyond exegesis, inhabiting the "symbolic world" of the text.[122] For this, we must become adept at "imagining the world Scripture imagines," for "People act on the basis of the imagined world in which they dwell."[123]

It is by cohabiting the world that Scripture imagines with other disciples who have been given Jesus' Spirit that we come to appreciate the way the biblical words go, and so acquire the discipline of Christian *phronēsis*. Here, too, it is less a matter of "using" Scripture than of having one's imagination — one's mind and heart — taken captive to God's word: "Scripture is the means by which individual and group identity is formed and reformed, and it is the means by which the community of believers seeks to transform the world around it by converting the world's imagination to conformity with the Word of God."[124]

Improvisation

Rightly to respond to God's word — to its assertions, commands, promises, warnings, etc. — requires more than repetition or rote memorization. Theology goes beyond what is written each time it does more than merely repeat the original Hebrew and Greek. To go "beyond" — to formulate doctrine, to meet new ethical challenges — is, at its best, not a faithless departure from biblical authority but its faithful, even creative, realization. The challenge of Christian discipleship and doctrine alike is to go beyond what is written in ways that nevertheless accord with the Scriptures. Our obedience in a long direction may be far removed from the original historical circumstances in which the Bible was written, but it is measured by the same normative judgments that undergird biblical discourse.

Improvisation puts feet on the imagination and thus provides an intriguing model for thinking about how disciples inhabit the world of the biblical text, follow the direction of doctrine, and integrate canon, conscience, church, and Comforter (John 14:26, ASV) into the pattern of theological authority.[125] Musical and dramatic improvisation alike depend more on memory and narrative skills than on

121. O'Donovan, "The Moral Authority of Scripture," in Bockmuehl and Torrance, eds., *Scripture's Doctrine*, 168.

122. See Richard B. Hays, *The Moral Vision of the New Testament: A Contemporary Introduction to New Testament Ethics* (San Francisco: Harper, 1996), 209.

123. Luke Timothy Johnson, "Imagining the World Scripture Imagines," *Modern Theology* 14 (1998): 3-18.

124. Green, *Imagining God*, 123.

125. I treat these matters at greater length in *The Drama of Doctrine: A Canonical-Linguistic Approach to Christian Theology* (Louisville: Westminster John Knox, 2005), 335-44.

novelty or ad-libbing; improvisation is a matter of building on what has gone on before, creatively continuing an initial premise (e.g., a theme or scene). Disciples have to improvise each time they decide what it means to have the mind of Christ in *this* situation, what it looks like to do the truth in *this* context, with *these* materials.

The true improviser trains "to act from habit in ways appropriate to the circumstance."[126] What comes to the fore is the importance not of following a single exegetical method but rather of becoming a peculiar people — disciples formed by biblical discourse to imagine their world as Scripture imagines it (i.e., as it really is "in Christ") and thus to speak and act with obedient freedom.[127] The Bible both depicts acts of apostolic improvisation and cultivates in its readers habits of heart and mind that enable them to contribute, creatively yet faithfully, to the ongoing drama of redemption.

A biblical example: Paul does not command but fully expects Philemon to improvise his response to his returning runaway slave not by punishing him, as the conventional social script would have it, but rather by welcoming him back as a brother in Christ. The whole epistle is an extended plea to Philemon to recognize what is fitting for him to do with regard to Onesimus given their mutual adoption "in Christ" into the family of God.[128]

A historical example: necessity is often the mother of doctrinal invention, and the Council of Nicea *improvised* a way beyond the crisis of Arianism that threatened to engulf the fourth-century church: *homoousios*. This non-biblical term preserves the basic judgment underlying much of what the Bible says about Jesus Christ, namely, that as God's Son he is "the same nature" as the Father. By improvising the term *homoousios,* the Nicene fathers said what had to be said in terms of Greek ontology to say who Jesus was, thus demonstrating their deep understanding of the biblical drama and divine *dramatis personae.*

Tom Wright likens the church to a company of players charged with performing a play whose final scene is sketched but whose penultimate scenes are missing: "It is an essential part of authentic Christian discipleship both to see the New Testament as the foundation for the ongoing (and still open-ended) fifth act and to recognize that it cannot be supplanted or supplemented."[129] It is

126. Samuel Wells, *Improvisation: The Drama of Christian Ethics* (Grand Rapids: Brazos, 2004), 65.

127. I believe that biblical interpreters need to employ multiple exegetical methods. While each method helps us appreciate a particular aspect of the text, no single method yields insight on all aspects and levels of Scripture's meaning.

128. For an extended analysis of Philemon along these improvisational lines, see my "Imprisoned or Free? Text, Status, and Theological Interpretation in the Master/Slave Discourse of Philemon," in *Reading Scripture with the Church: Toward a Hermeneutic for Theological Interpretation,* ed. A. K. M. Adam et al. (Grand Rapids: Baker, 2006), 51-93.

129. Wright, *The Last Word,* 126. Cf. his earlier article, "How Can the Bible Be Authoritative?" *Vox Evangelica* 21 (1991): 7-32.

important to know which Act one is playing. It would be entirely inappropriate, for example, to include a moment for slaying lambs and goats as sin offerings in a Sunday-morning worship service; that Act is past. Wright believes that the church now is in the ongoing, and open-ended, fifth act, as was the New Testament church. I agree, though I would add that the ending of the fifth act has already been scripted (see Revelation 20–22). Nothing is missing from our canonical script and transcript. *Everything we need faithfully to improvise the Christian way forward is there,* if we have eyes and ears to see and hear it.

Improvisation is ultimately a type of creative understanding. *To go beyond what is written in an improvisatory manner is not to produce innovations but rather progressively to discover the full meaning potential of the divine authorial discourse intrinsic to and implicit in the Bible.* Moving beyond the Bible to theology is a matter of improvisatory interpretation, an extended exegesis that leads the meaning out of the text even further.

Faithful improvisation is a function of Word and Spirit. It is the Spirit's ministry to illumine readers to see the sufficient potential of what is written for their own time and place: "We shall find what we need as we read, and shall not need to look elsewhere. But *what* we find there will equip us to see and to say things which, in God's masterful government of history, precisely our time, and no other, has been given to see and to say."[130] That prior generations of disciples have improvised, and hence discovered something of permanent value in the biblical text, is a key consideration for the pattern of theological authority. If the Spirit has led the church into further truth, then we must attend not only to Scripture but also to orthodox tradition: "[W]e cannot merely translate the language of Scripture into our own language, ignoring the intervening ages . . . we will only proclaim the gospel faithfully if we make an effort to understand how it has been passed on to us."[131] In short: we must be imitators not only of Paul, but also of Nicea and Chalcedon.[132]

Regula Scriptura: Ways of Rightness and Right of Way

Only let your manner of life be worthy of the gospel of Christ. (Phil. 1:27)

Kanōn is the Greek word for "rule." As its name is, so is its nature: the canonical Scriptures are the church's supreme rule for faith and life. To this point, however,

130. O'Donovan, "The Reading Church," 15.

131. Stephen Holmes, *Listening to the Past: The Place of Tradition in Theology* (Grand Rapids: Baker, 2002), 3.

132. As I shall argue below, however, there is a qualitative difference between apostolic and post-apostolic tradition. The former, as divinely commissioned and inspired testimony, must always be the judge of the latter.

we have offered what amounts only to a vision statement for conceiving biblical authority in the church. Conspicuous by its absence is any mention of the means by which to make this vision visible, a means with which to determine whether or not a particular formulation of doctrine or course of action accords with the normative biblical pattern. If Scripture is indeed to rule our faith and life, we must have some means of deciding whether a given improvisation is faithful or faithless. And, if church tradition is to have a place in the pattern of theological authority, we must have some means of deciding whether particular developments, including the Rule of Faith itself, are warranted. This section can only begin to address the all-important question of criteria. What is it that allows us to assert of a particular doctrine or ethical decision "It is meet and right so to do (and say)"?

The (Rightwise) Ways of God: The Pattern of Triune Communicative Action

Going beyond what is written rightly means making judgments about rightness and, ultimately, the righteousness of God. The substance of the theodrama concerns nothing less than God's right-doing.[133] God's right-doing is the heart of the gospel, the revelation of the righteousness of God (Rom. 1:17). The Bible provides a normative account of what God has done in Christ — of what it means and of what we must do in response. Scripture is God's rightful say-so about God's right doing.

God is the only real source of authority (Rom. 13:1). The Father has given the Son all authority on heaven and on earth (Matt. 28:18) and the Son, in turn, has commissioned the church to evangelize and make disciples under his authority. He has also promised to send the Spirit to help the church in its truth-proclaiming, witness-bearing task (John 14:15-26; 15:26–16:15). Everything proceeds from the speech and acts of the triune God. O'Donovan's gloss on Galatians 4:4 ("When the time had fully come, God sent forth his Son") is insightful: "In that message all the authority of the biblical texts finds its source."[134] Stated in terms of the present argument: all authority resides in the triune economy of communicative action. What carries authority are the rightwise ways of God.

How, then, can we move from theodrama to doctrine, sacred page to proposition, story to system so that we respond to new situations while nevertheless preserving the pattern of theological authority (i.e., the triune God speak-acting in the Scriptures)? By learning and participating in the pattern of God's own rightwise saying and doing. God revealed his will in former times by the prophets, but the locus of his definitive revelation is the speech-act of his Son (Heb. 1:2).

133. The gospel presupposes ontology (i.e., right-being), too, that is, understanding the *being* of the one who does right.

134. O'Donovan, "The Moral Authority of Scripture," 173.

Everything in theology is more or less an attempt to describe and understand the history of God's name as it converges on and coincides with the name "Jesus Christ." These names stand for the history of their bearers, the set of acts and events in which their being and identity come to light. Theology and Christology are but the unfolding of a drama: the drama of the name, and ways, of God.[135] This drama is the form and substance of the triune communicative action, the supreme standard to which all theology and ethics must correspond.

We do not have time to unfold the entire drama here. Suffice it to say that biblical narrative, prophecy, Psalms, wisdom, and apocalyptic alike all serve to fill out the name and ways of God. Of special note is the name the Lord reveals to Moses in Exodus 34:5-7: "a God merciful and gracious, slow to anger and abounding in steadfast love and faithfulness." This name takes on its distinctive meaning in light of its context (i.e., the Lord's forgiveness of Israel and covenant renewal). Thanks to what God says and does, Israel now sees both *who* the Lord is ("the one who brought you out of Egypt") and *what* he is like.[136]

The climax of the theodrama is, as we have seen, God's sending forth his Son. The prologue of the Fourth Gospel identifies Jesus as a new (and from a historical standpoint, *improvised*) revelation of God's glory. It further harkens back to the earlier revelation of God's name and ways in Exodus 34:6-7 ("steadfast love [*ḥesed*] and faithfulness [*'emet*]") by identifying Jesus as "full of grace and truth" (John 1:14). Indeed, we might say that the final response to Moses' request to God ("please show me now your ways" — Exod. 33:13) is the person and work of Jesus Christ. It is by coming to discern the shape and substance of God's communicative action that disciples have their minds and hearts — their capacity for right judgment — enabled and trained to extend and continue the pattern.[137]

Rightful Say-So and Do-So: The Question of Criteria

The high calling of Christian discipleship is so to witness to and participate in God's loving outreach to the world that we become "imitators of God" (Eph. 5:1).

135. A point made by John Webster in connection to Karl Barth (*Barth's Ethics of Reconciliation* [Cambridge: Cambridge University Press, 1995], 83). But why let Barth sing all the good evangelical tunes?

136. Graham Cole notes that Exod. 34:6-7 is "the nearest thing to a systematic statement of the being and attributes of God in the Hebrew Bible" ("Exodus 34, the Middoth, and the Doctrine of God: The Importance of Biblical Theology to Evangelical Systematic Theology" (unpublished manuscript).

137. This has profound implications for theological education, whose ultimate purpose is not merely to stockpile the student's inventory of knowledge *(scientia)* but to teach students how to think/see/judge theologically and desire to do what is rightwise *(sapientia)*. The goal is not simply to transmit knowledge but to cultivate understanding.

The challenge is to discern what is "meet and right" to say and do. As we have just seen, *rightness* is a function of what God has said and done: his "ways." It remains to consider criteria for discerning what is *meet*. Something is meet if it is fitting or befits, if it measures up.[138] Interestingly enough, the divine attributes derived from Exodus 34:6 are known as the *middôt* or "measures."

Nicholas Wolterstorff has recently proposed a definition of truth as that which "measures up" in being or excellence. True assertions measure up (i.e., correspond) to reality: what is. A true proposition is one that measures up to or "fits" the facts.[139] I want both to expand Wolterstorff's suggestion to include goodness and beauty and to qualify it by specifying God's communicative activity as the index of reality. God's triune communicative activity, especially as this pertains to the person and work of Christ and its canonical self-attestation, is the ultimate measure of truth, goodness, and beauty alike. To the extent that something fails to participate in God's communicative activity, then to that extent it fails to measure up: it lacks being.

The Bible's words are true, good, and beautiful.[140] Scripture is a key ingredient in the triune economy of communication: the divinely authorized, commissioned, and superintended words that communicate what we need in order to know, love, and follow the way of Jesus Christ with all our mind, heart, soul, and strength. We go beyond the Scripture rightly only when what we say and do measures up to the formal and material principle of theological authority: the triune communicative action of God. The canon is the formal principle, the ruler by which we determine whether what we say and do as disciples "measures up." Scripture is the norming norm, the "unmeasured measure."[141] The substance to which disciples are to measure up, and the material principle of authority, is the covenant that the Bible both constitutes and mediates. Truth involves *apprehending* covenantal fittingness (i.e., that which corresponds to the theodrama); goodness involves *acting* fittingly (i.e., in a way that corresponds to the theodrama); beauty involves *appraising* fittingness (i.e., the way the parts of the theodrama correspond to one another).

Is there any biblical warrant for thinking in terms of covenantal fittingness? There is indeed: "For it was fitting *(prepō)* that he, for whom and by whom all things exist, in bringing many sons to glory, should make the pioneer of their salvation perfect through suffering" (Heb. 2:10). We have in this single verse a kind of *précis* for the entire theodrama, alluding as it does to the creation, the people of God, the incarnation and death of Jesus, and the consummation — fellowship with God.

138. The origin of the term "meet" in Old English is *metan:* "measure." To "mete out" justice is to measure out the appropriate amount.

139. Nicholas Wolterstorff, "True Words," in *But Is It All True? The Bible and the Question of Truth,* ed. Alan G. Padgett and Patrick R. Keifert (Grand Rapids: Eerdmans, 2006), 34-43.

140. Strictly speaking, it is the Bible's *discourse* that is true, good, and beautiful.

141. O'Donovan, "The Reading Church."

Disciples may go beyond what is written, but only if they continue the same pattern of theodramatic action that the Son and Spirit have initiated and attested in history and the canon. The patterns of communicative action in canon rule the disciple's judgments about rightness *(ortho),* in all its forms: right desiring of beauty (the orthopathos and orthodoxa of the heart); right deliberating about truth (the orthodoxy of the head); right doing of the good (the orthopraxis of the hand). In all three cases, Scripture is useful, and authoritative, for training in "meetness" (i.e., covenantal fittingness).

The general criterion for discerning when and how it is proper to go beyond what is written is theodramatic fittingness. Yet we need practical reason — the ability to make right judgments about truth, goodness, and beauty — to discern whether our speech and action befit what God has said and done. Those who are mature will be able to do more than replicate or repeat biblical words and phrases or behaviors. Those whose minds have been nurtured by the "mind of the canon" will know what to say and do in new situations. They will be "workers in fittingness," participating here and now in diverse ways in the one thing God is doing in Christ to make all things new. Three further criteria assist workers in fittingness in their task.

Canon Sense

To learn canon sense is to cultivate what Athanasius refers to as the "mind of Scripture." Canon sense means knowing who and where you are in relation to the whole drama of redemption. No one had the mind of Scripture more than Jesus himself. Jesus knew the answer to the key questions — Who am I? What ought I to be doing? What time is it? — because he perfectly grasped the broader story of which he was the central part. To have canon sense is to be able to make judgments about what is meet and right to say and do in light of the biblical text. This criterion — canonical fittingness — grounds the others.

Catholic Sensibility

Disciples are to be imitators not only of God but "imitators of the churches of God in Christ Jesus" (1 Thess. 2:14). We are hardly the first to struggle with canon sense. William Whitaker acknowledges the importance of heeding earlier attempts to lead out the meaning of the Bible: "For we also say that the church is the interpreter of Scripture, and that the gift of interpretation resides only in the church: but we deny that it pertains to particular persons, or is tied to any particular see or succession of men." Jesus' promise that the Spirit will guide us into all truth (John 16:13) has reference not merely to this or that denomination or individual, but to the whole (*kath' holou* = "catholic") church.

In one important sense, however, the tradition too is fixed in writing. I refer, of course, to the *apostolic* tradition *(paradosis)* that Paul urges the Thessalonians, and by extension us, to maintain: "So then, brothers, stand firm and hold to the traditions that you were taught by us, either by our spoken word or by our letter" (2 Thess. 2:15; cf. 3:6). Indeed, Paul's whole apostolic ministry could be viewed as his delivering — traditioning, handing on — the message he had received about Christ in accordance with the Scriptures (1 Cor. 15:3). Furthermore, the apostles themselves are "ones sent" by Jesus Christ. Oscar Cullmann's point is therefore worth pondering: the apostolic tradition enshrined in the New Testament originates with the ascended Lord who sends his Spirit to the ones he sends into the world as his commissioned witnesses.[142] It follows that the risen Christ himself is the ultimate authorial agent of the apostolic tradition.[143]

Reading with the Spirit-led church, the community of the canon extended in space and time, can serve as a helpful subsidiary criterion. Church tradition provides a rich resource of case studies in how other performers have received the apostolic tradition and made judgments concerning canonical fittingness. Christians from all parts of the world can learn from the past and from other Christian communities how best to extend in new situations the same pattern of thinking, feeling, and acting instantiated by Christ and the apostles: "Theology is not simply about giving priority to the Bible; it is about valuing and engaging with those in the past who gave priority to the Bible."[144] Some of these exercises in catholic wisdom have achieved not only local but permanent gains in understanding, even if they are associated with particular places and times (e.g., Nicea, Chalcedon). Catholic fittingness means that our beliefs and practices measure up to the standard of the company of the gospel.[145]

Contextual Sensitivity

Whether the contemporary context deserves a place in the pattern of theological authority is a subtle query. Revisionists, as we have seen, tend to accord magiste-

142. Note that Paul says that he received the tradition concerning the Lord's Supper "from the Lord" (1 Cor. 11:23).

143. Oscar Cullmann, *La Tradition: Problème Exégétique, Historique et Théologique* (Paris: Delachaux et Niestlé, 1953). I am indebted to Yarnell's discussion in *Formation of Christian Doctrine,* 128-33.

144. Alister McGrath, "Engaging the Great Tradition: Evangelical Theology and the Role of Tradition," in *Evangelical Futures: A Conversation on Theological Method,* ed. John Stackhouse (Grand Rapids: Baker, 2000), 144.

145. While catholic tradition is often an invaluable guide to going beyond Scripture rightly, it too finally stands under the normative authority of the apostolic tradition enshrined in Scripture (i.e., the written gospel).

rial authority to the contemporary situation, and are willing to revise the teaching of Scripture in its light. It is better to see one's context as the stage and setting for new performances of the same ongoing drama of redemption, however, for there is no other theodrama, just as there is no other gospel (Gal. 1:7).

The Bible, says Miroslav Volf, is "God's word addressed to people of all times and places."[146] To receive this word, he says, I must receive it for what it is but also *as myself,* that is, as a word for me and my situation, not just a word for "them" back "then and there."[147] The challenge is to translate or transpose the same canonical pattern of communicative action into new cultural modalities.

I have argued that what gets handed on from one generation to the next — the apostolic tradition — is fundamentally a canonical pattern of seeing, thinking, feeling, judging, and acting. The church makes known and participates in the theodrama — the good news of God *doing* — by staging what for lack of a better term we could call *world-for-world translations* of the Bible, unfolding the world implied by the canonical text in terms of our own contemporary context. Dramatic transposition, like its musical counterpart, is a matter of preserving the same melodic line (speech) and harmony (action) in a different key (culture). To transpose or modulate is to change from one mode, key, or form to another while preserving the same subject matter. The mode of gesture, dress, etc. may be different when *Romeo and Juliet* is transposed into the twentieth-century New York City setting of *West Side Story,* for example, but the story is the same. Here, too, the Spirit's guidance is necessary as the church strives to discern contextual fittingness as it extends and unfolds what is written in new cultural and conceptual forms.[148]

Conclusion: Mapping the Mission — Toward a Critical Biblicism

Only let us hold true to what we have attained. (Phil. 3:16)

The Bible maps the great mystery of our faith, providing the orientation we need for our ongoing mission as the people of God: to continue walking the right way (i.e., the Way). And walk we must, for neither time nor little children stand still. The church is a company of pilgrims that has everything it needs to keep moving forward: most importantly, a canonical compass with a magnetic Spirit that keeps pointing toward Jesus Christ. To use the compass and arrive at one's destination, however, one must also learn rightly to read the lay of the land (context).

146. Miroslav Volf, *Captive to the Word: Engaging the Scriptures for Contemporary Theological Reflection* (Grand Rapids: Eerdmans, 2010), 26.

147. Volf, *Captive to the Word,* 36.

148. For a fuller treatment of fittingness to contemporary context, see my *Drama of Doctrine,* 259-63 and 319-24.

There is yet one more piece to place in the pattern of theological authority: church leaders, in particular "pastors and teachers" (Eph. 4:11). It is the special privilege and responsibility of pastors to lead congregations beyond what is written each time they preach. Sermons are not scholarly commentaries but pastoral summons to respond to God's word as befits its meaning and force. The point of the sermon is to move listeners beyond what is written, enabling them to follow the way the biblical words go by extending them into our world. That is the whole point of preaching: to invite congregations to participate in what Scripture is about. Theology serves preachers who seek to bring the word of God to bear on the here-and-now of the world, ministering understanding, and reality, to those who are beginning to see a great light (Isa. 9:2). Pastors must not only exposit the world of the text but also encourage their hearers to indwell the world thus set out.[149] Otherwise we will become like those who look into the mirror, only to forget what we see when we turn away (James 1:23-25).

The pattern of theological authority set forth in this essay acknowledges the supreme authority of Scripture while making a case, and place, for church tradition and conscience as instruments through which the Holy Spirit exercises a ministerial authority. Church tradition in particular opens up creative understandings that lead us "beyond" what is written, not by leaving the text "behind" but precisely by going "further up and further in."[150] What has magisterial authority in the pattern of theological authority is the voice of the triune God that commissions and authorizes the prophetic and apostolic testimony to the old and new covenants. The Spirit ministers this magisterial word to tradition and conscience by extending its meaning through corporate and individual judgments — cognitive and communicative "performances" — that issue in speech and action that is meet and right insofar as it accords with God's word embodied and enacted in the canonical Scriptures.

This is biblicism, to be sure, but it is hardly naïve. Here is no abbreviated but rather unabridged Protestant principle that works hand in hand with its Pauline and Puritan cousins. Call it *critical biblicism* (but do not confuse it with biblical criticism, its polar opposite). Note, first, that it is a form of *biblicism:* the position for which I have argued accords final authority to the Bible as the norm for all subsequent Christian communicative action, including beliefs and practices. The norm to which all other words, thoughts, and deeds must measure up is the pattern of judgments reflected in biblical discourse. But second, it is a *critical* biblicism. This means that it does not conflate our interpretations with the meaning of the biblical text. The text stands in judgment over our interpretations in an asymmetrical hermeneutical hierarchy.

149. This is the thrust of what Abraham Kuruvilla terms "pericopal theology" in his *Text to Praxis: Hermeneutics and Homiletics in Dialogue* (London: T. & T. Clark, 2009), chapter 4.

150. An important and recurring phrase in C. S. Lewis, *The Last Battle,* chapter 15.

Critical biblicism is critical, moreover, because it rejects "solo" *scriptura.* Critical biblicism is shorthand for the whole pattern of theological authority advocated in this chapter. It acknowledges the magisterial authority and normative place of prophetic and apostolic tradition (i.e., the Spirit speaking in Scripture) in the triune economy of communication while also acknowledging the vital, even indispensable, role of the Spirit's working through the ministerial authorities of church tradition and individual conscience. The way forward is not to eliminate one or more of these factors but rather to order them so that they preserve the pattern of triune communicative agency.

We are now in a position to respond to our initial query. Mother, may we therefore go beyond what is written after all? If going beyond means *against* the grain of the text, then certainly not. If, however, going beyond means proceeding *along* the grain of the text, following the way the words go, then, little children, we *must.*

Philosophical and Epistemological Topics

TWENTY-FIVE

Contemporary Religious Epistemology: Some Key Aspects

James Beilby

I have a very distinct memory from the summer of 2001. As I was frantically working to complete my dissertation on Alvin Plantinga's religious epistemology, I heard my three-year-old daughter singing "Jesus loves me, this I know, for the Bible tells me so" as she played in the next room. Needless to say, the contrast between my travel through the labyrinthine details of epistemological debates and the message of her song was striking. Yet it dawned on me that one of the challenging aspects of religious epistemology was to unpack the many complexities of this seemingly simple statement without dismissing or ignoring the truth of what my daughter said. The topic of this essay is not whether my daughter was right. I will assume that the Christian God exists and has revealed himself in a variety of ways, including in Scripture. Rather, I propose to ask how the epistemological question at the heart of my daughter's song should be understood — namely, how do we Christians know what we take ourselves to know about Scripture's teaching about Jesus Christ? To talk of the truthfulness and authority of Scripture inevitably raises fundamental issues in the realm of epistemology. The aim of this chapter is to sketch the terrain of current epistemological debates and show some of their bearing on serious reflection on the nature and truthfulness of Scripture.

Initial Considerations

Christianity is often described as a belief system. This is misleading, for a variety of reasons. First, Christianity is not just a set of beliefs. It includes, among other things, practices, attitudes, dispositions, and affections. But of course, Christian practices, attitudes, and affections are clearly understood only when they are seen as connected to a complex set of dispositions and commitments that might be labeled "Christian belief." Second, the notion of "Christian belief" might be taken to indicate a common, identical, and clearly definable set of beliefs that deserve the label "Christian." Of course, this is not the case. Even if there is a family resemblance among the beliefs of orthodox Christians, the differences between the beliefs of individual Christians are enormous. Compare the set of beliefs of my late grandmother and me. While we share a commitment to the core beliefs of Christianity, our approach to theological questions and our desire for in-depth analysis of those questions are wildly divergent. One might say that at the "what we believe" level there is great similarity, but at the "how did we get those beliefs" and "why we believe as we do" levels there are vast differences. Even with respect to core theological beliefs — the deity of Jesus Christ, for example — the beliefs of different Christians will be different in important respects. And even among Christians whose theological beliefs might be described as orthodox, these differences go beyond mere doctrinal disputes — for example, debates over the Two Minds and Kenotic Christology. The differences between individual Christians include the role an individual belief plays relative to other beliefs. For example, does one believe in the deity of Christ because one believes in the authority of Scripture or does one believe in the authority of Scripture because one believes in the deity of Christ? Other important differences between individual Christians include the willingness to accept evidence, differences in how evidence is treated, differences in the need for evidence, and differences in the type of evidence desired or needed. Because Christian beliefs are networked together in complex and individually unique ways, religious epistemology must be fine-grained. Generalizations are possible, but one must do the difficult work of applying theory to the lives of particular believers.

Unfortunately, it is typical to particularize religious epistemology primarily or even solely around the beliefs of idealized (and usually hypothetical) Christian academics. Doing so, however, gives the mistaken impression that understanding and resolving perennial theological debates is necessary for religious knowledge and that the proper environment for the formation of religious knowledge is the academy rather than the church. Religious epistemology can and should focus on academic matters, but it should also consider people like my grandmother, lest we end up with an account of religious knowledge that places the bar out of reach of 99 percent of Christians.

It is also important to focus our epistemological discussion on the right set of Christian beliefs. Too often Christians are content to merely ask if God exists. While considering God's existence is important, from a Christian perspective it is insufficient. For a religious epistemology to be *Christian,* we must extend our epistemological ruminations into theological arenas: What kind of God exists? Has he revealed himself? etc. In short, a Christian religious epistemology should ask what can be known about the gospel of Jesus Christ. In this endeavor, questions about the nature, truthfulness, and authority of Scripture will be paramount.

Finally, it is crucially important to acknowledge the many different layers of issues embedded in a consideration of "knowing" the gospel. I will consider four fundamental questions: (1) Is the concept of religious epistemology viable or are epistemological questions regarding the features of religious belief unanswerable? (2) How should the epistemic values at the heart of this discussion — justification, knowledge, etc. — be understood? (3) What theological or epistemological assumptions would lead one to the belief that scriptural knowledge is not possible? And are these assumptions reasonable themselves? (4) How does Scripture itself approach the concept of knowledge of God's teachings? And what reasons may be given for embracing the truthfulness of the gospel?[1]

The Viability of Religious Epistemology

Before seeking to understand the various debates within religious epistemology, it is appropriate to pause and acknowledge that there are those who think that the entire enterprise is misguided. There is, of course, no simple answer to the question: "Is religious epistemology viable?" And that is (at least partially) because there is no simple answer to the question: "What is religious epistemology?" In any given case, it is not always easy to see whether somebody is objecting to the very concept of epistemology, the particular epistemological approach, the very concept of religious belief, the particular theological details underpinning the religious belief, or a judicious blend of some or all of the above. I will survey some of the common objections.

Objections to Epistemology

It is not uncommon to hear pronouncements of the "death" of epistemology. Of course, many of these pronouncements are aimed not at epistemology per se, but at a particular brand or subset of epistemology. It is common to hear objections to foundationalism or the notion of *a priori* beliefs. Most decried are the epistemological heirs of Descartes. And, of course, the objection to the excessive epistemological optimism of the late Enlightenment is well taken. Certainty may be a valid category as a descriptor of a psychological state — one is psychologically certain with respect to a particular belief when one doesn't entertain the slight-

1. The first two questions are called *meta-epistemological questions,* because they involve an inquiry into the meaning and usage of fundamental epistemological concepts. The second two questions are *applied epistemological questions,* because they ask whether knowledge is present (or could be present) in a particular instance. Meta-epistemological questions are logically prior to applied epistemological questions, but the point of meta-epistemological questions is to help us answer applied epistemological questions. See Richard Fumerton, *Epistemology* (Malden, MA: Blackwell, 2006), 5-11.

est doubt about its truth value.[2] But certainty is not and has never been a valid epistemological category for human beings. It is simply not possible to eliminate all possibility that one might be wrong, even with respect to our most apparently obvious beliefs. But the failure of Descartes's quest for apodictic certainty doesn't suggest that epistemological questions as a whole should be abandoned any more than the existence of bad hermeneutics suggests that we should stop interpreting texts.

Others, such as W. V. O. Quine, argue that traditional epistemology should be abandoned and replaced with the methodologies of the natural sciences, particularly cognitive psychology. This approach, a species of Naturalized Epistemology called Replacement Naturalism, recommends that instead of asking philosophical questions about the nature of and conditions for justification and knowledge, we should study the physiological and psychological processes that take us from sensory stimulations to beliefs about the world. Quine says: "The stimulation of his sensory receptors is all the evidence anybody has had to go on, ultimately, in arriving at his picture of the world. Why not just see how this construction really proceeds? Why not settle for psychology?"[3] Normative questions such as "Is this evidence sufficient for knowledge?" are replaced by descriptive questions: "What belief is formed in this situation?"

Another "replacement project" is the "Replacement Pragmatism" of Richard Rorty which replaces traditional epistemological questions with a study of the usefulness of different claims, vocabularies, and constructs from varying communities, cultures, and disciplines.[4] Instead of asking whether beliefs are true, justified, or rational, Rorty would have us ask whether our beliefs contribute to human flourishing or make society more tolerant.

The proclamation of the death of epistemology, like most such proclamations — note, for example, the proclamation of the death of God in the 1960s — is more than a little premature. If anything, religious epistemology is enjoying a renaissance of sorts, buoyed not by a resurgence of Enlightenment optimism, but by a realization that questions about the epistemological quality of theological statements are extremely difficult to banish from the arena of scholarly discussion. While the varying replacement projects have been successful in demonstrating the importance of descriptive and utilitarian questions, fundamental questions remain about their ability to truly replace traditional epistemological questions. In particular, replacement naturalism is much more plausible as a "replacement"

2. For a consideration of varieties of certainty, see Baron Reed, "Certainty," in *The Stanford Encyclopedia of Philosophy* (hereafter *SEP*), ed. Edward N. Zalta (Fall 2008 edition), http://plato.stanford.edu/archives/fall2008/entries/certainty.

3. W. V. O. Quine, *Ontological Relativity and Other Essays* (New York: Columbia University Press, 1969), 75.

4. Richard Rorty, *Philosophy and the Mirror of Nature* (Princeton: Princeton University Press, 1979); *Contingency, Irony, and Solidarity* (Cambridge: Cambridge University Press, 1989).

given the assumption that "real knowledge" must be scientific. But that assumption is not widely embraced by those who are not metaphysical naturalists. Rorty's replacement pragmatism is similarly flawed. It sets aside and ignores the questions of traditional epistemology, but it does not provide adequate reasons to think that such questions are unanswerable or misguided. In fact, Rorty's assertions show the importance of traditional epistemological questions, since one might still want to ask whether various beliefs really do contribute to human flourishing and whether we are justified in believing that they do.

The Autonomy and Incommensurability of the Christian Narrative

A second objection to the practice of religious epistemology draws on the later work of Ludwig Wittgenstein.[5] In his *Philosophical Investigations,* Wittgenstein argued (or has been taken to argue) that there is no single concept of knowledge that underlies various disciplines. While there might be a "family resemblance" among the various concepts of knowledge, it is better to talk about knowledge in a discipline-specific sense and relative to the "language games" in which it occurs. Hence, the concept of religious knowledge differs in important senses from ethical knowledge and scientific knowledge, and mathematical knowledge.[6]

A wide range of theologians have sought to make a similar point. Some narrative theologians hold only that theological beliefs are best presented in narrative form. Others go farther, holding that theological statements *must* be given in narrative and this is because propositional theological statements fail to live up to their promise of representing religious reality to the mind.[7] Instead of propositions that describe reality, this latter variety of narrative theology (called a "pure narrative theology" by Comstock) offers a narrative that describes a

5. This fact alone makes this objection a complex one, for there is little agreement on how Wittgenstein is to be understood. I will, however, set aside matters of Wittgensteinian exegesis and focus solely on how some have used (or misused) his work.

6. Wittgenstein's insight has been applied to religious belief in (at least) two ways. (This distinction comes from Peter Forrest, "The Epistemology of Religion" in *SEP,* accessed May 28, 2010.) Some see Wittgenstein as pushing the *autonomy* of religious belief. On this view, religious utterances are evaluated as rational, justified, true only from within the form of life; external epistemological standards are irrelevant. Others find in Wittgenstein's statements an assertion of the *incommensurability* of religious forms of life. Religious beliefs have completely different ends and assumptions than scientific or metaphysical claims and consequently, it is pointless to judge religious beliefs by the standards of science or metaphysics. Doing so would be kind of like trying to explain why landing on Boardwalk when it is owned by someone else is a bad thing to someone who has never played Monopoly.

7. Gabriel Fackre, "Narrative Theology: An Overview," *Interpretation* 37 (1983): 340-52; Gary Comstock, "Two Types of Narrative Theology," *Journal of the American Academy of Religion* 55 (1987): 687-717.

person's or a community's experience. In a similar vein, Karl Barth, George Lindbeck, and Stanley Hauerwas (among others) have, each in different ways, expressed misgivings about the task of religious epistemology. It is not that these scholars argue that God does not exist, or exists only in our minds, or cannot be "known" (in some sense of that word); it is that the attempt to demonstrate or justify theological beliefs inevitably misconstrues the content of the gospel of Jesus Christ.[8]

Let us first note that there is an important sense in which the autonomy thesis is correct. Karl Barth's famous critique of natural theology and apologetics was aimed at those (like Friedrich Schleiermacher) who make Christian belief subservient to an external set of metaphysical and epistemological assumptions. They try to shoehorn the theological foot into a philosophical shoe it was never intended to fit. So there is an important sense in which religious epistemology can and should be autonomous. It should remain faithful to orthodox theological commitments. But, given such faithfulness, it is important to see that religious epistemological questions cannot be avoided.

The mistake of the "narrative theology" objection to religious epistemology is in seeing narratives as adequate replacements for justified beliefs. As Edward Oakes has said, such a position "relies far too much on its hopes for short-circuiting the very real challenges we face by living in modern society. No appeal to narrative can obviate these daunting challenges, at least if we take with full seriousness the task of making the Christian message both intelligible and compelling to a secular civilization that feels it can tune out that message because it feels so sure it has already superseded it."[9]

There are, I suggest, two important and often overlooked arguments for engaging in religious epistemology.[10] First, meaningful religious dialogue requires the willingness to engage the questions of religious epistemology. For authentic dialogue to occur between two parties with differing beliefs, each party must believe that (1) we are talking about the same issue and (2) our different perspectives are not merely a matter of personal preference. After all, how much dialogue can there really be between people who believe: *Both my belief and my dialogue partner's belief, a belief that contradicts mine, are true*? By way of illustration, try to imagine an extended, thoughtful, mutually informative discussion on "Which color is the prettiest?" Moreover, if you believe that you and your dialogue part-

8. For example, James William McClendon powerfully embodies this sort of approach in what he calls his "practical theory of religion." He focuses on the practices of religious adherents, not on their beliefs. Consequently, he begins his three-volume work in systematic theology not with doctrine but with ethics (*Systematic Theology,* vol. 1, *Ethics* [Nashville: Abingdon, 2002]).

9. Edward T. Oakes, "Apologetics and the Pathos of Narrative Theology," *Journal of Religion* 72 (1992): 48.

10. I develop these arguments more fully in chapter 6 of my *Thinking about Christian Apologetics: What It Is and Why We Do It* (Downers Grove, IL: InterVarsity, 2011).

ner have contradictory beliefs but do not talk about the fact that your beliefs are contradictory, if you ignore the reasons why you still hold your belief in the face of legitimate alternatives, have you really had a meaningful dialogue? A discourse that seeks only to understand a perspective but does not engage with the truth value, rationale, and reasons offered for that perspective is, in the words of Paul Griffiths, "pallid, platitudinous, and degutted. Its products are intellectual pacifiers for the immature: pleasant to suck on but not very nourishing."[11]

Second, religious epistemology is assumed by theological education. Without some capacity to engage epistemology questions that arise when teaching about the Good News of Jesus Christ, theological education quickly loses both its *theos* and its *logos* — "theological" education becomes less about God and more about humans and less about teaching and understanding and more about indoctrination and regurgitation. Former dean of Duke Divinity School, Dennis Campbell, says this brilliantly: "[In our educational efforts] it is not that we have failed to be global, or that we have failed to take adequate account of the setting, or of the oppressed, but that we are not sure that religion is ultimately significant, that Christianity is true, and that the proclamation of the gospel is critically important for everyone everywhere."[12]

Human Sinfulness/God's Transcendence

A third objection to religious epistemology builds on what might be called the epistemic distance between God and humans. This distance is created by two factors: human sinfulness, which robs us of the ability humans might have had to understand God's existence and nature, and divine transcendence, which even apart from human sinfulness eliminates our ability to understand God. While it has always been part of orthodox Christianity to affirm that God is not merely quantitatively greater than his creation, but qualitatively different, some theologians have taken these themes even farther, holding that God is strictly unknowable and incomprehensible. God's infinity, trinity, simplicity, the fact that he does not have a body, and his "not being a being like other beings in this world" are all held up as reasons why humans cannot refer to God using finite human language or have any true beliefs about God's nature. And, of course, if humans by definition are unable to say true things about God, the task of religious epistemology becomes extraneous at best.

First, a response to this objection to religious epistemology must not, as has

11. Paul J. Griffiths, *An Apology for Apologetics: A Study in the Logic of Interreligious Dialogue,* Faith Meets Faith Series (Maryknoll, NY: Orbis, 1991), xii.

12. Dennis M. Campbell, "Why Should Anyone Believe? Apologetics and Theological Education," *Christian Century* 106, no. 4 (February 1-8, 1989): 137.

too often been the case, downplay God's transcendence. God's nature is not like ours, and finite human minds cannot fully grasp or describe his being. Rather, our ability to refer to God, to speak about him, and say things that are true about his nature must be seen, like salvation, as a gift of God's grace. We can know God, despite his utterly transcendent nature, because he created us with the capacity to know him and because he has revealed himself to us — directly, in history and in speech, in writing, and through his Spirit. While Scripture is clear that humans cannot fully conceptualize God's nature, it assumes that we can know some things about God and holds humans accountable for false understandings of God. Our ability to know God, therefore, is not because God is intrinsically knowable, but because God has created us with such a capacity.

Second, it should be noted that this objection, whether focused on human sinfulness or divine transcendence, undercuts not just religious epistemology, but all forms of theology. In fact, if God is strictly unknowable then it is no more true to say that "God is good" than to say that "God is a ham sandwich." Consequently, the fact that Scripture speaks about God is itself a powerful response to this objection. Since Scripture teaches that God is good and not evil (or a ham sandwich), then Scripture's statement assumes that it is possible to conceptualize and even know something about God's nature. And with that assumption comes the task of religious epistemology, as we seek to know God faithfully.

Nature of Faith

A final objection to the viability of religious epistemology as it has been traditionally conceived is that it is inappropriate given the nature of Christian faith. The clearest articulation of this objection is Merold Westphal's. Westphal likens the task of traditional religious epistemology to a misguided lover who harms the relationship with her beloved by insisting on knowledge that will put her beloved at her disposal. "The movement 'beyond faith' to knowledge (is) not the ascent from that which is inferior . . . to that which is superior . . . ; (it is) rather the withdrawal from the site at which alone is possible a loving, trusting relation with a God before whom one might sing and dance."[13]

This objection includes but goes beyond the typical objection based on Mark 10:15. Speaking to his disciples, Jesus says: "I tell you the truth, whoever does not receive the Kingdom of God like a child will never enter it" (NET). The problem, according to Westphal, includes a lack of child-like trust, but it is not only that. The problem is with seeing faith as including insight into God's nature. Religious epistemology involves "thinking God's thoughts after him" and "dissipating the

13. Merold Westphal, *Overcoming Onto-Theology: Toward a Postmodern Christian Faith* (New York: Fordham University Press, 2001), 27.

darkness of mystery with the light of human knowledge."[14] Rather, says Westphal, the task of theology (and, one might assume, Christian epistemology) "is to serve the life of faith, not the ideals of knowledge as defined by the philosophical traditions."[15]

There is much to commend Westphal's argument. But his objection is an indictment not of religious epistemology per se, but of versions of religious epistemology that strive for demonstrable certainty and fail to acknowledge the limitations of human knowledge of God. For Westphal does not claim that the lover is completely in the dark about her beloved. She knows that he exists and (presumably) that his character makes him worthy of her love. So, while Westphal's admonition that religious epistemology must not be driven by values and ideals antithetical to the Christian faith is salutary, the necessity of religious epistemology is highlighted by Westphal's own example. For we must avoid creating our beloved in our own image. In the final analysis, there is no substitute for careful, faithful epistemological inquiry.

The Nature of Positive Epistemic Status

Rudolf Bultmann famously said that, given what modern humans know, "it is impossible to believe in the New Testament world of spirits and miracles."[16] More recently, but with more vitriol, Richard Dawkins, has dismissed belief in God as a cognitive virus, a virulent disease that destroys the ability to think clearly and carefully.[17] Of course, Christians demur. But what is being debated? There are two related but distinct issues. First, there are what might be called *de facto* considerations. Does God in fact exist? Are the central teachings of Christianity true? Second, there are *de jure* considerations. *De jure* objections are not objections to the truth of Christianity, but to its rational acceptability. (Of course, Dawkins and many others have both *de facto* and *de jure* objections to Christian belief.) A *de jure* objection to Christian belief holds that Christianity is irrational, unjustified, a product of wish-fulfillment, based on inadequate evidence, and so on. In each case, there is something wrong — epistemically and maybe even ethically — with holding the belief in question.

While *de facto* considerations are obviously crucially important for Christianity, my discussion of religious epistemology will focus on *de jure* questions and

14. Westphal, *Overcoming Onto-Theology,* 27.

15. Westphal, *Overcoming Onto-Theology,* 27. While Westphal clearly distances himself from certain philosophical ideals of knowledge, it might be fair to ask whether his approach owes too much to other philosophical traditions, such as existentialism.

16. Rudolf Bultmann, *Kerygma and Myth* (New York: Harper & Row, 1961), 5.

17. Richard Dawkins, "Viruses of the Mind," in *Dennett and His Critics: Demystifying Mind,* ed. Bo Dahlbom (Oxford: Blackwell, 1993), 13.

the relationship between *de jure* considerations and *de facto* considerations. But before one addresses the *de jure* considerations at the heart of religious epistemology, it is important to understand the epistemic feature or features Christian belief is claimed to have — or, for those who object to Christianity, the feature Christian belief is claimed to lack. However, the complexity of this matter is substantial. Not only is there no agreement on which variety of positive epistemic status should be the focus of conversation, there is no agreement on how each of these epistemic concepts should be understood. The idea of giving even a rough survey of all of these issues is laughable. Instead, I will offer a sketch of the basic structure of knowledge and then consider some of the important issues and debates surrounding the nature and structure of justification.

The Basic Structure of Knowledge

Knowledge comes in different varieties. First, there is *knowledge by acquaintance,* as in "I know the book in front of me." Second, there is *procedural knowledge,* or knowing how to do something, as in "I know how to drive a car with a manual transmission." Third, there is *propositional knowledge,* which is knowledge *that* something is the case: "I know that Minneapolis lies farther south than Moscow." In religious epistemology, the primary importance of knowledge by acquaintance comes in the arena of religious experience and the primary importance of procedural knowledge comes from a discussion of the role intellectual virtues might play in religious knowledge. That being said, most discussions of religious knowledge have focused primarily on propositional knowledge.[18]

Let's start with Plato's definition of propositional knowledge — "true belief plus some account."[19] Whether Plato himself was enthusiastic about this definition or not is less important than the fact that it has been a very influential way of looking at the concept of knowledge. For a person to know *p,* one must, first, believe that *p,* and, second, *p* must be true. In addition, since it is generally accepted that accidentally true belief is not knowledge, the person must have "some account" of why they believe that *p.* In other words, knowledge requires (1) an ontological component (truth), (2) a psychological component (belief), and (3) and an epistemological component (an account), some reason or set of reasons that support the belief in question for the person in question.

There is, of course, nothing like unanimity on these conditions. It is possible

18. I believe that an exclusive focus on propositional knowledge is problematic, but the increasingly common trend that ignores the role of propositional knowledge in Christian epistemology is also utterly mistaken.

19. *Theaetetus* 201d.

to find objections to any and all of them. It is not surprising, therefore, that Plato's *Theaetetus* is an aporetic dialogue — it is a dialogue that ends not with an answer, but an impasse. Nonetheless, Plato's three conditions are widely accepted as excellent starting points; and, among those who are comfortable with the task of epistemology in general, there is a general consensus that some version of each of these conditions is necessary for knowledge.

Thus, the crucial question in the study of knowledge is this — What must be added to true beliefs to convert them into knowledge? For at least the last century, the traditional epistemological position has been to identify this epistemological component with "justification," or "rationality," or perhaps some judicious mix of both. Rationality is a wide-ranging concept, but it is commonly used to indicate a state in which belief is permitted. A belief is rational if the person holding it does not simultaneously have reasons that count against that belief. A justified belief, on the other hand, is a belief for which the "knower" has sound reasons. There is great variety in such "reasons." These reasons for belief may work by themselves or in conjunction with a complex set of background beliefs. And they may produce beliefs through conscious inferences that can be clearly traced by the person in question or the belief may be "triggered" by cognitive processes of which she is only partially aware.[20]

Traditionally, both justification and rationality have been understood deontologically. In other words, for a person to be justified or rational with respect to a particular belief that person must not violate any epistemic duties, obligations, or responsibilities with respect to acquiring or maintaining the belief in question. While the notion of "epistemic duties" is fairly commonsense (hence the multitude of statements like "He has no reason to believe the way he does"), the nature and scope of these duties are not entirely precise. Common epistemic duties are "the avoidance of false beliefs and the maximization of true beliefs" and "pursuing your doxastic goals in an effective fashion." Other more controversial duties have been proposed, such as William Clifford's Principle: "It is wrong, always, everywhere, and for anyone to believe anything upon insufficient evidence."[21] Those who keep their intellectual duties with respect to a particular belief are said to be "justified" in that belief.

The definition of knowledge as "justified true belief" enjoyed the status of epistemological orthodoxy for many years. In 1963, however, Edmund Gettier wrote a three-page article that turned the epistemological world on its head.[22] In "Is Justified True Belief Knowledge?" Gettier highlighted an entire set of coun-

20. Robert Audi, *The Structure of Justification* (Cambridge: Cambridge University Press, 1993), 273.

21. William K. Clifford, "The Ethics of Belief," in *The Ethics of Belief and Other Essays,* ed. T. Madigan (Amherst, NY: Prometheus, 1999 [1877]), 70.

22. Edmund Gettier, "Is Justified True Belief Knowledge?" *Analysis* 23 (1963): 121-23.

terexamples to the definition of knowledge as justified true belief.[23] What Gettier showed is that justification, even when conjoined with true belief, was not sufficient for warrant, and therefore, that knowledge could not be merely justified true belief. Something more was needed. In Gettier's wake, two broad options have emerged. The first group deems Gettier's argument to be an indictment only of the completeness of the "justified true belief" account. Knowledge can and should still be understood as justified true belief, but a fourth condition must be added to mollify Gettier. These people might be labeled "Post-Gettier Optimists." "Post-Gettier Pessimists," on the other hand, deem Gettier to have exposed a fundamental flaw in traditional "justified true belief" accounts of knowledge; what is needed is not a fourth condition, but a fundamental change in perspective.[24] Since Gettier, the primary front on which this debate has raged has been the debate over the nature of justification.

Debates over the Nature of Justification

As we have seen, the traditional account of justification — and, therefore, the traditional account of the epistemic component of knowledge — is deontological in nature. Justification is about doing one's epistemic duties, seeking evidence, accepting only those beliefs that are based on good reasons. While a deontological conception of justification is not without its plausibility, it has come under increasing fire in contemporary philosophical circles. First, it isn't at all clear what these epistemic obligations are or where we get them. Second, a deontological account of justification seems to assume that our beliefs are under our direct control — a position known as *doxastic voluntarism.* Of course, I can bring it about that I believe something, such as when I look up the date of the last eruption of Krakatoa. But most of our beliefs — that I am sitting or that I see a cardinal outside my window — are not under our direct control. It is more accurate to say that I find myself with these beliefs than I form these beliefs. Deontological accounts of justification seemed designed for an academic setting, where beliefs are forged

23. A Gettier counterexample can be constructed by putting an epistemic agent in a setting in which he or she forms a belief characterized by simultaneous cases of epistemic bad luck and epistemic good luck. Take, for example, the act of looking at the clock on your office wall. The clock has always been reliable, so you form the belief: "It is now 11:34 a.m." However, unbeknownst to you, the clock's battery ran out last night (bad luck), but did so at exactly 11:34 p.m. (good luck). Therefore, even though your belief is true and justified (after all, you have ample evidence of the clock's reliability), your belief is only accidentally true and therefore does not count as knowledge for you.

24. The terms "Post-Gettier Optimist" and "Post-Gettier Pessimist" are Kevin Meeker's. See his *Knowledge and Norms: A Defense of Epistemic Justification* (Ph.D. dissertation, University of Notre Dame, 1998), 1-2.

in the fire of research, analysis, and debate. It is possible that the plausibility of deontological accounts of justification is a function of the academic setting in which individuals who debate things like the nature of justification reside. However, as William Alston notes,

> Controversial and difficult issues force themselves to our attention, especially if we are intellectuals, just because we spend so much of our time trying to resolve them. But if we survey the whole range of our cognitive operations, they will appear as a few straws floating on a vast sea of items about none of which we entertain the slightest doubt. By comparison, the controversial beliefs we have in religion, politics, philosophy, and the conduct of our affairs are negligible in number, however significant they may be individually.[25]

Questions regarding deontological accounts of justification have induced a pair of related "shifts in focus" in contemporary epistemology. Of course, not everybody has embraced these shifts. But among those who have become convinced that deontological justification is headed down a wrong path, two alternate routes have been popular. The first shifts the focus regarding justification from *epistemic responsibility* to *truth conductivity.*[26] On this view what is most important is not responsibility on the part of the epistemic agent, but the likelihood that beliefs so formed will be true. The second shift is related to the first and involves a shift in focus from duties to virtues. Instead of focusing legalistically on the list of things that must be done to justify a belief, virtue epistemology instead asks what sort of person forms justified beliefs.[27] What personal and intellectual characteristics does a person who is a reliable thinker possess? Notice that a focus on epistemological virtues is possible whether you construe justification as responsibility or truth-conductivity.

Notice that both of these shifts raise a deeper question regarding the role of reflective awareness on the part of the subject. This issue has become crystalized in the debate between two positions known as *internalism* and *externalism.* Very roughly, the battleground of the internalism/externalism debate concerns whether knowledge requires only that a person *has* a well-grounded belief or

25. William Alston, "The Deontological Conception of Epistemic Justification," in *Epistemic Justification: Essays in the Theory of Knowledge* (Ithaca, NY: Cornell University Press, 1989), 124-25.

26. Here I am assuming some version of a *realist* understanding of truth. Given an epistemic conception of truth, the truth-conditions for a belief are not external to the epistemic agent. For a powerful defense of a minimalist version of realism, see William Alston, *A Realist Conception of Truth* (Ithaca, NY: Cornell University Press, 1996).

27. Virtues could either be excellences of persons or excellences of cognitive systems. See John Greco, "Two Kinds of Intellectual Virtue," *Philosophy and Phenomenological Research* 60 (2000): 179-98.

whether it requires that the person in question be actually or potentially aware of at least one of the features that make their belief well grounded. Internalists demand that the features that ground or justify a belief be part of the actual or potential reflective awareness of the epistemic agent. The value of such reflective awareness is that the agent is in a position to explain why they know what they take themselves to know. Externalists reject this Awareness Requirement, focusing instead on the reliability or truth-conduciveness of cognitive faculties or belief-forming mechanisms and (often) replacing the term justification with warrant.[28] Consequently, for externalists, justification (or warrant) is a property of beliefs — belief *B* is warranted for person *P* — whereas, for internalists, justification is a property of persons — Person *P* is justified in believing belief *B*.

While adjudicating the internalism/externalism debate is beyond the scope of this essay, two things may be said to sketch a path beyond the impasse. The first involves reconsidering the relationship between knowledge and skepticism. The assumption that knowledge requires a particular kind of response to the skeptic — one that demonstrates with certainty that knowledge does, in fact, obtain — has a long pedigree. It is certainly the driving assumption of the Enlightenment and some find it to be a core assumption of medieval and even Greek philosophical thought. Regardless, whether one embraces an internalist or externalist epistemology, the assumption that knowledge requires certainty is worth reconsidering. Consider my belief that I see a pine tree out the window. The externalist construal of knowledge as the result of truth-conducive cognitive mechanisms gives an adequate account of my knowledge, a more plausible account than the internalist construal of my visual experience as reflectively accessible evidence for my belief. While I could be wrong — I could be in the Matrix or being deceived by a malevolent demon — I do not seriously entertain those options. I acknowledge them as logical possibilities but not as reasonable possibilities. It is infinitely more reasonable for me to believe "I see a pine tree" than "My vision is the result of demonic deception."

Second, it is possible to reconfigure the internalism/externalism debate as a debate not over the nature of knowledge, but as an affirmation that there are different levels or qualities of knowledge. Externalism does a better job of the knowledge of base-level cognitive activity, such as perceptual, introspective, memorial beliefs. It is strained at best to expect reflective awareness regarding the reasons that justify my belief that I had toast this morning. How do I know that I had toast? I just do. Yes, I have a decent track-record of remembering such things, but none of that gets to the bottom of why I know what I ate. But there

28. The term "cognitive faculties" is an odd one. Those who use the term do not intend to convey the idea that there is a portion of the brain that produces beliefs. Rather, a cognitive faculty is short for the entire complex psychological and physiological process that results in a person having a belief.

are many instances when we want more than this. In addition to warrant for our beliefs, we may want what might be called "articulate reflection" or "the ability to give an account of one's knowledge — that is, the ability to give reasons for believing what one rightly believes."[29] This requires the sort of cognitive access to those reasons that internalists find lacking in externalist accounts of warrant.

This acknowledgment of the value of reflective awareness does not call into question the viability of externalism, it only questions whether it answers all the questions that might be asked of it. Ernest Sosa draws a distinction between "animal knowledge" and "human" or "reflective" knowledge. Lorraine Code and Linda Zagzebski make similar distinctions between "knowing" and "knowing well" (Code) and "high-grade" and "low-grade" knowledge (Zagzebski).[30] Internalism can be taken as the insistence that a person who is able to reflect on the source and pedigree of their knowledge possesses something uniquely and genuinely valuable. And this value is not diminished if articulate reflection is not the "something" that divides knowledge from non-knowledge. One might hold, for instance, that articulate reflection is what divides knowledge from understanding. And it is obvious that understanding is a good thing from an epistemic point of view.

Debates over the Structure of Justification

Arguments over the nature of justification have been advanced with the development of meta-epistemology and the realization that there exist family resemblances and common themes in the various positions on the nature of justification.[31] One of the most recognized positions on the structure of justification has been called foundationalism — one of the dreaded "F-words" used in contemporary academic discourse (the other being "fundamentalist"). Used as a term of abuse, foundationalism has become code for elements of the Enlightenment, manifested most clearly (it is said) in René Descartes's quest for a method that would produce absolute certainty. As Nicholas Wolterstorff points out, "Foundationalism has been so widely condemned in recent years, and the term itself so indiscriminately tossed about, that the term has by now lost almost all determinate meaning. What remains is little more than pejorative connotations. To be

29. Philip R. Olson, "Comments on 'Naturalism and Normativity': What Is Epistemic Value Pluralism?" JanusBlog: The Virtue Theory Discussion Forum, accessed June 13, 2010.

30. Lorraine Code, *Epistemic Responsibility* (Hanover, NH: University Press of New England/Brown University Press, 1987); Linda Zagzebski, *Virtues of the Mind: An Inquiry into the Nature of Virtue and the Ethical Foundations of Knowledge,* Cambridge Studies in Philosophy (Cambridge: Cambridge University Press, 1996), 273-83.

31. Nicholas Wolterstorff, "Herman Bavinck: Proto Reformed Epistemologist," *Calvin Theological Journal* 41 (2010): 134.

called a foundationalist in the academy is rather like being called a child abuser in general society; people are horrified."[32] Sadly, most of the treatments of the term "foundationalist" do not even attempt to provide an analysis of the concept that goes beyond platitudes and superficialities.

Consequently, we must make a pair of distinctions with respect to foundationalism. First, there is a difference between *doxastic foundationalism* and *source foundationalism.*[33] Doxastic foundationalism is simply the notion that there is a unique sort of relationship among some of our beliefs — some beliefs provide an anchor in a certain sense for other beliefs. Some of our beliefs receive justification directly, from an experience; other beliefs receive justification indirectly, from inferences from other beliefs. Beliefs that receive direct justification are called *basic* beliefs and basic beliefs that are justified are called *properly basic* beliefs. Source foundationalism, on the other hand, involves the claim that "some of our sources of belief are privileged in the sense that (a) they can be rationally trusted in the absence of evidence of their reliability, and (b) it is irrational to rely on other sources of evidence unless they are somehow 'certified' by the privileged sources,"[34] positivism and rationalism. Examples of source foundationalism include logical positivism and rationalism.

Second, there is a difference between *classical foundationalism* and *modest foundationalism.* Classical foundationalists are characterized by a restrictive set of requirements for justified basic beliefs. A belief can only be *properly basic* or immediately justified if it is self-evident, evident to the senses, or about one's internal mental states. Modest foundationalism (sometimes called broad foundationalism) has a much less restrictive set of requirements for proper basicality. Memory beliefs, some subjective experiences, and intuitions are also candidates for proper basicality. Moreover, for the modest foundationalist, properly basic beliefs are *prima facie* justified, but they are not indefeasible. For this reason, while modest foundationalism is a variety of doxastic foundationalism, it is not a variety of source foundationalism.

Both source foundationalism and classical foundationalism have been used primarily as a means to guarantee truth. If one's foundational beliefs are indubitable and if the method used to "base" nonbasic beliefs on basic beliefs was free from error (based on sound deductive logic), then in principle one could demonstrate the truth of any belief one held. As such, source foundationalism has been viewed as a variety of *methodism* (not to be confused with the Christian denomination). Methodism is the requirement that prior to attaining knowledge,

32. Wolterstorff, "Herman Bavinck," 134.

33. Many have drawn attention to this distinction, but I am following Mike Rea's terminology ("Introduction," in *Analytic Theology: New Essays in the Philosophy of Theology,* ed. Oliver D. Crisp and Michael C. Rea [Oxford: Oxford University Press, 2009], 12-13).

34. Rea, "Introduction," 13.

one must specify criteria for knowledge, a method for attaining knowledge, and demonstrate that method to be reliable. The alternative to methodism is *particularism.* The particularist starts with clear instances of knowledge, such as the belief that *I had toast for breakfast this morning* or *3 + 2 = 5.* One may develop criteria for knowledge along the way, but the clear instances of knowledge are not validated by their meeting criteria for knowledge. Rather the criteria are validated by their congruence with clear instances of knowledge.[35]

Hence, the notion that there are only two options — foundationalism and non-foundationalism — must be rejected. There are, in fact, four options (and myriad variations on each of those four). First, one might accept both source foundationalism and doxastic foundationalism and, in so doing, embrace the quest for certainty that motivated both Descartes and the Classical Foundationalists. Second, one might reject both and in so doing reject the very distinction between basic and nonbasic beliefs. This position, known as *coherentism,* holds that coherence with other beliefs is the only way to justify beliefs. Third, one might reject doxastic foundationalism, but accept source foundationalism. An example of such a position would be a coherentist who held that science was the only means to knowledge. Fourth and finally, one might accept doxastic foundationalism but reject source foundationalism. This position retains the distinction between basic and nonbasic beliefs but acknowledges that basic beliefs are not certain and inferences of nonbasic beliefs from basic beliefs are not necessarily perfect.

One other category of views should be noted. Many who have been frustrated with the polarity between foundationalism and non-foundationalism have sought a via media. Susan Haack has developed a position known as foundherentism, which seeks to combine the respective strengths of foundationalism and non-foundationalism.[36] And it is increasingly common to hear discussion of "postfoundationalism."[37] Like other positions referred to with the "post" prefix, postfoundationalism is less of a position in its own right and more of a rejection of a position. Consequently, the term "postfoundationalism" has been used to refer to a wide range of positions. Some use the term to refer to any position that rejects classical foundationalism. Others use the term postfoundationalism as a synonym for coherentism. Perhaps the best use of the term, however, is to denote an approach that holds that the "entire debate between foundationalism and

35. J. P. Moreland and William Lane Craig, *Philosophical Foundations for a Christian Worldview* (Downers Grove, IL: InterVarsity, 2003), 100.

36. Susan Haack, *Evidence and Inquiry: Towards Reconstruction in Epistemology* (Oxford: Blackwell, 1993).

37. Noted post-foundationalists include J. Wentzel van Huyssteen and Philip Clayton. One of the most clear and complete accounts of "postfoundationalism" has been written by LeRon Shults. See his *The Postfoundationalist Task of Theology: Wolfhart Pannenberg and the New Theological Rationality* (Grand Rapids: Eerdmans, 1999), 25-81.

nonfoundationalism is based on an outdated epistemological dilemma."[38] Central to such an approach is a collapsing of the distinction between epistemology and hermeneutics. Foundherentism and postfoundationalism both clearly reject source foundationalism and classical foundationalism. And both emphasize the role of the epistemic community and the necessity of seeing justification as holistic and multidirectional rather than linear. But, as I have argued elsewhere, doxastic foundationalism is perfectly compatible with each of these insights.[39] Hence, it is best to see foundherentism and postfoundationalism as versions of the broad category I have labeled doxastic foundationalism.

While adjudicating these positions is not the task of this essay, it is worthwhile to consider a trio of arguments, one aimed at non-foundationalists and the other two aimed at foundationalists. Some hold that a high view of Scripture requires a commitment to foundationalism because non-foundationalism ends up watering down the concept of truth. Certainly many conceptual relativists are coherentists, but there is no necessity that coherentists accept conceptual relativism. This is because coherentism (like doxastic foundationalism) is a theory about justification, not truth. There is such a thing as the Coherence Theory of Truth, but that is a completely different animal. It is possible to hold to a Correspondence Theory of Truth and believe that coherence is the best way to understand the nature of justification. In fact, there is nothing that stops a coherentist or non-foundationalist from holding to the inerrancy of Scripture; it's just that their approach to explaining or justifying Scripture's inerrancy may be quite different from the foundationalist's method.

If non-foundationalism is mistakenly labeled as theologically liberal, foundationalism is often mistakenly labeled as "fundamentalist" or "modernist." One of the most common objections to foundationalisms is that they fail to acknowledge that all beliefs reside in an interpretive framework and that no belief enters the web of belief without being interpreted.[40] It is, however, not just obvious that all beliefs are interpreted and therefore that there is no givenness to experience.[41] But notice that even if it is granted that all beliefs are interpreted (in some

38. LeRon Shults, "Postfoundationalism," in *The Encyclopedia of Science and Religion,* vol. 2, ed. J. Wentzel Vrede van Huyssteen (New York: Macmillan Reference USA, 2003), 688.

39. James Beilby, "The Implications of Postmodernism for Theology: On Meta-narratives, Foundationalism, and Realism," *Princeton Theological Review* 12 (2006): 13.

40. LeRon Shults, for example, develops an argument against positions that "allow some beliefs to bypass experience or to enter the web 'neutrally,' without being interpreted." See his *The Postfoundationalist Task of Theology,* 44.

41. Suppose you are driving down the road and among the myriad of things that pass through your visual field is a road sign. Later someone comments that the road you were driving on will be closed for roadwork and you recall that the sign you saw indicated that fact. You experienced the sign and got its message (in some sense) even if your experience was nonconceptual and non-propositional. It is likely that many of the things we experience on a daily

sense), that does not amount to an objection to doxastic foundationalism, but only to source foundationalism. When I have the experience of seeing a tree, the resulting belief is embedded in a complex interpretive grid. There are beliefs and dispositions that cause me to label the object as a "tree" rather than a "shrub," that indicate that my experience is not the result of mischievous hologram-projectors that interpret my existence as being conceptually distinct from that of the tree, and so on. But none of this suggests that I base the justification of my belief that "I see a tree" on that network of belief or any particular belief within that network.[42] Consequently, there is no problem in holding both that all beliefs reside within an interpretive grid and that some beliefs are epistemologically basic. In other words, granting that experiences take place within interpretive grids does not entail coherentism; it only entails fallibilism.

Finally, some object that the orthodox conception of the reliability of Scripture (especially when combined with the Protestant affirmation of *sola scriptura*) entails a version of source foundationalism. Undoubtedly many Christians have (and still do) approach Scripture in a source foundational way. But while orthodox Christians are committed to holding that Scripture is unique in terms of its authority and veracity, that commitment alone does not entail source foundationalism. Recall that source foundationalism is a means to guarantee truth. Those who justify their interpretations of Scripture by appealing to the inerrancy of Scripture are source foundationalists. But thoughtful Christians should acknowledge a distinction between the truthfulness of Scripture and the truthfulness of a particular interpretation of Scripture. Those that do so are not necessarily source foundationalists.[43]

Objections to Christian Belief

Many acknowledge that religious epistemology is a viable task, but they find Christian belief to be epistemically lacking. Some of these have a *de facto* objection to Christian belief, others have a *de jure* objection, and many have both. Are these objections to Christian belief persuasive? In answering this question, we must keep in mind the importance of a fine-grained, person-specific approach to this question. While it is important to answer the universalized version of this question — could there be *any* Christian whose beliefs could have positive epis-

---

basis are similar. Note, however, that non-conceptual experience is no guarantee of truth. Just as it is possible to mis-interpret an experience, it is possible to mis-see.

42. Consequently, one might say that, in terms of semantics (my calling the object I see a "tree" rather than *der Baum* or *l'arbre* or "jwbusxzp"), there are no basic beliefs. But it would be a confusion to extend this insight beyond semantics.

43. I say "not necessarily" only because they might still approach other sources, such as science, in a source foundationalist manner.

temic status? — we should also shoulder the laborious task of particularizing this question to specific people in specific contexts and specific cultures.

There are a dizzying variety of objections to the epistemological status of Christian belief. Because this essay is on Christian *epistemology* (and because space and time are finite), I will set aside *de facto* objections and focus on some of the most prominent *de jure* objections.

Insufficient Evidence

Perhaps the most common *de jure* objection is that the evidence for Christian belief is insufficient. While this claim has been found in the mouths of many, including some who would retain the label "Christians," the *locus classicus* of this position is undoubtedly William Clifford.

On this matter, he is known for two things: a story and a principle.[44] Clifford's story tells of a shipowner who has doubts about the seaworthiness of his ship but still sells tickets for a transatlantic voyage, convincing himself that the ship is up to the task of the voyage. When the ship goes down in a storm, Clifford proclaims that even though the shipowner sincerely believed the ship was safe, he "had no right to believe on such evidence as was before him." And his epistemic culpability would be the same even if the ship and its passengers had survived the voyage. Thus, Clifford's famous principle: "It is wrong, always, everywhere, and for anyone to believe anything upon insufficient evidence."[45]

While Clifford does not single out proponents of religion, there can be little doubt that he had religious beliefs in mind as he told his story and formulated his principle. And even apart from Clifford's intentions, his principle has been taken by many as an effective exposé of the epistemological deficits of religious belief. Notice, however, that Clifford's Principle, taken by itself, does not threaten religious belief at all, for a religious believer might take the *sensus divinitatis,* the internal instigation of the Holy Spirit, or faith itself as evidence supportive of their belief. Rather, it is only when Clifford's Principle is conjoined with a particular set of assumptions about what constitutes "sufficient evidence" that it becomes toxic to Christian belief.

Some have suggested that all evidence must be scientific in nature, others that it must be empirical, and still others that it must be open to repeatability or

44. An excellent survey of Clifford's evidentialism is found in Andrew Chignell and Andrew Dole, "The Ethics of Religious Belief: A Recent History," in *God and the Ethics of Belief: New Essays in Philosophy of Religion,* ed. Andrew Dole and Andrew Chignell (Cambridge: Cambridge University Press, 2005), 1-7.

45. William K. Clifford, "The Ethics of Belief," in *The Ethics of Belief and Other Essays,* ed. Timothy J. Madigan (Amherst, NY: Prometheus, 1999), 77.

subsequent verification. But perhaps the most influential method is to link Clifford's Principle with a particular account of evidence or epistemic justification such as Classical Foundationalism.[46] The conjunction of Classical Foundationalism and Cliffordian Evidentialism requires the Christian either to demonstrate that God's existence is self-evident or evident to the senses or to show how it can be deduced from propositions that are. While some Christians have tried to shoulder this task, it is not difficult to see that this combination is a recipe for religious skepticism.

At the outset, it should be noted that the conjunction of Classical Foundationalism and Cliffordian Evidentialism does not only cause epistemic problems for religious belief. Given this high standard, it is extremely difficult to defend the epistemic status of belief in other minds, belief in the existence of the past, memory beliefs, and testimonial beliefs. So we are left with the infelicitous result of not knowing fairly obvious beliefs such as "my wife has a mind" and "I had toast for breakfast this morning." This has led many to reconsider the standard set by Clifford and Classical Foundationalism.

The problem with Classical Foundationalism has been thoroughly discussed. It is self-referentially incoherent; it cannot meet the standard it sets for itself.[47] A looser set of requirements for basic beliefs is required. But how much looser? A similar question can be asked of evidentialism. Clifford entreats us to believe only on the basis of evidence. Fine. But what counts as evidence? Suppose while golfing alone I hit an absolutely terrible shot — a purely hypothetical example, to be sure — and after hitting five trees and two small woodland creatures, my ball ends up on the green, two feet from the hole. Because there are no witnesses, the improbability of my experience (and my well-known proclivity to tell tall tales about my golf game) will make it very difficult to demonstrate to anybody else that the event happened as I said. But does that mean that I am not justified in my belief? Not at all.

The lesson to be learned here is that the epistemic status of our beliefs should not be conflated with our ability to demonstrate their truthfulness to others. William Lane Craig makes a nice distinction between *knowing the truth* and *showing the truth.*[48] I can know that my golf ball ended up where it did even if I cannot hope to convince anybody else of that fact. More generally, one cannot evaluate evidence claims apart from the complex context in which those beliefs are

46. Notice that I am not arguing that evidentialism is based on Classical Foundationalism. Rather, I am saying only that many of those who raise the *de jure* objection to Christianity have linked evidentialism and Classical Foundationalism.

47. Alvin Plantinga, "Reason and Belief in God," in *Faith and Rationality: Reason and Belief in God,* ed. Alvin Plantinga and Nicholas Wolterstorff (Notre Dame: University of Notre Dame Press, 1983), 59-63.

48. William Lane Craig, *Reasonable Faith: Christian Truth and Apologetics,* rev. edition (Wheaton, IL: Crossway, 1994), 31-48.

formed. The evaluation of evidence for religious beliefs will depend greatly on other beliefs one has. If one acknowledges the existence of a God who speaks, it will be possible to see God's hand in Saul's experience on the road to Damascus. Atheists and deists, however, must find a psychological explanation for Paul's experience, because given their background beliefs, that is the only reasonable explanation.

This has led Alvin Plantinga and others to ask whether belief in God could be properly basic for some people — for example, for my grandmother. Of course, skeptics will find such a claim to be outrageous. But apart from demonstrating the falsity of the background beliefs with which Christians evaluate evidence claims, it seems that Christians need not take their objections as the final word on the matter. This does not mean that evidence is in the eye of the beholder and it certainly does not mean that anything goes. It means that Christians need not make the success of their religious epistemology dependent on demonstrating the justification they have for their religious beliefs to one who is skeptical.

This epistemological stance reflects the fundamental conviction that our religious beliefs cannot be divorced from our affections, attitudes, desires, and epistemic goals. One who approaches Christian belief with an attitude of basic trust, with a willingness to learn and submit, is vastly more likely to see truthfulness in Christianity. And those who approach the gospel with basic distrust, with an attitude of "I will not be duped," are vastly less likely to see even the evidence that exists. Blaise Pascal said this well: "[In faith] there is enough light for those who desire only to see and enough darkness for those of a contrary disposition."[49]

Social Evidentialism and Public Epistemic Parity

The second *de jure* objection to Christian belief is closely related to the first. Whatever else it is, evidentialism is an epistemic principle the purpose of which is to make knowledge claims more objective. Consequently, many people have called attention to the fact that there is a communal or social intuition behind evidentialism. Gary Gutting has defended the notion of *social evidentialism,* drawing on the idea that the proper governance of one's beliefs relative to the available evidence has important social implications.[50] His claim is that the rationality of one's beliefs is connected in an important way with the beliefs of those who might be called your "epistemic peers." An epistemic peer is someone whose knowledge cannot be dismissed. According to Peter Forrest,

49. Blaise Pascal, *Pensées,* 149, trans. A. J. Krailsheimer, rev. edition (London: Penguin, 1995), 50.

50. Gary Gutting, *Religious Belief and Religious Skepticism* (Notre Dame: University of Notre Dame Press, 1982), esp. 79-108.

> [T]o be sure, sometimes those who disagree with you are your intellectual inferiors in some respect. Consider, for instance, someone who insisted that pi was precisely 22/7. Those who know of and can follow a proof that pi is an irrational number may justifiably dismiss that person as a mathematical ignoramus. The case of interest, however, is that in which no such inferiority is on public display. This is referred to as a situation of public epistemic parity.[51]

Suppose you are in a situation of public epistemic parity. You believe some religious belief *p* and your epistemic peer believes *~p*. According to Gutting, when persons find themselves in such a situation, they are obligated to produce adequate evidence for *p* or acknowledge that their reasons are insufficient to support full-fledged belief. But who decides the adequacy of evidence? And why assume that justification is a function of publicly demonstrable evidence? Note that social evidentialism is parasitic on evidentialism *simpliciter.* That is, the notion that one's beliefs depend on the acceptance of those beliefs by one's epistemic peers is only plausible given the assumption that beliefs require an evidential basis. The implication of this fact is that if evidentialism *simpliciter* is false, then social evidentialism is also false.

Moreover, the very idea of epistemic parity is a bit strained. Is there ever epistemic parity on matters as complex as religious belief? Gutting would undoubtedly respond that *sufficient* similarity of epistemic situations was good enough. But how is such similarity to be gauged? And who does the gauging? Moreover, the concept of epistemic parity also seems to either deny or discount the possibility of unique, private experiences. Consider Saul's best friend, Caiaphas. Even if they were in a "sufficiently similar" epistemic situation before Saul's trip to Damascus, wouldn't Saul's experience on that journey change things dramatically? And wouldn't Saul be unreasonable to withhold his new belief about the Risen Jesus because he could not convince his friend? Unique, private experiences matter. If it is acceptable for a skeptic to appeal to their private experience of never having any sorts of religious experiences, it seems okay for the Christian to appeal to their experience of having had religious experiences.

Finally, while it is crucially important to listen to and learn from people with whom you disagree, it is very difficult to argue as Gutting does without falling prey to special pleading. Peter van Inwagen recounts an interesting experience:

> A philosopher once told me that he could not accept Christianity or any other religion because there were many religions, each of them logically incompatible with the others, and it was impossible to determine which of them was correct. That is, when you think about it, a very odd thing for a *philosopher* to say, for, *mutatis mutandis,* it is an exact description of the situation in philoso-

51. Peter Forrest, "The Epistemology of Religion," *SEP,* accessed June 13, 2010.

> phy. And yet the oddness of what this philosopher was saying was something that had never occurred to him. (The fact that it had never occurred to him — a very intelligent and well-trained philosopher — is itself a very odd fact, one well worth reflecting on.)[52]

Public epistemic parity does perhaps create a burden for the believer to evaluate their reasons for believing. But if Gutting requires that their reasons must be deemed to be acceptable to their epistemic peers, then Gutting's social evidentialism has self-referential problems. For many of his epistemic peers reject his reasons for holding social evidentialism.

Cognitive Dysfunction

A third objection to Christian belief is actually a category of related objections. The common theme in this category is that religious beliefs are dysfunctional in some important respect or another. David Hume, Jean-Jacques Rousseau, Ludwig Feuerbach, and Friedrich Nietzsche have developed varieties of this objection, but the most famous versions come from Sigmund Freud and Karl Marx. Freud's argument is that religious beliefs "which are given out as teachings, are not precipitates of experience or end-results of thinking: they are illusions, fulfillments of the oldest, strongest and most urgent wishes of mankind."[53] Religious beliefs are wishes for protection. For Freud, the problem with such beliefs is not that they cannot be true, but that those who are thoughtful should realize that such beliefs are superstitious and that their dysfunction comes from the fact that they are not aimed at truth, but at creating an illusion of happiness.

Karl Marx's objection is similar. For Marx, religion is the "opium of the people," a tool designed to create a sense of happiness and complacency. "The abolition of religion as the *illusory* happiness of the people is required for their *real* happiness."[54] Marx seems to suspect that many in the ruling class realize the lie of religion, but they continue to propagate it to keep the oppressed working class under their control and thereby to retain their power and status. Members of the working class that buy the lie do so because the social structure in which they find themselves is so perverted as to give them no other lawful means of

52. Peter van Inwagen, "Some Remarks on Plantinga's Advice," *Faith and Philosophy* 16 (1999): 166-67.

53. Sigmund Freud, *The Future of an Illusion,* trans. and ed. James Strachey (New York: W. W. Norton, 1961), 30. Originally published as *Die Zukunft einer Illusion* (Leipzig: Internationaler Psychoanalytischer Verlag, 1927).

54. Karl Marx and Friedrich Engels, "Contribution to the Critique of Hegel's Philosophy of Right, Introduction," in *On Religion,* trans. Reinhold Niebuhr (Chico, CA: Scholars Press, 1964), 42.

hope. So, for Marx, the problem with religious beliefs is that it arises either from hypocrisy or social blindness. In either case, it cannot have anything approaching positive epistemic status.

One must first acknowledge that the religious belief of some who are (or claim to be) Christians is exactly as Freud and Marx suggest. They are motivated by psychological or social dysfunction; their beliefs say more about them than they do about religious reality. The problem for Freud and Marx is to demonstrate that all Christian belief falls prey to these objections. And to make that claim they would have to know the intentional states behind the religious beliefs of every believer or "know" ahead of time that all religious beliefs must have an origin in a defective psychological state because there is no non-dysfunctional origin of religious beliefs. The former is obviously impossible for anyone lacking omniscience and the latter is obviously question-begging.

For Christians who believe that God created humans to be in relationship with him, Freud and Marx's claim that religious beliefs originate in deep, basic human desires should not be troubling. It's just that there is nothing dysfunctional about John Calvin's *sensus divinitatis* or C. S. Lewis's God-shaped hole in the human heart. According to orthodox Christian belief, they are a part of how humans were created and, consequently, they do not distort religious reality, they have the capacity to reveal it.

Reasons for Christian Belief

When discussing reasons for Christian belief, a distinction between what I will term the *descriptive* and *evaluative* projects is immediately necessary. While the descriptive project merely asks "What reasons are there for belief?," the evaluative project goes farther, asking whether these reasons are sufficient. Both questions are important. It is difficult to completely and fairly engage the evaluative question without first answering the descriptive question, and it is shortsighted to engage the descriptive project without also engaging the evaluative project.

A second distinction is also important. As alluded to earlier in this essay, there is a crucial difference between *explaining how* one knows something and *showing that* one knows that thing. Consider my belief that I had toast for breakfast. The features that ground that belief and make it a candidate for knowledge are not the same features I might appeal to when asked by another what I ate this morning. While my knowing is based on a clear and distinct belief combined with the lack of any reasons to question that belief's veracity, such reasons are inaccessible to others. Consequently, if I am to show the truthfulness of my belief, I will have to appeal to very different grounds. Moreover, and most importantly, it certainly seems possible to know truths that cannot be shown to be true. To the degree that this is the case, showing the truth cannot be a necessary part of knowing the truth.

Key Scriptural Themes

Not surprisingly, Scripture has quite a bit to say about the knowledge of God. This is, of course, not to say that Scripture provides a system of religious epistemology. Very little of what Scripture says is formalized and most of it is descriptive rather than evaluative and focused on knowing rather than showing. Nonetheless, it is possible to discern in Scripture a number of closely connected epistemological concepts and principles.

1. *Knowledge of God is divinely instigated:* Scripture unswervingly depicts knowledge of God as possible because God desires to make it possible. Our knowledge of God is enabled, first, by the fact that God has created humans with a natural disposition to see his character in what he has created (Rom. 1:18-19). Second, God acts and speaks in human history.[55] Third, as God reaches down through creation and revelation, through the indwelling of the Holy Spirit, he enables humans to "reach up" and achieve knowledge that could not have been attained on our own. This theme, pervasive throughout the New Testament, is particularly clear in 1 Corinthians. "We have not received the spirit of the world, but the Spirit who is from God, so that we may know the things that are freely given to us by God" (2:12 NET) and "No one can say, 'Jesus is Lord,' except by the Holy Spirit" (12:3 NET). It is crucial to see, however, that the action of the Holy Spirit does not take place apart from human cognition. The human mind is engaged, not supplanted by the indwelling and action of the Holy Spirit.[56]

2. *Knowledge of God is participatory:* In Scripture, knowledge of God is attained by those who choose to make themselves available to God for his purposes. In the Old Testament (and especially the book of Deuteronomy), knowledge of God is attained through living the redemptive story in accord with God's teachings,[57] and both testaments emphasize the epistemologically decisive role of repentance. And this is why the fear of the Lord is the centerpiece of Israel's religious epistemology. Fear of the Lord puts one in the appropriate position to understand creation and humans within their divinely given possibilities and limits and therefore as aligned with God's purposes in creation.[58] Consequently, while questions regarding the epistemological status of the reasons that ground

55. For a thorough and profound study of the notion that God speaks, see Nicholas Wolterstorff, *Divine Discourse: Philosophical Reflections on the Claim That God Speaks* (Cambridge: Cambridge University Press, 1995).

56. Mary Healy, "Knowledge of the Mystery: A Study of Pauline Epistemology," in *The Bible and Epistemology: Biblical Soundings on the Knowledge of God,* ed. Mary Healy and Robin Parry (Milton Keynes: Paternoster, 2007), 148-49, 150 n. 57.

57. Ryan P. O'Dowd, "Memory on the Boundary," in Healy and Parry, eds., *The Bible and Epistemology,* 3-22; see esp. 20.

58. R. C. Van Leeuwen, "Wisdom Literature," in *Dictionary for Theological Interpretation of the Bible,* ed. Kevin Vanhoozer et al. (Grand Rapids: Baker, 2005), 849.

our religious beliefs have captivated the modern mind since the Enlightenment, Scripture subordinates such questions to "the more urgent question of how those who have seen and heard are being called to respond."[59] In other words, the scriptural approach to knowledge of God constitutes the antithesis to the epistemological heirs of the Enlightenment who hold detachment and objectivity to be the cardinal epistemic virtues and who seek knowledge without being affected by the process.[60]

3. *Knowledge of God is holistic:* Those whom Scripture describes as coming to know God, do so with all of their being. There is undoubtedly an intellectual dimension — would-be believers are called to receive and accept God's revelation. But this intellectual dimension is never divorced from a practical dimension in which God's commands are followed and one's life is changed. It is insufficient to merely say "yes" to the core truths of Christianity. One must allow those truths to affect one's values, emotions, and commitment to loving God and neighbor. Consequently, the scriptural account of knowledge of God can look confusing to one looking with one-dimensional eyes, for Scripture weaves together propositional knowledge (knowledge of truths), procedural knowledge (knowledge of how to do things), and especially personal knowledge (knowledge of persons). An implication of Scripture's holistic epistemology is that the means to knowledge of God are diverse. Arguments and experiences have important roles, but most important is a more relational avenue to knowledge: *testimony.* In some cases, God speaks directly; in others, indirectly through human or angelic messengers. But the most common instance of testimonial knowledge of God occurs when humans respond to God's call to announce the Good News, teach and disciple, and train up their children.

4. *Knowledge of God is particularistic:* This sense of particularism does not deny or mitigate the holistic nature of knowledge of God. We know God with our whole being, but our knowledge is never knowledge of the whole, knowledge from God's perspective, or knowledge that is at our disposal. Scripture does not first establish epistemological rules by which we may come to know God and only then give us the evidence by which God may be known.[61] The particularity of biblical epistemology also mitigates any and all attempts to mechanistically re-create situations of knowing. Just because one person comes to know God in a particular way at a particular time — whether it be via testimony, experience, or argument — does not mean that others' experience will be the same.

Of course, the biblical picture of knowledge of God will be, to say the least, deeply dissatisfying to the skeptic who demands assurance that Scripture is in

59. Murray Rae, "'Incline Your Eye So That You May Live': Principles of Biblical Epistemology," in Healy and Parry, eds., *The Bible and Epistemology,* 163.

60. Rae, "'Incline Your Eye So That You May Live,'" 164.

61. Rae, "'Incline Your Eye So That You May Live,'" 163.

fact true and who refuses to commit until such assurance is forthcoming. There is no neutral, detached path to knowledge of God. But neither does Scripture demonize the desire to evaluate the quality of one's reasons for believing. The Bereans, for example, "examined" *(anakrinō)* Paul's claims and were praised for doing so (Acts 17:11). Neither rationalism nor fideism can lay claim to the religious epistemology expressed in Scripture.

Methodological Foundations of Evaluative Religious Epistemology

It is crucial to see that evaluating the epistemological pedigree of the reasons offered for Christian beliefs is a complex matter. One cannot engage with the evaluative project by looking solely at surface-level evidence. One must seek to understand and evaluate deeper-level methodological and axiological assumptions on which the various epistemological debates turn. Consider an analogy drawn from the study of the Gospels. Suppose a person deems a particular passage in the Gospels to be historical. Understanding their claim requires asking a cascading series of deeper-level questions. At the first level, claims to historicity are built upon and assume particular criteria or accounts of how one might identify a historical statement of Jesus. At a second level, criteria of authenticity are built on and assume a particular account of the nature of history — What does it mean to say that something is historical? And, at a third level, definitions of historical method are built upon and assume philosophical or worldviewish commitments. These include assumptions about the constitution and knowability of reality.

Similarly, the epistemological debates sketched in this paper are built upon and assume various fundamental metaphysical perspectives. These perspectives weave together theology, philosophy, and axiology. These perspectives are also rarely examined in depth by Biblical and Theological scholars. And while philosophers typically spend more time in the rarified air of metaphysics, they are much less likely to extend the implications of their work to ground-level biblical and theological issues. (There is reason to hope that this trend is changing, and changing on both philosophical and biblical/theological fronts.) Consequently, one's epistemological evaluation of the possibility and nature of the knowledge of God will turn on a number of methodological/axiological issues. I will mention just a few.

1. *The nature of human beings:* One's assessment of the epistemological status of religious belief is affected to a significant degree by one's evaluation of the nature and origin of human beings. Those that see humans as the product of blind and purposeless causal processes will struggle to find definitive reasons for religious belief and will be much more likely to see the beliefs of Christians as arising from cognitive dysfunction of some sort (such as wish-fulfillment or projection). For if God does not exist, it is difficult to see the apparently hard-wired

sense of God as anything other than psychological dysfunction or epistemological immaturity. But if God does exist, then that very same hard-wired impulse is a reflection of the way that God created us and, in fact, reveals (even if only partially) an aspect of reality to us. For these (and other) reasons, Alvin Plantinga has persuasively argued that *de jure* objections to Christian belief — objections to the epistemological status of Christian beliefs — are not independent from *de facto* objections — objections to the truth of Christian belief. He says: "There aren't any *de jure* objections that do not depend on *de facto* objections. Everything really depends on the *truth* of Christian belief; but that refutes the common objection that Christian belief whether true or not, is intellectually unacceptable."[62] One important implication of Plantinga's recognition is this — just as Christian scholars have become convinced of the importance of a theological interpretation of Scripture, we need to emphasize the role of theology in epistemology. Theology is not something that is done after our epistemological spadework is finished, it must be done as a part of our epistemological endeavors.

2. *The role of natural theology:* There are two senses of "natural theology." Taken in the first sense, natural theology is a method and constitutes the attempt to ask what knowledge of God might be attained apart from special revelation. Romans 1:18-19 has been taken by many as suggesting that such a thing might be possible, and some see Acts 14:15-17 and 17:22-31 as examples of natural theology. The other sense of natural theology includes an assumption about what it takes to justify religious beliefs. Given this sense of natural theology, there is a requirement to produce adequate *non-circular* reasons for belief prior to commitment. Those committed to natural theology in the second sense will hold that a theological epistemology — one that starts and reasons from certain theological commitments — is not philosophically viable. One's stance on natural theology (taken in this sense) will significantly affect whether evidences for the Christian faith are approached with an "innocent until proven guilty" or "guilty until proven innocent" fashion. But it important to note that it is difficult to see why Christians must accept the requirement to produce adequate *non-circular* reasons for their religious beliefs. They might desire to do so, and it is perfectly reasonable to embrace natural theology in the first sense without accepting it in the second sense. In other words, it is possible to value the project of natural theology without treating religious beliefs as guilty till proven innocent.

3. *The purpose of religious knowledge:* Believers and unbelievers alike assume that God would give evidence of his existence to anyone who wanted it, regardless of their motives for wanting such evidence. This assumption makes perfect sense if the purpose of divine revelation were merely to make people aware of God's existence. But there are other, more scripturally plausible understandings

62. Alvin Plantinga, *Warranted Christian Belief* (New York: Oxford University Press, 2000), xiii. Plantinga develops this point further on 190-91.

of the purpose of the knowledge received from God about himself. In a series of recent works, culminating in his book *The Elusive God,* Paul Moser has sought to revolutionize the way Christians think about the task of religious epistemology by arguing that God is not content with our having true, justified beliefs about his existence but instead desires for us to enter into a life-transforming, filial relationship with him (cf. James 2:19).[63] Consequently, Moser contends that "we should expect evidence of divine reality to be purposefully available to humans, that is, available in a manner, and only in a manner, suitable to divine purposes in self-revelation."[64] In fact, God may deliberately hide himself from those who pridefully insist on personal detachment and expect (and will accept nothing less than) divine pyrotechnics as evidence of God's existence.[65]

4. *The ultimate goal of intellectual inquiry:* My college football coach used to say "Failure is not an event, but an opinion about what constitutes success." What constitutes success (or failure) in religious epistemology? There is, I submit, no single answer to this question. Rather, success or failure is a function of the goal one sets out to achieve. One might engage in religious epistemology with an apologetic goal. In that case, one would be successful if one demonstrated that the gospel was intellectually defensible. Or one might have an evangelistic goal, in which case success would require polemical usefulness. Or one might have a formational or educational goal, in which case it would be prudent to aim at understanding or integration. For a variety of reasons, Christian epistemology has focused on justification and knowledge. At one level, this is understandable — the need for apologetics has been and will continue to be profound. But it would be an egregious mistake to *reduce* the project of religious epistemology to talking about justification and knowledge. This requires a shift in thinking toward what is called *epistemic value pluralism* — the recognition that there are many different epistemic values.[66] From a scriptural perspective, as we saw in the previous section, values such as wisdom and understanding are intimately connected with knowledge of the gospel of Jesus Christ, as is the recognition that propositional

63. Paul Moser, *The Elusive God: Reorienting Religious Epistemology* (Cambridge: Cambridge University Press, 2008); Moser, "Reorienting Religious Epistemology: Cognitive Grace, Filial Knowledge, and Gethsemane Struggle," in *For Faith and Clarity: Philosophical Contributions to Evangelical Theology,* ed. James Beilby (Grand Rapids: Baker, 2006), 65-84; Moser, "Cognitive Idolatry and Divine Hiding," in *Divine Hiddenness: New Essays,* ed. Paul K. Moser and Daniel Howard-Snyder (Cambridge: Cambridge University Press, 2002), 120-48.

64. Moser, *The Elusive God,* x.

65. Michael Polanyi makes a related point, that all knowledge is personal in nature and depends on our personal commitments and fiduciary frameworks. See his *Personal Knowledge: Towards a Post-Critical Philosophy* (London: Routledge & Kegan Paul, 1958).

66. William Alston, "Epistemic Desiderata," *Philosophy and Phenomenological Research* 53 (1993): 527-51; Jonathan Kvanvig, *The Value of Knowledge and the Pursuit of Understanding,* Cambridge Studies in Philosophy (Cambridge: Cambridge University Press, 2007).

knowledge cannot be separated from procedural and personal knowledge. A biblical account of knowledge of God is never just knowledge for knowledge's sake, but a tightly woven tapestry of knowledge, understanding, and wisdom.

5. *The paradigm for success in religious epistemology:* This final point is related to the previous point. Christians must not only consider what success looks like in religious epistemology, we must be very thoughtful about our paradigms of epistemological success. Since questions surrounding religious knowledge are invariably convoluted, it is understandable that religious epistemologists seek to simplify matters wherever possible. There are two common ways of doing this. First, religious epistemologists are tempted to place emphasis not on the incredibly complex details of actual religious beliefs, with all of its denominational and cultural distinctives, but on bare religious belief. Second, there is a strong tendency to de-emphasize the beliefs and practice of the typical Christian and instead to focus on cases of ideal justification and idealized belief-forming situations.[67] The danger here, of course, is successfully articulating the possibility of religious knowledge, but having nobody who actually knows that their Redeemer lives, because nobody's situation is ideal. Nobody believes or accepts bare religious belief; nobody believes just that "God exists." Our religious beliefs are complicated (and often confused) in myriad ways. This does not suggest, of course, that a consideration of ideal epistemological situations is worthless. But, it is important for epistemologists to do the difficult and messy work of extending their reflection on those ideal situations to more typical situations.[68]

An Example: Alvin Plantinga's *Warranted Christian Belief*[69]

For the purposes of providing a concrete example, I will close this essay with a brief sketch of Alvin Plantinga's influential (and somewhat controversial) Christian religious epistemology. In his religious epistemology, Plantinga focuses on

67. This is what I take to be the suggestion of Andrew Chignell, who claims inspiration for his suggestion from Nicholas Wolterstorff. See Chignell's "Prolegomena to Any Future Non-doxastic Religion," *Religious Studies* 49 (2013): 197. It is also a part of my critique (albeit sympathetic critique) of Alvin Plantinga's religious epistemology in *Epistemology as Theology* (London: Ashgate, 2006), chapter 6, and "Plantinga's Model of Warranted Christian Belief," in *Alvin Plantinga,* Contemporary Philosophy in Focus, ed. Deane-Peter Baker (New York: Cambridge University Press, 2007), 146-47.

68. One of the more promising ways of doing this is to pick up on Nicholas Wolterstorff's suggestion that epistemologists engage the "philosophically significant aspects of the liturgy" (Chignell, "Prolegomena," 197).

69. In this section, I am drawing on and abbreviating a section from my "Plantinga's Model of Warranted Christian Belief," 125-65. And I am summarizing material Plantinga presents primarily in *Warranted Christian Belief,* chapters 6-9.

the externalist concept of warrant — the property that separates knowledge from mere true belief. Very briefly, a warranted belief, according to Plantinga, is one that is produced by a cognitive faculty that is functioning properly in the relevant respects, reliably aimed at true beliefs, and subject to no defeaters. There are a myriad of reasons Plantinga chooses to make warrant his focus, including his dissatisfaction with traditional internalist accounts of justification and knowledge. But paramount among his reasons is the fact that Plantinga's account of warrant as proper function allows him to integrate theological notions such as special revelation, the image of God, and the indwelling of the Holy Spirit into his religious epistemology.

Plantinga's religious epistemology is expressed in terms of two models: the A/C Model, which provides a general description of how Christian beliefs might be warranted, and the Extended A/C Model, which applies specifically to our post-lapsarian epistemic environment. While the A/C Model draws on a shared insight of Thomas Aquinas and John Calvin, much of the flavor of the model is Reformed, reflecting dependence on Calvin, Jonathan Edwards, and Abraham Kuyper. Crucial to the A/C Model is a description of the innate tendency for humans to see the hand of God in creation, a tendency that Calvin called the *sensus divinitatis.* This innate tendency is occasioned by a wide variety of circumstances that will likely vary from person to person.

The defining characteristic of Plantinga's religious epistemology — a feature that is decidedly more Calvinistic than Thomistic — is his insistence that the deliverances of the *sensus divinitatis* are not inferential beliefs.[70] One does not see a beautiful sunset and *infer* from that beauty that only God could have created all of this. Rather, the belief arises immediately and spontaneously. As such, there is epistemic parity between the deliverances of the *sensus divinitatis* and perceptual beliefs.[71] Both can be "properly basic" — fully appropriate from an epistemic point of view. In fact, they can be properly basic with respect to warrant — that is,

70. It would be a serious mistake to take Plantinga's reticence to base Christian belief in arguments as fideistic. Plantinga acknowledges that logical arguments *can be* sufficient to eliminate the warrant a believer has for aspects of the faith. The Christian, he says, "is not to hold [Christian] beliefs in such a way as to be invulnerable to criticism. . . . If I find good reason to modify my understanding of the Christian faith, then (so far forth) I should do so. 'Good reason' could come from many sources: logic, obvious ethical principles, common sense beliefs of various kinds, science and the like" ("Response to Keller," *Faith and Philosophy* 5 [1988]: 162).

71. When Plantinga claims there is epistemic parity between belief in God and, say, memory beliefs, he is not claiming that belief in God is *phenomenologically* identical to perceptual or memorial beliefs. What creates epistemic parity between beliefs about God and mundane perceptual beliefs, therefore, is two features: (1) *the cause of the beliefs* — they are both formed by properly functioning cognitive faculties, and (2) *the psychological response associated with the formation of those beliefs* — in both cases the beliefs seem appropriate, right, approved. See *Warranted Christian Belief,* 264.

despite not being based on arguments or evidence, they can meet the conditions necessary for warrant.

To account for our post-lapsarian context, Plantinga develops the Extended A/C Model. The Extended A/C Model acknowledges that human beings have fallen into sin and as a result the *sensus divinitatis* is both damaged and narrowed in the scope of its operation. In circumstances where we would have naturally formed beliefs about God, no theological beliefs are formed. Further, sin introduces in us not only a resistance but a hostility to the deliverances of the *sensus divinitatis;* we not only are unable to see what we ought to see, we do not desire to see those things.

As a response to sin, the Extended A/C Model includes a three-tiered process whereby humans become aware of the plan of salvation God has graciously made available. God's revelation of his plan of salvation typically proceeds first through Scripture, humanly authored, but divinely inspired. The second tier is the presence and action of the Holy Spirit. Through the internal instigation of the Holy Spirit, we come to see that the Bible is true and contains divine testimony. Finally, the principal work of the Holy Spirit is the production of the third element of the process, faith. Faith is a divine gift and includes both cognitive and affective dimensions. In the words of John Calvin, faith is "a firm and certain knowledge of God's benevolence towards us, founded upon the truth of the freely given promise in Christ, both revealed to our minds and sealed upon our hearts through the Holy Spirit."[72] While faith includes propositional and cognitive aspects, to have faith is not only to know God, it is also to have a proper affectional disposition toward God. Consequently, through the work of the Holy Spirit, the person with faith not only knows about God ("belief that" God exists), she also comes to trust, love, and serve God ("belief in" God).

Just as with regard to the *sensus divinitatis,* Plantinga claims that the deliverances of the internal instigation of the Holy Spirit can be fully rational and justified for the believer — she will be flouting no epistemic duties with regard to acquiring and maintaining her beliefs.[73] Further, Plantinga claims that the deliverances of the internal instigation of the Holy Spirit can "satisfy the conditions that are jointly sufficient and severally necessary for warrant."[74] First, the belief will be produced

72. *Institutes of the Christian Religion* (1536), 3.2.7, cited in *Warranted Christian Belief,* 244.

73. There is an important difference between the *sensus divinitatis* and the internal instigation of the Holy Spirit. Where the *sensus divinitatis* is a part of humanity's original cognitive equipment, the internal instigation of the Holy Spirit, whereby we come to realize the central truths of the gospel, is a special gift given by God that comes with salvation and is part of the process designed to produce faith. Hence, the internal instigation of the Holy Spirit is not a cognitive faculty in the same way that perception, memory, or even the *sensus divinitatis* is; it is a cognitive process or "a means by which belief, and belief on a certain set of topics, is regularly produced in regular ways" (*Warranted Christian Belief,* 256).

74. Plantinga, *Warranted Christian Belief,* 258.

by a properly functioning cognitive process. This cognitive process is specially designed by God to produce this very effect, just as vision is designed to produce certain kinds of perceptual beliefs. Second, Plantinga's environmental condition is met, since the Extended A/C Model was designed for a post-lapsarian context. Finally, this cognitive process is *successfully* aimed at the production of true beliefs. Of course, even if a person's belief in God meets Plantinga's conditions for warrant, that does not mean that her belief is beyond question. It is possible that an otherwise warranted belief can be defeated either by a defeater already present in a person's noetic structure or by a defeater that enters a person's noetic structure after the belief in question has already been accepted.

Crucial to understanding Plantinga's project is understanding of the function of a "model" in this context. According to Plantinga, a "model" is a set of propositions (or a state of affairs) that jointly describe how beliefs about God *could be* warranted.[75] His claim is that the Extended A/C Model is *epistemically possible.*[76] Consequently, since the Extended A/C Model explains how belief in God could have warrant, if the state of affairs described by the model obtains or is actual, then belief in God does in fact possess warrant. Plantinga's claims regarding the Extended A/C Model can therefore be summarized in the following conditional: *If the Extended A/C Model is true, then beliefs formed as described by the model are warranted.* Given this conditional claim, the truth of the antecedent — whether the Extended A/C Model is actually true — is obviously of crucial importance. Plantinga closes his book *Warranted Christian Belief* by addressing this question:

> But is [the Extended A/C Model] true? This is the really important question. And here we pass beyond the competence of philosophy, whose main competence, in this area, is to clear away certain objections, impedances, and obstacles to Christian belief. Speaking for myself, and of course not in the name of philosophy, I can say only that [the Extended A/C Model] does, indeed, seem to me to be true, and to be the maximally important truth.[77]

So while Plantinga believes the Extended A/C Model to be true, he *does not* argue that it is true. He says:

> The only way I can see to argue that Christian belief [is warranted] is to argue that Christian belief is, indeed, *true.* I don't propose to offer such an argument.

75. Plantinga, *Warranted Christian Belief,* 168.

76. An epistemically possible proposition, according to Plantinga, is "consistent with what we know, where 'what we know' is what all or most of the participants in the discussion can agree on" (*Warranted Christian Belief,* 168-69). For example, while the propositions *My computer has a mass greater than the solar system* and *China has a population of four* are broadly logically possible, they are not epistemically possible.

77. Plantinga, *Warranted Christian Belief,* 499.

> That is because I don't know of an argument for Christian belief that seems very likely to convince one who doesn't already accept its conclusion.[78]

Because Plantinga does not argue that Christianity is true, some will fail to see his project as viable. This would be a serious mistake, for it confuses reasons to think one knows God with reasons that could show a skeptic that one knows God. While there is nothing wrong with the project of showing the faith to be true (as long as one doesn't have unrealistic expectations about what might be accomplished), one should not assume that one doesn't really know God until one can provide reasons that satisfy the skeptic.

Of course, Plantinga's religious epistemology is not the final word on the matter. Plantinga himself did not intend it as such.[79] Consequently, it is possible to expand Plantinga's account in a variety of ways. First, it is possible to expand the role for the arguments of natural theology. Such arguments would not be necessary, but could still perform a variety of important functions including removing objections to the faith, providing intellectual grounding for one's theological commitments, and giving non-Christians reasons to take Christianity seriously.[80] Second, Plantinga's account could benefit from a more fine-grained account of the epistemological details of conversion and discipleship. Particularly helpful would be an account that offered an explanation of the role of human freedom in responding to or accepting the inward instigation of the Holy Spirit. In this respect, it would be helpful to develop Plantinga's insights along the lines of Christian procedural knowledge or doxastic practices. The work of William Abraham, especially his *Crossing the Threshold of Divine Revelation,* could be helpful in this regard.[81] Finally, Plantinga's religious epistemology could be expanded to include Paul Moser's notion of the purposiveness of divine self-revelation and divine hiddenness. On this expanded account, the failure of some to attain God's

78. Plantinga, *Warranted Christian Belief,* 200-201.

79. Plantinga's stated purpose for his religious epistemology is twofold. First, it is an exercise in apologetics, a demonstration that a set of objections to religious belief (*de jure* objections) are not successful. Arguing against the epistemological viability of Christianity is insufficient; the skeptic must shoulder the more difficult task of arguing against the truth of Christian belief. Second, it is an exercise in Christian philosophy, a philosophically nuanced explanation of how Christians might think about the warrant of their religious beliefs. See *Warranted Christian Belief,* xiii-xiv.

80. Plantinga himself acknowledges that arguments can perform each of these roles. He says: "[Arguments] can confirm and support belief reached in other ways; they may move fence-sitters closer to Christian belief; they can function as defeater-defeaters; and they can reveal interesting and important connections" ("Rationality and Public Evidence: A Reply to Swinburne," *Religious Studies* 37 [2001]: 217). So, while he does not integrate a robust role for arguments into his Extended A/C Model, it would be certainly possible to do so.

81. William Abraham, *Crossing the Threshold of Divine Revelation* (Grand Rapids: Eerdmans, 2006).

knowledge would be due to their unwillingness to seek God in a way that aligns with God's purposes in revealing himself. Such a notion would fit very well with Plantinga's account of the importance of the affective dimension of faith.

Despite its limitations, the strengths of Plantinga's religious epistemology are many. First, Plantinga makes it clear that knowledge of God does not require propositional evidence or arguments. His religious epistemology is applicable to more than just academics and, therefore, on his account my grandmother does know that her Redeemer lives. Second, Plantinga's account is robustly holistic, emphasizing the affective dimension of faith as well as the cognitive dimension. Faith is not only revealed to our minds, it must be sealed on our hearts. Third, Plantinga's account has a very clear explication of the divine role in knowledge of God. Not only does God create humans with a *sensus divinitatis,* he employs a pneumatological cognitive process to respond to our sinful situation. Fourth, Plantinga's argument that *de jure* objections are not independent of *de facto* objections also serves to draw attention to the interconnectedness of theology and philosophical matters in religious epistemology. Consequently, his work exposes the attempt to articulate a "purely agnostic" or "methodologically naturalistic" religious epistemology as either impossible or hopelessly tendentious. Religious epistemology must be theological. Finally and most important for the Scripture Project, Plantinga's approach is built squarely on the notion that God has spoken in Scripture. The object of knowledge, for Christians, is not a vague, semi-deistic creator, but the triune God himself, revealed in Jesus Christ and communicated through special revelation.

TWENTY-SIX

Non-Foundational Epistemologies and the Truth of Scripture

R. Scott Smith

It is commonplace for evangelical theologians, biblical scholars, and pastors to affirm a "high" view of Scripture, which includes its authority, infallibility, and inerrancy. For many, we have been taught to understand the Scriptures as our "foundation" for all knowledge, upon which all other beliefs we hold should be based in order for them to be justified. This view has had direct ties with the epistemological view, *foundationalism*. Generally, as a theory about the justification of our beliefs, it tries to account for how our beliefs should be structured so that justification can transfer from justified beliefs to other beliefs. More so, foundationalism distinguishes between "beliefs we justifiably accept on the evidential basis of other beliefs . . . versus those we justifiably accept in a basic way, that is, not entirely on the basis of the support they receive from other beliefs."[1]

But as we pass from the modern era into a more postmodern one, many have criticized modernity and how it has influenced the church, including how many tend to see the Scriptures as our foundation for knowledge. Indeed, foundationalism, especially when seen as a modern epistemology, has been roundly criticized, not only in the broader academy, but also by Christian scholars, including evangelicals, and "emergents."[2] On Cartesian foundationalism, the foundations must be certain, and we can know universal truths objectively. But this modern expression of foundationalism has been a target for much deserved criticism. Indeed, some have declared the "demise" of foundationalism altogether in philosophy and theology.[3]

1. J. P. Moreland in J. P. Moreland and William Lane Craig, *Philosophical Foundations for a Christian Worldview* (Downers Grove, IL: InterVarsity, 2003), 112.

2. As but two examples, see Brian McLaren, *A New Kind of Christian* (San Francisco: Jossey-Bass, 2001), 16-18, and Tony Jones, *Postmodern Youth Ministry* (Grand Rapids: Zondervan, for Youth Specialties, 2001), 18.

3. For instance, Stanley Grenz and John Franke claim that we have seen "the demise of foundationalism," in *Beyond Foundationalism: Shaping Theology in a Postmodern Context* (Louisville: Westminster John Knox, 2001), 47. They also quote from other philosophers and theolo-

Many competing epistemologies have been offered in light of foundationalism's "demise." *Non-foundational* epistemologies have been offered, chiefly *coherentism,* which generally is the view that what justifies a belief is its coherence with one's other beliefs. Until recently, this has been the major alternative to foundationalism. But now other responses have surfaced which I would tend to classify as *postfoundational.* These likewise reject foundationalism, but they also might well tend to reject a dichotomy between foundationalism and nonfoundationalism as a modern dichotomy, stressing instead a more holistic alternative. For instance, James K. A. Smith, Merold Westphal, and LeRon Shults argue in part out of the perceived collapse of the epistemology-hermeneutics distinction, as Jim Beilby argues in the previous chapter of this collection. These tend to embrace the influence of many continental thinkers, perhaps Heidegger and/or Derrida. Others, such as Nancey Murphy, follow the holisms she sees in the later Wittgenstein and J. L. Austin, stressing the importance of the relationship between communities, their particular founding narratives, and how we live and talk in them. But both groups agree that we never could gain a vantage point from which we could know reality directly; we can know it only from our particular, historically situated locations, which will be highly influenced by our embodiment, culture, and language. There is *Truth,* but only for God; and while we can know *truth,* we cannot gain a neutral, God's-eye view of reality, which would be pristine, perfect, exhaustive, and blind-to-nothing.

What should we think of these alternatives to foundationalism? What might their implications be for holding a high view of Scripture? To many Christians, the postfoundationalist views resonate deeply for at least a few reasons. First, they seem to place us on equal footing with others' views, which is a markedly different, apparently advantageous position to be in, especially after having to deal for so long with the claims of the superiority of science over religion. After all, if we all speak from our different language games and stories, then the naturalistic story that drives much of modern science is just another story told from its standpoint, which cannot give us the knowledge of Truth. Second, they seem to foster an epistemic humility, especially against modern arrogance about having certainty. Third, the postfoundationalist view that we cannot have a God's-eye view into Truth strikes many as true, especially in comparison with the modern confidence in knowing universal truths from an ahistorical viewpoint.

---

gians who agree, such as Merold Westphal: "That it is philosophically indefensible is so widely agreed that its demise is the closest thing to a philosophical consensus in decades" (Merold Westphal, "A Reader's Guide to 'Reformed Epistemology,'" *Perspectives* 7, no. 9 [Nov. 1992]: 10-11). Evangelical theologian D. A. Carson also seems to agree with a rejection of *modern* foundationalism, which I will distinguish later. He writes that "in its insistence on the inescapable entailments of human finitude, it [postmodernism] has done a reasonable job of destroying foundationalism." *Becoming Conversant with the Emerging Church* (Grand Rapids: Zondervan, 2005), 115.

I will argue that these scholars are right to reject modern-inspired foundationalism, but we will need to see whether that applies to *all* forms. Foundationalism is much older than its modern versions, and today a *modest* form is being advocated without reference to Descartes's certainty requirement. This new version will be crucial to examine.

First, I will proceed with a more careful description and assessment of the main elements of modern foundationalism, focusing on Descartes's version. We also should examine foundationalism's suggested replacements, particularly for their implications for our having a high view of Scripture. So, next, I will describe and then assess coherentism as the major form of non-foundationalism. Then I will do so with the more postfoundationalist views of Shults, Stanley Grenz and John Franke, Murphy, and Westphal and Smith. In that process, I will also consider a more modest foundationalism. I will argue that only one of these views about the justification of our beliefs allows us to uphold a high view of Scripture and withstand other scrutiny. Then I will conclude with a brief look at implications for the places God, Scripture, and we ourselves have in epistemology.

Modern Foundationalism and Its Critics

Though foundationalism can be traced back to Aristotle's work in his *Posterior Analytics,* book l, parts 2 and 3,[4] there are particular modern emphases that have been the focus of the aforementioned critics.[5] Beilby introduced *classical foundationalism* as the view that allows for only a limited range of beliefs to be justified and basic. For instance, to be properly basic, a belief must be self-evident, about one's own mental states, or evident to the senses. Moreover, according to him, classical foundationalism has been used as a means to *guarantee* truth.[6] In this sense, a classical foundationalism also may be characterized as a *strong foundationalism* in terms of the degree of strength a foundational belief must have. To guarantee truth, such beliefs must be *infallible, certain, indubitable,* or *incorrigible.*[7] For a belief to be infallible, it seems a person could not both (a) hold that belief and at the same time (b) be mistaken about it. According to J. P. Moreland, certainty can have two senses: "Sometimes it refers to a certain depth of psychological conviction with which a belief is held. On the other hand,

4. E.g., see http://classics.mit.edu/Aristotle/posterior.1.i.html, accessed January 24, 2011.

5. For an essay that examines the history of foundationalism, see Francis Remedios, "The Foundationalist Justification of Epistemic Principles," *Philosophical Inquiry* 12, no. 1-2 (1990): section 1.

6. Jim Beilby, "Contemporary Religious Epistemology: Some Key Aspects," chapter 25 in this collection.

7. Here, I will be following Moreland's discussion, *Philosophical Foundations for a Christian Worldview,* 113.

a belief is sometimes called *certain* in the sense that at least this must be true of it: accepting that belief is at least as justified as accepting any other belief whatsoever."[8] A belief is indubitable "when no one could have grounds for doubting" it.[9] Finally, incorrigibility can be used in the same sense as infallibility, but also to mean that someone could never be in a position to correct a particular belief.

Now Descartes's foundationalism seems to be the exemplar of the modern variety. He tried to doubt whatever he could, until he could find beliefs he thought he could not possibly doubt. Descartes found he could doubt almost everything, since it was conceivable he was being deceived by an evil demon.[10] Yet, he realized he was thinking, and to be able to think, he had to exist; he could not doubt that, or so he reasoned. Thus, Descartes's project was an attempt to find an unshakeable foundation for knowledge that *could not* be defeated by skeptical claims.

Grenz characterizes Descartes's project as leading to "a new conception of the human person" as a thinking substance and an "autonomous rational subject."[11] Grenz claims that by focusing on personal experience and knowledge, Descartes established (1) "the centrality of the human mind" for knowledge and (2) the emphasis upon "the reasoning subject rather than divine revelation as the starting point for knowledge and reflection."[12] Descartes also tried to introduce "the rigor of mathematical demonstration into all fields of knowledge," which stemmed from the view that mathematical truths are derived from reason, thereby providing a more sure foundation for knowledge than empirical observation.[13]

In *Beyond Foundationalism,* Grenz and Franke develop a more postmodern approach to theology that avoids critical philosophical errors that plague liberal and conservative Christian theology. They accept as axiomatic "the demise of foundationalism" and the myth that we can stand in an epistemically neutral vantage point and form a "single, universal set of criteria by means of which we can judge definitively the epistemic status of all beliefs."[14] Instead, there are no neutral starting points, definitions, or methodologies from which we may begin to do theology (16). Like Murphy, they assert that "experiences are always filtered by an interpretative framework" (49).

Thus they oppose modern values, which they describe as the pursuit of "cer-

8. Moreland, *Philosophical Foundations for a Christian Worldview,* 113.

9. Moreland, *Philosophical Foundations for a Christian Worldview,* 113.

10. To draw a present-day parallel, a skeptic might suggest that we could be a brain in a vat, and it is possible that a mad scientist is just stimulating us with electrical impulses, thus causing us to believe we are more than just brains, or that we are experiencing pleasure.

11. Stanley J. Grenz, *A Primer on Postmodernism* (Grand Rapids: Eerdmans, 1996), 64.

12. Grenz, *A Primer on Postmodernism,* 64-65.

13. Grenz, *A Primer on Postmodernism,* 64.

14. Stanley Grenz and John Franke, *Beyond Foundationalism: Shaping Theology in a Postmodern Context* (Louisville: Westminster John Knox, 2001), 47. Subsequent page references are given in parentheses in the text.

tain, objective, and universal knowledge, along with its dualism and its assumption of the inherent goodness of knowledge" (21-22).[15] Modern foundationalism sought to discover an approach to knowledge that would provide incontestable certainty about the truth of our beliefs that would be available to *any* rational person (23).

Interestingly, they draw connections between foundationalism and a correspondence view of truth.[16] To them, Descartes claimed

> to have established the foundations of knowledge by appeal to the mind's own experience of certainty. . . . Descartes was convinced that this epistemological program yields knowledge that is certain, culture- and tradition-free, universal, and reflective of a reality that exists outside the mind (this latter being a central feature of a position known as "metaphysical realism" or simply "realism"). (31)

Indeed, they see close correlations in the Enlightenment project between the adoption of foundationalism, a realist metaphysic, and a "strong preference for the correspondence theory of truth" (32).[17]

Other critics resonate with these views. For instance, Nancey Murphy contends that foundationalism is an attempt to provide "certain and universal knowledge" by appealing to universally accessible truths.[18] Foundationalism is particularly modern because it, like other modern views, is reductionistic, for it emphasizes individual propositions instead of the whole in which they are found. She claims that moderns tended to fall into two groups with respect to what counts as part of the foundations. First, empiricists appealed to claims about mental representations and supposedly universal experience. But she claims what dealt a death blow to this kind of foundationalism was the recognition that scientific facts, which draw heavily from observations, are theory-laden, and thus not universal and available to all.[19]

Second, for conservative Protestantism, Scripture is the foundation for theo-

15. By "dualism," I believe they mean a distinction that is drawn between basic and non-basic beliefs.

16. Roughly, on the correspondence theory, truth is a relation of correspondence (or matching) between a proposition and reality.

17. In contrast, they suggest that the demise of foundationalism and with it this trio of positions opens the door for a "chastened rationality," and a "transition from a realist to constructionist view of truth and the world" (23). This also ties to a rejection of the modern "metanarrative."

18. Nancey Murphy, *Anglo-American Postmodernity* (Boulder, CO: Westview, 1997), 26; see also her *Beyond Liberalism and Fundamentalism: How Modern and Postmodern Philosophy Set the Theological Agenda,* Rockwell Lecture Series, ed. Werner H. Kelber (Harrisburg, PA: Trinity Press International, 1996), 12-13. See also Grenz and Franke, *Beyond Foundationalism,* 23, 30.

19. Murphy, *Beyond Liberalism and Fundamentalism,* 91.

logical knowledge, but Murphy rejects this view as well. For one, she believes that Christian theologians' arguments do not provide the requisite certainty that the Bible is the written word of God. Also, Descartes's rationalist appeal to "clear and distinct ideas" fails to provide a certain foundation, for "what is indubitable in one intellectual context is all too questionable in another."[20]

Importantly, for her, the foundations end up "hanging from the balcony," since they are partly supported "from above," by theoretical, non-foundational beliefs.[21] We never have raw, theory-neutral observations. For rationalist foundations, there always are presupposition-laden intuitions in the philosophical arguments. If foundationalism's picture of linear reasoning and justification moves only from bottom to top, these counterexamples show that this picture oversimplifies how justification actually proceeds.[22]

For LeRon Shults, foundationalism and "antifoundationalism" simply are not the only alternatives in epistemology. There also is his postfoundationalist alternative, which he thinks avoids the pitfalls of absolutism and relativism. The Cartesian emphasis upon the individual human subject as a thinking thing mistakenly separates the self from its knowing. Instead, the knowing subject is embedded in, and not abstracted from, relations to self, others, and the world.[23] We live in light of the "turn to relationality," so "human knowing is no longer understood as wholly self-determined nor as undetermined, but rather as conditioned and mediated by the communal relations of the knower."[24] For these and other now-familiar reasons, foundationalism rests upon a mistake.

For Westphal, Descartes's foundationalist program works hand-in-hand with modernity's goals of achieving absolute clarity and certainty via what Westphal calls "Cartesian immediacy"; that is, the "mutually naked presence of thought and its object to each other," in which both remain "pure and unadulterated" in this mutual presence.[25] That is, "neither inference nor interpretation separates

20. Murphy, *Beyond Liberalism and Fundamentalism,* 91. To illustrate, she contrasts her differing presuppositions with those of Richard Swinburne over the possibility of his being changed into a crocodile and yet remaining the same person. As a Cartesian dualist, it seems possible to him that his soul could be embodied in a crocodile's body. Yet as a nonreductive physicalist, she believes our "mental and spiritual capacities arise out of the complex ordering of our physical selves in their social environment," so Swinburne's notion is inconceivable to her (93). Due to differing presuppositions, what seems basic to one might not to another.

21. Murphy, *Beyond Liberalism and Fundamentalism,* 92.

22. Murphy, *Beyond Liberalism and Fundamentalism,* 94; see also Murphy, *Anglo-American Postmodernity,* 26.

23. LeRon Shults, *Reforming Theological Anthropology* (Grand Rapids: Eerdmans, 2003), 31.

24. Shults, *Reforming Theological Anthropology,* 183-84.

25. Merold Westphal, "Postmodernism and Religious Reflection," *International Journal for Philosophy of Religion* 38 (1995): 128-29. Subsequent page references are given in parentheses in the text.

us from immaculate, immediate, infallible intuition . . . the object is totally here and at no distance that might dim or distort our view of it" (129). Moreover, such "pure presence" is concerned just with the present, without reference to a past "in which it is essentially indebted" or the future "in which it will be completed" (129). The Cartesian knower is not embedded in a context that mediates reality. According to Westphal, this "metaphysics of presence" is a claim of immediate access and presence to either meanings or facts. It is tied to a quest to make philosophy autonomous, placing theology in its service (130).

Instead, Westphal sees postmodernism as a critique of this metaphysics of presence. It denies any clear and distinct ideas and any unmediated, infallible access to the very presence of things themselves, which could serve as an ultimate grounding for our foundational beliefs. Foundationalism is false because we never could achieve such an unfettered viewpoint. As such postmodernism rejects this Cartesian aspiration (128-29).

Likewise, Smith thoroughly rejects the Cartesian aspirations to know objective, universal truths. We are inescapably finite, and so our viewpoints are finite. Therefore attempts to gain a God's-eye view betray a lustful pride to become like God. The Cartesian and Enlightenment optimism to know foundational, universal truths from our limited, creaturely standpoints is fueled by a lack of appreciation of the noetic effects of sin, which in turn tends to discredit appeals to a "neutral" reason.[26]

While these various concerns may be more theoretical, there also are other factors. Like Smith, Franke is concerned with foundationalist arrogance:

> It [truth] is a reality that continually reminds us that we are always in a position of dependence and in need of grace with respect to our knowledge of God, who is the source of all truth. The failure of humans to acknowledge our dependence on God and the ways in which we are prone to error, especially when our own interests are at stake, is all too common throughout history, including the history of the church. Such failure, no matter how well intentioned, inevitably leads to forms of oppression and conceptual idolatry.[27]

Similarly, Brian McLaren has tried to identify the operational and ethical effects of embracing modern foundationalism.[28] By having a set of beliefs that are absolutely true, he thinks we tend to view evangelism as encounters that win a per-

26. James K. A. Smith, *Who's Afraid of Postmodernism? Taking Derrida, Lyotard, and Foucault to Church* (Grand Rapids: Baker Academic, 2006), 28.

27. John R. Franke, *Manifold Witness: The Plurality of Truth,* Living Theology series, ed. Tony Jones (Nashville: Abingdon, 2009), 18.

28. For more of my thoughts about McLaren and the operational effects of modern foundationalism, see my *Truth and the New Kind of Christian: The Emerging Effects of Postmodernism in the Church* (Wheaton, IL: Crossway, 2005), 52-57.

son to Jesus by winning an argument. But then, we often fail to value a genuine friendship with a person. So, the methodology is *coercive, not loving,* and our faith tends to be treated as a rigid belief system that must be accepted, instead of a unique, joyful way of living, loving, and serving.[29]

Though some of these critics may realize that foundationalism has a longer history than just the modern period, nonetheless they all attack modern foundationalism. But to what extent should we agree with them? To begin, certainty is an unrealistic standard for knowledge. Surely there are many things we can know and yet not be certain (i.e., it is possible, or conceivable, that we could be mistaken) about them. For instance, as I write this, I know that I am married to Debbie Hubbard. It seems I know this with about as much justification as possible. Still, it is possible that that belief is false; she might have been killed in a traffic accident five minutes ago, but I am not aware of that.[30]

So we can hold beliefs that count as knowledge even without certainty. Also, often a belief's justification can be defeated. We may accept (i.e., believe) a propositional claim as true, and yet we may find more evidence later that it is false.

While we do not have to have certainty to have knowledge, that legacy still has had its effects, even in the church. Tony Jones, the former national coordinator for Emergent U.S., once remarked to me that "the problem is not with what philosophers believe [i.e., whether foundationalism requires certainty or not], but with the way pastors act. . . . [M]any EV pastors speak, preach, and write with a tone of such certainty that it is ultimately offputting to many 'seekers.' "[31] Also,

29. Brian McLaren, *More Ready Than You Realize* (Grand Rapids: Zondervan, 2002), 41-42.

30. To require that our beliefs be "bomb proof" in order to count as knowledge is *extremely* unrealistic; to hold this requirement plays right into skeptics' hands. A skeptic could always reply, "But isn't it just *possible* [no matter how unlikely] that you *could* be mistaken?" If we are honest with ourselves, we most likely should answer "yes." Does this mean the skeptic wins the argument? If we assert that we know that we aren't a brain in a vat because we know we ate breakfast this morning, the skeptic can demand a criterion: "But, how do you know that? Surely you *could* be deceived on that matter, *couldn't* you?" This position is known as *epistemic methodism.* If we take that bait and play by the skeptic's rules, we are doomed, for the skeptic can keep demanding a criterion for how we know anything, such that we cannot ever get started and know *anything.* The answer, therefore, is not to play the game of epistemic methodism. Instead, there are some things we simply know, without having to provide a criterion to anyone else to show how we know them. For example, I simply know my daughter is named Anna; that 2 + 2 = 4; that red is a color; that murder is wrong; and many more such things. There are particular things I simply do know (a view called *epistemic particularism*), and now the burden is on the skeptic to defeat my knowledge claim. I simply *rebut* the skeptical assertions; I don't have to shoulder the additional burden of *refuting* or *proving* him or her to be wrong. Nor do my knowledge claims require "bomb proof" certainty.

31. Tony Jones, private email correspondence, June 22, 2004; bracketed inserts mine. By "EV," I assume he means "evangelical."

some related attitudes have been passed down. For instance, too often believers can suffer from anxiety if they do not have certainty in their beliefs.[32]

Now, these critics argue against our abilities to know universal, *objective* truths. Here, let me distinguish objective truths and *our* being objective. The former concern is metaphysical — they would be true independently of our beliefs about them. Even if I don't believe that 2 + 2 = 4, it still is true. But the latter concern is epistemological; can *we* be objective? Their answer to *this* question has driven many of their contentions against foundationalism, and it has been stated in a number of interrelated ways (e.g., no one is neutral or unbiased; everyone has been shaped significantly by his or her upbringing, cultural-historical location, language, etc.; we are finite and thus have blinders; etc.). Unlike God, we are fallible and cannot access reality perfectly and pristinely.

None of these critics deny that there is a real world and truth (perhaps better put as *Truth* — i.e., Truth as only God knows it). So, their focus here is epistemic, and they are largely correct. Many postfoundationalists rightly diagnose the Cartesian aspirations as examples of gross human arrogance, an attempt to usurp God's throne by scaling to the peaks of knowledge by our reason, without God's aid through revelation. Indeed, after we acknowledge our finitude and fallenness, we are left facing this question: "Is there any way left for us to talk about knowing what is true or objectively real?"[33]

Finally, these postfoundationalists see a close relationship between foundationalism, truth, and our abilities to know it. They repudiate our abilities to know objective truths directly, not because they don't exist, but because of our limitations. If accurate, this line of argument would cut against *any* form of foundationalism. We will return to this point in an assessment of their positive views.

32. I went through a painful time of doubting a year after becoming a Christian, after having been challenged by two professors I respected about the basis for my Christian belief. This type of doubt can be the result of a mindset that if you have doubts as a believer, there is something wrong with you, for we are to accept the Bible as true simply by faith — that is, without other evidence. In *Truth and the New Kind of Christian,* 124-31, I discuss this period of my life and how I grew out of it, not by embracing postmodernism or postfoundationalist views, but by finding evidences for my belief, as well as finding committed, truthful, and gracious believers who dearly love the Lord.

33. Carson, *Becoming Conversant with the Emerging Church,* 104. He concurs that such postmodern insights have helped to successfully deconstruct modern foundationalism. He lists factors such as our acknowledgment of the "unavoidable finiteness of all human knowers, the cultural diversity of the human race, the diversity of factors that go into human knowing, and even the evil that lurks in the human breast and easily perverts claims of knowledge into totalitarian control and lust for power . . ."

Coherentism

The major non-foundational alternative to foundationalism is coherentism. As Beilby reminds us, this is a position about the way our beliefs should be structured so that they may be justified. It is not to be confused with a coherentist theory of truth or meaning.[34]

But let me also introduce Moreland's distinction between *strong* and *weak* coherentism. For Beilby, coherentism rejects both doxastic and source foundationalism, in which case "coherence with other beliefs is the *only* way to justify beliefs."[35] This matches with Moreland's strong coherentism, in which there is *no* role for sensory experiences to provide a role for justifying some beliefs. But in weak coherentism, coherence is just *one* determinant of justification. This position is compatible with a kind of foundationalism that allows for coherence to play a justificatory role, positively or negatively.[36] If right, this would not be a form of modern foundationalism. Therefore, even if we reject modern foundationalism, there still could be other forms to consider (which we will do later).

In general, it makes sense that one's beliefs should be coherent. Suppose I walk into my church's auditorium and seem to see a table up front set up with silver-colored trays filled with grape juice cups and broken pieces of crackers. I form the belief on the basis of that experience that I am seeing silver-colored trays on a table in the front of the church. Now suppose I need to go on several errands, and each time I come back in, I see the same things and form that same belief. In such a case, the coherence of all these beliefs with one another *further* increases the justification of my belief that there are indeed such trays on a table in the front of the church.

In the same case, suppose one of those times I form a belief that I am seeing gold-colored trays, which does not cohere with other beliefs in that set. Negatively, then, that degree of incoherence serves to count against the justification of my original belief.

Now, for the strong coherentist, since only beliefs confer justification, then it seems natural for strong coherentists to tend to affirm that all our experiences are theory-laden.[37] This is because there is no role for experience to provide justification for any beliefs, even perceptual ones. So, nothing in reality is simply *given,* or directly present, as it is to us in conscious awareness; to think that it could be is to embrace the "myth of the given." Such "givenness" would involve some sort of preconceptual and prejudgmental access to these aspects of reality. Instead, everything that is present before us in conscious awareness is "taken"

34. See also Moreland, *Philosophical Foundations for a Christian Worldview,* 121.
35. Beilby, p. 811 above.
36. Moreland, *Philosophical Foundations for a Christian Worldview,* 115, 123.
37. Moreland, *Philosophical Foundations for a Christian Worldview,* 124.

to be such-and-such, which will require that theories and an interpretive grid already are in place to even have experiences.

Now, it may not be *logically necessary* that a strong coherentist about justification must deny the givenness of all experience. Beilby acknowledges this when he says that a coherentist need not deny the correspondence theory of truth. Perhaps he offers a helpful way to help reconcile the two views. That is, conceivably a coherentist about justification could affirm the inerrancy of Scripture (which is a metaphysical claim about reality) in light of the correspondence theory of truth. But how that person will justify that belief about inerrancy will be very different than how a foundationalist would.

Nevertheless, on a strong coherentist view, it seems hard to conceive how one could maintain consistently a correspondence theory of truth. Offhand, it seems we could not know reality as it truly is, nor if our beliefs match up with it, if all experience is theory-laden. Yet, we do seem to experience some things directly, as in Beilby's example of seeing a road sign while driving down the road.[38]

Perhaps the strong coherentist could reply that we can have sensory experiences without having beliefs, but this is just a psychological fact and does not contribute to the justification of sensory beliefs. Still, this reply seems to miss the mark; if I pay close attention to my awarenesses, it seems I can see that my now having an experience of my laptop serves to justify my belief that it is here. My seeing, touching, and tasting an apple serves to justify my belief that an object with me is an apple. If so, descriptively this seems to fit better with a foundationalist account of how beliefs can be justified than a strong coherentist one.

Now let us consider *linear* and *holistic* coherentism. In the former, beliefs are justified by other ones in a circular chain. As Moreland observes, "*P* justifies *Q*, *Q* justifies *R*, and so on in a single, inferential line until a loop is completed."[39] A sufficiently rich and large loop confers justification on its members. In contrast, for holistic coherentism, for someone to be justified in believing some belief *B*, *B* must be coherent with all the other beliefs in that person's noetic structure. It is the coherence of the whole set of beliefs that confers justification.

Yet linear coherentism seems viciously circular. As the loop is completed, the chain from *Q* through *Z* in turn serves to justify *P*. But this will not work unless the whole chain is justified. This helps surface what seems to be the *essence* of foundationalism, as well as a critical weakness of this form of strong coherentism. As Moreland suggests, for foundationalism, there are basic beliefs (some of which can be properly basic) and nonbasic ones, and nonbasic beliefs can be justified on the basis of their relationship to basic ones.[40] Now, the basing relation is irre-

38. For now, I will not probe this position further, but I will address it when we assess the postfoundationalists' views.

39. Moreland, *Philosophical Foundations for a Christian Worldview*, 123.

40. Moreland, *Philosophical Foundations for a Christian Worldview*, 118.

flexive and asymmetrical; it is irreflexive in that some belief *B* cannot be justified by itself. A self-evident belief would not violate this condition; rather, it would be justified on the basis of an experienced obviousness or the like. Moreover, if two beliefs, *A* and *B*, are in the basing relationship, then while *A* can be based upon *B*, *B* cannot be based upon *A*. This means that foundationalism provides an answer to the "regress problem," but for linear coherentism, there is no way to account for these features of the basing relation, and justification ends up being viciously circular.[41]

Therefore, some coherentists have turned to holistic coherentism. This move may sidestep the problem of circularity, but it seems to raise other problems. First, if justification comes just from mutual coherence of a set of beliefs, then there is no real place for sensory experience or reason to serve as sources of justification. Nevertheless, it does seem that experience and truths of reason (e.g., laws of logic, mathematical truths) play a role in our beliefs' justification.

Second, holistic coherentism seems to isolate our theories and sets of beliefs from their relation to reality. It seems possible to have an internally coherent set of beliefs, yet one that has little if anything to do with reality. That is, there is no necessary connection between one's set of beliefs and reality. Still, one might reply that there is a place for the real world to influence our beliefs because its inputs help cause them. But by itself, that move is insufficient, for there still is no room for the world to play any *rational* role in justifying our beliefs; it merely helps cause them.

Third, conceivably there could be more than one equally coherent, yet mutually incompatible, belief sets, which poses a few problems. One, according to whose perspective are they internally coherent? Their proponents would not be advocating the coherence and justification of their respective belief sets from some neutral standpoint; internal coherence (i.e., from one's point of view) matters. But that seems to lead to relativism. It also seems there would not be a way to adjudicate between these competing "webs" of belief. Two, as Moreland argues, "The coherentist would have to say that the beliefs in each set are equally justified, but surely this is not the case."[42]

What then are the implications of strong coherentism for holding a high view of Scripture? While it is possible to be a strong coherentist in justification yet also a correspondence theorist about truth (and thereby affirm that Scripture, as one part of reality, is true in that sense), it seems that it would be hard to hold both together consistently. For on a strong coherentist view, there is no place for reality (including Scripture) to serve as a source of justification of our beliefs, even though Scripture is God's word, infallible, etc. That would seem to be a claim

41. From the "regress problem," we can see that the justification for our beliefs cannot be truly infinite; it has to start somewhere.

42. Moreland, *Philosophical Foundations for a Christian Worldview*, 127.

made from the standpoint of the web of beliefs of the one making that claim. Indeed, there would not be room for appeals to evidences in reality (e.g., from archeological findings) to serve to justify our beliefs that the Bible is infallible.

Thus we seem to lack any way to make good on our claims that the Bible is (uniquely) God's word, that salvation is found through Jesus Christ alone, etc. We would make those claims from the standpoint of our web of beliefs, but there could be equally internally coherent, yet incompatible, webs. If we do not have a way to adjudicate between competing webs (as it seems we do not on this view), then we seem to be without resources to make good on our claims.

These are just a few (yet crucial) problems with holding both to strong coherentism and a high view of Scripture. Yet perhaps the very distinction between foundational and non-foundational ways to justify our beliefs belies a *modern* kind of *dichotomy*. Instead, perhaps we should be considering something *post*-foundational, that is, a way to *transcend* modernity's categories. Both strong coherentism and foundationalism seem to presuppose a bifurcation of world and language, or epistemology and hermeneutics, something that various postmodern thinkers have argued against. So now I will turn to the various suggestions of postfoundationalists. I have already surfaced some of their arguments against foundationalism; here I will focus on their own positive reasons for their views.

Postfoundationalism(s)

LeRon Shults

Between 1999 and 2005, Shults addressed how to do Christian theology in light of the developments of late modernity, especially in terms of a response to postmodernity. For him, we always are socially situated, embedded in a vast network of relationships. Epistemologically, instead of seeing humans being mainly as autonomous knowing subjects, in which "the 'self' is dualistically separated from its 'knowing,'" and "the human subject is defined prior to and over and against the objects of its knowledge," Shults thinks that we need to see the self in light of the turn to relationality.[43] Metaphysically, humans are not to be understood on the basis of body-soul dualism, but a type of monism that embraces our essential relationality.[44] On that model, "human knowing is no longer understood

43. Shults, *Reforming Theological Anthropology,* 181. In this book, Shults has in mind the turn away from substance metaphysics (and body-soul dualism) to monism, in which our human *essence* is understood in terms of our relationships with ourselves, world, and others, including God (see also 31). Shults has recently become an atheist.

44. Shults, *Reforming Theological Anthropology,* 181.

as wholly self-determined nor as undetermined, but rather as conditioned and mediated by the embodied communal relations of the knower."[45] Put differently, we are completely embedded in creation; not even our minds escape this continuity.[46] Furthermore, God encompasses and conditions "all finite experience, quantitative and qualitative."[47] We are beings-in-relation, even with God, which for Shults results in his own nuanced version of panentheism. Our relationality in God entails that "we cannot step back from our relation to the *infinite* trinitarian God and compare this divine object to other objects."[48]

Shults situates his postfoundationalism as a middle option between two polar, "either-or" kinds of responses to postmodernity. At one extreme is the deconstructive approach, in which "the emphasis is primarily on engaging contemporary culture, with less interest in upholding or conserving the [Christian, Reformed] tradition."[49] He sees deconstructionism as being aligned with relativism and antifoundationalism. At the other extreme is a "*paleo*-constructive response, which would ignore or dismiss the challenges by appealing to an earlier premodern (or early modern) era in which truth and knowledge about God and humanity were allegedly unproblematic."[50] Foundationalism is most closely aligned with this approach, with an emphasis upon absolute, even dogmatic foundations and universal reasons.[51]

Shults claims these two "poles" structure the debate in response to postmodernity, yet he argues for a "linking of epistemology and hermeneutics," to embrace a middle, *postfoundationalist* way.[52] He quotes J. Wentzel van Huyssteen approvingly that the postfoundationalist wants to fully acknowledge contextuality, the epistemically crucial role of interpreted experience, and the way that tradition shapes the epistemic and non-epistemic values that inform our reflection about God and what some of us believe to be God's presence in this world. At the same time, however, a postfoundationalist notion of rationality in theological reflection claims to point creatively beyond the confines of the local community, group, or culture towards a plausible form of interdisciplinary conversation.[53]

Shults explores four conceptual couplets that, as posed, typify the foundationalism–non-foundationalism dichotomy: (1) experience and belief; (2) truth

45. Shults, *Reforming Theological Anthropology,* 183-84.

46. Shults, *Reforming Theological Anthropology,* 164.

47. LeRon Shults, *Reforming the Doctrine of God* (Grand Rapids: Eerdmans, 2005), 131.

48. Shults, *Reforming the Doctrine of God,* 164.

49. Shults, *Reforming Theological Anthropology,* 7.

50. Shults, *Reforming Theological Anthropology,* 7.

51. LeRon Shults, *The Postfoundationalist Task of Theology: Wolfhart Pannenberg and the New Theological Rationality* (Grand Rapids: Eerdmans, 1999), 25.

52. Shults, *Reforming Theological Anthropology,* 8.

53. J. Wentzel van Huyssteen, *Essays in Postfoundationalist Theology* (Grand Rapids: Eerdmans, 1997), 4, quoted in Shults, *The Postfoundationalist Task of Theology,* 26.

and knowledge; (3) individual and community; and (4) explanation and understanding.[54] To transcend these dualisms, he develops a form of relationality between each pair, to develop an "ideal type" of postfoundationalism. The first is that "interpreted experience engenders and nourishes all beliefs, and a network of beliefs informs the interpretation of experience" (43). In agreement with Susan Haack, he explains that "against the foundationalist . . . justification of belief is not one-directional, but against the non-foundationalist she wants experience (not merely other beliefs) to play a crucial role in justifying the rationality of belief" (49). Thus, "it is precisely the reciprocal relation between belief and experience that sets the postfoundationalist model apart from its rivals" (46).

Second, "the objective unity of truth is a necessary condition for the intelligible search for knowledge, and the subjective multiplicity of knowledge indicates the fallibility of truth claims" (43). Shults explains that "the goal is to maintain the foundationalist vision of truth," objectivity, and rationality, as ideals that drive our inquiry, to avoid fideism (50, 58). But, "the postfoundationalist does not claim to 'have' the truth," for we must also acknowledge the "provisional, contextual, and fallible nature of human reason," which protects against embracing a totalizing metanarrative (56, 58).

Third, "rational judgment is an activity of socially situated individuals, and the cultural community indeterminately mediates the criteria of rationality" (43). Individual and communal factors are "mutually conditioning elements in the shaping of rationality" (68). Referencing van Huyssteen approvingly, Shults suggests that the postfoundationalist attempts to take into account both the "nonfoundationalist sensitivity to the hermeneutical conditioning effected by being situated in a community of inquirers" and "the intuition of the foundationalist that it is the individual who actually *makes* a rational judgment" (60).

Fourth, "explanation aims for universal, transcontextual understanding, and understanding derives from particular contextualized explanations" (43). The danger for the non-foundationalist is relativism, by holding to a view that all understanding is conditioned, and "interpretation and language go all the way down and all the way back up" (70). On the other hand, for the foundationalist, the urge to find absolute explanations by following rules "which are or aim to be clearly true regardless of tradition or context" ignores the mediating influence of our contexts (69).[55]

Finally, for Shults, the postfoundationalist refuses either extreme: the modern concern for finding absolute foundations for justified true beliefs, or post-

54. Shults, *The Postfoundationalist Task of Theology*, 28. Subsequent page references from this work are given in parentheses in the text.

55. In Shults's view, "by emphasizing the back-and-forth movement between traditioned understanding and universally intended explanations, the postfoundationalist escapes relativism without retreating into absolutism" (72).

modern attempts to replace epistemologically adequate explanations (and even epistemology itself) with "mere hermeneutical understandings" (78). That is, they are "two differentiated yet mutually conditioning or reciprocally related movements" (79). Their two concerns are held together in a way that transcends the false dichotomy between foundationalism and non-foundationalism.

It seems that, as he sees it, someone could hold a high view of Scripture's authority. That is, Scripture seems authoritative in theology, even though it should be done in light of interdisciplinary dialogue. However, inerrancy could well be seen as a mistaken, modern stance, since it would presuppose that we can achieve a view from nowhere and compare the text we have with the text in itself. Still, in this period, Shults did not want to give up making and vigorously defending truth claims from the standpoint of the faith. Yet, on his views, Scripture seems true, perhaps in an eschatological sense, and inspired, but not necessarily propositionally.[56]

Stanley Grenz and John Franke

I will begin by exploring the work of Grenz and Franke in their joint book, *Beyond Foundationalism,* and then I will examine Franke's separately stated views. This is because they offer overlapping, yet differently focused, reasons. Moreover, though they will use the term "non-foundationalist," I believe they mean by this much of what Shults means by "postfoundationalist." They decidedly want to move past modern categories, and they also fit well with the values expressed by van Huyssteen for a postfoundationalist epistemology.

First, Grenz and Franke observe that coherentism and pragmatism (in terms of truth) helped us leave behind the preference of foundationalism for the correspondence theory of truth.[57] If justification is a matter of the internal coherence of one's beliefs, then whether or not they match up with reality makes no real difference. The linguistic turn also helped undermine the correspondence theory. The later Wittgenstein's work, which focused on meaning being a matter of the use of terms in a form of life, drew attention to the many different ways we use words, and not simply to make assertions and refer to entities. According to Grenz and Franke's understanding of Wittgenstein, "each use of language occurs within a separate and seemingly self-contained system complete with its own rules" (42). These "language games" are not autonomous; rather, they are embedded in local communities, or forms of life, each with their own formative language.

But the linguistic turn also helped theologians leave behind metaphysical

56. My thanks for Jim Beilby's suggestions in an email, February 8, 2011.

57. Grenz and Franke, *Beyond Foundationalism,* 42. Subsequent references to this work are given in parentheses in the text.

realism, which Grenz and Franke see as closely tied to foundationalism. This is because "for Wittgenstein, meaning and truth are not related — at least not directly or primarily — to an external world of 'facts' waiting to be apprehended" (42). Instead, they are internally related to the language of a given, local community, and that language serves as the grammar (the forming story for the behavior) of a community.

With the moves away from foundationalism and its related views of the correspondence theory of truth and metaphysical realism, Grenz and Franke set out to chart a "non-foundationalism" that rejects the Enlightenment's universality of reason, for reason is not neutral, nor is there a "single, universal set of criteria by means of which we can judge definitively the epistemic status of all beliefs" (47). Moreover, there is no uninterpreted experience that could serve as a foundation for knowledge: "experience does not precede interpretation. Rather, experiences are always filtered by an interpretive framework — a grid — that facilitates their occurrence" (49).

Language also plays a critical role, for "theology, we might conclude, explores the world-constructing, knowledge-forming, identity-forming 'language' of the Christian community" (53). But this does not mean that a language-independent world does not exist, for "there is, of course, a certain undeniable givenness to the universe apart from the human linguistic-constructive task." But this obvious truth does not dismiss the importance of social construction: "the simple fact is, we do not inhabit the 'world-in-itself'; instead, we live in a linguistic world of our own making" (53).

There is another sense in which the world is objective, in terms of its *eschatological reality.* Grenz and Franke firmly believe that Christians can know the world *as God wills it to be in the future.* This view is based on the biblical narrative's vision of what kind of world (and new community) God is creating, which will be realized in the future. From this perspective, the world gains its most fundamental sense of actuality, or objectivity.

By himself, Franke stresses some other factors that contribute to his "non-foundationalism," in particular his use of key elements of Karl Barth's theology. One of Franke's starting points is his assertion that we are "finite and situated in our understanding. All of our thoughts are shaped by the social and cultural settings that we inhabit."[58] Franke also makes a stronger claim: *if* (which I take to be rhetorical) "we are *thoroughly* situated and imbedded in our own social and historical settings, what are the implications for claims about truth?" (66; emphasis mine).

He first considers a metaphor that perhaps God "breaks through" our situatedness to reveal truth. But this implies that God negates our limitations from our finitude, which is just the result of our creatureliness. Instead, he opts for a second

58. Franke, *Manifold Witness,* 66. Subsequent references to this work are given in parentheses in the text.

interpretation of the character of revelation: God enters into our limitations and accommodates (or "adjusts," "descends") his revelation to our limited capacities. As he suggests, "even revelation does not provide human beings with a knowledge that directly corresponds to the knowledge of God, even with reference to the content of revelation itself" (67).[59] The "infinite mysteries of the divine reality" are "by their very nature" beyond "the capabilities of human beings to grasp" (67). Put differently, "human beings cannot handle the truth about God as it is in itself," due to the "infinite qualitative distinction" between us and God (67).[60]

So revelation is mediated, contextual, and uses means such as human nature, language, speech, and writing that are limited due to their creaturely character. But this does not mean that God is completely hidden from us; indeed, he is "genuinely" revealed (68). The mediated character of revelation suggests to Franke that we adopt the notion of "indirect revelation," according to which "revelation is indirect because it is always mediated through creaturely forms, and nothing can be known of God directly by the natural perception of human beings" (68). He connects these ideas to Barth's views of *veiling* and *unveiling;* that is, from our perspective, God's revelation through creaturely mediums serves as veils "that hide what is revealed from its intended recipients apart from the further action of God" (68).

Therefore, we cannot seize control of the epistemological process of knowing revelation; we are entirely dependent upon God for revealing more of himself by giving us "eyes" of faith. God gives us the "faith to understand what is hidden in the veil" (69). Since we do not have control over God's giving of revelation, we are always in a position of epistemic dependency upon God, and not one of mastery.

But there is another reason why we cannot seize control of the epistemological process. Though Franke denies there are epistemic foundations, there are *ontological* ones; non-foundationalism does not deny Truth's existence. However, Franke avers that these "foundations" are not "given" to us, as though they are not ours to control.[61] Citing Bruce McCormack, Franke says these foundations " 'always elude the grasp of the human attempt to know and to establish them from the human side' and they cannot be demonstrated or secured 'philosophically or in any other way.' "[62]

These theological points lead to a twofold critique of foundationalism. First, since we are finite, the modern ideals of objectivity, universality, and certainty of knowledge are not possible. Moreover, our epistemic dependency undercuts

59. See also John R. Franke, "Nonfoundationalism, Truth, and the Knowledge of God" *Philosophia Christi* 8 (2006): 297.

60. See also Franke, "Nonfoundationalism, Truth, and the Knowledge of God," 297.

61. Franke, "Nonfoundationalism, Truth, and the Knowledge of God," 299.

62. Franke, "Nonfoundationalism, Truth, and the Knowledge of God," 299-300, citing Bruce L. McCormack, "What Has Basel to Do with Berlin? Continuities in the Theologies of Barth and Schleiermacher," *The Princeton Seminary Bulletin* 23 (2002): 172.

all appeals to supposedly self-evident and non-inferential grounds for justifying our beliefs. Self-evident beliefs are undercut by our need to depend upon God for all knowledge of him. Non-inferential beliefs about God also seem false, for they would not be based upon what God has revealed. Second, foundationalism is not even desirable, for the modern idea of the inherent goodness of knowledge deeply underestimates our fallenness and the extent to which we can want to seize control of the epistemic process in order to empower ourselves.[63]

What then might be the implications of these views for holding to a high view of Scripture? At the time of these writings, Franke still is a member of the Evangelical Theological Society, as was Grenz, which requires inerrancy. Plus, Scripture, along with tradition and culture, is one of theology's sources.[64] It is authoritative "as the instrumentality of the Spirit," but not insofar as it is a book. Rather, "the biblical message spoken by the Spirit through the text is theology's norming norm."[65]

Nancey Murphy

Murphy's "holist" epistemology is tightly interwoven with her philosophy of language, not to mention her metaphysics. Her own self-described "Anglo-American" postmodern views reflect the importance of tradition and narrative as seen in Alasdair MacIntyre, the epistemic holism from W. V. O. Quine, and the emphases of J. L. Austin and the later Wittgenstein upon ordinary language use in local communities.[66]

For her, foundationalism should be replaced by a postmodern holist view of epistemic justification. She draws upon W. V. O. Quine's "image of knowledge as a web or net," such that "there are no sharp distinctions between basic (foundational) beliefs and nonbasic beliefs." Not only do the beliefs in the web reinforce each other in a variety of kinds of connections among themselves as well as to the whole, they also work in a top-down manner. For example, in philosophy of science, there are no data that are simply given; rather, all "facts" are made "by means of their interpretation" in light of other theoretical assumptions.[67]

Yet Quine provides too circumspect a view of what counts as knowledge to allow for how we can justify claims of other disciplines in which we are interested,

63. John Franke, *The Character of Theology: A Postconservative Evangelical Approach* (Grand Rapids: Baker Academic, 2005), 28. Notice his use of the term "postconservative" in the subtitle, and not "nonfoundational."

64. Grenz and Franke, *Beyond Foundationalism,* chapters 3-5.

65. Grenz and Franke, *Beyond Foundationalism,* 69.

66. While interpretation plays a significant role for her, the more continental approaches of Westphal and Smith emphasize the turn from epistemology to interpretation.

67. Murphy, *Anglo-American Postmodernity,* 27.

such as theology and ethics. And, there could be competing webs of beliefs, which raises the specter of relativism. So, Imre Lakatos allows Murphy to unpack her own views of philosophy of science and later apply them to theology and ethics when considered as sciences in their own right.[68] Lakatos provides a way to judge rationally between competing scientific research programs, even though the standards of rationality are internal to that program.[69] Nonetheless, this does not entail relativism, for competing programs can be compared on the basis of their abilities to change over time in response to problematic, or anomalous, empirical discoveries.[70]

To flesh out her epistemological holism, even for theology and ethics and as a broader theory of rationality, she appeals to the holist views of Alasdair MacIntyre. For him, rationality is found only within traditions, which are historically extended, socially embodied arguments about the nature of the good for that tradition.[71] Like Lakatos, traditions involve a historical dimension, and they are tied to communities, or, following Wittgenstein, "forms of life," with their respective languages. Traditions provide the context within which we "see" the world. We can think and perceive only by means of the categories and stories found in traditions, for there is no independent reality against which we may compare a text.[72] Nor can we compare reality with our favored conceptual scheme, for we do not have "some sort of direct insight into the nature of reality."[73] Indeed, MacIntyre thinks there are no theory-independent facts, for "facts . . . were a seventeenth-century invention."[74]

MacIntyre claims that specific types of claims make sense only in terms of historical reason.[75] This is what Murphy calls *diachronic* justification, or how we

68. This is the focus of chapter 9 of *Anglo-American Postmodernity.*

69. Murphy, *Beyond Liberalism,* 101.

70. For her, there is a hard core of any research program, and there are auxiliary hypotheses that surround and protect it. These auxiliary theses can be altered when falsifying data are found, but they work together over time, even as they are modified, to protect the core. Anomalies can be made consistent with the research program by theoretical adjustments. If these are made by ad hoc maneuvers, then over time the program has become degenerative. But if these are made such that new versions of the program account for anomalies and are supported by novel, unexpected facts, then the program is progressive. See her *Theology in the Age of Scientific Reasoning,* Cornell Studies in the Philosophy of Religion, ed. William P. Alston (Ithaca, NY: Cornell University Press, 1990), 59, 61. Importantly, it is the acceptability of the *whole* program that matters.

71. Alasdair MacIntyre, *After Virtue,* 2nd edition (Notre Dame: University of Notre Dame Press, 1984), 222.

72. Murphy, *Anglo-American Postmodernity,* 140.

73. Murphy, *Anglo-American Postmodernity,* 127.

74. Alasdair MacIntyre, *Whose Justice? Which Rationality?* (Notre Dame: University of Notre Dame Press, 1984), 357.

75. Murphy, *Anglo-American Postmodernity,* 58.

justify modifications within a tradition. A second aspect of justification is *synchronic.* MacIntyre provides a means to rationally assess why one tradition is rationally superior to a rival, even though rational standards are *internal* to a tradition.[76] Seeing the rational superiority of a tradition over another involves the comparison of their languages, such that "a tradition is vindicated by the fact that it has managed to solve its own major problems, while its competitor has failed to do so, and by the fact that it can give a better account of its rival's failures than can the rival itself."[77]

Seeing such rational superiority depends upon people in one tradition learning the language of another as a second, first language.[78] This can be done only by participation within that alien tradition. In this way, they can see the epistemic resources available in another tradition to help solve problems internal to their own.

In philosophy of language, like MacIntyre, Murphy embraces the holism in the later Wittgenstein, and she also draws upon J. L. Austin. Meaning is basically *use* in a linguistically shaped form of life, the whole in which words have their meaning. Furthermore, language and life are inextricable, such that language is not *about* the world; rather, language is *in* the world. She indicates that "the biblical narratives *create* a world, and it is within this world that believers are to live their lives and understand reality."[79] We do not "transcend" language to know how things are from some supposed neutral standpoint, which also would undercut foundationalism. Rather, as Wittgenstein observed, "the connection between 'language and reality' is made by definition of words, and these belong to grammar, so that language remains self-contained and autonomous."[80] Still, the world has a bearing on how we may talk, but the community's grammar will constrain the appropriate kinds of expressions.[81]

Applied to her views of Scripture, it seems that it would have much room for the same high place for its authority we have seen in Grenz and Franke. But perhaps more explicitly, Murphy can appeal to Scripture as the "grammar" of the Christian community, that is, its formative story that should govern how we use

76. Another way to put this is that standards of rationality "emerge from and are part of a history in which they are vindicated by the way in which they transcend the limitations of and provide remedies for the defects of their predecessors within the history of that same tradition" (MacIntyre, *Whose Justice?* 7).

77. Murphy, *Anglo-American Postmodernity,* 59.

78. E.g., see MacIntyre, *Three Rival Versions of Moral Enquiry* (Notre Dame: University of Notre Dame Press, 1990), 114.

79. Murphy, *Anglo-American Postmodernity,* 120; emphasis mine.

80. Ludwig Wittgenstein, *Philosophical Grammar,* ed. Rush Rhees, trans. Anthony Kenny (Berkeley and Los Angeles: University of California Press, 1974), §55.

81. Murphy, *Anglo-American Postmodernity,* 25.

our language (which is how we engage in verbal and nonverbal behavior).[82] But for her, the biblical texts contain contradictions.[83] Moreover, appeals to inerrancy seem misguided for the same reasons as I explored in regards to Shults.

Merold Westphal and James K. A. Smith

Finally, let us consider the more continental views of Westphal and Smith. Here I will examine their positive proposals vis-à-vis their critical interaction with one of the foremost defenders of foundationalism and the founder of *phenomenology,* Edmund Husserl.[84]

There are at least two main places in which Westphal discusses the failure of Husserl's project. In *Phenomenologies and Religious Truth,* Westphal portrays Husserl as advocating a "Cartesian dream of rigorous science"[85] by our ability to achieve a "complete and ultimate grounding on the basis of absolute insights, insights behind which one cannot go back any further" (109).[86] But these claims strike Westphal suspiciously, especially in light of our tendencies toward "situated self-deceptions" (110).

Worse, these Husserlian claims are mistaken, for Westphal claims that Heidegger has shown successfully that all experience has an as-structure; that is, "even at the level of ordinary sense perception and prior to any explicit assertion there is no 'mere seeing' but always the act that sees something *as* something" (112).[87] Westphal agrees that "only that which is taken can be given — which is to say that nothing is given free of interpretation" (112). If so, we can never achieve a foundation of certainties, or one for knowledge, period,

82. This seems to be the focus of one of Murphy's students, Brad Kallenberg.

83. Murphy, *Beyond Liberalism,* 93. Murphy also thinks that an appeal to the autographs' inerrancy is useless: "When conservative theologians were forced to admit that the biblical texts contained contradictions, a common move was to argue that only the original autographs were inerrant. This claim is incorrigible (since all of these are lost) but the incorrigibility comes at the cost of needing to ground theology on something inaccessible to contemporary theologians; the lost autographs are inerrant but useless."

84. By "phenomenology," I mean roughly a movement he founded that "focuses on a careful description and presentation of specific cases to see what can be learned from them" about some feature of reality (Moreland, *Philosophical Foundations for a Christian Worldview,* 139).

85. Merold Westphal, "Phenomenologies and Religious Truth," in *Phenomenology of the Truth Proper to Religion,* ed. Daniel Guerrière (Albany: State University of New York Press, 1990), 109. Subsequent page references from this work are given in parentheses in the text.

86. Quoting Edmund Husserl, *Cartesian Meditations: An Introduction to Phenomenology,* trans. Dorin Cairns (The Hague: Nijhoff, 1973), 2.

87. Westphal takes Heidegger's paragraph 32 of *Being and Time* as the "crucial transition" (111) to realizing that all seeing really involves interpretation, thereby eliminating any possibility for immediacy (the ability to directly access reality).

based on experiences (or beliefs based on those experiences) in which their objects are directly given. Instead, every interpretation presupposes an earlier one (112). Thus we find ourselves in something like Heidegger's hermeneutical circle, and "no reflection, no matter how methodologically rigorous, enables us to outflank life and escape our entanglement with it" (112). Thus foundationalism must be replaced.

Ironically, Westphal thinks Husserl's "transcendental phenomenology" finds its natural fulfillments in the hermeneutics of finitude due to the circle, and then in turn in the hermeneutics of suspicion, since we distort what we see due to hidden, devious desires. Whereas the hermeneutics of finitude are about our blindness from perspective, the hermeneutics of suspicion are about our blindness due to perversity (121). Our hidden desires shape "the intentionalities that give shape to human existence," so "the phenomenological project completes itself only when it incorporates into itself the kind of suspicion that carries the task of interpretation to this level" (120).

Westphal also attacks Husserl's use of the "phenomenological reduction," which involves his notion of "bracketing," for "the phenomenological reduction abandons the natural standpoint of empirical consciousness in the midst of a surrounding real world." Moreover, he thinks Husserl bracketed "the question of the relation of thought to reality," thereby forcing the phenomenologist "to focus on the ways in which the contents of consciousness, whatever their ontological status, are given to a pure or transcendental consciousness." However, for Westphal that move is fallacious, for that consciousness "intends a world of which it is not a part," and thus Husserl advocates the very thing that Westphal says we cannot do — extricate ourselves from our situatedness and avoid the effects of our fallenness. Thus, Husserl's "bracket" is an attempt to abandon the natural standpoint and achieve access to "a realm of pure consciousness where presuppositionless, apodictic intuitions of essences can occur."[88]

Westphal draws support by taking Kant's ideas of the noumenal and phenomenal worlds as being two ways of apprehending the one real world.[89] There is a real, noumenal world, which is the world as it is known by God. Kant's phenomenal world is the world as it is apprehended by us. To know reality in itself is to be God, for only he has an absolute, all-encompassing point of view.[90] But the human mind "is a receiving or interpreting apparatus that does two things: it

88. Merold Westphal, "Hermeneutics as Epistemology," in *The Blackwell Guide to Epistemology,* ed. John Greco and Ernest Sosa (Malden, MA: Blackwell, 1999), 419.

89. Westphal, "Hermeneutics as Epistemology," 419.

90. Westphal, "Christian Philosophers and the Copernican Revolution," in *Christian Perspectives on Religious Knowledge,* ed. C. Stephen Evans and Merold Westphal (Grand Rapids: Eerdmans, 1993), 167. See also Westphal, "Onto-theology, Metanarrative, Perspectivism, and the Gospel," in *Christianity and the Postmodern Turn,* ed. Myron B. Penner (Grand Rapids: Brazos, 2005), 151.

gives us real access to the real and, in so doing, it distorts it so that what it really is cannot be equated with the way we apprehend it."[91]

According to Westphal, there is objective "Truth," but only for God, for as finite and fallen creatures we can never achieve God's view; we always work from a standpoint of how the world appears to us.[92] Indeed, we "never get beyond appearances or phenomenal knowledge."[93] For us, there will be "a pluralistic account of the phenomenal world," for "the a prioris that define human cultures, paradigms, language games, and so forth are legion."[94]

Westphal also appeals to Derrida's claim that *"there is nothing outside the text."*[95] This is not a license to arbitrariness, for it signifies "textuality as a limit within which we have whatever freedom we have." Instead, Westphal unpacks Derrida's statement epistemologically and metaphysically. Epistemically, it means that "Being must always already be conceptualized," in that we do not have access immediately to things themselves. Furthermore, metaphysically the things themselves are *signs* and not what is signified, and as such they "essentially point beyond themselves."[96] Therefore, Westphal claims that "there is no signified that 'would place a reassuring end to the reference from sign to sign' by failing to refer beyond itself."[97]

For Derrida, there is always an absence "to" things, which somehow is present. What is not present is somehow essential to what is present. He denies that things, such as thoughts, facts, or linguistic utterances are wholes that are complete in themselves. Rather, from one re-presentation to another, there always will be *differance,* for nothing has an identity that can be circumscribed. Similarly, for Westphal our limited perspectives are "constituted to a significant degree by contingencies of linguistic usage and sociohistorical location," and they "hide" certain things from our view.[98] That is, our "points of view, by analogy with vi-

91. Westphal, "Of Stories and Languages," in *Christianity and the Postmodern Turn,* 232.

92. Westphal, "Christian Philosophers and the Copernican Revolution," 176. Thus, to claim that there is a mind- or language-independent world is not sufficient to demarcate realism from Westphal's "creative anti-realism."

93. Westphal, "Hermeneutics as Epistemology," 425.

94. Westphal, "Christian Philosophers and the Copernican Revolution," 176-77.

95. Jacques Derrida, *Of Grammatology,* trans. Gayatri Chakravorty Spivak (Baltimore: Johns Hopkins University Press, 1976), 158, quoted in Westphal, "Hermeneutics as Epistemology," 429.

96. Westphal, "Hermeneutics as Epistemology," 430. By *"sign,"* I mean basically "any information-carrying entity," such as linguistic tokens, pictures, road signs, and much more (W. Kent Wilson, "Theory of signs," *The Cambridge Dictionary of Philosophy,* 2nd edition, ed. Robert Audi [Cambridge: Cambridge University Press, 1999], 915).

97. Derrida, *Of Grammatology,* 49, as quoted by Westphal, "Hermeneutics as Epistemology," 430.

98. Westphal, "Onto-theology, Metanarrative, Perspectivism, and the Gospel," 151.

sion, enable us to see what can be seen from that site only by hiding from us what cannot be seen from there."[99]

Still, we can achieve a "fusion of horizons" (i.e., perspectives), in which we can mutually understand each other, sufficient for life together, despite our different perspectives from our finitude.[100] But, we are not even ideally human, due to our own sin.[101] Thus, we are not neutral, and all too often we are guilty of a will to power.

For Smith, too, there is no direct access, despite Husserl's claims to the contrary. Smith follows John Caputo, who claims that for Husserl, "to intuit the given means to know how to construe what presents itself, failing which there is only the flux."[102] But this does not mean that our interpretations are arbitrary. We all see the same material reality; the real world provides a limit to the range of interpretations, for they are interpretations "of the world." Since "the world is a fundamentally given, objective world that is shared by all, thought will be constituted differently by those who share it as a lifeworld."[103] There are such things as "empirical transcendentals" (though not to be understood as a priori ones) that are the world as given and experienced.[104] Texts, including the Scriptures, act similarly, so not just any interpretation goes. Indeed, Smith thinks that interpreting the world as creation is the *true* interpretation.[105]

Still, the mediated status of all experience and knowledge means that there will be a hermeneutical kind of pluralism, which is just the result of our finitude and created status. But there also is a deeper, "directional" pluralism, which is due to our fallenness, and this relates to our deep differences over fundamental issues, such as "what it means to be authentically human and how we fit into the cosmos."[106]

If we cannot escape our finitude, and our viewpoints are finite, then the modern foundationalist attempt to attempt to gain a God's-eye view by rising above all our situatedness actually betrays a lustful pride to become like God. The

99. Westphal, "Onto-theology, Metanarrative, Perspectivism, and the Gospel," 151.

100. Merold Westphal, "Positive Postmodernism as Radical Hermeneutics," in *The Very Idea of Radical Hermeneutics,* ed. Roy Martinez (Atlantic Highlands, NJ: Humanities Press, 1997), 55.

101. Westphal, "Of Stories and Languages," 232.

102. John Caputo, *Radical Hermeneutics: Deconstruction, Repetition and the Hermeneutical Project* (Bloomington: Indiana University Press, 1987), 43, quoted in Smith, *The Fall of Interpretation* (Downers Grove, IL: InterVarsity, 2000), 172.

103. Smith, *The Fall of Interpretation,* 171.

104. Smith, *The Fall of Interpretation,* 169.

105. James K. A. Smith, "Who's Afraid of Postmodernism? A Response to the 'Biola School,'" in *Christianity and the Postmodern Turn,* ed. Myron B. Penner (Grand Rapids: Brazos, 2005), 218.

106. Smith, *Who's Afraid of Postmodernism?* 50.

Enlightenment's optimism is fueled by a lack of appreciation of the noetic effects of sin, which in turn tends to discredit appeals to a supposedly neutral reason.[107] So, for Westphal and Smith, Husserl is a quintessential modern foundationalist who is arrogant in his pretensions to be able to know reality directly, without any mediating influences, and in particular in his attempt to develop his phenomenology into a rigorous science in which we can attain certainty.

What might be the implications of their views for Scripture? While not certain, it seems it would be hard to find a place for inerrancy, for similar reasons as we have seen above. Yet, Scripture seems to be authoritative for how Christian communities are to live out the gospel story, though I am unclear as to how authoritative it would be for their liturgies. Also, Smith claims the New Testament books themselves are "interpretations of a person and an event," and therefore "we never have 'the Scriptures themselves' . . . in any pure, unadorned sense."[108] This is in keeping with a rejection of scriptural foundationalism. So, directly accessing the meaning of the authors (the Spirit and the human authors) is an impossible task.

Assessing These Postfoundationalist Views

Despite some differences over particulars, there are clear patterns we may synthesize from these postfoundationalists' views. All affirm a real world that exists independently of our thoughts, stories, etc., and reality must include Scripture and God himself. Yet all reject the claim that we ever can achieve immediacy in relation to reality, to know it directly. Their stated reasons for this may be summarized in terms of our finitude and fallenness. As such, all our knowledge is provisional, fallible, and contextual. Unlike God's knowledge, ours never is pristine, blind-to-nothing, or objective, which also is due to our fallenness. And, as Grenz and Franke make explicit, foundationalism tends to be closely aligned with the correspondence theory of truth and metaphysical realism. But if we cannot access reality directly, the correspondence theory of truth becomes rather useless.

Let me summarize some key points about which these postfoundationalists seem quite correct.

First, there is much hubris in modern foundationalism. Searching for utter certainty in foundational beliefs is much too high a standard for knowledge, and it plays right into skeptics' hands.

Second, McLaren and others are right about several operational effects of modernity upon evangelicals. Subtly, some evangelicals are susceptible to

107. Smith, *Who's Afraid of Postmodernism?* 28.

108. Smith, *The Fall of Interpretation,* 53.

a "Christian rationalism" by elevating their reason to the place of authority in understanding and living out Scripture, thereby not really depending upon the Spirit. That implies that Christians would get skilled at living "out of their heads," without really paying attention to their hearts' attitudes and condition.[109] Obviously truth is very important, but it can be used as a weapon if not united with compassion. If in the process we forsake the cries of the hearts of those given to us to shepherd, in effect we send them to look outside the body of Christ for their love. But there Satan's affections will overtake them.[110]

Third, well-meaning evangelicals can be overtaken by evil, even when trying to defend truth. They can elevate their thoughts above God's, thereby becoming arrogant and worshiping their minds. Fourth, these factors can lead to the silencing of God's Spirit.[111] There can be a danger from stressing an intellectual assent to the truth if not coupled with humble hearts before God. In such cases, the heart still would be disconnected from the mind, and the heart from God, so that we are not loving God with all our being (cf. Jer. 17:9).

But *most of all,* it now should be obvious that these mediating factors these postfoundationalists discuss *do* play important roles in shaping us and our understandings of reality, of which modern thinkers simply have not taken much notice. But the conclusion our postfoundationalists reach is that therefore all our access to reality is mediated. *Indeed, this is their central reason why foundationalism of all kinds must be rejected.* Nevertheless, *must* it be one way or the other? *Could it be that we are indeed finite and significantly influenced by the many factors they claim, but we still can access reality directly, that is, accurately, just not pristinely, exhaustively, or neutrally?* This question is *the dividing issue;* its answer largely determines the fate of foundationalism and its rivals.

In what follows, I will return to the work of Husserl as the crucial way to address this issue. If the postfoundationalists are right, then his work, along with foundationalism, can be consigned permanently to the trash pile; but if his work, properly understood, is defensible and cogent, then postfoundationalism and non-foundationalism will be sadly mistaken. And those results will have profound implications for which views we should adopt in justifying our beliefs, including our beliefs in the truth of Scripture.

109. My thanks to Joe Gorra for this suggestion.

110. Of course, many in the body of Christ are deeply wounded by their own sin, but also by others' sin against them. From my readings and conversations, I think many "emergents" feel quite wounded by evangelicals.

111. As one source to look further into this idea, see Dallas Willard, *Hearing God: Developing a Conversational Relationship with God* (Downers Grove, IL: InterVarsity, 1999).

Husserl and a More Modest Foundationalism

As Franke realizes, there also is another form of foundationalism that is currently enjoying wide philosophical acceptance. It is a more modest form, and because of it, foundationalism as a philosophical view is far from dead. It is alive and well, according to leading epistemologists like Laurence BonJour (a former coherentist) and Paul Moser.[112]

Husserl provides perhaps the foremost account of how we can access reality directly, which makes a study of his views indispensable for the prospects of a modest foundationalism. If Westphal and Smith are accurate in their understanding, however, then we should reject Husserl's views. It is *true* that Husserl's later works, which originated after 1901, sought to develop a phenomenology that would be a rigorous science. Interestingly, Smith and Westphal cite from works written after (and sometimes *well* after) this date. Indeed, Smith and Westphal seem quite right to reject Husserl's later pretensions to achieve an exact, rigorous science of knowledge across all disciplines, which we could extend to theology. For instance, Husserl seems exceedingly overconfident when he claims that his philosophy can enable us to reach an "infinitude of knowledge previous to all deduction."[113] He seems audacious when he also claims that those who do not see his phenomenological claims about essences are blinded by their own prejudices, for he is an authority in phenomenology who "has really wandered in the trackless wilds of a new continent and undertaken bits of virgin cultivation."[114]

When Husserl claims that a rigorous body of knowledge entails that it is

112. Moser claims that there cannot be an endless regress, or chain, of beliefs. A set of beliefs must begin somewhere in terms of its justification. This argument "poses a serious challenge to non-foundationalist accounts of the structure of epistemic justification, such as epistemic coherentism. More significantly, foundationalism will then show forth as *one of the most compelling accounts of the structure of knowledge and justification. This explains, at least in part, why foundationalism has been very prominent historically and is still widely held in contemporary epistemology*" (Paul K. Moser, "Foundationalism," in *The Cambridge Dictionary of Philosophy,* 2nd edition, ed. Robert Audi [Cambridge: Cambridge University Press, 1999], 323, emphasis mine).

BonJour reasons that it "is doubtful that there is any very general agreement concerning the deficiencies of foundationalism; indeed, many of those who reject it do not seem to have any very definite argument in mind. Thus, as happens with rather alarming frequency in philosophy, *the movement away from foundationalism in the last three decades or so often looks less like a reasoned dialectical progression than a fashionable stampede*" (Laurence BonJour, "The Dialectic of Foundationalism and Coherentism," in Greco and Sosa, eds., *The Blackwell Guide to Epistemology,* 120; emphasis mine).

113. Edmund Husserl, *Ideas: General Introduction to a Pure Phenomenology,* trans. W. R. Boyce Gibson (London: Allen & Unwin, 1931), 12. This is a translation of *Ideen zu einer reinen Phänomenologie und phänomenologischen Philosophie,* first published in 1913.

114. Husserl, *Ideas: General Introduction to a Pure Phenomenology,* 23.

crystal clear, that all presuppositions are precisely analyzed, and that it has no theoretical doubt, Dallas Willard rightly rejects such hubris on the grounds that these are "demands which no science of *concrete* realities, whether physical or psychical, can possibly meet."[115] As he observes, "the quest for — and the pretensions of — *systematic* certainty, or certainty and rigor *throughout* the range of topics traditionally dealt with by philosophers is greatly at fault."[116]

So Husserl's later views attempted to achieve a modern-inspired philosophy as a rigorous science, but what about his views that originated *by* 1901? What seems to be absent from Westphal's and Smith's discussions is the Husserl who wrote before that time, who laid out his basic project in his *Logical Investigations.* If those views are cogent, then the question will be if they are impugned by his later hubris. I will attempt to sketch Husserl's early views, followed by applications to Westphal, Smith, and our other postfoundationalists' claims.

Husserl's Earlier Views

Husserl's project tries to answer how a mental act (thought, belief, experience, etc.) can reach beyond itself and be "together" (or, enter into a relation) with its intended object.[117] He begins with the metaphysical principle of determinacy, that every existent is a determinate whole — that is, it has specifiable parts and properties, even though we may not be able to know all of them as such.[118] This principle encompasses acts of consciousness just as much as it would physical objects, for they too are existents. Thus, mental acts are wholes with their parts and properties, just as intended objects (trees, persons — including God, concepts, Scripture, etc.) have theirs.

A crucial feature of mental acts is their "directedness" toward, or "selectivity" of, some intended object. Almost all mental acts have this property of *intentionality* (its ofness or aboutness), but of course that property of a mental act does not guarantee that the intended object actually exists in reality. Why? We can hallucinate that we are seeing something that does not really exist, such as Pegasus or the present-day king of France. Or, we can think of possible circumstances, or "states of affairs," that may or may not obtain in reality, such as my thought about where I left my glasses as being on the coffee table (when actually I may have left them on my dresser).

Husserl stresses this distinction between what is intended (e.g., my glasses)

115. Dallas Willard, *Logic and the Objectivity of Knowledge* (Athens: Ohio University Press, 1984), 259.

116. Willard, *Logic and the Objectivity of Knowledge* 270.

117. Of course, this issue relates to all areas of knowledge, including Scripture and God.

118. This will become evident with his treatment of physical objects in particular.

and the phenomenological content that is immanent as a property *of an experience.*[119] This is important because *mere intentional direction of a mental act is indifferent to the ontological status (or, actual existence) of the intended object.* If we have an experience of Pegasus, all that entails is that we are having "a certain presentational experience, which may be dismembered as one chooses" without turning up Pegasus.[120] So that experience of Pegasus is a whole with its parts, but Pegasus itself (the winged horse) is not a *part* thereof. If it were, then a winged horse would be a part of that experience itself.

Ontological Transcendence and Immanence

Here we may see an important distinction Husserl makes between *transcendence* and *immanence* in an *ontological* sense. Consider a cat and a thought about that cat. Ontological transcendence means that the intended object (the cat) with its parts and properties is *not* a part of the thought about that cat. On the other hand, ontological immanence focuses upon the parts and properties of (or, present in) that thought. Applying that distinction, Husserl draws an important conclusion, that the objects

> *are also unable to create differences among presentations*. . . . That a representation refers to a certain object in a certain manner, is not due to its acting on some external, independent object, "directing" itself to it in some literal sense, or doing something to it or with it, as a hand writes with a pen. It is due to nothing that stays outside of the presentation, but to its own inner peculiarity alone . . . a given presentation presents *this object in this manner* in view of its *peculiarly differentiated presentational characteristics.*[121]

Therefore, the mental act's own *intrinsic* parts and properties *alone* determine what its object (whether or not it is real) is and *how* that object is presented for the act.

For instance, suppose I pay attention to my thought about what I ate for breakfast. To be *that* particular thought, it does not seem it *could* be about anything else. Of course, I could think instead about a new car, my weight, etc., but those would be different thoughts, for they would have different intentional contents. Indeed, thoughts (and other mental states) seem to have intrinsic qual-

119. See Edmund Husserl, *Logical Investigations*, vol. 2, trans. J. N. Findlay (London: Routledge & Kegan Paul, 1970), 576-80.

120. Willard, *Logic and the Objectivity of Knowledge*, 220.

121. Husserl, *Logical Investigations*, 603. Subsequent page references from this work are given in parentheses in the text.

ities, such that they are essential to what they are. That is, they seem to have their intentionality *intrinsically.*

But "*the intentional essence does not exhaust the* [mental] *act phenomenologically*" (591). What then are other parts and properties of mental acts that have a bearing upon our verifying if our thought (or other mental act) is together with its intended object? First, there is the *directedness* of a given act upon a specific object (which he calls "matter") (737). So, acts present *this* particular thing, or judge *that* specific action, etc. (586). Mental acts also differ in their "quality," that is, *propositional attitudes* toward the object (e.g., they can be "presentative, judgemental, emotional, desiderative, etc."). Third, mental acts have *representing content* (their "sensa"). These are the same general types as sense-perceptible qualities, such as colors, flavors, smells, sounds, and more, even though Husserl did not limit what exists to what is sense-perceptible.[122] A mental act may remain the same in intentional content (e.g., it is of the coffee cup), yet the *vivacity* of its sensuous contents may increase or diminish; an object that now "appears with greater clearness and definiteness" also can become "lost in a mist," become "paler in colour etc." (591).

Husserl uses this account to draw two ideal types of limiting cases (739). One extreme is the *purely signitive* act, in which the more or less vivid sensum might be utterly different from the intended object. The other extreme is the *purely intuitive* act, in which every property of the intended object matches a sensum that instances that same property. Importantly, Husserl thought that the latter kind of act is impossible with physical objects (866).

We now can sketch Husserl's general schema of mental acts and how they can be together with their intended objects, if they obtain in reality. Mental acts are wholes with parts and properties, as are their intended objects (if they really exist). Determinate wholes can enter into relations, and second, from the general theory of relations, whatever relations obtain depend upon the properties of the relata. Since a thought and its intended object have their respective parts and properties, *the object is indifferent ontologically to the thought* and thus exists "in itself."[123] For a relation to obtain between the mental act and its intended object, the act's intentional property with its nature is "together with" the object's *intensional* properties[124] due to their *natures,* or, alternatively, their "natural affinity" for each other. For instance, it is the nature of my experience of my wife to be together with my wife, due to the properties of each. Or, the nature of my thought of my cat is to be of my cat, and it is together with it due to the intrinsic properties of each. This is how a mental act can "get outside itself" ontologically.

122. Clearly, this must be true since he affirmed the existence of essences.

123. On their differences, see, e.g., Husserl, *Logical Investigations,* 567.

124. By "intensional" properties, I mean the properties that a given "object" must have to be that kind of thing (like, the properties an apple must have to be an apple).

Fulfillment, and Epistemological Transcendence and Immanence

But how can we *know* if a given mental act of ours enters into a relation with its intended object? This brings us to a discussion of Husserl's notion of *fulfillment,* or verification. Through a series of increasingly closer examinations, an object that is thought of or referred to is found to be as it was thought to be. In the *ideal* case, the object's properties are found to match completely those in thought. This is *epistemological immanence;* in contrast, *epistemological transcendence* is when the intended object is not fully given.

Suppose I am walking down a long corridor of a shopping mall, and I see someone at a distance who looks as if she might be my wife. With my old glasses, I cannot see objects at a distance too clearly. But I can continue to move closer in the direction of that person and make more observations. Then I can start to see more clearly some other aspects of that person. For instance, I can see that the color of the person's dress is like the one my wife is wearing today. As I come closer, there can come a point when I can clearly see who it was, and then I can see if the person is my wife or not.

In the example, I had a series of experiences, and each one could help fulfill the subsequent one, such that I could see that a relationship obtained between each experience in the sequence, and each one helped me come *closer epistemically* to the same person. Eventually, I could see that a relationship of fulfillment obtained between my thought of my wife and my wife as she was presented in my experience. How could this be?

First, Husserl maintains that a relationship of fulfillment obtains between *concrete* experiences. The fulfilling experience must be an experience of the same thing, and even known to be that (696). Second, the process of fulfillment involves

> in an intuitive presentation a *varying amount of intuitive fullness. . . .* This talk of varying amount points . . . to possible gradients of fulfilment: proceeding along these, we come to know the object better and better, by way of a presentative content that resembles it ever more and more closely, and grasps it more and more vividly and fully. (745)

In order for one act to fulfill another, "the fulfilling act has a *superiority* which the mere intention lacks: *it imparts to the synthesis the fulness of 'self,' at least leads more directly to the thing itself*" (720).[125]

In the *ideal* case, the object is fully and directly present before us in conscious awareness, and we find that every property of the object present in experience

125. According to Willard's interpretation, Husserl understands this process of verification, and fulfillment itself, "under the term *'intuition,'* which makes the object intended to be 'itself' present" (Willard, *Logic and the Objectivity of Knowledge,* 231, emphasis mine).

matches the corresponding properties of the object as it was thought to be. That is the limit of "intuitiveness." Crucially, however, we must make two qualifications. First, fullness comes about "as the properties of the object intended, whatever they may be, come into intuitive view in the manner appropriate to properties of the type in question."[126] Second, fulfillment admits of degrees, and again this likely will tie closely to the kind of objects and their respective properties under consideration.

Husserl considered mainly three kinds of intentional objects: physical objects in the world; mental acts themselves; and universals. For physical objects, Husserl did not think we could achieve such fullness. Due to the kind of thing these objects are, they do not admit of being fully present in intuition at a single time. Moreover, sense perception is not infallible.

But for mental acts and universals (e.g., the property of intentionality itself; the fulfillment and truth relations themselves; a concept that many people may have in mind at any given time), *in principle* they *can* be presented in syntheses of fulfillment. As Husserl says, *"only the perception of one's actual experiences is indubitable and evident."*[127] *Even so,* though he thought it is possible for mental acts and universals to be fully present before us, that may not happen in actual experience, for they too can be represented inadequately.

Let me reiterate: *Husserl does not contend that in fulfillment we will have exhaustive, pristine, and blind-to-nothing knowledge.* We can be directly acquainted with an object as it is intended, but that does not mean we will know everything about it (or someone). Clearly, *only* God could know that. It seems utterly fallacious to level that charge at his earlier views.

But for all this talk of intuition of universals and essences (the *categorial intuition*), and how an intended object can be directly present before us in conscious awareness in a relationship of fulfillment, could it not be the case after all that the mind has *produced* that objectivity? I do not think so. Minds can produce mental acts, and we can compare experiences of the intended object, to see if a relationship of fulfillment obtains between them. But in a new whole (i.e., consisting of the fulfillment relationship between the intended object and the fulfilling mental act), the object's character as a part of *that* whole is not that of something "added to that thing by an act perceiving it as a part of the whole."[128] *Thus, the mental act directed upon some object does not do something to that object.*[129]

Still, how can a distinction *within* experience guarantee a transcendent *reach* beyond experience? Having a thought with its fulfilling intuition is a mental act; so, its mere existence does not guarantee a reach beyond a "circle" of ideas, ex-

126. Willard, *Logic and the Objectivity of Knowledge,* 229.

127. Husserl, *Logical Investigations,* 866.

128. Willard, *Logic and the Objectivity of Knowledge,* 236.

129. See also Husserl, *Logical Investigations,* 788.

periences, language, etc. Here we come to perhaps one of Husserl's most significant distinctions. *Generally* speaking, there is not a *necessary* connection between mental acts of an object and the object itself. A mental act's mere intentionality will not suffice for this, for we can think about many things without them having to exist. Conversely, the existence of an object does not entail that there would be any thoughts or experiences of it. *Their connection, therefore, is not existential.* Instead, if an act is of the *appropriate kind,* then the objectivity of the object *is* knowable. For instance, to examine an argument's validity we would not smell it, nor would we tune a violin by tasting the strings. Rather, there are constraints of an *essential* kind that determine which acts and objects can come together in a relationship of fulfillment, and wholes can enter into that relationship due to the kind of properties they have. *Thus, the connection between a mental act and its object is one of essences, not existence.*[130]

Husserl in Dialogue with the Postfoundationalists

Now let us see what insights Husserl's early views might afford us into the many claims of Westphal, Smith, and our other postfoundationalists. Then, I will pose some difficulties for their views.

Importantly, there seems to be no reason why Husserl's early views should be impugned by the hubris in his later ones. These are distinct and separable, for the early ones are able to stand on their own, had his later attitudes never even developed. Moreover, his early views show us three crucial things:

1. We can be directly acquainted with and know reality directly, albeit not infallibly, nor from some supposedly neutral standpoint, nor exhaustively.
2. Although there are limitations to different kinds of things we may know, still, in general, we can know things *accurately* as they are insofar as God has revealed them to us, whether that be through creation, Scripture, or his Spirit's speaking and disclosing himself to us now.
3. Therefore, his early views show us why a modest foundationalism is accurate.

130. So, if an object is fully present, "the object is not merely meant, but in the strictest sense *given,* and given as it is meant, and made one with our meaning-reference" (Husserl, *Logical Investigations,* 765). By this Husserl means that the specific act, with its matter and quality, and its intended object enter into a necessary relationship. That is, "given *this* specifically qualified experience indwelt by a certain meaning, the corresponding object must exist, and must be *as* it is thought to be" (Willard, *Logic and the Objectivity of Knowledge,* 202). Moreover, when an act transcendentally "reaches" beyond itself to its object (i.e., enters into the transcending relationship), it has two features that might seem at first glance to be paradoxical. That is, the object is immanent in the sense of being *in* the whole formed by that relationship between act and object. *But the object still retains its own essential qualities apart from that whole; thus it is transcendent to that whole.*

However, perhaps the most frequently stated objection to Husserl is that he mistakenly advocates that we abandon the *natural standpoint,* so that we can achieve a naked, immaculate, even certain gaze directly into reality. But this is *anything but* what he held. The natural standpoint is the belief in the existence of the natural world, and Husserl's philosophy is eminently practical, for his concern is what it is like to be naturally directed upon the world in which we live.[131] He focuses our attention on *concrete* (even mundane) cases and experiences and what is present in consciousness through them. Indeed, much of his attention is on how our mental acts can be together with everyday, *material* objects. Moreover, in the process of coming closer epistemically to some intended object, we would do this in the way appropriate to that kind of thing. So, for material objects, to be able to have a series of fulfilling experiences and find that an object is as it was thought to be requires that I am an embodied person, even to be able to go about this process.

Similarly, if I see some artifact, I would be foolish to ignore my own cultural and historical context. For instance, if I were to see a Coke bottle in the desert, I would be foolish to ignore my American, twentieth-century background, for I am able to see it *as* a Coke bottle because of that, unlike the main Kalahari bushman in *The Gods Must Be Crazy* (1980). So, quite emphatically to the contrary of Westphal and Smith, *to practice his methodology is to embrace, rather than flee from, our embodiment, particularity, and context.*

Moreover, it is *erroneous* to charge Husserl with believing we should expect to have certainty in our beliefs, or in our knowledge of our mind's connection with its objects. We have seen many examples where this simply is not the case, especially so with material objects. It is true that in our knowledge of universals and mental acts themselves, he thought that we *could* be infallible. But, *even in those cases,* we still can misrepresent them.

Finally, let me address the crucial charge that Husserl is wrong that we can have immediate access to things in themselves. Consider Smith's approving use of Caputo, who claims that for Husserl, to intuit the given is to know *how to interpret* what presents itself, failing which there is only the flux. There is an important truth embedded in the first part of this claim, for Husserl held that to experience either fulfillment or disappointment requires *concepts,* as well as experience(s). There is an important, indeed, crucial role for interpretation, to see something that is given *as* some kind of thing (e.g., a Coke bottle). To find something in experience *to be as I have thought it to be* does require concepts.

But the latter claim, that failing to know how to interpret what is given there is only the flux, seems radically mistaken. First, this is not Husserl's own claim. According to him, intended objects present themselves as wholes, although we can focus upon the parts of objects as presented in experience. Second, while we

131. For instance, see his *Ideas,* §§27-30.

may have difficulty or even be unable to identify (or classify) something given as such-and-such (for instance, we may not have any prior experiences of such a thing, like the Bushman with the Coke bottle), what ordinarily is given in experience is not accurately described as a flux. To pick Smith's case, when he looks outside his window and sees the tree that is transcendent to him, it presents itself for interpretation as an empirical transcendental. Neither Smith, myself, nor the Bushman would see a flux of discrete greenish and brownish color patches, unless perhaps we are experiencing a narcotic-induced hallucination.[132] But that is anything but an example of typical experience. So, descriptively, it is a mistake to maintain that apart from interpretation, there is only the flux in experience. Rather, objects present themselves, and they seem to do so as wholes, whether we are experiencing rocks, fish, people, houses, CPU chips, etc.

Of course, this claim is contrary to Derrida's, that beings have presence by naming or predication (which, of course, is done by us in language), yet they always have traces of their other. For him, even "things in themselves" are *signs* that essentially point beyond themselves.[133] His position seems affected by his interpretation of Husserl, that the objects of consciousness are *noemata,* such as appearances and experiences, not things like cats and trees (or essences).[134] But as we have seen, that is not Husserl's position. Moreover, descriptively, Derrida's claim seems mistaken. Suppose I am having an experience of a cat. If I focus upon that experience, I can become aware that it does point beyond itself to the cat, and this seems due precisely to its having intentionality. But if I focus my attention upon the cat, I can readily discover that it does *not* have any such property. As with this case, so it is with the *usual* cases of perception, in which the object of our mental act is *not* a noema, and therefore an epistemic progression can terminate in the thing itself.

Additionally, a series of interpretations has to start with something other than an interpretation, or else we have an infinite regress of interpretations without a way to start. An interpretation is of something, and the descriptions and arguments that Westphal and Smith offer, along with our other postfoundationalists, all want to claim that we are interpreting the external, real world. Moreover, interpretations require concepts, but concepts themselves must be acquired and formed. But how we are able even to start developing concepts on their views begs for an explanation, since, *ex hypothesi,* our access to *all* our intended objects requires interpretation. Frankly, I do not think there will be an

132. Seeing such discrete color patches is more like what we would expect on David Hume's theory.

133. By "sign," I mean something that represents something else.

134. Jacques Derrida, *Writing and Difference,* trans. Alan Bass (Chicago: University of Chicago Press, 1978), 135. "Noemata" (appearances) or "noema" would be (the directedness of) mental acts, such as appearances, experiences, beliefs, etc.

explanation forthcoming, for it seems it must require appeal to access to things in themselves.[135]

Now I will apply this issue to the views of our postfoundationalists. While they do agree with Husserl *that* there can be connections between our mental acts and objects in the real world, nonetheless they part company with him in terms of *how* that can happen. The kinds of relations that can obtain depend upon the properties of acts and their objects. So what kinds of properties would be involved for postfoundationalists so that a relation could obtain between a mental act and its intended object? Evidently, a thought would have its specific intentionality and its quality (some propositional attitude). As far as the intended

135. Still, a likely rebuttal will be that we *clearly* know that all experience is theory-laden, or requires interpretation. Here, let me take up the claim that Heidegger has shown conclusively that all experience has an as-structure. For him, we encounter the world of our everyday activity *as* "involved," or organized already for possibilities for action toward meeting practical purposes and human concerns. For Heidegger, the "world" is a dynamic set of meaning-giving relations and possibilities, and in that context things get their significance, such as being *useful to, needed for, helpful as,* and so on (see Martin Heidegger, *Being and Time,* trans. J. Macquarrie and E. Robinson [Malden, MA: Blackwell, 1962], 189).

By attempting to categorize all particular beings under concepts and thereby tending to ignore individuals' uniquenesses as historically embedded beings-in-a-situation, we tend to conceal important features of our lives as individuals. More fundamental than theorizing or reflection (or an abstract essence), we are beings in everyday contexts, and we always must conduct inquiry from our limited perspectives. We are beings in "thrown" situations, and we do not understand entities fully or immediately, or in their essence, but only in their significance in a situation.

There is much to appreciate about these points. Heidegger is right in that we learn many things by doing. I do not have much, if any, problem with his views about our learning by doing for practical purposes. Even so, Heidegger assumes our thoughts and experiences can be together with their entities (various tools, people, etc.). Yet *how* can he make good on that (valid) assumption? We already have seen how Husserl can do that — by drawing upon universals (such as in intentionality, and the intentional properties of the intended objects, if they obtain) and how they can be before the mind in conscious awareness. But for Heidegger, bringing universals into his account seems off limits, for in a life-world being is temporal and finite, and we have no access to what transcends (metaphysically at least) our life-situation. As I argued above, for Husserl, thoughts are intrinsically about their intended objects, even if these do not obtain. So, why a given thought "selects" its intended object cannot be due to its existence, but rather its essence. For if the connection was existential, then any time I have a thought about something it seems that "thing" must exist. But that is false.

Thus Heidegger does not seem to have a way to account for how his thoughts or experiences could be about all that he discusses. He seems to have no basis for his many thoughts and claims *about* real life, how entities gain their significance by their usefulness to us, and even that all experience already has an "as" structure built into it. Despite his good points about how we find tools as being useful to us in everyday life to achieve certain goals, and how we often learn the significance of a tool by using it, he still seems to lack a basis for making good on his many claims.

object is concerned, while logically it must have properties or else it would not exist, it seems that to specify any of these would require interpretation.

But if so, our question presses again firmly: *Why* would a mental act be together with, or select, its intended object? Following our postfoundationalists' views, it seems the best answer is that the thought of the object can enter into a relationship with the *object-as-interpreted-or-conceived.* After all, no author wants to say that we enter into a relationship with our interpretations per se; instead, we think about (and interpret) the *objects,* which exist in the real world.

Perhaps they might make a Wittgensteinian move and claim that the reason thoughts are together with their objects is due to how the people in a form of life use their language. Generally, however, this move will not work, for the mere existence of a thought with its specific intentionality will not guarantee that its intended object obtains. Likewise, the existence of the object would not guarantee there would be thoughts about it. It is just as we saw above — *connections between mental acts and their intended objects are due to their essences, not their existence.*[136]

But now we have come to a crucial point, one that stems from confusion over the nature of the object when it is intended in a thought. Surely our postfoundationalists would agree that thinking about a material object does not change its being, for we do not have that kind of power, nor do concepts enter into its ontological makeup. The object-as-interpreted *is* a conceptualization, but that act does not change the object itself. On their view, objects-as-interpreted are what they are to us in terms of how we have interpreted them; thus, they seem to be *internally related* to their interpretations, which in turn are tied to language. But Husserl's clarity in distinguishing the properties of mental acts from those of their intended objects shows that they are *externally related* to each other; each one is what it is apart from any whole of act-plus-object, which surely seems right.[137]

Thus, despite their claims that we are interpreting the real world as it presents itself to us, it seems that for our postfoundationalists, when we think, we actually

136. Of course, this point has major implications for another debate among theologians, biblical scholars, and philosophers; i.e., are humans one kind of thing (monism, which usually is explained in terms of physicalism), or two (dualism of body and soul)? For this same reason, if we are but physical things, it does not seem to me that we will be able to know reality. Nancey Murphy has written prolifically on anthropological monism; as one example, see *Bodies and Souls, or Spirited Bodies?* (New York: Cambridge University Press, 2006). Joel Green defends monism in his *Body, Soul, and Human Life: The Nature of Humanity in the Bible* (Grand Rapids: Baker Academic, 2008). For two critiques of these kinds of views, see my "Joel Green's Anthropological Monism: Biblical, Theological, and Philosophical Considerations," *Criswell Theological Review* 7 (2010): 19-36; and my *In Search of Moral Knowledge* (Downers Grove, IL: InterVarsity, 2014), ch. 6, esp. 155-56.

137. If parts are externally related to a whole, then those parts are "the same inside or outside of the whole and thus are indifferent" to the whole. If parts are internally related to a whole, the "parts lose identity when severed from the whole and thus are dependent on" the whole (Moreland, *Philosophical Foundations for a Christian Worldview,* 220).

engage with just our interpretations or conceptualizations, and not objects in reality. Indeed, it seems impossible that we could do otherwise. But if so, they have lost any ability to hold on to knowledge of reality, which would include God and Scripture.

Conclusion: God, Scripture, Our Selves, and Their Places in Epistemology

I have tried to show that only one kind of epistemic theory of justification works with our abilities to access reality directly — a *modest* kind of foundationalism, which rejects certainty, dogmatism, and even our supposed "unsituatedness." On the postfoundationalists' views, we cannot even start to know reality, nor can we truly access it, which must include Scripture, the creation, and God himself. This will undermine a high view of Scripture. Moreover, just like Christians who have been too influenced by modern foundationalism, postfoundationalism leaves us trying to wrest control of our knowledge and interpretation from the Lord, leaving us unable to listen to the Spirit himself.[138]

Despite recognizing our own self-deceptiveness and how we easily tend to elevate our hearts and minds above the Lord, this problem is not unique to modern foundationalism. Such arrogance is an equal-opportunity afflicter, regardless of one's epistemology. Surely there is hubris in Husserl's later writings, just as there can be among those who think they can know reality directly, especially if they teach with an air of invincible certainty in their interpretations. This attitude gives traction to many emergents' critiques of so-called modern Christians.

Now these results should inform significantly a theologically shaped epistemology, which is Franke's concern. Ironically, he denies that the ontological foundations of reality are given to us.[139] But this is true *only* in the sense that we cannot know them exhaustively. Instead, I have tried to show that we can know

138. Where does the postfoundationalist view leave us in terms of knowledge of Christian truth claims, such as that God has revealed himself through creation and special revelation? It seems that the prospects for our knowledge of God's intended meanings are dim indeed, for we could know "truths" only insofar as we have interpreted them. We *cannot* access the meaning the Spirit had in mind in giving revelation, nor what he has in mind today as he leads and guides his church. *Inevitably,* then, on their views we *must* elevate our own interpretations over the Lord's voice, all the while under the cloak of "humility." So Scripture will become a tool that we shape in our hands according to our hearts' desires. Ironically, this is hardly a humble approach, for it requires the same lustful elevation of heart and mind over the Lord that Adam and Eve exhibited in the garden. It is a naked grab for power and control over the epistemic and hermeneutical processes, rather than bowing humbly before the Lord.

139. I take him to mean "given" in the sense of our having direct access to them. Surely they are not given to us in the sense of being "handed over" to us, to control and do with as we like.

reality directly, although not exhaustively or perfectly. But who says we have to in order to know it *accurately*?

For example, when my daughter was quite young, I taught her what an apple is by showing and eating apples (red delicious, gala, etc.), as well as seeing pictures. Over time, from many exposures and noticings, she started to form the concept of an apple, so that she could identify other kinds of apples, even ones I had never seen before. Now, I have a more detailed concept of an apple than she does, for I have more experience, even from my work in the grocery business. But farmers or botanists have still richer concepts of apples. Though I *accommodated* her limited abilities to understand by simple examples and incomplete descriptions, nonetheless it seems she clearly came to know apples *accurately.* Why could it not be the same for God's revealing truth to us? Indeed, if we *cannot* access reality (even Scripture) directly, albeit in ways that are accommodated to our finite minds, we will not know reality; at best, we will know *only* our interpretations or conceptualizations, yet without any way to make good on our claims about reality to ourselves or others.

Or consider the conversion of Saul of Tarsus. As a Pharisee of the Pharisees, he did not have in his interpretive grid the concept of Jesus being the Lord. Yet somehow, when the resurrected Jesus appeared to him, he experienced a radical transformation into one who suddenly believed in him as the Lord. How can we explain this transformation? On the postfoundationalists' views, somehow (1) Saul had to acquire the concept of Jesus as Lord. But, (2) to have this experience, an interpretive grid already had to be in place. But his Pharisaical grid could not have yielded this concept. Still, he suddenly converted; why? It seems to me the best explanation is that Saul saw Jesus for who he truly is, which experience was so overwhelming it totally upset his conceptual framework. Does that mean he experienced Jesus *exhaustively*? Of course not; but he did experience him *accurately,* and that experience, with such powerful self-authentication, shook him and his paradigm to their cores.

Modest foundationalism need not undermine theological epistemology. Just because we are finite and have been shaped profoundly by our contexts, it does not follow that we cannot know reality directly and accurately. Furthermore, self-evident beliefs are *not* undercut by our need to depend upon God for all knowledge of him. They, too, are based upon what God has revealed.

What is crucial, therefore, is the heart attitude we bring to God's revelation. For there we are reaching into the very reality of the living God, whose communication should make us tremble. The fear of the Lord is the beginning of wisdom (Prov. 9:10), and, as with Solomon, wisdom requires having a "hearing heart" (1 Kgs. 3:9), one that listens to and depends upon the Spirit, the divine author of Scripture, especially as we come to read, interpret, and apply Scripture. But, the postfoundationalist or coherentist views necessitate that we cannot access the Spirit's voice or God's word (or its meaning) directly. It is hard to see therefore how one could maintain consistently a high view of Scripture if one also takes these epistemologies consistently. But modest foundationalists can account for how we can know what the Scriptures themselves say and what the authors meant, and thus they can affirm consistently a high view of Scripture. But whether we know and are living in the truth that has been revealed still requires a humble heart and mind before him.[140]

140. Let me also note that I think the way most postfoundationalists treat our situatedness is mistaken. Instead, we should understand it as *attentive influence.* See J. P. Moreland, "Two Areas of Reflection and Dialogue with John Franke," *Philosophia Christi* 8 (2006). Moreland explains that "people fall into ruts and adopt ways of seeing things according to which certain features are noticed and others are neglected" (311). So, "situatedness functions as a set of habit-forming background beliefs and concepts that direct our acts of noticing or failing to notice various features of reality" (311). Our "situatedness" thus affects *how* we attend to reality, but, with effort and sometimes help, we can change how we do that. This may require forming new habits. Otherwise, things like therapy, or even coming to see the extent to which language and culture influence us, would be impossible.

TWENTY-SEVEN

Authority and Truth

Michael C. Rea

Discussions of the authority of Scripture are commonly intertwined with discussions of the truthfulness of Scripture. A casual survey of the literature on biblical authority might well convey the impression that questions about the nature and scope of biblical authority *just are* questions about the nature and scope of biblical truthfulness.[1] In fact, however, these issues are very different — as we can see quite easily by attention to the fact that questions about the nature and scope of parental authority (say) are very different from questions about the nature and scope of parental truthfulness. Taking a low view of a parent's truthfulness might imply taking a low view of her authority in some particular domain. But the precise connection between authority and truthfulness in this case is hardly imme-

1. To see just how the impression might be conveyed, see (for example) Paul Achtemeier, *Inspiration and Authority* (Peabody, MA: Hendrickson, 1999), 148-50; Douglas Moo, ed., *Biblical Authority: Conservative Perspectives* (Grand Rapids: Kregel, 1997); Jack Rogers and Donald McKim, *The Authority and Interpretation of the Bible: An Historical Approach* (San Francisco: Harper & Row, 1979). Both the title of Moo's edited volume and the title of the book by Rogers and McKim convey the impression that each book is primarily about biblical *authority;* and yet the clear focus of each is, instead, the question of biblical truthfulness. In similar vein, Achtemeier moves very quickly within the space of two paragraphs from saying that "the Bible is authoritative . . . because it is true" to saying that "the divine authority of the Bible consists in propositional truth" (149).

This essay has benefited from discussion with my colleagues in this project (June 2010), and in the weekly discussion group of the Center for Philosophy of Religion at the University of Notre Dame in January 2011. For helpful comments I am particularly grateful to Billy Abraham, Alex Arnold, Robert Audi, Jim Beilby, Michael Bergmann, Henri Blocher, Jeff Brower, Don Carson, Graham Cole, Dan Doriani, Paul Draper, Simon Gathercole, Paul Helm, Michael Hickson, Peter Jensen, Matthew Lee, Richard Lints, Phil Long, Tom McCall, Sam Newlands, Ryan Nichols, Christina Brinks Rea, Todd Ryan, Amy Seymour, Jeff Snapper, Kevin Vanhoozer, Jerry Walls, and John Woodbridge. I have also benefited from helpful conversations with and unpublished work by Luke Potter on matters related to the discussion of metaphor in the second part of this essay.

diately obvious. Saying anything helpful about the connection would require us to get clear on what exactly we mean by calling a parent authoritative (no doubt distinguishing, along the way, various different ways in which a parent might be authoritative), what we mean by calling her truthful, and the like. So too, I think, with the relation between biblical authority and biblical truthfulness.

This essay is divided into three parts. In the first part, "Authority," I try to get clear about what we might mean in calling a text authoritative. In the second part, "Truth," I draw distinctions between different things that we might mean by saying that a text is truthful. My goal in both of these parts is to arrive at some general conclusions about *texts,* rather than specific conclusions about the Bible. Consequently, I try to refrain from making assumptions about (e.g.) biblical interpretation or about the truth of particular biblical texts. Indeed, for much of the discussion, the Bible is not even directly in view. In the third part, "Authority and Truth," I draw out some of the implications of the discussions in the first two parts for the question of how textual authority and textual truth are connected to one another. I also comment on the significance of these conclusions for discussions about the relation between biblical authority and biblical inerrancy.

Many people seem to think that if a text is authoritative, then what it says must be true. We shall see, however, that this is not quite correct. To say simply that a text is authoritative is, in fact, to say nothing at all definitive about whether it is, or even could be, true. Nor does it guarantee freedom from falsehoods. There are, however, connections to be drawn between certain kinds of authority and *reliability,* or likelihood of being true. Many also seem to think that if a text is truly authoritative over a person, then she must regard it as *perfectly* reliable, or inerrant. (Thus, for example, one sometimes hears arguments to the effect that if one thinks that the Bible makes mistakes, then one thereby treats human sources of evidence — reason, sense perception, scientific investigation, testimony from others, etc. — as authoritative over the Bible rather than the other way around.) We shall see, however, that there is no clear way to derive the claim that a text is perfectly reliable from the claim that it is authoritative over a person unless we also make substantive philosophical assumptions about the very nature of the text's author. What this means, then, is that a high view of biblical truthfulness — the view that the Bible is perfectly reliable, or close to it — stands or falls not with the claim that the Bible is authoritative (which a text may or may not be, regardless of how truthful it is), but rather with philosophical-theological claims about the nature of God and the divine authorship of Scripture.

Authority

Throughout this essay, as I have indicated, I shall be concerned first and foremost with questions about the authority and truthfulness of *texts.* This, of course, raises the question of what counts as a text. Books, articles, contracts, and written signs are paradigm examples. But where do we draw our boundaries? Are films texts? Photographs? Symphonies? Paintings? Dance performances? Ordinary artifacts or natural objects that signify or can be taken to signify something to somebody? Though I can see the attraction of drawing the lines liberally enough to allow a very wide range of communicative acts and objects to merit the label "text," for purposes here I shall simply follow Kevin Vanhoozer in defining a text as a "communicative action fixed by writing."[2]

We treat a wide variety of texts as authoritative, and we do so in different ways. In *Scrabble®*, the latest edition of the *Official Scrabble® Dictionary* is authoritative with respect to questions about which sequences of letters form admissible words and which do not. In a physics class, the assigned text is generally authoritative with respect to questions about physics. Homer's *Iliad* is authoritative with respect to questions about certain matters of Greek mythology. An uncontested will is authoritative with respect to questions about how a person's assets are to be distributed after her death. The United States Constitution is authoritative with respect to questions about the permissibility of a wide variety of executive, legislative, and judicial acts, election practices, and the like. Reflection on examples like these helps to shed light on what it might mean to say that a text is authoritative.

Note first that it would make little sense to say (e.g.) that the *Iliad,* or Jill's last will and testament, or the *Scrabble® Dictionary* is authoritative, *simpliciter.* Each of these texts has a *domain* within which it is authoritative. One might think that to say that a text is authoritative *simpliciter,* where not even the claim's context specifies a domain, is just to say that the text is authoritative in every domain within which a text might possibly be authoritative. If so, however, then no text — and certainly not the Bible — is authoritative *simpliciter.* For Jill's last will and testament is (we may suppose) the *only* text that is authoritative in the domain of questions about how precisely Jill's possessions are to be distributed after her death, and that text is authoritative in virtually no other domain. In light of this, one initial conclusion we might draw is that no ascription of authority to a text is complete without the specification of the domain within which it has authority. We may also conclude that unqualified ascriptions of authority are charitably interpreted as saying something other than that the text has authority in every domain within which a text might have authority.

Note, second, that there are different kinds of authority. The authority of a physics book is primarily *theoretical:* it is "belief-guiding" rather than action-guiding. The *Official Scrabble® Dictionary* and a last will and testament are partly

2. Kevin Vanhoozer, *Is There Meaning in This Text? The Bible, the Reader, and the Morality of Literary Knowledge* (Grand Rapids: Zondervan, 1998), 229. For a helpful survey of alternative characterizations, see also 103-13.

belief-guiding, but primarily action-guiding, albeit in different ways. Thus, their authority is primarily *practical.* Homer's *Iliad* is theoretically authoritative for us about (among other things) the contours of Greek mythology and ancient legends about the Trojan war. For the ancient Greeks it was theoretically authoritative in a different way: it provided authoritative information about (at least) the personalities and dispositions of the beings who (so it was thought) inhabited Olympus. In other words, for *us* the text is an authoritative source of information about *mythology;* for them, it was (to some degree) an authoritative source of information about *the gods.* It was also practically authoritative, insofar as it helped to define Greek ideals about courage and other virtues, for example.[3] Saying that a text is authoritative, then, is twice incomplete: not only do we need to specify the domain within which the text is authoritative, but we need to specify the kind of authority that the text has.

In the previous paragraph I indicated that there is a distinction to be drawn between practical and theoretical authority. It will be helpful in what follows to understand that distinction a bit more fully. Roughly speaking, practical authorities provide *decisive reasons for action* in the domains over which they are authoritative (tennis matches, state law, morality, etc.); theoretical authorities provide *decisive reasons for belief* in the domains over which they are authoritative (chemistry, mathematics, etc.).[4] *Authorities* are sources of information or directives. An authority might be a *communicator* (e.g., a speaker or institution); it might be *the product of a communicative act* (e.g., a text or a gesture); or it might even be something like a cognitive faculty (e.g., reason, or sensory experience).[5] A *decisive reason for action* is, among other things, a reason to ignore in one's deliberations alternative courses of action.[6] A *decisive reason for believing* a proposition is, among other things, a reason to disbelieve conflicting propositions and

3. Cf. Alasdair MacIntyre, *A Short History of Ethics: A History of Moral Philosophy from the Homeric Age to the Twentieth Century* (Notre Dame: University of Notre Dame Press, 1998), esp. chapters 1-2.

4. Here I follow Mark Murphy, who writes: "if A is a genuine practical authority over B in some domain, then in that domain A's telling B to φ is a decisive reason for B to φ. . . . If A has theoretical authority over B in some domain, then A must be a speaker and B must be one who can believe things for reasons; and if A tells B that it is the case that p, then A's telling B that it is the case that p is a reason for B to believe that p, a reason that is decisive from B's point of view" (Mark Murphy, "Authority," in *The Encyclopedia of Philosophy,* ed. Donald Borchert [Detroit: Macmillan Reference, 2006], 413). Whereas Murphy focuses on the authority of *speakers,* however, we are also, and primarily, concerned with the authority of *texts.*

5. I assume that it's not just metaphor to speak, for example, of "the authority of reason." I also assume that not just any object is a source of information or directives. Experience of a sofa, for example, is a source of information about the sofa; but (in the usual case) a sofa is not itself a source of information.

6. Cf. Murphy, "Authority," 413. On this point, Murphy follows Joseph Raz, *The Authority of Law* (Oxford: Oxford University Press, 1979).

perhaps also a reason to discontinue further investigation into the matter. Note, too, that reasons here are justifiers, not (necessarily) motivators. Having decisive reason to tell the truth, for example, is different from being motivated to tell the truth.[7] Likewise, having decisive reason to believe that you are an inferior chess player is different from being motivated to believe this. (It might seem odd to speak of motivation and stubbornness with respect to belief-formation, but that is only because many of us think of belief-formation as an involuntary matter. I don't want to take a position on that issue here.)

This is, of course, not a full account of the distinction. It tells us only what is necessary for practical and theoretical authority, not what is sufficient. We learn, for example, that *in order* for A to have practical authority over B, then A's directives *must* supply B with decisive reasons for action. But we don't learn anything to the effect that *whenever* a certain range of conditions are satisfied, A has practical authority over B. This much is fine for our purposes, however. We have no need right now for a full analysis of either kind of authority.

Still, we do need to attend to at least one complication. The complication has to do with cases in which authority is *defeated.* For instance: Dad tells Bart to go mow the lawn. Unbeknownst to Dad, Mom has told Bart to clean his room. Both Mom and Dad are authorities for Bart, but, given that mowing and cleaning preclude one another, Bart does not have *decisive* reason to take either course of action. Claire is told by her doctor that a trans-oceanic flight is safe at this stage in her pregnancy; but she is told by another doctor that it is not. Assuming she has no reason to distrust either doctor, both may be theoretical authorities for her with respect to this issue. But she does not have decisive reason for believing that the trans-oceanic flight is safe.

The two examples just mentioned — cases in which we have conflicting authorities — show that it isn't strictly true to say without qualification that authorities provide decisive reasons for belief or action. Problems also arise in cases where there is no overt conflict among authorities. Consider again the case of Claire, and her question about the trans-oceanic flight. Although doctors generally function as authorities for us in matters of health, we know enough about the prevalence of disagreement among doctors to *continue investigation* when we receive answers from our doctors that, for one reason or another, we are tempted to doubt. Thus, if Claire were sufficiently worried about the safety of the flight, reassurance from her doctor might fail to settle the matter for her even in the absence of an explicitly conflicting report from another doctor. Even while granting that her doctor is an authority on this matter, she might reasonably take herself to lack *decisive* reason for believing that it is safe to fly until she has consulted several doctors.

7. Cf. Jean Hampton, *The Authority of Reason* (Cambridge: Cambridge University Press, 1998), 85-92.

To handle these sorts of cases, we must add "no defeater" conditions to our account of the necessary conditions on practical and theoretical authority. Authorities are suppliers of reasons (more on this below), and reasons have the power to confer justification on beliefs or actions. In epistemology, a reason for a belief is said to be *defeated* whenever its power to confer justification is neutralized by some other belief or experience. The neutralizing belief or experience is then called a *defeater* for the reason. The defeater might be a reason to believe contrary to the original belief (i.e., it might be a rebutting defeater). Or it might be a reason to think that one's original set of reasons does not really support the belief, or indicate that it is true (i.e., it might be an undercutting defeater).[8] Similar might be said in the case of reasons for action.

An example will help to illustrate the distinction between rebutting and undercutting defeaters. Suppose Betty believes on the basis of Barney's testimony that Barney is a brilliant neurosurgeon. If she later learns that Barney has a pathological habit of lying about his profession in order to attract women, she will have an undercutting defeater for her reason (Barney's testimony) for believing that he is a neurosurgeon. If, on the other hand, she learns that Barney flunked out of college, has never been to medical school, and spends every day of the week working at the local rock quarry, she will have a rebutting defeater — that is, she will have reason to believe that Barney is *not* a brilliant neurosurgeon.

In the problem cases above, what we seem to encounter are situations wherein *authority* is defeated. Importantly, these are not cases in which an erstwhile authority has simply ceased to be one — as if, say, Claire's doctor was once an authority in the domain of medicine but has now entirely lost whatever authority she once had. Nor does it seem exactly right to say that the *reasons* supplied by the authority are defeated. The fact that Claire's doctor says that it is safe to take the flight is still a serious reason for thinking that it is safe to fly. (So it is not in that respect like the case of poseur-Barney's testimony.) It's just that the doctor's testimony no longer supplies *decisive* reason. In other words: *relative to the present context and the particular issue at hand* the doctor is no longer authoritative. Likewise in the other cases. Putting it just this way, however, suggests wrongly that authority might be an *entirely* situation-relative matter, and it still gives us no clear information about the circumstances under which authority is defeated. It will help, then, to seek a bit of further clarity.

In order to understand the phenomenon of authority-defeat and the circum-

8. For more precise characterizations, see Michael Bergmann, *Justification without Awareness* (Oxford: Oxford University Press, 2006), chapter 6; Alvin Plantinga, *Warranted Christian Belief* (New York: Oxford University Press, 2000), chapter 11; John L. Pollock and Joseph Cruz, *Contemporary Theories of Knowledge* (Lanham, MD: Rowman & Littlefield, 1999), 195-97. Bergmann and Plantinga treat beliefs as the objects of defeat whereas Pollock and Cruz treat reasons as the objects of defeat. As Bergmann explains, however, this is mostly just a terminological difference (Bergmann, *Justification without Awareness*, 159-60).

stances under which it occurs, we need first to understand three other concepts: the concept of one reason being *prior* to another, the concept of someone or something being a *source* or *supplier* of reasons, and the concept of a source of reasons being *more authoritative than* another. I'll take these in order.[9]

Suppose Fred has a reason — self-interested fear of consequences — to lie to his boss, and a different reason — the fact that lying is immoral — to tell the truth. Suppose further that he has no other reasons relevant to the decision whether to lie. One of these reasons *has priority* over the other if, and only if, it is more (practically) rational to act on the basis of one rather than the other.[10] Likewise with reasons for belief: one has priority over another if, and only if, it is more (epistemically) rational to believe on the basis of one rather than on the basis of the other.[11]

A source or supplier of reasons is, intuitively, an individual or a cognitive faculty or a text or some other entity from which we are able to acquire cognitive input that functions for us as a reason for belief or action. But it is a rather tricky matter to identify once and for all the list of things from which we are able to acquire cognitive input on a topic. There is a perfectly good sense, for example, in which God is a source of input on any topic whatsoever. God knows everything, after all; and God can reveal to us anything that can be understood by our finite minds. But there is also a perfectly good sense in which God is not a source of cognitive input on most topics. For example, one can't simply consult God to find

9. I am particularly grateful to Matthew Lee for pressing objections that helped me to see that clarification of these three concepts was necessary in order to understand authority-defeat. I am also grateful to him for helping me to make some of the relevant clarifications.

10. You might be tempted to object that whether it is more rational to act on the basis of reason R1 rather than on the basis of reason R2 depends on the circumstances. But, as I see it, any circumstances that would be relevant to how one should act would simply be additional *reasons.* Suppose, for the sake of argument (and contrary to philosophers like Thomas Aquinas) that there is an exception to the moral prohibition on lying: it is always wrong (and therefore irrational) to lie, except when doing so will protect innocent life, in which case it might be more rational to lie than to tell the truth. If this is true, then whether it is more rational for Fred to lie or tell the truth to his boss depends on whether the consequences of telling the truth will include loss of innocent life. But this doesn't at all show that circumstances make a difference to the question as to whether it is more rational for Fred to act *on the basis of* the reason supplied by morality or the reason supplied by his self-interested fear. Suppose innocent life *will* be lost if Fred tells the truth. In that case (assuming, again, that it might be rational to lie in order to protect innocent life), it might be more rational for Fred to act *in accord with* the reason supplied by his self-interested fear; but there is still no reason to think that it is more rational for him to act *on the basis* of that fear.

11. The distinction between practical and epistemic rationality may be understood as the distinction between what it is rational to *do* given the goal of furthering one's overall best interests and what it is rational to *believe* given the goal of believing in accord with the truth. Cf. Michael Rea, *World without Design* (Oxford: Oxford University Press, 2002), 139-44.

out how one's deceased relatives want their worldly possessions distributed. One can't expect God to adjudicate between theories in fundamental physics. Though God *has* that information, there is absolutely no reason to think that God is willing to distribute it on demand (or even in response to a lot of effort). It is this sense of being a source of reasons — the sense in which God is *not* a source of reasons in every domain — that I have in mind when I talk about sources of reasons in what follows. Roughly (and I don't think we can do much better than "roughly"), a source of reasons is an entity from which it is *physically* possible without miracles or special divine intervention to acquire reasons for belief or action.[12]

We can now say what it is for a source of reasons to be *more authoritative than* another. Authorities are dispute-settlers. They are, in other words, sources of reasons that have priority over reasons that we get from non-authoritative sources. But, of course, the reasons that come from one authority might well trump the reasons that come from another. Schoolteachers have authority over children: they supply reasons for the children to act that trump a lot of other reasons they might have for acting (reasons like *the desire to throw chalk, the belief that it would be amusing to make Billy cry,* etc.). But, dysfunctional cases aside, parents are more authoritative than schoolteachers: the reasons for action supplied by a parent have priority over reasons for action supplied by schoolteachers. For example, other things being equal, the fact that a fifth-grader's schoolteacher has assigned watching *The Matrix* as homework is reason for the fifth-grader to watch that movie. But that reason will be trumped by a parent's general prohibition on watching movies with an "R" rating. Likewise, *Scientific American* provides, in the domain covered by the natural sciences, reasons for belief that trump a lot of other reasons we might have for belief in that domain (reasons coming from untutored empirical intuition, for example, or testimony by non-experts). But the word of a Nobel prize–winning physicist speaking in earnest in her area of expertise trumps whatever conflicting reasons we might get from *Scientific American.* Thus, a bit more formally:

12. Note, too, that being a source or supplier of reasons is — for purposes here — not the same as being a source or supplier of *information about* reasons that one has, as it were, from other sources. A parent might inform her child that it is wrong to lie; but in so doing she is not, in the sense I have in mind, becoming the source or supplier of a reason to tell the truth. When a parent tells her child that it is wrong to lie, she is simply informing the child of the existence of a reason that is available and supplied, as it were, from another source. The reasons of which parents are sources are reasons that we might express with phrases like *because Mom told me not to lie* (a reason for telling the truth) or *because Mom told me that it is wrong to lie* (a reason for *believing* that it is wrong to lie, and so a reason for *believing* that one has, from another source, a reason to tell the truth).

The "More Authoritative Than" Relation

A is more authoritative than B (for a person C, in a domain D) if, and only if, A and B are both sources of reasons for belief or action for C in D, and the reasons supplied by A have priority for C in D over the reasons supplied by B.

We may now return to the notion of authority-defeat. Note first that this whole messy issue arose because we found cases wherein (1) we still want to say that someone — Claire's doctor, for example — is an authority in a domain, but (2) the authority in question has supplied reasons for belief or action that are not decisive in that domain. What ought to be clear by now is that these are cases where, for one reason or another, there are conflicting reasons supplied by other sources that are on a par with or have priority over the reasons supplied by the authoritative individual. But how can this occur, if an authority is, by definition, a supplier of *decisive* reasons?

The most natural response, I think, is to say (as indicated above) that *being an authority* is not an absolute matter: whether something counts as an authority depends a lot on context. This much is easily verified. For example, around my dinner table, I can say truthfully to one of my daughters that my thirteen-year-old son is an authority on how to play the French horn. I can say this truthfully in that context because he is, for us around the family table, *more authoritative* in that domain than any other source to which we have access. But, of course, if I were to go to the members of the music department at Notre Dame and announce that they should take heed, for my son Aaron is an authority on how to play the French horn, I would be saying something false. But in saying that *being an authority* is not an absolute matter, we are in no way committed to the view that all of the facts about authority are situation relative. We can (and should) say that the absolute facts about authority are facts expressed by claims of the form "X is *more authoritative than* Y (for individual S in domain D)." To be *an authority* in some domain, then, is just to be, in that domain, a source of reasons that is (objectively, absolutely) *more authoritative* for some contextually salient group of people than other contextually salient sources of reasons. In the case of Claire's doctor, we can still truthfully say that she is an authority in the domain of medicine because, in context, that boils down to something like the claim that Claire's doctor is more authoritative for non-doctors than sources of evidence that are neither doctors nor medical texts written by doctors, etc. But in the particular context of our example, the authority of Claire's doctor is defeated by the fact that she is *not* more authoritative in the domain of medicine than the other doctors who are giving conflicting opinions.

In light of all of this, we can now identify the following conditions under which authority-defeat occurs:

Authority-Defeat

A's authority (for a person B, in a domain D) is defeated at a time if, and only if (i) there are contexts relative to which it would be true to say that A is an authority for B in D, but (ii) at the time of defeat it is not rational for B to treat some statement or directive from A in D as decisive reason for belief or action.

Condition (ii) is satisfied in cases like our earlier examples involving conflicting directives from parents and conflicting information from medical authorities. It is also satisfied in cases where B acquires evidence independent of conflicts with other authorities for thinking that an erstwhile authority is no longer authoritative. Thus, for example, if B learns that A is morally corrupt in relevant ways, at least some of A's commands will no longer be decisive reasons for action; if B learns that A lacks expertise that B once thought she had, then there will be at least some contexts in which A's say-so is no longer decisive reason for belief; and so on.

Recall that we introduced the concept of authority-defeat because we needed it in order to flesh out our accounts of theoretical and practical authority. Now, we have already said that *being an authority* (and so, likewise, *having authority*) in a domain D is a context-relative matter: it is a matter of being, for some salient group of people, more authoritative than other salient sources. Employing this insight, as well as our understanding of authority-defeat, we can now say more clearly what it is for someone or something to have theoretical or practical authority over an individual in a domain:

Having Theoretical/Practical Authority

Where A is a source of reasons and B is someone who can believe or act on the basis of reasons, A has theoretical authority over B in D only if A's affirming something in D is, in the absence of authority-defeaters, decisive reason for B to believe what A affirms.

Likewise, A has practical authority over B in D only if A's telling B to do something that falls within D is, in the absence of authority-defeaters, decisive reason for B to do that thing.

We have now taken note of two features of authority: first, that it is domain-relative; second, that it comes (broadly speaking) in at least two varieties. Thus, in order to be clear about what we mean in calling a text authoritative, we must both specify a domain and specify the type of authority we have in mind. Before closing, there are two further bits of terminology that I'd like to introduce. First, we should note the distinction between *de facto* and *de jure* authority. Second, it will be helpful to have in what follows a concept of *foundational* authority.

The difference between *de facto* and *de jure* authorities corresponds roughly to the distinction between what we happen to *treat* as sources of decisive reasons and what are *in fact* sources of decisive reasons.[13] (Note that treating something as a source of decisive reasons doesn't necessarily involve *believing* it to be a source of such reasons. Parents are generally treated by small children as sources of decisive reasons even though small children typically lack the belief — by virtue of lacking the relevant concepts — that their parents are sources of such reasons.) Even atheists will agree that, for example, biblical assertions and injunctions are *de facto* authoritative for many people. It is undeniable that many people *treat* the Bible's say-so as decisive reason for belief or action. But there will be real controversy over the question whether biblical assertions and injunctions are *de jure* authoritative. For there is real controversy over the question whether the Bible's say-so provides anyone with *genuinely* decisive reasons for belief or action. Thus far, I have been treating an attribution of "genuine authority" as equivalent to an attribution of de jure authority, and I will continue to do so in what follows. Thus, A's taking a text as authoritative — its being a de facto authority for A — isn't, in my terminology, sufficient for its being genuinely authoritative over A. Accordingly, unless otherwise noted, in the remainder of this essay all talk of authority should be construed as talk of de jure authority.

The notion of *foundational authority* may be characterized as follows:

Foundational Authority

A is foundationally (theoretically/practically) authoritative over B in D if, and only if, A has (theoretical/practical) authority over B in D and there is no source of (epistemic/practical) reasons for B in D that is more authoritative than A.

Given this definition, it should be easy to see that there can be more than one foundational authority for a given person in a given domain. The reason is simply that more than one source can be such that there is no source *more* authoritative than it. Given the characterizations of authority-defeaters above, it should also be clear that foundational authorities can defeat one another. Foundational authorities can also suffer authority-defeat if other evidence comes to light — perhaps

13. To a certain extent, the distinction in view here could also be captured by the terms "subjective" and "objective" (replacing "*de facto*" and "*de jure*" respectively). But there are problems with these terms as well. For example, it seems rather odd to say that a text might be subjectively, but not objectively, authoritative for a nation, or for all of humanity at a time, whereas it sounds less odd to say that the same text is *de facto* authoritative but not *de jure* authoritative for a nation, or for all of humanity at a time.

even from less authoritative sources — that they are no longer to be treated as suppliers of decisive reasons for belief or action.[14]

So, it would seem that a very rough-and-ready answer to the question "What does it mean to call a text authoritative?" is something like this: To call a text (genuinely, *de jure*) authoritative is to say that, within some domain and for some individual or individuals, the text supplies reasons for belief or action (or both) that are, absent defeaters, decisive. Again, it doesn't follow from this that the supplied reasons *motivate* the relevant beliefs or actions. Nor does it even follow that the individual or group in question will recognize them as decisive. (*De jure* authorities might fail to be *de facto* authorities — as often happens, we might think, when people casually and habitually act contrary to state laws or common moral intuitions.) But they will, nonetheless, decisively justify the relevant beliefs or actions.

This characterization of *textual* authority comports well with a variety of formal, informal, and partial characterizations of *biblical* authority that one finds in the literature. Thus, for example, in discussing Jesus' view of the authority of the Old Testament, Edward J. Young writes:

> [Jesus] believed that both as a unit and in its several parts [the Old Testament] was finally and absolutely authoritative. To it appeal might be made as to the ultimate authority. Its voice was final. When the Scriptures spoke, man must obey.[15]

Here the idea seems to be that Scripture is a de jure foundational supplier of decisive reasons for action. Robert Gnuse takes a similar view, quoting with approval Robert Bryant:

> The basic definition of authority is to speak of that "which is acknowledged as rightly and worthily commanding loyalty and obedience."[16]

14. In the domain of theoretical authority, what I have elsewhere called basic sources of evidence will be in some ways akin to foundational authorities. (Cf. Rea, *World without Design,* 2.) To treat something as a basic source of evidence is to trust it as reliable even in the absence of evidence for its reliability. Our basic sources of evidence are *de facto* authorities for us and, in the typical case, they are treated as foundational (in the sense just described) as well. Of course, since we can treat hopelessly unreliable sources as basic, something's being a basic source of evidence for us doesn't guarantee that it is a genuine authority, much less a foundational authority. Still, treating something as a basic source of evidence will typically (though not necessarily) go hand in hand with believing it to be a foundational authority in some relatively wide domain.

15. Edward J. Young, "The Authority of the Old Testament," in *The Infallible Word: A Symposium by the Members of the Faculty of Westminster Theological Seminary,* ed. N. B. Stonehouse and Paul Wooley (Philadelphia: P&R, 1967), 59.

16. Robert Gnuse, *The Authority of the Bible: Theories of Inspiration, Revelation, and the*

Young, Bryant, and Gnuse are clearly (in these passages, anyway) focused on the practical authority of Scripture. But the literature is also replete with characterizations of Scripture as having what we are here calling theoretical authority. Thus, for example, Clark Pinnock assimilates the notion of scriptural authority to the notion of "primary evidence."[17] Similarly, John Woodbridge, in his own contribution to this collection, notes that one meaning for the Latin word *auctoritas* (from which our term "authority" is derived) is "the things which serve for the verification or establishing of a fact."[18] The clear suggestion in the text following this remark is that this meaning is part of what we invoke when we call Scripture authoritative.

On the other hand, there are other characterizations of biblical authority with which my own is inconsistent — such as, for example, characterizations according to which authority is equivalent to canonicity.[19] Being canonical, after all, has much less to do with being a de jure supplier of decisive reasons for belief and action and a lot more to do with being *regarded* by the church as being divinely inspired or as containing a record of divine revelation.

It should also now be clear that the bare claim that the Bible is authoritative does not tell us very much. We can also see that many of the questions about biblical authority that have vexed theologians over the centuries (but perhaps especially in the past two centuries) are more perspicuously characterized as, or at least dependent on, questions about the *domain* over which the Bible exercises authority (history? science? just "faith and practice"? or what?) and about the *type* of authority (*de jure, de facto,* foundational, non-foundational, theoretical, practical, etc.) that the Bible exercises. Does one challenge biblical authority if one thinks that one can use reason or science to discover factual errors in the biblical text? Does one challenge biblical authority if one tries to demythologize the Bible? Does one challenge biblical authority if one thinks that the Bible reflects an outmoded system of moral values that aren't binding on enlightened contemporary thinkers? In each case, the answer depends on what one takes the domain of biblical authority to be, and on whether one thinks that the Bible has practical authority, theoretical authority, or both.

We turn now to a discussion of what it means to say that a text is truthful, after which we draw some conclusions about the relations between authority and truth.

Canon of Scripture (New York: Paulist, 1985), 2, quoting Robert Bryant, *The Bible's Authority Today* (Minneapolis: Augsburg, 1968), 156.

17. Clark Pinnock, *The Scripture Principle: Reclaiming the Full Authority of the Bible,* 2nd edition (Grand Rapids: Baker Academic, 2006), 95.

18. John Woodbridge, "German Pietism and Scriptural Authority: The Question of Biblical Inerrancy," chapter 5 in the present volume.

19. See, e.g., N. B. Stonehouse, "The Authority of the New Testament," in Stonehouse and Wooley, *The Infallible Word,* 92-93.

Truth

Philosophers have worried quite a bit over the question of what it means to say that a sentence, or a belief, or a proposition is true. Our question here is far more complicated: we are asking what it means to say that a *text* is true — any text, including texts that go on for hundreds of pages, texts that consist of nothing more than pictures, texts that include literary tropes like metaphor and hyperbole, and so on. We cannot hope to do this question (or even the simpler first one) real justice here. But we can, I think, hope to say enough about truth to draw some interesting conclusions about the relationship between authority and truth.

Let me begin by saying a few words about the nature of truth. In the philosophical literature, the major theories about the nature of truth are primarily theories about what it is for a sentence, belief, or proposition to be true. They are not theories about truth in pictures, truth in metaphor, truth in literature, or anything of the sort. For this reason, an extended foray into the overgrown jungle of theories about truth is unlikely to be productive for present purposes. Those theories are simply too narrow; they will not help us (much) with questions about what it means to say that a metaphor, or a parable, or a psalm, or an epistle is true. Still, it will be helpful to be aware of two of the main divisions within that literature.

The first is that between *realist* and *anti-realist* conceptions of truth. To understand this division, and its import, we must first say what we mean by "realism." Realism has been characterized in many different ways. For purposes here, I'll adopt the following characterizations:[20]

Realism
Where "x" is a singular term, realism about x is the view that some particular thing is identical to x. Where "F" is the name of a kind (e.g., "unicorn"), property (e.g., "moral wrongness"), or relation (e.g., "causation"), realism about F (or about Fs) is the view that the following conditions hold: (i) Something is (an) F or stands in the F-relation to something else. (ii) If some particular thing is an F or

20. This formulation differs from the one I offered in "Realism in Theology and Metaphysics," in *Belief and Metaphysics*, ed. Conor Cunningham and Peter Candler (London: SCM, 2007), 324, by replacing some of the talk about *dependence* with talk about *partial constitution*. I take the present formulation to be a precisification of the earlier one, not a substantial alteration of it. Being an F is *partly constituted* by facts F1–Fn if, and only if, part of what it is to be F is for F1–Fn to obtain. So, for example, *x*'s being Fred's favorite food is at least partly constituted by facts about Fred's attitudes toward different foods, including *x*: i.e., at least part of *what it is for something to be Fred's favorite food* is for Fred to have a certain pro-attitude toward that thing and to have no equally strong pro-attitude toward any other food.

> stands in the F-relation to some other things, that fact does not depend upon the experiences that other creatures might have of those things, nor does it depend upon what other creatures think about them or about the conditions under which being an F or standing in the F-relation is exemplified.

Given these characterizations, one way to be an anti-realist about God (say) is to affirm that there is no such being as God; but another way is to say, for example, that "God exists" expresses a truth but that the truth it expresses *isn't* that there is something identical to God, but rather (say) the claim or "conviction that free and loving persons-in-community have a substantial metaphysical foundation, that there are cosmic forces working toward this sort of humanization."[21] Likewise, one way to be an anti-realist about statues is to say that there are none; but another way is to say that nothing counts as a statue unless it is believed to be one by creaturely observers. One way to be an anti-realist about beliefs, or about minds, is to believe that whether a person has a belief or a mind depends in some way upon how individuals other than that person think about or experience her. And so on.

Accordingly, anti-realism about *truth* will be the thesis that (i) nothing is true or (ii) something's being true depends in some way upon people's beliefs about the conditions under which something is true, or (iii) something's being true is at least partly constituted by facts about actual or hypothetical creaturely mental states.[22] For example, the view that p is true if, and only if, p is uncontroversial would count as a particularly radical version of anti-realism about truth. So too would the view that p is true if, and only if, p *would be* uncontroversial in a community of ideal rational agents.

It is sometimes thought that anti-realism about truth goes hand-in-hand with some sort of metaphysical anti-realism. But this is not correct. Metaphysical anti-realism is likewise characterized in many different ways. Sometimes it is treated as a view about the aims of metaphysics (roughly: metaphysical theories aren't aimed at truth). Sometimes it is treated as a view about commonsense and scientific kinds (roughly: anti-realism about all or most commonsense and scientific kinds is true). Sometimes it is treated as equivalent to the thesis that metaphysical theories aren't *objectively* true. And so on. We can capture the most important kinds of metaphysical anti-realism, I think, by saying that metaphysical anti-

21. Gordon Kaufmann, *The Theological Imagination: Constructing the Concept of God* (Philadelphia: Westminster, 1981), 49; quoted in Plantinga, *Warranted Christian Belief*, 41.

22. We might note that beliefs count as true and they *are* mental states, but it doesn't follow that their being true *depends* on mental states in the relevant sense. To say that the truth of my belief that p is "mind dependent" in the relevant sense is to say either that its being true depends on what other people think about the conditions under which a belief is true, or that the fact that my belief is true is partly constituted by facts about other people's mental states.

realism is the thesis that theories in metaphysics are not to be "interpreted realistically," where interpreting a theory realistically is to be understood as follows:

Interpreting a Theory Realistically

> To interpret a theory realistically is (a) to take it as having an objective truth-value (i.e., to take it as something other than a mere evocative metaphor or expression of tastes, attitudes, or values), and (b) to interpret it as being true only if realism about the objects and properties (supposedly) referred to in the theory is true.[23]

To be sure, some ways of being an anti-realist about truth will imply metaphysical anti-realism. For example, the view that nothing is true (because, e.g., the whole concept of truth is defective) counts as a version of anti-realism about truth, and it straightforwardly implies that no theory in metaphysics or any other discipline is to be interpreted realistically. But anti-realism about truth is also separable from metaphysical anti-realism. Suppose, for example, you think that p is true if and only if p is what would be believed by rational inquirers at the end of an ideal process of inquiry. This view implies anti-realism about truth. But one can hold this view while at the same time holding (for example) that God is the only rational inquirer capable of engaging in an ideal process of inquiry, that God believes that there are objective truths in metaphysics, and that God is also a realist about various commonsense and scientific kinds (e.g., the kinds "person" and "human being"). Thus, even though the view in question implies anti-realism about truth, it does *not* imply that truth in metaphysics is always subjective, or that no theory in metaphysics is to be interpreted realistically, or that anti-realism about commonsense and scientific kinds is true.[24] So it doesn't imply metaphysical anti-realism.

What goes for the relation between realism about truth and metaphysical realism goes also for the relation between realism about truth and theological realism. Theological realism is, in effect, a species of metaphysical realism: it is the thesis that theories in theology (or in some particular domain of theology — for example, Christian theology, or distinctively Presbyterian theology) are to be realistically interpreted (in the sense described above). And just as one might endorse anti-realism about truth without endorsing metaphysical anti-realism, so too one might endorse anti-realism about truth without endorsing theological anti-realism.

As noted above, the division between realism and anti-realism about truth is just the first of the divisions to which we must attend. The second is that be-

23. Cf. Rea, "Realism in Theology and Metaphysics," 324.

24. On this, cf. William Alston, *A Realist Conception of Truth* (Ithaca, NY: Cornell University Press, 1996); Michael Devitt, *Realism and Truth,* 2nd edition (Oxford: Basil Blackwell, 1991).

tween epistemic and non-epistemic conceptions of truth. Epistemic conceptions of truth maintain that there is a necessary connection between what is true and what would be believed under certain specified conditions by a certain kind of rational agent or agents. Epistemic conceptions of truth abound in the literature. To take just a few examples: C. S. Peirce says that "[t]he opinion which is fated to be ultimately agreed to by all who investigate, is what we mean by the truth";[25] William James claims that "[t]rue ideas are those that we can validate, corroborate, and verify";[26] and Brand Blanshard holds that "truth *consists* in coherence [of our ideas]."[27] Non-epistemic conceptions of truth, on the other hand, maintain that there is no necessary connection between truth and what would be believed by rational creatures.

The main import of this second division within the literature on truth for our purposes is just this: Whatever other links there are between authority and truth, epistemic conceptions of truth introduce additional and very direct connections. For example, undefeated theoretical authorities validate, corroborate, and verify our ideas, and, by definition, their assertions cohere with the assertions of all authorities to which they are not prior. Thus, it looks as if on the theories offered by James and Blanshard, undefeated authoritative assertions are automatically true.

Be that as it may, I propose to set aside consideration of epistemic accounts of truth in what follows. This is not because they are unworthy of attention, but rather because I have elsewhere already given them the attention that I think they deserve. Elsewhere, I have argued — developing a line of reasoning found in the work of Alvin Plantinga[28] — that epistemic accounts of truth imply something very much like theism.[29] Naturally, I am a fan of the implied consequence; but it is hard to take seriously a theory of *truth* that is so heavy-laden with ontological commitments. Better, I think, to look elsewhere for a theory of truth. Once we do so, however, we find that differences among theories of truth do not make for substantive differences in what we say about the relationship between authority and truth. And so we save ourselves the trouble of proceeding piecemeal, asking with respect to each theory of truth what the relationship between authority and truth is *if that theory is true.*

The third and final division to which I want to attend lies within the realist camp: the division between correspondence theories of truth and all the rest. The main thing that I want to note about this division is simply that it *exists:*

25. C. S. Peirce, "How to Make Our Ideas Clear," in *The Essential Peirce,* ed. N. Houser and C. Kloesel (Bloomington: Indiana University Press, 1878), 139.

26. William James, "Pragmatism's Conception of Truth," *Journal of Philosophy and Scientific Methods* 4 (1907): 142.

27. Brand Blanshard, *The Nature of Thought* (New York: Macmillan, 1940), 269.

28. Alvin Plantinga, "How to Be an Anti-Realist," *Proceedings and Addresses of the American Philosophical Association* (1982).

29. Michael Rea, "Theism and Epistemic Truth-Equivalences," *Noûs* 34 (2000): 291-301.

that is, some realist theories are correspondence theories, but not all of them are. It is sometimes thought that realism about truth goes hand-in-hand with a correspondence theory of truth. But this is a mistake. The confusion is especially important in the present context because it seems to be one to which Christian theologians, and especially evangelicals, are particularly prone. One often finds theologians taking a stand for the correspondence theory of truth, apparently in part because of the misguided belief that one *must* do so in order to preserve the (absolute) truth of core doctrines of the Christian faith. The basic idea seems to be that giving up the correspondence theory means giving up realism about truth which, in turn, means giving up realism in theology. We have already seen that the second link in this chain of reasoning is weak; but it is important to see that the first is as well.

The correspondence theory of truth comes in different varieties, all of which maintain that being true consists in the obtaining of a relation — the correspondence relation, whatever exactly that is — between truth-bearers (propositions, beliefs, or sentences usually) and something in the world (states of affairs, or facts, for example). But one need not believe in the existence of any sort of correspondence relation, nor need one even believe that truth has a substantive, analyzable nature, in order to be a realist about truth. A coherence theory of truth, for example, maintains (roughly) that being true is a matter of cohering with certain other beliefs or propositions. But it does not follow from this doctrine that being true is "mind dependent" in the sense specified by condition (ii) of the schematic characterization of "realism about F."[30] Similarly, William Alston has defended at length the thesis that realism about truth is consistent with minimalism about truth — the thesis, roughly, that there is nothing more to be said about the nature of truth beyond the so-called T-schema ("X is true if, and only if, *p*," where particular instances are obtained by replacing *"p"* with a declarative sentence and "X" with an expression referring to that sentence).[31] So, again, realism about truth does not require the correspondence theory.

So much for remarks about the nature of truth. I now turn to a more direct consideration of the main question of this section — the question of what it means to attribute truth (or falsity, for that matter) to a *text*. First some easy cases. If the text in question expresses a single proposition, then the text is true if and only if the proposition it expresses is true. If, on the other hand, the text is a sentence like "Stop!" or "Enter at your own risk," then attributing truth to the text is just a category error. But, of course, we are not here interested in the easy cases. What interests us here ultimately is the Bible — a text composed of smaller book-length works of various genres, which includes within it sentences of various grammat-

30. Though, of course, there are anti-realist ways of developing the coherence theory.

31. For discussion of the T-schema and its relation to Tarski's "Form T," see Alston, *A Realist Conception of Truth*, 30ff.

ical types, as well as various literary tropes like metaphor, allegory, hyperbole, and the like. What could it mean to say that a text like *that* is true?

Suppose someone were to tell you that Tolkien's *Lord of the Rings* is true — not that there are hobbits and elves and a place called Mordor, of course, but that, despite the non-existence of these sorts of things and despite the fact that the events narrated therein never took place, the text is nonetheless *true.* Or suppose someone were to hand you a book of sonnets and poetic lamentations, and suppose they were to tell you that the poems were true. Could anyone make sense of these claims?

What I want to suggest is that we can make sense of claims like this in much the same way in which we make sense of similar claims about interesting metaphors. The philosophical literature on metaphor is vast and complicated, but we don't need a full-blown theory of metaphor in order to appreciate roughly what it might mean to call a metaphor "true." Attention to two main points of agreement in the literature ought to suffice for present purposes.

Note first that there is a distinction to be drawn between the *semantic content* of a text and what the *speaker or author* means by the text (or, in other words, what the text "pragmatically conveys"). I don't have a theory about the relationship between semantics, pragmatics, and "what is said" by a text,[32] but we don't need any such theory in order to appreciate the basic point that what authors of metaphors typically mean by their words is something other than the bare semantic content of the metaphor. There is controversy in the literature over whether live metaphors typically (or ever) mean anything *determinate.* That is, there is controversy over whether what is conveyed by a metaphor is a definite proposition, or whether metaphors merely invite or stimulate certain kinds of reflection.[33] But there is general agreement that *if* metaphors convey anything determinate, what they convey goes beyond their semantic content.[34]

Accordingly (and this is our second point), so-called "metaphorical truth,"

32. For a start into this literature, with particular attention to metaphor, see Elisabeth Camp, "Contextualism, Metaphor, and What Is Said," *Mind and Language* 21 (2006): 280-309.

33. For example, compare, on the one hand, Donald Davidson, "What Metaphors Mean," in *On Metaphor,* ed. Sheldon Sacks (Chicago: University of Chicago Press, 1979), 29-46, and David Cooper, *Metaphor* (Oxford: Oxford University Press, 1986), with, on the other hand, Max Black, "Metaphor," *Proceedings of the Aristotelian Society* 55 (1954/55): 273-94; Black, "More about Metaphor," *Dialectica* 31 (1977): 431-57; Janet Martin Soskice, *Metaphor and Religious Language* (Oxford: Oxford University Press, 1985); and, more recently, Josef Stern, *Metaphor in Context* (Cambridge, MA: MIT Press, 2000); Stern, "Metaphor, Literal, Literalism," *Mind and Language* 21 (2006): 243-79; Elisabeth Camp, "Critical Study of Josef Stern's *Metaphor in Context,*" *Noûs* 39 (2005): 715-31; Camp, "Contextualism, Metaphor, and What Is Said"; and Camp, "Metaphor and That Certain 'Je Ne Sais Quoi,'" *Philosophical Studies* 129 (2006): 1-25.

34. See, e.g., Camp, "Contextualism, Metaphor, and What Is Said," 280-309, and "Metaphor and That Certain 'Je Ne Sais Quoi,'" 1-25; Stern, *Metaphor in Context.*

whatever it is, will attach to what is intentionally conveyed rather than to the semantic content. This, of course, is why metaphors that are semantically false — for example, "Juliet is the sun" — can nevertheless be assessed as true. If the author of a metaphor intentionally conveys propositional content by way of the metaphor, then the metaphor (as such) will be true if, and only if, the relevant proposition is true. On the other hand, if the author of the metaphor fails to convey propositional content (perhaps because metaphors as such generally lack such content), then either the author fails to convey any "metaphorical truth" or the metaphor's "truth" consists in its being insightful or revealing or otherwise interestingly illuminating by virtue of the sorts of reflections it stimulates.[35]

Return, now, to the cases we began with — cases wherein someone tells you, for example, that *The Lord of the Rings* is true, or that a book of poetry is true. It seems that we can understand these sorts of truth claims in roughly the way just described. Either we attribute to the speaker — the one who is telling us that the text is true — the view that the text intentionally *conveys a message* that is somehow different from the semantic content of the text, and that the message in question is genuinely true; or we attribute to the speaker the view that the metaphor intentionally invites lines of reflection that naturally lead to genuine insights, fruitful lines of research, and so on. If we buy into the view that the text conveys a true message, we employ our skills at literary analysis to try to extract the message and then to assess it as true or false. If we think that the text merely invites lines of reflection that lead to genuine insights, then we pursue the relevant lines of reflection.

This, then, is one way in which attributions of truth to a text require clarification. For all but the simple texts, however, there is a further way in which such attributions must be clarified. Consider, for starters, Benjamin Franklin's poem "Death Is a Fisherman":

> Death is a fisherman, the world we see
> His fish-pond is, and we the fishes be;
> His net some general sickness; howe'er he
> Is not so kind as other fishers be;
> For if they take one of the smaller fry,
> They throw him in again, he shall not die:
> But death is sure to kill all he can get,
> And all is fish with him that comes to net.

Someone might well attribute truth to this poem; and, indeed, one might well suppose that the poem conveys propositional truth (as opposed to *merely* stimulating interesting lines of reflection). But note that one can do so while dis-

35. On this, see David Cooper, *Metaphor* (Oxford: Oxford University Press, 1986), chapter 4.

agreeing with central features of the allegory. So, for example, it seems that the following represents one perfectly sensible, though hardly inevitable, response to the poem:

> The poem is quite true — Death is merciless and takes all who fall into his net; and Death seems like a fisherman in other respects as well (Death is predatory and so on). But it just doesn't seem right to say that "some general sickness" is his net. Death catches us in many ways.

Does the remark that "it doesn't seem right to say that 'some general sickness' is his net" negate the remark at the beginning of the speech — namely, that the poem is "quite true"? No. For, clearly enough, an attribution of truth to a text *need not mean that every single message conveyed by the text or by some part of the text is true.*

In fact, I suspect that it is relatively rare for attributions of truth to a complex text to mean anything more than that the central, or most important message conveyed by the text is true. (Obviously for a long or complex text, the central or most important message may be a longish conjunction of smaller messages.)[36] Suppose you read an intellectual biography of Sartre that devotes hundreds of pages to a description of his upbringing, early intellectual development, and philosophical career but, as regards his romantic life, offers only one sentence: "Sartre enjoyed a lifelong romance with Simone de Beauvoir, to whom he was ever faithful." Given that Sartre was notorious for his many mistresses, we would be reluctant to say of a biography like this that it is true, even if it were absolutely inerrant with respect to all of the other details of Sartre's life. The reason is that it gets wrong a fact that many of us will regard as pretty important. On the other hand, we probably would assess it as true if it were accurate on this and other salient details but included mistakes on such matters as the number of students attending some famous lecture of Sartre's, the precise date on which Sartre first met Camus, or the number of pages in the first edition of *Being and Nothingness* (so long as it was not mistaken by much). If asked how we could possibly say that *the text as a whole* is true when it contains manifest falsehoods, our reply would likely just be that the falsehoods simply aren't central — that is, they are not part of "the most important message" of the text. Moreover, it seems clear that *which* details count as part of the central message of a text (and so which details the text

36. In some cases it will be a bit of a stretch to speak of "the central message," even if we insist that we are thinking of it as a long conjunction of smaller such messages. You might, for example, say of a newspaper that it tells the truth. But it sounds odd to say that the paper has a central message — even one that is just the conjunction of the central messages of all of the stories. Point taken (and I thank Paul Draper for raising the point); but, despite the oddity, I am inclined to think that if one were to assert of a newspaper that it is true, or tells the truth, what one would probably mean is just that the "central message" (in the "longish conjunction" sense of the term) is true.

must get right in order to count as true) may shift from context to context. A time traveler who took Newton's *Principia* back to Egypt of 3,000 B.C.E. would not be lying if she said that everything in the *Principia* is true. But she would be lying (or confused) if she brought the text into a twenty-first-century graduate-level physics course and announced that everything in the text is true. The reason is that the ways in which the *Principia* goes wrong are not salient in a context where Newton's work is being introduced to Egyptians of the fourth millennium B.C.E., but they are highly salient in a twenty-first-century graduate-level physics course.

We may now formulate a recipe for assessing attributions of truth to biblical texts or to the Bible as a whole. For any such attribution, we must determine whether the claim is (1) that the (central, or most important) semantic content of the text is true, (2) that the text intentionally conveys a genuinely true message that is both the central or most important message conveyed by the text and also somehow differs from or goes beyond its semantic content, (3) that the text invites reflection that will naturally lead to genuine insight, or (4) some combination of these three. We must then employ our skills at literary analysis to uncover the central or most important message (which, again, will likely be a conjunction of smaller central and important messages), pursue the relevant lines of reflection, and so on. This means, of course, that there is real complexity involved in evaluating attributions of truth to texts — so much so that it is not clear that one says anything deeply informative when one says of a long and complicated text simply that it is true. Before we can even begin to evaluate such a claim, we need a lot more information — information about what is central to the text, about the proper interpretation of the literary tropes within the text, information about genre and much more. But I think that, rather than be troubled by such a conclusion, we ought to welcome and embrace it. No one is helped in their understanding or assessment of the Bible to be told, without further clarification, that the Bible, as a whole, is true. The really crucial questions, it seems, are questions about the parts.

Authority and Truth

We are now in a position to draw some conclusions about the relationship between attributions of authority and attributions of truth. First, it should be clear from the foregoing that to say without qualification that a text is authoritative is to say nothing definitive about whether it is true. The reason is that the text might be merely practically authoritative, and a merely practically authoritative text need not semantically express or pragmatically convey any propositional message. It need not even stimulate insightful lines of reflection. It might merely issue directives. (The Ten Commandments, for example, cannot sensibly be said to be true in any sense that we are interested in here.)

This is not to say, however, that truth is entirely irrelevant to practical authority. For example, it would be hard to take seriously a text's claim even to practical authority in the domain of morality if the text in question were filled with supposedly factual assertions to the effect that members of a particular race or gender are morally worthless, or if it went on for pages extolling the health benefits of cannibalism, or if it contained enough other misguided assertions as to lead one seriously to doubt the wisdom or sanity of its author. On the other hand, a text might have a great deal of merely practical authority and still be mistaken about a wide variety of facts, so long as its being so mistaken is consistent with the view that its author possesses sufficient wisdom and knowledge within the relevant domain to merit obedience. The point, then, is just that practical authority on its own is no guarantee of general truthfulness, both because it is possible that a merely practical authority makes no factual assertions, but also because it is possible that the factual assertions such an authority does make are entirely irrelevant to its status as a practical authority.

Second, it should also be clear that if a text has *theoretical authority* over an individual in some domain, then the text's assertions within that domain must be *reliable enough* to warrant belief in the absence of defeaters. (For purposes here, "what the text says" is just the conjunction of whatever it semantically asserts with whatever its author intentionally conveys;[37] and "reliability" is to be understood in terms of likelihood of truth.[38]) How reliable is "reliable enough"? That is hard to

37. Note too that what a text semantically *asserts* is not necessarily the same as what it semantically *expresses.* The proposition that Juliet is the sun, for example, is identical to the proposition that Juliet is the gaseous object around which Earth, Mars, Venus, and various other planets are in orbit. Romeo's metaphorical remark that Juliet is the sun semantically expresses this proposition — i.e., the proposition is its semantic content. But, obviously, his remark does not *assert* that proposition; it asserts a different proposition, which is pragmatically conveyed by the words, in context, "Juliet is the sun."

38. At the conference connected with this volume, it was pointed out that some have argued that "the biblical concept of truth" is very close to the concept of reliability. Supposedly, then, according to "the biblical concept," saying that something is true is roughly equivalent to saying that it is trustworthy, able to be relied upon, etc. If this view about truth is correct, then here we have a very close connection indeed between a kind of authority and truth *simpliciter;* and if it is indeed *the biblical concept,* then this might mean that Christians have good reason to endorse it. However, I am not persuaded by the arguments that purport to establish that this is *the* biblical concept. One problem is that those who give such arguments are not always careful to distinguish epistemic from non-epistemic conceptions of truth. So, for example, Roger Nicole sometimes characterizes "the biblical concept of truth" in a way that makes it sound like an epistemic conception, and sometimes characterizes it in a way that makes it sound more like a correspondence theoretic concept (Roger Nicole, "The Biblical Concept of Truth," in *Scripture and Truth,* ed. D. A. Carson and John Woodbridge [Leicester: Inter-Varsity, 1983], 412-18). Moreover, Thiselton explicitly claims that multiple conceptions may be found in scripture (Anthony Thiselton, "Does Lexicographical Research Yield 'Hebrew' and 'Greek'

say; but we seem to understand the concept well enough to employ it in everyday judgments. Tabloids are not reliable enough within the domain of "world news" to warrant belief. If you believe that Elvis Presley is still alive because you read in *The National Enquirer* that he was recently seen at a mall in Kentucky, your belief is not warranted. *The Wall Street Journal*, on the other hand, is reliable enough to warrant belief in this domain — and this despite the fact that it is hardly *perfectly* reliable. Note, in this connection, that it would be wholly implausible to say, in general, that if a text has theoretical authority over someone within some domain, then whatever it says to that person within the domain must be perfectly reliable. Theoretical authority implies reliability; it does not imply infallibility.

Third, we may conclude that if a text has *foundational theoretical authority* over S in D, then it must be at least as reliable as any other authority for S in D. For suppose this were not the case. Suppose, for example, you have two books (T1 and T2) about some historical event, one of which (T1) has foundational theoretical authority in that domain and the other of which (T2) doesn't. (Perhaps the first book contains the only surviving eyewitness account of the event, and there is no forensic evidence available about the event apart from the testimony of that source.) It follows from our earlier characterization of foundational authority that if T1 and T2 were to conflict in their assertions about the event, it would be more rational to believe in accord with T1 than with T2. But it is hard to see how this could be the case if T1 were *less reliable* than T2 in D. Thus, at a minimum, T1 must be at least as reliable in D as T2. Thus, if one understands attributions of authority to the Bible to be attributions of *foundational* practical authority or foundational theoretical authority in some domain, it follows that the Bible must be at least truthful enough to be *as reliable as* any other authority in that domain.

Thus far, our conclusions about the general connections between authority and truth — and so our conclusions about the connection between biblical authority and biblical truthfulness — have been rather milquetoast. In short, attributions of authority, depending on what exactly they amount to, might require a reasonably high degree of reliability in some interesting domain, but (so far) nothing like reliability across the board, and nothing even close to inerrancy. But religious believers are often inclined to make assumptions about God and God's relation to the biblical text that, given what else we have said here, would

---

Concepts of Truth [1978] and How Does This Research Relate to Notions of Truth Today? [New Summary]," in *Thiselton on Hermeneutics: Collected Works and New Essays* [Grand Rapids: Eerdmans, 2006]). These two facts cast some doubt, I think, on the idea that there is one single "biblical concept of truth." Indeed, one might reasonably be skeptical that the Bible offers a robust enough set of linguistic data to determine any such thing as *the* biblical concept of truth.

Even if it is true that "the biblical concept of truth" is connected with reliability in the way described above, however, it must further be noted that this is a different notion of reliability from the one I am invoking here — which is, again, a notion that is partly *definable* in terms of truth).

justify stronger conclusions. Importantly, however, many of these assumptions are negotiable.

Consider, for example, the following schema:

> (α) G is the author of T, and, necessarily, for any text τ authored by G and for any individual S other than G, τ has foundational authority over S in D.

Many Christians are willing to assume that α is true in the case where "G" is replaced with "God," "T" is replaced with "the Bible," and "D" is replaced with the name of some fairly large domain like "the domain of truths about God, morality, the human condition, and salvation" or, much more generally, "the domain defined by the text itself" — that is, the domain which is just the conjunction of every proposition that is semantically asserted or intentionally conveyed by the text. And if some instance of α is true, it follows that whatever T says within D is true and whatever directives T issues within D constitute (for everyone) decisive reasons for action. In other words, T is perfectly reliable. Here is the proof: Consider a possible world W1 in which G produces a text T1 that is authoritative over some individual S (≠ G) but less than perfectly reliable in D. Then there is a possible world W2 that differs from W1 in no relevant respect apart from these facts: (a) W2 contains, in addition to T1, a text T2 that is both authoritative over S and perfectly reliable in D; and (b) S knows that T2 is more reliable than T1.[39] In W2, then, T2 is clearly more authoritative than T1: reasons supplied by T2 have priority over reasons supplied by T1. But if that is so, then it is possible that there be someone (other than G) over which T1 does not have foundational authority, contrary to α.

Now let us consider the assumption β, generated from α by substituting "God" for "G," "the Bible" for "T," and "the domain defined by the text itself" for "D":

> (β) G is the author of the Bible, and, necessarily, for any text τ authored by God and for any individual S other than God, τ has foundational authority over S in the domain defined by the text itself.

Our fourth — and certainly more substantive — conclusion, then, is that β implies that the Bible is perfectly reliable within the domain defined by the text itself. Thus, if β is true, then every proposition that the Bible semantically asserts or intentionally conveys must be true, and all of its directives constitute decisive reason for action. Of course, β is not an implication of the bare claim that the

39. I assume that texts must be of finite length. Thus, there will be no text whose content is an infinitely long set of conjunctions that express in full detail the entire truth about a possible world.

Bible is authoritative, nor is it an implication of the bare claim that the Bible is true, nor is it even clearly implied by any passage in Scripture. It is, it would seem, just a philosophical-theological doctrine. It is an interesting question whether its second conjunct in particular could be shown to follow from any of the central tenets of classical theism, or from some plausible alternative version of theism such as open theism or process theism. But this is a question that will not be taken up here.

The fourth conclusion is naturally construed as drawing a connection between a certain view about the nature of the authority of Scripture — the view captured by β — and the *inerrancy* of Scripture. For a lot of evangelicals, the go-to document for an "official" statement of the doctrine of inerrancy is the *Chicago Statement on Inerrancy.* That document does a lot more than merely define the doctrine; but according to the portion of the document that looks most like a definition, "Scripture is without error or fault in all its teaching, no less in what it states about God's acts in creation, about the events of world history, and about its own literary origins under God, than in its witness to God's saving grace in individual lives."[40] This is pretty close to the claim that the Bible is perfectly reliable in whatever it semantically asserts or intentionally conveys, and also perfectly reliable in whatever directives it issues. If there is a difference at all, it will lie in the difference between the sum total of "what the Bible teaches" on the one hand and, on the other hand, the sum total of whatever the Bible says to us, along with whatever directives it issues. The Bible *teaches,* for example, that Jesus told his apostles to go unto all nations, baptizing them in the name of the Father, Son, and Holy Spirit. I am not so sure, however, that it *teaches* that we are to do the same. If anything, by including the teaching that Jesus said this, the divine author of the Bible *intentionally conveys to believers the directive that they are to do the same.* But that is no more one of the Bible's teachings than a command to "Stop!" is one of a policeman's teachings. Still, since I am inclined to think that believers in inerrancy would not want to exempt intentionally conveyed directives from the scope of what they take to be "without fault" in Scripture, I am inclined to think that this fourth conclusion here does indeed draw a connection between a certain view of biblical authority and the doctrine of biblical inerrancy.

Fifth, it is not clear that any (non-question-begging) assumption weaker than β will forge the same link between authority and inerrancy. We have already seen that a text can be foundationally authoritative for an individual in a domain without being perfectly reliable in that domain. β manages to connect authority with perfect reliability because it implies that there is an author who is such that any text of which he or she is the author would have to be *at least as reliable* in some domain as a text that is *perfectly reliable* in that domain. But that implication holds only when the author is necessarily such as to be the author *only* of texts that have

40. Norman Geisler, ed., *Inerrancy* (Grand Rapids: Zondervan, 1980), 494.

foundational authority of some kind. So it seems that those interested in maintaining a connection between scriptural authority and scriptural inerrancy will be best served by devoting their philosophical-theological energies to a defense of β.

Moreover, it is worth noting that the inerrancy doctrine itself has relatively few implications about what we actually ought to believe in light of Scripture. It is, after all, compatible with widely varying views about what (if any) propositional messages are asserted or conveyed by biblical texts. Suppose that what the biblical text says is just what the divine author of the text semantically asserts or intentionally conveys through the text. Then what the biblical text says depends heavily upon what God aims to do with it. If we think that God intends to teach us the sober historical facts about the genesis of life on Earth, the origins of Israel, and the conquest of Canaan, then we will have reason to take most of the declarative sentences in the Old Testament as genuinely asserting their semantic contents. If, on the other hand, we think that God's authorship of the Old Testament amounts primarily to God's having appropriated a variety of myths and hyperbolic tales to make rather general points about divine sovereignty, divine faithfulness, and the like, then we will have little reason at all to think that the same Old Testament texts say much of anything at all about the origins of life or of Israel, or about the conquest of Canaan. The claim that the Bible is perfectly reliable in whatever it says will imply that whatever it says is true; but it implies nothing at all about what the Bible actually says.

As I see it, then — and this is the sixth and final conclusion — our views about the nature and scope of biblical authority shed, all by themselves, relatively little light on the most interesting questions about the truthfulness of problematic passages in Scripture. Consequently, it is a mistake to treat the topic of biblical authority as somehow lying at the heart of debates about the reliability and inerrancy of Scripture. Far more pertinent to these latter debates are questions about the nature of God and divine authorship: In what sense is God an (or the) author of Scripture? What are God's aims in Scripture? What might be God's aims in this or that part of Scripture? Is God the sort of author about whom β is true? These are the questions that promise to shed the most light on the topics that really worry us. Of course, some of them — especially the last one — will involve us in questions about authority; but none of them are fundamentally about the nature of authority, and all of them seem to be questions different from those that have occupied so much of the literature.

TWENTY-EIGHT

The Idea of Inerrancy

Paul Helm

In this essay I attempt a careful treatment of how the word "inerrancy" is used in connection with Scripture, by both its friends and its opponents. My main aim is to attempt to offer clarifications of the concept of inerrancy and to draw out some implications of these. These are undertaken in the hope that they will help the understanding of both inerrancy-affirmer and inerrancy-denier alike.

Debates about the significance of biblical inerrancy cannot (in my view) be separated from issues in hermeneutics, but although hermeneutics is (mercifully) not my brief, I have nonetheless used biblical examples in what I hope is a fairly conventional way for the purposes of illustration. This, I also hope, makes what follows not as intolerably abstract as it would otherwise be.

"Inerrancy": Some Conceptual Remarks

An expression — an assertion, a sentence, a formula, a document, a part of a document — may be said to be inerrant if it is wholly true, without error. But not only may errors occur in what someone asserts; they may also occur in what someone does. So there are errors in cookery, in seamanship, in chess, in soccer, in etiquette, in driving an automobile, and so on. Where there are norms or rules, or well-worn practices, then it is possible to flout these, and to be in error. However, in this essay we shall not be overly concerned with errors that arise in what may, in a rough-and-ready way, be called practices, but with error in claims to assert the truth or truly report what is false.

A document may be possibly inerrant, or probably inerrant, or have a good chance of being inerrant, or may most certainly not be inerrant. A recent edition of the phone book may be probably inerrant, or partly inerrant, or it may have a

---

Thanks are due to Oliver Crisp for his comments on an earlier draft.

good chance of being inerrant. Last year's phone book is possibly inerrant, but probably not. A document may be necessarily inerrant.

Yet these claims about inerrancy and "inerrant" do not sound quite correct. For while we may say that what someone said is wholly true, it seems odd to say that it is inerrant, unerring. I believe that this is because "inerrant" and "unerring" are present participles. They denote a condition that lasts, or may last, through time. Because the words "inerrant" and "unerring" refer to a property that is held over a period of time, and continuously for that period, it is awkward to speak of someone or something being inerrant at one time. What you say may be wholly true without it or you being inerrant. A source of truth that was inerrant for a moment or two, or was intermittently inerrant, would hardly count as such.

So "inerrant" connotes more than "being wholly true." Why, otherwise, are defenders of inerrancy not content with asserting that the Bible is wholly true? For the phone directory to be not only wholly true but also inerrant, it has to be not only wholly true, but constantly or continuously wholly true, and even perhaps to carry some kind of guarantee or endorsement that it is so.

A memory man who gives nothing but correct answers to questions about the novels of Jane Austen whenever the questions may be asked has some reason to be called inerrant with respect to those novels. On his chosen topic he displays freedom from error for a time. Some source of information can be wholly true for a time, or wholly true for most of the time, or intermittently true. Inerrancy is best thought of as a stable or a fairly permanent feature of the source. So the force of calling a book or other authority inerrant, or infallible, is that being wholly true is a constant feature of that authority. The idea is that if the authority is inerrant then it can repeatedly be revisited and at each visit be regarded as being wholly true in what it asserts or reports as confidently as at the last visit. This is one of the senses — a temporal sense — in which an inerrant document cannot be false: so long as D, a document, is inerrant then there are no times when it is false. It has this in common with "infallibility"; an infallible authority is not merely one that is not failing now, but one that never fails, or never will fail. This may be qualified, as in the example about the novels of Jane Austen. "Infallible" is often used interchangeably with "inerrant," but sometimes writers wish to distinguish the two, preferring one or the other term.

If there is a distinction (as some claim) then insofar as "infallible" is thought of as a mark of the capacity of an authority unfailingly to guide the reader to a certain goal, then "infallibility" is certainly distinct from "inerrant," since the ability of a document or other piece of information to guide the reader successfully depends upon what the reader already believes, and whether the truths recorded are all such as to be relevant to a person being guided.[1] If so, then "infallible" is

1. On this distinction, see A. T. B. McGowan, *The Divine Spiration of Scripture* (Leicester:

an epistemic term or more of an epistemic term than is "inerrant," which has to do with truth bearing. If so, then inerrancy may be a sufficient condition of infallibility, thus understood, but it need not be a necessary condition, since a document may be an unfailing guide without being inerrant. A map may be an unfailing guide from London to Lowestoft even though part of it has been torn off, or if some matters having nothing to do with the London–Lowestoft route contain mistakes.

A document may be inerrant, wholly true over time, while nevertheless misleading a reader who comes to it with the wrong beliefs, including the wrong expectations. In what follows we shall leave the notion of infallibility to one side, and focus on inerrancy understood as the ability of a document to give wholly true information (about those matters it deals with) over time. Whether "A document gives wholly true information" is equivalent to "A document is wholly true" is a question that we shall come to.

There is a further distinction. An authority's inerrancy may be *de facto* or *de jure.* Were the memory man to suffer significant brain damage then he would in all likelihood cease to be inerrant. If we ask, why is a particular authority inerrant, why is it wholly true over time, the answer usually given is that this property of providing true information over time is grounded in some other property or properties it possesses. The "can" here is stronger than the *de facto* sense, "does not err at any time," for the property of a document lies in the nature of the powers of that source or grounding. So in such a case a document or other source does not just happen to be inerrant but it is necessarily so in virtue of its grounding. To say that a document is necessarily inerrant is not to say that it consists of nothing but necessary truths, but that it is conditionally or hypothetically necessarily true. If someone with perfect vision sincerely reports that the box is larger than the ball, then it necessarily follows that the box is larger than the ball, even though it is a contingent matter of fact that this is so.

So the sort of truth that we are concerned with in discussing the concept of inerrancy has a close relationship with the meaning of words and sentences that are, or are not, true, or inerrantly true, with lexicality and grammaticalness. And also with what, in writing or saying or otherwise uttering some words, some author or reporter or issuing agency intends, with meaning as intention.

But we are also concerned with meaning as convention. For example, there are conventions regarding degrees of exactness or vagueness. A writer may intend to express a certain truth by utilizing certain already-current conventions in speech or in a written language. Intention and convention come together in

Apollos, 2007), chapter 5. For discussion of its significance, see John D. Woodbridge, "Evangelical Identity and the Doctrine of Biblical Inerrancy," in *Understanding the Times: New Testament Essays in Honor of D. A. Carson on the Occasion of His 65th Birthday,* ed. Andreas J. Köstenberger and Robert W. Yarbrough (Wheaton: Crossway Books, 2011), 104-40.

the case of a person who makes an assertion by asking a question, but in a certain tone of voice, as in (to the children), "Isn't it time you did the washing up?" There may be certain conventions governing agency, conventions that are not narrowly literary, but which may express themselves in what is said or uttered. The truth conditions of such a statement may be detailed, even pedantic, or they may be less stringent. It would be rather unrealistic to suppose that inerrancy was always committed to the pedantic. But whether or not it is does not have to do with the meaning of "inerrant" but with the conventions governing the truth of those expressions said to be inerrant. I shall return to this point.

Can an inerrant author utter or contain errors? One certainly can. For example, suppose that it is true that the cat sat on the mat and I report this (referring to the same mat and the same cat) by writing "The cat sat on teh mat." There is an error. The second "the" has been misspelled. But provided that this is generally understood to be a misspelled "the," then the sentence containing the error can still be understood as expressing a truth, and therefore as being possibly inerrant, as being true over time. More significant on this point is the reporting of direct speech in a document. In the transcript of a trial it may be recorded that Joe Bloggs, the accused, said, "I was fifty miles away from the scene of the crime when it took place." But the transcript, in faithfully and accurately and truly reporting that claim, may be reporting what is false, and so the (let us suppose) inerrant report contains a falsehood. David once said "Now I shall one day perish by the hand of Saul" (1 Sam. 27:1). This is false. He did not perish by the hand of Saul. Jairus said of his daughter, "She is dead," when this was not, strictly speaking, true. So the Bible contains falsehoods. It is perfectly consistent with a document's being inerrant that it should contain many reports of falsehoods.

So it is necessary to beware of a fallacy, the fallacy of division, of believing that because something as a whole has a character, then necessarily each separate element has that character. The poem may rhyme, but it does not follow that each word in the poem rhymes with each other word. Not every thread of my tartan tie is tartan. There is another reason for noting the danger of committing this fallacy. A document that is wholly true may contain expressions that are neither true nor false: it may contain questions and commands and expletives, of which it makes no sense to assert that they are true. This fact requires us to consider speech-acts, which have become prominent in recent discussions of the status of the Bible.

We have seen that inerrancy as respects an authority that is said to possess it has to do with truth. And this naturally raises the question, what are the bearers of truth? If inerrancy is an alethic concept, what are the bearers of truth? In recent years it has been said that the bearer of truth is not the proposition, but the assertion, and this also signals a concern with speech-acts.

Inerrancy and the Bible

Having sketched some of the relevant conceptual features of "inerrancy" and its cognates, we shall now attempt to apply these to the peculiar features of the Bible.

The Grounding of Inerrancy

The traditional doctrine of biblical inerrancy is, I believe, a doctrine of necessary inerrancy. The epistemic vehicle of the good news of the gospel could have been a series of purely human, that is, uninspired, but veracious reports. Even a stalwart biblical inerrantist such as B. B. Warfield says

> [w]e may say that without a Bible we might have had Christ and all that he stands for to our souls. Let us not say that this might not have been possible. But neither let us forget that, in point of fact, it is to the Bible that we owe it that we know Christ and are found in him.[2]

If God in his wisdom had chosen such a vehicle for his revelation, and it is possible that he had, then this could have been a case of revelation through reports and testimonies that were in general true, true for the most part, but not inerrant.

If something has the character of God's word, then it follows that it too must be necessarily inerrant. The objection that this would make the Bible an object of worship, that it would divinize it, cannot be sustained.[3] God is all-knowing, and cannot err, and he is veracious. The character of the truth claims made by a word of God is warranted by the God whose word it is. The Bible is wholly true not in virtue of some benign coincidence or freak of history, though there could have been such a book, but because of who God, its primary author, is. So that the next time, and the time after that, and at any subsequent time that a person consults its pages, it follows that they will provide unfailing truth.

This is so in view of some divine and human concursus, a kind of concursus that is deeper and more mysterious than the ordering of a series of events to form a providential order. "Ordinary" concursus as we might call it is consistent with the occurrence of actions that in some sense flout God's will. This extraordinary concursus involves a "breathing out" of God's word from God himself so as to se-

2. B. B. Warfield, "The Inspiration of the Bible," in *Revelation and Inspiration* (New York: Oxford University Press, 1927), 72.

3. John Webster makes such an objection in his generally excellent treatment of Scripture, *Holy Scripture: A Dogmatic Sketch* (Cambridge: Cambridge University Press, 2003), 28. The creatureliness of Scripture is secured by its contingency. If it is inspired and inerrant, this is not because it is the result of a process of divinization.

cure that the inspired agent, though fully human, expresses what is both his own word, bearing the hallmark of his character and situation, and also God's word.

Inerrancy, Propositions, and Speech-Acts

The term "speech-act" arose from the work of the Oxford philosopher J. L. Austin in the 1950s. (*How to Do Things with Words,* published in 1962, after Austin's early death, is the seminal work.) However, we must not confuse the term with the thing. Appreciation of speech-acts is by no means an exclusively post-Austinian development in biblical interpretation.

In his work Austin focused upon what he called *performative* utterances: forms of utterance in which merely to say something is to do something. The standard example is the wedding ceremony. The saying of "I will" at the appropriate points *is* the wedding of the groom and the bride. Their words constitute the action of becoming man and wife. Such acting-by-speaking occurs because of words uttered with the appropriate intention, and also because of the existence of certain conventions — in the case of marriage, certain legal and moral conventions that govern the marriage service, making it the sort of occasion that it is. A more theologically central example is the nature of justification. When God justifies the ungodly he does so by *declaring* a person righteous. It is law-court language, as when a judge pronounces a person to be innocent of the charge against him. In declaring a person innocent a judge is not making a person innocent, nor is he describing what innocence is; he is making a declaration in the light of the evidence presented to the court. What is noticeable about such cases is that there is an identifiable framework, a convention, often backed by the law, which confers powers on certain people — a judge, a minister, and so on.

However, such conventions may also be very informal and tacit. In the course of a conversation to say "I promise" is usually taken to be the very act of promising. Saying "I resign" is, in certain circumstances, to resign, saying "apologize" is an apology, and so on. But of course the mere utterance of these words need not be cases of promising or resigning. Suppose a person uses the words "I promise" merely to clear his throat, or for pronunciation practice, then the words "I promise" are not a true performative. So not only do certain conventions, formal or informal, need to be in operation, but also the speakers must have a certain intention in speaking, and the hearer (or hearers), the ones addressed, must understand that intention in order for the speech-act (such as "I promise") to take proper effect, what Austin called *perlocutionary* effect, for someone to *be promised to.*[4] As already noted, there are many types of speech-act, including

4. Incidentally, sometimes we are told that the Lord's creative fiats in Genesis 1 are instances of performatives, but this is surely a mistake. In Genesis 1 the reason that God's saying is

asking questions, giving orders, and (most importantly for us) making assertions. But speech-acts do not correspond to grammatical mood in a consistent way. A question may be used to perform a speech-act having the force of a command, as in our earlier example: "Isn't it time you did the washing up?"; or an expression of thanks may be used to issue a request, as in "Thank you for not smoking." Assertions, including promises, may be tacitly conditional. But in the appropriate circumstances, saying "The cat is on the mat" is asserting that the cat is on the mat.

Arising from such reflections is Austin's distinction among the following: (1) the *locution,* for example, the words of the sign "Beware of the dog," or the uttered language; (2) the *illocution,* that is, the force of the words, what is intended by them in the circumstances/conventions in which they are uttered — say, to warn people about the presence of the fierce dog; and (3) the *perlocution,* that is, the success of the intended force, the success of the sign in warning people about the dog. (Incidentally, this example of the sign shows that speech-acts do not need to be precisely dateable events; they can have a permanent or at least an enduring character. This will be important in what follows.)

The doctrines of inerrancy or infallibility are sometimes said to be "propositionalist" in character, even to be concerned with the Bible when it is regarded as nothing other than a set of propositions. We shall examine this in a bit of detail in a moment or two. But we can at once see that this claim cannot be a matter of logic. For it is rightly asserted that Scripture is not a simple "list of propositions," but that it contains a great variety of types of speech-acts, not only statements, but questions, commands, vows, exclamations, and so forth. The exegete and the theologian need to take account of all such forms, and not to attempt to reduce Scripture to one form, the proposition, or to pay exclusive attention to that form, neglecting all else as mere "wrapping."

The focus of the proponents of a speech-act approach to Scripture, as opposed to a propositionalist approach, is to stress divine and human activity, especially speech-activity, in interrelation.[5] On some views, Scripture is the record of such speech and its interactive effects; on other, stronger views, of a more "theodramatic" kind, we ourselves may be caught up in this interaction; people who are presently living may be the conversation partners of God, agents in the drama.

There are reckoned to be at least two other advantages of this speech-act approach. One is to make clear that Scripture is richer than the propositionalist view may lead us to believe. For it is sometimes alleged that the propositionalist temptation is to regard the non-propositionalist elements simply as the pretty packaging of historical or doctrinal content, to be torn off and discarded.

---

his doing is not in virtue of the existence of any conventions, but solely because of his supreme power.

5. For an excellent treatment of Scripture from a "speech-act" perspective, see Timothy Ward, *Words of Life* (Leicester: Apollos, 2009), chapter 3.

A further claimed advantage to using the speech-act approach in understanding inerrancy is to help to determine the genre of particular books or parts of Scripture. The idea here is that particular books or parts of books in Scripture are written with different conventions or rules, though perhaps not consciously or explicitly so. The rules that govern the writing of apocalyptic, such as parts of the book of Revelation, and of Daniel and Ezekiel, are different from the conventions of a chronicle, or of prophecy, or of New Testament letter-writing, or of a proverb, or of the telling of a parable. These diverse forms, properly grasped in terms of their associated conventions, ought to set up different kinds of expectations in readers' minds as to how the language is to be taken, the place of repetition (in Hebrew poetry, for example), the nature of a greeting (in Paul), the use of numbers and symbols (in apocalyptic), and of invented storytelling (as in Jesus' parables).

What are we to say of this speech-act approach? The general idea that God's word is God's speech, the word of our Creator and Redeemer, seems correct. Through the various divinely appointed human agents, and through his Incarnate Son, God speaks to his people of the Old and New Testaments from time to time and in various ways, in the last days in his Son. In addition, the whole of divine revelation in Scripture, in which the Lord records the speech of some, inspires the speech of others, and in which he himself sometimes speaks, is confessed by the Christian church to be God's speech, God's word. So we might think of the whole of Scripture as being enclosed within speech marks, with other sets of speech marks occurring within the enclosing set. The entire Bible is in these senses "God's speech."

However, there is one general disadvantage to stressing that Scripture contains God's speech. Speaking is an event, though speech-acts may not be. Notices such as "Beware of the dog" and "Thank you for not smoking" may be assertions without being, strictly speaking, events. But typically, speech occurs at a time, lasts for so long, and then stops. It is an event every bit as much as coughing or raising and then lowering one's arm are events. The general danger is that, with this in mind, we approach Scripture in an overcontextualizing or overtemporal frame of mind, a tendency to think that the occasions of divine speech pass, and are replaced by others. To counter this tendency we must remember that there are vastly different kinds of events, even of speech events. The Coronation of the Monarch, with its speech component, has lasting effects, as does a declaration of war, or the enacting of legislation, or putting up of a notice. By contrast, casual conversation may be inconsequential chatter that immediately evaporates. The fact that there has been divine speech does not mean that its significance is confined to the occasion of the utterance, or even that its chief significance arises from its first occasion of utterance. We shall take up this point later on.

There is also the danger of exaggeration, to make out that the speech-act differs in meaning from the corresponding proposition. Consider this simple argument. "If the cat is on the mat, then Fido is on the mat. The cat is on the mat.

Therefore, Fido is on the mat." The first premise asserts a conditional proposition, put forward for consideration. But neither the antecedent nor the consequent is separately asserted. In the conclusion the consequent is asserted. But "the cat is on the mat," whether asserted or not, must have the same meaning, otherwise the argument would not be valid.[6] So the meaning of a statement must be other than the speech-act that it may be used to perform.

Can a document that contains vows, questions, jokes, expletives, greetings, etc., be inerrant? In order to steady our nerves at this point, it is helpful to remember that chief among the speech-acts is the assertion. I can use the sentence "The cat sat on the mat" to assert that the cat sat on the mat, and if I'm correct, and the cat did sit on the mat, then to say "The cat sat on the mat" is to make a wholly true assertion. If I'm wrong, because it was a dog that sat on the mat, then my assertion is errant, it errs, it is in error, it is false. Taking our cue from this, we might think of a letter of Paul's, say, as being one speech occasion, the entire epistle being enclosed in speech marks, and containing (even if not wholly consisting of) assertions. Some of these assertions, like the notices about the dog and about not smoking, may be of permanent or abiding importance.

But that may not satisfy everyone. What are we to say of a document or collection of documents, like the Bible, that contains vows, questions, commands, exclamations, and the like? It may be satisfactory to raise the question of inerrancy in the case of its assertions, but what about the vows and so on? Surely, if inerrancy has to do with truth, then if a question or a command cannot be true, it cannot be a candidate for being inerrant. Here I think we need to tread carefully. Take an example from John's Gospel where Jesus is reported as saying, "Fill the water jars up to the brim" (John 2:7). Here he gives a command or makes a request. It seems to make no sense to ask: Is "Fill the water jars up to the brim" true? Nevertheless, it is still possible to ask, Is it true that Jesus commanded those at the feast to fill the water jars up to the brim?

It may be thought that highlighting such forms of speech as questions, commands, vows, etc., as we have been doing moves us away somewhat from the idea of propositional revelation. As we have seen, it is sometimes said that inerrantism flattens or reduces the variegated linguistic phenomena of Scripture, and its varied genres, into "lists of propositions." If that is what happened in the past then that was unfortunate, though personally I rather doubt that it was what happened. For I do not think that the distinguishing of biblical literature into distinct genres, or noting various grammatical moods, is a modern development.

The Bible records other things than vows and requests. It reports and narrates and records. It records expressions that are not assertions, and that are assertions but not true assertions, and it records many occurrences that do not contain linguistic features at all. For example, it records, "The tomb was blocked

6. On this point see P. T. Geach, "Assertion," *Philosophical Review* 74 (1965): 449-65.

by a large stone." We might call this a state of affairs: it records the state of affairs of the tomb being blocked by a large stone. It seems to me that a wordless state of affairs, such as this, is rather like a wordy state of affairs such as, "Jesus said, 'Fill the jars up to the brim'" in this respect: that it neither is nor can be a case of propositional teaching such as we find in the ministries of, say, Jesus or Paul or Moses. Rather, these are cases of reporting or recording. The Bible records events of both kinds, wordy and wordless events, and if the Bible is inerrant, then these events may have been as they are recorded. We did notice earlier, however, that some reports contained in the Bible are false and that it is perfectly consistent with a doctrine of inerrancy that it should contain many falsehoods.

In some of what Jesus did he used words. He asserted that his Father is greater than himself. He rebuked Peter with the words "Get you behind me, Satan," and invited sinners with the words "Come unto me all you who labor and are heavy laden and I will give you rest." On one occasion he wept without (apparently) saying anything. So on the one hand he used words to rebuke and to invite. But on the other hand he did things that did not involve words. Jesus wept, and slept. The words he used in rebuking and inviting are of course not statements or assertions. To rebuke is not to assert or state anything, to invite is not to assert or state anything, any more than are promising or requesting. Jesus did all these non-assertoric things, and lots more besides, as did many others of the people of the Bible.

Although the idea of Scripture as divine speech is accurate and helpful, the claim that in view of Austin's work we are faced with a new choice about the nature of divine revelation — we must take either a speech-act view of divine revelation, or a propositional view — won't stand up to scrutiny. There are a number of reasons for this.

Behind the polarizing of speech-acts and propositions there is a misunderstanding of the terms "proposition" and "propositional" as these have been used in standard accounts by the proponents of propositional revelation. "Proposition" can be used as a term of art, equivalent to: *an expression that conveys a thought to which a truth value may be assigned.* So the sentence "The cat is on the mat" can be employed as a proposition in this sense, given a truth value, or assumed to have one, and it can then be used in logical arguments as we saw earlier. Likewise, the English sentence "The window is open" and the French sentence "La fenêtre est ouverte," when taken standardly, may be said to express the same proposition, the same thought, the same possible truth or falsehood. This is the logicians' sense of proposition, a thought that can be assigned a truth value. When used in this special sense the "proposition" may be considered in a way that abstracts from particular occasions of utterance. We may say such propositional language is occasion-indifferent — that is, neutral or occasion-indifferent. That's why it can be used and reused in logical argument.

For another thing, despite the charge that the propositionalist view of revelation and theology considers propositions to be "timeless" (a matter to be discussed in more detail shortly), as far as I am aware no practitioner of the allegedly dark art of "propositional theology" believes that "proposition" in "propositional revelation" is being used in this logicians' way.

Inerrancy, Indexicality, and Assertion

Speech-acts may focus attention on the direct speech in Scripture, on speech events, and may encourage us to think of Scripture as itself constituting God's direct speech to us. This being so, we must consider important features of speech, especially its indexicality. Speech-acts occur at a time and place, and may be about that time and place. Much of our everyday speech is not only an event, an act of speaking at a time; it is an act of speaking in which what is asserted is something that is contemporaneous with the speaking, or connected with what is contemporaneous. If I make the true assertion, at 5:38 a.m. on 9 May 2007, "The sun is rising now," the utterance is an event, a happening, and the utterance is true only at that time, just as if I say "The sunrise is clearer today than yesterday" I am comparing something that is contemporary with something that occurred somewhat earlier. What is true of time is true of place. There are many of these assertions in Scripture: "My time has not yet come," "Today you shall be with me in paradise," "Let us go hence," "Now is our salvation nearer than when we first believed." This is the phenomenon of indexicality, the fact that language may be about the very time (or the very place) of its utterance.

Why is it necessary to consider indexicality? Because, by and large, indexical speech-acts have a short life, they are soon spent; the occasion of their utterance passes. For Scripture to be a narrative that *abides,* not a set of speech-acts the force of which is soon lost, the interpretative framework of the narrative has to consist of abiding, non-indexical assertions. Very many different speech-acts to be found in Scripture presuppose such assertions, abiding assertions — the true assertions, or propositions, about the existence and character of God and of his ways, for example — that provide the bedrock of theological reflection on which Christian theology is based. For the speech of Scripture to be used theologically, and for its inerrancy to be a property that it possesses over time, then its indexical expressions must be framed by sets of non-indexical assertions the purpose of which is to give us the abiding theological significance of the indexical speech.

After Jesus raised the paralytic, the people who were there said, "We have seen extraordinary things today" (Luke 5:26). If this indexical expression has permanent value, it is so only as a report of an assertion.[7] Its first uttering was on

7. The distinction between what the Bible records or merely reports and what it proposes for belief and trust is routinely made. So (to take a seventeenth-century example) Francis Tur-

an occasion, and wholly about that occasion. But there are assertions that, though they first occurred on a particular occasion, in a distinct context, have permanent or enduring importance, to the end of time. They can be reasserted without any loss of meaning or force. So Jesus said, "I am the light of the world," and Paul said, "Christ Jesus came into the world to save sinners," and the writer of Hebrews said that Jesus is the same yesterday, today, and forever. These assertions initially occurred on different occasions, and they are true on the first occasion, but true also on all subsequent occasions when asserted with the original intention. These are not timeless propositions (whatever exactly timeless propositions are — see below), but they are assertions with a permanent illocutionary force, informing us of such things as fundamental features of Jesus' teaching and of the reason for his coming into the world. It is important therefore to bear in mind the distinction between the occasion of the first utterance of an assertion and what it is that makes that assertion true, if it is true. It is the assertion's truth conditions that warrant our reasserting it.

So anyone can see from these observations that there is more to the Bible than propositions. It presents actions through language — assertions, for example — and reports actions and states of affairs that are wordless. But are the non-propositional data simply the packaging of what is of real value, the proposition? Obviously not. Such data may be vital in building up an understanding of what, say, the New Testament teaches us about the person of Christ. Was Jesus a Stoic? No, he wept. Was he only a stern teacher? No, he graciously invited the weak and heavy laden to come to him. Was Jesus likely to be deflected from the course that he had set himself, the work that his heavenly Father had given him to do? No, he rebuked as Satanic temptations any suggestions that he might deviate from that path. Such information, the information conveyed to us in the speech-acts of Jesus, and his wordless states, help build up a faithful portrait of Jesus.

We need to bear in mind that, as regards requests or rebukes or invitations that are not assertions, as well as assertions, the language used in such activities, if it is intelligible language, embodies *thoughts.* Suppose I invite you to shut the window by saying "Please shut the window." In order for you kindly to comply with my request, why do you go over to the window and not to the door? Because the request contains or implies the thought that the window is open and not the thought that the door is open, even though the door may also in fact be open.

For although, as we have seen, vows, requests, commands, declarations, etc.,

---

retin says, "Again authenticity is either of history or of narrative or in addition to this of truth and of rule. According to the former, whatever is narrated in Scripture is most true as it narrates either what is good or what is bad, whether it be true or false. But those things are said to have the latter which are so true in themselves that they are given as a rule of faith and practice. All things in Scripture do not have the authenticity of rule (as those things which the wicked and the Devil are reported to have said), but all do have historical authenticity" (*Institutes of Elenctic Theology,* trans. G. M. Giger, ed. James T. Dennison Jr. [Phillipsburg, NJ: P&R, 1992], 1:62).

are not assertions, they do nonetheless have a propositional element. Consider Jesus' command "Fill the water jars up to the brim." This is a request, not an assertion. How did those to whom the request was addressed know what to do? Because they understood the request. And to understand the request means that they understood Jesus to be saying something like "Let it be the case *that the water jars are filled to the brim,*" and not "Let it be the case *that the water jars are half-filled*" or "Let it be the case *that the water jars are smashed to pieces.*" The italicized expressions are what we might call the thoughts of these three requests, or the propositional content of them. To understand a request and so intelligently (as contrasted with purely accidentally) to comply with it is to know what state of affairs would satisfy the request, and that is to know what would have to become the case for that request to be satisfied. Once the jars were filled to the brim, then Jesus' request or command had been satisfied. So although types of speech-act that are not assertions cannot be true, they can have occurred (and are capable of being inerrantly reported) and their propositional content indicates to those to whom the speech is addressed what state of affairs would count as satisfying them. A wholly inerrant document will unerringly record these speech-acts that are not assertions, even if in fact what is recorded did not in fact obtain.

Why are commands, or invitations, or promises (and so on) informative to those to whom they were originally addressed, and continue to be so for us? How is it that we can, where appropriate, cue into them, to obey or disobey the commands, or accept or reject the invitations, or believe or disbelieve the promises? Simply because the words of these types of sentences express or imply distinct *thoughts* that we are capable of understanding. Sometimes the thought implied is more complex than those we have just noticed. "Jesus was convinced that attempts to persuade him not to go to Jerusalem to fulfill the will of his Father were Satanic temptations," or something like it, is the thought that is implied in (and so, in a metaphorical sense, is what "lies behind") his rebuke of Peter.

So it is plainly false, demonstrably false, to suppose that the idea of biblical inerrancy requires or implies that the Bible consists of nothing but propositions, and that only the propositions or assertions that we find in Scripture are important. There is, besides assertions, the *thought-ful* content of types of sentences that are usually used to make requests, to rebuke, to invite, as well as (as we have seen) reports of wordless states of affairs.

The response to such non-propositional or non-assertoric sentences as they were originally uttered cannot simply have been to believe them. The appropriate response of Peter to the rebuke of Jesus was to be rebuked, and to take the necessary action to avoid further rebukes, which he was slow in doing, of course. The response of his hearers (and of countless others down the Christian centuries) to Jesus' invitation "Come unto me" is to go to him. Rebukes and invitations are not so much to be believed as to be complied with; but they are to be believed in the sense of being credited to their authors.

Inerrancy and Time

Does the idea of biblical assertions that can be reasserted time and time again reduce the Christian faith to being "timeless truth," or "abstract"? Those who say such things clearly regard timeless truth as a bad thing, something to be avoided at all costs. What follows is an attempt to understand why it is that "timeless truth" is so closely associated with the idea of revealed propositions or assertions, and why it is regarded as such a bogey. For it is hard to fathom what those with this distaste for the timelessness of truth really object to. It is difficult to find a critic who states what the problem is: what it would be for a theological assertion to express a timeless truth, and what's so bad about that. What follows is an attempt to answer this question for the critic by canvassing various possibilities.

In the mainstream Christian tradition — Augustine, Boethius, Anselm, Aquinas, Calvin, Edwards — God's existence is timeless, in the sense that he is outside time, without a past or future, existing in a timelessly eternal present. But it's surely not in this sense of timelessness, the timelessness of the eternal life of God, that some people think that "propositionalism" delivers a system of "timeless truth."

Still, if God is timelessly eternal then at least some propositions about him will be timelessly true in this very robust sense. *God is timeless* is itself presumably an example of a timeless truth, if it is a truth. And whatever is essential to God will, in turn, be robustly timeless in this sense — God is just, God is love, God is one in three, and so on. But I don't get the feeling that the excoriation of "timeless truth" is due to the thought that propositionalism (or assertoricism, as we might call it) commits one to the view that theological truth in general is timeless as the eternal God is (on some views) timeless.

On some views of divine sovereignty, events occur in time, assertions are made in time, but each such occurrence is eternally decreed to happen. Does a particular view of Scripture, that of regarding it basically and essentially as propositional revelation, entail such a view of God's will, of his plan? Clearly not. Does the "timeless" charge amount to saying that it does? I hope not. There are many who uphold the view that revelation is propositional who would vehemently deny that everything is eternally decreed by God. And it's possible that there are those who deny propositional revelation who nevertheless think that all things, including all assertions, are decreed by God. So it's hard to see that the "timeless" charge is that propositionalism leads to the view, or entails the view, that every revealed proposition is eternally or timelessly decreed by God, or that it leads to an exclusive focus on "eternal truths."[8]

8. It is puzzling why the connection between inerrancy and timeless or eternal truths is routinely made. For example, in *The Uses of Scripture in Recent Theology* (London: SCM, 1975) David H. Kelsey offers several short characterizations of B. B. Warfield's theological attitude to

Here's what I have come to think about the "timeless truth" charge. In saying that upholding the propositional or assertoric character of Scripture commits one to "timeless truth," what the objectors have in mind is not the robust timelessness of God's eternal existence, nor that associated with eternal divine decrees, but *tenselessness. Copper expands when heated* is a tenselessly true proposition. It is true at all times. Besides that, it is a general or universal truth about copper. At any and every time it is true that copper expands when heated. So it is not surprising to find objectors to propositional or assertoric views of revealed truth criticizing them for making possible a system of universal truths. That truth about copper is not true of some time rather than another (as "There is presently a copper coin on the table" is true of the present, or as "I bought the copper kettle last Thursday" is true of last Thursday). So my surmise is that what the objectors object to is timeless truth in the sense of tenseless truth with which (they think) propositionalism is saddled.

But if this is what is meant, that the shape of the Christian gospel is distorted by a doctrine of inerrancy that stresses propositions or assertions into something that is true of all times, tenselessly true, then this charge is also wide of the mark.

Let us briefly reconsider what we were discussing earlier. Events that occur at particular times, and statements about these events, are crucial to the Christian gospel. That Jesus Christ came into the world to save sinners, that he was crucified on Calvary, that he died and was buried, is true, and integral to our faith. The truth of this set of assertions (let's call it "A") is about some particular time, or times, the times of the birth, crucifixion, and death of the Savior, whenever exactly these times were.

Nevertheless, although A is true about a time or times when certain events occurred, either presupposing these times, or referring to them, the truth of A does not depend upon when A is stated, or reasserted. The sort of involvement that A has with time is not that associated with indexicality. Assertions about Christ such as those we have just noted are not utterances that are true only when they are uttered. Whenever people repeat A as part of their confession, and in whatever natural language they use, they make assertions that Christians believe to be true. Christians down the centuries, repeating A, have expressed the same truths. We may say this, then, that as regards the central affirmations of our faith, though their truth is bound up with the occurrence of certain events, that truth is not affected in any way, not altered or modified, by when they are asserted, or by any events subsequent to the events that A refers to. We might say of such

---

Scripture arising from his belief in its inerrancy. One of these is "a text book of doctrine having the force of *asserting* (infallibly) some eternal truths about objective states of affairs" (100). For further discussion, see Paul Helm, "Revealed Propositions and Timeless Truths," *Religious Studies* 8 (1972): 127-36.

assertions: once true, always true, permanently true.[9] The same is also true of some commands, of course: "You shall love your neighbor as yourself" does not lose its force as a command when suitably repeated today.

Is this what those who worry about the idea that "propositionalism" engenders "timeless propositions" have in mind, that the truths of the Christian faith are now forever true? Are they bothered by the thought that it is now true that A is true, and that it will always be? What would have happened to our faith if it were not true as long as time lasts that our Savior came into the world to save sinners? Jesus stopped being born, he stopped suffering, and so on, but the assertions "Jesus came into the world to save sinners," "Jesus suffered," etc., never stop being true, and their importance and efficacy are undiminished by the passage of time.

If the critics of propositionalism or assertoricism are not making the criticism that it leads to the truths of the Christian faith being always true, a criticism that, if it were sustained, would surely overthrow our faith, then I am stumped as to what it is they are saying. So I conclude that the timelessness charge is baseless. How it comes to have the prominence in the literature that it has is a complete mystery. (I suspect that it may be a carryover from the criticism of certain kinds of liberal theology that in their understanding of the Christian faith eliminate the central historical events of faith in favor of sets of abstractly presented moral ideals.)

Earlier we discussed and evaluated the current emphasis upon speech-acts. Speech-acts are events. Are events true? They happen, but are they true? Clearly not. Paul asserted "Christ Jesus came into the world to save sinners." Let's call this "B." Paul is asserting B was an event. And his asserting this at one particular time did not *make* B true. What makes B true is the fact of Jesus' coming into the world to save sinners. To focus on the fact that Paul uttered B, that B is a speech-act, and to concentrate on this feature, may distract us from the matter of truth. The great thing about the Christian gospel is that it is permanently true, true as long as time lasts, and so it can be freely reproduced and reiterated by translators and teachers and preachers.

If we focus on what Paul asserted in stating B, rather than on the fact that he asserted it, then we focus on the issue of the truth or falsity of the thought or propositional content of his assertion. What he asserted moves to the center of our attention, displacing interest in the fact that he asserted it. Of course it is not without interest and some importance that Paul asserted it, that this is a statement having apostolic authority, that he uttered it when he did and in the context that he did. No doubt all these factors contribute to the meaning of what he asserted, and so help us to determine what exactly is the truth that he uttered. Attention to these things is part of the process of establishing the meaning of what

9. Those with extra-sensitive mental antennae kindly note that for present purposes I eschew considering the sense in which the Creed may be said to be true *before* the events it refers to occur. I don't think this affects the present issue. In any case, one thing at a time.

he wrote and why he wrote it. But none of this affects the point of principle. In our endeavors to understand our faith we must repeatedly move from the assertions of Scripture and the conditions under which they originally occurred to what is asserted in them, their theological truth content, that which it is possible to reassert. We need repeatedly to take the step from context to content.

For the big, significant fact is not that Paul asserted B, but that B is true, and that what he asserted is today and will forever be true and so is, in that sense, timeless — or better, perhaps, it is time-indifferent. It is *permanently* true. To the extent that our attention is focused on the occurrence of events, utterances, or actions, to that extent we are distracted from issues of truth. Our attention is directed not to what is time-indifferent, or permanent, but instead to a certain time or times, the times of the utterances or actions. There is a world of difference between the expression "Paul wrote 'Jesus Christ came into the world to save sinners' at such a time and place for such and such readers," and the abiding truth that *Jesus Christ came into the world to save sinners.*

When we focus on the truth of what Paul asserted, rather than upon the fact that he asserted it, or facts about the fact of his asserting it, are we abstracting? Is what Paul asserted, that Jesus Christ came into the world to save sinners, abstract? As we have been seeing, there is a clear sense in which it is: for while nonetheless bearing in mind its apostolic authority, or perhaps taking this for granted, the assertion may be abstracted from or extended beyond Paul's original speech-act. When the preacher asserts B, or the congregation confesses B, then the truth of B is being "reissued," reaffirmed. Having abstracted this content, the fact of the matter is that Jesus came into the world to save sinners.

We can see from this that abstracting the cognitive content of the event from Paul's original assertion is not a failing. It is not a weakness of the idea of propositional or assertoric truth that such truths may be extended into other contexts than the first context of their utterance. Rather, their being abstractable or extendable is necessary if we are to be in the position of considering the truth of such assertions anew, and of asserting them today and tomorrow.

But in another sense such assertions are not abstract or timeless, for they are about a particular individual and about a particular time. In reasserting such assertions we are not watering them down. Nor are they made vague by repetition, as "Someone called" is vaguer than "Peter called," and "Peter called" is vaguer than "Your brother Peter called." Judged in this way, "Jesus Christ came into the world to save sinners" is a concrete, not an abstract, assertion. It is about a concrete person and what happened to him, or what he did, together with its significance. Of course it leaves other questions of detail to be answered, but then so does every similar utterance.

Does it follow that if there is an assertion that is true for all time, such as "God was in Christ reconciling the world unto himself," then we have a full grasp of its meaning? In knowing the truth of that, would we know God as he is in himself?

Why would that follow? Why are we in danger of upturning the creature-Creator relationship, as is sometimes suggested? May we not know in part, see through a glass darkly, and walk by faith not by sight? Of course we may, and must.[10] There is always more to be said and more to be understood. So, once again, it is hard to see what the charge that propositionalism turns divine revelation into timeless "abstract propositions" means, and why it is to be avoided.

Inerrancy, Convention, and Falsifiability

This last section of the essay makes some brief comments on the relation between the intention of a speaker and the meaning of what he says, and then considers what would have to be the case for the doctrine of biblical inerrancy to be disproved.

It is a commonplace of the Reformation's hermeneutical approach to Scripture to interpret its data literally, that is, in terms of the intention of the author. Knowing or discerning that intention is not a matter of divining a private mental act that has to occur prior to an action in order to make that action one with a particular intention and not, say, an action with an intention of a different kind, or a blunder or unintentional mistake. If discovering the intention involved such divination, then coming to understand the meaning of an expression would be an extremely hazardous undertaking. There may be such cases, but rarely, for in general, part of identifying the intention of a writer is identifying a particular literary convention and the writer's awareness of that convention.

If one thinks of the distinctions, for example, between poetry and prose, proverbs and parables, scientific and everyday speech, narrative history and apocalyptic, then it is obvious that understanding what a biblical author means requires that we discern as best we can what he intends, and that boils down to what he intends by employing this convention or that convention. It may be, of course, that important biblical passages do not fit any of the conventional conventions: Is Genesis 1–3 myth, or cosmology, or prehistory, or (as befits the uniqueness of the creation) something *sui generis*?

The range of illocutionary forces of what is written is limited by the writer's knowledge of the genre that he is writing in. Take the case of the depiction of animals in apocalyptic literature: it would be odd to critique this on the grounds that the writer was biologically inept. So the animals may change their appearance or species or behavior in ways that, as a matter of fact, are biologically impossible and still satisfy the conventions of apocalyptic.

Can a biblical author mean more than he intended to say? In saying that

10. On this, see the exchange between Merold Westphal, "Taking Plantinga Seriously," and Alvin Plantinga, "On Heresy, Mind and Truth," both in *Faith and Philosophy* 16 (1999).

Christ did not sin (1 Pet. 2:22) Peter asserted something that is compatible with Jesus' impeccability, that he could not sin, even though he may not have intended to do so. Similarly Paul, when he asserted that Jesus was in the form of God, may not have intended to say that Jesus could not sin. But it might be shown by combining these two that both Peter and Paul (assuming apostolic unison) *were committed* to Christ's impeccability, even though neither *committed himself* to this conclusion. In other words, reference to the intention of individual writers ought not to be made in a minimalist sense, since what they mean may have implications that, not being omniscient, they may not have been aware of.[11]

It is sometimes claimed that the doctrine of biblical inerrancy suffers the fate of death by a thousand qualifications, that it is so hedged about by caveats and conditions as to be unfalsifiable.[12] A number of things need to be said about this charge.

First, we argued earlier that the historic doctrine of inerrancy is that of the necessary inerrancy of Scripture. Scripture does not just happen, by a fluke, to be inerrant, but is so in virtue of the properties of God, its primary author, and his intention. It might be thought that this by itself seals it off against falsification. But this would be a mistake. For necessary inerrancy is what is claimed for Scripture, or what it claims for itself. This does not seal it off from possible falsification; and if it could be shown to err, then not only would it not be necessarily inerrant, it would not even be wholly true.

Second, the fact that a doctrine is presented in a careful, qualified fashion is not per se a sign of unfalsifiability. We need only to think of the way in which a doctrine such as Incarnation is qualified so as to avoid a series of errors, of Apollinarianism, or Monophysitism, or Nestorianism, and so on. The question is not whether a doctrine is carefully stated, but whether, granting the qualifications, there remains doctrinal substance to it.

Third, unfalsifiability depends upon genre. Take apocalypse: it is surely not possible to show inerrancy unless the writer is explicitly self-contradictory. Similarly with the teaching of Jesus, or of Paul. In the case of some genres, it is possible in principle to disprove inerrancy — were there to be no evidence for a Sea of Galilee, or of the nation of the Hittites, say.

Here we must touch again on genre. In their famous paper on Inspiration, A. A. Hodge and B. B. Warfield distinguish between exactness of expression and accuracy of expression.

11. The example of Christ's impeccability was suggested to me by Oliver Crisp's chapter, "Was Christ Sinless or Impeccable?" in *God Incarnate: Explorations in Christology* (London: T. & T. Clark, 2009), chapter 9.

12. I. H. Marshall, *Biblical Inspiration* (London: Hodder & Stoughton, 1982), 72-73, cited in McGowan, *The Divine Spiration of Scripture*, 106.

> There is a vast difference between exactness of statement, which includes an exhaustive rendering of details, an absolute literalness, which the Scriptures never profess, and accuracy, on the other hand, which secures a correct statement of fact or principles intended to be affirmed.[13]

Note the reference to intention, and so, by implication, to genre. Without this implied reference it is hard to uphold the distinction in the terms in which the authors draw it. Is "The sun is setting" exact? Obviously not. But is it literally true? Hardly not, either, unless the fact of which this is a correct statement is a fact not about the sun in its relation to the Earth, but how the sun in its relation to the Earth *appears.*

What would be required for an error to be established? According to A. A. Hodge and B. B. Warfield in the same article, for an error to be established it must be a proved error, an indubitable error, or a "proved mistake."[14] These seem to be three ways of saying the same thing about the relation between what Scripture asserts to be a fact about the world and what that fact actually is. There has not merely to be a discrepancy between the two, but for error to be established there has to be a contradiction between the biblical assertion and some independently established fact. As regards internal disharmony between one assertion of Scripture and another, harmonizing must be impossible for the charge to stand. That is, disharmony must be proved beyond doubt.[15] I suppose we have to add, given earlier remarks about genre, that the alleged contradiction must be between two accounts in the same genre.

The epistemic or evidential standards employed by Hodge and Warfield may seem to be rather high. For suppose that there were a number of discrepancies between two witnesses (each of whom was initially presumed to be wholly reliable) in their accounts of what happened; then the two accounts may not be formally self-contradictory. Nevertheless, it would be surprising if doubts were not raised in the mind about the reliability of one or other of the witnesses or of both of them.

There is not only the problem of what evidential standards one employs. There is the question of where the onus of proof lies. Is the onus on the skeptic to prove a contradiction, or on the upholder of inerrancy to prove consistency? Further, whether or not the Bible is accepted as true, let alone inerrant, with regard to all that it teaches, is obviously a matter of trust, and not of firsthand

13. A. A. Hodge and B. B. Warfield, "Inspiration," *Presbyterian Review* (1881), reprinted with the same pagination in *Inspiration,* with an introduction by Roger R. Nicole (Grand Rapids: Baker, 1979), 28-29.

14. These claims occur on pages 41, 44, and 45, respectively, of Hodge and Warfield, "Inspiration."

15. Hodge and Warfield, "Inspiration," 54.

verification. So there is the question of a person's attitude to such *prima facie* inconsistencies. All may agree that inerrancy entails consistency. Yet some might say, "If a document is inerrant then discrepancies ought to be reconcilable easily, and now." Others might rest content with "If a document is inerrant then there must be some way of reconciling discrepancies but at present I cannot see how." Still others might say, "If a document is inerrant then there must be some non-awkward or non-artificial way of harmonizing discrepancies." It is hard to see how these different attitudes can be adjudicated. More pertinently, it is hard to see how a policy of adjudicating discrepancies can itself form a part of a doctrine of inerrancy, any more than the listing of a set of books as canonical can itself be a part of that canon.

TWENTY-NINE

To Whom Does the Text Belong? Communities of Interpretation and the Interpretation of Communities

Richard Lints

In recent years, evangelicals appeared to have rediscovered the significance of the church.[1] Undoubtedly there are theological reasons for this, but it also arises from the increasing cultural distrust of individualism and the accompanying embrace of communities. This communal orientation has gone hand-in-hand with a yearning for post-partisan modes of biblical interpretation. If only we could put aside our individual biases and show greater respect for the wider church community we would have a more consensual grasp of the biblical text — or so the sentiment goes. But the irony is that the post-partisan impulse has not led to any lessening of interpretive fragmentation.[2] The privileging of communities over individuals has done little to mask the intractable differences among contemporary communities. A simple reaffirmation of the individual responsibilities of biblical interpreters is not likely to lessen the fragmentation either. Living with the dialectic between unity and diversity and between communities and individuals requires the wisdom of the gospel. Let me consider the turn to community and the dilemma to

1. Representative titles include: Mark Husbands and Daniel J. Treier, eds., *The Community of the Word: Toward an Evangelical Ecclesiology* (Downers Grove, IL: InterVarsity, 2005); John G. Stackhouse Jr., ed., *Evangelical Ecclesiology: Reality or Illusion?* (Grand Rapids: Baker Academic, 2003); Brad Harper and Paul Louis Metzger, *Exploring Ecclesiology: An Evangelical and Ecumenical Introduction* (Grand Rapids: Brazos, 2009); and Jonathan R. Wilson, *Why Church Matters: Worship, Ministry, and Mission in Practice* (Grand Rapids: Brazos, 2006).

2. In an earlier era, evangelical fragmentation concerned differences about doctrines of baptism, the millennium, or divine election. See David F. Wright, "Scripture and Evangelical Diversity with Special Reference to the Baptismal Divide," in *A Pathway into Holy Scripture,* ed. Philip Satterthwaite and David F. Wright (Grand Rapids: Eerdmans, 1994), 257-76. The contemporary post-partisan fragmentation focuses around differences of cultural engagement, political orientation, or ethnic and gender issues. As an example see Fernando Segovia, "Toward a Hermeneutics of the Diaspora: A Hermenuetics of Otherness and Engagement," in *Hispanic Christian Thought at the Dawn of the 21st Century,* ed. Alvin Padilla, Roberto Goizueta, and Eldin Villafañe (Nashville: Abingdon, 2005), 55-68.

which it gives rise in biblical interpretation before tackling a theological response to the problem.

The turn to community may not be as thorough as the turn to the subject in the era of the Enlightenment or the turn to language in early-twentieth-century philosophical circles, but it has crept into popular culture at a much faster rate than its two earlier counterparts.[3] The demise of the lonely solitary self of modernity and the rise of the community in postmodern times is nothing if not breathtaking in their respective speeds. Many observers are not persuaded that either trend is as well established as pop culture supposes, but there can be little doubt that trend watchers have rightly noticed how much more frequently the language of community appears in our ordinary discourse these days.[4]

Belonging to a community is important to most people today, or at least the appearances of belonging to a community is important. Sacrificing one's own will to power may not be easy as Nietzsche reminded us a century ago, but woe to the person who appears to lord it over others in these communally sensitive times of ours. The picture of the lonely soul bowling alone is not something anyone wants to be saddled with either.[5] We all want to belong to some group even if we also want to be careful about that group's hold on us. We want community without authority.

Communities at the beginning of the twenty-first century do not look much like traditional communities of tribe and clan and church of earlier times, nor of other parts of the globe. Communities of discourse today are more likely bound together by political views, by economic status, by leisure activities, or by educational backgrounds to name but a few of the variables that tie groups together. Communities are held together by common interests rather than by common traditions.[6] The notable exceptions here are ethnic communities in the West that

3. It should be mentioned that the "linguistic turn" in early-twentieth-century philosophical circles was predated by linguistic concerns in theological circles of both liberal and conservative persuasions in the nineteenth century. Of special interest to this volume is the overt attention given to language among adherents of inerrancy in the nineteenth century, Charles Hodge and B. B. Warfield. See the essay by Brad Seeman, "The Old Princetonians on Biblical Authority," in this collection. On the "linguistic turn" in twentieth-century philosophical circles, see especially the edited collection of essays by Richard Rorty, *The Linguistic Turn* (Chicago: University of Chicago Press, 1967).

4. In evangelical theological circles, Stanley Grenz was a central figure in drawing attention to the significance of community for theological discussion. See his *Theology for the Community of God* (Nashville: Broadman & Holman, 1994) and his *Created for Community: Connecting Christian Belief with Christian Living* (Grand Rapids: Baker, 1998) and *The Social God and the Relational Self: A Trinitarian Theology of the Imago Dei* (Louisville: Westminster John Knox, 2001).

5. Robert Putnam, *Bowling Alone: The Collapse and Revival of American Community* (New York: Simon & Schuster, 2000).

6. For the most influential sociological treatment of the paradoxes of community and

sustain peculiar traditions in the midst of a secularizing culture that is no respecter of traditions.

There is also plenty of evidence that we are not nearly as communal as we would like to believe about ourselves.[7] We are still a people who watch television in virtual isolation, who scan the Internet by ourselves, and who are fascinated by our own internal psychology. We may speak much about the praiseworthiness of community, but few are willing to count the costs of belonging to an actual living, breathing, enduring community. A colleague once remarked to me, "I love community. I just could never live in one." Along with most of our sports heroes, we want to be wanted but we would rather be free agents at the end of the day when it comes time for contract talks.

Why then do we talk so much more about community than we used to? And why is there a morally commendable tone attached to communities and not to individuals any longer? Why has the pendulum swung in the way it has and what difference might it make for interpreting the Bible? Let me suggest three well-rehearsed factors in this collective change of our cultural ethos before spelling out the implications for biblical interpretation. Each factor may in turn temper the attraction to the buzz surrounding community in our day, even if they may also help us faintly to hear the echo of the biblical depictions of community.

The Turn to Community

Two generations ago a host of conceptual battles were fought in the academy that moved the ideological playing field away from individually objective perceptions of reality toward context-dependent modes of understanding. Those context-dependent modes of understanding were construed in a variety of ways. Thomas Kuhn in the history of science pointed at the way in which socially constructed paradigms of research programs profoundly influenced not only which questions were asked by natural scientists, but also what counted as appropriate answers. Science was as dependent upon the assumptions of communities of scientists as it was on the hard evidence collected and analyzed by any individual scientist. The longstanding dogmas of the empiricist tradition surrounding epistemic objectivism were stridently challenged by empiricist-leaning philoso-

---

individualism see the enduring study of Robert Bellah et al., *Habits of the Heart: American Individualism and Commitment in American Life* (Berkeley: University of California Press, 1985).

7. George Rupp, "Communities of Collaboration: Shared Commitments/Common Tasks," in *On Community,* ed. Leroy Rouner (Notre Dame: University of Notre Dame Press, 1991), 192, writes, "The prominence of the theme of community in contemporary literature and social commentary itself testifies to the deep sense of its lack in the consciousness of cultural elites in the modern West."

phers at mid-century as well.[8] In the work of W. V. O. Quine and Wilfred Sellars, the language of objectivity was jettisoned and in its place belief systems became web-like in their structure, never touching reality simply at individual points of correspondence.[9] Beliefs were held because of socially reinforced mechanisms. The myth of the given was exposed as a figment of the Enlightenment imagination.[10] Peter Berger and Thomas Luckmann in turn argued that reality was socially constructed rather than simply being discovered by human inquiry.[11] Observation was as much socially approved interpretation as it was simple discovery of facts. Berger in particular was careful to highlight the relativist overtones implicit in the nascent sociology of knowledge, but in so doing he supposed that he was relativizing the relativizers.

There were also major changes in the global character of culture during the twentieth century that impacted the turn to community at the outset of the twenty-first century. During the twentieth century there was a sharp uptick in global economic activity. Unrelated to the shifts of conceptual paradigms, the economic boom, especially of the postwar years, brought a radical increase in international trade and with it the sharp increase in cross-cultural interactions. The globe was growing ever more intertwined as the consumer markets of North America and Western Europe spread their economic tentacles into parts heretofore unknown to them.[12] Ironically the globe grew smaller as diverse people groups came into far more pervasive and persistent contact.[13] The loss of the limitations of geography slowly cemented an American's sense of identity. The melting pot mythology of American history seemed ill-suited to the era of the civil rights and the second feminist movements, massive new waves of immigra-

8. Richard Rorty rehearses this story at the beginning of his influential work, *Philosophy and the Mirror of Nature* (Princeton: Princeton University Press, 1979).

9. See Quine, "Two Dogmas of Empiricism," in his *From a Logical Point of View* (Cambridge, MA: Harvard University Press, 1953). He famously wrote at the end of that essay, "For my part I do, qua lay physicist, believe in physical objects and not in Homer's gods; and I consider it a scientific error to believe otherwise. But in point of epistemological footing the physical objects and the gods differ only in degree and not in kind. Both sorts of entities enter our conception only as cultural posits."

10. See Sellars, *Science Perception and Reality* (London: Routledge & Kegan Paul, 1963 [orig. 1956]).

11. See Berger and Luckmann, *The Social Construction of Reality: A Treatise in the Sociology of Knowledge* (Garden City, NY: Doubleday, 1966).

12. It is safe to say that the phenomena of globalization have not been experienced in uniform fashion across the diverse cultural locations of the globe. There are multiple "globalizations" even as the pressures toward conformity of a single global reality grow stronger. See Peter L. Berger and Samuel P. Huntington, eds., *Many Globalizations: Cultural Diversity in the Contemporary World* (New York: Oxford University Press, 2002).

13. Cf. Mike Featherstone, ed., *Global Culture: Nationalism, Globalization and Modernity* (London: Sage, 1990).

tion and the demise of colonial sensibilities.[14] The reality was dawning that the melting pot did not mix so well. Self-definition grew out of an encounter and often against that encounter with the "other." In retrospect the identity politics that has so characterized the last half of the twentieth century was but a natural outcome of the forces of globalization. No one simply belonged to oneself. We were all part of a group, whether we realized it or not.

A final part of the story I want to mention here is the democratizing technologies of the latter half of the twentieth century, most especially television and the Internet. In a story still not fully told, these technologies greatly increased our power as individuals while also creating enormous pressures of conformity among individuals.[15] The flow of information grew in unprecedented amounts, but communities of special interests grew just as rapidly around commercially suitable needs.[16] An individual's sense of significance and security was growing ever closer to the sense of belonging to a peer issues group. The end of the mythology of individualism was intertwined with this growing mythology that belonging to a group was better than belonging to oneself.[17] The new social media of the last decade have only reinforced that portrait.

Understanding these historical, cultural, and conceptual contexts is important if we are to understand the appropriate ways in which the language of community intuitively functions in our context. Our context-dependent manner of understanding our context may also help us hear more clearly the manner in which the gospel spells out the virtues and vices of communities. Paying attention to our own cultural filters may help us to hear more clearly how the gospel is to be situated in our deeply fragmented but communal setting.

The Scriptures portray our identity in ways that should seem foreign to our modern Western ears. The corporate character of Israel's identity as God's people lacks the individual autonomy so prevalent in contemporary democracies. So it is that those who have been reconciled to God in Christ belong to each other

14. See William R. Hutchison, *Religious Pluralism in America: The Contentious History of a Founding Ideal* (New Haven: Yale University Press, 2003). See especially chapter 9, "Whose America Is It Anyway? The Sixties and Afterwards," 219-40.

15. See Albert Borgmann, *Technology and the Character of Contemporary Life: A Philosophical Inquiry* (Chicago: University of Chicago Press, 1984), and his *Power Failure: Christianity in the Culture of Technology* (Grand Rapids: Brazos, 2003).

16. See George Ritzer, *Explorations in the Sociology of Consumption: Fast Food, Credit Cards and Casinos* (London: Sage, 2001), and Gary Cross, *An All Consuming Century: Why Commercialism Won in Modern America* (New York: Columbia University Press, 2002).

17. Suzanne Keller has argued that communities in technologically advanced contexts will continue to thrive because of the intrinsic yearnings of people for roots. In her thirty-year longitudinal study of a planned community in New Jersey, she concluded that the yearning for roots survived all the democratizing pressures of technology, though in very different social forms than traditional communities. See her *Community: Pursuing the Dream, Living the Reality* (Princeton: Princeton University Press, 2003).

in peculiar premodern ways. In the New Testament relationships were defined by the uniqueness of the family tree to which they belonged, not according to inherited genes, but by virtue of a common theological inheritance. It is the great treasure of the gospel which the people of God in the new covenant inherited and which defined their life together.[18] Belonging to each other was not signaled by wearing the same clothes, or speaking the same language or living at similar addresses. Rather it was by sharing the common gift of the gospel in contextually similar and different ways.[19]

Now to the central concern of the essay: How does the turn to community impact positively and negatively the ways we ought to read the Scriptures? Does the existence of peculiar communities authorize the attendant peculiar interpretations of those communities? And conversely, how are diverse readings of the Bible to be rendered appropriate?

The Trinitarian Analogies

Christians confess that God exists as three-in-one and one-in-three. Three persons and one being. One God. Father, Son, and Holy Spirit. This entails that there is a communal dimension to the Godhead. Each of the persons stands in relationship to each of the other two as a community of divine persons. Yet in the mystery of the Godhead, there are not three individual Gods but one God in three persons. Immediately comes the caution of speaking too fully about the inter-Trinitarian life of the Godhead. Trying to remove the veil behind this great mystery tempts in either of two directions in the search for theological clarity about human communities.[20] It is possible to privilege the three persons of the triune God in such a fashion that individual (and communal) diversity always trumps the overarching unity of God. Likewise it is possible to privilege the oneness of God's being in such a fashion that there is no room for diversity of any interesting

18. See the powerful testimony of the Anglican Archbishop of Uganda, Henry Luke Orombi, "What Is Anglicanism?" *First Things* 175 (August/September 2007): 23-28. He testifies to the theological inheritance of Ugandan Anglicans, which carved out a peace among warring tribes grafted onto the same tree of grace by the gospel of Jesus Christ.

19. Cf. Simon Gathercole's contribution in this collection, "*E pluribus unum?* Apostolic Unity and Early Christian Literature," for a discussion of the unifying dimension of the gospel across the canon of Scripture.

20. Miroslav Volf writes, "[T]o think in Trinitarian ways means to escape the dichotomy between universalization and pluralization. If unity and multiplicity are equiprimal in God, then He is the ground of both unity and multiplicity. Since God is the one God, reality does not degenerate into individual scenes like a bad play; yet since the one God is a communion of the divine persons, the world drama does not degenerate into a boring monologue." *After Our Likeness: The Church as the Image of the Trinity* (Grand Rapids: Eerdmans, 1997), 193.

kind. Keeping the tension in the mystery of the triunity of God is difficult but important in order to prevent the theological pendulum from swinging too far to one side or the other.[21]

In addition, caution is necessary because analogies between the divine and the human are always delicate. There is a great conceptual chasm between the infinite, omniscient, and omnipotent God and finite and limited human agents. There is some analogy between the two because there is some reflection of God in human persons. The book of Genesis is clear that humans, created in the image of God, are "like" God. They are not God but they are like God in some respects. Like all analogies, this analogy breaks down if pressed too far. Knowing the limits to the analogy is key to understanding the analogy in the first place. When the rhetorical question is asked of Job in the whirlwind, "Have you an arm like God, and can you thunder with a voice like his?" (Job 40:9), the analogy moves in two directions, from Job to God and from God to Job. The "arms" of God is a reference by analogy that compares human strength to divine might. The "thunderous voice" is a reference by analogy, contrasting the power of divine speech to the impotence of Job. Quite obviously the analogies also break down if pressed too far. God is not an embodied person with arms, nor does Job have vocal cords capable of producing thunder. The conclusion is straightforward. Humans are like God in some respects, and different than God in some respects.

Affirming that God is a divine community encourages an affirmation that there is a reflection of communal life among humans, but there is also a sense in which it must not undermine important differences between the divine community and any and all human communities.[22] Human communities are not infinite. Human communities are always embodied. Human communities are always gendered. Human communities on this side of the grave are always to some extent corrupt. Recognizing similarities and differences is crucial to understanding the way in which human communities function both to illuminate the being of God in constructive ways and the potential of communities to distort the Creator's imprint.

God experiences diversity differently than we do as humans. There is no fundamental conflict of perspectives in the Godhead. This is grounded in the claim that God is one and in God there is no corruption. If we take seriously the human experience of Jesus, we must nonetheless affirm that there is a mystery in

21. See Colin Gunton, *The One, the Three and the Many: God, Creation and the Culture of Modernity* (Cambridge: Cambridge University Press, 1993). Gunton argues that Western theology until recently privileged the oneness of God as the means to protect the uniformity of culture. In late modernity, the pendulum has swung in the opposite direction to underwrite the embrace of cultural pluralism.

22. Ironically, one of the most influential treatments in the West of the analogy between divine and human communities can be found in the Eastern Orthodox theologian, John Zizioulas, *Being as Communion: Studies in Personhood and the Church* (Crestwood, NY: St. Vladimir's Seminary Press, 1985).

the tension between the desire of Jesus not to suffer on the cross and the desire of Jesus to be faithful to his Father's will regarding the cross. There are different perspectives between God the Father and God the Son at that juncture in redemptive history by virtue of the incarnate experience of the Son.[23] This does not entail a fundamental conflict of perspectives between the two. However the tension is explained, the consequence is that the divine community expresses a unity in diversity in its relationships as they are known on the pages of Scripture.

All interpretation is shaped by the unique experiences of the interpreter. Part of this unique experience is the social location and cultural context of the interpreter. What one sees is influenced by what one is expecting to see. Those expectations in turn are formed in the complex interplay of individual and social orientations. This part of the cultural narrative of human knowing is more familiar than it used to be.[24] However, that same cultural narrative appears to incline us to believe that all interpretations might be equally valid, or that one's interpretation should be insulated from criticism from other cultural locations.[25] But the wider story into which our own particular narratives of human knowing occur point in the opposite direction. All interpretations are not created equal. There are better and worse culturally influenced readings. Though there is no context-independent set of criteria for determining this, this should not tempt us toward interpretive relativism.[26]

23. See Oliver Crisp, *Divinity and Humanity: The Incarnation Reconsidered* (Cambridge: Cambridge University Press, 2007), for a helpful conceptual account of the relation of divinity to Christ's unique humanity.

24. There is convergence at this point in the story between evangelicals and liberation theologians. Both have decried the disinterested modes of interpretation at the heart of the academic study of the Bible in the West. But to the question, What does "involved interpretation" look like? the answers remain quite different. Liberation exegetes trained in the West think predominantly of the power relationships fostered by the Scriptures and those restrained in marginalized communities. Evangelicals by contrast have predominantly thought of the authority of Scripture to order the lives of believers. For a clear and straightforward treatment of "involved interpretation" of liberation exegesis see the collection of essays in the *Union Seminary Quarterly Review* 56, no. 1-2 (2002). Two essays in that collection to note are: Kah-Jin Jeffrey Kuan, "My Journey into Diasporic Hermeneutics," 50-54, and Archie C. C. Lee, "The Bible and Contextual Reading: Encountering Communities, Encountering Texts — A Response," 77-81.

25. For a radically pluralistic model of interpretation by which the canon means primarily what diverse communities think it means, see Dale Martin, *Pedagogy of the Bible: An Analysis and Proposal* (Louisville: Westminster John Knox, 2008).

26. Cf. J. Todd Billings, *The Word of God for the People of God* (Grand Rapids: Eerdmans, 2009). "It is a truism that there is no context free interpretation of Scripture. The historical critic who interprets the Bible from a library desk in Harvard Divinity School is just as shaped by the sociocultural context as the Masai Christian who takes a rest from herding cattle in Kenya to recollect a memorized passage of Scripture" (105). On the issue of hermeneutics and relativism see Anthony Thiselton, *Hermeneutics: An Introduction* (Grand Rapids: Eerdmans, 2009).

The Diverse Unities of Scripture

Mapping the unity and diversity of the Scriptures will aid us in thinking more clearly about theological models of interpretive differences.[27] The foundational act of divine wisdom revealed across the Scriptures is the organic ordering and executing of redemptive history. There is a center that holds throughout the canon and reaches climactic expression in the cross and resurrection of Jesus. This is the story of the gospel. That story is woven through the narration of the events and is the basis upon which the canon has an internal unity.[28] The entire complex of meaning surrounding Israel's temple is required to understand what happened on the cross. The giving of the Law at Sinai is required to understand the giving of the Spirit at Pentecost. The Old Covenant is required to understand the New Covenant. The myriad of narratives detailing the surprising interventions of God among his people is required to put the resurrection into context. It may fairly be said as well that all that happens after the cross and resurrection is related to these archetypal events by the authors of the New Testament. Followers of Jesus must die to themselves even as Jesus died. Baptism is a theological echo of the cross (Rom. 6:4) and resurrection is to be "heard" in the life of the Christian lived in God's presence (Rom. 6:5).

The glue that holds everything to the canonical center ought not to be characterized in simple or simplistic terms. The rich diversity of people, institutions, and events is woven into a fabric whose patterns are complex and ironic.[29] On one interpretive level, the Scriptures reveal a single story in and through an almost countless number of diverse episodes. How we understand the unity of the story in large measure depends upon our models of unity. If there are not rich enough theological resources to understand the unity and diversity of the story, inevitably the Scriptures will be flattened out and will lose their intended depth. If we, by contrast, avail ourselves of theological resources too strongly pluralizing the Scriptures, we will make the Scriptures so particular to their own contexts as to lose any of their intended traction in our lives.[30] Whatever unity

27. I recognize the circular nature of the argument at this point — viz., to understand the nature of differences of interpretation I am appealing to the nature of difference in the Scripture, but the nature of the difference in the Scripture is itself a matter of interpretative difference. The only proviso I add here is that the differences within the canon to which I point are not largely points of disagreement among broadly evangelical interpreters.

28. The story is rich and complex, but it is nonetheless a single story. Cf. Richard Bauckham, "Reading Scripture as a Coherent Story," in *The Art of Reading Scripture,* ed. Ellen Davis and Richard Hays (Grand Rapids: Eerdmans, 2003), 38-53.

29. A helpful summary exposition of this claim can be found in Craig Bartholomew and Michael Goheen, *The Drama of Scripture: Finding Our Place in the Biblical Story* (Grand Rapids: Baker Academic, 2004).

30. I take this to be Peter Stuhlmacher's criticism of certain practitioners of the historical-

and diversity we interpret the Scriptures having will in part be a function of our interpretive models.

Ultimately God is the "glue" that holds the Scripture together. But God is a being whose character belies easy oversimplifications. God's "voice" is not a monotone. God's mercy is a surprising dimension of God's justice. God faithfully acts as God has promised and God also acts contrary to expectations, forgiving when judgment was expected. God's promise to Abraham's particular descendants somehow is also a promise to all nations. God gives unbreakable laws and yet surprisingly suffers punishment on behalf of other guilty parties. God authorizes poetry and apocalyptic literature, and each is to be read very differently than Law.

The fact that we have such rich diversity of forms in the canon strongly argues that whatever models of unity are embraced, they must be sufficiently complex to account for the surprising diversity in the divine communication of redemption. Wisdom suggests that knowing the difference between gospel and epistle, between apocalyptic literature and historical narrative, is essential to understanding why all these diverse books belong to one canon.[31]

This intuition is also underwritten by the claim that the Scriptures do not hide an otherwise abstract and disembodied revelation. It is the living Word who speaks in and through the written Word as a life-giving Word. The Scriptures perform the task of enacting the gospel into the lives of diverse communities of believers.[32] This gospel gets situated in diverse contexts across many ages and people groups. In this regard the church is the fundamental community of interpreters in which the meaning of the Scriptures is discerned.[33] It is not a disinterested discernment, but a discernment that comes by means of being the community in which the gospel is enacted. In this respect there is a peculiar community called the church, which is given the responsibility to submit to the authority of Scriptures. Not just any community with religious concerns acts as

---

critical school of biblical interpretation. See his *Historical Criticism and Theological Interpretation of Scripture,* trans. Roy Harrisville (Philadelphia: Fortress, 1977). Stuhlmacher does not think it an option to abandon all historical enquiries of the Scripture, but rather that these enquiries cannot be an end in their own right.

31. See Barry Webb's contribution in this collection, "Biblical Authority and Diverse Literary Genres" (chapter 19), for a very helpful argument regarding the connection of the diversity of genres in the canon and the unity of the canon.

32. For exposition of performative notions of Scripture see Kevin Vanhoozer, *The Drama of Doctrine* (Louisville: Westminster John Knox, 1995), and Michael S. Horton, *Covenant and Eschatology* (Louisville: Westminster John Knox, 2001).

33. Nadine Pence Frantz speaks of the local church as the "reader of the text and active participant in the knowing of the text" in her "Biblical Interpretation in a 'Non-Sense' World: Text, Revelation, and Interpretive Community," *Brethren Life and Thought* 39, no. 3 (Summer 1994): 160.

the church. It is precisely those communities who belong to the gospel that may rightly be called the church.[34] Submitting to the Scriptures serves as the central interpretive impulse of the church and by which its interpretive framework ought to be different than other communities.

The church is, by extension, called to a unity-in-diversity and a diversity-in-unity. It is the conversation of interpretation within diverse ecclesial bodies that require attention at this point. And of course churches both local as well as connected across regions, nations, and continents carry on conversations of interpretation about the meaning of the Bible and its peculiar application in their midst. Churches of every stripe wrestle with how to manifest a unity-in-diversity within their own congregational boundaries. There is no more perplexing problem a pastor faces than building a sense of community that sustains a healthy balance of unity-in-diversity.[35] What may appear as homogeneity from outside the church's walls is in fact experienced as significant diversity within the lived experience of the congregation.

Maintaining the unity of the congregation while promoting an appropriate diversity has proven very difficult in this democratized era for pastors charged with serving as the focal point of an ecclesial identity. Tendencies are noticeable that either stress the unity of the church around the persona of the pastor (and thereby promote an enforced uniformity), or that stress a laissez-faire mode that results in a chaotic democracy of conflicts. Likewise the task of biblical interpretation carried on within the church tends toward these two poles. A uniformity of interpretation can be authorized by appeal to a uniform set of elite biblical interpreters. But so likewise is it possible to promote a chaotic democracy of biblical interpretation wherein every one is one's own interpreter.[36]

The goal of inhabiting a unity-in-diversity is not the sheer self-preservation of the church any more than paying attention to how others read the Scriptures is simply a function of intellectual courtesy. The gospel itself is implicit in this model of unity-in-diversity. The gospel is thick and rich and no single description will capture it fully.[37] It is the gospel for which the church exists and through

34. Discerning the identity of those communities who belong to the gospel from those who do not is fraught with difficulty and yet the task of discernment must be engaged. The biblical injunctions about false teachers and counterfeit gospels are too numerous to ignore. On the task of discernment, see Michael Horton, *People and Place: A Covenantal Ecclesiology* (Louisville: Westminster John Knox, 2008).

35. Cf. Douglas L. Fagerstrom and James W. Carlson, *The Lonely Pew: Creating Community in the Local Church* (Grand Rapids: Baker, 1993), and Lyle D. Vander Broek, *Breaking Barriers: The Possibilities of Christian Community in a Lonely World* (Grand Rapids: Brazos, 2002).

36. See George Marsden, "Everyone One's Own Interpreter? The Bible, Science and Authority in Mid-Nineteenth-Century America," in *The Bible in America,* ed. Mark Noll and Nathan Hatch (Oxford: Oxford University Press, 1982), 79-100.

37. It is important to avoid what Kevin Vanhoozer calls propositionalism on the one hand

which the church is to act. It is the nature of the gospel that the "dividing walls of hostility" are broken down in Christ. He is our "peace" in whom the many are fit into one body.[38] The gist of that argument is the same with respect to biblical interpretation. The variety of gifts is given for the well-being of the church, even as the well-being of the church depends upon the embrace of the one gospel in Christ. Gabriel Fackre puts it this way,

> Epistemology and ecclesiology are linked. Short of the final vision, illumination is given to the church in precisely the way the gift-ministries within the Body are called to relate to one another. There is a variety within the Body and we must acknowledge that.[39]

The important proviso in this is that the diverse parts of the body must understand each other well enough to benefit from each other in the task of biblical interpretation. This requires the difficult labors of listening enough across the divides to permit understanding, and also to affirm that understanding is possible across the divides. If diverse interpretive perspectives are framed as incommensurable there will be no way to bridge the divisions. There will be no way to communicate across the chasms of our differences.[40] Only to the extent that interpretive differences can be understood by the respective communities, will the differences potentially serve constructive purposes.

Different Kinds of Differences

The church ought to hold together two theological affirmations about how God works in relation to our diverse social locations and cultural contexts. By the power of the Spirit, interpretations across diverse social locations and cultural contexts may enrich each other even as they may also help expose the latent idolatries peculiar to each context. Differences of interpretation can be obstacles

---

and perspectivism on the other. Propositionalism supposes that reality can be adequately captured by descriptive propositions. Perspectivism, by contrast, supposes that reality is nothing more than an interpreter's own perspective. Vanhoozer defends aspectival realism, which supposes that while there are multiple aspects or dimensions to reality that can be known, no single description will capture all of them. Historical writing, poetry, and epistles are just three genres that truly express different aspects of the gospel in the Scriptures. See Vanhoozer, *The Drama of Doctrine: A Canonical Linguistic Approach to Christian Theology* (Louisville: Westminster John Knox, 2005). See especially chapter 9, "The Canonical-Linguistic Approach."

38. Cf. Eph. 2:11-16 and 4:1-16. In chapter 2, Paul writes of the "two becoming one," and in chapter 4, he writes of the body being held together by its many joints.

39. Gabriel Fackre, *The Doctrine of Revelation* (Grand Rapids: Eerdmans, 1999), 198.

40. See Adonis Vidu, *Theology After Neo-Pragmatism* (Milton Keynes: Paternoster, 2008).

to overcome or they may be pieces of a puzzle that belong together. As Todd Billings notes:

> Because of the Spirit's indigenizing work, scripture interpretation from diverse contexts can be received as mutual enrichment, gifts of the Spirit. Yet there is a second side to the Spirit's work through Scripture as well. All cultures have idols that resist God's transformation in the reading of Scripture; therefore a critique of culture is an important practice in receiving Scripture as God's word, discerning through Scripture the bounded character of the Spirit's work in Christ, which calls all cultures to continual conversion.[41]

It is clear that our human experience as individuals gives rise to tensions and conflicts between us in regard to our diverse perspectives. My experience of life as an American in the twenty-first century carries with it diverse perspectives from those who were Americans in the eighteenth century or those who are African or Asian in the twenty-first century. Some of these differences may manifest fundamental conflicts, though surely not all differences are of this ilk. There are differences that emerge from the diverse corruptions of our hearts while other differences are owing to the finite realities of our human nature and the manner in which our lives are always situated in historical contexts. We use the language of "bias" to represent the interpretations that arise from the corruptions of our hearts and the language of "perspective" to represent the interpretations that arise from our own unique historical and personal context.[42] Distinguishing between bias and perspective is a notoriously difficult project.

At times this issue has appeared problematic for Protestants. Without an infallible teaching magisterium, Protestant biblical interpretation lacks a uniform external control that distinguishes bias from perspective. The problem is not as troublesome as it may at first appear. The Scriptures are the final interpretive

41. Billings, *The Word of God for the People of God,* xv.

42. James K. A. Smith, *The Fall of Interpretation* (Downers Grove, IL: InterVarsity, 2000), and Merold Westphal, *Whose Community? Which Interpretation?* (Grand Rapids: Baker Academic, 2009). Both argue that evangelicals too strongly connect diverse epistemic perspectives with the doctrine of sin. They take particular issue with those evangelical thinkers who suppose that the goal of interpretation is an objectively adequate non-context-dependent interpretation. However, both Smith and Westphal seem to downplay the spectrum of differences between better and worse interpretations and thereby suggest that differences of interpretation are almost always owing to the peculiar (not peculiarly corrupt) perspective of the interpreter. But this belies the role that truth plays in distinguishing better (or worse) interpretations. Anthony Thiselton has argued that affirming truth which can be tested is not tied to (disreputable) classical foundationalism nor to epistemic objectivism. Knowing the truth need not require objectivism any more than having a perspective requires sinfulness. See Thiselton, *The Hermeneutics of Doctrine* (Grand Rapids: Eerdmans, 2007), especially section 7.2, "Does a Communal, Contingent, Hermeneutical Approach Exclude Epistemology?" 126-34.

court of appeal and therefore serve as their own internal control that distinguishes bias from perspective. If this is so, then the Scriptures subvert any external imposition of interpretive controls. Protestants do not lack an authorized interpreter, but rather lack the very obstacles that often impede access to the full canonical story.[43]

Recently the emerging church conversation has urged the wider Protestant evangelical movement to simply affirm the diversity of interpretations as a sign of the Spirit's work.[44] So John Franke writes,

> As Christian communities formed in a variety of cultural situations, they established traditions that became integral to their cultural and communal outlook. These traditions shaped their understanding of the Christian faith, their reading of the Bible, and the particular shape of their witness to the gospel. This plurality is part of the work of the Spirit in guiding the church into truth and serves as a defining mark of the Christian tradition.[45]

And surely evangelical Protestants have been slow to affirm the plurality of interpretative traditions within Protestantism. In the last half-century, ecumenical conflicts and conversations with Roman Catholics have put evangelicals on the defensive when it comes to defending the unity of the church.[46] This has sometimes led to an overspiritualizing of the unity of the church.[47] Franke and other emergents have rightly called the wider Protestant movement to think theologically about the plurality of church communities within Protestantism as not simply an obstacle to overcome but an expression of the situatedness of all ec-

43. For a thoughtful and irenic treatment of the differences between Protestant and Roman Catholic notions of biblical authority and interpretation see Chris Castaldo, *Holy Ground: Walking with Jesus as a Former Catholic* (Grand Rapids: Zondervan, 2009).

44. See Peter Rollins, *How (Not) to Speak of God* (Brewster, MA: Paraclete, 2006).

45. John Franke, *Manifold Witness: The Plurality of Truth* (Nashville: Abingdon, 2009), 33. It is worth noting that the emergent slogan "belonging before believing" arises naturally out of their commitment to the positive nature of ecclesial contextualization. However, the church ought to be at one and the same time at home in the world and a stranger to its world. Traversing this dialectic suggests that believing is sometimes necessary before belonging. See Rick Richardson, *Reimagining Evangelism* (Downers Grove, IL: InterVarsity, 2006), and Eddie Gibbs and Ryan K. Bolger, *Emerging Churches: Creating Christian Community in Postmodern Cultures* (Grand Rapids: Baker Academic, 2005).

46. Cf. Mark Noll and Carolyn Nystrom, *Is the Reformation Over? An Evangelical Assessment of Contemporary Roman Catholicism* (Grand Rapids: Baker Academic, 2004).

47. Geoffrey Wainwright makes this very point in his review of Noll and Nystrom, *Is the Reformation Over?* See Wainwright, "An Indifferent Reconciliation," *First Things* 156 (October 2005): 40. He expands on this criticism in his "Evangelical Truth and Ecclesial Unity," in *Ancient and Postmodern Christianity: Paleo-Orthodoxy in the 21st Century,* ed. Christopher Hall and Kenneth Tanner (Downers Grove, IL: InterVarsity, 2002), 183-98.

clesial bodies. The danger, however, is equating plurality with the ongoing work of the Spirit. Not all contextual differences are appropriate to the well-being of the church and therefore not all contextual differences ought to be attributed to the work of the Spirit.[48] Contextual distortions of the gospel are as frequent as contextual appropriations of the gospel. It is the gospel therefore that finally must serve as the criterion for better or worse contextualizations. It is the gospel that is the norm that ought to norm the cultural norms.

Contextualizations emerge because of the way in which God has created human agents as socially located. There is a unique unrepeatable quality to each of our human experiences by virtue of the distinctive nature of embodied persons in historical and cultural contexts. In this sense there is no difference between the humanity of Jesus and our humanity. Each is peculiarly embedded in a unique cultural location and the patterns of life reflect that reality. However, there is also an important difference between our humanity and the humanity of Jesus. On this side of paradise, our human experience is corrupted by our fallen condition and by the socially constructed networks of corruption in which we are located. Our fallen condition is both individual and communal.[49] Any adequate theory of contextualization must account for human communities being necessarily embodied as well as corrupted.[50]

Some differences among human communities are owing to the corruption of our nature and some are owing to the diverse social locations of the communities. The tension between the Son and the Father at the crucifixion points at the reality that differences are not always owing to corruptions. Sometimes personal differences complement each other, and other times our human differences arise

48. Gary Badcock, *The House Where God Lives: Renewing the Doctrine of the Church for Today* (Grand Rapids: Eerdmans, 2009), comes perilously close to attributing all significant ecclesiological change to the work of the Spirit. Without diminishing the work of the Spirit, we ought to be cautious in assuming that all change is good, and therefore ought to be cautious that all change is owing to the work of the Spirit.

49. The dialectic between systemic and individual corruptions may explain the sharp differences between recent theological communitarians (e.g., Stanley Hauerwas and Alasdair MacIntyre) and those who have defended individual human rights as fundamental restraint on communal corruptions (e.g., Nicholas Wolterstorff and Jeffrey Stout). Reading both sides of the debate may temper individualistic tendencies by evangelicals on one side and the unqualified embrace of communities on the other side. See Hauerwas, *A Community of Character: Toward a Constructive Christian Social Ethic* (Notre Dame: University of Notre Dame Press, 2005 [orig. 1981]) and *In Good Company: The Church as Polis* (Notre Dame: University of Notre Dame Press, 1995). See also Nicholas Wolterstorff, *Justice: Rights and Wrongs* (Princeton: Princeton University Press, 2008), and Jeffrey Stout, *Democracy and Tradition* (Princeton: Princeton University Press, 2004).

50. David Kelsey, *Eccentric Existence: A Theological Anthropology* (Louisville: Westminster John Knox, 2009), is a massive attempt at reckoning with human identity as essentially embodied without losing the distinctively theological character of personhood.

from sin and self-interest. If there is a common good that grows out of bonds to each other, there are also potential dangers when those bonds are corrupted. Protecting the common good while guarding against the corruptions of those common bonds is part and parcel of the wisdom of the gospel.[51]

Reading the Scriptures together in community and across communities pushes us to recognize both sides of this equation. We may not read the Scriptures as others do because we are peculiar individuals who see things differently because of those peculiarities. Some of those peculiarities emerge from our corruptions, some emerge from our distinctive experiences, and some emerge from our finite limitations.

Whatever else the meaning of a biblical text is, it is more complex and rich than ordinary discourse supposes but less complex than technical academic treatments sometimes suggest. It is also clearer than ordinary intuitions about clarity suppose. The clarity of the Bible has to do with how the words of Scripture actually accomplish the communicative task for which they were written. The Scriptures in the power of the Spirit provoke the appropriate response that enables us to call them "clear." The words are inspired by the Spirit of God and applied to our lives by the same Spirit. It is also the Spirit who illuminates the true nature of the gospel in our lives. Our trust in the clarity of Scripture, in other words, is the trustworthiness of the Spirit.[52]

Leaving aside for the moment the question as to whether texts have singular or plural meanings, it is safe to say that some texts are more difficult to understand than others because of the depth of their claims. Take, for example, a passage like the following:

> He is the image of the invisible God, the firstborn of all creation. For by him all things were created, in heaven and on earth, visible and invisible, whether thrones or dominions or rulers or authorities — all things were created through him and for him. And he is before all things, and in him all things hold together. (Col. 1:15-17)

51. Anthony Thiselton comments, "Many postmodern understandings of the human as corporately under bondage to forces of power beyond the control of the individual have more in common with biblical perspectives than the shallow liberal theological optimism that speaks only of the infinite value of an individual 'soul'" (*The Hermeneutics of Doctrine,* 196). See also Thiselton, *Interpreting God and the Postmodern Self: On Meaning, Manipulation, and Promise* (Edinburgh: T. & T. Clark, 1995). It should be added that evangelicals are no less optimistic than liberals when it comes to thinking about human nature.

52. See the essay in this collection by Mark Thompson, "The Generous Gift of a Gracious Father: Toward a Theological Account of the Clarity of Scripture" (chapter 20). He writes, "The clarity of Scripture is that quality of Scripture which, arising from the fact that it is ultimately God's effective communicative act, ensures the meaning of each biblical text, when viewed in the context of the canonical whole, is accessible to all who come to it in faith."

This bit of text is rich enough in its testimony to Jesus that it seems fair to say that interpreters over the centuries have not exhausted the depths of its claims.[53] What readers hear this text saying is influenced by how much of the remainder of the book of Colossians they are familiar with, how much of the remainder of the Pauline corpus they understand, and undoubtedly how much of the entire Canon they understand as background to this passage. Would it be true to say that no one reader has discovered the full richness of this text?[54] Of course. In this regard it would be better to have the eyes and ears of many readers across the centuries and across the globe to better grasp the wider breadth and depth of canonical backgrounds that explain the depth of this passage. Reading the book of Colossians with the aid of Chrysostom, Aquinas, Calvin, Wesley, J. B. Lightfoot, H. C. G. Moule, as well as contemporary interpreters in the West and among majority world Christians would surely increase our sensitivities to the wider range of these canonical backgrounds of the book.[55] Reading along with the community of interpreters across the ages and across the globe cannot but help us to see and hear more of the text than we would otherwise.

But the converse would not be false. It would not be the case that any reader in particular was so helpless outside of the full background of interpreters across the centuries and the wider breadth of the canonical background that they could not understand Colossians 1:15-17 or what the key claims of the passage were. Reading the Bible on their own may not grant them as much access to the meaning of the text as possible, but it would surely not leave them without hope of hearing the text in part.

What should be said about different (communal) readings of Colossians

53. See *Colossians, 1-2 Thessalonians, 1-2 Timothy, Titus, Philemon* in the Ancient Christian Commentary on Scripture Series, ed. Peter Gorday (Downers Grove, IL: InterVarsity, 2000) for a selection of voices from the early church on the richness of this text.

54. The "richness" of a text allows for the possibility of thinking of mutually enriching interpretations rather than only better or worse interpretations. There are surely better and worse interpretations, but there are also interpretations that help to recover aspects of reality not fully manifest in other interpretations. Metaphors for the richness of the biblical text might include its "symphonic quality" or its "aesthetic beauty." Like a great piece of music or art, the Bible possesses a depth that brings diverse elements into a coherent whole without rendering the parts the same. See the essay by Phil Long, "'Competing Histories, Competing Theologies?' Reflections on the Unity and Diversity of the Old Testament('s Readers)" (chapter 12 in this collection), for a wider discussion of the conceptual framework for understanding the unity of the Bible as an artistic unity. Long discusses artistic unity at much greater length in his *The Art of Biblical History* (Grand Rapids: Zondervan 1994). See also Vanhoozer, *The Drama of Doctrine,* on aspectival realism as another way to conceptualize this issue. See also Hans Urs von Balthasar, *Truth Is Symphonic: Aspects of Christian Pluralism,* trans. Graham Harrison (San Francisco: Ignatius, 1987).

55. Cf. John L. Thompson, *Reading the Bible with the Dead: What You Can Learn from the History of Exegesis That You Cannot Learn from Exegesis Alone* (Grand Rapids: Eerdmans, 2007).

1:15-17 that are in conflict with each other? Can this passage give rise to two subsequently diverse and contradictory renderings? It is not uncommon among some sects like the Jehovah's Witnesses to interpret the phrase "the firstborn of all creation" to be a claim about the creaturely status of Jesus, denying in essence that Jesus was prior to creation.[56] Those within the historic Trinitarian traditions of the church have read this passage not as a denial of Jesus' preexistence, but rather a reference to his authority over the created order by virtue of his status as "firstborn of all creation."[57] In dispute is the meaning of the phrase "firstborn of all creation" *(prōtotokos pasēs ktiseōs).* The controversy has to do with the genitive relation of "firstborn" to "all creation." If, for instance, the apostle Paul had used the phrase "firstborn of the father," the controversy over the eternal status of Jesus would not have been focused on this particular verse. But because the apostle connects the legal status of Jesus ("firstborn") with the whole of the cosmos ("over all creation"), the historic Christian church has steadfastly refused to consider Jesus merely a creature. In this instance, it should not be supposed that the meaning of the phrase is so variable that the language of "firstborn" might be both an affirmation and a denial of Jesus' preexistence. The accompanying "of all creation" provides adequate support to the preexistence claim of the Christian tradition. It might be the case that the phrase has other overtones as well, but it would be very odd indeed if the phrase supported both sides of the conflict.[58]

How do we account for these sorts of differences of interpretation across diverse communities? In this instance the differences emerge, at least in part, from the diverse interpretative intuitions of the different communities about Jesus. Belonging to one community or the other(s) would not authorize their particular reading of Colossians 1:15. It would simply confirm one's membership in the respective community. Settling the differences would not (ordinarily) be accomplished by appealing to one's interpretive community. Rather, the differences would be settled (if possible) by appeal to the words themselves in their immedi-

56. The claim is detailed at considerable length in many of the publications of the Watchtower Bible and Tract Society, the official publication arm of the Jehovah Witnesses. Online publications explicating the Jehovah Witness interpretation of Colossians 1:15 can be found at www.watchtower.org.

57. Representatively, see P. T. O'Brien, *Colossians and Philemon* (Waco, TX: Word, 1982).

58. It should be noted that there are some places where there are genuine ambiguities in the text and it would be wrong in those instances to arbitrarily choose how to interpret the ambiguity, except by appeal to wider literary contexts. Mark Thompson's essay in this collection helpfully clarifies what we mean by "clarity" and thus what we also mean by "ambiguity" with respect to the Scriptures. The Bible is not ambiguous in general about the major points of doctrine nor about the central story of the gospel. But this would not rule out ambiguities in the Bible on some exegetical points, some of which may impact how major doctrinal convictions are established. I am indebted to Simon Gathercole in personal correspondence for the reminder that taking ambiguity seriously rather than simply overlooking it is an exegete's rightful responsibility in interpreting the Scripture.

ate and wider literary contexts. The authority of the community's interpretation is grounded in the accuracy and adequacy of their understanding of the passage.

At this level of generalization, the "turn to community" does not much impact the nature of interpretation. The adequacy of interpretation is not better or worse because a community rather than an individual interprets the Scriptures. The adequacy of interpretation is a function in the first place of the meaning of the Scriptures to be interpreted and the reader's responsibility in reading them faithfully.[59] But lest we forget, the Scriptures are not a text simply "out there" to be interpreted. The Bible makes demands on its readers.[60] It is a text that seeks to interpret the reader even as readers seek to interpret the text. In this regard we must not merely read the Scriptures, but read them in relation to ourselves.[61] The Scriptures function in this regard as a world-absorbing text, drawing its readers into the rich orbit of its meaning and significance.[62]

Inhabiting the World Created by the Word

Christians across the ages have continued to read the Book long after they first became acquainted with it. There is always more to learn, and more of the Scriptures in which to be embedded. The church insisted that its theological goal was to inhabit the narrative of redemption as it was revealed in the canon, not merely to understand it. Why else continue to read the Scriptures day after day and year after year?

Christian communities assume that additional discernment is always possible as they consistently and persistently pay attention to the Scriptures.[63] There is

59. Kevin Vanhoozer marks out the difference between a reader's response and a reader's responsibility to the text. The former is not necessarily a function of the latter. See his "Imprisoned or Free? Text, Status and Theological Interpretation in the Master/Slave Discourse of Philemon," in *Reading Scripture with the Church,* ed. A. K. M. Adam, Stephen Fowl, Kevin Vanhoozer, and Francis Watson (Grand Rapids: Baker Academic, 2006), 51-93.

60. See the essay by Dan Doriani in this volume for an especially thoughtful exposition of this claim, "Take, Read" (chapter 35).

61. Miroslav Volf rightly recognizes that texts in general and the biblical texts in particular are not simply objects or things. They are social relations enacted between author and reader. The intended social relation is that of communication in the broadest sense. The consequence is that readers are called to "the task of decoding meaning and constructing plausible accounts of the meanings" intended in the act of communication. See his *Captive to the Word of God* (Grand Rapids: Eerdmans, 2010), 29.

62. The term is borrowed from Bruce Marshall, "Absorbing the World: Christianity and the Universe of Truth," in *Theology and Dialogue: Essays in Conversation with George Lindbeck,* ed. Bruce Marshall (Notre Dame: University of Notre Dame Press, 1990), 69-103.

63. Nicholas Wolterstorff, *Divine Discourse: Philosophical Reflections on the Claim That God Speaks* (Cambridge: Cambridge University Press, 1995), uses the language of "first hermeneutic" to reference the church's ongoing public reading of Scripture.

always the hope of a richer immersion in the narrative of redemption and greater absorption into the wisdom of the gospel. It is an ordinary practice that communities read the Scriptures together, in part to guard against the eccentricities of private interpretations, and in part to encourage the whole of the community being absorbed into the whole of the gospel.

If we become too intent on getting the meaning out of Scripture and into our world, the gospel too easily gets swallowed up in the patterns of our contemporary habits. It too quickly gets fragmented by the particularities of our circumstances and contexts. George Lindbeck has written,

> In those circles where the text itself is widely and assiduously studied — conservative Protestant, charismatic, base communities, and groups interested in spirituality — the reading is often so remote from the classic hermeneutic, so divisive and/or individualistic, that the kind of historical reconstructions which stay with the Christian mainstream seem preferable.[64]

Resisting that particularizing move is made by inverting the order of conformation in conscious and intentional ways. Reading communities must see themselves conformed to the Scriptures by contrast to drawing the Scriptures into the reader's own world. It is the Word that gives life to "life together." The Word creates the church within which individuals understand what it means to belong to others. The Word restrains selfishness without undermining individual significance.

A danger for the church in the West, as it is for majority world churches, is to overparticularize the gospel by confusing cultural norms with gospel norms. The gospel is always enculturated, but some enculturations tame the gospel in such a fashion that the gospel loses its prophetic distance from the culture. Thinking about this task from the perspective of the community of readers, the task is to find ways to let the Scriptures ask the questions as well as provide the answers. The wisdom of Scripture resides in the gospel itself, which means the Scriptures ought to interpret the Scriptures, by means of which the community of readers is interpreted by the Scriptures. What may have seemed confounding and confusing initially becomes wise and provocative over time.[65] It becomes wise and provocative, not because the Scriptures have changed, but because readers have been changed in their understanding of themselves in relation to the Scriptures.

An important corollary: the meaning of the gospel does not lie in the first

64. George Lindbeck, "Scripture, Consensus and Community," in *Biblical Interpretation in Crisis: The Ratzinger Conference on Bible and Theology,* ed. Richard John Neuhaus (Grand Rapids: Eerdmans, 1989), 88.

65. See Mark Thompson, *A Clear and Present Word: The Clarity of Scripture* (Downers Grove, IL: InterVarsity, 2006).

instance in the changes it occasions in the life of the reader; the central significance is contained in the actual redemptive acts of God's mercy. The Scriptures are a life-giving Word, and in this sense the church comes to know the Scriptures by living them. The Scriptures also provide plenty of counsel about what the church is *not* supposed to be like. The Bible restrains the unfettered self-interest of churches and the idolatries of religion and irreligion. The church is called to be different because it is united to its bridegroom, Christ.

It is likely that diverse parts of the redemptive drama will impact diverse readers in diverse manners. And over this diversity of responses the text cannot exercise temporal control. Different communities will read the Scriptures in different ways for a host of different reasons. This descriptive diversity lays no normative claim upon the church until there is an explanatory account of the differences that matter and the differences that do not matter. Noticing that the Scriptures are read in diverse ways by diverse peoples may amount to no more than that diverse people read in diverse ways.[66]

The Scriptures as Public and Personal

The church has confessed that the Scriptures are a public document whose interpretation is accountable to the wider church and the breadth of ecclesial traditions. The church has also confessed that the Scriptures are a covenant document articulating God's deeply personal and intimate love of the church across the ages and across the globe.[67] The sacred romance at the heart of the covenant relationship of God to his people cannot be reduced to a list of objective beliefs about either party to the covenant, though surely these core convictions cannot be excised out of the story either. The Scriptures are public and personal. No reading should be merely private, nor should any reading be strictly neutral and non-partisan.

The Bible commits us to an interaction of two diverse "ways-to-put-the-world-together" — ours and the Bible's. It is an interaction between the history of redemption and our own history. In this meeting, different communities of readers realize that as they ask questions of the Scriptures, questions are being asked of them and they are forced to reckon with an alternative "way-to-put-the-world-together." This compels readers to rethink many of their fundamental

66. Doriani, "Take, Read" (chapter 35 herein), argues that God is concerned not merely that his Word be read, but that it be read properly. As Doriani writes, "We must read with an eye for the suffering and glory of the Christ (Luke 24:26-27) and for the way of salvation by faith in Jesus (2 Tim. 3:15). We read for authoritative commands (James 1:22), but also for the Spirit rather than the letter of the law (2 Cor. 3:6)."

67. See Michael S. Horton, *Covenant and Eschatology* (Louisville: Westminster John Knox, 2002), for the best recent treatment of a covenantal account of biblical authority.

assumptions and ways of living, even diverse readers who are situated in very diverse historical and cultural contexts. Reading the Scriptures in the company of differently situated readers may aid in reckoning more fully with the Scripture's alternative "way-to-put-the-world-together." Conversely, readers may reinterpret the Scriptures on their terms, keeping any impact of the Scriptures to a minimum. The taken-for-granted character of ordinary life can prove an impediment to hearing the text as an adversary as well as a friend.[68] Sometimes reading the Scriptures proves too costly to the life of its readers and they simply dismiss the Book. But by the power of the Spirit, on occasion, some communities of readers "get it" and realize how life-changing the Book's message actually is. In this instance the wisdom of God breaks through.

The accountability to the wisdom of God is enhanced by the public conversation about the meaning of Scripture within communities and across communities.[69] But we feel the pinch when the public conversation gets messy and diverse interpretations become entrenched. The community of the saints is not always a communion of the saints, and the canon of Scripture too often gives way to innumerable canons within the canon. Retreating into the safety of one's own ecclesial tradition or communal enclave may be a natural response to this messiness, but it undermines the implicit accountability to read the text on its own terms, rather than ours.

We are aware that Wesleyan and Reformed interpreters do not interpret verses like Exodus 10:1 or John 3:16 in the same fashion. Protestants and Roman Catholics read the second chapter of James in different ways. African Christians tend to read the "principality and powers" passages in Ephesians 6 and Colossians 2 differently than American dispensationalists. None of these traditions of interpretation is warranted simply because they bear the weight of a particular community. The very differences of interpretation are accountable to the wider public conversation of the church universal.[70]

Being accountable to the wider body of Christ means that we should not

68. Markus Bockmuehl writes of the confrontation between the Scriptures and its readers such that the reader is "the object as much as the subject of analysis and interpretation." See his *Seeing the Word: Refocusing New Testament Study: Studies in Theological Interpretation* (Grand Rapids: Baker Academic, 2006), 147.

69. Stuhlmacher, among others, has argued for public accountability in hermeneutics. He refers to this as a hermeneutics of consent. It requires honest exegetical conversations with historians and with the history of interpretation, as well as with contemporary communities of interpretation who seek to live out the text, and finally with an openness to hear God speak through the Bible. Stuhlmacher refers to this dimension as an "openness to transcendence." See his *Historical Criticism and Theological Interpretation of Scripture,* 83-91.

70. Given human limitations, we ought to be careful about packing too much into anyone's ability to account for the full scope of the church universal and its varied and various commitments.

rest merely content in the tried and tested interpretations of our peculiar communities, for no one church or single tradition "owns" the Scripture. More particularly, it is God who "owns" the Scripture. It is fully the Divine Word and by authorization fully a human Word. It is through this Word that the formative identity of the gospel is enacted in the church. The corollary is that every church and each tradition over which that divine ownership extends, explicitly belongs to every other church and every other tradition over which divine ownership extends. Put another way, it is the gospel in all its canonical richness to which the churches and traditions belong and are thereby necessarily connected to each other.

This does not mean that we should sit lightly on any interpretative tradition simply because some community in the wider body of Christ disagrees with it. It requires that we "bump into" the differences we have with each other, which in turn requires that these differences are made intelligible across our diverse cultural and social locations. Being accountable to others is a difficult labor requiring both humility and confidence. At times it also requires the hard work of reconciliation. And if reconciliation is at the heart of the gospel it ought to be reflected in the ways different gospel communities deal with each other across their divisions. A chief challenge facing deeply polarized ecclesial communities is to read the Scriptures "with one another" and not merely "against each other."[71]

Dealing with Our Differences

Understanding those labors requires that we understand the natural and cultural intuitions we have about dealing with our differences. The social world of modernity is pluralized in countless directions and is experienced at many levels. Everything from politics and religion to economics, art, and music has been pluralized in our modern world. The contemporary is often marked out from the traditional purely by the pluralization of experience. The contemporary connotes a much higher volume of diversity — diversity of music, of religion, of vocation, of culture, of language. The sheer complexity of technology compounds the diversity that surrounds us. Consider how many diverse individuals fill our lives, as reflected in the size of an email address book or how many "friends" one has on Facebook. Consider how many television channels fill diverse niches of interest today. Consider the vast number of diverse locations we are transported to every day via the Internet. The emergence of these deep diversities in our lives has

71. See Gay Bryon, "Biblical Interpretation as an Act of Community Accountability," *Union Seminary Quarterly Review* 56 (2002): 55-58. Byron's central concern is the African American community of scholars, who have often been excluded from the academic guild of biblical interpreters.

the inevitable consequence of privileging diversity over unity in our collective consciousness.[72]

That embrace of deep diversity after two centuries of liberal democracy in the West has had unfortunate and unintentional consequences. It has legitimated an antinomian moment where our attentions are given to fragments and individual interests. Self-interest seems far too rampant, and we find it difficult to imagine other possibilities. Condemned to the intrinsic bias of our own perspective, we seem all too comfortable with the loss of a universal context for life. We tell it like it is, which translated means, "My perspective is all that really matters." When it comes to biblical interpretation this has proven disastrous.

The resurgence of tribal sympathies related to race, gender, and ethnicity appears as a natural reaction to the emptiness of one's own individual perspective. People have looked for social reinforcement of their own interpretations in homogenous communities when they cannot be found elsewhere. But the more this search is tribal in nature, the more fractured the church's common life becomes and the tendency to yet greater conflict is realized. In an age of global capitalism, corporate corruption, identity politics, and theocratic terrorism, our deep ecclesial conflicts of interpretation seem a natural if unfortunate outcome.

Recognition of the differences that race, gender, and ethnicity make, however, is not always tribal in its character. It has and can serve to undermine the arrogance of oppressive cultural structures that do not recognize their own idolatries. In the 1960s the civil rights movement cast grave doubts on the notion of an objective American perspective that could speak for all and that represented every citizen.[73] As America learned painfully through the struggle, not all perspectives were created equal and not all Americans experienced life in equal ways.[74] In that same era and as a result of the second feminist movement, we learned to appreciate the fact that a woman's experience was not in all respects identical to a man's experience. Gender made a difference, though it was not always clear what that difference was.[75]

72. The wide cultural embrace of diversity is merely a descriptive claim at one level. When it slips into normative mode the consequences are far-reaching. See D. A. Carson, *The Gagging of God: Christianity Confronts Pluralism* (Grand Rapids: Zondervan, 1995).

73. I discuss at greater length the demise of objectivity in the cultural and conceptual turmoil of the 1960s in my *Progressive and Conservative Religious Ideologies: The Tumultuous Decade of the 1960s* (London: Ashgate, 2010).

74. An especially valuable treatment of the civil rights movement as a distinctive theological movement can be found in Charles Marsh, "The Civil Rights Movement as Theological Drama — Interpretation and Application," *Modern Theology* 18 (2002): 231-50.

75. Possibly it was to see that sin emerged not only from the roots of pride but also from shame and insignificance. An early feminist theologian, Valerie Saiving, wrote in 1960, "[T]he temptations of woman as woman are not the same as the temptations of man as man, and the specifically feminine forms of sin . . . have a quality which can never be encompassed by

As we are now well aware, the resurgence of Christianity outside of the West has revitalized ecclesial notions of mission and evangelism.[76] Attached to that awareness has been the (slower) realization that Christianity is translatable across a virtually infinite set of cultural contexts.[77] This theological translatability entails that biblical interpretation likewise cannot be confined to any single set of culturally defined parameters. The task of reading the Bible across the myriad of cultural boundaries is a task intrinsic to the nature of the gospel itself. The accompanying danger of reading the text of Scripture in overly particularized ways will inevitably be realized, but this danger should not prevent the church from engaging the task itself.[78]

If it is true that we live in a time that privileges diversity over unity in the West, it is also true that we are not always clear about the nature of the differences that matter and why they matter. And even as we celebrate our diversities, we are drawn ever deeper into the cocoons of partisanship that protect us from these diversities.[79] A great irony of modern life is the ever-growing disparity between the descriptive diversity of contemporary culture and the actual homogeneity of the communities in which we experience day-to-day life. We are conscious of the conflicts between political parties, between fans of different sports teams, or between members of different educational establishments. We also know that what animates great rivalries is the homogeneity of the respective rival communities. Under the pressures of pluralization, we tend to socially migrate to safe havens of unity. Social conservatives tend to listen to socially conservative commentators. Social radicals tend to read other social radicals. We migrate toward homogenous communities as a response to the increase of diversity around us.[80]

---

such terms as 'pride' and 'will to power.' They are better suggested by such items as triviality, distractibility, and diffuseness; lack of an organizing center or focus; dependence on others for one's self-definition; tolerance at the expense of standards of excellence . . . in short, underdevelopment or negation of the Self." Saiving, "The Human Situation: A Feminine View," *JR* 40 (1960): 108.

76. The early work of Lesslie Newbigin was a particularly pungent theological call to recast the nature of mission from a "sending to foreign shores" notion to an "embedded *missio dei* in every culture" notion. See his *The Household of God* (New York: Friendship Press 1954), and *Trinitarian Faith and Today's Mission* (Richmond, VA: John Knox Press, 1964).

77. See Timothy Tennent, *Theology in the Context of World Christianity* (Grand Rapids: Zondervan, 2007).

78. Darryl Guder has written of the need for the "continuing conversion" of the church in its cross-cultural interactions. All cultural translations of the gospel bear some imprint of their social locations, which stand in need of correction and are only corrected as the gospel bumps up against them from another social location. See his *The Continuing Conversion of the Church* (Grand Rapids: Eerdmans, 2002).

79. I borrow this phrase from David Brooks, "Getting Obama Right," *New York Times*, March 12, 2010.

80. See Margaret Wheatley and Myron Kellner-Rogers, "The Paradox and Promise of

This is so in part because diversity can be painful when it is concretized in disagreement. Differences of taste may not matter in the abstract until such time as it comes to deciding what the family will eat for dinner — together. Differences of fashion seem harmless enough in most cases until such time as the family must be part of a common photograph. Different habits of cleanliness may not seem significant until husband and wife must learn to live with these differences on a daily basis. Differences matter when they make a difference of a certain sort.

Our experience of diversity is not always problematic. Marriages that work well often work because of deep respect of differences that bring out otherwise hidden virtues in each partner. Likewise diverse readings of great literature often illuminate the depths of meanings not illuminated by the simply private readings of an individual. Listening to diverse voices in a congregation may prevent the abuse of power when all authority is consolidated into the hands of a few. Most of us want to say, in other words, that diversity is sometimes a very positive experience.

Why should we not say the same thing about biblical interpretation? Some differences of interpretation may well be destructive and others may well be instructive. Some differences may illuminate the richness of the text; others may mask or distort that same richness, pointing instead to the conflicts of communities. There is no mechanical way to determine which differences make a difference until we enter into the conversation with the diverse communities of interpretation and allow those conversations to instruct us about the differences that make a difference.

Much has been written in the recent past about the theological significance of the "other"[81] — other nations, other communities, other people. In a time of increased scrutiny and anxiety about global conflicts, the language of the "other" has focused attention on the immensely important work of reconciliation in the context of these conflicts.[82] It has provided a way to think more clearly about the intensely personal cost of diversity and the impact of racial, ethnic, and cultural diversities upon our own personal identity. Luther's dictum that we should read the Scripture in the first instance as our adversary, reminds us that the Scripture is in important respect the ultimate "other."[83] It stands against us and challenges

Community," in *The Community of the Future,* ed. Frances Hesselbein (San Francisco: Jossey-Bass, 1998), 9-18.

81. One of the most powerful and poignant theological treatments of the "other" is Miroslav Volf, *Exclusion and Embrace: A Theological Exploration of Identity, Otherness, and Reconciliation* (Nashville: Abingdon, 1996).

82. For a theological account connecting the work of reconciliation with the nature of God see Kelly Kapic, *God So Loved, He Gave: Entering the Movement of Divine Generosity* (Grand Rapids: Zondervan, 2010).

83. In his essay in this collection, Robert Kolb remarks that for Luther, the Christian life is a life of repentance. God continually addresses his people with the law's demands. His Word

our normal assumptions about life.[84] In utterly unexpected ways, it also invites us into its world and manifests a strange hospitality to strangers.

Showing genuine theological hospitality to the "other" will not settle the conflicts of our interpretative square, but it will surely more nearly reflect the gospel we confess at the heart of the interpretative square.[85] It is no answer to say that we will simply permit diverse interpretations to continue onward toward the course of yet greater alienation and arbitrariness. Not listening to communities outside of our own provides only a false sense of security. For good or ill, we must recognize that messiness of the interpretative square is our plight and as Christians it is not ours to escape. Privileging communities above individuals or individuals above communities will not resolve this messiness. It is not a realistic option to suppose fundamental interpretive conflicts are going to be solved anytime soon. We must never give up the yearning to resolve our differences and to be reconciled across our conflicts. We must learn to live as faithful readers with and through our diverse interpretations.[86]

A pluralistic interpretive square is the only option beside oppression available to us today.[87] It is a square to which we are accountable, though it is the Scriptures themselves to which we are ultimately accountable in our interpretations. We can retreat from this interpretive messiness, or seek to dominate it, or learn to live with it wisely. Undoubtedly there are many evangelicals today rightfully wary about the fracturing of our theological cohesion. They are wary of its dilatory effects upon their churches. They are wary of the pretensions of "neutrality" so often articulated by the most ardent defenders of tolerance and diversity.

---

is not our ally at the outset, but our accuser. But as the law touches our conscience, the gospel brings salve to it as well. See Kolb, "The Bible in the Reformation and Protestant Orthodoxy" (chapter 3 herein). For a longer treatment of these themes see Robert Kolb, *Martin Luther, Confessor of the Faith* (Oxford: Oxford University Press, 2009).

84. See Robert Kolb, "The Relationship between Scripture and the Confession of the Faith in Luther's Thought," in *Kirkens bekjennelse I historisk og aktuelt perspektiv: Festskrift til Kjell Olav Sannes,* ed. Torleiv Austad, Tormod Engelsviken, and Lars Østner (Trondheim: Tapir, 2010), 53-62.

85. I am borrowing several clues from Martin Marty, *When Faiths Collide* (Oxford: Blackwell, 2005), though applying the hospitality of the gospel to the interpretive square rather than to the wider global religious square as Marty does.

86. In the analogous context of the political square, Nicholas Wolterstorff writes, "Yet we must live together. It is to politics and not to epistemology that we shall have to look for an answer as to how to do that. 'Liberal' politics has fallen on bad days recently. But to its animating vision of a society in which persons of diverse traditions live together in justice and friendship, conversing with each other and slowly altering their traditions in response to the conversation — to that, there is no viable alternative." *John Locke and the Ethics of Belief* (New York: Cambridge University Press, 1996), 246.

87. For the analogy to the wider public square see James W. Skillen, *Recharging the American Experiment: Principled Pluralism for Genuine Civic Community* (Grand Rapids: Baker, 1994).

Dealing with that diversity requires humility and wisdom. It requires a vigilance against resentment and cynicism. Dealing with interpretive diversity requires faith, hope, and charity. Those who read Scripture seriously must engage the interpretive world of diversity on its own God-given terms rather than the terms being dictated by our cultural elites. This requires us to think about it honestly and humbly. It requires the radically counterintuitive claim that we show hospitality to those with whom we have deep disagreements.[88] We engage our disagreement neither by seeking to dominate nor by being merely tolerant. We invite the outsider into the common wisdom of our interpretive traditions. We take their ideas seriously, not primarily to overthrow their ideas, but rather with the expectation that wisdom may be found in the strangest of places — even among those who disagree with us.

88. See Marty, *When Faiths Collide.*

THIRTY

Science and Scripture

Kirsten Birkett

> [A]stronomers investigate with great labour whatever the sagacity of the human mind can comprehend. Nevertheless, this study is not to be reprobated, nor this science to be condemned, because some frantic persons are wont boldly to reject whatever is unknown to them. For as astronomy is not only pleasant, but also very useful to be known: it cannot be denied that this art unfolds the admirable wisdom of God.[1]

As Christians throughout history have endeavored to deal with Scripture responsibly, they perpetually come up against the question: What do we do with knowledge from outside Scripture? How should we best understand the discoveries that Christians or non-Christians are making about the world around us?

It is inevitable that we will want to consider this extra-biblical knowledge in some way. After all, Christians want Scripture to look as good as possible. Apologetically, we want to demonstrate that Scripture stands up in the world of reason and truth, as understood by the non-Christian world. This has always been part of the Christian's desire to defend Scripture and to present it as the way to salvation. A defense of Scripture in itself will not save anyone, but it has a part to play in evangelism.

There are other reasons for our desire to grapple with extra-scriptural knowledge. Being human, we are curious, and want to know how the truths of Scripture fit in with whatever we regard as other truths that have been discovered. There is a great intellectual satisfaction in putting together a "big picture" of knowledge, reconciling all the information we have available to create a system of truth.

These are good impulses. The trouble is, they are a constant temptation to reinterpret Scripture in terms other than its own. In our desire to "reconcile"

1. John Calvin, *Commentary on Genesis* 1.16. See http://153.106.5.3/ccel/calvin/calcom01.vii.i.html, viewed 4 June 2010.

the Bible with other information, it is very easy to forget that Scripture provides a solid framework in its own terms. We must always be careful to maintain the integrity of Scripture, and understand it within its own interpretative grid.

This temptation is multiplied by the fact that every age tends to think that the discoveries or philosophy outside Scripture made in its own time must be true. It is the case now, as it ever was — in particular, the secular sciences are regarded by the majority of the Western population as essentially true and reliable (although it is perhaps curious for a discipline that holds that its very strength is that it is constantly revisable). It is not a new problem. Throughout history, there have been philosophies and discoveries outside Scripture that have drawn Christians into understanding the Bible in terms other than its own.

It is always a mistake, no matter how true we might suppose that extra-scriptural knowledge to be. Certainly, holding to a doctrine that might be called "common grace," we can accept that there is wisdom to be gained from the world. We are commanded by God to exercise dominion over his world, and God has uniquely gifted us amongst his creatures to be able to do so — and one part of that gift, it would seem, is the ability to observe creation and reason intelligently about it.[2] This is something for which we should be immensely grateful. It is a different thing to use that knowledge as our framework for interpreting Scripture — or worse still, for saying what Scripture "must" or "must not" be saying.

This essay looks at a number of ways in which we might be tempted to impose scientific views (in particular) on Scripture, and the dangers that might hold. Because it has always been a temptation, we will look at some historical background before coming to some modern examples.

But first, a cautionary tale.

When the Church Is Too Pro-Science: The Story of Galileo[3]

This might seem a surprising topic to pick as our cautionary tale for a pro-science church.[4] Most histories of science, especially of the more popular sort, consider Galileo to be a case study in what happens when the church is *anti*-science. After all, was not Galileo the hero of science, opposed and eventually imprisoned by a conservative and hidebound Catholic church?

It is true that in 1616 a board of theologians for the Roman Catholic Church

2. See my *Unnatural Enemies: An Introduction to Science and Christianity* (Sydney: Matthias Media, 1997), for a more extensive discussion of this point, and its connection to the biblical category of "wisdom."

3. The following section is based on my article, "Galileo: History v. Polemic," *Kategoria: A Critical Review of Modern Life* 1, no. 1 (1996): 13-42.

4. Thanks to the student at an Oak Hill College postgraduate seminar who suggested this way of seeing the Galileo story.

discussed the new Copernican theory, and came up with an official decree stating that to say the sun is at the center of the world and immovable is foolish and absurd, and formally heretical. Moreover, to say that the Earth moves was decreed similarly foolish and erroneous in the faith.

Sixteen years later Galileo faced the Inquisition on charges of heresy because of his belief in that same theory. He was ordered to abjure his heretical opinions — that is, to state that he firmly believed that the Earth did not move — and was sentenced to a prison term with penance. Galileo, the popular story has it, threatened with torture and the might of the Catholic Church, recanted and stated through clenched teeth that he did not believe that which he knew to be true. Yet, the story goes, the spirit of free thought could not be suppressed. As he left the room with its instruments of torture, he muttered, "and yet it turns."

There is no record that Galileo ever said anything so foolish, and indeed, this courtroom drama conceals the real struggle that was going on. This was not a battle between an anti-science church and a pro-science individual. On the contrary, it could be better characterized as a pro-science church, led by the academy that taught and embraced that science, against an eccentric maverick. The fact that Galileo's ideas turned out to be the more accurate does not change the true story: this is a case study in what happens when old science is threatened by new data, and the institutions that have endorsed that science are too slow to change.

Why were the institutions so slow to accept Galileo's ideas? Part of the answer is that it is in the nature of institutions to be conservative. When a large number of people have power and position depending upon the status quo, new ideas that challenge that status quo are naturally treated with suspicion. Indeed, it might be seen as intellectually responsible to do so; no one wants centuries of progress to be thrown out for a new and maverick idea. The universities of the time, just as universities now, were slow to accept an upstart new theory with little to back it up. For the church, the situation was even more fraught. The Catholic Church was following this issue against the background of Reformation and Counter-Reformation, having been shaken to the roots by Protestant demands for the individual's right to personal access to the Bible, and it is not surprising that somewhere along the line someone was charged with heresy. Had Galileo been a less abrasive character, had his involvement in academic politics been less prominent, and had the political situation been less volatile, it might not have happened at all.

The old theory was geocentrism, in which the Earth was at the center of the universe, with planets (including the sun and moon) and stars revolving around it. All physics, dynamics, and matter theory backed up the cosmology. The new theory was heliocentrism, with the sun at the center of the universe and the Earth, one of the planets, revolving around it. We, of course, know which theory won. The heroes of the story for twenty-first-century viewers are those who supported the heliocentric universe. At the beginning of the seventeenth century, however, the geocentric universe looked far more likely, or at least, that was what the scientists of the day thought.

In 1543, in the last year of his life, a modest Polish astronomer named Nicholas Copernicus published a speculative astronomical theory. It was in a work titled *De revolutionibus orbium coelestium* ("The revolution of the heavenly spheres"). It was different from the old Ptolemaic theory, in placing the sun rather than the Earth at the center of the universe. It was like the old theory in that all the planets moved in circles around the center.[5] Copernicus's theory was, from a purely scientific point of view, only marginally better than the old one. Of course he was right, but how could people know that at the time? Besides, he was not completely "right" — his commitment to circular motion meant that his theory necessarily had problems.

By 1600 only ten astronomers can be identified who thought Copernicus was right.[6] In other words, Copernican theory was not the great overnight revolution. It was a relatively unsuccessful addition to astronomical knowledge, which the majority of professional astronomers failed to take up. The church decision to reject it in 1616 was not at the time so very irrational.[7]

There is a deep and important reason why Copernican theory was not convincing as a new scientific theory. It had no physics to back it up. It is all very well to hypothesize that the Earth moves around the sun — and certain astronomical observations might thereby be better accounted for — but what makes the Earth move? Copernicus had no answers. He had no laws of motion, and no theory of gravity (that was to come two centuries later, when Isaac Newton finally developed his basic laws of physics). At the time, the only known physics was Aristotelian.[8]

Copernicus's theory did not fit into Aristotelian physics, and he did not have

5. For a summary of the Copernican system and the advantages it had over the Ptolemaic, see section 1 of Alexander Koyré, *The Astronomical Revolution: Copernicus, Kepler, Borelli* (Paris: Hermann; London: Methuen; Ithaca, NY: Cornell University Press, 1973).

6. Robert S. Westman, "The Astronomer's Role in the Sixteenth Century: A Preliminary Study," *History of Science* 28 (1980): 105-47, on 106.

7. See Jerzy Dobrzycki, ed., *The Reception of Copernicus' Heliocentric Theory* (Dordrecht and Boston: D. Reidel, 1972).

8. See Aristotle, *De Coelo*. An English translation is available in Milton K. Munitz, *Theories of the Universe: From Babylonian Myth to Modern Science* (New York: Free Press, 1957) — which also has excerpts from Copernicus and Ptolemy. For a summary of Aristotelian physics and cosmology, see Stephen Toulmin and June Goodfield, *The Fabric of the Heavens* (Harmondsworth, UK: Penguin, 1961), chapter 3; or Thomas S. Kuhn, *The Copernican Revolution: Planetary Astronomy in the Development of Western Thought* (Cambridge, MA, and London: Harvard University Press, 1957), chapter 3. For discussion of the clash between Aristotle's universe and the new science see William R. Shea, *Galileo's Intellectual Revolution* (London and Basingstoke: Macmillan, 1972), and Giorgio de Santillana, *The Crime of Galileo* (Melbourne, London, and Toronto: Heinemann, 1958).

a new physics in which to embed a new astronomy. This was a serious lack. The theory was not worthless, by any means. It had a mathematical elegance that Ptolemaic theory lacked — enough to impress Galileo, who was a very competent mathematician. Without proper physical laws, however, it could not hope to gain widespread acceptance among the academic community; in particular, among the physicists, or natural philosophers as they were known.

This clash with Aristotelian thought is something we must take seriously. It is hard to imagine now just how immense a challenge Copernican theory was. If it were true, the entire body of received knowledge about physics — laws of motion, theories of matter, the most fundamental ideas about what the universe is made of and why it behaves the way it does — would have to change. When Galileo began championing Copernican theory, he was not merely suggesting an interesting new technical piece of astronomy. He was, implicitly at first and later explicitly, challenging centuries of accepted knowledge.

Aristotle's system of knowledge was remarkably satisfying and complete. He was regarded as having solved essentially all the problems of the physical universe.[9] Aristotle's laws worked, they explained everything, and civilized humanity had recognized that for centuries. If there was to be any differing opinion, it could perhaps come from those who preferred Plato to Aristotle; but that an astronomer could come up with an entirely new theory was ridiculous, and that Galileo would actually defend such a theory and teach it to his students was very worrying. It was quite natural that his fellow academics opposed him. It was, after all, the duty of established scholars to protect the young from dangerous ideas.

Since Thomas Aquinas's adoption of Aristotelian philosophy into a comprehensive theological schema, the church had also been firmly wedded to Aristotelianism. The science was not the most important part of the system as far as theology went, but to question Aristotle was to question theology. The church was fully behind the universities in defending Aristotelian science. Its theology was so intertwined with Aristotelian thought that it was very difficult to extract — indeed, it eventually took centuries to do so.

It is probably fair to say that Galileo's academic enemies, unable to defeat him in logical argument or by social pressure, took the battleground to the church. Galileo had not allowed his opponents to silence him in the normal ways, so they looked to silence him through creating theological trouble. There is evidence of a deliberate strategy used against Galileo. Certain of Galileo's enemies formed the loosely organized group known as the "Liga," apparently led by Lodovico

9. Aristotelianism had embedded within it a different conception of the nature of knowledge. There was, it was assumed, a finite amount of knowledge to be gained about the universe, and Aristotle had pretty much done it. There was very little of our modern concept of the progress of knowledge. See Shea, *Galileo's Intellectual Revolution,* 31.

delle Colombe. The group also drew upon disgruntled clerics such as a certain Father Lorini who had received criticism from Galileo in the past, and the young Dominican Friar Tommaso Caccini (who may have simply delighted in stirring up trouble). These men openly accused Galileo of contradicting the Bible and set about creating popular suspicion against Galileo in order to catch the attention of the church authorities.

After various confrontations and accusations, Galileo wrote a long treatise addressed to the Grand Duchess Christina — a work of theology, explaining how the Bible should be interpreted, quoting from the church fathers to back up his argument.

It appears he had gone too far. Galileo had produced a treatise telling theologians how they ought to do theology. Coming from an astronomer, with no theological training, this was not likely to be well received. It also brought him into direct conflict with Cardinal Bellarmine, one of the most influential cardinals in the Inquisition and indeed perhaps in the church.

Here we come to another interesting aspect of the story. Cardinal Bellarmine, a Jesuit, had spent his life fighting Protestantism, and those who find themselves under attack tend to be much more rigid in their defense. He was the professor of Controversial Theology at the Collegio Romano, one of the major universities in Rome. He was a polemicist, not a speculative philosopher, and though he was intellectually quite capable of understanding Galileo's arguments, he was used to making definitive judgments in the "life-and-death" battle against heresy. Because he had spent his life fighting Protestants who claimed freedom to interpret the Bible as they wished, he was naturally very wary of an individual with no church authority, albeit a loyal Catholic, who wanted to reinterpret Scripture to accommodate his theories.[10]

Bellarmine had lectured in astronomy early in his career. His lectures give some insight into his character and reveal why he could not possibly have agreed with Galileo. Bellarmine considered theology to be far above astronomy. Indeed, in the face of eternity he could not understand why men were so interested in the mere physical structure of this ephemeral universe. He was happy to let astronomers disagree over technical details, and considered it not the place of theologians to be involved in such disputes. This was not a statement in favor of intellectual autonomy for astronomers — on the contrary, it reflects how unimportant he thought astronomy really was. It meant that theologians were free "to select among them the one which best corresponds to the Sacred Scripture."

Galileo's treatise challenged Bellarmine on his own ground, which was hardly tactful. Galileo quoted extensively from Augustine as part of his argument, in the confident tone of a professional. Bellarmine, a serious patristic scholar, would

10. See Richard S. Westfall, *Essays on the Trial of Galileo* (Rome: Vatican University Publications, 1989), chapter 1.

have known far more about Augustine's view of Scripture than Galileo, and would hardly have taken kindly to Galileo instructing him in what Augustine said. To make it worse, Galileo could not, or did not, hold back his sarcastic wit. He lampooned theologians as narrow-minded — not a good idea when Bellarmine was one of them.

The matter had become official and was dealt with quickly. Galileo came to Rome, and the matter of Copernican theory was considered by a panel of theologians (undoubtedly under Bellarmine's influence) for three days. Copernicus's book was condemned, and Galileo was told not to hold or defend the theory. Galileo himself was not officially mentioned in any condemnation, nor was he disciplined.

For the time being, it was over. Although Galileo was not discredited or humiliated, he had been silenced — a victory for his opponents. In the battle of new science against old science, old science had won this skirmish at least. The Aristotelians, who were not convinced about Copernicanism on scientific grounds, had finally seen it come to grief against church power — a power being wielded on behalf of science. In the end, Bellarmine, theologically so wedded to an old-world Aristotelian universe, was not about to accept the arguments of the new-world Galileo. Bellarmine saw no reason to change his belief that the Bible taught a stationary earth.

It would be sixteen years before Galileo was finally sentenced to house arrest under charges of heresy, and by then the story had become even more complicated.[11] Galileo's final downfall and condemnation were the result of a very messy political situation in which Galileo made the wrong enemies. It is hard to find one clear culprit, for there were many people involved in the political intrigues. But at no point did Galileo's story involve Christianity opposing science per se; it was the church *defending* Aristotelian science.

What happened when Protestants came across the Copernican theory is perhaps a more cheerful story. There was no widespread horror or outcry against Copernicanism in Protestant countries. It was accepted for what it was: an astronomical theory, of little interest to theologians, but with some technical points to recommend it to astronomers. It was not something to cause a great reaction. There is doubt about whether Calvin ever even heard of the theory.[12] It is unlikely he would have condemned it on biblical grounds. In his commentary on Psalm 136 he was of the opinion that the Holy Spirit "had no intention to teach astronomy."[13]

11. See my essay "Galileo: History v. Polemic" for details.

12. See Edward Rosen, "Calvin's Attitude toward Copernicus," *Journal of the History of Ideas* 21 (1960): 431-41; Robert White, "Calvin and Copernicus: The Problem Considered," *Calvin Theological Journal* 15 (1980): 233-43; and Christopher B. Kaiser, "Calvin, Copernicus and Castellio," *Calvin Theological Journal* 21 (1986): 5-31.

13. John Calvin, *Commentary on the Book of Psalms,* vol. 5, ed. and trans. James Anderson (Grand Rapids: Eerdmans, 1949), 184.

Luther made none but offhand comments about the theory.[14] Those who took the trouble to study Copernicanism were inclined to be mildly in favor of it, if anything. Melanchthon, who was responsible for widespread educational reform in Protestant Germany, encouraged astronomy and lectured on Copernicanism. His approach was cautious, but not reactionary; he developed what is known as the "Wittenberg position," which was influential in Protestant universities for several decades.[15] While he was not prepared to take on Copernicanism wholeheartedly, he acknowledged its technical improvements over the Ptolemaic theory and was content for his students to study it. It was possible for a member of a Protestant country to be far more enthusiastic — as was Rheticus, the German scholar who was "converted" to Copernicanism with as much zeal as he gave to religion. Though he did not have many followers, he was certainly not persecuted for his ideas, and indeed continued in a respectable academic career.

This is not the place to present a comprehensive account of the Protestant reaction to Copernican theory. There might, however, be some salutary lessons to be learned. The Protestant reaction provides a necessary counterpoint to Galileo's condemnation. It is not that Protestantism necessarily had a doctrinal bias toward believing that the earth moved; but if a Protestant did wish to accept and defend Copernican theory, he generally had freedom to do so. Protestantism, with its fundamental tenet of individual interpretation of the Bible, was not so entwined with what we might call the secular science of the day. Indeed, after Copernicanism had been suppressed by the Catholic Church, the story was spread far and wide in Protestant polemic against repressive Catholic institutions. All these factors gave Protestant countries an intellectual climate that could be more accepting of Copernicanism than otherwise.

Christians should never allow Christianity to be tied to a secular system of thought. Aristotelianism was very attractive and convincing as an intellectual system, and it gave Christianity a great intellectual boost when the two were "reconciled"; but Aristotelianism was not Christian, and Christianity should never have been made to depend upon it. The great Aristotelian synthesis left medieval Christianity irrevocably tied to an ultimately faulty philosophy. By the time the flaws in the philosophy were demonstrated, the upholders of the system supposed to be Christian were so steeped in Aristotelianism they were unable to cope with the changes. The result was that Christianity was discredited for something that has nothing to do with it.

The same danger potentially lies before us with theories of modern science, if

14. The one famous comment is recorded in Luther, "Table Talk," *LW* 54:358-59; for discussion of the likely veracity of this record, see Wilhelm Norlind, "Copernicus and Luther: A Critical Study," *Isis* 44 (1953): 273-76.

15. See Robert S. Westman, "The Melanchthon Circle, Rheticus, the Wittenberg Interpretation of the Copernican Theory," *Isis* 66 (1975): 165-93.

we are not careful. Modern empirical science is an excellent route to knowledge about our physical universe, and most likely a lot of what it promotes is true. Yet its very success lies in the contingent and revisable nature of its theories. Empirical science is a system that is only ever probably true — deliberately so — for by nature it must allow itself to be open to constant revision in the light of new evidence. Science advances by rejection of the old under scrutiny of the new. That is the strength and real value of scientific knowledge.

Christianity, if it really is based on infallible revelation from God, does not need to attach itself to that system and does so at its own peril. There is nothing wrong with demonstrating that any particular scientific theory is compatible with biblical revelation. Such demonstration, however, does not prove the Bible true and should never be made the grounds for accepting biblical truth. In time, the scientific theory will change. Christians must recognize the limits of revealed knowledge and not connect it to knowledge that is constantly under revision. That is the path to ridicule and disillusionment, when the science moves on and Christians are left behind.

Chronology, the Age of the Earth, and the Days of Genesis

When Scripture becomes wedded to one particular scientific view, it is no longer speaking in its own terms. It is too easy to allow the strictures of a scientific theory to dominate the discussion of biblical literature — which has, and must have, different disciplinary norms. The way in which science operates is different from the way in which biblical scholarship operates. In more recent years, we have seen this played out in the major issue of the last two centuries in science and religion debates: how to read Genesis in the light of modern geological and biological science.[16]

Here we enter our main battleground, which continues to dominate discussions of science and Christianity and shows no sign of diminishing. Whenever I speak on the topic, even (or especially) when I make no mention of biological theory or Genesis in my talk, I can guarantee that the first question to be asked will be about Genesis, evolution, and the age of the earth.

But before we get to the more recent debates, let us take a moment to understand our historical context. It is too easy to caricature those who accept a non-literal reading of, for instance, Genesis 1, to be seen as the innovators who have given in to a modern scientific worldview; whereas those who hold to the

16. As background to this discussion, I recommend that readers consult some of the excellent commentaries on Genesis: for instance, Bruce K. Waltke and Cathi J. Fredricks, *Genesis: A Commentary* (Grand Rapids: Zondervan, 2001), and Henri Blocher, *In the Beginning: The Opening Chapters of Genesis* (Leicester: Inter-Varsity, 1984).

strict six twenty-four-hour days are those faithful to the traditional and most obvious reading of the Scriptures. However, church history, and the history of the interpretation of Scripture, does not in itself back this up.

It can surprise listeners to find out that the "days" of Genesis 1 have been controversial since the days of the early church. It is an instance of the question of how to read Scripture in the light of non-scriptural philosophy, which has been around as long as Christianity itself. The non-scriptural philosophies have changed, but they pose an essential question: To what extent do we allow extra-biblical ideas to determine our reading of Scripture?[17]

Take, for instance, the views of the ancient writer Philo (20 B.C.E.–50 C.E.). In his reading of Genesis, the account of creation in the Bible is interpreted figuratively, as is necessary for it to fit into a largely Platonic schema of creation. Philo describes a two-stage creation, in which God first created the intelligible forms of things, then their sensible copies. On day one, God created the basic forms, and on days two to six, the derived forms and copies; on that sixth day, he also created the "noumenal" man (Gen. 1:26-27) and its copy, the "earthly" man (Gen. 2:7). Philo is quite emphatic that creation did not literally take six days — Moses wrote this way only to demonstrate the order with which it occurred.[18]

> He [Moses] says that in six days the world was created, not that its Maker required a length of time for His work, for we must think of God as doing all things simultaneously, remembering that "all" includes with the commands which he issues the thought behind them. Six days are mentioned because for the things coming into existence there was need of order.[19]

The patristic writer Origen (ca. 185-254) was extremely scathing of those who would take a literal approach to the creation accounts in Genesis.

> Now who is there, pray, possessed of understanding, that will regard the statement as appropriate, that the first day, and the second, and the third, in which also both evening and morning are mentioned, existed without sun, and moon, and stars — the first day even without a sky? And who is found so ignorant as to

17. Extra-biblical discoveries might, of course, prompt us to read Scripture in a new light, and see new aspects of it or come to new insights that we had previously overlooked. This is a different issue; it is not that the new discovery was necessary for us to find the truth of Scripture — if we had been doing our job properly, we would never have needed it.

18. Thanks to my former colleague Charles Anderson for letting me read in advance the manuscript of his book on Philo's views of creation: *Philo of Alexandria's Views of the Physical World,* WUNT 309 (Tübingen: Mohr Siebeck, 2011). For more, see Roberto Radice, "Philo's Theology and Theory of Creation," in *The Cambridge Companion to Philo,* ed. Adam Kamesar (Cambridge: Cambridge University Press, 2009), 124-46.

19. Philo, *On the Account of the World's Creation Given by Moses (De opificio mundi),* LCL.

> suppose that God, as if He had been a husbandman, planted trees in paradise, in Eden towards the east, and a tree of life in it, i.e., a visible and palpable tree of wood, so that anyone eating of it with bodily teeth should obtain life, and, eating again of another tree, should come to the knowledge of good and evil? No one, I think, can doubt that the statement that God walked in the afternoon in paradise, and that Adam lay hid under a tree, is related figuratively in Scripture, that some mystical meaning may be indicated by it.[20]

Augustine (354-430) had trouble with the notion of "days" of creation, not, as modern commentators do, because days are too short for the work of creation, but precisely the opposite — because days are too long! How could Scripture describe the work of an act of creation as taking a day, Augustine asked, when God's will can be made real in an instant? Augustine suggests various ways in which these texts could be read more figuratively as being more plausible.[21]

The question of the age of the earth and how to read Genesis in the light of extra-biblical evidence is, then, contrary to most popular thought, hardly a new one. Long before modern geology, the issue of the time spans and genealogies in Genesis, and indeed the question of how to read different kinds of biblical literature, were thoroughly discussed. How controversial such discussions were depended largely not on the content of the discussions themselves, but on how hard-pressed the commentators felt at the time. When people of the church feel under threat, for whatever reason, they tend to become far more rigid on what is allowable as fair discussion.

It is not surprising, then, that the question of interpreting Genesis in the light of secular discoveries has frequently been intertwined with what we might call "biblical criticism." This is generally thought of as a nineteenth-century discussion, where the Bible seemed to be under attack from historical criticism as much as science. However, these ideas too had been rehearsed in different forms far earlier in church history.[22]

To see how some of these questions were debated long before modern geol-

20. Origen, *De principiis* (translated from the Latin of Rufinus), 4.1.16. http://www.newadvent.org/fathers/04124.htm (viewed 17 December 2010).

21. Augustine, *Commentary on the Biblical Book of Genesis* 1.10.18, in *St. Augustine, the Literal Meaning of Genesis,* vol. 1, trans. and annotated by John Hammond Taylor, S.J., Ancient Christian Writers 41 (New York: Paulist, 1982). See also the introduction to *St. Augustine on Genesis* (New York: New City Press, 2004).

22. For an interesting excursion into this discussion, into which there is no space to go here, see Noel Malcolm, "Did Moses Write Genesis? Hobbes, Ezra and the Bible: The History of a Subversive Idea," in *Aspects of Hobbes* (Oxford: Clarendon, 2002), 383-431. This paper describes the ways in which authors in the seventeenth century arrived more or less independently at the idea that the Pentateuch was not written by Moses, based on ideas in Jewish and Christian biblical criticism that had been in existence since the first century C.E.

ogy seemed to stretch history into the far past, we look now to the early modern discipline of chronology, the attempt to establish a dated calendar for human history.

Renaissance scholars agreed that chronology — an accurate system of dating world events — was necessary to understand history. The question was, how were they to establish a true chronology? In particular, should they rely on the Bible alone, or on the literature of the pagan classical world as well? There were sharp arguments even when the Bible alone was considered — for instance, over the determination of the number, names, and order of the kings of ancient Israel. Trying to reconcile information coming in from a variety of pagan sources as well made the task a very difficult one. "You will find it easier to make the wolf agree with the lamb," Iacobus Curio said in 1557, "than to make all chronologers agree about the age of the world."[23] Up to and throughout the sixteenth century, chronology was a confusing and messy discipline. A major change came through the work of Joseph Scaliger, who managed to bring together a wide number of sources to clarify many issues in the field.[24]

Joseph Scaliger (1540-1609) was a French Calvinist, recognized in his day as being among the foremost of scholars. He was a professor at Calvin's college at Geneva from 1572 to 1574, and then spent twenty years working in France, preparing editions of classical works and essentially founding modern chronology. From 1593 he held a chair at Leiden in Holland where he embarked on considerable controversy with the Jesuits. For our purposes, his importance lies in his work with chronology.

In Geneva, where Scaliger had taught, questions over chronology and its use of extra-biblical texts were already contentious. His successor at the Geneva Academy, Mattheus Beroaldus, had published in 1575 a *Chronicum* that claimed to rest entirely on Scripture and denounced use of pagan sources as impious. Other Protestants used other sources. Some used forged works without realizing it. Scaliger, an expert in textual criticism among other things, was able to expose many forged sources, and in building his chronology used biblical material as well as that from other writers.

There had been two strands of work on chronology up to this time. Editors of classical texts and antiquarians tried to understand ancient references to dates and calendars. At the same time, astronomers, geographers, calendar reformers, and those studying the more mysterious Asian literature compiled more specialized treatises. Sometimes the traditions overlapped. Scaliger had done some work

23. I. Curio, *Chronologicarum rerum lib. II* (Basel, 1557), 8, quoted in Anthony Grafton, "Scaliger's Chronology: Philology, Astronomy, World History," in *Defenders of the Text: The Traditions of Scholarship in the Age of Science, 1450-1800* (Cambridge, MA, and London: Harvard University Press, 1991), 106.

24. The following material is largely taken from Grafton, "Scaliger's Chronology."

in the first, humanistic tradition. But his *Opus novum de emendatione temporum* (1583),[25] which revolutionized the field, was in the second, systematic tradition.

Scaliger's *De emendatione temporum* dealt in the first four books with the principal calendars, ancient and modern, solar and lunar. The fifth and sixth books gave his actual chronology, establishing important dates from the Creation to recent times. The seventh book presented texts and translations of medieval Jewish, Ethiopian, and Byzantine treatises on the calendar, known as computuses, and the eighth explained the bearing of this research on calendar reform. (Scaliger "proved" the "biblical" dating of the Flood by comparing it with a Babylonian text. However, he had falsified the evidence in his enthusiasm to find support for the Bible. This is a weakness of books 5 and 6.)

The state of calendars was truly confusing at the time; several different dating systems existed, and trying to match up dates from the Middle Ages, in different systems, was very difficult. Scaliger successfully put various sources together and managed to date historical events by astronomical methods. Incidentally, Copernicus's *De revolutionibus* (1543) transformed astronomy into a tool for historical research, accidentally, by repeating the wrong idea that the Babylonian king Nabonassar was the biblical Salmanassar. He was wrong, but this mistake set up some useful research. Paul Crusius in 1578, in his posthumously published *De epochis,* gave some correct dates, such as for the eclipse that dated Alexander's empire. This inspired Scaliger.

Scaliger was also innovative in that he consistently confronted the biblical history of Israel and other nations, and the patristic histories of early Christianity, with the evidence of nonbiblical texts. His aim was to show that the Bible was neither complete nor self-contained as a history of man. "The chronologer could not date the events it mentioned — far less work out the histories of the non-Jewish nations it described — without constantly referring to nonbiblical sources."[26] Scaliger was not being especially contentious in saying so, Grafton points out.

The general view that the Bible could not stand alone was well established in the 1580s. Guillaume Postel, Scaliger's first master in Oriental studies, had argued in 1551 that the full truth about antediluvian history would not be known until the Ethiopic Book of Enoch was available in Latin.[27]

Not only was the question of dating a real one in the Renaissance, but so was the question of whether Adam was really the first man. For instance, we have the story of Isaac La Peyrère.[28]

25. I have not been able to find an English translation of this work. Grafton's detailed work on the subject is in his *Joseph Scaliger,* vol. 1, *Textual Criticism and Exegesis* (London: Clarendon, 1983).

26. Grafton, *Joseph Scaliger,* 1:133.

27. Grafton, *Joseph Scaliger,* 1:133, citing G. Postel, *De originibus* (Basel, 1553), 72. Grafton adds that Postel was probably disappointed.

28. See Grafton, "Isaac La Peyrère and the Old Testament," in *Defenders of the Text.*

Isaac La Payrère came from a Calvinist family in Bordeaux. Around 1640 he wrote up an idea he had first had as a child: that the two creation stories of Genesis 1 and 2 in fact told of the creation of mankind as a whole (Genesis 1), and of the Jews (Genesis 2), the second coming much later. Men had lived before Adam, then, for millennia. This, La Peyrère contended, reconciled Bible chronology with the longer ones of the ancient pagans, the American Indians, and the Chinese.

The ideas circulated privately and were sympathetically received in Paris; but as the ideas spread they attracted violent criticism. The work was published anonymously in Holland, reprinted four times, and translated into English and Dutch. Calvinist Holland and Catholic France alike condemned it. La Peyrère was arrested by the Inquisition in Brussels. His master Conde secured his release at the price of his conversion to Catholicism. He had to publish a retraction and died a pauper.

However, many people used La Peyrère's theories. These included skeptics such as Spinoza, but La Peyrère's real concern had been positive — the conversion of the Jews.[29] La Peyrère wanted to reconcile pagan sources and scholarship with the Bible, to show that the Bible "is wonderfully reconciled with all prophane Records whether ancient or new, to wit, those of the Caldeans, Egyptians, Scythians and Chinensians."[30]

There had already been discussion of pagan sources that took history far beyond apparent biblical history. Scaliger had brought to light Berosus's account of the Babylonian *Urgeschichte*. He had also published and defended Manetho's lists of the kings of ancient Egypt. Josephus had described two columns of stone and brick on which ancient peoples had given their history. Greek writers from Xanthus of Lydia down to Hermippus and Hermodorus had dated Zoroaster to very early times indeed; Eudoxus put him 6000 years before Plato's death.

There are many more historical quirks we could follow concerning discussion over biblical literature and how to date it, among other things. But for the purposes of this essay, it is sufficient to note that long before modern geology or Darwin, church scholars were quite aware of claims to a long history of the earth and to various degrees were prepared to accept it.[31] This puts into context Colin Gunton's assertion that "belief in the doctrine of creation has never officially required belief in the literal truth of the book of Genesis."[32]

29. See Richard Popkin, *Isaac La Peyrère, 1596-1676* (Leiden: Brill, 1987).

30. Quoted in Grafton, *Joseph Scaliger,* 207; from I. La Peyrère, *Prae-Adamitae* (1655), chapter 7, 29; see also *Men before Adam* (London, 1656), 18.

31. To put this discussion in the context of the history of skeptical thought, see Richard Popkin, *The History of Scepticism from Savonarola to Bayle,* rev. edition (Oxford: Oxford University Press, 2003).

32. Colin E. Gunton, *The Triune Creator: A Historical and Systematic Study* (Grand Rapids

This provides us with background as we turn to some of our more modern controversies, and how more recent science has challenged Bible readers.

The Rise of Creationism: Scripture against Science

We turn now to a more recent episode when issues of secular science and its implications for the dating of history and biblical texts arose once more. Once more we find difficulties when Scripture is interpreted in the light of science, as exemplified in the movement that came to insist on six twenty-four-hour days of creation, no more than 10,000 years ago.

But why would we include a movement famous for its absolute dedication to Scripture, even over and against the findings of modern science, as an example of failing to let Scripture speak for itself? Surely creation scientists would seem to be the ones most committed to Scripture, against interpreting it according to science. However, the contention here is that interpretation in reaction can be just as problematical as interpretation in accordance with science. Moreover, with the rise of a comprehensive research program of "creation" science, and the emphasis on its scientific credentials particularly in American debates about education and the public acceptance of science, this movement runs the risk of letting its science dominate its reading of Scripture.

Of course, not all who hold to what is known as the "creationist" view these days would do so in reaction to science. There are well-argued, internal theological reasons put forward for this treatment of Genesis, given how important the theological themes of Genesis are for understanding Christ's work in salvation. Moreover, the issue of creation and evolution is a very difficult one to discuss, in a context where views are so polarized as to be recognized by codewords — namely "creation" and "evolution" — although there are anything but two sides to this issue. In particular, the debate has become so deeply riven in American society that there are no doubt all sorts of sensibilities being trampled by an Australian author often quite bewildered by the assumptions hidden within different opinions. The fact that histories are written by those who similarly take sides, and so are not untouched by the emotionally laden burden of aspects of the debate, also presents its own problem.

However, what we are looking at here is the relatively simpler problem of the rise of this movement known as "creationist," which was driven largely not from such theological convictions, but in reaction to what was perceived as the atheism of Darwinism, along with certain convictions about literal readings of

---

and Cambridge: Eerdmans, 1998), 155. This book is well worth reading for reflections upon a theological understanding of creation, including the relationship with developing and modern science.

Scripture. It is to these tendencies in the early days of the creationist movement that we turn now.[33]

Many histories have been written of the history of science leading up to Darwin's *The Origin of Species* and the subsequent controversies.[34] The nineteenth century saw not only a new era of discovery in geology, but also a great deal of discussion about evolution of various types. Darwin added to the discussion with his own theory of evolution — natural selection through descent with modification — which turned out to be a mechanism that survived, albeit altered, into the twenty-first century. Intertwined with the scientific developments preceding and following Darwin is a story of how scientific ideas were held alongside Scripture.

The problem was not nearly so polarized as it is now. The leading scientist Asa Gray, for instance, wanted Darwin to be willing to allow special supernatural origin for humans, since he had allowed it for the beginning of life on earth. Darwin went the opposite way; in 1868, in *Variation of Animals and Plants under Domestication,* he wrote "however much we may wish it, we can hardly follow Professor Asa Gray in his belief" in divinely guided evolution.[35] Aubrey Moore, Fellow of St John's College, Oxford, Curator of the Oxford Botanical Gardens, on the other hand, welcomed Darwin's theory because it gave God an intimate involvement in creation. "There are not, and cannot be, any Divine interpositions

33. This information is largely taken from Ronald L. Numbers, *The Creationists: From Scientific Creation to Intelligent Design,* exp. edition (Cambridge, MA, and London: Harvard University Press, 2006). See also Ronald L. Numbers, "The Creationists," in *God and Nature: Historical Essays on the Encounter between Christianity and Science,* ed. David C. Lindberg and Ronald L. Numbers (Berkeley: University of California Press, 1986), 391-423; for background information and a focus on the Scopes "Monkey" trial see Edward J. Larson, *Summer for the Gods: The Scopes Trial and America's Continuing Debate over Science and Religion* (New York: Basic Books, 1997).

34. Just a selection of accessible works can be mentioned here: Mark A. Noll, ed., *The Princeton Theology 1812-1921: Scripture, Science, and Theological Method from Archibald Alexander to Benjamin Breckinridge Warfield* (Grand Rapids: Baker, 1983); Jonathan Wells, *Charles Hodge's Critique of Darwinism: An Historical-Critical Analysis of Concepts Basic to the 19th Century Debate* (Lewiston, NY: Edwin Mellen, 1988); Jon H. Roberts, *Darwinism and the Divine in America: Protestant Intellectuals and Organic Evolution, 1859-1900* (Madison: University of Wisconsin Press, 1988); David N. Livingstone, *Darwin's Forgotten Defenders* (Grand Rapids: Eerdmans, 1987); David Hull, *Darwin and His Critics: The Reception of Darwin's Theory of Evolution by the Scientific Community* (Cambridge, MA: Harvard University Press, 1973); James R. Moore, *The Post-Darwinian Controversies: A Study of the Protestant Struggle to Come to Terms with Darwin in Great Britain and America, 1870-1900* (Cambridge: Cambridge University Press, 1979). For a summary of theories leading up to Darwin, see D. R. Oldroyd, *Darwinian Impacts: An Introduction to the Darwinian Revolution* (Kensington: New South Wales University Press, 1980). Two of the best biographies of Darwin are Adrian Desmond and James Moore, *Darwin* (London: Michael Joseph, 1991) and Janet Browne, *Charles Darwin,* vol. 1, *Voyaging,* and vol. 2, *The Power of Place* (London: Pimlico, 2003).

35. Quoted in Numbers, *The Creationists,* 17.

in nature, for God cannot interfere with Himself. His creative activity is present everywhere. There is no division of labour between God and nature, or God and law . . . for the Christian theologian the facts of nature are the acts of God."[36]

There were very few Victorian creationists in the modern, six-day sense. Even Charles Hodge, famous for his insistence that "Darwinism is atheism," accepted the great antiquity of the earth and a day-age theory.[37] Almost universally, post-Darwinian scientists and clerics who held to divine creation did not reject the antiquity of the Earth, deny the progressive nature of the fossil record, or attach geological significance to the Flood. No doubt many ordinary Christians held to recent six-day creation, but not published writers. Very few people used the Flood to explain the fossil record.[38]

George Frederick Wright, for instance, a clerical scientist and acknowledged geological expert, saw Genesis 1 as not being about timing at all, but as an anti-polytheistic document. Similarly, he considered that the genealogies of Genesis were about descent, not time. When in the 1880s he moved from Boston to be a professor of New Testament in Ohio, and faced the challenge of biblical criticism, he moved to a somewhat more "literalistic" view. For example, James Dwight Dana convinced him that the Mosaic account of creation was inspired cosmogony; otherwise the credibility of everything in the Bible was suspect. "Dana's persuasion — and the unrelenting aggression of biblical critics — apparently convinced Wright that this was indeed an accurate assessment."[39] However, Wright still insisted that creation and evolution were to be seen as "virtual synonyms, equally appropriate for describing a process of emergent evolution in which God 'created' humans from previously existing apelike creatures."[40]

36. Quoted in Denis Alexander, *Creation or Evolution: Do We Have to Choose?* (Oxford: Monarch Books, 2008), 172. (Since this writing, the book has appeared in a second edition, 2014. Page references herein are to the first edition.)

37. See Mark A. Noll and David Livingstone, eds., *Charles Hodge: What Is Darwinism? And Other Writings on Science and Religion* (Grand Rapids: Baker, 1994).

38. Exceptions were the brothers Eleazer Lord (1788-1871) and David Nevis Lord (1792-1880), vocal laymen who published works on six-day, 6,000-year-old creation. This view was always more prevalent among laypeople than clergy or scientists. See Alvar Ellegard, *Darwin and the General Reader: The Reception of Darwin's Theory of Evolution in the British Periodical Press, 1859-1872* (Chicago: University of Chicago Press, 1958-90).

39. Numbers, *The Creationists,* 39. Notice that it was in opposition to atheistic attacks, not just because of Scripture itself, that Wright changed his views.

40. Numbers, *The Creationists,* 49. Numbers sees Wright as an example of a Christian Darwinist who became a fundamentalist. I would question this description, based on Numbers's own research. Unless you are wedded to the idea that the two positions are incompatible, it doesn't seem that Wright changed much, except to revise his scientific views on Darwin as most scientists were doing around the turn of the century. In any case, there were a number of "fundamentalists" who accepted Darwin. See my "Darwin and the Fundamentalists," *Kategoria: A Critical Review of Modern Life* 2 (1996): 25-53.

In the 1880s and 1890s, according to Ronald Numbers, debate about evolution stopped being so scholarly and spilled over into more popular arenas, and those who objected to evolution on biblical grounds — primarily premillenarians — began to get alarmed. "The aggressive declarations of a few biologists, who announced their determination to drive the last vestiges of supernaturalism from science, also aroused fear and danger among the orthodox."[41] When after 1880 many scientists began to reject Darwin's account of evolution, critics felt emboldened to speak out.

However, it seems that the new fundamentalist movement was provoked to stronger anti-evolution activism by the "intolerance and insensitivity" of atheist schoolteachers, as evolution became a part of high school biology, in the unprecedented growth of public high schools. It was not that the theory of evolution itself was a new threat — even church-related colleges in the South had been teaching evolution for decades — although it grew slowly. What was new was the militant atheism, using the growth of public education to mock Christian ideas.

Then came World War I, which indirectly had a huge impact on the new creationist movement. In particular, it galvanized William Jennings Bryan, a politician (a Democrat presidential candidate, no less) who was to begin a formal creationist crusade against evolution. Bryan, appalled by the war, traced the source of the evil to Darwinism — in particular, the way in which Darwinian theory stunted the human conscience. Two books, *Headquarters Nights* by scientist Vernon Kellog (1917) (which recounted firsthand conversations with German officers that revealed Darwinism had persuaded the Germans to declare war) and Benjamin Kidd's *Science of Power* (1918) presented historical and philosophical links between Darwinism and German militarism. Scientists were worried, too, and responded by stressing the importance of cooperation in evolution. Bryan responded by trying to quash evolution itself.

At the same time, Bryan was seeing "an epidemic of unbelief" in the country's youth, and became convinced that it was evolution, when taught as a fact instead of a theory, that was the problem. Evolution caused the students to lose faith in the Bible. There was statistical evidence that going to college endangered traditional religious belief. A famous trial convinced him that murder was caused by belief in evolution.[42] Bryan launched his crusade nationwide against evolution, arguing that it was both unchristian and unscientific.

Bryan was against evolution, but he was not a strict creationist as the term would be understood today. He accepted evolution before Adam, and held a day-age interpretation of Genesis 1. However, he could not accept the social im-

41. Numbers, *The Creationists,* 51.

42. In opposition to this, Numbers points out, critics added that the outlaw Jesse James was a fundamentalist, and the states where evolution was not taught had more murders per capita than any others.

plications of an atheistic, evolutionary worldview; and above all else, he was a democrat by conviction. He resented a small, scientific elite determining what could be taught to forty million American Christians.

This is only a brief look at the history of a crusade that was to galvanize millions over the next century. Many of these, as already stated, have serious theological arguments to back up their reading of Scripture. However, the point to be made here is that at the start of the movement, the rise of creationism was spurred by the *atheistic* contention that the Bible and evolution could not both be true. Those who accepted this, repelled by evolutionist arrogance, took up creationism. It was perhaps misguided to see scientific evolution as a primary cause of social decay, but certainly it was part of a concerted atheist effort to see science as the lens through which all other knowledge must be understood.[43] When a large number of those who joined the movement were literalists anyway — something that statistically tended to go along with premillenarian views — it is not surprising that creationism developed as it did. People reacted against science to determine their view of the Bible; and those views became increasingly inflexible as the decades went on.

The Alternative: Evolution alongside Scripture

What of the other side — those who would hold that evolutionary science is true, and that Scripture can be read in a way that defers to this view? There are a great many Christians who write along these lines, but one particularly prominent scholar is chosen here. He is both a conservative Christian and an evolutionary scientist, so holds a high view of truth in both areas.

Evolutionary biologist Denis Alexander has made a large contribution to the science/religion debate throughout his career, as well as pursuing a successful career in biological science. He has provided many helpful examples of how to write about science in a scriptural context, and has defended Christianity strongly in his evangelistic ministry. His book *Rebuilding the Matrix*[44] is

43. There is another, very large story to be told, which we can only glimpse briefly here. Part of it is Thomas Huxley's determination, along with a number of other nineteenth-century scientists, to see science dominate Christianity as a social force. Another part is the rise of a number of secularist movements that attacked Christianity in politics, literature, and other arenas. We have also hardly mentioned the advent of biblical criticism in the nineteenth century, which seemed to be undermining the Bible on many fronts. Also, while evolutionary science itself did not necessarily attack biblical morality, the philosophies based on it (such as Spencerianism) did. To begin to enter these waters, see, for instance, Adrian Desmond, *Huxley: Evolution's High Priest* (London: Michael Joseph, 1997); and John Hedley Brooke, *Science and Religion: Some Historical Perspectives* (Cambridge: Cambridge University Press, 1991).

44. Denis Alexander, *Rebuilding the Matrix: Science and Faith in the 21st Century* (Oxford: Lion, 2001).

an excellent and balanced overview of the science-religion interface, covering aspects of the history and philosophy of science as well as cultural history. There is a wealth of material with which to interact, but for the purposes of this essay we will be looking at just one issue, precisely because it is so controversial: How does an evolutionary scientist deal with Genesis and the theological issues it addresses?

Alexander is commendably non-dogmatic in some of his stronger statements about how Scripture should be read in the light of science. Nonetheless, he does hold that science rules out certain readings and pushes us toward others. Even with his careful caveats, we are sometimes presented in Alexander's work with the idea that science determines what the Bible can or cannot say. Here, then, we have a way of thinking about the interaction between science and Scripture that tends toward science being the interpretive grid through which we read Scripture.

Alexander's book *Creation or Evolution: Do We Have to Choose?* is a discussion of evolutionary theory and an attempt at reconciling it with Scripture.[45] Alexander gives an overview of standard aspects of the theory. It is when he begins to look at objections to the theory that some interesting points emerge.[46]

Alexander points out that objecting to evolution on the basis that it relies on chance processes is an illegitimate position. He begins by talking about different kinds of "chance." Some things we can predict in principle but not in practice. Consider the example of fertilization of an ovum. In one sense fertilization is a truly chance process. Any one of millions of sperm could have fertilized that egg, in which case you would have been a different person. It is not possible for any scientist to predict, in practice, which sperm is going to be the one that fertilizes the egg. However, there is a clear causal path that leads to that sperm winning.

> Other things, it appears scientifically at least, we cannot predict in principle — for instance, quantum events. Some DNA mutations through failures in repair enzymes are the first kind. Mutation through radiation is unpredictable in theory, and in that sense evolution can be said to depend upon chance — but only to a limited extent. In any case, it doesn't matter for evolution how the difference in DNA arose. The whole process is bound by restraints and follows certain paths; it is not in the least random.[47]

45. See also Denis Alexander and Robert S. White, *Beyond Belief: Science, Faith and Ethical Challenges* (Oxford: Lion, 2004); and *Rebuilding the Matrix.*

46. For a more general discussion of such objections and answers to them, see Daniel C. Dennett and Alvin Plantinga, *Science and Religion: Are They Compatible?* (Oxford and New York: Oxford University Press, 2011).

47. In any case, as Christians, we know that God is sovereign over all processes. This is the way to think about evolution, Alexander says. God is sovereign over the law-like workings of

Alexander also critiques the young-earth theory on biological grounds: If you have a young earth, how are you going to account for predatory structures? They wouldn't have been needed in Eden, and must have evolved post-Fall. This forces evolution into, Alexander contends, a ridiculously small timescale. He also questions whether the idea of God creating fixed "kinds" in the language of Genesis 1, with some development within those kinds, can account for the biodiversity observed today. How many fixed "kinds" would need to be created at the start? There are 850,000 species of insect alone.

How then, should Genesis be read? Alexander has a very high view of Scripture, but insists that it must be read in the light of scientific views.

> First it should be emphasised that our shared inheritance with the apes is one of the most certain conclusions of contemporary biology. The reason for being so sure is because of . . . comparative genomics. . . . The record of our evolutionary past is indelibly inscribed within the DNA of every cell of our bodies. We are all walking genetic fossil museums![48]

For that reason, he insists that this must establish certain boundaries in our understanding of Genesis.[49]

Alexander is, however, carefully cautious when he discusses how the evolutionary picture fits with Adam and Eve. There are too many unknowns, he states. However, whatever the details of the fit, he preserves the evolutionary story; and adds that at some stage, the evolving humans became spiritual. Adam and Eve, however, are not the only historical problem that Genesis presents; there is also the status of the Fall — was it historical or not? — and the very real question of when death began. For if death came into the world through Adam, as Romans 5 states, what does that mean?

Alexander gives five models of what the connection between Genesis and evolution might be. Three are compatible with current scientific evolution, two not. Model A sees no place for a fit between the two accounts at all; there is no connection because Genesis was not written for that purpose. The Fall, then, is the "eternal story of everyman"; it describes the common human experience of alienation from God; but talk of evolutionary biology, and the physical death of

creation (Ps. 33:6-11), chance events (Prov. 16:33), or control of the weather (Ps. 148:8). I would think we can extend God's sovereignty to quantum events, so that there is actually nothing truly random or governed by chance in the universe.

This may also be an area for further study: What were the prevailing views on sovereignty in nineteenth-century English theology, and how did this affect responses to Darwinism?

48. Alexander, *Creation or Evolution,* 200. Hereafter, page references from this book will be given in parentheses in the text.

49. One might point out that "shared" DNA does not prove common ancestry; common ancestry is just a plausible (possibly the most plausible) explanation for it.

animals and humans is irrelevant to how the Fall "happened." Death was there all throughout history. Model B has an evolutionary history for humans with a gradual development of spiritual understanding, later written up in mythical form. The Fall is a historical process that happened over a long time as people became spiritual and consciously rejected God. The story was dramatized, personalized, and placed in an Ancient Near East context, presumably because that's where the writers were. Actual death happened throughout history, as in view A.

Model C, which Alexander endorses, supposes that at some point God revealed himself to a particular couple or community, the first *homo divinus.* The man was the federal head of humanity and is written up as such. Adam and Eve disobeyed God at a certain time and brought spiritual death, which is a broken relationship between humankind and God. As Adam was the federal head, then as Adam fell, so did humankind. Physical death, however, happened throughout history. Model D he describes as old-earth creationism; Adam and Eve were created directly from dust, with no direct continuity with other animals. Adam and Eve were created, lived in the Garden, and fell. There was animal and plant death before this, but the Fall meant both physical and spiritual death of humans. Otherwise they would have been immortal.

Model E is young-earth creationism. There was no death at all before Adam and Eve sinned. At the Fall there were also marked changes in the laws of science; for instance, the second law of thermodynamics came into effect, so there was now death and degradation in the physical world. Adam and Eve would never have died physically or spiritually without the Fall.

No doubt other authors would add more subtle distinctions and gradations between the views, but Alexander presents enough detail to describe where his view stands in relation to others. He holds tentatively to model C.

This, of course, requires a fairly non-literal reading of the text. He defends it on several fronts. The geography of Eden, for instance, is one issue; he points out that there is no such identifiable place as described in Genesis 2. Rivers are formed by tributaries drawing together, but the river from Eden separates into four rivers. Pishon and Cush have never been identified.[50] It is, then, he asserts, an image of a well-watered oasis, the source of blessing. Nowhere in Scripture is Eden referred to as a specific place. Spiritual death comes upon Adam and Eve immediately when they eat. Their lives are cursed, and tilling the ground,

50. Of course, he could not have known of the discoveries made possible by the latest Shuttle Imaging Radar. Farouk el-Baz, geologist and director of the Center for Remote Sensing at Boston University, has discovered beneath the sands traces of what he called the Kuwait River because the ancient bed heads east toward Kuwait (see his "A River in the Desert," *Discover* 14, no. 7 [July 1993]: 10). The connection with Pishon was made by James A. Sauer, "The River Runs Dry," *BAR* 22, no. 4 (1996): 52-54, 57, 64, and James K. Hoffmeier, in Hoffmeier, Gordon J. Wenham, and Kenton L. Sparks, *Genesis: History, Fiction, or Neither? Three Views on the Bible's Earliest Chapters* (Grand Rapids: Zondervan, 2015), 33-34.

meaning farming, would be difficult; there is no indication that there is any broader curse on the earth, or any physical change in the earth or heavens because of the Fall.

Elsewhere in Scripture, Alexander adds, when the Garden of Eden or the Fall narrative is mentioned, it tends to be interpreted figuratively. In Ezekiel 28 the King of Tyre "falls" as from Eden. Jeremiah has virtually a reversal of the creation narrative.

Many New Testament passages, Alexander goes on, are consistent with Adam being a real, federal head and death from the Fall being spiritual only. God always intended humans to die a physical death. Otherwise the command "be fruitful and multiply" could only have applied for a few thousand years until there was absolutely no room left on the earth.[51] Romans 8, with its reference to creation "groaning," is used to suggest a creation-wide effect of the Fall, but there is no evidence that Paul had Genesis 3 in mind when he wrote it. More likely it was Isaiah 24–27 about final judgment. The point of Romans 8 is to look forward, not back, to say the destiny of the earth is closely linked to the future of humankind. There is no evidence from here to support a discontinuity in the past.

What of the argument that it was Adam's sin that brought suffering into the world? Alexander answers that the Bible does not teach there was no pain before the Fall, and in any case, that would be impossible because pain is "actually essential to our health and well-being" (272).

"Those who deny the reality of physical pain, disease and death before the Fall are like ostriches with their heads in the sand. The reality will not go away" (274).

Again, whether or not he is right is not the point; rather, the point is that here science is driving interpretation. Alexander also considers that D and E are just not possible — not realistic in the light of either Scripture or science.

Alexander is not calling for a completely "mythical" understanding of Genesis; he believes that A and B do not emphasize enough that sin is about relationship with God being broken. Model C, however, he feels is consistent with both biblical and scientific data.

> It may be wrong and I would not wish to hold to it more than tentatively. But it provides, I believe, a reasonable working model for proposing an anthropological history lying behind the inspired, figurative, theological essay that Genesis

51. I fear this argument does not work. God could have limited families; or God could have brought the end of the world; or in a non-sinful, non-fallen world, we could have advanced in technology and developed space travel in a few thousand years . . . there are many alternative scenarios, albeit wildly speculative!

> 1–3 provides, and I for one am happy to hold to this model until a better one comes along. (274-75)

Let us return to the question of suffering before the Fall. To what degree did Adam's sin result in suffering for the rest of us? In Alexander's schema, it brought death to humans, because the evolved beings that existed, even with civilization to some extent, were not human; it was not until God established a special relationship, recorded figuratively in Genesis 2, that they became human. But Alexander holds that death and pain existed before then, on the grounds that biology insists that they did.

Biology is a package deal, he writes; you can't have life without pain. Life implies death. Survival brings pain. More specifically, mutations are essential for our existence and our diversity; yet mutations cause cancer and genetic diseases. Eating is necessary, but chemically it leads to DNA damage and aging. All life is in a food chain and interdependent.

Yet there is no "cruelty" in nature, Alexander holds, because animals don't have ethics; the baby seal tossed around to death by a shark is not being treated cruelly because the shark has no conscience. Alexander gives a strong warning against oversentimentalizing animals. Scripture does not do so. Animals are valuable to God in their own right and as an interdependent system. This is a world that was made good, that is, fit for purpose, but a tough world that needed subduing; it is a boot camp for moral and spiritual growth. It was always the precursor for the new heavens and new earth. So-called natural evil is not a result of moral evil, but in contrast to the age to come where there will be no pain or suffering.

Why does God make us go through so much suffering? Why any at all? Because, Alexander says, the end will be better. It may not make sense to us, but perhaps this amount of biological suffering really is necessary for a good end. Maybe there is some crucial insight or perspective that will make that obvious in the world to come. We can't say so definitely, "But even the possibility of an affirmative answer provides a very powerful theodicy" (292).

Alexander has his own diagnosis for why Christians are tempted to be against modern science.

> Occasionally Christians are found jumping on the "anti-science" bandwagon. One reason for this may be as a reaction against atheists who try to utilize their science to prop up their atheistic ideologies. But we should be careful not to throw out the baby with the bath water. Just because an atheist tries to use the prestige of a particular scientific theory to support their own particular philosophy does not mean that the theory in question is wrong. (292)

Alexander has some historical support for that, as we have seen. But a further caution bites harder:

> Another reason why Christians can become anti-science is because they really do not want certain scientific truths to be the case, perhaps because they do not fit into their favourite theological schemes or some special interpretation of certain biblical texts. But we have to be careful to take on board what is actually the case and not merely what we would like to be the case. Describing the properties of God's created order accurately is a Christian duty. (78)

Here we come to the crux of the matter. I have no argument with Alexander's promotion of science. However, is this a "duty"? Is it right to say, as he does, "Christians should be, and often are, at the forefront of promoting the international and cooperative nature of the scientific enterprise" (198)? Alexander has acted conscientiously on this basis, probably at personal cost, and can be praised for doing so; but in the end, it is obeying Scripture and understanding its commands in its own terms that is a Christian's duty. No secular pursuit of knowledge, however praiseworthy in its own right, has a greater ethical or epistemological claim.

Science Dominates Scripture

We now turn to a different scientist, and a very different way in which theology is reconciled with science, to finish our story. John Polkinghorne is famous for being both a senior published physicist and an Anglican clergyman. As well as writing well-received books and articles on science and Christianity, he has frequently spoken to audiences and appeared in the media as a leading figure in this area. As such, he has presented a powerful witness to Christianity, and has been a great asset in apologetics. His work has no doubt broken down many barriers for those who might previously have felt that science and Christianity cannot be reconciled.

It is not with any casualness, therefore, that his work is critiqued here. However, it may be that his very power as a scientific thinker has been less than beneficial to his published views on Scripture and how it is to be understood. For while Polkinghorne remains thoroughly orthodox in several ways, holding to the reality of the resurrection and the truth of relationship with God, his scientific views have led him to reinterpret certain key aspects of Scripture. Here, then, we have an example of a thinker whose science is leading his interpretation of the Bible, not the other way around.

This in itself is not terribly surprising when we see Polkinghorne's views of Scripture, particularly as it relates to the scientific endeavor. It is Polkinghorne's frequently stated view that the pursuits of science and theology have a great many things in common. Both, he insists, are ways of seeking a critical realism.

> [N]either science nor theology can be pursued without a measure of intellectual daring, for neither is based on incontrovertible grounds of knowledge. Yet both can, I believe, lay claim to achieving a critical realism. Each demands commitment to a corrigible point of view as a necessary starting-point in the search for truth. Each has to be open to the way things are and must conform its mode of inquiry to the nature of reality it encounters. . . . It has been said that science uses "universe-assisted logic"; theology must employ "liturgy-assisted logic."[52]

The desire for understanding motivates scientists. A similar desire is part of the inspiration for the religious quest. The two, however, must be different; you can't get anything as neat as a set of equations to describe God.

> The reality of God so far transcends our finite grasp that he will never be held by our intellects in such a way. Our encounter with him involves deeper levels within us than that of the rational mind alone and it demands a total response of obedience and worship. Nevertheless the search for understanding will be incomplete if it does not include within itself the religious quest, for otherwise it will leave fundamental questions of significance and purpose unaddressed and unanswered.[53]

One of the main differences between science and religion is how the question of certainty is approached. Mathematics is not absolutely certain, Polkinghorne states, but no one stays awake at night worrying about it. Science is somewhat less certain but the same holds. In religion, however, there seems to be not just widespread uncertainty, but intense disagreement, even between educated people. Why is it you can ask any competent person in three different continents what is the structure of matter and get the same answer, but ask the same people about God and you'll get three different answers?

The difference, Polkinghorne answers, is the degree of personal engagement demanded.[54] Science, although it requires humans to interpret it and involves

52. John Polkinghorne, *Reason and Reality: The Relationship between Science and Theology* (London: SPCK, 1991), 1. It is significant here that Polkinghorne, while upholding theology as a noble and truth-seeking pursuit, holds that it does not have an incontrovertible ground of knowledge (although in many ways evangelicals would hold that Scripture is this ground), and sees theology as employing "liturgy-assisted logic" rather than "scripture assisted."

53. John Polkinghorne, *Science and Creation: The Search for Understanding* (London: SPCK, 1988), xi.

54. I would disagree with his analysis. For one, by "competent" he means "educated," and not all will be educated about Christianity. Also, most Westerners will have been taught that the answer is a matter of private opinion and not "truth," so it doesn't matter whether you give the "right" answer.

tacit knowledge, and so is not entirely impersonal, is largely so. Art and ethics are more personal; they require more judgment and are more affected by personal experience, so there is less public agreement about them. An encounter with the divine is supremely personal; so "[h]ere the refracting power of culture will be powerfully present."[55] This is why Christians will see visions of the virgin Mary and Buddhists will see visions of Buddha. This to some extent solves the problem of the differences in world religions, although not all.[56]

The place of revelation in religion is a different issue again. Christian revelation, Polkinghorne states, is not Scripture, nor the creeds. The creeds are summaries of human experience, and they do not delineate God — to think so would be idolatry. Revelation is the person of Jesus, an astonishingly exciting way for God to reveal himself to finite humans without crushing them. That means we are not talking about detached propositions but a relationship with a person. Now Barth says encounter with God is only through Christ, and rational enquiry elsewhere will get you nowhere. Polkinghorne disagrees. But where is one to seek him, if he is everywhere? We can if we ask the right questions. There is an analogy here in science — gravity is everywhere, but we only notice when we start asking the right questions. Also, just as when studying a complex phenomenon in science, we need a simple situation where we can study it in isolation. There are particular moments in history where people can access experience of the divine in a way we call revelation.

This resonates with what Ian Barbour, another prominent writer in the science-religion field, considers to be the basis of a theology of nature, something he wants to develop. A theology of nature, he writes,

> starts from a religious tradition based on the religious experience of a historical community. Advocates of this approach hold that some traditional doctrines — especially doctrines of God and human nature — need to be reformulated in the light of current science.[57]

For Barbour, Christian Scripture is therefore important but not authoritative. "In the task of theological reformulation, I believe that we should take the Bible seriously but not literally."[58] He believes that Genesis speaks of truths, expressed "through a symbolic and poetic story," but that the words of the Bible are not to

55. Polkinghorne, *Reason and Reality,* 54.

56. I would add that Christianity requires something of us and so costs more to accept than mathematics; and we are sinful people, so we don't want the truth about God and will run away from it.

57. Ian Barbour, *Nature, Human Nature, and God* (London: SPCK, 2002), 3.

58. Barbour, *Nature, Human Nature, and God,* 3.

be considered revelation in themselves. "I believe that revelation occurred, not in the dictation of an infallible book, but in the lives of people."[59]

Similarly, for Polkinghorne a strength of religion is that it is based on experience: it is the codified summary of many experiences, just as science is. The difference between science and religion is that religious experience is of something far greater than us, so it's hard to describe and codify. Christianity is the *true* religion, in his view, because God made his greatest revelation through Christ. In Christ we find a whole lifetime of experience, whereas other religions are based on just human glimpses of the divine. But in Polkinghorne's writings, there is no overriding idea of the authority of Scripture, or that the truth of God is exclusively in Scripture, or even really that it is the word of God.

Polkinghorne is aware of objections to his view. He notes that evangelicals complain that he pays insufficient attention to the Bible, which they think judges questions of reason and reality. Polkinghorne has his own ideas on how Scripture is to be used, based on the history of the church.[60]

Christians have always had a mixture of respect and freedom in their response to the Bible, Polkinghorne says; after all, Jesus reinterpreted Jewish Scriptures, and when the New Testament writers appeal to Old Testament texts they do so in a ragtag way, suggesting they are reading the story of Jesus into the Old Testament rather than being controlled by what is there. This is, of course, not a conservative way of understanding New Testament use of Old Testament Scripture, but a considerably more liberal approach.

In its evidential role, Polkinghorne goes on, Scripture gives information about Jesus and the history of Israel, both of whom "represent uniquely important loci in which the divine nature and the divine purpose have been most clearly revealed."[61] How the evidence is weighed will be affected by how persuasive one finds the theological understanding offered as the interpretation of the results. Polkinghorne believes they provide sufficient foundation for Christian belief.

There is also a spiritual use of Scripture, where we do not sit in judgment on the character and historicity of the text, but we allow that text to sit in judgment on us, as "we seek to make it the inspiration and guide of a pilgrim life lived in the presence of God."[62] One aspect of this is using Scripture in liturgy. Psalms are

59. Barbour, *Nature, Human Nature, and God,* 4.

60. Polkinghorne is well aware that there is a tradition of Christian thought that assigns the Bible a supreme role, making it the arbiter of all theological inquiry. This conservative biblicism is often attractive to scientists, he says, particularly in their student days. But those scientists who go on to postgraduate study realize that "the search for truth involves more than the ability to scan the literature" (*Reason and Reality,* 61).

61. John Polkinghorne, *Science and the Trinity: The Christian Encounter with Reality* (London: SPCK, 2004), 38.

62. Polkinghorne, *Science and the Trinity,* 39.

especially important. There is also benefit in using a short passage of even a single verse, which is meditated upon and absorbed into the heart.

Scripture also has a contextual role, structuring the setting within which theological reflection takes place. The basic context of all Christian theological thinking is that provided by Scripture, and genre is extremely important.

> Those who attempt to read Genesis 1 and 2 as if these chapters were divinely dictated scientific texts, kindly provided by God to save us the trouble of attempting to read the book of nature for ourselves, are committing . . . an act of literary violence.[63]

Polkinghorne has a great deal more to say about his theories of Scripture, which may be found in various of his books.[64] But like many authors committed to a strong view of the role of science, he holds that Scripture is not authoritative in the way that a conservative reading would have it.

> Belief in the continuing work of the Holy Spirit undergirds a theological understanding of the fruitfully open meaning of scripture, for it allows for a process by which the unfolding of divine truth has occurred in the past and can continue to occur into the future.[65]

There are some things that just cannot be accepted by a scientifically educated person. For Polkinghorne, demon possession and such phenomena are simply not realistic, so we read that as an idiom of the time. Just as other ancient literature, Scripture can still speak to us across the centuries — testimony to the existence of a real human nature. The Bible has its contradictions and inconsistencies, but they all add to the rich tapestry of the whole. "The presence of clash and contradiction within the Bible is fatal to the theory of using it as a divinely-guaranteed textbook."[66]

How, then, must we read the Bible? "The clue lies, I believe, in the assimilation of our engagement with the Bible to our fundamental experience of open engagement with symbol" (67) — a description rather at odds with a conservative hermeneutic. The Bible is not to be tied down; it has multilayered meaning. The Old Testament does not contain prophecies that were later fulfilled, or types for which Christ is the anti-type; rather, it gives ideas and language to the New

63. Polkinghorne, *Science and the Trinity,* 44.

64. *Science and the Trinity* is a good source.

65. Polkinghorne, *Science and the Trinity,* 51.

66. Polkinghorne, *Reason and Reality,* 67. Hereafter, page references from this book will be given in parentheses in the text.

Testament writers as they express their own thoughts about Christ and their own encounter with God.

Nonetheless, Polkinghorne holds that the Bible is a great encouragement to him as a scientist. The ideas of creation by the word in the New Testament give a clear encouragement to the scientific thinker, particularly confidence in the rationality of the universe. Romans 1:19 gives encouragement to natural theology. The Old Testament, with the value it places on creation, encourages science.

Especially, Polkinghorne adds, Genesis 1–3 must be read correctly. The two creation accounts are different and the compiler never tried to reconcile them, suggesting that neither is to be taken literally. Genesis 3 in Polkinghorne's view is a myth about alienation from God, not an etiology for our condition — it can't be, since science hasn't discovered any rift in human history. "A discriminating use of biblical imagery is surely legitimate for us as we seek to integrate what we learn from the book of Scripture with what we learn from the book of nature" (73).

If that is Polkinghorne's view of Scripture, how does he see science? Polkinghorne's philosophy of science has a Kuhnian ring. Models in physics are heuristic devices and different from theories that are "candidates for verisimilitudinous descriptions" of reality. Models should aim to be theories, which should be unique. Theology, on the other hand, is unlikely to achieve "more than a collection of viable models, usable with discretion" — which would seem to imply that, in his view, science is more likely to be *right* than theology. Science sometimes uses metaphor to grasp a difficult concept; theology must do this much more so. "If mathematics is the natural language of physical science, symbol is the natural language of theology" (31). Symbol is the most intense metaphor, or maybe better than metaphor, as it has more vitality of its own. It is not just a sign; it carries "a cloud of allusion and suggestion" that enables individuals to respond to it in their own way. Like sacrament, symbol should not be reified — this is to be too Catholic — nor reduced to the mere sign — this is the mistake of the Reformed. He speaks sacramentally because worship is central to theology and the Eucharist is central to Christian worship.

Science and theology are, then, both investigations of what is (what exists), both the search for increasing verisimilitude in our understanding of reality. So underlying both science and theology is "rational inquiry into what our experience leads us to believe is actually the case" (5).

In science it is rational to assume the reasonableness of the world and to search for it. The coherence theory of truth and the correspondence of truth end up the same thing; what is intelligible is what is, and what is is intelligible. Polkinghorne rejects foundationalism, that there is a totally secure basis on which to construct knowledge. That leads to a propositional account of theology, with dogmatic formulae guaranteed by an unchallengeable authority. You cannot base your system on axioms because axioms come from somewhere; they are distilled from experience.

The best way to think about theology, like science, is the critically realist view. Religion will always be more culturally conditioned in its expression than science, because religion is more personal. Theology will always be more qualified in its attainment of verisimilitude because of the nature of the reality it examines. Yet there can still be some truth and truth claims in it. Theology cannot be experimental in the way that physics is, because its terms are broad, worldview ones, not specific predictions; also, God is not to be put to the test. But if theology is to maintain cognitive claims it must be empirical to the extent that its assertions are related to an understanding of experience.

Science does not need theology; it will answer its own questions.[67] Neither can science comment on theology's questions. But there is overlap, in the sense that theology *contains* science, and must listen to science (along with aesthetics and many other disciplines) because it is the overarching study of all things and puts all things in context. Theology answers those meta-questions that arise from science but which science cannot answer. It provides the ultimate quenching of the thirst for understanding (particularly expressed in the Thomist tradition). What science can do for theology is tell it what the physical world is actually like. Science places limitations on theology and stops ungrounded speculation.

Theology's gift to science is to answer two meta-questions. It explains the intelligibility of the universe: why the world is comprehensible, why mathematics describes it, and why our minds can understand it. Evolutionary survival alone does not account for all of this. Also, theology gives an explanation for the scientific discoveries of the peculiar "fine-tuning" of the universe. Conversely, there are three constraints that science places on theology. First, in origins: the doctrine of creation is ontological, not temporal, so theology never had a preference for Big Bang over steady-state theories; and it would not matter if Hawking's non-beginning were true.[68] Second, as regards the end: the universe is either going to fly apart or have the big crunch, but neither matters to theology, which always says there is hope beyond the physical, and we can hope that means cosmically as well as individually. Third, concerning chance and necessity: both are consonant with Christian theology, since God is both loving and faithful. In love he gives freedom to his creation; faithfulness means he provides lawlike necessity to give fruitful regularity to freedom.

Some of the implications of the strong relationships that Polkinghorne draws between Scripture and science start to emerge when he talks more specifically about causality and precisely how God interacts with his physical creation.

For all that most sensible thinkers would be anti-reductionistic — holding, for instance, that cells and social groups are as real as atoms — yet we still want

67. I assume that Polkinghorne means this in a fairly narrow sense; science does not need theology, for instance, to discover the chemical structure of some substance.

68. See Stephen Hawking, *A Brief History of Time* (London: Bantam Books, 1995).

to explain things in terms of a lower level. We think of emergence as one-way. We all accept at least structural reductionism; atoms are made of quarks and gluons, elements are made of atoms. We also think the universe started that way; first there were quarks, then nuclear matter, then atoms, then molecules, then single-celled organisms, then complex animals.

But maybe emergence works both ways, Polkinghorne says. Think of chaotic systems, in which behavior can be inherently unpredictable, because you can never know the initial circumstances with unlimited accuracy; a difference in one decimal point thirty places in can produce huge differences in outcome. A totally deterministic, simple equation can produce unpredictable complexity. At the same time, classes of chaotic systems act similarly. Large-scale order is generated that seems incomprehensible at the microscopic level.

But the systems are only unpredictable because we can't measure the exact initial conditions. If we could, would the weather actually be predictable? We always think that way — we always think of the lower controlling the higher. But is that just a problem of our limited intellect? A trick of intellectual perspective?

> That structured chaos can arise from deterministic equations is a mathematical fact. That act by itself does not settle the metaphysical question of whether the future is determined or, on the contrary, the world is open in its process. (39)

After all, in quantum physics it seems the higher level determines the lower; when the wave function collapses at observation, a new thing has been caused; the quantum event before collapse was genuinely random. Maybe chaotic behavior is similar; macro events are so sensitive to initial micro conditions that they are genuinely open, because in attempting prediction one would reach levels of required accuracy that are denied to us by Heisenberg's uncertainty principle.

What has this to do with God? The point is that for scientists, epistemology and ontology merge; what you know is what is there. That is why so many hold a genuinely indeterminate interpretation of quantum physics. So why not hold a genuinely unpredictable interpretation of chaos? It's what seems to be observably true. Polkinghorne appears to like this because he does not like a deterministic universe, as, say, a Calvinist might (which Polkinghorne is, self-confessedly, definitely not). For Polkinghorne, this is where perhaps genuine freedom for God to act as well as humans to act can be found.

> The picture which has been building up is that of a physical world liberated from the thrall of the merely mechanical but retaining those orderly elements which science has been so successful in exhibiting and understanding. (44)

This is, in Polkinghorne's view, what you would expect from a loving God who gives his creation both reliability and freedom.

The world, then, is a range of possible futures arising from initial conditions differing only infinitesimally from each other; the choice of path does not correspond to any physical act or any input of energy, but rather to a selection, to an input of information. This means there is genuinely top-down causation. This could be how God interacts with the world in relation to humanity and all other open processes. Others don't like this, seeing it as too detached and deistic; God is much more intimately involved in the world. But how? No one has been able to give any but the vaguest of accounts. What Polkinghorne wants to give is theology with physical sense.

> God is certainly not a cosmic tyrant; his interaction with his world can be expected to respect its freedom (including our own). His acts will be veiled within the unpredictability of complex process. They may be discernible by faith but they will not be demonstrable by experiment. (47)

This is similar to what authors sympathetic to the "process theology" tradition, such as Ian Barbour, write about God's action in the world.

> Here I join those who say that God is omniscient in knowing all that can be known, but this does not include choices that are unknowable until they are made. The "free-will defense" in theodicy asserts that the price of human freedom is the possibility of the choice of evil. Polkinghorne has used the term *free process defense* to refer to divine self-limitation in the nonhuman domain. I would prefer to speak of creativity rather than freedom in nature apart from humanity, but clearly similar issues are at stake concerning God's power and knowledge in human and nonhuman domains.[69]

If this is true — if God is necessarily limited in his foreknowledge and action in the world, as Polkinghorne says — then there are very definite implications for prayer and for the understanding of miracles. God's freedom to change the universe is, roughly speaking, in those parts of the universe described by quantum theory and chaos theory. They mean that we can pray for healing, perhaps rain, but not for the sun to stand still or for winter to become summer. We cannot know about the behavior of non-linear systems, and therefore the future is genuinely open. So not only does God not know the future, but when he wants to affect it he influences it through these systems by input of information.

God must not act "intermittently," is Polkinghorne's contention; God's action must be characterized by the most profound consistency. The regularities

69. Ian Barbour, *Nature, Human Nature, and God,* 108. This volume is also useful for gaining an overview of how admirers of process theology approach a number of different theological and scientific issues.

discerned by science are signals of God's reliability and faithfulness. But God must also have a range of possible action available to him, for if he cannot make specific response to individuals then it is not a personal relationship.

There is a problem, then, of how God acts. We can't expect God to change the seasons. The motions of the solar system are mechanical, with predictability over long periods of time. "Thus the succession of the seasons will be guaranteed by transcendent divine reliability and it would indeed be foolish to pray for their alteration."[70] Weather, on the other hand, is far more complex, so it is legitimate to pray for rain. God will only act, we speculate, in those things that are unpredictable anyway. But God's providence in providing parking spaces? To assume that God will provide help with such things is just facile. He does not "fussily intervene."

A biblical perspective, however, might question Polkinghorne's conclusion. God is the God of the falling sparrow, the one who counts hairs on the head. God is the one who "determines the number of the stars; he gives to all of them their names" (Ps. 147:4). This *is* a God who fussily intervenes — or rather, fussily governs every detail to his own, conscious and deliberate, plan.

What of miracle? Miracle in Polkinghorne's view is unexpected, made possible by an unprecedented regime, rather than a divine *tour de force.* The important thing about a miracle, Polkinghorne says, is its significance, not its power. God probably can, in one sense, suspend the laws of nature. But will the rationally coherent God actually change his mind? Will he really work against the grain of the natural law that he himself has ordained? And if *that* is what he does, why does he not do it more often? There seems to be plenty of scope for extra miracles to alleviate the sufferings of mankind.[71]

There is a problem, then, of God's *inaction,* "his apparent absence from those occasions when his powerful presence seems most needed and desired."[72] Polkinghorne here is separating himself from a more traditional perspective, in which miracles are seen as being important in their *signifying* role at least as much as, if not more than, their role in providing mercy. God's deliverance of mankind from suffering, while a crucial part of God's ministry to us, has an eschatological dimension — we are not yet in the time when God will alleviate all suffering.

Yet in Polkinghorne's view, miracles fall into a simpler schema. They happen maybe in two forms. The first is arranged coincidence, two entirely natural things arranged to happen at the same time (as may have happened in Jesus' stilling of the storm). The second is the truly extraordinary, like the resurrection.

70. John Polkinghorne, *Science and Providence: God's Interaction with the World* (London: SPCK, 1989), 31-32.

71. Polkinghorne, *Science and Providence,* 46.

72. Polkinghorne, *Science and Providence,* 17.

> This is the fundamental theological problem of miracle: how these strange events can be set within a consistent overall pattern of God's reliable activity; how we can accept them without subscribing to a capricious interventionist God, who is a concept of paganism rather than of Christianity.[73]

It makes theological sense to Polkinghorne that Jesus, Lord and Christ, could not be held by death. The miracle of the wedding at Cana is more problematical; it seems more capricious. The problem is, if God can do such miracles, then why didn't he stop the holocaust? "If God were a God who simply interferes at will with his creation, the charge against him would be unanswerable."[74] But if he is always consistent then "it is not clear that he is to be blamed for not overruling the wickedness of humankind." As we have seen before, this is typical of authors who would tend to privilege the scientific view of nature; but it fails to deal adequately with the biblical evidence of a God who is utterly sovereign over creation, and can manipulate it at will.

It is interesting at this point to compare Polkinghorne's views with another writer who is even further committed to the scientific view as authoritative. Arthur Peacocke developed his views over a lifetime of thought, and has been an extremely influential writer in the area of science and religion. His mature thought can be examined in the book completed literally on his deathbed, as he presented his conclusions in summary, ranging over a wide number of topics.[75]

Peacocke adheres to naturalism, in a particular sense: it is a naturalism that allows for theism, but not supernaturalism, that there is a being outside the universal web of cause-effect relations.

> This theology may be properly deemed to be "naturalistic" insofar as it assumes that the world of nature is real, that science unveils its realities, and that this natural world contains those entities, processes, and structures that are explicable and eventually rendered intelligible through the natural sciences — hence . . . no "supernatural" entities, no "miracles" that break the laws or regularities of nature discovered by science, no dualisms within the natural world.[76]

This world, Peacocke believes, owes its existence to a Creator God, who is real, personal, and has purposes for this world. But God "does not implement these purposes through 'miracles' that intervene in or abrogate the world's natural

73. Polkinghorne, *Science and Providence,* 51.

74. Polkinghorne, *Science and Providence,* 52.

75. Arthur Peacocke, *All That Is: A Naturalistic Faith for the Twenty-First Century* (Minneapolis: Fortress, 2007), Kindle edition: references are given to the Kindle location numbering system.

76. Peacocke, *All That Is,* location 238.

regularities, which continue to be explicated and investigated by the natural sciences."[77] How, then, could God influence particular events without contravening the regularities of science? Not, Peacocke believes, through the supernatural. Rather, emergent systems are the mode of divine creativity in nature. "Natural systems, it transpires, have an inbuilt capacity to produce new realities; hence any theistic understanding has to recognize that this is the mode and milieu of God's creative activity."[78]

This in itself, of course, is perfectly compatible with a conservative, biblical view of God's activity; but also biblical is the recognition that we must not limit God's activity to such processes. The discoveries of science might describe God's action, but in no way place limitations upon him. Note the force of Peacocke's "hence" in the above quotation: it implies not only that this reasoning from nature is valid, but that it is the only valid method — there is, here, no witness from Scripture.

This is, indeed, typical of Peacocke's writing — he insists that theology be brought in line with science, but not with Scripture. So his assertion that "a revived emphasis on the immanence of god as Creator 'in, with and under' the natural processes of the world unveiled by the sciences becomes imperative if theology is to be brought into accord with all that the sciences have revealed"[79] — one might also say that this is imperative if one is to be biblical, but that is not Peacocke's authority.

Peacocke's actual suggestions about a scientifically consistent theology are similar to Polkinghorne's in many ways. For instance, he makes much of the implications of those areas of science exploring apparently random or chaotic systems.

> For a theist, God must now be seen as acting creatively in the world often through what we call "chance" or random processes, thereby operating *within* the created order, each stage of which constitutes the launching pad for the next. The Creator unfolds the created potentialities of the universe in and through a process in which its possibilities and propensities became actualized. God may be said to have "gifted" the universe, and goes on doing so, with a "formational economy," which is the set of all of the dynamic capabilities of matter and material.[80]

So what is God's action in the world? It is something like "information flow," a pattern-forming influence. This could act at all levels, but perhaps most fully at the human level. Peacocke's ideas of seeing God's action at the human level are certainly interesting, and could be fruitful if explored within a biblical frame-

77. Peacocke, *All That Is,* location 247.
78. Peacocke, *All That Is,* location 281.
79. Peacocke, *All That Is,* location 391.
80. Peacocke, *All That Is,* location 386.

work, but as they stand are too constrained by what he sees as the authoritative testimony of science to be taken at face value.[81]

The trouble is that Peacocke continually limits the scope of God's activity: "[T]he processes revealed by the sciences are in themselves the action of God as Creator, such that God is not to be found as some kind of *additional* influence or factor added on to the processes of the world God is creating."[82] It is true that the processes revealed by the sciences are the action of God — but God is certainly also to be found elsewhere, as his own testimony reveals.

Like Polkinghorne, Peacocke is selective about what parts of traditional biblical theology he will retain; but interestingly, he is differently selective. The filter of science is not a sure one; or at least, it is not consistent between commentators. Polkinghorne is inclined to retain more of the biblical witness than Peacocke, but not as a ruling authority. Peacocke will allow some aspects of traditional theology — God as being a personal agent in the world, for instance — but only reinterpreted within his scientific categories. "[T]he traditional, indeed biblical, model of God as in some sense a 'personal' agent in the world, acting especially on persons, is rehabilitated — but now in the quite different metaphysical, non-dualist framework which is itself coherent with the worldview engendered by the sciences."[83]

Perhaps even more than Peacocke, Polkinghorne is clearly familiar with Scripture; his yearly discipline of reading the Bible through in accordance with the rules set down for Anglican clergy would put many a Christian to shame. Yet he has not let Scripture guide his science, but science guide his reading of Scripture. In doing so, he has lost crucial aspects of the understanding of God — ironic, for someone so clearly dedicated to discovering truth.

The problem with his views is, of course, that they simply go against Scripture. God is clearly described in the Bible as sovereign, and predetermining; he not only knows what happens in the future, but he makes it happen. Polkinghorne has attempted to understand God's interaction with the world in terms of contemporary scientific theory. However, though it protects some ideas of God that Polkinghorne appears to hold dear, it is not consistent with God's self-witness.

Conclusion

Simply put, the conclusion is this: when we let our interpretation of what Scripture says be led by philosophies found outside the Scripture, we are not giving Scripture its due as an integrated and coherent — although not exhaustive —

81. See locations 730-44.

82. Peacocke, *All That Is,* location 409.

83. Peacocke, *All That Is,* location 758.

guide to understanding reality. For while it is true that God has given us tremendous gifts to enable us to think, to investigate, and to control the world, while it is a noble and worthwhile thing to pursue truth outside of Scriptures, yet that is the knowledge that is always contingent and open to uncertainty. Scripture is our solid foundation; other knowledge should be understood and interpreted in its light, not the other way around.

What does this mean in practice? It means that we will approach Scripture reverently, contextually, and with all the literary tools available to help us understand what the text is actually saying, however ill that may fit with preconceptions. There are many volumes written on how to read Scripture, and this is not the place to rehearse basic Bible-reading techniques.[84] It is the place, however, to stress that a belief in the authority of Scripture may at times lead us to tension with whatever is the reigning extra-scriptural philosophy of the time. When that happens, we will hear other claims to knowledge gladly, and with full realization that God is capable of revealing truth through the gifts of intelligent observation and thought with which he blesses the human race, but with a healthy skepticism. Scripture sometimes says hard things, and our preconceptions — in any direction — can blind us to its truth. It takes study, and effort, and community perseverance in prayerful humility to read it accurately. For the purposes of this essay, the main message is: do not approach Scripture saying "but it *can't* mean that" — whatever "that" might be. It can. It can mean whatever God has written it to mean. External philosophies, even ones as successful in explanatory power as modern science, do not have the final say.

For a great many areas of knowledge, Scripture will say very little in terms of specifics. This appears to be the case with much of the detail of science. Polkinghorne is right that it is no accident that the Protestant doctrines of God's sovereignty and divine freedom were the background to the Scientific Revolution in the West: if God cannot be bound by our ideas, then we cannot assume anything about this creation, but must go out and investigate it to find out how it works. God gifts us and privileges us to be able to do so. The details are ours to discover; Scripture is not generally concerned with such things, and is not constrained by them.

Yet Scripture is very concerned with other aspects of reality that science needs. It is what grounds us in reality, in our knowledge that there is a real and good world to be investigated. It tells us of the rational and wise creator who made a world that is able to be understood and described intelligibly. It gives us

84. Gordon D. Fee and Douglas Stuart, *How to Read the Bible for All Its Worth* (Grand Rapids: Zondervan, 2003), is still a good introduction to this topic. More recent is J. Scott Duval and J. Daniel Hays, *Grasping God's Word: A Hands-On Approach to Reading, Interpreting, and Applying the Bible* (Grand Rapids: Zondervan, 2005), and Nigel Benyon and Andrew Sach, *Dig Deeper: Tools to Unearth the Bible's Treasure* (Nottingham: Inter-Varsity, 2005).

reason to believe in a predictable world characterized by consistent rationality. Incidentally, it provides the moral foundation for cooperation and honesty on which the international scientific endeavor completely depends.[85]

Without the foundation of Christian Scripture, although much of the world has forgotten it, science makes very little sense, and becomes very difficult to do.[86] Ultimately, science without Scripture is pointless; for only Scripture reveals the purpose for the universe that scientists study so avidly. It is here for the glory of Jesus Christ; and without that knowledge, science is ultimately an exercise in tedium, or at least frustration. For science's sake, as much as Scripture's, we must get them in the right order.

85. To that extent, those who try to defend science against the extremes of postmodern reinterpretations, such as Paul R. Gross and Norman Levitt in *Higher Superstition: The Academic Left and Its Quarrels with Science* (Baltimore: Johns Hopkins University Press, 1998), would find their best ally in Scripture.

86. For more on this theme, see Peter Jensen, *The Revelation of God* (London: Inter-Varsity, 2002), chapter 5, especially 113-17; also my own *Unnatural Enemies.*

Comparative Religions Topics

THIRTY-ONE

Knowing the Bible Is the Word of God Despite Competing Claims

Te-Li Lau

Christians accept the authority of the Bible and receive it as the word of God. This conviction, however, faces challenges in light of the religious diversity brought about by globalization and recent demographic movements. An awareness and familiarity with other religions lead many to claim that the Bible is only one sacred text or scripture among many others, all of which make claims to sacral authority or are imputed authority by their respective traditions. For example, the Bhagavad Gita claims to be a dialogue between the Hindu deity Krishna and Prince Arjuna, the Buddhist sutras the word of Buddha, the Qur'an the word of Allah, and the Book of Mormon the word of God. Given the similar claims to authority made in each of these different religious texts, how are we to adjudicate between them? Can they all be true? And if they are not all true,[1] why should one accept the Bible as the true word of God and not the Qur'an or the Book of Mormon?

In this essay, I argue that, despite rival claims, Christians can know that the Bible is the word of God in three interdependent ways: (1) through its explicit claims to be the word of God, (2) through its supporting implicit claims, and (3) through the testimony of the Holy Spirit. As I proceed through each section, I also make brief comparative moves with the Book of Mormon, the Qur'an, and the Buddhist sutras in order to highlight the Christian perspective. A concluding paragraph will relate these three means of knowing the Bible into a model of human knowledge and summarize the essay.

1. The central affirmations of these sacred texts are fundamentally opposed to one another such that not all of them can equally be the true word of God. Although some suggest that religious truth claims are personal or ineffable and therefore not subject to the logical rules of non-contradiction, Harold A. Netland, *Dissonant Voices: Religious Pluralism and the Question of Truth* (Grand Rapids: Eerdmans, 1991), 112-50, convincingly argues for the necessity of propositional and exclusive elements in religious truth.

Explicit Claims

The Bible

The Bible makes explicit assertions that it is the word of God.[2] In the OT, there are multiple records of the words that God spoke directly to individual men and women: Adam and Eve (Gen. 3:16-19), Moses (Exod. 3:4), Samuel (1 Sam. 3:10-14), Elijah (1 Kgs. 19:9-18), and Isaiah (Isa. 6:8-13). There are also hundreds of reports of prophetic speech that begin with "Thus says the Lord." When an OT prophet uses such a formula, he claims to be a messenger who communicates the authoritative words of God. Every word that he speaks must come from God or he would be a false prophet (cf. Num. 22:38; Ezek. 13:1-7). In addition to the words of God spoken directly or through an intermediary, the OT also contains the written words of God, the most famous being the Decalogue — the covenantal testimony written with the finger of God (Exod. 31:18; 34:1), functioning as a suzerainty treaty between God (the king) and Israel (the vassal state). Although written, the Decalogue and the rest of the OT are no less authoritative than the oral word of God. Thus, numerous passages such as Psalm 119 demand obedience to and praise of the divine written word.

The above does not show that *all* the OT is authoritative. The authority of the *entire* OT is, however, recognized by the NT as God's written word. Jesus, the supreme word of God, cites OT passages, even those that are not directly attributed to God in the OT, as the authoritative words of God (Matt. 19:5; cf. Gen. 2:24). Moreover, he speaks and acts in ways that fulfill many OT Scriptures (Mark 14:49; Matt. 5:17; 26:54; Luke 4:21; 24:44; John 13:18; 15:25), claiming that it cannot be set aside or proved false (John 10:35). The apostles' view of the OT is no less different. Paul considers all the OT Scripture to be "the very words of God" (Rom. 3:2), even in cases where the speaker is not God himself (see the Isa. 28:11-12 quotation in 1 Cor. 14:21); they are "breathed out by God" (2 Tim. 3:16) or "spoken by God." Similarly, Peter considers the ultimate source of every OT prophecy to rest in God. The prophets do not speak on their own initiative, but speak the words of God as they are carried along by the Holy Spirit (2 Pet. 1:21).

2. See also B. B. Warfield, *The Inspiration and Authority of the Bible* (Philadelphia: P&R, 1948), 299-348; John Murray, "The Attestation of Scripture," in *The Infallible Word,* 3rd edition, ed. Paul Woolley and Ned B. Stonehouse (Philadelphia: P&R, 1967), 1-54; John M. Frame, "Scripture Speaks for Itself," in *God's Inerrant Word,* ed. John W. Montgomery (Minneapolis: Bethany, 1974), 178-81; Wayne A. Grudem, "Scripture's Self-Attestation and the Problem of Formulating a Doctrine of Scripture," in *Scripture and Truth,* ed. D. A. Carson and John D. Woodbridge (Grand Rapids: Zondervan, 1983), 19-59; I. Howard Marshall, *Biblical Inspiration* (Grand Rapids: Eerdmans, 1983), 19-30; Sinclair B. Ferguson, "How Does the Bible Look at Itself?" in *Inerrancy and Hermeneutic: A Tradition, a Challenge, a Debate,* ed. Harvie M. Conn (Grand Rapids: Baker, 1988), 47-66.

As in the case of the OT's view of itself, no NT text claims authoritative status for the *entire* NT. This simply cannot happen since the canon was not recognized when the NT documents were being composed. Nonetheless, there is substantial internal evidence that the NT should be accorded the same status as the OT. Just as the OT prophets are messengers of God, the NT apostles are also chosen by God to function as messengers of his revelation. These apostles are adequate for the task since the Holy Spirit teaches and reminds the apostles of everything that Jesus, the Word of God, taught them (John 14:26). The proclamation of the gospel message by the apostles is thus understood not to be the words of men, but the very words of God (1 Thess. 2:13). The NT writers also understand that what they are writing is the word of God. Thus, when Paul writes to the Corinthian church concerning proper worship practices, he boldly claims that what he is writing is a "command of the Lord" (1 Cor. 14:37).[3] Finally, some NT writers consider other existing NT writings to be on par with OT Scripture. Paul links what is probably Luke 10:7 with Deuteronomy 25:4, introducing both of them with the formula "For the Scripture says" (1 Tim. 5:18).[4] Peter also writes that the ignorant and unstable twist Paul's writings "as they do the other Scriptures," thereby placing the Pauline writings in the category of Scripture, the authoritative word of God. The application of the technical term "Scripture" to these other texts demonstrates awareness that there were other documents circulating at that time which were also considered to be God's very word.

Comparative Work

The Bible's explicit claims to authority are not unique. The sacred texts of other religions such as Mormonism and Islam also claim to be the word of God. As a religion that rejects the notion of an eternal creator God, Buddhism affirms the authority of its sacred texts not on its status as the word of God, but on its status as the word of Buddha.

Latter-day Saints "believe the Book of Mormon to be the word of God" (A of F 8), and Joseph Smith affirmed it as "the most correct of any book on earth" (*HC* 4:461). This affirmation builds on the internal claims found within the Standard Works. For example, the Book of Mormon commends itself as the word of God. It contains direct speech from God to men using the formula "the Lord said,"

3. In 1 Corinthians 7:12, Paul distinguishes his ethical instruction from the Lord's. He nevertheless goes on to imply that this teaching is just as authoritative because he gives his "opinion as one who by the Lord's mercy is trustworthy" (7:25; cf. also 14:37).

4. Since "Scripture" typically refers to what is written and authoritative, the source of "the worker deserves his wages" is probably the Gospel of Luke rather than a circulating oral tradition.

"God said," or "the Lord God said" (see for example Ether 2:16, 20, 23; 2 Ne 4:4; 5:25, 30; Enos 1:12, 18; Mosiah 27:25; Alma 37:23). It also reports prophetic speech (God's word spoken by men) using the introductory formula "Thus saith the Lord" (Hel 13:8, 11; 2 Ne 5:22; 10:7; Jacob 2:23, 25). Moreover, Nephi claims that the book contains the "word of Christ" that was given to him from Christ (2 Ne 33:10-11). Moroni testifies that "these things are true" (Moro 7:35) and that the book was "written by way of commandment, and also by the spirit of prophecy and of revelation" (title page).[5] Furthermore, the text claims divine authority for itself. As it contains the gospel of Christ (Ether 4:3; Morm 7:8), those who do not listen to it will stand condemned on the last day (2 Ne 33:11, 14-15).

Apart from the internal claims of the Book of Mormon, the Doctrines and Covenants also affirms the truth of the Book of Mormon. The Doctrines and Covenants is a compilation of revelations primarily through Joseph Smith. In these revelations, Christ, speaking through Smith, affirms that the Book of Mormon contains the truth, the fullness of the gospel (20:9; 27:5; 42:12), and the word of God (19:26; see also 10:42; 11:22). It was given by inspiration (20:10); was translated by the gift, mercy, and power of God (1:29; 20:8; see also 135:3); contains scripture that was spoken by the manifestation of the Spirit (8:1); and has its origin in Christ himself (1:24). Moreover, Christ remarks that the text is sacred (10:9; 17:5-9) and is the work of God (10:23; see also 10:43). Furthermore, Christ also places the Book of Mormon on par with the Bible, making both of them normative for Mormon faith and practice (33:16; 84:57). Those who "receive it in faith . . . shall receive a crown of eternal life; but those who harden their hearts in unbelief, and reject it, it shall turn to their own condemnation" (20:14-16).

Muslims believe the Qur'an to be the revealed word from Allah in Arabic. This affirmation rests primarily on its numerous self-referential terms and claims:

1. The Qur'an, with the exception of Sura 1, takes the form of direct speech from Allah, using the first-person "I" or "We." This oracular nature and the lack of framing narratives within the Qur'an present the words of the Qur'an as the *ipsissima verba Dei* which directly confront the listener, be it Muhammad, specific groups of people, or all humanity. The Qur'an's self-reference as *al-Qur'an* or "The Recitation" further underscores this divine oral nature. Fazlur Rahman writes,

> Not only does the word *Qur'an,* meaning "recitation," clearly indicate [that the Qur'an asserts its own divine origin and does not include the words or ideas of Muhammad], but the text of the Qur'an itself states in several places that the Qur'an is *verbally revealed* and not merely in its "meaning" and "ideas."[6]

5. See also Ether 4:5; 8:1; 2 Ne 33:11; 3 Ne 30:1-2, which state that Christ commanded the prophets to write the things in the Book of Mormon.

6. Fazlur Rahman, *Islam,* 2nd edition (Chicago: University of Chicago Press, 1979), 30-31.

2. The Qur'an claims to be divine revelation that is sent down from Allah (32:2-3; 41:2-3). On the mystical Night of Power (97:1-5), Allah caused the Qur'an to be sent down in its entirety from the Heavenly Book above the seventh heaven to the heaven immediately above the earth.[7] From this staging area, the angel Gabriel approached Muhammad and imparted to him the first revelation of the Qur'an (53:1-10). As Muhammad received the revelation, he proclaimed what he heard with absolute fidelity. Thus, the Qur'an claims not to be an admixture of divine and human influence, but to contain the precise words of Allah without human intervention.[8] As the clear revelation from Allah, the Qur'an claims to be truth (32:3) and attests to its own authority, noting that those who follow its instructions will receive mercy (6:155), but those who disbelieve will be gathered and thrown into hell (4:140; see also 2:2-7, 120; 22:57; 72:17).

3. The Qur'an calls itself the *kitāb* more than seventy times (2:176, 231; 3:7; 4:105, 113; 6:155; 16:64; 21:10; 29:47). Although primarily translated as "Book" or "Scripture," the Qur'an uses *kitāb* in relationship to divine knowledge (22:70), divine authority (35:11), and revelation (2:53; 3:48; 5:48, 110; 7:2; 23:49; 41:45). These uses lead Daniel Madigan to assert that "when the Qur'an speaks of itself as *kitāb,* it seems to be talking not about the form in which it is sent down but rather about the authority it carries as a manifestation of the knowledge and command of God."[9]

In contrast to Christianity, Mormonism, and Islam, the Buddhist scriptural "canon" is vast and fluid.[10] What is considered canonical by one Buddhist tradition may be considered apocryphal by another. But despite the variations between the different schools, the primary and undisputed essence of any Buddhist scripture is the *buddhavacana* ("the word of Buddha").

The authority of Siddhartha Gautama's teaching stems from him being enlightened, achieving realization of the ultimate truths of reality and knowing things as they truly are. The Buddhist scriptures attest to the validity of Buddha's teaching. As the Buddha, he is "the Arahant (Holy One), the Fully-enlightened One, Wise, Upright, Happy, World-knowing, Supreme, the Bridler of men's wayward hearts, the Teacher of gods and men, the Exalted and Awakened One."[11] As

7. The Heavenly Book is the source and totality of all revelations including the Qur'an. It is also called the Mother of the Book (43:4), the Hidden Book (56:78), and Preserved Tablet (85:22).

8. See 75:16-19 where Muhammad is told not to rush ahead in his recitation but to repeat it exactly as God recites it ("When We have recited it, repeat the recitation and We shall make it clear").

9. Daniel Madigan, "Book," in *Encyclopedia of the Qur'an,* ed. Jane Dammen McAuliffe, 6 vols. (Leiden: Brill, 2001-6), 1:250.

10. There is no definitive Buddhist canon. I use "canon" here to indicate a loosely bounded set of texts that are considered authoritative.

11. *Dīgha Nikāya* 2.93 (ET *Dialogues of the Buddha,* trans. T. W. Rhys Davids, 3 vols. [London: Oxford University Press, 1899-1921], 2:99).

the Buddha, "What is to be known is known (by [him]), what is to be cultivated is cultivated (by [him]), what is to be left is left by [him]."[12] Consequently, all that he teaches is true and not false, for

> in the interval between the night . . . wherein the Tathāgata [a fully Self-awakened one] was enlightened in the supreme enlightenment, and the night wherein he passed away without any condition of rebirth remaining, — all that, in that interval, he speaks in discourse of conversation or exposition: — all that is so, and not otherwise.[13]

Moreover, the true Dharma or doctrine that he expounds is "good at its beginning, good in its middle, and good at its end, its meaning profound and recondite, its words subtle and refined, pure and without alloy, fully endowed with the marks of pure, white brahman-conduct."[14]

Gautama did not appoint a successor or a community to be the authoritative perpetuator of his teachings; neither did he leave behind a collection of his teachings. The teachings of the Buddha are therefore to be found in the remembrances of the disciples. Consequently, the sutras assert the authenticity of its tradition with the prefatory formula "Thus have I heard," thereby claiming that its content traces back to the master's teaching as heard by one of his disciples.[15]

In contrast to the Pali Canon, later Mahayana texts further attest to their own authority by their self-understanding as scripture and objects of deification. For example, the *Lotus Sutra* states,

> If there is a man who shall receive and keep, read and recite, explain, or copy in writing a single gāthā of the Scripture of the Blossom of the Fine Dharma, or who shall look with veneration on a roll of this scripture as if it were the Buddha himself, or who shall make to it sundry offerings . . . , or who shall even join palms in reverent worship of it . . . , be it known that this man or any other like him shall have made offerings to ten myriads of millions of Buddhas in former time.[16]

12. *Mahāvagga* in *Sutta Nipāta* (ET *The Dhammapada; The Sutta Nipāta,* ed. F. Max Müller, Sacred Books of the East 10 [Oxford: Clarendon, 1881], 130).

13. *Dīgha Nikāya* 3.135 (ET *Dialogues of the Buddha,* 3:127).

14. Leon Hurvitz, trans., *Scripture of the Lotus Blossom of the Fine Dharma,* Buddhist Studies and Translations 94 (New York: Columbia University Press, 1976), 12-13. This common formula is also found in *Dīgha Nikāya* 1.62 (ET *Dialogues of the Buddha,* 1:78).

15. It should be noted that the concept of *buddhavacana* and the sources of the Dharma extend beyond the teachings of the historical Gautama. See Étienne Lamotte, "Assessment of Textual Authenticity in Buddhism," trans. Sara Boin-Webb, *Buddhist Studies Review* 1 (1983): 4-15.

16. *Scripture of the Lotus Blossom,* 175. See also *Scripture of the Lotus Blossom,* 221, where the sutra claims that it is "venerable, Supreme among the multitude of scriptures."

Similarly, the *Diamond Sutra* claims that just four lines of its sutra are all-sufficient for deliverance, able to generate an "immeasurable and incalculable" heap of merit. The reason for such an exalted view of this sutra is "because from it has issued the utmost, right, and perfect enlightenment of the Tathagatas, Arhats, Fully Enlightened Ones, and from it have issued the Buddhas, the Lords."[17]

In light of how the Bible, the Qur'an, the Book of Mormon, and the Buddhist sutras all claim to be the word of God or Buddha, it is clear that such claims in and of themselves cannot persuasively establish the authority of the sacred text. Rather, other evidences must be evaluated. But if we believe that the Bible is the unique source of special revelation and the final authority for the Christian faith, then any Christian doctrine including a doctrine of Scripture can only be obtained and developed from Scripture. Consequently, any evidence that is evaluated must be evaluated according to biblical assumptions. Critics charge such an argument to be circular. While admitting the presence of a certain degree of circularity, we should note that such circularity is always inherent in questions of ultimate criterion or ultimate standards of truth.[18] One cannot argue for ultimate authority by appealing to another authority, as that would undermine the ultimate authority. As the status of the Bible as the Word of God is clearly an issue of ultimate authority, the validity of the Bible must rest on its own claims. Moreover, one must make a distinction between a narrow and broad circular argument. A narrow circular argument such as "the Bible is the word of God because it claims to be the word of God" will hardly be convincing. Nevertheless, a broad circular argument such as "the Bible is the word of God not only because of its explicit claim to be so, but also because it makes other claims that can be verified, makes prophetic predictions that have been fulfilled, presents credible accounts of eyewitness testimony, etc." should not be cavalierly dismissed. The latter argument is also circular since evidences and data are ultimately evaluated from a scriptural worldview or from scriptural presuppositions, but it is a broader argument as more data are presented for consideration.[19]

Implicit Claims

The above survey shows that it is difficult to accept the Bible's authority *solely* based on its explicit claims to be the Word of God since other sacred texts make similar claims. The Bible witnesses to itself; but the Bible is not *only* or *primarily* self-referencing. It is primarily about God and his plan of salvation for humanity

17. *Diamond Sutra* 8 (ET *Buddhist Wisdom: Containing the Diamond Sutra and the Heart Sutra,* trans. Edward Conze [London: G. Allen & Unwin, 1958], 35).

18. John M. Frame, *Apologetics to the Glory of God* (Phillipsburg, NJ: P&R, 1994), 9-14.

19. John M. Frame, *The Doctrine of the Knowledge of God* (Phillipsburg, NJ: P&R, 1987), 131.

from sin. In presenting this message of salvation, the Bible also makes other assertions that can be externally verified and that implicitly support its contention to be the Word of God. Due to space constraints, I only examine two areas: (1) the historical reliability of the Bible, and (2) the coherence and unity of its message.

Historical Reliability

Christianity is to a large degree different from other religions in that "its claim to reveal the truth relies not on private mystical revelations to a prophet or teacher (revelations that, because of their private nature, cannot be verified or falsified), but on public events."[20] These events are a matter of public record and can therefore be ascertained as any other historical event, affording us the ability to determine whether the historical truth claims are true of false. If these claims are properly evaluated and shown to be false, then the Bible's assertion to be the word of God is likewise false, contradicting its own claim that God cannot lie (2 Sam. 7:28; Titus 1:2; Heb. 6:18). If, however, the claims are shown to be true, then the Bible's assertion to be the word of God is not conclusively proven but compellingly supported. Due to space limitations, I will focus only on the historical reliability of the Gospels.

Before examining the truthfulness of the Gospels' historical claims, it may be helpful to note that the current Greek New Testament that we possess is a faithful reconstruction of the original autographs. Although we cannot be 100 percent certain that we have the exact wording in every case, "we have good reason to believe that what we have preserved in the several hundred manuscripts of the first millennium is the text that the writers of Scripture penned."[21] This confidence stems from several factors. (1) The earliest extant manuscript of the NT is much closer to the date of the original writing than any other ancient document. For example, P^{52} (which contains parts of John 18:31-33, 37-38) dates from the early second century, no more than a period of fifty years after the Gospel of John was written in the 80s.[22] (2) There is a profusion of manuscripts (approximately 5,700) that have survived to the present time, far exceeding that of any other ancient writing. Of the extant NT manuscripts, sixty contain the entire NT, the most important of which is Codex Sinaiticus, a fourth-century majuscule manuscript. (3) The majority of textual variants are related only to matters of spelling

20. Paul Barnett, *Is the New Testament Reliable?* rev. edition (Downers Grove, IL: InterVarsity, 2003), 9.

21. Craig A. Evans, "Textual Criticism and Textual Confidence: How Reliable Is Scripture?" in *The Reliability of the New Testament,* ed. Robert B. Stewart (Minneapolis: Fortress, 2011), 172.

22. For the dating of the Gospel of John to 80-85 C.E., see D. A. Carson, *The Gospel according to John* (Grand Rapids: Eerdmans, 1991), 82-87.

and grammar, and do not affect the meaning of the text. If we were to compare the NT textual history with that of a comparable ancient document, we would be "embarrassed by the wealth of material"[23] available to NT textual critics. For example, the *Jewish Wars* written by Josephus in the latter half of the first century has only seven important manuscripts, all of which date from the eleventh to the twelfth century. Moreover, the earliest and only papyrological evidence of Josephus (Pap. Graec. Vindobonensis 29810) dates to the late third century C.E. and contains no more than 112 words.[24]

The strong textual reliability of the NT argues against the claims made by some Mormons and Muslims that the text of the NT has been so corrupted that we are unsure of the contents of the original autographs.[25] Moreover, when Muslims tout the stability of the qur'anic textual history vis-à-vis the NT, one should remember that this is primarily because the Qur'an underwent a formal process of textual standardization for doctrinal, political, and liturgical reasons. This standardization process began in the first century after Muhammad's death and included the destruction of variant manuscripts during the reign of Uthman (*Sahih al-Bukhari,* 6.61.510). Such a process of textual standardization was not possible in the early church as it was persecuted in the first three centuries; nor was it deemed desirable even when Christianity became a state religion during the reign of Constantine.

Having determined that the present text we possess is a faithful reconstruction of the original autographs with a high degree of confidence, we can proceed to examine the historical reliability of the Gospels in two areas.[26]

23. Bruce M. Metzger and Bart D. Ehrman, *The Text of the New Testament: Its Transmission, Corruption, and Restoration,* 4th edition (New York: Oxford University Press, 2005), 51.

24. Tommaso Leoni, "The Text of Josephus's Works: An Overview," *Journal for the Study of Judaism in the Persian, Hellenistic and Roman Period* 40 (2009): 150-53.

25. The Qur'an asserts that Jews and Christians did not faithfully preserve the original message of the revelations they received. They distorted *(tahrif)* the meaning of various words, concealed some (2:42; 3:71), forgot others (5:13), and "substituted a different word from the one they had been given" (2:59). See also 2:79; 3:78; 4:46. In the Book of Mormon, 1 Ne 13:24-29 and Moses 1:40-41 assert that "plain and precious things" have been taken out of the gospel. This is usually understood in two ways. The first option takes the current NT text itself to be corrupt, a view that led Joseph Smith to produce a revised translation of the Bible called the Inspired Version. This view is, however, not tenable since there is no manuscript evidence to support the theological changes that Smith introduced. The second option, adopted by Mormon scholar Stephen Robinson, affirms that the biblical "texts are essentially correct in their present form." The "plain and precious things" that have been taken out of the Bible are not texts that were originally in the "*present* biblical books," but *other* inspired writings that were not included in the canon. See Craig Blomberg and Stephen E. Robinson, *How Wide the Divide? A Mormon and an Evangelical in Conversation* (Downers Grove, IL: InterVarsity, 1997), 63. Unfortunately, this claim also has no historical support. There are other early Christian writings or apocryphal documents, but none of them contains any distinctive Mormon doctrine.

26. There are other pressing historical issues, not least of which are the apparent contra-

One main support for the historical reliability of the Gospels is the Gospels' claim to be based on eyewitness testimony. Luke explicitly notes in the preface of his gospel that he consulted material from those who were eyewitnesses from the beginning (Luke 1:1-4); the Gospel of John claims to be written by an eyewitness (John 21:24-25); and the Gospel of Mark implicitly claims Peter as the eyewitness source.[27] Traditional form criticism challenges this claim, arguing instead that the Gospels are best seen not as the work of an individual author but the product of a community. Moreover, the oral traditions that circulated before the Gospels were written down cannot be traced to the testimonies of eyewitnesses, but are anonymous traditions shaped by a collective community. This collective community formed and structured the Jesus traditions with a view to how they would eventually function within the community. Consequently, the traditions have no biographical, chronological, or geographical value as they were created not only *for* the church but also *by* the church.

It is not possible to give a full rebuttal in short compass; nevertheless, a brief response can be sketched as follows:

First, although all four Gospels are anonymous in the sense that their names do not appear in the text of the work, Martin Hengel rightly argues that the traditional titles ("according to Matthew," "according to Mark," and so forth) are an attribution of authorship in much the same way that the Greek Old Testament is referred to as "according to the seventy" or "according to Symmachus." Moreover, the unanimity of the second-century attributions strongly suggests that these titles were attached to the Gospels from the beginning, and that the Gospels never circulated anonymously.[28]

Second, the time frame between the writing of the Gospels and the events they report is short. The Roman historian Tacitus writes that Jesus was executed during the reign of Tiberius at the hands of Pontius Pilate who governed Judea from 26 to 36 C.E.[29] Evidence from the Gospels and astronomy suggests that Jesus' death occurred either in 30 or 33 C.E. Assuming a date of 33 C.E., the time between Jesus' death and the writing of one of the earliest NT documents (1 Thessalonians) in 50 C.E. is seventeen years; and the time between Jesus' death and the writing of the earliest Gospel (Mark) in the late 50s or 60s is only perhaps

dictions between the accounts provided in the four Gospels. For discussions on these issues, see Craig Blomberg, *The Historical Reliability of the Gospels,* 2nd edition (Downers Grove, IL: InterVarsity, 2007); David Wenham and R. T. France, eds., *Gospel Perspectives,* 6 vols. (Sheffield: JSOT Press, 1980).

27. See Richard Bauckham, *Jesus and the Eyewitnesses: The Gospels as Eyewitness Testimony* (Grand Rapids: Eerdmans, 2006), 155-81.

28. Martin Hengel, *The Four Gospels and the One Gospel of Jesus Christ: An Investigation of the Collection and Origin of the Canonical Gospels* (Harrisburg, PA: Trinity Press International, 2000), 48-56; Martin Hengel, *Studies in the Gospel of Mark* (Philadelphia: Fortress, 1985), 64-84.

29. *Annals* 15.44.2-8.

a period of twenty-five to thirty-five years. This brief time interval suggests that eyewitnesses of Jesus' ministry were still present during the writing and circulation of the Gospels — eyewitnesses who could be interviewed to produce an accurate historical account, eyewitnesses who could challenge the claims made in the Gospels if they were false, and eyewitnesses who could ratify that the Jesus traditions go back to the historical Jesus. As Vincent Taylor remarks, "If the Form-Critics are right, the disciples must have been translated to heaven immediately after the Resurrection."[30]

Third, the presence of a theological *Tendenz* does not negate the historical reliability of the Gospels. On the contrary, it confirms our understanding of the Gospels as a testimony to the history and significance of Jesus. If God revealed himself uniquely in history, then the historical element requires a historiographic presentation, and the disclosure of God requires a witness to that event to speak of God. A testimony to such a revelatory event must therefore present empirical fact and theological interpretation with the result that fact and interpretation become inseparable.[31] Richard Bauckham draws a modern-day parallel to the Gospel testimony by noting that although the Holocaust and the history of Jesus are vastly different, the role of testimony in conveying both exceptional events is similar.[32] The uniqueness of both events invalidates Troeltsch's criteria of analogy, and the uniqueness of both events necessitates fact and interpretation in order to allow an outsider to access the truth of that event.

The presuppositions of form criticism cannot stand. It is better to affirm that

> in the period up to the writing of the Gospels, gospel traditions were connected with named and known eyewitnesses, people who had heard the teaching of Jesus from his lips and committed it to memory, people who had witnessed the events of his ministry, death, and resurrection and themselves had formulated the stories about these events that they told.[33]

Another main support for the historical reliability of the Gospels is the Gospels' claim that Jesus was crucified, buried, and resurrected. The fact of this historical event is so central to the early Christian faith that Christianity would crumble if the resurrection did not historically occur (1 Cor. 15:14). The historical reliability of Jesus' crucifixion is beyond dispute, accepted by even liberal historical Jesus scholars.[34] Some, however, question whether the resurrection of

30. Vincent Taylor, *The Formation of the Gospel Tradition,* 2nd edition (London: Macmillan, 1935), 41.

31. Bauckham, *Jesus and the Eyewitnesses,* 411.

32. Bauckham, *Jesus and the Eyewitnesses,* 499-505.

33. Bauckham, *Jesus and the Eyewitnesses,* 93.

34. John Dominic Crossan, *The Historical Jesus: The Life of a Mediterranean Jewish Peasant* (San Francisco: HarperSanFrancisco, 1992), 372, writes, "I take it absolutely for granted that

Jesus occurred as a historical event in the past, interpreting Jesus' resurrection in a spiritual, non-bodily sense. But such a reading is impossible. In 1 Corinthians 15:3-4, Paul notes that "Christ died for our sins . . . , that he was buried, that he was raised." If Christ's death and burial is bodily, then his resurrection must also be bodily. Moreover, there is no indication in Second Temple Judaism that resurrection could mean anything other than a bodily resurrection.[35]

The historical reliability of the resurrection has been written about in great detail,[36] and only brief remarks can be supplied here. We should first note that the resurrection is the only possible explanation why James, Peter, and Paul were willing to die as martyrs for their faith. These men had every reason not to believe in a risen Messiah. James was originally not a believer of Jesus (John 7:2-5); Peter's expectation of an apocalyptic kingdom of God was not realized with Jesus' arrival in Jerusalem (Luke 19:38; 22:38, 49-50; 24:21; John 12:13; 18:10; Acts 1:6); and Paul was a zealous persecutor of the early church. It is difficult to believe that each of them would serve Jesus for thirty years and die for their faith unless they were truly convinced that Jesus had risen from the dead. Moreover, C. F. D. Moule notes that if we are to explain the phenomena of the birth of early Christianity within Palestine in the first century, the most plausible and perhaps inescapable explanation is the "tremendous confirmatory event" of the resurrection.[37] The sole *raison d'être* of Christianity is the event of the resurrection; from the very first, the existence of Christianity either stands or falls by its conviction that Jesus rose from the dead.[38] This conviction is witnessed in the earliest documents of the church. Paul, for example, makes passing comments concerning the resurrection (1 Thess. 1:10; 4:14; Gal. 1:1; Phil. 3:10; Rom. 1:4; 4:24-25; 6:4-5, 9; 7:4; 8:11, 34; 10:9; 2 Cor. 4:14; 5:15) in support of his other arguments. He therefore *assumes* the resurrection to be a fundamental belief that is held by his readers. Furthermore, the reality of the resurrection is the only adequate explanation why Jewish Christians in the earliest Palestinian churches gather for worship on Sunday (the day of the resurrection) and uniformly consider the Lord's Day (Rev. 1:10) to be this day of the week.[39] Finally,

---

Jesus was crucified under Pontius Pilate. Security about the *fact* of the crucifixion derives not only from the unlikelihood that Christians would have invented it but also from the existence of two early and independent non-Christian witnesses to it, a Jewish one from 93-94 C.E. and a Roman one from the 110s or 120s C.E."

35. N. T. Wright, *The Resurrection of the Son of God* (Minneapolis: Fortress, 2003), 314.

36. See Michael Licona, *The Resurrection of Jesus: A New Historiographical Approach* (Downers Grove, IL: InterVarsity, 2010); Wright, *The Resurrection of the Son of God.*

37. C. F. D. Moule, *The Phenomenon of the New Testament: An Inquiry into the Implications of Certain Features of the New Testament* (Naperville, IL: A. R. Allenson, 1967), 3, 17.

38. Moule, *The Phenomenon of the New Testament,* 11.

39. Richard Bauckham, "The Lord's Day," in *From Sabbath to Lord's Day: A Biblical, Historical, and Theological Investigation,* ed. D. A. Carson (Grand Rapids: Zondervan, 1982), 232-40.

N. T. Wright argues convincingly that the two historically secure events of the empty tomb and the multiple appearances of the risen Jesus form the necessary and sufficient condition to explain the development of early Christian belief in the bodily resurrection of Jesus.[40]

History is of utmost importance to the Christian faith because the Bible does not only make claims about abstract or philosophical truth, but also claims concerning historical events that happened in space and time. Such historical truth claims are subject to external control and can be challenged or verified. If these historical truth claims (assuming that they are correctly interpreted) should be disproven, then there is no reason to accept its other truth claims, or specifically, its claim to be the word of God. If these historical truth claims (again, assuming that they are correctly interpreted) are verified, then the Bible's claim to be the word of God, although not proven, is nevertheless affirmed. In this section, I provided evidences that demonstrated the historical reliability of the Gospels. Similar evidences can be presented for the rest of the NT and for the OT.[41] Together, these evidences confirm the historicity of the biblical texts and give credibility to the Bible's claim to be the word of God.

Coherence and Unity of the Bible

Apart from making claims about history, the Bible also makes statements that affirm and presuppose its unity and coherence. Jesus considers himself the fulfillment of the Law and the Prophets (Matt. 5:17), and Acts 13:17-41 presents a summary of the biblical story from the Patriarchs to the proclamation of the good news by Jesus' followers. Moreover, the NT, not least the book of Revelation, makes numerous allusions and appeals to the authority of the OT. As the climax of prophecy, "Revelation offers in some sense an overview of the [biblical] story from the perspective of its end, but even here the end is anticipated from within the still-continuing

40. Wright, *The Resurrection of the Son of God,* 685-718.

41. For discussions on the reliability of Acts, see Colin J. Hemer, *The Book of Acts in the Setting of Hellenistic History,* ed. Conrad H. Gempf, WUNT 49 (Tübingen: J. C. B. Mohr, 1989); A. N. Sherwin-White, *Roman Society and Roman Law in the New Testament* (Oxford: Clarendon, 1963). For discussions on the historical reliability of the OT, see Kenneth A. Kitchen, *On the Reliability of the Old Testament* (Grand Rapids: Eerdmans, 2003); V. Philips Long, Gordon J. Wenham, and David W. Baker, eds., *Windows into Old Testament History: Evidence, Argument, and the Crisis of "Biblical Israel"* (Grand Rapids: Eerdmans, 2002); Iain W. Provan, V. Philips Long, and Tremper Longman, *A Biblical History of Israel* (Louisville: Westminster John Knox, 2003). For a critical appraisal of modern and postmodern approaches to Scripture, see James K. Hoffmeier and Dennis R. Magary, eds., *Do Historical Matters Matter to Faith?* (Wheaton, IL: Crossway, 2012).

story."[42] This implicit claim for the unity of the Bible is pertinent to our study. If the Bible is inspired by God and is the word of God such that there is a single divine author behind the multiplicity of human authors, one would expect to find a certain coherence and unity in the Bible. In other words, the presence of a demonstrable unity in the Bible supports the Bible's explicit claim to be the word of God.

There are, however, challenges to discerning a unity.

1. The Bible is a collection of books written by about forty human authors with a diversity of qualifications (kings, poets, physicians, tax collectors, shepherds, fishermen, priests) over a thousand years in locations as culturally diverse as Patmos, Babylon, Jerusalem, and Rome. It exhibits a variety of literary genres (historical, legal, prophetic, poetic, wisdom, Gospels, epistles, and apocalypses), and it is written to different audiences with different objectives in three different languages (Hebrew, Aramaic, and Greek). But despite the challenges, one can discern a unity in the Bible under various rubrics such as typology, covenant, Christ, intertextuality, NT use of the OT, and prophecy-fulfillment. But a broad proposal that ties all the various books of the Bible together is a salvation-historical approach that views the Bible as the gradual unfolding of God's plan of salvation for the world. If we follow the chronological sequence of the books, we see how successive narratives build on and refer to earlier ones, forming a coherent and unified story: a story that describes God's creation of the world and the heavens; the disobedience of man with its devastating consequences; the redemption of the world by God through the ministry of his prophets, and ultimately in the work and death of his only Son, Jesus Christ; and the consummation of God's salvific plan in the new creation of the new heavens and the new earth. There are no doubt subplots and literary genres within the biblical books that do not lend themselves easily to such a framework; nevertheless, they do not detract from the main storyline.

2. Some scholars assert that there is no theological unity within the Bible. Instead of a biblical theology *(eine gesamtbiblische Theologie),* there are biblical theologies. In some cases, even the possibility of an OT or NT theology is denied. At best, one can only speak of OT theologies (Yahwist, Deuteronomic, Priestly, deutero-Isaiah, and so on) or NT theologies (Paul, Luke, John, Q, and so on).[43] The issues are complex, dependent on the exegesis of multiple passages. Nevertheless, two points need to be emphasized.

The first is that, in moving between the two testaments, the progressive

42. Richard Bauckham, "Reading Scripture as a Coherent Story," in *The Art of Reading Scripture,* ed. Ellen F. Davis and Richard B. Hays (Grand Rapids: Eerdmans, 2003), 42.

43. Manfred Oeming, "Unitas Scripturae? Eine Problemskizze," in *Einheit und Vielfalt Biblischer Theologie,* ed. Ingo Baldermann et al., *Jahrbuch für Biblische Theologie* 1 (Neukirchen-Vluyn: Neukirchener Verlag, 1986), 50, writes, "On the other hand, through an increasingly more nuanced perception of the biblical voices it becomes clear that 'the Bible' emphatically does not contain a unified, coherent theology, but rather a plurality of theologies that must each be regarded individually" (thanks to Robert Yarbrough for this translation).

revelation of Scripture and the progressive redemption in salvation history call for both continuity and discontinuity in theological thought. For example, Romans 16:25-26 declares that the gospel is a mystery that has been hidden for ages past but now revealed and made known through the OT. In other words, the gospel has been hidden in times past and is now revealed; yet, the gospel has also been predicted in times past and is now fulfilled.[44] There are lines of continuity and discontinuity, but Paul betrays no tension in holding these two poles together.

The second point to be emphasized is that divergent theologies present in either the OT or NT need not be interpreted as contradictory theologies. It is better to envision a "basic unity [that] is developed in divergent directions, but without reaching positions that have to be labeled as 'contradictory' in nature."[45] For example, Ernest Käsemann concurs with Martin Luther that the doctrines of justification in Paul and James are "theologically irreconcilable."[46] Paul insists that justification comes by faith alone (Rom. 3:28); but James declares that a person is justified by works and not by faith alone (James 2:24). Without minimizing the theological tension that these two passages present, a better way to understand these passages is to note that Paul and James use the verb "justify" differently. Paul uses "justify" to denote the "initial declaration of a sinner's innocence before God; James to the ultimate verdict of innocence pronounced over a person at the last judgment."[47] Moreover, James, like Paul, considers works to be a consequence of a living faith, although a necessary component (compare James 1:25 to Rom. 2:13).[48] The ability to harmonize theologically divergent passages should not lead us to minimize the theological contributions made by Paul and James, nor should it lead us to neglect the occasional nature of their letters; nevertheless, it should caution us to dismiss disparate theologies as irreconcilable.

3. Postmodernists eschew any concept of a metanarrative, an overarching story that explains all of the religious phenomena in the Bible at the expense of

44. See D. A. Carson, "Mystery and Fulfillment: Toward a More Comprehensive Paradigm of Paul's Understanding of the Old and the New," in *Justification and Variegated Nomism,* vol. 2, *The Paradoxes of Paul,* ed. D. A. Carson, P. T. O'Brien, and Mark Seifrid (Tübingen: Mohr Siebeck, 2004), 393-436.

45. Peter Balla, "Are We Beyond New Testament Theology?" in *Moving Beyond New Testament Theology: Essays in Conversation with Heikki Räisänen,* ed. Todd Penner and Caroline Stichele (Göttingen: Vandenhoeck & Ruprecht, 2005), 37.

46. Ernst Käsemann, "Begründet der neutestamentliche Kanon die Einheit der Kirche?" in *Das Neue Testament als Kanon,* ed. Ernst Käsemann (Göttingen: Vandenhoeck & Ruprecht, 1970), 130.

47. Douglas J. Moo, *The Letter of James,* PNTC (Grand Rapids: Eerdmans, 2000), 141.

48. See Tim Laato, "Justification according to James: A Comparison with Paul," *TJ* 18 (1997): 43-84.

respecting the diverse outlooks and viewpoints in the respective books. They consider such grand narratives to be oppressive and symbols of authoritarian reductionism. Instead of focusing on the "great story," postmodernists prefer an atomistic approach that relishes the "little" stories. Thus, Walter Brueggemann insists that the proper focus of biblical study is "the specific text, without any necessary relation to other texts or any coherent pattern read out of or into the text."[49] Two responses should be noted here.

The first response is that, although the biblical story has been misused in history, it is inherently not oppressive or culturally repressive. On the contrary, it subverts the human will to autonomous power with its message of the cross.[50] Moreover, the biblical story does not obliterate cultural diversity but affirms it. Thus, when Paul remarks that there is no Greek, Jew, barbarian, or Scythian in the body of Christ (Col. 3:11), he is not denying cultural diversity but cultural privilege. The affirmation of cultural diversity is also seen in the urgency to translate Scripture into every language. Such translation is not only a practical necessity to fulfill God's mission, but is grounded in the very nature of the gospel, a gospel "to every nation, tribe, language, and people" (Rev. 14:6).[51] Such translatability cannot be said for the Qur'an. Muslims believe that the Qur'an cannot be reproduced in another language without losing its sacred character because Arabic is the privileged and revelatory language.

The second response is that, if the "little" stories are read in isolation from others in the biblical canon, what is the guiding rubric for interpreting them apart from the imagination that we bring into the text?[52] Moreover, when we detach and abstract the "little" stories from any perceptible plotline in Scripture, we domesticate these texts such that they lose their true significance and contribution. Thus, despite objections from the postmodernist camp, we must still ask whether there is a continuous storyline running through the entire Bible on which the canonical books hang and make their individual contribution. In our search for a central plotline, we should nevertheless not construct a canon within a canon nor should we smother the voices of the "little" stories under a rigidly constructed schema that ignores God's communicative acts in the diverse literary genres of Scripture; rather, we should allow the various texts to challenge our understanding of the Bible's central story. The tension between the "little"

49. Walter Brueggemann, *Texts under Negotiation: The Bible and Postmodern Imagination* (Minneapolis: Fortress, 1993), 58.

50. See Richard Bauckham, *Bible and Mission: Christian Witness in a Postmodern World* (Grand Rapids: Baker, 2003), for an example of how the biblical story subverts the exploitative story of global capitalism.

51. See Lamin O. Sanneh, *Translating the Message: The Missionary Impact on Culture*, 2nd edition (Maryknoll, NY: Orbis, 2009).

52. Brueggemann, *Texts under Negotiation*, 26-56, argues that "evangelical imagination" is needed to construct a better reality.

stories and the "great" story cannot be minimized, but must be maintained. It is only then that the unity of Scripture functions not as a rival, but as a compass that elicits the contribution of its multiple voices toward a single goal.[53]

Despite the diversity of literary genres, languages, and theological outlooks, the above section argues that it is possible to discern a basic unity within Scripture. The individual books of the Bible contribute to an unfolding story of God's redemption of the world, and this unifying plot in books written by different authors over a thousand years in different geographical and cultural regions attests that there is a unifying author; that author is God.

Other Sacred Texts

The implicit claims of the Book of Mormon, the Qur'an, and the Buddhist sutras can also be examined. Given the prominence of historical claims in Christianity, I will only examine the role of history in the authentication of Buddhist, Islamic, and Mormon sacred texts. At the outset, we should note that the significance of a historical event that defines the existence of a movement puts Christianity apart from Buddhism, Islam, and Mormonism, as these three religions arose to promote a certain ideology — Buddhism with its path to enlightenment, Islam with its forceful monotheism, and Mormonism with its reformation agenda. Even if we are to grant that there are key foundational events in these three religions, we should note that these events could be predicated on other human individuals. In other words, other human individuals could have functioned as the conduits of divine revelation. For example, the enlightenment of Gautama is not unique as there are others who have been enlightened; the revelation from Allah to Muhammad could very well be given to another human prophet; and the discovery of the gold plates by Joseph Smith could be undertaken by another individual.

History does not play an authenticating role in the Buddhist sutras since history and historical events are judged to be unimportant in Buddhism compared to the atemporal system of thought that is bound up with the absolute and timeless Dharma. As the Dharma exists independently of any person, the essence of the sutras is true regardless of whether they are the actual teachings of the historical Gautama. Thus, even though the earliest writings stemmed from the teachings of Gautama, later writings were added and authenticated by the understanding that his disciples who have been trained in the Dharma and realize its true nature teach nothing that contradicts it. The *Aṣṭasāhasrikāprajñāpāramitā sūtra* states,

53. Brevard S. Childs, *Biblical Theology of the Old and New Testaments: Theological Reflection on the Christian Bible* (Minneapolis: Fortress, 1993), 725.

> Whatever . . . the Lord's Disciples teach, all that is to be known as the Tathagata's work. For in the dharma, demonstrated by the Tathagata they train themselves, they realize its true nature, they hold it in mind. Thereafter nothing that they teach contradicts the true nature of dharma.[54]

The implication of this thought is that while Christian textual criticism focuses on the search for the autographs, Buddhism emphasizes charting the overall textual development rather than the search for a supposed *Urtext.*[55]

History also does not play a major authenticating role in the Qur'an since the Qur'an repeatedly emphasizes its own nature rather than historical events. The Qur'an generally does not name individuals or cities, and consistently uses techniques of generalization. Coupled with its oracular nature, the Qur'an lacks the concrete narratival feel present in the Gospels. There are narratives within the Qur'an. Nevertheless, these are often allusive, suggesting that the details of the story are of no primary consequence. This narratival ambiguity is seen in its account of the crucifixion of Jesus. One passage flatly denies that the Jews killed Jesus (4:157-58), but three passages affirm his death (3:55; 5:117; 19:33).[56]

The veracity of the Book of Mormon is inextricably tied to the story of the book's origin — the discovery of the gold plates and their translation by Joseph Smith. Several close associates of Smith testified that they saw and handled the plates, but the authenticity of the plates cannot be presently verified since Smith returned them to the angel. Without the physical evidence of the plates, LDS apologists and critics focus on the book's claim to be an authentic work by ancient people of Israelite descent. While most Mormons would admit that there is no concrete evidence, others note that "evidence can be adduced — largely external and circumstantial — that commands respect for the claims of the Book of Mormon concerning its ancient Near Eastern background."[57] Thomas Finley, however, challenges the evidence put forth by Mormon writers.[58] He notes that

54. ET *The Perfection of Wisdom in Eight Thousand Lines and Its Verse Summary,* trans. Edward Conze (Berkeley: Four Seasons Foundation, 1973), 83.

55. Lewis Lancaster, "Buddhist Literature: Its Canons, Scribes, and Editors," in *The Critical Study of Sacred Texts,* ed. Wendy O'Flaherty (Berkeley: Graduate Theological Union, 1979), 228.

56. For further discussion, see Todd Lawson, *The Crucifixion and the Qur'an: A Study in the History of Muslim Thought* (Oxford: Oneworld, 2009); A. H. Mathias Zahniser, *The Mission and Death of Jesus in Islam and Christianity* (Maryknoll, NY: Orbis, 2008).

57. Hugh Nibley, "Book of Mormon Near Eastern Background," in *Encyclopedia of Mormonism,* ed. Daniel H. Ludlow, 5 vols. (New York: Macmillan, 1992), 1:187.

58. Thomas J. Finley, "Does the Book of Mormon Reflect an Ancient Near Eastern Background?" in *The New Mormon Challenge: Responding to the Latest Defenses of a Fast-Growing Movement,* ed. Francis Beckwith, Carl Mosser, and Paul Owen (Grand Rapids: Zondervan, 2002), 337-66.

the nature of the metal plates mentioned in the Book of Mormon differs from that commonly found in ancient times. Moreover, the linguistic features of the Book of Mormon reflect those of a pseudo-translation imitating the style of the KJV rather than the translation of an ancient Semitic original.

Internal Testimony of the Holy Spirit

The previous two sections show that the Bible makes both explicit and implicit claims to be the word of God; Scripture is self-authenticating. As the word of God, Scripture is divine in its origin and character, bearing the marks of its divinity. But if Scripture clearly manifests itself to be divine, why is faith not the consequent result of everyone that is confronted with the claims of Scripture? The answer is that sin affects the perceptive faculty of all humanity so that, in our rebellion against God and in our self-interest, we misinterpret or suppress evidence, and are unable to accept Scripture for what it truly is (1 Cor. 2:14). If we are to perceive and approve the divine character of Scripture, nothing less than the work of the Holy Spirit is required.

The work of the Spirit in enabling us to hear Scripture as God's word can be seen in two parts: illumination and demonstration. First, the Holy Spirit illumines or opens our mind to behold the divine excellence that is contained in Scripture. He regenerates our noetic faculties such that we are able to hear the words of Scripture as God's personal message to us. In essence, the Spirit as the divine author of the text opens the text to us. Second, the Holy Spirit demonstrates or testifies to the truth of Scripture. In 1 Corinthians 2:4-14 and 1 Thessalonians 1:5, Paul attributes the persuasive and convicting power of the gospel to the testimony of the Holy Spirit. The testimony of the Spirit then provides us with the certainty that Scripture is indeed the word of God. Calvin remarks,

> If we desire to provide in the best way for our consciences — that they may not be perpetually beset by the instability of doubt or vacillation, and that they may not also boggle at the smallest quibbles — we ought to seek our conviction in a higher place than human reasons, judgments, or conjectures, that is, in the secret testimony of the Spirit.[59]

59. *Institutes* 1.7.4. All citations of Calvin's *Institutes* are from *Institutes of the Christian Religion* (1559), ed. John T. McNeill, trans. Ford Lewis Battles (Philadelphia: Westminster, 1960). Calvin's phrase ("in a higher place than human reason") should not be taken to mean that rational arguments are not necessary or that faith is a blind conviction. Rather, Calvin is asserting that the testimony of the Spirit is not an appeal to human reason but is a direct act of God.

The certainty afforded by the Holy Spirit is not a formal certainty; it is not self-evident or incorrigible in the sense that 1 + 1 = 2. Rather, it is a moral certainty that gives one cognitive rest or peace regarding the divine authority of Scripture.[60]

Scripture is self-authenticating; it attests to its own divinity. But we need the Spirit to illumine that self-attestation, and we need the Spirit to testify and assure us that that self-authentication is valid and true. In so doing, the Spirit does not provide new evidences, but testifies to the truth that is objectively inherent in the text. The Spirit then is not the *reason* for faith, but the *cause* of faith.[61] The *reason* for faith would be Scripture's self-attestation as seen in the explicit and implicit claims of Scripture to be the word of God as mentioned earlier in this essay. The Spirit is the *cause* of faith because he illumines our minds and furnishes us with the assurance that the claims of Scripture are true, making us perceive and accept the authoritative status of Scripture as the word of God. This does not mean that Scripture lacks intrinsic authority before the work of the Spirit. Scripture has objective authority in and of itself, as it is the inspired word of God. The Spirit, however, works existentially within an individual and establishes the subjective authority of Scripture with respect to that individual.

Certainty and Evidences

The above section suggests that the Holy Spirit works with and testifies to the self-authenticating explicit and implicit claims of Scripture. The relationship between the testimony of the Spirit and evidences is developed in a slightly different approach by Alvin Plantinga.[62] Plantinga appropriates Calvin's doctrine of the testimony of the Spirit and considers external proofs such as arguments from history, archeology, or reason to be epistemically weak, as they belong only to the realm of opinion or probability. For example, if the proposition *S* (Scripture is the word of God) is only externally verified, then the certainty of *S* is dependent on some other proposition or propositions (that Jesus rose from the dead, that there was a virgin birth, that there are no contradictions within the various Synoptic accounts, and so on). But the certainty of these dependent proposi-

60. R. C. Sproul, "The Internal Testimony of the Holy Spirit," in *Inerrancy,* ed. Norman Geisler (Grand Rapids: Zondervan, 1980), 344-47; Frame, *Doctrine of the Knowledge of God,* 152-58.

61. John M. Frame, *The Doctrine of the Word of God* (Phillipsburg, NJ: P&R, 2010), 312-14.

62. See Alvin Plantinga, *Warranted Christian Belief* (New York: Oxford University Press, 2000). Plantinga develops a model in which the great truths of the gospel are justified, rational, and warranted. One is entitled to believe these things without evidence or argument, in much the same way we believe that there is a past. This model, however, can be expanded such that the belief that the Bible is the word of God can also have warrant (see 375-80).

tions is only probable since they must be investigated with the same tools that historical-critical scholars use for evaluating the historicity of other historical events. Consequently, the problem with such an approach is the dwindling probability of *S* since we have to *multiply* (not add) the relevant probabilities of its dependent propositions.[63]

In contrast to the probabilities produced by the inferential processes of external verification, the testimony of the Spirit is certain, for it is a direct or one-step endorsement from God himself. The Spirit provides the same kind of certainty as direct sense perception, enabling one to see the truths of the gospel as immediately and as certainly as one sees the color black or white. Consequently, belief in the divinity of the gospel has warrant in the basic way, not dependent on propositional evidences external to Scripture or on any historical arguments for the truth of the gospel.[64] Believers are therefore within their epistemic rights to believe in the divine origin of Scripture even if they can't articulate explicit reasons for doing so. Believers "have a reason" for their belief even though they can't "give a reason" for it.[65]

Plantinga's model is cogent. It is important, nevertheless, to remember that it only offers epistemic permission, not epistemic obligation. It eliminates a reason for not believing Scripture, but provides no reason for believing so. One should therefore not discount the value of evidential arguments for several reasons: (1) The testimony of the Holy Spirit regarding the validity of Scripture can be accomplished by helping an individual properly assess the significance of the evidences. Thus, despite Plantinga's assertion that arguments are only probable, there is no reason why one cannot hold beliefs with full certitude even though one came to believe in them via arguments. (2) Plantinga's account asserts that it is possible to have a reason for one's belief without giving a reason for it. But all things being equal, it is more optimal to have a reason *and* to give a reason for one's belief. Not only can evidential arguments function as rebuttals or undercutters to a supposed defeater or overrider produced by a Muslim apologist,[66] they can also function as arguments for positive apologetics. (3) Evidential arguments *when* interpreted along Christian presuppositions and from a biblical worldview are not merely probable; they are demonstrative and they obligate assent, regardless of whether that certainty is subjectively experienced.[67] Evidential arguments should therefore not be discounted.

63. Plantinga, *Warranted Christian Belief,* 268-80, 378-79.

64. Plantinga, *Warranted Christian Belief,* 258-66.

65. For this distinction, see George I. Mavrodes, *Belief in God: A Study in the Epistemology of Religion,* Studies in Philosophy (New York: Random House, 1970), 11-16.

66. C. Stephen Evans, "Evidentialist and Non-evidentialist Accounts of Historical Religious Knowledge," *Philosophy of Religion* 35 (1994): 175-76.

67. Frame, *Doctrine of the Knowledge of God,* 142-44.

Mormonism, Islam, and Buddhism

The testimony of the Holy Spirit also plays a vital part in affirming the authenticity of the Book of Mormon.[68] Moroni exhorts his followers "that ye would ask God, the Eternal Father, in the name of Christ, if these things are not true; and if ye shall ask with a sincere heart, with real intent, having faith in Christ, he will manifest the truth of it unto you, by the power of the Holy Ghost. And by the power of the Holy Ghost ye may know the truth of all things" (Moro 10:4-5). When honest truth seekers cry out in their hearts to God concerning the truth of the things recorded in the Book of Mormon, he will "speak peace to [their minds] concerning the matter" (D&C 6:23). Despite the similar function, the content of the testimony of the Holy Spirit in Mormonism differs from evangelical Christianity. Evangelical Christians believe that the Spirit does not add to, modify, or contradict Scripture; the Spirit witnesses to the Word, not against it or in addition to it. Mormons, however, hold that the ultimate source of knowledge "is linked not to written words, not even to the writings of Moses or Isaiah or Malachi, not to the four Gospels or the epistles of Paul, but rather to the spirit of prophecy and revelation."[69] Consequently, the Spirit does not so much testify to the Bible, or the Book of Mormon, as to its ongoing revelation. But this creates the problem of a continuous circular argument. If new revelation is needed to attest to the revelation in the Book of Mormon, then further revelation is needed to attest to this new revelation.

Islam has no notion of the Holy Spirit. It nevertheless does have some form of subjective experience that attests to the Qur'an's divine character. The Qur'an notes how its recitation can generate an aesthetic response in the audience. During the early years of his prophetic calling, Muhammad regularly went to the Ka'ba to recite the revelations. Although some sneered at his recitations, others who were supposedly endowed with spiritual knowledge and insight would prostrate themselves or cry, recognizing that what they heard was the clear truth of God's word (5:83; 17:107-9; 32:15; 84:21). Another passage speaks of a tingling sensation in the skin and the softening of the heart (39:23). The sacrality of the qur'anic recitation is incipient in the Qur'an. Later Islamic thought, however, developed and embellished stories of spontaneous conversion, stories in which unbelievers and even those hostile to the prophet responded positively upon hearing the recitation of the Qur'an.[70] Regardless of how Muslims epistemologists

68. Craig J. Hazen, "The Apologetic Impulse in Early Mormonism," in *The New Mormon Challenge* (Grand Rapids: Zondervan, 2002), 56, suggests that the emphasis placed on the testimony of the Spirit by modern LDS apologists and scholars probably stems from the lack of "major objective confirmations . . . of key factual claims" concerning Mormonism.

69. Robert L. Millet, *A Different Jesus? The Christ of the Latter-Day Saints* (Grand Rapids: Eerdmans, 2005), 78.

70. See Navid Kermani, "The Aesthetic Reception of the Qur'ān as Reflected in Early

interpret this religious experience, we should note that the Christian appeal to the testimony of the Spirit is not an appeal to a person's experience, emotions, intellect, or inner consciousness — it is an appeal directly to God. This witness is not a witness borne *by* our consciousness, but a witness *to* our consciousness by the Spirit. The witness of the Spirit does provide a feeling or experience of cognitive rest, but the existence of this experience is not the premise of an argument, but the occasion, for the formation of our belief that Scripture is indeed the word of God.[71]

Buddhism also contains a subjective element in determining the authenticity of its texts, but this subjective dimension is different. Instead of an experience that validates the text, provisional authority is first imputed to a text by an individual in order to achieve an experience. As each individual has the potential for enlightenment, "each individual holds final responsibility for his own development and, ultimately, for what in Buddhist tradition is to be accepted as authentic and what is not."[72] One has to choose the appropriate text necessary for one's particular stage of development, but that text must be discarded at a certain point on one's path toward enlightenment. Some Buddhists, especially Zen Buddhists, do speak of self-authentication,[73] but what is self-authenticated is a particular experience (the state of enlightenment) that the text helps to bring about rather than the text itself.

Three Perspectives of Knowing Scripture as the Word of God

This essay argues that we know Scripture to be the word of God in three interdependent ways: through its explicit or direct claims to be the Word of God, its supporting implicit or indirect claims, and the internal testimony of the Holy Spirit. Taken together, these three ways fit a model of human knowledge advanced by John Frame. Frame proposes that human knowledge is tri-perspectival: it comprises the interdependence of the knowledge of God's norms, knowledge of our

---

Muslim History," in *Literary Structures of Religious Meaning in the Qur'ān,* ed. Issa J. Boullata (Richmond, VA: Curzon, 2000), 255-76.

71. Plantinga, *Warranted Christian Belief,* 258, 265.

72. Reginald A. Ray, "Buddhism: Sacred Text Written and Realized," in *The Holy Book in Comparative Perspective,* ed. Frederick Denny and Rodney Taylor (Columbia: University of South Carolina Press, 1985), 152.

73. Daisetz T. Suzuki, *The Essentials of Zen Buddhism: Selected from the Writings of Daisetz T. Suzuki* (Westport, CT: Greenwood Press, 1973), 164, writes that the *satori* (enlightenment) experience is authoritative in that "the knowledge realized by satori is final, that no amount of logical argument can refute it. Being direct and personal it is sufficient unto itself." See also Kenneth Kraft, *Eloquent Zen: Daitō and Early Japanese Zen* (Honolulu: University of Hawaii Press, 1992), 93.

situation, and knowledge of ourselves.[74] Human knowledge "is an application of God's revealed norms for thought (normative) to the facts of God's creation (situational) by a person qualified to make such applications (existential)."[75] When applied to our discussion, we come to know that Scripture is the word of God by its self-attestation (normative), by facts and evidences properly interpreted through Scripture (situational), and by the Spirit enabling us to evaluate truly the Bible's claims and evidences (existential). The explicit claims of Scripture lay out the normative perspective that Scripture is self-attesting. The implicit claims of Scripture probe the situational perspective, affirming that the evidence supports Scripture's contention to be the word of God. Finally, the testimony of the Holy Spirit falls within the existential perspective of our knowing, convincing us that Scripture is indeed the word of God.

These three perspectives overlap and interpenetrate one another, and all three perspectives need to be justified in order to have true knowledge. The normative perspective of Scripture's self-authentication is justified by Scripture itself. Despite the circularity, a broad circular argument will also be persuasive because it displays the internal coherence of its system. The situational perspective is justified as the claims of Scripture correspond to ultimate reality, the "real world" as understood from a Scriptural perspective. The existential perspective for believers is justified as the Holy Spirit removes their cognitive and affective blindness, causing them to perceive and accept Scripture as the word of God. With the justification of these three perspectives of knowing, Christians can truly know that the Bible is the word of God.

74. Frame, *Doctrine of the Knowledge of God,* 62-75.

75. Frame, *Doctrine of the Word of God,* 311.

THIRTY-TWO

Qur'anic Challenges for the Bible Reader

Ida Glaser

"What can we say about matters which are still outside our knowledge?"

So asks Martin Luther, rhetorically, in his introduction to Bibliander's Qur'an, 1543.[1] "I have wanted to get a look at a complete text of the Qur'an," he continues. He realized that much of what he had read was a Christian view that presented only a rather distorted version of the most negative (from a Christian perspective) aspects of Islam. He needed to read for himself the sources of Islam in order to find out what Muhammad really said, and to read Islamic literature in order to find out what Muslims really believed. His stated purpose was to refute Islam and to assist others to do so. He was less interested in calling Muslims to Christ — perhaps understandably given that, for him, Islam meant the Turks who were invading his country.[2]

The challenges raised by Islam for Christians today are not very different from those raised for Luther. First, will we read for ourselves the primary sources of the faith rather than relying on Christian critiques of those sources? After all, we would not recommend a Muslim to obtain understanding of the Bible only through Islamic apologetic writings. Second, will we examine what Muslims themselves say about their beliefs, rather than relying on Christian introductions to Islam? After all, we would not recommend a Muslim to learn about Christian faith from Muslims. Third, in a climate in which Islam is often seen as a threat to Christianity and to Western societies, can we keep a gospel focus in our relationships with Muslims? This latter challenge implies a challenge to think and act biblically, and therefore to read the Bible faithfully in the context of Islam.

1. Translation in S. Henrich and J. L. Boyce, "Two Prefaces on Islam: Preface to the *Libellus de ritu et moribus Turcorum* (1530) and Preface to *Bibliander's edition of the Qur'an* (1543)," in *Word and World* 16, no. 2 (1996), http://www2.luthersem.edu/Word&World/Archives/16-2_Islam/16-2_Boyce-Henrich.pdf.

2. For a discussion of Luther's views of Islam, see my *Crusade Sermons, Francis of Assisi and Martin Luther: What Does It Mean to 'Take Up the Cross' in the Context of Islam?* Crowther Centre Monograph 14 (Oxford: Church Mission Society, 2010), and bibliography therein.

This chapter will be restricted to the challenges raised by the Islamic scripture for the Christian reader of the Christian scripture: by the Qur'an for the Bible reader. These challenges are unique: while various Jews and Christians differ in interpretations of the Bible, and other major religions have texts that tell very different stories, the Qur'an offers its own version of the Bible story and claims authority over the biblical text. "Challenge 1," the first section below, approaches this by going straight to the primary source and listening to the challenges presented to the Bible reader in the Qur'an itself. We will find that there is a fundamental question concerning truth: Is the Qur'an from God, and should it be given priority over the Bible?

An examination of the Qur'an's truth claims from a biblical perspective makes it clear that there are important differences in how Muslims and Christians view their Books, which leads to our second section and the second challenge: that of developing an understanding of Muslims without which effective communication is impossible. Our final two sections concern related challenges: How might engagement with the Qur'an affect our reading of the Bible — and hence our lives?

The chapter's primary intent is to address challenges to Christian readers, since it is written by a Christian for a Christian readership, and Jesus Christ's own teaching exhorts us to challenge ourselves before we challenge others (Matt. 7:1-5). However, the process of Christian reflection on the Qur'an necessarily raises challenges to the Qur'an's view of itself, and for Muslims in their reading of it. We will note some of these reciprocal challenges in what follows.

Challenge 1: Truth — Reading the Bible in the Context of Qur'anic Claims

Luther's idea that the Qur'an was what Muhammad really said is already contentious from an Islamic perspective. While Muslims believe that Muhammad spoke the Qur'an, they do not see it, and neither does it see itself, as the words of Muhammad. It presents itself as the direct Word of God given to the prophet Muhammad. The Qur'an, like the Bible, presents One God who is both creator and judge, and to whom all creatures owe their worship; but, where the New Testament witnesses to Jesus, the Qur'an witnesses to itself.

The Qur'an's Claim to Divine Authority[3]

The claim to authority pervades the Qur'an. As the second Surah asserts:

3. As indicated in the section "Challenge 2" below, there is a long tradition of Islamic inter-

> This is the Scripture in which there is no doubt. (2:2)

The translator M. A. S. Abdel Haleem explains, "The Arabic construction *la rayba fihi* (there is no doubt in it) carries more than one meaning, including 'there is nothing dubious about/in it' and 'it is not to be doubted' as regards its origin or contents."

The Surah continues:

> This is the Scripture in which there is no doubt, containing guidance for those who are mindful of God, who believe in the unseen, keep up the prayer, and give out of what We have provided for them; those who believe in the revelation sent down to you [Muhammad], and in what was sent before you, those who have firm faith in the Hereafter. Such people are following their Lord's guidance and it is they who will prosper. As for those who disbelieve, it makes no difference whether you warn them or not: they will not believe. God has sealed their hearts and their ears, and their eyes are covered. They will have great torment.

Clearly, acceptance of the Qur'an and following its guidance is deemed the non-negotiable necessity for what, in Christian terms, might be called salvation. The claim is serious and demands our attention: rejecting it, we are told, leads to damnation. Such ideas permeate the Qur'an, and comprise its fundamental challenge to all peoples.

The nature of the authority claimed by the Qur'an is indicated by its self-descriptions, its most frequent characterizations of itself being as "guidance" (e.g., 17:9; 26:2; 34:6) and "warning" (e.g., 26:2). Other relevant descriptors include "book of wisdom" (10:1; 31:2; 36:2), "clear light" (4:174; 42:52), "clear evidence, guidance and mercy" (6:157), "glad tidings and warning" (17:9-10), and "healing and mercy" (17:82).

The Qur'an's claim to authority is closely linked with its claim to be truth. As indicated in Michael Rea's essay (chapter 27 in this collection), the link between authority and truth can be a complex one. In the Qur'an, there is frequent reference to truth in passages that exhort acknowledgment not only of the authority of the Qur'an, but also of the authority of Muhammad. This is often in the context of challenges to Muhammad's prophethood. There are two relevant Arabic roots:

---

pretations of the Qur'an, which need to be taken into account in any Christian reflection on the Qur'an's claims. Here, we shall attempt no more than to introduce the Christian reader to those claims by direct reference to the Qur'an itself. My reading, and that of the translation I have chosen (M. A. S. Abdel Haleem, *The Qur'an: A New Translation* [Oxford: Oxford University Press, 2004]), seeks to be consonant with a broad Islamic consensus unless otherwise stated. All qur'anic quotations in this chapter are from Haleem's translation.

ṢDQ has to do with speaking what is true,[4] and *ḤQQ* has a broader meaning that can embrace ideas of reality and necessity. In relation to the qur'anic revelation, the latter is used in describing the Truth that God sends to Muhammad, and the former in affirming that both God and Muhammad speak the truth. Relevant examples include:

> This scripture, free from all doubt, has been sent down from the Lord of the Worlds. Yet they say, "Muhammad has made it up." No indeed! It is the Truth *(ḥaqq)* from your Lord for you [Prophet], to warn a people who have had no one to warn them before, so that they may be guided. (32:2-3)[5]

> So who could be more wrong than the person who invents a lie about God and rejects the truth *(ṣidq)* when it comes to him? Is there not ample punishment for the disbelievers in Hell? It is the one who brings the truth *(ṣidq)* and the one who accepts it as true *(ṣaddaqa)* who are mindful of God. (39:32-33)[6]

The two roots are interestingly brought together in an admonitory passage that looks toward the Bible as well as toward the Qur'an. The affirmation of Muhammad is linked with a claimed continuity with former prophets:

> Whenever it was said to them, "There is no deity but God," they became arrogant, and said, "Are we to forsake our gods for a mad poet?" "No: he brought the truth *(al-ḥaqq)* and confirmed *(ṣaddaqa)* the earlier messengers; you will taste the painful torment, and be repaid only according to your deeds." (37:33-39)

This claim to authority and truth raises several questions:

Whence such authority? While Christians and Jews have lengthy discussions over the human as well as the divine origins of the various biblical books, the Qur'an claims to have come direct from God. The word translated "sent down" in Surah 2:4 above is from the Arabic root *NZL,* which the Qur'an uses frequently to describe its own origins (e.g., 2:213; 3:7; 4:113; 6:155; 17:105). The idea is quite literally "coming down," the word being used in modern Arabic for, for example, an airplane landing.

How did it come? Islamic tradition tells of Muhammad receiving it, bit by bit

4. The root ṢDQ is also the basis for vocabulary on free-will giving.

5. See also 34:6; 69:48-51.

6. Since this is in the context of a defense of the Qur'an, the one who "brings the truth" here is Muhammad. The root ṢDQ is also used in reference to the truth told by other prophets, such as Solomon (27:27) and Jesus (5:113).

from the age of forty until his death, by direct dictation from the angel Gabriel. The actual experiences of revelation differed:

> Narrated 'Aisha: (the mother of the faithful believers): Al-Harith bin Hisham asked Allah's Apostle "O Allah's Apostle! How is the Divine Inspiration revealed to you?" Allah's Apostle replied, "Sometimes it is (revealed) like the ringing of a bell, this form of Inspiration is the hardest of all and then this state passes off after I have grasped what is inspired. Sometimes the Angel comes in the form of a man and talks to me and I grasp whatever he says." 'Aisha added: Verily I saw the Prophet being inspired Divinely on a very cold day and noticed the Sweat dropping from his forehead (as the Inspiration was over). (Bukhari 1.1.2)

The *Hadith* tell of how Muhammad received the first revealed Surah by direct dictation from the Angel Gabriel:

> Narrated 'Aisha: (the mother of the faithful believers): The commencement of the Divine Inspiration to Allah's Apostle was in the form of good dreams which came true like bright day light, and then the love of seclusion was bestowed upon him. He used to go in seclusion in the cave of Hira where he used to worship (Allah alone) continuously for many days before his desire to see his family. He used to take with him the journey food for the stay and then come back to (his wife) Khadija to take his food like-wise again till suddenly the Truth descended upon him while he was in the cave of Hira. The angel came to him and asked him to read. The Prophet replied, "I do not know how to read."
>
> The Prophet added, "The angel caught me (forcefully) and pressed me so hard that I could not bear it any more. He then released me and again asked me to read and I replied, 'I do not know how to read.' Thereupon he caught me again and pressed me a second time till I could not bear it any more. He then released me and again asked me to read but again I replied, 'I do not know how to read (or what shall I read?).' Thereupon he caught me for the third time and pressed me, and then released me and said, 'Read in the name of your Lord, who has created (all that exists) has created man from a clot. Read! And your Lord is the Most Generous" (96.1, 96.2, 96.3). Then Allah's Apostle returned with the Inspiration and with his heart beating severely. (Bukhari 1.1.3)

Whence has it come? "By the Scripture that makes things clear, We have made it a Qur'an in Arabic so that you [people] may understand. It is truly exalted in the Source of Scripture kept with Us, and full of wisdom" (43:2-4). The phrase translated "Source of Scripture" is *umm il-kitāb,* literally "mother of the Book." This is generally identified with the "Preserved Tablet" *(lawḥ il-maḥfūẓ)* mentioned in Surah 85:

> This is truly a glorious Qur'an on a preserved Tablet. (Surah 85:21-22)

This is generally interpreted as referring to an eternal book that has always been in heaven with God. In the early Islamic centuries, there was heated discussion as to whether the Book, and therefore the Qur'an, was created or uncreated. This became a political as well as a theological issue, and blood was shed over it. The view that it was uncreated won, and has been uncontested since.[7] The orthodox position is stated by the great jurist, Abu Hanifa (d. 767) as follows:

> The Qur'an is the Word of God, and is his inspired Word and Revelation. It is the necessary attribute of God. It is not God, but still it is inseparable from God. It is written in a volume, it is read in a language, it is remembered in the heart, and its letters and its vowel points, and its writing are all created, for these are the works of man, but God's Word is uncreated. Its words, its writing, its letters, and its verses, are for the necessities of man, for its meaning is arrived at by their use, but the Word of God is fixed in the essence of God, and he who says that the Word of God is created is an infidel.[8]

Christians will immediately see that Islamic questions about the nature of the Qur'an are much more parallel with Christian questions about Jesus Christ than with Christian questions about the Bible: where Christians see Jesus as the eternal, uncreated Word that has come to earth in flesh, Muslims see the Qur'an as the eternal, uncreated Word that has come down as a book. The big difference is that, while Christians have continued to ask just how Jesus can be both human and divine, few Muslims have continued to ask the parallel question about the Qur'an.[9]

In sum, the Qur'an is seen as a direct dictated message from God: the question of accommodation of the divine Word to human language arises, but not the question of how human authorship relates to divine inspiration, because there is no human authorship. If this is its origin, the only question is whether the received words have been accurately transmitted. Hence the Islamic apologetical preoccupation with proving the purity of the text — and with questioning the biblical text. Some Muslims use the sorts of Christian discussions

7. See Richard C. Martin, "Createdness of the Qur'ān," in *Encyclopaedia of the Qur'ān,* ed. Jane Dammen McAuliffe (Washington, DC: Georgetown University; Leiden: Brill, 2010); Brill Online; Oxford University libraries; http://www.paulyonline.brill.nl/subscriber/entry?entry=q3_COM-00044 (accessed 20 April 2010). Martin notes that there were Christian debates about the doctrine of the Trinity contemporaneous with the Islamic debates about the createdness of the Qur'an.

8. Cited in "Qur'an," in *A Dictionary of Islam,* ed. T. P. Hughes (Lahore: Kazi Publications [repr. of 1885 original]), 484.

9. See "Settled Questions," pp. 1037-43 below.

about canon and text that are referred to in this volume in their anti-biblical polemic.[10] At the same time, critical discussions of the qur'anic text are unwelcome to them.

The Christian reader might, then, ask on what basis such a strong claim to authority is built. There are two foundational ideas here: inimitability and continuity with the Bible.[11]

The first foundational idea is inimitability. The Qur'an is, according to itself, God's revelation in God's language. So, although the Qur'an repeatedly affirms the prophethood of Muhammad, its primary witness is not to him but to itself. Further, the Qur'an's major truth claim *is* itself: it is self-authenticating in that its language, form, and content are evidently beyond human explanation. The best-known verse on the subject is this:[12]

> If you have doubts about the revelation We have sent down to Our servant, then produce a single surah like it — enlist whatever supporters you have other than God — if you truly [think you can]. If you cannot do this — and you never will — then beware of the Fire prepared for the disbelievers, whose fuel is men and stones. (2:23-24)

Many Muslims say that Muhammad's only miracle is the Qur'an. Its text is, they say on the basis of the above verse, inimitable *(i'jaz)*. The Qur'an speaks of Christians who were moved to tears by the recitation of its verses, and therefore embraced Islam.[13]

The second foundational idea is continuity with the Bible. A key aspect of the qur'anic claim to truth is that of continuity with previous scriptures. It is not only that, as in Surah 37:37 quoted above, Muhammad's truth affirms the previous messengers, but also that it affirms the previous books:

> The Scripture We have revealed to you [Prophet] is the Truth *(ḥaqq)* and confirms *(muṣaddiq)* the scriptures that preceded it. (35:31)

10. M. R. Kairanvi (also spelled Khairanawi), *Izhar ul-Ḥaqq* [*The Demonstration of Truth*], originally six volumes written in Arabic in 1864, then translated into Urdu, is the well-known pioneer of the use of modern biblical criticism in Islamic polemic. M. Bucaille, *The Bible, the Qur'an and Science* (Chicago: Kazi Publications, 2003 [French original, 1976]), is an influential current example.

11. Aspects of the life and personality of Muhammad are also cited by Muslims as indications of his authority and therefore of that of the Qur'an, but these will not be explored here, partly in order to keep this chapter's focus on the Qur'an, and partly because this sort of argument depends on the traditional accounts of Muhammad, and it is debatable how far these have been shaped by the beliefs they are being used to affirm.

12. See also 28:49; 11:13; 10:37-38; 17:88; 52:33-34.

13. 5:82-84.

The idea is that each prophet has essentially the same message about the unity of God and the necessity of following His guidance, and that successive revelations confirm previous ones. For example,

> We revealed the Torah with guidance and light . . . We sent Jesus, son of Mary, in their footsteps, to confirm the Torah that had been sent before him: We gave him the Gospel with guidance, light, and confirmation of the Torah already revealed — a guide and a lesson for those who take heed of God. . . . We sent you [Muhammad] the Scripture with the truth *(ḥaqq),* confirming *(muṣaddiq)* the Scriptures that came before it, and with final authority over them. (Surah 5:44, 46, 48)

The word translated "revealed" in verse 44 has the same root, *NZL,* that is used of the sending down of the Qur'an, and it is implied elsewhere that the previous Scriptures also originate in the Preserved Tablet (13:36-39). It is a common qur'anic theme that Muhammad is the final prophet in the series, and the Qur'an the final book that both confirms its predecessors and completes their message. The Qur'an is sometimes popularly described as the "Third Testament" or, more often, the "Final Testament" — the Old and New Testaments being the earlier ones.

The Qur'an's Direct Challenges to Christians

Not only does the Qur'an claim continuity with the Bible: it directly addresses Bible readers, both Jews and Christians, challenging them to accept its message and the prophethood of Muhammad. This is a common theme, especially in the Surahs originating in Muhammad's Medinan years, when one of his major challenges was dealing with the Medinan Jews and he had increasing contact with Christians. For the purposes of this and the following section, I will focus on just one surah, Surah 5: The Table. This Surah contains a variety of material that is generally classified as late Medinan, and much of it deals with Jews and Christians, the "People of the Book."[14]

Surah 5 contains some of the best-known verses about Jews and Christians and their relationship with the Bible. It contains the verses affirming the Torah and the gospel that we have just considered (44 and 46), and then urges Christians to use the gospel as their criterion:

> So let the followers of the Gospel judge according to what God has sent down in it. Those who do not judge by what God has revealed are lawbreakers. (5:47)

14. "People of the Book" is the literal translation of *Ahl il-Kitāb,* which is a common designation for Jews and/or Christians in the Qur'an. It is occasionally used of other groups.

What is this about? On the one hand, it looks back to an incident relating to *law.* Some Jews had come to Muhammad asking for his judgment on a legal issue, but apparently doing so with ill intent. The Qur'an asks why they should do so if they have their own Scriptures, and accuses them of "distorting the meanings of (revealed) words" (5:41-43; the Arabic word for "distortion" is *taḥrīf*). It goes on to detail a particular part of the Mosaic Law and Jesus' development of it.[15] This is the immediate context of our verse. On the other hand, the passage goes on to speak of the finality of Muhammad's revelation.

> We sent you [Muhammad] the Scripture with the truth, confirming the Scriptures that came before it, and with final authority over them: so judge between them by what God has sent down. (Surah 5:48)

The clear implication is that those who are faithful to the Bible will also accept the Qur'an. This is, again, the challenge to accept the Qur'an's authority on the basis of its continuity with biblical revelation.

The challenges, then, are not only to test the Qur'an's claims but also to follow our own Book. This involves the following:

- *Faithful interpretation and transmission of the Bible.* A key question is what "distorting the meanings of words" implies. While early commentators thought that wrong interpretation (perhaps deliberate) was meant, most present-day Muslims believe that the actual text of the Bible has been corrupted.[16] Christian discussions of the development of the New Testament canon and textual criticism are often cited in support of this view.
- *Acting by it.* The Qur'an frequently calls Jews and Christians to obey their Scriptures, and warns of the fearful consequences of not doing so. For example:

> If only the People of the Book would believe and be mindful of God, We would take away their sins and bring them into gardens of delight. If they had upheld

15. "In the Torah We prescribed for them a life for a life, an eye for an eye, a nose for a nose, an ear for an ear, a tooth for a tooth, an equal wound for a wound" (5:45; cf. Deut. 19:21; Matt. 5:38-42). This is one of the very few actual quotations from the Bible to be found in the Qur'an. The others are Ps. 37:1 cited in 21:105 and Matt. 19:24 cited in 7:40. 61:6 is said to refer to the promise of the Paraclete in John 14 and 16 — the Paraclete being interpreted by most Muslims as being Muhammad.

16. The Arabic word for corruption is *taḥrīf.* See Hava Lazarus-Yafeh, "Taḥrīf (a.)," in *Encyclopaedia of Islam,* 2nd edition, ed. P. Bearman, Th. Bianquis, C. E. Bosworth, E. van Donzel, and W. P. Heinrichs (Leiden: Brill, 2010); Brill Online: http://www.paulyonline.brill.nl/subscriber/entry?entry=islam_SIM-7317. G. D. Nickell, *Narratives of Tampering in the Earliest Commentaries of the Qur'an* (Leiden: Brill, 2011), explores the development of Islamic interpretation of this word in relation to the Bible.

> the Torah and the Gospel and what was sent down to them from their Lord, they would have been given abundance from above and from below: some of them are on the right course, but many of them do evil. (5:65-66)

> People of the Book, you have no true basis unless you uphold the Torah, the Gospel, and that which has been sent to you by your Lord. (5:68)

Some of the implications of such challenges are explored under "Challenge 3" and "Challenge 4" below; but, first, we address the challenge to accept the Qur'an and its prophet.

A Bible Reader's Response: Biblical Challenges for the Qur'an Reader

Not only does the Qur'an expect Jews and Christians to accept its claims on the basis of the Bible; it also tells Muslims to go to Bible readers in order to find confirmation of itself:

> So if you [Prophet] are in doubt about what We have revealed to you, ask those who have been reading the scriptures before you. The Truth has come to you from your Lord, so be in no doubt and do not deny God's signs. (10:94)

That is, the Qur'an is confirmed not only by reference to the previous scriptures, but also as it is recognized by the People of the Book. Such an interpretation is confirmed elsewhere:

> Truly, this Qur'an has been sent down by the Lord of the Worlds: the Trustworthy Spirit [generally understood to mean the Angel Gabriel] brought it down to your heart [Prophet], so that you could bring warning in a clear Arabic tongue. This was foretold in the scriptures of earlier religions. Is it not proof enough for them that the learned men of the Children of Israel have recognized it? (26:192-97)

Thus it is appropriate from a qur'anic as well as from an evangelical perspective that a Christian response to qur'anic challenges should start from the Bible and that we should judge the Qur'an's claims to truth on the basis of our own book. Since, as we shall see, there are some fundamental differences between the Bible and the Qur'an, the evaluation of the Qur'an on biblical grounds turns out to be very challenging to Muslim readers of the Qur'an.

The two major claims to be examined are those to inimitability and to continuity with the Bible.

Inimitability?

The claim to inimitability is difficult for the non-Arabic speaker to assess.[17] This can, in itself, be seen as a problem from a biblical perspective: Might God give a revelation for all humankind that could be assessed only by those speaking a particular language?

On the other hand, the Christian reader might suggest that the Qur'an itself can be read as saying that it was only ever meant for the Arabs. This can be argued from the above quotation from Surah 43:2-4 (p. 1017), but it is never understood thus by Muslims. This raises another issue: that of interpretation. In our assessment of the Qur'an, do we read it from our own perspective, or from that of its Muslim commentators? In responding to the challenges directed at us, it is logical to start from the former. Understanding how Muslims deal with the Qur'an is a distinct challenge, and will be discussed under the heading "Interpretative Questions" below (pp. 1039-43).

One aspect of qur'anic perfection often cited by Muslims is its self-consistency, explicitly claimed in 4:82:

> Will they not think about this Qur'an? If it had been from anyone other than God, they would have found much inconsistency in it.

Examination of this claim takes us, yet again, to questions of interpretation. Christian readers may point out contradictions in the Qur'an,[18] but Muslims may interpret them otherwise. An example from Surah 5 is one of the best-known apparent contradictions about Christians. On the one hand:

> You are sure to find the closest in affection towards the believers are those who say, "We are Christians," for there are among them people devoted to learning and ascetics. These people are not given to arrogance, and when they listen to what has been sent down to the Messenger, you will see their eyes overflowing with tears because they recognise the truth [in it]. (4:82)

On the other hand:

17. Arabic-speaking Christians have long questioned the claim. See S. Masood, *The Bible and the Qur'an: A Question of Integrity* (Carlisle: OM Publishing, 2001), chapter 8.

18. See, for example, http://www.answering-islam.org/Quran/Contra/. There is also a long tradition of Muslims pointing out apparent inconsistencies in the Bible, dating back to Ibn Hazm (d. 1064), whose arguments are summarized in J. W. Sweetman, *Islam and Christian Theology,* part 2, vol. 1 (London: Lutterworth, 1955), 178-262. See also C. Adang, *Muslim Writers on Judaism and the Hebrew Bible from Ibn Rabban to Ibn Hazm* (Leiden: Brill, 1996).

> You who believe, do not take the Jews and Christians as allies: they are allies only to each other. Anyone who takes them as an ally becomes one of them — God does not guide such wrongdoers. (4:51)

Perhaps the most obvious way of handling these verses is to see them as applying to different Christians. There are some Christians who will be friendly toward Muslims, but there are also those with whom alliance should not be made. The latter are explicitly described only a few verses later:

> You who believe, do not take as allies those who ridicule your religion and make fun of it — whether people who were given the Scripture before you, or disbelievers — and be mindful of God if you are true believers. When you make the call to prayer, they ridicule it and make fun of it: this is because they are people who do not reason. Say [Prophet], "People of the Book, do you resent us for any reason other than the fact that we believe in God, in what has been sent down to us, and in what was sent before us, while most of you are disobedient?" (4:57-59)

Handled in this way, these verses are not contradictory. Rather they help Muslims to discern which Christians are to be trusted, and underline the challenge to Christians to be faithful to their scriptures. At the same time, they clearly see the "good" Christians as those who accept Muhammad and his prophethood. From a qur'anic perspective, such is the assumed continuity with the previous scriptures that it seems inconceivable that anyone being faithful to those scriptures could reject Muhammad as prophet. To this issue of continuity we now turn.

Continuity?

The most obvious starting point here is to ask whether the content of the Qur'an affirms that of the Bible. We will explore this question briefly with reference to the central biblical figure of Jesus, but find that this but raises more interpretative questions: specific context has to be understood in the context of the whole worldview of the Qur'an. We therefore move on to a consideration of the form and emphases of the two books, and of how the Qur'an incorporates biblical material into its own framework. At this stage, we are still reading from a Christian perspective: as will be seen in the following sections, Muslim worldviews are affected by Muhammad and the early history of Islam as well as by the Qur'an.

Does the Qur'an Contradict the Bible?

Apparently Contradictory Statements about Jesus The Qur'an affirms many of the biblical assertions about Jesus. According to Surah 19:16-34, he was born of a virgin, a sign for humankind, a mercy from God, God's servant, and blessed wherever he is. Surah 3:45-55 adds that he is a Word from God, called the Messiah, honorable in this world and the next, a messenger to Israel, who healed the blind and the leper and raised the dead; and Surah 4:171 speaks of him as God's Word and a Spirit from him. Yet, as is well known, the Qur'an is as strong in its denials as in its affirmations.[19] Our Surah 5 includes the following:

> Those who say, "God is the Messiah, son of Mary," have defied God. The Messiah himself said, "Children of Israel, worship God, my Lord and your Lord." If anyone associates others with God, God will forbid him from the Garden, and Hell will be his home. No one will help such evildoers. Those people who say that God is the third of three are defying [the truth]: there is only One God. If they persist in what they are saying, a painful punishment will afflict those of them who persist. Why do they not turn to God and ask His forgiveness, when God is most forgiving, most merciful? The Messiah, son of Mary, was only a messenger; other messengers had come and gone before him; his mother was a virtuous woman; both ate food [like other mortals]. See how clear We make these signs for them; see how deluded they are. Say, "How can you worship something other than God, that has no power to do you harm or good? God alone is the All Hearing and All Knowing." Say, "People of the Book, do not overstep the bounds of truth in your religion and do not follow the whims of those who went astray before you — they led many others astray and themselves continue to stray from the even path." (Surah 5:72-77)

At first glance, this passage denies the divinity of Christ; and this is how most Muslims read it. However, it is possible to interpret it otherwise, and to suggest that what is being denied is not orthodox but heretical Christology. The formulations "God is the Messiah" (5:72) and "God is the third of three" (5:73) are not representative of orthodox views. A later formulation in the same Surah is even further from orthodoxy:

19. I have chosen here to explore affirmations and denials about the nature of Jesus. There are also affirmations and one denial concerning his crucifixion (19:33; 5:119-20; 3:55; cf. 4:157-58). For a brief discussion of Islamic interpretations of these texts from a Christian perspective, see Chawkat Moucarry, *Faith to Faith: Christianity and Islam in Dialogue* (Nottingham: Inter-Varsity, 2001), chapter 10. T. Lawson, *The Crucifixion and the Qur'an: A Study in the History of Muslim Thought* (Oxford: Oneworld, 2009), 1-25, places the Qur'anic denial in the context of seventh-century Christian Christological debate.

> When God says, "Jesus, son of Mary, did you say to people, 'Take me and my mother as two gods alongside God'?" he will say, "May You be exalted!" I would never say what I had no right to say — if I had said such a thing You would have known it: You know all that is within me, though I do not know what is within You, You alone have full knowledge of things unseen — I told them only what You commanded me to: "Worship God, my Lord and your Lord." (5:116-17)

The Christian reader then wants to ask about the sources of these formulations of Christian belief. The most obvious answer is to be found in the Christological controversies of the time. The seventh century was a time in which the full divinity of Christ had been firmly established, but there was much debate as to how the human and divine natures could relate. The debate took political form, so that the major groupings of Orthodox, Monophysite, and Nestorian believers also represented different power blocs that surrounded and impinged on the Arabian Peninsula.[20]

It is beyond the scope of this essay to explore how the various seventh-century Christologies can be traced in the Qur'an.[21] Suffice it to say that most of the qur'anic denials about Jesus can be read as entering into contemporary discussion and therefore denying heretical rather than orthodox interpretations. Further, qur'anic Christology, not least in Surah 5, addresses Jews as well as Arabs and Christians. It can therefore be seen as defending the messiahship of Jesus against Jewish denials.

Although such a reading implies the historical contingency of the text, which is problematic from an Islamic perspective, it illustrates the way in which the Qur'an can sometimes be interpreted as not contradicting the Bible even where it appears to do so.[22] However, such specific concerns about content need to be seen in the wider context of the forms, the emphases, and the overall shapes of the two scriptures, to which we now turn.

20. Orthodox belief was represented by the Byzantine empire and the desert monks in the northwest of Arabia and was probably also in what is now Yemen at the time of Muhammad. Monophysites, with their emphasis on Word Christology and the single nature of Jesus Christ, were across the Red Sea in Abyssinia (now Ethiopia) and had influence in Yemen. The Nestorians, who divided the human and divine natures of Christ, had communities in northeast Arabia and down the Gulf coast.

21. G. Parrinder, *Jesus in the Qur'an* (Oxford: Oneworld, 1996 [orig. 1965]), gives a helpful analysis of all the qur'anic material about Jesus and raises questions about how it relates to contemporary Christian views.

22. Christians have even argued that the Qur'an encourages them to retain their Christian faith (e.g., Paul of Antioch in the twelfth century: a translation of part of his *Risalah* can be found in J. M. Gaudeul, *Encounters and Clashes* [Rome: Pontificio Istituto di Studi Arabi e d'Islamistica, 2000], 2:271-75), or found ways of seeing Christ in many unexpected texts (e.g., G. Basetti-Sani, *The Qur'an in the Light of Christ* [Chicago: Franciscan Herald Press, 1977]).

Form As explored in Barry Webb's chapter (chapter 19 in this collection), the nature of the authority of a text is closely related to its form. The Qur'an is no exception: the authority it claims is tied both to the form by which the revelation is said to have been given and to the associated literary form in which it is now extant in the written book. However, just as the form of revelation described is different from that of the Bible, so the literary form of the Qur'an is very different from that of the Bible.

THE QUR'AN takes the form of *divine speech* in the Arabic language. — With the exception of the first Surah, it is written in the voice of God,[23] addressed sometimes to Muhammad, sometimes to specific groups, and sometimes to all humankind. Further, where the biblical books bear the stamps of their human authors, the Qur'an is said to have been directly dictated by the angel Gabriel, and its very words are therefore seen as being directly divinely given. Indeed the most common way of describing the coming of the Qur'an is *tanzīl:* which literally means that it has come down — as we have seen, from a heavenly prototype. Although Muslim thinkers have recognized the questions surrounding the idea of eternal speech in a particular human language, the question of "double agency" addressed in chapter 17 of this collection does not arise.

THE QUR'AN is almost entirely *hortatory.* — Although it contains narrative, nearly every story[24] is told as part of an argument or exhortation. The stories are most often used as illustration, as warning or as encouragement, or as indicating the pattern of divine and human action through history. In contrast, Barry Webb describes narrative as the Bible's "master" and "indispensable" genre.

THE QUR'ANIC MATERIAL has *no obvious principle for organization.* — While the ordering of the biblical canon is seen as but a convenient convention, the arrangement as well as the content of the Qur'an is seen as part of what God gave to Muhammad. However, it is difficult to discern the logic of its organization. The Surahs are arranged roughly in descending order of length, and, according to both traditional and scholarly dating, the shorter Surahs date to the earlier parts of Muhammad's career.[25] However, there are exceptions to this rule, and many

23. Surah 1: *al-Fātiḥah* (The Opening), is a prayer, used in every unit of the five daily Islamic prayers. Sometimes the Qur'anic voice can be interpreted as that of the angel Gabriel.

24. The exception is Surah 71, which comprises only a narrative about Noah. However, Noah's preaching in this Surah indicates that the story is being primarily told as a parallel to the opposition experienced by Muhammad in Mecca. The parallel between Noah and Muhammad is particularly evident in Surah 11:25-48. Surah 12, which tells the story of Joseph, is sometimes cited as a story in its own right, but it finishes with an exhortation to heed its lesson and accept the Qur'an (12:111).

25. But note the difficulty in dating the Qur'an discussed in n. 28 below. Even dating material by its relationship to events in the life of Muhammad is problematic: the extant accounts of

Surahs contain a mixture of material relating to different periods and occasions. Traditionally, most qur'anic exegesis has been done on a verse-by-verse basis. Only in recent times have commentators sought to elucidate the overall structure of more complex surahs.[26]

THE QUR'AN has a *single transmitter.* — While the Bible is a mixture of books produced at different times by different people, each with its own literary form, the Qur'an is believed to have been given to a single person — Muhammad — over a period of only twenty-three years. This one person combines the roles of prophet and political leader that are so carefully separated through most of biblical history.[27]

BOTH THE FORM and the content of the qur'anic material reflect the *three periods of Muhammad's prophethood.* — Muhammad's situation developed from Mecca, where he had few followers and much opposition, to Medina, where he was leading a community struggling to establish itself as a social and political entity. After the conquest of Mecca, he was the established leader of a community growing in political power. Meccan material[28] is generally characterized by short verses, and by exhortations to worship the one God and warnings of the consequences of rejection. Medinan material includes much that is addressed to specific community concerns, legal decisions, and discussions with Christians and Jews.

In testing the Qur'an's claim to be consistent with biblical revelation, an obvious question is, "Is there anything in the Bible that could be seen as a parallel to the Qur'an in form?" That is, can we find a single authored book that comprises God-given words? I think we have to answer, "No." While there are some apparent parallels in the prophetic books, none has the *tanzīl* quality claimed by the Qur'an. Prophets like Ezekiel, Jeremiah, and Isaiah put together a series of oracles

---

Muhammad date to at least a century after his death, and it is possible that some were composed in order to explain passages of the Qur'an. For an overview of the issues, see Gerhard Böwering, "Chronology and the Qur'ān," in McAuliffe, ed., *Encyclopaedia of the Qur'ān* (cf. Brill Online: http://www.paulyonline.brill.nl/subscriber/entry?entry=q3_COM-00034).

26. See, for example, M. Mir, *Coherence in the Qur'an: A Study of Islahi's Concept of Nazm in Tadabbur-i Qur'an* (Indianapolis: American Trust Publications, 1986).

27. The main biblical person in whom they are combined is Moses: it is interesting that the Qur'an both gives more space to Moses than to any other biblical character and keeps more closely to the biblical account of his life than to the accounts of most other biblical characters. Muslims see the "prophet like Moses" of Deut. 18:18 in Muhammad.

28. Distinguishing between Meccan and Medinan material is not always straightforward. We have noted the Islamic tradition of asking about the occasion of revelation for particular verses and Surahs, but this does not cover the whole of the Qur'an. There is also a traditional attribution of each Surah to Mecca or Medina, but many Surahs include material from different times. Western dating systems often depend in part on the idea that Meccan verses are short, thus making the observation in this paragraph potentially part of a circular argument.

received at different times and places. However, not one of them is completely lacking in human words. Even Obadiah, which is almost entirely words from God, includes an introductory statement that this is Obadiah's vision (Obad. 1:1), and each of the prophetic books bears the stamp of its human author. In contrast, every word in the Qur'an is presented as being spoken directly from God.

Further, the actual verbal form of the Qur'an is considered essential by Muslims. However, where the Qur'an emphasizes its nature as an Arabic text, and Muslims see it as untranslatable, the Bible's Old Testament includes Aramaic and the New Testament uses Greek translations of the Old. Few Christians have thought that there might be some kind of special heavenly language in which the biblical oracles were revealed: indeed, few have thought access to the original biblical languages essential to Christian discipleship. Rather, biblical translation has been a characteristic since the earliest times, and the right to translation into the vernacular something for which people have been willing to die. The untranslatability of the Qur'an not only makes it difficult for most of humankind to assess its truth claims: it is also symptomatic of its fundamental difference from the Bible in form.[29]

In judging by the Bible, then, we would have to say that, at the least, the Qur'an is a very unlikely form of divinely inspired writing. We might add that the qur'anic revelation claims only a single witness, that is, Muhammad is the only one said to have witnessed the revelation given by the angel. This is a problem from a biblical perspective, where it is important that even Jesus himself was affirmed by more than one witness (John 5:31ff.), and each of the prophets finds his place within the wider history of Israel, and is but one of the people who are speaking to Israel from God at their particular time.

Emphasis We have already seen one qur'anic emphasis that is quite different from that of the Bible: its claims about its own nature. Whereas the Bible only occasionally refers to itself, the Qur'an presents itself and its credentials throughout. Further study indicates that, while most ideas about the nature of God and of human beings in the Qur'an can be found somewhere in the Bible, the two books have very different emphases on many important matters. For example, the idea of God as loving can be found in the Qur'an,[30] but the pervasive Old Testament focus on *ḥesed* and the New Testament identity of God with love (e.g., 1 John 4:7-8) are absent.

29. See also Lamin Sanneh, *Translating the Message,* 2nd edition (Maryknoll, NY: Orbis, 2009), and the discussion in Barry Webb, chapter 19 in this collection, esp. the section titled "Authority and Translatability."

30. The root *ḤBB,* love, is used to speak of God loving some people and not others. However, there are two places where God is described as *wadūd,* which is usually translated as "loving" (11:90; 85:14).

Two other examples from Surah 5 underline the point and indicate two key differences in qur'anic and biblical worldviews.

The first concerns the law. The verses already quoted about judging by the gospel are in the context of a legal and not a theological issue. This is indicative of the Islamic emphasis on law, which is rooted in the Qur'an. As we saw from Surah 2:2, the Qur'an presents itself as a book of guidance: it reveals not God's self but God's will. This signals both the view that God is so different from human beings that he cannot reveal himself to us, and the view that guidance is what human beings need. Muslims see humanity not as fallen, but as ignorant or forgetful, and in need of the mercy of God not in redemption but in guidance.[31] Within the Qur'an, the emphasis on law becomes increasingly evident in the Medinan Surahs, as the early Muslim community develops and needs a great deal of regulation.

One comparison will suffice to illustrate the difference in emphasis in the Gospels. Surah 4 has extensive details about inheritance law. This contrasts with Jesus' response to the young man who wanted a judgment on how his father's property should be divided (Luke 12:13-14). Jesus responded with the enigmatic, "Human, who made me a judge or arbitrator over you?" and the parable of the rich fool. It is not only that Jesus prioritizes the ethical principles over the legal details, but that he sees the development of law as a human responsibility.

The Islamic emphasis on law often leads Christians to suppose that, while Christianity is a religion of grace, Islam is a religion of law. Again, this is a matter of emphasis. The Qur'an certainly stresses that human beings are dependent upon God's mercy, his forgiveness, and his favor. The Arabic words for the latter are sometimes translated as "grace,"[32] and are thus used in Arabic translations of the Bible. However, the different qur'anic emphasis implies that the word means something different than it might in biblical context. Our second example, again from Surah 5, points to the nature of this different meaning.

The second example deals with covenant breaking. The Qur'an acknowledges the key biblical idea of God's covenants, but these are described in terms of something taken from rather than something given to human beings:

> God took a pledge from the Children of Israel. . . . But they broke their pledge, so We distanced them [from Us] and hardened their hearts . . . We also took a pledge from those who say, "We are Christians," but they too forgot some of what they were told to remember, so We stirred up enmity and hatred among them until the Day of Resurrection. . . . (Surah 5:12, 14)

31. For an introduction to Islamic ideas of sin, see Chawkat Moucarry, *The Search for Forgiveness: Pardon and Punishment in Islam and Christianity* (Nottingham: Inter-Varsity, 2004), chapter 7.

32. There are several words from the root N'M associated with this idea. The Qur'an uses this root of God's favor toward human beings in sixty-four places.

While the Bible both predicts and describes God's judgment on covenant breakers, this is never the end of the story because biblical covenants are based on pledges from the loving God. The Qur'an asks how love and punishment can be reconciled:

> The Jews and the Christians say, "We are the children of God and His beloved ones." Say, "Then why does he punish you for your sins?" (5:18)

The biblical reconciliation of this tension is, of course, on the cross. The qur'anic question signals the very different qur'anic emphasis concerning God's love: in the Qur'an, God loves the good and not the bad,[33] and covenant breaking results in permanent loss of privilege. In the Bible, none is good, but God's love accomplishes his covenants. This signals a fundamental difference in what is meant by God's love, and therefore in how God and his relationship with human beings is understood.[34]

Reworking of Biblical Material We have noted that the Qur'an claims continuity with the Bible, and that it refers to many biblical characters. The question of continuity therefore becomes the most acute when we begin to read how the Qur'an uses this biblical material. Surah 5, being addressed to Jews and Christians, refers to the Mosaic covenant, to the spies who went into the promised land and to Israel's wilderness years. It tells of Mary and Jesus, and of the disciples' requesting a table of food that descended from heaven in response to Jesus' prayer. It also has the only qur'anic reference to the Cain and Abel story.

The very range of material included signals the fact that the Qur'an does not tell the biblical story chronologically. Indeed, rather than telling the stories, it uses the stories to illustrate its own points. One of the easiest examples to look at is the Cain and Abel story (Surah 5:27-34):

> [Prophet], tell them the truth about the story of Adam's two sons: each of them offered a sacrifice, and it was accepted from one and not the other. One said, "I will kill you," but the other said, "God only accepts the sacrifice of those who are mindful of Him. If you raise your hand to kill me, I will not raise mine to kill you. I fear God, the Lord of all worlds, and I would rather you were burdened with my sins as well as yours and became an inhabitant of the Fire: such is the evildoers' reward." But his soul prompted him to kill his brother: he killed him and became one of the losers. God sent a raven to scratch up the ground and

33. 2:190; 3:32, 140; 4:36; etc. Cf. 2:195, 222; 3:134, 146; passim.

34. See my "The Concept of Relationship as a Key to the Comparative Understanding of Christianity and Islam," *Themelios* 11, no. 2 (January 1986): 57-60, also available at http://www.medievalchurch.org.uk/pdf/islam_glaser.pdf.

> show him how to cover his brother's corpse and he said, "Woe is me! Could I not have been like this raven and covered up my brother's body?" He became remorseful. On account of [his deed], We decreed to the Children of Israel that if anyone kills a person — unless in retribution for murder or spreading corruption in the land — it is as if he kills all mankind, while if any saves a life it is as if he saves the lives of all mankind. Our messengers came to them with clear signs, but many of them continued to commit excesses in the land. Those who wage war against God and His Messenger and strive to spread corruption in the land should be punished by death, crucifixion, the amputation of an alternate hand and foot, left hand and right foot or vice versa, or banishment from the land: a disgrace for them in this world, and then a terrible punishment in the Hereafter, unless they repent before you overpower them — in that case bear in mind that God is forgiving and merciful.

If we compare this to the account in Genesis 4, we can see some parallels. Both stories are clearly about the two sons of Adam, one of whom has his sacrifice accepted and one of whom has his sacrifice rejected. The son whose sacrifice was accepted is then killed by the other, who is jealous of him. However, there are also significant differences. The stories have different contexts, and they include different information. The Qur'an has none of the biblical story of the birth of the brothers, neither does it tell us what happened to Cain after he killed his brother. However, it does tell us how Cain buried his brother, which the Bible does not. Perhaps the most obvious differences are in characterization, and in the conversations recorded. While the qur'anic story is clearly about Cain and Abel, and the discussion that is recorded is between the two of them, the biblical story is much more concerned with Cain and God. Abel says not a word.

These differences immediately raise concerns. First, *what are the sources of the Qur'an's version of the story?* In Islamic thinking of course the source of the story is the prototype — it comes straight from God by the angel Gabriel. However, such a divine origin is not necessary. For example, the story of the raven scratching the ground is similar to that found in Jewish commentary, where Adam and Eve wonder how to bury their dead son, and God shows them by showing a raven scratching the ground. Jewish discussion also asks about the conversation between Cain and Abel implied by Genesis 4:8,[35] and the legislation immediately following the story also has parallels in Jewish commentary on the Cain and Abel story.[36]

35. The Hebrew has only "Cain said to his brother Abel," which is an incomplete sentence.

36. An accessible summary of Jewish comment can be found in *Bereishis,* ed. Nosson Sherman and Meir Ziotowitz, Artscroll Tanach Series 1a (Brooklyn: Mesorah Publications, 1986), 148ff. The relevant classical midrash is in *Genesis Rabbah,* 22. The midrash cited in Q5:32 is *Tanchuma* B.10, which is commenting on the Mishnah, *Sanhedrin* 4:5.

Second, *what is the context of the story?* The immediate qur'anic context is two passages (starting at 5:15 and 5:19 respectively) telling the People of the Book that Muhammad is God's messenger. They are warned of wrong beliefs about Jesus, about arrogance, and by the example of the cowardly spies sent into Canaan by Moses. According to Islamic tradition, the occasion of revelation was a Jewish plot to kill Muhammad.[37] Thus the story is warning the "older brothers" (Jews and Christians) against jealousy of the younger brother (Muslims), as well as being used as an introduction to legal material on murder and mischief, which is usually interpreted as acts against Islam and the Muslim community.[38]

Third, *what are the theological implications?* What kind of relationship between God and human beings is being presented in these two versions of the story? Who is Cain, and who is Abel? The qur'anic version has none of the biblical concern for the guilty brother: rather, it implies a division of humanity into the guilty, who will be judged, and the innocent, who will be saved.

Fourth, *what is the overall narrative framework into which the story fits*? We have noted its context in Muhammad's life. From an Islamic perspective, although the Qur'an originates in the uncreated Preserved Tablet, it was spoken into a specific historical context, so Muslims as well as non-Muslims understand not only this story but the whole of the Qur'an through the framework of the life of Muhammad. That life is so linked to the eternal revelation that it is also the lens through which the rest of sacred history is viewed.

We have seen the claim that the Qur'an is continuous with biblical revelation. It is not, then, surprising that the Qur'an's view of sacred history is Muhammad-shaped. The Cain and Abel story is not part of a story of creation, fall, and redemption, but part of a story of the repeated sending of prophets for the guidance of ignorant and forgetful humanity.[39] Each prophet receives and transmits his message, some (Abraham, Moses, David, Jesus, and Muhammad) in the form of a book. Each provokes both belief and unbelief, resulting in judgment and hell for unbelievers and rescue and paradise for believers. Each time, the message gets forgotten or distorted, necessitating a further prophet, until the final, perfect revelation that will be preserved forever is given to Muhammad. The Cain and Abel story indicates an early division of humanity into those who respond positively and those who respond negatively to God's commands.

Finally, *what is the understanding of truth?* The qur'anic Cain and Abel story brings us back to the question of truth. It begins:

37. This is the common interpretation of 5:11, which gives the context for the Cain and Abel story.

38. Such interpretations are common in qur'anic commentary. Note the parallel Christian uses of the Cain and Abel story as a metaphor for Jewish rejection of Christ.

39. Biblical characters seen as prophets in the Qur'an include Adam, Enoch, Noah, Abraham, Lot, Isaac, Ishmael, Jacob, Joseph, Moses, Aaron, David, Solomon, Elijah, Elisha, Ezekiel, Job, Jonah, Zechariah (father of John the Baptist), John the Baptist, and Jesus.

> Tell them the truth about the story of Adam's two sons . . . (5:27)

The idea may be that the Qur'an explains the true meaning of the story, but it also implies that this is the true version of it — which means that previous versions may be wrong. This is explicit just a few verses earlier:

> People of the Book, our messenger has come to make clear to you much of what you have kept hidden of the Scripture and to overlook much. A light has now come to you from God, and a Scripture which makes things clear. (5:15)

What, Then, Is the Result of Considering the Qur'an Through Biblical Eyes?

We have seen just a small amount of the evidence that the Qur'an contains much material that has its origin in the Bible. However, that material appears to have been received orally, and includes much material from extra-biblical tradition and from contemporary controversy.[40] However, the material has been removed from the skeleton of biblical salvation history and re-formed around a skeleton of prophetic history as understood through the life of Muhammad. Even more seriously from a Christian perspective, the reshaping removes the Fall and therefore the need for redemption, so that there are few traces left of the central biblical theme of atonement.

Further, the form of the Qur'an indicates a concept of revelation that is both very limited when compared to biblical understandings, and difficult to reconcile with biblical models of prophethood. The idea of direct dictation implies a total dichotomy between the human and the divine, which in turn implies understandings of God and humanity that make the idea of incarnation both ludicrous and blasphemous.[41] In sum, our study has led us to the conclusion that, from a biblical perspective, the Qur'an cannot be a post-biblical revealed book. The process of "judging by the Bible" turns out to challenge fundamentally Islamic views of the Qur'an: Muslims are right in thinking that, if the Qur'an is entirely true, the biblical writings must have been changed.

A major implication of reading the Bible in this context is, then, that Christians should reexamine biblical authority in response to qur'anic challenges. If

40. There is an increasing literature on the relationship between the Qur'an and the Bible. G. S. Reynolds, *The Qur'an and Its Biblical Subtext* (London: Routledge, 2011), offers some detailed case studies of the qur'anic use of biblical and biblically related material.

41. My "Towards a Mutual Understanding of Christian and Islamic Concepts of Revelation," *Themelios* 7, no. 31 (982): 16-22 (or cf. also http://www.medievalchurch.org.uk/pdf/islamic-revelation_glaser.pdf), discusses the implications of the differing understandings of revelation for understandings of God, humanity, and salvation.

they conclude, as do the writers in this collection, that the Bible is reliable, there is another challenge to be faced: that of relating to people with whom they have fundamental disagreements, and of appropriately communicating their own understanding of revelation, and particularly of Jesus, to them.

It is important to start by noting that, despite the differences explored above, there are many ideas in the Qur'an that are in agreement with ideas in the Bible, and can therefore be used as a basis for both relationship and communication. It is even possible to find within the Qur'an themes that can be developed to point to the key biblical doctrines of the divinity of Christ, the crucifixion, and the atonement.[42] In order to utilize the various points of agreement, it is necessary to move out of the Christian thought-world of the current section and try to understand how Muslims view and read the Qur'an. This is our next challenge.

Challenge 2: Understanding — Seeing Islamic Perspectives

Many Christians find it difficult to understand why Muslims believe in the Qur'an, and have even more difficulty with some of the ways in which they build their lives upon it. Many Christians read Christian apologetics and critiques of Islam that appear, to them, obviously correct, and wonder why Muslims are not convinced by them. The challenge is, then, to go beyond a Christian reflection on the Qur'an and try to understand the Muslims who believe in it. What does the Qur'an mean to them? Why do they believe it? How do they handle it? And why does this result in what seems obvious to Christians being incomprehensible or simply wrong from an Islamic perspective?

Mutual Puzzlement

The journey toward understanding can, perhaps, be best approached from a recognition that puzzlement is mutual. On the one hand, many Christians are puzzled by the questions that Muslims *don't* ask of their Scripture. They ask none of the critical questions about who wrote it and why, about how it depends on other texts and how it is determined by its historical context. Instead, they ask questions about the pointing and pronunciation of the Arabic, and how the occasion of revelation assists understanding of the meaning.

42. For example, see Kenneth Cragg, *Mosque Sermons: A Listener for the Preacher* (Sawbridgeworth, UK: Melisende, 2008); and "The Qur'an and the Cross: Less Absent Than You Think," in *Jesus and the Cross: Reflections from Islamic Contexts,* ed. D. Singh (Oxford: Regnum, 2008), 177-86.

On the other hand, Muslims may be puzzled by the questions that Christians *do* ask, including many of the questions addressed by the essay in this collection. For example:

- historical and critical questions about the authorship and origin of texts confirm the idea that these are texts of human and not divine origin;
- textual criticism and questions about the development of the canon imply great uncertainty about the transmission of the divine message;
- discussions of the priorities of Scripture, tradition, and reason imply that Christians are not confident in their own Book.

The mutual puzzlement indicates the need for each to study the other's point of view if we are to develop mutual understanding. Such study indicates that the similarities and differences in thinking about Scripture not only reflect our respective views of God but also our common human nature. Three preliminary points illustrate this.

First, Muslims give as much attention to intelligent study of their Scripture as do Christians. Their questions about pronunciation and occasions of revelation can be seen as parallel to the Christian critical questions about the Bible, but based on the qur'anic view of direct divine authorship rather than the biblical view of divinely inspired human authorship. The historical issue is not, "What can we learn by taking into account the context out of which the text arose?," but, "What can we learn from taking into account the context into which the text was given?" The live textual questions are not about human reception of and witness to the text, but about the grammar and recitation of divine language.

Second, Muslims value the Qur'an as much as Christians value the Bible, and may report the effect of the Qur'an on their lives in terms that echo what Christians say about the Bible.[43] They may describe it in deeply emotional terms, saying that reading[44] it is a direct communication with God that affects their body as well as their heart and mind. They read it in their families and in daily devotions, and find in it guidance and encouragement for life. However, they emphasize the use of the original language much more than do even the biblical scholars among Christians: in fact, the Qur'an is believed to be untranslatable, so when Muslims speak about reading the Qur'an, they assume that it is being read in Arabic. Again, this reflects the view that the very Arabic words of the Qur'an are seen as the divine word.

43. Examples of Muslims and Christians speaking about their experience of reading their Scriptures can be found in M. Ingrave, ed., *Scriptures in Dialogue* (London: Church House Publishing, 2004), chapter 1.

44. When Muslims speak of "reading" the Qur'an, they often mean reciting it from memory rather than reading from the book.

Third, Muslim questions often relate to Trinitarian understandings of the Bible. Muslims do not have anything like the Christian idea of the role of the Holy Spirit in the production, reception, and interpretation of Scripture.[45] Therefore the idea that anything written by human beings could be entirely reliable can be incomprehensible. If something is divine, it cannot be human, and vice versa.

A related point is that Muslims have very different questions about how the Qur'an relates to Muhammad than Christians have about how the Bible relates to Jesus. The Qur'an is divine, and Muhammad is human: Islamic thinking excludes the possibility of the messenger being himself the divine Word. The idea that the Bible is not the Word of God that comes down from heaven in the sense that Jesus is the Word of God that comes down from heaven appears to them to undermine its authority.

This reflects a difference in understanding of the divine-human relationship that makes it difficult for Muslims to call God "Father." So different from humanity is God understood to be that he can only reveal his will and not himself.

In sum, how God speaks depends on who he is and on how he relates to those addressed.

Settled Questions

The different Muslim and Christian ideas about Scripture lead to different ways of dealing with the texts. In particular, they lead to different understandings of authority and of what can be questioned or changed. One way of understanding the differences in Muslim and Christian handlings of Scripture is the recognition that there are some questions that Christians continue to ask that have long been settled in traditional Islamic thinking. At the same time, Muslims live in the same post-Enlightenment, postmodern world that Christians live in, so the challenges to which the contributors to this collection respond are challenges that also face Muslims. Hence some of the current tensions within the Muslim world.

What I have called "settled questions" include issues around the text and the nature of the Book as well as around interpretation and authority.

The Text

Whereas biblical scholars continue to research the various early texts and translations, the traditional Islamic accounts indicate that Muslims settled on a single

45. The Arabic *Rūḥ ul-Qudūs,* literally translated as "the holy spirit," is commonly understood to refer to the angel Gabriel (see Qur'an 19:17). *Rūḥ ullah,* literally translated as "the spirit of God," is a title for Jesus (Qur'an 4:171). In each case, *Rūḥ* is understood as the created entity.

Arabic text of the Qur'an only about twenty years after the death of Muhammad.[46] Until the time of Uthman, the third Caliph (leader of the Muslim community), the text was largely transmitted orally, and there were numerous variations of pronunciation and even content.[47] Under Uthman, an authorized written text was produced and circulated, and variants were suppressed. Many Muslims see the preservation of the text since that time as evidence for the divine origin of the Qur'an. A popular children's book states:

> No other book in the world can match the Qur'an in respect of its recording and preservation. The astonishing fact about this book is that it has remained unchanged even to a dot over the last 1400 years. . . . The Qur'an exists today in its original form unaltered and undistorted. It is a living miracle in the sense that it has survived so many centuries without suffering any change.[48]

The earliest written Qur'ans were without vowels or diacritical points, so Muslims point out the emphasis on rigorous memorization of the whole Qur'an in the early Muslim community. It is the oral tradition as much as the written manuscripts that is seen as guaranteeing textual authenticity.

The Nature of the Book

Christians took centuries to reach an agreed doctrine of the full divinity of Christ and were continuing to debate the relationship between the human and divine

46. This follows traditional Sunni accounts of the development of Islam. There are, of course, scholarly debates about the historicity of these accounts. Scholars such as John Wansborough, Patricia Crone, and Michael Cooke have offered reconstructions that question whether the Qur'an reached its present form before the end of the seventh century (e.g., Patricia Crone and Michael Cooke, *Hagarism: The Making of the Islamic World* [Cambridge: Cambridge University Press, 1977]). A thorough critical study of the qur'anic text is being prepared by the *Corpus Coranicum* project in Germany (http://www.bbaw.de/bbaw/Forschung/Forschungsprojekte/Coran/). The history of Shi'ite discussion of possible errors and omissions is found in the first part of M. M. Bar-Asher's article, "Shīʿism and the Qur'an," in McAuliffe, ed., *Encyclopaedia of the Qur'ān* (cf. Brill Online, http://www.paulyonline.brill.nl/subscriber/entry?entry=q3_COM-00181).

47. A. von Denffer, *'Ulum al-Qur'an: Introduction to the Sciences of the Qur'an* (Markfield, UK: Islamic Foundation, 1994; available at http://web.youngmuslims.ca/online_library/books/ulum_al_quran/); chapter 2 gives an account from classical Islamic sources of how the Qur'an was collected and written down, and lists some of the variants that were in circulation at the time of Uthman. J. Burton, *The Collection of the Qur'an* (Cambridge: Cambridge University Press, 1977), is a non-Muslim analysis of classical Islamic texts on the subject.

48. G. Sarwar, *Islam Beliefs and Teachings*, 3rd edition (London: Muslim Educational Trust, 1984), 33.

natures at the time of Muhammad. Muslims took only 222 years from the death of Muhammad to reach the conclusion of their debates about the nature of the Qur'an mentioned above.

It is interesting that the debate came to a head at the instigation of political rather than religious leaders. It was the Caliph al-Ma'mun (died 833) who instituted the *miḥnah* (usually translated "inquisition") in which people were forced to accede to the createdness of the Qur'an. Historians suggest that the Caliph wanted to make the point that it was he, and not the religious scholars, who was in control of belief as well as the state. The scholars won, and a doctrine of accepting mysteries without question[49] was established.

The *miḥnah* lasted for about eighteen years, and it caused polarization between the philosophical Mu'tazilites and the scholars who favored the authority of the *Hadith.* From that time, it is not only specific doctrines but also such scholastic authority that has been largely unquestioned.[50] This is why debates about the nature of Scripture such as those that characterize Christian theology are largely absent from Islam.

Interpretative Questions

Like Christians, Muslims continue to discuss interpretation of their sacred text. However, where many Christians seek new ideas, most Muslims are suspicious of innovation, and precedence is of great importance. The Arabic word *bida'* refers to developing or believing ideas that have no precedence in the classical texts or accepted authorities: it is almost always seen as negative.[51] Thus, while the Qur'an may need to be applied afresh in new situations, there are agreed methods of interpretation and, in orthodox thinking, only those who have studied those methods have the right to interpret.[52] According to this sort of thinking,

49. The Arabic is *bila kayf,* literally "without why." The term was used by Ahmad Ibn Hanbal, one of the major protagonists in the *miḥnah.* It was first applied to accepting anthropomorphisms relating to God in the Qur'an, but then to accepting the uncreatedness of the Qur'an. The implication is that certain theological questions, like how the Qur'an can be uncreated and yet God be One, cannot be answered and should not be asked.

50. A helpful account of the issues surrounding the *miḥnah* can be found in F. Esack, *The Qur'an: A Short Introduction* (Oxford: Oneworld, 2002), chapter 5.

51. See also Wael B. Hallaq, "Innovation," in McAuliffe, ed., *Encyclopaedia of the Qur'ān* (cf. Brill Online http://www.paulyonline.brill.nl/subscriber/entry?entry=q3_SIM-00222).

52. S. Taji-Farouki, ed., *Modern Muslim Intellectuals and the Qur'an* (Oxford: Oxford University Press, 2004), is a collection of papers that gives a good overview of recent attempts to apply different hermeneutics to the Qur'an. Such attempts can be very controversial, and I shall not attempt to interact with them in this chapter.

before any current interpretation can be made, the following precedents need to be considered.[53]

Obviously, the Qur'an has first to be interpreted by itself. It is often possible to clarify one text by reference to another: for example, the different accounts of the Adam story[54] can be put together to give a complete picture. Where the Qur'an appears to contradict itself, a classical strategy has been the idea of abrogation — that the later ruling replaces the earlier.[55]

One of the best-known examples concerns alcohol. There are four relevant verses, believed to have been given in the following order:

> From the fruits of date palms and grapes you take sweet juice and wholesome provisions. There truly is a sign in this for people who use their reason. (16:67)

> They ask you [Prophet] about intoxicants and gambling: say, "There is great sin in both, and some benefit for people: the sin is greater than the benefit." (2:219)

> You who believe, do not come anywhere near the prayer if you are intoxicated, not until you know what you are saying. (4:43)

> You who believe, intoxicants and gambling, idolatrous practices, and [divining with] arrows are repugnant acts — Satan's doing — shun them so that you may prosper. With intoxicants and gambling, Satan seeks only to incite enmity and hatred among you, and to stop you remembering God and prayer. Will you not give them up? (5:90-91)

The accepted interpretation is that this represents a mercifully gradual introduction of a particularly challenging prohibition.

An alternative approach is to see different rulings as applying in different situations, as in the example of the verses concerning Christians cited above (pp. 1023-24). This raises the question of determining the context of the rulings within the life of Muhammad, and there is a large amount of tradition concerning *asbāb un-nuzūl* (occasions of revelation).[56] One of the key current areas in which this approach is being used is that of gender relationships: verses that imply male superiority are read as specific rulings ameliorating the superior male attitudes

53. This is closely parallel to methods of developing Islamic law: the sources are, first, the Qur'an; second, the *Hadith;* third, agreement of the accepted scholars; and only then reasoning from these to current application.

54. See Surah 2:31-37; 7:11-25; 20:116-24.

55. The idea can be found in the Qur'an itself (2:106).

56. http://www.altafsir.com/ includes a translation of the classical collection of *Asbab un-Nuzul* ("occasions of revelation") by al-Wahidi.

of seventh-century Arabia, while verses that imply gender equality are read as establishing basic principles.[57]

Second, the Qur'an is interpreted through the *Hadith.* These are essentially reports of what Muhammad said or did. The life of Muhammad is effectively a secondary revelation through which the Qur'an has to be understood. There are two important underlying concepts here:

- *Types of revelation:* Muslims distinguish two types of revelation. *Waḥy,* the sort of revelation through which Muhammad received the Qur'an, has verbal infallibility. *Ilhām* is closer to Christian ideas of inspiration, whereby the prophet's human characteristics are used in receiving and communicating the message. *Ilham* is seen as fallible because of its human dimension.
- *The doctrine of* ʿiṣma, *or prophetic infallibility.* All prophets are generally believed to be guarded from sin, although they can make mistakes of judgment. Muhammad in particular is seen as an example to be followed (Surah 33:21), this usually meaning not only his moral example but also the details of his practical life.

From an interpretative point of view, the problem is that this interpretative key is embedded in the life of a seventh-century politician, and there are aspects of Muhammad's political life and of seventh-century culture that, although they might have been admirable at the time, are problematic in the twenty-first century. It is not surprising, then, that some Muslims at the moment are reinterpreting and even reconsidering the *Hadith.* They were collected 200-300 years after the death of Muhammad,[58] and some argue that, as so much effort was put into those early collections, so today's Muslims should be using contemporary scholarship to reassess them.[59]

Third, there are various commentaries on the Qur'an that are considered authoritative by different groups of Muslims. We consider here just a few available in English translation.

57. See, for example, F. Mernissi, *Women and Islam: An Historical and Theological Enquiry* (Oxford: Blackwell, 1991).

58. The classical Sunni collections were made by Al-Bukhari (d. 256 A.H./870 C.E.), Muslim (d. 261 A.H./875 C.E.), Abu Dawud (d. 202 A.H./888 C.E.), Ibn Majah (d. 273 A.H./886 C.E.), Ut-Tirmidhi (d. 279/892 C.E.), and An-Nasa'i (d. 303 A.H./915 C.E.). Shiʿites recognize different collections, and, in practice, different Muslim groups refer to different shorter collections abstracted from their larger canons.

59. Mernissi, *Women and Islam,* takes this approach. D. Brown, *Rethinking Tradition in Modern Islamic Thought* (Cambridge: Cambridge University Press, 1996), explores a range of Muslim thinking about the *Hadith* in the context of the history of Islamic views of prophetic tradition.

We begin with commentaries from the classical era.[60] Perhaps the most influential is that of Al-Tabari (died 923 C.E.).[61] The importance of precedent can be seen from the way in which his work cites many *Hadith* and reports of what Jews, Christians, and previous Muslims have said without necessarily giving his own opinion. He often offers a range of options and concludes, "God knows best."

Some medieval commentators are popular with particular groups. For example, Ibn Kathir (d. 1373 C.E.) has a website dedicated to his commentary (http://www.tafsir.com/). This commentary is characterized by its use of Qur'an and *Hadith,* with little reference to earlier commentators. Such going back to the original sources appeals to the many English-educated Muslims who either do not know the classical Arabic literature or who judge its discussions irrelevant to the twenty-first century.

There are more recent commentaries, sometimes written in languages other than Arabic, that are used in particular localities. For example, the two major Sufi reform groups that emerged in nineteenth-century India and represent the majority of Pakistani Muslims in Britain each have a commentary originally written in Urdu.[62]

The twentieth-century commentaries of Maududi and Qutb[63] are of particular note, having been written by two of the main inspirations for current Islamist movements. Neither of these authors was educated in the traditional qur'anic sciences, and their commentaries make little reference to the classical works. The trend of going directly to the Qur'an and ignoring many of the traditional authorities is one of the factors that distances these writers and their followers from other Muslims.

All the above commentaries represent developments within Sunni Islam.

60. Classical commentaries on the Qur'an have limited availability in English. Online are the works of Ibn Kathir (d. 1373) http://www.tafsir.com/, and a growing collection of translations at http://www.altafsir.com/. Mahmoud Ayoub has produced the first two of a series of volumes that anthologize classical qur'anic commentaries: *The Qur'an and Its Interpreters* (Albany: State University of New York Press, 1984, 1992).

61. W. F. Madelung and A. Jones, eds., *The Commentary on the Qur'an by Abu Ja'far Muhammad b. Jarir Al-Tabari* (Oxford: Oxford University Press, 1987), is an English translation of the first part of this.

62. S. M. A. Reza Khan, *Al-Qur'ān Al-Ḥakīm,* is popular with Barelwis. S. A. Usmani, *Tafsir-e-Usmani,* translated as *The Noble Qur'an* (Lahore: Aalameen Publications, 1991), is popular with Deobandis.

63. S. A. A. Maududi, *Tafhīm Al-Qur'ān,* translated by Z. I. Ansari as *Towards Understanding the Qur'an* (Leicester: The Islamic Foundation, 2009-), several volumes, not yet complete. S. Qutb, *Fi Zilal al-Qur'an,* translated by M. A. Salahi and A. A. Shamis as *In the Shade of the Qur'an* (Leicester: The Islamic Foundation, 2007-), several volumes, not yet complete.

Shi'ites have their own interpretative methods and commentaries,[64] as do other, smaller Islamic movements.[65]

We see, then, that qur'anic interpretation is by no means as settled as might appear at first sight. First, different interpretative issues and strategies have been differently settled by different groups — the different *Hadith* collections and commentaries used by different groups being obvious examples. Second, traditional authorities can, in practice, be replaced by more recent authorities, or be very selectively used.

Non-Cognitive Uses of the Qur'an

> It is always wrapped in a specially stitched back; not only "it," but also anything leading to "it." Thus during my childhood my basic Arabic reader was always treated with enormous reverence. If our Arabic primers, perchance, fell to the ground they had to be hastily picked up, kissed, placed against our foreheads to renew our commitment to their sanctity, as if to say "please forgive me" in the same way that one would treat a dearly beloved baby.[66]

While qur'anic interpretation varies and develops, there are non-cognitive ways of treating the Qur'an that are common to all Muslim communities. It is a corollary of the view of the Qur'an as the directly given Word of God that the cognitive dimension of reading and interpretation is but one dimension of the importance of the Qur'an. Indeed, since most Muslims do not understand Arabic, the cognitive dimension may actually be less important than others. Perhaps the nearest Christian category for understanding this is that of sacrament, particularly the high ideas of the Holy Communion in some Christian traditions.

- Just as some Christians treat the consecrated bread and wine with great respect, Muslims treat the physical Qur'an with great respect. They keep the book on a high shelf, wrap it when they carry it out of doors, would not throw away or stand on a piece of paper with a qur'anic verse written on it, and do not handle the text when in a state of ritual impurity.
- Just as the Holy Communion is believed by many Christians to put them in touch with God even if they don't really understand it, so reciting the Qur'an is seen as giving blessing even though the Arabic is not understood.

64. The best-known modern Shi'ite commentary is that of Muhammad Hussain Ṭabāṭabā'ī, available in English translation at http://www.shiasource.com/al-mizan/.

65. For example, the Ahmadiyyas have the *Tafsīr Kabīr* of Mirza Mahmood Ahmad.

66. Esack, *The Qur'an,* 13.

- Just as some Christians put great emphasis on the details of liturgy and the beauty of music and vestments, so Muslims put great emphasis on correct pronunciation and beautiful recitation using traditional chants.

The *Hadith* give a glimpse of how the Qur'an is used.[67] They detail the benefits of reciting and memorizing the Qur'an.

> Allah's Apostle said, "The example of the person who knows the Qur'an by heart is like the owner of tied camels. If he keeps them tied, he will control them, but if he releases them, they will run away." (Bukhari)

> The Prophet said, "The most superior among you (Muslims) are those who learn the Qur'an and teach it." (Bukhari)

> The Prophet said, "The example of him (a believer) who recites the Qur'an is like that of a citron which tastes good and smells good. And he (a believer) who does not recite the Qur'an is like a date which is good in taste but has no smell. And the example of a dissolute wicked person who recites the Qur'an is like the *Raihana* (sweet basil) which smells good but tastes bitter. And the example of a dissolute wicked person who does not recite the Qur'an is like the colocynth which tastes bitter and has no smell. (Bukhari)

They extol the virtues of particular Surahs.

> "Tell him that Allah loves him," said he (Muhammad) about a man who recited it (Surah 1) in every Prayer because it described the Most-merciful. (Bukhari, Muslim)

> "Recite Surah (2) al-Baqarah: for to hold on to it is a *barakah* (blessing), to leave it is a regret." (Muslim)

> "Everything has a heart and the heart of the Qur'an is *Ya Sin* (Surah 36). Anyone who reads it, God will write down for him ten readings of the Qur'an." (Tirmidhi)

67. Bukhari, Muslim, and Tirmidhi are three of the classical collections of *Hadith.* Some of the examples below are cited in chapter 8 of K. Murad, *Way to the Qur'an* (Leicester: The Islamic Foundation, 1985, available online at http://islamworld.net/docs/WTQ/index.html). I have kept here to usages that are common to most Muslims. At the popular level, there are more magical uses of the Qur'an that are viewed as illegitimate by purists. A. A. Thanvi, *Bahishti Zewar* (trans. F. Uddin as *Heavenly Ornaments* [Delhi: The Taj Company, 1990], 491-94), gives a list of popular but fairly widely accepted verses and how they should be recited to deal with problems ranging from stammering to cholera.

Certain Surahs and verses are to be read in particular situations.

> Surah 59:22-24: if one recites these in the morning, "seventy thousand angels ask forgiveness for him until the evening, and if he recites it in the evening they do so until the morning." (Tirmidhi)
>
> On reciting Surah 2:255 when going to bed: He (Muhammad) confirmed that "a protector from Allah will then remain over you, and Satan will not come near you, until the morning." (Bukhari)
>
> "Whenever Allah's Apostle became sick, he would recite *Mu'awwidhat* (Surahs 113 and 114) and then blow his breath over his body. When he became seriously ill, I used to recite (these two Suras) and rub his hands over his body hoping for its blessings," reported Aishah. (Bukhari)

These non-cognitive dimensions of Muslim interactions with the Qur'an underline the observation made concerning "Challenge 1" above, that *the Qur'an in Islamic thinking is more parallel to Jesus in Christian thinking than to the Bible.* We there explored how the Qur'an is seen as the eternal Word that came down to Gabriel and thence to Muhammad, and noted the parallel with the Johannine description of Jesus as the eternal Word made flesh. It is, then, not surprising that, in some ways, Muslims respect the Qur'an as Christians respect Jesus Christ and that they seek blessing through contact with the Qur'an in ways that have parallels in Christians' seeking of blessing through contact with Jesus.

This is, I suggest, the single most important key to Christian understanding of Muslim views of the Qur'an. It is also at the heart of the difference between biblical and qur'anic concepts of revelation: Was the Word made flesh and blood or was the Word dictated as a book?

Toward Mutual Understanding?

I have argued that the aspects of Islamic thinking about the Qur'an that puzzle Christians can be seen as consequences of the view that the eternal Word has come to humanity as a book, and of the tradition that has developed on this basis. What about the aspects of Christian thinking about the Bible that puzzle Muslims? How can Muslims learn to begin by understanding Christian views of the Bible rather than by criticizing Christians and rejecting the Bible as corrupted? There are implied challenges here for Christians as well as for Muslims.

For *Christians,* the challenge is to deal with Islamic criticisms of the Bible in the context of the different understandings of the nature of Scripture explored above. It is tempting for evangelicals, with their high view of Scripture, to begin by defending the text; but that runs the danger of implying to the Muslim that the human process by which the Bible was formed is problematic. This has two major dangers. First, we can get pushed into defending the Bible as if it were the Qur'an, vying for "which is best" in an inappropriate way — inappropriate both because this can lead to unnecessary confrontation and because, in fact, it took longer for the accepted canon of New Testament to be formed than most scholars think it did for the accepted canon of the Qur'an to be formed, so the confrontational comparison does not necessarily favor the Bible. Second, we can miss discussion of the divine-human relationship in the production of the Bible, and therefore lose the opportunity of communicating the divine-human relationship that is at the heart of the biblical worldview and of the gospel.[68]

For *Muslims,* the challenge is to make the effort to understand how Christians (and Jews) regard the Bible. The problem here is not only that Islamic views of the Qur'an are so different from Christian views of the Bible, but also that there are clear Islamic views of what the Bible ought to be. The continuity between Qur'an and Bible discussed above works both ways. On the one hand, as I have argued, Christians should test the Qur'an by asking whether it is consonant with biblical views of revelation. The corollary is that, if one accepts the Qur'an, one would expect the Bible to be of the same kind as the Qur'an; and, indeed, the Qur'an sees the previous books as having been revelation *(waḥy)* sent down *(tanzīl)* in a similar manner to itself.[69] Taking the Bible seriously as it is rather than critiquing it against a qur'anic view of what it ought to be is, then, a difficult task.

There is a further implied challenge for Muslims: it is to deal with scholarship that reads the Qur'an as historically contingent rather than as eternally fixed. Christians and other non-Muslims, who see scriptures as human products even if they might also be divinely inspired, will naturally ask the same questions of the Qur'an as they do of the Bible. Currently, there are Muslims who see the importance of studying the historical situation into which the Qur'an was spoken, and who see non-Muslim qur'anic scholarship as helpful.[70] There are also some who are happy to apply all the critical human sciences to the Qur'an, but their approach is rejected by the majority.[71] Source criticism in particular continues to challenge the thinking of most Muslims, since it implies a human process as the determining factor in the production of the Qur'an.

68. See "Challenge 4" below.

69. E.g., 3:93; 16:43.

70. For example, Esack, *The Qur'an,* both uses and critiques non-Muslim qur'anic scholarship.

71. Muslim Rationalism, http://muslimrationalism.wordpress.com/, expresses the views of people who continue to identify themselves as Muslims but who see the Qur'an as a human book.

The quest for mutual understanding results, then, not only in progress toward appreciating each other's point of view on their scriptures, but also to each being challenged on the validity as well as the understanding of their own. We are now ready to return to the Qur'an's explicit challenges to Christians: to interpret and to live by the Bible.

Challenge 3: Interpretation — Reading the Bible in the Context of the Qur'an

We have seen that Islamic critiques of the Bible are rooted in the Qur'an's charge that Jews (and, by extension in Islamic thinking, Christians), are guilty of *taḥrīf* — of distorting their Books. There are many difficulties with the current prevalent Islamic view that this means the texts are distorted.[72] It seems that the initial charge was one of false interpretation or of deliberate misrepresentation. The challenge to Christians is then twofold: faithful interpretation of the Bible in Islamic contexts, and faithful communication of the nature and message of the Bible to Muslims. Responding to this challenge involves a rereading of the Bible and a rethinking of how we present our theology of Scripture in relation to Muslims. How might the encounter with the qur'anic challenges affect Christian thinking about the Bible? If the Word-made-flesh is at the heart of biblical revelation, how do we describe the Bible to Muslims? If the mechanism for the production of Scripture involved human agency and cannot be described as infallible *waḥy,* how can the Bible be totally reliable? And what difference might the encounter with the Qur'an and with Muslims make to our interpretation of the Bible?

How We Read[73]

First, I want to suggest that reading the Bible after reading the Qur'an can lead to an appreciation of its difference from the Qur'an, and thus to attention to aspects of the Bible that might otherwise be missed. We take as examples the ideas noted under the heading "A Bible Reader's Response" (pp. 1022-34 above).

72. For an Islamic treatment of these difficulties, see A. Saeed, *The Qur'an: An Introduction* (London: Routledge, 2008), esp. chapter 8, "The Qu'ran and Other Scriptures."

73. A broad overview of factors to be taken into consideration in reading the Bible in the context of Islam can be found in my "Using the Bible in the Context of Islam," in *Understanding and Using the Bible,* ed. C. J. H. Wright and J. Lamb (London: SPCK, 2009), chapter 7.

Form

In seeking to explain the nature of the Bible to Muslims, we realize that *the form is as much a part of the revelation as is the content.* It is, after all, logical that the form should be consistent with what is revealed. If what is being revealed is primarily a verbal message, then the form of the Qur'an is to be expected. We might then approach the Bible by asking what its mixed forms of writing and origin tell us about the nature of what is being revealed. This can revolutionize our thinking. Aspects of the Bible that have hitherto seemed problematic can become part of the Good News.

For example, Muslims often point out the differences between the four Gospels and say that this indicates inconsistency. Further, they say, only a small proportion of the New Testament records the actual words of Jesus. By this, they mean, first, that we have mostly not the message of Jesus but what other people have to say about him and, second, that even what we have is a Greek translation of an Aramaic original. There is a tendency to respond by trying to harmonize the Gospels and to demonstrate that the various writings about Jesus are consistent with his words. It is, I suggest, more fruitful to ask why we have the different Gospels and why we have, in these senses, so few words of Jesus.

The answer is, of course, that the primary revelation is not Jesus' message but Jesus' self. The Gospels function as witnesses to him — which is why we need more than one, and why it is good that John and the Synoptics clearly come from different perspectives. Further, the various dimensions of the person to whom the Gospels bear witness could not be adequately communicated through a single account: the truth about God cannot be contained in one univocal text.

The different Gospel accounts then become dynamic historical sources rather than flat conveyors of ideas. These are not divinely given accounts but divinely inspired human witnesses to the divine event: the humanity of the Gospels is as much a part of their nature as the Word of God as is their inspiration. As we read, for example, the different resurrection narratives, instead of asking how they can be harmonized (though that is a legitimate question) we can ask what they indicate about the nature of Scripture, and about the nature of the God who speaks through such human, historical documents.

In short, the differences in the forms of the Bible and the Qur'an raise all the questions dealt with in the chapters on genre in the current collection (17 and 19). On the one hand, such questions can make us look at the variety of biblical genres as problematic; but, on the other hand, they can help us to see that the form of the Bible is intrinsic to its nature as the revelatory Book of the triune God, so that what might appear to be problematic should rather be celebrated. The rich diversity of authority and of inspiration that is characterized by the diversity of literary form is part of the Good News.

Emphasis

Next, if we ask *what the form of the Bible tells us about its content,* we find that it reflects the difference in emphases of the two Books as noted under the heading "Continuity" (pp. 1024-31 above).

- If the Bible is largely narrative rather than exhortation, that implies an emphasis on the history of God's covenant interaction with his world rather than on his commands to his creatures.
- If it includes the prayers of God's people, that implies an emphasis on a two-way relationship between God and humanity rather than on prophetic words from God to people.
- If it includes human wisdom and questioning about death and suffering, that implies an emphasis on human response to God.
- If a large proportion of the Gospels is given to accounts of the crucifixion and resurrection, that implies an emphasis on God's finding a way to deal lovingly and justly with covenant breaking rather than on judgment of disobedience.

The comparison with different qur'anic emphases can then lead to an appreciation of biblical emphases, and to asking different questions of the biblical text. For example, the Islamic emphasis on law not only brings an appreciation of biblical ideas of grace but also challenges us to ask about the relationship between law and ethics, and between Christian faith and the law of the state in secular societies. It takes us back to ask again the purpose of the laws given to Israel, and the extent to which particular laws depend on circumstance and stage in history. More fundamentally, a system that denies the fall needs to ask more acute questions about the relationship between biblical views of the law, grace, and human fallenness.

Reworking of Biblical Material

Reading passages of the Bible alongside parallel qur'anic material not only raises the sorts of questions about the Qur'an raised above; it can also send us back to the Bible with new questions and lead to new insights.[74]

For example, the comparison between the biblical and qur'anic Cain and Abel stories might lead not only to an examination of the content of the Genesis conversation between God and Cain but to a reflection on the fact of that conversation. Why is Abel silent? Why does God speak not to the innocent brother

74. For further examples, see also my "Qur'anic Challenges for Genesis," *JSOT* 75 (1997): 3-19, and "Roles and Relationships: Reflections on the Khalifah and the Image of God," *Transformation* 15, no. 1 (1997): 18-23.

but to the guilty one? Jesus' reworking of the story in the parable of the Prodigal Son (Luke 15:11-32) then underlines God's love for the guilty. It also assures us that, far from dividing the world into the guilty and the innocent, the Cain and Abel story is about the destructive tendencies in all human beings.[75]

Issues Raised by Muslim Readings of the Bible

"Challenge 1" above presented a Christian reflection on the Qur'an, and "Challenge 2" sought understandings of Muslim thinking about the Qur'an and Christian thinking about the Bible. It remains to consider Muslim understandings of the Bible; and these open further aspects of the context and agenda for Christian biblical interpretation in Islamic contexts.

First, as already pointed out, Muslims reading the Bible see a very different book than the Qur'an and usually conclude that the original books given to Abraham, Moses, David, and Jesus have been lost or distorted. They therefore offer extensive critiques of the Bible, focusing on historical criticism of the text and on aspects that contradict Islamic understandings.

At the same time, the way that the Qur'an refers to biblical stories without telling them means that a few Muslims see the need to read the Bible in order to further their understanding of the Qur'an, and there is a long tradition of Islamic uses of the Bible as a tool for qur'anic interpretation. In the first Islamic centuries, much information came over into qur'anic commentary from Christian and Jewish converts, and a genre of "stories of the prophets" developed that drew on biblical as well as extra-biblical (for example, midrashic) accounts of the qur'anic prophets. At this stage, it seems that most Muslims saw the qur'anic accusations about the distortion of the Bible as referring to the distortion of the Bible's meaning by Jews and Christians.

As time went on, it became common to say that the biblical text itself had been distorted, and that is now the belief of most Muslims, and the Bible itself became less and less used. However, there are also some who see the extant biblical text as sufficiently reliable to augment their qur'anic studies.[76] More are

75. The parable of the prodigal son is also one of the biblical passages that speaks most eloquently to Muslims. See Colin Chapman, *Cross and Crescent: Responding to the Challenge of Islam* (Nottingham: Inter-Varsity, 2003), 311-14.

76. The pioneer of this approach in modern times was Sir Sayyed Ahmad Khan. In 1862, he published *The Mahomodan Commentary on the Holy Bible* on his private press in Ghazeepore, India. The second volume examines the parallels between Genesis 1–11 and the Qur'an and *Hadith;* the first examines the basis for so doing. It is a study of European critical biblical scholarship that argues for the general reliability of the Bible, and concludes that, while the extant text might not be entirely that originally given, it is edifying reading for Muslims and important for the interpretation of qur'anic passages that refer to it. A current example is Mustansir Mir;

happy to depend on the wealth of Islamic tradition that fills in the qur'anic gaps in the stories, but are nonetheless interested in reading biblical accounts, and in books authored by characters mentioned in the Qur'an.[77]

Second, Muslims are likely to look for material that is continuous with Islam: for biblical teaching that is similar to qur'anic teaching, and for explicit predictions concerning Muhammad and the Arabs. We have space here for but a few examples of the latter.

- *The prophet like Moses* (Deut. 18:18). The "prophet like Moses" is frequently asserted to be Muhammad. The Qur'an refers more to Moses than to any other prophet, and it is evident that Muhammad's life is seen as parallel to his. Muhammad's confrontation with the Meccans parallels Moses' confrontation with Pharaoh; as Moses led his people to freedom, so Muhammad led his people to Medina; Muhammad, like Moses, was both community leader and the recipient of divine messages and laws. Besides all this, Muslims point out that, like Muhammad and unlike Jesus, Moses married and had a family and died. Further, the verse says that the prophet will be "from amongst your brethren." Who, they ask, are the brethren of the Israelites, if not the Ishmaelites?
- *The altogether lovely* (Song of Solomon 5:16). The word translated "altogether lovely" here is *meḥmedīm* — which sounds like Muhammad. Wherever the root ḤMD appears in Hebrew, or even in Syriac versions, Muslims have found references to Muhammad.[78]
- *The paraclete* (John 14 and 16). The Qur'an speaks of Jesus predicting the coming of *aḥmad,* which is generally understood as referring to Muhammad. (Note: in Surah 61:6, *aḥmad* means "the praised one"; the root ḤMD is also the root of *muḥammad,* so that *aḥmad* is read as a personal name for Muhammad.) An obvious Christian reading of Surah 61:6 would be to suggest that the "praised one" predicted by Jesus was the Holy Spirit. Many Muslims, however, read the promise of the paraclete as a prediction of Muhammad. Their basis is a linguistic argument: *paraklētos,* they say, is a misreading of *periklytos,* which means "praised one," and would translate into Arabic as "Ahmad." Verses like John 16:13-15 are then interpreted in terms of Muhammad's receiving of the Qur'an.[79]

---

see his *Understanding the Islamic Scripture: A Study of Selected Passages from the Qur'an* (New York: Pearson Education, 2008).

77. In particular, the psalms of David are mentioned, and there are stories of Solomon's wisdom but none of his collected proverbs.

78. 'Ali b. Rabban al-Tabari (785-860) (not the Al-Tabari who wrote the famous commentary mentioned above), *The Book of Religion and Empire,* trans. A. Mingana (Manchester: Manchester University Press, 1922), 88-92, quoted in Gaudeul, *Encounters and Clashes,* 242, cites Ps. 45:2-5; 48:1-2; and 50:1-3.

79. This makes sense to Arabic speakers, because Arabic, like Hebrew, has consonantal

Third, Muslims are likely to come to the Bible with interests that are not on the agenda of most Christians. For example, the Islamic emphasis on law means that Muslims reading Acts might be more interested in the development of the food laws than in the preaching of the gospel. Other legal concerns might include dress, ritual purity, and inheritance laws. Additionally, Muslim cultures are often much nearer to biblical cultures than are those of the West, so Muslims may be particularly interested in the family structures of the Genesis patriarchs or in biblical accounts of hospitality. They may be as scandalized by the parable of the prodigal son and as puzzled by the parables of the Pharisee and the tax collector at prayer as would have been Jesus' first hearers. Moreover, ongoing public interest in *jihād* may lead to interest in how Christians have interpreted their war texts, not only today but historically. Relevant periods include those of the Byzantine Empire at the time of Muhammad, the Crusades, and Western colonialism. The interest in historical interpretations can be fed by Islamic views of the authority of tradition mentioned above. Finally, Islamic emphasis on social justice and organization may lead to Muslims being much more interested in how Christians put Jesus' teaching on wealth and poverty into practice than in how they understand justification by faith.

Agendas for Study

Thinking about the Bible in the context of the Qur'an, then, not only raises interpretative issues, but also alerts us to an agenda for urgent study that reflects the issues raised in this chapter. To the Islamic interests mentioned in the paragraph above, we might add:

- *Revelation:* The comparison with the Qur'an not only raises questions about how God speaks and the relationship between revelation and Scripture considered above, but prompts further study of the nature of prophethood. Further, the often-discussed question about the fate of those who have had no access to special revelation is modified in consideration of those who know something of biblical revelation but through a non-Christian lens.[80]
- *Power:* One of the reasons for the Islamic emphasis on law is the fact that the Qur'an reflects Muhammad's development of political power. This raises a

roots and a consonantal script, to which voweling was regularly added only after the time of Muhammad. It makes much less sense in the context of Greek, which, like English, includes vowels in ordinary script.

80. This might include Jews, who view the Bible through Talmud; Jehovah's Witnesses, who view it through the New World Translation; as well as Muslims, who view it through the Qur'an.

host of issues regarding the relationship between faith and power and between religious and political authority. We need better understanding of territory, of nations, and of the roots of violence. Key to this is an understanding of Israel: Why did God call a people and give them rule and land?

Such study will not only enable us to communicate with Muslims on matters that interest them, but also enhance our understanding of many of the current tensions in our world.

The question of how Christians should read the Bible in the context of the Qur'an raises the corollary: How should Muslims read the Qur'an in the context of the Bible? We have considered above something of how Muslims may read the Bible through a qur'anic lens, but what might happen if, as suggested above, they sought to read the Bible for what it is, and ask how that might affect their reading of the Qur'an?

Such questions raise another possibility: that of Christians and Muslims reading the Bible and the Qur'an together. The developing practice of "scriptural reasoning" offers a model for shared reading, whereby Christians can present their understanding of a biblical text and hear Muslim reflections on it, and Muslims can present their understanding of a qur'anic text and hear Christian reflections on it.[81] This is followed by a time of discussion on similarities and differences and of any issues raised. Thus there is a move from Christians reading the Bible in the context of the Qur'an to reading it in the context of both the Qur'an and its readers, and vice versa. Not surprisingly, such shared reading raises all the challenges explored in this chapter; but it does so in the context of relationships as well as of ideas.

Challenge 4:
Living Accordingly

Reading the Bible in the context of the Qur'an is not, then, simply an academic exercise. Just as most of the essays in this collection constitute a response to live human issues caused by twenty-first-century Western thinking, so this chapter is a response to live human issues caused by a book that is considered authoritative by nearly one quarter of the world's population, and, more fundamentally, to the commission of Christ to share the biblical gospel with all of humankind. I have tried in this chapter to model a way of faithfully reading the Bible in the context of another faith; and, as in any other context, faithful reading and faithful living go together. It is the living that takes us back to the Bible with new questions, and the reading that equips and challenges us for living.

81. The practice usually includes Jews, but some groups are for Christians and Muslims only. See www.scripturalreasoning.org, www.scripturalreasoning.org.uk.

We started by listening to what the Qur'an says to us, which is, by implication, what Muslims say to us, and then considered what we had heard on the basis of our own understanding of the Bible. We then tried to understand where Muslim people might be coming from, and went on to search the Bible to see what it might be saying to us in this context. In doing so, we raised the question of how Muslims might be reading the Bible, which gave us a further agenda for biblical study. The next step would be to take all this understanding into our relationships with Muslims, which would take us back to the study of Islam, to considering Islam from a biblical perspective, to trying to understand Muslims, and to reading the Bible with all this in mind.

I want to finish with two areas in which our study might determine our living.

First, it has raised many clues for effective communication with Muslims:

- There are points of agreement with which we can start.
- The Qur'an has accounts of the biblical characters that we can discuss.
- The calls to biblical faithfulness mean that we can explain to Muslims how we are trying to use the Bible as a basis of our lives.
- There are many Islamic interests that can be addressed from a biblical point of view.

Even the common Muslim objections to the Bible can lead to helpful discussion and explanation. Accusations about corruption of the text can be an occasion for explaining something of the history of the canon and of our understanding of the work of the Holy Spirit. More importantly, questions about the human nature of the Bible can be opportunities for talking about the compatibility between the human and the divine that is envisaged in the idea of "the image of God," and that makes possible the incarnation — the Word made flesh. Since the Qur'an speaks of Jesus as God's Word,[82] this is, arguably, the most important single idea for helping Muslims to understand Christian ideas of revelation.[83]

Second, the qur'anic challenge is not only about belief; it is also about how we live. We recall the exhortation to the People of the Book:

> If only the People of the Book would believe and be mindful of God, We would take away their sins and bring them into gardens of delight. If they had upheld

82. Surah 4:171.

83. John 1 has been used by Christians in discussion with Muslims from the earliest days. John of Damascus (675-753 C.E.), *The Discussion of a Christian and a Saracen* (available in N. A. Newman, ed., *Early Christian-Muslim Dialogue* [Hatfield, PA: Interdisciplinary Biblical Research Institute, 1993], 144-52), starts from the idea of Jesus as God's Word, and uses some of the Islamic discussion about the createdness of the Qur'an.

> the Torah and the Gospel and what was sent down to them from their Lord, they would have been given abundance from above and from below: some of them are on the right course, but many of them do evil. (Surah 5:65-66)

More specifically of Christians, the Qur'an says:

> We gave (Jesus) the Gospel and put compassion and mercy into the hearts of his followers. But monasticism was something they invented — We did not ordain it for them — only to seek God's pleasure, and even so, they did not observe it properly. (Surah 57:27)

The change of heart effected in the followers of Jesus is something unique in the Qur'an.[84] Many Muslims know something of the emphasis of Jesus on humility, poverty, and love.[85] They have a very powerful idea of the importance of following the prophet's example, so they expect Christians to follow the example of Jesus — and that includes following his example in their relationships with Muslims. The starting point in communication with Muslims is not words but life, not only in response to these qur'anic challenges, but also because the center of our faith is not a Word made book but the Word made flesh.

What might following the way of Jesus in relation to Muslims entail? It surely includes repenting of wrong attitudes toward Muslims, confessing the wrong done to Muslims by Christians in the past, and loving even those Muslims who act in enmity toward Christians, toward the Gospel, or toward our societies. And loving people means trying to see things from their point of view, giving them the same freedoms that we would want for ourselves, and being as much concerned for their welfare as for our own.

This way of Jesus is by no means as straightforward as it might seem: there are questions of reciprocity here. In the context of Christian-Muslim dialogue, it is often pointed out that there is an imbalance. While Christians may repent of and apologize for past sins, Muslims seldom do so, at least in public — not only because they would not wish to bring shame on Islam, but also because they may not agree that something done in the past was in error.[86] While Jesus told us to

84. The Qur'an most often speaks of God sealing or hardening or veiling people's hearts (e.g., 2:7; 5:13; 6:25; 6:46; 7:101; 8:12; passim) or putting fear into hearts (e.g., 3:151, 156). See also Jane Dammen McAuliffe, "Heart," in McAuliffe, ed., *Encyclopaedia of the Qur'ān* (cf. Brill Online http://www.paulyonline.brill.nl/subscriber/entry?entry=q3_COM-00081).

85. For Sufis in particular, Jesus is the exemplary ascetic. For a collection of traditional Muslim material on Jesus, see T. Khalidi, *The Muslim Jesus: Sayings and Stories in Islamic Literature* (Cambridge, MA: Harvard University Press, 2001).

86. This is particularly noticeable in relation to conquest and cultural colonialism. Christians usually view political conquest that was seen as "Christian" as an aberration, and Western Christians feel guilty about the propagation of Western culture alongside the gospel in colonial

love our enemies, the Qur'an has no such idea.[87] While Christians today would ask for freedom for all people to propagate as well as to believe their faith, Islamic law, while it protects non-Muslim minorities, criminalizes conversion from Islam and any activities that might lead to it.

There are implicit challenges here for Muslims: How far can a religion whose basis is in the establishment of political power at Medina and whose law is based on the assumption of superiority agree to cohabit with people of different convictions on an equal basis? Such challenges are much debated within twenty-first-century Islam. But this chapter is primarily addressed to the Bible reader. How will we respond to the Qur'an's challenge to live according to the compassion and mercy that God puts into our hearts? How far should our actions depend on whether others reciprocate? Will we follow the way of the Jesus of the New Testament even though Muslims follow the very different way of Muhammad? The Qur'an, as interpreted by most Muslims, denies that Jesus died on the cross:[88] the way of the Jesus of the New Testament leads directly to it.

times. In contrast, Muslims see the Islamic conquests as glorious affirmations of Islam, and the spreading of Arabic culture as intrinsic to Islam.

87. There are *Hadith* about loving one's neighbor, but even then the Muslim neighbor is generally given precedence over the non-Muslim neighbor in Islamic thought.

88. See n. 19 above.

THIRTY-THREE

Can Hindu Scriptures Serve as a "Tutor" to Christ?

Timothy C. Tennent

In 1974 Walter Buhlmann was one of the earliest writers to point out a major demographic shift that was taking place in the Majority World.[1] The rise of these new centers of Christian vibrancy has been a frequent theme in the writings of Andrew Walls, Kwame Bediako, and Lamin Sanneh, among others.[2] David Barrett, the well-known demographer and editor of the *World Christian Encyclopedia,* provided the statistical support for this shift in 1982. The 2010 publication of the *Atlas of Global Christianity* to commemorate the 100th anniversary of the 1910 Edinburgh World Missionary Conference is currently the most up-to-date analysis of this dramatic shift in global Christianity. Interestingly, although the number of Christians in the world has grown dramatically from 612 million in 1910 to 2.2 billion in 2010, the overall percentage of world population who identify themselves as Christian has declined slightly.[3] Therefore the most significant

1. Walter Buhlmann, *The Coming of the Third Church* (Maryknoll, NY: Orbis, 1978). A word about terminology is in order. The phrase "the non-Western world" should be abandoned because it defines Christians from Asia, Africa, and Latin America by what they are *not* rather than what they *are.* The expression "Third World" or *(Tiers Monde)* was coined in 1952 by the French demographer Alfred Sauvy. It quickly entered English as a helpful phrase to speak collectively about Africa, Asia, and Latin America. It was later popularized as a *political* expression for the non-aligned world during the Cold War. However, in the 1960s and 1970s, the expression "Third-World country" began to be used in an *economic* sense (often pejoratively) to refer to underdeveloped countries marked by poverty, corruption, and disease. The phrase "Majority World" is the preferred twenty-first-century term since it helps to highlight the basic point that Africa, Asia, and Latin America are where the majority of the world's Christians are now located.

2. See Andrew F. Walls, *The Missionary Movement in Christian History: Studies in the Transmission of Faith* (Maryknoll, NY: Orbis, 1996); Walls, *The Cross-Cultural Process in Christian History* (Maryknoll, NY: Orbis, 2002); Lamin Sanneh, *Whose Religion Is Christianity? The Gospel beyond the West* (Grand Rapids: Eerdmans, 2003); Kwame Bediako, *Christianity in Africa: The Renewal of a Non-Western Religion* (Maryknoll, NY: Orbis, 1995).

3. Todd M. Johnson and Kenneth R. Ross, eds., *Atlas of Global Christianity* (Edinburgh:

development of twentieth-century Christianity is not so much the growth of Christianity as a world religion, but *where* Christians are located in the world. The ethnic composition or "face" of Christianity has changed dramatically in the last one hundred years. At the turn of the twentieth century the typical "representative" Christian was a forty-seven-year-old European male; today the most representative Christian would be a twenty-seven-year-old African female. However, as late as the year 1990 when *Christian History* magazine listed the one hundred most significant events in the history of Christianity, there was not a single reference to any event taking place in the Majority World or initiated by Majority World Christians.[4] There seemed to be little awareness that one of the most dramatic developments in the history of Christianity was unfolding in the Majority World.

It was the publication of Philip Jenkins's books *The Next Christendom* and *The New Faces of Christianity* that served to dramatically increase the general awareness among Western Christians about the rise of the Majority World church.[5] Some specific examples of how the church is changing will, perhaps, help to illustrate this shift better. In 1900, there were over 380 million Christians in Europe and fewer than 10 million on the entire continent of Africa.[6] Today there are over 494 million Christians in Africa, comprising one-fifth of the entire Christian church. Throughout the twentieth century a net average gain of 16,500 people were coming to Christ every day in Africa. From 1970 to 1985, for example, the church in Africa grew by over six million people. During that same time an average of 4,300 people per day were leaving the church in Europe and North America.[7] To give a specific example as a way of grasping the scale and scope of this demographic shift, one could note, for example, that during the twentieth century China gained 2.87 million new Christians whereas Germany lost 248,000 Christians.[8]

The church is not just moving southward; it is also moving eastward. In Korea, for example, despite the fact that Christianity was not formally introduced

University of Edinburgh Press, 2009), 7. The actual overall percentage of Christians in the world has declined slightly from 34.8 to 33.2 percent between 1910 and 2010, because during the same 100-year period the population of the world grew from 1.7 billion to 6.9 billion people.

4. Philip Jenkins, *The Next Christendom: The Coming of Global Christianity,* 3rd edition (Oxford/New York: Oxford University Press, 2011), 4. See also *Christian History* 28 (1990): 51.

5. Jenkins, *The Next Christendom* and *The New Faces of Christianity: Believing the Bible in the Global South* (Oxford/New York: Oxford University Press, 2008).

6. The World Christian Database notes that there were 380,641,890 Christians in Europe and 9,938,588 Christians in Africa. See www.worldchristiandatabase.org.

7. Sanneh, *Whose Religion,* 15. Elizabeth Isichei says that the number leaving the church in the West was 7,500 per day. See Elizabeth Isichei, *A History of Christianity in Africa: From Antiquity to the Present* (Grand Rapids: Eerdmans, 1995), 1.

8. Johnson and Ross, eds., *Atlas of Global Christianity,* 61.

within the country itself until the eighteenth century, it is staggering to realize that today there are over 20 million Christians in South Korea alone. In fact, South Korea is widely regarded as the home of the modern church growth movement, which is exemplified by the remarkable story of the Yoido Full Gospel Church founded by Dr. "David" Paul Yonggi Cho (b. 1936). Founded in 1958 with only five people in a small living room, the church now claims over 700,000 members, making it easily the largest church in the world. Even as recently as the Cultural Revolution in China (1966-1976) there were only about one million Christians in China. Today the Chinese church comprises over 90 million believers, with an average growth rate of 16,500 per day.[9] India has been called the cradle of the world's religions, having given birth to Hinduism, Buddhism, Jainism, and Sikhism. Yet today, this land of exotic eastern religions is also the home of over 60 million Christians.[10] Church planting in India, particularly in the traditionally Hindu north, is taking place at a blistering pace. It is likely that by the year 2050 India will have over 100 million Christians.[11] It is vital that Christians begin to grapple with some of the theological implications of this geographic shift in Christianity's center of gravity.[12]

Christianity is growing quite dramatically in areas that are the traditional heartlands of major non-Christian religions. For centuries the church in the West has thrived within the larger context of Christendom where there were no other serious religious competitors or known sacred texts. Most Christians would live without ever actually meeting a Buddhist or a Muslim in person. The growth of Christianity was tied almost exclusively to the Christian birthrate. In contrast, today Christianity is growing in settings where Christianity is a minority religion flourishing under the shadow of another major world religion such as Hinduism or Islam. The word "scripture" does not automatically assume that the referent is the Christian Bible. The vast majority of new Christians are coming by conversion (not by birthrate) from some other major world religion.

9. David Barrett, George Kurian, and Todd Johnson, *World Christian Encyclopedia*, 2nd edition (New York: Oxford University Press, 2001), 191.

10. Todd M. Johnson, Sarah Tieszen, and Thomas Higgens, "Counting Christians in India, AD 52-2200," *Dharma Deepika*, forthcoming. This research was conducted at the Center for the Study of Global Christianity at Gordon-Conwell Theological Seminary, which produces the data for the *World Christian Encyclopedia*. This represents 6.15 percent of the population of India, far above the official 3 percent figure given by the government. However, the official figures disenfranchise millions of Christians who are counted as "tribals" or who are remaining within Hindu communities.

11. This is the current projection of the Center for the Study of Global Christianity. This represents 8.94 percent of the population of India.

12. For more on this see my *Theology in the Context of World Christianity: How the Global Church Is Influencing the Way We Think about and Discuss Theology* (Grand Rapids: Zondervan, 2007).

Key Questions

This demographic shift in world Christianity raises many issues that deserve reflective consideration, but several questions emerge that are particularly relevant to this collection of essays on Scripture. The purpose of this chapter is to explore our attitude toward the sacred texts of other religions. Furthermore, this chapter seeks to explore whether or not we should make use of these texts in communicating or teaching the gospel to those who currently belong to other non-Christian world religions. These questions naturally give rise to a host of fascinating questions. For example, as millions of new Christians from the Majority World pour into the church, how does their prior understanding of categories such as sacred text, authority, historicity, authorial intent, and canonicity (to name just a few) impact the concomitant notions in Christianity? Since non-Christian sacred texts such as the Qur'an, the Upanishads, and the *Lotus Sutra* provide the prevailing theological categories, stock images, religious vocabulary, and transcendent conceptions for millions across the Majority World, what kind of guidance can we give men and women seeking to communicate the gospel into these contexts? Is it advisable to make use of these texts in preaching and explaining the Christian gospel? Could the non-Christian philosophical or religious writings that are so prevalent in the Majority World raise important questions that are left either unanswered or are answered unsatisfactorily, but could be shown to be answered in and through the gospel of Jesus Christ? Could non-Christian sacred texts serve as a *preparatio evangelica* for the gospel? How should a believer regard the sacred texts of their pre-Christian past once they become Christians and embrace the Bible as the Word of God? As long as Christianity remained predominately a Western faith with no major non-Christian religions as near competitors, then these questions remained more remote. However, now that Christianity is growing so rapidly in the very contexts where Islam, Buddhism, and Hinduism are so deeply entrenched, these questions are becoming increasingly urgent to explore and reflect upon theologically. This chapter will, broadly speaking, explore the entire frontier between Christianity and other religions as it relates to our attitude toward their sacred texts. However, this chapter will seek to give special attention to Hindu texts for two reasons. First, this collection of essays contains excellent contributions concerning both Islam and Buddhism. Second, Hindu scriptures represent a collection of texts that, by most estimates, lie the farthest from the Christian tradition. Thus, if the principles can be set forth with Hindu scriptures they can far more easily be applied to those of other religious traditions.

Before these key questions can be properly addressed it is important to set all of these discussions within the larger framework of two substantial themes that will undoubtedly influence how we respond to the two key questions of this chapter. First, we must briefly survey the biblical attitude toward other religions and Yahweh's place "among the gods." This is important because, in many ways, our attitude toward their sacred texts is a subset of this larger theme. Second, any examination of the potential uses of sacred texts from other religions requires our ongoing reflection on the nature of revelation itself.

Attitude of the People of God Toward Other Religions

There are at least 239 places in Scripture that record the people of God coming into contact with people from other religious traditions.[13] While the overall missional nature of the biblical texts is obvious, it is also clear that the Scriptures do not advocate a single position or attitude toward other religions.[14] While the overwhelming message of these texts is one of conflict over against other gods and the worthlessness of false religions, there are some surprising moments of positive engagement. One need only compare and contrast three biblical accounts to bring home this message: Abraham in the Valley of Shaveh interacting positively with Melchizedek, king of Salem (Genesis 14); Elijah on Mt. Carmel confronting, challenging, and finally slaying the worshipers of Baal (1 Kings 18); and the apostle Paul on Mars Hill carefully reasoning with the religious leaders of Athens and quoting from their own texts to move them from an altar to an unknown God to a declaration of the known God of biblical revelation (Acts 17). However, despite the variation found in these accounts, among others, it remains unmistakably clear that biblical revelation declares that Yahweh and his revelation is without equal and is superior to that of other gods. To briefly summarize, there are at least three ways that Yahweh is portrayed as superior to other gods.

Sovereign over All Creation

First, he is declared to be sovereign over all creation (Isa. 40:12-26). Creation theology is not merely attested in the opening chapters of Genesis and then forgotten. Rather, it is a dominant theological theme that can be found in every major strand of Scripture (Genesis 1; Isaiah 40; Amos 4:13; Psalm 90, 104; Jeremiah 10; John 1; Acts 1; Colossians 1).[15] Yahweh is not regarded as merely Israel's sovereign, but as the ultimate ruler over all creation and everything in it. Jeremiah proclaims,

13. Terry Muck and Frances S. Adeney, *Christianity Encountering World Religions* (Grand Rapids: Baker Academic, 2009), 33. For a full list of the 239 texts see their appendix, 379-85.

14. For an excellent overview of the missional nature of the biblical texts, see Christopher J. H. Wright, *The Mission of God* (Downers Grove, IL: IVP Academic, 2006).

15. For a full survey of these texts see Thomas C. Oden, *The Living God*, vol. 1 (Peabody, MA: Prince Press, 2001), 225-316.

"Ah, Sovereign Lord, you have made the heavens and the earth by your great power and outstretched arm. Nothing is too hard for you" (Jer. 32:17). In a similar fashion, the psalmist proclaims that "the earth is the LORD's, and everything in it, the world and all who live in it" (Ps. 24:1). From a biblical perspective there are no human cultures or societies that lie outside his sovereign rule. Biblical revelation concerning *ex nihilo* creation separates Yahweh's role as creator from Hindu ideas about creation as well as a host of religious ideas that affirm the eternality of matter, pantheism, panentheism, or a wide array of dualistic ideas that posit some other eternally comparable power who stands next to God.

More Powerful Than All Other Gods

Second, Yahweh is more powerful than all other gods. Yahweh declares his plagues on Egypt as a sign to those who worship false gods that "there is no one like me in all the earth" (Exod. 9:14). David blessed Yahweh, declaring, "Yours, O LORD, is the greatness and the power and the glory and the victory and the majesty, for all that is in the heavens and the earth is yours. . . . In your hand are power and might, and in your hand it is to make great and to give strength to all" (1 Chron. 29:11-12).

Uniqueness of Covenant and Covenantal Relationship

Third, Yahweh is not only revealed to be superior in power and might; he is also revealed to be connected relationally to his people in a way that is unknown to the other nations: "What other nation is so great as to have their gods near them the way the Lord our God is near us whenever we pray to him?" (Deut. 4:7). The same text goes on to declare that the covenant Yahweh entered into with his people was also unique: "And what other nation is so great as to have such righteous decrees and laws as this body of laws I am setting before you today?" (Deut. 4:8).

Nature of Revelation

Yahweh is the only true and living God and is, therefore, the ultimate source of all revelation. Revelation literally means an "unveiling" or "disclosure" of something previously hidden. In the Christian understanding, revelation comes as God's gift and is a free-will act of his self-disclosure. The Bible speaks of revelation not so much in a theoretical sense, that is, as a doctrine of epistemology explaining how we *know* things, but in a more practical sense. God reveals truths about himself and about humanity so that we might know him and his saving purposes. In short, God's revelation allows us to capture a glimpse of the *missio Dei.*

Christians have long recognized that revelation occurs in a wide array of forms — in creation, in historical acts, in the incarnation, and in the Bible. In order to better understand revelation many theologians have made the distinction between general or natural revelation and special revelation. General revelation represents those features of God's self-disclosure that are *universally accessible.* The two most prominent examples of general revelation are the created order (Ps. 19:1) and human conscience (Rom. 2:14-15), since both are commonly shared by all humanity. Special revelation represents God's self-disclosure to particular people at particular times regarding his saving purposes, but it is not universally accessible. Examples of special revelation include such divine disclosures as the Mosaic Law, the incarnation of Jesus Christ, and the Bible. We also have examples in the Bible whereby God specifically reveals his divine, sovereign intentions to unbelievers such as Pharaoh, Nebuchadnezzar, or Cyrus. Pharaoh was given a dream of God's decree concerning Egyptian crops (Genesis 41). Nebuchadnezzar was given a dream about his reign in light of God's sovereignty (Daniel 2). Ezra declares that "the Lord stirred up the spirit of Cyrus king of Persia" to make a proclamation on behalf of Israel.

The relationship between general and special revelation is crucial to developing a theology of religions. There are many different views among theologians about the relationship of general revelation to special revelation. On one end of the spectrum are those who believe that special revelation is nothing more than specific and particularized symbolism of the general revelation that is universally known. At the other end of the spectrum are those who emphasize that true knowledge is found only in Christ and the Scriptures and all other claims to knowledge have no sure foundation and are utterly false.[16] One's understanding of revelation will, of course, always play a key role in how we understand many of the key issues raised in this chapter. We are now prepared to address the key questions of this study.

Upanishads as a Hindu Old Testament? — The Challenge Stated

In India, it is not uncommon to hear Indian Christian theologians referring to the Upanishads as *their* Old Testament. Such a statement must seem quite odd to an outsider, but the idea is that just as the Old Testament served to prepare the way and point people to Christ in the early Jewish context, so the Upanishads serve as a kind of *preparatio evangelica* for the gospel in the Indian context. Some In-

16. Daniel L. Migliore, *Faith Seeking Understanding: An Introduction to Christian Theology,* 2nd edition (Grand Rapids: Eerdmans, 2004), 30.

dian theologians have read the account of Jesus on the road to Emmaus where it is said that "he explained to them what was said in all the Scriptures concerning himself" (Luke 24:27) and applied it to Jesus' presence in India today whereby he walks by Indian Christians and explains to them how the Indian scriptures point to and bear witness to him.[17] Some Indian Christians even include readings from the Vedas or the Upanishads in Christian worship services.[18] In fact, A. J. Appasamy, who was a well-known Indian bishop of the Church of South India and considered one of the fathers of Indian Christian theology, published a book titled *Temple Bells* that was a collection of readings taken from a wide variety of Hindu sacred texts. The book was designed to be used devotionally and liturgically by Indian Christians. In his preface to *Temple Bells* Appasamy sets forth several reasons why Indian Christians should become acquainted with the sacred texts of Hinduism. Although published in 1930, the reasons Bishop Appasamy gives remain essentially unchanged even in the contemporary discourse.[19] First, he reminds the reader that Jesus "came to fulfill, not to destroy" (Matt. 5:17). Appasamy is writing in the nineteenth-century heyday of "fulfillment" theology, so this would strike a very concordant theme in his readers. He urges Christians to take special note of "the impulses, instincts, questions, longings and aspirations" that are reflected in these texts. Only by looking intently at the Hindu questions can we truly grasp how Jesus comes to India as the answer to, and the fulfillment of, the deepest longings of the Hindu heart.[20] Second, Bishop Appasamy points out that only by reading Hindu sacred texts can Christians become

17. See, for example, Pal Puthanangady, "The Attitude of the Early Church Towards Non-Christian Religions and Their Scriptures," in *Research Seminar on Non-Biblical Scriptures,* ed. D. S. Amalorpavadass (Bangalore: National Biblical, Catechetical and Liturgical Centre, 1974).

18. A. J. Appasamy, *The Gospel and India's Heritage* (New York: SPCK, 1942), 77. There are several articles on this in *Research Seminar on Non-Biblical Scriptures* (see previous note). See especially IV.14, "Reflections on Hindu Religious Texts," by Ignatius Puthiadam, S.J.; and III.2, "Reflections of a Christian on the Upanishads," by Sr. Vandana. See also M. Amaladoss, S.J., "Other Scriptures and the Christian," *Indian Theological Studies* 22, no. 1 (March 1985): 62-78.

19. The following four reasons may all be found in A. J. Appasamy, ed., *Temple Bells* (London: SCM, 1930), viii-ix. It should be noted that while Appasamy believed in the value of Christians knowing the Hindu scriptures he did not accept the idea that the Hindu Scriptures could in any way replace the Old Testament. He believed that the Hindu scriptures could "supplement, not supplant" the Old Testament. See A. J. Appasamy, *Christianity as Bhakti Marga* (Madras: Christian Literature Society for India, 1930), 166.

20. A number of well-known books have been written that seek to demonstrate how Jesus is the fulfillment of Hinduism. See, for example, Raimundo Panikkar, *The Unknown Christ of Hinduism* (Maryknoll, NY: Orbis, 1994); E. Stanley Jones, *Christ of the Indian Road* (Nashville: United Methodist Publishing House, 2001), and J. N. Farquhar, *The Crown of Hinduism* (London and New York: Oxford University Press, 1913).

acquainted with the "storehouse of terms, images and metaphors" that have become "a great charm for the Indian mind." Hindu religious and philosophical vocabulary, with all of their stock images and metaphors, continue to dominate Christian language discourse in India. For example, Krishna Mohan Banerjea, another pioneer of Indian theology, published his landmark book under the title *Christ the True Prajapati.* The book with its strange title remains unintelligible to someone who is not familiar with the importance of the *Prajapati* figure in the Hindu Vedas. *Prajapati* is a cosmic figure who sacrifices himself to create the world. Banerjea draws upon this powerful image that resides as a stock image in the consciousness of Indians and argues that Christ fulfills and completes the sacrificial figure of *Prajapati* by becoming the true and final sacrifice and the progenitor of a new, redeemed world. Third, Appasamy goes on to argue that the "loving, joyful abandon to God" that is conveyed through the devotion of Hindus can be an inspiration to Christians who are also called to be wholeheartedly devoted to God. Appasamy's doctoral research at Oxford University focused on reading John's Gospel in light of the Hindu devotional movement known as *bhaktism.*[21] Finally, Appasamy is convinced that only by reading Hindu sacred texts such as the Vedas, the Upanishads, and the Bhagavad-Gita can someone really understand the Bible. He argues that many of the traditional Eastern emphases that were "inherent in Christian thought" have been lost in the long sojourn of Christianity in the Western world. Now that Christianity is coming back to its home in Asia, the Christian texts can be read with greater clarity and power, for, as Appasamy writes, "it is when the Bible is placed in its old environment that it can be fully understood."[22]

Appasamy's reflections raise important questions about the relationship of a Christian believer to the sacred texts of their pre-Christian past. How does a well-defined canon like the Bible relate to non-canonical sacred materials? Can non-canonical materials that form the sacred texts of other religions be used as a *preparatio evangelica*? By not acquainting ourselves with their own pre-Christian texts, are we unwittingly contributing to promoting a kind of spiritual amnesia, whereby we assume that when someone comes to Christ, everything in their past must be jettisoned to make room for Christ? Should Christians make use of the sacred text of another religion if it helps them in communicating the Christian gospel? These are a few of the issues this chapter seeks to address that are not normally reflected on in a traditional theology class when considering issues of inspiration, revelation, and canonicity.

21. A. J. Appasamy, *The Johannine Doctrine of Life: A Study of Christian and Indian Thought* (London: SPCK, 1934). Later, Appasamy published his well-known book, *Christianity as Bhakti Marga,* now reprinted (Whitefish, MT: Kessinger, 2010), which is a more popularized version of his doctoral research.

22. Appasamy, ed., *Temple Bells,* ix.

The Canon of the New Testament and Its Relationship to Other Texts

Very early on the church held a virtual unanimity regarding the inspiration of the twenty-seven books that today comprise the New Testament.[23] Although there have been a few dissenting voices, the fact that Roman Catholics, Protestants, Anglicans, Pentecostals and Eastern Orthodox Christians virtually all agree on the extent of the New Testament canon is quite remarkable. My purpose here is not to focus on the canon of the New Testament per se, but rather to examine the ways in which the New Testament canon has come in contact with other sacred or authoritative texts. This is an issue that has been largely ignored in traditional seminary training in the West and yet is becoming increasingly important in today's global context. In the West, it is rare to find someone who has more than a cursory knowledge of the sacred texts of other religions. In contrast, because Christians in the Majority World are often in settings that are dominated by other religions, it is not uncommon to meet a Christian with a Muslim or Hindu or Buddhist background who has an intimate knowledge of another sacred text. Because there are so many facets to this issue I will begin by setting forth the four main ways in which the New Testament canon interacts with other sacred and/or authoritative texts. This chapter will then focus on the last two of the four because they represent the issues most neglected by evangelical scholarship.

Four Ways Our Canon Interacts with Other Sacred/Authoritative Texts

1. Old Testament in the New Testament

The first and most obvious way that the New Testament canon interacts with another sacred text is through the extensive quotation and application of texts from the Hebrew canon that appear in the New Testament. In the case of the New Testament canon the hundreds of quotations from the Law, Prophets, and Writings of the Jewish canon that we call the Old Testament are fully accepted and received without question as canonical within their new home in the New Testament because the entire corpus of inspired writings within Judaism was accepted *a priori* as inspired by the newly emerging Christians since the Christian church was birthed out of Judaism. The apostle Paul alone quotes the Old Testament eighty-one times. The most common type of Jewish text that is incorporated into the New Testament canon are texts the early Christians believed pointed to Jesus

23. For fuller discussions of canonicity see Bruce Metzger, *The Canon of the New Testament* (Oxford: Clarendon, 1987), and R. Laird Harris, *Inspiration and Canonicity of the Scriptures* (Greenville, SC: A Press, 1995).

Christ, thus demonstrating continuity between the Old Testament texts and the fulfillment now being proclaimed in Jesus Christ. Therefore, texts such as Psalm 2, Psalm 16:10, Psalm 110, and Isaiah 53 are quoted in the New Testament and applied to Jesus Christ. The Christian use of the Old Testament texts is particularly interesting because the early followers of Christ quoted from this canon as a means to authenticate and bring legitimacy to their message. So, in some ways, the full acceptance of the New Testament canon was, in part, contingent upon the idea that the New Testament proclamation was consistent with, and a fulfillment of, the pre-Christian sacred writings they had already received and accepted as Jewish believers. This is the source of the idea that the entire New Testament is hidden in the Old Testament and the entire Old Testament is revealed in the New Testament.[24] This is an area that has received considerable attention by Christian scholarship and so does not concern us in this chapter.

2. *Non-Canonical "Jesus Material" Used in the Canonical Texts*

A second way the New Testament canon interacts with authoritative sources is the way in which authoritative source material about the life and teachings of Jesus Christ eventually appears in the received canonical texts. It has long been observed, for example, that Matthew and Luke seem to share a common source not available to Mark. This source has often been called "Q" after the German word *Quelle,* meaning source. The existence of "Q" is, of course, a conjecture, but it remains one of the leading explanations for the structure and wording similarities between Matthew and Luke.[25] We have other examples where the Apostolic tradition (*paradosis,* i.e., "passing down" or "handing down") is apparently larger than what was eventually included in the Gospels. The apostle John makes his well-known statement in the last verse of his Gospel that if everything Jesus did were written down then "even the whole world would not have room for the books that would be written" (John 21:25). The apostle Paul also quotes "the words of the Lord Jesus himself" when he said, "it is more blessed to give than to receive" (Acts 20:35) although that saying of Jesus never appears in any of the four canonical Gospels. Similarly, the account of the woman caught in adultery in John chapter 8 does not appear in the earliest manuscripts of John's Gospel, but is widely accepted as an authentic story of Jesus. Apparently, part of the Holy Spirit's work of inspiring the writers of the Gospels was helping them in their

24. This is also the source of the saying *universa scriptura de solo Christo est ubique* (everywhere the whole of Scripture is about Christ alone).

25. For an extensive discussion concerning hypotheses regarding sources for and relationships between the Synoptic Gospels see E. P. Sanders and Margaret Davies, *Studying the Synoptic Gospels* (Philadelphia: Trinity Press International, 1989).

selection of which texts to use in conveying their gospel message. This is also an area that has received considerable scholarly attention and, therefore, will not be under consideration here.

3. *Non-Canonical, Non-Christian Texts in the New Testament*

The third way the New Testament canon interacts with other sacred or authoritative texts is actually an extension of the second, but it is important for our purposes here to treat separately. This is the borrowing, use, and adaptation of non-canonical sources that have no natural connection to the Christian movement (as the Jesus material did) but eventually find their way into biblical text. This is important not only because it has not received sufficient attention by evangelical scholars, but because there are several ways this area under consideration is being used and applied today by Christians in the Majority World that deserve careful scrutiny and reflection.

Every student of the Old Testament is familiar with examples in the Old Testament where a rather strange non-canonical text is quoted. For example, Numbers 21:14 quotes from the *Book of the Wars of the Lord* which is no longer extant but appears to be an ancient collection of war songs that were used to worship God in times of conflict. Other examples include Joshua's command for the sun to stand still during his conflict with the Amorites (Josh. 10:12-13) and David's mourning of Jonathan's death (2 Sam. 1:17-27). In both instances they quote from the *Book of Jashar,* a text that was never received as part of the Jewish canon. These quotes, although non-canonical, seem to come from sources that arise out of the experience and worship of the People of God in a way similar to the "Q" document noted above.

In the New Testament we encounter several examples similar to what we have observed in the Old Testament. However, we also observe some distinctively new elements. Perhaps the best-known quotation in the New Testament of a non-canonical source occurs in the Book of Jude. Jude recounts in some detail a dispute between the archangel Michael and the Devil over the body of Moses. This dispute is not recorded in the canonical texts of Judaism, but the early church fathers wrote that the account was recorded in a Jewish work known as the *Assumption of Moses,* which is no longer extant. Later in his Epistle, Jude quotes from the *Book of Enoch* as follows:

> Enoch, the seventh from Adam, prophesied about these men: "See, the Lord is coming with thousands upon thousands of his holy ones to judge everyone, and to convict all the ungodly of all the ungodly acts they have done in the ungodly way, and of all the harsh words ungodly sinners have spoken against him." (Jude 14-15)

The Book of Enoch is a pseudonymous text written from the perspective of the famous patriarch Enoch who, according to Genesis, "walked with God; then he was no more, because God took him away" (5:24).[26] Jude quotes from a vision that Enoch had about the blessings that God has promised the righteous and the corresponding judgment upon the wicked (*1 Enoch* 1:9).[27] *The Book of Enoch* enjoyed wide popularity in the first century and Jude clearly assumes his readers are familiar with this non-canonical text. However, all of these quotations arise from well-known pseudepigraphical materials.

In the New Testament, however, we also encounter several examples of non-canonical material becoming part of the New Testament canon which find their origin in sources that have no connection with the life and experience of the people of God. On several occasions the apostle Paul quotes Greek poets who were popular in the first century. For example, Acts 17 records Paul's arrival in Athens where he is invited to the Areopagus to preach (Acts 17:16-34). His audience is Greek, not Jewish. Thus, rather than drawing from Jewish sources, either canonical or pseudepigraphical, Paul draws from popular allusions to their own Greek poets. In Acts 17:28 Paul quotes from "what appears to be the fourth line of a quatrain" from a poem popularly believed to be by the seventh-century B.C.E. Cretan poet Epimenides when he declares, "in him we live and move and have our being."[28] In the same verse Paul goes on to say, "As some of your own poets have said, 'we are his offspring,'" a quotation from the Cilician poet Aratus.[29] Later, when writing to the church in Corinth, Paul quotes from a well-known Greek comedy *Thais,* written by the Greek poet Menander, when he says, "bad company corrupts good character" (1 Cor. 15:33). Finally, one of the most memorable secular quotations used by Paul is from the poet Epimenides, a native of Crete, who wrote, "Cretans are always liars, evil brutes, [and] lazy gluttons," which Paul quotes in Titus 1:12.

The broad response to these texts, whether they are found in the Old or the New Testament, or their original source is from other religious or secular sources, has been to affirm that their presence in the canon of the New Testament in no

26. This Enoch is not to be confused with the Enoch in the lineage of Cain spoken of in Genesis 4:17. The Enoch quoted in Jude is in the lineage of Seth and is mentioned in Genesis 5:18-24 and 1 Chronicles 1:3. *The Book of Enoch,* as well as Jude, refers to him as the "seventh from Adam" (see *1 Enoch* 60:8 and 93:3).

27. Jude quotes from the Greek version of the text, which originally was in Aramaic. Earlier in Jude he assumes his readers are also aware of the punishment on the fallen angels recorded in *1 Enoch* 6–11.

28. F. F. Bruce, *The Book of Acts,* NICNT (Grand Rapids: Eerdmans, 1988), 338. The precise authorship of this line of Greek poetry is incidental to the argument of this research.

29. The quote appears in Aratus's *Phaenomena* as well as in Cleanthes (331-233 B.C.E.) in his *Hymn to Zeus.* The complete verse is as follows: "The sea is full of him; so are the harbors. In every way we have all to do with Zeus, for we are truly his offspring."

way should be taken to imply either the authority or the inspiration of the texts from which these quotations are taken. Nevertheless, once they are part of the received text of the New Testament they now fully share in the authority and inspiration of the Scriptures.

This trustworthy answer has served evangelical students in the West for many generations because for such a long time there were no major rivals to Christianity in the West. However, in the Majority World where preaching Christianity more closely resembles the first-century context, it has become incumbent upon evangelists, pastors, and scholars alike to demonstrate how Christianity is similar to or contrasts with the major world religion(s) with which people are already intimately acquainted. In the New Testament church we observed how vital it was to demonstrate the continuity between the Hebrew canon and the Christian proclamation. We accept the extensive presence of the Old Testament canon in the New Testament without question. However, we have observed how the Jewish connection was irrelevant to the Greeks, which at least partly explains Paul's quotations from non-canonical sources.

Many Christians in the Majority World have taken Paul's quotation of Greek poets or John's use of *logos* as an important precedent, modeling for us how we should communicate the gospel when we are in an Islamic, Buddhist, Hindu, secular, or any other setting where people are unfamiliar with biblical texts, prophecies, and expectations. Is this a legitimate application of Pauline or Johannine practice? Should we encourage insightful quotations from the Islamic Qur'an, the Hindu Upanishads, the Buddhist Tipitaka, or the Sikh Granth, if it will help us better to communicate the gospel in the varying contexts in which Christian witness takes place today? I raise this question because many make a strong distinction between a pastor quoting from an inspiring poem or a popular movie (which is accepted without question) and quoting from a text that is regarded as sacred by another religion. Quoting from the latter implies to some that the authority of that book in its entirety is accepted, thus unwittingly eroding confidence in the sole authority of the Bible. Is there a difference between quoting from a source that no one considers inspired and quoting from a source like the Qur'an, which is revered by the followers of Islam to be the absolute, inerrant Word of Almighty God? These are some of the questions that must be explored further in this chapter.

4. *Biblical Texts Appearing in the Canon of Another Religion*

The fourth and final way in which the biblical canon interacts with other sacred texts is the appearance of biblical texts (or allusions to those texts) in the sacred texts of non-Christian religions. Since the texts of most of the world's major religions pre-date the rise of Christianity, this is mainly a feature found in Islam and

Sikhism, the two most prominent world religions that emerged after Christianity, as well as the cult of Mormonism.[30] The best example among non-Christian world religions is to be found in the Islamic Qur'an, which contains hundreds of references to biblical texts, mostly from the Old Testament. Because the Bible was not translated into Arabic until after the death of Muhammad, we do not find many precise quotations of the Bible in the Qur'an. Nevertheless, the open use and adaptation of canonical materials is quite extensive. For example, as in the biblical account, Allah creates the earth in six days (Surah 25:59), culminating in the creation of the first man Adam. He and his wife eat the forbidden fruit and become aware of their nakedness (20:115-222). Allah sends Moses to confront Pharaoh, inflict the plagues on Egypt, and lead the Israelites out of Egypt by parting the Red Sea (26:9-75). Allah gives Moses the Ten Commandments on two tablets of stone, which, as in the biblical account, are subsequently broken (7:143-50). Throughout the Qur'an, many of the Ten Commandments are repeated, including the command to "serve no other gods" (24:55), the prohibition against making idols (4:116), the commands not to covet (4:32) or murder (6:151), and the command to honor your father and mother (6:151). In the Qur'an, one can read about familiar Old Testament stories such as Noah building the ark (11:25-49), King David's adultery with Bathsheba (28:21-25), the Queen of Sheba's visit to Solomon (27:22-44), and Jonah being swallowed by the great fish (37:139-48).[31]

The reliance of the Qur'an on the Jewish canon is quite extensive, but examples can also be found where the Qur'an is clearly influenced by the canon of the New Testament, although like the Old Testament, mostly through oral contact with people who were acquainted with the Scriptures rather than any intimate knowledge of the precise wording of particular texts. For example, the Qur'an affirms that Jesus was born without sin to the Virgin Mary (Surah 19:15-22). His ministry is foretold by John the Baptist, and he is a worker of many miracles (3:49, 50; 43:63). Jesus is also given several honorific titles that are also found in the Christian Scriptures such as the Word (3:39; 4:171) and the Messiah (3:45).

When Muslims who have an intimate knowledge of the Qur'an come to a saving faith in Jesus Christ and begin to read the Bible, they will quite naturally notice many of the parallels noted above, as well as some of the striking differences between the two texts that I have not taken time to highlight here.[32] But

30. The *Book of Mormon* also contains numerous allusions and citations that find their origin in either the Old or New Testaments. However, this research is limited to the texts of the world's major non-Christian world religions.

31. It is beyond the purpose of this essay to explore many of the places where the Qur'an contradicts some of the details of the Old Testament texts or is silent about key events in Israel's history. For more on this see my *Christianity at the Religious Roundtable: Evangelicalism in Conversation with Hinduism, Buddhism, and Islam* (Grand Rapids: Baker Academic, 2002), 177, and the chapter by Ida Glaser in this collection (chapter 32, above).

32. One of the differences that surprises Muslim-background readers of the Bible is that

certainly the issue is raised: How do we respond to the presence of inspired, canonical material that shows up in the Qur'an? Can the Qur'an be considered a trustworthy or reliable witness to truths that are consistent with biblical revelation? Do statements in the Qur'an which, for example, affirm that the Israelites crossed the Red Sea or that Jesus was born of a virgin become in any way "less true" or "less inspired" once they appear in the larger context of the Qur'an, whose inspiration and canonicity we roundly reject? These are a few of the questions that, along with those noted above, must be considered.

Canonicity, Revelation, and Inspiration in Other Religions

Before we can adequately address the questions that we have posed, it is important for students unfamiliar with non-Christian religions to recognize that terms such as canonicity, revelation, and inspiration have distinctively Christian connotations that sometimes do not have a clear parallel in other religious traditions. Thus, when Hindus, Buddhists, or Muslims use terms such as "revelation" and "inspiration," they frequently understand the terms quite differently than the way they are understood within the boundaries of historic Christian discourse. This, in turn, sometimes influences the way Christians with a Hindu or Buddhist or Islamic background have understood and written about these questions. It is vital, therefore, that we begin this part of our study with an overview of how these key terms are understood among those belonging to the major non-Christian religions. This chapter assumes that the reader has a general understanding of how these terms are used within the Christian tradition.[33]

Hinduism

Hindus accept neither the human authorship nor the historical origin of their most sacred texts. True knowledge (or what we would identify as the content of revelation) is eternally reverberating throughout the universe as a resonating sound known as *anāhata śabda,* that is, the "unstruck sound." This sound, which resonates eternally throughout the universe, is symbolized by the sound *"OM"* (pronounced AUM) and does not require, though it may not exclude, its being associated with the self-disclosure of a personal God. The way this sacred sound gets translated into textual form begins with unknown meditating sages who, at

---

Abraham (almost) offered up Isaac, rather than Esau, on the sacred mountain (see Gen. 22:1-18). For more on this, see my *Christianity at the Religious Roundtable,* 176-77.

33. For a basic introduction to these terms see Harris, *Inspiration and Canonicity of the Scriptures.*

the dawn of each of the unending creation cycles, rehear the knowledge that then forms the core content of the sacred oral tradition. This oral tradition was later written down and codified into sacred texts such as the four Vedas *(Rig, Sama, Yajur, Atharva),* and their famous philosophical/religious appendices known as the Upanishads.

There are several crucial points that need to be considered when examining the core Hindu sacred materials. First, the four Vedas should not be understood as four separate "books" containing independent, discrete data. Rather, they should be seen as more like four recensions of a common set of core material. This is particularly true of the first three Vedas. For example, there are 1,549 stanzas in the Sama Veda, but 1,474 of them are derived from the Rig Veda. The Sama Veda takes the basic hymns of the Rig Veda and reworks them into chants. Second, because of the sacredness of the earliest Vedic material, additional material gained authority by attaching itself as an appendage to the core material. The highest level of Hindu sacred material falls into four headings known as Samitas (Vedas), Brahmanas (commentary on the Vedas), Aranyakas (treatises by forest dwellers), and the Upanishads (philosophical and speculative material). Each of these subsequent strands is attached to the Vedas as extended appendices. Third, all of this material is collectively known as *sruti,* which means "that which is heard." This represents the highest form of revelation in Hinduism. Unlike Christian sacred texts, it is not rooted in history, but is eternally resonating in the universe as the "unstruck sound." However, there is no certainty that the sages have heard the full content of the "unstruck sound" or if it is even possible, so the resulting *sruti* canon leaves room for the possibility of further revelation as long as it does not contradict what has already been heard. That which is not yet "heard" is sometimes collectively referred to as the mysterious "fifth Veda."

Hindus also have a large collection of sacred materials that they recognize as having both human authorship and a particular historical origin. This material is known as *smrti,* which means "that which is remembered," and forms a lower, second-tier body of texts. This material includes such important texts as the philosophic *Sutras,* the Law Books, the *Puranas,* and the two great epics, *Mahabharata* (including *Bhagavad-Gita*) and *Ramayana. Smrti* is considered authoritative because it is held to be consistent with *sruti* and, indeed, much of the *smrti* material represents authoritative expositions of *sruti.* The line that separates *sruti* from *smrti* and *smrti* from non-authoritative texts is not absolutely fixed since Hindus are not in complete agreement as to what constitutes the *sruti* texts. Furthermore, there are also significant differences about what material can appropriately be considered *smrti.*[34]

34. Some, for example, include only the *Samhitas,* i.e., the original Rig, Sama, Yajur, and Atharva Vedas without the Brahmanas and Aranyaka supplementary material. There are also different views about the relationship of the Upanishads to the earliest Vedic material.

Sruti

Samhitas	**+ Brahmanas**	**+ Aranyakas**	**+ Upanishads**
Sacred Manual	*Prose Commentary*	*Forest Dweller Treatises*	*Speculative Treatises*
Rig (hymns)	composed by	(four stages of life)	108 classical
Sama (chant)	Brahmins	►student	18 principal
Yajur (sacred Formulas)		►householder	
Atharva (spells/esoteric)		►forest dweller	
		►Sannyasi (world renouncer)	

Smrti

Sectarian texts	**Epics**	**Songs/Poetical**
Maha-Puranas (old Stories) Agni, Bhagavata, Bhavishya, Brahma, Brahmavaivarta, Garuda, Harivamsa, Kurma, Linga, Markandeya, Matsya, Narada, Padma, Shiva, Sikanda, Vamana, Varaha, Vayu and Vishnu	Ramayana	Tevaram (Saivite)
	Mahabharata Bhagavadgita	Divya Prabandha (Vaishnavite)
		Ramcharitmanas of Tulsidas
Gitagovinda Bhaktisutras		
Upa-Puranas (smaller sects) Kula-Puranas (origins of castes)		

From this survey, what can we conclude about Hindu views regarding words such as inspiration, revelation, and canonicity? First, it is clear that the Christian canon is what Paul Hiebert would call a "bounded set," that is, it is fixed, whereas the Hindu canon is more of a "fuzzy set" since there is not complete agreement on whether the Vedas should be given priority over the Upanishads or even precisely which Upanishads should be accepted as *smrti,* and which should be rejected as sectarian documents.[35] Second, the most sacred texts in Hinduism *(sruti)* are not regarded as the result of any acts of divine personal, self-disclosure, as in Christianity. The "unstruck sound" is eternal, but non-personal. Indeed, most of the theistic self-disclosure forms of "revelation" occur in the lower-tier *smrti* texts.

35. See chapter 6, "The Category Christian in the Mission Task," in Paul G. Hiebert, *Anthropological Reflections on Missiological Issues* (Grand Rapids: Baker Books, 1994), 107-36.

Perhaps the best example of this would be the *Bhagavad-Gita,* which is believed to be the personal self-disclosure of Krishna to one of his devotees, Arjuna. Third, because the highest tier of Hindu sacred texts is eternal, they are not believed by Hindus to be related to any particular historical contexts, as is the case in the entire Christian canon.

Islam

Islamic views of canonicity, inspiration, and revelation are dramatically different from those of Hindus, but also have several important differences with the historic Christian view. Muslims believe that revelation is rooted in the divine will whereby Allah chooses to reveal his will to the human race. Like Christianity, Islam accepts propositional revelation. In other words, the content of the revelation has been perfectly recorded in truth statements that have been written down in the Arabic Qur'an (39:28; 43:3, 4). The 114 chapters or Surahs of the Qur'an, comprising 6,236 verses known as *ayat,* were revealed to one person, Muhammad (48:28, 29), through one mediator, the angel Gabriel (2:97), over a twenty-two-year period of time (610-632 C.E.). Muslims believe that all of the words contained in the revelation have been fixed on a heavenly tablet since before the world was created. This heavenly tablet is called in Surah 85:22 the "Preserved Tablet" to distinguish it from earlier revelations, which were not in Arabic and have become corrupted. The contents are thus recited to Muhammad who takes them down like dictation from the heavenly tablet, which is also known as the Mother of the Book:

> We have made it a Qur'an in Arabic, that you may be able to understand. And verily, it is in the Mother of the Book, with Us, high (in dignity), full of wisdom. (Surah 43:3-4)

The Qur'an is specifically in Arabic since "the twenty-eight letters of the Arabic alphabet form the language of the Divine Breath *(Nafs-al-Rahmān)* itself."[36] The contents of the Qur'an, therefore, represent a "bounded set."

The Arabic language makes clear distinctions between words for inspiration such as *ilham* or *wahl* as opposed to the term *tanzil* (sending down).[37] *Ilham* or *wahl* could happen to any spiritual person, like a great theologian or cleric, whose natural insights and creativity are heightened. Many people can be said to be inspired in this way. Prophetic utterances are also widely accepted in Islam. All

36. Sam Bhajjan, "The Muslim Understanding of the Scripture," in *Research Seminar on Non-Biblical Scriptures,* ed. D. S. Amalorpavadass (Bangalore: NBCLC, 1974), 493.

37. Keith Ward, *Religion and Revelation* (Oxford: Oxford University Press, 1994), 174.

Muslims believe that Allah has sent many prophets into the world and, in fact, to many different nations of the world.[38] For Muslims, the important point is not that Muhammad was the *only* prophet God ever sent, but that he was the *last* of a long line of prophets. Muhammad is considered the "seal" of the prophets, since the highest and most complete revelation was given to him. This is why the greatest form of revelation in Islam, known as *tanzil,* occurs only with the Qur'an. *Tanzil* means "sending down" and refers specifically to that revelation which was directly transmitted from the Preserved Tablet into the mind of Muhammad — although, remarkably, the Qur'an also applies the word *tanzil* to the Torah, the Psalms, and the Gospel *(Injil),* which along with the Qur'an have their ultimate source in the Preserved Tablet. However, Muslims regard these non-Quranic texts to be currently in a corrupted state that no longer reflects the purity of the original revelation.[39]

Just as Hindus have two separate categories of revelation, *sruti* and *smrti,* so Muslims, in practice, accept guidance from the Qur'an as well as the example of Muhammad *(sunna),* which has been codified in various collections of narratives known as *Hadith.* Both Sunni and Shiite Muslims accept the idea that the example of Muhammad, known as *sunna,* is an important source for guiding the Islamic community, particularly since the Qur'an is silent about many of the practical social and religious details that are essential for Islamic catechesis and the formation of a comprehensive legal code, known as *Sharia.* After Muhammad's death many stories began to circulate about events in the life of Muhammad, Muhammad's practice, and a number of pithy sayings of Muhammad that revealed his wit and wisdom. Eventually these stories were collected together into short narratives known as *Hadith.* Soon it became clear that many of the circulating *Hadith* were obviously spurious and had been invented to meet a particular religious or social need. Therefore Islam developed an elaborate system for verifying and authenticating *Hadith* by a very careful scrutiny of the sources, which traces the saying from the Prophet or one of his immediate companions to the point where it was written down as *Hadith.* This list of sources is known as the chain of *isnad* and

38. Traditionally, Islam accepts 124,000 prophets.

39. Muslim scholars are divided between those who believe that this Tablet has been eternally in the presence of Allah and those who believe that the revelation is the creation of Allah. The Mu'tazilah believe that the Qur'an must be created or Islam would be forced to accept that Allah is not the only eternal reality in the universe. The Ash'arite, in contrast, affirm speech as one of the eternal attributes of Allah and therefore affirm an eternal, uncreated Qur'an. Most Sunni Muslims accept a view of the Qur'an's eternality, whereas a minority (such as the Ismaili sect of Shiite Islam) believe that the Qur'an is a creation of Allah. For more on this debate about the Qur'an being created or uncreated see W. Montgomery Watt, *Islamic Philosophy and Theology* (Edinburgh: University of Edinburgh Press, 1985), 12-13, 35, 48, 58-59. This debate is important because an uncreated Qur'an would dramatically downplay the importance of the relationship of the Qur'an to the history of the Arab peoples.

is the closest Muslims come to practicing a form of textual criticism, which is forbidden for the Qur'an but was essential for establishing a reliable collection of *Hadith.*[40] Today, there are six collections of *Hadith* that the Sunni accept; the oldest and most reliable is the collection by al-Bukhari containing 7,300 *Hadith.*[41] Shiite Muslims have five collections of *Hadith* that they accept.[42]

With this brief overview, it should now be clear that Muslims have a more complex understanding of revelation than is generally thought. At the highest tier the text of the Qur'an stands as the embodiment of divine revelation. For Muslims, the Qur'an transcends human history and most believe its texts to be eternal. All faithful Muslims believe in the inerrancy of every word in the Qur'an, the text of which is beyond question and, indeed, cannot even be translated from Arabic into any other language without a loss in the beauty, meaning, and power of the Qur'an. At the second tier, Muslims believe in the revelatory nature of the *sunna,* which has been authenticated in various collections of *Hadith.* However, these passages are different from the Qur'an for three main reasons. First, the *Hadith* are not considered eternal since they find their origin firmly rooted in the life of Muhammad. Second, the *Hadith* do not constitute a "bounded set" for all Muslims everywhere, since various groups within Islam accept as authoritative different collections of *Hadith,* some of which support various sectarian beliefs or practices that other groups do not accept. Third, according to Muslims, Muhammad received the Qur'an as the direct revelation from Allah (through Gabriel). Muhammad is not considered a source of revelation, but merely the conduit through which it came. He heard it, he recited it, and, eventually, it was written down. Muhammad is a passive conduit. To suggest any influence from Muhammad is blasphemous. In contrast, Muhammad's life is the active and positive source of the *Hadith.* Muslims believe that because Muhammad is the greatest example of someone who fully submitted to Allah, his life, words, and actions *(sunna)* remain an important guide to Muslims throughout the world.

40. According to Islamic tradition, some disputes broke out among Islamic leaders about the proper reading of certain texts in the Qur'an. The third Caliph, 'Uthman (644-656), ordered an authentication of the text of the Qur'an that was eventually copied and sent throughout the Islamic realm. All textual variations were then destroyed.

41. The following six collections are accepted by Sunni Muslims: Bukhari (256 A.H.), Muslim (261 A.H.), Tirmizi (279 A.H.), Abu Daoaod (275 A.H.), An-Nasaer (303 A.H.), and Ibn Majaah (273 A.H.). The dates refer to the Islamic calendar, which began in 630 C.E. Although the al-Bukhari collection contains 7,300 *Hadith,* there are many duplications or very similar *Hadith,* but with different chains of *isnad.* Thus, al-Bukhari's collection contains 2,762 unique *Hadith.*

42. The Shiite accept the following five collections: Kafi (329 A.H.), Sheikh Ali (381 A.H.), Tahzib (466 A.H.), Istibsar (466 A.H.), and Ar-Razi (406 A.H.). Sometimes the *Hadith* in the Shiite collection are identical to the Sunni collection, but the *isnad* is established through respected Shiite leaders. However, there are some significant differences in the *Hadith* themselves since the Shiite place less weight on the reliability of the Companions of the Prophet than do the Sunni.

Buddhism

Unlike the Islamic Qur'an or the Christian Bible, Buddhists do not have a single sacred text that all the Buddhist faithful accept as authoritative in a final sense. In fact, there are actually thousands of sacred texts, known as sutras, in Buddhism. However, understanding how the diverse sacred textual traditions of Buddhism emerged requires some basic knowledge of the history of Buddhism.

The teaching of the Buddha is known generally as the *Dharma*. The basic message of the *Dharma* is to set forth a "middle way" (between extreme asceticism and materialistic consumption) which leads to enlightenment. The core content of the *Dharma* is attributed to some very early expositions by Buddha to his disciples known as "turning the wheel of *Dharma*" and is not understood as having any reference to a sovereign, objective God. Today, these early sermons include the four noble truths, the Eightfold Path, and the doctrines of dependent arising *(pratitya-samutpada)* and no-self *(anatman)*. The content of this teaching represents the core teachings of Buddhism. This teaching is non-theistic, denies the reality of the self, and rejects all ultimate first-causes.

The basic teaching or *Dharma* of Buddha became codified into a canon in the years following the death of the Buddha (456 B.C.E.) According to tradition, one of the Buddha's closest followers, known as Mahākāśyapa, called a Council of the Elders to discuss the movement. He questioned several of the Buddha's disciples who were able to recite from memory all of the discourses of the Buddha as well as the rules of the monastic life. Eventually, these teachings, along with some early theoretical discussions, were brought together into three collections known as *pitaka,* or baskets. The Basket of Discipline *(Vinaya Pitaka)* sets forth all of the rules of monastic Buddhism. The Basket of Discourses *(Sūtra Pitaka)* records the teachings of the Buddha. The Basket of Higher Teachings *(Abhidharma Pitaka)* contains profound discussions concerning philosophy and moral psychology. These three "baskets," known collectively as the *Tipitaka,* represent the closest thing to a Buddhist canon. In fact, they are often referred to as the Pali Canon, since they were originally written down in the Pali language. The earliest Buddhist tradition, known as *Therevada* (Way of the Elders), regards this canon as closed and final.

While most Buddhists accept the canonicity of the *Tipitaka,* the vast majority also believe that additional, and more advanced, teachings have been preserved in other sutras besides those found in the *Tipitaka.*[43] This view is held by the largest branch of Buddhism, known as *Mahayana.* The word *Mahayana* means "great vehicle" and is the popular, lay form of Buddhism that represents nearly 80 percent of all Buddhists in the world. The *Mahayana* believe that the Buddha

43. I say most because, for example, the Chinese Buddhists only accept four of the five sections of the *Tipitaka* — although one of the most important and popular divisions of the fifth section, the *Dhammapada,* does appear as a separate sutra in China.

turned the wheel of *Dharma* a second time and left teachings that are not found in the *Tipitaka*. In other words, the canon is effectively reopened by Mahayana Buddhists, and thousands of new sutras are added to the original Pali Canon.

Mahayana Buddhists resolve the "problem" of an expanding canon in two ways. First, some Mahayana groups will create a hierarchy of teachings that progressively reveals deeper and deeper insights into Buddhism, finally culminating in the particular text most revered by that group. Second, many Mahayana Buddhists will frankly admit that Buddhist teachings are dramatically different, even contradictory, but that the Buddha, like a great doctor, understood that different medicines were necessary to treat various diseases. In the same way, various teachings are tailor-made to fit various problems related to human ignorance and desire, which, according to Buddhists, must be extinguished.[44]

The notion of an expanding Buddhist canon is further complicated in several ways. First, some Mahayana Buddhists believe that because a particular sutra contains or surpasses all of the insights of all the other sutras, there is no point in studying any other text. This effectively means that different Buddhist groups may revere totally different sets of sacred texts. Second, sometimes particular commentaries on or summaries of certain sutras are revered as authoritative, thereby blurring the line between a sacred text and a commentary on a sacred text.

While a comprehensive survey of Mahayana sacred texts is beyond the scope of this study, it may be helpful and illustrative of the points made so far to introduce a few examples of how these principles work out in some of their most important texts. The earliest body of sacred literature in Mahayana is known as the *Prajnaparamita Sūtras,* meaning the Perfection of Wisdom teachings. These sutras date back to around the first century. However, over the next several hundred years some important summarizing works appeared which claimed to distill all the wisdom of the *Prajnaparamita* into condensed form. The two most famous summaries, known as the *Diamond Sutra* and the *Heart Sutra,* are among the most influential and famous texts within Mahayana Buddhism. They are frequently revered quite apart from the original texts that they summarize. Other famous sutras emphasize very different methods of liberation. For example, the famous *Lankavatara Sutra* emphasizes the importance of meditation in achieving liberation. In contrast, the *Lotus Sutra* emphasizes the role and assistance of certain enlightened beings known as Bodhisattvas who dwell in a transcendent realm and who can be called upon to assist a Buddhist in their path toward enlightenment. For many East Asian Buddhists, the *Lotus Sutra* is so revered that Buddhist scholar Paul Williams remarks that, for them, "it is the nearest Buddhist equivalent to a Bible."[45]

There are several aspects of how terms like "inspiration," "revelation," and "canonicity" are understood in Buddhism that must now be highlighted. First, it

44. This is known as the doctrine of expedient means.

45. Paul Williams, *Mahayana Buddhism* (London: Routledge, 1989), 141.

is clear that the textual canon of Buddhism is remarkably fluid when compared with Christianity and Islam. Indeed, even when compared with the sacred texts of Hinduism, Buddhism is far more fluid because in Hinduism all sacred texts are built on the foundation of the Vedas *(Samhitas)* and acknowledge its seminal authority. In contrast, Buddhism has developed several different lineages of textual traditions that effectively operate in isolation from one another. Second, because Buddhism is non-theistic, whatever texts are received as authoritative are not understood as the self-disclosure of an objective, transcendent God, but rather as the enlightened teachings of a Buddha.[46] Once the doctrine of God is rejected, it is not difficult to begin to grasp how dramatically this influences how words like "revelation" and "inspiration" are understood. For example, the entire content of Buddhist teachings is the result of sustained discipline and meditative skills developed through self-denial by the Buddha over hundreds of lifetimes until, finally, in an extreme meditative state, he grasped the insights that form the basis of Buddhist teachings.

Focusing the Questions: Two Categories of Questions

With this general background, we are now in a position to explore the questions raised earlier in the chapter. Essentially, all of the questions that were raised fall into two distinct categories. The first category seeks to understand how we regard those examples when our canonical texts have been incorporated into the sacred text of another religion. While there is evidence of some Christian influence in some of the texts of Hinduism and Buddhism that emerged after the onset of the Christian era, our focus is on Islam, since this is a major and undeniable feature of the Qur'an. The second category, which we will focus on more extensively, deals broadly with whether or not we should make use of the sacred texts of Hinduism, Buddhism, or Islam in communicating the gospel to those who are already familiar with these texts. If so, can any of these texts or any portions of these texts be regarded as inspired or in any way arising through some kind of revelation?

The Presence of Inspired, Revelatory Material in the Qur'an

The first category of questions relates to the relationship of biblical, canonical material to the sacred texts of other religions. Even if we reject the inspiration of the Qur'an, we still have to reflect on how we regard those portions of the inspired texts of Christians (Old and New Testaments) that have been incorporated into

46. Buddhism is in agreement in the rejection of theism, but is divided over whether there was only one Buddha or many buddhas.

the Qur'an. It is important to remember that Muslims do not believe that a single verse of the Qur'an was in any way influenced or taken from either Jewish or Christian sources. The Qur'an is verbally given to the Prophet Muhammad as a kind of dictation from the Preserved Tablet in heaven. Muhammad memorized it and, later, recited it to his followers who eventually, according to Muslims, wrote the recitations down exactly as they had heard them. It is therefore impossible for Muslims to make the distinction between what God revealed earlier in the Jewish Torah that Muhammad accepts as authoritative and incorporates into the Qur'an and what was revealed particularly to Muhammad that is unique to the Qur'an. In Islam the entire text of the Qur'an, all 6,236 verses of it, is viewed as a single unit in complete isolation from any of our texts. The Qur'an is *tanzil,* that is, a sending-down of Divine Truth, and should not, in their view, be confused with or discussed alongside of any other texts or lesser forms of "inspiration."

So despite the remarkable and extensive presence of Jewish and Christian writings that make their way into the Qur'an, there is no meaningful way to discuss this with a Muslim in an Islamic context. From the Christian point of view, since these texts had been taken out of their Christological and ecclesiological context when they were brought into the Qur'an, these texts may no longer be spoken of as either inspired or revealed, even though those particular statements which the Qur'an has incorporated into its text without distortion remain trustworthy and true.

Using Their Texts in a Christian Context

We are now prepared to examine the second category of questions related to the use and/or acceptance of the non-biblical sacred texts of other religious traditions. In December of 1974 Roman Catholic scholars in India convened a week-long conference in Bangalore titled Research Seminar on Non-Biblical Scriptures. The papers and official statements from the conference were eventually published in a book containing more than 700 pages.[47] The central question that brought the conference together was this: Can we use the scriptures of other religions in our worship? This, in turn, led the conference to address a number of related questions, including whether or not the scriptures of non-Christians can be considered inspired or revealed. Many of the papers that appeared in the conference publication were also published in various academic journals that, in turn, generated considerable discussion on the topic, at least within India. In fact, it should not surprise us that the Research Seminar on Non-Biblical Scriptures was convened in India by Indian scholars, or that one of the most important

47. D. S. Amalorpavadass, *Research Seminar on Non-Biblical Scriptures* (Bangalore: NBCLC, 1974).

books published on the subject, titled *Inspiration in the Non-Biblical Scriptures,* was published by the Indian Jesuit, Ishanand Vempeny.[48] We have already noted that it was the Indian bishop of the Church of South India, A. J. Appasamy, who as early as 1930 published a collection of readings from Hindu religious literature to be used devotionally and liturgically by Christians. The reason is that one cannot live as a Christian in India and not be aware of the presence of 700 million Hindus whose religion has permeated virtually every aspect of Indian life and culture. Being a Christian minority in a country dominated by some other religion was the context of the early church as well as the context of most Christians in Asia today. Increasingly, Western Christians must learn important lessons from our Asian brothers and sisters in Christ who have hundreds of years of experience in facing what has become a relatively new phenomenon in the Western world. What lessons can we learn from Asian Christians? Two main lessons will be explored that will help prepare us to address the central questions.

Two Lessons from Asian Christians

1. Avoid Broad Condemnation or Naïve Acceptance of Non-Christian Texts

Asian Christians are generally more nuanced in their attitude toward non-Christian sacred texts. In the West, Christians tend toward two extreme views. On the one side there are the liberal Christians who have drunk deeply at the well of relativism. They are content to put all the world's sacred texts on the same shelf as equal partners. For them, the Upanishads are just as likely to yield spiritual light as the Sermon on the Mount. On the other side are the conservative Christians who have far less exposure to the actual texts of other religions and tend to react defensively to the suggestion of any spiritual light outside of the Bible. Far from yielding any spiritual insights, they point out that the Qur'an is a satanic book that does not acknowledge the full deity of Jesus Christ and has helped to lead millions of Muslims into condemnation. Likewise, the Hindu Upanishads are full of evil, spiritual darkness and deception and should be discarded to make room for the salvific message of the New Testament. To be fair, there are some who accept that one or two pearls might be found in these texts in the midst of heaps and heaps of worthless rubbish, but, generally speaking, Christians tend toward these two extreme views.

48. Ishanand Vempeny, S.J., *Inspiration in the Non-Biblical Scriptures* (Bangalore: Theological Publications in India; Poona: Sakal Press, 1973). Evangelical scholarship in the West has begun to discuss these issues in more detail. See, for example, Gerald McDermott, *Can Evangelicals Learn from World Religions?* (Downers Grove, IL: InterVarsity, 2000).

Without a doubt, both of these extreme views are also found in India, but there is, comparatively speaking, a more substantial group in the middle who reject both extremes. Interestingly, both the liberal and the conservative extremes are rejected on the same grounds; namely, for being insufficiently Christocentric. The liberal view is rejected because it tends to relativize and downplay the uniqueness and centrality of Jesus Christ in the Christian message. The conservative extreme is also rejected because it tends to lock Jesus Christ up inside the covers of a book and forget that he is also "the light which gives light to every man" (John 1:9). Practically speaking, this places Christology as a subset of bibliology. Instead, they argue that there are rays of light present in the sacred texts of India which, however dim, ultimately point to and find their fulfillment in Jesus Christ. This leads us, quite naturally, into the second basic lesson that we can learn from our Christian brothers and sisters who live in Asia.

2. *Christ Does Not Arrive in Any Culture as a Stranger*

Asians insist that Christ does not arrive in Asia as a stranger. Asians do not have to experience spiritual amnesia when they receive Jesus Christ as their Lord and Savior. Ishanand Vempeny in his *Inspiration in the Non-Biblical Scriptures* opens the book by retelling the story of the Islamic sacking of Alexandria. Reportedly, the Arab commander Amrouh did not know what to do with the Alexandrian library, which contained the literary masterpieces of the Western world and was considered the largest library in the world, even though portions of it had been destroyed by fire earlier. However, according to the Islamic legend, Caliph Umar gave the order to destroy the library because, he said, "The Qur'an contains all the truths that are worthwhile. Let every other book be reduced to ashes."[49] Although the account is probably an apocryphal caricature, it does illustrate an attitude that conveys the idea that the only way to fully affirm the worth of Holy Scripture is to insist that all other books are worthless. This notion is rejected, not only by Vempeny, but by many Indian Christians with a Hindu background who are trying to understand how Christ not only demolished the false doctrines and evil idolatry of their Hindu past, but how, at the same time, Christ came to fulfill and complete longings and aspirations that they had held as Hindus. Having taught in India over the last twenty years and having many students, colleagues, and friends who are Hindu-background Christians, I can say that when many of them look back on their past life in Hinduism and reflect on it as a Christian, they are aware of profound discontinuity as well as surprising continuity. When they look back on their past, they see not only deliverance from demonic deception, but also, quite remarkably, evidence of little windows of God's grace in preparing

49. Vempeny, *Inspiration in the Non-Biblical Scriptures,* xvi.

them, and drawing them, even while they were still Hindus, for the day when they would receive the full light and glory of the Christian gospel and live their new lives in the presence of the risen Christ.

These admonitions from our Indian brothers and sisters should at least give us grounds to consider the possibility of using non-biblical texts in the context of Christian worship or preaching, even if we are predisposed toward rejecting the idea. Nevertheless, for an evangelical fully committed to the final authority of the Bible, it is important that the biblical basis for such a practice be clearly and convincingly set forth. Is it biblical for Christians to quote Hindu sacred texts when communicating the gospel to Hindus?

Biblical Basis Explored: An Imaginative Journey from Text to Context

Earlier in the chapter we examined several passages where the apostle Paul quotes from well-known Greek poets and playwrights. It was argued that Paul quoted from these texts because he was preaching to Greeks who would not be easily persuaded by quotations from what they would have considered strange Jewish prophets who had anticipated the coming of a Jewish messiah. They were not Jews, and therefore the coming of a Jewish messiah would seem quite irrelevant to them. Even though the Old Testament is the inspired Word of God that provides the most trustworthy preparation for and anticipation of the coming of Christ, Paul, surprisingly, elected to utilize quotations from sources that he neither accepted as generally authoritative nor believed were inspired by God, but which he nevertheless used because it helped to corroborate his message in the hearts and minds of his pagan audience. The challenge, of course, is making the leap from the first century to the twenty-first century. Can Paul's practice become an example for us to follow today?

In order to answer this, let us begin by using a bit of imagination in order to apply this biblical account to a more contemporary situation. What if the apostle Paul were preaching the gospel to Hindus in India, rather than to Hellenistic pagans in the Roman empire? What if we found the apostle Paul standing in the holy city of Varanasi on the banks of the Ganges River rather than on top of Mars Hill in Athens? In some ways the scene would be very familiar to Paul. If you are standing on top of Mars Hill the most imposing visual site is the massive Parthenon, the great temple of the goddess Athena, which is immediately to the southeast of Mars Hill. Likewise, if Paul were in Varanasi and he stood on the banks of the Ganges River, the most imposing visual site is the great Kashi Vishwanath Temple of Lord Shiva, the god of the Ganges River.[50] It is believed that

50. Kashi is the ancient name of modern day Varanasi, a city the British called Benares. Vishwanath means Lord of All.

the Ganges River flows from Shiva's hair and anyone who dips in these sacred waters will have their sins washed away. For centuries Hindus have made the long and arduous pilgrimage to this city, considered the holiest city in India, and, like Athens, one of the oldest cities on earth. The Scripture records that on Mars Hill Paul saw dozens of altars with inscriptions to various gods and goddesses, including one with the inscription, "to an unknown god" (Acts 17:28). Likewise, if Paul were in the city of Varanasi and walked along the banks of the Ganges he would see hundreds of shrines and temples and altars to various gods and goddesses in the Hindu pantheon. While in Athens, the Scriptures tell us that Paul got into a dispute with a group of Epicurean and Stoic philosophers who were two of the major intellectual rivals of that time (Acts 17:18). If Paul were to stay long in Varanasi he would soon find himself in a dispute with philosophers who teach at the famous Benares Hindu University located in Varanasi. Followers of the great philosophers Sankara and Ramanuja still debate the nature of God, the reality of the world, and the best path to salvation. Finally, Paul's Hindu audience in Varanasi would be just as ignorant of Jewish promises and prophets found in the Old Testament as were those "men of Athens" who heard Paul's message on Mars Hill.

In such a situation, would it not be just as unlikely that the apostle Paul would try to convince Hindus of the gospel by quoting from foreign Jewish prophets about whom they knew nothing? If Paul were to walk around Varanasi for long he would notice that the Hindus, like the Athenians, are very religious. They take great pride in the outward religious displays of sacrifice, self-denial, pilgrimage, and so forth. One of the most important messages for a Hindu to hear is that outward ritual and outward religiosity have no benefit, because God looks into our hearts. Paul might quote the well-known text from 1 Samuel 16:7, "The Lord does not look at the things man looks at. Man looks at the outward appearance, but the Lord looks at the heart." But then, to corroborate this text I can certainly see the apostle Paul going on to say, "for even as your own poet, Tukārām has said, *'the shell of the coconut is hard, but the inside is excellent. In accordance with this, remember that purity inside is what we aim at . . . the value of a thing depends on its inner qualities.'*"[51] Quoting Tukārām in such a context does not give an exalted or inspired status to Tukārām's poem any more than Paul's quotation of Epimenides' poem *Cretica* gave it any kind of special status. Yet it serves as a powerful indigenous corroboration of the biblical text that brings the message of Jesus Christ into their worldview, rather than insisting that they relate to Christ as a stranger.

51. J. N. Fraser and K. B. Marathe, *The Poems of Tukarama,* vol. III, p. 197, as quoted in A. J. Appasamy, *Temple Bells,* 84. Tukārām was a seventeenth-century Marati poet-saint from Maharashtra. Tukārām was a devotee of the god Krishna, and his poems are filled with love and adoration of Krishna. They are used as sacred texts in the *bhakti* tradition of Hinduism.

Guidelines for Use of Non-Biblical Sacred Texts

I do believe that the biblical account in Acts 17 provides a convincing precedent for the use of non-biblical sacred texts in certain *limited* contexts. However, I would like to suggest three guidelines in the use of such texts. First, the use of these texts should be limited to *evangelistic outreach* where the audience is predominately non-Christian and is acquainted with the texts that are being quoted. Paul's quotation of these texts on Mars Hill is clearly in an evangelistic context. His audience would probably not be familiar with a Jewish prophetic writing such as *Isaiah,* but were well acquainted with a text like *Hymn to Zeus* from which Paul quotes. The context of Paul's use of these texts on Mars Hill seems to be a good rule of thumb to follow today as well.

Second, these texts should only be used to provide a *corroborative witness* to a biblical message, rather than an independent testimony in isolation from the biblical witness. As Christians, we do not accept the final authority of the Upanishads any more than Paul accepted the final authority of the *Hymn to Zeus.* However, this fact does not exempt these texts from being used in a way that serves to corroborate a biblical message. In a courtroom, sometimes even convicted felons are called upon to testify because they heard or saw something that helps to advance the prosecution's case. In the same way, a Christian may find it advantageous to call upon external witnesses outside the Bible to assist in corroborating the biblical message. For example, if you were preaching to Hindus and wanted to demonstrate the inner longing all men and women have for truth and eternity, it would help to quote what is widely believed to be one of the best-known prayers in India, taken from the Upanishads:

> From the unreal, lead me to the real!
> From darkness, lead me to the light!
> From death, lead me to immortality. (Brihad-Aranyaka Upanishad 1.3.28)[52]

Such a text could serve as a corroborative witness to Paul's point in Acts 14 when he declared that even among the pagans, God has "not left himself without a witness" (Acts 14:17). Using a non-biblical sacred text as a corroborative witness serves to sharpen the biblical message and helps to demonstrate that Jesus does not arrive in India as a stranger, but in answer to the prayers of Hindu hearts.

Third, any non-biblical sacred text that is quoted should be lifted out of its original setting and clearly reoriented within a new *Christocentric setting.* Both Epimenides and Aratus were, like Tukārām, non-Christian poets committed to the worship of false gods. Epimenides' poem, which Paul quotes from in Acts 17,

52. S. Radhakrishnan, ed., *The Principal Upanishads* (Amherst, NY: Humanity Books, 1992), 162.

is, in its original context, words on the lips of Minos, Zeus's son, and was given in praise of Zeus. Minos declares, "But thou art not dead; thou livest and abidest forever, *for in thee we live and move and have our being.*"[53] Paul clearly rejected that Zeus was alive and "abidest forever," but he boldly applies it to the Christian gospel, calling on pagans to reach out and receive God's grace in their lives. The original quote from Aratus was also in honor of Zeus. The original line of the poem is as follows: "It is with Zeus that every one of us in every way has to do, *for we are also his offspring.*"[54] However, in its new setting Paul uses the quote to demonstrate that the entire human race is under the rule of the living God of biblical revelation and that he is calling the whole world to account and will judge the world by and through Jesus Christ (Acts 17:28-31). This is the basic pattern of the apostle Paul, whether he is quoting from the sacred biblical Scriptures or from a pagan source. He imports the text out of its original context and reorients it within a new, distinctively Christian setting.

Using these texts in this limited fashion clearly conveys that these texts are not regarded as inspired or revelatory in the Christian sense of the word. The Christian understanding of inspiration and special revelation cannot be understood in isolation from the broader theological framework of Christology and ecclesiology. All inspired texts must ultimately bear witness to Christ, who is the Word made flesh. Furthermore, all inspired texts in the Christian sense of the word are those that have been given to serve the community of God's redeemed people, the church, which is the Body of Christ. This is how even a partial quotation from the *Hymn to Zeus* can become part of the inspired text of the New Testament. It is only because it has been reoriented within this larger Christological and ecclesiological framework. Conversely, even if John 3:16 were incorporated into the sacred text of another religion it would no longer be regarded as inspired because it would no longer lie within the larger context of Christian revelation. The entire Christian understanding of special revelation is predicated on our larger understanding of Christ who embodies and fulfills all other revelation and the purpose of that revelation, which is to call forth the redeemed community, the body of Christ.

It is therefore impossible to speak about Christian views of inspiration and revelation outside of the larger context of Christology and ecclesiology. The Upanishads or the Qur'an or the Tipitaka do not bear witness to Christ and do not serve the church and therefore cannot be regarded as inspired. This does not mean, of course, that these texts contain only error. On the contrary, God has

53. As quoted in Richard N. Longenecker, "The Acts of the Apostles," *The Expositor's Bible Commentary,* vol. 9 (Grand Rapids: Zondervan, 1981), 476; italics mine, to emphasize the portion that Paul quotes.

54. Longenecker, "The Acts of the Apostles," 476; italics mine, to emphasize the portion that Paul quotes.

made certain truths about himself known universally, which is why, as noted above, Paul can declare that God has not left himself without a witness. In fact, it seems that God has provided at least two universal witnesses to himself. The first is the external witness that is heard through the glorious proclamation of creation: "the heavens declare the glory of God" (Ps. 19:1). The second is an internal witness heard through the voice of conscience, which demonstrates that "the requirements of the law are written on their [gentile] hearts" (Rom. 2:15).[55] We should expect that insights derived from these two universal witnesses might be reflected in the world of literature, including non-Christian sacred texts. We would be surprised if they did not. Wherever such texts help to corroborate the Christian message, we rejoice, but because the overall contexts of these sacred texts are not specifically related to either Christ or to the church, we cannot consider them inspired or revealed in the special Christian sense of those words.

Conclusion

This chapter has sought to examine two questions. First, how should we regard the presence of material borrowed from the Bible that has been incorporated into the sacred texts of other religions, particularly Islam? Second, can Christians make use of sacred textual material from other religions in worship, preaching and teaching in Christian settings? We have concluded that while we should not use these texts liturgically, Christians can and, indeed, *should* make use of appropriately selected materials from the sacred or secular traditions that surround us as long as certain guidelines are followed. This chapter has also sought to establish that a doctrine of revelation and inspiration is unintelligible for the Christian apart from the larger framework of Christology and ecclesiology. Therefore even though the sacred texts of other traditions sometimes make statements that are true and insightful, inspirational, and even spiritually edifying, these texts cannot be regarded as inspired or revelatory since they lack the proper Christological and ecclesiological context. This even applies to the biblical material itself, which in the case of the Qur'an has been taken out of its original biblical setting and set within the context of the Qur'an. Even though these specific texts remain true in their original setting, they can no longer be regarded as inspired or revelatory when they are taken out of their original context and taken to mean something quite different.

55. I am following the widespread interpretation that this text refers to gentile *unbelievers*. However, I acknowledge that some major writers such as Augustine and Barth, among others, argue, less persuasively, that this text refers to gentile *Christians,* understanding the phrase "by nature" to modify "do not have the law."

THIRTY-FOUR

Buddhist Sutras and Christian Revelation

Harold Netland and Alex G. Smith

It was the nineteenth-century pioneer of comparative religions Max Müller (1823-1900) who, in speaking of the value of the study of other religions, came up with the oft-quoted dictum: "He who knows one knows none."[1] While this should not be pressed too far, there is some wisdom here. One can, of course, have a fully adequate understanding of the Christian faith without studying Zoroastrianism or Baha'i. But Müller's point was that often in studying another religion one comes to see one's own tradition in a fresh light.

The point can be illustrated by considering one thing that many religions share, namely, commitment to a particular text or set of texts as especially authoritative. For Christians, the sacred scripture is the Bible. But if by "scripture" we mean written texts that are regarded as especially authoritative for a particular religious tradition, then each of the world religions includes an authoritative scripture.[2] It is easy to assume that the nature and function of sacred scripture in the various religions is essentially the same. Thus, Christians might take it for granted that adherents of other religions view their sacred texts much as Christians regard the Bible. But this is mistaken. Sacred texts are understood in rather different ways and serve different purposes in religions such as Judaism, Christianity, Islam, Hinduism, Buddhism, or Sikhism.

The Buddhist and Christian understandings of scripture are especially divergent, since the broader worldviews within which the respective views of sacred texts are embedded are so different. This chapter will explore in a general way the place of scripture in Buddhism and then conclude by contrasting Buddhist perspectives with some Christian beliefs concerning divine revelation. Examination of the role of authoritative texts in a religion such as

1. As cited in John R. Hinnells, "Why Study Religions?" in *The Routledge Companion to the Study of Religion,* ed. John R. Hinnells (New York: Routledge, 2005), 14.

2. See William A. Graham, "Scripture," in *The Encyclopedia of Religion,* 2nd edition, vol. 12, ed. Lindsay Jones (Farmington Hills, MI: Thomson Gale, 2005), 81-94.

Buddhism will highlight the distinctive place of divine revelation within the Christian faith.

Overview of Buddhism

Buddhism is a diverse family of religious and philosophical traditions which, although emerging originally in India, have developed over the past 2,500 years in many different cultures.[3] Buddhism quickly spread from its homeland into south, central, and east Asia. As Buddhist teaching was embraced by people in very different cultural and religious settings Buddhism itself changed, resulting in the enormous variety in teachings and practices among contemporary Buddhists. But all Buddhist traditions claim to trace their beliefs and practices in some sense back to the enlightenment of Gautama the Buddha and to the teachings deriving from this experience.

The Traditional Narrative

Siddhartha Gautama (or Sakyamuni, the sage of the *sakya* clan) lived in either the sixth or fifth century B.C.E., in what is now the border region of India and Nepal. Western scholars generally accept the dates 563-483 B.C.E. for Gautama's life, whereas Chinese and Japanese scholars often place him in the fifth century B.C.E. The Japanese scholar Hajime Nakamura, for example, argued for 466-386 B.C.E.[4] Questions about Gautama's life are complicated by the fact that written accounts of his life do not appear until some 400 years after his death. But the traditional narratives tell of young Gautama being brought up in a life of luxury.[5] Gautama rejected his palace life, however, and embarked upon a quest to discover the causes and cure to suffering. After experimentation with various ascetic meditative disciplines, Gautama became fully enlightened or awakened. The Buddha (the Awakened One), as he was now called, is said to have grasped the fundamen-

3. Helpful introductions to Buddhism include Donald S. Lopez Jr., *The Story of Buddhism: A Concise Guide to Its History and Teachings* (New York: HarperCollins, 2001); Donald W. Mitchell, *Buddhism: Introducing the Buddhist Experience,* 2nd edition (New York: Oxford University Press, 2008); and Richard H. Robinson and Willard L. Johnson, *The Buddhist Religion,* 4th edition (Belmont, CA: Wadsworth, 1997).

4. See Mitchell, *Buddhism,* 11; Hajime Nakamura, *Gotama Buddha* (Tokyo: Buddhist Books International, 1977), 12-14; Nakamura, *Gotama Buddha: A Biography Based upon the Most Reliable Texts,* vol. 1, trans. Gaynor Sekimori (Tokyo: Kosei, 2000); and David Edward Shaner, "Biographies of the Buddha," *Philosophy East and West* 37, no. 3 (July 1987): 306-22.

5. See, for example, the account in the *Buddhcarita* 4, in *Buddhist Scriptures,* ed. and trans. Edward Conze (New York: Penguin, 1959), 4-5.

tal causes of suffering and how to make them cease. Over the next forty-five years, the Buddha traveled widely, teaching and attracting many disciples.

The heart of the Buddha's teaching is the Four Noble Truths.[6] The First Truth states that all existence is characterized by *dukkha* (P),[7] that is, suffering, pain, or discontent. Even the most intense pleasures are temporary and all of existence involves a haunting unsatisfactoriness. The Second Truth holds that the root cause of such suffering is *tanha* (P), or thirst, craving, or desire. It is not simply wrong desires that produce suffering; desire itself results in pain. According to the Third Truth, when desire or craving ceases then suffering ceases as well. The Fourth Truth puts forward the Noble Eightfold Path, which provides the way to eliminate desire and suffering. The eight constituents of the Path are grouped into three divisions: morality (right speech, right action, right livelihood), concentration (right mindfulness, right effort, and right concentration), and wisdom (right understanding and right thought).

The Four Noble Truths exhibit an elegant simplicity and logical structure. An initial diagnosis of the cause of suffering is followed by a prescription for the cure. Both diagnosis and cure are based upon a sophisticated metaphysic that presupposes multiple rebirths regulated by the principle of *karma* (S) and the teachings of *anatta* (P), or absence of self, and *anicca* (P), or impermanence. Like most Indian religious and philosophical systems, the Buddha accepted the idea of multiple rebirths regulated by *karma.* Unlike Hindus and Jains, however, he taught a radical notion of the impermanence of everything apart from *nirvana* (S). What exists is in continual flux and beings are continually being reborn, with the conditions of one's rebirth being determined by previous dispositions and actions.

A consequence of the teaching on impermanence is the denial of the reality of a substantial, enduring soul or person. It was the Buddha's teaching on *anatta,* the denial of an enduring person or soul, that set his teachings apart from that of the Brahmins and Jains. But if there is no soul or enduring person, what then is reborn? The Buddha taught that what is passed on from one life to another is the cumulative karmic effects of actions and dispositions which, in the next life, combine under appropriate conditions to form again the illusion of an enduring self. When the fires of desire and the conditions producing rebirth are eliminated, there is no more birth and what obtains is *nirvana,* the only reality that is permanent and unconditioned. The soteriological goal of early Buddhism was attaining *nirvana* by eliminating the causal conditions for rebirth.

6. A concise expression of the Four Noble Truths is given in the Buddha's first sermon, as found in the *Samyutta-Nikaya,* in *A Source Book in Indian Philosophy,* ed. Sarvepalli Radhakrishnan and Charles A. Moore (Princeton: Princeton University Press, 1957), 65.

7. Technical Buddhist terms will be transliterated from either Pali or Sanskrit, followed by "P" indicating Pali or "S" indicating Sanskrit.

In time, of course, Buddhists developed complex elaborations of these basic teachings, involving highly technical discussions of epistemology and ontology. Many schools developed, with Buddhism eventually evolving into three very broad traditions — the Theravada, Mahayana, and Vajrayana or Tibetan traditions. As we shall see, there are significant differences between them. Furthermore, running across all three traditions is the important distinction between "high" or philosophical Buddhism and "folk" Buddhism. The former refers to the intellectually sophisticated philosophical Buddhism practiced by scholars and monks, whereas the latter denotes the Buddhism of the laity, the ordinary men and women who often understand little of the doctrinal subtleties. Folk Buddhism typically combines Buddhist teachings with an assortment of folk religious beliefs and practices, including an enchanted world of spirits, gods, ghosts, demons, and magical forces that would be frowned upon by high Buddhism.

In order to understand global Buddhism today, we must make a further distinction that applies to the three broad traditions as well as to philosophical and folk Buddhism: earlier or premodern Buddhism throughout Asia must be distinguished from forms of Buddhism, both in Asia and the West, that are coming to grips with modernization and globalization. All of this makes for enormous diversity within what we commonly refer to simply as "Buddhism."

Buddhism has always been a missionary religion, moving beyond India first into what is today Sri Lanka and southeast Asia, then throughout north and east Asia. Buddhist teachings and practices were transmitted by merchants who came to India for business, converted to Buddhism and then returned to their homes with the new teaching.[8] According to tradition, King Asoka, the great third-century B.C.E. Mauryan ruler who converted to Buddhism, sent proclaimers of the Buddhist message to rulers in Syria, Egypt, and Macedonia in the West, and to Sri Lanka and southeast Asia to the south.[9] From the Indian subcontinent, Buddhism moved north into China sometime during the first century C.E., and then on into Korea in the fourth century. It was introduced into Japan in the sixth century and into Tibet in the seventh century. Although for over two millennia it was found exclusively in Asia, in the nineteenth and twentieth centuries Buddhism became established in North America and Europe, and it is today a genuinely global religion. Before considering Buddhist approaches to the scrip-

8. See Akira Hirakawa, *A History of Indian Buddhism: From Sakyamuni to Early Mahayana,* trans. and ed. Paul Groner (Honolulu: University of Hawaii Press, 1990), 76-77. On the movement of Buddhist missionaries from Asia to the rest of the world in the twentieth century see *Buddhist Missionaries in the Era of Globalization,* ed. Linda Learman (Honolulu: University of Hawaii Press, 2005).

9. Mitchell, *Buddhism,* 70-72. Richard Gombrich calls Asoka "the most important Buddhist layman in history," for "it was his patronage which made [Buddhism] a world religion" (Richard Gombrich, *Theravada Buddhism: A Social History from Ancient Benares to Modern Colombo* [London: Routledge & Kegan Paul, 1988], 127).

tures, we will highlight briefly the three major Buddhist schools and then note the emergence of what is now called Buddhist modernism.

Theravada Buddhism

Although no current Buddhist school can trace its origin directly to the time of Gautama, Theravada Buddhism is generally accepted as reflecting more closely the teachings of the early Buddhist community than other forms of Buddhism. It is found today in Sri Lanka, Burma, Thailand, Laos, and Kampuchea as well as in immigrant communities in the West.

Theravada Buddhism tends to be more conservative and less innovative doctrinally than other forms of Buddhism. For example, Theravada Buddhists accept the Pali Canon (see further below) as faithfully conveying the teachings of Gautama and thus as fully authoritative for Buddhist belief and practice. Mahayana Buddhists, by contrast, while acknowledging the authority of the Pali Canon also recognize many other *sutras* (S)[10] and commentaries as equally, and sometimes more, authoritative than the Pali texts.

While generally discouraging metaphysical speculation, the Theravada tradition emphasizes the Four Noble Truths and the Path of Purification, as outlined in the Noble Eightfold Path, as the way to enlightenment and *nirvana.* The one who follows the Path of Purification successfully is an *arahat* (P), or "worthy one," free from all defilements, and will not be reborn. Buddhists give special reverence to the Three Refuges or the Three Jewels — the Buddha, the *Dharma* (S; *Dhamma,* P), and the *Sangha* (S). One formally identifies oneself as a Buddhist with the public profession of the following formula:

> I go to the Buddha for refuge.
> I go to the *Dharma* for refuge.
> I go to the *Sangha* for refuge.

The contrast between those who seek refuge from suffering in unsatisfactory places and those who find refuge in the Buddha, the *Dharma,* and the *Sangha,* is expressed in the *Dhammapada (Sayings of Dhamma),* one of the most popular texts of Theravada Buddhism.

10. The term "sutra" can be used in either a general or a more specific sense. In a general sense "sutra" refers to texts from the Hindu Vedas as well as Buddhist writings, which are characterized by short, pithy verses conveying profound meanings. In a more technical sense "sutra" refers to the second of three collections of Buddhist writings (the *Tripitaka*) comprising the Pali Canon. A source of much Buddhist doctrine and moral teaching, the sutras include the discourses of the Buddha as well as other narrative material. See Kogen Mizuno, *Buddhist Sutras: Origin, Development, Transmission* (Tokyo: Kosei, 1982), 13-17.

Many for refuge go
To mountains and to forests,
To shrines that are groves or trees —
Humans who are threatened by fear.

This is not a refuge secure,
This refuge is not the highest.
Having come to this refuge,
One is not released from all misery.

But who to the Buddha, Dhamma,
And Sangha as refuge has gone,
Sees with full insight
The Four Noble Truths;

Misery, the arising of misery,
And the transcending of misery,
The Noble Eightfold Path
Leading to the allaying of misery.

This, indeed, is a refuge secure.
This is the highest refuge.
Having come to this refuge,
One is released from all misery.[11]

But who is the Buddha, and what are the *Dharma* and the *Sangha*? The term "Buddha" is not a proper name but rather is a descriptive title meaning Awakened One or Enlightened One. The term has become associated with Siddhartha Gautama after his enlightenment, but Buddhism from the earliest times has maintained that there were other Buddhas prior to Gautama and there will be others to come in the future. Mahayana Buddhism in particular postulates the reality of many Buddhas currently existing in other parts of this universe or in other universes. "The key role of a perfect Buddha is, by his own efforts to rediscover the timeless truths and practices of the *Dharma* . . . at a time when they have been lost to society."[12]

Theravada Buddhism has emphasized the humanity of Gautama the Buddha, discouraging speculation about his metaphysical status after attaining enlighten-

11. *The Dhammapada* 14.188-92, trans. John Ross Carter and Mahinda Palihawadana (New York: Oxford University Press, 1987), 35.

12. Peter Harvey, "Buddha," in *Encyclopedia of Buddhism,* ed. Damien Keown and Charles S. Prebish (London: Routledge, 2010), 93.

ment. Gautama was born as a human but, because of the perfections developed through his many previous lives, he was a human with extraordinary abilities that culminated in his enlightenment. Once enlightened, however, the Buddha was no longer merely a human, "as he had perfected and transcended his humanness."[13] He was beyond humans and the gods.[14] Sri Lankan scholar K. N. Jayatilleke notes,

> The idea that the Buddha was a "mere human being" is also mistaken. For when the Buddha was asked whether he was a human being, a Brahma (God) or Mara (Satan), he denied that he was any of them and claimed that he was Buddha, i.e. an Enlightened Being who had attained the Transcendent. This does not, however, make the Buddha unique for it is a status that any human being can aspire to attain.[15]

The term *Dharma* has various meanings in Indian religious and philosophical thought and is often translated into English as "truth," "universal moral order," "norm," "religion," "righteousness," "doctrine," "duty," or "proper conduct." In Buddhism *Dharma* refers to the teachings of the Buddha, who has discovered the eternal truth and has passed this on to others. "The *Dharma* itself, however, is transhistorical and exists whether or not it has been perceived by anyone or disseminated as a body of teachings over time by the Sangha."[16] The *Sangha* is the monastic community comprising the disciples of the Buddha who have committed themselves to living out the teachings of the Buddha. So the Three Refuges reflect the interrelationship between the eternal truth, the Buddha who discovers and passes on this truth, and the monastic community that maintains and practices this truth.

Theravada Buddhism, unlike some later forms of Mahayana Buddhism, insists that the individual is responsible for his or her own liberation or enlightenment. The Buddha did proclaim the *Dharma* and thus he can be said to assist all sentient beings. But it is up to each individual to grasp the truth, to appropriate it, and thereby to attain *nirvana*. Moreover, attaining enlightenment is something relatively few, and only those in a monastic community who have properly mastered the necessary disciplines under a qualified mentor, can hope to realize in this life. The laity must be content with trying to improve their condition of rebirth in the next life, eventually positioning themselves for possibly attaining *nirvana*.

13. Harvey, "Buddha," 93.

14. Buddhism does not deny the reality of gods and other supernatural beings, but it includes them within the causal nexus determining all existents and renders them irrelevant to attaining enlightenment. See U. Thittila, "The Fundamental Principles of Theravada Buddhism," in *The Path of the Buddha: Buddhism Interpreted by Buddhists,* ed. Kenneth W. Morgan (New York: Ronald Press Company, 1956), 71.

15. K. N. Jayatilleke, *The Message of the Buddha,* ed. Ninian Smart (New York: Free Press, 1974), 53.

16. Damien Keown, "Dharma," in Keown and Prebish, eds., *Encyclopedia of Buddhism,* 271.

Hope for a good rebirth has resulted in the importance of *punyu* (P) or merit in Theravada Buddhism. Traditional Buddhist cosmology includes many levels of heavens and hells, inhabited by gods, demigods, humans, animals, ghosts, and hell beings.[17] Rebirth is determined by the relative weight of "good *karma*" or meritorious actions over "bad *karma*." Many kinds of actions have become recognized as meritorious, so that their practice enhances one's standing in rebirth. The laity in Theravada traditionally are meticulous in giving alms to monks, practicing morality, respecting elders, listening to preaching, or even having one's son undergo ordination as a monk so as to enhance their lot in the next life. An elaborate system for attaining and transferring merit (what Gombrich calls "spiritual cash") has developed, so that merit can even be transferred from the living to those who have died.[18]

Mahayana Buddhism

From roughly 100 B.C.E. to 100 C.E. a new Buddhist movement emerged that identified itself as the Mahayana, or Great Vehicle, in contrast with what it somewhat pejoratively referred to as the Hinayana, or Lesser Vehicle. Mahayana Buddhism is today the dominant form of Buddhism in China, Korea, Vietnam, and Japan and is also found in the West. Like Theravada, Mahayana Buddhism claims to represent the original teaching of the Buddha.

Mahayana promised a more generous approach than the traditionalists offered. Whereas Theravada Buddhism restricted the path to liberation to the few who could master the requisite disciplines within a monastic community, Mahayana opened the way to many, offering a vast multitude of spiritual guides and saviors to assist in deliverance from suffering. Chief among these benevolent beings are the *bodhisattvas* (S). *Bodhisattvas* are supernatural beings who became the object of popular devotion and prayer, and who, out of compassion, come to the aid of sentient beings caught up in the cycle of rebirth.[19] *Bodhisattvas* have experienced enlightenment but they have taken a special vow to assist others to attain enlightenment rather than enter *nirvana* themselves. The *bodhisattva* came to represent the ideal of compassion and became the object of meditation, supplication, and even worship.

As Buddhism spread throughout Asia it encountered cultures and religious

17. See Lopez, *The Story of Buddhism*, 19-24.

18. Gombrich, *Theravada Buddhism*, 124-27; see also Alex G. Smith, "Transfer of Merit in Folk Buddhism," in *Sharing Jesus Holistically with the Buddhist World*, ed. David Lim and Steve Spaulding (Pasadena, CA: William Carey Library, 2005), 99-124.

19. See Paul Williams, *Mahayana Buddhism: The Doctrinal Foundations*, 2nd edition (New York: Routledge, 2009), 55-62; and Mitchell, *Buddhism*, 119-32.

traditions quite different from those of the Indian subcontinent. Buddhism in northern Asia has been remarkably flexible in adapting to new environments in China, Tibet, Korea, and Japan.[20] As it spread throughout eastern Asia, Buddhism was influenced by indigenous religious beliefs and practices. Moreover, the notions of rebirth and *karma,* so central to Indian religious and philosophical thought, were lacking in the Chinese context. Release from rebirth was thus not the burning issue for Chinese, who had a much more positive view of life, nature, and society. Consequently, one finds in the Mahayana tradition as it developed in China, Korea, and Japan a decreasing emphasis upon the notion of *nirvana* as release from rebirth and greater emphasis upon the idea of enlightenment in this life.

A further innovation in Mahayana Buddhism concerns the elaborate teachings on the Three Bodies of Buddha, three distinguishable, but closely related, levels or dimensions of the "Buddha essence."[21] According to this doctrine, the historical Gautama Buddha was a human manifestation of an underlying, all-inclusive Buddha essence, the *Dharmakaya* (S), or Law Body. The *Dharmakaya,* synonymous with *Tathata* (S) or "Thusness," is the nondual, formless reality underlying the phenomenal world and includes all the perfections of the eternal *Dharma.* On a second level, however, the Buddha essence is manifest as the Body of Bliss, or *Sambhogakaya* (S), and it is here that *bodhisattvas* and Buddhas apprehend and enjoy the Buddha essence. Finally, there is the Transformation Body, or the *Nirmanakaya* (S), in accord with which Buddhas appear at select moments in time to teach the *Dharma* to sentient beings. In this sense the historical Gautama can be regarded as a historical, human manifestation of the *Dharmakaya.*

The doctrine of the Buddha's Bodies is also related to another prominent Mahayana theme, the *Tathagata-garba* (S) or "womb or embryo of the Buddha." A number of Mahayana sutras written between 200 and 350 C.E., including the *Tathagata Sutra,* speak of the "womb" or "embryo" of the Buddha. All living beings are said to possess or participate in the *Tathagata-garba,* the universal Buddha nature. "It was taught that all living beings already possess this innate essence of Buddhahood; they just do not realize this fact."[22] The idea that all living beings are potential Buddhas because of their participation in the universal Buddha nature has been a prominent — and controversial[23] — theme in Chinese and Japanese Mahayana schools.

20. See Kenneth K. S. Ch'en, *The Chinese Transformation of Buddhism* (Princeton: Princeton University Press, 1973).

21. See Williams, *Mahayana Buddhism,* chapter 8; and Paul J. Griffiths, *On Being Buddha: The Classical Doctrine of Buddhahood* (Albany: State University of New York Press, 1994).

22. Mitchell, *Buddhism,* 148.

23. See the essays in *Pruning the Buddha Tree: The Storm over Critical Buddhism,* ed. Jamie Hubbard and Paul L. Swanson (Honolulu: University of Hawaii Press, 1997), for an overview of the contemporary debate among Japanese Buddhists over whether the *Tathagata-garba* doctrine is authentically Buddhist.

Vajrayana and Tibetan Buddhism

Roughly five centuries after the emergence of Mahayana, yet another movement within Indian Buddhism emerged — Vajrayana ("Thunderbolt" or "Diamond Vehicle") Buddhism, or Buddhist Tantra. The term *tantra* (S) refers to Buddhist texts concerned with rituals or instructions that open the mind to esoteric Buddhist teachings and practices.[24] Indian Tantrism provided Buddhists with a way in which the long and arduous path to liberation could be shortened, as one learns to harness supernormal or magical powers. Tantric practices "included physical postures of body and hands called *mudras,* the use of magical phrases called *mantras,* the invoking and visualization of deities, breathing exercises, the movement of subtle forms of energy through psychic channels in the body, the cultivation of sensual bliss through sexual rituals."[25] These esoteric practices were said not only to provide special powers in this life but also to aid in the pursuit of *nirvana.* Buddhist traditions that adopted the *tantra* texts became known as Vajrayana Buddhism, and have been especially influential in Tibetan Buddhism.

Buddhism was introduced into Tibet in the seventh century C.E. The indigenous Tibetan Bon religion had been shamanistic and animistic, involving sacrificial rituals, magicians/diviners, and worship of various deities.[26] Initially severely persecuted, Buddhism was almost stamped out, but it became established once again in the eleventh century and from that point on it coexisted with Bon folk religion. In the eleventh century monks who had earlier fled Tibet returned and built a monastery. Over time, Indian sutras were translated and studied, and a tradition of careful scholarship of Buddhist texts was established. Tibetan Buddhism became distinguished by its commitment to rigorous scholarship and philosophical acumen, discipline, and Tantric practices.[27] Over time four major schools of Tibetan Buddhism developed — the Geluk, Sakya, Kagyu, and Nyingma schools. The various schools are united in their acceptance of a common Tibetan Buddhist canon and their common ancestry in Indian Mahayana and Vajrayana Buddhism.

The Geluk tradition is best known in the West, because of its association with the Dalai Lama. Tibetan Buddhism is well known for its teaching of *tulku* (Tibetan) reincarnation, according to which some *lamas* (Tibetan for "guru") who have already attained lamahood in a previous life are said to reincarnate. The current Dalai Lama, Tenzin Gyatso (b. 1935), is the fourteenth Dalai Lama and is regarded in Tibetan Buddhism as not only a reincarnation of previous Dalai Lamas but also an incarnation of the Buddha Avalokitesvara.

24. Lopez, *The Story of Buddhism,* 213; and Mitchell, *Buddhism,* 153-58.

25. Mitchell, *Buddhism,* 154-56.

26. See Per Kvaerne, "The Religions of Tibet," in *The Religious Traditions of Asia,* ed. Joseph Kitagawa (New York: Macmillan, 1989), 196-98.

27. Kvaerne, "The Religions of Tibet," 191.

Buddhist Modernism

Until recent times Buddhism was found almost exclusively in Asia, but the *Dharma* has now come to the West. While there are today only about four million Buddhists in the United States,[28] the religious and cultural impact of Buddhism has been far greater than the numbers alone would indicate.[29] No single event was as significant for the public acceptance of Buddhism in America as the World's Parliament of Religions, held in Chicago in 1893. For the Parliament, given extensive positive coverage by the press, provided a prominent platform from which Hindu and Buddhist spokesmen could address Western audiences, and "it set in motion the first Buddhist missions to the United States."[30] But the Japanese at the Parliament were not simply passing on the pristine, ancient *Dharma*. The Japanese delegation was deeply influenced by the social crises of late-nineteenth-century Japan, as it embarked upon modernization, and by the effort of Japanese progressives to produce a "new Buddhism" (*shin bukkyo,* Japanese) that is thoroughly modern and scientific. Japanese Buddhists saw it as their mission "to convince intellectuals that Japanese Buddhism was the equal of Western philosophy, superior to Western religion and completely in accord with Western science."[31]

The Japanese, along with many others both in Asia and the West, were crafting what is sometimes called "Buddhist modernism." David McMahan has demonstrated that what is known today as Buddhism — not only in the West but also in modernizing Asian societies — is not simply a faithful transmission of the ancient teachings, but rather a fresh kind of Buddhism shaped through encounters with Western colonialism, Christian missions, and modernization.

> What many Americans and Europeans often understand by the term "Buddhism," however, is actually a modern hybrid tradition with roots in the European Enlightenment no less than the Buddha's enlightenment, in Romanticism and transcendentalism as much as the Pali canon, and in the clash of Asian cultures and colonial powers as much as in mindfulness and meditation.[32]

28. See Richard Hughes Seager, *Buddhism in America* (New York: Columbia University Press, 1999), 10-11; and Robert Wuthnow and Wendy Cage, "Buddhists and Buddhism in the United States: The Scope and the Influence," *Journal for the Scientific Study of Religion* 43 (2004): 364.

29. On Buddhism in the West see James William Coleman, *The New Buddhism: The Western Transformation of an Ancient Tradition* (New York: Oxford University Press, 2001); and *Westward Dharma: Buddhism Beyond Asia,* ed. Charles S. Prebish and Martin Baumann (Berkeley: University of California Press, 2002).

30. Seager, *Buddhism in America,* 37.

31. Judith Snodgrass, *Presenting Japanese Buddhism to the West: Orientalism, Occidentalism, and the Columbian Exposition* (Chapel Hill: University of North Carolina Press, 2003), 9.

32. David L. McMahan, *The Making of Buddhist Modernism* (New York: Oxford University Press, 2008), 5.

McMahan identifies three developments that define Buddhist modernism — detraditionalization, demythologization, and psychologization.[33] Detraditionalization involves the modern tendencies to elevate reason, experience, and intuition over traditional practices and authority structures, so that Buddhist practice becomes individualized and privatized, a matter of personal choice. With demythologization, traditional Buddhist beliefs regarded as problematic under modernity — belief in the many levels of hell, meritorious actions, rebirth not only as humans but also as animals or hungry ghosts, the existence of an array of demons, spirits, and gods — are ignored or reinterpreted in non-literal terms. Similarly, during the past century Buddhism has become especially linked to Western psychology, with Buddhist metaphysical claims being translated into psychoanalytic language and the interior life of the mind. Buddhism becomes a form of spiritual therapy that can be practiced quite apart from accepting the traditional doctrines it has advanced.[34]

Buddhist modernism is found not only in the West but also among well-educated Buddhists throughout Asia. Jay Garfield points out that as Asian societies become more globalized they are being influenced by Western values and beliefs sometimes at odds with traditional Buddhist ways.

> [T]he effect of Western influence upon Buddhist Asia is not negligible: it is issuing in the dramatic, rapid transformation of those cultures. Asian Buddhist cultures are not only absorbing Western technologies and popular culture but also Western approaches to Buddhism itself, and this is often mediated by Western Buddhist texts and Western translations of Asian Buddhist texts. . . . The intra-Buddhist multi-traditional syncretism that so often characterizes Western Buddhism is finding its way into Asia, and interpretations of Buddhist doctrine and scripture mediated by Western science, political theory, popular psychology, and philosophy are increasingly familiar to Asian Buddhists scholars, monastics, and lay practitioners.[35]

An especially interesting case is the transformation of Buddhism in nineteenth-century Ceylon, resulting in what has been called Protestant Buddhism.[36] Provoked by both British colonialist policies and Christian mis-

33. McMahan, *The Making of Buddhist Modernism,* 42-59.

34. For a good example of Buddhist modernism see Stephen Batchelor, *Buddhism without Beliefs: A Contemporary Guide to Awakening* (New York: Riverhead Books, 1997); Batchelor, "Life as a Question, Not a Fact," in *Why Buddhism? Westerners in Search of Wisdom,* ed. Vickie Mackenzie (London: Element, 2002), 142-62.

35. Jay L. Garfield, "Translation as Transmission and Transformation," in *TransBuddhism: Transmission, Translation, Transformation,* ed. Nalini Bhushan, Jay L. Garfield, and Abraham Zablocki (Amherst: University of Massachusetts Press, 2009), 90.

36. See Richard Gombrich and Gananath Obeyesekere, *Buddhism Transformed: Religious*

sionary practices, and guided by the virulently anti-Christian pioneers of the Theosophical Society, Madame Blavatsky and Colonel Henry Steel Olcott, Buddhism in Ceylon enjoyed a resurgence of popularity and redefined itself as a tradition of ancient wisdom that is fully compatible with modern science and tolerant of all faiths. But even as Buddhism provided a protest movement against Western colonialism and Christian missions, it was itself heavily influenced by Protestant Christianity, especially in the increased significance given the laity and the greater emphasis placed upon the written text in modern Buddhism. In 1881 the Theosophist Olcott published in English *A Buddhist Catechism,* which was his attempt to combine elements from a variety of Buddhist traditions in one work, which would set out the basic tenets that all Buddhists in the world should be able to accept. *A Buddhist Catechism* would eventually go through more than forty editions and be translated into over twenty languages, and it was used in Sri Lankan schools into the late twentieth century.[37] Gombrich observes, "This document . . . deserves to rank as a Theosophical rather than a Buddhist creed. But this is not widely realized, notably in Britain, where the connections between Theosophy and organized Buddhism have been intimate."[38]

Thus, when we think about Buddhist understandings of sacred texts we must bear in mind the great diversity within Buddhism. The disagreements over which texts are authoritative are not simply between adherents of Theravada, Mahayana, and Vajrayana traditions, but also between traditionalists and modernists within each of these movements. Garfield argues that globalization and the translation of many Buddhist texts into English are creating a very different way of understanding and utilizing written texts among Buddhists today. For example, whereas traditionally schools such as Theravada, Mahayana, and Vajrayana have each had their own set of authoritative texts, today it is not unusual to find texts from these diverse traditions included together in anthologies in English translation. As Westerners, who are not rooted in any particular historical Buddhist tradition, read these texts indiscriminately what emerges is a kind of intra-Buddhist syncretism or mixing of traditions that historically have been distinct.

Moreover, in traditional Asian Buddhist communities the written text was utilized only within certain contexts. Donald Lopez reminds us that "the vast majority of Buddhists across Asia have been illiterate." This has implications for how Buddhists have regarded the written text.

Change in Sri Lanka (Princeton: Princeton University Press, 1988); and Gombrich, *Theravada Buddhism,* chapter 7.

37. Stephen Prothero, *The White Buddhist: The Asian Odyssey of Henry Steel Olcott* (Bloomington: Indiana University Press, 1996), 101.

38. Gombrich, *Theravada Buddhism,* 186.

> Thus, it is misleading to think of the Buddhist book solely as something to be read. Sutras were placed on altars and worshiped with offerings of flowers and incense, as the sutra itself often prescribed. Laypeople sought to accrue merit and avert misfortune by paying monks to come into their homes and chant sutras. Regardless of whether the audience (or the reader) could understand the content, the word of the Buddha was being heard, and this carried the power of a magic spell. . . . In China, some monasteries had halls devoted exclusively to the recitation of sutras. Laypeople could purchase certificates representing a given number of recitations of a sutra. Those certificates could then be offered (through burning) in services for deceased relatives. . . . Whether or not the text was comprehended, this was considered a meritorious act.[39]

Not even all monks were literate, and many monastic communities had only a few written texts. In Buddhism the written text has generally been regarded as ancillary to oral tradition. "One reads a text with a teacher: the text is an occasion for the transmission of an oral lineage, and most of what is important, what is to be learned, is in that oral transmission."[40] Garfield contends that the approach to Buddhist texts found in the West today, and increasingly in Asia as well, is "making it possible for students or practitioners of Buddhism to engage with its literary tradition independently of a teacher or an authority," and that in so doing "[w]e are creating, in the act of translation, a new Buddhism, both in the West and in traditionally Buddhist Asian cultures." He suggests that what is emerging is "a new Western Buddhist canon."[41] All of this makes it difficult to speak about *the* Buddhist perspective on sacred texts, for there are multiple perspectives that share certain features while differing in other respects.

Buddhist Canons

The Word of the Buddha

As we have seen, Buddhism traditionally has maintained that there have been many Buddhas apart from the historic Gautama. But Buddhists insist that there is a basic continuity in the enlightenment experiences and teachings of the many Buddhas; what Gautama taught is fundamentally the same as what is taught by other Buddhas. The common teaching of all the Buddhas is rooted in the *buddhavacana* (S), or the word of the Buddha, which is itself an expression of the eternal

39. Lopez, *The Story of Buddhism*, 188-89.
40. Garfield, "Translation as Transmission and Transformation," 97-98.
41. Garfield, "Translation as Transmission and Transformation," 98-99.

Dharma.[42] The word of the Buddha is inherent in all genuine enlightenment experiences and the teachings of authoritative Buddhist texts.

But Theravada and Mahayana traditions interpret the *buddhavacana* in different ways. For Theravada Buddhism, "only sutras held to be directly spoken by, or in the presence of and with the approval of the Buddha, constitute *Buddhavaccana.*" Mahayana Buddhism, however, with its many authoritative texts written much later than those accepted by the Theravada tradition, adopts a more flexible understanding of the word of the Buddha. For Mahayanists, "anything in accordance with what the Buddha said, anything that conduces to realization or to liberation, is also *Buddhavaccana.*"[43] The word of the Buddha has been understood in Mahayana in four senses. The first refers to the teaching preached by Gautama the Buddha in his earthly life. But the Buddha was also understood to appear and to teach in a non-physical body, or the *Sambhoga-kaya,* as when he is said to have preached the seven books of the Pali *Abhidharma* to his deceased mother in a heavenly realm.[44] Furthermore, *buddhavacana* also applies to what was not spoken directly by the Buddha himself but by enlightened disciples of the Buddha. And finally, the word of the Buddha can also be preached by sages, gods, and apparitional beings. "Thus Buddha's word means both that which was spoken in a very literal way by the 'historical,' meaning physically human, Buddha, and equally, that which is spoken with the mind of enlightenment, whether by Buddha Sakyamuni in a non-physical form, by another buddha, or by someone else."[45]

The multifaceted nature of the *buddhavacana* made it almost inevitable that there would be questions about the authenticity of oral and written claims concerning the teaching of the Buddha. Buddhists engaged in extensive epistemological and hermeneutical discussions of criteria for recognizing the authentic word of the Buddha. Final authority for Buddhist teaching is found in a complex interplay among three factors: (1) an individual who apprehends the way things actually are (a Buddha), (2) a text (written or oral) that is in continuity with the teaching of Buddhas, and (3) the *Sangha* or Buddhist community, which provides the hermeneutical context for apprehending the word of the Buddha.[46]

Buddhism does have its authoritative scriptures, although the list of such texts and the ways in which they are held to be significant vary with Buddhist schools and historical eras. Unlike Christianity and Islam, in Buddhism there is no single book or collection of texts that is authoritative for everyone. Regional, linguistic, and sectarian considerations have resulted in the compilation of separate

42. See Reginald Ray, "Buddhism: Sacred Text Written and Realized," in *The Holy Book in Comparative Perspective,* ed. Frederick M. Denny and Rodney L. Taylor (Columbia: University of South Carolina Press, 1985), 150-51.

43. Garfield, "Translation as Transmission and Transformation," 100.

44. Ray, "Buddhism," 151.

45. Ray, "Buddhism," 151.

46. Ray, "Buddhism," 154.

canons, with few texts that are commonly accepted across all traditions. There are three major Buddhist canonical collections (Pali, Chinese, and Tibetan), each comprising many books with varying criteria for inclusion. The Chinese canon alone requires nearly 100,000 pages in its printed form.[47]

The Pali Canon

According to Buddhist tradition, after the death of Gautama some five hundred of the Buddha's disciples who had attained enlightenment gathered together at Rajagrha to standardize an authoritative body of teachings to serve as a guide for the monastic community.[48] The teachings were recited orally and a set of authoritative teachings were acknowledged and committed to memory. The teachings were eventually divided into three groups, which together comprise the *Tipitaka* (P; *Tripitaka,* S) or Triple Basket. The *Sutta Pitaka* includes the discourses or sermons of the Buddha, the *Vinaya Pitaka* consists of the monastic codes, and somewhat later the philosophical and logical analyses of the *Abhidhamma Pitaka* were also added.

About a hundred years after the First Council a Second Council, held at Vaisali, was convened to address disputes over interpretation of the rules for life in the monastic community. A Third Council was called by King Asoka around 250 B.C.E. to clarify further proper interpretation of the Buddha's teachings. Tradition maintains that a Fourth Council was held in Sri Lanka around 29 B.C.E., at which time the canon, which had been transmitted orally to this point, was put into writing in the Pali language. These texts comprise the Pali Canon. Theravada Buddhism accepts the Pali Canon as faithfully conveying the teachings of Gautama the Buddha and thus as fully authoritative for Buddhist belief and practice, although it was not until the fifth century C.E. that a final list of texts for the Pali Canon was agreed upon.[49]

Mahayana Canons

It is sometimes said that Mahayana is distinguished more by its vastly expanded sacred literature than by any particular doctrine or practice.[50] Although all Bud-

47. Lewis Lancaster, "Buddhist Books and Texts: Canon and Canonization," in *Encyclopedia of Religion,* 2nd edition, vol. 2, ed. Lindsay Jones (Farmington Hills, MI: Thomson Gale, 2005), 1251-52.

48. Karen C. Lang, "Canons and Literature," in Keown and Prebish, eds., *Encyclopedia of Buddhism,* 197; Mizuno, *Buddhist Sutras,* 18-23, 112-14.

49. Lancaster, "Buddhist Books and Texts," 1252.

50. Robinson and Johnson, *The Buddhist Religion,* 84.

dhists accept in theory the authority of the Pali Canon, Mahayanists also accept many other sutras as authoritative — texts that are largely rejected by the Theravadins. Mahayana schools recognize sutras written in Sanskrit and then translated into Chinese and Tibetan, as well as original texts composed in China and Japan. The new sutras began appearing about the first century C.E. and were said to convey the more advanced teaching of the Buddha which, it was said, was only hinted at in the earlier Pali texts. Thus the later Mahayana texts are held by Mahayanists to represent the final, mature doctrine of the Buddha which was revealed only to his most astute followers.

Since the new Mahayana texts appeared after the Pali texts, Mahayanists naturally had to defend their claim that the later texts contain the original teachings of Gautama. Karen Lang summarizes the approach adopted by the Mahayanists:

> The creators of these new Mahayana *sutras* disputed the mainstream canons' claims to represent a complete collection of the Buddha's teaching. These *sutras* were presented in the form of dialogues between Sakyamuni Buddha and his disciples that took place in various regions in central India, often on Vulture Peak. The anonymous creators of these Mahayana *sutras* and the *Dharma* preachers *(dharmabhanakas)* who memorized and recited them in public regarded these works as the Buddha's word on the ground that "Whatever is well spoken is the word of the Buddha." The Buddha to these anonymous authors and *Dharma* preachers revealed some of these *sutras* in meditations, visions, and dreams. Other *sutras,* the *Perfection of Insight* scriptures *(Prajnaparamita Sutras),* claimed to be the teachings entrusted by the Buddha to semi-divine beings, the serpent-like *nagas,* until the time came when there were people receptive to their profound, deep teachings. Each *sutra* proclaimed its own unique authoritative status and the vast quantities of merit that the devout could acquire from hearing, preaching, copying, and preserving these texts.[51]

The vastness of the Mahayana canon is partially a function of its views on the transmission of the *Dharma.* As Lewis Lancaster puts it, "Because the Buddhist canons represent the written part of a religion that teaches the constant availability of the insights of enlightenment and holds that the teaching of its founder, Sakyamuni, need not be the only expression of the highest teaching, it is not surprising to find canons of large size."[52]

Among the more influential Mahayana texts are the *Prajnaparamita Sutras (Perfection of Wisdom Sutras),* written roughly from the first century through the eighth century, which include the popular *Diamond Sutra* and *Heart*

51. Lang, "Canons and Literature," 201.
52. Lancaster, "Buddhist Books and Texts," 1258.

Sutra.[53] In these texts we find dominant Mahayana themes such as the importance of cultivating wisdom (*prajna,* S), or the correct understanding of the way things really are; "emptiness" (*sunyata,* S) as characteristic of all constituents of existence; and the *bodhisattva* path of compassion. Also significant are the *Vimalakirti-Nirdesa-Sutra (Sutra Expounded by Vimalakirti),* composed around the first century C.E., which presents the doctrine of the "emptiness" or "suchness" (*tathata,* S) of all things, and the *Lankavatara Sutra (Sutra on the Descent into Lanka),* composed around the fourth century C.E., with its subtle discussion of the operations of the mind. The *Mulamadhyamakakarika (Fundamental Wisdom of the Middle Way)* by the second-century C.E. Indian Buddhist philosopher Nagarjuna, with its teaching that everything is *sunya* (S) or "empty" of a fixed, independent nature, has had an enormous influence on subsequent Mahayana thought.

One of the most popular and revered Mahayana texts is the *Saddharma-pundarika-Sutra (Lotus Sutra),* written around 200 C.E. The *Lotus Sutra* touches upon many key Mahayana themes, including the Buddha as a sublime being with supernatural powers; the use of "skillful means" (*upaya-kausala,* S) in Buddhist teaching; and the many Buddhas and compassionate *bodhisattvas* who appear for the betterment of human beings. The Larger and Smaller *Sukhavati-Vyuha-Sutras (Land of Bliss/Happiness Sutras),* composed around the second century C.E., form the basis for the Pure Land traditions, one of the most popular Mahayana movements.

With the later rise of the Vajrayana tradition, an additional set of texts came to be accepted as authoritative. A new genre of Buddhist writings, *tantra,* emerged during the fifth through eleventh centuries C.E. Like other Mahayana works, the *tantras* claimed to be based upon insights gained from meditation, visions, and dreams.[54] The teachings of the *tantras* were regarded as esoteric and hidden from those not properly initiated into their meanings by a qualified teacher.

We can speak of the Chinese and Tibetan traditions as comprising distinct canons within the broader set of authoritative Mahayana scriptures. Various schools within Mahayana and Vajrayana Buddhism adopted different scriptures as authoritative, or gave different weight to particular texts, so that relatively few texts have been accepted as fully authoritative by all schools. A complete canon of Chinese Buddhist texts was not available until 984 C.E., when the Chinese-language scriptures were printed with wooden printing blocks.[55] This edition then was transmitted to Korea, Vietnam, and Japan. The first Japanese editions of the Chinese canon appeared in the seventeenth century, and the 1924-34 Taisho

53. On the Mahayana texts see Williams, *Mahayana Buddhism,* 29-54; and Mitchell, *Buddhism,* 103-19.

54. Lang, "Canons and Literature," 202.

55. Lang, "Canons and Literature," 203.

Shinshu Daizokyo edition (in eighty-five volumes) has become the standard reference for the Chinese canon. Beginning in the seventh century, large numbers of Buddhist scriptures from India and China were translated into Tibetan. Early in the fourteenth century, Tibetan scholars compiled translations from the previous five hundred years and determined which of these to include in an authoritative Tibetan canon.[56] The last major editing of the Tibetan canon, commissioned by the thirteenth Dalai Lama, resulted in the Lhasa edition of 1931.[57]

In addition to the officially recognized canonical texts, there are many other Buddhist writings concerning the Buddha, monastic rules, rituals, and guides to living that are used by monks and laity, thus forming a kind of practical or informal canon.

> Ritual manuals guide monks and nuns in the performance of consecration rituals, which bring together the lay and monastic communities in consecration of a temple, a *stupa,* or an image. Laypeople also invite monastics to chant ritual texts for protection against illness and misfortune, but also as blessings for new houses, new businesses, and new marriages. The most important ritual activities that Buddhist monastics perform for the laity concern the dead and the dying, and all Buddhist monastic institutions instruct their members in the proper recitation of ritual texts at funeral and memorial services.[58]

Thus, while written scriptures play a prominent role in Buddhist teaching and practice there is enormous variety within Buddhism on which texts are authoritative and how we are to understand the significance of such texts.

Buddhist Scriptures and Christian Revelation

In both Buddhism and Christianity written texts are accepted as authoritative, but the ways in which Buddhists and Christians regard their respective scriptures are quite different. The differences are neither minor nor incidental. They stem from the very different worldviews, especially the ontological and metaphysical commitments, of Buddhism and Christianity.

The Christian faith, for example, is based upon the conviction that God has spoken to humankind in an understandable manner and that this divine revelation is available to us in the writings known as the Bible. The Bible is regarded as God's special revelation to humankind in written form and thus as divinely inspired. To be sure, the divine inspiration of Scripture does not negate the very real human

56. Lang, "Canons and Literature," 203-4.
57. Lancaster, "Buddhist Books and Texts," 1256.
58. Lang, "Canons and Literature," 205.

contribution to Scripture. But Christians insist that God superintended the process of writing in such a way that the very words in the Bible, while reflecting the style and intent of the human authors, are the very words that God intended.

One of the more significant statements of the biblical understanding of divine revelation is found in the opening verses of the Letter to the Hebrews: "Long ago, at many times and in many ways, God spoke to our fathers by the prophets, but in these last days he has spoken to us by his Son, whom he appointed the heir of all things, through whom he also created the world" (Heb. 1:1-2; cf. John 1:1-3, 14). These verses touch upon three important respects in which the Christian understanding of divine revelation is fundamentally different from Buddhist perspectives on authoritative texts. First, divine revelation in the Christian sense presupposes a creator God who speaks and who reveals himself in an intelligible manner to humankind. Second, God's self-revelation takes place within and through the historical process, thereby giving history special significance. Third, the apex of God's self-revelation is the Incarnation in Jesus of Nazareth, so that the life, death, and resurrection of Jesus Christ are themselves revelatory. This means that Jesus has a relation to the Bible and the Christian faith that is very different from that of Gautama to Buddhist texts.

Scriptures without Divine Revelation

Perhaps the greatest difference between Christian and Buddhist understandings of scripture is the fact that in Buddhism there is no God to reveal and inspire scripture.[59] Buddhism traditionally has denied the reality of an eternal creator God.

It is not unusual in the West today to hear that Buddhism is not atheistic and that it simply does not commit itself on the question of God's existence. Some contend that rather than atheistic Buddhism is agnostic, thereby raising the possibility that perhaps Buddhism and Christianity really are not incompatible with respect to God's existence.[60] It is true that in the past two hundred years there

59. On differences between Buddhism and Christianity see Keith E. Yandell and Harold Netland, *Buddhism: A Christian Exploration and Appraisal* (Downers Grove, IL: InterVarsity, 2009), 175-212.

60. See Paul Knitter, *Without Buddha I Could Not Be a Christian* (Oxford: Oneworld, 2009); Perry Schmidt-Leukel, "The Unbridgeable Gulf? Towards a Buddhist-Christian Theology of Creation," in *Buddhism, Christianity and the Question of Creation: Karmic or Divine?* ed. P. Schmidt-Leukel (Aldershot, UK: Ashgate, 206), 109-78. For a fascinating discussion of whether Buddhism is compatible with the idea of a creator God see Perry Schmidt-Leukel, "'Light and Darkness' or 'Looking Through a Dim Mirror'? A Reply to Paul Williams from a Christian Perspective"; José Ignacio Cabezón, "A Response to Paul Williams' *The Unexpected Way*"; and Paul Williams, "Buddhism, God, Aquinas and Morality: An Only Partially Repentant Reply to Perry Schmidt-Leukel and José Cabezón," all in *Converging Ways? Conversion and*

have been those, both in Asia and the West, who present Buddhism as possibly compatible with theism. This is especially evident with certain forms of Buddhist modernism. For example, Shaku Soen, the Japanese emissary to the 1893 Parliament of Religions, in a lecture titled "The God-Concept of Buddhism," claimed that Buddhism "is not atheistic" and that it "certainly has a God, the highest reality and truth, through which and in which this universe exists."[61]

But there can be little question that historically Buddhism has denied the reality of an eternal creator God. Paul Williams, a leading scholar of Buddhism and formerly a practicing Buddhist who converted to Roman Catholicism, states, "Buddhists do not believe in the existence of God. There need be no debating about this. In practicing Buddhism one never finds talk of God, there is no role for God, and it is not difficult to find in Buddhist texts attacks on the existence of an omnipotent, all-good Creator of the universe."[62] A careful examination of both the implications of Buddhist metaphysics and the Buddhist texts themselves reveals that Buddhism rules out the possibility of there being a creator God. Williams observes, "To portray Buddhism as agnostic in this way seems to me a modern strategy. In ancient times Buddhists were quite clear that they denied the existence of a personal creator God as taught in rival theistic systems."[63]

Consider, for example, the basic Buddhist teaching that, *nirvana* aside, *nothing* enjoys independent existence, that is, an existence not dependent on the existence and activity of something else. This, of course, rules out the Christian understanding of God, since *nirvana* is not a personal being capable of action. It is not surprising, then, that Buddhist thinkers throughout the ages have rejected theism as incompatible with Buddhist metaphysics. The Sri Lankan Buddhist

---

Belonging in Buddhism and Christianity, ed. John D'Arcy May (Sankt Ottien, Germany: EOS Klosterverlag, 2007), 67-154.

61. As quoted in McMahan, *The Making of Buddhist Modernism,* 67.

62. Paul Williams, *The Unexpected Way: On Converting from Buddhism to Catholicism* (Edinburgh: T. & T. Clark, 2002), 25. There are some forms of Mahayana Buddhism, especially the Pure Land traditions, that do resemble theism in some respects. And certainly on the level of folk Buddhism there are many who do regard the Buddha as a kind of deity and who worship him accordingly. But the dominant Buddhist traditions have clearly rejected theism.

63. Williams, *The Unexpected Way,* 25. On Buddhist critiques of theism see Gunapala Dharmasiri, *A Buddhist Critique of the Christian Concept of God* (Antioch, CA: Golden Leaves Publishing Company, 1988); Arvind Sharma, *The Philosophy of Religion: A Buddhist Perspective* (Delhi: Oxford University Press, 1995), chapters 1-3; Paul Williams, "Aquinas Meets the Buddhists: Prolegomenon to an Authentically Thomas-ist Basis for Dialogue," in *Aquinas in Dialogue: Thomas for the Twenty-First Century,* ed. Jim Fodor and Christian Bauerschmidt (Oxford: Blackwell, 2004), 87-117; Jayatilleke, *The Message of the Buddha,* chapter 8; A. L. Herman, "Religions as Failed Theodicies: Atheism in Hinduism and Buddhism," in *Indian Philosophy of Religion,* ed. Roy W. Perrett (Dordrecht: Kluwer, 1989), 35-60; and especially Parimal G. Patil, *Against a Hindu God: Buddhist Philosophy of Religion in India* (New York: Columbia University Press, 2009).

scholar K. N. Jayatilleke says that if by "God" we mean a Supreme Being, creator of everything else apart from God, then "In denying that the universe is a product of a Personal God, who creates it in time and plans a consummation at the end of time, Buddhism is a form of atheism."[64] Similarly Walpola Rahula asserts that, "According to Buddhism, our ideas of God and Soul are false and empty."[65] The Dalai Lama states,

> The entire Buddhist worldview is based on a philosophical standpoint in which the central thought is the principle of interdependence, how all things and events come into being purely as a result of interactions between causes and conditions. Within that philosophical worldview it is almost impossible to have any room for an atemporal, eternal, absolute truth. Nor is it possible to accommodate the concept of a divine Creation.[66]

In sum, unlike claims made about the sacred writings of theistic religions, Buddhists do not hold that the sutras are divinely inspired revelation. While authoritative, they are not revealed by God. How then should we understand the word of the Buddha or *buddhavacana*? While the word of the Buddha is something that the Buddhas, either in human form, as with Gautama, or in spiritual form can communicate to others, this is not a matter of a personal creator God revealing himself and his will to humankind. The content of the word of the Buddha is the *Dharma,* the eternal truth, which is available to anyone who attains enlightenment.

The Scriptures and History

The ways in which Christians and Buddhists think about history and the relation of history to the authoritative scriptures is also very different. Two significant contrasts will be briefly noted. First, Christianity and Buddhism understand the significance of the flow of history in very different ways. Whereas the Christian faith sees history moving in a linear direction from a definite starting point in the past to a climactic consummation in the future, Buddhism adopts a more cyclical view that has no particular beginning or end. In Christianity, the universe began with the creative act of God (Gen. 1:1), and with the creation of the first human beings we have the origin of history as we know it. The Bible concludes with a glo-

64. Jayatilleke, *The Message of the Buddha,* 105.

65. Walpola Rahula, *What the Buddha Taught,* rev. edition (New York: Grove Press, 1974), 52.

66. His Holiness the Dalai Lama, *The Good Heart: A Buddhist Perspective on the Teachings of Jesus,* ed. Robert Kiely, trans. Geshe Thupten Jinpa (Boston: Wisdom Publications, 1996), 82.

rious vision of a new and restored creation — "a new heaven and a new earth" — in which evil and death, which have ravaged God's creation since the introduction of sin and rebellion against God (Genesis 3), are conquered (Revelation 20–21). There is a definite direction or *telos* to human history as it moves progressively toward this culmination. Furthermore, since there is a singularity to historical events history has significance. It is within the historical movement of peoples and events that God speaks and reveals himself progressively to humankind. The pinnacle of God's self-revelation — the Incarnation in Jesus of Nazareth in the first century — takes place within a specific historical context.

Buddhism, by contrast, denies that there is a definite beginning to the entire series of universes. Masao Abe states, "Since there is no God in Buddhism, there is no creation or last judgment, but rather Emptiness. Thus, for Buddhism, history has neither beginning nor end."[67] History is not proceeding, under the sovereign direction of an omnipotent God, to a definite goal. "Unlike so many other traditions, the Buddhist scriptures contain no classic account of an end time, an apocalypse, an eschaton."[68] Rather, history is part of the beginningless and ongoing processes of birth, death, and rebirth.

Moreover, Mahayana Buddhism in particular distinguishes between two levels of truth or reality, with the processes and events of history being relegated to the lower level of reality. The distinction is basic to the work of the great Mahayana philosopher Nagarjuna:

> The Buddha's teaching of the Dharma
> Is based on two truths:
> A truth of worldly convention
> And an ultimate truth.
>
> Those who do not understand
> The distinction drawn between these two truths
> Do not understand
> The Buddha's profound truth.[69]

Conventional truth, which includes historical events and processes, applies to the ordinary world of experience. But since it describes a world that lacks inherent existence it cannot be about what is truly ultimate. Jay Garfield explains the relation between the two truths:

67. Masao Abe, *Zen and Western Thought,* ed. William R. LaFleur (Honolulu: University of Hawaii Press, 1985), 214.

68. Lopez, *The Story of Buddhism,* 33.

69. *The Fundamental Wisdom of the Middle Way: Nagarjuna's Mulamadhyakakarika* 24.8-9; translation and commentary by Jay L. Garfield (New York: Oxford University Press, 1995), 68.

> The term translated here as "truth of worldly convention" (Tib: *kun-rdzob bden-pa,* Skt: *samvrti-satya*) denotes a truth dependent upon tacit agreement, an everyday truth, a truth about things as they appear to accurate ordinary investigation, as judged by appropriate human standards. The term "ultimate truth" (Tib: *dam-pa'i don gyi bden-pa,* Skt: *paramartha-satya*) denotes the way things are independent of convention, or to put it another way, the way things turn out to be when we subject them to analysis with the intention of discovering the nature they have from their own side, as opposed to the characteristics we impute to them.[70]

Although the ultimate truth is said not to deny conventional truth, it reveals the true nature of what is apprehended on the conventional level. But the *Dharma,* the eternal truth about the way things actually are, knowledge of which is essential to attaining *nirvana* and liberation, transcends the space-time world of conventional truth, including "truths" about history.

Second, in light of the above, it is not surprising that the historicity of the events attributed to Jesus in the Bible carries an importance for Christian faith that is not paralleled in Buddhism. Both Jesus of Nazareth and Gautama the Buddha were actual historical figures, but the relation between Jesus and history is different from that of Gautama to history, and the significance of each figure varies with the two religions.[71] Peter Harvey observes that "Buddhism is less focused on the person of its founder than is, for example, Christianity. The emphasis in Buddhism is upon the *teachings* of the Buddha(s), and the 'awakening' of human personality that these are seen to lead to."[72] Some scholars argue that the tendency to focus upon Gautama as the founder of Buddhism is a modern one, influenced in part by the Christian view of the importance of Jesus to Christian faith. Judith Snodgrass, for example, claims that "until the emergence of modern Buddhism in the mid-nineteenth century, no Asian Buddhists regarded [Gautama] as the founder of the religion or as the only Buddha. Sakyamuni was understood to be but one of a series of Buddhas born into the world to teach the eternal dharma."[73]

For Buddhists, the problem of the historicity of events attributed to Gautama first emerged with the proliferation of the Mahayana writings and the new teachings that were at variance with earlier Theravada teachings. The issue became especially problematic for Japanese Buddhism in the late nineteenth century, as Japan encountered modern historiography and attacks from Christian mission-

70. *The Fundamental Wisdom of the Middle Way,* 297-98.

71. On the relation of the historical Gautama to Buddhism see Whalen Lai, "The Search for the Historical Sakyamuni in Light of the Historical Jesus," *Buddhist Christian Studies* 2 (1982): 77-91.

72. Harvey, "Buddha," 93; emphasis in original.

73. Judith Snodgrass, "Discourse, Authority, Demand: The Politics of Early English Publications on Buddhism," in Bhushan et al., eds., *TransBuddhism,* 22.

aries who argued that the Mahayana did not represent the authentic teaching of the Buddha.[74] While many Buddhists continued to insist that Mahayana teachings are implicit in earlier Pali sutras, Sensho Murakami (1851-1929), a monk and scholar in the Pure Land tradition, readily acknowledged that Mahayana was not the teaching of the historical Gautama. Although a devout Buddhist, Murakami claimed that "Shakyamuni Buddha as he appears in Mahayana sutras and in treatises on those sutras is not the historical Buddha but a figure larger than life, a superhuman being."[75] But in admitting this Murakami was not suggesting that Mahayana teachings are therefore illegitimate or false. To the contrary, he claimed that Mahayana teachings were timelessly true regardless of whether Gautama actually spoke the words attributed to him in the Mahayana texts.[76] Murakami "hoped to demonstrate the concord between true Buddhism and the spirit of the Buddha's teachings and thus show that even teachings that had not actually been preached by the Buddha could be identified with him."[77] The *Dharma,* the truth Mahayana teaches, is eternal and transcends any particular expression of it. Murakami's views initially were controversial, but his general approach has been widely accepted by Buddhist modernists. Kogen Mizuno summarizes the current perspective among Japanese Buddhists scholars:

> The question of whether or not the Buddha preached Mahayana doctrines is no longer discussed much in Japan for two reasons. First, it has been accepted that it simply is not possible to prove that Mahayana doctrines are the direct teaching of the historical Buddha; and second, although the Mahayana sutras were compiled more than five centuries after the death of Shakyamuni, they do embody his original teachings and contain more profound teachings than the [earlier] Agama sutras. For these reasons Japanese Buddhologists came to a tacit agreement some time ago that Mahayana sutras are the word of the Buddha.[78]

The issue of religious truth and historicity emerged in a conversation between the Protestant theologian Paul Tillich and Japanese Buddhists during Tillich's 1960 visit to Japan. Tillich asked some Buddhist scholars: "If some historian should make it probable that a man of the name Gautama never lived, what would be the consequence for Buddhism?" After noting that the historicity of Gautama Buddha has never been a central issue for Buddhism, one scholar stated, "Accord-

74. See Lai, "The Search for the Historical Sakyamuni in Light of the Historical Jesus"; and Notto R. Thelle, *Buddhism and Christianity in Japan: From Conflict to Dialogue, 1854-1899* (Honolulu: University of Hawaii Press, 1987), chapter 5.

75. Mizuno, *Buddhist Sutras,* 130.

76. Lai, "The Search for the Historical Sakyamuni in Light of the Historical Jesus," 80-81.

77. Mizuno, *Buddhist Sutras,* 130.

78. Mizuno, *Buddhist Sutras,* 133.

ing to the doctrine of Buddhism, the *dharma kaya* [the body of truth] is eternal, and so it does not depend upon the historicity of Gautama."[79]

We can see here a major difference between Christianity and Buddhism. Although most Buddhists would insist that the teachings of contemporary Buddhist schools are consistent with what the historical Gautama taught, they also would acknowledge that the truth of Buddhist teachings is distinct from and does not depend upon the historical accuracy of Buddhist texts portraying the life and teachings of Gautama.

Christian faith, by contrast, is inextricably rooted in the historical person of Jesus so that Christian teachings cannot be separated from his life, death, and resurrection. The teachings of the Christian faith are not simply eternal truths that are unrelated to events in history. They grow out of and depend upon what Jesus of Nazareth actually said and did. In particular, the Christian faith rests upon the actual resurrection of Jesus Christ from the dead, not simply upon some timeless truth about life after death (Rom. 1:4; 1 Cor. 15:26-58). Whereas it is possible to think of Buddhist teachings apart from the historical person of Gautama (it is possible that another individual at another time would have attained enlightenment and proclaimed the *Dharma*), the Christian faith cannot be conceived apart from the life, teachings, death, and resurrection of Jesus of Nazareth.

Suspicion of the Written Text

There is within Buddhism considerable ambivalence concerning the written text. On the one hand, Buddhist texts have been the object of veneration and Buddhist monks have been meticulous in copying and studying the sutras. Highly technical and sophisticated commentaries on authoritative texts abound. Perhaps no text is more venerated than the Mahayana text *Saddharmapundarika-Sutra,* or the *Lotus Sutra.* Disciples of the thirteenth-century Japanese Buddhist Nichiren (1222-1282), for example, regard the *Lotus Sutra* as the most perfect expression of the Buddhist *Dharma* and superior to all other sutras. Nichiren's followers chant the *Daimoku* (Japanese), a sacred formulation of adoration of the *Lotus Sutra* (*namu myoho renge kyo* (Japanese), "I take refuge in the Lotus of the Wonderful Law"), which is said to encapsulate all of truth in a single invocation. Only teachings and practices based upon the *Lotus Sutra* are to be accepted, with other Buddhist schools rejected as heretical.

At the same time, the written word is not the ultimate authority for most Buddhists, and there is in many Buddhist traditions a strong suspicion of the written text.

79. "Tillich Encounters Japan," ed. Robert W. Wood, *Japanese Religions* 2 (May 1961): 48-50.

> Buddhism avers that the sacred text has, in and of itself, no particular value. Its worth depends entirely on what is done with it, and at best, the sacred text is never more than an aid that must be abandoned by each individual at a certain point on his journey toward the Buddhist goal of enlightenment.[80]

Suspicion of verbal formulations and the written text is especially pronounced in Zen. Although its roots are in Indian Buddhism, Zen was shaped definitively through its encounter with Taoism in China.[81] Zen maintains that the core of what the Buddha realized in his enlightenment was communicated directly and non-verbally from Gautama to one of his disciples, and has been passed on directly from master to disciple ever since. According to a famous Zen tradition,

> Once when the World Honored One [Gautama the Buddha] was staying on the Mount of the Vulture, he held up a flower before the assembled ones. All fell silent. Only the venerable Kasyapa broke into a smile. The Honored One then spoke: "The eye of the true Dharma, the wonderful Mind of Nirvana, the true formless Form, the mysterious Gate of the Dharma, which rests not upon words and letters, and a special transmission . . . outside the scriptures; this I hand over to the great Kasyapa."[82]

In other words, the most mature teaching of Gautama is not what is contained in the Pali texts but is something much more profound, something inexpressible in human words. Enlightenment in Zen is said to be a direct, intuitive insight into the true nature of reality, an understanding that transcends dualities, conceptualization, and verbalization.

Tradition maintains that this "wonderful Mind of Nirvana" was then transmitted non-verbally through twenty-eight Indian patriarchs, the last of whom was the legendary Bodhidharma (ca. 470-543 C.E.). Although the historicity of Bodhidharma is questioned by scholars, tradition attributes to him the famous four-line stanza said to express the heart of Zen:

> A special transmission outside the scriptures,
> Not founded upon words and letters;
> By pointing directly to [one's] mind
> It lets one see into [one's own true] nature and [thus] attain Buddhahood.[83]

80. Ray, "Buddhism," 148.

81. For the historical development of Zen see Heinrich Dumoulin, *Zen Buddhism: A History,* vol. 1, *India and China,* and vol. 2, *Japan,* trans. James W. Heisig and Paul Knitter (New York: Macmillan, 1988, 1990).

82. From the *Mumonkan,* as cited in Heinrich Dumoulin, *Zen Enlightenment: Origin and Meaning* (New York: Weatherhill, 1979), 16.

83. As cited in Dumoulin, *Zen Buddhism: A History,* 1:85.

In China this tradition, heavily influenced by Taoism, became known as Ch'an Buddhism.[84] Both Ch'an and Taoism were deeply suspicious of words, maintaining that ultimate reality is inexpressible. For example, the Taoist classic the *Tao Te Ching* begins with these enigmatic words:

> The way [Tao] that can be spoken of
> Is not the constant way;
> The name that can be named
> Is not the constant name.
> The nameless was the beginning of heaven and earth;
> The named was the mother of the myriad creatures.[85]

The Tao is said to be "forever nameless." The Taoist sage "practices the teaching that uses no words. . . . One who knows does not speak; one who speaks does not know."[86] Zen, under the influence of Taoism, is simply a more radical expression of tendencies already well established in much of Mahayana thought that push one beyond reliance upon words, logical categories, and the written text.

The contrast with Christian thought here is significant. To be sure, there is in the Christian tradition recognition of the limitations of human thought and language when it comes to the divine. Christian theologians have consistently emphasized the transcendence of God, and there is an important sense in which God is beyond the scope of human conceptual and linguistic categories. It does not follow from this, however, that none of our concepts or terms can be applied meaningfully to God. It is the witness of Scripture that God has spoken to humankind and that because of God's self-revelation we can have partial, but adequate, knowledge of God. In particular, it is the Incarnation that reveals God to us (John 1:14, 18; 14:9; Col. 1:15, 19; 2:9). Because God has spoken, meaningful and coherent descriptions of God's nature and activity can be formulated in human linguistic and conceptual categories, although such descriptions have their limitations and must be interpreted appropriately. For Christians, it is the written text, the Bible, that provides access to the Incarnation and is the repository of God's special self-revelation. It is the claim that the eternal creator God has spoken to humankind that sets the Christian faith apart from Buddhist approaches to the sutras.

84. *Ch'an* is a Chinese rendering of the Sanskrit term *Dhyana* (meditation); *Zen* is the Japanese adaptation of *Ch'an*.

85. *Lao Tzu: Tao Te Ching* 1.1-2, trans. D. C. Lau (Harmondsworth, UK: Penguin, 1963), 57.

86. *Lao Tzu: Tao Te Ching* 1.1-2, trans. Lau, 91, 58, 117.

Thinking Holistically

THIRTY-FIVE

Take, Read

Daniel M. Doriani

The title of this chapter, "Take, Read," comes to us not from Scripture but from the account of one Scripture-mediated struggle with God. Augustine of Hippo's dramatic reading of Romans 13:13-14 makes two foundational points: it is imperative to take and read, but it is difficult to take and read. As a command, "take, read" summons everyone, including pastors and theologians, to take and read Scripture while giving ourselves to God's aim in ordaining it, that by reading we might know, love, trust, and follow the triune God (Jer. 9:24; Ezek. 36:28; Heb. 8:11; passim). We might wish for an uncomplicated plan for using the Bible: take, read, comprehend, believe, obey. But the story of Augustine suggests that reading is no simple thing.

The Story of Augustine

According to the *Confessions,* Augustine attended church when duties permitted, read the lives of the saints, conversed with believers, and made "Scriptures . . . the subject of deep study" for perhaps a decade before his conversion. He was, at the same time, such a "slave of lust" that he could not live without a concubine, even while he awaited his formal marriage.[1] His desire for success in worldly affairs was just as strong. A decisive change began when a leading Roman official named Ponticianus visited Augustine's rented home in Hippo. When Ponticianus noticed a copy of Romans lying open, he regaled them with the story of Anthony, a prominent man who became a solitary monk. More than that, Ponticianus told how the story of Anthony had led to his own conversion and the conversion of his friends. The story filled Augustine with affection for Ponticianus, but reproach for himself.[2]

1. Augustine, *Confessions,* trans. Henry Chadwick (Oxford: Oxford University Press, 1991), 53 (4.2.2), 109 (6.15.25).

2. Augustine, *Confessions,* 141-44 (8.5-6.12-15).

Augustine suffered spiritual torment, for he wanted to become a new man, yet he feared a conversion that deprived him of his two enthralling mistresses, his concubine, and his career. His "conscience complained" and he gnawed at himself as Ponticianus spoke. Augustine "was violently overcome by a fearful sense of shame."[3] Yet "the agony of hesitation" continued, even after he realized that God grants the resources necessary for obedience. Weeping and groaning, Augustine stole from the villa he shared with his friend and fellow seeker Alypius, threw himself down under a fig tree, and cried, "How long, how long. . . . Why not an end to my impure life in this very hour?"[4]

At that moment, he heard a child chanting, "Take, read, take, read." Although he realized it must be part of a child's game, he chose to interpret it as a divine command. Augustine had carried a copy of Romans with him from the house. He opened it at random and read: "Not in riots and drunken parties, not in eroticism and indecencies, not in strife and rivalry, but put on the Lord Jesus Christ, and make no provision for the flesh in its lusts." He concludes, "I neither wished nor needed to read further." At once, certainty flooded his heart and the gloom of doubt vanished. A few minutes later, the estimable Alypius joined him in resolving to follow Christ.[5] Augustine quit his career in rhetoric and began to study the Word full time with a band of friends. Soon enough Augustine was ordained as priest and, before long, as bishop.

Clearly, Augustine did not "Take, read" as a naïf. He studied, meditated, and, after a fashion, understood the Bible for years before he yielded himself to the God of the Bible. The command to take and read had its effect because Augustine had already learned the content of the faith, the doctrine and demands of the gospel, as stated in Romans. If anything, Augustine's case suggests that a naïve reader cannot simply take up the Bible, read it, comprehend it, and follow it.

This chapter considers the way theologians, pastors, and scholars read Scripture from a personal rather than a strictly academic perspective.[6] It studies the commitments and dispositions we have before interpretation begins, the way we do or do not appropriate what we read, and the effect of these on teaching, preaching, and living.

As we study the interpretation, canonicity, authorship, inspiration, authority, and transmission of Scripture, scholars necessarily treat the Bible as an object of their study. Yet before we study the Bible as an object, scholars and pastors must know that we are the objects of God's study. We search for the meaning of the words and the words; meanwhile "the Lord searches every heart" (1 Chron.

3. Augustine, *Confessions,* 144-47 (8.7-8.16-19).

4. Augustine, *Confessions,* 147, 151-52 (8.8-12.20, 27-28).

5. Augustine, *Confessions,* 152-53 (8.12.29-30).

6. I use the terms "theologian," "teacher," "pastor," and "scholar" almost interchangeably; all are exegetes and teachers, although their spheres of labor do vary.

28:9). "The lamp of the LORD searches the spirit of a man" (Prov. 20:27; cf. Ps. 7:9; Rom. 8:27; Rev. 2:23). God's word "judges the thoughts and attitudes of the heart" (Heb. 4:12). As we read the Bible, it reads us.

The Bible is normative and more, for it is the norm above all norms, the source that tests and directs all our private and professional activity. Because we have an inspired, infallible, inerrant, perspicuous word from God, it is possible to proclaim "the Bible says" and "God says" and to say both with authority. Our view of Scripture makes real preaching possible; the same cannot be said for every other view.

Some theologians judge unguided reading to be dangerous; everyone believes some preparation is necessary for the most constructive reading. Eugene Peterson says, "It is not sufficient to place a Bible in a person's hand and command, 'Read it.'" That is as foolish and dangerous as putting car keys into an adolescent's hands and saying, "Drive it."[7] The point is defensible but misleading. God gave the Bible *to us;* it is *for us,* individually and corporately. It presents a habitable text, a narrative world, a relational world, that offers a good (and real) place to live in the present and a source of God-centered hope for the future (Rom. 15:4).[8] The Bible is indeed a dangerous book, but it also generates joy in the reading and rereading, in the discovery, the sharing, and the proclamation of life-giving truth. And without minimizing the complexities of interpretation, we must confess that if the Spirit removes the veil that covers unregenerate eyes, Scripture is clear enough that readers can grasp its basic truths and believe.

Besides, the Bible is hardly the only document that is prone to misreading and theologians are hardly the only scholars who disagree. The Internet teems with such distortions of other people's work that we have to wonder if the respondents are fully literate. Even academic exchanges and book reviews regularly cry, "But that's not what I said/meant."

So it is possible, if not necessarily *easy,* to take and read the Bible — or other literature. For example, in 2009 the world panicked over the H1N1 flu, which briefly threatened to become a death-dealing pandemic. Since flu vaccines were a familiar feature of medical care, the public was full of hope for a life-saving vaccine. Epidemiologists warned that it takes time to develop and mass-produce safe vaccines. Before long, the press began to notice alternative views of the flu and epidemiology. Vaccine skeptics began to get some attention. These researchers found serious flaws in studies that allegedly prove the value of flu vaccines. Specifically, some studies claimed that a flu vaccine reduces the likelihood of death in the elderly by 50 percent, possibly more. An eminent researcher declared, "For a vaccine to reduce mortality by 50 percent . . . means it has to prevent deaths not just from influenza, but also from falls, fires, heart disease, strokes, and car

7. Eugene Peterson, *Eat This Book* (Grand Rapids: Eerdmans, 2006), 81.

8. My phrasing is shaped by a fellow contributor to this collection, Mark Thompson.

accidents. That's not a vaccine, that's a miracle." Surely, some researchers proposed, the vaccinated and unvaccinated must also differ in education, lifestyle, or general health. Indeed, a set of meticulously crafted studies concluded that the entire benefit of flu vaccines could be explained by the "healthy user effect." But the response was hardly scientific. The scientific community told the skeptics not to ask such questions, adding that it could damage their careers. Thus, most refused to believe the studies; they refused to take, read, and become disciples. As Thomas Kuhn showed, scientists initially resist evidence that calls prevailing theories into question.[9] Scientists cannot "read" data that lead to unsettling, unorthodox conclusions.[10]

Apparently dedicated Christians can also experience sudden loss of reading skill. Men and women who long espouse orthodox biblical views on topics such as divorce or abortion suddenly change their position when love for their spouse evaporates or a teenage girl gets pregnant. This is no surprise. Indeed, the Bible itself leads us to expect recalcitrant readers.

The Bible Takes Sustained Interest in the Way It Is Read

It is possible to "take and read" under the right conditions and occasionally the Bible mentions what those are: We must read with an eye for the suffering and glory of the Christ (Luke 24:26-27) and for the way of salvation by faith in Jesus (2 Tim. 3:15). We read for authoritative commands (James 1:22), but also for the Spirit rather than the letter of the law (2 Cor. 3:6).

There are many valid ways to read the Bible. It should be read grammatically, historically, theocentrically, Christocentrically, redemptively, and covenantally.[11] We should read holistically, seeking the message of the whole Bible, while searching for the distinctive themes of each of its sixty-six books. We read repeatedly, accumulating knowledge as we go. We read the Bible for insight into every sphere of life: psychology, education, history, aesthetics, economics, politics, family, and ethics.[12] Scripture addresses every facet of the human person: the body, mind, will, and emotions. It addresses every realm of human responsibility: our duties, character, goals or life purposes, and foundational beliefs. It shapes the way we see the world and the way we live out our vocations.

The Bible is that rare work that takes direct and sustained interest in guiding

9. Thomas Kuhn, *The Structure of Scientific Revolutions* (Chicago: University of Chicago Press, 1962).

10. Shannon Brownlee and Jeanne Lenzer, "Shots in the Dark: Does the Vaccine Matter?" *The Atlantic* 304, no. 4 (November 2009): 44-54.

11. It is beyond the scope of one essay to attempt to define these concepts and practices.

12. On the spheres touched by salvation, see Albert Wolters, *Creation Regained,* 2nd edition (Grand Rapids: Eerdmans, 2005), 73-81.

the people who read it. Most canonical books address the question in some way. The Psalms command God's people to meditate on the word and so to find life, wisdom, light, righteousness, direction, and blessing (Ps. 1:1-2; 19:7-11; 119:1-16, passim). In Proverbs, Solomon implores his readers to "treasure up my commandments" and so to find blessed life (Prov. 2:1; 7:1). James exhorts people, "Do not merely listen to the word, and so deceive yourselves. Do what it says" (James 1:22).[13] Further, a surprising number of texts show how Scripture should *not* be read.

This interest in assisting and correcting the work of its readers is unusual. The books within arm's reach in my home library (an unscientific survey, I confess) make the point. In the academic and theological books, most authors spell out their primary and secondary aims in the preface or introduction. This is an ancient tradition, already practiced by Plato and Josephus. But after a few comments on method and the intended audience, the reader is on his own. Volumes on history and social analysis are similar. Most have a short statement about purposes and goals: Stephen Ambrose's account of D-Day will make full use of 1,380 interviews of combatants.[14] Andrew Cherlin promises to explain the gap between the high marriage ideals that Americans express and their disappointing practices — nearly the highest divorce rate on earth.[15] After the preface and a few remarks on how to draw conclusions from the author's work, readers must fend for themselves. Novels do even less to guide their readers, other than clues about genre: When one begins, "This book is largely concerned with hobbits" the reader knows he has a fantasy, and takes it from there.[16] Dense as they are, my volumes on poetry by Billy Collins and Ted Kooser also expect me to find my way. Older works by Plato, Aristotle, Josephus, Philo, and an anonymous Buddhist volume are essentially the same.[17]

But the Bible is different, for three reasons. First, God wants those who read the Bible to know him and become disciples as a result of their reading (Jer. 31:34; John 10:4). It both inculcates and commands love of God, covenant loyalty, faith in Jesus, and obedience to him. Second, the Bible's writers are constantly aware that their work will encounter willful rejection (Jer. 36:23), wanton distortion (2 Pet. 3:16), and ordinary misunderstanding (1 Cor. 5:10-11). Third, the Bible's Author and authors have chosen to reach their goals not by straightforward lecture, proceeding proposition by proposition, but through songs and poems, dark

13. The NIV is periphrastic, but it captures the terseness of the command.

14. Stephen Ambrose, *D-Day* (New York: Simon & Schuster, 1994), 8.

15. Andrew Cherlin, *The Marriage-Go-Round* (New York: Knopf, 2009), 3-4.

16. J. R. R. Tolkien, *The Lord of the Rings: The Fellowship of the Ring* (New York: Ballantine Books, 1973), 19.

17. Josephus does orient readers to his themes with prefaces to *Antiquities* and *Wars*. Philo is constantly concerned with right interpretation of Scripture, but not with the right interpretation of his own work.

sayings, and half-interpreted stories. Jesus interprets some parables (Matt. 13:3-43), but lets us figure out how to read other parables as pictures of the kingdom, of kingdom ethics, and of the King himself (e.g., 13:37).[18] We readers don't take dictation; we swim in metaphor.

Eugene Peterson's book on Jesus and language, *Tell It Slant,* commandeers lines from an Emily Dickinson poem, which begins, "Tell all the Truth but tell it slant — " and continues, "The Truth must dazzle gradually . . . Or every man be blind."[19]

Peterson rightly observes that Jesus commonly "tells it slant," not straight. His teaching overflows with metaphor, simile, exaggeration, proverb, riddle, paradox, irony, and uninterpreted parables.[20] He asks loaded questions, expecting answers, while refusing to give a straight answer to half the questions people put to him. "He wasn't so much handing out information as reshaping our imaginations."[21] Some biblical literature is more linear, more propositional; Paul's letters come to mind. But so much is not: apocalyptic literature, poetic prophecies. While some narratives spell out their meaning, a great number in Genesis, Judges, Samuel, and Kings stretch out, page after page, without a first-order declaration of their message. Stanley Fish, sometime radical reader-response theorist, asserts that "it is the reader who 'makes' literature."[22] We deny the assertion but we see why someone might apply it to Scripture.

Yet the Bible is not like the elitist poetry that delights in baffling its readers. God aims to make disciples through his words. When John says he wrote his account of Jesus' signs "that you may believe that Jesus is the Christ, the Son of God, and that by believing you may have life in his name" (John 20:30-31), he does not intend to declare the purpose of the entire Bible, but it's not bad as a starting point. In the poem "Keeper of the Word Hoard," L. D. Brodsky declares: "I am the words I say / They define my ascending declensions / Identify my person and case . . ."[23] Brodsky has another purpose, but the concept applies, *mutatis mutandis,* to God's self-revelation. We know him both from his deeds and from the words he says out, words that interpret his purposes when he did this

18. Craig Blomberg, *Interpreting the Parables* (Downers Grove, IL: InterVarsity, 1990), esp. 313-24. As with the parables, dense apocalyptic interrupts itself to offer *occasional* hints on proper interpretation of its symbols (e.g., Rev. 1:20; 12:7-12).

19. Emily Dickinson, *The Complete Poems,* ed. Thomas H. Johnson (Boston: Little, Brown & Company, 1955), 506.

20. Robert Stein, *The Method and Message of Jesus' Teaching,* rev. edition (Louisville: Westminster John Knox, 1994), 4-59.

21. Eugene Peterson, *Tell It Slant* (Grand Rapids: Eerdmans, 2008), 12.

22. Stanley Fish, *Is There a Text in This Class?* (Cambridge, MA: Harvard University Press, 1980), 67.

23. L. D. Brodsky, "Keeper of the Word Hoard," in *The World Waiting to Be* (St. Louis: Time Being Books, 2008), 35.

or that. Indeed, God effectively speaks twice and acts once. For he first foretells his acts, partially explaining them, then he acts, and after that he elucidates their meaning more fully.[24]

We justly say the Lord wants readers to understand his word. Yet "whenever Moses is read, a veil lies over their minds," a veil that is removed "when a man turns to the Lord" (2 Cor. 3:15-16). Further, Jesus occasionally *chooses* to be cryptic: "For those outside everything is in parables." Matthew explains this is "*because* seeing they do not see" — that is, sometimes parables are punitive. But Mark explains that parables are causative, too. Jesus spoke in parables "*so that* they may indeed see but not perceive" (Mark 4:12).[25] Scripture affirms both, seeing them as complementary truths. Exodus 4–9 asserts both that Pharaoh hardened his own heart (Exod. 8:15, 32; 9:34) and that God hardened his heart (Exod. 4:21; 7:3; 14:8). The same held in Jesus' day. People hardened their hearts to Jesus' word, for they did not want to hear it — "Because I tell the truth, you do not believe me!" (John 8:45). Yet Jesus also hardened them, punishing unbelief by withdrawing his word. God enlightens "those whom he has freely chosen." Others are blinded, yet the blame remains theirs, because "this blindness is voluntary."[26]

Clearly, the Bible must guide its readers. The literature is engaging but cryptic, of supreme importance, yet not inclined to bald declarations of all its purposes. Because readers can innocently misinterpret what is difficult and wantonly pervert what is clear, it is no surprise that the Bible also tells us how *not* to read it.

Jesus Critiques the Misreading of Scripture

On five occasions, Jesus chides Jewish leaders for misreading Scripture, using the rhetorical formula "Have you not read?"[27] Jesus is questioning neither the teachers' literacy nor their reading habits. He knows they have *read* the Scriptures; he means they failed to grasp their *meaning*.[28] On four of these occasions,

24. Gerhardus Vos, *Biblical Theology* (Grand Rapids: Eerdmans, 1945), 6-7.

25. Matthew 13:13 says Jesus spoke in parables *because* (*hoti*) seeing they do not see, so that parables punish sin. Mark 4:12 says Jesus spoke in parables *so that* (*hina*) seeing they might not see, making parables a reflection of God's decision.

26. John Calvin, *Commentary on a Harmony of Matthew, Mark and Luke,* trans. William Pringle (Grand Rapids: Baker, 2003), 2:107-8.

27. In all, the question appears ten times in five passages, for it is repeated in Matthew 12, and four times the question is doubled in parallel passages. The list: Matthew 12:3, 5 // Mark 2:25; Luke 6:3; Matthew 19:4; Matthew 21:16 // Mark 12:10; Matthew 21:42 // Mark 12:26; Matthew 22:31 (no parallel). The verb *anaginōskō*, ordinarily "I read," appears each time, but the phrasing varies slightly. It is *ouk anegnōte* in Matthew 12:3, 5; 19:4; 22:31, and Mark 12:26; but *oudepote anegnōte* in Matthew 21:16; 21:42; Mark 2:25; *oude . . . anegnōte* appears in Mark 12:10, Luke 6:3.

28. The question has precursors in prophetic and rabbinic literature. Rabbis distinguished

their failure hinges on Scripture's testimony to Jesus. The fifth passage, where we begin, chides the Pharisees for following the letter and failing to seek the intent of Scripture.

In Matthew 19, the Pharisees ask, "Is it lawful for a man to divorce his wife for any and every reason?" (Matt. 19:3). Jesus replies, "Have you not read" that God created humankind male and female, to become one flesh (19:4-6)? Some Pharisees had indeed misread Moses, turning regulations intended to restrain divorce into permission for men to divorce their wives at their volition. They misread Scripture by dwelling on the grounds for dissolving a marriage rather than the ways for restoring it.[29] They read for legal, casuistic rules concerning the grounds for divorce and missed their intent — that husband and wife remain together living as one flesh.

Remaining instances turn on a failure to see that the law and the prophets testify to Jesus. In Matthew 12 the Pharisees charge him with breaking the Sabbath when he permits his disciples to pluck grain from fields as they walk along. By way of reply, he asks, "Have you not read" how David and his companions entered the tabernacle and ate the consecrated bread, which was unlawful, because they were hungry (12:3)? That is, just as human need outweighed sacrificial regulations in David's day, so too something or someone outweighs Sabbath regulations in Jesus' day. He continues, "Have you not read" that on the Sabbath priests toil in the temple and yet remain innocent (12:5)? Jesus' point is twofold. First, the law knows priorities. Human need supersedes Sabbath regulations as does God's service. Furthermore, Jesus declares, "One greater than the temple is here" (12:6). That is, if priests are permitted to serve in the space *representing* the presence of God, the disciples may do what is necessary to assist the anointed one, who *is* the presence of God.

Matthew 22 (// Mark 12:26) is similar, although the focus is on the Father, not

between reading and interpreting, between what a text says and what a reader learns. David Daube, *The New Testament and Rabbinic Judaism* (Peabody, MA: Hendrickson, 1956), 427-32.

29. *The Mishnah,* trans. Herbert Danby (London: Oxford University Press, 1933), 307-21, devotes pages to regulating divorce, but includes nothing about preserving marriage. Here is part of a law regulating bills of divorce (Gittin 2:3-6, pp. 308-9):

> It may be written with anything: ink, red dye, gum, copperas, or whatsoever is lasting; but it may not be written with . . . fruit juice or whatsoever is not lasting. It may be written on anything — on an olive leaf, or on a cow's horn (and he must give her the cow). . . . All are qualified to write a bill of divorce, even a deaf mute, an imbecile or a minor. All are qualified to bring a bill of divorce, excepting a deaf mute, an imbecile, a minor, a blind man or a Gentile. . . . If it was received from the husband by a minor who (later) became of age, or by a deaf mute whose senses (later) become sound, or by an imbecile who became sane . . . it is still valid. But if (given by) one of sound senses who then became a deaf mute and again became of sound senses, . . . or by one who was sane who then became an imbecile and again became sane, it is valid. . . . If at the beginning and at the end an act is performed knowingly, it is valid.

the Son. When the Sadducees deny the bodily resurrection, Jesus asks, "Have you not read what God said [in Exod. 3:6], 'I am the God of Abraham, and the God of Isaac and the God of Jacob'?" (Matt. 22:29-32; cf. Acts 7:32). Jesus admonishes them because they failed to realize that Exodus 3 signifies that the patriarchs belong to God and God identifies himself with them. They are alive, for the Lord "is not the God of the dead but of the living" (Matt. 22:32b).[30] This reading does not ask too much of the Sadducees. Philo and 4 Maccabees, roughly contemporary sources, use an argument like that found in Matthew 22 and Mark 12.[31] Thus both Pharisees and Sadducees fail to read Scripture, although the Lord expects us to read and understand (e.g., Acts 13:27; Eph. 3:4; Rev. 1:3).

Jesus' remarks on misreading follow many in the prophets. Indeed, the prophets both *declare* that their words will not be received and *show* how that failure came to pass. For example, at the time of his call, Isaiah learns that Israel will essentially reject his ministry. The people will "be ever hearing, but never understanding" until hearts are hard and the nation ruined (Isa. 6:9-12). In the immediately following passage, Ahaz demonstrates the point (7:1-12). Jesus cites Isaiah 6 to explain why he speaks in parables: "Because seeing they do not see, and hearing they do not hear, nor do they understand. . . . [T]he prophecy of Isaiah is fulfilled . . . 'You will indeed hear but never understand, and you will indeed see but never perceive, for this people's heart has grown dull' " (Matt. 13:13-15). Similarly, the first oracle that the LORD gives Jeremiah prophesies that the people will reject him and his message and deny their guilt (2:23, 35). And they do just that. They say, "The prophets are but wind and the word is not in them" (5:13), so they refuse to listen to him (6:10-19). Because they trust in the temple and its rituals, they disregard Jeremiah's warnings (6:14; 7:4) and then plot against him (26:1-11; 11:18-19). Because they hate his message, they question his loyalty, imprison him, and lower him into a muddy cistern (37:1–38:6). Ezekiel and Amos suffer the same disregard (Ezek. 2:3-7; Amos 7:10-17). Even when they act with power, prophets are ill-received, as we see in the lives of Moses (Exod. 17:3-4; 32:1-6; Num. 12:1-2; 14:1-10), Elijah (1 Kgs. 18:17; 19:2), and Elisha (2 Kgs. 2:23-25).

The New Testament adds more cases of bad listening. A rich young man thinks Scripture might tell him what he must *do* to gain eternal life (Matt. 19:16ff.). Herod Antipas listens to John as a kind of intellectual stimulation, but kills him because of a rowdy party (Mark 6:14-29). Stephen is stoned after a provocative speech (Acts 7:54-60). The Athenians hear Paul as a curiosity, but scorn him when he questions their presuppositions (17:22-32). Paul's trials recount a bitter tale of

30. Exodus 3:6, Mark 12:26, and Acts 7:32 lack the copula, but Matthew 22:32 has the verb *eimi* in the present tense; he *is* their God.

31. Craig Keener, *A Commentary on the Gospel of Matthew* (Grand Rapids: Eerdmans, 1999), 528-29; N. T. Wright, *The Resurrection of the Son of God* (Minneapolis: Fortress, 2003), 424-25.

bad listening. Felix cannot hear Paul because he hopes for a bribe (24:10-26). Festus listens with an ear attuned to politics rather than truth or justice. Agrippa acts surprised that Paul would try to convince him of anything (25:23–26:28). Given all these cases of misreading, how should we read?

We Read to Find the Great Themes of Scripture

Above all, the ideal reader will follow the stated purposes of Scripture. A quest for a single statement of Scripture's purpose is roughly like a quest for "the best food." But we can identify a series of statements that, taken together, show the purpose of Scripture. We may begin with the call of Abraham, which may be the first statement of God's grand mission. As we know, Genesis 12 says that God called Abraham that he might be blessed and bless the nations. Further, his faithful instruction of his household would be a vital means to that end (Gen. 12:1-3; 22:16-18). Exodus 19–20 and Deuteronomy 6–7 teach readers that God chooses and redeems by grace alone. Because he first loved us, we should love him with heart, soul, mind, and strength. We should hold fast to the truth and the life of the covenant and pass this on to our children. Since many subsequent texts expand these points we may trust that they are central.[32] Thus Jeremiah says Israel and all nations should know God (Jer. 24:7; 31:34). Indeed all the nations shall know "that the LORD is God and there is no other" (1 Kgs. 8:60; Isa 45:5-6, 14, 18, 22; Mark 12:32; see also Isa. 43:10-12; 49:6; Acts 13:47).

From the beginning, the Bible shows that the nations will come to know these things not through a theological treatise, but by a narrative that threads its way through Scripture, the story of salvation, the drama of a loving Father seeking and restoring lost children. After Adam's rebellion, God promises a child who will crush the deceiver (Gen. 3:15). That son of Abraham will bless the nations (Gen. 12:1-3). That son of David will rule forever (2 Sam. 7:8-16). As the Lord says, "You will be my people, and I will be your God" (Jer. 11:4; 30:22; Ezek. 36:28; cf. Exod. 6:7).

In Jesus the promise comes to fruition. He ransoms people from every nation and reconciles them to himself. Jesus himself declares and the apostles repeat that his death and resurrection, his suffering and glory, constitute the climax of redemption (Luke 24; Acts 4:12; Rom. 8:17; Heb. 2:9-10; 1 Pet. 2:19-25). Various books of the Bible have purpose statements that sound a bit different yet cohere with the passages just cited. Thus John wrote "that you may believe that Jesus is the Christ, the Son of God, and that by believing you may have life in his name" (John 20:30-31; cf. 1 John 5:13). With the same goal, Paul presents his essential gospel in

32. Christopher Wright, *The Mission of God* (Downers Grove, IL: InterVarsity, 2006), 61-68, 191-221.

more than one epistle, in more than one way. We could cite "The righteous will live by faith" or "Christ Jesus came into the world to save sinners, of whom I am the foremost" (Rom. 1:17; 1 Tim. 1:15 ESV). We might just as sensibly quote texts such as Romans 3:21-28 or Galatians 2:15-20 or various other passages. We must expect the canonical writers to express the most foundational idea — there is a personal and active, creating and redeeming God, and he expects us to respond to him in faith and obedience — in any number of ways. Thus Jeremiah will say "let him who boasts boast about this: that he understands and knows me, that I am the LORD" (Jer. 9:23-24), and Jesus will say "If you love me, you will keep my commandments" (John 14:15 ESV) and they will essentially mean the same thing.

From these passages it is a short step to statements about the expansion of the gospel and discipleship. So Matthew records Jesus' charge to the apostles, to make disciples in all nations (Matt. 28:18-20). Paul adds that his disciples must entrust the things they heard him say "to reliable men who will also be qualified to teach others" (2 Tim. 2:2).

These principles show both insiders and novices how to navigate the sprawl of Scripture. Whatever we think we find as we read Scripture, it must cohere with these themes, explaining, developing, supporting, or expanding them.

We Read to Appropriate the Great Themes of Scripture

Since it is vital to discover and align our reading with the great themes of Scripture, the Bible insists that we also appropriate those themes. Psalm 1, paradigmatic as it is, blesses the man who delights in the law, meditates on it day and night (Ps. 1:1-3).[33] The Psalms invite (rather than command) us to savor the sweetness of the word, to treasure it, and to let its light search deep internally and guide us externally (19:7-14; 119:1-24, 105). Paul says Scripture "is able to make you wise for salvation through faith in Christ Jesus" (2 Tim. 3:15). He then specifies that Scripture has four functions: teaching, rebuking, correcting, training in righteousness (3:14-17). These four functions fall into two categories, creed and conduct. When Paul says Scripture is useful for teaching and refutation, he means Scripture as creed shapes our creeds and refutes doctrinal errors, which promote sin (3:1-9; 4:1-5). Regarding conduct, to say Scripture corrects is to say it rebukes sin. And to say it trains in righteousness is to say it promotes godly deeds. Therefore, we must read Scripture for orthodoxy and orthopraxy, for they are inseparable.[34]

33. Mark Futato, *Interpreting the Psalms: An Exegetical Handbook* (Grand Rapids: Kregel, 2007), 58-75. Futato argues that Psalms 1 and 2 introduce the purposes of Psalms.

34. Paul exhorts the church to guard the gospel and to do good works with roughly equal frequency. He never asserts the primacy of orthodoxy over orthopraxy. Dead orthodoxy and blind activism are equally problematic (cf. Rev. 2:1-7; Luke 10:38-42).

Still, while large portions of Scripture seem quite clear, obstacles remain. Ignorance, lack of training, and the sheer density of the content cause some mistakes, but there is a spiritual aspect to flawed reading, too. Peter links the two problems when he says Paul's letters "contain some things that are hard to understand, which ignorant and unstable people distort, as they do the other Scriptures, to their own destruction" (2 Pet. 3:16).

If we may focus on the spiritual dimension, Scripture reveals sin, confronts idols, and lays our secrets bare (Heb. 4:12-13). Proverbs 9:8 says, "Rebuke a wise man and he will love you," but not everyone is wise. Fools hate a rebuke. Thus the prophets say the word is sweet as honey when they eat it (Ezek. 3:3; Rev. 10:9); yet it becomes bitter or sour in the stomach, because it summons repentance and threatens judgment (10:10). Worse, the people who so desperately need to repent refuse to listen. They disregard the message and punish the messenger (Ezek. 3:1-27; Rev. 11:3-10; cf. Isa. 6:1-12; Jeremiah 20).

Some sayings are hard; they drive the unregenerate and the superficial away (John 6:60). Indeed, rebellion against the word is inevitable among unbelievers, unless God draws them: "The sinful mind is hostile to God. It does not submit to God's law, nor can it do so" (Rom. 8:7, cf. John 6:37). Again, "The man without the Spirit does not accept the things that come from the Spirit of God, for they are foolishness to him, and he cannot understand them, because they are spiritually discerned" (1 Cor. 2:14). By contrast, Jesus tells his disciples, "The knowledge of the secrets of the kingdom of heaven has been given to you, but not to them" (Matt. 13:11). The best reading is the result of God's supernatural gift. Nonetheless, we can do analytical work, the better to see how to take and read to greatest effect.

Reading the Bible and the World

Christian pastors and scholars read two texts, the Bible and the world (or culture), and they do so with two goals: their own edification and the edification of their hearers, the congregation or class.[35] A teacher is like a spiritual midwife. We do not give birth but our instruction can assist as God creates — or deepens — spiritual life through the word. Like a midwife, a teacher might be superfluous if all goes well. Men and women can read the Bible for profit without assistance (1 John 2:27). But when complications arise people need interpreters to explain the ancient text to contemporary audiences. We can present the interpreter's task through this model:[36]

35. I use "teacher," "reader," and "interpreter" interchangeably; "pastor" and "scholar" are nearly so, for both are exegetes and teachers, although their spheres of labor differ.

36. This portion of the chapter adapts some themes from my monograph, *Putting the*

Figure 1: A model of the interpreter's task

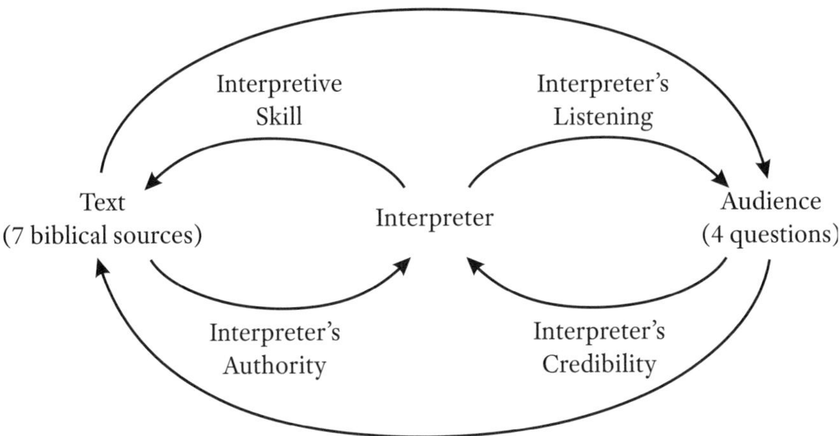

Clearly, the scholar (2) reads the text of Scripture (1). But it is also his responsibility to apply Scripture to his hearers (3) and to humanity in general. He must show how the Bible answers their valid questions, such as: What are my duties; that is, what do I owe God and man? What is godly character and how can I find or pursue it? To what goals or causes should I give my energy? How can I see my life and my world as God does?

By dint of study of the geography, customs, language, and worldview of biblical ages, pastors gain interpretive skill (4); they can discover the original message or intent of Scripture. But if they hope to present the truth to good effect, scholars must also be listeners (5), hearing what individuals, groups, and cultures want to know and what they have to say.[37] For this process to be effective, the interpreter must submit to the Bible's authority, following it wherever it goes (6), whether he particularly likes it or not. Finally, audiences will be more likely to gain from teachers whom they judge to be credible (7) — wise, loving, and good.

Of these seven, I will try to address those that bear most directly on the quest to take and read, beginning with credibility. Let us admit at once that this point creates a problem. A preacher is like a cardiologist with heart disease. We commit the very sins that we decry. The vain preach humility, the temperamental and the obese urge self-control, and the grasping teach contentment. Nonetheless credibility is essential. At point after point, Jesus incarnates the character he blessed. He says, "Blessed are the merciful," and he constantly shows mercy. He says, "Take up your cross and follow me," and he takes up his cross soon enough.

Truth to Work: The Theory and Practice of Biblical Application (Phillipsburg, NJ: P&R, 2001), 18-24, 59-77.

37. Kevin Vanhoozer, Charles Anderson, and Michael Sleasman, *Everyday Theology: How to Read Cultural Texts and Interpret Trends* (Grand Rapids: Baker, 2007).

Even Paul, the chief of sinners, could say, "Whatever you have learned or received or heard from me, or seen in me — put it into practice. And the God of peace will be with you" (Phil. 4:9; cf. 1 Tim. 1:15).

Robert Dabney said that if a speaker has intelligence but not integrity, "the plausibility of what he advances will be felt; but the more ability he shows, the more will the people fear to commit themselves to his opinions; for they have no guarantee . . . that he is not employing these forces of his genius . . . to . . . injure them." But if the people are convinced of a preacher's knowledge and affection and his desire for his hearers' benefit, then he has their ear. "Eloquence may dazzle and please; holiness of life convinces."[38]

How might we attain such holiness of life? Beyond our most visible sins, our brokenness also causes us to misuse Scripture. We are ignorant, blind, and stubborn, and that complicates the process of interpreting and teaching. We are never mere conduits for data. Our sources have taught us "facts" that may be falsehoods. And sometimes we want to avoid or obscure the biblical message. What can we do? Among other things, we need to read the Bible in life-giving ways.

Reading That Promotes Life — *Lectio Divina*

Every occupation has its hazards; the work of pastors and theologians is no different. Lazy students and recalcitrant parishioners may seem like the prime danger, but the misuse of Scripture is a greater problem. Eugene Peterson rightly says,

> We pick up the Bible and find that we have God's word in our hands, *our* hands. We can now handle it. It is easy enough to suppose that we are in control of it, that we can use it, that we are in charge of applying it wherever, whenever, and to whomever we wish.[39]

The danger is all the greater when we read the Bible professionally — preparing lessons from the posture of expert and crafting sermons from the posture of spiritual guide. We dream that we can master the text, and then use the results of our study to master others.

Peterson proposes the ancient and venerable plan for reading known as *lectio divina,* which has four elements: "*Lectio* (we read the text), *meditatio* (we meditate the text), *oratio* (we pray the text), and *contemplatio* (we live the text)."[40] Faithful God-centered and Christ-centered reading will also become doxological.

38. Robert Dabney, *Sacred Rhetoric* (Carlisle, PA: Banner of Truth Trust, 1870, 1979), 261-63.

39. Peterson, *Eat This Book,* 81-82.

40. Peterson, *Eat This Book,* 91.

While we can detect a natural progression through the four steps, *lectio divina* is not linear. A pastor or scholar may pray before, during, and after reading. As we read the passage again and again, reading and meditation blur.[41] "The process is more like a looping spiral in which all four elements are repeated, but in varying sequences and configurations."[42]

This ancient approach stands in contrast to a view, favored for decades by certain Protestants, that segregates exegesis from the preacher's work of the text's current meaning (or "application") and the disciple's commitment to *live* the text.[43] Krister Stendahl epitomized this view, saying, "[W]hen the biblical theologian becomes primarily interested with the present meaning, he implicitly or explicitly loses his enthusiasm . . . for the descriptive task." Biblical theology can only advance, he continued, when interpreters retain a sense of "the distance and the strangeness of biblical thought," and accept "that our only concern is to find out what these words meant," using methods agreeable to "believer and agnostic alike." Only when interpreters refrain from mingling the two phases can the Bible "exert the maximum of influence."[44]

Stendahl rightly insists on the quest for the original meaning of the text. Earlier, Martin Luther said the believer meditates on God's law, while "perverted people . . . twist the Scriptures . . . and by their own fixed meditation compel the Scriptures" to agree with their empty opinions.[45] Certainly, we should be resolute in determining the original meaning before moving on to contemporary uses. Yet our theory should describe, not rule out, what skilled teachers actually do when they apply Scripture.[46] We reply, therefore, that Stendahl's sharp disjunction between interpretation and application, use, or response breaks down in practice. For one thing, teachers begin to develop hunches (at the least) about the implications of a passage long before they finish interpreting it. When they do, they may redouble their exegetical work, as they try to judge if their hunch is correct or not.

Furthermore, Scripture itself links exegesis and application. Jesus repeatedly

41. Meditation here has the typically Christian sense of extended contemplation of an idea, rather than the Buddhist sense of emptying the mind of ideas.

42. Peterson, *Eat This Book,* 91.

43. I use "application," "implication," "use," and "response" almost interchangeably. The term "application" can be imprecise, not least because it leads to a disjunction between "original meaning" and "significance" or "application," which I address below.

44. Krister Stendahl, "Biblical Theology, Contemporary," in *Interpreter's Bible Dictionary,* ed. George A. Buttrick et al. (Nashville and New York: Abingdon, 1962), 1:419-22.

45. Martin Luther, "Psalm 1," in *First Lectures on the Psalms,* in *Luther's Works,* vol. 10, ed. Hilton C. Oswald (St. Louis: Concordia, 1975), 18.

46. Anthony Thistelton, *The Two Horizons* (Grand Rapids: Eerdmans, 1980), 357-58, 372. Cf. Ludwig Wittgenstein, *Philosophical Investigations,* trans. G. E. M. Anscombe (New York: Macmillan, 1973), 11, 14, 23.

rebukes Jewish leaders for what we might call a failure to *apply* Scripture, while he actually chides them for failing to *read* it (Matt. 12:1-8), to know it (Matt. 22:23-33), and to understand it (Luke 24:44-47).[47] Consider the lawyer who stands up to test Jesus, asking, "What shall I do to inherit eternal life?" Jesus replies, "What is written in the law? How do you read it?" (Luke 10:25-26 ESV). The question is not "*What* do you read" but "*How* do you read?" (*pōs anaginōskeis;*). Jesus' question refers to the lawyer's heart intent, not his skills.

Speech-act theory offers a helpful way of thinking through the distinction between hearing the word and responding faithfully to it. Speech-act theory notices that the distinction between speaking and doing is overdrawn, for we *do things with words* — we promise, pardon, warn, urge action, and much more. Speech-act theory therefore distinguishes the *locution,* the words spoken or written, from the *illocution,* the author's aims, goals, or intended effects as he or she spoke or wrote. Next, we consider whether hearers or readers respond as the author intended (the *perlocution*).[48] Did he or she believe the promise, receive forgiveness, heed the warning, or act obediently? One advantage of this scheme is that it is more refined than the traditional meaning-application distinction (in part because it distinguishes the different senses of "meaning").[49]

For reasons like this, John Frame wants to erase the distinction between meaning and implications. He says, "The meaning of Scripture is its application."[50] That is, we understand Scripture only when we know how to use it. Try, for example, to separate the *meaning* from the *application* of the eighth commandment. Suppose someone duplicates copyrighted materials, cheats on his taxes, and misrepresents products that he sells. If he claimed he obeyed the law since he never *stole* anything, we would not say he failed to *apply* the command; we would say he did not *understand* it. Frame holds that theology, rightly conceived, never seeks to discover abstract "truth-in-itself." Theology is "the application of the Word of God by persons to all areas of life" to promote godliness and spiritual health.[51]

Frame certainly helps us correct Stendahl's sharp claim that "our only concern is to find out what these words meant" and that only then can the word have

47. Notice implicit rebukes in John 5:36-40; 7:37-42; 10:24-39. Similarly, in Matthew 2, the scribes know where the Christ was born, yet fail to go to worship him.

48. To illustrate, "Is there any salad?" is a locution that, if spoken at a dinner table, has the illocutionary force of requesting salad, leading to the perlocutionary response of someone passing a salad bowl.

49. Speech-act theory has been put to especially fruitful theological use by Kevin Vanhoozer in, for example, *The Drama of Doctrine* (Louisville: Westminster John Knox, 2005), 63-68, passim.

50. John Frame, *The Doctrine of the Knowledge of God* (Phillipsburg, NJ: P&R, 1987), 67, 97.

51. Frame, *The Doctrine of the Knowledge of God,* 81-84.

"influence." Yet there is a distinction between the meaning and the implications of texts. Frame rightly argues that one should not claim to understand "Thou shalt not steal" if one embezzles funds or steals ideas. But by choosing a limpid command he makes the situation look simpler than it is. Many a passage, indeed, many a law, demands painstaking labor before we can be sure of its sense, let alone its penumbra of implications. For example, why does Moses thrice forbid cooking a kid in its mother's milk (Exod. 23:19; 34:26; Deut. 14:21)? And how might the commands to honor boundary stones bear on current theories of property and economics (Deut. 19:14; 27:17; Prov. 22:28)? Some enthusiastic capitalists detect a direct endorsement of a free market economy, a conclusion that runs afoul of laws and prophecies that prohibit the accumulation of land and property (Lev. 25:13-43; Deut. 15:12-18; 24:19-22; Isa. 5:8; Mic. 2:8-9).[52]

When Frame relaxes or blurs the boundaries between meaning, theology, and application, he stands with Calvin, who, being a biblical theologian, knew that theological formulations are never ends in themselves. In the *Institutes,* Calvin constantly, deliberately moves from biblical theology to the use or benefits of biblical truth. For example, as Book 12, chapter 15 explores the offices of Christ, prophet, priest, and king, he repeatedly pauses to name the "heavenly benefits" or "efficacy" of the doctrines. Because Christ is king, the church is "secure in . . . frightful storms" and assured of "everlasting preservation . . . no matter how many strong enemies plot to overthrow the church."[53] Even when Calvin does not explicitly draw implications from biblical doctrine, he puts his pronouns to effortless and subtle use. Thus, in explicating the work of Christ as priest, he says God's righteousness "bars *our* access" to God; that Jesus' sacrifice "blotted out *our own* guilt"; that by Jesus' intercessory work "*we* obtain favor."[54] This approach pervades the *Institutes.* After presenting the biblical doctrine of God's sovereignty, he pens an entire chapter, eighteen pages of impassioned pastoral counsel, titled "How We May Apply This Doctrine to Our Greatest Benefit."[55] He even insists on the "usefulness" and "very sweet fruit" of the doctrine of predestination.[56]

The concept of a seamless transition from truth to its "use" should hold for the ethical passages in Scripture too. Imagine an exposition of Matthew 5:22: "Anyone who says to his brother, 'Raca' is answerable to the Sanhedrin. But anyone who says 'You fool' will be in danger of the fires of hell." Naturally, the teacher is obligated to explain what "Raca" and "Fool" mean:

52. Christopher Wright, *Old Testament Ethics for the People of God* (Downers Grove, IL: InterVarsity, 2004), 85-97.

53. John Calvin, *Institutes of the Christian Religion,* trans. F. L. Battles (Philadelphia: Westminster, 1960), 2.15.2-5.

54. Calvin, *Institutes* 2.15.6; emphasis mine.

55. Calvin, *Institutes* 1.17.1-11.

56. Calvin, *Institutes* 3.21.1-2.

> The term "Raca" expresses contempt for the head — something like "You stupid idiot!" "Fool" shows contempt for the character. It means, "You scoundrel." "Raca" means "You have no brains." "Fool" means "You have no heart." Together, they imply, "You're worthless. Good for nothing." When someone cuts us off in traffic and we mutter "idiot!"; when someone fails us and we whisper, "He's worthless," Jesus calls it murder. We're saying they don't deserve to live. Even Christian parents can talk this way. By this standard, most of us are murderers — and the carnage may not remain internal. Murder in the heart permits murderous actions such as abortion, euthanasia and neglect of the poor. People take lives of the unborn and neglect the needy because they make a judgment: "This life has no value. They might as well be dead." Jesus says such thoughts, even without action, make us liable to judgment.[57]

Through close reading, we can detect where the speaker shifted from exegesis to its uses or implications, but the boundary is permeable. Stated another way, if someone said, "I won't call anyone 'Fool' but I see no problem with 'worthless,'" we would have to say they misunderstood Jesus.

This phenomenon, readily observable in the work of skilled preachers and teachers, returns us to the *lectio divina.* It advocates that we *read* the text as skillfully as possible. But we also *meditate;* when we do we enter the world of the text and become empathetic with it. Luther says that to meditate is "to think carefully, deeply, and diligently . . . to muse in the heart." The one who meditates is "moved in the innermost self," asks questions and longs for understanding. When we delight in the law "meditation will come of its own accord."[58] Peterson says we also *pray* the text because we realize "God has spoken to me; I must answer." If we read and pray the text we can also *live* the text in the noisy demands and dull duties of life.[59] As we shall see, efforts to live the text normally drive us to reread it. Then the cycle begins again, for the goal is never reading alone. If we merely read words, they become marks on a page, saying the same thing over and over. But if God gives us ears to hear (Matt. 13:9, 16), we can read, meditate, pray, and live the word. The word remains fresh as we constantly put new questions to it, so we can live it.

I experienced this reading-meditating-living nexus in a surprising way while teaching one week at a seminary in northern India. One morning I read and considered the proverb, "A gentle answer turns away wrath" (Prov. 15:1). We had some free time that afternoon, so our hosts, Americans who had lived in India for decades, took us to visit a deserted British cemetery in the southern Himalayas. After we had walked around for a while, a custodian rushed at us, shouting vehe-

57. See Daniel Doriani, *Matthew* (Phillipsburg, NJ: P&R, 2008), 144.

58. Martin Luther, "Psalm 1," in *Psalms,* in *Luther's Works,* 10.17.

59. Peterson, *Eat This Book,* 92-117.

mently, "What are you doing here, you trespassers! Grave robbers! How did you break in? This cemetery is closed. Get out of here or I will set my dogs on you!"

To my astonishment, our polite, soft-spoken host bellowed right back, roaring our innocence. They stood inches apart shouting on top of each other, spraying each other with saliva. After a minute, the clamor diminished, though both men still yelled. In another minute, the tone become milder still, even genial. Momentarily, we had an invitation to tea! When we were alone again, I asked my friend to explain why he had shouted at the custodian and how, it seemed, the yelling had calmed him. He explained: "The caretaker doesn't have much to do; it's his job to shout a little. I yelled back because that's how you establish sincerity and innocence here. If I backed down, he would have decided that we *were* trespassers."

The proverb "A gentle answer turns away wrath" came to mind. Obviously, my host had turned away wrath; his loud protest had served as a gentle or "gentling" answer, in his cultural context.[60] Deliberately exercising self-control, he had yelled in order to turn away wrath. Because my friend had learned to live or contextualize the proverb in his society, I reconsidered and surmised that the proverb's intent is not to monitor volume, but to turn away wrath. A whisper can be inflammatory and a shout can be calming. Since this was more insightful guess than exegetical conclusion, I asked my peers (my interpretive community) if they concurred (they did). I also recalled occasions when whispers caused wrath and shouts brought calm. I scanned dozens of Proverbs and saw that many aim for a goal or result, not just a behavior. For example, the proverbs on fools aim to warn readers neither to be a fool nor to trust one. Next, standard lexical study showed that the term translated "gentle" *(rak)* means tender or soft, but not necessarily "quiet." Finally, I consulted a skilled commentator who said the phrase "gentle answer" may connote "a response that in both substance and style soothes and comforts the listener."[61] Thus he agreed that the proverb speaks to the *goal* of speech more than the *decibels.*

This case study illustrates the multifaceted character of interpretation. We make use of certain technical skills, but we also come to texts with our needs, questions, and heartaches. As we read, something touches upon a life issue and we begin to apply the text to ourselves before we finish reading exegetically. Listeners, likewise, fasten upon a teacher's most incidental and unplanned side comments, if they connect with burning life issues. A good sermon, people often say, is one that gives them something to think about. That "something" typically touches their relationships, aspirations, or secrets. Therefore reading, in the fullest sense, requires technical skill, accumulated knowledge, artful analysis, and

60. In fact, both this encounter and the discourse on "raca" and "fool" could both be considered exercises in contextualization.

61. Bruce Waltke, *The Book of Proverbs: Chapters 1–15,* NICOT (Grand Rapids: Eerdmans, 2004), 613.

spiritual concentration or alertness. When we want to *heed* the word, we see better how to *read* the word.[62]

But the quest to read, contemplate, pray, and live the text occurs in a world that disrupts the process in both internal and external ways. Our efforts to read Scripture are hampered by our individual or idiosyncratic sins on one side and by corporate or cultural problems on the other. Internally, sins of laziness and distraction intrude. And focus dissipates when we read texts that challenge cherished beliefs or fond habits of sin. (How *did* the medieval church justify its accumulation of vast wealth?) Externally, every culture clashes with God's ideals, making it more difficult to take, read, and live the text. When a reader's native culture finds elements of the biblical worldview or lifestyle absurd, it is harder to read the Bible at that point.

Reading and the Culture

In ways we can never fully detect, we operate within our culture's dominant thought world. It can be easy to see where ideas clash, but it may be harder to resist anti-Christian patterns of thought. Every culture has answers to questions such as: What topics are interesting or difficult enough to merit our attention? What counts as a valid reply to the questions of the day?

For example, Western culture currently scorns supernatural explanations of dramatic events. We no longer see plagues as acts of God. After an earthquake, we do *not* say, "God wants to warn of impending judgment" and "the will of God" does not *count* as a valid explanation of such events. Our era says it is fitting to offer *scientific* explanations of disease and disaster. In 2004 and 2009, strong earthquakes caused massive destruction and loss of life in Indonesia and Haiti, respectively. In 1755 a far more powerful earthquake struck near Lisbon, capital of Portugal, on a Sunday morning.[63] Many thousands perished while gathered for worship. In Lisbon alone, about 50,000 died from the buildings that collapsed and the tsunami that arrived thirty minutes later. Religious Europeans — and almost all were religious — took the event as a sign of God's wrath or as a warning of impending judgment. Voltaire denied the notion that there could be divine justice in earthquakes or "volcanoes seething." In his "Poem on the Lisbon Disaster," Voltaire asked:

62. Gadamer says that the understanding of a text is tested by one's ability to see its significance for new situations. See Hans-Georg Gadamer, *Truth and Method,* 2nd edition, trans. Joel Weinsheimer and Donald G. Marshall (New York: Continuum, 1997), 277-305. Of judicial and biblical law he says, "To understand the order means to apply it to the specific situation to which it is relevant" (298).

63. The Indonesia and Haiti earthquakes were roughly 7 on the Richter scale, whereas seismologists estimate the Lisbon quake had to be nearly 9, hence almost 100 times more powerful.

What crime, what sin, had those young hearts conceived
That lie, bleeding and torn, on mother's breast?
Did fallen Lisbon deeper drink of vice than London, Paris or sunlit Madrid?
In these men dance; at Lisbon yawns the abyss.[64]

Voltaire privately believed that earthquakes prove that God is either nonexistent or indifferent to humanity. He publicly argued that capricious quakes cannot represent God's justice. Voltaire's voice, once so lonely, has won the day. The victory of antisupernaturalist explanations is so thorough that I have seen mature pastors groan reflexively when "unsophisticated" Christians dare to connect such disasters to God's judgment. Yet they might rescind their reaction if they remember that the Bible *does* view them as signs in Isaiah 29:6, Ezekiel 38:19, Matthew 24:7, 27:54, and Revelation 6:12, 11:13 (et passim). Nonetheless, we are viscerally inclined to adopt the naturalistic explanation of earthquakes.[65] Indeed, our perspective may be so far from the eighteenth-century worldview that we struggle to attain "a wholly reliable understanding of what the Europeans" felt when the Lisbon quake struck.[66] And if it is a struggle to reach the eighteenth century, how much more the ages of Scripture? The questions people ask and the criteria for plausible answers vary from culture to culture.

What seems interesting, what seems to require comment, and what seems reasonable depends on our basic commitments, our worldview, and the community within which we live and think.[67] It cannot be a surprise that prevailing convictions and habits make it difficult for audiences to hear and accept what the Bible says about gender roles and sexual morality. That complicates the teacher's work. Some, knowing this, shirk the more difficult questions.

Character and Reading

The culture of higher education allows professors to challenge the culture, and biblical theology requires pastors to be bold, but that is easier said than done. Church leaders can easily let misguided fears or craving for praise or success

64. F. M. A. de Voltaire, *Poèmes sur le Désastre de Lisbonne et sur La Loi Naturelle avec des Prefaces, des Notes etc.* (Genève, n.d. [1756]), in *Selected Works of Voltaire,* trans. Joseph McCabe (London: Watts & Co., 1911), 1-2.

65. The dominance of naturalism is visible everywhere. A best-selling historical novel, Ken Follett's *World without End* (New York: Dutton, 2007), meticulously reconstructs the *material* world of the fourteenth century, but the author cannot let his hero think of collapsed cathedral walls or bridges in supernatural terms.

66. A. J. Conyers, *The Eclipse of Heaven* (Downers Grove, IL: InterVarsity, 1992), 15.

67. See D. A. Carson, *The Gagging of God* (Grand Rapids: Zondervan, 1996), and Lesslie Newbigin, *The Gospel in a Pluralist Society* (Grand Rapids: Eerdmans, 1989).

debilitate their preaching and teaching. If the congregation is full of wealthy, powerful, or attractive people, it is tempting to minimize warnings about greed, the abuse of power, and vanity. It is all too easy to say next to nothing of the sins visible in one's own church — gluttony, laziness, deception, pride, or premarital cohabitation. How bold it seems to denounce the errors of absent opponents and to flatter our allies.[68] When we lack the courage to address local sins, we may blind ourselves to those sins. If we refuse to say what we see in Scripture, we may find that we can no longer see it. Thus sin corrupts the reading of Scripture. Thus I suggest that the courage to declare whatever we find in the word is an aspect of "reading."

Preachers and teachers need godly character to let the Bible say what it means, to see the world as it is, and to address the difference. The temptation to cowardly silence assails us weekly, as our preparations urge us to say things that may offend. If the subject is murder, we must say it is murder to call people good-for-nothing idiots, even if saying so indicts dozens in the audience. If the subject is sexual purity, we must say extramarital sex is a thieving lie, as well as adultery, since extramarital sex is a life-uniting act that has no life-uniting intent.[69] Whenever we rebuke sins such as materialism or careerism, we know that many will feel pangs of guilt, or will silently or even angrily disagree. Some of those people feed us and our families.

Peer pressure may also induce us to adjust our remarks. Imagine a gathering dominated by secular people. The topic of homosexuality comes up and someone asks our opinion. The desire to sound reasonable, to be likable, can feel overwhelming. But if God has spoken and appointed teachers to declare his word on his behalf, then we must declare the truth, whether that feels comfortable or not. We are heralds for the one God who has spoken through Jesus, the prophets, and the apostles, so we must be a faithful steward of the mysteries of God (1 Cor. 4:1-2). We should ask *how* we might speak, to be persuasive, but not *whether* we should speak. The courage to speak is, again, an aspect of "reading."

The Right Posture toward Scripture Strengthens Our Reading

The last section assumes a view of Scripture, which I want to explore briefly, so we can see its bearing on the question of reading. Consider therefore the postures

68. Luke Timothy Johnson warns teachers about sins they can commit while expounding the word. Public speech before a frequently captive audience can, he says, tempt us "to virtually every form of evil speech: arrogance and domination over students; anger and pettiness at contradiction or inattention; slander and meanness toward absent opponents; flattery of students for the sake of vainglory" (*The Letter of James,* AB 37a [New York: Doubleday, 1995], 263).

69. Lewis Smedes, *Sex for Christians* (Grand Rapids: Eerdmans, 1994), 109-36.

an interpreter may take toward Scripture. First, the critical reader stands *over* the Bible as the judge of its truth claims. Second, a reader may stand beside the Bible, roughly as a peer, in dialogue. Third, pastors and scholars may stand under the authority of God, expressed in his word. In short, readers can stand over, under, or beside the Bible.

The Reader Is over the Text, as Critic: The Reader Has the Last Word

Critics may profess admiration or animosity for biblical religion. They may regard it as a noble spiritual system or as a naïve or repressive element of a superannuated worldview. They may long for a simple pre-critical faith or they may wish to liberate society from an oppressive orthodoxy. Regardless, critics say, no thinking citizen can trust an alien authority that posits a three-story universe with angels in heaven, demons in hell, and mankind in between. For modern man, this mythical view of the world is literally incredible.[70] A return to simple pre-scientific faith is impossible. Furthermore, the critic says, even if someone should choose such a faith, it is *their* decision. Like it or not, each individual is the final arbiter of his beliefs.

The Reader Is Beside the Text, in Dialogue: The Reader Has the Last Word, but Hesitates to Say So

On this view, readers of Scripture have existential encounters with past believers and their experience of God. Thus, when someone hears Scripture, his world meets another world and no one can prejudge the result. The reader may be changed by the text, or he may, perhaps reluctantly, reject it.[71] If we define a critic as someone who is willing, in principle, to say, "The Bible says 'x' and the Bible is wrong," the existential position is still critical. Yet this view shares the conservatives' belief in the power of the Bible to surprise, transform, and lay the heart bare. It holds, with conservatives, that while the Bible can insist on its authority, it ordinarily operates by "a non-violent appeal" to the imagination.[72] Thus this is truly an intermediate position.[73]

70. Rudolf Bultmann, "New Testament and Mythology," in *Kerygma and Myth: A Theological Debate,* ed. Hans Werner Bartsch, trans. R. M. Fuller (New York: Harper & Row, 1961), 1-44; John Macquarrie, *Jesus Christ in Modern Thought* (Philadelphia: Trinity Press International, 1990), 70, and many others.

71. Gadamer, *Truth and Method,* 302ff.; Thistelton, *The Two Horizons,* 307-10.

72. Paul Ricoeur, "Toward a Hermeneutic of the Idea of Revelation," *HTR* 70 (1977): 37.

73. While dialogue is the wrong posture toward Scripture, it is apt for the relation between pastor and church or teacher and class. The Second Helvetic Confession does say that

The Reader Is Below the Text, in Submission: The Text, or, the Lord Who Wrote It, Gets the Last Word

This reader bows to the God who reveals himself in Scripture and accepts whatever it says. If the Bible overthrows a cherished conviction, we say, "I stand corrected." Facing a difficult text, we may redouble our exegetical work, but if we confirm that it means what it seems, then we yield to the Lord, who speaks with authority.[74] So we are willing to submit to Scripture.

But there is a difficulty with this view. To confess "I submit to Scripture" is one thing; actual submission is another. Sadly, this view can be perverted by this series of notions:

> I believe whatever the Bible says.
> Whatever the Bible says, I believe.
> I know what the Bible says.
> Therefore, what I believe *is* what the Bible says.
> Therefore, if the Bible seems to say something I don't believe, it must not really mean that.

While the professor may glimpse this line of illogic in the academy, it is all too evident in churches that affirm the authority of Scripture. In Bible studies, people glibly assert what they believe, however thin the biblical evidence, because they once heard it from some authority. Meanwhile they ignore all that clashes with their beliefs. Thus they profess the authority of Scripture but function as if impervious to it.

The essential point for our study is this: it is possible for putatively submissive teachers to think they have the Bible's message under control and so to seal their ears. They are unwilling to read with true openness for they are too committed to their own opinions. *They blind themselves to anything that contradicts them, since their pledge to submit to Scripture would obligate them to believe and do things they want neither to believe nor do.* Meanwhile, the "dialogical" or existential teacher

---

the preaching of the word of God is the word of God, but Bullinger certainly did not believe that every sermon has the same authority as Scripture. Because sin and ignorance infect every teacher, the listening church should heed 1 Thessalonians 5:22, "Test all things, hold fast to what is good."

74. Critics sometimes accuse conservatives of biblicism, which makes sense to them since they separate God from the Bible. But if the Bible is God's word, the charge falls away. To submit to Scripture is to submit to the Lord who reveals himself in it. Notice Romans 9:17, which begins, "For the Scripture says to Pharaoh, 'I raised you up for this very purpose . . .' " This is from Exodus 9:16, where *God* speaks to Pharaoh. Thus for Paul "Scripture says" = "God says." Believers respond to the Author through his word. Yet it would be a deadly error if someone related to Scripture in itself and missed God himself.

may be more willing to read what the Bible actually says since he (erroneously) claims the right to reject it.

There is a better way to read. First, whenever we read a passage, however familiar it seems, we should confess that we do not understand it as fully as possible. Second, we should remind ourselves that we probably do not believe this passage as purely as we should. Therefore, third, we must be willing to let every passage correct our thoughts and our deeds.

So, then, we are prepared to read well if we believe that the living God has spoken in Scripture, giving us truth that supersedes human wisdom and corrects human misconceptions and misdeeds. To read the Bible well, scholars and pastors need linguistic, analytical skills and historical knowledge, but we also need faith. In addition, we need to read the world well.

Understanding of the World Deepens Our Reading

The better we read the culture, the better we will read the Bible, and so fulfill the task of pastors and theologians, which is to lead God's people to hear his word and to participate in the divine life, individually and corporately.

John Frame says, "The law is necessary to understand the world" and "The world is necessary to understand the law." That is, we must know something about the world or we cannot apply the law.[75] I cannot understand, that is, *apply,* the command "You shall not steal" if I don't know what property is mine and what is my neighbor's. I must study animals, plants, and minerals so I know how to tend and subdue the earth. We don't know what Scripture means — we don't know how to live it — unless we understand the world, for "the meaning of Scripture is its application."[76] Therefore, to read the Bible properly we need skill at reading the world.

In *Everyday Theology,* Kevin Vanhoozer provides categories and questions that enhance an interpreter's ability to read a culture, to "catch" more of what is happening. We catch more if we describe phenomena in thick, multi-perspectival, non-reductionistic ways. This holds for high culture — serious books, movies, operas, and paintings — but also for "everyday" culture — entities such as a prom or a grocery store checkout line. A reductionist may see proms in terms of social and economic power. But the prom is also a social and historical event, one that affirms friendships and inaugurates or solidifies relationships. To apply Scripture to "the prom" in a credible way, we need a handle on the several aspects of what a prom is.[77]

75. Frame, *The Doctrine of the Knowledge of God,* 66-67.
76. Frame, *The Doctrine of the Knowledge of God,* 66-68.
77. Vanhoozer et al., *Everyday Theology,* 45-46, 63ff.

Vanhoozer restates the familiar distinction between the locution, the illocution, and the perlocution of a text, then reformulates it as "the world behind, of, and in front of the cultural text." This is "general hermeneutics." Vanhoozer continues: "Just as various types of literary criticism can focus on authors or texts or readers, respectively, so various schools of cultural criticism emphasize either the producers, the cultural products themselves, or the consumer of these products."[78] Thus when we review a movie, we know we should consider its message and artistic merits, but Vanhoozer would also consider why its creators made it and how they intended to affect their consumers.

Take James Cameron's 2009 film *Avatar.* Behind the text we have Cameron's technical genius as a director and as inventor of camera systems. Behind the text we also have Cameron the egotist, the man with well-known anti-Christian and anti-American views. In the film itself we have a dazzling visual experience joined to a pedestrian plot and dull dialogue that fail to enhance Cameron's subtle-as-a-sledgehammer nativist message. All this serves sales, Cameron's name, and, possibly, his personal views. This analysis is painfully short, but it explains why some culturally aware believers thought the film was good-old Hollywood entertainment and others judged it abominable.

To the point of this essay, analytical tools such as these help us read/obey commands such as "Test the spirits to see whether they are from God" (1 John 4:1 ESV) and "Test everything; hold fast what is good" (1 Thess. 5:21 ESV). The better we read the culture, the better we will read the Bible and so fulfill the task of pastors and theologians: to mediate God's word to God's people so they can participate in the divine life. The teacher's goal is to form the speech, thought, judgment, and behavior of the church, collectively and in its individual members. As Vanhoozer says elsewhere, "Theology exists" that we may understand "what God has said/done in the world for us and . . . what the church must say/do for God in response."[79]

Character and Reading

Some reading skills are intellectual and philosophical; others have more to do with wisdom and character. Some skills help us listen to the culture and our communal life; others help us listen to individuals and so to mediate, as midwife, God's word to them. Several character traits foster the art of listening to individuals.[80] *Love* wholly attends to others in their sin and neediness. It quenches

78. Vanhoozer et al., *Everyday Theology,* 44-53, quote on 48.

79. Kevin Vanhoozer, "A Drama of Redemption Model," in *Four Views on Moving beyond the Bible to Theology,* ed. Gary Meadors (Grand Rapids: Zondervan, 2009), 161.

80. Jesus repeatedly shows an ability to read minds: see Matthew 9:4; 12:25; Luke 5:22;

the desire to tell our story, to show our analytical skill and pithy wisdom, and to speak last. *Truthfulness* leads us to see and address the situation as it is, not as we prefer to imagine it. *Wisdom* knows how to cut through blather and excuses until we hear the truth. *Mercy* listens tenderly, so that we diagnose in order to render aid, not to criticize. *Patience* listens quietly to the story of people just like us, and people utterly unlike us. These traits deepen our listening, so that our reading-for-teaching acquires authenticity and drills real issues in real terms, so that people do not say "I enjoyed your talk" — a troubling compliment for preachers who hope to create some constructive misery — but rather, "I know exactly what you mean."

Humility also makes us better readers. A preacher is a diagnostician who detects in himself a deadly yet curable disease that he finds in his patients. The herald of grace is a sinner saved by grace. We "hold out the gospel in contaminated hands."[81] Therefore, we should approach every text penitently, *confessing* our need for its rebuke and correction, and *behaving* meekly as well. Humility assists communication, but it deepens interpretation even more. Humility leads us to read Scripture from inside the covenant of grace, so that as we read the text, the text reads us. When we have wrestled with sin, and lost a round or two, a realism, an awareness of the difficulty of faithfulness, suffuses our work.

But, to come to *lectio divina* from another angle, character has yet another role. Specifically, when we take our sin seriously and let it humble us, it will lead to a hunger and a thirst for righteousness (Matt. 5:6). That hunger will make us better interpreters. When we first begin to read-for-teaching, most of us have a simple, unarticulated model of the way it goes. Its basis lies in the activities that might appear on a weekly work report, together with a statement of the purpose of that work: pastors or scholars have a topic (by choice or assignment). They study it, then arrange what they know so that it is an acceptable discourse, whether sermon or lecture. The people listen, learn, and, one hopes, change their practices. The model is linear.

Figure 2: A naïve model of interpretation

Study → Knowledge → Lectures, sermons → Audience edification: knowledge, practice

This model is not completely invalid. It is true, for both teachers and hearers, that *what we know shapes what we do.* As Paul says, "Do not be conformed to the pattern of this age, but be transformed by the renewing of your mind" (Rom. 12:2a). But this model does not recognize that *what we* ***do*** *also affects what we*

6:8; 7:39-40; 9:47; John 2:25. Perhaps this was God-given prophetic insight or a manifestation of his omniscience. But he often chose not to exercise his divine prerogatives (Matt. 24:36), so perhaps his selfless ability to focus on others enabled him to read minds.

81. Cornelius Plantinga, "Preaching Sin to Reluctant Hearers," *Perspectives* 12 (December 1997): 11-12.

know. As Paul immediately adds, "Then you will be able to test and approve what God's will is" (12:2b). That is, when we try to obey the word, we put it to the test. When it passes the test, we know it better because experience has confirmed it.

When he was teaching at the feast of tabernacles and the crowds were debating whether Jesus was a good man or a deceiver, Jesus said, "If anyone wills to do God's will, he will know whether my teaching is from God or whether I speak on my own" (John 7:17, author's translation). Jesus says the central issue is volitional not intellectual: If the crowd wants to *do* God's will, they will recognize that Jesus' teaching comes from God (John 7:14-18). That is, the crowd objected to Jesus' teaching not because flawed study methods misled them, but because they did not want to follow him. Jesus' word of truth is self-authenticating for those who commit themselves to it. Thus, a renewed mind promotes godly action, but godly action also renews the mind and brings conviction of the truth (cf. Mal. 3:10). As the saying goes, "Do, and you will know."

Everyone realizes that people gain knowledge gradually, typically by coming at something again and again. Two thinkers, Friedrich Schleiermacher and Maurice Blondel, analyzed how the process works. Schleiermacher's contribution today has the label "the Hermeneutical Spiral."[82]

The Hermeneutical Spiral

The phrase "the hermeneutical spiral" evokes the idea of open-ended movement. A reader has a certain position before he or she encounters a text, but the text opens new vistas for those who are willing to learn and even to change their views. Yet views change slowly; a text may not do all its work in one sitting. Instead, readers spiral ever nearer to the author's meaning by refining their understanding when they repeatedly return to it.

One scholar described it this way: "I am . . . spiraling nearer and nearer to the text's intended meaning as I refine my hypotheses and allow the text to continue to challenge and correct those alternative interpretations, then to guide my delineation of its significance for today."[83] This idea has merit, but it sounds too narrowly cerebral. It misses the link between knowing and doing (just above). It misses the earlier lesson that life forces us to consider relevance long before we finish the mental process. The earlier account of the shouting in India makes this point.

82. The original term (from Friedrich Schleiermacher, *Hermeneutics: The Handwritten Manuscripts*) was hermeneutical *circle*, but the image of a circle is too static; *spiral* better expresses the idea of refinement and movement. See Thiselton, *The Two Horizons*, 327-56; Grant Osborne, *The Hermeneutical Spiral* (Downers Grove, IL: InterVarsity, 1991), 6-8, 366-415.

83. Osborne, *The Hermeneutical Spiral*, 6. Osborne's position is subtle, but hermeneutical theorists can give the impression that protracted cogitation precedes application.

Figure 3: The hermeneutical spiral

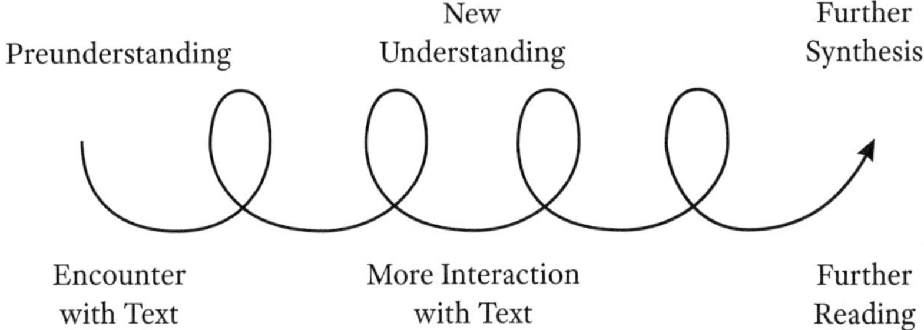

Adjusting the Hermeneutical Spiral

The philosopher-theologian Maurice Blondel observed that interpreters gain understanding of Scripture through attempts to apply it, not merely by round after round of reflective reading. As we attempt to obey the Scripture we understand it better, even if the exegesis is incomplete.

Blondel observes that humans both ponder and act. Aside from customary or habitual actions, we are planners. After premeditated actions we ask, "Did I act correctly? Did I obtain my goal or not? Could I have been more effective, more virtuous?" There is typically a gap between the goal and the result of our plans. In sophisticated projects, we rarely achieve precisely what we intend. The gap between our self-imposed demands and our success then prompts us to ask, "What went wrong? How can I avoid repeating my errors? How can I build on my success?" As we attempt to close the gap between plans and results, we progress toward our goal.[84]

As we read the Bible, we encounter many worthy goals: to turn away wrath, to do justice, to show mercy. The attempt to *fulfill* a text by reaching its goals helps us grasp what it means. Consider Titus 3:10: "Warn a divisive person once, and then warn him a second time. After that, have nothing to do with him." Surely the pastor whose church is roiled by gossip and slander will most carefully consider several questions: Who is a divisive person? How do we effectively warn him? What does it mean to "have nothing to do with him"? The pastor will work hard to read both the text and the world. Thus the desire to live the Bible helps him understand it.

84. Maurice Blondel, "Letter to Pere Auguste Valensin," quoted in *Introduction to Maurice Blondel: The Letters on Apologetics and History and Dogmatics,* trans. and ed. Alexander Dru and Illtyd Trethowan (London: Harvill Press, 1964), 96; John Macquarrie, "Maurice Blondel," in *Encyclopedia of Philosophy* (New York: Macmillan, 1967), 1:323-24.

Figure 4: A new model: knowledge and action stimulate each other

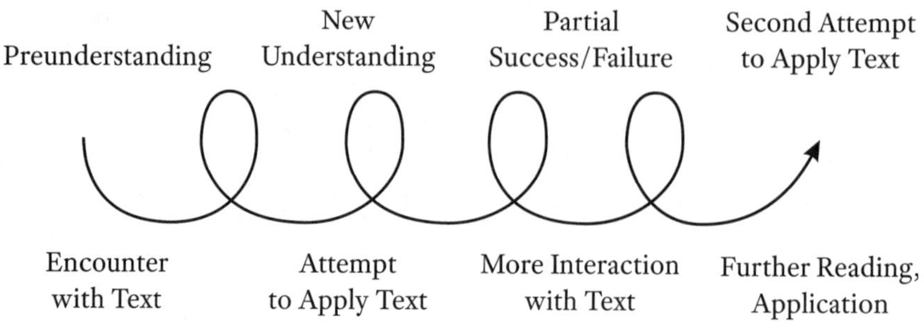

Conversely, if we refuse to practice what we know, we sever motives for reading well. If anything, inaction causes us to avoid knowledge, because it stirs our guilt. On the other hand, proper actions confirm halting steps in the right direction. An upward spiral develops, as small successes breed confidence, and confidence prepares us for the next challenge.

Wise theologians know this. Calvin said pupils of Scripture must "apply themselves teachably" to the word and "reverently embrace" its witness. He concluded, "[N]ot only faith . . . but *all right knowledge of God is born of obedience.*" So for Calvin the quest for obedience advances the knowledge of God and his word.[85] Similarly, Luther said interpretation requires "the experience of the heart" as well as skill with Scripture.[86] Wesley said that only the Bible could establish a doctrine but that experience does "confirm a doctrine which is grounded on Scripture."[87]

More recently, Gordon Fee said, "The ultimate aim of all true exegesis is spirituality," first for interpreters, then for their hearers.[88] Before exegesis starts, we give the text permission to bring us up short, to astonish and admonish us. Through exegesis we invite the text and its Author to exegete our soul and the souls of our hearers.[89] Similarly, Moises Silva said we cannot help but bring our failures and questions to the Bible:

> It is proper and even necessary to approach the Bible with a strong sense of our needs. The problems faced in the gospel ministry often alert us to truths

85. Calvin, *Institutes* 1.6.2.

86. Martin Luther, in Gerhard Maier, *Biblical Hermeneutics,* trans. Robert Yarbrough (Wheaton, IL: Crossway, 1994), 70.

87. John Wesley, *The Works of John Wesley* (Grand Rapids: Zondervan, 1872), 5:132-33, cf. 129.

88. Gordon Fee, "Exegesis and Spirituality: Reflections on Completing the Exegetical Circle," *Crux* 31, no. 4 (Dec. 1995): 30.

89. Fee, "Exegesis and Spirituality," 31, 34.

in Scripture that might otherwise remain veiled to us. Proper exegesis consists largely of asking the right questions from the text, and the life of the church can provide us with those very questions.[90]

So spiritual formation both precedes and follows interpretation. A feedback loop connects knowledge and practice: knowledge guides Christian living, but Christian living also verifies knowledge. A passion for righteousness spurs teachers on to deeper study, and enriches the hermeneutical spiral.[91] As we speak hard truths in love, we learn what "speaking the truth in love" means (Eph. 4:15). When we respectfully submit to a difficult or foolish boss we learn what it means to submit to a harsh master (1 Pet. 2:18). Thus a practical question may sensitize us to aspects of the text we might otherwise miss. It is possible that the question, "How does this apply; what does it mean *now*?" can lead to deeper inquiry into the question, "What did it mean *then*?"

True knowing entails doing. After he washed the disciples' feet, Jesus said, "Do you understand what I have done for you? . . . Now that I, your Lord and Teacher, have washed your feet, you also should wash one another's feet. . . . Now that you know these things, you will be blessed if you do them" (John 13:4-17). James, as we saw, says, "Do not merely listen to the word, and so deceive yourselves. Do what it says" (James 1:22). With diagnostic sarcasm, he extols those who affirm orthodox theology without acting on it: "You believe that God is one; you do well. Even the demons believe [that] — and shudder!" (2:19 ESV). The author of Hebrews chided the church, because their failure to practice what they knew had dulled their minds, so they could hardly follow his teaching. He concludes, "Solid food is for the mature, who by *constant use* have trained themselves to distinguish good from evil" (Heb. 5:11-14). They should have matured by applying their prior Christian experience to their current crisis.[92] If they had even tried, their imperfect attempts would have prepared them for their new struggle.[93]

People do not genuinely understand the Bible unless they can apply it. If a congregation has a flawless ecclesiology, but ignores visitors from other social and ethnic groups, do they understand the church? If a man memorizes Ephesians 5:25 but domineers his wife at every turn, does he "know" what it says?

90. Moises Silva, *Has the Church Misread the Bible?* (Grand Rapids: Zondervan, 1987), 22.

91. Dan McCartney and Charles Clayton, *Let the Reader Understand: A Guide to Interpreting and Applying the Bible* (Wheaton, IL: Bridgepoint, 1994), 254-55.

92. William Lane, *Hebrews 1–8,* WBC (Dallas: Word, 1991), 131, 139.

93. Frame, *The Doctrine of the Knowledge of God,* 154.

Blessed Reading

It is indeed vital to read the Bible expectantly, anticipating that we will find answers to life's questions as we keep turning Scripture over in our minds. A personal story makes the point. One day, after a frustrating attempt at disciplining our then eleven-year-old daughter, my wife said, "I don't know what to do. She's too old to spank and grounding punishes me as much as it punishes her. Take away privileges? She hardly watches television, and her activities are constructive. What is left?" Like a good scholar I promised to look into it. Eight weeks later my wife was still awaiting my reply when I reread Exodus 21:18-25 and noticed something I had previously overlooked in the *lex talionis*, "eye for eye, tooth for tooth." I knew that the law seeks justice and forbids vindictiveness and revenge: "If you hit me, I'll kill you" (per Gen. 4:23-24). But reading as a parent, I saw a principle that held promise for our disciplinary problem: let the punishment fit the crime and be proportional to it. The principle of proportional discipline implies that food crimes deserve food punishments. If a child, misbehaving, knocks over his juice three consecutive days, he can go without juice for three days. Property offenses deserve property discipline. If a child leaves her book bag on the floor several days, she can carry her books to school in a grocery bag for several days. If children refuse to stay in bed, they can stay up, doing nothing for a while. Children readily see the justice and learn from this. Recently my children, now in their twenties, were reminiscing about childhood blessings; they fondly mentioned this very principle because it seemed so fair and because they never suffered arbitrary "grounding." Thus a desire to be a godly parent led to an expectant sort of reading of Scripture, which produced a lifelong, multigenerational blessing. That is what the word can do.

Now it seems fitting to close with a short study of the way the Bible itself says the Word should work. Many passages present themselves as options, but James 1 seems fitting for scholars and teachers.

James Describes Godly Reading (James 1:18-25)

James 1:18 says God "chose to give us birth through the word of truth, that we might be a kind of firstfruits of all he created." This is another aspect of a point made just above. While the regenerate are able to grasp the word, the means God uses to regenerate is the "word of truth" (1:18). The phrase "word of truth" appears five times in the New Testament. In Paul, the phrase clearly means "the gospel" in each case (e.g., Eph. 1:13; Col. 1:5b-6a ESV). The gospel is the word of truth that gives us life. As Peter says, "For you have been born again, not of perishable seed, but of imperishable, through the living and enduring word of

God. . . . And this word is the good news that was preached to you" (1 Pet. 1:23, 25b ESV).[94]

James continues, "Everyone should be quick to listen, slow to speak and slow to become angry. For man's anger does not bring about the righteous life that God desires" (1:19b-20). Obviously, we learn more by listening than by speaking, and it's hard to hear a thing when we are angry. But the context seems to indicate that James is talking about listening to the word, not listening in general. His point, then, is that anger leads away from righteousness because the angry do not listen to God.

Therefore, James continues, we should "put away all filthiness and rampant wickedness and receive with meekness the implanted word, which is able to save your souls" (1:21 ESV). The order of James's commands is unexpected. We hear *second* that we should receive the word "with meekness." That is, we listen well, shun argument, and become docile and teachable before the word.[95] But it seems that this should be the *first* command, for no one can obey the first commandment and "put away filth and wickedness" on his own. One must hear and heed the first command and receive the implanted word "which is able to save your souls" (1:21 ESV). *Then* we can put away wickedness. Surely moral reform is not a precondition to hearing the word. The word, implanted in our heart, enables us to put off wickedness. Why does James have the opposite order?

By "put away filth" James means we must put off the old, sinful way of life. In Scripture, filthy clothes represent sin (Isa. 64:6; Zech. 3:3-4). To change clothes is to convert and reform (Zech. 3:4-9; Eph. 4:22-24; 5:26-27). But how does this happen? As he said in 1:18, God gives birth to us through the word of truth, the gospel. The word discloses our true condition — our "moral filth and rampant wickedness." So it describes our need of God's mercy and, by the gospel ("the word of truth"), directs us to that mercy.

Rereading James 1:21, we wonder why it says "put away all filthiness" *before* it says "receive . . . the implanted word, which is able to save your souls." Surely, the theologian thinks, James has the wrong order. First we receive the word, which saves the soul, and *then* we put away moral filth. But James is addressing "beloved brothers" (1:19), who were already born of (or birthed by, *apokyeō*) the gospel (1:18). Second, James seems to be speaking pastorally and experientially. As the eye sees things, a desire to break free from wickedness often precedes an interest in God's word. New converts often say (in the slang of the day) that a desire to get their lives in order led them to go to church or read the Bible.

Yes, the Holy Spirit imparts every genuine desire for reform. Nonetheless,

94. The verb in this sentence is *euangelizomai*, "preach the gospel" or "preach the good news." Unlike most translations, the NIV fails to show that the word that is preached is the gospel.

95. The Greek is *prautēs* — meekness, gentleness, or humility. Cf. Matt. 5:5; 11:29; 21:5.

unbelievers still ought to aspire to lay aside wickedness. As should we, if we would be good listeners. Notice that James says "receive the implanted word," not "work at removing sin." We put away moral filth and "live as believers" in Christ (2:1) when the implanted word takes root within us and purifies us (1:21, 27). It brings conviction of sin and assurance of mercy. It instills faith and creates new life, so that good fruit grows. This will not be easy, for wickedness is "rampant"; it grows prolifically, like noxious weeds, against which we wage war.

The church's chief weapon against sin is the word, which does three things. First, it gives us birth, so we become God's first fruits, uniquely dedicated to him (1:18; cf. Exod. 23:19; 34:26; Deut. 26:2; passim). Second, it promotes righteousness (1:20). Third, it saves our souls (1:21). Whatever we find in our studies, we must remember that the word aims to bring life and holiness.

However zealous the church may be about small groups and service teams, it is entirely possible to form happy relationships and remain utterly lost. On the other hand, everyone who preaches to large congregations, writes books, teaches at conferences, or posts messages knows that total strangers write and say, "Your message changed my life. As you spoke, it seemed that you were reading my mind. How did you know?" We didn't know, but God knew and chose to express his truth in his word. That word of God, applied by the Spirit, saves lives and redirects behavior. As we redeclare that word (cf. Matt. 16:19; 18:18), it saves from past sinfulness, it saves in this present life, and it saves for our future life with God.

Therefore, while teachers of the word labor to present it to others, James says that we ourselves must listen to the word (James 1:19), receive it (1:21), and do what it says (1:22-25). But scholars and pastors are prone to professionalize their reading of Scripture, applying it to everyone but themselves. Consider how that may happen to a potential pastor called Jason.

When Jason converts and becomes serious about the faith, his initial style of reading will be *naïve and devotional.* He devours Scripture, underlines everything, and feels that God is speaking directly to him.

In time, Jason becomes a *sophisticated and devotional* reader. He still feels that God speaks to him in the text, but he has learned some rules of interpretation. He reads texts in their contexts, understands that biblical truth unfolds progressively, and reads Bible dictionaries and commentaries. He begins to appraise the quality of his sources. He realizes that each Bible translation has a strategy and begins to use that awareness to get at the original text.

Next Jason goes to seminary, where he becomes a *technical reader.* He toils at the Greek and Hebrew text and consults scholarly sources. He respects the distance between his world and the Bible's. His zeal for cultural backgrounds grows. He pursues what the word originally *meant* and may begin to neglect what it means today, to *him.*

After ordination, Jason knows that his study has the edification of the church as its goal. He continues to read technically, but his study now has a definite use in view. As he preaches, he both shares and proclaims his findings to his church. So he becomes a *technical and functional* reader. He organizes his discoveries and offers them to others, but his soul may be detached at a personal level. He is teaching the church but he profits less.

Jason needs therefore to become a *technical and devotional* reader. Every technical skill remains, but he returns to his first love and immerses himself in the word again, letting it speak directly to his heart. He finds what Paul Ricoeur calls a "second naiveté." Jason is both technically astute and meek. He both receives God's word and expounds it. In this way, he finds strength to endure trials (1:12), to check the growth of sin (1:21), and to know he is blessed by a living faith (1:25).

Since the word both saves the soul and removes wickedness (1:21), James adds that we must "be doers of the word, and not hearers only, deceiving yourselves" (1:22 ESV). The NIV paraphrases crisply, "Do not merely listen to the word, and so deceive yourselves. Do what it says." The verb *ginomai*, rendered "*be* doers" could be translated "*become* doers," since the more active "become" fits James's usage in 1:12, 2:4, 2:10, and 2:11.[96] Reading that fails to lead to obedience is self-deceptive. "For if anyone is a hearer of the word and not a doer, he is like a man who looks intently at his natural face in a mirror. For he looks [intently] at himself and goes away and at once forgets what he was like" (1:22-24 ESV). But if we truly hear the word, we obey it (1:25; Rom. 2:13). In subsequent chapters James insists that knowledge must lead to practice; faith must lead to deeds (2:14-26). Those who are wise must *show it* by their life (3:13). Anyone who knows the good he ought to do and does not do it, sins (4:17).

If we fail to connect creed and conduct, James says, we *deceive* or *defraud* ourselves (1:22). Both translations are plausible contextually and lexically. We *deceive* ourselves if we say we hear the word, but don't follow it. We *defraud* ourselves if we fail to heed the word, for we rob ourselves of the fruit of obedience.

Again, James compares the careless reader to a man who peers into a mirror only to forget what his face looks like (1:23-24). Scripture truly is a mirror for the soul. We gaze in a physical mirror to inspect and perhaps improve our physical appearance. So we should gaze into Scripture to inspect and improve our spiritual condition. James concludes: "But the one who looks into the perfect law, the law of liberty, and perseveres, being no hearer who forgets, but a doer who acts, he will be blessed in his doing" (1:25 ESV).

Since Scripture, as mirror, discloses our sin and the promise of grace, we ought to remember what we see and amend what is amiss. But we gaze carelessly. When I was in seminary, my pastor had unruly hair and he sometimes used pins and barrettes in the morning to tame it. One morning he inserted a large silver barrette to control his hair, but forgot to remove it. When he got home that night, his wife gaped. He had gone through the day and seen hundreds of people

96. Johnson, *The Letter of James,* 206.

with that barrette firmly in place, for he looked in the mirror and forgot what he saw. He suffered transitory embarrassment, but we will fare far worse if we gaze at the word and fail to remedy our sin. Paul says, "Watch your life and doctrine closely. Persevere in them, because if you do, you will save both yourself and your hearers" (1 Tim. 4:16). Let us therefore take and read this mirror to the soul, see our flaws, and turn afresh to the Lord, who loved us and gave himself for us. We should read to know him, love him, and follow him.

FAQs

THIRTY-SIX

Summarizing FAQs

D. A. Carson

In the following FAQs (Frequently Asked Questions), the first number refers to the chapter where the question is discussed; the second figure (i.e., after the period) is the question number.

1.1 Why is the authority of Scripture so hotly debated today?

We live in a time when many competing voices scramble to impose their own understandings of life, culture, spirituality, and much else — the "age of authenticity," in the words of Charles Taylor, when what makes us "authentic" is that we adopt an intrinsic suspicion of authorities so that we can be free to be ourselves. From the Bible's perspective, this is, in part, a reprehensible flight from God, a form of idolatry.

1.2 Why are the issues surrounding the Bible's authority so complicated?

A good deal of the complexity is bound up with the range of disciplines that affect how we understand biblical authority. These include disputes about how the Bible's authority has been understood at various points in church history, what truth is, the nature of revelation, principles of interpretation, how different literary genres in the Bible have different ways of making their own rhetorical appeals, text criticism, epistemology, and much, much more.

1.3 Isn't the word "inerrancy" pretty useless, since it has to be defined very carefully and technically for it to be deployed at all?

There are very few words in the pantheon of theological vocabulary that *don't* have to be carefully defined if accurate communication and serious discussion are to take place. Consider, after all, "God," "justification," "apocalyptic," "Spirit," "regeneration," "sanctification," and many more. That a word, to be useful in theological debate, must be defined carefully (e.g., inerrancy has nothing necessary to do with precision, and certainly understands that the sacred Scriptures are written in a wide diversity of sentences and clauses, not all of which are propositions), is no reason not to use it.

2.1 What role did Scripture play in the writings of the patristic period?

Scripture lay at the very center of the intellectual and spiritual life of the Christians of the early centuries of the Christian church.

2.2 Wasn't the formation of the New Testament canon a rather late development?

A careful reading of the primary sources shows that the notion of canon, as a given set of inspired and authoritative writings, was well established in the second century.

2.3 Didn't the fathers apply the term "inspiration" to writings other than the writings of the New Testament?

Yes, once in a while they did — but then they deployed other terms to show that only the biblical writings were authoritative and free from error.

3.1 Did Luther and Calvin provide substantial innovation as they worked out their doctrine of Scripture?

Both Reformers were heirs to the high view of Scripture they received from the early church and from medieval scholars. Their contribution, so far as their understanding of the nature of Scripture is concerned, largely lay in freeing up the Bible from its domestication by certain ecclesiastical traditions and by scarcely constrained allegorizing. Theologically, there is a Christ-centeredness and a justification-centeredness in their handling of Scripture that sets them apart, but such exegesis did not exclude attention to the Bible as the authority for other matters in the church's and believer's life.

3.2 Doesn't Luther's well-known comment that James is "an epistle of straw" demonstrate that he was prepared to dismiss Scripture when it didn't suit his theology?

On the contrary. In the same Prefaces, Luther insists that James is "a good book because it sets up no human teaching but vigorously promulgates the law of God." But Luther tended to evaluate the weight of any biblical text by the clarity with which it expounded Christ and justification. Hence his characterization of James as an "epistle of straw."

3.3 How similar are the views of Luther and Calvin on the doctrine of Scripture?

Both of these Reformers embraced the absolute authority of God's Word, from which the Holy Spirit, who brought the texts into being through human authors, still speaks. Slight differences emerge in their formulations: Luther, for instance, was significantly influenced by Ockham, and Calvin was not. Again, Luther does not use the word "inspiration" as much as Calvin, but he does insist that the Holy Spirit was truly present in the origin and is truly present in the use of Scripture.

4.1 Weren't the scientists of the seventeenth century, such as Kepler, Galileo, and Newton (like Copernicus a century earlier), essentially an early species of secularists whose scientific methods left them free to challenge the authority of Scripture?

No. All these men were Christians or Deists who continued to reverence Scripture. But hermeneutically they tended to argue that when it comes to the natural order the Bible tends to speak phenomenologically (to use the word we prefer today). And some of these scientists cited Scripture, with all its authority, to justify learning about God and his ways by studying the natural order God had made.

4.2 Didn't theologians systematically try to marginalize the scientists?

In the seventeenth century, the Westminster divines were themselves moving in the direction of recognizing secondary causes in nature. In the *Westminster Confession of Faith,* chapter 5 (on Providence), God is identified as the "first cause"; indeed, the divines affirmed that while "God the great Creator of all things does uphold, direct, dispose, and govern all creatures, actions, and things, from the greatest even to the least, by His most wise and holy providence, . . . yet, by the same providence, He orders them to fall out, according to the nature of second causes, either necessarily, freely, or contingently." The supporting footnote cites half a dozen biblical texts that depict ordinary cause-and-effect relationships in the natural order. In other words, they went out of their way to incorporate the findings and foci of scientists within a larger theological framework.

4.3 So when did a more skeptical approach to the Scriptures begin to surface among scientists?

Well into the eighteenth century — and even then the evidence is quite mixed.

5.1 Is it not the case that many Christians in the Pietist-Methodist-Holiness-Pentecostal traditions trace at least some of their roots to Spener and other German Pietists? And that includes their views on Scripture?

Yes, that much is certainly true.

5.2 Is it not the case that Spener and other early Pietists rejected inerrancy, owing in part to their reaction against Lutheran orthodoxy?

It is true that this position is often asserted, not least in the writings of Donald Dayton. But careful perusal of the primary sources themselves shows it simply isn't the case. The early Pietists, by their own testimony, were solidly in the inerrantist camp. They did not reject Lutheran views of Scripture; rather, they constantly criticized Lutherans for not living up to their own theology.

6.1 Is it not true to say that the Wesleyan tradition on Scripture descends from Pietism, such that Pietist views on Scripture controlled the stances of the early Wesleyans?

There was much more crossover of traditions than is sometimes envisaged. In other words, early Wesleyans were shaped not only by Pietism but also by Scholasticism and other traditions — and all of those traditions were committed to the classic traditional understanding of the nature of Scripture.

6.2 Why then do many Wesleyans explicitly reject the traditional stance on inerrancy?

Some do so because they misread the primary documents of Pietism (see FAQs 5.1 and 5.2 above), or because they distance themselves from the mainstream Wesleyan heritage on this subject. Others reject the traditional Wesleyan stance on Scripture because they think it is incompatible with the Free Will Defense. William Lane Craig has demonstrated, however, that their logic is not unassailable.

6.3 Haven't some Wesleyans (especially William Abraham) argued that, since the Bible has been given for purposes of transformation rather than information (which seems to be the focus of attention in inerrantist formulations), the emphases of the traditional position on truth are fatally misdirected?

Indeed, that is one of the arguments sometimes deployed. The argument expresses a legitimate concern, but it does not undermine the traditional view in any way. On the contrary, it encourages us to appreciate the classical view even more. A small analogy helps: a physician acquires a body of knowledge in order to heal people — but it is altogether desirable that that body of knowledge be true and reliable if real healing is to take place. One cannot legitimately sideline the importance of the truthfulness of Scripture by observing, rightly, that the *purpose* of Scripture is more than truth-telling.

7.1 Who are the "Old Princetonians," and why are they brought up in connection with debates over the nature of Scripture?

The expression "Old Princetonians" refers to the remarkably learned and influential theologians and biblical scholars at Princeton Seminary in the nineteenth century (including Archibald Alexander, Charles Hodge, and Benjamin B. Warfield — the latter working into the beginning of the twentieth century). It is commonly alleged that in their defensive stance against the inroads into the doctrine of Scripture in their day, they ended up introducing innovations into the doctrine, including the affirmation of inerrancy, that were unknown before them.

7.2 What, more precisely, are the Old Princetonians alleged to have done?

Under the influence of Scottish Common Sense Realism and a Baconian view of science, the Old Princetonians allegedly viewed the Bible as a repository of inerrant truths, which simply needed to be carefully gathered together in a scientific fashion so as to compile a reliable systematic theology.

7.3 Are the charges against the Old Princetonians justified?

While they were men of their time who undoubtedly made mistakes, the Old Princetonians rightly understood their defense of inerrant Scripture to stand within the classic and common heritage of the church. In their day, novel critiques of church teaching were being consolidated on Kantian or Hegelian foundations. Their defense faithfully restated church teaching and included pointed critiques of Baconianism and Scottish Common Sense Realism. As Seeman puts it, "The Princetonian reaffirmation and defense of the church's teaching on biblical authority is not beholden to an indefensible epistemological stance." Not only so, but both Hodge and Warfield display remarkable profundity in sorting through how systematic theology is responsibly constructed — a far cry from seeing it as mechanical compilation of facts.

8.1 What is meant by "accommodation"?

In the fathers, the Middle Ages, and Calvin, the topic of accommodation arose partly out of reflection on the ways in which an infinite and holy God could communicate with his finite and sinful image-bearers (he could do so by "accommodating" himself to their limitations), and partly as a way to explain apparent contradictions in the text of Scripture (the language is frequently accommodated to the understanding of common human beings — e.g., by describing some things in phenomenological language, which of course we still do today when we say things such as "The sun will rise this morning at 5:39 a.m.").

8.2 Is that how accommodation is commonly understood today?

In the late Enlightenment, while some followed Spinoza and simply rejected biblical authority, many scholars maintained some sort of notion of biblical authority but under the influence of Socinus, whose views of accommodation included the assertion that the many ostensible errors in Scripture were no more than God's "accommodation" to flawed human beings. Those who presuppose this more recent view of accommodation, with its ready embrace of many kinds of error, are misleading when they say that accommodation has always been part of sophisticated treatments of Scripture. Although formally true, the statement hides the way the notion of accommodation has changed in recent centuries. Discussion of the topic has become complex. Arguably Calvin saw accommodation as a theological category tied to God's grace toward us, and exemplified in some ways in the incarnation. That is a far cry from seeing it as a merely rhetorical and exegetical device.

9.1 How come Karl Barth's views of Scripture have come back to be the focus of so much attention today?

There are at least three reasons. First, Barth was certainly the most prolific and perhaps creative theologian of the twentieth century, so it is no wonder that people study his writings. Second, Barth's thought is profoundly God-centered, profoundly Christ-centered, profoundly grace-centered. And third, his view of Scripture, though not quite in line with traditional confessionalism, is reverent, subtle, and complex, so scholars keep debating exactly what he was saying.

9.2 Doesn't Barth say that the Bible isn't the Word of God, but becomes the Word of God when it is received by faith?

In fact, he can affirm both; the question is, What does he mean? The "becoming" language is for Barth tied up with his insistence that the initial revelation of the Word and its revelation to the individual believer are tied up together in one gracious whole. The same is true with Barth's treatment of inspiration. He refuses to speak of the Bible as itself inspired, but links together what is traditionally called the inspiration of Scripture and the illumination of the believer into one whole.

9.3 Doesn't Barth claim to stand in line with the Reformers, so far as his view of Scripture is concerned?

Yes, he does, but he is clearly mistaken. Comparison with Calvin, for example, casts up not a few instances where Calvin happily speaks of the inspiration of Scripture, the text itself being God-breathed, regardless of whether or how believers receive it. Barth prefers to speak of the out-breathing of the Spirit of God in both the text and the believer, thus distancing himself both from the exegesis of Scripture and from the Reformed tradition. He appears to recognize his distance from Calvin in *CD* II/2, §3e.

9.4 Does Barth allow that there are errors in Scripture?

Yes, he does, though he refuses to identify them (but cf. his treatment of the fall of angels in 2 Peter and Jude, *CD* III/3, §51, where he finds a theological error in Scripture). For Barth, this seems to be part of the humanness of Scripture, though he insists that God's revelatory authority encompasses the whole, errors and all. That in turn inevitably raises questions about how passages of Scripture that include errors (not identified) can be said to carry the revelatory authority of God.

10.1 Does the Roman Catholic Church share the same view of Scripture that you have been describing as "classic" or "traditional"?

Yes. Indeed, across many centuries and until quite recently, Catholicism has been one of the mainstays in holding that the Bible is uniquely inspired by God, and inerrant. But that is not the whole picture. Catholicism has also held that tradition has an authority comparable to that of Scripture, and in any case the Magisterium, the teaching authority of the church, alone determines what Scripture and tradition mean. Thus, so far as understanding the nature of Scripture goes, the Reformers' argument with Rome was not so much over the nature of Scripture as over its exclusive sufficiency.

10.2 What do you mean by "until quite recently"? Have the views of Catholicism as to the nature of Scripture changed?

For the last century or so, Catholicism has gradually recognized more of the human dimensions of Scripture than had formerly been the case. Vatican II, however, signaled a more dramatic shift. Influenced in part by liberal Protestantism, the Catholic Church in Vatican II (1962-65) tended to preserve much of the traditional language, while allowing to stand in Scripture a lot of things that an earlier generation would have understood to be errors.

10.3 Is this proving divisive in the Roman Catholic Church?

Arguably not as divisive as in various forms of Protestantism, in part because the Magisterium preserves its voice of authority as to the teachings of the church, regardless of changes in the way Scripture is perceived.

11.1 Is there scholarly consensus on when the Old Testament canon was more or less stable?

No. There is a sharp division between the "minimalists" and the "maximalists." The former hold that the Old Testament canon did not begin to form until the second century C.E. and was still being disputed two centuries later; the maximalists argue that the Old Testament canon was stable by the second century B.C.E., and rabbinic discussions after Christ were essentially confirmatory.

11.2 What is the nature of the evidence that these two positions are fighting over?

There is not as much evidence as we'd like, but the crucial text is Josephus's *Against Apion,* written toward the end of the first century C.E. Without actually listing the books in the canon, Josephus pretty clearly speaks of the books of the Hebrew canon as being in place a couple of centuries earlier. Later rabbinic discussions tend in the same direction. Minimalists tend to attack the credibility of Josephus and debate the meaning of the rabbinic sources; maximalists not only take Josephus at face value but also find efforts to explain away his clear words simply not credible.

12.1 Why do the substantive differences among scholars regarding the history of Israel matter to our Christian faith?

They matter for two reasons: (1) A great deal of biblical Christianity is cast as a *historical* religion — that is, God has revealed himself to us through events that take place in history, in the space-time continuum. The supreme example is the resurrection of Christ. The apostle makes clear that if Christ did not really rise from the dead, then our entire faith is a farce. The history of Israel is in one sense a useful test case of how Christians think about history and God's self-disclosure in that history. In the OT the supremely important redemptive event is the exodus. (2) Biblical texts that purport to tell us what happened in the past are the passages where the divine revelation meshes with the ordinary claims of reliable reportage. If Scripture cannot be trusted where its claims can most readily be verified or falsified, why should it be trusted in other arenas?

12.2 Then the more pressing question becomes, Why do these substantive differences regarding the history of Israel exist? Why can't scholars agree on such matters?

The question is a good one, and too seldom directly discussed by the scholars themselves. Very often there is a profound difference in their respective "control beliefs." For example, some scholars are deeply committed to philosophical naturalism, eschewing all appeals to supernatural influence or power in discussion of matters alleged to be in the "historical" arena; others are convinced that any discussion of the God of the Bible must allow for him to act in ways that are frankly supra-natural. These controlling beliefs inevitably influence how we read the biblical texts.

12.3 In order to preserve discussion, might it not be a good thing for the supernaturalists to engage in some discussion on a kind of "as if" basis — that is, to play by the rules of the philosophical naturalists, not because they espouse them, but "as if" they were right in order to see how far the study of the texts can take us on this reduced basis?

That is often done, and certainly on a limited basis such study can produce useful results. On the other hand, to play by such restricted rules all the time is, from any Christian perspective, to act out unbelief, to adopt a kind of tacit atheism, or to admit, implicitly, that God's ostensible saving acts in history did not really take place in the space-time continuum after all. The price to pay is too high.

13.1 Does it make any sense to affirm that the Bible is inerrant in the original, when we do not possess the autographa?

That is one of the most frequently repeated objections of Bart Ehrman and others. The objection has a certain superficial plausibility, but on closer inspection it turns on the multivalence of such terms as "Bible," "text," and "original."

13.2 What do you mean by the "multivalence" of these expressions?

That is simply a way of saying that these words mean slightly different things in different contexts. For example, "Bible" can refer to a collection of books that constitute holy Scripture; alternatively, it can refer to a particular copy. "Original" can refer to the original language(s) of Scripture, or it can refer to an autograph. "Text" can refer to the actual manuscript on which something is written or printed, or it can refer to the message encoded in the words without reference to anything concrete.

13.3 What difference does this make for discussions about inerrancy?

Ehrman and others object that when evangelicals affirm the inerrancy of the text, they (evangelicals) are asserting the inerrancy of something they do not possess, viz. the original text. But sophisticated treatments of inerrancy by evangelicals do not make that claim. Like Warfield, when they speak of the "text" they are referring to the immaterial definition, the message of the Scriptures. In other words, the Ehrman objection is attacking a straw man. The same sort of mistake is made with respect to several expressions, and sometimes, sad to say, by evangelicals themselves.

14.1 Haven't many scholars demonstrated that in its origins Christianity was highly diverse, theologically speaking, and that unity of doctrine was gradually and rigidly enforced by the group that viewed itself alone as orthodox, a process that took three or four centuries?

Certainly that stance has its vociferous proponents. It became popular owing to a book by Walter Bauer in the 1930s, and today its most prominent popularizer is doubtless Bart Ehrman. But the actual evidence runs in the other direction: it is not that from many theological stances one arose triumphant, but from one shared theological vision many diverse heresies sprang up.

14.2 What evidence supports your claim?

First, within the pages of the New Testament, careful exegesis shows there is far more theological unity than is sometimes alleged. It has been shown that the apostles were the people closest to Jesus and they were stamped by him such that the differences in their stances, compared with second-century figures who had no immediate access to Jesus, were relatively small. Second, all four of the NT Gospels have discernible connections with specific apostles. By contrast, later documents, such as the *Gospel of Judas* and the *Gospel of Mary,* have no traceable and credible connections with the apostles. Third, it is possible to follow this theological trajectory, the trajectory of the "proto-orthodox" who preserve the apostolic tradition, in marked contrast to the literature of other groups whose inspiration demonstrably does not connect with the apostolic tradition.

15.1 Isn't the "canon" of biblical books a rather arbitrary collection?

The fundamental question is whether God is a self-disclosing God, a God whose revelation extends to writings that he reveals. If one answers this question in the affirmative, then questions about the canon are inexorable: one wants to know *which* books are God-revealed. As Graham Cole puts it, "The existence of a canon is a corollary of inspired special revelation."

15.2 When was the present order of the books in our canon established?

The order was established by the church during the first few centuries, and disagreements about which order is best continued for many centuries. We do not claim that the order of the biblical books enjoys divine sanction the way we claim that the content of the biblical books enjoys divine sanction.

16.1 How should we think of the relationship between God and his Word?

Although it is transparent that God and his Word are not ontologically identical, nevertheless Scripture repeatedly and in highly diverse ways insists that to believe God's Word is to believe God, to obey God's Word is to obey God, to disobey God's Word is to disobey God, and so forth.

16.2 Isn't it possible to believe the gospel without being too fussed about believing everything in the Bible?

Certainly it is possible; people do it all the time. But it is not possible to do it with any consistency — or, to put the matter more dramatically, sooner or later one wonders if it is the gospel that is truly being believed. For the consistent pattern of OT witness, of apostolic witness, of the teaching of Jesus himself, ties not only the gospel but appropriate response to the gospel to the shape of God's self-disclosure in his Word.

16.3 Aren't such demands a bit out of favor with contemporary demands for authentic freedom?

Yes, but that's part of the point. "Freedom" from the authority of God's gracious and transforming self-disclosure soon turns out to be no freedom at all, but a tacit slavery to the shibboleths of our age and culture — in a word, to idolatry. Contrast that with the effort and self-sacrifice of a William Tyndale, whose determined effort to translate the Bible was motivated, finally, by his conviction that what he was doing was putting into English nothing less than *the Word of God*!

17.1 The notion of two authors, divine and human, standing behind the Scriptures is intrinsically difficult. How should we begin to think about these things?

The challenge is to be faithful to the biblical language itself. If one pits the human author against the divine Author, then if the importance of one is underscored the other is correspondingly diminished, and many proposed models have been guilty of that mistake. Sometimes the discussion has turned on words that have been misunderstood. For example, across the centuries many spoke of Scripture being "dictated" by God, which some might initially think reduces the human writer to a secretary taking dictation, or to a transcription machine. But the best of those theologians who used the language of dictation (for instance, Calvin) chose the Latin *dictare* not to describe the means of delivery but to stress the result: the words of Scripture are indeed God's words. At the same time, they were fully insistent on the contribution that the human authors made, way beyond mere transcription. As Henri Blocher puts it, "The One God — Father, Son/Word, and Holy Spirit — is able to 'breathe out' the discourse of human authors as his own."

17.2 But are not some models for thinking about this "dual authorship" better than others?

Yes, certainly. Although in recent decades, many have argued that there is not one safe and comprehensive model for understanding the relationship between God and the human authors of Scripture, the multiplication of many models *within* Scripture tends to end up with different degrees of faithfulness, of truth-telling, of authority. Careful and painstaking exegesis and theological reflection show that the model of the biblical prophet has a certain overarching coherence to it, and it can be strengthened by reflection on the model of the apostle.

18.1 Aren't the "pre-history" chapters of the Bible — Genesis 1–11 — cast as myths?

Everything depends on what you mean by "myth"! Because the so-called *usus loquendi,* the way "myth" is used in common speech, associates myth with the non-historical, attempts at sidestepping this reality by appealing to sophisticated definitions are self-defeating. Indeed, a careful, taxonomical analysis of the uses of "myth" in relation to related concepts demonstrates just how fuzzily and imprecisely the term is commonly used.

18.2 Doesn't the creation account in Genesis sound very much like (for instance) the Babylonian *Enuma Elish* and other ancient Near Eastern creation myths?

Certainly there are some interesting parallels. But responsible inferences drawn from these parallels demand that we evaluate not only the differences between Genesis and the Babylonian myths but also possible explanations of their ostensible similarities. Careful study discloses massive differences in worldview between Genesis and *Enuma Elish.*

19.1 In their treatments of biblical authority, haven't Christians paid too little attention to the Bible's diverse literary genres?

This is a fair comment. Most serious treatments of the Bible's authority have developed in confessional and ecclesiastical settings; many of the best treatments of the Bible's literary genres developed in university settings. In recent years, however, much more attention has been paid to some of the relationships between authority and literary genre, not least (and with somewhat different results) in the writings of Brevard S. Childs and Kevin J. Vanhoozer.

19.2 How is the authority of Scripture related to Scripture's diverse literary genres?

For example, the Bible's ordering narrative, its "storyline," not only orders the rest of the biblical material but establishes what did, in fact, happen and how the narrative leads to the historical revelation of Jesus Christ. Where law makes demands, where prophecy exhorts, rebukes, threatens, and predicts, each genre not only has its own way of making its appeal, but underscores the authority of God in making the demands or issuing the (for example) rebuke. Careful study demonstrates not only how each genre "works" but also how each contributes to the whole to provide a unified revelation.

19.3 Are there any advantages bound up with the Bible's highly diverse literary genres?

Yes, certainly. The Bible's diversity, as Barry Webb puts it, "tells us that the authority of the Bible is the kind of authority that fully engages with our humanity. It speaks to us from within our humanity, and not just from outside it (as in creation, for example). It is not an authority of raw power, but one that fully recognizes and engages with our weakness, struggle, and sinfulness. In other words it is a gracious rather than coercive authority." In this respect the Bible is very different from the Qur'an. The latter pictures a God who cannot participate in humanity without somehow threatening his own Deity; the God of the Bible not only interacts at many levels with human beings (reflected in the diverse literary genres) but also interacts supremely by becoming a human being, for he is the God "who not only gave us a book and prophet, but gave us himself."

20.1 What is meant by "the clarity of Scripture"? After all, many people find the Bible to be pretty obscure.

It does not mean that every part of Scripture is equally easy to understand, or that there is no need for teachers, or that every opinion about what the text means is equally valuable. Rather, it should be thought of (as Mark Thompson's title puts it) as "the generous gift of a gracious Father." Language itself is a gift from God, and God has chosen to lay out his redemptive purposes in language he gave to his image-bearers. The incarnate Son of God repeatedly presupposes the clarity of Scripture, not least when he repeatedly asks the question, "Have you not read . . . ?" And the Spirit himself is involved both in the provision of God's Word and in its reception. In sum: "The clarity of Scripture is that quality of Scripture which, arising from the fact that it is ultimately God's effective communicative act, ensures the meaning of [this] text . . . is accessible to all who come to it in faith" (Thompson).

20.2 But can't the clarity of Scripture be abused? Don't we *need* some sort of authoritative office, like the Catholic Magisterium, to teach us what is clearly being said when there are so many differences of opinion?

The Bible shows that even an apostle can get things wrong (Galatians 2), so there is no sure hope there. The clarity of Scripture does not mean that there are no disputes in interpretation, but (1) that the resolution of such disputes lies in the study of the Scriptures themselves, not in any other authority, and (2) that the causes of the disputes are largely attributed to our finiteness, sinfulness, cultural biases, traditionalism, and the like, rather than to some identifiable fault in Scripture itself.

21.1 Do some of the postconservative theologians offer a helpful way forward?

Postconservatives vary quite a lot among themselves, so one needs to be careful about generalizations. Careful reading of John Franke and Stanley Grenz suggests that they share in common, among other things, a rejection of classic foundationalism and a considerable sympathy for the cultural-linguistic turn that characterizes the so-called Yale school. The price paid in unacknowledged subjectivism of various kinds is very high.

21.2 Yet is it not the case today that most philosophers reject foundationalism?

There is more diversity today than some acknowledge, not least because there are many mediating positions. Many today think of themselves as "modest" or "soft" foundationalists, and the line between their positions and those of "modest" or "soft" non-foundationalists is very thin.

22.1 Isn't it a bit circular to try to establish Jesus' view of the Scriptures by appealing to the Gospels, which are part of the Scriptures?

Certainly one wants to avoid "vicious circularity." But there is a softer circularity that is unavoidable whenever one considers anything claiming supreme authority in any realm. If to justify that supreme authority one is forced to appeal to some external authority, then arguably that external authority displaces the first — which calls for us to establish *its* authority, with the same tension. One tumbles into an infinite regression. Many scholars acknowledge the inevitability of some kind of "soft" circularity — indeed, its desirability. (See also 31.2.)

22.2 So among the countless opinions regarding the reliability of the Gospels, how can you construct a historically credible approach to finding Jesus' views on the authority of (antecedent) Scripture?

There are several ways it could be done. The way adopted by Craig Blomberg is this: he adopts a four-pronged criterion that "looks for that which is *both* plausible within a Jewish context in Israel during the first third of the first century, *yet* dissimilar enough from conventional Jewish thought or practice that the average ancient Jew (or Jewish-Christian) is not likely to have invented it, *and* plausible within the context of Jesus' first followers, *yet* dissimilar enough from subsequent early Christianity that the average ancient Jewish (or gentile) Christian probably didn't make it up. When elements in the Gospels reasonably well satisfy all four parts of this criterion, a powerful case can be made that the teaching or action in question goes back to the historical Jesus." The result, carefully working through many passages, confirms that Jesus' view of what we now call the Old Testament simply could not have been higher.

23.1 Do not many scholars dismiss any notion of inerrancy, or even inspiration, on the ground that the NT writers use the OT very (shall we say) "creatively" — that is, with no apparent respect for the OT context? Don't these realities set aside all possibility of cognitive coherence in the Bible?

Certainly many contemporary scholars adopt some form of this line of argument. Sometimes the argument is tinged with antisupernaturalism; more commonly, perhaps, scholars argue that, although there is some kind of revelation or inspiration behind the text of Scripture, it is not the sort that guarantees factual reliability and cognitive truth.

23.2 Their argument seems like a good one. How would you respond?

The NT use of the OT is variegated and complex. Sometimes the NT writers simply use OT language without intending to claim anything more than a linguistic connection to the OT passage. Where a connection *is* intended, it may belong to several kinds: for instance, direct fulfillment of a specific prediction; a subtle contextual "echo"; some kind of carefully defined *sensus plenior* ("fuller sense"); a typological connection of some kind; and more. When these sorts of connections are carefully explored, the way the NT writers use the OT is a great deal more credible than the use of the OT in some of the parallel Judaisms of the first century.

24.1 What are the dangers in trying to move from Scripture to the construction of systematic theology? How does the Bible address, say, moral questions that are nowhere directly addressed in its pages (e.g., stem cell research) and forms of government never envisaged (e.g., representative democracy)?

Such questions are both perennial and challenging. One danger is the simple conflation of what Scriptures actually say with our own interpretations of those Scriptures, without grappling with the distance in time and culture from the Scriptures' settings to ours. No less dangerous are attempts to build entire structures on a restrictive selection of biblical passages, ignoring what else the Bible may say that is pertinent to the subject.

24.2 But how *should* we move from Scripture to theology?

Many suggestions have been put forward: for example, merely add up all that Scripture teaches; "principlize" from concrete examples to universal, abstract principles; follow the trajectories of Scripture rather than what Scripture explicitly says; and many more. In each case, whatever the merits of the proposal, there are also dangers to avoid. For example, if one follows the "principlizing" option, it is easy to make the abstract principles, which are possible inferences from the text, more authoritative than the concrete particulars of the text. What we must see is that, whereas Scripture has supreme authority, God has also given us teachers, the long history of the church, the Spirit himself, not to mention our minds and hearts, not so much to work out principles by which we master the text, but that we might be mastered by the text, living under it, breathing it, living it out, as we seek faithfulness to the whole counsel of God.

24.3 Do you have a name for this approach?

Kevin Vanhoozer says, "Call it *critical biblicism* (but do not confuse it with biblical criticism, its polar opposite). Note, first, that it is a form of *biblicism:* the position for which I have argued accords final authority to the Bible as the norm for all subsequent Christian communicative action, including beliefs and practices. The norm to which all other words, thoughts, and deeds must measure up is the pattern of judgments reflected in biblical discourse. But second, it is a *critical* biblicism. This means that it does not conflate our interpretations with the meaning of the biblical text. The text stands in judgment over our interpretations in an asymmetrical hermeneutical hierarchy."

24.4 So are we supposed to go "beyond what is written" or not?

Certainly not in the sense prohibited by the apostle Paul in 1 Corinthians 4:6. The context shows that most assuredly we are not to go beyond Scripture in any way that boasts before God, acting as if we are wiser than he, behaving outside the privileges and constraints of the gospel. Rather, instead of running against the grain of the biblical text, we run along with the grain, working out and living out its matrices and mandated inferences. Christians are familiar with such developments in (for example) the fourth-century formulations of the doctrine of the Trinity.

25.1 What are we to make of the widespread cynicism over the ability to know anything about God?

Epistemology — the study of knowledge and how we know, or think we know — is a perennially challenging subject. It lurks not only behind the most sophisticated discussions of what we mean by the knowledge of God, but also behind "Jesus loves me this I know/For the Bible tells me so." Precisely because the topic is currently in such disarray, it is helpful to read a survey of some of the key aspects currently being debated (or ignored!).

25.2 What is the value of epistemology?

There are many. Among them is the focus on what constitutes justified or warranted belief. I may believe the moon is made of green cheese, but is the belief warranted? I may believe that Jesus is the only way to God, but is that belief justified? One soon learns the wide range of questions — cognitive, moral, human finiteness and sinfulness, evidence, reason, the *sensus divinitatis,* revelation, faith — that are bound up with the discipline.

26.1 Isn't it possible to reject foundationalism utterly and still hold to inerrancy?

Such an alignment is not very common, but clearly it is possible, since some scholars do hold to both positions. Whether such an alignment is entirely coherent is a different matter.

26.2 Should we then defend foundationalism as an epistemological stance that makes the defense of a high view of Scripture more coherent?

We should not defend Cartesian foundationalism because requiring certainty is an unrealistic expectation for justification of belief in a high view of Scripture. But there are ways of defending a modest foundationalism that enables us to be justified in having knowledge of true things beyond the cultural-linguistic parameters that we must use to say them. One key way of getting at these matters is to follow the phenomenology of the early Husserl.

27.1 Do the authority and truth of any text stand or fall together?

Not necessarily, or at least not without taking care to explain what we mean by both terms. For example, a text may be authoritative in one domain, but be quite mistaken in another; a text may be truthful in all it says, yet exercise little authority in the lives of its readers.

27.2 Is there no connection between authority and truth?

Yes, certainly, but such connections are most helpfully teased out after one has carefully thought through the different ways in which we speak of authority and of truth, and then bring them together carefully.

28.1 Doesn't a word such as "inerrancy" lose its attractiveness and utility if it has to be buttressed by endless qualifications, distinctions, and definitions?

Such qualifications and distinctions surround almost every weighty term used in theological discourse — including, for example, "God," "justification," "truth," "Spirit," "grace," and so on. In each case one can provide a simple definition, but in the cut-and-thrust of subsequent exchanges it is unsurprising that detailed and sometimes technical distinctions must be made.

28.2 So what simple definition of "inerrancy" might be advanced?

In Paul Helm's words, "An expression — an assertion, a sentence, a formula, a document, a part of a document — may be said to be inerrant if it is wholly true, without error."

29.1 Today there is increasing talk of "interpretive communities." What does this expression mean?

The situation is admittedly complex. In the West, where so much individualism reigns, there is more and more talk of various communities. Interpretive communities are communities in which certain interpretations or structures of interpretation are largely dominant. In one sense, interpretive communities are inescapable: individuals who think their interpretations are exclusively their own are simply failing to recognize how they, too, are culturally situated, and therefore in some measure reflect the views of a larger "community." But an interpretive community may be intentional: that is, in some particular community (for example, a denomination) there may be planned discussion among many people before a communally agreed interpretation (such as a statement of faith) is agreed. The willingness to listen to diverse interpretations across interpretive communities becomes ever more attractive at a time when Christians are becoming more and more aware of global Christianity.

29.2 So, then, are all interpretations by diverse communities equally valid, equally faithful?

You've just put your finger on the danger. On the one hand, it is an act of both realism and humility to recognize that no individual, and no single community, has all the truth about any individual biblical passage or theme. Listening to one another is bound to result in richer interpretations than would otherwise be the case — and sometimes it issues in straightforward correction. But on the other hand, one cannot help but recall the many warnings in the Bible regarding false doctrine, false Christs, false gospels. Not all interpretations are created equal, and just because some interpretation or other is espoused and protected by a particular community, it does not follow that it is faithful to Scripture. And so we return to careful listening to others, and to rereading of the Bible, eager to be corrected if that means greater fidelity — and eager, too, not to stand over Scripture as if we are the final judges, when in reality Scripture must stand over us and be our judge.

30.1 Isn't it true that Christians who defend the truthfulness of Scripture are in a long and losing conflict with science?

Although it sounds counterintuitive, one might instead argue that Christians have commonly assigned *too much* prestige and authority to the science and the philosophy of their own day, tending to domesticate their understanding of Scripture by the dominant outlook of their time. It was precisely *because* Christians agreed with the outlook of their time that the church, in line with natural philosophers, was convinced that Aristotle's view of the world and Ptolemy's understanding of the movement of the heavenly bodies were right, and so therefore was dragged into the movement to condemn Galileo. It is easy enough to find other parallels.

30.2 When science and the Bible seem to be in conflict, how should Christians proceed? How should they think things through?

Scripture has final authority. But it does not follow that the particular interpretation of Scripture that we favor on this or that point has final authority, so it is important to walk with humility and listen well. The history of science also reminds us that scientific theories are not only revisable in theory (that is the way science works) but have often been revised in fact. So it is important for Christians, however deeply they are enmeshed in current scientific commitments, not to become intimidated by every theory that claims to be scientific. Meanwhile we must let both Scripture and the various sciences speak in their own terms, and avoid adding to the hermeneutical muddle by forcing Scripture to address the science of the day.

31.1 At a deep level, aren't the holy books of scriptures of various world religions really saying the same thing?

Although that view is very common in the Western world, owing not least to the West's commitment to certain forms of pluralism, it really cannot be responsibly defended. These various scriptures say so many mutually contradictory things, not only at the level of detail but on the most profound conceptual matters, that it makes no sense to claim they are really saying the same thing. Christ is the Son of God, or he is not, or we are all sons of God in the same sense; there is one God, or there are many Gods; there is one God, *simplex* (Islam), or there is one God, *complex* (the Trinitarianism of Christianity); there is an unbridgeable gulf between the Creator and the creature, or we human beings are all on the way to being Gods ourselves; we are saved by our works, or we are saved by sheer grace; and so on, and so on. Moreover, those who claim that all these holy books are really saying the same thing are not only insulting the intelligence of the devout believers in the various traditions, but they make it impossible to engage in serious conversation across religious lines, for serious conversation refuses to paper over differences, but instead engages them.

31.2 Aren't the Bible's self-attesting claims a form of circular argument that is essentially self-defeating?

They are circular, but not viciously circular. Some degree of circularity is inevitable when establishing belief in an *ultimate* authority, for if instead one established the authority of the Bible on the basis of a greater authority external to the Bible, the Bible itself would not be the supreme authority. (See also 22.1.)

31.3 Since the holy books of other religions make self-attesting claims in a fashion not dissimilar from the claims the Bible makes, how can one legitimately claim exclusive authority for the Bible?

The self-attesting voice of Scripture is attached to witnesses that stand or fall together. For example, much of the revelation of the Bible is tied to historical events supported by plausible historical verification. In other words, the Bible is *not only* self-referential, but constantly refers to events outside itself, events that in some measure can be studied. This is very substantially different from what is possible in other holy books. One can offer a similar argument for the work of the Spirit in bearing witness to Scripture.

32.1 Do Muslims view the Qur'an, their holy book, in much the same ways in which Christians view the Bible, their holy book?

The similarities are superficial. Transparently, each of the two religions has a book taken to be holy and authoritative by their respective adherents. Nevertheless the differences are more pervasive and more important than the similarities. For example, the Bible was written by many human authors, in three languages, over a period of about a millennium and a half. Although it is made up of many literary genres, collectively the biblical books trace out an "arc of history" from creation to the consummation. Christians hold that the human authors were so borne along by the Holy Spirit that the resulting text is truly "God breathed." By contrast, Muslims hold that the words of the Qur'an, all in Arabic, are the very words of God without human mediation: Muhammad is not viewed as inspired or contributing a distinctive vocabulary or the like. No notion of "double authorship" exists: the words of the Qur'an are the words of God, and Muhammad was simply God's instrument, over an approximately twenty-two-year period, to memorize and write down what God gave him through the angel Gabriel. Structurally, the Qur'an, far from tracing out an "arc of history" through the many experiences of men and women, presents itself in 114 Surahs (chapters) of broadly descending length, the large majority of the material made up of God's direct address to human beings, commonly in commanding and exhortatory focus.

32.2. At least both sides have one set text, one holy book each, don't they?

Yes and no. Protestant Christians and Muslims would certainly appeal, respectively, to the Bible and to the Qur'an as final authority. But Muslims also appeal to the

Hadith, traditions that convey the life and devotion of Muhammad as the supreme exemplar of Islam, binding on Muslims everywhere — though Muslims do not agree on which of the *Hadith* are binding. But although the *Hadith* are authoritative and binding, in Muslim thought they are not the Word of God — that is, they do not share with the Qur'an the property of being God's own dictated words.

32.3 How, then, are Christians and Muslims to converse freely and knowledgeably with one another?

Both sides frequently display little understanding of the others' beliefs and commitments; misunderstandings abound. The first step is always to learn what the other side actually believes — often in categories very different from what is presupposed.

33.1 In Hindu belief, where is revelation located? Do not Hindus have holy books?

Timothy Tennent explains, "Hindus accept neither the human authorship nor the historical origin of their most sacred texts. True knowledge (or what we would identify as the content of revelation) is eternally reverberating throughout the universe as a resonating sound known as *anāhata śabda,* that is, the 'unstruck sound.' This sound, which resonates eternally throughout the universe, is symbolized by the sound *'OM'* (pronounced AUM) and does not require, though it may not exclude, it being associated with the self-disclosure of a personal God. The way this sacred sound gets translated into textual form begins with unknown meditating sages who, at the dawn of each of the unending creation cycles, rehear the knowledge that then forms the core content of the sacred oral tradition. This oral tradition was later written down and codified into sacred texts such as the four Vedas (*Rig, Sama, Yajur, Atharva*), and their famous philosophical/religious appendices known as the Upanishads." In theory, this corpus is expandable. Hindus also have a large collection of sacred texts that have both historical origin and human authorship. These are of various kinds — epics, philosophy, and other materials that are thought not to be contradicted by the first tier. The first tier is regarded as non-personal and eternal; the second tier often discloses things about particular deities (e.g., the *Bhagavad-Gita* is viewed as the personal disclosure of the god Krishna).

33.2 Is it appropriate for Christians to view the Hindu sacred writings as a sort of Hindu equivalent to the Old Testament — a kind of preparation for Christ and the new covenant?

Yes and no. No, because Christians insist that only the OT is the God-breathed precursor to the new covenant Scriptures, given by the personal-transcendent God to prepare human beings for the incarnation, atoning death, resurrection, ascension, and return of the unique and eternal Son of God. On the other hand, it is a bit sweeping to dismiss the Hindu sacred texts as useless folly when in his own day the apostle Paul could cite pagan texts to buttress the points he was making, even if he fills those texts with new meaning when he uses them in a Christian context. Although Christians will continue to think of the sacred texts of Hinduism as providing a way of thinking of reality that is fundamentally and deeply flawed, not a few individual passages may reflect a heart-longing and a religious sensibility that make communication and witness more comprehensible than initial consideration of the fundamentally opposed worldviews might imagine.

34.1 Do Buddhists possess their own "Bible," their own sacred writings?

As Harold Netland and Alex Smith put it, "Buddhism does have its authoritative scriptures, although the list of such texts and the ways in which they are held to be significant varies with Buddhist schools and historical eras. Unlike Christianity and Islam, in Buddhism there is no single book or collection of texts that is authoritative for everyone. Regional, linguistic, and sectarian considerations have resulted in the compilation of separate canons, with few texts that are commonly accepted across all traditions. There are three major Buddhist canonical collections (Pali, Chinese, and Tibetan), each comprising many books with varying criteria for inclusion. The Chinese canon alone requires nearly 100,000 pages in its printed form."

34.2 Do Buddhists hold that all these sacred writings convey revealed truth?

The category of "revelation" does not fit Buddhism. Although Buddhist experts disagree over whether Buddhists are atheists or agnostics, all of them agree that there is no place in Buddhism for an omnipotent, personal, Creator God (as in Christianity and Islam), and thus there is no revelation if that word is meant to convey the content that such a God discloses to people in his creation. While authoritative, the sutras cannot be thought of as divine revelation. The content of the sacred writings is *Dharma,* the eternal truth that is available to anyone who gains enlightenment by the means specified by the various branches of Buddhism.

35.1 Doesn't a collection of essays like the ones in this volume sport the risk of making the Bible something that we examine, that we study, that we master, that we defend — instead of being God's revelation to us, something we must understand and trust and obey, something to which we submit as we submit to God himself?

Yes, that is exactly right. These are not the only dangers, of course. For example, it remains important to understand how the Bible has been viewed across the history of the church, and it is crucial to talk about the Bible's truthfulness and authority, especially in the context of a culture that denies these things. But we are not treating the Bible aright if we defend its truth yet distance ourselves from its claims, demands, and promises. James reminds us that we can believe the Bible's witness to true things about God and yet not be farther advanced than the devils who do no less.

35.2 Then what is the way ahead?

Our reading will be deepened when we understand the world and ourselves better; when we love God and hunger to be conformed to his Word; when we keep trying to apply the Scriptures to ourselves and others in responsible ways; when faith and obedience become increasingly instinctive. None of these developments runs along a one-way axis (e.g., more Bible knowledge produces more obedience). Rather, these various components in living Bible study manage to cycle round in a beautiful spiral in which Christian virtues are both the fruit and the enablers of faithful Bible reading.

The Authors

James Beilby
Professor of Systematic and Philosophical Theology,
Bethel University, St. Paul, MN

Kirsten Birkett
Lecturer in Ethics and Philosophy, Oak Hill Theological College
Research Fellow, Latimer Trust

Henri A. G. Blocher
Professor of Theology and Dean Emeritus,
Faculté Libre de Théologie Evangélique, Vaux-sur-Seine
Former Gunther Knoedler Professor of Systematic Theology,
Wheaton College Graduate School

Craig L. Blomberg
Distinguished Professor of New Testament, Denver Seminary

D. A. Carson
Research Professor of New Testament, Trinity Evangelical Divinity School

Graham A. Cole
Dean and Vice President of Education, and Professor of Biblical and
Systematic Theology, Trinity Evangelical Divinity School

Stephen G. Dempster
Professor of Religious Studies, Crandall University, Moncton, NB

Daniel M. Doriani
Professor of Theology and Vice President for Special Academic Projects, Covenant Theological Seminary

Simon Gathercole
Senior Lecturer in New Testament, Faculty of Divinity, University of Cambridge

David Gibson
Minister, Trinity Church, Aberdeen, Scotland

Ida Glaser
Director of the Centre for Muslim-Christian Studies, Oxford
Associate Tutor at Wycliffe Hall, Oxford (seconded to both by Crosslinks)

Paul Helm
Formerly Professor of the History and Philosophy of Religion, King's College, London

Charles E. Hill
John R. Richardson Professor of New Testament and Early Christianity, Reformed Theological Seminary in Orlando

Peter F. Jensen
Former Principal, now Emeritus Faculty, Moore Theological College
Former Archbishop of Sydney

Robert Kolb
Missions Professor of Systematic Theology Emeritus, Concordia Seminary, Saint Louis

Anthony N. S. Lane
Professor of Historical Theology, London School of Theology

Te-Li Lau
Associate Professor of New Testament, Trinity Evangelical Divinity School

Richard Lints
Vice-President for Academic Affairs, Andrew Mutch Distinguished Professor of Theology, Gordon-Conwell Theological Seminary

V. Philips Long
Professor of Old Testament, Regent College, Vancouver

Thomas H. McCall
Director, Carl F. H. Henry Center for Theological Understanding, and Professor of Biblical and Systematic Theology, Trinity Evangelical Divinity School

Douglas J. Moo
Wessner Chair of Biblical Studies, Wheaton College

Andrew David Naselli
Assistant Professor of New Testament and Biblical Theology, Bethlehem College & Seminary

Harold Netland
Professor of Philosophy of Religion and Intercultural Studies, Trinity Evangelical Divinity School

Osvaldo Padilla
Associate Professor of Divinity, Beeson Divinity School, Samford University, Birmingham, AL

Michael C. Rea
Director, Center for Philosophy of Religion, and Professor of Philosophy, University of Notre Dame

Bradley N. Seeman
Associate Professor of Philosophy, Taylor University

Alex G. Smith
Advocate and International Trainer in the Buddhist World, OMF International

R. Scott Smith
Professor of Ethics and Christian Apologetics, Biola University

Rodney L. Stiling
Associate Professor of History, Seattle Pacific University

Glenn S. Sunshine
Professor of Early Modern European History, Central Connecticut State University

Timothy C. Tennent
President and Professor of World Christianity, Asbury Theological Seminary

Mark D. Thompson
Principal and Head of Theology, Moore Theological College, Sydney

Kevin J. Vanhoozer
Research Professor of Systematic Theology,
Trinity Evangelical Divinity School

Bruce K. Waltke
Professor Emeritus of Biblical Studies, Regent College
Distinguished Professor Emeritus of Old Testament,
Knox Theological Seminary

Barry G. Webb
Senior Research Fellow Emeritus in Old Testament,
Moore Theological College, Sydney

Peter J. Williams
Warden, Tyndale House, Cambridge

John D. Woodbridge
Research Professor of Church History, Trinity Evangelical Divinity School

Index of Ancient Names

Index of Modern Names

Index of Subjects

Index of Scripture References

NEW TESTAMENT

Matthew

2 Corinthians

Galatians